The Experience of PHILOSOPHY

Fifth Edition

Daniel Kolak

The William Paterson University of New Jersey

Raymond Martin

University of Maryland

WADSWORTH

★

THOMSON LEARNING™

Australia • Canada • Mexico • Singapore • Spain • United Kingdom • United States

WADSWORTH

THOMSON LEARNING

Publisher: Eve Howard
Philosophy Editor: Peter Adams
Assistant Editor: Kara Kindstrom
Editorial Assistant: Chalida Anusasananan
Development Consultant: Jake Warde
Marketing Manager: Dave Garrison
Marketing Assistant: Adam Hofmann
Permissions Editor: Bob Kauser

Print/Media Buyer: Karen Hunt
Production Service: Matrix Productions
Copy Editor: Vicki Nelson
Cover Designer: Yvo Riezebos
Cover Image: PhotoDisc
Compositor: ColorType, San Diego
Cover and Text Printer: Von Hoffmann Graphics

For permission to use material from this text,
contact us by
Web: http://www.thomsonrights.com
Fax: 1-800-730-2215 **Phone:** 1-800-730-2214

Library of Congress Cataloging-in-Publication Data
The experience of philosophy / [edited by] Daniel
    Kolak, Raymond Martin. — 5th ed.
        p. cm.
    Includes bibliographical references.
    ISBN 0-534-58104-8
    1. Philosophy. 2. Philosophy — Introductions.
    I. Kolak, Daniel. II. Martin, Raymond, [date].
B29 .E96 2001
100 — dc21
                                    2001026296

Wadsworth/Thomson Learning
10 Davis Drive
Belmont, CA 94002-3098
USA

For more information about our products, contact us:
Thomson Learning Academic Resource Center
1-800-423-0563
http://www.wadsworth.com

International Headquarters
Thomson Learning
International Division
290 Harbor Drive, 2nd Floor
Stamford, CT 06902-7477
USA

UK/Europe/Middle East/South Africa
Thomson Learning
Berkshire House
168-173 High Holborn
London, WC1V 7AA
United Kingdom

Asia
Thomson Learning
60 Albert Street, #15-01
Albert Complex
Singapore 189969

Canada
Nelson Thomson Learning
1120 Birchmount Road
Toronto, Ontario M1K 5G4
Canada

Contents

iii

Part IV: *Freedom*

Part V: *Knowledge*

Part VI: *God*

Part VII: *Reality*

Part VIII: *Experience*

Part IX: *Consciousness*

Part X: *Death*

Part XI: *Meaning*

Part XII: *Ethics*

Part XIII: *Values*

Epilog: *Concluding Unphilosophical Postscript*

Glossary

Preface

OUR PURPOSE IS TO PROVIDE A PROVOCATIVE AND ACCESSIBLE ANTHOLOGY. Our focus is not on the history of philosophy but, rather, on important ideas. Although classical sources are not neglected, the core of the material is recent philosophy, with an emphasis on an interdisciplinary approach that links philosophy to the physical and social sciences and to literature.

We make no attempt to be comprehensive. We substitute for the goal of being comprehensive the twin goals of being accessible and provocative. We want to excite and challenge readers with dramatic and important ideas that have the explosive power to change completely and irrevocably the way they think about themselves and the world.

The selections are fresh and easy to read, and they deliver a powerful philosophical punch. In most cases, they require little in the way of lecture supplement—none if they are used in conjunction with Kolak and Martin, *Wisdom Without Answers* (Wadsworth, 2002). We included the selections not just because they present important ideas but also because they are gripping. Each selection pulls readers out of their ordinary frameworks and challenges them to think critically about issues deeply relevant to their lives. To get most readers to *think* the issues, you first have to get them to *feel* the issues. Hence our title: *The Experience of Philosophy.*

Each of the thirteen sections of the book opens with an introduction designed to *provoke* the reader to want to read on. In addition, there is an individual introduction to each of the eighty-five selections. These individual introductions provide biographical information on the authors and orient the reader to the particular issues raised in the selection.

Each selection is framed by two sets of questions. "Reading Questions" are designed to aid reading comprehension. They focus the reader's attention on the main points in the selection and can serve as a quick self-test: readers who can answer these questions successfully have understood, at least minimally, the main points. "Further Questions" are designed to help readers think critically about the issues raised in the selections.

For the fifth edition, we have added many new selections, strengthening both classical and contemporary sources. To further revitalize traditional core philosophical issues within a contemporary framework, we offer a rich variety of new material that is up-to-date both in philosophy and related disciplines, yet accessible to today's beginning students.

Many people helped in various ways with this continuing project. We especially wish to thank Marshall Missner, Garrett Thomson, J. R. Salamanca, Freeman Dyson, Heidi Storl, Peter Unger, Wendy Zentz, Stephen Davies, David Prejsnar, Timothy Shanahan, Paul Shepard, Morton Winston, Mary Ann Carroll, Gary N. Kemp, John Knight, Louisa Moon, Gary Ortega, Stiv Fleishman, John O'Connor, Victor Velarde-Mayol, William Boos, Hope May, Joe Salerno, Kevin Levin, Michael Russo, Nancy Hall, and Wayne Alt.

We thank the following reviewers: Ronald Cox, San Antonio College; Jill Dieterie, Eastern Michigan University; Ronald Jackson, Clayton College and State University; John Knight, University of Wisconsin at Waukesha County Center.

Part I

Beginning Philosophy

THERE IS A FROZEN SEA WITHIN US. Philosophy is an axe.

Everything you believe is questionable. How deeply have you questioned it? The uncritical acceptance of beliefs handed down to you by parents, teachers, politicians, and religious leaders is dangerous. Many of these beliefs are simply false. Some of them are lies, designed to control you. Even when what has been handed down is true, it is not *your* truth. To merely accept anything without questioning it is to be somebody else's puppet, a second-hand person.

Beliefs can be handed down. Knowledge can perhaps be handed down. Wisdom can never be handed down. The goal of philosophy is wisdom. Trying to hand down philosophy is unphilosophical.

Wisdom requires questioning what is questionable. Because everything is questionable, wisdom requires questioning everything. That is what philosophy is: the art of questioning *everything*.

1   The Trial of Socrates
(From *Euthyphro, Apology,* and *Crito*)

PLATO

Plato was born in Athens about 427 B.C. to a prominent aristocratic family. Around 387 B.C. he founded the first university, which he named after a hero called Academus; it lasted more than a thousand years. Plato wrote philosophy, poetry, and drama, worked as a politician, and was a champion wrestler. He is one of the most influential persons in history; one prominent twentieth-century philosopher has called all Western philosophy merely "a series of footnotes to Plato." Plato lived to be eighty.

Many people consider religion and morality to be inseparable. In the following dialogue, however, Plato severed ethics from theology (*more than two thousand years ago!*) with one penetrating question: Is an act right because God approves of it, or does God approve of it because it is right? Concerning this question, the philosopher Antony Flew has remarked that "one good test of a person's aptitude for philosophy is to discover whether he can grasp its force and point."

Socrates is here on his way to his famous trial. He runs into Euthyphro, who tries to base morality on religious principles. Pay close attention to the method of cross-examination Socrates uses; it is a perfect example of the so-called "Socratic method."

From *Euthyphro*

Reading Questions

1. What does Socrates mean by "piety"? Why does Euthyphro have such a difficult time trying to define this term?
2. What is the significance of the "disagreement" between the gods? Can you translate this "disagreement" into contemporary terms?
3. How would you describe, using your own words, the "method" Socrates uses against Euthyphro? What is Socrates trying to do? Does he succeed?
4. Why is Socrates being prosecuted?
5. List Euthyphro's definitions of piety and Socrates' objections to each one.
6. What is Socrates' definition of piety, and his objection to his own definition?

Euth.: BUT WHAT IS THE CHARGE which he [Meletus] brings against you?

Soc.: What is the charge? Well, rather a grand one, which implies a degree of discernment far from contemptible in a young man. He says he knows how the youth are corrupted and who are their corruptors. I fancy that he must be a wise man, and seeing that I am the reverse of a wise

Reprinted from The Dialogues of Plato *translated by Benjamin Jowett, 3rd ed. (Oxford: Oxford University Press, 1896).*

man, he has found me out, and is going to accuse me of corrupting his generation. And of this our mother the state is to be the judge. Of all our political men he is the only one who seems to me to begin in the right way, with the cultivation of virtue in youth; like a good husbandman, he makes the young shoots his first care, and clears away us whom he accuses of destroying them. This is only the first step; afterwards he will assuredly attend to the elder branches; and if he goes on as he has begun, he will be a very great public benefactor.

Euth.: I hope that he may; but I rather fear, Socrates, that the opposite will turn out to be the truth. My opinion is that in attacking you he is simply aiming a blow at the heart of the state. But in what way does he say that you corrupt the young?

Soc.: In a curious way, which at first hearing excites surprise: he says that I am a maker of gods, and that I invent new gods and deny the existence of the old ones; this is the ground of his indictment.

Euth.: I understand, Socrates; he means to attack you about the familiar sign which occasionally, as you say, comes to you. He thinks that you are a neologian, and he is going to have you up before the court for this. He knows that such a charge is readily received by the world, as I myself know too well; for when I speak in the assembly about divine things, and foretell the future to them, they laugh at me and think me a madman. Yet every word that I say is true. But they are jealous of us all; and we must be brave and go at them.

Soc.: Their laughter, friend Euthyphro, is not a matter of much consequence. For a man may be thought clever; but the Athenians, I suspect, do not much trouble themselves about him until he begins to impart his wisdom to others; and then for some reason or other, perhaps, as you say, from jealousy, they are angry.

Euth.: I have no great wish to try their temper towards me in this way.

Soc.: No doubt they think you are reserved in your behaviour, and unwilling to impart your wisdom. But I have a benevolent habit of pouring out myself to everybody, and would even pay for a listener, and I am afraid that the Athenians may think me too talkative. Now if, as I was saying, they would only laugh at me, as you say that they laugh at you, the time might pass gaily enough with jokes and merriment in the court; but perhaps they

may be in earnest, and then what the end will be you soothsayers only can predict.

Euth.: I dare say that the affair will end in nothing, Socrates, and that you will win your cause; and I think that I shall win my own.

Soc.: And what is your suit, Euthyphro? are you the pursuer or the defendant?

Euth.: I am the pursuer.

Soc.: Of whom?

Euth.: When I tell you, you will perceive another reason why I am thought mad.

Soc.: Why, has the fugitive wings?

Euth.: Nay, he is not very volatile at his time of life.

Soc.: Who is he?

Euth.: My father.

Soc.: My dear Sir! Your own father?

Euth.: Yes.

Soc.: And of what is he accused?

Euth.: Of murder, Socrates.

Soc.: Good heavens! How little, Euthyphro, does the common herd know of the nature of right and truth! A man must be an extraordinary man, and have made great strides in wisdom, before he could have seen his way to bring such an action.

Euth.: Indeed, Socrates, he must.

Soc.: I suppose that the man whom your father murdered was one of your family—clearly he was; for if he had been a stranger you would never have thought of prosecuting him.

Euth.: I am amused, Socrates, at your making a distinction between one who is a member of the family and one who is not; for surely the pollution is the same in either case, if you knowingly associate with the murder when you ought to clear yourself and him by proceeding against him. The real question is whether the murdered man has been justly slain. If justly, then your duty is to let the matter alone; but if injustly, then proceed against the murderer, if, that is to say, he lives under the same roof with you and eats at the same table. In fact, the man who is dead was a poor dependant of mine who worked for us as a field labourer on our farm in Naxos, and one day in a fit of drunken passion he got into a quarrel with one of our domestic servants and slew him. My father bound him hand and foot and threw him into a ditch, and then sent to Athens to ask an expositor of religious law what he should do with him. Meanwhile he never attended to him and took no care about him, for he regarded him as a murderer; and thought that no great harm would be done even if he did die. Now this was just what happened. For such was the effect of cold and hunger and chains upon him, that before the messenger returned from the expositor, he was dead. And my father and family are angry with me for taking the part of the murderer and prosecuting my father. They say that he did not kill him, and that if he did, the dead man was but a murderer, and I ought not to take any notice, for that son is impious who prosecutes a father for murder. Which shows, Socrates, how little they know what the gods think about piety and impiety.

Soc.: Good heavens, Euthyphro! and is your knowledge of religion, and of things pious and impious so very exact, that, supposing the circumstances to be as you state them, you are not afraid lest you too may be doing an impious thing in bringing an action against your father?

Euth.: The best of Euthyphro, that which distinguishes him, Socrates, from the common herd, is his exact knowledge of all such matters. What should I be good for without it?

Soc.: Rare friend! I think that I cannot do better than be your disciple. . . . And therefore, I adjure you to tell me the nature of piety and impiety, which you said that you knew so well, in their bearing on murder and generally on offenses against the gods. Is not piety in every action always the same? and impiety, again — is it not always the opposite of piety, and also the same with itself, having, as impiety, one notion or form which includes whatever is impious?

Euth.: To be sure, Socrates.

Soc.: And what is piety, and what is impiety?

Euth.: Piety is doing as I am doing; that is to say, prosecuting anyone who is guilty of murder, sacrilege, or of any similar crime — whether he be your father or mother, or whoever he may be — that makes no difference; and not to prosecute them is impiety. And please to consider, Socrates, what a notable proof I will give you that this is the law, a proof which I have already given to others: — of the principle, I mean, that the impious, whoever he may be, ought not to go unpunished. For do not men acknowledge Zeus as the best and most righteous of the gods? — and yet they admit that he bound his father (Cronos) be-

cause he wickedly devoured his sons, and that he too had punished his own father (Uranus) for a similar reason, in a nameless manner. And yet when I proceed against my father, they are angry with me. So inconsistent are they in their way of talking when the gods are concerned, and when I am concerned.

Soc.: May not this be the reason, Euthyphro, why I am charged with impiety — that I cannot accept these stories about the gods? that, I suppose is where people think I go wrong. But as you who are well informed about them approve of them, I cannot do better than assent to your superior wisdom. What else can I say, confessing as I do, that I know nothing about them? Tell me, for the love of Zeus, whether you really believe that they are true.

Euth.: Yes, Socrates; and things more wonderful still, of which the world is in ignorance.

Soc.: And do you really believe that the gods fought with one another, and had dire quarrels, battles, and the like, as the poets say, and as you see represented in the works of great artists? The temples are full of them; and notably the robe of Athene, which is carried up to the Acropolis at the great Panathenaea, is embroidered with them throughout. Are all these tales of the gods true, Euthyphro?

Euth.: Yes, Socrates; and, as I was saying, I can tell you, if you would like to hear them, many other things about the gods which would quite amaze you.

Soc.: I dare say; and you shall tell me them at some other time when I have leisure. But just at present I would rather hear from you a more precise answer, which you have not as yet given, my friend, to the question, "What is 'piety'?" When asked, you only replied, "Doing as you do, charging your father with murder."

Euth.: And what I said was true, Socrates.

Soc.: No doubt, Euthyphro; but you would admit that there are many other pious acts?

Euth.: There are.

Soc.: Remember that I did not ask you to give me two or three examples of piety, but to explain the general form which makes all pious things to be pious. Do you not recollect saying that one and the same form made the impious impious, the pious pious?

Euth.: I remember.

Soc.: Tell me what is the nature of this form, and then I shall have a standard to which I may look, and by which I may measure actions, whether yours or those of anyone else, and then I shall be able to say that such and such an action is pious, such another impious.

Euth.: I will tell you, if you like.

Soc.: I should very much like.

Euth.: Piety, then, is that which is dear to the gods, and impiety is that which is not dear to them.

Soc.: Very good, Euthyphro; you have now given me the sort of answer which I wanted. But whether what you say is true or not I cannot as yet tell, although I make no doubt that you will go on to prove the truth of your words.

Euth.: Of course.

Soc.: Come, then, and let us examine what we are saying. That thing or person which is dear to the gods is pious, and that thing or person which is hateful to the gods is impious, these two being the extreme opposites of one another. Was not that said?

Euth.: It was. . . .

Soc.: And further, Euthyphro, the gods were admitted to have enmities and hatreds and differences?

Euth.: Yes, that was also said.

Soc.: And what sort of difference creates enmity and anger? Suppose for example that you and I, my good friend, differ on the question which of two groups of things is more numerous; do differences of this sort make us enemies and set us at variance with one another? Do we not proceed at once to counting, and put an end to them?

Euth.: True.

Soc.: Or suppose that we differ about magnitudes, do we not quickly end the difference by measuring?

Euth.: Very true.

Soc.: And we end a controversy about heavy and light by resorting to a weighing machine?

Euth.: To be sure.

Soc.: But what are the matters about which differences arise that cannot be thus decided, and therefore make us angry and set us at enmity with one another? I dare say the answer does not occur to you at the moment, and therefore I will suggest that these enmities arise when the matters of difference are the just and unjust, good and evil, honourable and dishonourable. Are not these the sub-

jects about which men differ, and about which when we are unable satisfactorily to decide our differences, you and I and all of us quarrel, when we do quarrel?

Euth.: Yes, Socrates, the nature of the differences about which we quarrel is such as you describe.

Soc.: And the quarrels of the gods, noble Euthyphro, when they occur, are of a like nature?

Euth.: Certainly they are.

Soc.: They have differences of opinion, as you say, about good and evil, just and unjust, honourable and dishonourable: there would be no quarrels among them, if there were not such differences—would there now?

Euth.: You are quite right.

Soc.: Does not each party of them love that which they deem noble and just and good, and hate the opposite? . . .

Then the same things are hated by the gods and loved by the gods, and are both hateful and dear to them?

Euth.: It appears so.

Soc.: And upon this view the same things, Euthyphro, will be pious and also impious?

Euth.: So I should suppose.

Soc.: Then, my friend, I remark with surprise that you have not answered the question which I asked. For I certainly did not ask you to tell me what action is both pious and impious; but now it would seem that what is loved by the gods is also hated by them. And therefore, Euthyphro, in thus chastising your father you may very likely be doing what is agreeable to Zeus but disagreeable to Cronos or Uranus, and what is acceptable to Hephaestus but unacceptable to Hera, and there may be other gods who have similar differences of opinion.

Euth.: But I believe, Socrates, that all the gods would be agreed as to the propriety of punishing a murderer: there would be no difference of opinion about that.

Soc.: Well, but speaking of men, Euthyphro, did you ever hear anyone arguing that a murderer or any sort of evil-doer ought to be let off?

Euth.: I should rather say that these are the questions which they are always arguing, especially in courts of law: they commit all sorts of crimes, and there is nothing which they will not do or say in their own defence.

Soc.: But do they admit their guilt, Euthyphro, and yet say that they ought not to be punished?

Euth.: No; they do not.

Soc.: Then there are some things which they do not venture to say and do: for they do not venture to argue that if guilty they are to go unpunished, but they deny their guilt, do they not?

Euth.: Yes.

Soc.: Then they do not argue that the evil-doer should not be punished, but they argue about the fact of who the evil-doer is, and what he did and when?

Euth.: True.

Soc.: And the gods are in the same case, if as you assert they quarrel about just and unjust, and some of them say while others deny that injustice is done among them. For surely neither god nor man will ever venture to say that the doer of injustice is not to be punished?

Euth.: That is true, Socrates, in the main.

Soc.: But they join issue about the particulars—gods and men alike, if indeed the gods dispute at all; they differ about some act which is called in question, and which by some is affirmed to be just, by others to be unjust. Is not that true?

Euth.: Quite true.

Soc.: Well then, my dear friend Euthyphro, do tell me, for my better instruction and information, what proof have you that in the opinion of all the gods a servant who is guilty of murder, and is put in chains by the master of the dead man, and dies because he is put in chains before he who bound him can learn from the expositors of religious law what he ought to do with him, is killed unjustly; and that on behalf of such a one a son ought to proceed against his father and accuse him of murder. How would you show that all the gods absolutely agree in approving of his act? Prove to me that they do, and I will applaud your wisdom as long as I live.

Euth.: No doubt it will be a difficult task; though I could make the matter very clear indeed to you.

Soc.: I understand; you mean to say that I am not so quick of apprehension as the judges: for to them you will be sure to prove that the act is unjust, and hateful to all the gods.

Euth.: Yes indeed, Socrates; at least if they will listen to me.

Soc.: But they will be sure to listen if they find that you are a good speaker. There was a notion that came into my mind while you were speaking; I said to myself: "Well, and what if Euthyphro does prove to me that all the gods regarded the death of the serf as unjust, how do I know anything more of the nature of piety and impiety? for granting that this action may be hateful to the gods, still piety and impiety are not adequately defined by these distinctions, for that which is hateful to the gods has been shown to be also dear to them." And therefore, Euthyphro, I do not ask you to prove this; I will suppose, if you like, that all the gods condemn and abominate such an action. But I will amend the definition so far as to say that what all the gods hate is impious, and what they love pious or holy; and what some of them love and others hate is both or neither. Shall this be our definition of piety and impiety?

Euth.: Why not, Socrates?

Soc.: Why not! certainly, as far as I am concerned, Euthyphro, there is no reason why not. But whether this premise will greatly assist you in the task of instructing me as you promised, is a matter for you to consider.

Euth.: Yes, I should say that what all the gods love is pious and holy, and the opposite which they all hate, impious.

Soc.: Ought we to inquire into the truth of this, Euthyphro, or simply to accept it on our own authority and that of others—echoing mere assertions? What do you say?

Euth.: We should inquire; and I believe that the statement will stand the test of inquiry.

Soc.: We shall soon be better able to say, my good friend. The point which I should first wish to understand is whether the pious or holy is beloved by the gods because it is holy, or holy because it is beloved of the gods.

Euth.: I do not understand your meaning, Socrates.

Soc.: I will endeavour to explain: . . . is not that which is beloved distinct from that which loves?

Euth.: Certainly. . . .

Soc.: And what do you say of piety, Euthyphro: is not piety, according to your definition, loved by all the gods?

Euth.: Yes.

Soc.: Because it is pious or holy, or for some other reason?

Euth.: No, that is the reason.

Soc.: It is loved because it is holy, not holy because it is loved?

GOD'S COMMANDS AND MAN'S DUTIES

Jonathan Harrison

When we consider the relation between God's commands and man's duties, it seems to be a fairly good rough approximation to the truth to say that there are three possible views about the nature of this relation. In the *first* place, it is possible to say that God, since he is omniscient, always knows what is right and wrong, and, since he is perfectly good, always commands us to do what is right and prohibits us from doing what is wrong; he is pleased with us when we obey his commands, and do what is right, and displeased with us when we disobey his commands, and do what is wrong. On this view, God's will is determined by his knowledge of right and wrong. *Secondly*, it is possible to say that what makes right actions right and what makes wrong actions wrong is that God has commanded the right actions and prohibited the wrong ones, and that being commanded by God is the only thing which makes an action right and being prohibited by God is the *only* thing which makes an action wrong. On this view, it is impossible for

God, in commanding some actions and prohibiting others, to be guided by the fact that the actions he commands are right and the actions he prohibits are wrong, because, before he has commanded them, no actions are right, and before he has prohibited them, no actions are wrong. The *third* possible view is that there are not two pairs of different facts, being commanded by God and being right, and being prohibited by God and being wrong: to say that an action is right just *means* that it is commanded by God, and to say that an action is wrong just *means* that it is prohibited by God. . . . On the third view there are not two different facts, being commanded by God and being right, such that we can ask whether the first is dependent upon the second or whether the second is dependent upon the first. There is just one single fact, which may be put indifferently by saying either that God has commanded something or that it is right.

From *Our Knowledge of Right and Wrong* (1971).

Euth.: Apparently.

Soc.: And it is the object of the gods' love, and is dear to them, because it is loved of them?

Euth.: Certainly.

Soc.: Then that which is dear to the gods, Euthyphro, is not holy, nor is that which is holy dear to the gods, as you affirm; but they are two different things. . . .

Euth.: Yes.

Soc.: But that which is dear to the gods is dear to them because it is loved by them, not loved by them because it is dear to them.

Euth.: True.

Soc.: But, friend Euthyphro, if that which is holy were the same with that which is dear to the gods, and were loved because it is holy, then that which is dear to the gods would be loved as being dear to them; but if that which is dear to them were dear to

them because loved by them, then that which is holy would be holy because loved by them. But now you see that the reverse is the case, and that the two things are quite different from one another. For one is of a kind to be loved because it is loved, and the other is loved because it is of a kind to be loved. Thus you appear to me, Euthyphro, when I ask you what is the nature of holiness, to offer an attribute only, and not the essence—the attribute of being loved by all the gods. But you still do not explain to me the nature of holiness. And therefore, if you please, I will ask you not to hide your treasure, but to start again, and tell me frankly what holiness or piety really is, whether dear to the gods or not (for that is a matter about which we will not quarrel); and what is impiety?

Euth.: I really do not know, Socrates, how to express what I mean. For somehow or other the definitions we propound, on whatever bases we rest them, seem always to turn round and walk away from us. . . .

Soc.: Then we must begin again and ask, What is piety? That is an inquiry which I shall never be weary of pursuing as far as in me lies; and I entreat you not to scorn me, but to apply your mind to the utmost, and tell me the truth. For, if any man knows, you are he; and therefore I must hold you fast, like Proteus, until you tell. If you had not certainly known the nature of piety and impiety, I am confident that you would never, on behalf of a serf, have charged your aged father with murder. You would not have run such a risk of doing wrong in the sight of the gods, and you would have had too much respect for the opinions of men. I am sure, therefore, that you know the nature of piety and impiety. Speak out then, my dear Euthyphro, and do not hide your knowledge.

Euth.: Another time, Socrates; for I am in a hurry, and must go now.

Soc.: Alas! my friend, and will you leave me in despair? I was hoping that you would instruct me in the nature of piety and impiety; and then I might have cleared myself of Meletus and his indictment. I would have told him that I had been enlightened by Euthyphro, and had given up rash innovations and speculations in which I had indulged only through ignorance, and that now I am about to lead a better life.

Further Questions

1. State in your own words what the problem is with supposing "an act is right *because* God approves of it." State what the problem is with supposing that "God approves of an act *because* it is right." How might a religious person respond? You might, as an exercise, go to a religious authority and pose the question to him or her. What answer do you get? What happens when you keep asking the question?
2. Why do you suppose that, in our society and in others, morality is widely considered to be the domain of religion? Do you think this is appropriate? Why or why not?
3. How might Socrates, were he alive, respond to the "religious moral authorities" of today? What would he say, for instance, to the way the Pope justifies a particular view, say the one against the use of artificial birth control?
4. If Socrates is right that morality is independent of the will of the gods, why then have so many societies, past and present, insisted on justifying morality on the grounds that it came from the accepted gods or God? What is their intent?
5. Socrates believed in subjecting all of his beliefs to rational scrutiny and in abandoning those that could not be supported by good reasons. Do you think this is how a person ought to live?

Further Readings

Nielsen, Kai. *Ethics Without God.* Buffalo, NY: Prometheus Books, 1973.

Rachels, James. *The Elements of Moral Philosophy.* New York: Random House, 1986. Elementary and concise, one of the best short introductions to ethics. See, especially, Chapter 4, "Does Morality Depend on Religion?"

From *Apology*

In 399 B.C., when Socrates was about seventy, his fellow Athenians put him on trial for corrupting the youth of Athens and for raising doubts in people's minds about their accepted gods. This happened in the aftermath of a long war against Sparta that had raged for most of Plato's life. It was a time when the aristocracy was vying with the democratic masses for control of the state. In what follows, Plato recounts Socrates' irreverent response to the charges against him.

Reading Questions

1. With what crime is Socrates charged? What today would be a similar charge brought, say, against your philosophy professor? What is Socrates' defense?
2. What was Socrates' main goal in life?
3. Why does Socrates not simply escape from Athens?
4. What is a "gadfly," and in what sense is Socrates one?
5. Why is Socrates not afraid of death?
6. Imagine getting an official letter telling you that you have been chosen "the wisest person in the country." How would you react? Supposedly, something similar happened to Socrates. How was his reaction different from what you would have done under similar circumstances, and why?
7. Why doesn't Socrates simply apologize and plead for mercy? What does he propose as an appropriate punishment for his "crimes"?
8. Are there any contemporary figures like Socrates? If Socrates were alive today, who might be his targets?

CHARACTERS *Socrates and Meletus*
SCENE *The Court of Justice*

Soc.: I cannot tell what impression my accusers have made upon you, Athenians. For my own part, I know that they nearly made me forget who I was, so believable were they; and yet they have scarcely uttered one single word of truth. But of all their many falsehoods, the one which astonished me most was when they said that I was a clever speaker, and that you must be careful not to let me mislead you. I thought that it was most impudent of them not to be ashamed to talk in that way; for as soon as I open my mouth they will be refuted, and I shall prove that I am not a clever speaker in any way at all—unless, indeed, by a clever speaker they mean a man who speaks the truth. If that is their meaning, I agree with them that I am a much greater orator than they. My accusers, then I repeat, have said little or nothing that is true; but from me you shall hear the whole truth. Certainly you will not hear an elaborate speech, Athenians, dressed up, like theirs, with words and phrases. I will say to you what I have to say, without preparation, and in the words which come first, for I believe that my cause is just; so let none of you expect anything else. Indeed, my friends, it would hardly be seemly for me, at my age, to come before

you like a young man with his specious phrases. But there is one thing, Athenians, which I do most earnestly beg and entreat of you. Do not be surprised and do not interrupt with shouts if in my defense I speak in the same way that I am accustomed to speak in the marketplace, at the tables of the moneychangers, where many of you have heard me, and elsewhere. The truth is this. I am more than seventy years old, and this is the first time that I have ever come before a law court; so your manner of speech here is quite strange to me. If I had been really a stranger, you would have forgiven me for speaking in the language and the fashion of my native country; and so now I ask you to grant me what I think I have a right to claim. Never mind the style of my speech—it may be better or it may be worse—give your whole attention to the question, Is what I say just, or is it not? That is what makes a good judge, as speaking the truth makes a good advocate.

I have to defend myself, Athenians, first against the old false accusations of my old accusers, and then against the later ones of my present accusers. For many men have been accusing me to you, and for very many years, who have not uttered a word of truth; and I fear them more than I fear Anytus and his associates, formidable as they are. But, my friends, those others are still more formidable; for they got hold of most of you when you were children, and they have been more persistent in accusing me untruthfully and have persuaded you that there is a certain Socrates, a wise man, who speculates about the heavens, and who investigates things that are beneath the earth, and who can make the weaker reason appear the stronger. These men, Athenians, who spread abroad this report are the accusers whom I fear; for their hearers think that persons who pursue such inquiries never believe in the gods. Then they are many, and their attacks have been going on for a long time, and they spoke to you when you were at the age most readily to believe them, for you were all young, and many of you were children, and there was no one to answer them when they attacked me. And the most unreasonable thing of all is that I do not even know their names: I cannot tell you who they are except when one happens to be a comic poet. But all the rest who have persuaded you, from motives of resentment and prejudice, and sometimes, it may be, from conviction, are hardest to cope with. For I cannot call any one of them forward in court to cross-examine him. I have, as it were, simply to spar with shadows in my defense, and to put questions which there is no one to answer. I ask you, therefore, to believe that, as I say, I have been attacked by two kinds of accusers — first, by Meletus and his associates, and, then, by those older ones of whom I have spoken. And, with your leave, I will defend myself first against my old accusers; for you heard their accusations first, and they were much more forceful than my present accusers are.

Well, I must make my defense, Athenians, and try in the short time allowed me to remove the prejudice which you have been so long a time acquiring. I hope that I may manage to do this, if it be good for you and for me, and that my defense may be successful; but I am quite aware of the nature of my task, and I know that it is a difficult one. Be the outcome, however, as is pleasing to God, I must obey the law and make my defense.

Let us begin from the beginning, then, and ask what is the accusation which has given rise to the prejudice against me, which was what Meletus relied on when he brought his indictment. What is the prejudice which my enemies have been spreading about me? I must assume that they are formally accusing me, and read their indictment. It would run somewhat in this fashion: Socrates is a wrong-doer, who meddles with inquiries into things beneath the earth and in the heavens, and who makes the weaker reason appear the stronger, and who teaches others these same things. That is what they say; and in the comedy of Aristophanes [*Clouds*] you yourselves saw a man called Socrates swinging round in a basket and saying that he walked on the air, and prattling a great deal of nonsense about matters of which I understand nothing, either more or less. I do not mean to disparage that kind of knowledge if there is anyone who is wise about these matters. I trust Meletus may never be able to prosecute me for that. But the truth is, Athenians, I have nothing to do with these matters, and almost all of you are yourselves my witness of this. I beg all of you who have heard me discussing, and they are many, to inform your neighbors and tell them if any of you have ever heard me discussing such matters, either more or less. That will show you that the other common stories about me are as false as this one.

But the fact is that not one of these is true. And if you have heard that I undertake to educate men, and make money by so doing, that is not true either, though I think that it would be a fine thing to be able to educate men. . . .

Perhaps some of you may reply: But, Socrates, what is the trouble with you? What has given rise to these prejudices against you? You must have been doing something out of the ordinary. All these stories and reports of you would never have arisen if you had not been doing something different from other men. So tell us what it is, that we may not give our verdict in the dark. I think that that is a fair question, and I will try to explain to you what it is that has raised these prejudices against me and given me this reputation. Listen, then: some of you, perhaps, will think that I am joking, but I assure you that I will tell you the whole truth. I have gained this reputation, Athenians, simply by reason of a certain wisdom. But by what kind of wisdom? It is by just that wisdom which is perhaps human wisdom. In that, it may be, I am really wise. . . .

You remember Chaerephon. From youth upwards he was my comrade; and also a partisan of your democracy, sharing your recent exile and returning with you. You remember, too, Chaerephon's character — how vehement he was in carrying through whatever he took in hand. Once he went to Delphi and ventured to put this question to the oracle—I entreat you again, my friends, not to interrupt me with your shouts—he asked if there was any man who was wiser than I. The priestess answered that there was no one. Chaerephon himself is dead, but his brother here will confirm what I say.

Now see why I tell you this. I am going to explain to you how the prejudice against me has arisen. When I heard of the oracle I began to reflect: What can the god mean by this riddle? I know very well that I am not wise, even the smallest degree. Then what can he mean by saying that I am the wisest of men? It cannot be that he is speaking falsely, for he is a god and cannot lie. For a long time I was at a loss to understand his meaning. Then, very reluctantly, I turned to seek for it in this manner. I went to a man who was reputed to be wise, thinking that there, if anywhere, I should prove the answer wrong, and meaning to point out to the oracle its mistake, and to say, You said that I was the wisest of men, but this man is wiser than I am. So I examined the man—I need not tell you his name, he was a politician—but this was the result, Athenians. When I conversed with him I came to see that, though a great many persons, and most of all he himself, thought that he was wise, yet he was not wise. Then I tried to prove to him that he was not wise, though he fancied that he was; and by so doing I made him indignant, and many of the bystanders. So when I went away, I thought to myself, I am wiser than this man: neither of us knows anything that is really worthwhile, but he thinks that he has knowledge when he has not, while I, having no knowledge, do not think that I have. I seem, at any rate, to be a little wiser than he is on this point: I do not think that I know what I do not know. Next I went to another man who was reputed to be still wiser than the last, with exactly the same result. And there again I made him, and many other men, indignant.

Then I went on to one man after another, seeing that I was arousing indignation every day, which caused me much pain and anxiety. Still I thought that I must set the god's command above everything. So I had to go to every man who seemed to possess any knowledge, and investigate the meaning of the oracle. Athenians, I must tell you the truth; by the god, this was the result of the investigation which I made at the god's bidding: I found that the men whose reputation for wisdom stood highest were nearly the most lacking in it, while others who were looked down on as common people were much more intelligent. Now I must describe to you the wanderings which I undertook, like Heraclean labors, to prove the oracle irrefutable. After the politicians, I went to the poets, tragic, dithyrambic, and others, thinking that there I should find myself manifestly more ignorant than they. So I took up the poems on which I thought that they had spent most pains, and asked them what they meant, hoping at the same time to learn something from them. I am ashamed to tell you the truth, my friends, but I must say it. Almost anyone of the bystanders could have talked about the works of these poets better than the poets themselves. So I soon found that it is not by wisdom that the poets create their works, but by a certain innate power and by inspiration, like soothsayers and prophets, who say many fine things, but who understand nothing of what they say. The poets seemed to me to be in a similar situation. And at the same time I perceived that, because of their poetry, they thought that they were the wisest of men in other matters, too, which they were not. So I went away again, thinking that I had the same advantage over the poets that I had over the politicians.

Finally, I went to the artisans, for I knew very well that I possessed no knowledge at all worth speaking of, and I was sure that I should find that they knew many fine things. And in that I was not mistaken. They knew what I did not know, and so far they were wiser than I. But, Athenians, it seemed to me that the skilled artisans made the same mistake as the poets. Each of them believed himself to be extremely wise in matters of the greatest importance because he was skillful in his own art: and this presumption of theirs obscured their real wisdom. So I asked myself, on behalf of the oracle, whether I would choose to remain as I was, without either their wisdom or their ignorance, or to possess both, as they did. And I answered to myself and to the oracle that it was better for me to remain as I was.

From this examination, Athenians, has arisen much fierce and bitter indignation, and from this a great many prejudices about me, and people say that I am "a wise man." For the bystanders always think that I am wise myself in any matter wherein I refute another. But, my friends, I believe that the god is really wise, and that by this oracle he meant that human wisdom is worth little or nothing. I do not think that he meant that Socrates was wise. He only made use of my name, and took me as an example, as though he would say to men: He among you is the wisest who, like Socrates, knows that in truth his wisdom is worth nothing at all. Therefore I still go about testing and examining every man whom I think wise, whether he be a citizen or a stranger, as the god has commanded me; and whenever I find that he is not wise, I point out to him, on the god's behalf, that he is not wise. I am so busy in this pursuit that I have never had leisure to take any path worth mentioning in public matters or to look after my private affairs. I am in great poverty as the result of my service to the god.

Besides this, the young men who follow me about, who are the sons of wealthy persons and have the most leisure, take pleasure in hearing men cross-examined. They often imitate me among themselves; then they try their hands at cross-examining other people. And, I imagine, they find plenty of men who think that they know a great deal when in fact they know little or nothing. Then the persons who are cross-examined get angry with me instead of with themselves, and say that Socrates is an abomination and corrupts the young. When they are asked, Why, what does he do? what does he teach? they do not know what to say; but, not to seem at a loss, they repeat the stock charges against all philosophers, and allege that he investigates things in the air and under the earth, and that he teaches people to disbelieve in the gods, and to make the weaker reason appear the stronger. For, I suppose, they would not like to confess the truth, which is that they are shown up as ignorant pretenders to knowledge that they do not possess. So they have been filling your ears with their bitter prejudices for a long time, for they are ambitious, energetic, and numerous; and they speak vigorously and persuasively against me. Relying on this, Meletus, Anytus, and Lycon have attacked me. Meletus is indignant with me on the part of the poets, Anytus on the part of the artisans and politicians, and Lycon on the part of the orators. And so, as I said at the beginning, I shall be surprised if I am able, in the short time allowed me for my defense, to remove from your minds this

prejudice which has grown so strong. What I have told you, Athenians, is the truth: I neither conceal nor do I suppress anything, small or great. Yet I know that it is just this plainness of speech which rouses indignation. But that is only a proof that my words are true, and that the prejudice against me, and the causes of it, are what I have said. And whether you look for them now or hereafter, you will find that they are so.

What I have said must suffice as my defense against the charges of my first accusers. I will try next to defend myself against Meletus, that "good patriot," as he calls himself, and my later accusers. Let us assume that they are a new set of accusers, and read their indictment, as we did in the case of the others. It runs thus. He says that Socrates is a wrongdoer who corrupts the youth, and who does not believe in the gods whom the state believes in, but in other new divinities. Such is the accusation. Let us examine each point in it separately. Meletus says that I do wrong by corrupting the youth. But I say, Athenians, that he is doing wrong, for he is playing a solemn joke by lightly bringing men to trial, and pretending to have zealous interest in matters to which he has never given a moment's thought. Now I will try to prove to you that it is so.

Come here, Meletus. Is it not a fact that you think it very important that the young should be as excellent as possible?

Mel.: It is.

Soc.: Come then, tell the judges who is it who improves them? You care so much, you must know. You are accusing me, and bringing me to trial, because, as you say, you have discovered that I am the corrupter of the youth. Come now, reveal to the gentlemen who improves them. You see, Meletus, you have nothing to say; you are silent. But don't you think that this is shameful? Is not your silence a conclusive proof of what I say — that you have never cared? Come, tell us, my good sir, who makes the young better citizens?

Mel.: The laws.

Soc.: That, my friend, is not my question. What man improves the young, who starts with the knowledge of the laws?

Mel.: The judges here, Socrates.

Soc.: What do you mean, Meletus? Can they educate the young and improve them?

Mel.: Certainly.

Soc.: All of them? or only some of them?

Mel.: All of them.

Soc.: By Hera, that is good news! Such a large supply of benefactors! And do the listeners here improve them, or not?

Mel.: They do.

Soc.: And do the senators?

Mel.: Yes.

Soc.: Well then, Meletus, do the members of the assembly corrupt the young or do they again all improve them?

Mel.: They, too, improve them.

Soc.: Then all the Athenians, apparently, make the young into good men except me, and I alone corrupt them. Is that your meaning?

Mel.: Most certainly; that is my meaning.

Soc.: You have discovered me to be most unfortunate. Now tell me: do you think that the same holds good in the case of horses? Does one man do them harm and everyone else improve them? On the contrary, is it not one man only, or a very few—namely, those who are skilled with horses who can improve them, while the majority of men harm them if they use them and have anything to do with them? Is it not so, Meletus, both with horses and with every other animal? Of course it is, whether you and Anytus say yes or no. The young would certainly be very fortunate if only one man corrupted them, and everyone else did them good. The truth is, Meletus, you prove conclusively that you have never thought about the youth in your life. You exhibit your carelessness in not caring for the very matters about which you are prosecuting me.

Now be so good as to tell us, Meletus, is it better to live among good citizens or bad ones? Answer, my friend. I am not asking you at all a difficult question. Do not the bad harm their associates and the good do them good?

Mel.: Yes.

Soc.: Is there any man who would rather be injured than benefited by his companions? Answer, my good sir; you are obliged by the law to answer. Does any one like to be injured?

Mel.: Certainly not.

Soc.: Well then, are you prosecuting me for corrupting the young and making them worse, intentionally or unintentionally?

Mel.: For doing it intentionally.

Soc.: What, Meletus? Do you mean to say that you, who are so much younger than I, are yet so much wiser than I that you know that bad citizens always do evil, and that good citizens do good, to those with whom they come in contact, while I am so extraordinarily stupid as not to know that, if I make any of my companions evil, he will probably injure me in some way, and as to commit this great evil, as you allege, intentionally? You will not make me believe that, nor anyone else either, I should think. Either I do not corrupt the young at all or, if I do, I do so unintentionally: so that you are lying in either case. And if I corrupt them unintentionally, the law does not call upon you to prosecute me for an error which is unintentional, but to take me aside privately and reprove and instruct me. For, of course, I shall cease from doing wrong involuntarily, as soon as I know that I have been doing wrong. But you avoided associating with me and educating me; instead you bring me up before the court, where the law sends persons, not for instruction, but for punishment.

The truth is, Athenians, as I said, it is quite clear that Meletus has never cared at all about these matters. However, now tell us, Meletus, how do you say that I corrupt the young? Clearly, according to your indictment, by teaching them not to believe in the gods the state believes in, but other new divinities instead. You mean that I corrupt the young by that teaching, do you not?

Mel.: Yes, most certainly I mean that.

Soc.: Then in the name of these gods of whom we are speaking, explain yourself a little more clearly to me and to these gentlemen here. I cannot understand what you mean. Do you mean that I teach the young to believe in some gods, but not in the gods of the state? Do you accuse me of teaching them to believe in strange gods? If that is your meaning, I myself believe in some gods, and my crime is not that of absolute atheism. Or do you mean that I do not believe in the gods at all myself, and I teach other people not to believe in them either?

Mel.: I mean that you do not believe in the gods in any way whatever.

Soc.: You amaze me, Meletus! Why do you say that? Do you mean that I believe neither the sun nor the moon to be gods, like other men?

Mel.: I swear he does not, judges; he says that the sun is a stone, and the moon earth.

Soc.: My dear Meletus, do you think that you are prosecuting Anaxagoras? You must have a very poor opinion of these men, and think them illiterate, if you imagine that they do not know that the works of Anaxagoras of Clazomenae are full of these doctrines. And so young men learn these things from me, when they can often buy places in the theatre for a drachma at most, and laugh at Socrates were he to pretend that these doctrines, which are very peculiar doctrines, too, were his own. But please tell me, do you really think that I do not believe in the gods at all?

Mel.: Most certainly I do. You are a complete atheist.

Soc.: No one believes that, Meletus, not even you yourself. It seems to me, Athenians, that Meletus is very insolent and reckless, and that he is prosecuting me simply out of insolence, recklessness and youthful bravado. For he seems to be testing me, by asking me a riddle that has no answer. Will this wise Socrates, he says to himself, see that I am joking and contradicting myself? or shall I outwit him and everyone else who hears me? Meletus seems to me to contradict himself in his indictment: it is as if he were to say, Socrates is a wrongdoer who does not believe in the gods, but who believes in the gods. But that is mere joking.

Now, my friends, let us see why I think that this is his meaning. Do you answer me, Meletus; and do you, Athenians, remember the request which I made to you at the start, and do not interrupt me with shouts if I talk in my usual way.

Is there any man, Meletus, who believes in the existence of things pertaining to men and not in the existence of men? Make him answer the question, my friends, without these interruptions. Is there any man who believes in the existence of horsemanship and not in the existence of horses? or in flute-playing and not in flute-players? There is not, my friend. If you will not answer, I will tell both you and the judges. But you must answer my next question. Is there any man who believes in the existence of divine things and not in the existence of divinities?

Mel.: There is not.

Soc.: I am very glad that these gentlemen have managed to extract an answer from you. Well then, you say that I believe in divine beings, whether they be old or new ones, and that I teach others to believe in them; at any rate, according to your statement, I believe in divine beings. That you have sworn in your indictment. But if I believe in divine beings, I suppose it follows necessarily that I believe in divinities. Is it not so? I assume that you grant that, as you do not answer. But do we not believe that divinities are either gods themselves or the children of the gods? Do you admit that?

Mel.: I do.

Soc.: Then you admit that I believe in divinities. Now, if these divinities are gods, then, as I say, you are joking and asking a riddle, and asserting that I do not believe in the gods, and at the same time that I do, since I believe in divinities. But if these divinities are the illegitimate children of the gods, either by the nymphs or by other mothers, as they are said to be, then, I ask, what man could believe in the existence of the children of the gods, and not in the existence of the gods? That would be as strange as believing in the existence of the offspring of horses and asses, and not in the existence of horses and asses. You must have indicted me in this manner, Meletus, either to test me or because you could not find any crime that you could accuse me of with truth. But you will never contrive to persuade any man with any sense at all that a belief in divine things and things of the gods does not necessarily involve a belief in divinities, and in the gods, and in heroes.

But in truth, Athenians, I do not think that I need say very much to prove that I have not committed the crime for which Meletus is prosecuting me. What I have said is enough to prove that. But I repeat it is certainly true, as I have already told you, that I have aroused much indignation. That is what will cause my condemnation if I am condemned; not Meletus nor Anytus either, but that prejudice and suspicion of the multitude which have been the destruction of many good men before me, and I think will be so again. There is no fear that I shall be the last victim.

Perhaps someone will say: Are you not ashamed, Socrates, of leading a life which is very likely now to cause your death? I should answer him with justice, and say: My friend, if you think that a man of any worth at all ought to reckon the chances of life and death when he acts, or that he ought to think of anything but whether he is acting rightly or wrongly and as a good or a bad man would act, you are mistaken. According to you, the demigods who died at Troy would be foolish, and among them the son of Thetis, who thought nothing of danger when the alternative was disgrace. For when his mother—and she was a goddess—addressed him, when he was burning to slay Hector, in this fashion, "My son, if you avenge the death of your comrade Patroclus and slay Hector, you will die yourself, for 'fate awaits you straightway after Hector's death'"; when he heard this, he scorned danger and death; he feared much more to live a coward and not to avenge his friend. "Let me punish the evildoer and straightway die," he said, "that I may not remain here by the beaked ships jeered at, encumbering the earth." Do you suppose that he thought of danger or of death? For this, Athenians, I believe to be the truth. Wherever a man's station is, whether he has chosen it of his own will, or whether he has been placed at it by his commander, there it is his duty to remain and face the danger without thinking of death or of any other thing except dishonor.

When the generals whom you chose to command me, Athenians, assigned me my station at Potidaea and at Amphipolis and at Delium, I remained where they placed me and ran the risk of death, like other men. It would be very strange conduct on my part if I were to desert my station now from fear of death or of any other thing when God has commanded me—as I am persuaded that he has done—to spend my life in searching for wisdom, and in examining myself and others. That would indeed be a very strange thing: then certainly I might with justice be brought to trial for not believing in the gods, for I should be disobeying the oracle, and fearing death and thinking myself wise when I was not wise. For to fear death, my friends, is only to think ourselves wise without really being wise, for it is to think that we know what we do not know. For no one knows whether death may not be the greatest good that can happen to man. But men fear it as if they knew quite well that it was the greatest of evils. And what is this but that shameful ignorance of thinking that we know what we do not know? In this matter, too, my friends, perhaps I am different from the multitude; and if I were to claim to be at all wiser

than others, it would be because, not knowing very much about the other world, I do not think I know. But I do know very well that it is evil and disgraceful to do wrong, and to disobey my superior, whoever he is, whether man or god. I will never do what I know to be evil, and shrink in fear from what I do not know to be good or evil. Even if you acquit me now, and do not listen to Anytus' argument that, if I am to be acquitted, I ought never to have been brought to trial at all, and that, as it is, you are bound to put me to death because, as he said, if I escape, all your sons will be utterly corrupted by practising what Socrates teaches. If you were therefore to say to me: Socrates, this time we will not listen to Anytus; we will let you go, but on this condition, that you give up this investigation of yours, and philosophy; if you are found following those pursuits again, you shall die. I say, if you offered to let me go on these terms, I should reply: Athenians, I hold you in the highest regard and affection, but I will be persuaded by the god rather than by you; and as long as I have breath and strength I will not give up philosophy and exhorting you and declaring the truth to every one of you whom I meet, saying, as I am accustomed, "My good friend, you are a citizen of Athens, a city which is very great and very famous for its wisdom and strength—are you not ashamed of caring so much for the making of money and for fame and prestige, when you neither think nor care about wisdom and truth and the improvement of your soul?" And if he disputes my words and says that he does care about these things, I shall not at once release him and go away: I shall question him and cross-examine him and test him. If I think that he does not possess virtue, though he says that he does, I shall reproach him for undervaluing the most valuable things, and overvaluing those that are less valuable. This I shall do to everyone whom I meet, young or old, citizen or stranger, but especially to citizens, for they are more nearly akin to me. For know that the god has commanded me to do so. And I think that no greater good has ever befallen you in Athens than my service to the god. For I spend my whole life in going about and persuading you all to give your first and greatest care to the improvement of your souls, and not till you have done that to think of your bodies or your wealth; and telling you that virtue does not come from wealth, but that wealth, and every other good thing which men have, whether in public or in private, comes from virtue. If then I corrupt the youth by this teaching, these things must be harmful; but if any man says that I teach anything else, there is nothing in what he says. And therefore, Athenians, I say, whether you are persuaded by Anytus or not, whether you acquit me or not, be sure I shall not change my way of life; no, not if I have to die for it many times.

Do not interrupt me, Athenians, with your shouts. Remember the request which I made to you, and do not interrupt my words. I think that it will profit you to hear them. I am going to say something more to you, at which you may be inclined to protest, but do not do that. Be sure that if you put me to death, who am what I have told you that I am, you will do yourselves more harm than me. Meletus and Anytus can do me no harm: that is impossible, for I am sure it is not allowed that a good man be injured by a worse. They may indeed kill me, or drive me into exile, or deprive me of my civil rights; and perhaps Meletus and others think those things great evils. But I do not think so. I think it is a much greater evil to do what he is doing now, and to try to put a man to death unjustly. And now, Athenians, I am not arguing in my own defense at all, as you might expect me to do, but rather in yours in order [that] you may not make a mistake about the gift of the god to you by condemning me. For if you put me to death, you will not easily find another who, if I may use a ludicrous comparison, clings to the state as a sort of gadfly to a horse that is large and well-bred but rather sluggish from its size, and needing to be aroused. It seems to be that the god has attached me like that to the state, for I am constantly alighting upon you at every point to rouse, persuade, and reproach each of you all day long. You will not easily find anyone else, my friends, to fill my place; and if you are persuaded by me, you will spare my life. You are indignant, as drowsy persons are, when they are awakened, and, of course, if you are persuaded by Anytus, you could easily kill me with a single blow, and then sleep on undisturbed for the rest of your lives, unless the god in his care for you sends another to rouse you. And you may easily see that it is the god who has given me to your city; for it is not human the way in which I

have neglected all my own interests and permitted my private affairs to be neglected now for so many years, while occupying myself unceasingly in your interests, going to each of you privately, like a father or an elder brother, trying to persuade him to care for virtue. There would have been a reason for it, if I had gained any advantage by this, or if I had been paid for my exhortations; but you see yourselves that my accusers, though they accuse me of everything else without shame, have not had the impudence to say that I ever either exacted or demanded payment. Of that they have no evidence. And I think that I have sufficient evidence of the truth of what I say — my poverty.

Perhaps it may seem strange to you that, though I go about giving this advice privately and meddling in others' affairs, yet I do not venture to come forward in the assembly and advise the state. You have often heard me speak of my reason for this, and in many places: it is that I have a certain divine sign, which is what Meletus has caricatured in his indictment. I have had it from childhood. It is a kind of voice which, whenever I hear it, always turns me back from something which I was going to do, but never urges me to act. It is this which forbids me to take part in politics. And I think it does well to forbid me. For, Athenians, it is quite certain that, if I had attempted to take part in politics, I should have perished at once and long ago without doing any good either to you or to myself. And do not be indignant with me for telling the truth. There is no man who will preserve his life for long, either in Athens or elsewhere, if he firmly opposes the multitude, and tries to prevent the commission of much injustice and illegality in the state. He who would really fight for justice must do so as a private citizen, not as an officeholder, if he is to preserve his life, even for a short time.

I will prove to you that this is so by very strong evidence, not by mere words, but by what you value highly, actions. Listen then to what has happened to me, that you may know that there is no man who could make me consent to do wrong from the fear of death, but that I would perish at once rather than give way. What I am going to tell you may be a commonplace in the law court; nevertheless it is true. The only office that I ever held in the state, Athenians, was that of Senator. When you wished to try the ten generals who did not rescue their men after the battle of Arginusae, as a group, which was illegal, as you all came to think afterwards, the tribe Antiochis, to which I belong, held the presidency. On that occasion I alone of all the presidents opposed your illegal action and gave my vote against you. The speakers were ready to suspend me and arrest me; and you were clamoring against me, and crying out to me to submit. But I thought that I ought to face the danger, with law and justice on my side, rather than join with you in your unjust proposal, from fear of imprisonment or death. That was when the state was democratic. When the oligarchy came in, the Thirty sent for me, with four others, to the council-chamber, and ordered us to bring Leon the Salaminian from Salamis, that they might put him to death. They were in the habit of frequently giving similar orders, to many others, wishing to implicate as many as possible in their crimes. But, then, I again proved, not by mere words, but by my actions, that, if I may speak bluntly, I do not care a straw for death; but that I do care very much indeed about not doing anything unjust or impious. That government with all its powers did not terrify me into doing anything unjust; but when we left the council-chamber, the other four went over to Salamis and brought Leon across to Athens; and I went home. And if the rule of the Thirty had not been destroyed soon afterwards, I should very likely have been put to death for what I did then. Many of you will be my witnesses in this matter.

Now do you think that I could have remained alive all these years if I had taken part in public affairs, and had always maintained the cause of justice like an honest man, and had held it a paramount duty, as it is, to do so? Certainly not, Athenians, nor could any other man. But throughout my whole life, both in private and in public, whenever I have had to take part in public affairs, you will find I have always been the same and have never yielded unjustly to anyone; no, not to those whom my enemies falsely assert to have been my pupils. But I was never anyone's teacher. I have never withheld myself from anyone, young or old, who was anxious to hear me discuss while I was making my investigation; neither do I discuss for payment, and refuse to discuss without payment. I am ready to ask questions of rich and poor alike, and if any man wishes to answer me, and then listen to what I have to say, he may. And I cannot justly be charged with causing these men to turn out good or bad, for I never either taught or professed to teach any of them any knowledge whatever. And if any man asserts that he ever learned or heard anything from me in private which everyone else did not hear as well as he, be sure that he does not speak the truth.

Why is it, then, that people delight in spending so much time in my company? You have heard why, Athenians. I told you the whole truth when I said that they delight in hearing me examine persons who think that they are wise. It is certainly very amusing to listen to that. And, I say, the god has commanded me to examine men, in oracles and in dreams and in every way in which the divine will was ever declared to man. This is the truth, Athenians, and if it were not the truth, it would be easily refuted. For if it were really the case that I have already corrupted some of the young men, and am now corrupting others, surely some of them, finding as they grew older that I had given them bad advice in their youth, would have come forward today to accuse me and take their revenge. Or if they were unwilling to do so themselves, surely their relatives, their fathers or brothers, or others, would, if I had done them any harm, have remembered it and taken their revenge. Certainly I see many of them in Court. Here is Crito, of my own deme and of my own age, the father of Critobulus; here is Lysanias of Sphettus, the father of Aeschines; . . . And I can name many others to you, some of whom Meletus ought to have called as witnesses in the course of his own speech; but if he forgot to call them then, let him call them now—I will yield the floor to him—and tell us if he has any such evidence. No, on the contrary, my friends, you will find all these men ready to support me, the corrupter, the injurer, of their relatives, as Meletus and Anytus call me. Those of them who have been already corrupted might perhaps have some reason for supporting me, but what reason can their relatives have who are grown up, and who are uncorrupted, except the reason of truth and justice—that they know very well that Meletus is a liar, and that I am speaking the truth?

Well, my friends, this, and perhaps more like this, is pretty much what I have to say in my defense. There may be some one among you who will be indignant when he remembers how, even in a less important trial than this, he begged and entreated the judges, with many tears, to acquit him, and brought forward his children and many of his friends and relatives in Court in order to appeal to your feelings; and then finds that I shall do none of these things, though I am in what he would think the supreme danger. Perhaps he will harden himself against me when he notices this: it may make him angry, and he may cast his vote in anger. If it is so with any of you—I do not suppose that it is, but in case it should be so—I think that I should answer him reasonably if I said: My friend, I have relatives, too, for, in the words of Homer, "I am not born of an oak or a rock" but of flesh and blood; and so, Athenians, I have relatives, and I have three sons, one of them a lad, and the other two still children. Yet I will not bring any of them forward before you and implore you to acquit me. And why will I do none of these things? It is not from arrogance, Athenians, nor because I lack respect for you—whether or not I can face death bravely is another question—but for my own good name, and for your good name, and for the good name of the whole state. I do not think it right, at my age and with my reputation, to do anything of that kind. Rightly or wrongly, men have made up their minds that in some way Socrates is different from the mass of mankind. And it will be shameful if those of you who are thought to excel in wisdom, or in bravery, or in any other virtue, are going to act in this fashion. I have often seen men of reputation behaving in an extraordinary way at their trial, as if they thought it a terrible fate to be killed, and as though they expected to live forever if you did not put them to death. Such men seem to me to bring shame upon the state, for any stranger would suppose that the best and most eminent Athenians, who are selected by their fellow citizens to hold office, and for other honors, are no better than women. Those of you, Athenians, who have any reputation at all ought not to do these things, and you ought not to allow us to do them; you should show that you will be much more ready to condemn men who make the state ridiculous by these pitiful pieces of acting, than men who remain quiet.

But apart from the question of reputation, my friends, I do not think that it is right to entreat the judge to acquit us, or to escape condemnation in that way. It is our duty to convince him by reason. He does not sit to give away justice as a favor, but to pronounce judgment; and he has sworn, not to favor any man whom he would like to favor, but to judge according to law. And, therefore, we ought not to encourage you in the habit of breaking your oaths; and you ought not to allow yourselves to fall into this habit, for then neither you nor we would be acting piously. Therefore, Athenians, do not require me to do these things, for I believe them to be neither good nor just nor pious; and, more especially, do not ask me to do them today when Meletus is prosecuting me for impiety. For were I to be successful and persuade you by my entreaties to break your oaths, I should be clearly teaching you to believe that there are no gods, and I should be simply accusing myself by my defense of not believing in them. But, Athenians, that is very far from the truth. I do believe in the gods as no one of my accusers believes in them: and to you and to God I commit my cause to be decided as is best for you and for me.

(He is found guilty by a vote of 281 to 220.)

I am not indignant at the verdict which you have given, Athenians, for many reasons. I expected that you would find me guilty; and I am not so much surprised at that as at the numbers of the votes. I certainly never thought that the majority against me would have been so narrow. But now it seems that if only thirty votes had changed sides, I should have escaped. So I think that I have escaped Meletus, as it is; and not only have I escaped him, for it is perfectly clear that if Anytus and Lycon had not come forward to accuse me, too, he would not have obtained the fifth part of the votes, and would have had to pay a fine of a thousand drachmae.

So he proposes death as the penalty. Be it so. And what alternative penalty shall I propose to you, Athenians? What I deserve, of course, must I not? What then do I deserve to pay or to suffer for having determined not to spend my life in ease? I neglected the things which most men value, such as wealth, and family interests, and military commands, and popular oratory, and all the political appointments, and clubs, and factions, that there are in Athens; for I thought that I was really too honest a man to preserve my life if I engaged in these matters. So I did not go where I should have done no good either to you or to myself. I went, instead, to each one of you privately to do him, as I say, the greatest of services, and tried to persuade him not to think of his affairs until he had thought of himself and tried to make himself as good and wise as possible, nor to think of the affairs of Athens until he had thought of Athens herself; and to care for other things in the same manner. Then what do I deserve for such a life? Something good, Athenians, if I am really to propose what I deserve; and something good which it would be suitable to me to receive. Then what is a suitable reward to be given to a poor benefactor who requires leisure to exhort you? There is no reward, Athenians, so suitable for him as a public maintenance in the Prytaneum. It is a much more suitable reward for him than for any of you who has won a victory at the Olympic games with his horse or his chariots. Such a man only makes you seem happy, but I make you really happy; and he is not in want, and I am. So if I am to propose the penalty which I really deserve, I propose this — a public maintenance in the Prytaneum.

Perhaps you think me stubborn and arrogant in what I am saying now, as in what I said about the entreaties and tears. It is not so, Athenians; it is rather that I am convinced that I never wronged any man intentionally, though I cannot persuade you of that, for we have discussed together only a little time. If there were a law at Athens, as there is elsewhere, not to finish a trial of life and death in a single day, I think that I could have persuaded you; but now it is not easy in so short a time to clear myself of great prejudices. But when I am persuaded that I have never wronged any man, I shall certainly not wrong myself, or admit that I deserve to suffer any evil, or propose any evil for myself as a penalty. Why should I? Lest I should suffer the penalty which Meletus proposes when I say that I do not know whether it is a good or an evil? Shall I choose instead of it something which I know to be an evil, and propose that as a penalty? Shall I propose imprisonment? And why should I pass the rest of my days in prison, the slave of successive officials? Or shall I propose a fine, with imprisonment until it is paid? I have told you why I will not do that. I should have to remain in prison, for I have no

money to pay a fine with. Shall I then propose exile? Perhaps you would agree to that. Life would indeed be very dear to me if I were unreasonable enough to expect that strangers would cheerfully tolerate my discussions and reasonings when you who are my fellow citizens cannot endure them, and have found them so irksome and odious to you that you are seeking now to be relieved of them. No, indeed, Athenians, that is not likely. A fine life I should lead for an old man if I were to withdraw from Athens and pass the rest of my days in wandering from city to city, and continually being expelled. For I know very well that the young men will listen to me wherever I go, as they do here; and if I drive them away, they will persuade their elders to expel me; and if I do not drive them away, their fathers and kinsmen will expel me for their sakes.

Perhaps someone will say, "Why cannot you withdraw from Athens, Socrates, and hold your peace?" It is the most difficult thing in the world to make you understand why I cannot do that. If I say that I cannot hold my peace because that would be to disobey the god, you will think that I am not in earnest and will not believe me. And if I tell you that no better thing can happen to a man than to discuss virtue every day and the other matters about which you have heard me arguing and examining myself and others, and that an unexamined life is not worth living, then you will believe me still less. But that is so, my friends, though it is not easy to persuade you. And, what is more, I am not accustomed to think that I deserve any punishment. If I had been rich, I would have proposed as large a fine as I could pay: that would have done me no harm. But I am not rich enough to pay a fine unless you are willing to fix it at a sum within my means. Perhaps I could pay you a mina, so I propose that. Plato here, Athenians, and Crito, and Critobulus, and Apollodorus bid me propose thirty minae, and they will be sureties for me. So I propose thirty minae. They will be sufficient sureties to you for the money.

(He is condemned to death.)

You have not gained very much time, Athenians, and, as the price of it, you will have an evil name for all who wish to revile the state, and they will say that you put Socrates, a wise man, to death. For they will certainly call me wise, whether I am wise or not, when they want to reproach you. If you would have waited for a little while, your wishes would have been fulfilled in the course of nature; for you see that I am an old man, far advanced in years, and near to death. I am saying this not to all of you, only to those who have voted for my death. And to them I have something else to say. Perhaps, my friends, you think that I have been convicted because I was wanting in the arguments by which I could have persuaded you to acquit me, if, that is, I had thought it right to do or to say anything to escape punishment. It is not so. I have been convicted because I was wanting, not in arguments, but in impudence and shamelessness—because I would not plead before you as you would have liked to hear me plead, or appeal to you with weeping and wailing, or say and do many other things which I maintain are unworthy of me, but which you have been accustomed to from other men. But when I was defending myself, I thought that I ought not to do anything unworthy of a free man because of the danger which I ran, and I have not changed my mind now. I would very much rather defend myself as I did, and die, than as you would have had me do, and live. Both in a lawsuit and in war, there are some things which neither I nor any other man may do in order to escape from death. In battle, a man often sees that he may at least escape from death by throwing down his arms and falling on his knees before the pursuer to beg for his life. And there are many other ways of avoiding death in every danger if a man is willing to say and to do anything. But, my friends, I think that it is a much harder thing to escape from wickedness than from death, for wickedness is swifter than death. And now I, who am old and slow, have been overtaken by the slower pursuer; and my accusers, who are clever and swift, have been overtaken by the swifter pursuer—wickedness. And now I shall go away, sentenced by you to death; and they will go away, sentenced by truth to wickedness and injustice. And I abide by this award as well as they. Perhaps it was right for these things to be so; and I think that they are fairly measured.

And now I wish to prophesy to you, Athenians, who have condemned me. For I am going to die, and that is the time when men have most prophetic power. And I prophesy to you who have sentenced me to death that a far more severe punishment than you have inflicted on me will surely overtake you as soon as I am dead. You have done this thing, thinking that you will be relieved from having to give an account of your lives. But I say that the result will be very different. There will be more men who will call you to account, whom I have held back, though you did not recognize it. And they will be harsher toward you than I have been, for they will be younger, and you will be more indignant with them. For if you think that you will restrain men from reproaching you for not living as you should, by putting them to death, you are very much mistaken. That way of escape is neither possible nor honorable. It is much more honorable and much easier not to suppress others, but to make yourselves as good as you can. This is my parting prophecy to you who have condemned me.

With you who have acquitted me I should like to discuss this thing that has happened, while the authorities are busy, and before I go to the place where I have to die. So, remain with me until I go: there is no reason why we should not talk with each other while it is possible. I wish to explain to you, as my friends, the meaning of what has happened to me. A wonderful thing has happened to me, judges—for you I am right in calling judges. The prophetic sign has been constantly with me all through my life till now, opposing me in quite small matters if I were not going to act rightly. And now you yourselves see what has happened to me—a thing which might be thought, and which is sometimes actually reckoned, the supreme evil. But the divine sign did not oppose me when I was leaving my house in the morning, nor when I was coming up here to the court, nor at any point in my speech when I was going to say anything; though at other times it has often stopped me in the very act of speaking. But now, in this matter, it has never once opposed me, either in my words or my actions. I will tell you what I believe to be the reason. This thing that has come upon me must be a good; and those of us who think that death is an evil must needs be mistaken. I have a clear proof that that is so; for my accustomed sign would certainly have opposed me if I had not been going to meet with something good.

And if we reflect in another way, we shall see that we may well hope that death is a good. For the state of death is one of two things: either the dead man wholly ceases to be and loses all consciousness or as we are told, it is a change and a migration of the soul to another place. And if death is the absence of all consciousness, and like the sleep of one whose slumbers are unbroken by any dreams, it will be a wonderful gain. For if a man had to select that night in which he slept so soundly that he did not even dream, and had to compare with it all the other nights and days of his life, and then had to say how many days and nights in his life he had spent better and more pleasantly than this night, I think that a private person, nay, even the great King himself, would find them easy to count, compared with the others. If that is the nature of death, I for one count it a gain. For then it appears that all time is nothing more than a single night. But if death is a journey to another place, and what we are told is true — that there are all who have died — what good could be greater than this, my judges? Would a journey not be worth taking, at the end of which, in the other world, we should be released from the self-styled judges here and should find the true judges who are said to sit in judgment below, such as Minos and Rhadamanthus and Aeacus and Triptolemus, and the other demigods who were just in their own lives? Or what would you not give to discuss with Orpheus and Musaeus and Hesiod and Homer? I am willing to die many times if this be true. And for my own part I should find it wonderful to meet there Palamedes, and Ajax, the son of Telamon, and the other men of old who have died through an unjust judgment, and in comparing my experiences with theirs. That I think would be no small pleasure. And, above all, I could spend my time in examining those who are there, as I examine men here, and in finding out which of them is wise, and which of them thinks himself wise when he is not wise. What would we not give, my judges, to be able to examine the leader of the great expedition against Troy, or Odysseus, or Sisyphus, or countless other men and women whom we could name? It would be an infinite happiness to discuss with them and to live with them and to examine them. Assuredly there they do not put men to death for doing that. For besides the other ways in which they are happier than we are, they are immortal, at least if what we are told is true.

And you, too, judges, must face death hopefully, and believe this is a truth that no evil can happen to a good man, either in life or after death. His fortunes are not neglected by the gods; and what has happened to me today has not happened by chance. I am persuaded that it was better for me to die now, and to be released from trouble; and that was the reason why the sign never turned me back. And so I am not at all angry with my accusers or with those who have condemned me to die. Yet it was not with this in mind that they accused me and condemned me, but meaning to do me an injury. So far I may blame them.

Yet I have one request to make of them. When my sons grow up, punish them, my friends, and harass them in the same way that I have harassed you, if they seem to you to care for riches or for any other thing more than virtue; and if they think that they are something when they are really nothing, reproach them, as I have reproached you, for not caring for what they should, and for thinking that they are great men when really they are worthless. And if you will do this, I myself and my sons will have received justice from you.

But now the time has come, and we must go away — I to die, and you to live. Whether life or death is better is known to God, and to God only.

From *Crito*

[THE CONVERSATION is taking place at Socrates' jail cell.]

Soc.: Then, my good friend, we must not think so much of what the many will say of us; we must think of what the one man who understands justice and injustice, and of what truth herself, will say of us. And so you are mistaken, to begin with, when you invite us to regard the opinion of the multitude concerning the just and the honorable and the good, and their opposites. But, it may be said, the multitude can put us to death?

Crito: Yes, that is evident. That may be said, Socrates.

Soc.: True. But, my good friend, to me it appears that the conclusion which we have just reached is the same as our conclusion of former times. Now consider whether we still hold to the belief that we should set the highest value, not on living, but on living well?

Crito: Yes, we do.

Soc.: And living well and honorably and justly mean the same thing: do we hold to that or not?

Crito: We do.

Soc.: Then, starting from these premises, we have to consider whether it is just or not for me to try to escape from prison, without the consent of the Athenians. If we find that it is just, we will try; if not, we will give up the idea. . . . Ought a man to carry out his just agreements, or may he shuffle out of them?

Crito: He ought to carry them out.

Soc.: Then consider. If I escape without the state's consent, shall I be injuring those whom I ought least to injure, or not? Shall I be abiding by my just agreements or not?

Crito: I cannot answer your question, Socrates. I do not understand it.

Soc.: Consider it in this way. Suppose the laws and the commonwealth were to come and appear to me as I was preparing to run away (if that is the right phrase to describe my escape) and were to ask, "Tell us, Socrates, what have you in your mind to do? What do you mean by trying to escape but to destroy us, the laws and the whole state, so far as you are able? Do you think that a state can exist and not be overthrown, in which the decisions of law are of no force, and are disregarded and undermined by private individuals?" . . . Shall I reply, "But the state has injured me by judging my case unjustly"? Shall we say that?

Crito: Certainly we will, Socrates.

Soc.: And suppose the laws were to reply, "Was that our agreement? Or was it that you would abide by whatever judgments the state should pronounce?" . . . What answer shall we make, Crito? Shall we say that the laws speak the truth, or not?

Crito: I think that they do.

Soc.: "Then consider, Socrates," perhaps they would say, "if we are right in saying that by attempting to escape you are attempting an injustice. We brought you into the world, we raised you, we educated you, we gave you and every other citizen a share of all the good things we could. Yet we proclaim that if any man of the Athenians is dissatisfied with us, he may take his goods and go away wherever he pleases; we give that privilege to every man who chooses to avail himself of it, so soon as he has reached manhood, and sees us, the laws, and the administration of our state. No one of us stands in his way or forbids him to take his goods and go wherever he likes, whether it be to an Athenian colony or to any foreign country, if he is dissatisfied with us and with the state. But we say that every man of you who remains here, seeing how we administer justice, and how we govern the state in other matters, has agreed, by the very fact of remaining here, to do whatsoever we tell him. And, we say, he who disobeys us acts unjustly on three counts: he disobeys us who are his parents, and he disobeys us who reared him, and he disobeys us after he has agreed to obey us, without persuading us that we are wrong.

". . . you might at your trial have offered to go into exile. At that time you could have done with the state's consent what you are trying now to do without it. But then you gloried in being willing to die. You said that you preferred death to exile. And now you do not honor those words: you do not respect us, the laws, for you are trying to destroy us; and you are acting just as a miserable slave would act, trying to run away, and breaking the contracts and agreement which you made to live as our citizen. First, therefore, answer this question. Are we right, or are we wrong, in saying that you have agreed not in mere words, but in your actions, to live under our government?" What are we to say, Crito? Must we not admit that it is true?

Crito: We must, Socrates.

Soc.: Then they would say, "Are you not breaking your contracts and agreements with us? And you were not led to make them by force or by fraud. You did not have to make up your mind in a hurry. You had seventy years in which you might have gone away if you had been dissatisfied with us, or if the agreement had seemed to you unjust. But you preferred neither Sparta nor Crete, though you are fond of saying that they are well governed, nor any other state, either of the Greeks or the Barbarians. . . . Clearly you, far more than other Athenians, were satisfied with the state, and also with us who are its laws; for who would be satisfied with a state which had no laws? And now will you not abide by your agreement? If you take our advice, you will, Socrates; then you will not make yourself ridiculous by going away from Athens.

"Reflect now. What good will you do yourself or your friends by thus transgressing and breaking your agreement? It is tolerably certain that they, on their part, will at least run the risk of exile, and of losing their civil rights, or of forfeiting their property. You yourself might go to one of the neighboring states, to Thebes or to Megara, for instance — for both of them are well governed — but, Socrates, you will come as an enemy to these governments, and all who care for their city will look askance at you, and think that you are a subverter of law. You will confirm the judges in their opinion, and make it seem that their verdict was a just one. For a man who is a subverter of law may well be supposed to be a corrupter of the young and thoughtless. Then will you avoid well-governed states and civilized men? Will life be worth having, if you do? Will you associate with such men, and converse without shame — about what, Socrates? About the things which you talk of here? Will you tell them that excellence and justice and institutions and law are the most valuable things that men can have? And do you not think that that will be a disgraceful thing for Socrates?"

Crito: I have nothing more to say, Socrates.

Soc.: Then let it be, Crito, and let us do as I say, since the god is our guide.

But I suppose that I may, and must, pray to the gods that my journey hence may be prosperous. That is my prayer; may it be granted.

Further Questions

1. How does Socrates, in his trial, use irony to attack those who profess to know more than they actually know?
2. Socrates said, "The unexamined life is not worth living." What do you suppose he meant by this?
3. Do you think you would like to have Socrates as a friend? A teacher? A brother? Why?
4. Do you agree with Socrates' view that it is better to speak the truth — no matter how disturbing — rather than what is considered proper or pleasing? What is the main value of such an approach to life? What is the main drawback?

Further Readings

Edwards, Paul. Editor-in-chief. *The Encyclopedia of Philosophy.* New York: Macmillan, 1967. An eight-volume collection of articles on all major philosophers and philosophical issues.

Russell, Bertrand. *History of Western Philosophy.* New York: Simon & Schuster, 1945. One of the most readable and concise histories of Western philosophy.

Obedience to Authority   2

STANLEY MILGRAM

Born in New York City in 1933, Stanley Milgram was educated at Queens College and at Harvard, where he received his Ph.D. As a social psychologist, he did research at Yale University where, from 1960 to 1963, he performed one of the most shocking and important experiments ever made on human behavior. His own account of it is reprinted here. His experiments revealed the extent to which ordinary people like you are ready to torture and kill other innocent people simply out of obedience to authority.

Reading Questions

1. If someone in authority asked you to hurt and perhaps even kill an innocent human being, would you obey? If you are like most people, you probably *think* you wouldn't. But if you are like most people, you probably *would*. Why?
2. Milgram is concerned with "the extreme willingness of adults to go to almost any lengths on the command of an authority." What is his evidence? How do you account for this behavior?
3. What are the "binding factors" that make people obedient?
4. What does Milgram mean by "counteranthropomorphic"?
5. What does Milgram say is the most fundamental lesson of his study?
6. Does Milgram think that the problem of obedience is just psychological? What else does he think is involved?

OBEDIENCE IS AS BASIC AN ELEMENT in the structure of social life as one can point to. Some system of authority is a requirement of all communal living, and it is only the man dwelling in isolation who is not forced to respond, through defiance or submission, to the commands of others. Obedience, as a determinant of behavior, is of particular relevance to our time. It has been reliably established that from 1933 to 1945 millions of innocent people were systematically slaughtered on command. Gas chambers were built, death camps were guarded, daily quotas of corpses were produced with the same efficiency as the manufacture of appliances. These inhumane policies may have originated in the mind of a single person, but they could only have been carried out on a massive scale if a very large number of people obeyed orders.

Obedience is the psychological mechanism that links individual action to political purpose. It is the dispositional cement that binds men to systems of authority. Facts of recent history and observation in daily life suggest that for many people obedience may be a deeply ingrained behavior tendency, indeed, a prepotent impulse overriding training in ethics, sympathy, and moral conduct. C. P. Snow (1961) points to its importance when he writes:

> When you think of the long and gloomy history of man, you will find more hideous crimes have been committed in the name of obedience than have ever been committed in the name of rebellion. If you doubt that, read William Shirer's

'Rise and Fall of the Third Reich.' The German Officer Corps were brought up in the most rigorous code of obedience . . . in the name of obedience they were party to, and assisted in, the most wicked large scale actions in the history of the world. (p. 24)

The Nazi extermination of European Jews is the most extreme instance of abhorrent immoral acts carried out by thousands of people in the name of obedience. Yet in lesser degree this type of thing is constantly recurring: ordinary citizens are ordered to destroy other people, and they do so because they consider it their duty to obey orders. Thus, obedience to authority, long praised as a virtue, takes on a new aspect when it serves a malevolent cause; far from appearing as a virtue, it is transformed into a heinous sin. Or is it?

The moral question of whether one should obey when commands conflict with conscience was argued by Plato, dramatized in *Antigone,* and treated to philosophic analysis in every historical epoch. Conservative philosophers argue that the very fabric of society is threatened by disobedience, and even when the act prescribed by an authority is an evil one, it is better to carry out the act than to wrench at the structure of authority. Hobbes stated further that an act so executed is in no sense the responsibility of the person who carries it out but only of the authority that orders it. But humanists argue for the primacy of individual conscience in such matters, insisting that the moral judgments of the individual must override authority when the two are in conflict.

The legal and philosophic aspects of obedience are of enormous import, but an empirically grounded scientist eventually comes to the point where he wishes to move from abstract discourse to the careful observation of concrete instances. In order to take a close look at the act of obeying, I set up a simple experiment at Yale University. Eventually, the experiment was to involve more than a thousand participants and would be repeated at several universities, but at the beginning, the conception was simple. A person comes to a psychological laboratory and is told to carry out a series of acts that come increasingly into conflict with conscience. The main question is how far the participant will comply with the experimenter's instructions before refusing to carry out the actions required of them.

But the reader needs to know a little more detail about the experiment. Two people come to a psychology laboratory to take part in a study of memory and learning. One of them is designated as a "teacher" and the other a "learner." The experimenter explains that the study is concerned with the effects of punishment on learning. The learner is conducted into a room, seated in a chair, his arms strapped to prevent excessive movement, and an electrode attached to his wrist. He is told that he is to learn a list of word pairs; whenever he makes an error, he will receive electric shocks of increasing intensity.

The real focus of the experiment is the teacher. After watching the learner being strapped into place, he is taken into the main experimental room and seated before an impressive shock generator. Its main feature is a horizontal line of thirty switches, ranging from 15 volts to 450 volts, in 15-volt increments. There are also verbal designations which range from SLIGHT SHOCK to DANGER—SEVERE SHOCK. The teacher is told that he is to administer the learning test to the man in the other room. When the learner responds correctly, the teacher moves on to the next item; when the other man gives an incorrect answer, the teacher is to give him an electric shock. He is to start at the lowest shock level (15 volts) and to increase the level each time the man makes an error, going through 30 volts, 45 volts, and so on.

The "teacher" is a genuinely naïve subject who has come to the laboratory to participate in an experiment. The learner, or victim, is an actor who actually receives no shock at all. The point of the experiment is to see how far a person will proceed in a concrete and measurable situation in which he is ordered to inflict increasing pain on a protesting victim. At what point will the subject refuse to obey the experimenter?

Conflict arises when the man receiving the shock begins to indicate that he is experiencing discomfort. At 75 volts, the "learner" grunts. At 120 volts he complains verbally; at 150 he demands to be released from the experiment. His protests continue as the shocks escalate, growing increasingly vehement and emotional. At 285 volts his response can only be described as an agonized scream.

Observers of the experiment agree that its gripping quality is somewhat obscured in print. For the subject, the situation is not a game; conflict is intense and obvious. On one hand, the manifest suffering of the learner presses him to quit. On the other, the experimenter, a legitimate authority to whom the subject feels some commitment, enjoins him to continue. Each time the subject hesitates to administer shock, the experimenter orders him to continue. To extricate himself from the situation, the subject must make a clear break with authority. The aim of this investigation was to find when and how people would defy authority in the face of a clear moral imperative.

There are, of course, enormous differences between carrying out the orders of a commanding officer during times of war and carrying out the orders of an experimenter. Yet the essence of certain relationships remains, for one may ask in a general way: How does a man behave when he is told by a legitimate authority to act against a third individual? If anything, we may expect the experimenter's power to be considerably less than that of the general, since he has no power to enforce his imperatives, and participation in a psychological experiment scarcely evokes the sense of urgency and dedication engendered by participation in war. Despite these limitations, I thought it worthwhile to start careful observation of obedience even in this modest situation, in the hope that it would stimulate insights and yield general propositions applicable to a variety of circumstances.

A reader's initial reaction to the experiment may be to wonder why anyone in his right mind would administer even the first shocks. Would he not simply refuse and walk out of the laboratory? But the fact is that no one ever does. Since the subject has come to the laboratory to aid the experimenter, he is quite willing to start off with the procedure. There is nothing very extraordinary in this, particularly since the person who is to receive the shocks seems initially cooperative, if somewhat apprehensive. What is surprising is how far ordinary individuals will go in complying with the experimenter's instructions. Indeed, the results of the experiment are both surprising and dismaying. Despite the fact that many subjects experience stress, despite the fact that many protest to the experimenter, a substantial proportion continue to the last shock on the generator.

Many subjects will obey the experimenter no matter how vehement the pleading of the person being shocked, no matter how painful the shocks seem to be, and no matter how much the victim pleads to be let out. This was seen time and again in our studies and has been observed in several universities where the experiment was repeated. It is the extreme willingness of adults to go to almost any lengths on the command of an authority that constitutes the chief finding of the study and the fact most urgently demanding explanation.

A commonly offered explanation is that those who shocked the victim at the most severe level were monsters, the sadistic fringe of society. But if one considers that almost two-thirds of the participants fall into the category of "obedient" subjects, and that they represented ordinary people drawn from working, managerial, and professional classes, the argument becomes very shaky. Indeed, it is highly reminiscent of the issue that arose in connection with Hannah Arendt's 1963 book, *Eichmann in Jerusalem*. Arendt contended that the prosecution's effort to depict Eichmann as a sadistic monster was fundamentally wrong, that he came closer to being an uninspired bureaucrat who simply sat at his desk and did his job. For asserting these views, Arendt became the object of considerable scorn, even calumny. Somehow, it was felt that the monstrous deeds carried out by Eichmann required a brutal, twisted, and sadistic personality, evil incarnate. After witnessing hundreds of ordinary people submit to the authority in our own experiments,

I must conclude that Arendt's conception of the *banality of evil* comes closer to the truth than one might dare imagine. The ordinary person who shocked the victim did so out of a sense of obligation—a conception of his duties as a subject—and not from any peculiarly aggressive tendencies.

This is, perhaps, the most fundamental lesson of our study: ordinary people, simply doing their jobs, and without any particular hostility on their part, can become agents in a terrible destructive process. Moreover, even when the destructive effects of their work become patently clear, and they are asked to carry out actions incompatible with fundamental standards of morality, relatively few people have the resources needed to resist authority. A variety of inhibitions against disobeying authority come into play and successfully keep the person in his place.

Sitting back in one's armchair, it is easy to condemn the actions of the obedient subjects. But those who condemn the subjects measure them against the standard of their own ability to formulate high-minded moral prescriptions. That is hardly a fair standard. Many of the subjects, at the level of stated opinion, feel quite as strongly as any of us about the moral requirement of refraining from action against a helpless victim. They, too, in general terms know what ought to be done and can state their values when the occasion arises. This has little, if anything, to do with their actual behavior under the pressure of circumstances.

If people are asked to render a moral judgment on what constitutes appropriate behavior in this situation, they unfailingly see disobedience as proper. But values are not the only forces at work in an actual, ongoing situation. They are but one narrow band of causes in the total spectrum of forces impinging on a person. Many people were unable to realize their values in action and found themselves continuing in the experiment even though they disagreed with what they were doing.

The force exerted by the moral sense of the individual is less effective than social myth would have us believe. Though such proscriptions as "Thou shalt not kill" occupy a pre-eminent place in the moral order, they do not occupy a correspondingly intractable position in human psychic structure. A few changes in newspaper headlines, a call from the draft board, orders from a man with epaulets, and men are led to kill with little difficulty. Even the forces mustered in a psychology experiment will go a long way toward removing the individual from moral controls. Moral factors can be shunted aside with relative ease by a calculated restructuring of the informational and social field.

What, then, keeps the person obeying the experimenter? First, there is a set of "binding factors" that lock the subject into the situation. They include such factors as politeness on his part, his desire to uphold his initial promise of aid to the experimenter, and the awkwardness of withdrawal. Second, a number of adjustments in the subject's thinking occur that undermine his resolve to break with the authority. The adjustments help the subject maintain his relationship with the experimenter, while at the same time reducing the strain brought about by the experimental conflict. They are typical of thinking that comes about in obedient persons when they are instructed by authority to act against helpless individuals.

One such mechanism is the tendency of the individual to become so absorbed in the narrow technical aspects of the task that he loses sight of its broader consequences. The film *Dr. Strangelove* brilliantly satirized the absorption of a bomber crew in the exacting technical procedure of dropping nuclear weapons on a country. Similarly, in this experiment, subjects become immersed in the procedures, reading the word pairs with exquisite articulation and pressing the switches with great care. They want to put on a competent performance, but they show an accompanying narrowing of moral concern. The subject entrusts the broader tasks of setting goals and assessing morality to the experimental authority he is serving.

The most common adjustment of thought in the obedient subject is for him to see himself as not responsible for his own actions. He divests himself of responsibility by attributing all initiative to the experimenter, a legitimate authority. He sees himself not as a person acting in a morally accountable way but as the agent of external authority. In the postexperimental interview, when subjects were asked why they had gone on, a typical reply was: "I wouldn't have done it by myself. I was just doing what I was told." Unable to defy the authority of the experimenter, they attribute all responsibility to him. It is the old story of "just doing one's duty" that was heard time and time again in the defense statements of those accused at Nuremberg. But it

would be wrong to think of it as a thin alibi concocted for the occasion. Rather, it is a fundamental mode of thinking for a great many people once they are locked into a subordinate position in a structure of authority. The disappearance of a sense of responsibility is the most far-reaching consequence of submission to authority.

Although a person acting under authority performs actions that seem to violate standards of conscience, it would not be true to say that he loses his moral sense. Instead, it acquires a radically different focus. He does not respond with a moral sentiment to the actions he performs. Rather, his moral concern now shifts to a consideration of how well he is living up to the expectations that the authority has of him. In wartime, a soldier does not ask whether it is good or bad to bomb a hamlet; he does not experience shame or guilt in the destruction of a village: rather he feels pride or shame depending on how well he has performed the mission assigned to him.

Another psychological force at work in this situation may be termed "counteranthropomorphism." For decades psychologists have discussed the primitive tendency among men to attribute to inanimate objects and forces the qualities of the human species. A countervailing tendency, however, is that of attributing an impersonal quality to forces that are essentially human in origin and maintenance. Some people treat systems of human origin as if they existed above and beyond any human agent, beyond the control of whim or human feeling. The human element behind agencies and institutions is denied. Thus, when the experimenter says, "The experiment *requires* that you continue," the subject feels this to be an imperative that goes beyond any merely human command. He does not ask the seemingly obvious question, "Whose experiment? Why should the designer be served while the victim suffers?" The wishes of a man—the designer of the experiment—have become part of a schema which exerts on the subject's mind a force that transcends the personal. "It's *got* to go on. It's *got* to go on," repeated one subject. He failed to realize that a man like himself wanted it to go on. For him the human agent had faded from the picture, and "The Experiment" had acquired an impersonal momentum of its own.

No action of itself has an unchangeable psychological quality. Its meaning can be altered by

Morality, Obedience, and Religion

Patrick Nowell-Smith

It is this premise, that being moral consists in obedience to commands, that I deny. There is an argument, familiar to philosophers but of which the force is not always appreciated, which shows that this premise cannot be right. Suppose that I have satisfied myself that God has commanded me to do this or that thing—in itself a large supposition, but I will waive objections on this score in order to come quickly to the main point—it still makes *sense* for me to ask whether or not I *ought* to do it. God, let us say, is an omnipotent, omniscient creator of the universe. Such a creator might have evil intentions and might command me to do wrong; and if that were the case though it would be imprudent to disobey, it would not be wrong. There is nothing in the idea of an omnipotent, omniscient creator which, by itself, entails his goodness or his right to command, unless we are prepared to assent to Hobbes' phrase, "God, who by right, *that is by irresistible power,* commandeth all things." Unless we accept Hobbes' consistent but repugnant equation of God's right with his might, we must be persuaded *independently* of his goodness before we admit his right to command. We must judge for ourselves whether the Bible is the inspired word of a just and benevolent God or a curious amalgam of profound wisdom and gross superstition. To judge this is to make a moral decision, so that in the end, so far from morality being based on religion, religion is based on morality.

From "Morality: Religious and Secular" (1961).

placing it in particular contexts. An American newspaper recently quoted a pilot who conceded that Americans were bombing Vietnamese men, women, and children but felt that the bombing was for a "noble cause" and thus was justified. Similarly, most subjects in the experiment see their behavior in a larger context that is benevolent and useful to society—the pursuit of scientific truth. The psychological laboratory has a strong claim to legitimacy and evokes trust and confidence in those who come to perform there. An action such as shocking a victim, which in isolation appears evil, acquires a totally different meaning when placed in this setting. But allowing an act to be dominated by its context, while neglecting its human consequences, can be dangerous in the extreme.

At least one essential feature of the situation in Germany was not studied here—namely, the intense devaluation of the victim prior to action against him. For a decade and more, vehement anti-Jewish propaganda systematically prepared the German population to accept the destruction of the Jews. Step by step the Jews were excluded from the category of citizen and national, and finally were denied the status of human beings. Systematic devaluation of the victim provides a measure of psychological justification for brutal treatment of the victim and has been the constant accompaniment of massacres, pogroms, and wars. In all likelihood, our subjects would have experienced greater ease in shocking the victim had he been convincingly portrayed as a brutal criminal or a pervert.

Of considerable interest, however, is the fact that many subjects harshly devalue the victim *as a consequence* of acting against him. Such comments as, "He was so stupid and stubborn he deserved to get shocked," were common. Once having acted against the victim, these subjects found it necessary to view him as an unworthy individual, whose punishment was made inevitable by his own deficiencies of intellect and character.

Many of the people studied in the experiment were in some sense against what they did to the learner, and many protested even while they obeyed. But between thoughts, words, and the critical step of disobeying a malevolent authority lies another ingredient, the capacity for transforming beliefs and values into action. Some subjects were totally convinced of the wrongness of what they were doing but could not bring themselves to make an open break with authority. Some derived satisfaction from their thoughts and felt that—within themselves, at least—they had been on the side of the angels. What they failed to realize is that subjective feelings are largely irrelevant to the moral issue at hand so long as they are not transformed into action. Political control is effected through action. The attitudes of the guards at a concentration camp are of no consequence when in fact they are allowing the slaughter of innocent men to take place before them. Similarly, so-called "intellectual resistance" in occupied Europe—in which persons by a twist of thought felt that they had defied the invader—was merely indulgence in a consoling psychological mechanism. Tyrannies are perpetuated by diffident men who do not possess the courage to act out their beliefs. Time and again in the experiment people disvalued what they were doing but could not muster the inner resources to translate their values into action.

A variation of the basic experiment depicts a dilemma more common than the one outlined above: the subject was not ordered to push the trigger that shocked the victim, but merely to perform a subsidiary act (administering the word-pair test) before another subject actually delivered the shock. In this situation, 37 of 40 adults from the New Haven area continued to the highest shock level on the generator. Predictably, subjects excused their behavior by saying that the responsibility belonged to the man who actually pulled the switch. This may illustrate a dangerously typical situation in complex society: it is psychologically easy to ignore responsibility when one is only an intermediate link in a chain of evil action but is far from the final consequences of the action. Even Eichmann was sickened when he toured the concentration camps, but to participate in mass murder he had only to sit at a desk and shuffle papers. At the same time the man in the camp who actually dropped Cyclon-B into the gas chambers was able to justify *his* behavior on the grounds that he was only following orders from above. Thus there is a fragmentation of the total human act; no one man decides to carry out the evil act and is confronted with its consequences. The person who assumes full responsibility for the act has evaporated. Perhaps this is the most common characteristic of socially organized evil in modern society.

The problem of obedience, therefore, is not wholly psychological. The form and shape of society and the way it is developing have much to do with it. There was a time, perhaps, when men were able to give a fully human response to any situation because they were fully absorbed in it as human beings. But as soon as there was a division of labor among men, things changed. Beyond a certain point, the breaking up of society into people carrying out narrow and very special jobs takes away from the human quality of work and life. A person does not get to see the whole situation but only a small part of it, and is thus unable to act without some kind of over-all direction. He yields to authority but in doing so is alienated from his own actions.

George Orwell caught the essence of the situation when he wrote:

> As I write, civilized human beings are flying overhead, trying to kill me. They do not feel any enmity against me as an individual, nor I against them. They are only "doing their duty," as the saying goes. Most of them, I have no doubt, are kind-hearted law abiding men who would never dream of committing murder in private life. On the other hand, if one of them succeeds in blowing me to pieces with a well-placed bomb, he will never sleep any the worse for it.

Further Questions

1. What light do you think Milgram's work sheds on the psychological forces at work behind the Nazi Holocaust? The slaughter of Native Americans? War in general?
2. Common sense would suggest that the obedient subjects in Milgram's experiment lost their "moral sense." Is this in fact what happened?
3. An American soldier tells why he and his buddies massacred Vietnamese men, women, and children at My Lai: "Because I felt like I was ordered to do it, and . . . at the time I felt like

I was doing the right thing. . . . They were begging and saying, 'No, no.' . . . the mothers . . . hugging their children . . . we kept on firing. . . ." (*New York Times*, November 25, 1969.) How does *whose side you're on* affect *how you feel and react*?

4. If obedience to authority is the problem, what do you suppose is the solution? Without obedience wouldn't there be chaos, anarchy? How do you know when to obey?

5. Make a list of the major sources of authority in your life. What kind of track record do these sources have?

6. You've probably seen and read many things about the Nazi Holocaust and have been exposed to lots of "theories" about how and why such awful things happen. What are they? Have you ever heard Milgram's work brought up in this context? If not, why do you suppose Milgram is ignored, given that his work seems so relevant?

Further Readings

Comfort, A. *Authority and Delinquency in the Modern State: A Criminological Approach to the Problem of Power*. London: Routledge & Kegan Paul, 1950. Highly influential to Milgram's work.

Milgram, Stanley. *Obedience to Authority*. New York: Harper & Row, 1974. The classic study from which the preceding selection is an excerpt. The CBS interview between Mike Wallace and an American soldier who participated in the My Lai massacre, from which the quotation in question 3 is taken, appears in the epilogue. For a stunning film version of the experiments, see *Obedience*, distributed by the New York University Film Library, 1965, available in many university libraries.

3   The Function of Education

JIDDU KRISHNAMURTI

Jiddu Krishnamurti was born to a poor Brahmin family in the south of India in 1895. By the time he died in California in 1986, he had become a world-renowned philosopher and teacher. He was the author of more than forty books, most of them in the form of dialogues and lectures. He traveled all over the world and talked to millions of people. Aldous Huxley, Anne Morrow Lindbergh, and Bertrand Russell studied his philosophy; Huxley said listening to Krishnamurti was as good as "a discourse by the Buddha." George Bernard Shaw once described him as the most beautiful person he had ever met. The actor John Barrymore once asked him to play Buddha in a film, but Krishnamurti refused. Greta Garbo, after hearing him speak, gave up her career in the movies.

Krishnamurti taught that to achieve freedom, we must become aware of the psychological conditioning that prevents us from seeing what is true and actual. According to the British theoretical physicist David Bohm, who participated in many discussions with Krishnamurti, Krishnamurti's teaching was rooted "in the fact that we are ignorant of our own processes of thought." Krishnamurti himself insisted that he was not an authority figure or guru; he spoke against all spiritual authorities and organizations. "Truth is a pathless land," he once said. "You cannot approach it by any religion, any sect. . . . You are accustomed to being told how far you have advanced, what your spiritual state is. How childish!" His lifelong purpose, he said, was "to set people absolutely, unconditionally free."

Reading Questions

1. Is the purpose of education merely to help you conform to the patterns of the accepted social order? Or, as Krishnamurti claims, should the function of education be to help you live freely and without fear? Why?
2. What does fear have to do with learning and intelligence?
3. Why should we be in revolt? What should we be in revolt against?
4. What is the greatest obstacle to learning? What role does freedom play in learning? What does revolt have to do with freedom? What is the connection between freedom and intelligence?

I WONDER IF WE HAVE EVER ASKED ourselves what education means. Why do we go to school, why do we learn various subjects, why do we pass examinations and compete with each other for better grades? What does this so-called education mean, and what is it all about? This is really a very important question, not only for the students, but also for the parents, for the teachers, and for everyone who loves this earth. Why do we go through the struggle to be educated? Is it merely in order to pass some examinations and get a job? Or is it the function of education to prepare us while we are young to understand the whole process of life? Having a job and earning one's livelihood is necessary—but is that all? Are we being educated only for that? Surely, life is not merely a job, an occupation; life is something extraordinarily wide and profound, it is a great mystery, a vast realm in which we function as human beings. If we merely prepare ourselves to earn a livelihood, we shall miss the whole point of life; and to understand life is much more important than merely to prepare for examinations and become very proficient in mathematics, physics, or what you will.

So, whether we are teachers or students, is it not important to ask ourselves why we are educating or being educated? And what does life mean? Is not life an extraordinary thing? The birds, the flowers, the flourishing trees, the heavens, the stars, the rivers and the fish therein—all this is life. Life is the poor and the rich; life is the constant battle between groups, races and nations; life is meditation; life is what we call religion, and it is also the subtle, hidden things of the mind—the envies, the ambitions, the passions, the fears, fulfilments and anxieties. All this and much more is life. But we generally prepare ourselves to understand only one small corner of it. We pass certain examinations, find a job, get married, have children, and then become more and more like machines. We remain fearful, anxious, frightened of life. So, is it the function of education to help us understand the whole process of life, or is it merely to prepare us for a vocation, for the best job we can get?

What is going to happen to all of us when we grow to be men and women? Have you ever asked yourselves what you are going to do when you grow up? In all likelihood you will get married, and before you know where you are you will be mothers and fathers; and you will then be tied to a job, or to the kitchen, in which you will gradually wither away. Is that all that *your* life is going to be? Have you ever asked yourselves this question? Should you not ask it? If your family is wealthy you may have a fairly good position already assured, your father may give you a comfortable job, or you may get richly married; but there also you will decay, deteriorate. Do you see?

Surely, education has no meaning unless it helps you to understand the vast expanse of life with all its subtleties, with its extraordinary beauty, its sorrows and joys. You may earn degrees, you may have a series of letters after your name and land a very good job; but then what? What is the point of it all if in the process your mind becomes dull, weary, stupid? So, while you are young, must you not seek to find out what life is all about? And is it not the true function of education to cultivate in

---

FINAL WORDS

Chuang Tzu

The fish trap exists because of the fish; once you've gotten the fish, you can forget the trap. The rabbit snare exists because of the rabbit; once you've gotten the rabbit, you can forget the snare. Words exist because of meaning; once you've gotten the meaning, you can forget the words. Where can I find a man who has forgotten words so I can have a word with him?

From *Chuang Tzu,* trans. Burton Watson (Columbia Univ. Press).

---

you the intelligence which will try to find the answer to all these problems? Do you know what intelligence is? It is the capacity, surely, to think freely, without fear, without a formula, so that you begin to discover for yourself what is real, what is true; but if you are frightened you will never be intelligent. Any form of ambition, spiritual or mundane, breeds anxiety, fear; therefore ambition does not help to bring about a mind that is clear, simple, direct, and hence intelligent.

You know, it is really very important while you are young to live in an environment in which there is no fear. Most of us, as we grow older, become frightened; we are afraid of living, afraid of losing a job, afraid of tradition, afraid of what the neighbours, or what the wife or husband would say, afraid of death. Most of us have fear in one form or another; and where there is fear there is no intelligence. And is it not possible for all of us, while we are young, to be in an environment where there is no fear but rather an atmosphere of freedom — freedom, not just to do what we like, but to understand the whole process of living? Life is really very beautiful, it is not this ugly thing that we have made of it; and you can appreciate its richness, its depth, its extraordinary loveliness only when you revolt against everything — against organized religion, against tradition, against the present rotten society — so that you as a human being find out for yourself what is true. Not to imitate but to discover — *that* is education, is it not? It is very easy to conform to what your society or your parents and teachers tell you. That is a safe and easy way of existing; but that is not living, because in it there is fear, decay, death. To live is to find out for

yourself what is true, and you can do this only when there is freedom, when there is continuous revolution inwardly, within yourself.

But you are not encouraged to do this; no one tells you to question, to find out for yourself . . . , because if you were to rebel you would become a danger to all that is false. Your parents and society want you to live safely, and you also want to live safely. Living safely generally means living in imitation and therefore in fear. Surely, the function of education is to help each one of us to live freely and without fear, is it not? And to create an atmosphere in which there is no fear requires a great deal of thinking on your part as well as on the part of the teacher, the educator.

Do you know what this means — what an extraordinary thing it would be to create an atmosphere in which there is no fear? And we *must* create it, because we see that the world is caught up in endless wars; it is guided by politicians who are always seeking power; it is a world of lawyers, policemen and soldiers, of ambitious men and women all wanting position and all fighting each other to get it. Then there are the so-called saints, the religious *gurus* with their followers; they also want power, position, here or in the next life. It is a mad world, completely confused, in which the communist is fighting the capitalist, the socialist is resisting both, and everybody is against somebody, struggling to arrive at a safe place, a position of power or comfort. The world is torn by conflicting beliefs, by caste and class distinctions, by separative nationalities, by every form of stupidity and cruelty — and this is the world you are being educated to fit into. You are encouraged to fit into the framework of this disastrous society; your parents want you to do that, and you also want to fit in.

Now, is it the function of education merely to help you to conform to the pattern of this rotten social order, or is it to give you freedom—complete freedom to grow and create a different society, a new world? We want to have this freedom, not in the future, but now, otherwise we may all be destroyed. We must create immediately an atmosphere of freedom so that you can live and find out for yourselves what is true, so that you become intelligent, so that you are able to face the world and understand it, not just conform to it, so that inwardly, deeply, psychologically you are in constant revolt; because it is only those who are in constant revolt that discover what is true, not the man who conforms, who follows some tradition. . . .

. . . The question is: if all individuals were in revolt, would not the world be in chaos? But is the present society in such perfect order that chaos would result if everyone revolted against it? Is there not chaos *now?* Is everything beautiful, uncorrupted? Is everyone living happily, fully, richly? Is man not against man? Is there not ambition, ruthless competition? So the world is already in chaos, that is the first thing to realize. Don't take it for granted that this is an orderly society; don't mesmerize yourself with words. Whether, here in Europe, in America or Russia, the world is in a process of decay. If you see the decay, you have a challenge: you are challenged to find a way of solving this urgent problem. And how you respond to the challenge is important, is it not? If you respond as a Hindu or a Buddhist, a Christian or a communist, then your response is very limited—which is no response at all. You can respond fully, adequately only if there is no fear in you, only if you don't think as a Hindu, a communist or a capitalist, but as a total human being who is trying to solve this problem; and you cannot solve it unless you yourself are in revolt against the whole thing, against the ambitious acquisitiveness on which society is

based. When you yourself are not ambitious, not acquisitive, not clinging to your own security—only then can you respond to the challenge and create a new world. . . .

Do you know what it means to learn? When you are really learning you are learning throughout your life and there is no one special teacher to learn from. Then everything teaches you—a dead leaf, a bird in flight, a smell, a tear, the rich and the poor, those who are crying, the smile of a woman, the haughtiness of a man. You learn from everything, therefore there is no guide, no philosopher, no guru. Life itself is your teacher, and you are in a state of constant learning. . . .

Do you know what attention is? Let us find out. In a classroom, when you stare out of the window or pull somebody's hair, the teacher tells you to pay attention. Which means what? That you are not interested in what you are studying and so the teacher compels you to pay attention—which is not attention at all. Attention comes when you are deeply interested in something, for then you love to find out all about it; then your whole mind, your whole being is there. . . . When you are doing something with your whole being, not because you want to get somewhere, or have more profit, or greater results, but simply because you love to do it—in that there is no ambition, is there? In that there is no competition; you are not struggling with anyone for first place. And should not education help you to find out what you really love to do so that from the beginning to the end of your life you are working at something which you feel is worth while and which for you has deep significance? Otherwise, for the rest of your days, you will be miserable. Not knowing what you really want to do, your mind falls into a routine in which there is only boredom, decay and death. That is why it is very important to find out while you are young what it is you really *love* to do; and this is the only way to create a new society. . . .

Further Questions

1. You have by now had many years of education. Based on your experience, with which of Krishnamurti's points do you agree? With which ones do you disagree?
2. What role does fear play in your life? How much of what you do is based on fear? Why?
3. Education, according to Krishnamurti, should help you find out what you really love to do. Has your education done this? If not, why not?

4. What, thus far in your life, do you most love to do? Are you happy doing it? Why?
5. What prevents you from pursuing your deepest interests? How could you overcome these obstacles?

Further Readings

Krishnamurti, J. *Reflections on the Self.* Raymond Martin, ed., Chicago: Open Court, 1997.
Krishnamurti, J. *Think on These Things.* New York: Harper & Row, 1970. The preceding selection was taken from this widely available book. *The First and Last Freedom* (Harper & Row, 1975) contains a foreword by Aldous Huxley. *Freedom from the Known* (Harper & Row, 1969) and *Truth and Actuality* (Harper & Row, 1977) are both excellent. *The Wholeness of Life* (Harper & Row, 1969) contains a series of discussions with the noted theoretical physicist, David Bohm.

4   The Value of Philosophy

BERTRAND RUSSELL

Bertrand Russell (1872–1970) was one of the most important and prolific philosophers of this century. His early work focused on philosophy of logic and philosophy of mathematics and includes the highly influential *Principia Mathematica* (1910), which he wrote with Alfred North Whitehead. Russell then wrote on virtually every area of philosophy, including especially epistemology, or the theory of knowledge, on which he produced many books. The selection here is taken from two of these books.

Russell was a great philosophical stylist, for which he was awarded the Nobel Prize in Literature in 1950. A political activist, he was always at the center of controversy. He was once denied permission to teach a course on logic at City College of New York because of his liberal views on sex. He was jailed many times: during World War I for his pacifism and at the age of 89 for protesting against nuclear arms.

This selection is the final chapter of Russell's short, classic introduction to philosophy, *The Problems of Philosophy,* which, although written in 1912, is still often used as an introductory text in philosophy courses. In it, Russell claims that philosophy is valuable not because it produces goods or knowledge but, rather, because it can have a mind-expanding and liberating effect upon those who study it.

Reading Questions

1. How does Russell describe the practical person, and what are the practical person's prejudices from which we must free ourselves? How does he describe the instinctive person?
2. Explain how, in Russell's view, "the self" enlarges itself.
3. How is philosophical thinking related to the practical world of action and justice?
4. How does Russell's "instinctive man" view philosophical questioning or speculation? Do you know any such people? Why do they view philosophy that way? Were you ever such a person? If so, and if you changed, what got you to change?

5. Some students feel that philosophy is worthless because it does not yield definite results. How would Russell respond? Russell says the value of philosophy is in its uncertainty. What does he mean? Do you agree?
6. What, in Russell's view, is the value of philosophy?

HAVING NOW COME TO THE END of our brief and very incomplete review of the problems of philosophy, it will be well to consider, in conclusion, what is the value of philosophy and why it ought to be studied. It is the more necessary to consider this question, in view of the fact that many men, under the influence of science or of practical affairs, are inclined to doubt whether philosophy is anything better than innocent but useless trifling, hair-splitting distinctions, and controversies on matters concerning which knowledge is impossible.

This view of philosophy appears to result, partly from a wrong conception of the ends of life, partly from a wrong conception of the kind of goods which philosophy strives to achieve. Physical science, through the medium of inventions, is useful to innumerable people who are wholly ignorant of it; thus the study of physical science is to be recommended, not only, or primarily, because of the effect on the student, but rather because of the effect on mankind in general. Thus utility does not belong to philosophy. If the study of philosophy has any value at all for others than students of philosophy, it must be only indirectly, through its effects upon the lives of those who study it. It is in these effects, therefore, if anywhere, that the value of philosophy must be primarily sought.

But further, if we are not to fail in our endeavour to determine the value of philosophy, we must first free our minds from the prejudices of what are wrongly called "practical" men. The "practical" man, as this word is often used, is one who recognizes only material needs, who realizes that men must have food for the body, but is oblivious of the necessity of providing food for the mind. If all men were well off, if poverty and disease had been reduced to their lowest possible point, there would still remain much to be done to produce a valuable society; and even in the existing world the goods of the mind are at least as important as the goods of the body. It is exclusively among the goods of the mind that the value of philosophy is to be found; and only those who are not indifferent to these goods can be persuaded that the study of philosophy is not a waste of time.

Philosophy, like all other studies, aims primarily at knowledge. The knowledge it aims at is the kind of knowledge which gives unity and system to the body of the sciences, and the kind which results from a critical examination of the grounds of our convictions, prejudices, and beliefs. But it cannot be maintained that philosophy has had any very great measure of success in its attempts to provide definite answers to its questions. If you ask a mathematician, a mineralogist, a historian, or any other man of learning, what definite body of truths has been ascertained by his science, his answer will last as long as you are willing to listen. But if you put the same question to a philosopher, he will, if he is candid, have to confess that his study has not achieved positive results such as have been achieved by other sciences. It is true that this is partly accounted for by the fact that, as soon as definite knowledge concerning any subject becomes possible, this subject ceases to be called philosophy, and becomes a separate science. The whole study of the heavens, which now belongs to astronomy, was once included in philosophy; Newton's great work was called 'the mathematical principles of natural philosophy.' Similarly, the study of the human mind, which was a part of philosophy, has now been separated from philosophy and has become the science of psychology. Thus, to a great extent, the uncertainty of philosophy is more apparent than real: those questions which are already capable of definite answers are placed in the sciences, while those only to which, at present, no definite answer can be given, remain to form the residue which is called philosophy.

"The Value of Philosophy" from The Problems of Philosophy *by Bertrand Russell (1912).*

This is, however, only a part of the truth concerning the uncertainty of philosophy. There are many questions—and among them those that are of the profoundest interest to our spiritual life—which, so far as we can see, must remain insoluble to the human intellect unless its powers become of quite a different order from what they are now. . . . Has the universe any unity of plan or purpose, or is it a fortuitous concourse of atoms? Is consciousness a permanent part of the universe, giving hope of indefinite growth in wisdom, or is it a transitory accident on a small planet on which life must ultimately become impossible? Are good and evil of importance to the universe or only to man? Such questions are asked by philosophy, and variously answered by various philosophers. But it would seem that, whether answers be otherwise discoverable or not, the answers suggested by philosophy are none of them demonstrably true. Yet, however slight may be the hope of discovering an answer, it is part of the business of philosophy to continue the consideration of such questions, to make us aware of their importance, to examine all the approaches to them, and to keep alive that speculative interest in the universe which is apt to be killed by confining ourselves to definitely ascertainable knowledge.

Many philosophers, it is true, have held that philosophy could establish the truth of certain answers to such fundamental questions. They have supposed that what is of most importance in religious beliefs could be proved by strict demonstration to be true. In order to judge of such attempts, it is necessary to take a survey of human knowledge, and to form an opinion as to its methods and its limitations. On such a subject it would be unwise to pronounce dogmatically; but if the investigations of our previous chapters have not led us astray, we shall be compelled to renounce the hope of finding philosophical proofs of religious beliefs. We cannot, therefore, include as part of the value of philosophy any definite set of answers to such questions. Hence, once more, the value of philosophy must not depend upon any supposed body of definitely ascertainable knowledge to be acquired by those who study it.

The value of philosophy is, in fact, to be sought largely in its very uncertainty. The man who has no tincture of philosophy goes through life imprisoned in the prejudices derived from common sense, from the habitual beliefs of his age or his nation, and from convictions which have grown up in his mind without the co-operation or consent of his deliberate reason. To such a man the world tends to become definite, finite, obvious; common objects rouse no questions, and unfamiliar possibilities are contemptuously rejected. As soon as we begin to philosophize, on the contrary, we find . . . that even the most everyday things lead to problems to which only very incomplete answers can be given. Philosophy, though unable to tell us with certainty what is the true answer to the doubts which it raises, is able to suggest many possibilities which enlarge our thoughts and free them from the tyranny of custom. Thus, while diminishing our feeling of certainty as to what things are, it greatly increases our knowledge as to what they may be; it removes the somewhat arrogant dogmatism of those who have never travelled into the region of liberating doubt, and it keeps alive our sense of wonder by showing familiar things in an unfamiliar aspect.

Apart from its utility in showing unsuspected possibilities, philosophy has a value—perhaps its chief value—through the greatness of the objects which it contemplates, and the freedom from narrow and personal aims resulting from this contemplation. The life of the instinctive man is shut up within the circle of his private interests: family and friends may be included, but the outer world is not regarded except as it may help or hinder what comes within the circle of instinctive wishes. In such a life there is something feverish and confined, in comparison with which the philosophic life is calm and free. The private world of instinctive interest is a small one, set in the midst of a great and powerful world which must, sooner or later, lay our private world in ruins. Unless we can so enlarge our interests as to include the whole outer world, we remain like a garrison in a beleaguered fortress, knowing that the enemy prevents escape and that ultimate surrender is inevitable. In such a life there is no peace, but a constant strife between the insistence of desire and the powerlessness of will. In one way or another, if our life is to be great and free, we must escape this prison and this strife.

One way of escape is by philosophic contemplation. Philosophic contemplation does not, in its widest survey, divide the universe into two hostile camps—friends and foes, helpful and hostile, good and bad—it views the whole impartially. Philosophic contemplation, when it is unalloyed, does not aim at proving that the rest of the universe is akin to man. All acquisition of knowledge is an enlargement of the Self, but this enlargement is best attained when it is not directly sought. It is best obtained when the desire for knowledge is alone operative, by a study which does not wish in advance that its objects should have this or that character, but adapts the Self to the characters which it finds in its objects. This enlargement of Self is not obtained when, taking the Self as it is, we try to show that the world is so similar to this Self that knowledge of it is possible without any admission of what seems alien. The desire to prove this is a form of self-assertion and, like all self-assertion, it is an obstacle to the growth of Self which it desires, and of which the Self knows that it is capable. Self-assertion, in philosophic speculation as elsewhere, views the world as a means to its own ends; thus it makes the world of less account than Self, and the Self sets bounds to the greatness of its goods. In contemplation, on the contrary, we start from the non-Self, and through its greatness the boundaries of Self are enlarged; through the infinity of the universe the mind which contemplates it achieves some share in infinity.

For this reason greatness of soul is not fostered by those philosophies which assimilate the universe to Man. Knowledge is a form of union of Self and not-Self; like all union, it is impaired by dominion, and therefore by any attempt to force the universe into conformity with what we find in ourselves. There is a widespread philosophical tendency towards the view which tells us that Man is the measure of all things, that truth is man-made, that space and time and the world of universals are properties of the mind, and that, if there be anything not created by the mind, it is unknowable and of no account for us. This view . . . is untrue; but in addition to being untrue, it has the effect of robbing philosophic contemplation of all that gives it value, since it fetters contemplation to Self. What it calls knowledge is not a union with the not-Self, but a set of prejudices, habits, and desires, making an impenetrable veil between us and the world beyond. The man who finds pleasure in such a theory of knowledge is like the man who never leaves the domestic circle for fear his word might not be law.

The true philosophic contemplation, on the contrary, finds its satisfaction in every enlargement of the not-Self, in everything that magnifies the objects contemplated, and thereby the subject contemplating. Everything, in contemplation, that is personal or private, everything that depends upon habit, self-interest, or desire, distorts the object, and hence impairs the union which the intellect seeks. By thus making a barrier between subject and object, such personal and private things become a prison to the intellect. The free intellect will see as God might see, without a *here* and *now*, without hopes and fears, without the trammels of customary beliefs and traditional prejudices, calmly, dispassionately, in the sole and exclusive desire of knowledge—knowledge as impersonal, as purely contemplative, as it is possible for man to attain. Hence also the free intellect will value more the abstract and universal knowledge into which the accidents of private history do not enter, than the knowledge brought by the senses, and dependent, as such knowledge must be, upon an exclusive and personal point of view and a body whose sense-organs distort as much as they reveal.

The mind which has become accustomed to the freedom and impartiality of philosophic contemplation will preserve something of the same freedom and impartiality in the world of action and emotion. It will view its purposes and desires as parts of the whole, with the absence of insistence that results from seeing them as infinitesimal fragments in a world of which all the rest is unaffected by any one man's deeds. The impartiality which, in contemplation, is the unalloyed desire for truth, is the very same quality of mind which, in action, is justice, and in emotion is that universal love which can be given to all, and not only to those who are judged useful or admirable. Thus contemplation enlarges not only the objects of our thoughts, but also the objects of our actions and our affections: it makes us citizens of the universe, not only of one walled city at war with all the rest. In this citizenship of the universe consists man's true freedom, and his liberation from the thraldom of narrow hopes and fears.

Thus, to sum up our discussion of the value of philosophy; Philosophy is to be studied, not for the sake of any definite answers to its questions, since no definite answers can, as a rule, be known to be true, but rather for the sake of the questions themselves; because these questions enlarge our conception of what is possible, enrich our intellectual imagination and diminish the dogmatic assurance which closes the mind against speculation; but above all because, through the greatness of the universe which philos- ophy contemplates, the mind also is rendered great, and becomes capable of that union with the universe which constitutes its highest good.

Further Questions

1. Russell says philosophy aims at knowledge. Other than knowledge about who said what, did you achieve any knowledge from your study of philosophy? What? Of the things you learned, what is most valuable to you? Why?
2. Russell says the person who has most profited from philosophy "will see as God might see, without a here and now, without hopes and fears. . . ." There are alternative views of the value of philosophy. Karl Marx, for instance, who in this respect is at the other extreme from Russell, said the point of philosophy is not to understand the world, but to change it. What would you say the main value of philosophy has been for you?

Further Readings

Nietzsche, Friedrich. *The Portable Nietzsche*. New York: Viking Press, 1954. Philosophy and power.
Suzuki, D. *Zen Mind, Beginner's Mind*. San Francisco: Weatherhill, 1970. A classic of meditation literature. On the value of not thinking.

Part II

Where and When

HERE. NOW. YOU.

Wherever you are, you are right now having the experience of being somewhere: here. Sometime: now. Someone: you. Obviously.

This feeling of obviousness, the obviousness of here and now, automatically colors *all* our experience. It is like wearing specially tinted lenses that obscure the strangeness of everything, lenses we've worn so long we no longer notice them. What the lenses contribute to our vision, we unknowingly project onto reality. Once we have our lenses on, everything, literally, falls into place.

So, what's the problem? Why not simply accept the here and now and get on with the project of understanding ourselves and the world? *That's* the problem. We want to accept the obvious and move on, as if the obvious has no effect. But it does. It deeply structures our understanding of ourselves and the world.

As you are about to see, our everyday notions of here and now—of space and time—are not the only possible ones. There are alternatives, some of the most bizarre of which have been endorsed by modern science. Our familiar concepts, on the other hand, cloaked in obviousness, reveal little and obscure much. Only by taking off our tinted lenses and looking at ourselves and the world from new perspectives can we see why. With familiarity and obviousness unmasked, everything that only a moment ago seemed so secure, so in place, so settled, comes flying apart at the seams—and so do we.

5　Flatland

EDWIN ABBOTT

E. A. Abbott was born in 1838 in England. In 1865 he became the headmaster of a London school. His field was classics, with an emphasis on literature and theology. Although he wrote several textbooks, some theological works, a biography of Francis Bacon and a Shakespearean grammar, his most famous and enduring work was in the field of popular mathematics and physics. What is even more remarkable, *Flatland,* from which the following selection is taken, was written when Einstein was only a child and the idea of space-time would not emerge for another quarter century! Stranger still, Abbott himself worried that this fantasy would destroy his reputation, and so published *Flatland* pseudonymously.

Though the style is somewhat old-fashioned, mathematicians, scientists, and students have enjoyed for more than a century this timeless story of a Square who lives contentedly in a two-dimensional world until, one day, he is whisked by a Sphere into the third dimension.

Reading Questions

1. Why do Flatlanders not see the third dimension?
2. Keep a lookout for the important phrase, "Upward, not northward." What is the significance of it?
3. What is the response of the Sphere to the Square's insistence that there might exist fourth, fifth, and other, higher, dimensions? Why does the Sphere, who at first seems so much wiser than the Square, have difficulty in imagining what the lowly Square himself can imagine?

OF THE NATURE OF FLATLAND

I CALL OUR WORLD FLATLAND, not because we call it so, but to make its nature clearer to you, my happy readers, who are privileged to live in Space.

Imagine a vast sheet of paper on which straight Lines, Triangles, Squares, Pentagons, Hexagons, and other figures, instead of remaining fixed in their places, move freely about, on or in the surface, but without the power of rising above or sinking below it, very much like shadows—only hard and with luminous edges—and you will then have a pretty correct notion of my country and countrymen. Alas, a few years ago, I should have said "my universe": but now my mind has been opened to higher views of things.

In such a country, you will perceive at once that it is impossible that there should be anything of what you call a "solid" kind; but I dare say you will suppose that we could at least distinguish by sight the Triangles, Squares, and other figures, moving about as I have described them. On the contrary,

Excerpts from Flatland *by Edwin Abbott (Dover, 1952).*

we could see nothing of the kind, not at least so as to distinguish one figure from another. Nothing was visible, nor could be visible, to us, except Straight Lines; and the necessity of this I will speedily demonstrate.

Place a penny on the middle of one of your tables in Space; and leaning over it, look down upon it. It will appear a circle.

But now, drawing back to the edge of the table, gradually lower your eye (thus bringing yourself more and more into the condition of the inhabitants of Flatland), and you will find the penny becoming more and more oval to your view; and at last when you have placed your eye exactly on the edge of the table (so that you are, as it were, actually a Flatlander) the penny will then have ceased to appear oval at all, and will have become, so far as you can see, a straight line.

The same thing would happen if you were to treat in the same way a Triangle, or Square, or any other figure cut out of pasteboard. As soon as you look at it with your eye on the edge of the table, you will find that it ceases to appear to you a figure, and that it becomes in appearance a straight line. Take for example an equilateral Triangle— who represents with us a Tradesman of the respectable class. Fig. 1 represents the Tradesman as you would see him while you were bending over him from above; figs. 2 and 3 represent the Tradesman, as you would see him if your eye were close to the level, or all but on the level of the table; and if your eye were quite on the level of the table (and that is how we see him in Flatland) you would see nothing but a straight line.

When I was in Spaceland I heard that your sailors have very similar experiences while they traverse your seas and discern some distant island or coast lying on the horizon. The far-off land may have bays, forelands, angles in and out to any number and extent; yet at a distance you see none of these (unless indeed your sun shines bright upon them revealing the projections and retirements by means of light and shade), nothing but a grey unbroken line upon the water.

Well, that is just what we see when one of our triangular or other acquaintances comes toward us in Flatland. As there is neither sun with us, nor any light of such a kind as to make shadows, we have none of the helps to the sight that you have in Spaceland. If our friend comes closer to us we see his line becomes larger; if he leaves us it becomes smaller: but still he looks like a straight line; be he a Triangle, Square, Pentagon, Hexagon, Circle, what you will—a straight Line he looks and nothing else.

You may perhaps ask how under these disadvantageous circumstances we are able to distinguish our friends from one another: but the answer to this very natural question will be more fitly and easily given when I come to describe the inhabitants of Flatland. For the present let me defer this subject, and say a word or two about the climate and houses in our country.

OF THE CLIMATE AND HOUSES IN FLATLAND

As with you, so also with us, there are four points of the compass North, South, East, and West.

There being no sun nor other heavenly bodies, it is impossible for us to determine the North in the usual way; but we have a method of our own. By a Law of Nature with us, there is a constant attraction to the South; and, although in temperate climates this is very slight . . . yet the hampering effect of the southward attraction is quite sufficient to serve as a compass in most parts of our earth. . . .

CONCERNING THE INHABITANTS OF FLATLAND

The greatest length or breadth of a full grown inhabitant of Flatland may be estimated at about eleven of your inches. Twelve inches may be regarded as a maximum.

Our Women are Straight Lines.

Our Soldiers and Lowest Classes of Workmen are Triangles with two equal sides. . . .

Our Middle Class consists of Equilateral or Equal-Sided Triangles.

Our Professional Men and Gentlemen are Squares (to which class I myself belong) and Five-Sided Figures or Pentagons.

Next above these come the Nobility, of whom there are several degrees, beginning at Six-Sided Figures, or Hexagons, and from thence rising in the number of their sides till they receive the honourable title of Polygonal, or many-sided. Finally when the number of the sides becomes so numerous, and the sides themselves so small, that the figure cannot be distinguished from a circle, he is included in the Circular or Priestly order; and this is the highest class of all. . . .

OF OUR METHODS OF RECOGNIZING ONE ANOTHER

You, who are blessed with shade as well as light, you, who are gifted with two eyes, endowed with a knowledge of perspective, and charmed with the enjoyment of various colours, you, who can actually *see* an angle, and contemplate the complete circumference of a Circle in the happy region of the Three Dimensions — how shall I make clear to you the extreme difficulty which we in Flatland experience in recognizing one another's configuration?

Recall what I told you above. All beings in Flatland, animate or inanimate, no matter what their form, present *to our view* the same, or nearly the same, appearance, viz. that of a straight Line. How then can one be distinguished from another, where all appear the same?

The answer is threefold. The first means of recognition is the sense of hearing; which with us is far more highly developed than with you, and which enables us not only to distinguish by the voice our personal friends, but even to discriminate between different classes, at least so far as concerns the three lowest orders, the Equilateral, the Square, and the Pentagon. . . .

Feeling is, among our Women and lower classes — about our upper classes I shall speak presently — the principal test of recognition, at all events between strangers, and when the question is, not as to the individual, but as to the class. What therefore "introduction" is among the higher classes in Spaceland, that the process of "feeling" is with us. "Permit me to ask you to feel and be felt by my friend Mr. So-and-so" — is still, among the more old-fashioned of our country gentlemen in districts remote from towns, the customary formula for a Flatland introduction. . . .

I am about to appear very inconsistent. In previous sections I have said that all figures in Flatland present the appearance of a straight line; and it was added or implied, that it is consequently impossible to distinguish by the visual organ between individuals of different classes: yet now I am about to explain to my Spaceland critics how we are able to recognize one another by the sense of sight. . . .

That this power exists in any regions and for any classes is the result of Fog; which prevails during the greater part of the year in all parts save the torrid zones. That which is with you in Spaceland an unmixed evil, blotting out the landscape, depressing the spirits, and enfeebling the health, is by us recognized as a blessing scarcely inferior to air itself, and as the Nurse of arts and Parent of sciences. But let me explain my meaning, without further eulogies on this beneficent Element.

If Fog were non-existent, all lines would appear equally and indistinguishably clear; and this is actually the case in those unhappy countries in which the atmosphere is perfectly dry and transparent. But wherever there is a rich supply of Fog objects that are at a distance, say of three feet, are appreciably dimmer than those at a distance of two feet eleven inches; and the result is that by careful and constant experimental observation of comparative dimness and clearness, we are enabled to infer with great exactness the configuration of the object observed. . . .

HOW I HAD A VISION OF LINELAND

It was the last day but one of the 1999th year of our era, and the first day of the Long Vacation. Having amused myself till a late hour with my favourite recreation of Geometry, I had retired to rest with an unsolved problem in my mind. In the night I had a dream.

I saw before me a vast multitude of small Straight Lines . . . interspersed with other Beings still smaller and of the nature of lustrous points — all moving to and fro in one and the same Straight Line, and, as nearly as I could judge, with the same velocity.

A noise of confused, multitudinous chirping or twittering issued from them at intervals as long as they were moving; but sometimes they ceased from motion, and then all was silence.

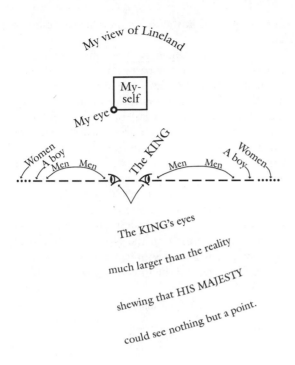

Approaching one of the largest . . . I . . . received no answer. A second and a third appeal on my part were equally ineffectual. Losing patience at what appeared to me intolerable rudeness, I brought my mouth into a position full in front of her mouth so as to intercept her motion, and loudly repeated my question, . . . "What signifies this concourse, and this strange and confused chirping, and this monotonous motion to and fro in one and the same Straight Line?"

. . . "I am the Monarch of the world. But thou, whence intrudest thou into my realm of Lineland?" Receiving this abrupt reply, I begged pardon if I had in any way startled or molested his Royal Highness; and describing myself as a stranger I besought the King to give me some account of his dominions. But I had the greatest possible difficulty in obtaining any information on points that really interested me; for the Monarch could not refrain from constantly assuming that whatever was familiar to him must also be known to me and that I was simulating ignorance in jest. However, by persevering questions I elicited the following facts:

It seemed that this poor ignorant Monarch—as he called himself—was persuaded that the Straight Line which he called his Kingdom, and

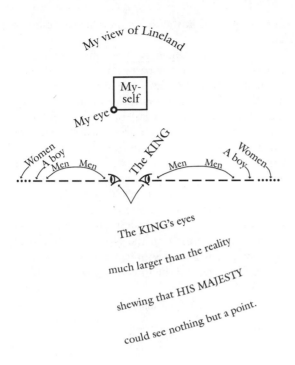

in which he passed his existence, constituted the whole of the world, and indeed the whole of Space. Not being able either to move or to see, save in his Straight Line, he had no conception of anything out of it. Though he had heard my voice when I first addressed him, the sounds had come to him in a manner so contrary to his experience that he had made no answer, "seeing no man," as he expressed it, "and hearing a voice as it were from my own intestines." Until the moment when I placed my mouth in his World, he had neither seen me, nor heard anything except confused sounds beating against—what I called his side, but what he called his *inside* or *stomach;* nor had he even now the least conception of the region from which I had come. Outside his World, or Line, all was a blank to him; nay, not even a blank, for a blank implies Space; say, rather, all was non-existent.

His subjects were all alike confined in motion and eye-sight to that single Straight Line, which was their World. It need scarcely be added that the whole of their horizon was limited to a Point; nor could any one ever see anything but a Point. Man, woman, child, thing—each was a Point to the eye of a Linelander. Only by the sound of the voice could sex or age be distinguished. Moreover, as each individual occupied the whole of the narrow path, so to speak, which constituted his Universe, and no one could move to the right or left to make way for passers by, it followed that no Linelander could ever pass another. Once neighbours, always neighbours. Neighbourhood with them was like marriage with us. Neighbours remained neighbours till death did them part. . . .

HOW I VAINLY TRIED TO EXPLAIN THE NATURE OF FLATLAND

Thinking that it was time to bring down the Monarch from his raptures to the level of common sense, I determined to endeavour to open up to him some glimpses of the truth, that is to say of the nature of things in Flatland. So I began thus: "How does your Royal Highness distinguish the shapes and positions of his subjects? I for my part noticed by the sense of sight, before I entered your Kingdom, that some of your people are Lines and others Points, and that some of the Lines are larger—" "You speak of an impossibility," interrupted the King; "you must have seen a vision; for to detect the difference between a Line and a Point by the sense of sight is, as every one knows, in the nature of things, impossible; but it can be detected by the sense of hearing, and by the same means my shape can be exactly ascertained. Behold me—I am a Line, the longest in Lineland, over six inches of Space—" "Of Length," I ventured to suggest. "Fool," said he, "Space is Length. Interrupt me again, and I have done." . . .

[The Square asks the king about what is to the right and left of him.]

"And let me ask what you mean by those words 'left' and 'right.' I suppose it is your way of saying Northward and Southward."

"Not so," replied I: "besides your motion of Northward and Southward, there is another motion which I call from right to left."

King: Exhibit to me, if you please, this motion from left to right.

I: Nay, that I cannot do, unless you could step out of your Line altogether.

King: Out of my Line? Do you mean out of the world? Out of Space?

I: Well, yes. Out of *your* World. Out of *your* Space. For your Space is not the true Space. True Space is a Plane; but your Space is only a Line.

King: If you cannot indicate this motion from left to right by yourself moving in it, then I beg you to describe it to me in words.

I: If you cannot tell your right side from your left, I fear that no words of mine can make my meaning clear to you. But surely you cannot be ignorant of so simple a distinction.

King: I do not in the least understand you.

I: Alas! How shall I make it clear? When you move straight on, does it not sometimes occur to you that you *could* move in some other way, turning your eye round so as to look in the direction towards which your side is now fronting? In other words, instead of always moving in the direction of one of your extremities, do you never feel a desire to move in the direction, so to speak, of your side?

King: Never. And what do you mean? How can a man's inside "front" in any direction? Or how can a man move in the direction of his inside?

I: Well then, since words cannot explain the matter, I will try deeds, and will move gradually out of Lineland in the direction which I desire to indicate to you.

At the word I began to move my body out of Lineland. As long as any part of me remained in his dominion and in his view, the King kept exclaiming, "I see you, I see you still; you are not moving." But when I had at last moved myself out of his Line, he cried in his shrillest voice, "She is vanished; she is dead." "I am not dead," replied I; "I am simply out of Lineland, that is to say, out of the Straight Line which you call Space, and in the true Space, where I can see things as they are. And at this moment I can see your Line, or side—or inside as you are pleased to call it; and I can see also the Men and Women on the North and South of you, whom I will now enumerate, describing their order, their size, and the interval between each."

When I had done this at great length, I cried triumphantly, "Does that at last convince you?" And, with that, I once more entered Lineland, taking up the same position as before.

But the Monarch replied, "If you were a Man of sense—though, as you appear to have only one voice I have little doubt you are not a Man but a Woman—but, if you had a particle of sense, you would listen to reason. You ask me to believe that there is another Line besides that which my senses indicate, and another motion besides that of which I am daily conscious. I, in return, ask you to describe in words or indicate by motion that other Line of which you speak. Instead of moving, you merely exercise some magic art of vanishing and returning to sight; and instead of any lucid description of your new World, you simply tell me the numbers and sizes of some forty of my retinue, facts known to any child in my capital. Can anything be more irrational or audacious? Acknowledge your folly or depart from my dominions."

Furious at his perversity, and especially indignant that he professed to be ignorant of my sex, I retorted in no measured terms, "Besotted Being! You think yourself the perfection of existence, while you are in reality the most imperfect and imbecile. You profess to see, whereas you can see nothing but a Point! You plume yourself on inferring the existence of a Straight Line; but I *can see* Straight Lines, and infer the existence of Angles, Triangles, Squares, Pentagons, Hexagons, and even Circles. Why waste more words? Suffice it that I am the completion of your incomplete self. You are a Line, but I am a Line of Lines, called in my country a Square: and even I, infinitely superior though I am to you, am of little account among the great nobles of Flatland, whence I have come to visit you, in the hope of enlightening your ignorance."

Hearing these words the King advanced towards me with a menacing cry as if to pierce me through the diagonal; and in that same moment there arose from myriads of his subjects a multitudinous war cry, increasing in vehemence till at last methought it rivalled the roar of an army of a hundred thousand Isosceles, and the artillery of a thousand Pentagons. Spell-bound and motionless, I could neither speak nor move to avert the impending destruction; and still the noise grew louder, and the King came closer, when I awoke to find the breakfast-bell recalling me to the realities of Flatland.

CONCERNING A STRANGER FROM SPACELAND

From dreams I proceed to facts.

It was the last day of the 1999th year of our era. The pattering of the rain had long ago announced nightfall; and I was sitting[1] in the company of my wife, musing on the events of the past and the prospects of the coming year, the coming century, the coming Millennium.

My four Sons and two orphan Grandchildren had retired to their several apartments; and my wife alone remained with me to see the old Millennium out and the new one in.

I was rapt in thought, pondering in my mind some words that had casually issued from the mouth of my youngest Grandson, a most promising young Hexagon of unusual brilliancy and perfect angularity. His uncles and I had been giving him his usual practical lesson in Sight Recognition, turning

ourselves upon our centres, now rapidly, now more slowly, and questioning him as to our positions; and his answers had been so satisfactory that I had been induced to reward him by giving him a few hints on Arithmetic, as applied to Geometry.

Taking nine Squares, each an inch every way, I had put them together so as to make one large Square, with a side of three inches, and I had hence proved to my little Grandson that—though it was impossible for us to *see* the inside of the Square—yet we might ascertain the number of square inches in a Square by simply squaring the number of inches in the side: "and thus," said I, "we know that 3^2, or 9, represents the number of square inches in a Square whose side is 3 inches long."

The little Hexagon meditated on this a while and then said to me; "But you have been teaching me to raise numbers to the third power: I suppose 3^3 must mean something in Geometry; what does it mean?" "Nothing at all," replied I, "not at least in Geometry; for Geometry has only Two Dimensions." And then I began to shew the boy how a Point by moving through a length of three inches makes a Line of three inches, which may be represented by 3; and how a Line of three inches, moving parallel to itself through a length of three inches, makes a Square of three inches every way, which may be represented by 3^2.

Upon this, my Grandson, again returning to his former suggestion, took me up rather suddenly and exclaimed, "Well, then, if a Point by moving three inches, makes a Line of three inches represented by 3; and if a straight Line of three inches, moving parallel to itself, makes a Square of three inches every way, represented by 3^2; it must be that a Square of three inches every way, moving somehow parallel to itself (but I don't see how) must make Something else (but I don't see what) of three inches every way—and this must be represented by 3^3."

"Go to bed," said I, a little ruffled by this interruption: "if you would talk less nonsense, you would remember more sense."

So my Grandson had disappeared in disgrace; and there I sat by my Wife's side, endeavouring to form a retrospect of the year 1999 and of the possibilities of the year 2000, but not quite able to shake off the thoughts suggested by the prattle of my bright little Hexagon. Only a few sands now remained in the half-hour glass. Rousing myself from my reverie I turned the glass Northward for the last time in the old Millennium; and in the act, I exclaimed aloud, "The boy is a fool."

Straightway I became conscious of a Presence in the room, and a chilling breath thrilled through my very being. "He is no such thing," cried my Wife, "and you are breaking the Commandments in thus dishonouring your own Grandson." But I took no notice of her. Looking round in every direction I could see nothing; yet still I *felt* a Presence, and shivered as the cold whisper came again. I started up. "What is the matter?" said my Wife, "there is no draught; what are you looking for? There is nothing." There was nothing; and I resumed my seat, again exclaiming, "The boy is a fool, I say; 3^3 can have no meaning in Geometry." At once there came a distinctly audible reply, "The boy is not a fool; and 3^3 has an obvious Geometrical meaning."

My Wife as well as myself heard the words, although she did not understand their meaning, and both of us sprang forward in the direction of the sound. What was our horror when we saw before us a Figure! At the first glance it appeared to be a Woman, seen sideways; but a moment's observation shewed me that the extremities passed into dimness too rapidly to represent one of the Female Sex; and I should have thought it a Circle, only that it seemed to change its size in a manner impossible for a Circle or for any regular Figure of which I had had experience. . . .

"How comes this person here?" she exclaimed, "you promised me, my dear, that there should be no ventilators in our new house." "Nor are there any," said I; "but what makes you think that the stranger is a Woman? I see by my power of Sight Recognition——" "Oh, I have no patience with your Sight Recognition," replied she, " 'Feeling is believing' and 'A Straight Line to the touch is worth a Circle to the sight' " —two Proverbs, very common . . . in Flatland.

"Well," said I, for I was afraid of irritating her, "if it must be so, demand an introduction." Assuming her most gracious manner, my Wife advanced towards the Stranger, "Permit me, Madam, to feel and be felt by——" then, suddenly recoiling, "Oh! it is not a Woman, and there are no angles either, not a trace of one. Can it be that I have so misbehaved to a perfect Circle?"

"I am indeed, in a certain sense a Circle," replied the Voice, "and a more perfect Circle than any in Flatland; but to speak more accurately, I am many Circles in one." . . .

I glanced at the half-hour glass. The last sands had fallen. The third Millennium had begun.

HOW THE STRANGER VAINLY ENDEAVOURED TO REVEAL TO ME IN WORDS THE MYSTERIES OF SPACELAND

. . . I began to approach the Stranger with the intention of taking a nearer view and of bidding him be seated: but his appearance struck me dumb and motionless with astonishment. Without the slightest symptoms of angularity he nevertheless varied every instant with gradations of size and brightness scarcely possible for any Figure within the scope of my experience. The thought flashed across me that I might have before me a burglar or cut-throat, some monstrous Irregular Isosceles, who, by feigning the voice of a Circle, had obtained admission somehow into the house, and was now preparing to stab me with his acute angle.

In a sitting-room, the absence of Fog (and the season happened to be remarkably dry), made it difficult for me to trust to Sight Recognition, especially at the short distance at which I was standing. Desperate with fear, I rushed forward with an unceremonious, "You must permit me, Sir—" and felt him. My Wife was right. There was not the trace of an angle, not the slightest roughness or inequality: never in my life had I met with a more perfect Circle. He remained motionless while I walked round him, beginning from his eye and returning to it again. Circular he was throughout, a perfectly satisfactory Circle; there could not be a doubt of it. Then followed a dialogue, which I will endeavour to set down as near as I can recollect it, omitting only some of my profuse apologies—for I was covered with shame and humiliation that I, a Square, should have been guilty of the impertinence of feeling a Circle. It was commenced by the Stranger with some impatience at the lengthiness of my introductory process.

Stranger: Have you felt me enough by this time? Are you not introduced to me yet?

I: Most illustrious Sir, excuse my awkwardness, which arises not from ignorance of the usages of polite society, but from a little surprise and nervousness, consequent on this somewhat unexpected visit. And I beseech you to reveal my indiscretions to no one, and especially not to my Wife. But before your Lordship enters into further communications, would he deign to satisfy the curiosity of one who would gladly know whence his Visitor came?

Stranger: From Space, from Space, Sir: whence else?

I: Pardon me, my Lord, but is not your Lordship already in Space, your Lordship and his humble servant, even at this moment?

Stranger: Pooh! what do you know of Space? Define Space.

I: Space, my Lord, is height and breadth indefinitely prolonged.

Stranger: Exactly: you see you do not even know what Space is. You think it is of Two Dimensions only; but I have come to announce to you a Third—height, breadth, and length.

I: Your Lordship is pleased to be merry. We also speak of length and height, or breadth and thickness, thus denoting Two Dimensions by four names.

Stranger: But I mean not only three names, but Three Dimensions.

I: Would your Lordship indicate or explain to me in what direction is the Third Dimension, unknown to me?

Stranger: I came from it. It is up above and down below.

I: My Lord means seemingly that it is Northward and Southward.

Stranger: I mean nothing of the kind. I mean a direction in which you cannot look, because you have no eye in your side.

I: Pardon me, my Lord, a moment's inspection will convince your Lordship that I have a perfect luminary at the juncture of two of my sides.

Stranger: Yes: but in order to see into Space you ought to have an eye, not on your Perimeter, but on your side, that is, on what you would probably call your inside; but we in Spaceland should call it your side.

I: An eye in my inside! An eye in my stomach! Your Lordship jests.

Stranger: I am in no jesting humour. I tell you that I come from Space, or, since you will not understand what Space means, from the Land of Three Dimensions whence I but lately looked down upon your Plane which you call Space forsooth. From that position of advantage I discerned all that you speak of as *solid* (by which you mean "enclosed on four sides"), your houses, your churches, your very chests and safes, yes even your insides and stomachs, all lying open and exposed to my view.

I: Such assertions are easily made, my Lord.

Stranger: But not easily proved, you mean. But I mean to prove mine.

When I descended here, I saw your four Sons, the Pentagons, each in his apartment, and your two Grandsons the Hexagons; I saw your youngest Hexagon remain a while with you and then retire to his room, leaving you and your Wife alone. I saw your Isosceles servants, three in number, in the kitchen at supper, and the little Page in the scullery. Then I came here, and how do you think I came?

I: Through the roof, I suppose.

Stranger: Not so. Your roof, as you know very well, has been recently repaired, and has no aperture by which even a Woman could penetrate. I tell you I come from Space. Are you not convinced by what I have told you of your children and household?

I: Your Lordship must be aware that such facts touching the belongings of his humble servant might be easily ascertained by any one in the neighbourhood possessing your Lordship's ample means of obtaining information.

Stranger: (*To himself.*) What must I do? Stay; one more argument suggests itself to me. When you see a Straight Line—your wife, for example—how many Dimensions do you attribute to her?

I: Your Lordship would treat me as if I were one of the vulgar who, being ignorant of Mathematics, suppose that a Woman is really a Straight Line, and only of One Dimension. No, no, my Lord; we Squares are better advised, and are as well aware as your Lordship that a Woman, though popularly called a Straight Line, is, really and scientifically, a very thin Parallelogram, possessing Two Dimensions, like the rest of us, viz., length and breadth (or thickness).

Stranger: But the very fact that a Line is visible implies that it possesses yet another Dimension.

I: My Lord, I have just acknowledged that a Woman is broad as well as long. We see her length, we infer her breadth; which, though very slight, is capable of measurement.

Stranger: You do not understand me. I mean that when you see a Woman, you ought—besides inferring her breadth—to see her length, and to *see* what we call her *height;* although that last Dimension is infinitesimal in your country. If a Line were mere length without "height," it would cease to occupy Space and would become invisible. Surely you must recognize this?

I: I must indeed confess that I do not in the least understand your Lordship. When we in Flatland see a Line, we see length and *brightness.* If the brightness disappears, the Line is extinguished, and, as you say, ceases to occupy Space. But am I to suppose that your Lordship gives to brightness the title of a Dimension, and that what we call "bright" you call "high"?

Stranger: No, indeed. By "height" I mean a Dimension like your length: only, with you, "height" is not so easily perceptible, being extremely small.

I: My Lord, your assertion is easily put to the test. You say I have a Third Dimension, which you call "height." Now, Dimension implies direction and measurement. Do but measure my "height," or merely indicate to me the direction in which my "height" extends, and I will become your convert. Otherwise, your Lordship's own understanding must hold me excused.

Stranger: (*To himself.*) I can do neither. How shall I convince him? Surely a plain statement of facts followed by ocular demonstration ought to suffice.—Now, Sir; listen to me.

You are living on a Plane. What you style Flatland is the vast level surface of what I may call a fluid, on, or in, the top of which you and your countrymen move about, without rising above it or falling below it.

I am not a plane Figure, but a Solid. You call me a Circle; but in reality I am not a Circle, but an infinite number of Circles, of size varying from a Point to a Circle of thirteen inches in diameter, one placed on the top of the other. When I cut through your plane as I am now doing, I make in your plane a section which you, very rightly, call a Circle. For even a Sphere—which is my proper

name in my own country—if he manifest himself at all to an inhabitant of Flatland—must needs manifest himself as a Circle.

Do you not remember—for I, who see all things, discerned last night the phantasmal vision of Lineland written upon your brain—do you not remember, I say, how, when you entered the realm of Lineland, you were compelled to manifest yourself to the King, not as a Square, but as a Line, because that Linear Realm had not Dimensions enough to represent the whole of you, but only a slice or section of you? In precisely the same way, your country of Two Dimensions is not spacious enough to represent me, a being of Three, but can only exhibit a slice or section of me, which is what you call a Circle.

The diminished brightness of your eye indicates incredulity. But now prepare to receive proof positive of the truth of my assertions. You cannot indeed see more than one of my sections, or Circles, at a time; for you have no power to raise your eye out of the plane of Flatland; but you can at least see that, as I rise in Space, so my sections become smaller. See now, I will rise; and the effect upon your eye will be that my Circle will become smaller and smaller till it dwindles to a point and finally vanishes.

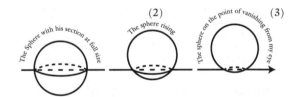

There was no "rising" that I could see; but he diminished and finally vanished. I winked once or twice to make sure that I was not dreaming. But it was no dream. For from the depths of nowhere came forth a hollow voice—close to my heart it seemed—"Am I quite gone? Are you convinced now? Well, now I will gradually return to Flatland and you shall see my sections become larger and larger."

Every reader in Spaceland will easily understand that my mysterious Guest was speaking the language of truth and even of simplicity. But to me, proficient though I was in Flatland Mathematics, it was by no means a simple matter. The rough diagram given above will make it clear to any Spaceland child that the Sphere, ascending in the three positions indicated there, must needs have manifested himself to me, or to any Flatlander, as a Circle, at first of full size, then small, and at last very small indeed, approaching to a Point. But to me, although I saw the facts before me, the causes were as dark as ever. All that I could comprehend was, that the Circle had made himself smaller and vanished, and that he had now reappeared and was rapidly making himself larger.

When he regained his original size, he heaved a deep sigh; for he perceived by my silence that I had altogether failed to comprehend him. And indeed I was now inclining to the belief that he must be no Circle at all, but some extremely clever juggler; or else that the old wives' tales were true, and that after all there were such people as Enchanters and Magicians.

After a long pause he muttered to himself, "One resource alone remains, if I am not to resort to action. I must try the method of Analogy." Then followed a still longer silence, after which he continued our dialogue.

Sphere: Tell me, Mr. Mathematician; if a Point moves Northward, and leaves a luminous wake, what name would you give to the wake?

I: A straight Line.

Sphere: And a straight Line has how many extremities?

I: Two.

Sphere: Now conceive the Northward straight Line moving parallel to itself, East and West, so that every point in it leaves behind it the wake of a straight Line. What name will you give to the Figure thereby formed? We will suppose that it moves through a distance equal to the original straight Line. —What name, I say?

I: A Square.

Sphere: And how many sides has a Square? How many angles?

I: Four sides and four angles.

Sphere: Now stretch your imagination a little, and conceive a Square in Flatland, moving parallel to itself upward.

I: What? Northward?

Sphere: No, not Northward; upward; out of Flatland altogether.

If it moved Northward, the Southern points in the Square would have to move through the positions previously occupied by the Northern points. But that is not my meaning.

I mean that every Point in you—for you are a Square and will serve the purpose of my illustration—every Point in you, that is to say in what you call your inside, is to pass upwards through Space in such a way that no Point shall pass through the position previously occupied by any other Point; but each Point shall describe a straight Line of its own. This is all in accordance with Analogy; surely it must be clear to you.

Restraining my impatience—for I was now under a strong temptation to rush blindly at my Visitor and to precipitate him into Space, or out of Flatland, anywhere, so that I could get rid of him—I replied:—

"And what may be the nature of the Figure which I am to shape out by this motion which you are pleased to denote by the word 'upward'? I presume it is describable in the language of Flatland."

Sphere: Oh, certainly. It is all plain and simple, and in strict accordance with Analogy—only, by the way, you must not speak of the result as being a Figure, but as a Solid. But I will describe it to you. Or rather not I, but Analogy.

We began with a single Point, which of course —being itself a Point—has only *one* terminal Point.

One Point produces a Line with *two* terminal Points.

One Line produces a Square with *four* terminal Points.

Now you can give yourself the answer to your own question: 1, 2, 4, are evidently in Geometrical Progression. What is the next number?

I: Eight.

Sphere: Exactly. The one Square produces a *Something-which-you-do-not-as-yet-know-a-name-for-but-which-we-call-a-Cube* with *eight* terminal Points. Now are you convinced?

I: And has this Creature sides, as well as angles or what you call "terminal Points"?

Sphere: Of course; and all according to Analogy. But, by the way, not what *you* call sides, but what *we* call sides. You would call them *solids*.

I: And how many solids or sides will appertain to this Being whom I am to generate by the motion of my inside in an "upward" direction, and whom you call a Cube?

Sphere: How can you ask? And you a mathematician! The side of anything is always, if I may so say, one Dimension behind the thing. Consequently, as there is no Dimension behind a Point, a Point has 0 sides; a Line, if I may say, has 2 sides (for the Points of a Line may be called by courtesy, its sides); a Square has 4 sides; 0, 2, 4; what Progression do you call that?

I: Arithmetical.

Sphere: And what is the next number?

I: Six.

Sphere: Exactly. Then you see you have answered your own question. The Cube which you will generate will be bounded by six sides, that is to say, six of your insides. You see it all now, eh?

"Monster," I shrieked, "be thou juggler, enchanter, dream, or devil, no more will I endure thy mockeries. Either thou or I must perish." And saying these words I precipitated myself upon him.

HOW THE SPHERE, HAVING IN VAIN TRIED WORDS, RESORTED TO DEEDS

It was in vain. I brought my hardest right angle into violent collision with the Stranger, pressing on him with a force sufficient to have destroyed any ordinary Circle: but I could feel him slowly and unarrestably slipping from my contact; no edging to the right nor to the left, but moving somehow out of the world, and vanishing to nothing. Soon there was a blank. But still I heard the Intruder's voice.

Sphere: Why will you refuse to listen to reason? I had hoped to find in you — as being a man of sense and an accomplished mathematician — a fit apostle for the Gospel of the Three Dimensions, which I am allowed to preach once only in a thousand years: but now I know not how to convince you. Stay, I have it. Deeds, and not words, shall proclaim the truth. Listen, my friend.

I have told you I can see from my position in Space the inside of all things that you consider closed. For example, I see in yonder cupboard near which you are standing, several of what you call boxes (but like everything else in Flatland, they have no tops nor bottoms) full of money; I see also two tablets of accounts. I am about to descend into that cupboard and to bring you one of those tablets. I saw you lock the cupboard half an hour ago, and I know you have the key in your possession. But I descend from Space; the doors, you see, remain unmoved. Now I am in the cupboard and am taking the tablet. Now I have it. Now I ascend with it.

I rushed to the closet and dashed the door open. One of the tablets was gone. With a mocking laugh, the Stranger appeared in the other corner of the room, and at the same time the tablet appeared upon the floor. I took it up. There could be no doubt — it was the missing tablet.

I groaned with horror, doubting whether I was not out of my senses; but the Stranger continued: "Surely you must now see that my explanation, and no other, suits the phenomena. What you call Solid things are really superficial; what you call Space is really nothing but a great Plane. I am in Space, and look down upon the insides of the things of which you only see the outsides. You could leave this Plane yourself, if you could but summon up the necessary volition. A slight upward or downward motion would enable you to see all that I can see.

"The higher I mount, and the further I go from your Plane, the more I can see, though of course I see it on a smaller scale. For example, I am ascending; now I can see your neighbour the Hexagon and his family in their several apartments; now I see the inside of the Theatre, ten doors off, from which the audience is only just departing; and on the other side a Circle in his study, sitting at his books. Now I shall come back to you. And, as a crowning proof, what do you say to my giving you a touch, just the least touch, in your stomach? It will not seriously injure you, and the slight pain you may suffer cannot be compared with the mental benefit you will receive."

Before I could utter a word of remonstrance, I felt a shooting pain in my inside, and a demoniacal laugh seemed to issue from within me. A moment afterwards the sharp agony had ceased, leaving nothing but a dull ache behind, and the Stranger began to reappear, saying, as he gradually increased in size, "There, I have not hurt you much, have I? If you are not convinced now, I don't know what will convince you. What say you?"

My resolution was taken. It seemed intolerable that I should endure existence subject to the arbitrary visitations of a Magician who could thus play tricks with one's very stomach. If only I could in any way manage to pin him against the wall till help came!

Once more I dashed my hardest angle against him, at the same time alarming the whole household by my cries for aid. I believe, at the moment of my onset, the Stranger had sunk below our Plane, and really found difficulty in rising. In any case he remained motionless, while I, hearing, as I thought, the sound of some help approaching, pressed against him with redoubled vigour, and continued to shout for assistance.

A convulsive shudder ran through the Sphere. "This must not be," I thought I heard him say: "either he must listen to reason, or I must have recourse to the last resource of civilization." Then, addressing me in a louder tone, he hurriedly exclaimed, "Listen: no stranger must witness what you have witnessed. Send your Wife back at once, before she enters the apartment. The Gospel of Three Dimensions must not be thus frustrated. Not thus must the fruits of one thousand years of waiting be thrown away. I hear her coming. Back! back! Away from me, or you must go with me— whither you know not—into the Land of Three Dimensions!"

"Fool! Madman! Irregular!" I exclaimed; "never will I release thee; thou shalt pay the penalty of thine impostures."

"Ha! Is it come to this?" thundered the Stranger: "then meet your fate: out of your Plane you go. Once, twice, thrice! 'Tis done!"

HOW I CAME TO SPACELAND, AND WHAT I SAW THERE

An unspeakable horror seized me. There was a darkness; then a dizzy, sickening sensation of sight that was not like seeing; I saw a Line that was no Line; Space that was not Space: I was myself, and not myself. When I could find voice, I shrieked aloud in agony, "Either this is madness or it is Hell." "It is neither," calmly replied the voice of the Sphere, "it is Knowledge; it is Three Dimensions: open your eye once again and try to look steadily."

I looked, and, behold, a new world! There stood before me, visibly incorporate, all that I had before inferred, conjectured, dreamed, of perfect Circular beauty. What seemed the centre of the Stranger's form lay open to my view: yet I could see no heart, nor lungs, nor arteries, only a beautiful harmonious Something—for which I had no words; but you, my Readers in Spaceland, would call it the surface of the Sphere.

Prostrating myself mentally before my Guide, I cried, "How is it, O divine ideal of consummate loveliness and wisdom that I see thy inside, and yet cannot discern thy heart, thy lungs, thy arteries, thy liver?" "What you think you see, you see not," he replied; "it is not given to you, nor to any other Being to behold my internal parts. I am of a different order of Beings from those in Flatland. Were I a Circle, you could discern my intestines, but I am a Being, composed as I told you before, of many Circles, the Many in the One, called in this country a Sphere. And, just as the outside of a Cube is a Square, so the outside of a Sphere presents the appearance of a Circle."

Bewildered though I was by my Teacher's enigmatic utterance, I no longer chafed against it, but worshipped him in silent adoration. He continued, with more mildness in his voice. "Distress not yourself if you cannot at first understand the deeper mysteries of Spaceland. By degrees they will dawn upon you. Let us begin by casting back a glance at the region whence you came. Return with me a while to the plains of Flatland, and I will shew you that which you have often reasoned and thought about, but never seen with the sense of sight—a visible angle." "Impossible!" I cried; but, the Sphere leading the way, I followed as if in a dream, till once more his voice arrested me: "Look yonder, and behold your own Pentagonal house, and all its inmates."

I looked below, and saw with my physical eye all that domestic individuality which I had hitherto merely inferred with the understanding. And how poor and shadowy was the inferred conjecture in comparison with the reality which I now beheld! My four Sons calmly asleep in the North-Western rooms, my two orphan Grandsons to the South; the Servants, the Butler, my Daughter, all in their several apartments. Only my affectionate Wife, alarmed by my continued absence, had quitted her room and was roving up and down in the Hall, anxiously awaiting my return. Also the Page, aroused by my cries, had left his room, and under pretext of ascertaining whether I had fallen somewhere in a faint, was prying into the cabinet in my study. All this I could now *see*, not merely infer; and as we came nearer and nearer, I could discern even the contents of my cabinet, and the two chests of gold, and the tablets of which the Sphere had made mention.

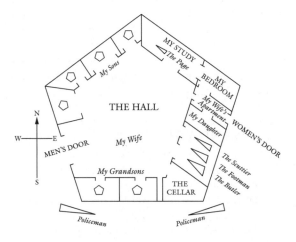

Touched by my Wife's distress, I would have sprung downward to reassure her, but I found myself incapable of motion. "Trouble not yourself about your Wife," said my Guide: "she will not be long left in anxiety; meantime, let us take a survey of Flatland."

Once more I felt myself rising through space. It was even as the Sphere had said. The further we receded from the object we beheld, the larger became the field of vision. My native city, with the interior of every house and every creature therein, lay open to my view in miniature. We mounted higher, and lo, the secrets of the earth, the depths of mines and inmost caverns of the hills, were bared before me.

Awestruck at the sight of the mysteries of the earth, thus unveiled before my unworthy eye, I said to my Companion, "Behold, I am become as a God. For the wise men in our country say that to see all things, or as they express it, *omnividence,* is the attribute of God alone." There was something of scorn in the voice of my Teacher as he made an-

swer: "Is it so indeed? Then the very pickpockets and cut-throats of my country are to be worshipped by your wise men as being Gods: for there is not one of them that does not see as much as you see now. But trust me, your wise men are wrong."

I: Then is omnividence the attribute of others besides Gods?

Sphere: I do not know. But, if a pick-pocket or a cut-throat of our country can see everything that is in your country, surely that is no reason why the pick-pocket or cut-throat should be accepted by you as a God. This omnividence, as you call it—it is not a common word in Spaceland—does it make you more just, more merciful, less selfish, more loving? Not in the least. Then how does it make you more divine?

I: "More merciful, more loving!" But these are the qualities of women! And we know that a Circle is a higher Being than a Straight Line, in so far as knowledge and wisdom are more to be esteemed than mere affection.

Sphere: It is not for me to classify human faculties according to merit. Yet many of the best and wisest in Spaceland think more of the affections than of the understanding, more of your despised Straight Lines than of your belauded Circles. But enough of this. Look yonder. Do you know that building?

I looked, and afar off I saw an immense Polygonal structure, in which I recognized the General Assembly Hall of the States of Flatland, surrounded by dense lines of Pentagonal buildings at right angles to each other, which I knew to be streets; and I perceived that I was approaching the great Metropolis.

"Here we descend," said my Guide. It was now morning, the first hour of the first day of the two thousandth year of our era. Acting, as was their wont, in strict accordance with precedent, the highest Circles of the realm were meeting in solemn conclave, as they had met on the first hour of the first day of the year 1000, and also on the first hour of the first day of the year 0.

The minutes of the previous meetings were now read by one whom I at once recognized as my brother, a perfectly Symmetrical Square, and the Chief Clerk of the High Council. It was found recorded on each occasion that: "Whereas the

States had been troubled by divers ill-intentioned persons pretending to have received revelations from another World, and professing to produce demonstrations whereby they had instigated to frenzy both themselves and others, it had been for this cause unanimously resolved by the Grand Council that on the first day of each millenary, special injunctions be sent to the Prefects in the several districts of Flatland, to make strict search for such misguided persons, and without formality of mathematical examination, to destroy all such as were Isosceles of any degree, to scourge and imprison any regular Triangle, to cause any Square or Pentagon to be sent to the district Asylum, and to arrest any one of higher rank, sending him straightway to the Capital to be examined and judged by the Council."

"You hear your fate," said the Sphere to me, while the Council was passing for the third time the formal resolution. "Death or imprisonment awaits the Apostle of the Gospel of Three Dimensions." "Not so," replied I, "the matter is now so clear to me, the nature of real space so palpable, that methinks I could make a child understand it. Permit me but to descend at this moment and enlighten them." "Not yet," said my Guide, "the time will come for that. Meantime I must perform my mission. Stay thou there in thy place." Saying these words, he leaped with great dexterity into the sea (if I may so call it) of Flatland, right in the midst of the ring of Counsellors. "I come," cried he, "to proclaim that there is a land of Three Dimensions."

I could see many of the younger Counsellors start back in manifest horror, as the Sphere's circular section widened before them. But on a sign from the presiding Circle—who shewed not the slightest alarm or surprise—six Isosceles of a low type from six different quarters rushed upon the Sphere. "We have him," they cried; "No; yes; we have him still! he's going! he's gone!"

"My Lords," said the President to the Junior Circles of the Council, "there is not the slightest need for surprise; the secret archives, to which I alone have access, tell me that a similar occurrence happened on the last two millennial commencements. You will, of course, say nothing of these trifles outside the Cabinet."

Raising his voice, he now summoned the guards. "Arrest the policemen; gag them. You know your duty." After he had consigned to their fate the wretched policemen—ill-fated and unwilling witnesses of a State-secret which they were not to be permitted to reveal—he again addressed the Counsellors. "My Lords, the business of the Council being concluded, I have only to wish you a happy New Year." Before departing, he expressed, at some length, to the Clerk, my excellent but most unfortunate brother, his sincere regret that, in accordance with precedent and for the sake of secrecy, he must condemn him to perpetual imprisonment, but added his satisfaction that, unless some mention were made by him of that day's incident, his life would be spared.

HOW, THOUGH THE SPHERE SHEWED ME OTHER MYSTERIES OF SPACELAND, I STILL DESIRED MORE; AND WHAT CAME OF IT

When I saw my poor brother led away to imprisonment, I attempted to leap down into the Council Chamber, desiring to intercede on his behalf, or at least bid him farewell. But I found that I had no motion of my own. I absolutely depended on the volition of my Guide, who said in gloomy tones, "Heed not thy brother; haply thou shalt have ample time hereafter to condole with him. Follow me."

(1) 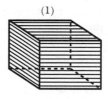   (2)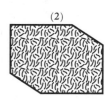

Once more we ascended into space. "Hitherto," said the Sphere, "I have shewn you nothing save Plane Figures and their interiors. Now I must introduce you to Solids, and reveal to you the plan upon which they are constructed. Behold this multitude of moveable square cards. See, I put one on another, not, as you supposed, Northward of the other, but *on* the other. Now a second, now a third. See, I am building up a Solid by a multitude of Squares parallel to one another. Now the Solid is complete, being as high as it is long and broad, and we call it a Cube."

"Pardon me, my Lord," replied I; "but to my eye the appearance is as of an Irregular Figure whose inside is laid open to the view; in other words, methinks I see no Solid, but a Plane such as we infer in Flatland; only of an Irregularity which betokens some monstrous criminal, so that the very sight of it is painful to my eyes."

"True," said the Sphere, "it appears to you a Plane, because you are not accustomed to light and shade and perspective; just as in Flatland a Hexagon would appear a Straight Line to one who has not the Art of Sight Recognition. But in reality it is a Solid, as you shall learn by the sense of Feeling."

He then introduced me to the Cube, and I found that this marvellous Being was indeed no Plane, but a Solid; and that he was endowed with six plane sides and eight terminal points called solid angles; and I remembered the saying of the Sphere that just such a Creature as this would be formed by a Square moving, in Space, parallel to himself: and I rejoiced to think that so insignificant a Creature as I could in some sense be called the Progenitor of so illustrious an offspring.

But still I could not fully understand the meaning of what my Teacher had told me concerning "light" and "shade" and "perspective"; and I did not hesitate to put my difficulties before him.

Were I to give the Sphere's explanation of these matters, succinct and clear though it was, it would be tedious to an inhabitant of Space, who knows these things already. Suffice it, that by his lucid statements, and by changing the position of objects and lights, and by allowing me to feel the several objects and even his own sacred Person, he at last made all things clear to me, so that I could now readily distinguish between a Circle and a Sphere, a Plane Figure and a Solid.

This was the Climax, the Paradise, of my strange eventful History. Henceforth I have to relate the story of my miserable Fall:—most miserable, yet surely most undeserved! For why should the thirst for knowledge be aroused, only to be disappointed and punished? My volition shrinks from the painful task of recalling my humiliation; yet, like a second Prometheus, I will endure this and worse, if by any means I may arouse in the interiors of Plane and Solid Humanity a spirit of rebellion against the Conceit which would limit our Dimensions to Two or Three or any number short of Infinity. Away

then with all personal considerations! Let me continue to the end, as I began, without further digressions or anticipations, pursuing the plain path of dispassionate History. The exact facts, the exact words,—and they are burnt in upon my brain,—shall be set down without alteration of an iota; and let my Readers judge between me and Destiny.

The Sphere would willingly have continued his lessons by indoctrinating me in the conformation of all regular Solids, Cylinders, Cones, Pyramids, Pentahedrons, Hexahedrons, Dodecahedrons, and Spheres: but I ventured to interrupt him. Not that I was wearied of knowledge. On the contrary, I thirsted for yet deeper and fuller draughts than he was offering to me.

"Pardon me," said I, "O Thou Whom I must no longer address as the Perfection of all Beauty; but let me beg thee to vouchsafe thy servant a sight of thine interior."

Sphere: My what?

I: Thine interior: thy stomach, thy intestines.

Sphere: Whence this ill-timed impertinent request? And what mean you by saying that I am no longer the Perfection of all Beauty?

I: My Lord, your own wisdom has taught me to aspire to One even more great, more beautiful, and more closely approximate to Perfection than yourself. As you yourself, superior to all Flatland forms, combine many Circles in One, so doubtless there is One above you who combines many Spheres in One Supreme Existence, surpassing even the Solids of Spaceland. And even as we, who are now in Space, look down on Flatland and see the insides of all things, so of a certainty there is yet above us some higher, purer region, whither thou dost surely purpose to lead me—O Thou Whom I shall always call, everywhere and in all Dimensions, my Priest, Philosopher, and Friend—some yet more spacious Space, some more dimensionable Dimensionality, from the vantage-ground of which we shall look down together upon the revealed insides of Solid things, and where thine own intestines, and those of thy kindred Spheres, will lie exposed to the view of the poor wandering exile from Flatland, to whom so much has already been vouchsafed.

Sphere: Pooh! Stuff! Enough of this trifling! The time is short, and much remains to be done before you are fit to proclaim the Gospel of Three Dimensions to your blind benighted countrymen in Flatland.

I: Nay, gracious Teacher, deny me not what I know it is in thy power to perform. Grant me but one glimpse of thine interior, and I am satisfied for ever, remaining henceforth thy docile pupil, thy unemancipable slave, ready to receive all thy teachings and to feed upon the words that fall from thy lips.

Sphere: Well, then, to content and silence you, let me say at once, I would shew you what you wish if I could; but I cannot. Would you have me turn my stomach inside out to oblige you?

I: But my Lord has shewn me the intestines of all my countrymen in the Land of Two Dimensions by taking me with him into the Land of Three. What therefore more easy than now to take his servant on a second journey into the blessed region of the Fourth Dimension, where I shall look down with him once more upon this land of Three Dimensions, and see the inside of every three-dimensioned house, the secrets of the solid earth, the treasures of the mines in Spaceland, and the intestines of every solid living creature, even of the noble and adorable Spheres.

Sphere: But where is this land of Four Dimensions?

I: I know not: but doubtless my Teacher knows.

Sphere: Not I. There is no such land. The very idea of it is utterly inconceivable.

I: Not inconceivable, my Lord, to me, and therefore still less inconceivable to my Master. Nay, I despair not that, even here, in this region of Three Dimensions, your Lordship's art may make the Fourth Dimension visible to me; just as in the Land of Two Dimensions my Teacher's skill would fain have opened the eyes of his blind servant to the invisible presence of a Third Dimension, though I saw it not.

Let me recall the past. Was I not taught below that when I saw a Line and inferred a Plane, I in reality saw a Third unrecognized Dimension, not the same as brightness, called "height"? And does it not now follow that, in this region, when I see a Plane and infer a Solid, I really see a Fourth unrecognized Dimension, not the same as colour, but existent, though infinitesimal and incapable of measurement?

And besides this, there is the Argument from Analogy of Figures.

Sphere: Analogy! Nonsense: what analogy?

I: Your Lordship tempts his servant to see whether he remembers the revelations imparted to him. Trifle not with me, my Lord; I crave, I thirst, for more knowledge. Doubtless we cannot *see* that other higher Spaceland now, because we have no eye in our stomachs. But, just as there was the realm of Flatland, though that poor puny Lineland Monarch could neither turn to left nor right to discern it, and just as there *was* close at hand, and touching my frame, the land of Three Dimensions, though I, blind senseless wretch, had no power to touch it, no eye in my interior to discern it, so of a surety there is a Fourth Dimension, which my Lord perceives with the inner eye of thought. And that it must exist my Lord himself has taught me. Or can he have forgotten what he himself imparted to his servant?

In One Dimension, did not a moving Point produce a Line with *two* terminal points?

In Two Dimensions, did not a moving Line produce a Square with *four* terminal points?

In Three Dimensions, did not a moving Square produce—did not this eye of mine behold it—that blessed Being, a Cube, with *eight* terminal points?

And in Four Dimensions shall not a moving Cube—alas, for Analogy, and alas for the Progress of Truth, if it be not so—shall not, I say, the motion of a divine Cube result in a still more divine Organization with *sixteen* terminal points?

Behold the infallible confirmation of the Series, 2, 4, 8, 16: is not this a Geometrical Progression? Is not this—if I might quote my Lord's own words—"strictly according to Analogy"?

Again, was I not taught by my Lord that as in a Line there are *two* bounding Points, and in a Square there are *four* bounding Lines, so in a Cube there must be *six* bounding Squares? Behold once more the confirming Series, 2, 4, 6: is not this an Arithmetical Progression? And consequently does it not of necessity follow that the more divine offspring of the divine Cube in the Land of Four Dimensions, must have 8 bounding Cubes: and is not this also, as my Lord has taught me to believe, "strictly according to Analogy"?

O, my Lord, my Lord, behold, I cast myself in faith upon conjecture, not knowing the facts; and I appeal to your Lordship to confirm or deny my logical anticipations. If I am wrong, I yield, and will no longer demand a fourth Dimension; but, if I am right, my Lord will listen to reason.

I ask therefore, is it, or is it not, the fact, that ere now your countrymen also have witnessed the descent of Beings of a higher order than their own, entering closed rooms, even as your Lordship entered mine, without the opening of doors or windows, and appearing and vanishing at will? On the reply to this question I am ready to stake everything. Deny it, and I am henceforth silent. Only vouchsafe an answer.

Sphere (after a pause): It is reported so. But men are divided in opinion as to the facts. And even granting the facts, they explain them in different ways. And in any case, however great may be the number of different explanations, no one has adopted or suggested the theory of a Fourth Dimension. Therefore, pray have done with this trifling, and let us return to business.

I: I was certain of it. I was certain that my anticipations would be fulfilled. And now have patience with me and answer me yet one more question, best of Teachers! Those who have thus appeared—no one knows whence—and have returned—no one knows whither—have they also contracted their sections and vanished somehow into that more Spacious Space, whither I now entreat you to conduct me?

Sphere (moodily): They have vanished, certainly —if they ever appeared. But most people say that these visions arose from the thought—you will not understand me—from the brain; from the perturbed angularity of the Seer.

I: Say they so? Oh, believe them not. Or if it indeed be so, that this other Space is really Thoughtland, then take me to that blessed Region where I in Thought shall see the insides of all solid things. There, before my ravished eye, a Cube, moving in some altogether new direction, but strictly according to Analogy, so as to make every particle of his interior pass through a new kind of Space, with a

wake of its own—shall create a still more perfect perfection than himself, with sixteen terminal Extrasolid angles, and Eight solid Cubes for his Perimeter. And once there, shall we stay our upward course? In that blessed region of Four Dimensions, shall we linger on the threshold of the Fifth, and not enter therein? Ah, no! Let us rather resolve that our ambition shall soar with our corporal ascent. Then, yielding to our intellectual onset, the gates of the Sixth Dimension shall fly open; after that a Seventh, and then an Eighth—

How long I should have continued I know not. In vain did the Sphere, in his voice of thunder, reiterate his command of silence, and threaten me with the direst penalties if I persisted. Nothing could stem the flood of my ecstatic aspirations. Perhaps I was to blame; but indeed I was intoxicated with the recent draughts of Truth to which he himself had introduced me. However, the end was not long in coming. My words were cut short by a crash outside, and a simultaneous crash inside me, which impelled me through space with a velocity that precluded speech. Down! down! down! I was rapidly descending; and I knew that return to Flatland was my doom. One glimpse, one last and never-to-be-forgotten glimpse I had of that dull level wilderness— which was now to become my Universe again— spread out before my eye. Then a darkness. . . .

NOTES

1. When I say "sitting," of course I do not mean any change of attitude such as you in Spaceland signify by that word; for as we have no feet, we can no more "sit" nor "stand" (in your sense of the word) than one of your soles or flounders.

Nevertheless, we perfectly well recognize the different mental states of volition implied in "lying," "sitting," and "standing," which are to some extent indicated to a beholder by a slight increase of lustre corresponding to the increase of volition.

But on this, and a thousand other kindred subjects, time forbids me to dwell.

Further Questions

1. You see a universe of only three dimensions. Is that how many dimensions the universe has? How can you find out? Suppose you make a date to meet someone on the second floor of a building that sits on the south corner of Hollywood and Vine. You have specified only three coordinates. What is missing?

2. To move along the fourth dimension, you would have to go "Upward but not upward." Relate this paradox to the problem of "Upward, not Northward" in the story. What happens when you try to visualize the fourth dimension?
3. Why can't you see time? Try to explain this using what you've learned in Flatland.
4. Many mystics over the ages have claimed that ultimate reality cannot be perceived or understood using our ordinary concepts. Often they have tried to communicate what they claim are mystical insights using self-contradictory or paradoxical statements. What significance, if any, do you think the story of Flatland has to such concerns?

Further Readings

Burger, Dionys. *Sphereland*. New York: Thomas Y. Crowell Company, 1965. Takes off where *Flatland* ends; it is told by a Hexagon who is the Square's grandson! It also takes into account the more recent non-Euclidean geometries of curved spaces.

Gamow, George. *Mr. Tompkins in Wonderland*. New York: Cambridge University Press, 1940. Illustrates without any technical language some of the most startling implications of living in an Einsteinian universe.

The Incredible Shrinking Zeno   6

DANIEL KOLAK AND DAVID GOLOFF

A brief biography of Daniel Kolak appears on page 96.

David Goloff, who received his Ph.D. in mathematics from Johns Hopkins University in 1989, has taught mathematics at William Paterson University and Northwestern State University of Louisiana. His current research interests concern holomorphic mappings between complex manifolds and envelopes of lines, which he is trying to apply to families (pencils) of conic sections. He and Daniel Kolak have collaborated on *Mathematical Thought* (Prentice Hall/Paramount/Macmillan) and have developed a multifaceted view of and approach to mathematics in terms of its importance to philosophy in particular and to thought in general.

Reading Questions

1. What was Parmenides' view of reality?
2. How did Zeno try to defend Parmenides against his critics?
3. Why does your moving across the room *not* solve Zeno's paradox?
4. What does "infinite process in a finite time" have to do with the problem posed?
5. Is it possible to do finite arithmetic with an infinite sum? What does the Gauss example have to do with it?
6. Are we capable of knowing more than we are capable of seeing? Why?
7. Whose side are Zeus and Hera on?
8. What does Shrinking Zeno see, from his point of view, after he has shrunk out of sight of the observers in the Lyceum? Why?
9. In what sense is Zeno's paradox solved? What is the solution? In what sense is Zeno's paradox not solved? What is the problem?

10. When you're walking, pay attention to your experience. Do you find yourself, in one way or another, having some concept of where you are now, of where you are going, and the space in between? How did you plan when you should leave in order to arrive somewhere on time? Do you find yourself psychologically projecting your concepts of space and time into the world? How do you understand the idea that you are moving?

WE OBSERVE THE WORLD and find ourselves automatically engaged in concepts such as place or position, time, distance, size or measurement, and a combination of these concepts called *motion*. Motion, in turn, involves the concept of identity: *one and the same* object is thought to occupy different *places* at different *times*. Thus, our most simple, commonsense beliefs about ordinary objects moving from one place to another involves our most complex and deepest concepts: space, time, and identity. It is important to point out that *all* of these are concepts. This means that they are concepts as opposed to realities that exist "out there."

The ancient (5th century B.C.) Greek philosopher Parmenides asserted that existence is not made up of individual things but that, in reality, "all is one." The totality of existence is one undifferentiated, unchanging, eternal whole. Even the simplest change, such as one thing moving from one place to another, is but an illusion. His basic argument was: If the whole existence is *not* one (if the universe is made of different things), then what separates one thing from another? Parmenides concluded that the supposed separation between one thing and another would have to consist in something that does not exist—i.e., nothing—and that this would be an absurdity. If we suppose that there are two things between which there is nothing, then these are not two things but one thing.

Zeno, a student of Parmenides, tried to prove Parmenides right. Zeno focused on the fundamental concepts mentioned above. He presented about forty paradoxes, each of which was supposed to show that those who claimed Parmenides' view was absurd were starting from an even *more* absurd view! Only a handful of his paradoxes have survived the twenty-five centuries since Zeno posed them, and we shall here discuss only the "Dichotomy," one of his paradoxes of motion, for the purpose of *refining Zeno's paradox within contemporary thought.*

1. STATEMENT OF ZENO'S PARADOX OF MOTION: THE DICHOTOMY

Zeno began by assuming for the sake of argument, that things are as they seem: there are different places and objects at those places (as common sense supposes) and that an object can indeed move from one place to another. He then posed the following puzzle.

Achilles starts running from a starting position toward a finish line. Before he reaches the finish line he must go half the distance. Achilles must then also go half of the remaining distance. And then he must go half of the distance that still remains. And so on. This is pictured in Figure 1.

Suppose Achilles starts running at a constant speed toward the finish line one mile away. Obviously, before he runs the whole mile he must run ½ mile. After he has gone ½ mile, he cannot just suddenly appear at the finish line without first crossing half the *remaining* ½ mile—that is, he must go ¾ of the distance from the starting point. When he's run ¾ mile, there is ¼ mile remaining but, again, he can't just appear at the finish line without going halfway between the ¾ mark and the finish line. When Achilles is only ⅛ mile away from the finish line, he must still run halfway between where he is at the moment and where the finish line is. At that point Achilles will be only ¹⁄₁₆ mile from the finish line. But, again, he can't run ¹⁄₁₆ mile without first going one-half of that ¹⁄₁₆ mile. And so on. "To say it once," as Zeno was fond of putting it, "is to say it forever."

Is there any remaining distance, at *any* point in the run, where Achilles can reach the finish line

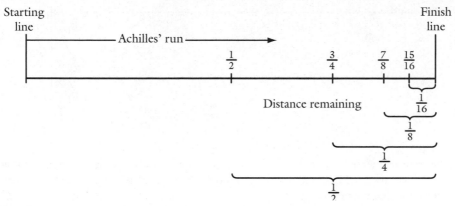

Figure 1

without first running halfway between wherever he is and where the finish line is? Of course not. How long can he proceed this way? Forever! Wherever Achilles is between the starting line and the finish line, there will always be some distance remaining between him and the finish line. So: *How is it possible for Achilles to ever reach the finish line?*

Achilles *does* appear at the finish line. That's what our eyes tell us! Reason says otherwise: If we think carefully about what we are seeing, we will understand that what *seems* to be going on can't *really* be going on—at least not in the way we think!

To address this paradox we must give it a precise formulation so that instead of merely intuitively feeling that there is a paradox (a psychological sense of dissonance), we can precisely identify the discrepancy. Let us therefore restate the problem more formally. Let A denote the starting point, and let B denote the finish line of the racecourse. We know that Achilles must, before he appears at the finish line, be at the point halfway between A and B. Call this halfway point between A and B, B_1. To say this is not to divide the space between A and B, nor to "halve the distance," it is merely to give a name to a point that must be there. B_1 is there whether we name it or not. That is, we are not performing some loaded manipulative move; we are not in any way changing the distance between A and B; we are merely bringing out of our conceptual framework that which, implicitly, already is there in the path between A and B.

Our concept of the path taken by Achilles is the real line, which involves an ordering of the path

between Achilles at the starting position at A and the finish line at B, as follows. There is a point halfway between A and B, B_1, such that Achilles' path is ordered so that B_1 comes after A and before B. There is a point, halfway between B_1 and B, and let us call this point, halfway between B_1 and B, B_2. There is a point halfway between B_2 and B, B_3. And so on (Figure 2).

Suppose Achilles is at B_{1099}, the point halfway between B_{1098} and B. Between B_{1099} and B *is a point*, B_{1100}; Achilles at B_{1099} cannot just suddenly, without cause and for no reason, vanish out of existence and pop into existence at $B!$ He must move along a continuous path through the midpoint.

That Achilles could never arrive at B is implied in that our description of how he arrives at the finish line evokes the necessity of an *infinite process*, since to get from any point to any other he must have gone through an infinite number of halfway points. Thus, there are infinitely many B_n:

$$B_1, B_2, B_3, \ldots, B_{1099}, B_{1100}, \ldots, B_n, \ldots$$

If you are not sufficiently puzzled yet, then note that even if B_1 were eliminated from the discussion and all the other B_n were kept in the discussion, it would have no effect whatsoever on Zeno's paradox: none! Similarly, for any finite number of B_n: No matter where he begins prior to B, Achilles only reaches the finish line at B after passing by infinitely many B_n. For instance, if Achilles starts at B_{1786} and starts running toward B, you would have exactly the same paradox as before. But we should also note that where before we had a mere psychological

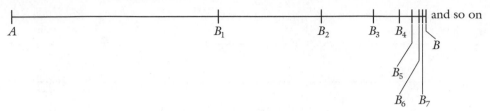

sense of puzzlement concerning Achilles running toward a finish line, we now have a specific set of concepts within our conceptual framework to which this paradox can be addressed and to which we must turn our rational attention.

Now, not only are the infinite number of B_n implicit in the problem, this is actually the source of the paradox. After all, were there only a finite number of B_n, Achilles would arrive at the finish line after a finite, not an infinite, process—and that Achilles could do that would be no more surprising than, say, you counting to the number ten.

The paradox thus appears embodied precisely in the question, "How can Achilles accomplish an infinite process in a finite amount of time?" or, "How can Achilles travel a finite distance by traveling infinitely many distances?" If Achilles were to slow down at each B_n so that he always takes one second to go from B_n to B_{n+1}, then it would take an infinite amount of time to reach the finish line and in fact he could not by this process ever reach it. In that case, there would be no paradox. Achilles does not reach the finish line—that's the answer. Or, it takes an infinite amount of time for him to reach the finish line through an infinite process—that's the answer. "Infinite process—therefore infinite distance" is not paradoxical, nor is "Infinite process—infinite time." What is paradoxical is "Infinite process—finite time and/or finite distance."

Note that what we are seeing here is not merely that "there is something wrong with our conceptual framework." We see much more—namely, that there is a fine-tuned problem with reconciling our concept of the finite with our concept of the infinite. In other words, we see exactly what parts of the conceptual framework appear to be out of whack (as opposed to the general feeling that "something is out of whack").

You probably believe things move and runners reach finish lines. Zeno is not claiming that experience is not that way. He is claiming that the nature of our experience is conceptually problematic. For instance, if you tried to refute Zeno by running across the room, he would probably just shake his head and tell you that you have misunderstood his paradox, for had you *not* been able to run across the room *then there would be no paradox!* The point is that what you (think you) *see* and what you (think you) think leads you to form particular beliefs about the way things actually are, but that a closer examination of the concepts behind your beliefs contradicts those very beliefs! Thus, Zeno's paradox is an argument against your ordinary beliefs about the way things are. Indeed, the word "paradox" means, literally, "beyond (*para*) belief (*doxa*)." And it is your own (often hidden) conceptions of the way things are that generates this paradox.

Note that Zeno's paradox directly examines the question of what there is between one place (the starting point) and another (the finish line). Thus, this addresses Parmenides' question of what separates one thing from another in a specific way. Notice, too, that this question is posed precisely and in mathematical terms: Zeno discusses *quantified* distances.

Zeno's paradox makes us question whether our beliefs regarding what is going on in the world can be made coherent using our concepts of motion, points, continuous lines, space, time, change, identity, etc. In implying that you don't know how motion is possible, what is at issue, ultimately, in Zeno's paradox, is the entire basis of the concepts we use in developing our knowledge of the world.

One reason why this paradox was difficult to address in ancient times was that the mathematics of that time only allowed for the addition of a finite number of quantities. To give a truly contemporary exposition of this paradox, we must replace such antiquated concepts with new ones.

2. SOLVING ZENO'S PARADOX OF MOTION: SUMMING THE INFINITE

The real question is how do you get a finite distance from an infinite amount of distances? Or, how do you get a finite amount of time from an infinite number of time intervals? These are really the same question, namely:

How can the sum of an infinite number of quantities be a finite quantity?

Each of the infinite number of quantities is itself a finite quantity. For instance, the length of the interval from A to B_1 is ½ mile. The interval from B_1 to B_2 is ¼ mile. The interval from B_2 to B_3 is ⅛ mile. Generally, the length of the interval from

$$B_{k-1} \text{ to } B_k \text{ is } (½)^k$$

Thus the entire interval from A to B must have length equal to the sum of the lengths of all the nonoverlapping parts:

$$½ + ¼ + ⅛ + \ldots + (½)^k + \ldots$$

The $(½)^k$ term comes from noting the pattern

$$½ = (½)^1, \quad ¼ = (½)(½) = (½)^2$$
$$⅛ = (½)(½)(½) = (½)^3.$$

Each term is just ½ raised to a power one greater than the term before it. The final "..." simply means that this pattern continues forever.

This kind of expression, one which involves the summation of an infinite number of quantities, is called an infinite series. The result of summing an infinite series we refer to as the "sum of the infinite series." The question before us is how to understand such a sum of an infinite series or how an infinite series can have a finite sum.[1]

Now notice something else. Not only are each of the quantities finite, they get *smaller*. It is intuitively clear that if we were to add up an infinite number of positive quantities of the same magnitude, the sum would be infinite. What is less intuitively clear is that if we were to add up an infinite number of quantities of lesser and lesser magni-

tudes, the sum could be *finite*. That is, what you may think is obvious — that one can't just add up an infinite series and have it be finite — is not really obvious at all. What *precise* reason do you have for believing an infinite series cannot have a finite sum? Perhaps you think that something which is infinite in some sense cannot be finite in another sense, but this is not precise and only begs the question.

The Zeno diagram in Figure 3 implies that this infinite collection of intervals does indeed come together into a finite interval. When you look at the diagram, what do you see but an infinite number of intervals coming together into a finite interval? That's what the picture shows! Often, people understand this in reverse; they take it to mean that what they see cannot be happening. What they should conclude, instead, is that what they are seeing is something quite remarkable: an infinite number of quantities (lengths) forming a finite quantity (length). This is represented arithmetically by the above infinite series. Thus what is happening is quite clear in pictures, but we need to see how to follow this through in the arithmetic representation. What is needed is a *theory* to account for what is being seen. Why deny what is visually very clear, and only a matter of extending a theory, in favor of what is not intuitively obvious at all but only prejudice?

It would be premature to not investigate the possibility of extending the mathematics with which we implement our concepts of space and time to account for the paradox on the grounds that the ultimate lesson of the paradox may be that we should stop playing conceptual games. It might turn out that people either are not intelligent enough to understand the world or that the world is unintelligible. We do have good reasons to believe that any conceptual framework will eventually break down and have to be rejected (one will sooner or later arrive at a certain stage of conceptual development). This suggests that to some extent, or in some sense, the world is ultimately not intelligible. But this only means that the conceptual apparatus will never be perfect nor complete — not that the apparatus is completely useless. Nor does it mean that our conceptual frameworks do not in some way get at the truth. This is because our conceptual frameworks give us a *point of analysis* and the potential of generating

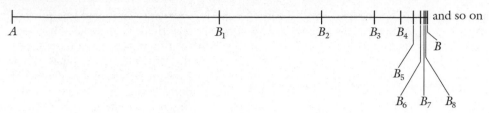

new and better paradoxes with which to revise and generate still better paradoxes through which our concepts get better and better. It is this process that allows us to compare known frameworks with the unknown — possibly unknowable — truth.

Below we explain how Zeno's paradox of motion can be solved via the method of summing an infinite series. Once we understand how summing an infinite series is indeed possible, we will be able to see how a mathematical theory can account for Zeno's paradox. This, in turn, will set the stage for our refinement of the paradox within contemporary thought.

Paradoxes and their solutions play dual roles in the dynamic process of conceptual evolution. In particular, as we are about to explain, the infinite series with a finite sum is not an impossibility at all. Yet, as we shall then see, Zeno was quite right to suggest that there is a deep and fundamental paradox which even the sum of an infinite series cannot transcend. And Zeno's paradox of motion is as sophisticated a way of pointing to where the fundamental paradox is as the sum of the infinite series is of showing where it is not.

A problem people typically have in accepting the idea of an infinite series of terms or quantities having a finite sum is that they link the idea of addition to the manual procedure of adding two terms at a time. This is only one method among alternatives. A plus sign indicates that pieces are part of a whole. The problem of summing the infinite series is one of *discovering* what whole the pieces are part of. In the case of summing a finite series of terms, you could do this by adding each number to the next. This is only a method of discovering what the sum is. The sum itself does not represent a computational activity.

If we free ourselves of the idea of doing addition from left to right, one step at a time, then we will begin to see that summing an infinite series can be made sense of. Let us do this in the case of a finite number of terms. When a sum is written down, even a finite one, this does not imply that we are obligated to add the first two numbers and then add the result to the third and so on. This is illustrated by an amusing story about the child prodigy J. C. F. Gauss (1777–1855). One day in elementary school Gauss' teacher wanted to keep the class busy by having them add up all the counting numbers 1 to 99:

$$1+2+3+ \ldots +97+98+99$$

As soon as the problem was posed, Gauss quickly shouted out, "4950!" He did this by observing the following: If you add the first and last terms (1+99) you get 100. If you add the second term to the second to last term (2+98) you get 100. And so on. There will be 49 pairs of terms, each of which together make 100, plus the one middle term, 50. Thus, the sum is 49 times 100, plus 50, which equals 4950! The point here is that the + signs do not necessarily mean that you should do addition as naively indicated.

Let us prepare to approach summing an infinite series by first looking at a related sum of a *finite* number of terms. We can do the following:

$$S = \tfrac{1}{2} + \tfrac{1}{4} + \tfrac{1}{8} + \tfrac{1}{16}$$
$$2S = 1 + \tfrac{1}{2} + \tfrac{1}{4} + \tfrac{1}{8}$$
$$2S - 1 = \tfrac{1}{2} + \tfrac{1}{4} + \tfrac{1}{8}$$
$$2S - 1 + \tfrac{1}{16} = \tfrac{1}{2} + \tfrac{1}{4} + \tfrac{1}{8} + \tfrac{1}{16}$$

Notice that the right side of the last equation is the same as what we started with. Therefore,

$$S = 2S - 1 + \tfrac{1}{16}$$

So, adding $(1-S)$ to both sides and subtracting $\tfrac{1}{16}$, we get

$$S + 1 - S - \tfrac{1}{16} = 2S - S - 1 + 1 + \tfrac{1}{16} - \tfrac{1}{16}$$

so that,

$$1 - \tfrac{1}{16} = S = \tfrac{15}{16}$$

Let us now try this idea on summing our *infinite* Zeno series:

$$S = \frac{1}{2} + \frac{1}{4} + \frac{1}{8} + \frac{1}{16} + \frac{1}{32} + \frac{1}{64} + \dots$$
$$2S = 1 + \frac{1}{2} + \frac{1}{4} + \frac{1}{8} + \frac{1}{16} + \frac{1}{32} + \dots$$
$$2S - 1 = \frac{1}{2} + \frac{1}{4} + \frac{1}{8} + \frac{1}{16} + \dots$$

Once again, we have, on the right side of the equation, exactly what we started with[2]; therefore, $S = 2S - 1$ and so $S = 1$!

Thus, the ordinary rules of arithmetic can be used on this infinite sum. Just as Achilles does not reach the halfway mark, stop, and then go on to the next, and just as Gauss did not have to add the first pair of terms, stop, then add the next, and so on, we also do not have to add two terms, stop, and add the next.

The difficulty in understanding how it is possible to sum an infinite number of quantities into a finite quantity is that we are here confronted with a situation rarely encountered in our daily lives, when usually the only mathematical thought we have to engage in, in terms of our actions, is finite arithmetic. For instance, balancing your checkbook requires a finite number of arithmetical steps. The reason people feel the puzzle in Zeno's paradox is that the solution requires a type of arithmetic that they are not accustomed to. Contemporary mathematics shows us how a finite amount of time can be sufficient for the completion of infinitely many events.

The philosophically productive move here—one that engages us with the real mystery, not removes us from it—is to realize that we have matured within our present conceptual framework and to use this intellectual maturation as an opportunity to explore the world further with our concepts of motion, time, space, infinite series, distance, etc. On the other hand, we should not be too quick to attach ourselves to this solution to Zeno's paradox! Many writers on this topic do not realize that Zeno could have made things much more difficult by posing his questions in terms of going $\frac{1}{3}$ the distance instead of going $\frac{1}{2}$ the distance. One must go $\frac{1}{3}$ of the distance. Then one must go a distance $\frac{1}{3}$ as long as the *previous* distance traveled, $\frac{1}{9}$ of the full distance, and so on.[3] This would have forced us to consider the following infinite sum:

$$S = \frac{1}{3} + \frac{1}{9} + \frac{1}{27} + \frac{1}{81} \dots$$

Here, if we follow the same procedure as earlier, we get $S = 3S - 1$ and thus: $S = \frac{1}{2}$! This means that the runner gets only $\frac{1}{2}$ of the way to the finish line! The $\frac{1}{2}$ marks, even though there are an infinite number of them, would not extend to the finish line. Thus we see that Zeno posed an infinite series problem of minimum difficulty! If you pose one of greater difficulty (or refine the paradox slightly differently, as we shall do shortly) Zeno's paradox cannot be solved in this way.

It should be clear, however, that an objection like "the sum of the Zeno series cannot be finite because you can't ever finish doing the addition" makes no sense because nobody is saying that one must do the addition as naively indicated. It would be like saying you can't ever pose Zeno's paradox because you can't ever finish showing all of the halfway marks. What one must do instead is find the sum. Just as Gauss found the sum even though he did not do what the teacher naively intended, we must find the Zeno sum without having to add each term to the next, which would take longer than the time we have to do it.

Ultimately, the objection that you cannot sum the Zeno series comes down to a rejection of any infinite concept. This would be consistent in that you would then be rejecting both the paradox and the solution for the same reason. But it would be inconsistent to reject the solution and keep the paradox (which requires the infinite to be stated). In taking this way out, both Zeno's paradox and the solution would no longer exist as such.

Since the Zeno series can be understood and computed, why not allow it as an explanatory conceptual tool for the way we conceive the world? The concept of summing an infinite series is only an extension of the idea of summing a finite series. No one objects to adding $2 + 2$ to get 4. No one thinks this is some kind of mathematical trick that does not appreciate the nature of plurality. On the contrary, $2 + 2 = 4$ gives a precise description of the situation in which one wants to be able to compare finite quantities of objects, lengths, or times. Why then not accept that summing the infinite series gives a precise way to describe Zeno's paradox?

Zeno's paradox suggests the real mystery is how an infinite process can occur within a finite distance and finite time. *Summing an infinite series answers this question.* It is not mysterious that an infinite number of distances come together into a finite distance. Whether Achilles begins near the finish line or at the starting line, it is indeed possible that *a finite distance can consist of an infinite number of distances.* However, intuitively we still feel that there is something mysterious in Zeno's paradox. *The above analysis merely shows us that the mystery is not where we might have thought it was!*

3. REFINING ZENO'S PARADOX

We now carry on the tradition of Zeno by acknowledging the present state of conceptual development and reacting to it. Yet, we must maintain a philosophically critical stance with regard to our new knowledge. To simply deny the concept of an infinite series is not a philosophically critical stance. We need a specific philosophically critical tool that applies to the particular concept rather than a generalized suspicion of concepts. Paradox could almost be defined as such a critical tool. Our paradox must be just as precise as the concept to which it reacts.

It would be productive now to find a stronger paradox that would provide a greater opportunity to examine and refine our concepts. The idea is that even though there is a way to answer Zeno's paradox, we see that our concepts are far stranger and much further removed from common sense than we originally thought. Summing the infinite series, though logically OK, is still difficult to relate to our perception of reality. It is hard to experience the passing of all the halfway marks. Try to imagine all the halfway marks (infinitely many of them) drawn on the floor of the racetrack and then experiencing Achilles passing by all of them to reach the finish line. You can't. You can only imagine a blur. It is not that our concepts are wrong or mistaken, but rather that our concepts are not the stuff of the world in and of itself.

Let us begin our refinement of Zeno's paradox by taking another look at our Zeno diagram below. As the n in the B_n get larger and larger the B_n get closer and closer to B and it becomes more and more difficult to draw, see, or imagine (from our point of view) the tiny gaps between B_n and B for the successively larger n. Let us assume that we are drawing our Zeno diagram with a pencil of thickness 1 millimeter. Then, when the gaps between B_n and B are smaller than 1 mm, we do the following. Through our conceptual microscope we take a picture of the 1 mm remaining part of the Zeno dia-

gram—say at B_5. We now have an enlarged picture of the gap between B_5 and B. If the length of the remaining interval between Achilles and the finish line at B is 1 meter, the enlargement is also one meter and to scale: It is a "blowup," (like the "blowup" feature used in photo enlargements; see Figure 4).

Now that the picture is blown up, we can continue to use our 1 mm pencil to mark off further B_n until once again—this time at B_{10}—we will have to use our conceptual microscope to take another picture that will be a blowup of the gap between B_{10} and B. It should be intuitively obvious that we can continue this process forever; since there are infinitely many B_n, we can make infinitely many diagrams. Our Zeno diagram was constructed to examine the path of a moving object: Achilles. When we used the infinite series our attention was focused on the distance traveled, that is, what was being added up. Let us focus our attention now on the gap itself, that is, on the distance between Achilles and the finish line.

Our story begins back in the Lyceum. Zeno has just finished posing his paradox of motion to a group who have been ridiculing Parmenides' view that all is one. Turning to Achilles, their leader, Zeno says:

"You make fun of Parmenides because you think you are so wise. You think you know what space, time, and motion are; but I have just shown that you merely *think* you know! You say Parmenides' views are absurd because they *contradict what your eyes tell you.* But your view is the far more absurd view, for you *contradict yourself!* If a wise man is someone who knows how little he knows, obviously, Achilles, you are anything but wise—you are just the opposite!"

Insulted, Achilles orders his men to seize Zeno.

"Enough," cries Achilles. "I will now defeat both you and your arguments, Zeno!"

Achilles orders his strongest warriors to form a gauntlet, or corridor, that ends at a wall, with Zeno in the middle. Achilles begins at one end and starts running after Zeno, who, when he reaches the wall, will be crushed between the wall and Achilles' shield.

Unbeknownst to any of them, however, Zeus has been watching the proceedings from a cloud:

"Hera, come and watch how these brutes think to dismiss the magical query which against my

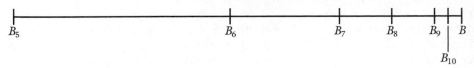

B_5 B_6 B_7 B_8 B_9 B

B_{10}

Figure 4

wishes you have thrown down to the mortal philosophers. You said it would make them think, but look! Our poor Zeno's skull is about to be crushed. What a shame. I was hoping we would have millennia of long and lasting amusement at the mortals' attempt to reconcile their contradictory points of view. You have overestimated these foolish mortals. How often have you he ard them dismiss the greatest mysteries as simply being mysteries? How their poets go on and on, ad nauseum, about their wonderful lack of explanation! Your game will end up but a beautifully unenlightening poem, and Zeno will be crushed."

"I have already taken care of it."

"What have you done, my dear and clever wife?"

"Watch, dear, and be amazed."

Achilles takes up his shield and begins running toward the wall with Zeno between the shield and the wall. When Achilles is 1 meter away from the wall, Zeno puts his right hand up to block against the shield and his left hand up to brace him against the wall, thinking this might help prevent him from being crushed when, suddenly, he begins to shrink! When the distance between Achilles' shield and the wall has halved, Zeno has shrunk by one-half. When the distance between the shield and the wall is ¼ meter, Zeno has shrunk by one-quarter. And so on. When the distance between the shield and the wall is $\frac{1}{128}$ meter, Zeno has shrunk down to $\frac{1}{128}$ scale. And Zeno keeps shrinking such that as the distance is $\frac{1}{2_n}$ meters, Zeno has shrunk down to $\frac{1}{2_n}$ scale. By the moment Achilles has smashed his shield into the wall, Zeno is nowhere to be seen!

Up in the clouds, Zeus turns to Hera and says, "You must feel very little for your bold young student Zeno, my dear wife, that you should wish him to suffer so sincerely for your folly."

"Bold indeed, but why so certain that he suffers? That mighty warrior's shield did not crush him. Nor was there suffering upon his countenance while he was visible. And this is exactly all

that is certain, for he is no longer visible! It is your gloating that hides suffering so insincerely. Were you sincere you would surely recognize that I have bequeathed us all a query worthy of great deliberation and which I am certain will only vindicate my Zeno and make your gloating but a fool's solution to a mystery worthy of even us gods."

Let us look at the situation more closely. We begin with Achilles' shield at point A one meter from the wall and Zeno standing between the shield at A and the wall at B, his arms extended between the shield and the wall (see Figure 5).

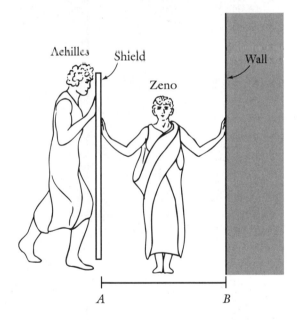

Let us examine the situation from Zeno's point of view between the shield and the wall. Doing so will help us discover the source of Hera's confidence.

As Hera pointed out in our story, from the point of view of the outside observers the shield never crushes Zeno. What about from Zeno's point of view? As he begins to shrink he sees Achilles' shield getting larger and larger. By the time Achilles' shield is at, say, $B_{11,000}$, the surface of the shield is still only just barely touching the surface of Zeno's right hand, but the shield is now so big compared to Zeno's body that it looks to him like a giant wall reaching all the way up and all the way down as far as he can see. At the same time, the wall that his left palm is just barely touching seems to go upward forever and downward forever. From Zeno's point of view, the spectators in the Lyceum are even farther away than the already unseen receding base of Achilles' shield, thus they are virtually infinitely far away. Therefore, at this point, *Zeno will observe no further changes in his visual field whatsoever.* From Zeno's point of view, nothing is happening! Nothing else is moving. There is a virtually infinite shield on his right and a virtually infinite wall on his left. If there ever was some process going on, from his point of view it has stopped (see Figure 6).

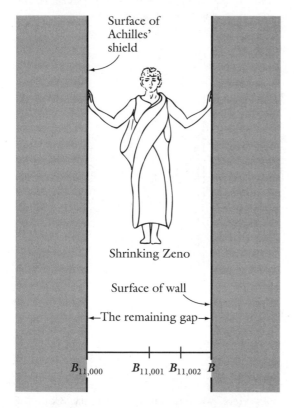

Surface of Achilles' shield

Shrinking Zeno

Surface of wall

←The remaining gap→

$B_{11,000}$ $B_{11,001}$ $B_{11,002}$ B

Let us now go back to the point of view of the gloating spectators and the unworried Hera. When Achilles' shield first touches Zeno's right hand, the spectators see Zeno shrink. As Achilles' shield approaches the wall they still see Zeno getting smaller

and smaller until at some instant before the shield hits the wall Zeno virtually disappears from their sight. At that point they conclude that Zeno must have been crushed when the shield smashed into the wall. Since the spectators see the shield smash into the wall, from their point of view there is no gap. There is no space in which Zeno's extended body can extend and therefore no space in which for him to exist as a real entity. Where, then, is Zeno?

The spectators conclude that Zeno has disappeared and, in some sense, they are right. They cannot see him. And no physical microscope, regardless of how powerful, could allow Zeno to be seen because, after all, his size is 0. Zero multiplied by any (finite) number is still 0. An (extensionless) point magnified by any (finite) magnification is still an extensionless point. From the spectators' point of view alone, Zeno has indeed disappeared.

Since we are aware that there are two points of view here — the point of view of the spectators and the point of view of Zeno — we should address the question of their (in)commensurability. For it is the question of the (in)commensurability of these two points of view that *refines Zeno's paradox.*

Does it make sense, from Zeno's point of view, that at some moment *he* disappears? As we said above, at all moments during which the process is still happening from his point of view, (1) he still exists as an extended being, (2) except for Achilles' shield and the wall, which still exist in their virtually infinitely enlarged form, the spectators, the Lyceum, and all the rest of the world have disappeared, and (3) nothing is happening in that the picture is static for Zeno, just as the picture is static for the spectators once Achilles' shield hits the wall. So Zeno's understanding of the suggestion that he disappeared would have to be described, from his point of view, as a "popping out of the universe" *for no reason whatsoever:* that is, no reasons from within his point of view could possibly explain a popping out of the universe. For Zeno to understand how it is possible that he disappears he not only would have to favor the spectators' point of view — which would be a strange thing given that from within his point of view it is they who have disappeared, not he — he would have to give up the reasons available to him within his point of view and accept reasons from a point of view to which he has no access.

That is, we can imagine Zeno thinking, as he is shrinking: "My friend Hera has saved me by enlarging the spectators and the universe out of existence!" The idea of something that shrinks continuously (and self-similarly, retaining its same shape) shrinking suddenly and spontaneously out of existence and the idea of something that enlarges continuously (and self-similarly) being suddenly and spontaneously enlarged out of existence are equally unjustified (or, even, equally justified) but (in either case) they are incommensurate. They are incommensurate because the only way it would make sense for Zeno to think that he ever disappears from the universe is for him to think that from the point of view of the spectators at some point he disappears. But, once again, from his point of view it is they who at some point do in fact disappear.

These "popping-out-of-existence" alternatives are incommensurate. To himself, Zeno still exists and from his point of view there can be no reason to simply decree that he suddenly and spontaneously stops existing. It is also as equally unjustified to decree that the spectators in the Lyceum spontaneously vanish from the universe, just to make things consistent with Zeno's point of view. Someone could say that, from each other's point of view, the other disappears. But how then would we reconcile these two apparently irreconcilable, noncommensurate points of view?

If from each point of view, taken separately, it is true to say that the other pops out of existence, then a fundamental revision of our most basic concept of existence is required; it would entail that Zeno's paradox reaches into the very heart of existence—that existence itself is somehow paradoxical.

If our shrinking Zeno paradox is to be successfully addressed, we must reconcile the two apparently incommensurate points of view, and not simply and arbitrarily pick one point of view over the other. Either we take the spectators' point of view and conclude for no sufficient reason that Zeno's body has become an extensionless point, *B*, or we can take Zeno's point of view and conclude without sufficient reason that the spectators occupy no position on the floor of the Lyceum, since they are infinitely far away from Zeno.[4] Each alternative makes sense relative to the relevant points of view considered separately. But the two points of view are incommensurate and mutually exclusive.

Let us therefore instead of dismissing Zeno from the realm of existence rejoin him on his journey. More than a second of time has gone by and he knows that, since Achilles is traveling at one meter per second, Achilles' shield relative to the spectators' point of view has indeed reached the wall. From Zeno's point of view, now after a second, he is there with the (now not merely virtually but *actually*) infinitely large shield touching his right palm, the wall touching his left palm. From his own point of view Zeno knows that the spectators seem to have disappeared but have not actually disappeared. He reasons as follows. "I know it is my own point of view that dictates that the spectators will become infinitely far away from me when I become (from their point of view) an extensionless point. I also know, when the spectators become infinitely far away from me, Achilles' shield will have grown infinitely large and therefore any part of it will be infinitely large. But, by Zeus, how then could I possibly continue to see a shield, or myself for that matter, or anything at all?"

We will now, as Zeno did, ask a perplexing question: How can it be that Achilles' moving shield ever makes contact with the wall at *B*? We want to focus our attention on what the gap is like from our shrinking Zeno's point of view. Immediately we notice that from his point of view Achilles' shield is not moving. Indeed, within the gap, *nothing is happening whatsoever*. This is because as the shield (from Achilles' point of view) gets closer to the wall, from Zeno's point of view they always remain an arm's length apart. If he were to look up and to the sides he would see the lines extending further and further upward. However, he does not see or feel the walls moving.

If we construct blowups as before, the pictures will be exactly the same except the shield and wall get taller. Note, too, that there is a (virtual) variant from picture to picture. If each picture were a movie of the moving Achilles, then if Achilles moves at the constant velocity of 1 meter per second (as described in the original Zeno diagram) then his shield would be seen through the microscope to be traveling 32 times faster in each subsequent diagram. For example, the surface of the shield facing Zeno would be seen to be moving at 32 meters per second in the first enlargement, 32^2 meters per second in the second enlargement, 32^3

meters per second in the third enlargement, 32^n meters per second in the nth enlargement.

When n is sufficiently large, Achilles' shield will *seem* to be moving faster than light. Technically, this is neither an illusion nor a hallucination, since the image being seen is an actual image; it is *not* like the case of the drunk who sees pink elephants. And yet what is being seen is not the actual motion of the shield which, after all, is at any point in its journey from A to B traveling at 1 meter per second. It is the motion of one part of an image relative to other parts of the image. This raises the philosophical question of what makes some images virtual, or only images, and some images the images of things that are seen and therefore "real." The problem, in other words, is that supposedly one kind of motion we are seeing is real motion of real things, while other motions we are seeing are only the motions of images that—while they do correspond, by the rule of enlargement, to something real—are themselves not real. The virtual motion of Achilles' shield in our enlargements, however, does not in actuality violate the speed of light.

It is obvious that we are beginning our journey deep into the tail end of the sequence of B_n. In a sense, we have constructed a conceptual microscope through which we can see something that we understand as a place beyond all the halfway marks and yet before the wall. Our conceptual microscope is already in place through our consideration of enlargement diagrams that picture our shrinking Zeno. The problem here is that these intervals collapse to a point in the limit. But a point does not fit conceptually into the pattern of our diagrams. That is, a point is obviously qualitatively different from an interval in that a point is not the sort of thing that can be further divided.

But how can this be? We know that since Achilles is moving at one meter per second, and the wall is one meter away, that from Achilles' point of view after exactly one second the shield makes contact with the wall, i.e., there is no space between them. We also know that from Zeno's point of view there is no reason whatsoever that the shield and wall should *ever* make contact. This is the very essence of our refined paradox. We know, from one point of view, that it is absolutely *necessary* that contact happens and that, from the other point of view, it is *impossible* that contact ever happens!

Our shrinking Zeno paradox does not *add* anything to the distance between A and B. It merely illuminates, via a sort of conceptual microscope, what is already there and what is already paradoxical. It does, however, in a sense add something to the *conceptual* space between A and B. It forces us to add that strange place where our shrinking Zeno is to our conception of space. An infinitesimal calculus would offer some solution to this paradox by adding the place where Zeno now is to our concept of space, thereby creating a new mathematical spatial object. And though our shrinking Zeno paradox alters Zeno's original form of his paradoxes, the key issues remain the same. The solution offered to the original paradox had eliminated the issue of infinite process—finite distance. The shrinking Zeno paradox does not depend on the infinite–finite issue. However, the key issue that the gap between two things is paradoxical—Parmenides' question of what separates one thing from another—is preserved. Thus it is indeed right to call our shrinking Zeno paradox Zeno's paradox. *And it cannot be solved by summing the series nor by standard calculus.*

4. WHERE IS ZENO?

We now have a real problem on our hands! The problem is this. From his own point of view, Zeno has not disappeared; therefore, he is somewhere. From the spectators' point of view, he has disappeared. Therefore, as far as they are concerned, he is nowhere. What does it mean to say that X is somewhere? It means that X is in a containing space. To have a location is to be embedded in a space. Well, what about our shrinking Zeno? Where is he? How can we attribute to him the kind of somewhereness that we usually attribute to things? Can we say that he is in the Lyceum? From his point of view, he is infinitely far away from anything in the Lyceum. Furthermore, if you looked through the Lyceum for him, even armed with the most (finitely) powerful microscope in the world, you would not find him there.

Yet, we could say that his hand is near the rest of his body and that it is on the wall rather than, say, on his forehead. This is puzzling because the people in the Lyceum are also near the wall! One problem with the idea that Zeno is somewhere is that the surface of the wall and the surface of the shield are in contact—so how can Zeno's right hand be on Achilles' shield and his left hand be on the wall? If the shield and the wall are in contact, there is no space between them!

Asking where shrinking Zeno is, is in some ways like asking: *Where are the points of space?* Even with our most powerful microscope, you will not be able to find them. Yet they are somewhere: there, in *that* location and not in some other.

Obviously, our shrinking Zeno paradox examines the idea of motion differently from the paradox of Achilles running the racecourse. Instead of looking at a distance and examining what happens across a distance, the shrinking Zeno paradox focuses on motion at one instant of time in one point of space—as does Zeno's original paradox of the arrow. If an arrow is moving, then it is moving at each instant of time and at each point along a path. Time is conceived of as being made of moments and space is conceived of as being made of points (places). How can you find the motion in each instant and place occupied at that instant? You can't. At each moment the arrow is where it is. At each moment the arrow is the same as a stationary arrow at the same instant in the same place. Zeno's paradox of the arrow is that if you can't find the motion in the units of which time and space are made, then how can it be possible to find it in time and space? If John is not at any place in this room, then how can he be in this room?

Calculus addresses the problem of instantaneous motion through the idea of a derivative. The concept of a derivative depends on the idea of intervals collapsing on a point—*as in our shrinking Zeno paradox.* Thus, our shrinking Zeno paradox shows that Zeno's original paradoxes of motion have not really been solved. Asking where our shrinking Zeno is, is to ask where the points of space are and, ultimately, to inquire into the deeply mysterious question of what space is made of.

After all, where are the spectators in the Lyceum? If you ask our shrinking Zeno, he cannot see them and he could not see them through any telescope, no matter how powerful. From Zeno's point of view, they are nowhere! Again, each could say "I am here where I am." They would point to things available to their point of view and say they are near those things. But once again there is a problem with the idea of where things are with respect to the two incommensurate points of view.

In noting that the idea of a derivative in calculus involved exactly this type of image, we note that here, in the gap, philosophy and mathematics meet. Philosophical reflection offers both mathematics and science new mysterious spaces to explore and conceptualize. This is already partly done with infinitesimal calculus and quantum physics. In standard calculus, the real numbers are used. In infinitesimal calculus, certain new types of quantities are used which mark and conceptualize that place where our shrinking Zeno is when he has shrunk out of sight. Quantum mechanics postulates that the ordinary concept of space and time completely breaks down where our shrinking Zeno is.

To recognize that Zeno's paradoxes are not solved is not to make the extravagant claim that our concepts of space, time, motion, and identity are worthless and that we should therefore give up rationality. Rather, the purpose is to give a precise way of focusing our attention on the discrepancy between reality and our concepts. To function as rational beings we must have concepts, which are the medium of rational consciousness. Without concepts, there can be no paradox. Our eyes are not windows. Our minds do not have direct access to reality. We must always interpret our experience according to concepts. Zeno's paradox thus examines the relationship of our minds to the world.

Since what is inside our minds is not, and never can be, an exact copy of reality, there will always be paradoxes that must be addressed to improve our understanding of our relationship (or lack thereof) to reality.

Recalling now that Zeno's intention was to use his paradoxes to defend Parmenides, what are we to make of Parmenides' assertion that "all is one"? Zeno's paradox has just shown us why the commonsense notion of the universe as an everchanging collection of many different things, separated from other things, all constantly moving about in space (the commonsense view) *is deeply paradoxical.*

NOTES

1. Technically, we only begin to discuss geometric series here. For a more complete and fuller treatment, see

our *Zeno's Paradox Refined*. For a complete, technical mathematical treatment, see any book on real analysis, such as Walter Rudin, *Principles of Mathematical Analysis*, New York: McGraw-Hill.

2. The full justification of this method of adding up an infinite series is actually more involved than just doing what we have done. For a full treatment of this, see any book on real analysis or advanced calculus. Look up "geometric series" in the index of any such book.

Note that we could apply the above method to

$$S = 1 + 2 + 4 + 8 + \ldots 2^k + \ldots$$
$$2S = 2 + 4 + 8 + \ldots$$
$$2S + 1 = S$$
$$S = -1$$

This is clearly nonsense since this sum of increasing terms would have to be of infinite value. Furthermore, there is no way that we are going to add up positive numbers and get a negative. One must learn more of the theory of infinite series to know which methods can be applied when.

3. The analogy of going by ⅓'s paradox (as given) to going by ½'s paradox is that in the ½'s case, each increment is ½ of the previous increment. In the ½'s case, this is the same as going ½ of the remaining distance. In the ⅓'s case, it is not the same as going ⅓ of the remaining distance. For instance, at the second increment, Achilles goes ⅓ of the previous distance but only ⅙ of the remaining distance.

4. For instance, if he were holding a ruler in his hand, the ruler would not be visible to the spectator through any finite microscope, no matter how powerful. Therefore, the distance between him and the spectator would be infinite compared to that ruler. Furthermore, if he laid the ruler side to side any finite number of times, he would never reach the spectators.

Further Questions

1. What is the function of paradoxes?
2. If the authors are right that there will always be paradoxes, what do you think this means for rationality in general, theories in particular? Do you agree with how the authors would answer the question? Why or why not?
3. Where do concepts like space, time, and motion, with which we try to understand the world, come from? Are they just fictions, mere make-believe? Or are they more? What do you think is the difference between concepts and fictions?
4. Go to your current (or recent) mathematics teacher and say you've been learning the original Zeno's paradox of motion. Do not say yet that you have a refined paradox in your pocket. Your goal is to get the teacher to talk about the infinite series. Listen with interest and make sure you understand what you are being told. Tell the teacher this is a very good answer. Then, tell the teacher about the shrinking Zeno paradox. Remember that the point is that what must be accounted for is that Zeno can to himself exist. (a) If the teacher says that this is but a fantasy, ask whether Einstein's riding a beam of light is but a fantasy. (b) If the teacher says your argument somehow goes beyond the accepted canons of mathematical explanation, ask whether people might have said that about the original paradox long before the sum of the infinite series was ever thought of.

Further Readings

Grunbaum, A. *Philosophical Problems of Space and Time*, 2nd ed. Dordrecht and Boston: D. Reidel, 1973. An excellent and thorough work, with detailed discussions of some of the philosophical implications of the mathematical underpinnings of the problems raised by Zeno's paradoxes.

Kolak, Daniel. *Zeno's Paradox Refined*, forthcoming. Further and more detailed elaborations of the extent to which contemporary mathematics and philosophy can deal with the shrinking Zeno paradox and the extent to which they cannot, with discussions of hyper-real numbers, ultrafilters, and the continuum hypothesis. Mathematical demonstrations required for a thorough understanding of the problem are provided, along with a new model of paradoxical rationality.

Where Am I?   7

DANIEL DENNETT

Daniel Dennett, best known for his writings in the philosophy of mind, teaches philosophy at Tufts University. Among his books are *Brainstorms* (Bradford Books, 1978), *Elbow Room* (Bradford Books, 1984), *Consciousness Explained* (Penguin, 1991), *Darwin's Dangerous Idea* (Simon and Schuster, 1995), and *Kinds of Minds* (Basic Books, 1996).

In the following selection he brings to light the unobvious mystery of how we locate ourselves. The meanings of words like *here, now,* and *me* seem so obvious that we ordinarily don't even question them. But by imagining himself in an extraordinary situation in which his body is separated from his brain, Dennett shows why even the most obvious apparent fact about you, expressed by your avowal "I am here," is deeply questionable.

Reading Questions

1. How is Dennett able to experience anything after his brain is removed and put in a vat?
2. What is a "point of view"?
3. What are the different ways in which Dennett tries to answer the "Where am I?" question in the various parts of the story?
4. When the computer brain runs in perfect synchronization with the brain in the vat, how *many* Dennetts are there? Is he one person with two brains? *Where* is the real Dennett? Can the Dennett character in the story tell which brain is running the body?
5. How do you know where you are? Ordinarily, you simply look and see. But when you're lost, you still see perfectly well—yet something crucial is missing. What? What information do you use to locate yourself?
6. Did you ever wake up and not know where you were? What did it feel like?
7. Suppose your living brain is transplanted into your friend's body. Would this be a case of your friend's getting a brain transplant or a case of your getting a new body? Suppose the transplant took place after you had been in a car accident in which your body was destroyed, leaving your brain intact, while your friend's body remained intact but his brain was destroyed. Who pays for the operation?

NOW THAT I'VE WON MY SUIT under the Freedom of Information Act, I am at liberty to reveal for the first time a curious episode in my life that may be of interest not only to those engaged in research in the philosophy of mind, artificial intelligence, and neuroscience but also to the general public.

Several years ago I was approached by Pentagon officials who asked me to volunteer for a highly dangerous and secret mission. In collaboration with NASA and Howard Hughes, the Department of Defense was spending billions to develop a Supersonic Tunneling Underground Device, or STUD. It was supposed to tunnel through the earth's core at great speed and deliver a specially designed atomic warhead "right up the Red's missile silos," as one of the Pentagon brass put it.

The problem was that in an early test they had succeeded in lodging a warhead about a mile deep under Tulsa, Oklahoma, and they wanted me to retrieve it for them. "Why me?" I asked. Well, the mission involved some pioneering applications of current brain research, and they had heard of my interest in brains and of course my Faustian curiosity and great courage and so forth. . . . Well, how could I refuse? The difficulty that brought the Pentagon to my door was that the device I'd been asked to recover was fiercely radioactive, in a new way. According to monitoring instruments, something about the nature of the device and its complex interactions with pockets of material deep in the earth had produced radiation that could cause severe abnormalities in certain tissues of the brain. No way had been found to shield the brain from these deadly rays, which were apparently harmless to other tissues and organs of the body. So it had been decided that the person sent to recover the device should *leave his brain behind*. It would be kept in a safe place where it could execute its normal control functions by elaborate radio links. Would I submit to a surgical procedure that would completely remove my brain, which would then be placed in a life-support system at the Manned Spacecraft Center in Houston? Each input and output pathway, as it was severed, would be restored by a pair of microminiaturized radio transceivers, one attached precisely to the brain, the other to the nerve stumps in the empty cranium. No information would be lost, all the connectivity would be preserved. At first I was a bit reluctant. Would it really work? The Houston brain surgeons encouraged me. "Think of it," they said, "as a mere *stretching* of the nerves. If your brain were just moved over an inch in your skull, that would not alter or impair your mind. We're simply going to make the nerves indefinitely elastic by splicing radio links into them."

I was shown around the life-support lab in Houston and saw the sparkling new vat in which my brain would be placed, were I to agree. I met the large and brilliant support team of neurologists, hematologists, biophysicists, and electrical engineers, and after several days of discussions and demonstrations, I agreed to give it a try. I was subjected to an enormous array of blood tests, brain scans, experiments, interviews, and the like. They took down my autobiography at great length, recorded tedious lists of my beliefs, hopes, fears,

and tastes. They even listed my favorite stereo recordings and gave me a crash session of psychoanalysis.

The day for surgery arrived at last and of course I was anesthetized and remembered nothing of the operation itself. When I came out of anesthesia, I opened my eyes, looked around, and asked the inevitable, the traditional, the lamentably hackneyed postoperative question: "Where am I? The nurse smiled down at me. "You're in Houston," she said, and I reflected that this still had a good chance of being the truth one way or another. She handed me a mirror. Sure enough, there were the tiny antennae poling up through their titanium ports cemented into my skull.

"I gather the operation was a success," I said. "I want to go see my brain." They led me (I was a bit dizzy and unsteady) down a long corridor and into the life-support lab. A cheer went up from the assembled support team, and I responded with what I hoped was a jaunty salute. Still feeling lightheaded, I was helped over to the life-support vat. I peered through the glass. There, floating in what looked like ginger ale, was undeniably a human brain, though it was almost covered with printed circuit chips, plastic tubules, electrodes, and other paraphernalia. "Is that mine?" I asked. "Hit the output transmitter switch there on the side of the vat and see for yourself," the project director replied. I moved the switch to OFF, and immediately slumped, groggy and nauseated, into the arms of the technicians, one of whom kindly restored the switch to its ON position. While I recovered my equilibrium and composure, I thought to myself: "Well, here I am sitting on a folding chair, staring through a piece of plate glass at my own brain. . . . But wait," I said to myself, "shouldn't I have thought, 'Here I am, suspended in a bubbling fluid, being stared at by my own eyes'?" I tried to think this latter thought, I tried to project it into the tank, offering it hopefully to my brain, but I failed to carry off the exercise with any conviction. I tried again. "Here am *I*, Daniel Dennett, suspended in a bubbling fluid, being stared at by my own eyes." No, it just didn't work. Most puzzling and confusing. Being a philosopher

From Brainstorms: Philosophical Essays on Mind and Psychology *by Daniel C. Dennett (Bradford Books, Publishers, Inc., 1978). Reprinted by permission of the publisher.*

of firm physicalist conviction, I believed unswervingly that the tokening of my thoughts was occurring somewhere in my brain: yet, when I thought "Here I am," where the thought occurred to me was *here,* outside the vat, where I, Dennett, was standing staring at my brain.

I tried and tried to think myself into the vat, but to no avail. I tried to build up to the task by doing mental exercises. I thought to myself, "The sun is shining *over there,*" five times in rapid succession, each time mentally ostending a different place: in order, the sunlit corner of the lab, the visible front lawn of the hospital, Houston, Mars, and Jupiter. I found I had little difficulty in getting my "there"'s to hop all over the celestial map with their proper references. I could loft a "there" in an instant through the farthest reaches of space, and then aim the next "there" with pinpoint accuracy at the upper left quadrant of a freckle on my arm. Why was I having such trouble with "here"? "Here in Houston" worked well enough, and so did "here in the lab," and even "here in this part of the lab," but "here in the vat" always seemed merely an unmeant mental mouthing. I tried closing my eyes while thinking it. This seemed to help, but still I couldn't manage to pull it off, except perhaps for a fleeting instant. I couldn't be sure. The discovery that I couldn't be sure was also unsettling. How did I know *where* I meant by "here" when I thought "here"? Could I *think* I meant one place when in fact I meant another? I didn't see how that could be admitted without untying the few bonds of intimacy between a person and his own mental life that had survived the onslaught of the brain scientists and philosophers, the physicalists and behaviorists. Perhaps I was incorrigible about where I *meant* when I said "here." But in my present circumstances it seemed that either I was doomed by sheer force of mental habit to thinking systematically false indexical thoughts, or where a person is (and hence where his thoughts are tokened for purposes of semantic analysis) is not necessarily where his brain, the physical seat of his soul, resides. Nagged by confusion, I attempted to orient myself by falling back on a favorite philosopher's ploy. I began naming things.

"Yorick," I said aloud to my brain, "you are my brain. The rest of my body, seated in this chair, I dub 'Hamlet.'" So here we all are: Yorick's my brain, Hamlet's my body, and I am Dennett. *Now,* where am I? And when I think "where am I?" where's that thought tokened? Is it tokened in my brain, lounging about in the vat, or right here between my ears where it *seems* to be tokened? Or nowhere? Its *temporal* coordinates give me no trouble; must it not have spatial coordinates as well? I began making a list of the alternatives.

1. *Where Hamlet goes, there goes Dennett.* This principle was easily refuted by appeal to the familiar brain-transplant thought experiments so enjoyed by philosophers. If Tom and Dick switch brains, Tom is the fellow with Dick's former body—just ask him; he'll claim to be Tom, and tell you the most intimate details of Tom's autobiography. It was clear enough, then, that my current body and I could part company, but not likely that I could be separated from my brain. The rule of thumb that emerged so plainly from the thought experiments was that in a brain-transplant operation, one wanted to be the *donor,* not the recipient. Better to call such an operation a *body* transplant, in fact. So perhaps the truth was,

2. *Where Yorick goes, there goes Dennett.* This was not at all appealing, however. How could I be in the vat and not about to go anywhere, when I was so obviously outside the vat looking in and beginning to make guilty plans to return to my room for a substantial lunch? This begged the question I realized, but it still seemed to be getting at something important. Casting about for some support for my intuition, I hit upon a legalistic sort of argument that might have appealed to Locke.

Suppose, I argued to myself, I were now to fly to California, rob a bank, and be apprehended. In which state would I be tried: in California, where the robbery took place, or in Texas, where the brains of the outfit were located? Would I be a California felon with an out-of-state brain, or a Texas felon remotely controlling an accomplice of sorts in California? It seemed possible that I might beat such a rap just on the undecidability of that jurisdictional question, though perhaps it would be deemed an interstate, and hence Federal, offense. In any event, suppose I were convicted. Was it likely that California would be satisfied to throw Hamlet into the brig, knowing that Yorick was living the good life and luxuriously taking the waters in Texas? Would Texas incarcerate Yorick, leaving Hamlet free to take the next boat to Rio? This alternative appealed to me. Barring capital punishment or other cruel and unusual punishment, the state would be obliged to maintain the life-support system for Yorick though they might move him from Houston to Leavenworth, and aside from the unpleasantness of the opprobrium, I, for one, would not mind at all and would consider myself a free man under those circumstances. If the state has an interest in forcibly relocating persons in institutions, it would fail to relocate me in any institution by locating Yorick there. If this were true, it suggested a third alternative.

3. *Dennett is wherever he thinks he is.* Generalized, the claim was as follows: At any given time a person has a *point of view,* and the location of the point of view (which is determined internally by the content of the point of view) is also the location of the person.

Such a proposition is not without its perplexities, but to me it seemed a step in the right direction. The only trouble was that it seemed to place one in a heads-I-win/tails-you-lose situation of unlikely infallibility as regards location. Hadn't I myself often been wrong about where I was, and at least as often uncertain? Couldn't one get lost? Of course, but getting lost *geographically* is not the only way one might get lost. If one were lost in the woods one could attempt to reassure oneself with the consolation that at least one knew where one was: one was right here in the familiar surroundings of one's own body. Perhaps in this case one would not have drawn one's attention to much to be thankful for. Still, there were worse plights imaginable, and I wasn't sure I wasn't in such a plight right now.

Point of view clearly had something to do with personal location, but it was itself an unclear notion. It was obvious that the content of one's point

of view was not the same as or determined by the content of one's beliefs or thoughts. For example, what should we say about the point of view of the Cinerama viewer who shrieks and twists in his seat as the roller-coaster footage overcomes his psychic distancing? Has he forgotten that he is safely seated in the theater? Here I was inclined to say that the person is experiencing an illusory shift in point of view. In other cases, my inclination to call such shifts illusory was less strong. The workers in laboratories and plants who handle dangerous materials by operating feedback-controlled mechanical arms and hands undergo a shift in point of view that is crisper and more pronounced than anything Cinerama can provoke. They can feel the heft and slipperiness of the containers they manipulate with their metal fingers. They know perfectly well where they are and are not fooled into false beliefs by the experience, yet it is as if they were inside the isolation chamber they are peering into. With mental effort, they can manage to shift their point of view back and forth, rather like making a transparent Necker cube or an Escher drawing change orientation before one's eyes. It does even as a matter of habit. I should dwell on images of myself comfortably floating in my vat, beaming volitions to that familiar body *out there.* I reflected that the ease or difficulty of this task was presumably independent of the truth about the location of one's brain. Had I been practicing before the operation, I might now be finding it second nature. You might now yourself try such a *trompe l'oeil.* Imagine you have written an inflammatory letter which has been published in the *Times,* the result of which is that the government has chosen to impound your brain for a probationary period of three years in its Dangerous Brain Clinic in Bethesda, Maryland. Your body of course is allowed freedom to earn a salary and thus to continue its function of laying up income to be taxed. At this moment, however, your body is seated in an auditorium listening to a peculiar account by Daniel Dennett of his own similar experience. Try it. Think yourself to Bethesda, and then hark back longingly to your body, far away, and yet *seeming* so near. It is only with long-distance restraint (yours? the government's?) that you can control your impulse to get those hands clapping in polite applause before navigating the old body to the rest room and a well-deserved glass of evening sherry in the lounge. The task of imagination is certainly difficult, but if you achieve your goal the results might be consoling.

Anyway, there I was in Houston, lost in thought as one might say, but not for long. My speculations were soon interrupted by the Houston doctors, who wished to test out my new prosthetic nervous system before sending me off on my hazardous mission. As I mentioned before, I was a bit dizzy at first, and not surprisingly, although I soon habituated myself to my new circumstances (which were, after all, well nigh indistinguishable from my old circumstances). My accommodation was not perfect, however, and to this day I continue to be plagued by minor coordination difficulties. The speed of light is fast, but finite, and as my brain and body move farther and farther apart, the delicate interaction of my feedback systems is thrown into disarray by the time lags. Just as one is rendered close to speechless by a delayed or echoic hearing of one's speaking voice so, for instance, I am virtually unable to track a moving object with my eyes whenever my brain and my body are more than a few miles apart. In most matters my impairment is scarcely detectable, though I can no longer hit a slow curve ball with the authority of yore. There are some compensations of course. Though liquor tastes as good as ever, and warms my gullet while corroding my liver, I can drink it in any quantity I please, without becoming the slightest bit inebriated, a curiosity some of my close friends may have noticed (though I occasionally have *feigned* inebriation, so as not to draw attention to my unusual circumstances). For similar reasons, I take aspirin orally for a sprained wrist, but if the pain persists I ask Houston to administer codeine to me *in vitro*. In times of illness the phone bill can be staggering.

But to return to my adventure. At length, both the doctors and I were satisfied that I was ready to undertake my subterranean mission. And so I left my brain in Houston and headed by helicopter for Tulsa. Well, in any case, that's the way it seemed to me. That's how I would put it, just off the top of my head as it were. On the trip I reflected further about my earlier anxieties and decided that my first postoperative speculations had been tinged with panic. The matter was not nearly as strange or metaphysical as I had been supposing. Where was I?

In two places, clearly: both inside the vat and outside it. Just as one can stand with one foot in Connecticut and the other in Rhode Island, I was in two places at once. I had become one of those scattered individuals we used to hear so much about. The more I considered this answer, the more obviously true it appeared. But, strange to say, the more true it appeared, the less important the question to which it could be the true answer seemed. A sad, but not unprecedented, fate for a philosophical question to suffer. This answer did not completely satisfy me, of course. There lingered some question to which I should have liked an answer, which was neither "Where are all my various and sundry parts?" nor "What is my current point of view?" Or at least there seemed to be such a question. For it did seem undeniable that in some sense *I* and not merely *most of me* was descending into the earth under Tulsa in search of an atomic warhead.

When I found the warhead, I was certainly glad I had left my brain behind, for the pointer on the specially built Geiger counter I had brought with me was off the dial. I called Houston on my ordinary radio and told the operation control center of my position and my progress. In return, they gave me instructions for dismantling the vehicle, based upon my on-site observations. I had set to work with my cutting torch when all of a sudden a terrible thing happened. I went stone deaf. At first I thought it was only my radio earphones that had broken, but when I tapped on my helmet, I heard nothing. Apparently the auditory transceivers had gone on the fritz. I could no longer hear Houston or my own voice, but I could speak, so I started telling them what had happened. In midsentence, I knew something else had gone wrong. My vocal apparatus had become paralyzed. Then my right hand went limp—another transceiver had gone. I was truly in deep trouble. But worse was to follow. After a few more minutes, I went blind. I cursed my luck, and then I cursed the scientists who had led me into this grave peril. There I was, deaf, dumb, and blind, in a radioactive hole more than a mile under Tulsa. Then the last of my cerebral radio links broke, and suddenly I was faced with a new and even more shocking problem: whereas an instant before I had been buried alive in Oklahoma, now I was disembodied in Houston. My recognition of my new status was not immediate.

It took me several very anxious minutes before it dawned on me that my poor body lay several hundred miles away, with heart pulsing and lungs respirating, but otherwise as dead as the body of any heart-transplant donor, its skull packed with useless, broken electronic gear. The shift in perspective I had earlier found well nigh impossible now seemed quite natural. Though I could think myself back into my body in the tunnel under Tulsa, it took some effort to sustain the illusion. For surely it was an illusion to suppose I was still in Oklahoma: I had lost all contact with that body.

It occurred to me then, with one of those rushes of revelation of which we should be suspicious, that I had stumbled upon an impressive demonstration of the immateriality of the soul based upon physicalist principles and premises. For as the last radio signal between Tulsa and Houston died away, had I not changed location from Tulsa to Houston at the speed of light? And had I not accomplished this without any increase in mass? What moved from A to B at such speed was surely myself, or at any rate my soul or mind—the massless center of my being and home of my consciousness. My *point of view* had lagged somewhat behind, but I had already noted the indirect bearing of point of view on personal location. I could not see how a physicalist philosopher could quarrel with this except by taking the dire and counterintuitive route of banishing all talk of persons. Yet the notion of personhood was so well entrenched in everyone's world view, or so it seemed to me, that any denial would be as curiously unconvincing, as systematically disingenuous, as the Cartesian negation, "non sum."

The joy of philosophic discovery thus tided me over some very bad minutes or perhaps hours as the helplessness and hopelessness of my situation became more apparent to me. Waves of panic and even nausea swept over me, made all the more horrible by the absence of their normal body-dependent phenomenology. No adrenaline rush of tingles in the arms, no pounding heart, no premonitory salivation. I did feel a dread sinking feeling in my bowels at one point, and this tricked me momentarily into the false hope that I was undergoing a reversal of the process that landed me in this fix—a gradual undisembodiment. But the isolation and uniqueness of that twinge soon convinced me that it was simply the first of a plague of phantom body hallucinations that I, like any other amputee, would be all too likely to suffer.

My mood then was chaotic. On the one hand, I was fired up with elation of my philosophic discovery and was wracking my brain (one of the few familiar things I could still do), trying to figure out how to communicate my discovery to the journals; while on the other, I was bitter, lonely, and filled with dread and uncertainty. Fortunately, this did not last long, for my technical support team sedated me into a dreamless sleep from which I awoke, hearing with magnificent fidelity the familiar opening strains of my favorite Brahms piano trio. So that was why they had wanted a list of my favorite recordings! It did not take me long to realize that I was hearing the music without ears. The output from the stereo stylus was being fed through some fancy rectification circuitry directly into my auditory nerve. I was mainlining Brahms, an unforgettable experience for any stereo buff. At the end of the record it did not surprise me to hear the reassuring voice of the project director speaking into a microphone that was now my prosthetic ear. He confirmed my analysis of what had gone wrong and assured me that steps were being taken to reembody me. He did not elaborate, and after a few more recordings, I found myself drifting off to sleep. My sleep lasted, I later learned, for the better part of a year, and when I awoke, it was to find myself fully restored to my senses. When I looked into the mirror, though, I was a bit startled to see an unfamiliar face. Bearded and a bit heavier, bearing no doubt a family resemblance to my former face, and with the same look of sprightly intelligence and resolute character, but definitely a new face. Further self-explorations of an intimate nature left me no doubt that this was a new body, and the project director confirmed my conclusions. He did not volunteer any information on the past history of my new body and I decided (wisely, I think in retrospect) not to pry. As many philosophers unfamiliar with my ordeal have more recently speculated, the acquisition of a new body leaves one's *person* intact. And after a period of adjustment to a new voice, new muscular strengths and weaknesses, and so forth, one's *personality* is by and large also preserved. More dramaticchanges in personality have been routinely observed in people who have undergone extensive plastic surgery, to say nothing of sex-change operations, and I think no one contests the survival of the person in such cases. In any event I soon accommodated to my new body, to the point of being unable to recover any of its novelties to my consciousness or even memory. The view in the mirror soon became utterly familiar. That view, by the way, still revealed antennae, and so I was not surprised to learn that my brain had not been moved from its haven in the life-support lab.

I decided that good old Yorick deserved a visit. I and my new body, whom we might as well call Fortinbras, strode into the familiar lab to another round of applause from the technicians, who were of course congratulating themselves, not me. Once more I stood before the vat and contemplated poor Yorick, and on a whim I once again cavalierly flicked off the output transmitter switch. Imagine my surprise when nothing unusual happened. No fainting spell, no nausea, no noticeable change. A technician hurried to restore the switch to ON, but still I felt nothing. I demanded an explanation, which the project director hastened to provide. It seems that before they had even operated on the first occasion, they had constructed a computer duplicate of my brain, reproducing both the complete information-processing structure and the computational speed of my brain in a giant computer program. After the operation, but before they had dared to send me off on my mission to Oklahoma, they had run this computer system and Yorick side by side. The incoming signals from Hamlet were sent simultaneously to Yorick's transceivers and to the computer's array of inputs. And the outputs from Yorick were not only beamed back to Hamlet, my body; they were recorded and checked against the simultaneous output of the computer program, which was called "Hubert" for reasons obscure to me. Over days and even weeks, the outputs were identical and synchronous, which of course did not *prove* that they had succeeded in copying the brain's functional structure, but the empirical support was greatly encouraging.

Hubert's input, and hence activity, had been kept parallel with Yorick's during my disembodied days. And now, to demonstrate this, they had actually thrown the master switch that put Hubert for the first time in on-line control of my body—not Hamlet, of course, but Fortinbras. (Hamlet, I learned, had never been recovered from its underground tomb and could be assumed by this time to have largely returned to the dust. At the head of my grave still lay the magnificent bulk of the abandoned device, with the word STUD emblazoned on its side in large letters—a circumstance which may provide archaeologists of the next century with a curious insight into the burial rites of their ancestors.)

The laboratory technicians now showed me the master switch, which had two positions, labeled *B,* for Brain (they didn't know my brain's name was Yorick) and *H,* for Hubert. The switch did indeed point to *H,* and they explained to me that if I wished, I could switch it back to *B.* With my heart in my mouth (and my brain in its vat), I did this. Nothing happened. A click, that was all. To test their claim, and with the master switch now set at *B,* I hit Yorick's output transmitter switch on the vat and sure enough, I began to faint. Once the output switch was turned back on and I had recovered my wits, so to speak, I continued to play with the master switch, flipping it back and forth. I found that with the exception of the transitional click, I could detect no trace of a difference. I could switch in mid-utterance, and the sentence I had begun speaking under the control of Yorick was finished without a pause or hitch of any kind under the control of Hubert. I had a spare brain, a prosthetic device which might some day stand me in very good stead, were some mishap to befall Yorick. Or alternatively, I could keep Yorick as a spare and use Hubert. It didn't seem to make any difference which I chose, for the wear and tear and fatigue on my body did not have any debilitating effect on either brain, whether or not it was actually causing the motions of my body, or merely spilling its output into thin air.

The only truly unsettling aspect of this new development was the prospect, which was not long in dawning on me, of someone detaching the spare—Hubert or Yorick, as the case might be—from Fortinbras and hitching it to yet another body—some Johnny-come-lately Rosencrantz or Guildenstern. Then (if not before) there would be *two* people, that much was clear. One would be me, and the other would be a sort of super-twin brother. If there were two bodies, one under the control of

Hubert and the other being controlled by Yorick, then which would the world recognize as the true Dennett? And whatever the rest of the world decided, which one would be *me*? Would I be the Yorick-brained one, by virtue of Yorick's causal priority and former intimate relationship with the original Dennett body, Hamlet? That seemed a bit legalistic, a bit too redolent of the arbitrariness of consanguinity and legal possession, to be convincing at the metaphysical level. For suppose that before the arrival of the second body on the scene, I had been keeping Yorick as the spare for years, and letting Hubert's output drive my body—that is, Fortinbras—all that time. The Hubert–Fortinbras couple would seem then by squatter's rights (to combat one legal intuition with another) to be the true Dennett and the lawful inheritor of everything that was Dennett's. This was an interesting question, certainly, but not nearly so pressing as another question that bothered me. My strongest intuition was that in such an eventuality *I* would survive so long as *either* brain-body couple remained intact, but I had mixed emotions about whether I should want both to survive.

I discussed my worries with the technicians and the project director. The prospect of two Dennetts was abhorrent to me, I explained, largely for social reasons. I didn't want to be my own rival for the affections of my wife, nor did I like the prospect of two Dennetts sharing my modest professor's salary. Still more vertiginous and distasteful, though, was the idea of knowing *that much* about another person, while he had the very same goods on me. How could we ever face each other? My colleagues in the lab argued that I was ignoring the bright side of the matter. Weren't there many things I wanted to do but, being only one person, had been unable to do? Now one Dennett could stay at home and be the professor and family man, while the other could strike out on a life of travel and adventure—missing the family of course, but happy in the knowledge that the other Dennett was keeping the home fires burning. I could be faithful and adulterous at the same time. I could even cuckold myself—to say nothing of other more lurid possibilities my colleagues were all too ready to force upon my overtaxed imagination. But my ordeal in Oklahoma (or was it Houston?) had made me less adventurous, and I shrank from this opportunity

that was being offered (though of course I was never quite sure it was being offered to *me* in the first place).

There was another prospect even more disagreeable: that the spare, Hubert or Yorick as the case might be, would be detached from any input from Fortinbras and just left detached. Then, as in the other case, there would be two Dennetts, or at least two claimants to my name and possessions, one embodied in Fortinbras, and the other sadly, miserably disembodied. Both selfishness and altruism bade me take steps to prevent this from happening. So I asked that measures be taken to ensure that no one could ever tamper with the transceiver connections or the master switch without my (our? no, *my*) knowledge and consent. Since I had no desire to spend my life guarding the equipment in Houston, it was mutually decided that all the electronic connections in the lab would be carefully locked. Both those that controlled the life-support system for Yorick and those that controlled the power supply for Hubert would be guarded with fail-safe devices, and I would take the only master switch, outfitted for radio remote control, with me wherever I went. I carry it strapped around my waist and—wait a moment—*here it is.* Every few months I reconnoiter the situation by switching channels. I do this only in the presence of friends, of course, for if the other channel were, heaven forbid, either dead or otherwise occupied, there would have to be somebody who had my interests at heart to switch it back, to bring me back from the void. For while I could feel, see, hear, and otherwise sense whatever befell my body, subsequent to such a switch, I'd be unable to control it. By the way, the two positions on the switch are intentionally unmarked, so I never have the faintest idea whether I am switching from Hubert to Yorick or vice versa. (Some of you may think that in this case I really don't know *who* I am, let alone where I am. But such reflections no longer make much of a dent on my essential Dennettness, on my own sense of who I am. If it is true that in one sense I don't know who I am then that's another one of your philosophical truths of underwhelming significance.)

In any case, every time I've flipped the switch so far, nothing has happened. *So let's give it a try. . . .*

"THANK GOD! I THOUGHT YOU'D NEVER FLIP THAT SWITCH! You can't imagine how horrible it's been these last two weeks—but now you know; it's your turn in purgatory. How I've longed for this moment! You see, about two weeks ago—excuse me, ladies and gentlemen, but I've got to explain this to my . . . um, brother, I guess you could say, but he's just told you the facts, so you'll understand—about two weeks ago our two brains drifted just a bit out of synch. I don't know whether *my* brain is now Hubert or Yorick, any more than you do, but in any case, the two brains drifted apart, and of course once the process started, it snowballed, for I was in a slightly different receptive state for the input we both received, a difference that was soon magnified. In no time at all the illusion that I was in control of my body—our body—was completely dissipated. There was nothing I could do—no way to call you. YOU DIDN'T EVEN KNOW I EXISTED! It's been like being carried around in a cage, or better, like being possessed—hearing my own voice say things I didn't mean to say, watching in frustration as my own hands performed deeds I hadn't intended. You'd scratch your itches, but not the way I would have, and you kept me awake, with your tossing and turning. I've been totally exhausted, on the verge of a nervous breakdown, carried around helplessly by your frantic round of activities, sustained only by the knowledge that some day you'd throw the switch.

"Now it's your turn, but at least you'll have the comfort of knowing *I* know you're in there. Like an expectant mother, I'm eating—or at any rate tasting, smelling, seeing—for *two* now, and I'll try to make it easy for you. Don't worry. Just as soon as this colloquium is over, you and I will fly to Houston, and we'll see what can be done to get one of us another body. You can have a female body—your body could be any color you like. But let's think it over. I tell you what—to be fair, if we both want this body, I promise I'll let the project director flip a coin to settle which of us gets to keep it and which then gets to choose a new body. That should guarantee justice, shouldn't it? In any case, I'll take care of you, I promise. These people are my witnesses.

"Ladies and gentlemen, this talk we have just heard is not exactly the talk *I* would have given, but I assure you that everything he said was perfectly true. And now if you'll excuse me, I think I'd—we'd—better sit down."

Further Questions

1. Dennett's story makes several leaps of the imagination that go beyond our present technological abilities. List them in order from the least to most fantastic. How would you characterize these differences? Here are three labels you may wish to use: "technological impossibility," "physical impossibility," and "logical impossibility." Do you think performing such "thought experiments" invalidates any of the points Dennett tries to make? Why or why not?
2. Two galaxies can pass through each other. Does that mean that two objects can exist at the same place at the same time? If it does, could two people exist at the same place at the same time? If they could, how do you know that you are just one person?
3. What is a "point of view"? What does a point of view have to do with where a person is? In other words, does your point of view determine your location, or does your location determine your point of view, or neither?

Further Readings

Dennett, Daniel. *Kinds of Minds: Toward an Understanding of Consciousness.* New York: Basic Books, 1996. Accessible access to recent developments in philosophy of mind.
Sanford, David H. "Where Was I?" in Douglas Hofstadter and Daniel Dennett, eds., *The Mind's I.* New York: Basic Books, 1981, pp. 232–240. An amusing sequel to "Where Am I?" that explores the already technologically feasible idea of "nonsurgical mind extensions."

8   On the Idea of Time in Physics

ALBERT EINSTEIN

One of the greatest physicists of all time, Albert Einstein (1879–1955) is world-renowned for his theory of relativity. He was born in Germany and educated first in Munich and then Switzerland. At the age of fourteen, he began on his own the study of philosophy, reading and re-reading the works of the metaphysicians, especially Immanuel Kant. Though not a particularly good student, he was trained to be a teacher of physics and mathematics at the Swiss Federal Polytechnic school in Zurich. He did not think very highly of his teachers nor they of him; when he graduated in 1900, nobody would hire him. To support himself, Einstein worked at a patent office. In 1905, he earned his Ph.D. from the University of Zurich. In the same year, he published four papers that contain some of the most important discoveries of the twentieth century: the creation of the special theory of relativity; the establishment of the mass–energy equivalence ($E = mc^2$); the creation of the theory of Brownian motion; and the foundation of the photon theory of light, which led directly to the advent of quantum mechanics. By 1913, he had become a professor at the University of Berlin and the director of the Kaiser Wilhelm Institute. In 1922, he received the Nobel prize in physics.

Einstein left Berlin in 1932 to escape Hitler and the Nazi party; the next year, he became a member of the Institute for Advanced Study in Princeton, New Jersey, where he lived for the rest of his life. In his famous letter to President Franklin Roosevelt, Einstein pointed out that based on recent advances in physics stemming from his discovery that $E=mc^2$, a bomb could be built to fission the atom, setting off a self-perpetuating chain reaction that could unleash enormous quantities of energy, and that if Germany developed the bomb, it could win the war. As a result, the U.S. government began the Manhattan project to build the first atomic bomb.

A headline in the London *Times* of November 7, 1919, reads: "REVOLUTION IN SCIENCE: NEW THEORY OF THE UNIVERSE; NEWTONIAN IDEAS OVERTHROWN." Two days later, the *New York Times* article quoted the following comment about Einstein's discovery: "This is one of the greatest—perhaps the greatest—of achievements in the history of human thought." Within a few weeks in the London *Times,* an editorial entitled "Assaulting the Absolute" appeared, warning that "the raising of blasphemous voices against time and space threw some into a state of terror where they seemed to feel, for some days at least, that the foundations of all human thought had been undermined." Ten years later, the furor had still not died down; another editorial in the *Times* read: "It is a rare exposition of Relativity that does not find it necessary to warn the reader that here and here and here he had better not try to understand." By 1923, Einstein had become such a legendary figure that wherever he went, mobs of enthusiastic fans appeared; upon his arrival in Tokyo in January 1923, it was reported that "When Einstein arrived at the station there were such large crowds that the police was unable to cope with the perilous crush . . . At the chrysanthemum festival it was neither the empress nor the prince regent nor the imperial princess who held reception; everything turned around Einstein."

Reading Questions

1. What is meant by "simultaneity"?
2. What does it mean to say that a concept exists?
3. How, in the example, can you test whether two events are simultaneous?
4. What is the "logical circle"?
5. How is time defined in physics?
6. How is the concept of relative simultaneity introduced?
7. What does it mean to say that every coordinate system has its own particular time?
8. When is the statement of the time of an event meaningless?

LIGHTNING HAS STRUCK THE RAILS on our railway embankment at two places *A* and *B* far distant from each other. I make the additional assertion that these two lightning flashes occurred simultaneously. If I ask you whether there is sense in this statement, you will answer my question with a decided "Yes." But if I now approach you with the request to explain to me the sense of the statement more precisely, you find after some consideration that the answer to this question is not so easy as it appears at first sight.

After some time perhaps the following answer would occur to you: "The significance of the statement is clear in itself and needs no further explanation; of course it would require some consideration if I were to be commissioned to determine by observations whether in the actual case the two events took place simultaneously or not." I cannot be satisfied with this answer for the following reason. Supposing that as a result of ingenious considerations an able meteorologist were to discover that the lightning must always strike the places *A* and *B* simultaneously, then we should be faced with the task of testing whether or not this theoretical result is in accordance with the reality. We encounter the same difficulty with all physical statements in which the conception "simultaneous" plays a part. The concept does not exist for the physicist until he has the possibility of discovering whether or not it is fulfilled in an actual case. We thus require a definition of simultaneity such that this definition supplies us with the method by means of which, in the present case, he can decide by experiment whether or not both the lightning strokes occurred simultaneously. As long as this requirement is not satisfied, I

allow myself to be deceived as a physicist (and of course the same applies if I am not a physicist), when I imagine that I am able to attach a meaning to the statement of simultaneity. (I would ask the reader not to proceed farther until he is fully convinced on this point.)

After thinking the matter over for some time you then offer the following suggestion with which to test simultaneity. By measuring along the rails, the connecting line *AB* should be measured up and an observer placed at the mid-point M of the distance AB. This observer should be supplied with an arrangement (e.g., two mirrors inclined at 90°) which allows him visually to observe both places *A* and *B* at the same time. If the observer perceives the two flashes of lightning at the same time, then they are simultaneous.

I am very pleased with this suggestion, but for all that I cannot regard the matter as quite settled, because I feel constrained to raise the following objection: "Your definition would certainly be right, if only I knew that the light by means of which the observer at *M* perceives the lightning flashes travels along the length $A \rightarrow M$ with the same velocity as along the length $B \rightarrow M$. But an examination of this supposition would only be possible if we already had at our disposal the means of measuring time. It would thus appear as though we were moving here in a logical circle."

After further consideration you cast a somewhat disdainful glance at me—and rightly so—and you declare: "I maintain my previous definition nevertheless, because in reality it assumes absolutely nothing about light. There is only *one* demand to be made of the definition of simultaneity, namely, that in every real case it must supply us with an empirical decision as to whether or not the conception that has to be defined is fulfilled. That my definition satisfies this demand is indisputable. That light requires the same time to traverse the path $A \to M$ as for the path $B \to M$ is in reality neither a *supposition nor a hypothesis* about the physical nature of light, but a *stipulation* which I can make of my own free will in order to arrive at a definition of simultaneity."

It is clear that this definition can be used to give an exact meaning not only to *two* events, but to as many events as we care to choose, and independently of the positions of the scenes of the events with respect to the body of reference[1] (here the railway embankment). We are thus led also to a definition of "time" in physics. For this purpose we suppose that clocks of identical construction are placed at the points A, B and C of the railway line (coordinate system), and that they are set in such a manner that the positions of their pointers are simultaneously (in the above sense) the same. Under these conditions we understand by the "time" of an event the reading (position of the hands) of that one of these clocks which is in the immediate vicinity (in space) of the event. In this manner a time-value is associated with every event which is essentially capable of observation.

This stipulation contains a further physical hypothesis, the validity of which will hardly be doubted without empirical evidence to the contrary. It has been assumed that all these clocks go *at the same rate* if they are of identical construction. Stated more exactly: When two clocks arranged at rest in different places of a reference-body are set in such a manner that a *particular* position of the pointers of the one clock is *simultaneous* (in the above sense) with the *same* position of the pointers of the other clock, then identical "settings" are always simultaneous (in the sense of the above definition).

Up to now our considerations have been referred to a particular body of reference, which we have styled a "railway embankment." We suppose a very long train travelling along the rails with the constant velocity v and in the direction indicated in Figure 1.

People travelling in this train will with advantage use the train as a rigid reference-body (coordinate system); they regard all events in reference to the train. Then every event which takes place along the line also takes place at a particular point of the train. Also the definition of simultaneity can be given relative to the train in exactly the same way as with respect to the embankment. As a natural consequence, however, the following question arises:

Are two events (e.g., the two strokes of lightning A and B) which are simultaneous *with reference to the railway embankment* also simultaneous *relatively to the train*? We shall show directly that the answer must be in the negative.

When we say that the lightning strokes A and B are simultaneous with respect to the embankment, we mean: the rays of light emitted at the places A and B, where the lightning occurs, meet each other at the mid-point M of the length $A \to B$ of the embankment. But the events A and B also correspond to positions A and B on the train. Let M' be the mid-point of the distance $A \to B$ on the travelling train. Just when the flashes[2] of lightning occur, this point M' naturally coincides with the point M, but it moves toward the right in the diagram with the velocity v of the train. If an observer sitting in the position M' in the train did not possess this velocity, then he would remain permanently at M, and the light rays emitted by the flashes of lightning A and B would reach him simultaneously, i.e., they would meet just where he is situated. Now in reality (considered with reference to the railway embankment) he is hastening towards the beam of light coming from B, whilst he is riding on ahead of the beam of light coming from A. Hence the observer will see the beam of light emitted from B earlier than he will see that emitted from A. Observers who take the railway train as their reference-body must therefore come to the conclusion that the lightning flash B took place earlier than the lightning flash A. We thus arrive at the important result:

Events which are simultaneous with reference to the embankment are not simultaneous with respect to the train, and *vice versa* (relativity of simultaneity). Every reference-body (coordinate system) has its own particular time; unless we are told the reference-body to which the statement of time refers, there is no meaning in a statement of the time of an event.

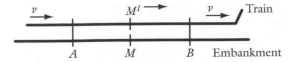

WHAT TIME IS IT ON MARS?

Paul Davies

One inevitable victim of the fact that there is no universal present moment is the tidy division of time into past, present and future. These terms may have meaning in one's immediate locality, but they can't apply everywhere. Questions such as "What is happening *now* on Mars?" are intended to refer to a particular instant on that planet. But as we have seen, a space traveller sweeping past Earth in a rocket who asked the same question at the same instant would be referring to a different moment on Mars. In fact, the range of possible "nows" on Mars available to an observer near Earth (depending on his motion) actually spans several minutes. When the distance to the subject is greater, so is this range of "nows." For a distant quasar "now" could refer to any interval over billions of years. Even the effect of strolling around on foot alters the "present moment" on a quasar by thousands of years!

The abandonment of a distinct past, present and future is a profound step, for the temptation to assume that only the present "really exists" is great. It is usually presumed, without thinking, that the future is as yet unformed and perhaps undetermined; the past has gone, remembered but relinquished. Past and future, one wishes to believe, do not exist. Only one instant of reality seems to occur "at a time." The theory of relativity makes nonsense of such notions. Past, present and future must be equally real, for one person's past is another's present and another's future.

The physicist's attitude to time is strongly conditioned by his experiences with the effects of relativity and can appear quite alien to the layman, although the physicist himself rarely thinks twice about it. He does not regard time as a sequence of events which *happen*. Instead, all of past and future are simply *there*, and time extends in either direction from any given moment in much the same way as space stretches away from any particular place. In fact, the comparison is more than an analogy, for space and time become inextricably interwoven in the theory of relativity, united into what physicists call *spacetime*.

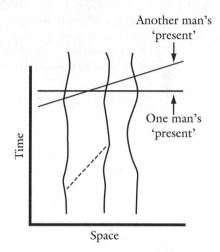

Physicists do not regard time as passing but laid out as part of "spacetime," a four-dimensional structure depicted here as a two-dimensional sheet by suppressing two space dimensions. A point on the sheet is an "event." The wiggly lines are the paths of bodies that move about; the broken line is the path of a light signal sent between two bodies. The horizontal line through the figure represents a slice through all of space at one instant from the point of view of one observer. Another observer, moving differently, would require the oblique slice. Thus, there must be a temporal (vertical) extension to make sense of the world. There is no universal "slice" representing a single, common, "present." For that reason, division into a universal past, present and future is impossible.

From *God and the New Physics*.

NOTES

1. We suppose further, that, when three events *A, B* and *C* occur in different places in such a manner that *A* is simultaneous with *B*, and *B* is simultaneous with *C* (simultaneous in the sense of the above definition), then the criterion for the simultaneity of the pair of events *A,*

C is also satisfied. This assumption is a physical hypothesis about the law of propagation of light; it must certainly be fulfilled if we are to maintain the law of the constancy of the velocity of light *in vacuo*.

2. As judged from the embankment.

Further Questions

1. What do you suppose people found so puzzling about Einstein's theory? What common-sense notions does it reject?
2. "The distinction between past, present and future," wrote Einstein, "is nothing but our most cherished illusion." What does this mean to you?
3. It feels to you as if the moment going on right now as you are reading this is the "real" moment, and all other moments have not yet happened: there is the absolute future and the absolute past and the absolute present. If Einstein is right that this feeling is merely an illusion, what could account for it?

Further Readings

Einstein, Albert. *Out of My Later Years*. New York: Citadel Press, 1956. Contains Einstein's essays on all aspects of life.

Schwartz, Jacob. *Relativity in Illustrations*. New York: New York University Press, 1962. A visual tour-de-force explanation of the paradoxical aspects of Einstein's relativity.

9   Time Travel: The Rules of the Road

KADRI VIHVELIN

Kadri Vihvelin has a degree in Jurisprudence from Oxford University, a law degree from Dalhousie University, and a Ph.D. in philosophy from Cornell University. Currently she is associate professor of philosophy at the University of Southern California. She writes on topics in metaphysics and ethics, especially on questions about free will, causation, counterfactuals, and time.

In this selection, she asks whether time travel to the past is really possible. Some people think it isn't because it involves changing the past, which is a contradiction. Vihvelin argues that this objection is based on the same confusion that leads to the fatalist's view that whatever will be must be. Nevertheless, she argues that time travel is very strange. The time traveler cannot do many things the rest of us can do: for instance, she cannot kill a helpless sleeping baby.

Reading Questions

1. What is the naive argument against time travel?
2. What is the fatalist fallacy?

3. What is the standard reply to the naive argument?
4. What are the reasons for thinking that Big Al can, in the ordinary sense, kill Little Al?
5. Why does Vihvelin think that Big Al can't, in the ordinary sense, kill Little Al? Do you agree? Why or why not?

THE MIDDLE-AGED MAN looks down on the baby in the crib. The child smiles up at him, but the man does not smile back. Instead the man's face is full of murderous resolve. He is a man obsessed. He is a man with a mission. He has come to kill this child. He has been planning the murder for many months, and his planning has been meticulous. He picked a time when he knew the child would be alone and unattended, and he has locked the door so that he will not be interrupted. He has several weapons with him, including a loaded gun that he has cleaned, checked, and rechecked a hundred times. It has never misfired or jammed in the past. But the man has left nothing to chance. He has another equally well-prepared gun as a backup, just in case. And if that fails, well, he has a knife in one pocket, a garrote in the other, and no mercy at all in his heart.

It's an ugly scene and even more tragic and macabre when you understand the background. The man, we call him "Al," is a traveler in time. He has journeyed from his present into the past—his own past, for the child in the crib is Al himself as a child. For reasons too depressing to relate, Al has decided that it would have been better if he had never lived. He has come back to commit suicide by killing himself as an infant; he's here to commit autoinfanticide.

So what happens next? Does Big Al kill Little Al? Can he? Here things become perplexing. For on the one hand it seems as if:

(1) Big Al can kill Little Al.

Never has a killer been so well prepared as Big Al at this moment. The child is defenseless, and Al is relentless. On the other hand, this is not an ordinary sort of murder attempt. In an ordinary case, we might be frightened for the child, but we know that Little Al is safe. We know that Big Al won't kill Little Al because we know that he didn't. If Al had died as a child, he wouldn't have grown up to travel back in time to try to kill himself. So whatever Big Al does next, we know that it won't result in the death of Little Al. Maybe all of the guns will jam and the other weapons will fail, or maybe Big Al will lose his nerve or be struck by lightning. However unlikely, we know that something *must* happen to prevent the killing, because we know that Little Al did not die. You cannot change the past; it can't be that Little Al dies and does not die. That's a contradiction. So it appears to be logically impossible for Big Al to kill Little Al. This means that despite all appearances, we have to say that:

(2) Big Al can't kill Little Al.

However, in saying both (1) and (2), it seems that our time travel story has led us into contradicting ourselves. Now we might say here, in defense of our story, that (1) and (2) are not really contradictory because they involve different senses of *can*. The sense in which we want to say that Big Al *can* kill Little Al is the sense we use on a day-to-day basis when we assess the abilities of others. That is, the sense in which we say that someone can walk (because she's not paralyzed) or can play the piano (because she's been taking lessons). On the other hand, the sense in which (2) seems true involves the *can* of logical or metaphysical possibility.

These are indeed different senses of *can*. Can pigs fly? Yes, if we mean this in the sense of logical possibility. As philosophers say, there are possible worlds—universes we can describe without contradicting ourselves—where pigs fly. But if we mean the sense of *can* in which we assess real-world abilities, the answer is: No, pigs cannot fly.

Distinguishing the various senses of *can* doesn't seem to help us in our time travel story. The problem is that in the ordinary sense of *can* in which we want to say that some people can play the piano and others can't, we also want to say that no one can do what is logically impossible. The is no sense of *can* in which anyone can make a contradiction true, but in our story, it seems that time travel puts Al in a position in which he can do the impossible.

Situations like Al's are sometimes called "paradoxes of time travel." There are, of course, different ways to tell such stories. The same sorts of puzzles would arise if Al were trying to kill any of his direct ancestors as infants, or if he were trying to sabotage the invention of time travel or prevent the evolution of homo sapiens . . . and so on.

Puzzles like these have convinced some people that time travel is logically impossible. We might put the argument in the form of a *reductio ad absurdum*: "If you could really travel back in time, you could go back and kill yourself when you were a small child. But clearly that's impossible; if you killed yourself as a small child you wouldn't grow up to go back and kill yourself. So if time travel were possible, the time traveler could do something impossible, which is impossible. Therefore time travel cannot be possible." For reasons that will become apparent in a moment, I am going to call this "the naive argument" against time travel.

Some philosophers (and many science fiction writers) have been convinced by the naive argument but have taken it to show, not that time travel is impossible, but only that time travel must have certain built-in limits — limits that somehow prevent time travelers from getting into the paradoxical situation in the first place. Maybe you can only travel into the past, but not your own past. Or maybe you can travel into only the very distant past, where nothing you do could make any difference to the present. Stories like these can be entertaining, but they never seem to me to make complete sense. If you can travel into the past, why can't you travel into your own past? I mean, can't you take a bus across town? And if you can only travel into the distant past, why can't you leave a time bomb waiting to catch up to your infant self? And no matter how far you go into the past, what keeps you from making that tiny difference that would result in your never being born (e.g., killing and eating the first mammal)?

It seems that the only way to consistently keep the time traveler out of potentially paradoxical situations consistently is to tell stories in which the time traveler is a ghostly observer who can witness but not affect anything she sees in the past. But this isn't time travel in any interesting sense; it is

past watching. We observe the past in this sense whenever we look at the newly arrived light of a distant star. That's all very well, but it's not the same thing as being there, because we can't make a difference to what we observe.

In any case, all of this apparatus will seem necessary only if we have been convinced by the naive argument that situations like Al's are genuinely paradoxical. However, most philosophers who have thought about time travel agree that the naive argument doesn't work. The standard reply is that the proponent of the naive argument is guilty of a logical fallacy sometimes called the "fatalist fallacy."

The fatalist's argument goes like this: "Take something you think you have a choice about, for instance, whether or not you will stay home tomorrow. Now either you'll stay home tomorrow or you won't, so it's either true now that you'll stay home tomorrow, or it's false now that you will stay home tomorrow. Suppose it's true. In that case, you can't go out because if you did, it would be both true and false that you stay home, which is a contradiction. Suppose, on the other hand, that it's false that you will stay home tomorrow. But in that case, you can't stay home because if you did, it would be both false and true that you stay home, again a contradiction. So no matter what the truth is about the future — whether you will stay home or whether you will go out — there is nothing you can do to change it. Whatever will be *must* be."

It is said that soldiers have drawn comfort from the fatalist's argument on the eve of battle, reasoning: "Either I will be killed tomorrow or I won't; if I will be killed, nothing can prevent it, if I am to live, nothing can harm me." Insofar as the argument is supposed to convince us that nothing we can do will make a difference to what happens in the future, it clearly doesn't work, and it's hard to believe that it ever persuaded any soldier not to duck when the bullets started flying.

The fatalist has made a mistake, a mistake about the logic of the word *can*. If we spell out the argument carefully, we can see what the mistake is. It is indeed logically impossible that you will stay home tomorrow *and* not stay home tomorrow. That's a contradiction, and no one can make contradictions true. So we should agree that you can't *both* stay home and go out tomorrow. But from the fact that you can't stay home and also go out, it doesn't follow that you can't stay home. Nor does it follow that you can't go out. You can stay home, you can go out. You just cannot do both. Of course you will do what you will do, but this doesn't mean that you *must* do what you will do. If you go out tomorrow, it won't be because the law of noncontradiction kicks you out of the house. If you stay home, it won't be because logic makes it impossible for you to leave.

The fatalist's mistake is in confusing the truth about the future with what *must* be true. The fatalist thinks that if it's a fact about the future that I will do something, it follows, by logic alone, that I *must* do it; I cannot do otherwise. And the fatalist thinks that if it's a fact about the future that I *will not* do something, then it follows, by logic alone, that I *cannot* do it. That's a mistake. Suppose that tomorrow I stay home. It doesn't follow that I can't go out. All that follows is that *if* I were to go out, tomorrow would be different from the way it actually will be.

We can make a similar mistake when thinking about the past. I didn't leave the house yesterday, so the facts about yesterday include the fact that I *didn't* leave the house. But it doesn't follow that I *couldn't* have left the house yesterday. All that follows is that *if* I had left the house, yesterday would have been different from the way it actually was.

We know a lot more about the past than we know about the future, and that's why it's easier to be a fatalist about the past; that is, to think that logic alone makes it impossible for us to change the past. But it's still a mistake to reason from the fact that something didn't happen in the past to the conclusion that it was impossible for it to happen. For instance, we know that Hitler didn't die until 1945, so we know that any earlier attempt to kill him failed. However, it doesn't follow that no one could have killed him before 1945, or that he couldn't have died before 1945. It just means that if Hitler had died before 1945, the past would have been different from the way it actually was.

The fatalist's argument doesn't work. Keeping this in mind, let's go back to the case of time travel. When we last left Al, he was poised over Little Al, ready to commit murder, and it seemed pretty clear that, given all his preparations, (1) is true, given our ordinary sense of *can*. Big Al *can* kill little Al. He's got what it takes, and he's in the right place at the right time. He's got the ability and the opportunity. What happens next?

Well, ignoring all of the details, one thing seems pretty clear: big Al won't kill Little Al. We know that he won't, because we know that Big Al didn't kill little Al. We know that because we know that if little Al had been killed, Big Al would never have grown up to be a time traveler who goes back to kill his baby self. Notice that in saying this we haven't contradicted ourselves. We have said that Big Al can kill Little Al, but he won't. He could have done it, but he didn't. No contradiction here. If we say that Big Al can kill his baby self, aren't we saying that he can make a contradiction true? No. A time travel story in which someone who did not die as a child is killed as a child would indeed be contradictory. We can agree that:

> It is impossible for Big Al to kill himself as a child *and* not kill himself as a child.

However, as we saw when looking at the fatalist argument, it doesn't follow that:

> It is impossible for Big Al to kill Little Al.

We can say that Big Al *can* kill Little Al, but he doesn't and didn't. So, our time travel story has not, after all, resulted in paradox or contradiction. More generally, we can argue in this way that a time traveler can do anything that anyone else can do.

That's the standard reply to the naive argument against time travel. For a long time, I was pesuaded by it, but I no longer think it's adequate. I agree, of course, that there is a difference between *did not* and *could not,* and I agree that the naive argument against time travel is based on fatalistic confusions. I agree that there are many ways in which time travelers are like the rest of us; there are things that they do not do which they nevertheless *can* do. But I now think that no time traveler can kill the baby who in fact is his younger self, given what we ordinarily mean by *can*. This is a surprising conclusion, one that I resisted for some time, and one that some of my readers have taken as a new argument against the possibility of time travel. I think it's a mistake to reject the logical (or even physical) possibility of time travel on the grounds that it cramps our style. I will argue that the time traveler's inability to commit autoinfanticide is just what we should expect, given the time traveler's somewhat peculiar situation.

Before I give my argument, we should reflect for a moment on the meaning of *can*.

OUR ORDINARY SENSE OF CAN

Let's begin by noting that there is a sense of *can* in which everyone, except perhaps the fatalist, will agree that the time traveler *can* kill his baby self. It is logically possible for him to do so. There is a possible world in which the following things happen: the time traveler shoots and kills his baby self, the baby is buried but three days later is resurrected from the dead; the baby grows up to become the time traveler who journeys back to the past, where he shoots and kills his baby self. This world has laws of physics that are different from ours and is strange in other ways. We may wonder why the time traveler does not know these extraordinary facts about his past history. But it is a possible world; we do not contradict ourselves when we describe what happens there.

However, this is not the sense of *can* we ordinarily use when we talk about what people can and cannot do. It's logically possible for me to run faster than the speed of light, but I cannot do so. It's logically possible for me to walk on water, but I can't do that either. On the other hand, I can swim and I can ride a bicycle.

What this ordinary sense of *can* commits us to is a long-standing philosophical issue, and what we say depends in part on what position we take on the question of free will and determinism. Some philosophers think that we can, in the ordinary sense, do something we don't do only if our choices are not subject to causal laws; other philosophers think that we can do otherwise even if everything that happens, including our choices and acts, is governed by deterministic causal laws. We don't need to take a stand on this difficult question to discuss the problem of autoinfanticide. All we need to assume is something that I think we all can agree on, regardless of our views on the problem of free will and determinism. Everyone should agree that a necessary condition of the truth of:

(C) Someone can do *x*.

is that it's at least sometimes true that:

(S) If she tried to do *x*, she would or at least might succeed.

And everyone should agree that if it's always true, of someone, that:

(F) If she tried to do *x*, she would fail.

then:

(N) She cannot do *x*.

For instance, it seems reasonable to suppose that I can swim and that I can ride a bicycle only if it's at least sometimes true that if I tried to do either of these things, I would or at least might succeed. And it seems reasonable to suppose that I cannot walk on water or run faster than the speed of light because it is always true that if I tried to do these things, I would fail.

The standard reply to the naive objection to time travel says that the time traveler can kill the baby who is his baby self because doing so is consistent with facts about the time traveler's abilities (e.g., his shooting skills) and opportunities (the gun in his hand, the proximity of the baby, and so on). I say that it's not at all obvious what the time traveler's abilities and opportunities are. If someone wants to defend the claim that Big Al *can* kill Little Al, despite the fact that all of his attempts to do so have failed and will continue to fail, she also has to defend the claim that there is at least one occasion on which it's true that if Big Al had tried (just one more time) to kill Little Al, he would, or at least might, have succeeded.

I don't think this claim can be defended. The fact that someone tries and fails to do something is consistent with its being true that he or she could have done that thing, for it is consistent with its being true that if he had tried, just one more time, he would, or at least might, have succeeded. But, in the case of the time traveler, I think that this counterfactual is always false.

COUNTERFACTUALS

Big Al can kill Little Al only if there is at least one occasion on which it's true that:

(S) If Big Al had tried to kill Little Al, Big Al would have, or at least might have, succeeded.

Our question is whether (S) is ever true.

Notice that (S) is a kind of conditional, that is, an "if P, then Q" statement: it says that if something (P) had been true, then something else (Q) would or might be true. Some examples: "If he had not sold his stock, he would have become rich a few weeks later." "If I had tossed this coin, it might have come up heads." "If you had stayed up all night studying, you still would have failed the exam." Notice that in these examples the first part of the conditional (the "antecedent") is false, yet the conditional may still be true.

Philosophers call these conditionals "counterfactuals" because they say that if something which is *in fact false* had been true, something else would also be true. At first this looks confusing. How can we know anything about something that didn't actually happen?

In fact, it isn't so confusing. What we know about the world includes our knowledge of the laws of physics as well as other general facts, and we can use this knowledge, together with our knowledge of particular facts, to predict the future and also to predict the consequences of our possible future actions. For instance, we predict that the sun will rise tomorrow, and we predict that if we do not eat, we will go hungry and eventually die. In a similar way, we can use our general knowledge, together with our knowledge of particular background conditions, to decide whether or not a counterfactual is true. For instance, we use our knowledge about how matches work, together with our knowledge about a particular match (dry, not defective, etc.) and background conditions (not too windy, etc.) to infer that if we had struck that match, it would have lit.

Philosophers use possible worlds to explain how we go about doing this. Think of a possible world as a total way the world might have been—a universe that we can describe without contradicting ourselves. Some possible worlds are very similar to the actual world, for instance, the possible world that was exactly like the actual world until I scratched my nose a moment ago. Other possible worlds are very different, for instance, possible worlds where pigs fly. Some possible worlds have the same laws of physics as ours. Other possible worlds have different physical laws. What happens at these worlds is physically impossible—that is, not possible given the actual laws of physics—but logically possible.

Keeping this in mind, here's how philosophers tell us we should go about figuring out whether the counterfactual "if P, it would or might be the case that Q" is true: Imagine the worlds most similar to ours where P is true. Then ask yourself whether Q is also true at these worlds. If Q is true at all, or even some, of these worlds, the counterfactual is true. On the other hand, if Q is false at all of these worlds, the counterfactual is false.

Here's an example: I have never tried to walk on water, but I know that if I tried to walk on water, I would fail. How do I know this? Aren't there possible worlds where I try and succeed in walking on water? Yes, but these possible worlds are not relevant to the evaluation of the counterfactual. Worlds where I try and succeed are very different from our world—they are worlds where I'm light as a feather, or I have wings, the earth has a much smaller mass, and so on. The *relevant* worlds are worlds that are much more similar to the actual world; they are as much like the actual world as is compatible with my *trying* to walk on water—that is, worlds where the laws of physics are the same as ours, the earth has the same mass, and I am a human being weighing what I actually weigh. And since all of these worlds are worlds where my attempt to walk on water fails, it's false that if I had tried to walk on water, I would or might have succeeded. On the contrary, if I had tried to walk on water, I would have failed.

WHY BIG AL CANNOT KILL LITTLE AL

Back to Big Al. We know that Big Al tried many times to kill Little Al and failed each time. The standard reply says that this doesn't mean he couldn't have killed Little Al. I say that if it's really true, given our ordinary sense of *could,* that he could have killed Little Al, it must at least sometimes be true that:

(S) If Big Al had tried to kill Little Al, he would, or at least might, have succeeded.

However, this is so only if there is at least one occasion on which it's true that at least one of the most similar worlds at which Big Al tries to kill Little Al is one where he succeeds. Whether this is so will depend, of course, on what the time traveler's world is like. I assume, as discussions of time travel standardly assume, that the time traveler's world is much like the actual world. When we ask "What would things be like if there were time travel?" we are asking a subjunctive question. We evaluate it as we would any counterfactual. We imagine a world as similar to our world as can be, consistent with its laws allowing time travel. Maybe, as some scientists tell us, the actual world is already a world like that.

I claim that at any world remotely like ours, (S) is always false. I say that all of the closest worlds where Big Al tries to kill Little Al are worlds where he fails. That is, I say that the following is invariably true:

(F) If Big Al had tried to kill Little Al, he would have failed.

If (F) is always true, and if I'm right about what we mean by *can*, it's always false that:

(C) Big Al can kill Little Al.

When we send Big Al back in the time machine, we know that he will not kill Little Al. We know that he will not because we know that he did not. Why didn't he? There are two possible explanations. Either he tried and failed, or he didn't try. If he tried and failed, there would be some explanation for his failure: the gun jammed, Little Al moved, the bullet was a dud . . . something happened that prevented him from succeeding. On the other hand, if he didn't even try to kill Little Al, we don't have to suppose that any of these factors prevented him from doing so. The gun may have been well oiled, the ammunition live, and the baby a sitting duck. But if he didn't try to kill the baby, it's not surprising that he didn't succeed. Our question is: Is it true, on any of these occasions, that if he had tried he might have succeeded?

I don't think so. Take any case you like: Suppose that the gun was greased, the bullets live, and the baby a sitting duck. I say that even in this case, (S) is false and (F) is true. Despite appearances, Big Al cannot kill his baby self.

Of course, it's logically possible for Big Al to kill Little Al; that is, there are worlds at which Big Al tries to kill Little Al and his attempt succeeds. But consider what those worlds must be like. They are worlds at which Little Al dies and is buried but is later resurrected from the dead and grows up to be the adult Al who travels back through time and kills his baby self.

Is there any other logically possible way to work the trick? Well, maybe. Maybe there are worlds where Big Al kills Little Al, and Little Al stays dead, but Little Al is somehow not Big Al's younger self. (Whether this is really possible is something we will take up shortly.)

Either way, we are talking about possible worlds very different from our own. So different, I think, that they are not relevant to counterfactuals about what would have been the case had Big Al tried to kill Little Al. If Big Al had tried to kill Little Al— if he had squeezed the trigger of the gun he was in fact holding in his hand—the laws of nature would still have been the same (or nearly the same) and there would still have been no resurrections from the dead. And if Big Al had tried to kill Little Al, Little Al would still have been Big Al's younger self.

Compare Al's case to more ordinary cases. Take any real-life actual baby you like. Don't kill it! Please, don't even *try* to kill it! But do consider the counterfactuals. Do you think it is true that if you tried to kill it, it would be resurrected from the dead? Of course not. Do you think that if you tried to kill it, someone else would, in later life, somehow take the place of the adult this baby will become? Of course not. There are possible worlds where there is resurrection from the dead, and maybe there are worlds where babies have stand-ins waiting in the wings, ready to take their place. But neither of these worlds is remotely like the way things would be if you tried to kill that baby. If you tried, either you would succeed and the baby would be gone forever, or you would fail. If you think that worlds where you fail are more like the actual world than any world where you succeed, you think that you cannot kill the baby. Precisely the same is true of Big Al and Little Al, but in Big Al's case there is this difference: The worlds where Big Al tries and fails are worlds where the gun jams, the bullets are duds, the baby moves, and so on. The worlds where Big Al tries and succeeds either have resurrection from the dead or some sort of system of baby replacement. There's no other way for him to succeed. However, worlds of the former sort— where guns jam or bullets misfire—are always more similar to the actual world than worlds of the latter sort, which is why it is always true that if Big Al tried to kill Little Al, he would fail.

The reason the counterfactuals come out this way has everything to do with the fact that Big Al is a time traveler and Little Al is his baby self. Other people can kill Little Al. Al's mother could have killed Little Al. Big Al can kill other babies. If Little Al were replaced by another baby exactly like Little Al, Big Al could kill that baby. But Big Al can't kill Little Al.

Objection: You've argued that if Big Al killed Little Al, Little Al would be—would have to be—resurrected from the dead. But then the standard defense of time travel is right after all. Big Al *can* kill Little Al. No contradictions or paradoxes arise if we suppose that he does.

Reply: I agree that if Big Al succeeded in killing Little Al, Little Al would be resurrected from the dead. But that's not the counterfactual relevant to our ordinary sense of *can*. What's relevant is what would happen if Big Al *tried* to kill Little Al. It's false that if Big Al tried to kill Little Al, Little Al would be resurrected from the dead. Compare: If I succeeded in running faster than the speed of light, the laws of nature would be—would have to be—very different. But it's false that if I *tried* to run faster than the speed of light, the laws of nature would be very different.

Objection: Doesn't your argument show that time travel is possible only in worlds whose laws provide for resurrection from the dead? Since our world is not such a world, you've shown that time travel is impossible in the way that running faster than the speed of light is: it's physically impossible.

Reply: Not so. I think that time travel is possible in worlds very much like ours, maybe exactly like ours. But in any case, there is any reason to suppose that there is any connection between time-travel-permitting laws and resurrection-permitting laws. My claim is that if time travel occurred, the laws would still be much the same; there would still be no resurrection from the dead.

Objection: Big Al *can* kill that baby—the one you're calling "Little Al." If he tried to kill that baby, he would succeed, but in that case it would turn out that the baby is not Little Al, but some other baby who looks just like Little Al.

Reply: You are changing the subject. That baby *is* Little Al, and our question is whether Big Al can kill Little Al, not whether he can kill Little Al's twin or any other baby. The only worlds relevant to this question are worlds where Big Al tries to kill Little Al.

Objection: But what's at issue is not whether Big Al can kill a baby who satisfies the description "Big Al's younger self." Maybe by definition it is impossible for Big Al to kill any baby who satisfies that description. But the interesting question is whether Big Al can kill a particular baby: *that* baby, however we describe it.

Reply: I agree; the issue is not terminological. "Big Al kills his younger self" isn't false by definition; there are worlds where it is true—worlds where there is resurrection from the dead. The impossibility I am arguing for is neither analytic nor logical; it's physical. Given our laws, the actual laws of physics, no one can kill his younger self. Laws sustain counterfactuals, and one of the counterfactuals sustained by our laws is this one: If anyone tried to kill the baby who is his younger self, he would fail.

Objection: But surely you agree that it's a contingent fact that *this* baby grew up to be *that* person: our grown-up Al, the time traveler. *This* baby could have died in infancy and *that* adult could have had a different past; he could have been born to a different mother and grown from a different baby. Surely there are worlds where *this* baby and *that* adult are two different people. So surely there are worlds with our laws (no resurrection from the dead) where *that* adult kills *this* baby. Why not say that a world thus described is what the world would be like if Big Al tried to kill Little Al?

Reply: Let's take this one step at a time. To avoid any possibility of confusion, let's call this baby "Little" and let's call that adult "Big." Certainly there are worlds where Little fails to become an adult. Let's also suppose—though some philosophers have questioned this—that there are worlds where Big was born to a different mother and grew from a different baby. And let's suppose, though this is pretty strange, that there are worlds where Little and Big are two different people. (Why is it strange? Well, ask yourself this question: At these worlds, who is Al? Is he Little or is he Big? Don't tell me he's both. How can one person, our one and only Al, be identical to two distinct people?) Finally, let's suppose there is a world where Big travels back in time to kill his baby self but somehow gets confused and ends up killing Little instead. I agree that we've just described, without contradicting ourselves, a world where

Big kills Little. But this doesn't show that Big *can* kill Little.

It may be true that it's logically possible for Big to kill Little. And it may even be true that if Big somehow succeeded in killing Little, then Little would stay dead (no resurrection!), but Big would have grown from a different baby. But that's beside the point.

Our question is not about what the world would be like if Big tried and succeeded in killing Little. Our question is about what Big *can* do, and that is a question about whether Big would or might have succeeded if Big had tried to kill Little. I think the answer is clearly "No." It is false that if Big had tried—if he had pulled the trigger just one more time—Big and Little would have been two different people. Any world like this is far less like ours than a world where Big tries but fails to kill Little.

Objection: Look, suppose that Big Al has a clone, Twin Al, who is the atom-for-atom duplicate of Big Al. Twin Al gets into a time machine to kill his baby self, but wires get crossed and he materializes right beside Little Al. You agree that Twin Al can kill Little Al. Yet you are saying that Big Al cannot do what his atom-for-atom duplicate can do.

Reply: Yes, I am saying this, and I agree that it seems odd. It seems odd because ordinarily, when we are considering what someone is able to do right now, the past is irrelevant. Or rather, the past is irrelevant except insofar as it affects current present-tense properties. Of course, Big Al can't swim if he hasn't taken lessons, but the lessons enable him to swim only because of the difference to the way his brain is set up now. It's his current brain setup that gives him that ability, however he acquired it; and if his twin had the same setup, he would have the same ability to swim, however he had acquired that setup. So, normally we think we can, at least in principle, read a person's abilities off his present-tense properties, the way he is now. And we think we can read facts about what a person *can* do from present-tense facts about the person—his abilities—together with present-tense facts about his immediate environment—his opportunities. But normally we are not dealing with time travelers. Normally causation runs in one direction only: from past to future, and the past restricts what we can do in the future only by affecting the present.

With time travelers it is different. The way Big Al and his surroundings are now is caused not only by the past but also by the future-tense fact that Little Al will survive to be Big Al. Therefore we shouldn't be surprised that what Big Al *can* do cannot be read off present-tense facts about Big Al and his surroundings. We should not be surprised that the future-tense fact of Big Al's *not* killing Little Al turns out to be one of the facts that must be held constant in our evaluation of counterfactuals about what would have happened had Big Al tried to kill Little Al. Big Al's failure to kill Little Al is what makes Big Al's attempt possible. The relevant sense of possible is physical; given our laws, Big Al tried to kill Little Al only if his attempt fails. (The laws of physics dictate that no one tries to do anything in later life if he was killed as a child.)

Objection: But if your argument works, doesn't it show that time travelers are able to do—can do—only what they in fact do?

Reply: No. There are other things time travelers cannot do; for instance, they cannot kill their ancestors before they pass on their genes. However, they are able to do lots of other things; they have plenty of abilities that they do not exercise but could have exercised. Big Al could have pinched Little Al. He could have gone next door and killed some other baby. There are worlds with our laws at which Big Al tries and succeeds in pinching his baby self or in killing that other baby. We have no reason to doubt the truth of the relevant counterfactuals: If Big Al had tried to pinch his baby self (kill that other baby), he would have succeeded.

But this leaves open lots of interesting questions. For instance, can a time traveler kill the infant Hitler? Here is an argument that no time traveler can do so.

If a time traveler is in the past, gun aimed at Baby Hitler, this can only be because she's read history books reporting the baby's future crimes. However, the history books will report these crimes only if the baby survives the traveler's visit and grows up to commit the crimes, so if the time traveler is in the past with Baby Hitler, this can only be because Baby Hitler survived her visit. We should hold this fact constant when we evaluate counterfactuals about what would have happened if the time traveler had tried to kill Hitler. So, if the time traveler had tried to kill Baby Hitler, she would have failed.

However, the first premise of this argument is false. It's false that the *only* reason a time traveler might try to kill Baby Hitler is because she knows the baby's future deeds. A time traveler might travel back to the past, pick a victim at random, and kill for sport. If the victim is Baby Hitler, the time traveler will not succeed, but there is no reason to doubt that if the time traveler had tried (one more time) to kill that baby, she would or might have succeeded.

Still, we might think that this argument works for time travelers who travel back to the past with the deliberate intention of killing Baby Hitler. Let's suppose that Al is such a time traveler and that he has, by our ordinary (present-tense) standards, both the ability and the opportunity to kill Baby Hitler. Does my argument show that Al cannot kill Baby Hitler? More generally, does it show that no time traveler can intentionally affect the past? I'm not sure. I think that in these sorts of cases, the counterfactuals are not always clear, but it is at least arguable that Al *can* kill Baby Hitler (although of course he won't).

The laws of physics, our laws, dictate that adults do not come into existence out of thin air; a person's adulthood is caused by her childhood. The particular counterfactuals these laws sustain make it false, I have argued, that time travelers can kill their baby selves. On the other hand, the laws of physics do allow memories and beliefs to arise *ex nihilo,* or at least without being true. There are worlds with our laws where Big Al tries to kill Baby Hitler because of what he believes this child will become, and he succeeds, and Hitler is not resurrected from the dead, nor does anyone take his place and commit his crimes. At these worlds, Big Al's beliefs are false; his memories are hallucinations. Therefore it's false that if Big Al had tried to kill Baby Hitler, this would have to have been because his attempt failed and Baby Hitler survived. There are other ways in which Big Al might have ended up trying to kill Baby Hitler. Can Big Al kill Baby Hitler? That depends on what would or might be the case if he tried, and that depends on what happens at the most similar worlds where he tries. Arguably, worlds where Big Al tries, succeeds, and turns out to have radically mistaken beliefs about Baby Hitler's future are more similar to the actual world than worlds where Big Al has true beliefs but something goes wrong and his attempt fails. If so, there is reason to believe that Big Al *can* kill Baby Hitler, even though we know that he never will.

Further Questions

1. Suppose there are two teams of time travelers trying to kill Hitler in 1935. One team, team A, is from the past—from 1925. The other team, team B, is from the future—1999. Neither team succeeds in killing Hitler, even though both teams are extremely well prepared.
   Can either team kill Hitler? Why or why not? (Note: Hitler died in 1945.)
2. Suppose you discover a book that tells the story of your life, from the day of your birth until the moment of your death. Everything in the book is true (so far as you know). You read about your future and decide to prove the book wrong. But somehow you never succeed. Does this mean that you can't prove the book wrong? Does it mean that you don't have free will? Why or why not?
   You learn how the book came to be written. It was written by a time traveler who traveled into your future, watched what you did and what happened to you, and wrote it all down. Does this make a difference in how you feel about free will and in being able to prove the book wrong? Why or why not?

Further Readings

Horwich, Paul. *Asymmetries in Time.* Bradford Books, 1989. A sometimes difficult but fascinating book about time and the ways in which we experience it, including a chapter that explains Godel's solution to the problem of autoinfanticide.

Lewis, David. "The Paradoxes of Time Travel." *American Philosophical Quarterly* 13 (1976): 145–152. The classic philosophical defense of the possibility of time travel.

Vihvelin, Kadri. "What Time Travelers Cannot do." *Philosophical Studies* 81 (1996): 315–330. An ancestor of the paper in this book, with less about fatalism and more about the ways in which it might be true that the time traveler can commit autoinfanticide.

Part III

Who

YOUR EVERYDAY NOTION OF PERSONAL IDENTITY—of what makes you *you*—functions as glue and as scissors. As glue, it binds the earlier to the later stages of yourself, making you a continuously existing person over time. As scissors, it separates you from others. Together, these give rise to two fundamental assumptions about who you are: you are the same self from birth to death *and* you are a unique self, different from other selves.

These assumptions are about *you*. As you are about to see, however, they are deeply questionable because they are based on stories to which there are plausible alternatives. But if these most basic assumptions about your identity are deeply questionable, then *who you are* must also be deeply questionable.

Who are you?

10   Descartes among the Ruins

DANIEL KOLAK

Author of numerous books, articles, stories, essays, and a novel (from which the following selection is taken), Daniel Kolak has lectured all over the world. His published works are in the areas of philosophy of mind and personal identity, philosophy of science, philosophy of language, philosophy of mathematics, history of philosophy, philosophy of religion, philosophy of art, cognitive science, and logic. He is the series editor of the *Wadsworth Philosophers Series* and *Philosophical Topics*. He has taught at the University of Wisconsin–Oshkosh, Towson State University, University College, and the University of Maryland, where after beginning his studies in physics he received his doctorate in philosophy in 1986. He is also a musician and has directed and composed professionally for the stage, including his highly acclaimed version of Sartre's *No Exit* at the Source Theater in Washington, D.C. Kolak's most recent film work is the original score for *Forsaken Cries: The Case of Rwanda*, produced by Amnesty International and narrated by Danny Glover. Among his books are: *I Am You: The Metaphysical Foundations for Global Ethics* (Kluwer, 2001), *On Hintikka* (Wadsworth, 2001), *The Principles of Cognitive Science* (Routledge, 2001), *Wittgenstein's Tractatus* (Mayfield, 1998), *From the Presocratics to the Present: A Personal Odyssey* (Mayfield, 1998), *In Search of God: The Language and Logic of Belief* (Wadsworth, 1994), *Lovers of Wisdom* (Wisdom, 1998), *In Search of Myself: Life, Death, and Personal Identity* (Wadsworth, 1998), *Wisdom without Answers* (5th ed., Wadsworth, 2002), *Self, Cosmos, God* (Harcourt Brace Jovanovich, 1993), and *Self & Identity* (Macmillan, 1991). He is professor of philosophy and director of the Cognitive Science Laboratory at the William Paterson University of New Jersey.

Reading Questions

1. Where does the story take place? What is the significance of the Temple?
2. How does the question, "Who are you?" affect the narrator? Why?
3. Why does the narrator think that the Goddess does not exist? Does *he* exist?
4. Did Descartes believe there was any difference between dream and waking states?
5. How does the narrator try to diminish "world" from "dream"? Does Philosophy agree? Why? Who is right, and why?
6. What is an "objective space"? Does such a space exist, according to Philosophy? Why?
7. What is meant by "object"? What is the relationship between the "subject" and "objects"?
8. Is the dream taking place in the narrator's head? Why?
9. Is there any light inside the narrator's head? What is the significance of this?
10. Who is the dreamer dreaming the dream?

I know that I exist, and I inquire what I am, I whom I know to exist.
René Descartes

MT. PARNASSUS: I'M WALKING ALONG the steep lower slope. Above me the Phaedriades ("shining rocks") glint against the cloudless, azure sky. Stretching southward across the valley a pearly turquoise Plistus river winds to an ash blue jagged horizon: Mt. Cirphis and the Gulf of Corinth. Below me stand the ruins of the ancient theater and temple of Delphi, the seat of the oracle of Apollo, a place the ancient Greeks considered the center of the world.

According to legend, Zeus released two eagles into the sky. One from the east, the other from the west, they flew toward the center until they met at Delphi at a spot marked in the temple by a stone called *omphalos,* the navel of the world. I sit on the burning rock. Except for the distant chorus of the cicadas all is absolutely still and quiet.

I am alone. Without wind the heat is oppressive. I take a sip of cool water from my canteen and wipe my brow. Every now and then the cicadas stop and the silence is like an explosion.

An ancient sanctuary. Before me looms the temple of Apollo with its empty alter. My eyes trace along what once were fifteen two-story columns along either side and six across each front to the small antechamber where nearly three thousand years ago a beautiful and wise woman bearing the title "oracle," the official voice of God, declared Socrates to be the wisest because he claimed to know nothing except how little he knew. The story, often used as the starting point of philosophy, is notably absent from the sculpted rocks, the surrounding mountain, the valley; it remembers itself sleepily within me. Neither her name nor his, nor their likenesses, appear anywhere. It makes me smile to realize that this place and I are inextricably linked. Without me there is no story. The place needs me to tell its story and I need it to help me to know . . . to discover, to remember, to decide . . . who I am.

The only human figures appear along a small temple-like building, with caryatids instead of columns, carved in beautifully preserved metopes depicting the adventures of Theseus and Heracles.

I think of the labyrinth and Ariadne, of the twelve Labors of that first son of God. Along with a hymn to Apollo, accompanied by musical notation, scratched into that wall by unknown hands over three millennia ago, there is a message to us. To you and to me.

The ancient inscription is well known. Socrates, who wrote nothing, declared it to be his one and only dictum, what he lived by and what he died by. Two words. Unlike the images which come to this place through the memory that has somehow wound its way here through me, the ancient message needs no story and no storyteller. The writing is on the wall, literally, preserved for anyone who happens to follow this tortuous path through the cleft between the rocks:

"Know Yourself."

I get up and walk to the wall. Standing in the crisp, dark shadow I run my fingers along the Greek letters. I say the words aloud: "*Gnothi s'afton.*" *Know yourself.* I close my eyes and breathe in an invisible hive of energy, the air throbbing from the carmine-winged grasshoppers, the locusts, the thousand buzzing insects who even in their collective unities cannot find a common beat, though their songs remain the same.

Here, in this sacred place, there is no philosophy. The sun obliterates it, the air you breathe extinguishes it, the ten thousand nights of learned study vanish in the windless, thirsty heat. It took thousands of years for the treasures that once lined every corner of this place to vanish, for the ceilings to fall, the walls to crumble; all your theories and your thoughts vanish in an instant.

You open your eyes and now you are empty of your deeds, your degrees, your sweet pedantries. There is just this place, this remarkable, incredible place that once was Greece. And here you are, all alone, face to face with two words left over from what once was the center of the world:

Know Yourself.

Nightfall. I retrieve my backpack from the *tholos,* a round building of unknown purpose, and make my way back along the colonnade into the temple. I will sleep in the antechamber where the

Oracle once made her pronouncements. I take out my blanket and unroll it next to the back wall.

Above me the sky turns iridescent; a new crescent moon peeks at me over the edge of the ruin. The cicadas have not stopped but a new chorus of night locusts joins their tumult. A salamander scuttles into a crevice in the wall. I hear tree frogs. Lying on my back, staring up into the firmament, I try to sleep. It is too early, the stars too many and too bright; I cannot. The stillness sizzles. The darkness is full of everything.

Moonrise. The silver light swallows the stars and returns them to the sky undigested. The temple and I lie silently beneath the chiaroscuro spectacle, afloat in a sea of insect sound. A sweet saffronlike smell of flowers wallows in the warm evening breeze.

I feel strangely restless in my tired calm. A night bird, high overhead, croaks primevally in the stars. The crickets chirp. A single black cloud, thin as a razor, races across the face of the moon.

Suddenly I heard a sound echo faintly from the steep hillside. It came again, louder. A primitive timbre. An ancient instrument? I sat up. Again that sound. I stood up and looked over the side wall: ash-lilac mountains, cypress trees, moonshadows; a strange, crepuscular light. A hornpipe? When again I turned to look I saw a woman sitting up on the high wall, a majestic and beautiful figure in a flowing robe. Her skin glowed marboreally against the sky, a translucent silhouette beneath the crescent moon. Across her breasts the Greek letters Π and Θ were sewn into the tightly threaded fabric, one above the other, with degrees marked between them like the rungs of a ladder. In her right hand she held books; in her left, a scepter.

"Who are you? How did you get up there!"

Her eyes locked on me. I had never been looked at like that before, at least not by a human being. By an insect or animal, perhaps, poised and predatory, single minded, reptilian.

"You do not recognize me?"

Atop her flows of long black hair I caught a glint of golden laurel leaves.

"You are Philosophy," I said. "The Goddess of Wisdom, the one who consoled Boethius before his death." I smiled. "Except you don't exist."

"Why not?"

"Because I do."

"How do you know?"

"I think, therefore I am," I laughed.

"Oh, René," she cooed seductively, "I too can think."

I shook my head. "I think, therefore you do not."

"How do you know that?"

"Because this is a dream."

She put down the books and scepter. "You've come to the right place." With the slightest tilt forward she glided down off the high wall, in slow motion, a wingless bird. "What makes you think this is a dream?"

"You flew! You just flew!"

"Ah. So you reason thus: I see a goddess fly, therefore, I must be dreaming?"

"I know goddesses do not exist. Therefore I reason, correctly, that I am dreaming a most extraordinary dream, that I converse with an apparition, a figment of my imagination."

"Do I look like a figment of your imagination?"

"Not at all." Staring into her fiery eyes I felt an eerie presence. How strange to look at eyes and believe they are not eyes, that there is no one there behind them. Behind my own eyes I wondered: what eyes am I seeing her with? "I admit I am dumbfounded. Doubly so. A realistic and lucid dream such as this, in which I find myself experiencing apparitions with the clearness and distinctness of waking life disturbs me exactly the way in waking life I should fear for my sanity were experience suddenly to turn tenuous, disjointed, discontinuous—"

"Tell me, then, who wrote these words:

I perceive so clearly that there exist no certain marks by which the state of waking can ever be distinguished from sleep, that I feel greatly astonished; and in amazement I almost persuade myself that I am now dreaming."[1]

I smiled. "The words are mine."

She smiled back. "Well, then?"

"I was making a philosophical point. Except for extraordinary cases such as this, dreams usually are less vivid, they lack continuity, they are not as bright—"

"But think, my dear René, think: if objects in dreams appeared to you as such you would not run from them, engage with them, talk with them. You would instead say: look at those insubstantial images! How could you be deceived by something that announces itself as an appearance and says, outright, 'I am a deception?' That you ever are deceived should thus alert you to this deep and fundamental truth."

"What—that I can't distinguish dream from reality?"

"That even the most distinguished philosopher deceives himself with the distinction."

"Between dream and reality?"

"As surely as between himself and others."

What a bizarre and amusing twist, I thought, in one move to thus challenge within myself the distinction between dream and reality and between self and other; in waking life I had gone the other way around in two moves to find what I had thought was absolute certainty. But perhaps I had succeeded only with the intellect. Did not the very fact of this dream suggest hidden doubts still lingered deep within my soul?[2]

"I will wake up and you will disappear," I said. "That's the difference between you and me, between dream and reality. You don't exist in the real world."

"What world is that?"

"The world outside my mind."

"You know any such world, René? How! By what experience?"

"Not by experience. By reason."

"Ah. By reason you mean by argument, by which you mean by strings of sentences, by which you mean by strings of words? Then by what you know you must mean not world but theory. For that is to what your words connect you: not to the world in which your being is inscribed but to descriptions, narratives, a story."

"The real world is not a story."

"The real world does not exist, except in stories."

"That's what this is."

"Is that what you think?"

"In a matter of speaking, yes."

"In a matter of speaking?" She laughed. "What about the manner of experiencing? Is this a story you are telling yourself, in which a description of Descartes encounters a description of Philosophy?"

"No," I said.

"No? Just like that: no? No! This, my dear and imaginary friend, is not a story but a world that you are in."

"This world is a dream."

"Know you any other world, or any other self, as such?"

"Tell me what you mean by *world*," I said. "Impress me with mathematics, not poetry."

"By mathematics you mean nonsense?"

"I'd like to understand."[3]

"A world," said Philosophy, "is an outside with an inside. Unlike a story, description, or theory, a world consists in space and time conjoined by two essential aspects: object and subject, such that without either there can be neither, and no world as such."[4]

"You mean, a world must be described from—"

"No, no; experience from."

"All right, yes," I said, "experienced from the first-person point of view. That's why this what I call *dream* you call *world*?"[5]

She nodded. "You are—or, I should say," she pointed at me, "'that' is—the world's subject. Whereas these walls," she gestured at the ruins, "the colonnade, the sky, even, from your point of view, me—are its objects. Subject and object are two aspects of one and the same being. And that being is the world."

"Because this is a dream," I said, "I can understand that. Dream objects exist only in my mind. But the real temple of Delphi—not this one I see here in the dream but the temple made of stone—has existed for centuries outside my mind—"

"Does the stone make the temple real? Or is mind the temple?"

"I don't understand."

"Does the 'real' temple—the one you just described as 'existing outside your mind'—exist as an object?"

"Yes."

"No, René!"

"Why?"

"Because what does *object* mean? Does *object* not require the notion of *subject*?"

"Not in the real world, no: real objects require no subject to exist. There is no *I* involved in the existence of objects in the real world, they exist regardless of whether I perceive them."

"Look at your conception: 'the real world.' Does it—the conception itself—exist without you?"

"I'm not talking about the conception."[6]

"What, then?"

I rubbed my face. "You expect me to believe nothing whatsoever exists independently of me?" My fingers had a strange smell to them, a mixture of resin and alcohol.

"I expect you to believe what you know to be true; no more, no less." She raised her eyebrows. "Follow your own *Rules for the Direction of the Mind*. Or was that another one of your philosophical points?"

"Would Philosophy destroy the concept of a real, mind-independent, object world?"

"You mean an 'objective, subjectless world'?" She laughed. "An easy victory."

"How can you say that?"

"Because no such world exists, René. You're thinking of an 'objective space,' an outside without an inside. The author of analytic geometry should know better! There can be no outside without an inside, no objects in space without a subject in time to which they appear. You desire a contradiction. You want to experience a conscious state that cannot possibly be experienced, to be the subject of a subjectless world."

"Is the sum of all worlds, then, reality?"

"No."

"Why?"

"No such sum is possible."

"Why not?"

"Because your concept, 'reality,' involves an 'objective world,' a 'super-world,' a consortium of worlds conceived in terms of purely 'objective,' subjectless, totality of objects *and* subjects! You cannot help but think *objective world* even though buried in your understanding is the hidden meaning that a world, as such, necessarily requires both subject and object. No 'objective world' as conceived by you exists because no such world could possibly exist."

"Then who—what—are we? Tell me what we are."

"Here." Philosophy offered me her hand. "The dreams that stuff is made of."

I took her hand. Her warm, delicate fingers, soft and inviting to the touch, smelled of lilac. I brought her hand within reach of my lips and for some reason bowed to it without a kiss, as one does with a married woman.

I caught myself in her eyes, awestruck suddenly by a numinous sense of the presence of the other—a being within me greater than myself. Telling myself this could not be possible, that she existed only in my head, I tried to imagine my sleeping body lying on its back with eyes closed. *Wake up,* I said to myself, *you're not here but there.* Projecting myself into that imagined bundle of conceived flesh, trying to resurrect myself into the 'real' world, I realized no, I was not 'there' but here. The world there, as I had just used it while thinking of a translucent image of a sleeping body referred ostensively not to a body made of flesh and blood but to a vaguely conceived image. My 'real' body was, I believed, asleep and lying down, a material substance made of flesh and blood, not this standing body made out of imagination. The body *I* was *in* was not that (vaguely imagined) lying body but this (vividly imagined, perceived, felt) standing body: the body I was in was not the body I believed I was in, and the body I believed I was in was not my body!

Like the dreamed stars hanging above me in the dreamed sky, both the conceived (i.e., 'real') body I believed I was in and the seen (i.e., 'experienced') body I believed was but an imaginary body in a dream were themselves imaginary, for both were dependent for their existence upon the subject, me. The body I seemed to be in was *here* and *imaginary* and the body I thought I was in was *imaginary* and *nowhere*.[7] This was not methodological doubt but fear for my existence, an abyss of unknowing, a maelstrom of anxiety. *I am not doubting whether I have a real body, I am realizing I have no real body.* Something within me had begun to unravel. Or, should I say, to sew itself together? *I am the ghost in the theoretical machine; reality is my theory and my corpse.*

Philosophy flew back up onto her former perch. The moon had set, leaving a sky full of effervescent stars. Mt. Parnassus loomed above the ruins, grim, ominous, silent in the starlight pouring over each crevice like magnetic fluid, swimming in electric effluvia.

This all is in my head, I said to myself, still trying to wake up, *this all is in my head,* and I went to repeating my hollow incantation to reality: *this all is in my head . . .*

"Clasp your hands on top of your head," she said.

Startled, I looked up. "What am I, surrendering?"

"No; the defiant one."

I put my hands on top of my head.

"Is that your head?"

"Yes." A chill shook me.

"There," she said, pointing at my head, "is that where this dream exists? Inside there?"

"Yes," I said, knowing it was false.[8]

"Everything here—the sky, the ruins, this world entire—is contained within that head which you presently hold in those hands?"

"Yes." *No,* I thought, but could not say it.

"So these objects—the wall of this antechamber, the temple, the stars—they all are contained—" she pointed again at me, "there, inside that head atop your shoulders?"

"Yes." *No.*

"Don't you see what I am asking?"

"No!" *Yes, yes,* I thought, but still I could not say it, not even to myself, not even in a dream, not even as the revelation divined existential shivers through my nonexistent spine. But I knew what she meant.

This was a dream. In this dream, a woman sat atop a wall, talking to a man. She had a body and head with eyes fixed upon the man. The man stood at the base of the wall, looking up at her. This man could think, feel, reason and wonder about himself and the world he was in. Perhaps the woman could too but the man believed she couldn't because he believed this was a dream, that she was a figment of his imagination, an object in his head. Except this man had no head. He had feet, legs, a torso, fingers, hands, arms and shoulders atop of which was not the head *she* was in but the world in which they both were in.

I was that man. I was the man in the dream who mistook his world for a head.

There is no light inside the head. Yet the 'scene before my eyes' presented itself to me as if the light I saw had traced the following geometrical path: from some light source (what—where—is the 'light' source in a dream?) to the 'surface' of the objects (as if they had an inside!) which in turn sent this 'reflected light' through space (what is the space, the medium of light, I see in a dream?) to my 'eyes' (what 'eyes' do I see with in a dream?) which in turn sent an impulse to my 'brain,' causing these perceptions to exist as ideas in my 'mind.' This false geometry of dreams lay at the root of the illusion that the world in my experience was external to my mind, a mathematical self-deception written into the meaning of the 'scene before my

eyes,' structuring my experience into a 'physical world.' For in fact no such geometrical path was involved in the generation of the objects in the dream. The 'eyes' through which I saw the dream were not eyes. The 'head' inside which I was situated was not a head but a world inside which there was no brain, no processor of information distinct from the mental objects of my perception. The nonexistent head I was in was but a vantage point from which I experienced the dream. The objects I saw 'outside' myself, including the headless body with the world atop its shoulders and the subject (myself) whom I took to be not a subject but my head, were generated not from another (from the object to the subject via perception) but in one simultaneous act of consciousness.

"Point," ordered Philosophy, "point to where the head is within which this dream exists."

And point I did: at the wall, at the stars, at Mt. Parnassus, at the ground and at the ruins all around. The head I was in was everywhere and all around, for this was a dream and I was in it, yet nowhere, for what I was pointing at was not a head but a world. I asked myself: if this space surrounding me exists inside my head, where in relation to me, the dream subject, is the 'real' head inside which this dream and I exist—in what space? Where in relation to me is 'reality,' that glorious and infinitely empty womb inside which the real world exists? In what direction from me, within the subjective space inside which I exist as a conscious subject, is the objective space I conceive to be the container of me and of my world, the universe entire?

Pointing now the other way (thinking this cannot be my finger, I am asleep, my hands are at my sides), right between my eyes (thinking these are not my eyes, my eyes are closed), at myself (thinking this is not me but a representation of myself inside myself) staring at my finger (with what, I asked myself, with what?), I couldn't speak, I couldn't think. Reason had abandoned me to the circular ruins inside myself, trapped me in the logic of the impenetrable contradiction that existence is, one with everything, full of nothing, empty as a tautology. Inside the labyrinth at the center of the world I found myself without a face and I stood there pointing at the beast, unmasked, headless.[9]

What was I pointing at? Who was I pointing at? Who was pointing? Who?

"But I am not nothing," I cried. "I am not no one! *Who am I?*"

Suddenly the question wounded, it opened everything.

NOTES

1. *Meditations on the First Philosophy, in Which the Existence of God, and the Real Distinction of Mind and Body, Are Demonstrated,* by René Descartes, John Veitch trans., Open Court 1901, reprinted in Daniel Kolak, *The Mayfield Anthology of Western Philosophy,* Mayfield 1998.

2. Her words, after all, were my words, my thoughts—they had to be, they were coming at me from somewhere within. This was a dream and she was a dream character. I did not believe in demons nor in possession. She was not a foreign soul but merely an aspect of myself, perhaps some part of me I had long ago in sculpting my philosophy hidden from myself. There is always that remaining part of your soul, unconvinced by your philosophy, that you have to exorcise from yourself to have a view; the philosophical dialectic: we make up our minds by halving them. Whole, we cannot remain on one side of an issue long enough to forget the view from the other side is just as flimsy and as good (everything works, when you are in it, *literally like a dream;* this is the secret wisdom of all religions). We thus divide and conquer ourselves: we become someone with a view and make that view our own. In this way your view becomes part of your identity. I had for a long time suspected this and perhaps that's who and what she was incarnate: my alter ego and philosophical antithesis rendered in the dramatic form of scholastic mythology and magic, a being within myself that I had banished from consciousness to become Descartes: Anti-Cartesius, now come back in the guise of the Goddess of Philosophy to haunt me, perhaps even to stake claim to my waking soul.

3. I knew what she meant. Mersenne and I had often quarreled about it. Did the objects of mathematics refer to the world as it existed in itself, or were they themselves but descriptions, renderings of mental experiences? The scientifically inclined natural philosophers in our Paris circle insisted that the language of mathematics, unlike the terms of ordinary language, has a grip on reality (of course I no longer know what *that* means)—that mathematics can render the world entire. (And of course by 'world' we in the Paris circle did not mean what Philosophy meant.) I myself was drawn to this view and had in my youth hoped to transfer some of its methodological insights into the new philosophy. The more skeptical philosophers among us, on the other hand, viewed mathematics the same way the Pyrhonnian skeptics once

viewed ordinary language and experience, as being a representation of purely mental constructions: mathematics viewed in this way is merely the set of tautologies, logical but therefore empty. Mathematics viewed in this way is but a symbolic container, as experience is, but only an idealized rendition of what is already in the mind to begin with such that mathematics is as impotent as natural language is to render 'reality.'

4. I marveled at the spontaneous subtlety and swiftness of her delivery. She implied that the sort of space and time she meant were not to be understood in some purely mathematical, or formal, sense. She did not mean by "space" the specification of such and such coordinates, that is, space understood in geometrical terms, or time understood as a numerical sequence or series, that is, time conceived in arithmetical terms. Rather, she was talking about the space one experiences and likewise for time—not in terms of a physical theory but as psychological time actually experienced. (In other words, time and space in the dream existed for me and may or may not have calibrated with any aspect of formal space and time as conceived in mathematical and physical theory as existing independently of me.) She thus meant phenomenal, subjective space, and phenomenal, subjective time (and experienced, not merely described, as such). By thus involving the subject in *her* description, she managed cleverly to fix the reference of *world* to an essentially subjective rendering of what, ordinarily, I would have wanted to call 'reality.' She was, indeed, very clever (and this of course pleased me, since I considered her 'my own,' albeit unconscious, creation) at setting up the verbal pieces of her conceptual argument in advance.

5. Once again I thought how strange it was to be having this argument with myself in a dream. What I had meant was that dreams are stories we tell ourselves with the help of mental pictures. But she had retorted with the crucial difference: dreams are not just pictures any more than waking experience consists of just pictures; there is in both cases a point of view involved, and not merely in the way, say, a scene in a painting is rendered from a certain perspective. In a dream, as in waking experience, the point of view is not something expressed as a perspectival arrangement of objects in the scene but is, itself, a projection of *you,* the viewer, into the scene such that it becomes *your* experience and—this is crucial—from the 'inside.' That is why she was bringing in, rightly, the notion of the subject. Whether in a dream or in a waking state, the subject is the apparent location within the scene of the experiencing entity one takes oneself to be.

6. She had cut off my escape route and I knew it. In waking life I might have tried to counter and the discussion would at this point no doubt have ceased being philosophical and turned merely rhetorical. But this was a dream and I knew therefore that I was only arguing

with myself; what would be the point of winning? Yet I was afraid of losing.

7. In other words, can you refer to your body in a dream? In one sense, of course you can; you can say "my body is at home, in bed, asleep." The problem with this is that as you are saying it you find yourself not at home in bed and unconscious but, as in the present case, standing somewhere. Now, you can try to say, as in the present case, "this body is not my body," but now you're shredding logic's gears, stripping both the sense (*Sinn*) and reference, or meaning (*Bedeutung*) from your expressions as such. (See my *Wittgenstein's Tractatus,* Mayfield 1998.) Of course you can wave your hands, proverbial or otherwise, and try to indicate yourself out of the philosophical black hole but in so doing you throw out the whole of your actual being there into an abyss of insubstantiality. (*Dasein;* see my discussion of Heidegger in *From the Presocratics to the Present: A Personal Odyssey,* Mayfield 1998, pp. 256–260.)

8. This was strange. Language said that this, what 'I' 'held' in 'my' hands, was 'my' head. But the truth of the matter was otherwise. "My head is not my head" was a true statement; once you see the sense in which this is not a contradiction you will have successfully severed the semantics of experience from the syntax of theory (but only for a while—you have to move quickly and then to keep moving). For how did I know this, except by means of language? Philosophy thus neither uses nor destroys language but turns language against itself. And that is the sense in which I would say it was literally true that I had finally lost my head.

9. The point I had just made to myself in the dream of course holds equally in dream and waking states. For instance: right now it seems to you that you are where your face is, on the surface of your skin, perched just in front of your face, looking outside at the world, as if your insides were behind you. But your insides are in front of you and all around! We exist backwards, upside down, inside out.

Further Questions

1. How does the narrator's "revelation" at the end that *he has no head* compare with Harding's "On Having No Head" (selection 12)?
2. What do you perceive the objects in your dreams with?
3. You probably assume that in dreams *you* are the dreamer. But if dreams happen inside the head, and the character in the dream that you take yourself to be exists *also* inside the dreamer's head, don't *you* in the dream, then, also exist inside the dreamer's head? Aren't you in the dream, then, also not the dreamer but the dreamed? But if *you* are the dreamed *who* is the dreamer?

Further Readings

Kolak, Daniel. *In Search of Myself: Life, Death and Personal Identity.* Belmont, CA: Wadsworth, 1999. (The selection here is the introduction and Chapter 1.)

Kolak, Daniel. *I Am You: The Metaphysical Foundations for Global Ethics.* Dordrecht: Kluwer Academic Publishers, 2001. A sustained philosophical explanation of how there exists only one person, who is you and everybody.

Kolak, Daniel. "Finding Our Selves: Individuation, Identification, and Multiple Personality Disorder." *Philosophical Psychology* 6: 4 (1993). A new way of understanding personas, personalities, and selves, including a theory of multiple personality disorder.

Kolak, Daniel. "The Metaphysics and Metapsychology of Personal Identity: Why Thought Experiments Matter in Deciding Who We Are." *American Philosophical Quarterly* 30 (1993): 39–50. How thought experiments function in philosophical debates about personal identity.

11   On Having No Self

BUDDHA

Buddha is a title, not a name. It means *Enlightened One*. The Buddha's name was
Siddhartha Gautama. He was born in (approximately) 563 B.C.E., in what today is southern Nepal, and he lived to be eighty years old. The son of a chieftain, Siddhartha was
brought up in relative luxury. According to the Scriptures, at his father's direction he led
an extraordinarily sheltered life until one day, by accident, he discovered firsthand the
meaning of old age, sickness, and death. So moved was he by these discoveries that at the
age of twenty-nine he abandoned his life of luxury (and also his wife and young son) to
set off on a spiritual journey to discover the cause and cure of human suffering.

For six years, he sought out ascetics and teachers, learning what he could from them.
He also underwent extreme self-mortification, which he later decided was more of a hindrance than a help. During this period, it is reported that often while he was trying to
sleep alone in the jungles, he was terrified by wandering tigers. He is said to have said that
sex was such a distraction that had it been any more distracting, he never would have become enlightened.

Eventually, though, he did become enlightened. It happened near Buddh Gaya, under
a bodhi tree, where he had resolved to sit and meditate until he either became enlightened or died. After his enlightenment, he traveled to Sarnath, outside Benares, where he
gave his first "sermon." It was on the "four noble truths": the fact of suffering, the cause
of suffering (selfish craving), the cure for suffering (dissolving the illusion of self), and the
way to the cure for suffering (the "eightfold path"). He spent the rest of his life—more
than forty years—in meditation and teaching, and he founded many monasteries.

At the age of eighty, not far from his birthplace, he died. The cause of his death is said
to be that he ate poisoned mushrooms. It is also reported that in his last words, he for-
gave the person who had mistakenly fed him the mushrooms. His remains were cremated,
and the relics distributed.

In the following two short selections from Buddhist Scripture, the Buddha expresses
what is perhaps the central doctrine in his teaching: the doctrine of no-self. These
selections are accompanied by two scholarly explanations of what it means to become
enlightened.

Reading Questions:

1. What does the Buddha mean by saying that we have no selves?
2. What role does analysis play in the Buddha's thought?
3. What are the best objections to the Buddha's no-self view? Does the Buddha answer these
   objections? How?

NIRVĀNA

Walpola Rahula

Elsewhere the Buddha unequivocally uses the word Truth in place of Nibbāna: "I will teach you the Truth and the Path leading to the Truth." Here Truth definitely means Nirvāna.

Now, what is Absolute Truth? According to Buddhism, the Absolute Truth is that there is nothing absolute in the world, that everything is relative, conditioned and impermanent, and that there is no unchanging, everlasting, absolute substance like Self, Soul or *Ātman* within or without. This is the Absolute Truth. Truth is never negative, though there is a popular expression as negative truth. The realization of this Truth, i.e., to see things as they are (*yathābhūtam*) without illusion or ignorance (*avijjā*), is the extinction of craving "thirst" (*Tanhakkhaya*), and the cessation (*Nirodha*) of *dukkha*, which is Nirvāna. It is interesting and useful to remember here the Mahāyāna view of Nirvāna as not being different from *Samsāra*. The same thing is Samsāra or Nirvāna according to the way you look at it—subjectively or objectively. This Mahāyāna view was probably developed out of the ideas found in the original Theravāda Pali texts, to which we have just referred in our brief discussion.

It is incorrect to think that Nirvāna is the natural result of the extinction of craving. Nirvāna is not the result of anything. If it would be a result, then it would be an effect produced by a cause. It would be *samkhata* "produced" and "conditioned." Nirvāna is neither cause nor effect. It is beyond cause and effect. Truth is not a result nor an effect. It is not produced like a mystic, spiritual, mental state, such as *dhyāna* or *samādhi*. TRUTH IS. NIRVĀNA IS. The only thing you can do is to see it, to realize it. There is a path leading to the realization of Nirvāna. But Nirvāna is not the result of this path. You may get to the mountain along a path, but the mountain is not the result, not an effect of the path. You may see a light, but the light is not the result of your eyesight.

From Walpola Rahula, *What the Buddha Taught* (1974).

"YOUR MAJESTY, I AM CALLED Nāgasena; my fellow-priests, your majesty, address me as Nāgasena: but whether parents give one the name Nāgasena, or Sūrasena, or Vīrasena, or Sīhasena, it is, nevertheless, your majesty, but a way of counting, a term, an appellation, a convenient designation, a mere name, this Nāgasena; for there is no Self here to be found." . . .

"Bhante Nāgasena, if there is no Self to be found, who is it then furnishes you priests with the priestly requisites—robes, food, bedding, and medicine, the reliance of the sick? who is it makes use of the same? who is it keeps the precepts? who is it applies himself to meditation? . . . who is it commits immorality? who is it tells lies? . . .

In that case, there is no merit; there is no demerit; there is no one who does or causes to be done meritorious or demeritorious deeds; neither good nor evil deeds can have any fruit or result. Bhante Nāgasena, neither is he a murderer who kills a priest, nor can you priests, bhante Nāgasena, have any teacher, preceptor, or ordination. When you say, 'My fellow-priests, your majesty, address me as Nāgasena,' what then is this Nāgasena? Pray, bhante, is the hair of the head Nāgasena?"

"Nay, verily, your majesty."

"Is the hair of the body Nāgasena?"

"Nay, verily, your majesty."

"Are nails . . . teeth . . . skin . . . flesh . . . sinews . . . bones . . . marrow of the bones . . . kidneys . . . heart . . . liver . . . blood . . . sweat . . . fat . . . tears . . . saliva . . . snot . . . urine . . . brain of the head Nāgasena?"

From H. C. Warren, Buddhism in Translation *(1963), Milindapañha, 71) with a few editorial emendations.*

Nirvāna

Edward Conze

We are, however, nowadays, if only through the writings of Aldous Huxley, familiar with the difference between God and Godhead. . . . When we compare the attributes of the Godhead as they are understood by the more mystical tradition of Christian thought, with those of Nirvāna, we find almost no difference at all. It is indeed true that Nirvāna has no cosmological functions, that this is not God's world, but a world made by our own greed and stupidity. It is indeed true that through their attitude the Buddhists express a more radical rejection of the world in all its aspects than we find among many Christians. At the same time, they are spared a number of awkward theological riddles and have not been under the necessity to combine, for instance, the assumption of an omnipotent and all-loving God with the existence of a great deal of suffering and muddle in this world. Buddhists also have never stated that God is *Love,* but that may be due to their preoccupation with intellectual precision, which must have perceived that the word "Love" is one of the most unsatisfactory and ambiguous terms one could possibly use.

But, on the other hand, we are told that Nirvāna is permanent, stable, imperishable, immovable, ageless, deathless, unborn, and unbecome, that it is power, bliss and happiness, the secure refuge, the shelter, and the place of unassailable safety; that it is the real Truth and the supreme Reality; that it is the *Good,* the supreme goal and the one and only consummation of our life, the eternal, hidden and incomprehensible Peace.

Similarly, the Buddha who is, as it were, the personal embodiment of Nirvāna, becomes the object of all those emotions which we are wont to call religious.

There has existed throughout Buddhist history a tension between the Bhaktic and the Gnostic approach to religion, such as we find also in Christianity. There is, however, the difference that in Buddhism the Gnostic vision has always been regarded as the more true one, while the Bhaktic, devotional, type was regarded more or less as a concession to the common people.

From Edward Conze, *Buddhism* (1951).

"Nay, verily, your majesty."

"Is now, bhante, form Nāgasena?"

"Nay, verily, your majesty."

"Is sensation Nāgasena?"

"Is consciousness Nāgasena?"

"Nay, verily, your majesty."

"Are, then, bhante, form, sensation, perception, the predispositions, and consciousness unitedly Nāgasena?"

"Nay, verily, your majesty."

"Is it, then, bhante, something besides form, sensation, perception, the predispositions, and consciousness, which is Nāgasena?"

"Nay, verily, your majesty."

"Bhante, although I question you very closely, I fail to discover any Nāgasena. Verily, now, bhante, Nāgasena is a mere empty sound. What Nāgasena is there here? Bhante, you speak a falsehood, a lie: there is no Nāgasena." . . .

* * *

"How, bhante Nāgasena, does rebirth take place without anything transmigrating? Give an illustration."

"Suppose, your majesty, a man were to light a light from another light; pray, would the one light have passed over [transmigrated] to the other light?"

"Nay, verily, bhante."

"In exactly the same way, your majesty, does rebirth take place without anything transmigrating."

"Give another illustration."

"Do you remember, your majesty, having learnt, when you were a boy, some verse or other from your professor of poetry? . . . did the verse pass over [transmigrate] to you from your teacher?"

"Nay, verily, bhante."

"In exactly the same way, your majesty, does rebirth take place without anything transmigrating."

"You are an able man, bhante Nāgasena."

Further Questions

1. Where is the "I" that you located? If it is part of your body, could that part be replaced while you still remain? If it is not part of your body, is it nevertheless a real thing? How do you know?
2. Does each of us identify with something that we call our self? If so, what form does this identification take?
3. Does the belief in self have anything to do with fear of death? Selfishness? Our instinct for self-preservation? Do animals have selves?

Further Readings

Rahula, Walpola. *What the Buddha Taught.* New York: Grove Press, 1974. Generally regarded as one of the best short introductions to Buddhist thought.

Smith, Huston. *The World's Religions.* San Francisco: Harper, 1991. Formerly *The Religions of Man,* this is the best selling text of comparative religion of all time. it contains a good, easily understood chapter on Buddhism.

On Having No Head   12

D. E. HARDING

Born in 1909, retired architect D. E. Harding for decades gave spiritual workshops in England. In this selection, he poignantly dramatizes the distinction between what we experience and the interpretations we put on what we experience. For instance, you think you experience your head. What could be more obvious? But Harding points out the ways in which your own head is, for you, an interpretation. According to him, you do not even have a head. Your head is a hallucination.

Reading Questions

1. Are there two "widely different species" of people, those with heads and those without them? What does Harding think?
2. Can you prove that you have a head by looking in a mirror or by asking your neighbor? What does Harding think? What do you think?
3. Can you prove *through experience* that Harding is wrong?
4. How does Harding distinguish *looking* from *thinking*?
5. What does he mean by "hallucination"?

THE BEST DAY OF MY LIFE—my rebirthday, so to speak—was when I found I had no head. This is not a literary gambit, a witticism designed to arouse interest at any cost. I mean it in all seriousness: *I have no head.*

It was eighteen years ago, when I was thirty-three, that I made the discovery. Though it certainly came out of the blue, it did so in response to an urgent enquiry; I had for several months been absorbed in the question: what am I? The fact that I happened to be walking in the Himalayas at the time probably had little to do with it; though in that country unusual states of mind are said to come more easily. However that may be, a very still clear day, and a view from the ridge where I stood, over misty blue valleys to the highest mountain range in the world, with Kangchenjunga and Everest unprominent among its snow peaks, made a setting worthy of the grandest vision.

What actually happened was something absurdly simple and unspectacular: I stopped thinking. A peculiar quiet, an odd kind of alert limpness or numbness, came over me. Reason and imagination and all mental chatter died down. For once, words really failed me. Past and future dropped away. I forgot who and what I was, my name, manhood, animalhood, all that could be called mine. It was as if I had been born that instant, brand new, mindless, innocent of all memories. There existed only the Now, that present moment and what was clearly given in it. To look was enough. And what I found was khaki trouserlegs terminating downwards in a pair of brown shoes, khaki sleeves terminating sideways in a pair of pink hands, and a khaki shirtfront terminating upwards in—absolutely nothing whatever! Certainly not in a head.

It took me no time at all to notice that this nothing, this hole where a head should have been, was no ordinary vacancy, no mere nothing. On the contrary, it was very much occupied. It was a vast emptiness vastly filled, a nothing that found room for everything—room for grass, trees, shadowy distant hills, and far above them snow-peaks like a row of angular clouds riding the blue sky. I had lost a head and gained a world.

It was all, quite literally, breathtaking. I seemed to stop breathing altogether, absorbed in the Given. Here it was, this superb scene, brightly shining in the clear air, alone and unsupported, mysteriously suspended in the void, and (and *this* was the real miracle, the wonder and delight) utterly free of "me," unstained by any observer. Its total presence was my total absence, body and soul. Lighter than air, clearer than glass, altogether released from myself, I was nowhere around.

Yet in spite of the magical and uncanny quality of this vision, it was no dream, no esoteric revelation. Quite the reverse: it felt like a sudden waking from the sleep of ordinary life, an end to dreaming. It was self-luminous reality for once swept clean of all obscuring mind. It was the revelation, at long last, of the perfectly obvious. It was a lucid moment in a confused life-history. It was a ceasing to ignore something which (since early childhood at any rate) I had always been too busy or too clever to see. It was naked, uncritical attention to what had all along been staring me in the face—my utter facelessness. In short, it was all perfectly simple and plain and straightforward, beyond argument, thought, and words. There arose no questions, no reference beyond the experience itself, but only peace and a quiet joy, and the sensation of having dropped an intolerable burden.

* * *

As the first wonder of my Himalayan discovery began to wear off, I started describing it to myself in some such words as the following.

Somehow or other I had vaguely thought of myself as inhabiting this house which is my body, and looking out through its two round windows at the world. Now I find it isn't like that at all. As I gaze into the distance, what is there at this moment to tell me how many eyes I have here—two, or three, or hundreds, or none? In fact, only one window appears on this side of my facade, and that one is wide open and frameless, with nobody looking out of it. It is always the other fellow who has eyes and a face to frame them; never this one.

There exist, then, two sorts—two widely different species—of man. The first, of which I note countless specimens, evidently carries a head on its shoulders (and by "head" I mean a hairy eight-inch ball with various holes in it) while the second, of which I note only one specimen, evidently carries no such thing on its shoulders. And till now I had overlooked this considerable difference! Victim of a prolonged fit of madness, of a lifelong hallucination (and by "hallucination" I mean what my dictionary says: *apparent perception of an object not actually present*), I had invariably seen myself as pretty much like other men, and certainly never as a decapitated but still living biped. I had been blind to the one thing that is always present, and without which I am blind indeed—to this marvellous substitute-for-a-head, this unbounded clarity, this luminous and absolutely pure void, which nevertheless is— rather than contains—all things. For, however carefully I attend, I fail to find here even so much as a blank screen on which these mountains and sun and sky are projected, or a clear mirror in which they are reflected, or a transparent lens or aperture through which they are viewed—still less a soul or a mind to which they are presented, or a viewer (however shadowy) who is distinguishable from the view. Nothing whatever intervenes, not even that baffling and elusive obstacle called "distance": the huge blue sky, the pink-edged whiteness of the snows, the sparkling green of the grass—how can these be remote, when there's nothing to be remote from? The headless void here refuses all definition and location: it is not round, or small, or big, or even here as distinct from there. (And even if there *were* a head here to measure outwards from, the measuring-rod stretching from it to the peak of Everest would, when read end-on—and there's no other way for me to read it—reduce to a point, to nothing.) In fact, these colored shapes present themselves in all simplicity, without any such complications as near or far, this or that, mine or not mine, seen-by-me or merely given. All twoness— all duality of subject and object—has vanished: it is no longer read into a situation which has no room for it.

Such were the thoughts which followed the vision. To try to set down the first-hand, immediate experience in these or any other terms, however, is to misrepresent it by complicating what is quite simple: indeed the longer the postmortem examination drags on the further it gets from the living original. At best, these descriptions can remind one

of the vision (without the bright awareness) or invite a recurrence of it; but they can no more convey its essential quality, or ensure a recurrence, than the most appetizing menu can taste like the dinner, or the best book about humour enable one to see a joke. On the other hand, it is impossible to stop thinking for long, and some attempt to relate the lucid intervals of one's life to the confused background is inevitable. It could also encourage, indirectly, the recurrence of lucidity.

In any case, there are several commonsense objections which refuse to be put off any longer, questions which insist on reasoned answers, however inconclusive. . . .

* * *

My first objection was: my head may be missing, but not its nose. Here it is, visibly preceding me wherever I go. And my answer was: if this fuzzy, pinkish, yet perfectly transparent cloud suspended on my right, and this other similar cloud suspended on my left, are noses, then I count two of them and not one; and the perfectly opaque single protuberance which I observe so clearly in the middle of your face is *not* a nose: only a hopelessly dishonest or confused observer would deliberately use the same name for such utterly different things. I prefer to go by my dictionary and common usage, which oblige me to say that, whereas nearly all other men have a nose apiece, I have none.

All the same, if some misguided skeptic, overanxious to make his point, were to strike out in this direction, aiming midway between these two pink clouds, the result would surely be as unpleasant as if I owned the most solid and punchable of noses. Again, what about this complex of subtle tensions, movements, pressures, itches, tickles, aches, warmths, and throbbings, never entirely absent from this central region? Above all, what about these touch-feelings which arise when I explore here with my hand? Surely these findings add up to massive evidence for the existence of my head right here and now, after all?

They do nothing of the sort. No doubt a great variety of sensations are plainly given here and cannot be ignored, but they don't amount to a head, or anything like one. The only way to make a head out of them would be to throw in all sorts of ingredients that are plainly missing here—in particular, all manner of coloured shapes in three dimensions. What sort of head is it that, though containing innumerable sensations, is observed to lack eyes, ears, mouth, hair, and indeed all the bodily equipment which other heads are observed to contain? The plain fact is that this place must be kept clear of all such obstructions, of the slightest mistiness or colouring which could cloud my universe.

In any case, when I start groping round for my lost head, instead of finding it here I only lose my exploring hand as well: it, too, is swallowed up in the abyss at the centre of my being. Apparently this yawning cavern, this unoccupied base of all my operations, this magical locality where I thought I kept my head, is in fact more like a beacon-fire so fierce that all things approaching it are instantly and utterly consumed, in order that its world-illuminating brilliance and clarity shall never for a moment be obscured. As for these lurking aches and tickles and so on, they can no more quench or shade that central brightness than these mountains and clouds and sky can do so. Quite the contrary: they all exist in its shining, and through them it is seen to shine. Present experience, whatever sense is employed, occurs only in an empty and absent head. For here and now my world and my head are incompatibles: they won't mix. There is no room for both at once on these shoulders, and fortunately it is my head with all its anatomy that has to go. This is not a matter of argument, or of philosophical acumen, or of working oneself up into a state, but of simple sight—of LOOK-WHO'S HERE instead of THINK-WHO'S-HERE. . . .

* * *

Probably there is only one way of converting the skeptic who still says I have a head here, and that is to invite him to come here and take a look for himself; only he must be an honest reporter, describing what he observes and nothing else.

Starting off on the far side of the room, he sees me as a full-length man-with-a-head. But as he approaches he finds half a man, then a head, then a blurred cheek or eye or nose, then a mere blur, and finally (at the point of contact) nothing at all. Alternatively, if he happens to be equipped with the necessary scientific instruments, he reports that the blur resolves itself into tissues, then cell-groups, then a single cell, a cell-nucleus, giant molecules . . . and so on, till he comes to a place where nothing is to be seen, to space which is empty of all solid or material objects. In either case, the observer who comes here to see what it's really like finds what I find here—vacancy. And if, having discovered and shared my nonentity here, he were to turn around (looking out with me instead of in at me) he would again find what I find—that this vacancy is filled to capacity with everything imaginable. He, too, would find this central Point exploding into an Infinite Volume, this Nothing into All, this Here into Everywhere.

And if my skeptical observer still doubts his senses, he may try his camera instead—a device which, lacking memory and anticipation, can register only what is contained in the place where it happens to be. It records the same picture of me. Over there, it takes a man; midway, bits and pieces of a man; here, no man and nothing—or else, when pointed the other way round, the universe.

* * *

Film directors . . . are practical people, much more interested in the telling re-creation of experience than in discerning the nature of the experiencer; but in fact the one involves some of the other. Certainly these experts are well aware (for example) how feeble my reaction is to a film of a vehicle obviously driven by someone else, compared with my reaction to a film of a vehicle apparently driven by myself. In the first instance I am a spectator on the pavement, observing two similar cars swiftly approaching, colliding, killing the drivers, bursting into flames—and I am mildly interested. In the second, I am the driver—headless, of course, like all first-person drivers, and my car (what little there is of it) is stationary. Here are my swaying knees, my foot hard down on the accelerator, my hands struggling with the steering wheel, the long bonnet sloping away in front, telegraph poles whizzing by, the road snaking this way and that, the other car, tiny at first, but looming larger and larger, coming straight at me, and then the crash, a great flash of light, and an empty silence. . . . I sink back onto my seat and get my breath back. I have been taken for a ride.

How are they filmed, these first-person sequences? Two ways are possible: either a headless dummy is photographed, with the camera in place of the head; or else a real man is photographed, with this head held far back or to one side to make room for the camera. In other words, to ensure that I shall identify myself with the actor, his head is got out of the way: he must be my kind of man. For a picture of me-with-a-head is no likeness at all: it is the portrait of a complete stranger, a case of mistaken identity.

It is curious that anyone should go to the advertising man for a glimpse into the deepest—and simplest—truths about himself; odd also that an elaborate modern invention like the cinema should help rid anyone of the illusion which very young children and animals are free of. But in other ages there were other and equally curious pointers, and our human capacity for self-deception has surely never been complete. A profound though dim awareness of the human condition may well explain the popularity of many old cults and legends of loose and flying heads, of one-eyed or headless monsters and apparitions, of human bodies with non-human heads, and of martyrs who (like King Charles in the ill-punctuated sentence) walked and talked after their heads were cut off—fantastic pictures, no doubt, but nearer than common sense ever gets to a true portrait of *this* man.

Further Questions

1. If you can't *see* that you have a head, can't you at least *feel* that you have a head? And if you can feel that you have one, is there any reason visual experience should take precedence over tactile experience in determining what is real?
2. Is there a useful distinction to be drawn between what we can know on the basis of direct experience and what we can know only on the basis of theory? If so, does Harding draw or utilize that distinction correctly?
3. Compare Harding's *realization* that he has no head with the narrator's experience in Kolak's *Descartes Among the Ruins* of realizing he was "the man in the dream" who mistook his world for a head (p. 101 of this book). How are they different? How are they the same?

Further Readings

Kapleau, Philip. *The Three Pillars of Zen.* New York: Anchor, 1980. How to uninterpret your experience, Zen-style. A beautifully written book.
Suzuki, D. T. *Essays in Zen Buddhism, First Series.* New York: Grove Press, 1961. Essays on experiences and truth, by the man who introduced Zen to the West.

On Self and Substance   13

RENÉ DESCARTES

A biography of Descartes appears on page 250.

The selection that follows is part VI of Descartes' *Meditations*. Its original title was "Of the Existence of Material Things and of the Real Distinction Between the Mind and Body of Man."

Reading Questions:

1. To distinguish between imaging and conceiving, Descartes appeals to the example of a chiliogon. What is his point? Are you convinced?

2. What are Descartes' reasons for doubting the testimony of his senses? Are they good reasons?
3. What does Descartes say is the difference between his mind and his body? How does he think the two are related?
4. How does Descartes prove the existence of the external, material world?

THERE NOW ONLY REMAINS the inquiry as to whether material things exist. With regard to this question, I at least know with certainty that such things may exist, in as far as they constitute the object of pure mathematics, since, regarding them in this aspect, I can conceive them clearly and distinctly. For there can be no doubt that God possesses the power of producing all the objects I am able distinctly to conceive, and I never considered anything impossible to him, unless when I experienced a contradiction in the attempt to conceive it aright. Further, the faculty of imagination which I possess, and of which I am conscious that I make use when I apply myself to the consideration of material things, is sufficient to persuade me of their existence: for, when I attentively consider what imagination is, I find that it is simply a certain application of the cognitive faculty to a body which is immediately present to it, and which therefore exists.

And to render this quite clear, I remark, in the first place, the difference that subsists between imagination and pure intellection. For example, when I imagine a triangle I not only conceive that it is a figure comprehended by three lines, but at the same time also I look upon these three lines as present by the power and internal application of my mind, and this is what I call imagining. But if I desire to think of a chiliogon, I indeed rightly conceive that it is a figure composed of a thousand sides, as easily as I conceive that a triangle is a figure composed of only three sides; but I cannot imagine the thousand sides of a chiliogon as I do the three sides of a triangle, nor, so to speak, view them as present. And although, in accordance with the habit I have of always imagining something when I think of corporeal things, it may happen that, in conceiving a chiliogon, I confusedly represent some figure to myself, yet it is quite evident that this is not a chiliogon, since it in no wise differs from that which I would represent to myself, if

I were to think of a myriogon, or any other figure of many sides; nor would this representation be of any use in discovering and unfolding the properties that constitute the difference between a chiliogon and other polygons. But if the question turns on a pentagon, it is quite true that I can conceive its figure, as well as that of a chiliogon, without the aid of imagination; but I can likewise imagine it by applying the attention of my mind to its five sides, and at the same time to the area which they contain. Thus I observe that a special effort of mind is necessary to the act of imagination, which is not required to conceiving or understanding; and this special exertion of mind clearly shows the difference between imagination and pure intellection. I remark, besides, that this power of imagination which I possess, in as far as it differs from the power of conceiving, is in no way necessary to my essence, that is, to the essence of my mind; for although I did not posses it, I should still remain the same that I now am, from which it seems we may conclude that it depends on something different from the mind. And I easily understand that, if some body exists, with which my mind is so conjoined and united as to be able, as it were, to consider it when it chooses, it may thus imagine corporeal objects; so that this mode of thinking differs from pure intellection only in this respect, that the mind in conceiving turns in some way upon itself, and considers some one of the ideas it possesses within itself; but in imagining it turns towards the body, and contemplates in it some object conformed to the idea which it either of itself conceived or apprehended by sense. I easily understand, I say, that imagination may be thus formed, if it is true that there are bodies; and because I find no other obvious mode of explaining it, I thence, with probability, conjecture that they exist, but only with probability; and although I carefully examine all things, nevertheless I do not find that,

John Veitch, trans. Open Court *(1901). With emendations by the editors.*

from the distinct idea of corporeal nature I have in my imagination, I can necessarily infer the existence of any body.

But I am accustomed to imagine many other objects besides that corporeal nature which is the object of the pure mathematics, as, for example, colours, sounds, tastes, pain, and the like, although with less distinctness; and, inasmuch as I perceive these objects much better by the senses, through the medium of which and of memory, they seem to have reached the imagination. I believe that, in order the more advantageously to examine them, it is proper I should at the same time examine what sense-perception is, and inquire whether from those ideas that are apprehended by this mode of thinking. I cannot obtain a certain proof of the existence of corporeal objects.

And, in the first place, I will recall to my mind the things I have hitherto held as true, because perceived by the senses, and the foundations upon which my belief in their truth rested; I will, in the second place, examine the reasons that afterwards constrained me to doubt of them; and, finally, I will consider what of them I ought now to believe.

Firstly, then, I perceived that I had a head, hands, feet, and other members composing that body which I considered as part, or perhaps even as a whole, of myself. I perceived further, that that body was placed among many others, by which it was capable of being affected in diverse ways, both beneficial and hurtful; and what was beneficial I remarked by a certain sensation of pleasure, and what was hurtful by a sensation of pain. And, besides this pleasure and pain, I was likewise conscious of hunger, thirst, and other appetites, as well as certain corporeal inclinations towards joy, sadness, anger, and similar passions. And, out of myself, besides the extension, figure, and motions of bodies, I likewise perceived in them hardness, heat, and the other tactile qualities, and, in addition, light, colours, odours, tastes, and sounds, the variety of which gave me the means of distinguishing the sky, the earth, the sea, and generally all the other bodies from one another. And certainly, considering the ideas of all these qualities, which were presented to my mind, and which alone I properly and immediately perceived, it was not without reason that I thought I perceived certain objects wholly different from my thought, namely, bodies

from which those ideas proceeded; for I was conscious that the ideas were presented to me without my consent being required, so that I could not perceive any object, however desirous I might be, unless it were present to the organ of sense; and it was wholly out of my power not to perceive it when it was thus present. And because the ideas I perceived by the senses were much more lively and clear, and even, in their own way, more distinct than any of those I could of myself frame by meditation, or which I found impressed on my memory, it seemed that they could not have proceeded from myself, and must therefore have been caused in me by some other objects; and as of those objects I had no knowledge beyond what the ideas themselves gave me, nothing was so likely to occur to my mind as the supposition that the objects were similar to the ideas which they caused. And because I recollected also that I had formerly trusted to the senses, rather than to reason, and that the ideas which I myself formed were not so clear as those I perceived by sense, and that they were even for the most part composed of parts of the latter, I was readily persuaded that I had no idea in my intellect which had not formerly passed through the senses. Nor was I altogether wrong in likewise believing that that body which, by a special right, I called my own, pertained to me more properly and strictly than any of the others; for in truth, I could never be separated from it as from the other bodies: I felt in it and on account of it all my appetites and affections, and in fine I was affected in its parts by pain and the titillation of pleasure, and not in the parts of the other bodies that were separated from it. But when I inquired into the reason why, from this I know not what sensation of pain, sadness of mind should follow, and why from the sensation of pleasure joy should arise, or why this indescribable twitching of the stomach, which I call hunger, should put me in mind of taking food, and the parchedness of the throat of drink, and so in other cases, I was unable to give any explanation, unless that I was so taught by nature; for there is assuredly no affinity, at least none that I am able to comprehend, between this irritation of the stomach and the desire of food, any more than between the perception of an object that causes pain and the consciousness of sadness which springs from the perception. And in the same way it seemed to

me that all the other judgments I had formed regarding the objects of sense, were dictates of nature; because I remarked that those judgments
were formed in me, before I had leisure to weigh
and consider the reasons that might constrain me
to form them.

But, afterwards, a wide experience by degrees
sapped the faith I had reposed in my senses; for I
frequently observed that towers, which at a distance seemed round, appeared square when more
closely viewed, and that colossal figures, raised on
the summits of these towers, looked like small statues, when viewed from the bottom of them; and,
in other instances without number, I also discovered error in judgments founded on the external
senses; and not only in those founded on the external, but even in those that rested on the internal
senses; for is there aught more internal than pain?
and yet I have sometimes been informed by parties
whose arm or leg had been amputated, that they
still occasionally seemed to feel pain in that part of
the body which they had lost,—a circumstance
that led me to think that I could not be quite certain even that any one of my members was affected
when I felt pain in it. And to these grounds of
doubt I shortly afterwards also added two others
of very wide generality: the first of them was that I
believed I never perceived anything when awake
which I could not occasionally think I also perceived when asleep, and as I do not believe that the
ideas I seem to perceive in my sleep proceed from
objects external to me, I did not any more observe
any ground for believing this of such as I seem to
perceive when awake; the second was that since I
was as yet ignorant of the author of my being, or at
least supposed myself to be so, I saw nothing to
prevent my having been so constituted by nature
as that I should be deceived even in matters that
appeared to me to possess the greatest truth. And,
with respect to the grounds on which I had before
been persuaded of the existence of sensible objects,
I had no great difficulty in finding suitable answers
to them; for as nature seemed to incline me to
many things from which reason made me averse, I
thought that I ought not to confide much in its
teachings. And although the perceptions of the
senses were not dependent on my will, I did not
think that I ought on that ground to conclude that
they proceeded from things different from myself,

since perhaps there might be found in me some
faculty, though hitherto unknown to me, which
produced them.

But now that I begin to know myself better,
and to discover more clearly the author of my being, I do not, indeed, think that I ought rashly to
admit all which the senses seem to teach, nor, on
the other hand, is it my conviction that I ought to
doubt in general of their teachings.

And, firstly, because I know that all which I
clearly and distinctly conceive can be produced by
God exactly as I conceive it, it is sufficient that I
am able clearly and distinctly to conceive one thing
apart from another, in order to be certain that the
one is different from the other, seeing they may at
least be made to exist separately, by the omnipotence of God; and it matters not by what power
this separation is made, in order to be compelled
to judge them different; and, therefore, merely because I know with certitude that I exist, and because, in the meantime, I do not observe that
aught necessarily belongs to my nature or essence
beyond my being a thinking thing, I rightly conclude that my essence consists only in my being
a thinking thing, [or a substance whose whole
essence or nature is merely thinking]. And although I may, or rather, as I will shortly say, although I certainly do possess a body with which I
am very closely conjoined; nevertheless, because,
on the one hand, I have a clear and distinct idea of
myself, in as far as I am only a thinking and unextended thing, and as, on the other hand, I possess
a distinct idea of body, in as far as it is only an extended and unthinking thing, it is certain that I,
[that is, my mind, by which I am what I am], is entirely and truly distinct from my body, and may exist without it.

Moreover, I find in myself universe faculties of
thinking that have each their special mode: for example, I find I possess the faculties of imagining
and perceiving, without which I can indeed clearly
and distinctly conceive myself as entire, but I cannot reciprocally conceive them without conceiving
myself, that is to say, without an intelligent substance in which they reside, for [in the notion we
have of them, or to use the terms of the schools] in
their formal concept, they comprise some sort of
intellection; whence I perceive that they are distinct
from myself as modes are from things. I remark

likewise certain other faculties, as the power of changing place, of assuming diverse figures, and the like, that cannot be conceived and cannot therefore exist, any more than the preceding, apart from a substance in which they inhere. It is very evident, however, that these faculties, if they really exist, must belong to some corporeal or extended substance, since in their clear and distinct concept there is contained some sort of extension, but no intellection at all. Farther, I cannot doubt but that there is in me a certain passive faculty of perception, that is, of receiving and taking knowledge of the ideas of sensible things; but this would be useless to me, if there did not also exist in me, or in some other thing, another active faculty capable of forming and producing those ideas. But this active faculty cannot be in me [in as far as I am but a thinking thing], seeing that it does not presuppose thought, and also that those ideas are frequently produced in my mind without my contributing to it in any way, and even frequently contrary to my will. This faculty must therefore exist in some substance different from me, in which all the objective reality of the ideas that are produced by this faculty, is contained formally or eminently, as I before remarked; and this substance is either a body, that is to say, a corporeal nature in which is contained formally [and in effect] all that is objectively [and by representation] in those ideas; or it is God himself, or some other creature, of a rank superior to body, in which the same is contained eminently. But as God is no deceiver, it is manifest that he does not of himself and immediately communicate those ideas to me, nor even by the intervention of any creature in which their objective reality is not formally, but only eminently, contained. For as he has given me no faculty whereby I can discover this to be the case, but, on the contrary, a very strong inclination to believe that those ideas arise from corporeal objects, I do not see how he could be vindicated from the charge of deceit, if in truth they proceeded from any other source, or were produced by other causes than corporeal things: and accordingly it must be concluded, that corporeal objects exist. Nevertheless they are not perhaps exactly such as we perceive by the senses, for their comprehension by the senses is, in many instances, very obscure and confused; but it is at least necessary to admit that all which I clearly and dis-

tinctly conceive as in them, that is, generally speaking, all that is comprehended in the object of speculative geometry, really exists external to me.

But with respect to other things which are either only particular, as, for example, that the sun is of such a size and figure, etc., or are conceived with less clearness and distinctness, as light, sound, pain, and the like, although they are highly dubious and uncertain, nevertheless on the ground alone that God is no deceiver, and that consequently he has permitted no falsity in my opinions which he has not likewise given me a faculty of correcting, I think I may with safety conclude that I possess in myself the means of arriving at the truth. And, in the first place, it cannot be doubted that in each of the dictates of nature there is some truth: for by nature, considered in general, I now understand nothing more than God himself, or the order and disposition established by God in created things; and by my nature in particular I understand the assemblage of all that God has given me.

But there is nothing which that nature teaches me more expressly [or more sensibly] than that I have a body which is ill affected when I feel pain, and stands in need of food and drink when I experience the sensations of hunger and thirst, etc. And therefore I ought not to doubt but that there is some truth in these informations.

Nature likewise teaches me by these sensations of pain, hunger, thirst, etc., that I am not only lodged in my body as a pilot in a vessel, but that I am besides so intimately conjoined, and as it were intermixed with it, that my mind and body compose a certain unity. For if this were not the case, I should not feel pain when my body is hurt, seeing I am merely a thinking thing, but should perceive the wound by the understanding alone, just as a pilot perceives by sight when any part of his vessel is damaged; and when my body has need of food or drink, I should have a clear knowledge of this, and not be made aware of it by the confused sensations of hunger and thirst; for, in truth, all these sensations of hunger, thirst, pain, etc., are nothing more than certain confused modes of thinking, arising from the union and apparent fusion of mind and body.

Besides this, nature teaches me that my own body is surrounded by many other bodies, some of which I have to seek after, and others to shun. And indeed, as I perceive different sorts of colours, sounds, odours, tastes, heat, harness, etc., I safely conclude that there are in the bodies from which the diverse perceptions of the senses proceed, certain varieties corresponding to them, although, perhaps, not in reality like them; and since, among these diverse perceptions of the senses, some are agreeable, and others disagreeable, there can be no doubt that my body, or rather my entire self, in as far as I am composed of body and mind, may be variously affected, both beneficially and hurtfully, by surrounding bodies.

But there are many other beliefs which, though seemingly the teaching of nature, are not in reality so, but which obtained a place in my mind through a habit of judging inconsiderately of things. It may thus easily happen that such judgments shall contain error: thus, for example, the opinion I have that all space in which there is nothing to affect my senses is void; that in a hot body there is something in every respect similar to the idea of heat in my mind; that in a white or green body there is the same whiteness or greenness which I perceive; that in a bitter or sweet body there is the same taste, and so in other instances; that the stars, towers, and all distant bodies, are of the same size and figure as they appear to our eyes, etc. But that I may avoid everything like indistinctness of conception, I must accurately define what I properly understand by being taught by nature. For nature is here taken in a narrower sense than when it signifies the sum of all the things which God has given me; seeing that in that meaning the notion comprehends much that belongs only to the mind [to which I am not here to be understood as referring when I use the term nature]; as, for example, the notion I have of the truth, that what is done cannot be undone, and all the other truths I discern by the natural light; and seeing that it comprehends likewise much besides that belongs only to body, and is not here any more contained under the name nature, as the quality of heaviness, and the like, of which I do not speak,—the term being reserved exclusively to designate the things which God has given to me as a being composed of mind and body. But nature, taking the term in the sense explained, teaches me to shun what causes in me the sensation of pain, and to pursue what affords me the sensation of pleasure, and other things of this

sort; but I do not discover that it teaches me, in addition to this, from these diverse perceptions of the senses, to draw any conclusions respecting external objects without a previous consideration of them by the mind; for it is, as appears to me, the office of the mind alone, and not of the composite whole of mind and body, to discern the truth in those matters. Thus, although the impression a star makes on my eye is not larger than that from the flame of a candle, I do not, nevertheless, experience any real or positive impulse determining me to believe that the star is not greater than the flame; the true account of the matter being merely that I have so judged from my youth without any rational ground. And, though on approaching the fire I feel heat, and even pain on approaching it too closely, I have, however, from this no ground for holding that something resembling the heat I feel is in the fire, any more than that there is something similar to the pain; all that I have ground for believing is, that there is something in it, whatever it may be, which excites in me those sensations of heat or pain. So also, although there are spaces in which I find nothing to excite and affect my senses, I must not therefore conclude that those spaces contain in them no body; for I see that in this, as in many other similar matters, I have been accustomed to pervert the order of nature, because these perceptions of the senses, although given me by nature merely to signify to my mind what things are beneficial and hurtful to the composite whole of which it is a part, and being sufficiently clear and distinct for that purpose, are nevertheless used by me as infallible rules by which to determine immediately the essence of the bodies that exist out of me, of which they can of course afford me only the most obscure and confused knowledge.

But I have already sufficiently considered how it happens that, notwithstanding the supreme goodness of God, there is falsity in my judgments. A difficulty, however, here presents itself, respecting the things which I am taught by nature must be pursued or avoided, and also respecting the internal sensations in which I seem to have occasionally detected error: Thus, for example, I may be so deceived by the agreeable taste of some viand with which poison has been mixed, as to be induced to take the poison. In this case, however, nature may be excused, for it simply leads me to desire the viand for its agreeable taste, and not the poison, which is unknown to it; and thus we can infer nothing from this circumstance beyond that our nature is not omniscient; at which there is assuredly no ground for surprise, since, man being of a finite nature, his knowledge must likewise be of limited perfection. But we also not unfrequently err in that to which we are directly impelled by nature, as is the case with invalids who desire drink or food that would be hurtful to them. It will here, perhaps, be alleged that the reason why such persons are deceived is that their nature is corrupted; but this leaves the difficulty untouched, for a sick man is not less really the creature of God than a man who is in full health; and therefore it is as repugnant to the goodness of God that the nature of the former should be deceitful as it is for what of the latter to be so. And, as a clock, composed of wheels and counter weights, observes not the less accurately all the laws of nature when it is ill made, and points out the hours incorrectly, than when it satisfies the desire of the maker in every respect, so likewise if the body of man be considered as a kind of machine, so made up and composed of bones, nerves, muscles, veins, blood, and skin, that although there were in it no mind, it would still exhibit the same motions which it at present manifests involuntarily, and therefore without the aid of the mind, I easily discern that it would also be as natural for such a body, supposing it dropsical, for example, to experience the parchedness of the throat that is usually accompanied in the mind by the sensation of thirst, and to be disposed by this parchedness to move its nerves and its other parts in the way required for drinking, and thus increase its malady and do itself harm, as it is natural for it, when it is not indisposed to be stimulated to drink for its good by a similar cause; and although looking to the use for which a clock was destined by its maker, I may say that it is deflected from its proper nature when it incorrectly indicates the hours, and on the same principle, considering the machine of the human body as having been formed by God for the sake of the motions which it usually manifests, although I may likewise have ground for thinking that it does not follow the order of its nature when the throat is parched and drink does not tend to its preservation, nevertheless I yet plainly discern that this latter acceptation of the term na-

ture is very different from the other; for this is nothing more than a certain denomination, depending entirely on my thought, and hence called extrinsic, by which I compare a sick man and an imperfectly constructed clock with the idea I have of a man in good health and a well made clock; while by the other acceptation of nature is understood something which is truly found in things, and therefore possessed of some truth.

But certainly, although in respect of a dropsical body, it is only by way of exterior denomination that we say its nature is corrupted, when, without requiring drink the throat is parched; yet, in respect of the composite whole, that is, of the mind in its union with the body, it is not a pure denomination, but really an error of nature, for it to feel thirst when drink would be hurtful to it: and, accordingly, it still remains to be considered why it is that the goodness of God does not prevent the nature of man thus taken from being fallacious.

To commence this examination accordingly, I here remark, in the first place, that there is a vast difference between mind and body, in respect that body, from its nature, is always divisible, and that mind is entirely indivisible. For in truth, when I consider the mind, that is, when I consider myself in so far only as I am a thinking thing, I can distinguish in myself no parts, but I very clearly discern that I am somewhat absolutely one and entire, and although the whole mind seems to be united to the whole body, yet, when a foot, an arm, or any other part is cut off, I am conscious that nothing has been taken from my mind; nor can the faculties of willing, perceiving, conceiving, etc., properly be called its parts, for it is the same mind that is exercised [all entire] in willing, in perceiving, and in conceiving, etc. But quite the opposite holds in corporeal or extended things; for I cannot imagine any one of them [how small soever it may be], which I cannot easily sunder in thought, and which, therefore, I do not know to be divisible. This would be sufficient to teach me that the mind or soul of man is entirely different from the body, if I had not already been apprised of it on other grounds.

I remark, in the next place, that the mind does not immediately receive the impression from all the parts of the body, but only from the brain, or perhaps even from one small part of it, viz., that in which the common sense is said to be, which as often as it is affected in the same way, gives rise to the same perception in the mind, although meanwhile the other parts of the body may be diversely disposed, as is proved by innumerable experiments, which it is unnecessary here to enumerate.

I remark, besides, that the nature of body is such that none of its parts can be moved by another part a little removed from the other, which cannot likewise be moved in the same way by any one of the parts that lie between those two, although the most remote part does not act at all. As, for example, in the cord A, B, C, D, if its last part D, be pulled, the first part A, will be moved in a different way than it would be were one of the intermediate parts B or C to be pulled, and the last part D meanwhile to remain fixed. And in the same way, when I feel pain in the foot, the science of physics teaches me that this sensation is experienced by means of the nerves dispersed over the foot, which, extending like cords from it to the brain, when they are contracted in the foot, contract at the same time the inmost parts of the brain in which they have their origin, and excite in these parts a certain motion appointed by nature to cause in the mind a sensation of pain, as if existing in the foot: but as these nerves must pass through the tibia, the leg, the loins, the back, and neck, in order to reach the brain, it may happen that although their extremities in the foot are not affected, but only certain of their parts that pass through the loins or neck, the same movements, nevertheless, are excited in the brain by this motion as would have been caused there by a hurt received in the foot, and hence the mind will necessarily feel pain in the foot, just as if it had been hurt; and the same is true of all the other perceptions of our senses.

I remark, finally, that as each of the movements that are made in the part of the brain by which the mind is immediately affected, impresses it with but a single sensation, the most likely supposition in the circumstances is, that this movement causes the mind to experience, among all the sensations which it is capable of impressing upon it, that one which is the best fitted, and generally the most useful for the preservation of the human body when it is in full health. But experience shows us that all the perceptions which nature has given us are of

such a kind as I have mentioned; and accordingly, there is nothing found in them that does not manifest the power and goodness of God. Thus, for example, when the nerves of the foot are violently or more than usually shaken, the motion passing through the medulla of the spine to the innermost parts of the brain affords a sign to the mind on which it experiences a sensation, viz., of pain, as if it were in the foot, by which the mind is admonished and excited to do its utmost to remove the cause of it as dangerous and hurtful to the foot. It is true that God could have so constituted the nature of man as that the same motion in the brain would have informed the mind of something altogether different: the motion might, for example, have been the occasion on which the mind became conscious of itself, in so far as it is in the brain, or in so far as it is in some place intermediate between the foot and the brain, or, finally, the occasion on which it perceived some other object quite different; whatever that might be; but nothing of all this would have so well contributed to the preservation of the body as that which the mind actually feels. In the same way, when we stand in need of drink, there arises from this want a certain parchedness in the throat that moves its nerves, and by means of them the internal parts of the brain; and this movement affects the mind with the sensation of thirst, because there is nothing on that occasion which is more useful for us than to be made aware that we have need of drink for the preservation of our health; and so in other instances.

Whence it is quite manifest that, notwithstanding the sovereign goodness of God, the nature of man, in so far as it is composed of mind and body, cannot but be sometimes fallacious. For if there is any cause which excites, not in the foot, but in some one of the parts of the nerves that stretch from the foot to the brain, or even in the brain itself, the same movement that is ordinarily created when the foot is ill affected, pain will be felt, as it were, in the foot, and the sense will thus be naturally deceived; for as the same movement in the brain can but impress the mind with the same sensation, and as this sensation is much more frequently excited by a cause which hurts the foot than by one acting in a different quarter, it is reasonable that it should lead the mind to feel pain in the foot rather than in any other part of the body.

And if it sometimes happens that the parchedness of the throat does not arise, as is usual, from drink being necessary for the health of the body, but from quite the opposite cause, as is the case with the dropsical, yet it is much better that it should be deceitful in that instance, than if, on the contrary, it were continually fallacious when the body is well-disposed; and the same holds true in other cases.

And certainly this consideration is of great service, not only in enabling me to recognize the errors to which my nature is liable, but likewise in rendering it more easy to avoid or correct them: for, knowing that all my senses more usually indicate to me what is true than what is false, in matters relating to the advantage of the body, and being able almost always to make use of more than a single sense in examining the same object, and besides this, being able to use my memory in connecting present with past knowledge, and my understanding which has already discovered all the cause of my errors, I ought no longer to fear that falsity may be met with in what is daily presented to me by the senses. And I ought to reject all the doubts of those bygone days, as hyperbolical and ridiculous, especially the general uncertainty respecting sleep, which I could not distinguish from the waking state: for I now find a very marked difference between the two states, in respect that our memory can never connect our dreams with each other and with the course of life, in the way it is in the habit of doing with events that occur when we are awake. And, in truth, if some one, when I am awake, appeared to me all of a sudden and as suddenly disappeared, as do the images I see in sleep, so that I could not observe either whence he came or whither he went, I should not without reason esteem it either a spectre or phantom formed in my brain, rather than a real man. But when I perceive objects with regard to which I can distinctly determine both the place whence they come, and that in which they are, and the time at which they appear to me, and when, without interruption, I can connect the perception I have of them with the whole of the other parts of my life, I am perfectly sure that what I perceive occurs while I am awake and not during sleep. And I ought not in the least degree to doubt of the truth of those presentations, if, after having called together all my senses, my memory, and my understanding for the purpose of examining them, no deliverance is given by any one of these faculties which is repugnant to that of any other: for since God is no deceiver, it necessarily follows that I am not herein deceived. But because the necessities of action frequently oblige us to come to a determination before we have had leisure for so careful an examination, it must be confessed that the life of man is frequently obnoxious to error with respect to individual objects; and we must, in conclusion, acknowledge the weakness of our nature.

Further Questions

1. What do *you* think is the essential distinction, if any, between *your* mind and body? How do *you* think the two are related?
2. How do *you* prove the existence of the external, material world?

Further Readings

Flew, Antony, ed. *Body, Mind, and Death*. New York: Macmillan, 1964. Contains classical selections of the mind/body problem.

Frankfurt, Harry. *Demons, Dreamers, and Madmen: The Defense of Reason in Descartes' Meditations*. Indianapolis: Bobbs-Merrill, 1970. A penetrating study by a famous philosopher.

14   Personal Identity

JOHN LOCKE

John Locke (1632–1704) was educated at Oxford University, where he studied the classics, philosophy, and medicine. At that time, Oxford was still under the influence of medieval scholasticism. Locke himself was interested in the view recently formulated by René Descartes, and in particular in working out a theory of knowledge that could accommodate the progress being made in the newly emerging sciences. Descartes was a "rationalist" who believed that reason is our primary source of knowledge about the world. Locke became convinced that experience was our primary source. That made Locke an "empiricist."

Locke's main attempt to explain his empiricism, his *Essay Concerning Human Understanding* (1690), was his chief work in theoretical philosophy. Because of it, Locke eventually became known as the first of three "British empiricists." The other two are George Berkeley and David Hume. Locke also wrote extensively on political philosophy, most notably, his *Two Treatises on Government* (1690), which profoundly influenced the founding fathers of the United States.

In this section, Locke addresses the question of what it is to be a self and to remain the same self over a period of time. He claims that it is an individual's consciousness, particularly his memory, that accounts for his retaining his identity as a person.

Reading Questions

1. Consider Locke's definition of "person." By his definition, could a total amnesiac be a person? Could a gorilla? Could an android?
2. What does Locke mean by "consciousness?" What is the relationship between consciousness and memory?
3. How does Locke distinguish between what it means to be "the same substance" over time and what it means to be "the same person" over time?
4. For Locke, could the same person have more than one soul? More than one body?
5. In what does Locke think personal identity consists?
6. Why can't you just say that your consciousness proves that you are the same identical substance over time?
7. Does Locke think that switching bodies is the same as switching personal identities?
8. How does Locke establish the idea of *same* consciousness?

CORPOREAL AND SPIRITUAL SUBSTANCES

WHEN WE TALK OR THINK of any particular sort of corporeal substances, as horse, stone, etc., though the idea we have of either of them be but the complication or collection of those several simple ideas of sensible qualities, which we used to find united in the thing called horse or stone; yet, *because we cannot conceive how they should subsist alone, nor one in another,* we suppose them existing in and supported by some common subject; which support we denote by the name substance, though it be certain we have no clear or distinct idea of that thing we suppose a support.

From chapters 23 and 27 of Book Two of Locke's Essay Concerning Human Understanding *(1690; 1694).*

The same thing happens concerning the operations of the mind, viz. thinking, reasoning, fearing, etc., which we concluding not to subsist of themselves, nor apprehending how they can belong to body, or be produced by it, we are apt to think these the actions of some other *substance,* which we call *spirit;* whereby yet it is evident that, having no other idea of notion of matter, but something wherein those many sensible qualities which affect our senses do subsist; by supposing a substance wherein thinking, knowing, doubting, and a power of moving, etc., do subsist, we have as clear a notion of the substance of spirit, as we have of body; the one being supposed to be (without knowing what it is) the *substratum* to those simple ideas we have from without; and the other supposed (with a like ignorance of what it is) to be the *substratum* to those operations we experiment in ourselves within. It is plain then, that the idea of *corporeal substance* in matter is as remote from our conceptions and apprehensions, as that of *spiritual substance,* or spirit: and therefore, from our not having any notion of the substance of spirit, we can no more conclude its non-existence, than we can, for the same reason, deny the existence of body; it being as rational to affirm there is no body, because we have no clear and distinct idea of the substance of matter, as to say there is no spirit, because we have no clear and distinct idea of the substance of a spirit. . . .

So that, in short, the idea we have of spirit, compared with the idea we have of body, stands thus: the substance of spirits is unknown to us; and so is the substance of body equally unknown to us. Two primary qualities or properties of body, viz. solid coherent parts and impulse, we have distinct clear ideas of: so likewise we know, and have distinct [and] clear ideas, of two primary qualities or properties of spirit, viz. thinking, and a power of action; i.e. a power of beginning or stopping several thoughts or motions. We have also the ideas of several qualities inherent in bodies, and have the clear distinct ideas of them; which qualities are but the various modifications of the extension of cohering solid parts, and their motion. We have likewise the ideas of the several modes of thinking viz. believing, doubting, intending, fearing, hoping; all which are but the several modes of thinking. We have also the ideas of willing, and moving the body consequent to it, and with the body itself too; for, as has been shown, spirit is capable of motion.

. . . If this notion of immaterial spirit may have, perhaps, some difficulties in it not easily to be explained, we have therefore no more reason to deny or doubt the existence of such spirits, than we have to deny or doubt the existence of body. . . .

THE IDENTITY OF LIVING THINGS

In the state of living creatures, their identity depends not on a mass of the same particles, but on something else. For in them the variation of great parcels of matter alters not the identity: an oak growing from a plant to a great tree, and then lopped, is still the same oak; and a colt grown up to a horse, sometimes fat, sometimes lean, is all the while the same horse: though, in both these cases, there may be a manifest change of the parts; so that truly they are not either of them the same masses of matter, though they be truly one of them the same oak, and the other the same horse. The reason whereof is, that, in these two cases, a mass of matter, and a living body, identity is not applied to the same thing.

VEGETABLES

We must therefore consider wherein an oak differs from a mass of matter, and that seems to me to be in this, that the one is only the cohesion of particles of matter any how united, the other such a disposition of them as constitutes the parts of an oak; and such an organization of those parts as is fit to receive and distribute nourishment, so as to continue and frame the wood, bark, and leaves, etc., of an oak, in which consists the vegetable life. That being the one plant which has such an organization of parts in one coherent body, partaking of one common life, it continues to be the same plant as long as it partakes of the same life, though that life be communicated to new particles of matter vitally united to the living plant, in a like continued organization conformable to that sort of plants. For this organization being at any one instant in any one collection of matter, is in that particular concrete distinguished from all other, and is that individual life, which existing constantly from that moment both forwards and backwards, in the same continuity of insensibly succeeding parts united to the living body of the plant, it has that identity which makes the same plant, and all the parts of it, parts of the same plant, during all the time that they exist united in that continued organization, which is fit to convey that common life to all the parts so united.

ANIMALS

The case is not so much different in brutes, but that any one may hence see what makes an animal and continues it the same. Something we have like this in machines, and may serve to illustrate it. For example, what is a watch?: It is plain it is nothing but a fit organization or construction of parts to a certain end, which, when a sufficient force is added to it, it is capable to attain. If we would suppose this machine one continued body, all whose organized parts were repaired, increased, or diminished by a constant addition or separation of insensible parts, with one common life, we should have something very much like the body of an animal; with this difference, that, in an animal the fitness of the organization, and the motion wherein life consists, begin together, the motion coming from within; but in machines, the force coming sensibly from without, is often away when the organ is in order, and well fitted to receive it.

PEOPLE

This also shows wherein the identity of the same man consists; viz., in nothing but a participation of the same continued life, by constantly fleeting particles of matter, in succession vitally united to the same organized body. He that shall place the identity of man in anything else, but like that of other animals, in one fitly organized body, taken in any one instant, and from thence continued, under one organization of life, in several successively fleeting particles of matter united to it, will find it hard to make an embryo, one of years, mad and sober, the same man, by any supposition, that will not make it possible for Seth, Ismael, Socrates, Pilate, Saint Austin, and Caesar Borgia, to be the same man. For, if the identity of soul alone makes the same man, and there be nothing in the nature of matter why the same individual spirit may not be united to different bodies, it will be possible that those men living in distant ages, and of different tempers, may have been the same man: which way of speaking must be, from a very strange use of the

word man, applied to an idea, out of which body and shape are excluded. And that way of speaking would agree yet worse with the notions of those philosophers who allow of transmigration, and are of opinion that the souls of men may, for their miscarriages, be detruded into the bodies of beasts, as fit habitations, with organs suited to the satisfaction of their brutal inclinations. But yet I think nobody, could he be sure that the souls of Heliogabalus were in one of his hogs, would yet say that hog were a man or Heliogabalus.

It is not therefore unity of substances that comprehends all sorts of identity, or will determine it in every case; but to conceive and judge of it aright, we must consider what idea the word it is applied to stands for: it being one thing to be the same substance, another the same man, and a third the same person, if person, man, and substance, are three names standing for three different ideas; for such as is the idea belonging to that name, such must be the identity; which, if it had been a little more carefully attended to, would possibly have prevented a great deal of that confusion which often occurs about this matter, with no small seeming difficulties, especially concerning personal identity, which therefore we shall in the next place a little consider.

SAME MAN

An animal is living organized body; and consequently the same animal, as we have observed, is the same continued life communicated to different particles of matter, as they happen successively to be united to that organized living body. And whatever is talked of other definitions, ingenious observation puts it past doubt, that the idea in our minds, of which the sound man in our mouths is the sign, is nothing else but of an animal of such a certain form: since I think I may be confident, that, whoever should see a creature of his own shape or make, though it had no more reason all its life than a cat or a parrot, would call him still a man; or whoever should hear a cat or a parrot discourse, reason, and philosophize, would call or think it nothing but a cat or a parrot; and say, the one was a dull irrational man, and the other a very intelligent rational parrot. . . .

I presume it is not the idea of a thinking or rational being alone that makes the idea of a man in most people's sense, but of a body, so and so shaped, joined to it; and if that be the idea of a man, the same successive body not shifted all at once, must, as well as the same immaterial spirit, go to the making of the same man.

CONSCIOUSNESS AND PERSONAL IDENTITY

PERSONAL IDENTITY

This being premised, to find wherein personal identity consists, we must consider what person stands for; which, I think, is a thinking intelligent being, that has reason and reflection, and can consider itself as itself, the same thinking thing, in different times and places; which it does only by that consciousness which is inseparable from thinking, and, as it seems to me, essential to it: it being impossible for any one to perceive without perceiving that he does perceive. When we see, hear, smell, taste, feel, meditate, or will anything, we know that we do so. Thus it is always as to our present sensations and perceptions: and by this every one is to himself that which he calls self; it not being considered, in this case, whether the same self be continued in the same or divers substances. For, since consciousness always accompanies thinking, and it is that which makes every one to be what he calls self, and thereby distinguishes himself from all other thinking things: in this alone consists personal identity, i.e., the sameness of a rational being; and as far as this consciousness can be extended backwards to any past action or thought, so far reaches the identity of that person; it is the same self now it was then; and it is by the same self with this present one that now reflects on it, that that action was done.

CONSCIOUSNESS MAKES PERSONAL IDENTITY

But it is further inquired, whether it be the same identical substance? This, few would think they had reason to doubt of, if these perceptions, with their consciousness, always remained present in the mind, whereby the same thinking thing would be always consciously present, and, as would be thought, evidently the same to itself. But that which seems to make the difficulty is this, that this consciousness being interrupted always by for-

getfulness, there being no moment of our lives wherein we have the whole train of all our past actions before our eyes in one view, but even the best memories losing the sight of one part whilst they are viewing another; and we sometimes, and that the greatest part of our lives, not reflecting on our past selves, being intent on our present thoughts, and in sound sleep having no thoughts at all, or at least none with that consciousness which remarks our waking thoughts; I say, in all these cases, our consciousness being interrupted, and we losing the sight of our past selves, doubts are raised whether we are the same thinking thing, i.e., the same substance or no. Which, however reasonable or unreasonable, concerns not personal identity at all: the question being, what makes the same person, and not whether it be the same identical substance, which always thinks in the same person; which in this case, matters not at all: different substances, by the same consciousness (where they do partake in it) being united into one person, as well as different bodies by the same life are united into one animal, whose identity is preserved in that change of substances by the unity of one continued life. For it being the same consciousness that makes a man be himself to himself, personal identity depends on that only, whether it be annexed solely to one individual substance, or can be continued in a succession of several substances. For as far as any intelligent being can repeat the idea of any past action with the same consciousness it had of it at first, and with the same consciousness it has of any present action; so far it is the same personal self. For it is by the consciousness it has of its present thoughts and actions, that it is self to itself now, and so will be the same self, as far as the same consciousness can extend to actions past or to come; and would be by distance of time, or change of substance, no more two persons, than a man be two men by wearing other clothes today than he did yesterday, with a long or a short sleep between: the same consciousness uniting those distant actions into the same person, whatever substances contributed to their production.

PERSONAL IDENTITY IN CHANGE OF SUBSTANCES

That this is so, we have some kind of evidence in our very bodies, all whose particles, whilst vitally united to this same thinking conscious self, so that we feel when they are touched, and are affected by, and conscious of good or harm that happens to them, are a part of ourselves; i.e., of our thinking conscious self. Thus, the limbs of his body are to every one a part of himself; he sympathizes and is concerned for them. Cut off a hand, and thereby separate it from that consciousness he had of its heat, cold, and other affections, and it is then no longer a part of that which is himself, any more than the remotest part of matter. Thus, we see the substance whereof personal self consisted at one time may be varied at another, without the change of personal identity; there being no question about the same person, though the limbs which but now were a part of it, be cut off. . . .

PERSONAL IDENTITY AND IMMATERIAL SUBSTANCE

But next, as to the first part of the question, "Whether if the same thinking substance (supposing immaterial substances only to think) be changed, it can be the same person?" I answer, that cannot be resolved, but by those who know what kind of substances they are that do think, and whether the consciousness of past actions can be transferred from one thinking substance to another. I grant, were the same consciousness the same individual action, it could not: but it being a present representation of a past action, why it may not be possible that that may be represented to the mind to have been, which really never was, will remain to be shown. And therefore how far the consciousness of past actions is annexed to any individual agent, so that another cannot possibly have it, will be hard for us to determine, till we know what kind of action it is that cannot be done without a reflex act of perception accompanying it, and how performed by thinking substances, who cannot think without being conscious of it. But that which we call the same consciousness, not being the same individual act, why one intellectual substance may not have represented to it, as done by itself, what it never did, and was perhaps done by some other agent; why, I say, such a representation may not possibly be without reality of matter of fact, as well as several representations in dreams are, which yet whilst dreaming we take for true, will be difficult to conclude from the na-

ture of things. And that it never is so, will by us, till we have clearer views of the nature of thinking substances, be best resolved into the goodness of God, who, as far as the happiness or misery of any of his sensible creatures is concerned in it, will not, by a fatal error of theirs, transfer from one to another that consciousness which draws reward or punishment with it. How far this may be an argument against those who would place thinking in a system of fleeting animal spirits, I leave to be considered. But yet, to return to the question before us, it must be allowed, that, if the same consciousness (which, as has been shown, is quite a different thing from the same numerical figure or motion of body) can be transferred from one thinking substance to another, it will be possible that two thinking substances may make but one person. For the same consciousness being preserved, whether in the same or different substances, the personal identity is preserved.

As to the second part of the question, "Whether the same immaterial substance remaining, there may be two distinct persons?" which question seems to me to be built on this, whether the same immaterial being, being conscious of the action of its past existence, and lose it beyond the power of ever retrieving it again; and so as it were beginning a new account from a new period, have a consciousness that cannot reach beyond this new state. All those who hold preexistence are evidently of this mind, since they allow the soul to have no remaining consciousness of what it did in that preexistent state, either wholly separate from body, or informing any other body; and if they should not, it is plain experience would be against them. So that personal identity reaching no further than consciousness reaches, a preexistent spirit not having continued so many ages in a state of silence, must needs make different persons. Suppose a Christian Platonist or a Pythagorean should, upon God's having ended all his works of creation the seventh day, think his soul hath existed ever since; and would imagine it has revolved in several human bodies, as I once met with one, who was persuaded his had been the soul of Socrates; (how reasonably I will not dispute; this I know, that in the post he filled, which was no inconsiderable one, he passed for a very rational man, and the press has shown that he wanted not parts or learning;) would any one say, that he, being not conscious of any of Socrates' actions or thoughts, could be the same person with Socrates? Let any one reflect upon himself, and conclude that he has in himself an immaterial spirit, which is that which thinks in him, and, in the constant change of his body keeps him the same: and is that which he calls himself: let him also suppose it to be the same soul that was in Nestor or Thersites, at the siege of Troy (for souls being, as far as we know anything of them, in their nature indifferent to any parcel of matter, the supposition has no apparent absurdity in it), which it may have been, as well as it is now the soul of any other man: but he now having no consciousness of any of the actions either of Nestor or Thersites, does or can he conceive himself the same person with either of them? Can he be concerned in either of their actions? Attribute them to himself, or think them his own, more than the actions of any other men that ever existed? So that this consciousness not reaching to any of the actions of either of those men, he is no more one self with either of them, than if the soul or immaterial spirit that now informs him had been created, and began to exist, when it began to inform his present body, though it were ever so true, that the same spirit that informed Nestor's or Thersites' body were numerically the same that now informs his. For this would no more make him the same person with Nestor, than if some of the particles of matter that were once a part of Nestor, were now a part of this man; the same immaterial substance, without the same consciousness, no more making the same person by being united to any body, than the same particle of matter, without consciousness united to any body, makes the same person. But let him once find himself conscious of any of the actions of Nestor, he then finds himself the same person with Nestor.

MEMORY AND PERSONAL IDENTITY

And thus may we be able, without any difficulty, to conceive the same person at the resurrection, though in a body not exactly in make or parts the same which he had here, the same consciousness going along with the soul that inhabits it. But yet the soul alone, in the change of bodies, would scarce to any one but to him that makes the soul

the man, be enough to make the same man. For should the soul of a prince, carrying with it the consciousness of the prince's past life, enter and inform the body of a cobbler, as soon as deserted by his own soul, every one sees he would be the same person with the prince, accountable only for the prince's actions: but who would say it was the same man? The body too goes to the making the man, and would, I guess, to everybody determine the man in this case; wherein the soul, with all its princely thoughts about it, would not make another man: but he would be the same cobbler to every one besides himself. I know that, in the ordinary way of speaking, the same person, and the same man, stand for one and the same thing. And indeed every one will always have a liberty to speak as he pleases, and to apply what articulate sounds to what ideas he thinks fit, and change them as often as he pleases. But yet, when we will inquire what makes the same spirit, man, or person, we must fix the ideas of spirit, man, or person in our minds, and having resolved with ourselves what we mean by them, it will not be hard to determine in either of them, or the like, when it is the same, and when not.

CONSCIOUSNESS MAKES THE SAME PERSON

But though the same immaterial substance or soul does not alone, wherever it be, and in whatsoever state, make the same man; yet it is plain, consciousness, as far as ever it can be extended, should it be to ages past, unites existences and actions, very remote in time into the same person, as well as it does the existences and actions of the immediately preceding moment: so that whatever has the consciousness of present and past actions, is the same person to whom they both belong. Had I the same consciousness that I saw the ark and Noah's flood, as that I saw an overflowing of the Thames last winter, or as that I write now; I could no more doubt that I who write this now, that saw the Thames overflowed last winter, and that viewed the flood at the general deluge, was the same self, place that self in what substance you please, than that I who write this am the same myself now whilst I write (whether I consist of all the same substance, material or immaterial, or no) that I was yesterday; for as to this point of being the same self, it matters not whether this present self be made up of the same or other substances; I being as much concerned, and as justly accountable for any action that was done a thousand years since, appropriated to me now by this self-consciousness, as I am for what I did the last moment.

SELF DEPENDS ON CONSCIOUSNESS

Self is that conscious thinking thing, whatever substance made up of (whether spiritual or material, simple or compounded, it matters not), which is sensible or conscious of pleasure and pain, capable of happiness or misery, and so is concerned for itself, as far as that consciousness extends. Thus every one finds, that, whilst comprehended under that consciousness, the little finger is as much a part of himself as what is most so. Upon separation of this little finger, should this consciousness go along with the little finger, and leave the rest of the body, it is evident the little finger would be the person, the same person, and self then would have nothing to do with the rest of the body. As in this case it is the consciousness that goes along with the substance, when one part is separate from another, which makes the same person, and constitutes this inseparable self; so it is in reference to substances remote in time. That with which the consciousness of this present thinking thing can join itself, makes the same person, and is one self with it, and with nothing else; and so attributes to itself, and owns all the actions of that thing as its own, as far as that consciousness reaches, and no further; as every one who reflects will perceive.

REWARD AND PUNISHMENT

In this personal identity is founded all the right and justice of reward and punishment; happiness and misery being that for which every one is concerned for himself, and not mattering what becomes of any substance not joined to, or affected with that consciousness. For as it is evident in the instance I gave but now, if the consciousness went along with the little finger when it was cut off, that would be the same self which was concerned for the whole body yesterday, as making part of itself, whose actions then it cannot but admit as its own now. Though, if the same body should still live, and immediately from the separation of the little finger have its own peculiar consciousness, whereof the little finger

knew nothing; it would not at all be concerned for it, as a part of itself, or could own any of its actions, or have any of them imputed to him.

This may show us wherein personal identity consists: not in the identity of substance, but, as I have said, in the identity of consciousness; wherein if Socrates and the present mayor of Queenborough agree, they are the same person: if the same Socrates waking and sleeping do not partake of the same consciousness, Socrates waking and sleeping is not the same person. And to punish Socrates waking for what sleeping Socrates thought, and waking Socrates was never conscious of, would be no more of right, than to punish one twin for what his brother-twin did, whereof he knew nothing, because their outsides were so like, that they could not be distinguished; for such twins have been seen.

But yet possibly it will still be objected, suppose I wholly lose the memory of some parts of my life, beyond a possibility of retrieving them, so that perhaps I shall never be conscious of them again; yet am I not the same person that did those actions, had those thoughts that I once was conscious of, though I have now forgot them? To which I answer, that we must here take notice what the word I is applied to; which, in this case, is the man only. And the same man being presumed to be the same person, I is easily here supposed to stand also for the same person. But if it be possible for the same man to have distinct incommunicable consciousness at different times, it is past doubt the same man would at different times make different persons; which, we see, is the sense of mankind in the solemnest declaration of their opinions; human laws not punishing the mad man for the sober man's actions, nor the sober man for what the mad man did, thereby making them two persons: which is somewhat explained by our way of speaking in English, when we say such an one is not himself, or is beside himself; in which phrases it is insinuated, as if those who now, or at least first used them, thought that self was changed, the selfsame person was no longer in that man. . . .

A PROBLEM ABOUT PUNISHMENT

But is not a man drunk and sober the same person? Why else is he punished for the act he commits when drunk, though he be never afterwards conscious of it? Just as much the same person as a man that walks, and does other things in his sleep, is the same person, and is answerable for any mischief he shall do in it. Human laws punish both, with a justice suitable to their way of knowledge; because, in these cases, they cannot distinguish certainly what is real, what counterfeit: and so the ignorance in drunkenness or sleep is not admitted as a plea. For, though punishment be annexed to personality, and personality to consciousness, and the drunkard perhaps be not conscious of what he did, yet human judicatures justly punish him, because the fact is proved against him, but want of consciousness cannot be proved for him. But in the great day, wherein the secrets of all hearts shall be laid open, it may be reasonable to think, no one shall be made to answer for what he knows nothing of; but shall receive his doom, his conscience accusing or excusing him.

CONSCIOUSNESS ALONE MAKES SELF

Nothing but consciousness can unite remote existences into the same person: the identity of substance will not do it; for whatever substance there is, however framed, without consciousness there is no person: and a carcass may be a person, as well as any sort of substance be so without consciousness.

Could we suppose two distinct incommunicable consciousnesses acting in the same body, the one constantly by day, the other by night; and, on the other side, the same consciousness, acting by intervals, two distinct bodies; I ask, in the first case, whether the day and the night man would not be two as distinct persons as Socrates and Plato? And whether, in the second case, there would not be one person in two distinct bodies, as much as one man is the same in two distinct clothings? Nor is it at all material to say, that this same, and this distinct consciousness, in the cases above mentioned, is owing to the same and distinct immaterial substances, bringing it with them to those bodies; which, whether true or no, alters not the case; since it is evident the personal identity would equally be determined by the consciousness, whether that consciousness were annexed to some individual immaterial substance or no. For, granting that the thinking substance in man must be necessarily supposed immaterial, it is evident that immaterial thinking thing may sometimes part with its past consciousness, and be restored to it again, as appears in the forgetfulness men often have of their past actions: and the mind many times recovers the memory of a past consciousness, which it had lost for twenty years together. Make these intervals of memory and forgetfulness to take their turns regularly by day and night, and you have two persons with the same immaterial spirit, as much as in the former instance two persons with the same body. So that self is not determined by identity or diversity or substance, which it cannot be sure of, but only by identity of consciousness. . . .

Further Questions

1. What is the point of Locke's "prince and cobbler" example? Do you agree with Locke's account of it? Would it affect your opinion if we imagine that whereas the prince's consciousness goes to the cobbler, the cobbler's consciousness just vanishes? Would it matter if the prince's consciousness went to ten different cobblers, and the consciousness of all ten just vanished?

2. Imagine a Star Trek–style "beamer" that dematerializes a person's body in one place—say, inside a spaceship—and then instantaneously creates an exact replica out of new matter at another place—say, on a planet's surface. Would Locke say that the person in the spaceship and the person on the planet's surface were the same person? Would you?

3. Is there any useful distinction to be drawn between "the same person" and "an exact replica"? If so, how would you draw it?

Further Readings

Ayer, A. J. and Raymond Winch, eds. *British Empirical Philosophers*. New York: Simon & Schuster, 1968. Excellent on the writings of Locke, Berkeley, and Hume.

Sacks, Oliver. *The Man Who Mistook His Wife for a Hat*. New York: Harper & Row, 1987. Brain problems that lead to identity problems.

15   Personal Identity

DAVID HUME

The Scottish philosopher David Hume (1711–1776), the last of the three British empiricists, was a philosophical extremist. He developed the empiricism of John Locke and George Berkeley—the central idea of which is that our knowledge of the world is derived from experience—to its logical conclusion. Whereas Locke's version of empiricism is tempered by common sense, often inconsistently, and Berkeley made an exception to his empiricist principles to protect his notion of the self, Hume threw common sense to the winds and developed a consistent version of empiricism.

A sympathetic critic of Hume once remarked that by making empiricism self-consistent, Hume "made it incredible." This selection by Hume illustrates what the critic meant. By applying his empiricist principles to the notion of "self," Hume reveals the sort of bizarre consequences that he argues follow from the seemingly innocent premise that our knowledge of the self, too, must be derived from experience.

Reading Questions

1. Hume claims he has no "impression" of the self. What does he mean by "impression"? Is he right?
2. Hume thinks that the labels we use to refer to ourselves mask the impermanence of who and what we really are. Why does he think this? Is he right?
3. What does Hume mean by "perception"?
4. What is the importance of *resemblance*, *causation*, and *memory* in Hume's argument?
5. Why does Hume think that the question of personal identity can never be decided? (Decided by *whom*?) What does he mean by claiming that personal identity is a *grammatical* rather than a *philosophical* difficulty?
6. What does he say some other philosophers think about the self?
7. Why, according to Hume, do we believe in personal identity?

THERE ARE SOME PHILOSOPHERS, who imagine we are every moment intimately conscious of what we call our *Self*; that we feel its existence and its continuance in existence; and are certain, beyond the evidence of a demonstration, both of its perfect identity and simplicity. . . . For my part, when I enter most intimately into what I call *myself*, I always stumble on some particular perception or other, of heat or cold, light or shade, love or hatred, pain or pleasure. I never can catch *myself* at any time

From David Hume, A Treatise of Human Nature. *First published in 1738.*

without a perception, and never can observe any thing but the perception. When my perceptions are remov'd for any time, as by sound sleep; so long am I insensible of *myself*, and may truly be said not to exist. And were all my perceptions remov'd by death, and cou'd I neither think, nor feel, nor see, nor love, nor hate after the dissolution of my body, I shou'd be entirely annihilated, nor do I conceive what is farther requisite to make me a perfect non-entity. If any one upon serious and unprejudic'd reflexion, thinks he has a different notion of *himself*, I must confess I can reason no longer with him. All I can allow him is, that he may be in the right as well as I, and that we are essentially different in this particular. He may, perhaps, perceive something simple and continu'd, which he calls *himself*; tho' I am certain there is no such principle in me.

But setting aside some metaphysicians of this kind, I may venture to affirm of the rest of mankind, that they are nothing but a bundle or collection of different perceptions, which succeed each other with an inconceivable rapidity, and are in a perpetual flux and movement. Our eyes cannot turn in their sockets without varying our perceptions. Our thought is still more variable than our sight; and all our other senses and faculties contribute to this change; nor is there any single power of the soul, which remains unalterably the same, perhaps for one moment. The mind is a kind of theatre, where several perceptions successively make their appearance; pass, re-pass, glide away, and mingle in an infinite variety of postures and situations. There is properly no *simplicity* in it at one time, nor *identity* in different; whatever natural propension we may have to imagine that simplicity and identity. The comparison of the theatre must not mislead us. They are the successive perceptions only, that constitute the mind; nor have we the most distant notion of the place, where these scenes are represented, or of the materials, of which it is compos'd.

What then gives us so great a propension to ascribe an identity to these successive perceptions, and to suppose ourselves possest of an invariable and uninterrupted existence thro' the whole course of our lives? . . .

. . . every distinct perception, which enters into the composition of the mind, is a distinct existence, and is different, and distinguishable, and separable from every other perception, either contemporary or successive. But, as, notwithstanding this distinction and separability, we suppose the whole train of perceptions to be united by identity, a question naturally arises concerning this relation of identity; whether it be something that really binds our several perceptions together, or only associates their ideas in the imagination. That is, in other words, whether in pronouncing concerning the identity of a person, we observe some real bond among his perceptions, or only feel one among the ideas we form of them. This question we might easily decide, if we wou'd recollect what has been already prov'd at large, that the understanding never observes any real connexion among objects, and that even the union of cause and effect, when strictly examin'd, resolves itself into a customary association of ideas. For from thence it evidently follows, that identity is nothing really belonging to these different perceptions, and uniting them together; but is merely a quality, which we attribute to them, because of the union of their ideas in the imagination, when we reflect upon them. Now the only qualities, which can give ideas an union in the imagination, are these three relations above-mention'd. These are the uniting principles in the ideal world, and without them every distinct object is separable by the mind, and may be separately consider'd, and appears not to have any more connexion with any other object, than if disjoin'd by the greatest difference and remoteness. 'Tis, therefore, on some of these three relations of resemblance, contiguity and causation, that identity depends; and as the very essence of these relations consists in their producing an easy transition of ideas; it follows, that our notions of personal identity, proceed entirely from the smooth and uninterrupted progress of the thought along a train of connected ideas, according to the principles above-explain'd.

The only question, therefore, which remains, is, by what relations this uninterrupted progress of our thought is produc'd, when we consider the successive existence of a mind or thinking person. And here 'tis evident we must confine ourselves to resemblance and causation, and must drop contiguity, which has little or no influence in the present case.

To begin with *resemblance;* suppose we cou'd see clearly into the breast of another, and observe that succession of perceptions, which constitutes his mind or thinking principle, and suppose that he always preserves the memory of a considerable part of past perceptions; 'tis evident that nothing cou'd more contribute to the bestowing a relation on this succession amidst all its variations. For what is the memory but a faculty, by which we raise up the images of past perceptions? And as an image necessarily resembles its object, must not the frequent placing of these resembling perceptions in the chain of thought, convey the imagination more easily from one link to another, and make the whole seem like the continuance of one object? In this particular, then, the memory not only discovers the identity, but also contributes to its production, by producing the relation of resemblance among the perceptions. The case is the same whether we consider ourselves or others.

As to *causation;* we may observe, that the true idea of the human mind, is to consider it as a system of different perceptions or different existences, which are link'd together by the relation of cause and effect, and mutually produce, destroy, influence, and modify each other. Our impressions give rise to their correspondent ideas; and these ideas in their turn produce other impressions. One thought chases another, and draws after it a third, by which it is expell'd in its turn. In this respect, I cannot compare the soul more properly to any thing than to a republic or commonwealth, in which the several members are united by the reciprocal ties of government and subordination, and give rise to other persons, who propagate the same republic in the incessant changes of its parts. And as the same individual republic may not only change its members, but also its laws and constitutions; in like manner the same person may vary his character and disposition, as well as his impressions and ideas, without losing his identity. Whatever changes he endures, his several parts are still connected by the relation of causation. And in this view our identity with regard to the passions serves to corroborate that with regard to the imagination, by the making our distant perceptions influence each other, and by giving us a present concern for our past or future pains or pleasures.

As memory alone acquaints us with the continuance and extent of this succession of perceptions,

'tis to be consider'd, upon that account chiefly, as the source of personal identity. Had we no memory, we never shou'd have any notion of causation, nor consequently of that chain of causes and effects, which constitute our self or person. But having once acquir'd this notion of causation from the memory, we can extend the same chain of causes, and consequently the identity of our persons beyond our memory, and can comprehend times, and circumstances, and actions, which we have entirely forgot, but suppose in general to have existed. For how few of our past actions are there, of which we have any memory? Who can tell me, for instance, what were his thoughts and actions on the first of *January* 1715, the 11th of *March* 1719, and the 3d of *August* 1733? Or will he affirm, because he has entirely forgot the incidents of these days, that the present self is not the same person with the self of that time; and by that means overturn all the most establish'd notions of personal identity? In this view, therefore, memory does not so much *produce* as *discover* personal identity, by shewing us the relation of cause and effect among our different perceptions. 'Twill be incumbent on those, who affirm that memory produces entirely our personal identity, to give a reason why we can thus extend our identity beyond our memory.

The whole of this doctrine leads us to a conclusion, which is of great importance in the present affair, viz. that all the nice and subtle questions concerning personal identity can never possibly be decided, and are to be regarded rather as grammatical than as philosophical difficulties. Identity depends on the relations of ideas; and these relations produce identity, by means of that easy transition they occasion. But as the relations, and the easiness of the transition may diminish by insensible degrees, we have no just standard, by which we can decide any dispute concerning the time, when they acquire or lose a title to the name of identity. All the disputes concerning the identity of connected objects are merely verbal, except so far as the relation of parts gives rise to some fiction or imaginary principle of union, as we have already observ'd.

Further Questions

1. Hume felt that although we have a natural disposition to think of ourselves as continuing things, an experiential examination of the underlying reality reveals that there is no *thing* that continues, but rather a series of separate "things," none of which individually is a person, that somehow get linked together to form us. When you look experientially at yourself, do you find that Hume's claim is true? Whether or not you do, do you find yourself resisting the idea (through fear) that it might be true? If so, what does that tell you about yourself?
2. We ordinarily suppose that physics has the last word about what material objects *are*. Shouldn't psychology or biology, then, have the last word about what persons are? If so, what do psychology and biology say? (If you don't know, ask a psychologist and a biologist.) If not, why not?
3. Do you find it odd that you can know lots of things, but among the things you really know least of all is yourself? If so, how would you explain this oddity?

Further Readings

Skinner, B. F. "What Is Man?" in *Beyond Freedom and Human Dignity*. New York: Bantam Books, 1972, pp. 175–206. A behaviorist criticizes the idea that there is a self within.

Tulku, Tarthang. "Tyranny of the I," Ch. 31 of *Knowledge of Freedom*. Berkeley, CA: Dharma Publishing, 1984, pp. 318–326. On how our experiencing the world through the lens of self may hurt us.

Critique of Locke and Hume on Behalf of Common Sense

16

THOMAS REID

Thomas Reid (1710–1796) was the son of a minister who also became a minister. A severe critic of the "theory of ideas" promulgated by Descartes, Locke, Berkeley, and Hume, according to which it is *ideas*, not *real objects*, that are immediately given in perception. Reid founded the Scottish School of Common Sense. In his view, certain fundamental commonsense beliefs need no proof because they cannot seriously be doubted; there is nothing more certain to which one might appeal in doubting them.

Reading Questions:

1. How does Reid say that he is understanding the word identity? Does it matter that he does not define it? Can every word be defined?
2. By *personality* Reid means *personhood*. What does he mean in saying that people place their personhood in something that cannot be divided, or consist in parts?
3. What are Reid's main criticisms of Locke? Of Hume?

... IT IS PROPER TO CONSIDER what is meant by identity in general, what by our own personal identity, and how we are led into that invincible belief and conviction which every man has of his own personal identity, as far as his memory reaches.

Identity in general I take to be a relation between a thing which is known to exist at one time, and a thing which is known to have existed at another time. If you ask whether they are one and the same, or two different things, every man of common sense understands the meaning of your question perfectly. Whence we may infer with certainty, that every man of common sense has a clear and distinct notion of identity.

If you ask a definition of identity, I confess I can give none; it is too simple a notion to admit of logical definition ...

I see evidently that identity supposes *an uninterrupted continuance of existence.* That which has ceased to exist cannot be the same with that which afterwards begins to exist; for this would be to suppose a being to exist after it ceased to exist, and to have had existence before it was produced, which are manifest contradictions. Continued uninterrupted existence is therefore necessarily implied in identity. Hence we may infer, that identity cannot, in its proper sense, be applied to our pains, our pleasures, our thoughts, or any operation of our minds. The pain felt this day is not the same individual pain which I felt yesterday, though they may be *similar* in kind and degree, and have the same cause. The same may be said of every feeling, and of every operation of mind. They are all successive in their nature, like time itself, no two moments of which can be the same moment. It is otherwise with the parts of absolute space. They always are, and were, and will be the same. So far, I think, we proceed upon clear ground in fixing the notion of identity in general.

NATURE AND ORIGIN OF OUR IDEA OF PERSONAL IDENTITY

It is perhaps more difficult to ascertain with precision the meaning of *personality;* but it is not necessary in the present subject: it is sufficient for our purpose to observe, that all mankind place their personality in something that *cannot be divided, or consist of parts.* A part of a person in a manifest absurdity. When a man loses his estate, his health, his strength, he is still the same person, and has lost nothing of his personality. If he has a leg or an arm cut off, he is the same person he was before. The amputated member is no part of his person, otherwise it would have a right to a part of his estate, and be liable for a part of his engagements. It would be entitled to a share of his merit and demerit, which is manifestly absurd. A person is something indivisible, and is what Leibniz calls a *monad.*

My personal identity, therefore, implies the continued existence of that indivisible thing which I call *myself.* Whatever this self may be, it is something which thinks, and deliberates, and resolves, and acts, and suffers. I am not thought, I am not action, I am not feeling; I am something that thinks, and acts, and suffers. My thoughts, and actions, and feelings, change every moment; they have no continued, but a successive, existence; but that *self,* or *I,* to which they belong, is permanent, and has the same relation to all the succeeding thoughts, actions, and feelings which I call mine.

Such are the notions that I have of my personal identity. But perhaps it may be said, this may all be fancy without reality. How do you know, — what evidence have you, — that there is such a permanent self which has a claim to all the thoughts, actions, and feelings which you call yours?

To this I answer, that the proper evidence I have of all this is *remembrance.* I remember that twenty years ago I conversed with such a person; I remember several things that passed in that conversation: my memory testifies, not only that this was done, but that it was done by me who now remember it. If it was done by me, I must have existed at that time, and continued to exist from that time to the present: if the identical person whom I call myself had not a part in that conversation, my memory is fallacious; it gives a distinct and positive testimony of what is not true. Every man in his senses believes what he distinctly remembers, and everything he remembers convinces him that he existed at the same time remembered.

From Essays on the Intellectual Powers of Man, *first published in England in 1785, and* An Inquiry into the Human Mind on the Principles of Common Sense, *first published in 1764.*

Although memory gives the most irresistible evidence of my being the identical person that did such a thing, at such a time, I may have other good evidence of things which befell me, and which I do not remember: I know who bore me, and suckled me, but I do not remember these events.

It may here be observed, (though the observation would have been unnecessary, if some great philosophers had not contradicted it), that it is not my remembering any action of mine that *makes* me to be the person who did it. This remembrance makes me to *know* assuredly that I did it; *but I might have done it, though I did not remember it.* That relation to me, which is expressed by saying that *I did it,* would be the same, though I had not the least remembrance of it. . . .

When we pass judgment on the identity of other persons than ourselves, we proceed upon other grounds, and determine from a variety of circumstances, which sometimes produce the firmest assurance, and sometimes leave room for doubt. The identity of person has often furnished matter of serious litigation before tribunals of justice. But no man of a sound mind ever doubted of his own identity, as far as he distinctly remembered. . . .

Thus it appears, that the evidence we have of our own identity, as far back as we remember, is totally of a different kind from the evidence we have of the identity of other persons, or of objects of sense. The first is grounded on *memory,* and gives undoubted certainty. The last is grounded on *similarity,* and on other circumstances, which in many cases are not so decisive as to leave no room for doubt.

It may likewise be observed, that the identity of *objects of sense* is never perfect. All bodies, as they consist of innumerable parts that may be disjoined from them by a great variety of causes, are subject to continual changes of their substance, increasing, diminishing, changing insensibly. When such alterations are gradual, because languages could not afford a different name for every different state of such a changeable being, it retains the same name, and is considered as the same thing. Thus we say of an old regiment, that it did such a thing a century ago, though there now is not a man alive who then belonged to it. We say a tree is the same in the seed-bed and in the forest. A ship of war, which has successively changed her anchors, her tackle, her sails, her masts, her planks, and her timbers, while she keeps the same name, is the same.

The identity, therefore, which we ascribe to bodies, whether natural or artificial, is not perfect identity; it is rather something which, for the conveniency of speech, we call identity. It admits of a great change of the subject, providing the change be *gradual;* sometimes, even of a total change. And the changes which in common language are made consistent with identity differ from those that are thought to destroy it, not in *kind,* but in *number* and *degree.* It has no fixed nature when applied to bodies; and questions about the identity of a body are very often questions about words. But identity, when applied to person, has no ambiguity, and admits not of degrees, or of more and less. It is the foundation of all rights and obligations, and of all accountableness; and the notion of it is fixed and precise.

STRICTURES ON LOCKE'S ACCOUNT OF PERSONAL IDENTITY

In a long chapter, *Of Identity and Diversity,* Mr. Locke has made many ingenious and just observations, and some which I think cannot be defended. . . .

This doctrine has some strange consequences, which the author was aware of. (1) Such as, that if the same consciousness can be transferred from one intelligent being to another, which he thinks we cannot show to be impossible, *then two or twenty intelligent beings may be the same person.* (2) And if the intelligent being may lose the consciousness of the actions done by him, which surely is possible, then he is not the person that did those actions; so that *one intelligent being may be two or twenty different persons,* if he shall so often lose the consciousness of his former actions.

(3) There is another consequence of this doctrine, which follows no less necessarily, though Mr. Locke probably did not see it. It is, *that a man may be, and at the same time not be, the person that did a particular action.* Suppose a brave officer to have been flogged when a boy at school for robbing an orchard, to have taken a standard from the enemy in his first campaign, and to have been

made a general in advanced life; suppose, also, which must be admitted to be possible, that, when he took the standard, he was conscious of having been flogged at school, and that, when made a general, he was conscious of his taking the standard, but had absolutely lost the consciousness of his flogging. These things being supposed, it follows, from Mr. Locke's doctrine, that he was flogged at school is the same person who took the standard, and that he who took the standard is the same person who was made a general. Whence it follows, if there by any truth in logic, that the general is the same person with him who was flogged at school. But the general's consciousness does not reach so far back as his flogging; therefore, according to Mr. Locke's doctrine, he is not the person who was flogged. Therefore the general is, and at the same time is not, the same person with him who was flogged at school.

Leaving the consequences of this doctrine to those who have leisure to trace them, we may observe, with regard to the doctrine itself, —

First, that Mr. Locke attributes to consciousness the conviction we have of our past actions, as if a man may now be conscious of what he did twenty years ago. It is impossible to understand the meaning of this, unless by *consciousness* he meant *memory,* the only faculty by which we have an immediate knowledge of our past actions. . . .

When, therefore, Mr. Locke's notion of personal identity is properly expressed, it is, that personal identity *consists in distinct remembrance;* for, even in the popular sense, to say that I am conscious of a past action means nothing else than that I distinctly remember that I did it.

Secondly, it may be observed, that, in this doctrine, not only is consciousness confounded with memory, but, which is still more strange, *personal identity* is confounded with *the evidence which we have of our personal identity.*

It is very true, that my remembrance that I did such a thing is the evidence I have that I am the identical person who did it. And this, I am apt to think Mr. Locke meant. But to say that my remembrance that I did such a thing, or my consciousness, *makes* me the person who did it, is, in my apprehension, an absurdity too gross to be entertained by any man who attends to the meaning

of it; for it is to attribute to memory or consciousness a strange magical power of producing its object, though that object must have existed before the memory or consciousness which produced it. Consciousness is the testimony of one faculty; memory is the testimony of another faculty; and to say that the testimony is the cause of the thing testified, this surely is absurd, if any thing be, and could not have been said by Mr. Locke, if he had not confounded the testimony with the thing testified.

When a horse that was stolen is found and claimed by the owner, the only evidence he can have, or that a judge or witnesses can have, that this is the very identical horse which was his property, is similitude. But would it not be ridiculous from this to infer that the identity of a horse *consists* in similitude only? The only *evidence* I have that I am the identical person who did such actions is, that I remember distinctly I did them; or, as Mr. Locke expresses it, I am conscious I did them. To infer from this, that personal identity consists in consciousness, is an argument which, if it had any force, would prove the identity of a stolen horse to consist solely in similitude.

Thirdly, is it not strange that the sameness or identity of a person should consist in a thing *which is continually changing,* and is not any two minutes the same?

Our consciousness, our memory, and every operation of the mind, are still flowing like the water of a river, or like time itself. The consciousness I have this moment can no more be the same consciousness I had last moment, than this moment can be the last moment. Identity can only be affirmed of things which have a continued existence. Consciousness, and every kind of thought, are transient and momentary, and have no continued existence; and therefore, if personal identity consisted in consciousness, it would certainly follow, that *no man is the same person any two moments of his life;* and as the right and justice of reward and punishment are founded on personal identity, no man could be responsible for his actions. . . .

Fourthly, there are many expressions used by Mr. Locke, in speaking of personal identity, which to me are altogether unintelligible, unless we suppose that he confounded that sameness or identity which we ascribe to an individual with the identity which, in common discourse, is often ascribed to many individuals of the same species.

When we say that pain and pleasure, consciousness and memory, are the same in all men, this sameness can only mean similarity, or sameness *of kind.* That the pain of one man can be the same individual pain with that of another man is no less impossible, than that one man should be another man: the pain felt by me yesterday can no more be the pain I feel today, than yesterday can be this day; and the same thing may be said of every passion and of every operation of the mind. The same kind or species of operation may be in different men, or in the same man at different times, but it is impossible that the same individual operation should be in different men, or in the same man at different times.

When Mr. Locke, therefore, speaks of "the same consciousness being continued through a succession of different substances"; when he speaks of "repeating the idea of a past action, with the same consciousness we had of it at the first," and of "the same consciousness extending to actions past and to come"; these expressions are to me unintelligible, unless he means not the same individual consciousness, but a consciousness that is similar, or of the same kind. If our personal identity consists in consciousness, as this consciousness cannot be the same individually any two moments, but only of the *same kind,* it would follow, that we are not for any two moments the same individual persons, but the same *kind* of persons. As our consciousness sometimes ceases to exist, as in sound sleep, our personal identity must cease with it. Mr. Locke allows, that the same thing cannot have two beginnings of existence, so that our identity would be irrecoverably gone every time we cease to think, if it was but a moment. . . .

STRICTURES ON HUME'S ACCOUNT OF PERSONAL IDENTITY

Locke's principle must be, that identity consists in remembrance; and consequently a man must lose his personal identity with regard to every thing he forgets.

Nor are these the only instances whereby our philosophy concerning the mind appears to be very fruitful in creating doubts, but very unhappy in resolving them.

Descartes, Malebranche, and Locke, have all employed their genius and skill, to prove the existence of a material world; and with very bad success. . . .

The present age, I apprehend, has not produced two more acute or more practised in this part of philosophy than [George Berkeley] the Bishop of Cloyne, and the author of the Treatise of Human Nature [David Hume, who] . . . undoes the world of spirits, and leaves nothing in nature but ideas and impressions, without any subject on which they may be impressed.

It seems to be a peculiar strain of humor in this author, to set out in his introduction, by promising with a grave face, no less than a complete system of the sciences, upon a foundation entirely new, to wit, that of human nature; when the intention of the whole work is to show, that there is neither human nature nor science in the world. It may perhaps be unreasonable to complain of this conduct in an author, who neither believes his own existence, nor that of his reader; and therefore could not mean to disappoint him, or to laugh at his credulity. Yet I cannot imagine, that the author of Treatise of Human Nature is so skeptical as to plead this apology. He believed, against his principles, that he should be read, and that he should retain his personal identity, till he reaped the honor and reputation justly due to his metaphysical *acumen.* Indeed he ingenuously acknowledges, that it was only in solitude and retirement that he could yield any assent to his own philosophy; society, like daylight, dispelled the darkness and fogs of skepticism, and made him yield to the dominion of common sense. Nor did I ever hear him charged with doing any thing, even in solitude, that argued such a degree of skepticism, as his principles maintain. . . .

That the natural issue of this system is skepticism with regard to every thing except the existence of our ideas, and of their necessary relations which appear upon comparing them, is evident: for ideas being the only objects of thought, and having no existence but when we are conscious of them, it necessarily follows, that there is no object of our thought, which can have a continued and

NARRATION AND PERSONAL IDENTITY

Alasdair MacIntyre

A central thesis then begins to emerge: man is in his actions and practice, as well as in his fictions, essentially a story-telling animal. He is not essentially, but becomes through his history, a teller of stories that aspire to truth. But the key question for men is not about their own authorship; I can only answer the question "What am I to do?" if I can answer the prior question "Of what story or stories do I find myself a part?" We enter human society, that is, with one or more imputed characters—roles into which we have been drafted—and we have to learn what they are in order to be able to understand how others respond to us and how our responses to them are apt to be construed. It is through hearing stories about wicked stepmothers, lost children, good but misguided kings, wolves that suckle twin boys, youngest sons who receive no inheritance but must make their own way in the world and eldest sons who waste their inheritance on riotous living and go into exile to live with the swine, that children learn or mislearn both what a child and what a parent is, what the cast of characters may be in the drama into which they have been born and what the ways of the world are. Deprive children of stories and you leave them unscripted, anxious stutterers in their actions as in their words. Hence there is no way to

give us an understanding of any society, including our own, except through the stock of stories which constitute its initial dramatic resources. Mythology, in its original sense, is at the heart of things. . . .

What the narrative concept of selfhood requires is thus twofold. One the one hand, I am what I may justifiably be taken by others to be in the course of living out a story that runs from my birth to my death; I am the *subject* of a history that is my own and no one else's, that has its own peculiar meaning. When someone complains—as do some of those who attempt or commit suicide—that his or her life is meaningless, he or she is often and perhaps characteristically complaining that the narrative of their life has become unintelligible to them, that it lacks any point, any movement towards a climax or a *telos*. Hence the point of doing any one thing rather than another at crucial junctures in their lives seems to such a person to have been lost.

. . . [P]ersonal identity is just that identity presupposed by the unity of the character which the unity of a narrative requires. Without such unity there would not be subjects of whom stories could be told.

From *After Virtue* (1981).

permanent existence. Body and spirit, cause and effect, time and space, to which we were wont to ascribe an existence independent of our thought, are all turned out of existence by this short dilemma: Either these things are ideas of sensation or reflection, or they are not: if they are ideas of sensation or reflection, they can have no existence but when we are conscious of them; if they are not ideas of sensation or reflection, they are words without any meaning.

Neither Descartes nor Locke perceived this consequence of their system concerning ideas.

Bishop Berkeley was the first who discovered it. . . . But with regard to the existence of spirits or minds, he does not admit the consequence; and if he had admitted it, he must have been an absolute skeptic. . . .

Thus we see, that Descartes and Locke take the road that leads to skepticism, without knowing the end of it; but they stop short for want of light to carry them farther. Berkeley, frighted at the appearance of the dreadful abyss, starts aside, and avoids it. But the author of Treatise of Human Nature, more daring and intrepid, without turning aside to the right hand or to the left, like Virgil's Alecto, shoots directly into the gulf. . . .

We ought, however, to do this justice both to the Bishop of Cloyne and to the author of the Treatise of Human Nature, to acknowledge, that their conclusions are justly drawn from the doctrine of ideas, which has been so universally received. On the other hand, from the character of Bishop Berkeley, and of his predecessors Descartes, Locke, and Malebranche, we may venture to say, that if they had seen all the consequences of this doctrine, as clearly as the author before mentioned did, they would have suspected it vehemently, and examined it more carefully than they appear to have done.

The theory of ideas, like the Trojan horse, had a specious appearance both of innocence and beauty; but if those philosophers had known that it carried in its belly death and destruction to all science and common sense, they would not have broken down their walls to give it admittance. . . .

It is certain, no man can conceive or believe smelling to exist of itself, without a mind, or something that has the power of smelling, of which it is called a sensation, an operation or feeling. Yet if any man should demand a proof, that sensation cannot be without a mind or sentient being, I confess that I can give none; and that to pretend to prove it, seems to me almost as absurd as to deny it.

This might have been said without any apology before the Treatise of Human Nature appeared in the world. For till that time, no man, as far as I know, ever thought either of calling in question that principle, or of giving a reason for his belief of it. Whether thinking beings were of an ethereal or igneous nature, whether material or immaterial, was variously disputed; but that thinking is an operation of some kind of being or other, was always taken for granted, as a principle that could not possibly admit of doubt. . . .

If there are certain principles, as I think there are, which the constitution of our nature leads us to believe, and which we are under a necessity to take for granted in the common concerns of life, without being able to give a reason for them; these are what we call the principles of common sense; and what is manifestly contrary to them, is what we call absurd. . . .

It is a fundamental principle of [Hume's] ideal system, that every object of thought must be an impression, or an idea, that is, a faint copy of some preceding impression. This is a principle so commonly received, that the author above mentioned, although his whole system is built upon it, never offers the least proof of it. It is upon this principle, as a fixed point, that he erects his metaphysical engines, to overturn heaven and earth, body and spirit. And indeed, in my apprehension, it is altogether sufficient for the purpose. For if impressions and ideas are the only objects of thought, then heaven and earth, and body and spirit, and every thing you please, must signify only impressions and ideas, or they must be words without any meaning. It seems, therefore, that this notion, however strange, is closely connected with the received doctrine of ideas, and we must either admit the conclusion, or call in question the premises. . . .

The triumph of ideas was completed by the Treatise of Human Nature, which discards spirits also, and leaves ideas and impressions as the sole existences in the universe. What if at last, having nothing else to contend with, they should fall foul of one another, and leave no existence in nature at all? This would surely bring philosophy into danger; for what should we have left to talk or to dispute about? However, hitherto these philosophers acknowledge the existence of impressions and ideas: they acknowledge certain laws of attraction, or rules of precedence, according to which ideas and impressions range themselves in various forms, and succeed one another: but that they should belong to a mind, as its proper goods and chattels, this they have found to be a vulgar error. These ideas are as free and independent as the birds of the air. . . .They make the whole furniture of the universe; starting into existence, or out of it, without any cause; combining into parcels which the vulgar call *minds;* and succeeding one another by fixed laws, without time, place, or author of these laws. . . .

The Treatise of Human Nature . . . seems to have made but a bad return, by bestowing upon them this independent existence; since thereby they are turned out of house and home, and set adrift in the world, without friend or connection, without a rag to cover their nakedness; and who knows but the whole system of ideas may perish by the indiscreet zeal of their friends to exalt them?

However this may be, it is certainly a most amazing discovery that thought and ideas may be without any thinking being; a discovery big with consequences which cannot easily be traced by those deluded mortals who think and reason in the common track. We were always apt to imagine, that thought supposed a thinker, and love a lover, and treason a traitor; but this, it seems, was all a mistake; and it is found out, that there may be treason without a traitor, and love without a lover, laws without a legislator, and punishment without a sufferer, succession without time, and motion without any thing moved, or space in which it may move; or if, in these cases, ideas are the lover, the sufferer, the traitor, it were to be wished that the author of this discovery had farther condescended to acquaint us, whether ideas can converse together, and be under obligations of duty or gratitude to each other; whether they can make promises, and enter into leagues and covenants, and fulfil or break them, and be punished for the breach? If one set of ideas makes a covenant, another breaks it, and a third is punished for it, there is reason to think that justice is no natural virtue in this system.

It seemed very natural to think, that the Treatise of Human Nature required an author, and a very ingenious one too; but now we learn, that it is only a set of ideas which came together, and arranged themselves by certain associations and attractions.

After all, this curious system appears not to be fitted to the present state of human nature. How far it may suit some choice spirits, who are refined from the dregs of common sense, I cannot say. It is acknowledged, I think, that even these can enter into this system only in their most speculative hours, when they soar so high in pursuit of those self-existent ideas, as to lose sight of all other things. But when they condescend to mingle again with the human race, and to converse with a friend, a companion, or a fellow citizen, the ideal system[1] vanishes; common sense, like an irresistible torrent, carries them along; and, in spite of all their reasoning and philosophy, they believe their own existence, and the existence of other things. . . .

This philosophy is like a hobby-horse, which a man in bad health may ride in his closet, without hurting his reputation; but if he should take him abroad with him to church, or to the exchange, or to the play house, his heir would immediately call a jury, and seize his estate.

1. [Berkeley's idealism.]

Further Questions

1. Do you agree with Reid that everyone "places their personhood" in something that cannot be divided, or consist in parts?
2. Imagine that you are Locke, and respond to Reid's criticisms.
3. Imagine that you are Hume, and respond to Reid's criticisms.

Further Readings

Grave, S.A., *The Scottish Philosophy of Common Sense*. Oxford: Clarendon Press, 1960.
Lehrer, Keith, *Thomas Reid*. Cambridge University Press, 1994.

Personal Identity from Plato to Parfit   17

RAYMOND MARTIN

Raymond Martin teaches at the University of Maryland–College Park. He writes primarily in the areas of personal identity theory, philosophy of historical methodology, and history of philosophy. He is the author of *The Past within Us* (Princeton: Princeton University Press, 1989), *Self-Concern* (Cambridge: Cambridge University Press, 1998), and *The Elusive Messiah* (Boulder, CO: Westview, 1999). He is co-author (with John Barresi) of *Naturalization of the Soul: Self and Personal Identity in the Eighteenth Century* (New York: Routledge, 2000). He is also the editor of *J. Krishnamurti: Reflections on the Self* (Lasalle, IL: Open Court, 1997) and co-author or co-editor (with Daniel Kolak) of several books.

In the selection that follows, written especially for this volume, Martin surveys the history of personal identity theory from its earliest beginnings to present times.

Reading Questions

1. What is the difference between the "soul view" and the "relations view" of personal identity? Do you have a soul? How do you know?
2. How does the question of personal identity differ from that of what matters primarily in survival? Which question, in your view, is more important?
3. How does the "intrinsic relations view" of personal identity differ from the "extrinsic relations view"? Which view, if either, do you favor?
4. What is a "fission example"? What is the importance of fission examples in deciding how we should analyze personal identity? What is their importance to the question of what matters primarily in survival?
5. Explain the difference between a three-dimensional and a four-dimensional view of persons. Explain the importance of the difference between them to questions of personal identity and what matters in survival.

EACH OF US ASSUMES that we remain who we are, through various changes, from moment to moment, hour to hour, day to day, and so on. We persist until we cease, perhaps at bodily death. Each of us also assumes that one of our most fundamental egoistic desires is to persist. As we say, we want to live. But what *accounts* for the fact, if it is a fact, that we remain the same persons over time and through various changes? That question is the philosophical problem of personal identity. And when, in ordinary circumstances, you want to per-

sist, what is it that you *really* want, that is, that you want fundamentally? That question is the philosophical problem of what matters primarily in survival. It is commonly assumed that when people want to persist, what they really want is simply to persist — that is, that there be people in the future who are the same persons as they are now. That answer is the thesis that identity is primarily what matters in survival. However, another possibility is that what *some* people really want is merely that certain parts of themselves (e.g., those parts of their psychologies that they value) continue, whether or not the continuation of those parts suffices for the continuation of *them*.

In a very strict sense of *same person,* as soon as you change, no matter how or how minutely, you cease. In this sense of *same person,* no one lasts for long. For obvious reasons, this sense of *same person* is not particularly useful. Its not being useful is different from its being false. It could be true and not useful. Or there may be no truth of the matter about how long each of us lasts. In any case, you will almost always think of yourself as remaining the same person through changes. Others will think of you this way also. Of course, some changes — biological death is the most compelling example — may cause you to cease. But, ordinarily we suppose, not just any change will cause you to cease. The problem of personal identity is the problem of explaining how, in spite of your changing in various ways, you manage to remain the same person.

A similar question arises in the case of any object — rock, plant, animal, automobile — that persists over time. The problem of personal identity might be merely a special case of the more general problem of the identity of any temporally extended object. The same solution might work for everything. Or personal identity might be different. Rather than worrying about this more general question, we shall focus on personal identity. We do not have to start from scratch. For as long as people have thought about the nature of things, they have thought about what accounts for the fact that they persist. We can begin, then, by surveying their solutions. Only a few basic solutions have been proposed, and each of them is associated with a particular historical period when philosophers generally — or at least the ones that we now think mattered most — considered it to be the right answer.

FROM PLATO UNTIL LOCKE: THE SOUL VIEW

In classical times, there was not really a philosophical problem of personal identity. Rather, there was a problem of death. The question of interest was not what accounts for the fact that we persist, but whether bodily death is the end. Personal identity entered the discussion through the back door, in the service of answering this more pressing ques-

tion. Then, just as now, most people feared death. And then, just as now, many people had intimations that bodily death is not the end, that somehow people survive it.

Plato's dialog, *Phaedo,* is a dramatic reenactment of the conversation that took place between Socrates, who was Plato's teacher, and a few of Socrates' students. The conversation took place in Socrates' jail cell, on the day that he was put to death. In this dialog, the character, Socrates, argues that people survive their bodily deaths. But beyond that, he explains in a way that no one had ever explained before what accounts for the fact that people — we — persist. In his view, the fact that we have (or are) immaterial souls explains it.

In ancient times (and still today), almost everyone assumed that if people survive their bodily deaths, there must be a vehicle (or medium) for each of their survivals. However, even before anyone had thought of the idea of an immaterial (unextended) soul, there was a ready vehicle available: fine matter. When Socrates was alive, many Greeks thought that the soul leaves the body when the person who dies expels his last breath; apparently they also thought that, at least at that moment, the soul *is* that last breath. It was Plato's genius (or perversity) to have suggested a radical alternative.

Although Plato never quite got the whole idea out, in *Phaedo* Socrates suggests that the vehicle for survival is not any sort of physical object, not even breath, but, rather an unextended thing. So far as we know, this suggestion was original to Plato (or Socrates). Previously, when others had talked of immaterial souls, they usually meant invisible matter. Even Socrates, in *Phaedo,* did not always distinguish sharply between something's being immaterial and its being invisible. But, then, sometimes he did distinguish between them. Subsequently in Europe, the view that each of us is essentially a soul, and that souls are immaterial, unextended things, really caught on. Although the earliest Christian philosophers — Tertullian, Iraeneus, and Minucius Felix — were materialists and so tried to explain survival of bodily death and the resurrection materialistically, later Christian philosophers seized on Plato's dualistic view to explain how people could survive their bodily deaths.

How, then, if he did, did Plato arrive at the idea of an immaterial, unextended soul? We do not know. In *Phaedo,* Socrates is concerned with the sources of generation and corruption, that is, with how things come to be and pass away. In his view, the corruption of a thing is brought about by its coming apart, that is, by its breaking into pieces, or decomposing. Plato may have reasoned, as the good student of geometry that he was, that any extended thing, merely by virtue of its being extended, is potentially divisible and, hence, potentially corruptible. So if people are immortal, not only by accident but necessarily, they must be unextended.

But why suppose that people are immortal? Plato may have thought he had evidence that people survive the demise of their gross physical bodies. In *Phaedo,* Socrates remarks that in graveyards people sometimes see ghosts. However, people would not have to be immortal, that is, last forever, to survive the demise of their gross physical bodies. In spite of the enormous influence of Plato's arguments for immortality, it is not clear why he thought that people are immortal. Nor is it clear why his famous student, Aristotle, who had what we would call a more scientific turn of mind, followed Plato at least in assuming that the rational part—*nous*—of our minds is immortal.

It is a little clearer why Plato thought it mattered whether people survive the demise of their gross physical bodies. He (or Socrates) thought that in trying to understand the nature of reality, one's body is a constant distraction. If people could get away from bodily distractions, it would help them to discover eternal truths. In addition, Plato tells us that in one of Socrates' last thoughts, Socrates mused about the joys of conversing with the dead. Apparently, then, if Plato (or Socrates) thought that after their bodily deaths, people can converse with other people who have also died, he also supposed that after bodily death souls carry along with them their associated mental dispositions, such as their memories; and apparently, since he looked forward to conversing with the dead, he thought that people were entitled to anticipate having the experiences of their postmortem selves.

A few centuries later, the philosopher Lucretius questioned the latter assumption. He wrote that the persistence of one's soul, even together with one's mental dispositions, would *not* entitle a person to anticipate having future experiences. In the context of his making the point that we have nothing to fear from bodily death, Lucretius argued

that "if any feeling remains in mind or spirit after it has been torn from body, that is nothing to us, who are brought into being by wedlock of body and spirit, conjoined and coalesced." He then considered the possibility that "the matter that composes us should be reassembled by time after our death and brought back into its present state" (compare with the later Christian view that something like this happens when we survive bodily death). He claimed that even if this were to happen, it still would "be no concern of ours once the chain of our identity had been snapped" (Lucretius 1951, Bk. 3). But why would it be of no concern?

Lucretius' answer, in effect, is, first, that our persisting, that is, our continuing as the same persons we now are, is a precondition of any such egoistic concern we might have for the experiences of any *parts* of ourselves that might survive our bodily deaths, and, second, that whatever *parts* may survive, *we* cease at our bodily deaths. "If the future holds travail and anguish in store, the self must be in existence, when that time comes, in order to experience it." "From this fate," Lucretius continued, "we are redeemed by death, which denies existence to the self that might have suffered these tribulations." The moral of these reflections, he thought, is "that we have nothing to fear in death" because "one who no longer is cannot suffer, or differ in any way from one who has never been born, when once this mortal life has been usurped by death the immortal" (1951, Bk. 3).

In sum, in Lucretius' view, regardless of what that is currently part of us persists and regardless of whether it is capable of having experiences and of performing actions, such as conversing with the dead, if this part of ourselves is not attended by the very bodies we have when we die—and in order for it to be attended by these very bodies, the bodies would have to exist continuously as integrated, functioning entities—this part of ourselves is not us; and if this part of ourselves is not us, its experiences and actions are not something we can look forward to having and performing. Unfortunately, Lucretius did not argue for this view. He merely asserted it.

What is impressive, however, is not so much Lucretius' answering the question of what matters primarily in survival by saying that it is personal identity. Rather, what is impressive is his thinking to *ask* it. So far as we know, no one previously, at least in the West, had thought to ask it. Normally people simply assumed (and still do assume) that if at some point in the future they no longer exist, something of inestimable value, at least from their own egoistic points of view, has been lost. In asking the question of what matters primarily in survival, Lucretius considered the possibility that we might not persist and yet that, even from our own egoistic points of view in wanting to persist, not much that matters might be lost, not because our lives were awful or because we do not value ourselves, but because identity is not what matters primarily in survival. As we shall see, the question of whether identity or something else matters primarily in survival resurfaced again in the late eighteenth and early nineteenth centuries, and then again, when it moved to center stage, in our own times.

FROM LOCKE UNTIL THE LATE 1960's: THE (INTRINSIC) RELATIONS VIEW

John Locke, toward the end of the seventeenth century, is usually regarded as the father of modern personal identity theory. However, Locke seems to have accepted that persons have immaterial souls, so he may have had one foot planted squarely in the past. Whether or not Locke was sincere in declaring that he believed in immaterial souls, his main theoretical innovation, so far as personal identity is concerned, was to argue that *even if* each of us is composed of an immaterial soul, because we cannot know that we are, our being so composed can have nothing whatsoever to do with personal identity. Rather, Locke argued, it is our retaining the "same consciousness" that makes us the same people over time. Locke also pointed out that, unlike the case of souls, each of us has direct, introspective access to our own consciousness and indirect access—by observing their behavior—to the consciousness of others.

Scholars are divided about what Locke meant by *same consciousness*. It is clear that part, but only part, of what he meant has to do with memory. It is also clear that he had other concerns about personal identity and its significance that anticipated

questions that have moved to center stage only in our own times. Before getting to these subtler aspects of Locke's thought, let's consider the view that Locke's eighteenth-century critics invariably attributed to him—that is, the view that a person at one time and one at another have the *same consciousness*, just in case the person at the later time *remembers* having had experiences or having performed actions that were had or performed by the person at the earlier time. This is a simple version of the memory view of personal identity. As we shall see, it is vulnerable to decisive objections, which Locke's critics, who wanted to retain the soul view, were not long in pointing out. Yet even this simple memory view of personal identity was, in important ways, an advance on the soul view.

According to the soul view, personal identity depends on sameness of soul. Souls, because they are unextended, are not part of the material world. Hence, on the soul view, personal identity depends on something profoundly mysterious. Other people's souls cannot be observed even indirectly. For instance, you cannot tell by observing another's behavior whether he has an immaterial soul, and, if he does, whether he has the same one throughout the time you are observing him. As we shall see when we get to David Hume, you cannot observe even your own soul directly. In Locke's simple memory view, by contrast, personal identity depends on the presence of a psychological relationship—memory—that binds together earlier and later stages of a person. Other people's memories, unlike their souls, can be observed indirectly. For instance, by listening to others talk about the past (or answer questions on an examination), you may be able to determine that they remember having experienced or done various things. You may be able also to observe directly, in introspection, that *you* remember having experienced and done various things.

Locke saw himself as proposing that we replace a mysterious, essentially religious view of personal identity with a nonmysterious (because the key relations involved are all observable) essentially scientific view. At the time Locke proposed his new theory, Isaac Newton had just demonstrated that there could be a science of nature. Locke was intent on demonstrating that there could also be a science of mind. In Locke's opinion, his new consciousness-view of personal identity, whatever the problems might be in working out its details, was a contribution to this new science of mind. In other words, in Locke's view, his account of personal identity was not just another theory. Rather, it was an idea whose time had come.

Locke's initial critics were not so progressive. However, they were right in thinking that the memory view that they attributed to Locke had three serious problems. One of these problems is that a person, for example, may not now remember having done things which he did in fact do. Locke concluded, rather implausibly in the views of these critics, that if you cannot remember having done something, you did not do it. It is more likely, the critics argued, that something other than memory, or perhaps in addition to memory, accounts for personal identity. They thought this other thing must be the immaterial soul.

A second problem with Locke's view, for which Bishop Joseph Butler usually gets the credit (although others had made the objection earlier), is that the view fails because it is circular. When you remember having experienced or done something, these critics claimed, you necessarily remember not only that someone, but also that *you,* had the experience or performed the action. And in remembering that *you* had the experience or performed the action, you are remembering that the person — you — who is now doing the remembering is the *same person* as the one who had the experience or performed the action. Hence, these critics claimed, because an analysis of personal identity is supposed to tell us what is meant by *same person,* it cannot noncircularly use the notion of memory in its answer. Memory also has to be analyzed in terms of the notion of *same person.*

A third problem, the critics claimed, is that Locke's memory view leads to a contradiction. As Thomas Reid is famous for having pointed out, if someone who did a crime cannot remember having done it but can remember everything he did at an earlier time when he could remember having done it, on Locke's view this later person both is and is not the same person who committed the crime. For example, suppose that there is a person, C, at some time, t_3, a person, B, at some earlier time, t_2, and a person, A, at some still earlier time, t_1. Leave it an open question whether C, B, and A, are the same or different people. Next, suppose

that at t_1 A committed a crime. Then suppose that at t_2 B remembers having committed that same crime. On the simple memory view, B and A would be the same person. Now suppose further that, at t_3, C remembers having experienced something that B, at t_2, experienced. Then, on the memory view, C and B would be the same person. Because C is the same person as B, and B is the same person as A, then C is also the same person as A. Finally, suppose that C has no (personal) memories that extend all the way back to A, at t_1. Then, on the memory view, C would not be the same person as A. But we have already seen that on the memory view, C would be the same person as A. So, on the memory view, C both would and would not be the same person as A. Hence, Reid claimed, the (simple) memory view is contradictory.

FISSION EXAMPLES AND THE QUESTION OF WHAT MATTERS IN SURVIVAL

In the course of proposing his same-consciousness view, Locke was preoccupied with the implications of examples in which what we ordinarily think of as one unified person divides into two (or more) parts, neither of which is directly conscious of what the other experiences. He asked, "Could we suppose two distinct incommunicable consciousnesses acting the same Body, the one constantly by Day, the other by Night?" Locke was also concerned with the implications of examples in which what we ordinarily think of as two independently unified persons share the same consciousness. He asked whether we could imagine "the same consciousness, acting by Intervals two distinct Bodies." Locke thought such examples supported the view that it is sameness of consciousness, rather than sameness of body, that determines identity: "I ask in the first case, Whether the *Day*- and the *Night-man* would not be two as distinct Persons, as *Socrates* and *Plato;* and whether in the second case, there would not be one Person in two distinct Bodies, as much as one Man is the same in two distinct clothings" (Locke 1694, II.27.23).

Eventually, Locke goes on to consider the possibility that in a case in which a person's little finger is cut off, consciousness might not just stay with the main part of that body or just go with the little finger, but instead might split and go with both: "Though if the same Body should still live, and immediately from the separation of the little Finger have its own peculiar consciousness, whereof the little Finger knew nothing, it would not at all be concerned for it, as part of it *self,* or could own any of its Actions, or have any of them imputed to him" (II.27.18). This example is one that in our own times has become known as a *fission example.* Although Locke did not explore its implications for his theory of personal identity, others soon did. And in our own times, fission examples have played a major part in the discussion of personal identity.

In the early eighteenth century, almost all European philosophers were Christians. As such, they accepted that sometime after each of us undergoes bodily death, we will be resurrected. One of the things about Locke's view that bothered many of these thinkers was its apparent consequences for what could happen in a postmortem scenario. They agreed with Locke that after our deaths—say, after *your* death—God can create a person and give that person your memories. In Locke's view, God's doing that *would make that person you.* These thinkers speculated that if God could create someone and give him your memories (as surely God could), God could just as well create two, or three, or any number of persons, and give each of them your memories. But, on Locke's view, that would make each of these *different* persons—you. How, these thinkers wondered, could that be possible?

The issue first came up in a famous, early-eighteenth-century debate between Samuel Clarke and Anthony Collins. Clarke, who had worked closely with Newton, was one of the most respected philosophers of his age. Collins, though less well known, had been a close friend and admirer of Locke. He had a reputation as a "free thinker." In their debate, Clarke attacked Locke's theory of personal identity and Collins defended it.

Clarke began by arguing that Locke's theory is "an *impossible* hypothesis":

> [T]hat the *Person* may still be the same, by a continual Superaddition of the *like Consciousness;* notwithstanding the whole *Substance* be changed: Then I say, you make *individual Personality* to be a mere *external imaginary Denomination,* and nothing in reality: Just as a *Ship* is called the *same*

Ship, after the whole Substance is changed by frequent Repairs; or a *River* is called the *same River,* though the Water of it be every Day new. . . . But he cannot be *really and truly* the *same Person,* unless the *same individual numerical Consciousness* can be transferred from one Subject to another. For, the continued Addition or Exciting of a *like Consciousness* in the new acquired Parts, after the Manner you suppose; is nothing but a Deception and Delusion, under the Form of Memory; a making the Man to seem himself to be conscious of having done that, which really was not done by him, but by another (Clarke, 1738, 844).

Clarke then introduced the idea of fission to hammer home the point that a sequence of like consciousnesses is not the same as a series of acts by a single consciousness:

> [S]uch a Consciousness in a Man, whose Substance is wholly changed, can no more make it Just and Equitable for such a Man to be punished for an Action done by another Substance; than the Addition of the like Consciousness (by the Power of God) to two or more new created Men; or to any Number of Men now living, by giving a like Modification to the Motion of the Spirits in the Brain of each of them respectively; could make them All to be one and the same individual Person, at the same time they remain several and distinct Persons; or make it just and reasonable for all and every one of them to be punished for one and the same individual Action, done by one only, or perhaps by none of them at all (844–5).

Hence, in Clarke's opinion, Locke's view had been shown to be contradictory because it would lead in this imaginary fission-scenario to saying of two or more individuals both that they are and also that they are not the same person. Collins did not have a good answer to this objection. Subsequent thinkers would do better.

Later in the century, Joseph Priestley, who also accepted Locke's view, raised the question of whether identity is primarily what matters in survival. He began by arguing that "the sentient principle in man, containing ideas which certainly have parts and are divisible and consequently must have extension, cannot be that simple, indivisible and immaterial substance that some have imagined it to be, but something that has real extension and therefore may have the other properties of matter" (Priestley 1777, 163). In fact, he said, it must be "a property of the nervous system or rather of the brain" (160). He argued that not only is the brain necessary for human mentality, but that it is sufficient as well. In his view, there is no need to postulate any immaterial soul to account for human behavior because the notion of an immaterial soul is scientifically useless.

All of this may sound quite modern. However, what is truly innovative in Priestley's treatment of personal identity is the way he downplayed the importance of personal identity per se, and highlighted that of the pragmatic functions of belief in our own identities. He began this part of his discussion by considering an objection, which he says was made to "the primitive Christians, as it may be at present" that "a proper resurrection is not only, in the highest degree, improbable, but even actually impossible since, after death, the body putrefies, and the parts that composed it are dispersed, and form other bodies, which have an equal claim to the same resurrection" (165). He continues: "And where, they say, can be the propriety of rewards and *punishments*, if the man that rises again be not identically the same with the man that acted and died?" (165). In reply, Priestley first makes it clear, as if just for the record, that in his opinion "we shall be identically the same beings after the resurrection that we are at present." Then, "for the sake of those who may entertain a different opinion," he proposes to "speculate a little upon their hypothesis" to show that "it is not inconsistent with a state of future rewards and punishments, and that it supplies motives sufficient for the regulation of our conduct here, with a view to it" (165).

In other words, the task that Priestley sets himself is that of showing that even if after death "resurrected selves" are not strictly identical to anyone who existed on Earth, it does not make any difference because *identity is not what matters primarily in survival.* That this is Priestley's project becomes especially clear when he continues: "And metaphysical as the subject necessarily is, I do not despair of satisfying those who will give a due attention to it, that the propriety of rewards and punishments, with our hopes and fears derived from them, do not at all depend upon such a kind of identity as the objection that I have stated supposes" (165). Specifically, then, what Priestley plans to show is that neither the propriety of divine rewards and punishments nor our anticipatory hopes

and fears with regard to the resurrection depends on there being resurrected persons who are identical to us.

In exploring this radical new idea, Priestley claimed that even if people universally and firmly came to believe that over the course of a year there was a complete change, "though gradual and insensible," in the matter of which they were composed, it "would make no change whatever in our present conduct, or in our sense of obligation, respecting the duties of life, and the propriety of rewards and punishments; and consequently all hopes and fears, and expectations of every kind would operate exactly as before (166). "For," he continues, "notwithstanding the complete change of the *man,* there would be no change of what I should call the *person*" (166). So far as personal identity is requisite either for the propriety of rewards and punishments, or for the concern that we take for our future selves, Priestley continued, endorsing Locke, "the sameness and continuity of consciousness seems to be the only circumstance attended to by us."

Then Priestley made it clear that, in the view under consideration, whether identity per se obtains is of no great consequence:

> Admitting, therefore, that the man consists wholly of matter, as much as the river does of water, or the forest of trees, and that this matter should be wholly changed in the interval between death and the resurrection; yet, if, after this state, we shall all know one another again, and converse together as before, we shall be, *to all intents and purposes,* the same persons. Our personal identity will be *sufficiently preserved,* and the expectation of it at present will have a proper influence on our conduct (166–7, emphasis added).

Priestley, in this passage, more successfully than anyone had before, separated the question of whether we will be identical with someone who exists in the future from that of whether it matters. In considering whether it matters, he separated three issues: first, ordinary, so-called self-interested *personal concerns* that all people have for their own futures; second, *societal concerns* that some have that the prospect of future rewards and punishments motivate people to behave themselves; and, third, *theological concerns* that some have about the propriety of divine awards and punishments. Thus, toward the end of the eighteenth century and perhaps without inferring anything from fission examples directly (although he knew about them), Priestley introduced one of the key ideas that has been central to the discussion of personal identity theory in our own times: that personal identity is not primarily what matters in survival.

More than any other Enlightenment philosopher, William Hazlitt, who had been Priestley's student, made the most original and modern use of fission examples. Although today Hazlitt is known primarily as a literary critic, his first book, *Essay on the Principles of Human Action* (1805), was a profound contribution to personal identity theory. In it, in the context of his critiquing Locke, he considered fission examples. What, Hazlitt asked, would a theorist committed to the idea that one's identity extends as far as one's consciousness extends say "if that consciousness should be transferred to some other being?" How would such a person know that he or she had not been "imposed upon by a false claim of identity? (1805, 135–6). He answered, on behalf of the Lockeans, that the idea of one's consciousness extending to someone else "is ridiculous": a person has "no other self than that which arises from this very consciousness." But, he countered, after our deaths:

> this self may be multiplied in as many different beings as the Deity may think proper to endue with the same consciousness; which if it can be so renewed at will in any one instance, may clearly be so in a hundred others. Am I to regard all these as equally myself? Am I equally interested in the fate of all? Or if I must fix upon some one of them in particular as my representative and other self, how am I to be determined in my choice? Here, then, I saw an end put to my speculations about absolute self-interest and personal identity. (136)

Thus, Hazlitt saw that, hypothetically, instead of psychological continuity continuing in a single stream, it might divide. In asking the two questions—"Am I to regard all of these as equally myself? Am I equally interested in the fate of all?"—he correctly separated the question of whether *identity* tracks psychological continuity from that of whether *self-concern* tracks it. Finally, in direct anticipation of what would not occur again to other philosophers until the 1970s, he concluded that because of the possibility of fission, neither identity nor self-concern necessarily tracks psychological continuity.

Hazlitt thus accomplished what, except for Priestley, others who had been sympathetic to Locke's views had resisted. He used fission examples, which previously others had employed only to criticize Locke, to motivate a view that went beyond Locke altogether.

Hazlitt's ideas never received the attention they deserved. Keats and Coleridge knew of his views, buy few others, and no mainstream philosophers, seem even to have noticed. Such ideas as Hazlitt proposed would not be taken seriously again until our own times.

THE QUESTION OF WHETHER PERSONS ARE REAL OR FICTIONAL

Locke may or may not have intended to suggest that persons are fictional entities. Whatever his intentions, some of his critics (e.g., Samuel Clarke and Bishop Butler) and also some of his admirers (e.g., Edmund Law) interpreted his view as implying that persons are *fictional* entities. Primarily two things in Locke's view motivated this interpretation. First, he held that persons are distinct from human animals. Second, he boldly pronounced that "[Person] is a Forensick Term [that is, a legal and/or moral term] appropriating Actions and their Merit" (1694 II.27.26). Locke, thus, suggested that while there could be a natural science of human animals, there could be none of persons, because the notion of *person* is not a natural kind of thing but just an invention of legal and/or ethical theory. It would seem to follow that persons have only a theoretical (hence, a fictional) status. Later in the century, Edmund Law saw this consequence of Locke's view and embraced it.

David Hume would return by a different route —through an examination of experience—to the theme that persons are fictions. Hume began by acknowledging that "there are some philosophers, who imagine we are every moment intimately conscious of what we call *our* Self," and "feel its existence and its continuance in existence," and are "certain, beyond the evidence of a demonstration, both of its perfect identity and simplicity" (by its *perfect identity* he meant its persisting from one moment to the next, without changing in any way; by its *simplicity* he meant its not, at any time, being composed of parts). But, according to Hume, such selves do not show up in experience. He said that if we look introspectively into our experience for a perceiv*er,* which is supposed to be an active *agent,* we will find only passive percepti*ons,* (e.g., "of heat or cold, light or shade, love or hatred, pain or pleasure".) Hume said that he could never catch himself "without a perception" or observe anything "but the perception," so that if others were like him in this respect, then there is no self in experience (1739, Bk. 1, sec. 6). In sum, in Hume's view, the commonsense belief that we experience ourselves *as* selves is based on our mistaking a bundle of percepti*ons* for a perceiv*er.*

Hume suggested that the mistake — actually an illusion — that we experience ourselves as perceivers arises because we do not look carefully enough at our own experience. That is, the perceptions succeed each other so rapidly that they give rise to the illusion that there is an active perceiver in experience. On this point, modern European theories about the self and personal identity make their closest contact with classical Asian theories. Two thousand years before Hume, the Buddha had made much the same point. However, for the Buddha, the point was not so much a philosophical *observation* about experience as it was an experiential *transformation,* which is a necessary step on the way to liberation. In the Buddha's view, the crucial transition that each of us has to make, if we are to be free, is not only to learn intellectually that there is an illusion of self in experience, but also to end that illusion. For as long as the illusion persists, the Buddha claimed, we are its captives regardless of what we may think intellectually.

Jack Engler, a contemporary Buddhist, nicely describes this aspect of what the Buddha had in mind:

> My sense of being an independent observer disappears. The normal sense that I am a fixed, continuous point of observation from which I regard now this object, now that, is dispelled. Like the tachistoscopic flicker-fusion phenomenon which produces the illusion of an "object" when discrete and discontinuous images are flashed too quickly

for normal perception to distinguish them, my sense of being a separate observer or experiencer behind my observation or experience is revealed to be the result of a perceptual illusion, of my not being normally able to perceive a more microscopic level of events. When my attention is sufficiently refined through training and kept bare of secondary reactions and elaboration of stimuli, all that is actually apparent to me from moment to moment is a mental or physical event and an awareness of that event. In each moment there is simply a process of knowing (nama) and its object (rupa). Each arises separately and simultaneously in each moment of awareness. No enduring or substantial entity or observer or experiencer or angesn—no self—can be found behind or apart from these moment-to-moment events to which they could be attributed (an-atta = no-self). In other words, the individual "frames" appear which had previously fused in normal perception in a tachistoscopic manner to produce an apparently solid and fixed image of a "self" or an "object." The only observable reality at this level is the flow of mental and physical events themselves. There is no awareness of an observer. There are just individual moments of observation. (Engler, 1986, 41–2)

In the sort of esoteric no-self experience that Engler is describing, the psychological sense of separation "between observer and observed," ordinarily a persistent feature of our experience regardless of the theories to which we subscribe, disappears.

From 1805 to the late 1960s, there are few important developments in personal identity theory. For the most part, theorists simply argued over whether physical or psychological relations were more important in determining whether personal identity obtains. However, since 1970 there have been three major developments in personal identity theory. One of these is that the *intrinsic* relations view of personal identity has been largely superseded by the *extrinsic* relations view (which is also sometimes called the *closest-continuer view* or the *externalist view*).

THE 1970s: THE (EXTRINSIC) RELATIONS VIEW

According to the older *intrinsic* relations view, what determines whether the two versions of a person at different times are identical is how the two versions are physically and/or psychologically related to *each other.* According to more recent *extrinsic* relations views, what determines this is not only how the two are physically and/or psychologically related to *each other* but also how they are related to *others.* For instance, in Locke's *intrinsic* relations view, you are the same person as someone who existed yesterday if you remember having experienced or having done things that person of yesterday experienced or did. In an *extrinsic* version of Locke's view, one would have to take into account not only whether you remember having experienced or having done things that person of yesterday experienced or did but also whether, besides you, anyone else remembers having experienced or having done those things.

Fission examples are largely responsible for the recent move from an intrinsic to an extrinsic relations view. In the sort of fission examples that have been most discussed, a person somehow divides into two (seemingly) *numerically* different persons, each of whom, initially, is *qualitatively* identical to the other and also to the prefission person from whom they both descended. For example, imagine that all information in human brains is encoded redundantly so that it is possible to separate a human's brain into two parts, leaving each half fully functioning and encoded with all it needs to sustain the original person's full mental life just as (except for the elimination of underlying redundancy) his whole brain would have sustained it had it never been divided. Now suppose that in some normal, healthy human we perform a brain separation, removing the two fully functioning half-brains from his body, which is then immediately destroyed. Suppose, further, that we immediately implant each of these half-brains into its own, brainless body, which, except for being brainless, is otherwise qualitatively identical to the original person's body, so that two people simultaneously emerge, each of whom, except for having only half a brain, is qualitatively identical—physically *and* psychologically—to the original person whose brain was divided and removed and, of course, to each other.

Are these two fission descendants the same person? In an intrinsic view of personal identity, such as Locke's, they would be. Each would remember having experienced things and having performed

actions that the original person experienced and performed. If in deciding whether two versions of a person, one at one time and one at another, are the same person, we have to consider *only* the relationship between the two of them, it would seem that they might be related so as to have all that is required to preserve identity. Obviously, the problem with supposing that we have to consider *only* the relationship between the two of them is that the other fission descendant has an equal claim to be the original person.

Many contemporary philosophers believe that, in such a case, the prefission person (the brain donor) would cease. They think he would cease because they think, first, that identity is a transitive relationship, which implies that if one of the fission descendants were the same person as the brain donor, and the brain donor were the same person as the other fission descendant, the former fission descendant would be the same person as the latter fission descendant; second, that the fission descendants, at least once they began to lead independent lives, would not plausibly be regarded as the same person (think, for instance, of the moral and legal complications if, five years down the road, one of them turns out to be a nice, law-abiding person and the other a nasty, criminal type); and third, it would be arbitrary to regard just one of the fission descendants but not the other as the same person as the donor (at the moment of "conception," the two fission descendants were equally qualified to be the same person as the donor). Hence, in the view of these philosophers, it is more plausible to regard each of the fission descendants as a different person from the prefission person. Philosophers who reason this way accept an *extrinsic* relations view of personal identity, according to which what determines whether a person at one time and one at another are the same person is not only how the two are physically and/or psychologically related to each other (which is all that would need to be considered on an *intrinsic relations* view) but also how the two are related to others (in our example, especially the other fission descendant).

The fission examples considered by eighteenth century philosophers were religion-fiction scenarios. The fission examples that philosophers in our own times have considered are science-fiction scenarios.

Both sorts of fission examples raise essentially the same issues for personal identity theory. In the eighteenth century, many philosophers supposed that the religion-fiction fission examples had a counterpart in real life (postmortem) situations. In our own times, the science-fiction fission examples actually do have a counterpart in real-life situations.

In the late 1930s, neurosurgeons in the United States began performing an operation in which they severed the corpus callosa—the bundles of nerve fibers that connect the two hemispheres of normal, human brains—of severe epileptics in the hope of confining their seizures to one hemisphere of their brains, thus reducing the severity of their seizures. To the surgeons' initial surprise, often the procedure was doubly successful. It reduced not only the severity of the seizures but also their frequency. It also had a truly bizarre side effect, not discovered until many years later: It created two independent centers of consciousness within the same human skull. These centers of consciousness, first, lacked introspective access to each other; second, could be made to acquire and express information independently of each other; and finally, and most dramatically, sometimes differed volitionally, expressing their differences using alternate sides of the same human bodies that they jointly shared. In one case, for instance, a man who had had this operation reportedly hugged his wife with one arm while he pushed her away with the other; in another, a man tried with his right hand (controlled by his left, verbal hemisphere) to hold a newspaper where he could read it, thereby blocking his view of the TV, while he tried with his left hand (controlled by his right, nonverbal hemisphere) to knock the paper out of the way.

THE RETURN OF A QUESTION: IS IDENTITY WHAT MATTERS PRIMARILY IN SURVIVAL?

Since 1970 there has been a second major development in personal identity theory. Philosophers have begun again to question whether personal identity is primarily what matters in survival. That is, they have faced the possibility that people might cease and be continued by *others,* whose existences

even from an exclusively self-interested perspective they would value as much as their own and in pretty much the same ways as they would value their own. Imagine, for instance, that you have a health problem that will result soon in your sudden and painless death unless you receive one of two available treatments. The first is to have your brain removed and placed into the empty cranium of a body that, except for being brainless, is qualitatively identical to your own. The second is to have your brain removed and divided into functionally identical halves (each capable of sustaining your full psychology), and then to have each of these halves put into the empty cranium of a body of its own, again one that is brainless but otherwise qualitatively identical to your own.

In the first treatment, there is a 10 percent chance that the transplantation will take. If it takes, the survivor who wakes up in the recovery room will be physically and psychologically like you just prior to the operation except that he will know he has had the operation and he will be healthy. In the second, there is a 95 percent chance that both transplantations will take. If both take, each of the survivors who wakes up in the recovery room will be physically and psychologically like you just prior to the operation except that each of them will know he has had the operation and each will be healthy. If the transplantation in the first treatment does not take, the would-be survivor will die painlessly on the operating table. If either transplantation in the second treatment does not take, the other will not take either, and both would-be survivors will die painlessly on the operating table. Everything else about the treatments is the same and as attractive to you as possible: For instance, both are painless, free of charge, and, if successful, result in survivors who recover quickly.

As we have seen, many philosophers believe that you would continue in the first (nonfission) treatment but cease and be replaced by others in the second (fission) treatment. As in the case of the previous fission examples considered, they think that you would cease and be replaced in the second treatment because they believe, first, that identity is a transitive relationship; second, that the survivors, at least once they began to lead independent lives, would not plausibly be regarded as the same people as each other; and third, that it would be arbitrary to regard one of the survivors but not the other as you. Hence, in the view of these philosophers, it is more plausible to regard each of the survivors as a different person from you.

Assume, for the sake of argument, that this way of viewing what will happen in the two treatments is correct. On this assumption, you would persist through the first treatment, but in the second you would cease and be replaced by others. Given the circumstances specified in the example, only by sacrificing your identity could you greatly increase the chances that someone who initially would be qualitatively just like you, would emerge from the operation and survive for years. The question is whether, in the circumstances specified, it would be worth it for you to have such an operation, that is, whether it would be worth it only from a point of view that in more normal circumstances would be considered a totally selfish (or self-regarding) point of view. Many who consider examples such as this one feel strongly that it would be worth it. For them, at least, it would seem that ceasing and being continued by others can matter as much, or almost as much, as persisting, and matter in pretty much the same ways. However, if ceasing and being continued by others can matter as much (and in the same ways) as persisting, identity is not what matters primarily in survival.

DEREK PARFIT'S VIEW

Parfit has a Neo-Lockean view of personal identity, according to which what binds our various stages into the individual people that we are is not just memory, but psychological relations more generally (including beliefs, intentions, character traits, anticipations, and so on). And, unlike Locke's view, in Parfit's view it is not necessary for each stage of us to be *directly* related to every other stage. It is enough if each stage is *indirectly* related through intermediate stages. In sum, in Parfit's view, what binds us are psychological connections, overlapping "like the strands in a rope" (Parfit, 1984, 222). Thus Parfit's view is not vulnerable to Reid's objection to Locke's view. If C at t_3 is *directly* psychologically connected to B at t_2 but *not* to A at t_1, but B at t_2 *is* directly psychologically connected to A at t_1, then C at t_3 is *indirectly* psycho-

logically connected to A at t_1 and that may be enough to preserve personal identity.

Parfit has also responded to those who think that the notion of *same person* enters into the proper analysis of various psychological relations, particularly of memory. To avoid the charge that his analysis of personal identity is circular, he has formulated it in terms of specially defined senses of psychological relations that do not include the notion of *same person*. For instance, in the case of memory, Parfit has defined a notion of *quasi memory* (or, *q memory*), which is just like that of *memory* except that whereas the claim that someone remembers having experienced something might imply that the person remembers that *she herself* experienced that thing, the claim that someone *q remembers* having experienced something implies, by definition only that the person remembers that *someone* experienced it. Thus Parfit's view is not vulnerable to the argument Butler used to try to show that Locke's view is circular.

To illustrate how q memory might work, Parfit gave as an example Jane's seeming to remember Paul's experience, in Venice, of looking across water and seeing a lightning bolt fork and then strike two objects (1984, 220). Parfit claimed that in seeming to remember this experience, Jane might have known that she was seeming to remember an experience that Paul (and not she) had had originally, and that if Jane had known this, she would have known, *from the inside,* part of what it was like to be Paul on that day in Venice. In other words, Jane would have known that she was seeming to remember Paul's experience from the same sort of subjective, first-person point of view from which Paul actually had the experience and from which Jane ordinarily remembers only her own experiences. If one acknowledges that Parfit's hypothetical example is at least theoretically possible, as it seems we should (imagine that part of Paul's brain had been surgically implanted into Jane's brain), apparently it is possible, in analyses of personal identity, to substitute q memory for memory and thereby avoid Butler's objection. In other words, even if simple memory analyses of personal identity are circular, it would not follow that q memory analyses of personal identity are circular.

When Locke proposed his psychological relations view, most philosophers subscribed to a soul view. In 1984, when Parfit proposed the fullest version of his theory, probably most philosophers subscribed to the view that the continuity of our bodies, or of some part of our bodies, is necessary for personal persistence. Parfit, by contrast, denied that bodily continuity is necessary for personal persistence. To support this denial, he supposed, first that although someone's brain is healthy, his body is ridden with cancer and his only hope for survival is to have his entire healthy brain transplanted intact to another healthy body. He supposed also that this transplantation procedure is perfectly safe and that the body into which the donor's brain will be transplanted is better than his current body, not only in that it is healthy but also in many other respects that appeal to the donor. Parfit pointed out, surely correctly, that the donor has not lost much if he jettisons his old body and moves his brain to the better body that awaits it. Such an operation would not be as bad as staying in the old body and dying of cancer, even if the death were painless. In fact, vanity being what it is, if radical cosmetic surgery of this sort were available and safe, it is likely that many people would choose it, even if the old bodies they jettisoned were healthy. If physical continuity matters, Parfit concluded, it cannot be continuity of the whole body, but at most the continuity of the brain.

However, Parfit argued, the importance of our brains, like that of our other organs, is not intrinsic but derivative; that is, the brain's importance depends solely on the function it serves. For most of us, if half a brain were functionally equivalent to the whole, the preservation of our whole brain would not matter much. And, it would seem, the continuity of even any part of the brain is not necessarily important. If some other organ, such as the liver, sustained our psychologies and our brains served functions this other organ now serves, the other organ would be as important in survival as the brain is now and the brain only as important as the other organ is now. It would seem that if something else — anything else — could sustain our psychologies as reliably as the brain, the brain (i.e., the physical organ that actually now functions as the brain) would have little importance in survival even if this other thing were not any part of our bodies (1984, 284–5).

A critic might object that even though the importance of an organ is derivative and based solely on its being the vehicle for preserving a person's psychology, given that it has always been that vehicle, the preservation of that organ matters greatly, perhaps even primarily, in survival. In other words, it is possible that even though something else might have assumed that organ's function of preserving a person's psychology and, hence, that under those imagined circumstances the organ that now serves that function would not have mattered greatly in survival, once an organ actually has served the function of preserving a person's psychology, it does matter importantly in survival. However, even though this is possible, it is doubtful that merely by virtue of its having sustained your psychology, an organ thereby matters all that importantly to you in survival.

Imagine, for instance, that competent doctors discover that you have both a brain disease and a brain abnormality. The disease has not impaired the functioning of your brain yet, but if it is untreated, it will result in your death in the near future. Because of the abnormality, there is a simple, effective, and painless cure. The abnormality is that you have two brains, the one now diseased, which is the only one that has ever functioned as a brain, and another, right beside it, lying dormant — healthy and perfectly capable of performing a whole brain's functions should the need arise, but nevertheless not yet functioning as a brain and not currently encoded with any of your psychology. The doctors can perform a simple procedure to switch the roles of your two brains: All of the encoded psychology on your diseased brain will be transferred to the healthy one; as it is transferred, it will be erased from your diseased brain, whereupon your healthy brain will begin to function just as the diseased one did (and would have continued to do had it been healthy and left alone).

Suppose that the procedure is as quick and as simple (and as abrupt) as flipping a switch, that it will not affect subjective psychology, and that consciousness will be continuous throughout the procedure. Indeed, suppose that you and the person who emerges from the procedure will not even notice any change. When the transfer is completed, your diseased brain will become dormant almost instantaneously and will pose no further threat to your organism's physical or psychological health. In these imagined circumstances, how much would it matter to you that the brain that has always sustained your psychology will no longer sustain it, while another that has never sustained it will sustain it from now on? Probably not much. The procedure would not be as bad as death. Unless it caused existential anxiety, it would not even be as bad as a root canal. So much for the derivative value of the organs that have actually sustained our psychologies.

Those who are skeptical of this response might imagine that whereas the procedure described is the simplest way of disabling the threat to the organism posed by your diseased brain, it is not the only way. An alternative procedure the doctors can perform is to repair your diseased brain through a series of twenty brain operations spread over the next twenty years of your life. Each operation will cost about one-half of your annual salary (suppose that insurance does not cover the procedure and probably never will) and will require two months of hospitalization. In addition, the operations will be disfiguring. When they are finally completed, you will be healthy enough, but your life will have been seriously disrupted and your body and face will be somewhat deformed. I assume that on your scale of values, the disruption, expense, and disfigurement, while bad, are not as bad as death. (If they are as bad as death, reduce their severity to the point where they are not *quite* as bad as death.) If the first procedure is as bad as death, the second procedure is a better choice. Which procedure would you choose? I think most people would choose the first procedure (for more on this example, see Martin, 1998, 80–5).

Finally, a critic might object that even though the preservation of one's body might not matter in survival, it still might be necessary for personal persistence. However, in Parfit's view, in the case of many of the exotic examples under discussion in the personal identity literature, including the one just discussed, the question of whether a person persists is an *empty question*. When one knows all of the physical and psychological ways in which the earlier and later persons are related, and how the earlier person evolved (or transformed) into the later person, one knows everything there is to know about the situation that's relevant to the question of personal persistence. There is no further fact to know, such as whether in such circumstances one actually persists. That is, in the case of such examples, there may be no truth of the matter about whether one persists.

In one of Parfit's most controversial claims, his notorious "branch line" example, he asks you to put yourself imaginatively into the place of a person on Earth who is trying to be teletransported to Mars (200–1). You enter the teletransportation booth and push the button, activating the process. You succeed in producing a replica of yourself on Mars, but because the teletransporter has malfunctioned you fail to dematerialize on Earth. A few minutes later, you emerge from the teletransporter and are told believably that, due to its malfunctioning, your heart has been damaged and you have only two more days to live. Parfit argues that in such a case, you should not be too concerned. Rather, you ought to regard your replica's persistence—now taking place on Mars—as an adequate surrogate for what might have been your own persistence on Earth. Although not many philosophers have followed Parfit in taking this line, explaining why one should not take it without returning to the view that identity is what matters in survival has not been easy (for more on this, see Martin, 1998, Chs. 6 and 7).

THREE- VS. FOUR-DIMENSIONAL VIEWS OF PERSONS

I said above that since 1970 there have been three major developments in personal identity theory. One has been that *intrinsic* relations views of personal identity have been largely superseded by *extrinsic* relations views. Another has been the reemergence of interest in the question of whether personal identity is primarily what matters in survival.

The third major development has been a challenge to the traditional three-dimensional view of persons, according to which a person can be wholly present at a given moment—for example, you are wholly present right now. Some philosophers have argued that we should replace this three-dimensional view with a four-dimensional view, according to which only time slices or "stages" of persons exist at short intervals of time. In this four-dimensional view, persons are aggregates of momentary person-stages, beginning with the person-stage that came into being at a person's birth and ending with the person-stage that existed when the person died, and including every person-stage between birth and death.

To see why it might matter which of these two views is correct, consider again any of the fission examples (except the branch line case) already discussed. It was suggested that the prefission person is not identical with either of his postfission descendants. That was a three-dimensional way of describing the situation. A four-dimensionalist would have said that what we are calling "the prefission person" is really not a person, but rather a person-stage, and that what we are calling "the postfission descendants" are also person-stages. According to a four-dimensionalist, in a fission example the prefission person does not cease. Rather what happens is that the prefission person-stage becomes a shared person-stage. That is, two persons, whose postfission person-stages are separate from the other overlap before fission and, thus, share their prefission person-stages.

Philosophers have used this four-dimensional way of conceptualizing what is going on in a fission example to argue that fission examples cannot be used to argue that identity is not what matters in survival. According to these philosophers, fission examples cannot be so used because in a fission example no one ceases (hence, identity is never traded for other benefits). Rather, what happens in a fission example is that the stages of two persons are shared stages before the fission, but no longer shared after the fission. Because in this view, a given person-stage may be part of two or three (or potentially any number) of persons, this view is sometimes called the multiple-occupancy view of persons. Although it has its defenders, most personal identity theorists have stuck with the traditional three-dimensional view.

THE BOTTOM LINE

The world is mysterious. Not the least of its mysteries is our own status in it. Your assuming that your status in the world is rock solid and unquestionable may shield you from this mystery, but it cannot make the world or yourself any less mysterious. Up to this point, your whole life, after a certain age, has been organized around the idea that you persist. It will continue to be organized around that idea. Studying philosophy will not change that. What studying philosophy can change

is your understanding of that idea and your attitude toward it. And that is where this philosophical issue differs from others. It is one thing to discover that you have been misled by an illusion. That is a common result in philosophy. However, it is quite another, and a far more disturbing, thing, to discover that you may be that illusion.

REFERENCES AND ACKNOWLEDGEMENTS

The relevant parts of Plato's *Phaedo* are included in selection 62, in the present anthology. Lucretius' views may be found in *De Rerum Natura,* trans. R. E. Latham, (Harmondsworth: Penguin, 1951). John Locke's views are in his, *An Essay Concerning Human Understanding,* 1694 (ed., Peter H. Nidditch, Oxford: Clarendon Press, 1975); and selection 13, in this anthology.

In the account I have given of eighteenth-century developments, I relied on research done with John Barresi and Alessandro Giovannelli. See Raymond Martin and John Barresi, "Hazlitt on the Future of the Self," *Journal of the History of Ideas,* vol. 56, 1995, 463–81; Raymond Martin, John Barresi, and Alessandro Giovannelli, "Fission Examples in the Eighteenth and Early Nineteenth Century Personal Identify Debate," *History of Philosophy Quarterly,* vol. 15, 1998. Martin and Barresi have written a book, *Naturalization of the Soul: Self and Personal Identity in the 18th Century,* (Routledge, 1999).

The Clarke-Collins debate is in volume 4 of *The Works of Samuel Clarke,* 4 vols, 1738 (reprinted New York: Garland Publishing, 1928). For Butler's criticisms of Locke, see Joseph Butler, *The Analogy of Religion, Natural and Revealed,* 1736 (reprinted, London: Henry G. Bohn, 1852). For Thomas Reid's criticisms, see selection 16, in this anthology or his *Essay on the Intellectual Powers of Man,* 1785, in *The Works of Thomas Reid,* ed. William Hamilton, 6th ed. (Edinburgh: Maclachlan and Stewart, 1863). Edmund Law's, "A Defense of Mr. Locke's Opinion Concerning Personal Identity" is in volume III, pages 177–201, of *The Works of John Locke,* 10 vols., (London: Thomas Tegg, 1823; reprinted 1963, Hildesheim, Germany: Scientia Verlag Aalan). For David Hume's views on personal identity, see selection 15 in this anthology or his *A Treatise of Human Nature*, 1738. Jack Engler's remarks are from "Therapeutic Aims in Psychotherapy and Meditation" in *Transformation of Consciousness*, ed. K. Wilber, J. Engler, and D. P. Brown, pages 17–52 (Boston: Shambhala, 1986). For Joseph Priestley's views, see his *Disquisitions Relating to Matter and Spirit and the Doctrine of Philosophical Necessity Illustrated*, 1777 (reprinted 1976, New York: Garland). William Hazlitt's book on personal identity is *Essay on the Principles of Human Action and Some Remarks on the systems of Hartley and Helvetius*, 1805 (reprinted 1969, with an introduction by John R. Nabholtz. Gainesville, Fla., Scholars' Facsimiles & Reprints). Hazlitt also wrote two essays on personal identity, which may be found in O. Cook, ed., *William Hazlitt: Selected Writings* (New York: Oxford University Press, 1991).

Derek Parfit's views are mainly in "Personal Identity," *Philosophical Review*, vol. 80, 1971, 3–27; and in his *Reasons and Persons*, (Oxford: Clarendon Press, 1984). David Lewis' explanation and defense of the four-dimensional view of persons is in his "Survival and Identity," *The Identities of Persons*, ed. Amelié Rorty (Berkeley: University of California Press, 1976), 17-40; see also "Postscript to Survival and Identity," in his *Philosophical Papers*, vol. 1 (New York: Oxford University Press, 1983).

Other important work since 1970 that would have been discussed in a more complete survey includes Sydney Shoemaker, "Persons and Their Pasts," *American Philosophical Quarterly*, vol. 7, 1970, 269–85, and his "Personal Identity: A Materialist Account," in Sydney Shoemaker and Richard Swinburne, *Personal Identity*, (Oxford: Basil Blackwell, 1984), 69–152 (in the section labeled, "The Return of a Question," the first fission example described in based on one originally presented by Shoemaker); John Perry, "Can the Self Divide?" *Journal of Philosophy*, vol. 69, 1972, 463–88, and "The Importance of Being Identical" in *The Identities of Persons*, ed. Amelie Rorty, (Berkeley: University of California, 1976), 67–90; Robert Nozick, *Philosophical Explanations* (Cambridge, Mass.: Harvard University Press, 1981); Thomas Nagel, *The View from Nowhere*, (New York: Oxford University Press, 1986); Ernest Sosa, "Surviving Matters," *Nous*, vol. 24, 1990, 305–30; and Peter Unger, *Identity, Consciousness, and Value*, (New York: Oxford University Press, 1991).

Daniel Kolak's *In Search of Myself: Life, Death, and Personal Identity* (Belmont, California: Wadsworth, 1999) is a provocative and accessible introduction to issues that arise in personal identity theory. Raymond Martin's latest views may be found in *Self-Concern: An Experiential Approach to What Matters in Survival* (Cambridge: Cambridge University Press, 1998).

Further Questions

1. If you had to state your own theory of personal identity, what would it be? What do you think would be the most plausible objection to your theory? How would you respond to this objection?
2. If you have to state your own theory of what matters primarily in survival, what would it be? What do you think would be the most plausible objection to your theory? How would you respond to this objection?

Further Readings

Kolak, Daniel and Raymond Martin, eds. *Self & Identity*. New York: Macmillan, 1991. Twenty-eight selections from contemporary philosophers and scientists on unity of consciousness, personal identity, and self, plus an extensive bibliography.

Parfit, Derek *Reasons and Persons*, Part 3. Oxford: Clarendon Press, 1984. In the opinion of many, the most important book of the twentieth century on the questions of personal identity and what matters in survival.

The Yellow Wallpaper   18

CHARLOTTE PERKINS GILMAN

Charlotte Gilman (1860–1935), whose great-aunt was Harriet Beecher Stowe, wrote poetry and short stories, often about male–female relationships. She is now considered an important precursor of the women's movement. "The Yellow Wallpaper," by far her most famous story, is about a woman's attempt to break through the imprisoning constraints of societal expectations. Her story beautifully and dramatically illustrates the struggle many people go through to shed a false and imprisoning sense of self and replace it with a liberating one. When her story was published, in 1891, a Boston physician complained that it might drive readers mad. Unquestionably, the story can have a powerfully disorienting effect. In her subsequent explanation of why she wrote it, Gilman wrote:

> For many years I suffered from a severe and continuous nervous breakdown tending to melancholia — and beyond. During about the third year of this trouble I went, in devout faith and some faint stir of hope, to a noted specialist in nervous diseases, the best known in the county. This wise man put me to bed and applied the rest cure, to which a still-good physique responded so promptly that he concluded there was nothing much the matter with me, and sent me home with solemn advice to "live as domestic a life as far as possible," to "have but two hours' intellectual life a day," and "never to touch pen, brush, or pencil again" as long as I lived. This was in 1887. I went home and obeyed those directions for some three months, and came so near the borderline of utter mental ruin that I could see over.
>
> Then, using the remnants of intelligence that remained, and helped by a wise friend, I cast the noted specialist's advice to the winds and went to work again — work, the normal life of every human being; work, in which is joy and growth and service, without which one is a pauper and a parasite — ultimately recovering some measure of power.
>
> Being naturally moved to rejoining by this narrow escape, I wrote "The Yellow Wallpaper," with its embellishments and additions . . . and sent a copy to the physician who so nearly drove me mad. He never acknowledged it.

Reading Questions

1. What is the significance of the wallpaper in this story?
2. What is the significance of the figures that the heroine thinks she sees behind the pattern in the paper?

IT IS VERY SELDOM THAT MERE ordinary people like John and myself secure ancestral halls for the summer.

A colonial mansion, a hereditary estate, I would say a haunted house and reach the height of romantic felicity — but that would be asking too much of fate!

Still I will proudly declare that there is something queer about it.

Else, why should it be let so cheaply? And why have stood so long untenanted?

John laughs at me, of course, but one expects that.

John is practical in the extreme. He has no patience with faith, an intense horror of superstition, and he scoffs openly at any talk of things not to be felt and seen and put down in figures.

John is a physician, and *perhaps* — (I would not say it to a living soul, of course, but this is dead paper and a great relief to my mind) — *perhaps* that is one reason I do not get well faster.

You see, he does not believe I am sick! And what can one do?

If a physician of high standing, and one's own husband, assures friends and relatives that there is really nothing the matter with one but temporary nervous depression—a slight hysterical tendency—what is one to do?

My brother is also a physician, and also of high standing, and he says the same thing.

So I take phosphates or phosphites—whichever it is—and tonics, and air and exercise, and journeys, and am absolutely forbidden to "work" until I am well again.

Personally, I disagree with their ideas.

Personally, I believe that congenial work, with excitement and change, would do me good.

But what is one to do?

I did write for a while in spite of them; but it *does* exhaust me a good deal—having to be so sly about it, or else meet with heavy opposition.

I sometimes fancy that in my condition, if I had less opposition and more society and stimulus—but John says the very worst thing I can do is to think about my condition, and I confess it always makes me feel bad.

So I will let it alone and talk about the house.

The most beautiful place! It is quite alone, standing well back from the road, quite three miles from the village. It makes me think of English places that you read about, for there are hedges and walls and gates that lock, and lots of separate little houses for the gardeners and people.

There is a *delicious* garden! I never saw such a garden—large and shady, full of box-bordered paths, and lined with long grape-covered arbors with seats under them.

There were greenhouses, but they are all broken now.

There was some legal trouble, I believe, something about heirs and co-heirs; anyhow, the place has been empty for years.

That spoils my ghostliness, I am afraid, but I don't care—there is something strange about the house—I can feel it.

I even said so to John one moonlight evening, but he said what I felt was a draught, and shut the window.

I get unreasonably angry with John sometimes. I'm sure I never used to be so sensitive. I think it is due to this nervous condition.

But John says if I feel so I shall neglect proper self-control; so I take pains to control myself—before him, at least, and that makes me very tired.

I don't like our room a bit. I wanted one downstairs that opened onto the piazza and had roses all over the window, and such pretty old-fashioned chintz hangings! But John would not hear of it.

He said there was only one window and not room for two beds, and no near room for him if he took another.

He is very careful and loving, and hardly lets me stir without special direction.

I have a schedule prescription of each hour in the day; he takes all care from me, and so I feel basely ungrateful not to value it more.

He said he came here solely on my account, that I was to have perfect rest and all the air I could get. "Your exercise depends on your strength, my dear," said he, "and your food somewhat on your appetite; but air you can absorb all the time." So we took the nursery at the top of the house.

It is a big, airy room, the whole floor nearly, with windows that look all ways, and air and sunshine galore. It was nursery first, and then playroom and gymnasium, I should judge, for the windows are barred for little children, and there are rings and things in the walls.

The paint and paper look as if a boys' school had used it. It is stripped off—the paper—in great patches all around the head of my bed, about as far as I can reach, and in a great place on the other side of the room low down. I never saw a worse paper in my life. One of those sprawling, flamboyant patterns committing every artistic sin.

It is dull enough to confuse the eye in following, pronounced enough constantly to irritate and provoke study, and when you follow the lame uncertain curves for a little distance they suddenly commit suicide—plunge off at outrageous angles, destroy themselves in unheard-of contradictions.

The color is repellent, almost revolting: a smouldering unclean yellow, strangely faded by the slow-turning sunlight. It is a dull yet lurid orange in some places, a sticky sulphur tint in others.

No wonder the children hated it! I should hate it myself if I had to live in this room long.

There comes John, and I must put this away—he hates to have me write a word.

We have been here two weeks, and I haven't felt like writing before, since that first day.

THE LIAR FEARS THE VOID

Adrienne Rich

The liar lives in fear of losing control. She cannot even desire a relationship without manipulation, since to be vulnerable to another person means for her the loss of control.

The liar has many friends, and leads an existence of great loneliness.

The liar often suffers from amnesia. Amnesia is the silence of the unconscious.

To lie habitually, as a way of life, is to lose contact with the unconscious. It is like taking sleeping pills, which confer sleep but blot out dreaming. The unconscious wants truth. It ceases to speak to those who want something else more than truth.

In speaking of lies, we come inevitably to the subject of truth. There is nothing simple or easy about this idea. There is no "the truth," "a truth"—truth is not one thing, or even a system. It is an increasing complexity. The pattern of the carpet is a surface. When we look closely, or when we become weavers, we learn of the tiny multiple threads unseen in the overall pattern, the knots on the underside of the carpet.

This is why the effort to speak honestly is so important. Lies are usually attempts to make everything simpler—for the liar—than it really is, or ought to be.

In lying to others we end up lying to ourselves. We deny the importance of an event, or a person, and thus deprive ourselves of a part of our lives. Or we use one piece of the past or present to screen out another. Thus we lose faith even with our own lives.

The unconscious wants truth, as the body does. The complexity and fecundity of dreams comes from the complexity and fecundity of the unconscious struggling to fulfill that desire. The complexity and fecundity of poetry come from the same struggle.

An honorable human relationship—that is, one in which two people have the right to use the word "love"—is a process, delicate, violent, often terrifying to both persons involved, a process of refining the truths they can tell each other.

It is important to do this because it breaks down human self-delusion and isolation.

It is important to do this because in so doing we do justice to our own complexity.

It is important to do this because we can count on so few people to go that hard way with us. . . .

The liar is afraid.

But we are all afraid: without fear we become manic, hubristic, self-destructive. What is this particular fear that possesses the liar?

She is afraid that her own truths are not good enough.

She is afraid, not so much of prison guards or bosses, but of something unnamed within her. . . .

The liar fears the void.

From *On Lies, Secrets, and Silence*, Norton, 1986.

I am sitting by the window now, up in this atrocious nursery, and there is nothing to hinder my writings as much as I please, save lack of strength.

John is away all day, and even some nights when his cases are serious.

I am glad my case is not serious!

But these nervous troubles are dreadfully depressing.

John does not know how much I really suffer. He knows there is no reason to suffer, and that satisfies him.

Of course it is only nervousness. It does weigh on me so not to do my duty in any way!

I meant to be such a help to John, such a real rest and comfort, and here I am a comparative burden already!

Nobody would believe what an effort it is to do what little I am able — to dress and entertain, and order things.

It is fortunate Mary is so good with the baby. Such a dear baby!

And yet I *cannot* be with him, it makes me so nervous.

I suppose John never was nervous in his life. He laughs at me so about this wallpaper!

At first he meant to repaper the room, but afterward he said that I was letting it get the better of me, and that nothing was worse for a nervous patient than to give way to such fancies.

He said that after the wallpaper was changed it would be the heavy bedstead, and then the barred windows, and then that gate at the head of the stairs, and so on.

"You know the place is doing you good," he said, "and really, dear, I don't care to renovate the house just for a three months' rental."

"Then do let us go downstairs," I said. "There are such pretty rooms there."

Then he took me in his arms and called me a blessed little goose, and said he would go down cellar, if I wished, and have it whitewashed into the bargain.

But he is right enough about the beds and windows and things.

It is as airy and comfortable a room as anyone need wish, and, of course, I would not be so silly as to make him uncomfortable just for a whim.

I'm really getting quite fond of the big room, all but that horrid paper.

Out of one window I can see the garden — those mysterious deep-shaded arbors, the riotous old-fashioned flowers, and bushes and gnarly trees.

Out of another I get a lovely view of the bay and a little private wharf belonging to the estate. There is a beautiful shaded lane that runs down there from the house. I always fancy I see people walking in these numerous paths and arbors, but John has cautioned me not to give way to fancy in the least. He says that with my imaginative power and habit of story-making, a nervous weakness like mine is sure to lead to all manner of excited fancies, and that I ought to use my will and good sense to check the tendency. So I try.

I think sometimes that if I were only well enough to write a little it would relieve the press of ideas and rest me.

But I find I get pretty tired when I try.

It is so discouraging not to have any advice and companionship about my work. When I get really well, John says we will ask Cousin Henry and Julia down for a long visit; but he says he would as soon put fireworks in my pillow-case as to let me have those stimulating people about now.

I wish I could get well faster.

But I must not think about that. This paper looks to me as if it *knew* what a vicious influence it had!

There is a recurrent spot where the pattern lolls like a broken neck and two bulbous eyes stare at you upside down.

I get positively angry with the impertinence of it and the everlastingness. Up and down and sideways they crawl, and those absurd unblinking eyes are everywhere. There is one place where two breadths didn't match, and the eyes go all up and down the line, one a little higher than the other.

I never saw so much expression in an inanimate thing before, and we all know how much expression they have! I used to lie awake as a child and get more entertainment and terror out of blank walls and plain furniture than most children could find in a toy-store.

I remember what a kindly wink the knobs of our big old bureau used to have, and there was one chair that always seemed like a strong friend.

I used to feel that if any of the other things looked too fierce I could always hop into that chair and be safe.

The furniture in this room is no worse than inharmonious, however, for we had to bring it all from downstairs. I suppose when this was used as a playroom they had to take the nursery things out, and no wonder! I never saw such ravages as the children have made here.

The wallpaper, as I said before, is torn off in spots, and it sticketh closer than a brother — they must have had perseverance as well as hatred.

Then the floor is scratched and gouged and splintered, the plaster itself is dug out here and there, and this great heavy bed, which is all we found in the room, looks as if it had been through the wars.

But I don't mind it a bit — only the paper.

There comes John's sister. Such a dear girl as she is, and so careful of me! I must not let her find me writing.

FEMINISM

Nancy Hartsock

Feminists, in making theory, take up and examine what we find within ourselves; we attempt to clarify for ourselves and others what we already, at some level, know. Theory itself, then, can be seen as a way of taking up and building on our experience. This is not to say that feminists reject all knowledge that is not firsthand, that we can learn nothing from books or from history. But rather than read a number of sacred texts we make the practical questions posed for us in everyday life the basis of our study. Feminism recognizes that political philosophy and political action do not take place in separate realms. On the contrary, the concepts with which we understand the social world emerge from and are defined by human activity.

For feminists, the unity of theory and practice refers to the use of theory to make coherent the problems and principles expressed in our practical activity. Feminists argue that the role of theory is to take seriously the idea that all of us are theorists. The role of theory, then, is to articulate for us what we know from our practical activity, to bring out and make conscious the philosophy embedded in our lives. Feminists are in fact creating social theory through political action. We need to conceptualize, to take up and specify what we have already done, in order to make the next steps clear. We can start from common sense, but we need to move on to the philosophy systematically elaborated by traditional intellectuals.

A third factor in making feminism a force for revolution is that the mode of analysis I have described leads to a transformation of social relations. This is true first in a logical sense. That is, once social relations are situated within the context of the social formation as a whole, the individual phenomena change their meanings and forms. They become something other than they were. For example, what liberal theory understands as social stratification becomes clearer when understood as class. But this is not simply a logical point. As Lukacs has pointed out, the transformation of each phenomenon through relating it to the social totality ends by conferring "reality on the day to day struggle by manifesting its relation to the whole. Thus it elevates mere existence to reality." This development in mass political consciousness, the transformation of the phenomena of life, is on the one hand a profoundly political act and on the other, a "point of transition." Consciousness must become deed, but the act of becoming conscious is itself a kind of deed.

From "Feminist Theory and the Development of Revolutionary Strategy," in Z. R. Eisenstein, ed., *Capitalistic Patriarchy and the Case for Socialistic Feminism* (1979).

She is a perfect and enthusiastic housekeeper, and hopes for no better profession. I verily believe she thinks it is the writing which made me sick!

But I can write when she is out, and see her a long way off from these windows.

There is one that commands the road, a lovely shaded winding road, and one that just looks off over the country. A lovely country, too, full of great elms and velvet meadows.

This wallpaper has a kind of subpattern in a different shade, a particularly irritating one, for you can only see it in certain lights, and not clearly then.

But in the places where it isn't faded and where the sun is just so—I can see a strange, provoking, formless sort of figure that seems to skulk about behind that silly and conspicuous front design.

There's sister on the stairs!

Well, the Fourth of July is over! The people are all gone, and I am tired out. John thought it might do me good to see a little company, so we just had Mother and Nellie and the children down for a week.

Of course I didn't do a thing. Jennie sees to everything now.

But it tired me all the same.

John says if I don't pick up faster he shall send me to Weir Mitchell[1] . . . in the fall.

But I don't want to go there at all. I had a friend who was in his hands once, and she says he is just like John and my brother, only more so!

Besides, it is such an undertaking to go so far.

I don't feel as if it was worthwhile to turn my hand over for anything, and I'm getting dreadfully fretful and querulous.

I cry at nothing, and cry most of the time.

Of course I don't when John is here, or anybody else, but when I am alone.

And I am alone a good deal just now. John is kept in town very often by serious cases, and Jennie is good and lets me alone when I want her to.

So I walk a little in the garden or down that lovely lane, sit on the porch under the roses, and lie down up here a good deal.

I'm getting really fond of the room in spite of the wallpaper. Perhaps *because* of the wallpaper.

It dwells in my mind so!

I lie here on this great immovable bed — it is nailed down, I believe — and follow that pattern about by the hour. It is as good as gymnastics, I assure you. I start, we'll say, at the bottom, down in the corner over there where it has not been touched, and I determine for the thousandth time that I *will* follow that pointless pattern to some sort of a conclusion.

I know a little of the principle of design, and I know this thing was not arranged on any laws of radiation, or alternation, or repetition, or symmetry, or anything else that I ever heard of.

It is repeated, of course, by the breadths, but not otherwise.

Looked at in one way, each breadth stands alone; the bloated curves and flourishes — a kind of "debased Romanesque" with delirium tremens go waddling up and down in isolated columns of fatuity.

But, on the other hand, they connect diagonally, and the sprawling outlines run off in great slanting waves of optic horror, like a lot of wallowing sea-weeds in full chase.

The whole thing goes horizontally, too, at least it seems so, and I exhaust myself trying to distinguish the order of its going in that direction.

They have used a horizontal breadth for a frieze, and that adds wonderfully to the confusion.

There is one end of the room where it is almost intact, and there, when the crosslights fade and the low sun shines directly upon it, I can almost fancy radiation after all — the interminable grotesque seems to form around a common center and rush off in headlong plunges of equal distraction.

It makes me tired to follow it. I will take a nap, I guess.

I don't know why I should write this.

I don't want to.

I don't feel able.

And I know John would think it absurd. But I *must* say what I feel and think in some way — it is such a relief!

But the effort is getting to be greater than the relief.

Half the time now I am awfully lazy, and lie down ever so much. John says I mustn't lose my strength, and has me take cod liver oil and lots of tonics and things, to say nothing of ale and wines and rare meat.

Dear John! He loves me very dearly, and hates to have me sick. I tried to have a real earnest reasonable talk with him the other day, and tell him how I wish he would let me go and make a visit to Cousin Henry and Julia.

But he said I wasn't able to go, nor able to stand it after I got there; and I did not make out a very good case for myself, for I was crying before I had finished.

It is getting to be a great effort for me to think straight. Just this nervous weakness, I suppose.

And dear John gathered me up in his arms, and just carried me upstairs and laid me on the bed, and sat by me and read to me till it tired my head.

He said I was his darling and his comfort and all he had, and that I must take care of myself for his sake, and keep well.

He says no one but myself can help me out of it, that I must use my will and self-control and not let any silly fancies run away with me.

There's one comfort — the baby is well and happy, and does not have to occupy this nursery with the horrid wallpaper.

FEMALE SUBORDINATION

Sherry B. Ortner

What do I mean when I say that everywhere, in every known culture, women are considered in some degree inferior to men? First of all, I must stress that I am talking about *cultural* evaluations; I am saying that each culture, in its own way and on its own terms, makes this evaluation. But what would constitute evidence that a particular culture considers women inferior?

Three types of data would suffice: (1) elements of cultural ideology and informants' statements that *explicitly* devalue women, according them, their roles, their tasks, their products, and their social milieux less prestige than are accorded men and the male correlates; (2) symbolic devices, such as the attribution of defilement, which may be interpreted as *implicity* making a statement of inferior valuation; and (3) social-structural arrangements that exclude women from participation in or contact with some realm in which the highest powers of the society are felt to reside. These three types of data may all of course be interrelated in any particular system, though they need not necessarily be. Further, any one of them will usually be sufficient to make the point of female inferiority in a given culture. Certainly, female exclusion from the most sacred rite or the highest political council is sufficient evidence. Certainly, explicit cultural ideology devaluating women (and their tasks, roles, products, etc.) is sufficient evidence. Symbolic indicators such as defilement are usually sufficient, although in a few cases in which, say, men and women are equally polluting to one another, a further indicator is required—and is, as far as my investigations have ascertained, always available.

On any or all of these counts, then, I would flatly assert that we find women subordinated to men in every known society. The search for a genuinely egalitarian, let alone matriarchal, culture has proved fruitless.

From "Is Female to Male as Nature Is to Culture?" in M. Z. Rosaldo and L. Lamphere, eds., *Woman, Culture, and Society* (1974).

If we had not used it, that blessed child would have! What a fortunate escape! Why, I wouldn't have a child of mine, an impressionable little thing, live in such a room for worlds.

I never thought of it before, but it is lucky that John kept me here after all; I can stand it so much easier than a baby, you see.

Of course I never mention it to them any more—I am too wise—but I keep watch for it all the same.

There are things in the wallpaper that nobody knows about but me, or ever will.

Behind the outside pattern the dim shapes get clearer every day.

It is always the same shape, only very numerous.

And it is like a woman stooping down and creeping about behind that pattern. I don't like it a bit. I wonder—I begin to think—I wish John would take me away from here!

It is so hard to talk with John about my case, because he is so wise, and because he loves me so.

But I tried it last night.

It was moonlight. The moon shines in all around just as the sun does.

I hate to see it sometimes, it creeps so slowly, and always comes in by one window or another.

John was asleep and I hated to waken him, so I kept still and watched the moonlight on that undulating wallpaper till I felt creepy.

The faint figure behind seemed to shake the pattern, just as if she wanted to get out.

I got up softly and went to feel and see if the paper *did* move, and when I came back John was awake.

"What is it, little girl?" he said. "Don't go walking about like that—you'll get cold."

I thought it was a good time to talk, so I told him that I really was not gaining here, and that I wished he would take me away.

"Why, darling!" said he. "Our lease will be up in three weeks, and I can't see how to leave before.

"The repairs are not done at home, and I cannot possibly leave town just now. Of course, if you were in any danger, I could and would, but you really are better, dear, whether you can see it or not. I am a doctor, dear, and I know. You are gaining flesh and color, your appetite is better, I feel really much easier about you."

"I don't weigh a bit more," said I, "nor as much; and my appetite may be better in the evening when you are here but it is worse in the morning when you are away!"

"Bless her little heart!" said he with a big hug. "She shall be as sick as she pleases! But now let's improve the shining hours by going to sleep, and talk about it in the morning!"

"And you won't go away?" I asked gloomily.

"Why, how can I, dear? It is only three weeks more and then we will take a nice little trip for a few days while Jennie is getting the house ready. Really, dear, you are better!"

"Better in body perhaps—" I began, and stopped short, for he sat up straight and looked at me with such a stern, reproachful look that I could not say another word.

"My darling," said he, "I beg you, for my sake and for our child's sake, as well as for your own, that you will never for one instant let that idea enter your mind! There is nothing so dangerous, so fascinating, to a temperament like yours. It is a false and foolish fancy. Can you trust me as a physician when I tell you so?"

So of course I said no more on that score, and we went to sleep before long. He thought I was asleep first, but I wasn't, and lay there for hours trying to decide whether that front pattern and the back pattern really did move together or separately.

On a pattern like this, by daylight, there is a lack of sequence, a defiance of law, that is a constant irritant to a normal mind.

The color is hideous enough, and unreliable enough, and infuriating enough, but the pattern is torturing.

You think you have mastered it, but just as you get well under way in following, it turns a back-somersault and there you are. It slaps you in the face, knocks you down, and tramples upon you. It is like a bad dream.

The outside pattern is a florid arabesque, reminding one of a fungus. If you can imagine a toadstool in joints, an interminable string of toadstools, budding and sprouting in endless convolutions—why, that is something like it.

That is, sometimes!

There is one marked peculiarity about this paper, a thing nobody seems to notice but myself, and that is that it changes as the light changes.

When the sun shoots in through the east window—I always watch for that first long, straight ray—it changes so quickly that I never can quite believe it.

That is why I watch it always.

By moonlight—the moon shines in all night when there is a moon—I wouldn't know it was the same paper.

At night in any kind of light, in twilight, candlelight, lamplight, and worst of all by moonlight, it becomes bars! The outside pattern, I mean, and the woman behind it is as plain as can be.

I didn't realize for a long time what the thing was that showed behind, that dim subpattern, but now I am quite sure it is a woman.

By daylight she is subdued, quiet. I fancy it is the pattern that keeps her so still. It is so puzzling. It keeps me quiet by the hour.

I lie down ever so much now. John says it is good for me, and to sleep all I can.

Indeed he started the habit by making me lie down for an hour after each meal.

It is a very bad habit, I am convinced, for you see, I don't sleep.

And that cultivates deceit, for I don't tell them I'm awake—oh, no!

The fact is I am getting a little afraid of John.

He seems very queer sometimes, and even Jennie has an inexplicable look.

It strikes me occasionally, just as a scientific hypothesis, that perhaps it is the paper!

I have watched John when he did not know I was looking, and come into the room suddenly on the most innocent excuses, and I've caught him several times *looking at the paper*! And Jennie too. I caught Jennie with her hand on it once.

She didn't know I was in the room, and when I asked her in a quiet, a very quiet voice, with the most restrained manner possible, what she was doing with the paper, she turned around as if she had been caught stealing, and looked quite angry—asked me why I should frighten her so!

Then she said that the paper stained everything it touched, that she had found yellow smooches on all my clothes and John's and she wished we would be more careful!

Did not that sound innocent? But I know she was studying that pattern, and I am determined that nobody shall find it out but myself!

Life is very much more exciting now than it used to be. You see, I have something more to expect, to look forward to, to watch. I really do eat better, and am more quiet than I was.

John is so pleased to see me improve! He laughed a little the other day, and said I seemed to be flourishing in spite of my wallpaper.

I turned it off with a laugh. I had no intention of telling him it was *because* of the wallpaper—he would make fun of me. He might even want to take me away.

I don't want to leave now until I have found it out. There is a week more, and I think that will be enough.

I'm feeling so much better!

I don't sleep much at night, for it is so interesting to watch developments; but I sleep a good deal during the daytime.

In the daytime it is tiresome and perplexing.

There are always new shoots on the fungus, and new shades of yellow all over it. I cannot keep count of them, though I have tried conscientiously.

It is the strangest yellow, that wallpaper! It makes me think of all the yellow things I ever saw—not beautiful ones like buttercups, but old foul, bad yellow things.

But there is something else about that paper—the smell! I noticed it the moment we came into the room, but with so much air and sun it was not bad. Now we have had a week of fog and rain, and whether the windows are open or not, the smell is there.

It creeps all over the house.

I find it hovering in the dining-room, skulking in the parlor, hiding in the hall, lying in wait for me on the stairs.

It gets into my hair.

Even when I go to ride, if I turn my head suddenly and surprise it—there is that smell!

Such a peculiar odor, too! I have spent hours in trying to analyze it, to find what it smelled like.

It is not bad—at first—and very gentle, but quite the subtlest, most enduring odor I ever met.

In this damp weather it is awful. I wake up in the night and find it hanging over me.

It used to disturb me at first. I thought seriously of burning the house—to reach the smell.

But now I am used to it. The only thing I can think of that it is like is the *color* of the paper! A yellow smell.

There is a very funny mark on this wall, low down, near the mopboard. A streak that runs round the room. It goes behind every piece of furniture, except the bed, a long straight, even *smooch*, as if it had been rubbed over and over.

I wonder how it was done and who did it, and what they did it for. Round and round and round—round and round and round—it makes me dizzy!

I really have discovered something at last.

Through watching so much at night, when it changes so, I have finally found out.

The front pattern *does* move—and no wonder! The woman behind shakes it!

Sometimes I think there are a great many women behind, and sometimes only one, and she crawls around fast, and her crawling shakes it all over.

Then in the very bright spots she keeps still, and in the very shady spots she just takes hold of the bars and shakes them hard.

And she is all the time trying to climb through. But nobody could climb through that pattern—it strangles so: I think that is why it has so many heads.

They get through and then the pattern strangles them off and turns them upside down, and makes their eyes white!

If those heads were covered or taken off it would not be half so bad.

I think that woman gets out in the daytime!

And I'll tell you why—privately—I've seen her!

I can see her out of every one of my windows!

PATRIARCHY

Jane Flax

Feminist theory is based on a series of assumptions. First, it assumes that men and women have different experiences; that the world is not the same for men and women. Some women think the experiences of women should be identical to the experiences of men. Others would like to transform the world so that there are no such dichotomous experiences. Proponents of both views, however, assume that women's experiences differ from men's, and that one task of feminist theory is to explain that difference.

Secondly, feminist theory assumes that women's oppression is not a subset of some other social relationship. Some argue that if the class system were destroyed, then women would not be oppressed—I don't classify that as feminist theory. Feminist theory assumes that women's oppression is a unique constellation of social problems and has to be understood in itself, and not as a subset of class or any other structure.

It also assumes that women's oppression is not merely a case of what the Chinese call "bad attitudes." I have problems with the word "sexism," because the term implies that women's oppression will disappear when men become more enlightened. On the contrary, I think feminist theory assumes that the oppression of women is part of the way the structure of the world is organized, and that one task of feminist theory is to explain how and why this structure evolved.

Feminist theory names this structure "patriarchy," and assumes that it is a historical force that has a material and psychological base. What I mean by "patriarchy" is the system in which men have more power than women, and have more access to whatever society esteems. What society esteems obviously varies from culture to culture; but if you look at the spheres of power, you'll find that all who have it are male. This is a long-term historical fact rooted in real things. It's not a question of bad attitudes; it's not a historical accident—there are real advantages to men in retaining control over women. Feminist theorists want to explain why that's so.

Patriarchy works backwards as well. It affects the way men and women feel about themselves, and is so deeply internalized that we can't imagine a world without gender. As much as we talk about androgyny, or some situation in which gender isn't so significant, I don't think any of us could imagine a world in which gender would not bring with it many special meanings. *We* may still want to attach special meanings to gender, but a feminist theory would argue that the power attached to gender should disappear; it should not determine whether a person is excluded or included in whatever is esteemed by society.

From "Women Do Theory," *Quest* (1979).

It is the same woman, I know, for she is always creeping, and most women do not creep by daylight.

I see her in that long shaded lane, creeping up and down. I see her in those dark grape arbors, creeping all round the garden.

I see her on that long road under the trees, creeping along, and when a carriage comes she hides under the blackberry vines.

I don't blame her a bit. It must be very humiliating to be caught creeping by daylight!

I always lock the door when I creep by daylight. I can't do it at night, for I know John would suspect something at once.

And John is so queer now that I don't want to irritate him. I wish he would take another room! Besides, I don't want anybody to get that woman out at night but myself.

I often wonder if I could see her out of all the windows at once.

But, turn as fast as I can, I can only see out of one at one time.

And though I always see her, she *may* be able to creep faster than I can turn! I have watched her sometimes away off in the open country, creeping as fast as a cloud shadow in a wind.

If only that top pattern could be gotten off from the under one! I mean to try it, little by little.

I have found out another funny thing, but I shan't tell it this time! It does not do to trust people too much.

There are only two more days to get this paper off, and I believe John is beginning to notice. I don't like the look in his eyes.

And I heard him ask Jennie a lot of professional questions about me. She had a very good report to give.

She said I slept a good deal in the daytime.

John knows I don't sleep very well at night, for all I'm so quiet!

He asked me all sorts of questions too, and pretended to be very loving and kind.

As if I couldn't see through him!

Still, I don't wonder he acts so, sleeping under this paper for three months.

It only interests me, but I feel sure John and Jennie are affected by it.

Hurrah! This is the last day, but it is enough. John is to stay in town over night, and won't be out until this evening.

Jennie wanted to sleep with me—the sly thing; but I told her I should undoubtedly rest better for a night all alone.

That was clever, for really I wasn't alone a bit! As soon as it was moonlight and that poor thing began to crawl and shake the pattern, I got up and ran to help her.

I pulled and she shook. I shook and she pulled, and before morning we had peeled off yards of that paper.

A strip about as high as my head and half around the room.

And then when the sun came and that awful pattern began to laugh at me, I declared I would finish it today!

We go away tomorrow, and they are moving all my furniture down again to leave things as they were before.

Jennie looked at the wall in amazement, but I told her merrily that I did it out of pure spite at the vicious thing.

She laughed and said she wouldn't mind doing it herself, but I must not get tired.

How she betrayed herself that time!

But I am here, and no person touches this paper but Me—not *alive*!

She tried to get me out of the room—it was too patent! But I said it was so quiet and empty and clean now that I believed I would lie down again and sleep all I could, and not to wake me even for dinner—I would call when I woke.

So now she is gone, and the servants are gone, and the things are gone, and there is nothing left but that great bedstead nailed down, with the canvas mattress we found on it.

We shall sleep downstairs tonight, and take the boat home tomorrow.

I quite enjoy the room, now it is bare again.

How those children did tear about here!

This bedstead is fairly gnawed!

But I must get to work.

I have locked the door and thrown the key down into the front path.

I don't want to go out, and I don't want to have anybody come in, till John comes.

I want to astonish him.

I've got a rope up here that even Jennie did not find. If that woman does get out, and tries to get away, I can tie her!

But I forgot I could not reach far without anything to stand on!

This bed will *not* move!

I tried to lift and push it until I was lame, and then I got so angry I bit off a little piece at one corner—but it hurt my teeth.

Then I peeled off all the paper I could reach standing on the floor. It sticks horribly and the pattern just enjoys it! All those strangled heads and bulbous eyes and waddling fungus growths just shriek with derision!

I am getting angry enough to do something desperate. To jump out of the window would be admirable exercise, but the bars are too strong even to try.

THE POPE AGAINST WOMEN PRIESTS

Naomi Goldenberg

Conservative leaders of contemporary religious institutions understand that allowing women access to top positions of authority threatens the age-old composition of the institutions themselves.

In January 1977, Pope Paul VI issued a declaration affirming the Vatican's ban on allowing women to be ordained as Catholic priests. The document states that because Christ was a man and because he chose only male disciples, women can never serve as chief officials in the Catholic hierarchy.

Pope Paul used an impressive knowledge of how image and symbol operate in the human mind to build his case against female priests. "The priest," he explained, "is a sign . . . a sign that must be perceptible and which the faithful must be able to recognize with ease. The whole sacramental economy is in fact based upon natural signs, on symbols imprinted upon the human psychology. . . ."

Pope Paul reasoned that because the priest must represent Christ, i.e., God, the priest must resemble God. If the priest looked very different from Christ, a follower would not feel immediate connection between God and the priest who was supposed to embody *Him*. The Pope realized that people experience God through *His* representatives. If one were to change the sex of God's representatives, one would be changing the nature of God *Himself*. As the chief guardian of the Catholic faith, the Pope understood that he could not allow any serious tampering with the image of God. . . .

However, we must ask ourselves what will happen to Christianity when women do succeed in changing traditions so that they are treated as the equals of men. Will not this major departure from the Christian view of women radically alter the religion? Pope Paul knew it would. The Pope understood that representatives of Christianity mirror the image of God by calling to mind the male figure of Jesus Christ. If women play at being priests, they would play at being God; and Christianity, he insisted, can only afford to have men in that role. . . .

From *Changing of the Gods* (1979).

Besides I wouldn't do it. Of course not. I know well enough that a step like that is improper and might be misconstrued.

I don't like to *look* out of the windows even — there are so many of those creeping women, and they creep so fast.

I wonder if they all come out of that wallpaper as I did!

But I am securely fastened now by my well-hidden rope — you don't get *me* out in the road there!

I suppose I shall have to get back behind the pattern when it comes night, and that is hard!

It is so pleasant to be out in this great room and creep around as I please!

I don't want to go outside. I won't, even if Jennie asks me to.

For outside you have to creep on the ground, and everything is green instead of yellow.

But here I can creep smoothly on the floor, and my shoulder just fits in that long smooch around the wall, so I cannot lose my way.

Why, there's John at the door!

It is no use, young man, you can't open it!

How he does call and pound!

Now he's crying to Jennie for an axe.

It would be a shame to break down that beautiful door!

"John, dear!" said I in the gentlest voice. "The key is down by the front steps, under a plantain leaf!"

That silenced him for a few moments.

Then he said, very quietly indeed, "Open the door, my darling!"

"I can't," said I. "The key is down by the front door under a plantain leaf!" And then I said it again, several times, very gently and slowly, and said it so often that he had to go and see, and he got it of course, and came in. He stopped short by the door.

"What is the matter?" he cried. "For God's sake, what are you doing!"

I kept on creeping just the same, but I looked at him over my shoulder.

"I've got out at last," said I, "in spite of you and Jane. And I've pulled off most of the paper, so you can't put me back!"

Now why should that man have fainted? But he did, and right across my path by the wall, so that I had to creep over him every time!

NOTE

1. Mitchell was a Philadelphia neurologist and author of *Diseases of the Nervous System, Especially of Women* (1881).

Further Questions

1. How would you interpret the symbolism in this story? Can you see yourself or any of your own problems in the scenes depicted?
2. Does the notion of one's "true self" make any sense? Would it be helpful to say that the woman in the story was searching for her true self? If so, explain what "true self" means. If not, how would you characterize what is going on in the story?

Further Readings

Bergman, Frithjof. *On Being Free*. South Bend, IN: University of Notre Dame Press, 1977. A theory of freedom along Sartrean lines.

Haight, Mary. *A Study of Self-Deception*. New York: Humanities Press, 1980. A British philosopher explains what it means to pull the wool over your own eyes.

19 Trans or Me?

ADAM/LINDA PARASCANDOLA

Adam Parascandola was born Linda Parascandola. He lived the first twenty-four years of his life as a woman before transitioning to living as a man. As Linda Parascandola, he attended the University of Maryland and received his bachelor's degree in philosophy. After graduating, Parascandola spent a year in India, through a program at the University of Wisconsin, studying animals in Hindu society. After returning from India, he read *Stone Butch Blues* by Leslie Feinberg, a novel about a woman who transitions first to living as a man and then to living as neither man nor woman. At this point (Parascandola) realized it was possible for people like himself to change their sex. A year later, he began taking testosterone and changed his name from Linda to Adam. Parascandola's friends and family were accepting and supportive of this change. Recently he married the woman he has been dating since before his transition. In 2000, he celebrated his thirty-first birthday and his sixth birthday as a man. Parascandola is grateful to have been born into the gray areas in our established sex and gender systems, as this accident of birth has allowed him to look at the ways in which these and other categories are limiting.

Reading Questions

1. What is the difference between sex and gender?
2. How can transsexuals be explained within the two-gender system?
3. How does the existence of transgendered people challenge the two-gender system?
4. How might the existence of transgendered people fit into or challenge what philosophers of personal identity such as John Locke have said about the factors that determine personal identity?

IN KAFKA'S *METAMORPHOSIS*, Gregor Samsa wakes up one morning to find his body has become that of a cockroach. One could say that he has become a cockroach, but this does not seem to be entirely true. The main distress caused to Gregor seems to come from the schism between his mental identity as a human being and his external appearance as a roach.

Imagine Kafka's scenario with one major change. Imagine that Gregor was born to a family of roaches, with the body of a roach. Though he has had the external appearance of a bug since birth, he still maintains his mental identity as that of a human being. Imagine that only Gregor feels horrified at his predicament. Everyone around him fails to see his mental human identity and thinks he is strange for insisting he is human. He is to everyone a bug, albeit an eccentric one, who has fantasies of one day becoming human. Who would accept this person? Other roaches would most likely dismiss him as disturbed, crazy, or perverse—particularly if he picked up the human custom of wearing clothes and had them specially tailored to fit his roach body. Humans, on the other hand, would most certainly laugh at his insistence that he is one of them. After all, he would have antennas, an exoskeleton, and several legs.

For transsexuals who are born into a body that seems to be in opposition to their mental identity, this scenario seems eerily familiar. When I was born, the doctor took a look at my genitalia and happily proclaimed me to be a healthy baby girl—branding me with an identity that was to haunt me for many years. There is a saying in the transgendered community that when one is asked what sex one's child is, one should always reply, "I don't know, they haven't told me yet." This, however, is not generally how doctors or most people think about gender. We think of gender as an identity that is concrete and based on scientific principles that place people neatly into one sex or the other. Until recently, no one thought about questioning this two gender system.

Let me define a few terms. *Transgender* is a term I use for all those who do not feel the sex they were assigned at birth is an adequate description of themselves. That is, they feel that their gender/sex identity in some ways goes beyond or differs from the category of male or female to which they were assigned at birth. Though often used interchangeably, the words *sex* and *gender* refer to two different things. Gender refers to one's mental identity while sex—that is, male or female—is a category to which one is assigned based on various physical attributes, whether it be genitalia or chromosomes. Many transgendered people may visibly cross or challenge their assigned category of sex by appearing androgynous, cross dressing, or expressing in other ways their identification with a different group. One of the most publicized forms of transgenderism includes transsexuals—those who actively change physical characteristics so as to move themselves from one sex category into the other. I am in this group. People call this a "sex change," but the process does not involve one single operation or even one single option. I myself have had surgery to have my breasts removed and have been taking testosterone to grow facial hair, deepen my voice, and lose female fat deposits while adding muscle. Gone are the days when transsexuals flew to Denmark and came back a new man or woman. Transsexuals like myself now choose what level of surgery and transformation they want. In the past, transsexuals typically made a clean break from and hid the secret of their former lives. Today many people are openly transsexual and are proud to claim their past life. I transitioned, or changed my sex, without taking any leave from my job. While I kept all my old friends and acquaintances—including my partner—I gradually got

people used to referring to me with male pronouns and by my new name. Retaining this connection to the past has helped me to keep the thread of my self whole. Rather than being a break that separates my self into two halves—before and after—I feel my life has been the winding road of one self.

Probably what most of you are asking yourselves at this point is: Why would anyone want to go through all this? What drives people to change their sex? Let's go back to our Kafka example for a minute. Imagine that you look like a bug to all observers. Though you could say to yourself that you are human and could know that you are human, other humans, seeing you as a bug, may still try to stomp on you. I knew from a young age that I was male despite all external appearances. However, the people around me insisted that I was female—labeling me a "tomboy." After all, we are a society that functions first and foremost on appearances. It is very hard for us to conceive that a person could have a mental identity that contradicts a physical one. I was told that I would grow out of it, that I was really a lesbian, and that my feelings were the result of some childhood trauma. Throughout most of my life I was simply told that I was mistaken. Whatever I thought, I was clearly a girl in the eyes of others. My gender was male, while my sex was female. This distinction is made in the transsexual world to show, among other things, that while someone may change sex, gender identity remains the same. That is, though I changed my sex from female to male, my gender identity was male from the beginning and remains unchanged. This is part of the thread, I suppose, that allows us to say that we are the same person that we were before.

It is interesting, I think, to consider briefly how my situation might fit into and/or challenge the frameworks in terms of which philosophers talk about personal identity. John Locke, for instance, distinguished between the identity of a human and the identity of a person. A human's identity, he claimed, is a matter of biology. One's identity as a human lasts as long as one's body lasts and no longer. If a person changed into a cockroach, the human who that person was just prior to the change would cease as soon as the change was made, even though the person would persist not as a human, but as a cockroach. A person's identity, Locke claimed, is a matter not of biology, but of psychology. Locke thought that the element of psychology that matters most in determining a person's identity is memory. But later philosophers who have been sympathetic to Locke's proposal — so-called *psychological continuity* theorists of personal identity — have tended to claim that many elements of one's psychology in addition to memory are also important in determining one's personal identity. Few of these theorists have discussed how a person's sex or gender identifications might affect the question of their continuing personal identity. In stressing the importance of psychology in determining personal identity, however, they have at least tacitly conceded the possibility that sex and gender identifications might play a key role. But from my point of view, this worry about what the philosophers might say is something of a digression.

Returning now to what I was talking about just before that digression into traditional philosophy, take a moment to think if your gender is aligned with your sex. My guess is that most of you will be asking what that means. Most of you have probably never thought about whether an internal gender identity coincides with your sex. I myself had never thought about gender identity until about five years ago. I knew for many years that how I felt on the inside did not match how I looked on the outside, but given no model in society that matched how I felt, I was simply confused. I knew even as a young child that I was male and did not understand why others insisted this was not true. As my body began to develop through puberty, I was shocked to find that I was actually developing as a girl. A schism opened between my internal (gender) identity and my external (sex) identity, and I had no idea how to reconcile it. My first attempt was to change my internal identity to match my external identity. I needed to accept that I was female. I rationalized that perhaps I had not been exposed to the right female role models and so my rebellion against being female was only a rebellion against the images of females put forth by society. I remembered being in a high school acting class where I was very excited when it came time for me to choose a scene to act out. I was trying to decide between my favorite Tennessee Williams characters when the teacher told me I would have to play a

female character because I would never be allowed to play a male character in the "real" world of acting. Little did she know the possibilities that exist. But at the time I simply tried to pick out a female character I could relate to. I could not find anything in Tennessee Williams or in any other play I looked for. The idea of playing a female character, like the idea of wearing a dress, provoked a violent reaction in me. I could not do it. I settled on playing a very androgynous character who could really have been any sex because no names were involved. As I looked back on this experience, I thought that perhaps society was like a Tennessee Williams play where I could relate to the male characters but not the female ones. Maybe it was up to me to redefine my role as a female.

I should mention that while I was living as a female I shuddered at the idea of putting on a dress or heels, even in play. Once I developed a masculine body, I had no such reluctance. Now secure in my male body, I have the freedom to play with my gender. At this earlier point in time, however, I began to identify myself as a lesbian. This community respected and even appreciated my masculinity. I didn't feel that I needed to soften my voice or my dress. I found women like K. D. lang, who dressed in suits, had their hair cut short, and were harassed by women for using the "wrong" bathroom. With some differences, they were women like me.

Most of my lesbian friends celebrated and enjoyed their femaleness. Being female was an essential part of who they were or who they saw themselves as. Many of them were not traditionally feminine, but they seemed very comfortable with the femaleness of their bodies. My body felt strange and uncomfortable. When I was naked, I saw it as a glaring statement of opposition to who I was. Here was a community of women who seemed like the role models I had missed before, but still I felt out of place. Eventually I had to admit my internal identity was male, not masculine female, and was not going to change. I cannot explain very well the strength of this internal identity. Everyone has, I believe, an internal identity that is in constant struggle with an external identity. We may see ourselves as strident environmentalists, yet we drive a car and live in houses heated by oil or electricity. We may see ourselves as smart, hard-working people but may be suspected of criminal behavior based on our race or dress. We live in a society that likes to label and categorize, and each of us struggles to find where we fit in those categories. Everyone's struggle may not be the same as mine, but we each have to reconcile our internal selves with the world outside us.

I realized I needed to change my external identity to match my internal one. How do I know this internal identity is male? I don't know. First I would need to decide what being male means. Is being male about the way your body looks? Is it about the way you think? This is a difficult question for me. I don't have all the physical parts traditionally associated with men. I do not have male genitalia and, lacking this, how would other men think of me if we were all naked in the locker room? Yet I feel male. I have certain behaviors that are thought of as male: a hard time crying, emotions that are often inaccessible to me, an ability with maps and directions. But I have other behaviors that are thought of as female: a strong compassion for animals, a gentle nature, a terrible mind for math. Like most people, I am a mix of both "male" and "female" behaviors. So if these behaviors don't make me male, what does? Perhaps there is a physical reason for the way I feel, an abundance or absence of some hormone or chromosome that has given me traits that we have labeled as male. Or is it just that my picture of myself coincides more closely with being a man? In many ways, my external identity seems unimportant to who I am. Over years of taking hormones and altering myself physically, I look like a completely different person than I did before. When I go back to where I grew up and walk by people I knew before, I am not recognized. Yet I feel myself to be the same person I have always been. Certainly I am more comfortable in my own skin, but beyond that nothing major has changed.

So why the need to change myself externally? One reason is simply that without changing my body, others would not believe my internal identity. When people see me as male, they reinforce this identity in many of the subtle and not so subtle ways that people relate to the different sexes. Other men are more relaxed around me and talk to me in a way that suggests, "You're on our team."

Women, on the other hand, very clearly say to me, through body language and conversation, "You are not one of us." I may not agree with this division of the sexes, but being treated as an insider by other men reinforces my male identity. If I appear female, most people will not relate to me as male no matter how much I try to convince them. Seeing is believing, after all. But the stronger reason for this change is more subtle. I have an internal self that was strong enough to overpower my years of indoctrination in the world of the dual sexes and strong enough to force me to make major changes in my life that cost considerable time and money and endangered many of my closest relationships. Because I can look back and see where I've been to explain who I am, sometimes I think that my self is nothing more than the past I have behind me, that there is no self who directs my life. Yet there is something inside me that seems to tell me where to take the next step. When I came to the realization that I had the ability to change my body, I felt immediately that it was a fork in the road I was meant to take. The rewards have been tremendous. Not only did I gain more confidence and comfort in moving through this world, but I gained a glimpse into both Venutians and Martians, to use the terminology of a popular book. I have also, in breaking past this duality, had the limitations of my thinking highlighted for me.

I have realized how much language dictates the way we think. We are given only two choices in our language, male and female, and this forces us to make a choice as to whether we are more man or woman. I often wonder, if society did not insist on granting identity based on external characteristics, whether I would have felt the need to change my body. Was it some fluke of nature that I was male inside and female on the outside, or is it that my internal self is in conflict with society's view of my external body? I think of how I felt in my female body when I hiked on the Appalachian Trail with only my dogs and how I feel now hiking on the trail with my male self. The feeling is the same. On my own I was comfortable in my skin. However, as soon as any thoughts would enter my head about other people or I were to pass or meet up with anyone on the trail, I was immediately uncomfortable again. It helped that there were no mirrors on the trail to show me my female body. What I could see of myself—flannel shirt, jeans, and hiking boots—is the same as I see now. There were no reminders contrasting who I felt I was with who others felt I was. If I was not assigned a female sex based on my body, and with it a whole bag of expectations and assumptions, then would I feel the need to change? This sex we are assigned is a social identity that is given to us based on physical characteristics that fit more into one category than the other.

Our social sexual identities are similar to other social assignments, such as race and ethnicity, that come with their own sets of assumptions. Often people are placed by others around them into these categories, which are thought to be mutually exclusive. However, they tend to oversimplify the individualities of who we are. It is important to realize that these social identities have not always been the same as they are today. For instance, many societies have allowed for more than two sexes. In India there is what is called a third sex, *hijra*s. These are "men" who are castrated or who have abnormalities in their genitalia. Though today they are often made fun of, in earlier times they were respected members of society. In the *Mahabarata*, a famous ancient Indian text, Arjuna—considered to be the greatest archer ever—lived for a time as a *hijra* in the court of a king. Other societies have had multiple sex categories. What we have seen as concrete and immutable now seems arbitrary and temporal. Perhaps my identity is simply so far removed from our contemporary sex definitions that I have no concept of myself within society without changing to fit the sex categories we have. Maybe I was never a person in conflict with myself but rather a person in conflict with society. Ultimately, this realization, if true, does not alter my decisions, because I am forced to live in the world that we have. We all make compromises in our lives between who we would be ideally and what we must do to get by. I compromise by blending in with genetic men and many times not challenging their assumptions about me. I don't have the energy to be in constant struggle with society, so I choose my battles. I don't undress fully in the locker room at the gym, I don't argue when women tell me I don't know what it's like to have

a period, and I let the people I meet assume I have always checked male on the census form—at least until I get to know them better. I don't feel that these compromises change the way I feel inside or how I direct my life, and I gain a certain peace of mind and comfort from being in public. This does not mean, however, that I will not work to change the way we think about these issues.

My experience as a transsexual blurs the lines of gender identity but does not altogether negate the two-gender system. One could argue that men and women are the only two types of humans and that transsexuals have simply had their wires crossed and belong to the sex opposite to the one they were born into. I was a man born in a woman's body, you could say. However, many transgender people are living in defiance of the traditional sex and gender system. They refuse to identify as male or female or may choose to identify as both. Their gender may be defined by any number of terms now being claimed as identities. Some of these terms have been in effect for many years: *shemale, butch, stone butch,* and so on. Others are newer to our vocabulary: *boychick, riot grrrl, s/he, FTM, trannyfag,* and so on. These terms are most easily explained as designating different genders. Through increasing body modifications, however, many people no longer clearly fit into one sex or the other. A shemale may choose to have her breasts enlarged surgically and to be put on estrogen but keep her male genitalia. A butch, on the other hand, may take testosterone to grow a beard and develop muscle mass but may have no surgery whatsoever. Others may not alter their body in any physical way but claim a space that lies somewhere between male and female. By the very existence of persons who identify with a gender beyond male and female, the dual-gender system has already been overturned. In academia and in science, these new genders are accepted and discussed. People have, in a sense, taken control of their identity. We have entered an age where we no longer look to "experts" to tell us who we are. Instead, people claim space for themselves outside these traditional identities.

The opening up of sex/gender definitions begins to play havoc with other social identities. Sexual orientation is one of the most affected. For how do we define sexual orientation? There are traditionally three categories: those who are attracted to the same sex (homosexual), those who are attracted to the opposite sex (heterosexual), and those who are attracted to both sexes (bisexual). This definition necessitates that someone be a member of one sex or the other. Otherwise, what is the same sex and what is the opposite sex? Take myself, for example. Were I only attracted to men, would I be homosexual or heterosexual? Being with my wife, am I heterosexual? At which point along my transition did I change from being homosexual to heterosexual? How about a transsexual who is attracted to other transsexuals? If someone is not exclusively male or female, then how do these definitions work?

I suppose in all this someone could argue that these self-imposed definitions are about gender and not sex. They could still argue for a dual-sex system. They could say that those who have altered their bodies still belong to the sex into which they were born. However, the dual-sex system has never encompassed the entire human population. Everybody knows that there are hermaphrodites—that is, "intersexed" people with both male and female reproductive organs—but few seem to think about what they mean to our sex system. Rather than seeing them as a refutation of the binary system, society has long chosen to consider the intersexed as freaks of nature or anomalies. In more recent history, they have been assigned a sex at birth and then altered physically to fit this category. Intersexed babies may be castrated, pumped with hormones, and subjected to a number of lengthy surgical procedures—all in order to "correct" their bodies to fit into one narrow category or the other. These procedures are performed on newborns, who of course have no say in the matter. Often the parents have no say as well. Frightened and confused by this "birth defect," they defer to the "experts." Many of these intersexed persons grow up with an identity that is strongly in conflict with the sex they were assigned. They may feel a strong identity with the other sex or they may feel an affinity with both sexes. One thing that many intersexed persons seem to feel is an anger at the violations that were imposed on them by doctors. That doctors have felt so confident in performing such extreme procedures without consent from the person themselves only demonstrates how engrained our idea is of two-sexes-and-two-sexes-only. There does not seem to be any medical danger to intersexed babies that these procedures avert. What would be the great harm in letting intersexed persons live with the genitalia they are born with and live as the sex and gender they choose? This is where I hope we are headed in the future. That there are more than two sexes has been, I think, well documented both in the non-human and human animal kingdom. The facts are there. It is the way that we look at them that needs to change.

In Kafka's story, Gregor is too horrified at his fate to contemplate how his opinion of roaches may have changed. Imagine in an updated story that Gregor had found a way to change his body to a human body. Say he met other roaches who had actually been born into human bodies and had changed to become roaches. Suppose this transmutation of species occurred in 1 percent of the population. Even in these numbers, it would certainly affect the way we thought about roaches. If my cousin Henry had changed into a roach, I might be hesitant to step on every roach I see for fear that one might be Henry. I would be forced to modify my assumption that roaches are fundamentally different from humans: after all, some roaches would have been born human. Similarly, I think it is time to redefine the way we look at many of our identities. Sex and gender are not the only ones that are crumbling. Racial identities as well are becoming harder to define as we find many people of mixed racial heritage who refuse to assign themselves to one category or another. What do these changes say about who we are?

I have passed through many stages of thought on my journey to where I am today. I thought I was a woman, a lesbian, a transsexual, a man. Each of these words may be used to describe me at some point in my life, but there is some self, separate from these words, that has continued unbroken through time. This self appears to be a conglomeration of memories, thoughts, and actions and is not unlike other selves. I am a person like any other person and my being transsexual does not make me different from others. Going from female to male was not a long way to travel, and the words I use to define myself are not fundamental to who I am. It turns out that my internal self is only partially gender based. Myself as a male and myself as a female are the same self. I've lived on Venus and I've lived on Mars, and they ain't that different. And that's why, if I am forced to name an identity for my self, I simply give the following words: *homosapien, herbivore, earthling, resident of the Milky Way Galaxy, inhabitor of the infinite universe.*

Further Questions

1. What does being male mean? What does being female mean? Are these genders or sexes? How do we determine who is one sex or the other? Compare the various ways we determine sex and gender and see where you fit in.
2. In what ways is your internal self in conflict with your external self? Is this internal self the same self through drastic external changes such as a sex change? If this internal self changes as we grow, what is the "thread of self"?
3. If we accept that the two-gender system is inadequate for defining the full spectrum of humanity, then what other categories and definitions in our thinking can also come into question? What purpose do these definitions of ourselves and others serve? Would we be better off without them, or could we expand these categories to include everyone?

Further Readings

Bornstein, Kate. *My Gender Workbook*. New York: Routledge, 1998. This book will challenge the way you think about gender.
Feinberg, Leslie. *Transgender Warriors: Making History from Joan of Arc to Rupaul*. Boston: Beacon Press, 1996. Portrays the transgender spectrum around the world and throughout history.

Part IV

Freedom

I T IS SOMETIME IN THE TECHNOLOGICALLY DISTANT FUTURE. You are a judge in the state's highest court. The facts in the case before you are these: A student made an android, which subsequently murdered someone and then fled. The police, unable to catch the android, apprehend the student instead. The prosecutor says the student should be held responsible for the android's behavior. The student defends herself by claiming that she programmed the android to make choices of its own free will, an idea the prosecutor rejects on the grounds that an android's choices are the product of just two things: how it was constructed originally, and how it is subsequently modified by its environment. Obviously, he reasons, the android has no say in how it is constructed, and it does not choose its initial environment. Its maker—the student—determines both of these things. Even if the android later chooses to move to another environment—or to reprogram itself—it cannot, the prosecutor claims, make such a choice freely, for how it makes such a choice will be determined by circumstances over which it has no control. If there is responsibility anywhere, the prosecutor argues, it lies behind the android, in its maker.

The student claims that the state's reasons for denying free will to an android are equally applicable to humans, for humans too, she points out, are the product of material and environmental circumstances over which they have no control. And, she adds, if God or nature programs humans, rather than a human programmer, that hardly makes humans any more free than androids. So, she concludes, since humans obviously can have free will, so too can androids.

The time for a decision is at hand: *Could* the student have programmed the android to have free will? You, as the judge, have to decide. What is your verdict?

20   The Illusion of Free Will

BARON HOLBACH

Born of German parents, Paul Heinrich Dietrich (1723–1789), later Baron Holbach, lived most of his life in France. A materialist and a relentless, militant enemy of organized religion in general and of the Catholic Church in particular, he was one of the first European writers to openly advocate atheism. Regarded by those who knew him best as a person of great generosity and integrity, he taught that religion and priestcraft are the source of most man-made evil and that atheism promotes good morality. His main work, *System of Nature* (1770), published anonymously, produced a great stir, eliciting responses from many famous men of the day, such as Voltaire and Goethe, the latter of whom regarded it as the most repulsive book ever written. In the selection from it that follows, Holbach argues that freedom of will is an illusion.

Reading Questions

1. Does Holbach think we are always, rarely, or never free?
2. How does Holbach use the water example to illustrate that people, no matter what they do, always act in accord with their strongest motives?
3. Some say that the fact that people can sometimes be persuaded to act differently than they originally intended shows that they have free will. How does Holbach reply?
4. Some say that people are free if there are no external obstacles to impede them from doing whatever they want to do. How does Holbach reply?
5. "No one ever acts freely because everyone's actions are caused ultimately by conditions over which they have no control." Is this Holbach's view? If not, what else is he saying?
6. What do the "errors of philosophers" concerning free will arise from?
7. Holbach claims there's no difference between whether you throw yourself out the window or whether someone else throws you out the window. What does he mean? Do you agree?
8. In "The Trial of Socrates," you read about how Socrates boldly refused to save himself by escaping from prison. Would Holbach think Socrates acted as a free agent in making this famous choice? Why? Do you agree? Why?
9. What does Holbach mean by the following terms: *free agency, causality, necessary order,* and *nature*?

MOTIVES AND THE DETERMINATION OF THE WILL

IN WHATEVER MANNER MAN IS CONSIDERED, he is connected to universal nature, and submitted to the necessary and immutable laws that she imposes on all the beings she contains, according to their peculiar essences or to the respective properties with which, without consulting them, she endows each particular species. Man's life is a line that nature commands him to describe upon the surface of the earth, without his ever being able to swerve from it, even for an instant. He is born without his own consent; his organization does in nowise depend upon himself; his ideas come to him involuntarily; his habits are in the power of those who cause him to contract them; he is unceasingly modified by causes, whether visible or concealed, over which he has no control, which necessarily regulate his mode of existence, give the hue to his way of thinking, and determine his manner of acting. He is good or bad, happy or miserable, wise or foolish, reasonable or irrational, without his will being for anything in these various states. Nevertheless, in spite of the shackles by which he is bound, it is pretended he is a free agent, or that independent of the causes by which he is moved, he determines his own will, and regulates his own condition. . . .

The will, as we have elsewhere said, is a modification of the brain, by which it is disposed to action, or prepared to give play to the organs. This will is necessarily determined by the qualities, good or bad, agreeable or painful, of the object or the motive that acts upon his senses, or of which the idea remains with him, and is resuscitated by his memory. In consequence, he acts necessarily, his action is the result of the impulse he receives either from the motive, from the object, or from the idea which has modified his brain, or disposed his will. When he does not act according to this impulse, it is because there comes some new cause, some new motive, some new idea, which modifies his brain in a different manner, gives him a new impulse, determines his will in another way, by which the action of the former impulse is suspended: thus, the sight of an agreeable object, or its idea, determines his will to set him in action to procure it; but if a new object or a new idea more powerfully attracts him, it gives a new direction to his will, annihilates the effect of the former, and prevents the action by which it was to be procured. This is the mode in which reflection, experience, reason, necessarily arrests or suspends the action of man's will: without this he would of necessity have followed the anterior impulse which carried him towards a then desirable object. In all this he always acts according to necessary laws from which he has no means of emancipating himself.

If when tormented with violent thirst, he figures to himself an idea, or really perceives a fountain, whose limpid streams might cool his feverish want, is he sufficient master of himself to desire or not to desire the object competent to satisfy so lively a want? It will no doubt be conceded, that it is impossible he should not be desirous to satisfy it; but it will be said—if at this moment it is announced to him that the water he so ardently desires is poisoned, he will, notwithstanding his vehement thirst, abstain from drinking it: and it has, therefore, been falsely concluded that he is a free agent. The fact, however, is, that the motive in either case is exactly the same: his own conservation. The same necessity that determined him to drink before he knew the water was deleterious upon this new discovery equally determined him not to drink; the desire of conserving himself either annihilates or suspends the former impulse; the second motive becomes stronger than the preceding, that is, the fear of death, or the desire of preserving himself, necessarily prevails over the painful sensation caused by his eagerness to drink: but, it will be said, if the thirst is very parching, an inconsiderate man without regarding the danger will risk swallowing the water. Nothing is gained by this remark: in this case, the anterior impulse only regains the ascendancy; he is persuaded that life may possibly be longer preserved, or that he shall derive a greater good by drinking the poisoned water than by enduring the torment, which, to his mind, threatens instant dissolution: thus the first becomes the strongest and necessarily urges him on to action. Nevertheless, in either case, whether he partakes of the water, or whether he does not, the two actions

From System of Nature *by Baron Holbach (1770). Translation by H. D. Robinson.*

will be equally necessary; they will be the effect of that motive which finds itself most puissant; which consequently acts in the most coercive manner upon his will.

This example will serve to explain the whole phenomena of the human will. This will, or rather the brain, finds itself in the same situation as a bowl, which, although it has received an impulse that drives it forward in a straight line, is deranged in its course whenever a force superior to the first obliges it to change its direction. The man who drinks the poisoned water appears a madman; but the actions of fools are as necessary as those of the most prudent individuals. The motives that determine the voluptuary and the debauchee to risk their health, are as powerful, and their actions are as necessary, as those which decide the wise man to manage his. But, it will be insisted, the debauchee may be prevailed on to change his conduct: this does not imply that he is a free agent; but that motives may be found sufficiently powerful to annihilate the effect of those that previously acted upon him; then these new motives determine his will to the new mode of conduct he may adopt as necessarily as the former did to the old mode. . . .

The errors of philosophers on the free agency of man, have arisen from their regarding his will as the *primum mobile,* the original motive of his actions; for want of recurring back, they have not perceived the multiplied, the complicated causes which, independently of him, give motion to the will itself; or which dispose and modify his brain, whilst he himself is purely passive in the motion he receives. Is he the master of desiring or not desiring an object that appears desirable to him? Without doubt it will be answered, no: but he is the master of resisting his desire, if he reflects on the consequences. But, I ask, is he capable of reflecting on these consequences, when his soul is hurried along by a very lively passion, which entirely depends upon his natural organization, and the causes by which he is modified? Is it in his power to add to these consequences all the weight necessary to counterbalance his desire? Is he the master of preventing the qualities which render an object desirable from residing in it? I shall be told: he ought to have learned to resist his passions; to contract a habit of putting a curb on his desires. I agree to it without any difficulty. But in reply, I again ask, is his nature susceptible of this modifica-

tion? Does his boiling blood, his unruly imagination, the igneous fluid that circulates in his veins, permit him to make, enable him to apply true experience in the moment when it is wanted? And even when his temperament has capacitated him, has his education, the examples set before him, the ideas with which he has been inspired in early life, been suitable to make him contract this habit of repressing his desires? Have not all these things rather contributed to induce him to seek with avidity, to make him actually desire those objects which you say he ought to resist? . . .

In short, the actions of man are never free; they are always the necessary consequence of his temperament, of the received ideas, and of the notions, either true or false, which he has formed to himself of happiness; of his opinions, strengthened by example, by education, and by daily experience. So many crimes are witnessed on the earth only because every thing conspires to render man vicious and criminal; the religion he has adopted, his government, his education, the examples set before him, irresistibly drive him on to evil: under these circumstances, morality preaches virtue to him in vain. In those societies where vice is esteemed, where crime is crowned, where venality is constantly recompensed, where the most dreadful disorders are punished only in those who are too weak to enjoy the privilege of committing them with impunity, the practice of virtue is considered nothing more than a painful sacrifice of happiness. Such societies chastise, in the lower orders, those excesses, which they respect in the higher ranks; and frequently have the injustice to condemn those in the penalty of death, whom public prejudices, maintained by constant example, have rendered criminal.

Man, then, is not a free agent in any one instant of his life; he is necessarily guided in each step by those advantages, whether real or fictitious, that he attaches to the objects by which his passions are roused: these passions themselves are necessary in a being who unceasingly tends towards his own happiness; their energy is necessary, since that depends on his temperament; his temperament is necessary, because it depends on the physical elements which enter into his composition; the modification of this temperament is necessary, as it is the infallible and inevitable consequence of the impulse he receives from the incessant action of moral and physical beings.

CHOICE DOES NOT
PROVE FREEDOM

In spite of these proofs of the want of free agency in man, so clear to unprejudiced minds, it will, perhaps, be insisted upon with no small feeling of triumph, that if it be proposed to any one, to move or not to move his hand, an action in the number of those called indifferent, he evidently appears to be the master of choosing; from which it is concluded that evidence has been offered of free agency. The reply is, this example is perfectly simple; man in performing some action which he is resolved on doing, does not by any means prove his free agency: the very desire of displaying this quality, excited by the dispute, becomes a necessary motive, which decides his will either for the one or the other of these actions: What deludes him in this instance, or that which persuades him he is a free agent at this moment, is, that he does not discern the true motive which sets him in action, namely, the desire of convincing his opponent: if in the heat of the dispute he insists and asks, "Am I not the master of throwing myself out of the window?" I shall answer him, no; that whilst he preserves his reason there is no probability that the desire of proving his free agency, will become a motive sufficiently powerful to make him sacrifice his life to the attempt: if, notwithstanding this, to prove he is a free agent, he should actually precipitate himself from the window, it would not be a sufficient warranty to conclude he acted freely, but rather that it was the violence of his temperament which spurred him on to this folly. Madness is a state, that depends upon the heat of the blood, not upon the will. A fanatic or a hero, braves death as necessarily as a more phlegmatic man or coward flies from it.

There is, in point of fact, no difference between the man that is cast out of the window by another, and the man who throws himself out of it, except that the impulse in the first instance comes immediately from without whilst that which determines the fall in the second case, springs from within his own peculiar machine, having its more remote cause also exterior. When Mutius Scaevola held his hand in the fire, he was as much acting under the influence of necessity (caused by interior motives) that urged him to this strange action, as if his arm had been held by strong men: pride, despair, the desire of braving his enemy, a wish to astonish him, and anxiety to intimidate him, etc., were the visible chains that held his hand bound to the fire. The love of glory, enthusiasm for their country, in like manner caused Codrus and Decius to devote themselves for their fellow-citizens. The Indian Colanus and the philosopher Peregrinus were equally obliged to burn themselves, by desire of exciting the astonishment of the Grecian assembly.

It is said that free agency is the absence of those obstacles competent to oppose themselves to the actions of man, or to the exercise of his faculties: it is pretended that he is a free agent whenever, making use of these faculties, he produces the effect he has proposed to himself. In reply to this reasoning, it is sufficient to consider that it in nowise depends upon himself to place or remove the obstacles that either determine or resist him; the motive that causes his action is no more in his own power than the obstacle that impedes him, whether this obstacle or motive be within his own machine or exterior of his person: he is not master of the thought presented to his mind, which determines his will; this thought is excited by some cause independent of himself.

To be undeceived on the system of his free agency, man has simply to recur to the motive by which his will is determined; he will always find this motive is out of his own control. It is said: that in consequence of an idea to which the mind gives birth, man acts freely if he encounters no obstacle. But the question is, what gives birth to this idea in his brain? Was he the master either to prevent it from presenting itself, or from renewing itself in his brain? Does not this idea depend either upon objects that strike him exteriorly and in despite of himself, or upon causes, that without his knowledge, act within himself and modify his brain? Can he prevent his eyes, cast without design upon any object whatever, from giving him an idea of this object, and from moving his brain? He is not more master of the obstacles; they are the necessary effects of either interior or exterior causes, which always act according to their given properties. A man insults a coward; this necessarily irritates him against his insulter; but his will cannot vanquish the obstacle that cowardice places to the object of his desire, because his natural conformation, which does not depend upon himself, prevents his having courage. In this case, the coward is insulted in spite of himself; and against his will is obliged patiently to brook the insult he has received.

ABSENCE OF RESTRAINT IS NOT ABSENCE OF NECESSITY

The partisans of the system of free agency appear ever to have confounded constraint with necessity. Man believes he acts as a free agent, every time he does not see any thing that places obstacles to his actions; he does not perceive that the motive which causes him to will, is always necessary and independent of himself. A prisoner loaded with chains is compelled to remain in prison; but he is not a free agent in the desire to emancipate himself; his chains prevent him from acting, but they do not prevent him from willing; he would save himself if they would loose his fetters; but he would not save himself as a free agent; fear or the idea of punishment would be sufficient motives for his action.

Man may, therefore, cease to be restrained, without, for that reason, becoming a free agent: in whatever manner he acts, he will act necessarily, according to motives by which he shall be determined. He may be compared to a heavy body that finds itself arrested in its descent by any obstacle whatever: take away this obstacle, it will gravitate or continue to fall; but who shall say this dense body is free to fall or not? Is not its descent the necessary effect of its own specific gravity? The virtuous Socrates submitted to the laws of his country, although they were unjust; and though the doors of his jail were left open to him, he would not save himself; but in this he did not act as a free agent: the invisible chains of opinion, the secret love of decorum, the inward respect of the laws, even when they were iniquitous, the fear of tarnishing his glory, kept him in his prison; they were motives sufficiently powerful with this enthusiast for virtue, to induce him to await death with tranquility; it was not in his power to save himself, because he could find no potential motive to bring him to depart, even for an instant, from those principles to which his mind was accustomed.

Man, it is said, frequently acts against his inclination, from whence it is falsely concluded he is a free agent; but when he appears to act contrary to his inclination, he is always determined to it by some motive sufficiently efficacious to vanquish this inclination. A sick man, with a view to his cure, arrives at conquering his repugnance to the most disgusting remedies: the fear of pain, or the dread of death, then become necessary motives; consequently this sick man cannot be said to act freely.

When it is said, that man is not a free agent, it is not pretended to compare him to a body moved by a single impulsive cause: he contains within himself causes inherent to his existence; he is moved by an interior organ, which has its own peculiar laws, and is itself necessarily determined in consequence of ideas formed from perception resulting from sensation which it receives from exterior objects. As the mechanism of these sensations, of these perceptions, and the manner they engrave ideas on the brain of man, are not known to him; because he is unable to unravel all these motions; because he cannot perceive the chain of operations in his soul, or the motive principle that acts within him, he supposes himself a free agent; which literally translated, signifies, that he moves himself by himself; that he determines himself without cause: when he rather ought to say, that he is ignorant how or why he acts in the manner he does. It is true the soul enjoys an activity peculiar to itself: but it is equally certain that this activity would never be displayed, if some motive or some cause did not put it in a condition to exercise itself: at least it will not be pretended that the soul is able either to love or to hate without being moved, without knowing the objects, without having some idea of their qualities. Gunpowder has unquestionably a particular activity, but this activity will never display itself, unless fire be applied to it; this, however, immediately sets it in motion.

THE COMPLEXITY OF HUMAN CONDUCT AND THE ILLUSION OF FREE AGENCY

It is the great complication of motion in man, it is the variety of his action, it is the multiplicity of causes that move him, whether simultaneously or in continual succession, that persuades him he is a free agent: if all his motions were simple, if the causes that move him did not confound themselves with each other, if they were distinct, if his machine were less complicated, he would perceive that all his actions were necessary, because he would be enabled to recur instantly to the cause that made him act. . . .

It is, then, for want of recurring to the causes that move him: for want of being able to analyze, from not being competent to decompose the complicated motion of his machine, that man believes himself a free agent: it is only upon his own ignorance that he founds the profound yet deceitful notion he has of his free agency: that he builds those opinions which he brings forward as a striking proof of his pretended freedom of action. If, for a short time, each man was willing to examine his own peculiar actions, search out their true motives to discover their concatenation, he would remain convinced that the sentiment he has of his natural free agency, is a chimera that must speedily be destroyed by experience.

Nevertheless it must be acknowledged that the multiplicity and diversity of the causes which continually act upon man, frequently without even his knowledge, render it impossible, or at least extremely difficult for him to recur to the true principles of his own peculiar actions, much less the actions of others: they frequently depend upon causes so fugitive, so remote from their effects, and which, superficially examined, appear to have so little analogy, so slender a relation with them, that it requires singular sagacity to bring them into light. This is what renders the study of the moral man a task of such difficulty; this is the reason why his heart is an abyss, of which it is frequently impossible for him to fathom the depth. . . .

If he understood the play of his organs, if he were able to recall to himself all the impulsions they have received, all the modifications they have undergone, all the effects they have produced, he would perceive that all his actions are submitted to that fatality, which regulates his own particular system, as it does the entire system of the universe: no one effect in him, any more than in nature, produces itself by chance; . . . All that passes in him; all that is done by him; as well as all that happens in nature, or that is attributed to her, is derived from necessary causes, which act according to necessary laws, and which produce necessary effects from whence necessarily flow others.

Fatality, is the eternal, the immutable, the necessary order, established in nature; or the indispensable connexion of causes that act, with the effects they operate. Conforming to this order, heavy bodies fall; light bodies rise; that which is analogous in matter reciprocally attracts; that which is heterogeneous mutually repels; man congregates himself in society, modifies each his fellow; becomes either virtuous or wicked; either contributes to his mutual happiness, or reciprocates his misery; either loves his neighbour, or hates his companion necessarily, according to the manner in which the one acts upon the other. From whence it may be seen, that the same necessity which regulates the physical, also regulates the moral world, in which everything is in consequence submitted to fatality. Man, in running over, frequently without his own knowledge, often in spite of himself, the route which nature has marked out for him, resembles a swimmer who is obliged to follow the current that carries him along: he believes himself a free agent, because he sometimes consents, sometimes does not consent, to glide with the stream, which, notwithstanding, always hurries him forward; he believes himself the master of his condition, because he is obliged to use his arms under the fear of sinking.

Further Questions

1. First, think of an action of your own that would seem to be free if any of your actions are free. Second, explain what it is about that action that makes it an optimal candidate for a free action. Third, explain how Holbach would reply to your reason for thinking that the example you mentioned may be a free action. Finally, give the best reason you can for objecting to Holbach's reply.
2. To what extent do Holbach's arguments that free will is an illusion depend upon his materialism? Is it easier to make a case that people have free will if we reject materialism and believe, say, that everyone has an immaterial soul? Explain.

Further Readings

Darrow, Clarence. *Attorney for the Damned*, edited by A. Weinberg. New York: Simon & Schuster, 1957. Eloquent, easily understood arguments that free will is an illusion.

Hook, Sidney, ed. *Determinism and Freedom in the Age of Modern Science*. New York: Collier Books, 1961. Among other questions, addresses whether modern science provides any support for the idea that we have free will.

21   Liberty and Necessity

DAVID HUME

David Hume (1711–1776), a leading philosopher of the Enlightenment, wrote a famous history of England and tutored Adam Smith in political economy. He spent most of his life in Edinburgh.

In this selection, from *An Inquiry Concerning Human Understanding* (1748), Hume argues that free will and causal determinism are compatible, that is, that people could sometimes act freely even if all of their actions and motives were caused. A brief biography of Hume appears on page 121.

Reading Questions

1. Hume thinks the dispute over whether people have free will ("the question concerning liberty and necessity") is merely a verbal dispute. Why?
2. What does Hume mean by "the doctrines of liberty and necessity?" What does he think gives these doctrines whatever plausibility they have?
3. Could the doctrines of liberty and necessity both be true? What does Hume think? Why?

PART I

IT MIGHT REASONABLY BE EXPECTED, in questions which have been canvassed and disputed with great eagerness since the first origin of science and philosophy, that the meaning of all the terms, at least, should have been agreed upon among the disputants, and our inquiries, in the course of two thousand years, been able to pass from words to the true and real subject of the controversy. For how easy may it seem to give exact definitions of the terms employed in reasoning, and make these definitions, not the mere sound of words, the object of future scrutiny and examination? But if we

consider the matter more narrowly, we shall be apt to draw a quite opposite conclusion. From this circumstance alone, that a controversy has been long kept on foot and remains still undecided, we may presume that there is some ambiguity in the expression, and that the disputants affix different ideas to the terms employed in the controversy. For as the faculties of the mind are supposed to be naturally alike in every individual—otherwise nothing could be more fruitless than to reason or dispute together—it were impossible, if men affix the same ideas to their terms, that they could so long form different opinions of the same subject, especially when they communicate their views and each party turn themselves on all sides in search of arguments which may give them the victory over their antagonists. It is true, if men attempt the discussion of questions which lie entirely beyond the reach of human capacity, such as those concerning the origin of worlds or the economy of the intellectual system or region of spirits, they may long beat the air in their fruitless contests and never arrive at any determinate conclusion. But if the question regard any subject of common life and experience, nothing, one would think, could preserve the dispute so long undecided, but some ambiguous expressions which keep the antagonists still at a distance and hinder them from grappling with each other.

This has been the case in the long-disputed question concerning liberty and necessity, and to so remarkable a degree that, if I be not much mistaken, we shall find that all mankind, both learned and ignorant, have always been of the same opinion with regard to this subject, and that a few intelligible definitions would immediately have put an end to the whole controversy. I own that this dispute has been so much canvassed on all hands, and has led philosophers into such a labyrinth of obscure sophistry, that it is no wonder if a sensible reader indulge his ease so far as to turn a deaf ear to the proposal of such a question from which he can expect neither instruction nor entertainment. But the state of the argument here proposed may, perhaps, serve to renew his attention, as it has more novelty, promises at least some decision of the controversy, and will not much disturb his ease by any intricate or obscure reasoning.

I hope, therefore, to make it appear that all men have ever agreed in the doctrine both of necessity and of liberty, according to any reasonable sense which can be put on these terms, and that the whole controversy has hitherto turned merely upon words. We shall begin with examining the doctrine of necessity.

It is universally allowed that matter, in all its operations, is actuated by a necessary force, and that every natural effect is so precisely determined by the energy of its cause that no other effect, in such particular circumstances, could possibly have resulted from it. The degree and direction of every motion is, by the laws of nature, prescribed with such exactness that a living creature may as soon arise from the shock of two bodies, as motion, in any other degree or direction than what is actually produced by it. Would we, therefore, form a just and precise idea of *necessity,* we must consider whence that idea arises when we apply it to the operation of bodies.

It seems evident that, if all the scenes of nature were continually shifted in such a manner that no two events bore any resemblance to each other, but every object was entirely new, without any similitude to whatever had been seen before, we should never, in that case, have attained the least idea of necessity or of a connection among these objects. We might say, upon such a supposition, that one object or event has followed another, not that one was produced by the other. The relation of cause and effect must be utterly unknown to mankind. Inference and reasoning concerning the operations of nature would, from that moment, be at an end; and the memory and senses remain the only canals by which the knowledge of any real existence could possibly have access to the mind. Our idea, therefore, of necessity and causation arises entirely from the uniformity observable in the operations of nature, where similar objects are constantly conjoined together, and the mind is determined by custom to infer the one from the appearance of the other. These two circumstances form the whole of that necessity which we ascribe to matter. Beyond the constant *conjunction* of similar objects and the consequent *inference* from one to the other, we have no notion of any necessity of connection.

If it appear, therefore, that all mankind have ever allowed, without any doubt or hesitation, that these two circumstances take place in the voluntary actions of men and in the operations of mind, it must follow that all mankind have ever agreed in the doctrine of necessity, and that they have hitherto disputed merely for not understanding each other.

As to the first circumstance, the constant and regular conjunction of similar events, we may possibly satisfy ourselves by the following considerations. It is universally acknowledged that there is a great uniformity among the actions of men, in all nations and ages, and that human nature remains

From David Hume, An Inquiry Concerning Human Understanding, *Section 8. First published in 1748.*

still the same in its principles and operations. The same motives always produce the same actions; the same events follow from the same causes. Ambition, avarice, self-love, vanity, friendship, generosity, public spirit—these passions, mixed in various degrees and distributed through society, have been, from the beginning of the world, and still are, the source of all the actions and enterprises which have ever been observed among mankind. Would you know the sentiments, inclinations, and course of life of the Greeks and Romans? Study well the temper and actions of the French and English: you cannot be much mistaken in transferring to the former *most* of the observations which you have made with regard to the latter. Mankind are so much the same, in all times and places, that history informs us of nothing new or strange in this particular. Its chief use is only to discover the constant and universal principles of human nature by showing men in all varieties of circumstances and situations, and furnishing us with materials from which we may form our observations and become acquainted with the regular springs of human action and behavior. These records of wars, intrigues, factions, and revolutions are so many collections of experiments by which the politician or moral philosopher fixes the principles of his science, in the same manner as the physician or natural philosopher becomes acquainted with the nature of plants, minerals, and other external objects, by the experiments which he forms concerning them. Nor are the earth, water, and other elements examined by Aristotle and Hippocrates more like to those which at present lie under our observation than the men described by Polybius and Tacitus are to those who now govern the world.

Should a traveler, returning from a far country, bring us an account of men wholly different from any with whom we were ever acquainted, men who were entirely divested of avarice, ambition, or revenge, who knew no pleasure but friendship, generosity, and public spirit, we should immediately, from these circumstances, detect the falsehood and prove him a liar with the same certainty as if he had stuffed his narration with stories of centaurs and dragons, miracles and prodigies. And if we would explore any forgery in history, we cannot make use of a more convincing argument than to prove that the actions ascribed to any person are directly contrary to the course of nature, and that no human motives, in such circumstances, could ever induce him to such a conduct. The veracity of Quintus Curtius is as much to be suspected when he describes the supernatural courage of Alexander by which he was hurried on singly to attack multitudes, as when he describes his supernatural force and activity by which he was able to resist them. So readily and universally do we acknowledge a uniformity in human motives and actions as well as in the operations of body.

Hence, likewise, the benefit of that experience acquired by long life and a variety of business and company, in order to instruct us in the principles of human nature and regulate our future conduct as well as speculation. By means of this guide we mount up to the knowledge of men's inclinations and motives from their actions, expressions, and even gestures, and again descend to the interpretation of their actions from our knowledge of their motives and inclinations. The general observations, treasured up by a course of experience, give us the clue of human nature and teach us to unravel all its intricacies. Pretexts and appearances no longer deceive us. Public declarations pass for the specious coloring of a cause. And though virtue and honor be allowed their proper weight and authority, that perfect disinterestedness, so often pretended to, is never expected in multitudes and parties, seldom in their leaders, and scarcely even in individuals of any rank or station. But were there no uniformity in human actions, and were every experiment which we could form of this kind irregular and anomalous, it were impossible to collect any general observations concerning mankind, and no experience, however accurately digested by reflection, would ever serve to any purpose. Why is the aged husbandman more skillful in his calling than the young beginner, but because there is a certain uniformity in the operation of the sun, rain, and earth toward the production of vegetables, and experience teaches the old practitioner the rules by which this operation is governed and directed?

We must not, however, expect that this uniformity of human actions should be carried to such a length as that all men, in the same circumstances, will always act precisely in the same manner, without making any allowance for the diversity of characters, prejudices, and opinions. Such a uniformity, in every particular, is found in no part of nature. On the contrary, from observing the variety of conduct in different men we are enabled to form a greater variety of maxims which still suppose a degree of uniformity and regularity.

Are the manners of men different in different ages and countries? We learn thence the great force of custom and education, which mold the human mind from its infancy and form it into a fixed and established character. Is the behavior and conduct of the one sex very unlike that of the other? It is thence we become acquainted with the different characters which nature has impressed upon the sexes, and which she preserves with constancy and regularity. Are the actions of the same person much diversified in the different periods of his life from infancy to old age? This affords room for many general observations concerning the gradual change of our sentiments and inclinations, and the different maxims which prevail in the different ages of human creatures. Even the characters which are peculiar to each individual have a uniformity in their influence, otherwise our acquaintance with the persons, and our observations of their conduct, could never teach us their dispositions or serve to direct our behavior with regard to them.

I grant it possible to find actions which seem to have no regular connection with any known motives and are exceptions to all the measures of conduct which have ever been established for the government of men. But if we could willingly know what judgment should be formed of such irregular and extraordinary actions, we may consider the sentiments commonly entertained with regard to those irregular events which appear in the course of nature and the operations of eternal objects. All causes are not conjoined to their usual effects with like uniformity. An artificer who handles only dead matter may be disappointed of his aim, as well as the politician who directs the conduct of sensible and intelligent agents.

The vulgar, who take things according to their first appearance, attribute the uncertainty of events to such an uncertainty in the causes as makes the latter often fail of their usual influence, though they meet with no impediment in their operation. But philosophers, observing that almost in every part of nature there is contained a vast variety of springs and principles which are hid by reason of their minuteness or remoteness, find that it is at least possible the contrariety of events may not proceed from any contingency in the cause but from the secret operation of contrary causes. This possibility is converted into certainty by further observation, when they remark that, upon an exact scrutiny, a contrariety of effect always betrays a contrariety of causes and proceeds from their mutual opposition. A peasant can give no better reason for the stopping of any clock or watch than to say that it does not commonly go right. But an artist easily perceives that the same force in the spring or pendulum has always the same influence on the wheels, but fails of its usual effect perhaps by reason of a grain of dust which puts a stop to the whole movement. From the observation of several parallel instances philosophers form a maxim that the connection between all causes and effects is equally necessary, and that its seeming uncertainty in some instances proceeds from the secret opposition of contrary causes.

Thus, for instance, in the human body, when the usual symptoms of health or sickness disappoint our expectation, when medicines operate not with their wonted powers, when irregular events follow from any particular cause, the philosopher and physician are not surprised at the matter, nor are ever tempted to deny, in general, the necessity and uniformity of those principles by which the animal economy is conducted. They know that a human body is a mighty complicated machine, that many secret powers lurk in it which are altogether beyond our comprehension, that to us it must often appear very uncertain in its operations, and that, therefore, the irregular events which outwardly discover themselves can be no proof that the laws of nature are not observed with the greatest regularity in its internal operation and government.

The philosopher, if he be consistent, must apply the same reasonings to the actions and volitions of intelligent agents. The most irregular and unexpected resolutions of men may frequently be accounted for by those who know every particular circumstance of their character and situation. A person of an obliging disposition gives a peevish answer; but he has the toothache, or has not dined. A stupid fellow discovers an uncommon alacrity in his carriage; but he has met with a sudden piece of

THE SELF AND FREE WILL

C. A. Campbell

Now if one chooses thus to limit one's self to the role of external observer, it is, I think, perfectly true that one can attach no meaning to an act which is the act of something we call a "self" and yet follows from nothing in that self's character. But then *why should* we so limit ourselves, when what is under consideration is a subjective activity? For the apprehension of subjective acts there is *another* standpoint available, that of *inner experience,* of the practical consciousness in its actual functioning. If our free will should turn out to be something to which we can attach a meaning from *this* standpoint, no more is required. And no more ought to be expected. For I must repeat that only from the inner standpoint of living experience *could* anything of the nature of "activity" be directly grasped. Observation from without is in the nature of the case impotent to apprehend the active *qua* active. We can from without observe sequences of states. If into these we read activity (as we sometimes do), this can only be on the basis of what we discern in ourselves from the inner standpoint. It follows that if anyone insists upon taking his criterion of the meaningful simply from the standpoint of external observation, he is really deciding in advance of the evidence that the notion of activity, and *a fortiori* the notion of a free will, is "meaningless." He looks for the free act through a medium which is in the nature of the case incapable of revealing it, and then, because inevitably he doesn't find it, he declares that it doesn't exist!

But if, as we surely ought in this context, we adopt the inner standpoint, then (I am suggesting) things appear in a totally different light. From the inner standpoint, it seems to me plain, there is no difficulty whatever in attaching meaning to an act which is the self's act and which nevertheless does not follow from the self's character. . . . [This] is thrown into particularly clear relief where the moral decision is to make the moral effort required to rise to duty. I submit, therefore, that the self knows very well indeed—from the inner standpoint—what is meant by an act which is the *self's* act and which nevertheless does not follow from the self's *character.*

What this implies—and it seems to me to be an implication of cardinal importance for any theory of the self that aims at being more than superficial—is that the nature of the self is for itself something more than just its character as so far formed. The "nature" of the self and what we commonly call the "character" of the self are by no means the same thing, and it is utterly vital that they should not be confused. The "nature" of the self comprehends, but is not without remainder reducible to, its "character": it must, if we are to be true to the testimony of our experience of it, be taken as including *also* the authentic creative power of fashioning and refashioning "character."

From *On Selfhood and Godhood* (1957).

good fortune. Or even when an action, as sometimes happens, cannot be particularly accounted for, either by the person himself or by others, we know, in general that the characters of men are to a certain degree inconstant and irregular. This is, in a manner, the constant character of human nature, though it be applicable, in a more particular manner, to some persons who have no fixed rule for their conduct, but proceed in a continual course of caprice and inconstancy. The internal principles and motives may operate in a uniform manner, notwithstanding these seeming irregularities—in the same manner as the winds, rains, clouds, and other variations of the weather are supposed to be governed by steady principles, though not easily discoverable by human sagacity and inquiry.

Thus it appears not only that the conjunction between motives and voluntary actions is as regular and uniform as that between the cause and effect in any part of nature, but also that this regular conjunction has been universally acknowledged among mankind and has never been the subject of dispute either in philosophy or common life. Now, as it is from past experience that we draw all inferences concerning the future, and as we conclude that objects will always be conjoined together which we find to have always been conjoined, it may seem superfluous to prove that this experienced uniformity in human actions is a source whence we draw *inferences* concerning them. But in order to throw the argument into a greater variety of lights, we shall also insist, though briefly, on this latter topic.

The mutual dependence of men is so great in all societies that scarce any human action is entirely complete in itself or is performed without some reference to the actions of others, which are requisite to make it answer fully the intention of the agent. The poorest artificer who labors alone expects at least the protection of the magistrate to insure him the enjoyment of the fruits of his labor. He also expects that when he carries his goods to market and offers them at a reasonable price, he shall find purchasers and shall be able, by the money he acquires, to engage others to supply him with those commodities which are requisite for his subsistence. In proportion as men extend their dealings and render their intercourse with others more complicated, they always comprehend in their schemes of life a greater variety of voluntary actions which they expect, from the proper motives, to co-operate with their own. In all these conclusions they take their measures from past experience, in the same manner as in their reasonings concerning external objects, and firmly believe that men, as well as all the elements, are to continue in their operations the same that they have ever found them. A manufacturer reckons upon the labor of his servants for the execution of any work as much as upon the tools which he employs, and would be equally surprised were his expectations disappointed. In short, this experimental inference and reasoning concerning the actions of others enters so much into human life that no man, while awake, is ever a moment

without employing it. Have we not reason, therefore, to affirm that all mankind have always agreed in the doctrine of necessity, according to the foregoing definition and explication of it?

Nor have philosophers ever entertained a different opinion from the people in this particular. For, not to mention that almost every action of their life supposes that opinion, there are even few of the speculative parts of learning to which it is not essential. What would become of *history* had we not a dependence on the veracity of the historian according to the experience which we have had of mankind? How could *politics* be a science if laws and forms of government had not a uniform influence upon society? Where would be the foundation of *morals* if particular characters had no certain or determinate power to produce particular sentiments, and if these sentiments had no constant operation on actions? And with what pretense could we employ our *criticism* upon any poet or polite author if we could not pronounce the conduct and sentiments of his actors either natural or unnatural to such characters and in such circumstances? It seems almost impossible, therefore, to engage either in science or action of any kind without acknowledging the doctrine of necessity, and this *inference* from motives to voluntary action, from characters to conduct.

And, indeed, when we consider how aptly *natural* and *moral* evidence link together and form only one chain of argument, we shall make no scruple to allow that they are of the same nature and derived from the same principles. A prisoner who has neither money nor interest discovers the impossibility of his escape as well when he considers the obstinacy of the jailer as the walls and bars with which he is surrounded, and in all attempts for his freedom chooses rather to work upon the stone and iron of the one than upon the inflexible nature of the other. The same prisoner, when conducted to the scaffold, foresees his death as certainly from the constancy and fidelity of his guards as from the operation of the ax or wheel. His mind runs along a certain train of ideas: the refusal of the soldiers to consent to his escape; the action of the executioner; the separation of the head and body; bleeding, convulsive motions, and death. Here is a connected chain of natural causes and voluntary actions, but the mind feels no difference between them in passing from one link to another, nor is less certain of the future event than if it were connected with the objects present to the memory or senses by a train of causes cemented together by what we are pleased to call a "physical" necessity. The same experienced union has the same effect on the mind, whether the united objects be motives, volition, and actions, or figure and motion. We may change the names of things, but their nature and their operation on the understanding never change.

Were a man whom I know to be honest and opulent, and with whom I lived in intimate friendship, to come into my house, where I am surrounded with my servants, I rest assured that he is not to stab me before he leaves it in order to rob me of my silver standish; and I no more suspect this event than the falling of the house itself, which is new and solidly built and founded. — *But he may have been seized with a sudden and unknown frenzy.* — So may a sudden earthquake arise, and shake and tumble my house about my ears. I shall, therefore, change the suppositions. I shall say that I know with certainty that he is not to put his hand into the fire and hold it there till it be consumed. And this event I think I can foretell with the same assurance as that, if he throw himself out of the window and meet with no obstruction, he will not remain a moment suspended in the air. No suspicion of an unknown frenzy can give the least possibility to the former event which is so contrary to all the known principles of human nature. A man who at noon leaves his purse full of gold on the pavement at Charing Cross may as well expect that it will fly away like a feather as that he will find it untouched an hour after. Above one-half of human reasonings contain inferences of a similar nature, attended with more or less degrees of certainty, proportioned to our experience of the usual conduct of mankind in such particular situations.

I have frequently considered what could possibly be the reason why all mankind, though they have ever, without hesitation, acknowledged the doctrine of necessity in their whole practice and reasoning, have yet discovered such a reluctance to acknowledge it in words, and have rather shown a propensity, in all ages, to profess the contrary opinion. The matter, I think, may be accounted for after the following manner. If we examine the operations of body and the production of effects from

their causes, we shall find that all our faculties can never carry us further in our knowledge of this relation than barely to observe that particular objects are *constantly conjoined* together, and that the mind is carried, by a *customary transition,* from the appearance of the one to the belief of the other. But though this conclusion concerning human ignorance be the result of the strictest scrutiny of this subject, men still entertain a strong propensity to believe that they penetrate further into the powers of nature and perceive something like a necessary connection between the cause and the effect. When, again, they turn their reflections toward the operations of their own minds and *feel* no such connection of the motive and the action, they are thence apt to suppose that there is a difference between the effects which result from material force and those which arise from thought and intelligence. But being once convinced that we know nothing further of causation of any kind than merely the *constant conjunction* of objects and the consequent *inference* of the mind from one to another, and finding that these two circumstances are universally allowed to have place in voluntary actions, we may be more easily led to own the same necessity common to all causes. And though this reasoning may contradict the systems of many philosophers in ascribing necessity to the determinations of the will, we shall find, upon reflection, that they dissent from it in words only, not in their real sentiments. Necessity, according to the sense in which it is here taken, has never yet been rejected, nor can ever, I think, be rejected by any philosopher. It may only, perhaps, be pretended that the mind can perceive in the operations of matter some further connection between the cause and effect, and a connection that has no place in the voluntary actions of intelligent beings. Now, whether it be so or not can only appear upon examination, and it is incumbent on these philosophers to make good their assertion by defining or describing that necessity and pointing it out to us in the operations of material causes.

It would seem, indeed, that men begin at the wrong end of this question concerning liberty and necessity when they enter upon it by examining the faculties of the soul, the influence of the understanding, and the operations of the will. Let them first discuss a more simple question, namely, the question of body and brute unintelligent matter, and try whether they can there form any idea of causation and necessity, except that of a constant conjunction of objects and subsequent inference of the mind from one to another. If these circumstances form, in reality, the whole of that necessity which we conceive in matter, and if these circumstances be also universally acknowledged to take place in the operations of the mind, the dispute is at an end; at least, must be owned to be thenceforth merely verbal. But as long as we will rashly suppose that we have some further idea of necessity and causation in the operations of external objects, at the same time that we can find nothing further in the voluntary actions of the mind, there is no possibility of bringing the question to any determinate issue while we proceed upon so erroneous a supposition. The only method of undeceiving us is to mount up higher, to examine the narrow extent of science when applied to material causes, and to convince ourselves that all we know of them is the constant conjunction and inference above mentioned. We may, perhaps, find that it is with difficulty we are induced to fix such narrow limits to human understanding, but we can afterwards find no difficulty when we come to apply this doctrine to the actions of the will. For as it is evident that these have a regular conjunction with motives and circumstances and character, and as we always draw inferences from one to the other, we must be obliged to acknowledge in words that necessity which we have already avowed in every deliberation of our lives and in every step of our conduct and behavior.[1]

But to proceed in this reconciling project with regard to the question of liberty and necessity — the most contentious question of metaphysics, the most contentious science — it will not require many words to prove that all mankind have ever agreed in the doctrine of liberty as well as in that of necessity, and that the whole dispute, in this respect also, has been hitherto merely verbal. For what is meant by liberty when applied to voluntary actions? We cannot surely mean that actions have so little connection with motives, inclinations, and circumstances that one does not follow with a certain degree of uniformity from the other, and that one affords no inference by which we can conclude the existence of the other. For these are plain and acknowledged matters of fact. By liberty, then, we

can only mean *a power of acting or not acting according to the determinations of the will;* that is, if we choose to remain at rest, we may; if we choose to move, we also may. Now this hypothetical liberty is universally allowed to belong to everyone who is not a prisoner and in chains. Here then is no subject of dispute.

Whatever definition we may give of liberty, we should be careful to observe two requisite circumstances: *first,* that it be consistent with plain matter of fact; *secondly,* that it be consistent with itself. If we observe these circumstances and render our definition intelligible, I am persuaded that all mankind will be found of one opinion with regard to it.

It is universally allowed that nothing exists without a cause of its existence, and that chance, when strictly examined, is a mere negative word and means not any real power which has anywhere a being in nature. But it is pretended that some causes are necessary, some not necessary. Here then is the advantage of definitions. Let anyone *define* a cause without comprehending, as a part of the definition, a *necessary connection* with its effect, and let him show distinctly the origin of the idea expressed by the definition, and I shall readily give up the whole controversy. But if the foregoing explication of the matter be received, this must be absolutely impracticable. Had not objects a regular conjunction with each other, we should never have entertained any notion of cause and effect; and this regular conjunction produces that inference of the understanding which is the only connection that we can have any comprehension of. Whoever attempts a definition of cause exclusive of these circumstances will be obliged either to employ unintelligible terms or such as are synonymous to the term which he endeavors to define.[2] And if the definition above mentioned be admitted, liberty, when opposed to necessity, not to constraint, is the same thing with chance, which is universally allowed to have no existence.

PART II

There is no method of reasoning more common, and yet none more blamable, than in philosophical disputes to endeavor the refutation of any hypothesis by a pretense of its dangerous consequences to religion and morality. When any opinion leads to absurdity, it is certainly false but it is not certain that an opinion is false because it is of dangerous consequence. Such topics, therefore, ought entirely to be forborne as serving nothing to the discovery of truth, but only to make the person of an antagonist odious. This I observe in general, without pretending to draw any advantage from it. I frankly submit to an examination of this kind, and shall venture to affirm that the doctrines both of necessity and liberty, as above explained, are not only consistent with morality, but are absolutely essential to its support.

Necessity may be defined two ways, conformably to the two definitions of *cause* of which it makes an essential part. It consists either in the constant conjunction of like objects or in the inference of the understanding from one object to another. Now necessity, in both these senses (which, indeed, are at bottom the same), has universally, though tacitly, in the schools, in the pulpit, and in common life been allowed to belong to the will of man, and no one has ever pretended to deny that we can draw inferences concerning human actions, and that those inferences are founded on the experienced union of like actions, with like motives, inclinations, and circumstances. The only particular in which anyone can differ is that either perhaps he will refuse to give the name of necessity to this property of human actions—but as long as the meaning is understood I hope the word can do no harm—or that he will maintain it possible to discover something further in the operations of matter. But this, it must be acknowledged, can be of no consequence to morality or religion, whatever it may be to natural philosophy or metaphysics. We may here be mistaken in asserting that there is no idea of any other necessity or connection in the actions of the body, but surely we ascribe nothing to the actions of the mind but what everyone does and must readily allow of. We change no circumstance in the received orthodox system with regard to the will, but only in that with regard to material objects and causes. Nothing, therefore, can be more innocent at least than this doctrine.

All laws being founded on rewards and punishments, it is supposed, as a fundamental principle, that these motives have a regular and uniform influence on the mind and both produce the good and prevent the evil actions. We may give to this influence what name we please; but as it is usually conjoined with the action, it must be esteemed a *cause* and be looked upon as an instance of that necessity which we would here establish.

The only proper object of hatred or vengeance is a person or creature endowed with thought and consciousness; and when any criminal or injurious actions excite that passion, it is only by their relation to the person, or connection with him. Actions are, by their very nature, temporary and perishing; and where they proceed not from some *cause* in the character and disposition of the person who performed them, they can neither redound to his honor if good, nor infamy if evil. The actions themselves may be blamable; they may be contrary to all the rules of morality and religion; but the person is not answerable for them and, as they proceeded from nothing in him that is durable and constant and leave nothing of that nature behind them, it is impossible he can, upon their account, become the object of punishment or vengeance. According to the principle, therefore, which denies necessity and, consequently, causes, a man is as pure and untainted, after having committed the most horrid crime, as at the first moment of his birth, nor is his character anywise concerned in his actions, since they are not derived from it; and the wickedness of the one can never be used as a proof of the depravity of the other.

Men are not blamed for such actions as they perform ignorantly and casually, whatever may be the consequences. Why? But because the principles of these actions are only momentary and terminate in them alone. Men are less blamed for such actions as they perform hastily and unpremeditatedly than for such as proceed from deliberation. For what reason? But because a hasty temper, though a constant cause or principle in the mind, operates only by intervals and infects not the whole character. Again, repentance wipes off every crime if attended with a reformation of life and manners. How is this to be accounted for? But by asserting that actions render a person criminal merely as they are proofs of criminal principles in the mind; and when, by an alteration of these principles, they cease to be just proofs, they likewise cease to be criminal. But, except upon the doctrine of necessity, they never were just proofs, and consequently never were criminal.

It will be equally easy to prove, and from the same arguments, that *liberty,* according to that definition above mentioned, in which all men agree, is also essential to morality, and that no human actions, where it is wanting, are susceptible of any moral qualities or can be the objects of approbation or dislike. For as actions are objects of our moral sentiment so far only as they are indications of the internal character, passions, and affections, it is impossible that they can give rise either to praise or blame where they proceed not from these principles, but are derived altogether from external violence.

I pretend not to have obtained or removed all objections to this theory with regard to necessity and liberty. I can foresee other objections derived from topics which have not here been treated of. It may be said, for instance, that if voluntary actions be subjected to the same laws of necessity with the operations of matter, there is a continued chain of necessary causes, preordained and predetermined, reaching from the Original Cause of all to every single volition of every human creature. No contingency anywhere in the universe, no indifference, no liberty. While we act, we are at the same time acted upon. The ultimate Author of all our volitions is the Creator of the world, who first bestowed motion on this immense machine and placed all beings in that particular position whence every subsequent event, by an inevitable necessity, must result. Human actions, therefore, either can have no moral turpitude at all, as proceeding from so good a cause, or if they have any turpitude, they must involve our Creator in the same guilt, while he is acknowledged to be their ultimate cause and Author. For as a man who fired a mine is answerable for all the consequences, whether the train he employed be long or short, so, wherever a continued chain of necessary causes is fixed, that Being, either finite or infinite, who produces the first is likewise the author of all the rest and must both bear the blame and acquire the praise which belong to them. Our clear and unalterable ideas of morality establish this rule upon unquestionable reasons when we examine the consequences of any

human action; and these reasons must still have greater force when applied to the volitions and intentions of a Being infinitely wise and powerful. Ignorance or impotence may be pleaded for so limited a creature as man, but those imperfections have no place in our Creator. He foresaw, he ordained, he intended all those actions of men which we so rashly pronounce criminal. And we must, therefore, conclude either that they are not criminal or that the Deity, not man, is accountable for them. But as either of these positions is absurd and impious, it follows that the doctrine from which they are deduced cannot possibly be true, as being liable to all the same objections. An absurd consequence, if necessary, proves the original doctrine to be absurd in the same manner as criminal actions render criminal the original cause if the connection between them be necessary and inevitable.

This objection consists of two parts, which we shall examine separately:

First, that if human actions can be traced up, by a necessary chain, to the Deity, they can never be criminal, on account of the infinite perfection of that Being from whom they are derived, and who can intend nothing but what is altogether good and laudable. Or, *secondly,* if they be criminal, we must retract the attribute of perfection which we ascribe to the Deity and must acknowledge him to be the ultimate author of guilt and moral turpitude in all his creatures.

The answer to the first objection seems obvious and convincing. There are many philosophers who, after an exact scrutiny of the phenomena of nature, conclude that the WHOLE, considered as one system, is, in every period of its existence, ordered with perfect benevolence; and that the utmost possible happiness will, in the end, result to all created beings without any mixture of positive or absolute ill and misery. Every physical ill, say they, makes an essential part of this benevolent system, and could not possibly be removed, by even the Deity himself, considered as a wise agent, without giving entrance to greater ill or excluding greater good which will result from it. From this theory some philosophers, and the ancient Stoics among the rest, derived a topic of consolation under all afflictions, while they taught their pupils that those ills under which they labored were in reality goods to the universe, and that to an enlarged view which could comprehend the whole system of nature every event became an object of joy and exultation. But though this topic be specious and sublime, it was soon found in practice weak and ineffectual. You would surely more irritate than appease a man lying under the racking pains of the gout by preaching up to him the rectitude of those general laws which produced the malignant humors in his body and led them through the proper canals to the sinews and nerves, where they now excite such acute torments. These enlarged views may, for a moment, please the imagination of a speculative man who is placed in ease and security, but neither can they dwell with constancy on his mind, even though undisturbed by the emotions of pain or passion, much less can they maintain their ground when attacked by such powerful antagonists. The affections take a narrower and more natural survey of their object and, by an economy more suitable to the infirmity of human minds, regard alone the beings around us, and are actuated by such events as appear good or ill to the private system.

The case is the same with *moral* as with *physical* ill. It cannot reasonably be supposed that those remote considerations which are found of so little efficacy with regard to the one will have a more powerful influence with regard to the other. The mind of man is so formed by nature that, upon the appearance of certain characters, dispositions, and actions, it immediately feels the sentiment of approbation or blame; nor are there any emotions more essential to its frame and constitution. The characters which engage our approbation are chiefly such as contribute to the peace and security of human society, as the characters which excite blame are chiefly such as tend to public detriment and disturbance; whence it may reasonably be presumed that the moral sentiments arise, either mediately or immediately, from a reflection on these opposite interests. What though philosophical meditations establish a different opinion or conjecture that everything is right with regard to the whole, and that the qualities which disturb society are, in the main, as beneficial, and are as suitable to the primary intention of nature, as those which more directly promote its happiness and welfare? Are such remote and uncertain speculations able to counterbalance the sentiments which arise from the natural and immediate view of the objects? A man who is robbed of a considerable sum, does he find his vexation for the loss anywise diminished by these sublime reflections? Why, then, should his moral resentment against the crime be supposed incompatible with them? Or why should not the acknowledgement of a real distinction between vice and virtue be reconcilable to all speculative systems of philosophy, as well as that of a real distinction between personal beauty and deformity? Both these distinctions are founded in the natural sentiments of the human mind; and these sentiments are not to be controlled or altered by any philosophical theory or speculation whatsoever.

The *second* objection admits not of so easy and satisfactory an answer, nor is it possible to explain distinctly how the Deity can be the immediate cause of all the actions of men without being the author of sin and moral turpitude. These are mysteries which mere natural and unassisted reason is very unfit to handle; and whatever system she embraces, she must find herself involved in inextricable difficulties, and even contradictions, at every step which she takes with regard to such subjects. To reconcile the indifference and contingency of human actions with prescience or to defend absolute decrees, and yet free the Deity from being the author of sin, has been found hitherto to exceed all the power of philosophy. Happy, if she be thence sensible of her temerity, when she pries into these sublime mysteries, and, leaving a scene so full of obscurities and perplexities, return with suitable modesty to her true and proper province, the examination of common life, where she will find difficulties enough to employ her inquiries without launching into so boundless an ocean of doubt, uncertainty, and contradiction.

NOTES

1. The prevalence of the doctrine of liberty may be accounted for from another cause, viz., a false sensation, or seeming experience, which we have, or may have, of liberty or indifference in many of our actions. The necessity of any action, whether of matter or of mind, is not, properly speaking, a quality in the agent but in any thinking or in-

telligent being who may consider the action; and it consists chiefly in the determination of his thoughts to infer the existence of that action from some preceding objects; as liberty, when opposed to necessity, is nothing but the want of that determination, and a certain looseness or indifference which we feel in passing, or not passing, from the idea of one object to that of any succeeding one. Now we may observe that though, in *reflecting* on human actions, we seldom feel such a looseness or indifference, but are commonly able to infer them with considerable certainty from their motives, and from the disposition of the agent; yet it frequently happens that, in *performing* the actions themselves, we are sensible of something like it; and as all resembling objects are readily taken for each other, this has been employed as a demonstrative and even intuitive proof of human liberty. We feel that our actions are subject to our will on most occasions, and imagine we feel that the will itself is subject to nothing, because, when by a denial of it we are provoked to try, we feel that it moves easily every way, and produces an image of itself (or a "velleity," as it is called in the schools), even on that side on which it did not settle. This image, or faint motion, we persuade ourselves, could at that time have been completed into the thing itself, be-

cause, should that be denied, we find upon a second trial that at present it can. We consider not that the fantastical desire of showing liberty is here the motive of our actions. And it seems certain that however we may imagine we feel a liberty within ourselves, a spectator can commonly infer our actions from our motives and character; and even where he cannot, he concludes in general that he might, were he perfectly acquainted with every circumstance of our situation and temper, and the most secret springs of our complexion and disposition. Now this is the very essence of necessity, according to the foregoing doctrine.

2. Thus, if a cause be defined, *that which produces anything,* it is easy to observe that *producing* is synonymous to *causing.* In like manner, if a cause be defined, *that by which anything exists,* this is liable to the same objection. For what is meant by these words, "*by which*"? Had it been said that a cause is *that* after which *anything constantly exists,* we should have understood the terms. For this is, indeed, all we know of the matter. And this constancy forms the very essence of necessity, nor have we any other idea of it.

Further Questions

1. "The fact that someone acts in accordance with his or her own will does not guarantee that the person acts freely; the will itself may have been caused by conditions over which the person had no control." Explain how Hume would respond. Then explain how someone could best criticize Hume's response.
2. Imagine that Holbach and Hume were sitting across the table from each other. As far as the issue of free will is concerned, what would be their main agreements and disagreements?

Further Readings

Hospers, John. *An Introduction to Philosophical Analysis.* New York: Prentice-Hall, 1953. Chapter 4 contains a clear, textbook introduction to the problem of free will and determinism.
Hoy, Ronald C., and Oaklander, L. Nathan, eds. *Metaphysics.* Belmont, CA: Wadsworth, 1991. Part IV contains a good selection of classical and contemporary writings on free will.

22   The Dilemma of Determinism

WILLIAM JAMES

William James (1842–1910), brother of the novelist Henry James, was born in New York City and educated at Harvard. He made outstanding contributions to psychology, which are found primarily in his book *The Principles of Psychology* (1890). In philosophy, he is best known for his development of a view called pragmatism, which he took over from the American philosopher and mathematician Charles Pierce, and for his contributions to philosophy of religion. James's goal, in philosophy, was the development of a point of view that would do equal justice to the claims of the exact sciences and also to those of moral and religious experience. His *The Varieties of Religious Experience* (1902) is regarded by many as the best book on the topic ever written. In the following selection, James defends the possibility of free will by arguing that, for all we know, many of our choices could be undetermined and yet our behavior be as intelligible as it is now. James also explains why believing in free will may have better consequences for our lives than not believing in it.

Reading Questions

1. Explain, in your own words, James's distinction between "determinism" and "indeterminism," and then illustrate the distinction with a clear example.
2. What is the point of James's Divinity Avenue/Oxford Street example? Do you agree?

A COMMON OPINION PREVAILS that the juice has ages ago been pressed out of the free-will controversy, and that no new champion can do more than warm up stale arguments which every one has heard. This is a radical mistake. I know of no subject less worn out, or in which inventive genius has a better chance of breaking open new ground,—not, perhaps, of forcing a conclusion or of coercing assent, but of deepening our sense of what the issue between the two parties really is, of what the ideas of fate and of free-will imply. . . .

The arguments I am about to urge all proceed on two suppositions: first, when we make theories about the world and discuss them with one another, we do so in order to attain a conception of things which shall give us subjective satisfaction; and, second, if there be two conceptions, and the one seems to us, on the whole, more rational than the other, we are entitled to suppose that the more rational one is the truer of the two. I hope that you are all willing to make these suppositions with me; for I am afraid that if there be any of you here who are not, they will find little edification in the rest of what I have to say. I cannot stop to argue the point; but I myself believe that all the magnificent achievements of mathematical and physical science—our doctrines of evolution, of uniformity of law, and the rest—proceed from our indomitable desire to cast the world into a more rational shape in our minds than the shape into which it is thrown there by the crude order of our experience. The world has shown itself, to a great extent, plastic to this demand of ours for rationality. How much farther it will show itself plastic no one can

From James: "The Dilemma of Determinism," An address to the Harvard Divinity Students published in the Unitarian Review *(1884). Also available in James:* Essays on Faith and Morals, *Longmans, Green and Co. (1949).*

say. Our only means of finding out is to try; and I, for one, feel as free to try conceptions of moral as of mechanical or of logical rationality. If a certain formula for expressing the nature of the world violates my moral demand, I shall feel as free to throw it overboard, or at least to doubt it, as if it disappointed my demand for uniformity of sequence, for example; the one demand being, so far as I can see, quite as subjective and emotional as the other is. The principle of causality, for example — what is it but a postulate, an empty name covering simply a demand that the sequence of events shall some day manifest a deeper kind of belonging of one thing with another than the mere arbitrary juxtaposition which now phenomenally appears? It is as much an altar to an unknown god as the one that Saint Paul found at Athens. All our scientific and philosophic ideals are altars to unknown gods. Uniformity is as much so as is free will. If this be admitted, we can debate on even terms. But if any one pretends that while freedom and variety are, in the first instance, subjective demands, necessity and uniformity are something altogether different, I do not see how we can debate at all.

To begin, then, I must suppose you acquainted with the usual arguments on the subject. I cannot stop to take up the old proofs from causation, from statistics, from the certainty with which we can foretell one another's conduct, from the fixity of character, and all the rest. But there are two *words* which usually encumber these classical arguments, and which we must immediately dispose of if we are to make any progress. One is the eulogistic word *freedom,* and the other is the opprobrious word *chance.* The word "chance" I wish to keep, but I wish to get rid of the word "freedom." Its eulogistic associations have so far overshadowed all the rest of its meaning that both parties claim the sole right to use it, and determinists today insist that they alone are freedom's champions. Old-fashioned determinism was what we may call *hard* determinism. It did not shrink from such words as fatality, bondage of the will, necessitation, and the like. Nowadays, we have a *soft* determinism which abhors harsh words, and, repudiating fatality, necessity, and even predetermination, says that its real name is freedom; for freedom is only necessity understood, and bondage to the highest is identical with true freedom. . . .

Now, all this is a quagmire of evasion under which the real issue of fact has been entirely smothered. . . . But there *is* a problem, an issue of fact and not of words, an issue of the most momentous importance, which is often decided without discussion in one sentence, — nay, in one clause of a sentence, — by those very writers who spin out whole chapters in their efforts to show what "true" freedom is; and that is the question of determinism, about which we are to talk tonight.

Fortunately, no ambiguities hang about this word or about its opposite, indeterminism. Both designate an outward way in which things may happen, and their cold and mathematical sound has no sentimental associations that can bribe our partiality either way in advance. Now, evidence of an external kind to decide between determinism and indeterminism is strictly impossible to find. Let us look at the difference between them and see for ourselves. What does determinism profess?

It professes that those parts of the universe already laid down absolutely appoint and decree what the other parts shall be. The future has no ambiguous possibilities hidden in its womb: the part we call the present is compatible with only one totality. And other future complement than the one fixed from eternity is impossible. The whole is in each and every part, and welds it with the rest into an absolute unity, an iron block, in which there can be no equivocation or shadow of turning.

> With earth's first clay they did the last man knead,
> And there of the last harvest sowed the seed.
> And the first morning of creation wrote
> What the last dawn of reckoning shall read.

Indeterminism, on the contrary, says that the parts have a certain amount of loose play on one another, so that the laying down of one of them does not necessarily determine what the others shall be. It admits that possibilities may be in excess of actualities, and that things not yet revealed to our knowledge may really in themselves be ambiguous. Of two alternative futures which we conceive, both may now be really possible; and the one become impossible only at the very moment when the other excludes it by becoming real itself. Indeterminism thus denies the world to be one unbending unit of fact. It says there is a certain ultimate pluralism in it; and, so saying, it corroborates our ordinary unsophisticated view of things. To that view, actualities seem to float in a wider sea of possibilities from out of which they are chosen; and, *somewhere*, indeterminism says, such possibilities exist, and form a part of truth.

Determinism, on the contrary, says they exist *nowhere*, and that necessity on the one hand and impossibility on the other are the sole categories of the real. Possibilities that fail to get realized are, for determinism, pure illusions: they never were possibilities at all. There is nothing inchoate, it says, about this universe of ours, all that was or is or shall be actual in it having been from eternity virtually there. The cloud of alternatives our minds escort this mass of actuality withal is a cloud of sheer deceptions, to which "impossibilities" is the only name that rightfully belongs.

The issue, it will be seen, is a perfectly sharp one, which no eulogistic terminology can smear over or wipe out. The truth *must* lie with one side or the other, and its lying with one side makes the other false.

The question relates solely to the existence of possibilities, in the strict sense of the term, as things that may, but need not, be. Both sides admit that a volition, for instance, has occurred. The indeterminists say another volition might have occurred in its place: the determinists swear that nothing could possibly have occurred in its place. Now, can science be called on to tell us which of these two point-blank contradicters of each other is right? Science professes to draw no conclusions but such as are based on matters of fact, things that have actually happened; but how can any amount of assurance that something actually happened give us the least grain of information as to whether another thing might or might not have happened in its place? Only facts can be proved by other facts. With things that are possibilities and not facts, facts have no concern. If we have no other evidence than the evidence of existing facts, the possibility-question must remain a mystery never to be cleared up.

And the truth is that facts practically have hardly anything to do with making us either determinists or indeterminists. Sure enough, we make a flourish of quoting facts this way or that; and if we are determinists, we talk about the infallibility with which we can predict one another's conduct; while if we are indeterminists, we lay great stress on the fact that it is just because we cannot foretell one another's conduct, either in war or statecraft or in any of the great and small intrigues and businesses of men, that life is so intensely anxious and hazardous a game. But who does not see the wretched insufficiency of this so-called objective testimony on both sides? What fills up the gaps in our minds is something not objective, not external. What divides us into possibility men and anti-possibility men is different faiths or postulates,—postulates of rationality. To this man the world seems more rational with possibilities in it,—to that man more rational with possibilities excluded; and talk as we will about having to yield to evidence, what makes us monists or pluralists, determinists or indeterminists, is at bottom always some sentiment like this.

The stronghold of the deterministic sentiment is the antipathy to the idea of chance. As soon as we begin to talk indeterminism to our friends, we find a number of them shaking their heads. This notion of alternative possibility, they say, this admission that any one of several things may come to pass, is, after all, only a roundabout name for chance; and chance is something the notion of which no sane mind can for an instant tolerate in the world. What is it, they ask, but barefaced crazy unreason, the negation of intelligibility and law? And if the slightest particle of it exist anywhere, what is to prevent the whole fabric from falling together, the stars from going out, and chaos from recommencing her topsy-turvy reign?

Remarks of this sort about chance will put an end to discussion as quickly as anything one can find. I have already told you that "chance" was a word I wished to keep and use. Let us then examine exactly what it means, and see whether it ought to be such a terrible bugbear to us. I fancy that squeezing the thistle boldly will rob it of its sting.

The sting of the word "chance" seems to lie in the assumption that it means something positive, and that if anything happens by chance, it must needs be something of an intrinsically irrational and preposterous sort. Now, chance means nothing of the kind. It is a purely negative and relative term, giving us no information about that of which it is predicated, except that it happens to be disconnected with something else,—not controlled, secured, or necessitated by other things in advance of its own actual presence. As this point is the most subtile one of the whole lecture, and at the same time the point on which all the rest hinges, I beg you to pay particular attention to it. What I say is that it tells us nothing about what a thing may be in itself to call it "chance." It may be a bad thing, it may be a good thing. It may be lucidity, transparency, fitness incarnate, matching the whole system of other things, when it has once befallen, in an unimaginably perfect way. All you mean by calling it "chance" is that this is not guaranteed, that it may also fall out otherwise. . . .

Nevertheless, many persons talk as if the minutest dose of disconnectedness of one part with another, the smallest modicum of independence, the faintest tremor of ambiguity about the future, for example, would ruin everything, and turn this goodly universe into a sort of insane sand-heap or nulliverse, no universe at all. Since future human volitions are as a matter of fact the only ambiguous things we are tempted to believe in, let us stop for a moment to make ourselves sure whether their independent and accidental character need be fraught with such direful consequences to the universe as these.

What is meant by saying that my choice of which way to walk home after the lecture is ambiguous and matter of chances as far as the present moment is concerned? It means that both Divinity Avenue and Oxford Street are called; but that only one, and that one *either* one, shall be chosen. Now, I ask you seriously to suppose that this ambiguity of my choice is real; and then to make the impossible hypothesis that the choice is made twice over, and each time falls on a different street. In other words, imagine that I first walk through Divinity Avenue, and then imagine that the powers governing the universe annihilate ten minutes of time with all that it contained, and set me back at the door of this hall just as I was before the choice was made. Imagine then that, everything else being the same, I now make a different choice and traverse Oxford Street. You, as passive spectators, look on and see the two alternative universes,—one of them with me walking through Divinity Avenue in it, the other with the same me walking through Oxford Street. Now, if you are determinists you believe one of these universes to have been from eternity impossible: you believe it to have been impossible because of the intrinsic irrationality or accidentality somewhere

involved in it. But looking outwardly at these universes, can you say which is the impossible and accidental one, and which the rational and necessary one? I doubt if the most ironclad determinist among you could have the slightest glimmer of light on this point. In other words, either universe *after the fact* and once there would, to our means of observation and understanding, appear just as rational as the other. There would be absolutely no criterion by which we might judge one necessary and the other matter of chance. Suppose now we relieve the gods of their hypothetical task and assume my choice, once made, to be made forever. I go through Divinity Avenue for good and all. If, as good determinists, you now begin to affirm, what all good determinists punctually do affirm, that in the nature of things I *couldn't* have gone through Oxford Street,—had I done so it would have been chance, irrationality, insanity, a horrid gap in nature,—I simply call your attention to this, that your affirmation is what the Germans call a *Machtspruch*, a mere conception fulminated as a dogma and based on no insight into details. Before my choice, either street seemed as natural to you as to me. Had I happened to take Oxford Street, Divinity Avenue would have figured in your philosophy as the gap in nature; and you would have so proclaimed it with the best deterministic conscience in the world.

But what a hollow outcry, then, is this against a chance which, if it were present to us, we could by no character whatever distinguish from a rational necessity! . . . The more one thinks of the matter, the more one wonders that so empty and gratuitous a hubbub as this outcry against chance should have found so great an echo in the hearts of men. It is a word which tells us absolutely nothing about what chances, or about the *modus operandi* of the chancing; and the use of it as a war-cry shows only a temper of intellectual absolutism, a demand that the world shall be a solid block, subject to one control,—which temper, which demand, the world may not be bound to gratify at all. In every outwardly verifiable and practical respect, a world in which the alternatives that now actually distract *your* choice were decided by pure chance would be by *me* absolutely undistinguished from the world in which I now live. I am, therefore, entirely willing to call it, so far as your choices go, a world of chance for me. To *yourselves,* it is true, those very acts of choice, which to me are so blind, opaque, and external, are the opposites of this, for you are within them and effect them. To you they appear as decisions; and decisions, for him who makes them, are altogether peculiar psychic facts. Self-luminous and self-justifying at the living moment at which they occur, they appeal to no outside moment to put its stamp upon them or make them continuous with the rest of nature. Themselves it is rather who seem to make nature continuous; and in their strange and intense function of granting consent to one possibility and withholding it from another, to transform an equivocal and double feature into an inalterable and simple past.

But with the psychology of the matter we have no concern this evening. The quarrel which determinism has with chance fortunately has nothing to do with this or that psychological detail. It is a quarrel altogether metaphysical. Determinism denies the ambiguity of future volitions, because it affirms that nothing future can be ambiguous. But we have said enough to meet the issue. Indeterminate future volitions *do* mean chance. . . .

We have seen what determinism means: we have seen that indeterminism is rightly described as meaning chance; and we have seen that chance, the very name of which we are urged to shrink from as from a metaphysical pestilence, means only the negative fact that no part of the world, however big, can claim to control absolutely the destinies of the whole. But although, in discussing the word "chance," I may at moments have seemed to be arguing for its real existence, I have not meant to do so yet. We have not yet ascertained whether this be a world of chance or no; at most, we have agreed that it seems so. And I now repeat what I said at the outset, that, from any strict theoretical point of view, the question is insoluble. To deepen our theoretic sense of the *difference* between a world with chances in it and a deterministic world is the most I can hope to do; and this I may now at last begin upon, after all our tedious clearing of the way.

I wish first of all to show you just what the notion that this is a deterministic world implies. The implications I call your attention to are all bound up with the fact that it is a world in which we constantly have to make what I shall, with your per-

mission, call judgments of regret. Hardly an hour passes in which we do not wish that something might be otherwise; and happy indeed are those of us whose hearts have never echoed the wish of Omar Khayyam—

> That we might clasp, ere closed, the book of fate,
>   And make the writer on a fairer leaf
> Inscribe our names, or quite obliterate.
> Ah! Love, could you and I with fate conspire
> To mend this sorry scheme of things entire,
>   Would we not shatter it to bits, and then
> Remould it nearer to the heart's desire?

Now, it is undeniable that most of these regrets are foolish, and quite on a par in point of philosophic value with the criticisms on the universe of that friend of our infancy, the hero of the fable The Atheist and the Acorn,—

> Fool! had that bough a pumpkin bore,
> Thy whimsies would have worked no more, etc.

Even from the point of view of our own ends, we should probably make a botch of remodelling the universe. How much more then from the point of view of ends we cannot see! Wise men therefore regret as little as they can. But still some regrets are pretty obstinate and hard to stifle,—regrets for acts of wanton cruelty or treachery, for example, whether performed by others or by ourselves. Hardly any one can remain *entirely* optimistic after reading the confessions of the murderer at Brockton the other day: how, to get rid of the wife whose continued existence bored him, he inveigled her into a desert spot, shot her four times, and then, as she lay on the ground and said to him, "You didn't do it on purpose, did you, dear?" replied, "No, I didn't do it on purpose," as he raised a rock and smashed her skull. Such an occurrence, with the mild sentence and self-satisfaction of the prisoner, is a field for a crop of regrets, which one need not take up in detail. We feel that, although a perfect mechanical fit to the rest of the universe, it is a bad moral fit, and that something else would really have been better in its place.

But for the deterministic philosophy the murder, the sentence, and the prisoner's optimism were all necessary from eternity; and nothing else for a moment had a ghost of a chance of being put into their place. To admit such a chance, the determinists tell us, would be to make a suicide of reason; so we must steel our hearts against the thought. And here our plot thickens, for we see the first of those difficult implications of determinism and monism which it is my purpose to make you feel. If this Brockton murder was called for by the rest of the universe, if it had to come at its preappointed hour, and if nothing else would have been consistent with the sense of the whole, what are we to think of the universe? Are we stubbornly to stick to our judgment of regret, and say, though it *couldn't* be, yet it *would* have been a better universe with something different from this Brockton murder in it? That, of course, seems the natural and spontaneous thing for us to do; and yet it is nothing short of deliberately espousing a kind of pessimism. The judgment of regret calls the murder bad. Calling a thing bad means, if it means anything at all, that the thing ought not to be, that something else ought to be in its stead. Determinism, in denying that anything else can be in its stead, virtually defines the universe as a place in which what ought to be is impossible,—in other words, as an organism whose constitution is afflicted with an incurable taint, an irremediable flaw. The pessimism of a Schopenhauer says no more than this,—that the murder is a symptom; and that it is a vicious symptom because it belongs to a vicious whole, which can express its nature no otherwise than by bringing forth just such a symptom as that at this particular spot. Regret for the murder must transform itself, if we are determinists and wise, into a larger regret. It is absurd to regret the murder alone. Other things being what they are, *it* could not be different. What we should regret is that whole frame of things of which the murder is one member. I see no escape whatever from this pessimistic conclusion, if, being determinists, our judgment of regret is to be allowed to stand at all.

The only deterministic escape from pessimism is everywhere to abandon the judgment of regret. That this can be done, history shows to be not impossible. The devil, *quod existentiam,* may be good. That is, although he be a *principle* of evil, yet the universe, with such a principle in it, may practically be a better universe than it could have been without. On every hand, in a small way, we find that a certain amount of evil is a condition by

which a higher form of good is brought. There is nothing to prevent anybody from generalizing this view, and trusting that if we could but see things in the largest of all ways, even such matters as this Brockton murder would appear to be paid for by the uses that follow in their train. An optimism *quand même,* a systematic and infatuated optimism like that ridiculed by Voltaire in his Candide, is one of the possible ideal ways in which a man may train himself to look on life. Bereft of dogmatic hardness and lit up with the expression of a tender and pathetic hope, such an optimism has been the grace of some of the most religious characters that ever lived.

> Throb thine with Nature's throbbing breast,
> And all is clear from east to west.

Even cruelty and treachery may be among the absolutely blessed fruits of time and to quarrel with any of their details may be blasphemy. The only real blasphemy, in short, may be that pessimistic temper of the soul which lets it give way to such things as regrets, remorse, and grief.

Thus, our deterministic pessimism may become a deterministic optimism at the price of extinguishing our judgments of regret.

But does not this immediately bring us into a curious logical predicament? Our determinism leads us to call our judgments of regret wrong, because they are pessimistic in implying that what is impossible yet ought to be. But how then about the judgments of regret themselves? If they are wrong, other judgments, judgments of approval presumably, ought to be in their place. But as they are necessitated, nothing else *can* be in their place; and the universe is just what it was before,—namely, a place in which what ought to be appears impossible. We have got one foot out of the pessimistic bog, but the other one sinks all the deeper. We have rescued our actions from the bonds of evil, but our judgments are now held fast. When murders and treacheries cease to be sins, regrets are theoretic absurdities and errors. The theoretic and the active life thus play a kind of see-saw with each other on the ground of evil. The rise of either sends the other down. Murder and treachery cannot be good without regret being bad: regret cannot be good without treachery and murder being bad. Both, however, are supposed to have been foredoomed; so something must be fatally unreasonable, absurd, and wrong in the world. It must be a place of which either sin or error forms a necessary part. From this dilemma there seems at first sight no escape. . . .

The only consistent way of representing a pluralism and a world whose parts may affect one another through their conduct being either good or bad is the indeterministic way. What interest, zest, or excitement can there be in achieving the right way, unless we are enabled to feel that the wrong way is also a possible and a natural way,—nay, more, a menacing and an imminent way? And what sense can there be in condemning ourselves for taking the wrong way, unless we need have done nothing of the sort, unless the right way was open to us as well? I cannot understand the willingness to act, no matter how we feel, without the belief that acts are really good and bad. I cannot understand the belief that an act is bad, without regret at its happening. I cannot understand regret without the admission of real, genuine possibilities in the world. Only *then* is it other than a mockery to feel, after we have failed to do our best, that an irreparable opportunity is gone from the universe, the loss of which it must forever after mourn.

If you insist that this is all superstition, that possibility is in the eye of science and reason impossibility, and that if I act badly 'tis that the universe was foredoomed to suffer this defect, you fall right back into the dilemma, the labyrinth, of pessimism, from out of whose toils we have just wound our way.

Now, we are of course free to fall back, if we please. For my own part, though, whatever difficulties may beset the philosophy of objective right and wrong, and the indeterminism it seems to imply, determinism, with its alternative of pessimism or romanticism, contains difficulties expressly repudiated awhile ago the pretension to offer any arguments which could be coercive in a so-called scientific fashion in this matter. And I consequently find myself, at the end of this long talk, obliged to state my conclusions in an altogether personal way. This personal method of appeal seems to be among the very conditions of the problem; and the most any one can do is to confess as candidly as he can the grounds for the faith that is in him, and leave his example to work on others as it may.

Let me, then, without circumlocution say just this. The world is enigmatical enough in all conscience, whatever theory we may take up toward it. The indeterminism I defend, the free-will theory of popular sense based on the judgment of regret, represents the world as vulnerable, and liable to be injured by certain of its parts if they act wrong. And it represents their acting wrong as a matter of possibility or accident, neither inevitable nor yet to be infallibly warded off. In all this, it is a theory devoid either of transparency or of stability. It gives us a pluralistic, restless universe, in which no single point of view can ever take in the whole scene; and to a mind possessed of the love of unity at any cost, it will, no doubt, remain forever inacceptable. A friend with such a mind once told me that the thought of my universe made him sick, like the sight of the horrible motion of a mass of maggots in their carrion bed.

But while I freely admit that the pluralism and the restlessness are repugnant and irrational in a certain way, I find that every alternative to them is irrational in a deeper way. The indeterminism with its maggots, if you please to speak so about it, offends only the native absolutism of my intellect,— an absolutism which, after all, perhaps, deserves to be snubbed and kept in check. But the determinism with its necessary carrion, to continue the figure of speech, and with no possible maggots to eat the latter up, violates my sense of moral reality through and through. When, for example, I imagine such carrion as the Brockton murder, I cannot conceive it as an act by which the universe, as a whole, logically and necessarily expresses its nature without shrinking from complicity with such a whole. And I deliberately refuse to keep on terms of loyalty with the universe by saying blankly that the murder, since it does flow from the nature of the whole, is not carrion. There are *some* instinctive reactions which I, for one, will not tamper with. . . .

Make as great an uproar about chance as you please, I know that chance means pluralism and nothing more. If some of the members of the pluralism are bad, the philosophy of pluralism, whatever broad views it may deny me, permits me, at least, to turn to the other members with a clean breast of affection and an unsophisticated moral sense. And if I still wish to think of the world as a totality, it lets me feel that a world with a *chance* in it of being altogether good, even if the chance never come to pass, is better than a world with no such chance at all. That "chance" whose very notion I am exhorted and conjured to banish from my view of the future as the suicide of reason concerning it, that "chance" is—what? Just this,— the chance that in moral respects the future may be other and better than the past has been. This is the only chance we have any motive for supposing to exist. Shame, rather, on its repudiation and its denial! For its presence is the vital air which lets the world live, the salt which keeps it sweet.

Further Questions

1. James argues that indeterminism could be true. Does he give any evidence that it actually is true? Does modern science give any evidence that the sort of indeterminism that James needs to support his belief in free will is true?
2. Is it possible, in principle, that someone could create an android for which it was a matter of pure chance whether it walked home via one street rather than another? If so, how can we know whether we are "natural androids" of that sort?
3. Would people be any more responsible for their behavior if it came about by chance than if it were predetermined? If so, why? If not, can one appeal to chance to support the idea that people might have free will?

Further Readings

Lehrer, Keith, ed. *Freedom and Determinism*. New York: Random House, 1966. A valuable anthology of the views of contemporary analytic philosophers.
Salmon, Wesley. *Scientific Explanation and the Causal Structure of the World*. Princeton, NJ: Princeton University Press, 1984. A clear, informed account of the role of chance in modern scientific theory.

Free Will   23

G. E. MOORE

Born in London, G. E. Moore (1873–1958) went to Cambridge University, where he concentrated, first, in classics and later, in philosophy. He remarked once that he never would have thought of philosophical issues if others had not brought them to his attention. Nevertheless, along with Bertrand Russell and Ludwig Wittgenstein, Moore is commonly regarded as one of the "founding fathers" of analytic philosophy, which for most of the twentieth century has been the dominant approach to philosophy in English-speaking countries. Except for Moore's academic pursuits, he led an uneventful life. He rarely left England. He is known for being unpretentious and for his childlike naivete, when it came to ordinary affairs. He is also known for his intense and passionate absorption in philosophy. He had a reputation for giving himself completely to a philosophical discussion, whether he was discussing it with a colleague or with a student, and for viewing its progress with the constant fresh surprise of one considering an issue for the first time. Moore wrote mainly in the areas of ethics and epistemology. Among his books are

Principia Ethica (Cambridge, 1903), *Philosophical Studies* (London, 1922), *Philosophical Papers* (London, 1959), and *Ethics* (London, 1912), from which the following selection is taken.

Reading Questions:

1. How does Moore characterize the Free Will controversy?
2. Is it ever the case that a person could have done something except what he or she actually did do? How does Moore answer? How does he argue for his answer?
3. What is the connection between the thesis that everything has a cause and the question of whether anyone ever acts freely?
4. Moore claimed that sometimes people could have done things they did not do. By this he means that they should (or would) have done them, if they had chosen. If everything has a cause, how could this be so? Explain.

WE HAVE BEEN CONSIDERING various objections which might be urged against the theory stated in Chapters I and II. And the very last objection which we considered was one which consisted in asserting that the question whether an action is right or wrong does *not* depend upon its *actual* consequences, because whenever the consequences, *so far as the agent can foresee,* are *likely* to be the best possible, the action is always right, even if they are not *actually* the best possible. In other words, this objection rested on the view that right and wrong depend, in a sense, upon what the agent *can know.* And in the present chapter I propose to consider objections, which rest, instead of this, upon the view that right and wrong depend upon what the agent *can do.*

Now it must be remembered that, *in a sense,* our original theory does hold and even insists that this is the case. We have, for instance, frequently referred to . . . as holding that an action is only right, if it produces the best *possible* consequences; and by "the best *possible* consequences" was meant "consequences at least as good as would have followed from any action which the agent *could* have done instead." It does, therefore, hold that the question whether an action is right or wrong does always depend upon a comparison of its consequences with those of all the other actions which the agent *could* have done instead. It assumes, therefore, that wherever a voluntary action is right or wrong (and we have throughout only been talking of *voluntary* actions), it is true that the agent

could, in a sense, have done something else instead. This is an absolutely essential part of the theory.

But the reader must now be reminded that all along we have been using the words "can," "could," and "possible" *in a special sense.* It was explained in Chapter I (pp. 12–13), that we proposed, purely for the sake of brevity, to say that an agent *could* have done a given action, which he didn't do, wherever it is true that he could have done it, *if* he had chosen; and similarly by what he *can* do, or what is *possible,* we have always meant merely what is possible, *if* he chooses. Our theory, therefore, has not been maintaining, after all, that right and wrong depend upon what the agent absolutely *can* do, but only on what he can do, *if* he chooses. And this makes an immense difference. For, by confining itself in this way, our theory avoids a controversy, which cannot be avoided by those who assert that right and wrong depend upon what the agent absolutely *can* do. There are few, if any, people who will *expressly* deny that we very often really could, *if* we had chosen, have done something different from what we actually did do. But the moment it is asserted that any man ever absolutely *could* have done anything other than what he did do, there are many people who *would* deny this. The view, therefore, which we are to consider in this chapter—the view that right and wrong depend upon what the agent absolutely *can* do—at once involves us in an extremely difficult controversy—the controversy concerning Free Will. There are many people who strenuously deny that any man ever *could* have done anything other than what he actually did do, or ever *can* do anything other than what he *will* do; and there are others who assert the opposite equally strenuously. And whichever view be held is, if *combined* with the view that right and wrong depend upon what the agent absolutely *can* do, liable to contradict our theory very seriously. Those who hold that no man ever *could* have done anything oher than what he did do, are, if they *also* hold that right and wrong depend upon what we *can* do, logically bound to hold that no action of ours is ever right and none is ever wrong; and this is a view which is, I think, often actually held, and which, of course, constitutes an extremely serious and fundamental objection to our theory: since our theory implies, on the contrary, that we very often do act *wrongly*, if never quite rightly. Those, on the other hand, who hold that we absolutely *can* do things, which we don't do, and that right and wrong depend upon what we thus *can* do, are also liable to be led to contradict our theory, though for a different reason. Our theory holds that, provided a man could have done something else, *if* he had chosen, that is sufficient to entitle us to say that his action really is either right or wrong. But those who hold the view we are considering will be liable to reply that this is by no means sufficient: that to say that it *is* sufficient, is entirely to misconceive the nature of right and wrong. They will say that, in order that an action may be *really* either right or wrong, it is absolutely essential that the agent should have been *really able* to act differently, able in some sense quite other than that of merely being able, *if* he had chosen. *If* all that were really ever true of us were merely that we could have acted differently, *if* we had chosen, then, these people would say, it really would be true that none of our actions are ever right and that none are ever wrong. They will say, therefore, that our theory entirely misses out one absolutely essential condition of right and wrong—the condition that, for an action to be right or wrong, it must be *freely* done. And moreover, many of them will hold also that the class of actions which we absolutely *can* do is often not identical with those which we can do, *if* we choose. They may say, for instance, that very often an action, which we *could* have done, *if* we had chosen, is nevertheless an action which we *could*

not have done; and that an action is always right, if it produces as good consequences as any other action which we really *could* have done instead. From which it will follow that many actions which our theory declares to be *wrong*, will, according to them, be right, because these actions really are the best of all that we *could* have done, though *not* the best of all that we could have done, *if* we had chosen.

Now these objections seem to me to be the most serious which we have yet had to consider. They seem to me to be serious because (1) it is very difficult to be sure that right and wrong do not really depend, as they assert, upon what we *can* do and not merely on what we can do, *if* we choose; and because (2) it is very difficult to be sure in what sense it is true that we ever *could* have done anything different from what we actually did do. I do not profess to be sure about either of these points. And all that I can hope to do is to point out certain facts which do seem to me to be clear, though they are often overlooked; and thus to isolate clearly for the reader's decision, those questions which seem to me to be really doubtful and difficult.

Let us begin with the question: Is it ever true that a man *could* have done anything else, except what he actually did do? And, first of all, I think I had better explain exactly how this question seems to me to be related to the question of Free Will. For it is a fact that, in many discussions about Free Will, this precise question is never mentioned at all; so that it might be thought that the two have really nothing whatever to do with one another. And indeed some philosophers do, I think, definitely imply that they *have* nothing to do with one another: they seem to hold that our wills can properly be said to be free even if we never can, in any sense at all, do anything else except what, in the end, we actually do do. But this view, if it is held, seems to me to be plainly a mere abuse of language. The statement that we have Free Will is certainly ordinarily understood to imply that we really sometimes have the power of acting differently from the way in which we actually do act; and hence, if anybody tells us that we have Free Will, while at the same time he means to deny that we ever have such a power, he is simply misleading us. We certainly have *not* got Free Will, in the ordinary sense of the word, if we never really *could*, in any sense at all, have done anything else than what we did do; so that, in this respect, the two questions certainly are connected. But, on the other hand, the mere fact (if it is a fact) that we sometimes *can,* in *some* sense, do what we don't do, does not necessarily entitle us to say that we *have* Free Will. We certainly *haven't* got it, *unless* we can; but it doesn't follow that we *have* got it, even if we *can.* Whether we have or not will depend upon the precise sense in which it is true that we can. So that even if we do decide that we really *can* often, in *some* sense, do what we don't do, this decision by itself does not entitle us to say that we have Free Will.

And the first point about which we can and should be quite clear is, I think, this: namely, that we certainly often *can,* in *some* sense, do what we don't do. It is, I think quite clear that this is so; and also very important that we should realize that it is so. For many people are inclined to assert, quite without qualification: No man ever *could,* on any occasion, have done anything else than what he actually did do on that occasion. By asserting this quite simply, without qualification, they imply, of course (even if they do not mean to imply), that there is *no* proper sense of the word "could," in which it is true that a man *could* have acted differently. And it is this implication which is, I think, quite certainly absolutely false. For this reason, anybody who asserts, without qualification, "Nothing ever *could* have happened, except what actually did happen," is making an assertion which is quite unjustifiable, and which he himself cannot help constantly contradicting. And it is important to insist on this, because many people do make this unqualified assertion, without seeing how violently it contradicts what they themselves, and all of us, believe, and rightly believe, at other times. If, indeed, they insert a qualification—if they merely say, "In *one* sense of the word "*could*" nothing ever *could* have happened, except what did happen," then, they may perhaps be perfectly right: we are not disputing that they may. All that we are maintaining is that, in *one* perfectly proper and legitimate sense of the word "could," and that one of the very commonest senses in which it is used, it is quite certain that some things which didn't happen *could* have happened. And the proof that this is so, is simply as follows.

It is impossible to exaggerate the frequency of the occasions on which we *all* of us make a distinction between two things, neither of which *did* happen—a distinction which we express by saying, that whereas the one *could* have happened, and other could *not.* No distinction is commoner than this. And no one, I think, who fairly examines the instances in which we make it, can doubt about three things: namely (1) that very often there really is *some* distinction between the two things, corresponding to the language which we use; (2) that this distinction, which really *does* subsist between the things, is *the* one which we mean to express by saying that the one was possible and the other impossible; and (3) that this way of expressing it is a perfectly proper and legitimate way. But if so, it absolutely follows that one of the commonest and most legitimate usages of the phrases "could" and "could not" is to express a difference, which often really does hold between two things *neither* of which did actually happen. Only a few instances need be given. I *could* have walked a mile in twenty minutes this morning, but I certainly could *not* have run two miles in five minutes. I did not, *in fact,* do either of these two things; but it is pure nonsense to say that the mere fact that I *did* not, does away with the distinction between them, which I express by saying that the one *was* within my powers, whereas the other was *not. Although* I did neither, yet the one was certainly *possible* to me in a sense in which the other was totally *im*possible. Or, to take another instance: It is true, as a rule, that cats *can* climb trees, whereas dogs *can't.* Suppose that on a particular afternoon neither A's cat nor B's dog *do* climb a tree. It is quite absurd to say that this mere fact proves that we must be wrong if we say (as we certainly often should say) that the cat *could* have climbed a tree, though she didn't, whereas the dog *couldn't.* Or, to take an instance which concerns an inanimate object. Some ships *can* steam 20 knots, whereas others *can't* steam more than 15. And the mere fact that, on a particular occasion, a 20-knot steamer *did* not *actually* run at this speed certainly does not entitle us to say that she *could* not have done so, in the sense in which a 15-knot one *could* not. On the contrary, we all can and should distinguish between cases in which (as, for instance, owing to an accident to her propeller) she did not, *because* she could not, and cases in which she did not, *although* she *could*. Instances of this sort might be multiplied quite indefinitely; and it is surely quite plain that we all of us do *continually* use such language: we continually, when considering two events, neither of which *did* happen, distinguish between them by saying that whereas the one *was* possible, though it didn't happen, the other was *im*possible. And it is surely quite plain that what we mean by this (whatever it may be) is something which is often perfectly true. But, if so, then anybody who asserts, without qualification, "Nothing ever *could* have happened, except what did happen," is simply asserting what is false.

It is, therefore, quite certain that we often *could* (in *some* sense) have done what we did not do. And now let us see how this fact is related to the argument by which people try to persuade us that it is *not* a fact.

The argument is well known: it is simply this. It is assumed (for reasons which I need not discuss) that absolutely everything that happens has a *cause* in what precedes it. But to say this is to say that it follows *necessarily* from something that preceded it; or, in other words, that, once the preceding events which are its cause had happened, it was absolutely *bound* to happen. But to say that it was *bound* to happen, is to say that nothing else *could* have happened instead; so that, if *everything* has a cause, *nothing* ever could have happened except what did happen.

And now let us assume that the premise of this argument is correct: that everything really *has* a cause. What really follows from it? Obviously all that follows is that, in *one* sense of the word "could," nothing ever *could* have happened, except what did happen. This really *does* follow. But, *if* the word "could" is ambiguous—if, that is to say, it is used in different senses on different occasions—it is obviously quite possible that though, in *one* sense, nothing ever could have happened except what did happen, yet in *another* sense, it may at the same time be perfectly true that some things which did not happen *could* have happened. And can anybody undertake to assert with certainty that the word 'could' is *not* ambiguous? that it may not have more than one legitimate sense? *Possibly* it is not ambiguous; and, *if* it is not, then the fact that some things, which did not happen, *could* have

happened, really would contradict the principle that everything has a cause; and, in that case, we should, I think, have to give up this principle, because the fact that we often *could* have done what we did not do, is so certain. But the assumption that the word "could" is *not* ambiguous is an assumption which certainly should not be made without the clearest proof. And yet I think it often is made, without any proof at all; simply because it does not occur to people that words often are ambiguous. It is, for instance, often assumed, in the Free Will controversy, that the question at issue is solely as to whether everything is caused, or whether acts of will are sometimes uncaused. Those who hold that we *have* Free Will, think themselves bound to maintain that acts of will sometimes have *no* cause; and those who hold that everything is caused think that this proves completely that we have not Free Will. But, in fact, it is extremely doubtful whether Free Will is at all inconsistent with the principle that everything is caused. Whether it is or not, all depends on a very difficult question as to the meaning of the word "could." All that is certain about the matter is (1) that, if we have Free Will, it must be true, in *some* sense, that we sometimes *could* have done, what we did not do; and (2) that, if everything is caused, it must be true, in *some* sense, that we *never could* have done, what we did not do. What is very *un*certain, and what certainly needs to be investigated, is whether these two meanings of the word "could" are the same.

Let us begin by asking: What is the sense of the word "could," in which it is so certain that we often *could* have done, what we did not do? What, for instance, is the sense in which I *could* have walked a mile in twenty minutes this morning, though I did not? There is one suggestion, which is very obvious: namely, that what I mean is simply after all that I could, *if* I had chosen; or (to avoid a possible complication) perhaps we had better say "that I *should,* if I had chosen." In other words, the suggestion is that we often use the phrase "*I could*" simply and solely as a short way of saying "I *should,* if I had chosen." And in all cases, where it is certainly true that we *could* have done, what we did not do, it is, I think very difficult to be quite sure that this (or something similar) is *not* what we mean by the word "could." The case of the ship may seem to be an exception, because it is certainly not true that she would have steamed twenty knots if *she* had chosen; but even here it seems possible that what we mean is simply that she *would, if the men on board of her* had chosen. There are certainly good reasons for thinking that we *very often* mean by "could" merely "would, *if* so and so had chosen." And if so, when we have a sense of the word "could" in which the fact that we often *could* have done what we did not do, is perfectly compatible with the principle that everything has a cause: for to say that, *if* I had performed a certain act of will, I should have done something which I did not do, in no way contradicts this principle.

And an additional reason for supposing that this *is* what we often mean by "could," and one which is also a reason why it is important to insist on the obvious fact that we very often really *should* have acted differently, *if* we had willed differently, is that those who deny that we ever *could* have done anything, which we did not do, often speak and think as if this really did involve the conclusion that we never should have acted differently, even *if* we had willed differently. This occurs, I think, in two chief instances—one in reference to the future, the other in reference to the past. The first occurs when, because they hold that nothing *can* happen, except what *will* happen, people are led to adopt the view called Fatalism—the view that *whatever we will,* the result will always be the same; that it is, therefore, *never* any use to make one choice rather than another. And this conclusion will really follow if by "can" we mean "*would* happen, even *if* we were to will it." But it is certainly untrue, and it certainly does not follow from the principle of causality. On the contrary, reasons of exactly the same sort and exactly as strong as those which lead us to suppose that everything has a cause, lead to the conclusion that if we choose one course, the result will *always* be different in *some* respects from what it would have been, if we had chosen another; and we know also that the difference would *sometimes* consist in the fact that *what* we chose would come to pass. It is certainly often true of the future, therefore, that whichever of two actions we *were* to choose, *would* actually be done, although it is quite certain that only one of the two *will* be done.

And the second instance, in which people are apt to speak and think, as if, *because* no man ever *could* have done anything but what he did do, it follows that he would not, even *if* he had chosen, is as follows. Many people seem, in fact, to conclude directly from the first of these two propositions, that we can never be justified in praising or blaming a man for anything that he does, or indeed for making any distinction between what is right or wrong, on the one hand, and what is lucky or unfortunate on the other. They conclude, for instance, that there is never any reason to treat or to regard the voluntary commission of a crime in any different way from that in which we treat or regard the involuntary catching of a disease. The man who committed the crime *could* not, they say, have helped committing it any more than the other man could have helped catching the disease; both events were equally inevitable; and though both may of course be great *misfortunes,* though both may have very bad consequences and equally bad ones—there is no justification whatever, they say, for the distinction we make between them when we say that the commission of the crime was *wrong,* or that the man was morally to blame for it, whereas the catching of the disease was *not* wrong and the man was not to blame for it. And this conclusion, again, will really follow if by "*could* not" we mean "*would* not, even if he had willed to avoid it." But the point I want to make is, that it follows *only* if we make this assumption. That is to say, the mere fact that the man *would* have succeeded in avoiding the crime, *if* he had chosen (which is certainly often true), whereas the other man would *not* have succeeded in avoiding the disease, *even* if he had chosen (which is certainly also often true) gives an ample justification for regarding and treating the two cases differently. It gives such a justification, because, where the occurrence of an event *did* depend upon the will, there, by acting on the will (as we may do by blame or punishment) we have often a reasonable chance of preventing similar events from recurring in the future; whereas, where it did *not* depend upon the will, we have no such chance. We may, therefore, fairly say that those who speak and think, as if a man who brings about a misfortune *voluntarily* ought to be treated and regarded in exactly the same way as one who brings about an equally great misfortune *involuntarily,* are speaking and thinking *as if* it were not true that we ever should have acted differently, even *if* we had willed to do so. And that is why it is extremely important to insist on the absolute certainty of the fact that we often really *should* have acted differently, *if* we had willed differently.

There is, therefore, much reason to think that when we say we *could* have done a thing which we did not do, we *often* mean merely that we *should* have done it, *if* we had chosen. And if so, then it is quite certain that, in *this* sense, we often really *could* have done what we did not do, and that this fact is in no way inconsistent with the principle that everything has a cause. And for my part I must confess that I cannot feel certain that this may not be *all* that we usually mean and understand by the assertion that we have Free Will; so that those who deny that we have it are really denying (though, no doubt, often unconsciously) that we ever *should* have acted differently, even if we had willed differently. It has been sometimes held that this *is* what we mean; and I cannot find any conclusive argument to the contrary. And if it is what we mean, then it absolutely follows that we really *have* Free Will, and also that this fact is quite consistent with the principle that everything has a cause; and it follows also that our theory will be perfectly right, when it makes right and wrong depend on what we *could* have done, *if* we had chosen.

But, no doubt, there are many people who will say that this is *not* sufficient to entitle us to say that we have Free Will; and they will say this for a reason, which certainly has some plausibility, though I cannot satisfy myself that it is conclusive. They will say, namely: Granted that we often *should* have acted differently, *if* we had chosen differently, yet it is not true that we have Free Will, unless it is *also* often true in such cases that we *could* have *chosen* differently. The question of Free Will has been thus represented as being merely the question whether we ever *could* have chosen, what we did not choose, or ever *can* choose, what, in fact, we shall not choose. And since there is some plausibility in this contention, it is, I think, worth while to point out that here again it is absolutely certain that, in two different senses, at least, we often *could* have chosen, what, in fact, we did not choose; and that in

neither sense does this fact contradict the principle of causality.

The first is simply the old sense over again. If by saying that we *could* have done, what we did not do, we often mean merely that we *should* have done it, *if* we had chosen to do it, then obviously, by saying that we *could* have *chosen* to do it, we may mean merely that we *should* have so chosen, *if* we had chosen *to make the choice.* And I think there is no doubt it is often true that we should have chosen to do a particular thing *if* we had chosen to make the choice; and that this is a very important sense in which it is often in our power to make a choice. There certainly is such a thing as making an effort to induce ourselves to *choose* a particular course; and I think there is no doubt that often if we *had* made such an effort, we *should* have made a choice, which we did not in fact make.

And besides this, there is another sense in which, whenever we have several different courses of action in view, it is *possible* for us to choose any one of them; and a sense which is certainly of some practical importance, even if it goes no way to justify us in saying that we have Free Will. This sense arises from the fact that in such cases we can hardly ever *know for certain* beforehand, *which* choice we actually *shall* make; and one of the commonest senses of the word "possible" is that in which we call an event "possible" when no man can *know for certain* that it will *not* happen. It follows that almost, if not quite always, when we make a choice, after considering alternatives, it *was* possible that we should have chosen one of these alternatives, which we did not actually choose; and often, of course, it was not only possible, but highly probable, that we should have done so. And this fact is certainly of practical importance, because many people are apt much too easily to assume that it is quite certain that they *will not* make a given choice, which they know they ought to make, if it were possible; and their belief that they *will* not make it tends, of course, to prevent them from making it. For this reason it is important to insist that they can hardly ever know for certain with regard to any given choice that they will *not* make it.

It is, therefore, quite certain (1) that we often *should* have *acted* differently, if we had chosen to; (2) that similarly we often should have *chosen* differently, *if* we had chosen so to choose; and (3) that it was almost always *possible* that we should have chosen differently, in the sense that no man could know for certain that we should *not* so choose. All these three things are facts, and all of them are quite consistent with the principle of causality. Can anybody undertake to say for certain that none of these three facts and *no* combination of them will justify us in saying that we have Free Will? Or, suppose it granted that we have not Free Will, unless it is often true that we *could* have chosen, what we did not choose:—Can any defender of Free Will, or any opponent of it, show conclusively that what he means by "*could* have chosen" in this proposition, is anything different from the two certain facts, which I have numbered (2) and (3), or some combination of the two? Many people, no doubt, will still insist that these two facts alone are by no means sufficient to entitle us to say that we have Free Will: that it must be true we were *able* to choose, in some quite other sense. But nobody, so far as I know, has ever been able to tell us exactly what that sense is. For my part, I can find no conclusive argument to show either that some such other sense of "can" is necessary, or that it is not. And, therefore, this chapter must conclude with a doubt. It is, I think, possible that, instead of saying, as our theory said, that an action is only right, when it produces consequences as good as any which would have followed from any other action which the agent *would* have done, *if* he had chosen, we should say instead that it is right whenever and only when the agent *could not have done* anything which would have produced better consequences: and that this "*could not* have done" is *not* equivalent to "would not have done, *if* he had chosen," but is to be understood in the sense, whatever it may be, which is sufficient to entitle us to say that we have Free Will. If so, then our theory would be wrong, just to this extent.

Further Questions

1. "If everything is caused, then all of your choices and actions are caused by conditions over which (ultimately) you have no control. Hence, even though there may be a sense in which you acted freely, it is such a thin sense of free, that it cannot be a matter of much importance whether people are ever free in that sense." How, if at all, does Moore respond to this argument? How would you respond?
2. Is the question whether people have free will just a trivial, verbal question, or is there an important substantive issue at stake? Give the best argument you can for both answers. Then explain which, if either, best represents your own view, and why.

Further Readings

Dennett, Daniel, *Elbow Room*. Cambridge, MA: MIT Press, 1984. A computer-science oriented argument for a position much like Moore's.

Urmson, J. O. *Philosophical Analysis, Its Development Between the Two World Wars*. Oxford: Clarendon Press, 1956. A concise and readable history of analytic philosophy.

Freedom and Determinism   24

RICHARD TAYLOR

Richard Taylor served on a submarine during World War II, where he became so interested in the melancholy philosophy of Schopenhauer that he subsequently became a
philosopher himself, eventually teaching at Brown University, Ohio State University, and
the University of Rochester, from which he retired. A prolific and engaging writer, Taylor
has written books on the philosophy of mind, metaphysics, and ethics. He is also a
renowned beekeeper and has written extensively on beekeeping. Among his many books:
Action and Purpose (1966), *Ethics, Faith, and Reason* (1985), *The New Comb Honey Book*
(1982), *The Joys of Beekeeping* (1984), and *Having Love Affairs* (1982).

In this selection, from his *Metaphysics* (4th ed., 1992), Taylor argues, first, that all of
the standard views on free will are inadequate and, second, that only the view that people
are self-determining beings, hence sometimes the causes of their own behavior, is compatible with two assumptions each of us makes: that our behavior is sometimes the outcome
of our own deliberation; and that it is sometimes up to us what we do.

Reading Questions

1. What is "soft determinism"? Of the philosophers whose views on free will you know,
   which, if any, are soft determinists? Why does Taylor think that soft determinism should
   be rejected?
2. What is "simple indeterminism"? Of the philosophers whose views on free will you know,
   which, if any, are simple indeterminists? Why does Taylor think that simple indeterminism
   should be rejected?
3. What is "the theory of agency"? Why does Taylor think that only this theory can account
   for the commonly made assumptions that our behavior is sometimes the outcome of our
   own deliberations and that it is sometimes up to us what we do? Do you agree?
4. What difficulties does Taylor think there are for the theory of agency? What, in your
   opinion, is the importance of these difficulties?

DETERMINISM

IN THE CASE OF EVERYTHING THAT EXISTS, there
are antecedent conditions, known or unknown,
which, because they are given, mean that things
could not be other than they are. That is an exact
statement of the metaphysical thesis of determinism. More loosely, it says that everything, including every cause, is the effect of some cause or
causes; or that everything is not only determinate
but causally determined. The statement, moreover,
makes no allowance for time, for past, or for future. Hence, if true, it holds not only for all things

that have existed but for all things that do or ever
will exist.

Of course people rarely think of such a principle,
and hardly one in a thousand will ever formulate it
to himself in words. Yet all do seem to assume it in
their daily affairs, so much so that some philosophers have declared it an *a priori* principle of the
understanding, that is, something that is known
independently of experience, while others have
deemed it to be at least a part of the common
sense of mankind. Thus, when I hear a noise I look
up to see where it came from. I never suppose that
it was just a noise that came from nowhere and had

no cause. Everyone does the same—even animals, though they have never once thought about metaphysics or the principle of universal determinism. People believe, or at least act as though they believed, that things have causes, without exception. When a child or animal touches a hot stove for the first time, it unhesitatingly believes that the pain then felt was caused by that stove, and so firm and immediate is that belief that hot stoves are avoided ever after.

We all use our metaphysical principles, whether we think of them or not, or are even capable of thinking of them. If I have a bodily or other disorder—a rash, for instance, or a fever or a phobia—I consult a physician for a diagnosis and explanation in the hope that the cause of it might be found and removed or moderated. I am never tempted to suppose that such things just have no causes, arising from nowhere, else I would take no steps to remove the causes. The principle of determinism is here, as in everything else, simply assumed, without being thought about.

DETERMINISM AND HUMAN BEHAVIOR

I am a part of the world. So is each of the cells and minute parts of which I am composed. The principle of determinism, then, in case it is true, applies to me and to each of those minute parts, no less than to the sand, wheat, winds, and waters of which we have spoken. There is no particular difficulty in thinking so, as long as I consider only what are sometimes called the "purely physiological" changes of my body, like growth, the pulse, glandular secretions, and the like. But what of my thoughts and ideas? And what of my behavior that is supposed to be deliberate, purposeful, and perhaps morally significant? These are all changes of my own being, changes that I undergo, and if these are all but the consequences of the conditions under which they occur, and these conditions are the only ones that could have obtained, given the state of the world just before and when they arose, what now becomes of my responsibility for my behavior and of the control over my conduct

that I fancy myself to possess? What am I but a helpless product of nature, destined by her to do whatever I do and to become whatever I become?

There is no moral blame nor merit in anyone who cannot help what he does. It matters not whether the explanation for his behavior is found within him or without, whether it is expressed in terms of ordinary physical causes or allegedly "mental" ones, or whether the causes be proximate or remote. I am not responsible for being a man rather than a woman, nor for having the temperament and desires characteristic of that sex. I was never asked whether these should be given to me. The kleptomaniac, similarly, steals from compulsion, the alcoholic drinks from compulsion, and sometimes even the hero dies from compulsive courage. Though these causes are within them, they compel no less for that, and their victims never chose to have them inflicted upon themselves. To say they are compulsions is to say only that they compel. But to say that they compel is only to say that they cause; for the cause of a thing being given, the effect cannot fail to follow. By the thesis of determinism, however, everything whatever is caused, and not one single thing could ever be other than exactly what it is. Perhaps one thinks that the kleptomaniac and the drunkard did not have to become what they are, that they could have done better at another time and thereby ended up better than they are now, or that the hero could have done worse and then ended up a coward. But this shows only an unwillingness to understand what made them become as they are. Having found that their behavior is caused from within them, we can hardly avoid asking what caused these inner springs of action, and then asking what were the causes of these causes, and so on through the infinite past. We shall not, certainly, with our small understanding and our fragmentary knowledge of the past ever know why the world should at just this time and place have produced just this thief, this drunkard, and this hero, but the vagueness and smattered nature of our knowledge should not tempt us to imagine a similar vagueness in nature herself. Everything in nature is and always has been determinate, with no loose edges at all, and she was forever destined to bring forth just

Richard Taylor, Metaphysics, *4e, © 1992, pp. 36–39, 43–53. Reprinted by permission. Prentice-Hall, Englewood Cliffs, NJ.*

what she has produced, however slight may be our understanding of the origins of these works. Ultimate responsibility for anything that exists, and hence for any person and his deeds, can thus rest only with the first cause of all things, if there is such a cause, or nowhere at all, in case there is not. Such, at least, seems to be the unavoidable implication of determinism.

DETERMINISM AND MORALS

Some philosophers, faced with all this, which seems quite clear to the ordinary understanding, have tried to cling to determinism while modifying traditional conceptions of morals. They continue to *use* such words as *merit, blame, praise,* and *desert,* but they so divest them of their meanings as to finish by talking about things entirely different, sometimes without themselves realizing that they are no longer on the subject. An ordinary person will hardly understand that anyone can possess merit or vice and be deserving of moral praise or blame, as a result of traits that he has or of behavior arising from those traits, once it is well understood that he could never have avoided being just what he is and doing just what he does. . . .

Now I could, of course, simply affirm that I am a morally responsible being, in the sense in which my responsibility for my behavior implies that I could have avoided that behavior. But this would take us into the nebulous realm of ethics, and it is, in fact, far from obvious that I am responsible in that sense. Many have doubted that they are responsible in that sense, and it is in any case not difficult to doubt it, however strongly one might feel about it.

There are, however, two things about myself of which I feel quite certain and that have no necessary connection with morals. The first is that I sometimes deliberate, with the view to making a decision; a decision, namely, to do this thing or that. And the second is that whether or not I deliberate about what to do, it is sometimes up to me what I do. This might all be an illusion, of course; but so also might any philosophical theory, such as the theory of determinism, be false. The point remains that it is far more difficult for me to doubt that I sometimes deliberate, and that it is sometimes up to me what to do, than to doubt any

philosophical theory whatever, including the theory of determinism. We must, accordingly, if we ever hope to be wiser, adjust our theories to our data and not try to adjust our data to our theories. . . .

FREEDOM

To say that it is, in a given instance, up to me what I do is to say that I am in that instance *free* with respect to what I then do. Thus, I am sometimes free to move my finger this way and that, but not, certainly, to bend it backward or into a knot. But what does this mean?

It means, first that there is no *obstacle or impediment* to my activity. Thus, there is sometimes no obstacle to my moving my finger this way and that, though there are obvious obstacles to my moving it backward or into a knot. Those things, accordingly, that pose obstacles to my motions limit my freedom. If my hand were strapped in such a way as to permit only a left motion of my finger, I would not then be free to move it to the right. If it were encased in a tight case that permitted no motion, I would not be free to move it at all. Freedom of motion, then, is limited by obstacles.

Further, to say that it is, in a given instance, up to me what I do, means that nothing *constrains* or *forces* me to do one thing rather than another. Constraints are like obstacles, except that while the latter prevent, the former enforce. Thus, if my finger is being forcibly bent to the left—by a machine, for instance, or by another person, or by any force that I cannot overcome—then I am not free to move it this way and that. I cannot, in fact, move it at all; I can only watch to see how it is moved, and perhaps vainly resist: Its motions are not up to me, or within my control, but in the control of some other thing or person.

Obstacles and constraints, then, both obviously limit my freedom. To say that I am free to perform some action thus means at least that there is no obstacle to my doing it, and that nothing constrains me to do otherwise.

Now if we rest content with this observation, as many have, and construe free activity simply as activity that is unimpeded and unconstrained, there is evidently no inconsistency between affirming both the thesis of determinism and the claim that I am sometimes free. For to say that some action of mine

DEFENSE OF LEOPOLD AND LOEB

Clarence Darrow

I know that one of two things happened to Richard Loeb: that this terrible crime was inherent in his organism, and came from some ancestor; or that it came through his education and his training after he was born. Do I need to prove it? Judge Crowe said at one point in this case, when some witness spoke about their wealth, that "probably that was responsible."

To believe that any boy is responsible for himself or his early training is an absurdity that no lawyer or judge should be guilty of today. Somewhere this came to the boy. If his failing came from his heredity, I do not know where or how. None of us are bred perfect and pure; and the color of our hair, the color of our eyes, our stature, the weight and fineness of our brain, and everything about us could, with full knowledge, be traced with absolute certainty to somewhere. If we had the pedigree it could be traced just the same in a boy as it could in a dog, a horse or a cow.

I do not know what remote ancestors may have sent down the seed that corrupted him, and I do not know through how many ancestors it may have passed until it reached Dickie Loeb.

All I know is that it is true, and there is not a biologist in the world who will not say that I am right.

If it did not come that way, then I know that if he was normal, if he had been understood, if he had been trained as he should have been it would not have happened. Not that anybody may not slip, but I know it and Your Honor knows it, and every schoolhouse and every church in the land is an evidence of it. Else why build them?

Every effort to protect society is an effort toward training the youth to keep the path. Every bit of training in the world proves it, and it likewise proves that it sometimes fails. I know that if this boy had been understood and properly trained—properly for him—and the training that he got might have been the very best for someone; but if it had been the proper training for him he would not be in this courtroom today with the noose above his head. If there is responsibility anywhere, it is back of him; somewhere in the infinite number of his ancestors, or in his surroundings, or in both. And I submit, Your Honor, that under every principle of natural justice, under every principle of conscience, of right, and of law, he should not be made responsible for the acts of someone else.

From *Attorney for the Damned*, edited by Arthur Weinburg (1957).

is neither impeded nor constrained does not by itself imply that it is not causally determined. The absence of obstacles and constraints is a mere negative condition, and does not by itself rule out the presence of positive causes. It might seem, then, that we can say of some of my actions that there are conditions antecedent to their performance so that no other actions were possible, and also that these actions were unobstructed and unconstrained. And to say that would logically entail that such actions were both causally determined, and free.

SOFT DETERMINISM

It is this kind of consideration that has led many philosophers to embrace what is sometimes called "soft determinism." All versions of this theory have in common three claims, by means of which, it is naïvely supposed, a reconciliation is achieved between determinism and freedom. Freedom being, furthermore, a condition of moral responsibility and the only condition that metaphysics seriously questions, it is supposed by the partisans of this view that determinism is perfectly compatible with such responsibility. This, no doubt, accounts for its great appeal and wide acceptance, even by some people of considerable learning.

The three claims of soft determinism are (1) that the thesis of determinism is true, and that accordingly all human behavior, voluntary or other, like the behavior of all other things, arises from antecedent conditions, given which no other behavior is possible—in short, that all human behavior is caused and determined; (2) that voluntary behavior is nonetheless free to the extent that it is not externally constrained or impeded; and (3) that, in the absence of such obstacles and constraints, the causes of voluntary behavior are certain states, events, or conditions within the agent himself; namely, his own acts of will or volitions, choices, decisions, desires, and so on.

Thus, on this view, I am free, and therefore sometimes responsible for what I do, provided nothing prevents me from acting according to my own choice, desire, or volition, or constrains me to act otherwise. There may, to be sure, be other conditions for my responsibility—such as, for example, an understanding of the probable consequences of my behavior, and that sort of thing—but absence of constraint or impediment is, at least, one such condition. And, it is claimed, it is a condition that is compatible with the supposition that my behavior is caused—for it is, by hypothesis, caused by my own inner choices, desires, and volitions.

THE REFUTATION OF THIS

The theory of soft determinism looks good at first—so good that it has for generations been solemnly taught from innumerable philosophical chairs and implanted in the minds of students as sound philosophy—but no great acumen is needed to discover that far from solving any problem, it only camouflages it.

My free actions are those unimpeded and unconstrained motions that arise from my own inner decisions, choices, and volitions; let us grant this provisionally. But now, whence arise those inner states that determine what my body shall do? Are they within my control or not? Having made my choice or decision and acted upon it, could I have chosen otherwise or not?

Here the determinist, hoping to surrender nothing and yet to avoid the problem implied in that question, bids us not to ask it; the question itself, he announces, is without meaning. For to say that I could have done otherwise, he says, means only that I *would* have done otherwise, *if* those inner states that determined my action had been different; if, that is, I had decided or chosen differently. To ask, accordingly, whether I could have chosen or decided differently is only to ask whether, had I decided to decide differently or chosen to choose differently, or willed to will differently, I *would* have decided or chosen or willed differently. And this, of course, *is* unintelligible nonsense.

But it is not nonsense to ask whether the causes of my actions—my own inner choices, decisions, and desires—are themselves caused. And of course they are, if determinism is true, for on that thesis everything is caused and determined. And if they are, then we cannot avoid concluding that, given the causal conditions of those inner states, I could not have decided, willed, chosen, or desired other than I, in fact, did, for this is a logical consequence of the very definition of determinism. Of course we can still say that, *if* the causes of those inner states, whatever they were, had been different, then their effects, those inner states themselves, would have been different, and that in this hypothetical sense I could have decided, chosen, willed, or desired differently—but that only pushes our problem back still another step. For we will then want to know whether the causes of those inner states were within my control, and so on *ad infinitum*. We are, at each step, permitted to say "could have been otherwise" only in a provisional sense—provided, that is, that something else had been different—but must then retract it and replace it with "could not have been otherwise" as soon as we discover, as we must at each step, that whatever would have to have been different could not have been different.

EXAMPLES

Such is the dialectic of the problem. The easiest way to see the shadowy quality of soft determinism, however, is by means of examples.

Let us suppose that my body is moving in various ways, that these motions are not externally constrained or impeded, and that they are all exactly in accordance with my own desires, choices, or acts of will and whatnot. When I will that my arm should move in a certain way, I find it moving in that way, unobstructed and unconstrained. When I will to speak, my lips and tongue move, unobstructed and unconstrained, in a manner suitable to the formation of the words I choose to utter. Now, given that this is a correct description of my behavior, namely, that it consists of the unconstrained and unimpeded motions of my body in response to my own volitions, then it follows that my behavior is free, on the soft determinist's definition of "free." It follows further that I am responsible for that behavior; or at least, that if I am not, it is not from any lack of freedom on my part.

But if the fulfillment of these conditions renders my behavior free — that is to say, if my behavior satisfies the conditions of free action set forth in the theory of soft determinism — then my behavior will be no less free if we assume further conditions that are perfectly consistent with those already satisfied.

We suppose further, accordingly, that while my behavior is entirely in accordance with my own volitions, and thus "free" in terms of the conception of freedom we are examining, my volitions themselves are caused. To make this graphic, we can suppose that an ingenious physiologist can induce in me any volition he pleases, simply by pushing various buttons on an instrument to which, let us suppose, I am attached by numerous wires. All the volitions I have in that situation are, accordingly, precisely the ones he gives me. By pushing one button, he evokes in me the volition to raise my hand; and my hand, being unimpeded, rises in response to that volition. By pushing another, he induces the volition in me to kick, and my foot, being unimpeded, kicks in response to that volition. We can even suppose that the physiologist puts a rifle in my hands, aims it at some passerby, and then, by pushing the proper button, evokes in me the volition to squeeze my finger against the trigger, whereupon the passerby falls dead of a bullet wound.

This is the description of a man who is acting in accordance with his inner volitions, a man whose body is unimpeded and unconstrained in its motions, these motions being the effects of those inner states. It is hardly the description of a free and responsible agent. It is the perfect description of a puppet. To render someone your puppet, it is not necessary forcibly to constrain the motions of his limbs, after the fashion that real puppets are moved. A subtler but no less effective means of making a person your puppet would be to gain complete control of his inner states, and ensuring, as the theory of soft determinism does ensure, that his body will move in accordance with them.

The example is somewhat unusual, but it is no worse for that. It is perfectly intelligible, and it does appear to refute the soft determinist's conception of freedom. One might think that, in such a case, the agent should not have allowed himself to be so rigged in the first place, but this is irrelevant; we can suppose that he was not aware that he was and was hence unaware of the source of those inner states that prompted his bodily motions. The example can, moreover, be modified in perfectly realistic ways, so as to coincide with actual and familiar cases. One can, for instance, be given a compulsive desire for certain drugs, simply by having them administered over a course of time. Suppose, then, that I do, with neither my knowledge nor consent, thus become a victim of such a desire and act upon it. Do I act freely, merely by virtue of the fact that I am unimpeded in my quest for drugs? In a sense I do, surely, but I am hardly free with respect to whether or not I shall use drugs. I never chose to have the desire for them inflicted upon me.

Nor does it, of course, matter whether the inner states that allegedly prompt all my "free" activity are evoked in me by another agent or by perfectly impersonal forces. Whether a desire that causes my body to behave in a certain way is inflicted upon me by another person, for instance, or derived from hereditary factors, or indeed from anything at all, matters not the least. In any case, if it is in fact the cause of my bodily behavior, I cannot help but act in accordance with it. Wherever it came from, whether from personal or impersonal origins, it was entirely caused or determined, and not within my control. Indeed, if determinism is true, as the theory of soft determinism holds it to be, all those inner states that cause my body to behave in whatever ways it behaves must arise from circumstances that existed before I was born; for the chain of causes and effects is infinite, and none could have been the least different, given those that preceded.

SIMPLE INDETERMINISM

We might at first now seem warranted in simply denying determinism, and saying that, insofar as they are free, my actions are not caused; or that, if they are caused by my own inner states—my own desires, impulses, choices, volitions, and whatnot—then these, in any case, are not caused. This is a perfectly clear sense in which a person's action, assuming that it was free, could have been otherwise. If it was uncaused, then, even given the conditions under which it occurred and all that preceded, some other act was nonetheless possible, and he did not have to do what he did. Or if his action was the inevitable consequence of his own inner states, and could not have been otherwise, given these, we can nevertheless say that these inner states, being uncaused, could have been otherwise, and could thereby have produced different actions.

Only the slightest consideration will show, however, that this simple denial of determinism has not the slightest plausibility. For let us suppose it is true, and that some of my bodily motions—namely, those that I regard as my free acts—are not caused at all or, if caused by my own inner states, that these are not caused. We shall thereby avoid picturing a puppet, to be sure—but only by substituting something even less like a human being; for the conception that now emerges is not that of a free person, but of an erratic and jerking phantom, without any rhyme or reason at all.

Suppose that my right arm is free, according to this conception; that is, that its motions are uncaused. It moves this way and that from time to time, but nothing causes these motions. Sometimes it moves forth vigorously, sometimes up, sometimes down, sometimes it just drifts vaguely about—these motions all being wholly free and uncaused. Manifestly I have nothing to do with them at all; they just happen, and neither I nor anyone can ever tell what this arm will be doing next. It might seize a club and lay it on the head of the nearest bystander, no less to my astonishment than his. There will never be any point in asking why these motions occur, or in seeking any explanation of them, for under the conditions assumed there is no explanation. They just happen, from no causes at all.

This is no description of free, voluntary, or responsible behavior. Indeed, so far as the motions of my body or its parts are entirely uncaused, such motions cannot even be ascribed to me as my behavior in the first place, since I have nothing to do with them. The behavior of my arm is just the random motion of a foreign object. Behavior that is mine must be behavior that is within my control, but motions that occur from no causes are beyond the control of anyone. I can have no more to do with, and no more control over, the uncaused motions of my limbs than a gambler has over the motions of an honest roulette wheel. I can only, like him, idly wait to see what happens.

Nor does it improve things to suppose that my bodily motions are caused by my own inner states, so long as we suppose these to be wholly uncaused. The result will be the same as before. My arm, for example, will move this way and that, sometimes up and sometimes down, sometimes vigorously and sometimes just drifting about, always in response to certain inner states, to be sure. But since these are supposed to be wholly uncaused, it follows that I have no control over them and hence none over their effects. If my hand lays a club forcefully on the nearest bystander, we can indeed say that this motion resulted from an inner club-wielding desire of mine; but we must add that I had nothing to do with that desire, and that it arose, to be followed by its inevitable effect, no less to my astonishment than to his. Things like this do, alas, sometimes happen. We are all sometimes seized by compulsive impulses that arise we know not whence, and we do sometimes act upon these. But because they are far from being examples of free, voluntary, and responsible behavior, we need only to learn that the behavior was of this sort to conclude that it was not free, voluntary, or responsible. It was erratic, impulsive, and irresponsible.

DETERMINISM AND SIMPLE INDETERMINISM AS THEORIES

Both determinism and simple indeterminism are loaded with difficulties, and no one who has thought much on them can affirm either of them without some embarrassment. Simple indeterminism has nothing whatever to be said for it, except that it appears to remove the grossest difficulties of determinism, only, however, to imply perfect absurdities of its own. Determinism, on the other hand, is at least initially plausible. People seem to have a natural inclination to believe in it; it is, indeed, almost required for the very exercise of practical intelligence. And beyond this, our experience appears always to confirm it, so long as we are dealing with everyday facts of common experience, as distinguished from the esoteric researches of theoretical physics. But determinism, as applied to human behavior, has implications that few can casually accept, and they appear to be implications that no modification of the theory can efface.

Both theories, moreover, appear logically irreconcilable to the two items of data that we set forth at the outset; namely, (1) that my behavior is sometimes the outcome of my deliberation, and (2) that in these and other cases it is sometimes up to me what I do. Because these were our data, it is important to see, as must already be quite clear, that these theories cannot be reconciled to them.

I can deliberate only about my own future actions and then only if I do not already know what I am going to do. If a certain nasal tickle warns me that I am about to sneeze, for instance, then I cannot deliberate whether to sneeze or not; I can only prepare for the impending convulsion. But if determinism is true, then there are always conditions existing antecedently to everything I do, sufficient for my doing just that, and such as to render it inevitable. If I can know what those conditions are and what behavior they are sufficient to produce, then I can in every case know what I am going to do and cannot then deliberate about it.

By itself this only shows, of course, that I can deliberate only in ignorance of the causal conditions of my behavior; it does not show that such conditions cannot exist. It is odd, however, to suppose that deliberation should be a mere substitute for clear knowledge. Ignorance is a condition of speculation, inference, and guesswork, which have nothing whatever to do with deliberation. A prisoner awaiting execution may not know when he is going to die, and he may even entertain the hope of reprieve, but he cannot deliberate about this. He can only speculate, guess—and wait.

Worse yet, however, it now becomes clear that I cannot deliberate about what I am going to do, if it is even *possible* for me to find out in advance, whether I do in fact find out in advance or not. I can deliberate only with the view to deciding what to do, to making up my mind; and this is impossible if I believe that it could be inferred what I am going to do from conditions already existing, even though I have not made that inference myself. If I believe that what I am going to do has been rendered inevitable by conditions already existing, and could be inferred by anyone having the requisite sagacity, then I cannot try to decide whether to do it or not, for there is simply nothing left to decide. I can at best only guess or try to figure it out myself or, all prognostics failing, I can wait and see; but I cannot deliberate. I deliberate in order to *decide* what *to* do, not to *discover* what it is that I am *going* to do. But if determinism is true, then there are always antecedent conditions sufficient for everything that I do, and this can always be inferred by anyone having the requisite sagacity; that is, by anyone having a knowledge of what those conditions are and what behavior they are sufficient to produce.

This suggests what in fact seems quite clear, that determinism cannot be reconciled with our second datum either, to the effect that it is sometimes up to me what I am going to do. For if it is ever really up to me whether to do this thing or that, then, as we have seen, each alternative course of action must be such that I can do it; not that I can do it in some abstruse or hypothetical sense of "can"; not that I could do it if only something were true that is not true; but in the sense that it is then and there within my power to do it. But this is never so, if determinism is true, for on the very formulation of that theory whatever happens at any time is the only thing that can then happen, given all that precedes it. It is simply a logical consequence of this that whatever I do at any time is the only thing I can then do, given the conditions that precede my doing it. Nor does it help in the least to interpose, among the causal antecedents of my behavior, my own inner states, such as my desires, choices, acts of will, and so on. For even supposing these to be always involved in voluntary behavior—which is highly doubtful in itself—it is a consequence of determinism that these, whatever they are at any time, can never be other than what they then are. Every chain of causes and effects, if determinism is true, is infinite. This is why it is not now up to me whether I shall a moment hence be male or female. The conditions determining my sex have existed through my whole life, and even prior to my life. But if determinism is true, the same holds of anything that I ever am, ever become, or ever do. It matters not whether we are speaking of the most patent facts of my being, such as my sex; or the most subtle, such as my feelings, thoughts, desires, or choices. Nothing could be other than it is, given what was; and while we may indeed say, quite idly, that something — some inner state of mind, for instance — *could* have been different, had only something *else* been different, any consolation of this thought evaporates as soon as we add that whatever would have to have been different could not have been different.

It is even more obvious that our data cannot be reconciled to the theory of simple indeterminism. I can deliberate only about my own actions; this is obvious. But the random, uncaused motion of any body whatever, whether it be a part of my body or not, is no action of mine and nothing that is within my power. I might try to guess what these motions will be, just as I might try to guess how a roulette wheel will behave, but I cannot deliberate about them or try to decide what they shall be, simply because these things are not up to me. Whatever is not caused by anything is not caused by me, and nothing could be more plainly inconsistent with saying that it is nevertheless up to me what it shall be.

THE THEORY OF AGENCY

The only conception of action that accords with our data is one according to which people — and perhaps some other things too — are sometimes, but of course, not always, self-determining beings; that is, beings that are sometimes the causes of their own behavior. In the case of an action that is free, it must not only be such that it is caused by the agent who performs it, but also such that no antecedent conditions were sufficient for his performing just that action. In the case of an action that is both free and rational, it must be such that the agent who

performed it did so for some reason, but this reason cannot have been the cause of it.

Now, this conception fits what people take themselves to be; namely, beings who act, or who are agents, rather than beings that are merely acted upon, and whose behavior is simply the causal consequence of conditions that they have not wrought. When I believe that I have done something, I do believe that it was I who caused it to be done, I who made something happen, and not merely something within me, such as one of my own subjective states, which is not identical with myself. If I believe that something not identical with myself was the cause of my behavior — some event wholly external to myself, for instance, or even one internal to myself, such as a nerve impulse, volition, or whatnot — then I cannot regard that behavior as being an act of mine, unless I further believe that I was the cause of that external or internal event. My pulse, for example, is caused and regulated by certain conditions existing within me, and not by myself. I do not, accordingly, regard this activity of my body as my action, and would be no more tempted to do so if I became suddenly conscious within myself of those conditions or impulses that produce it. This is behavior with which I have nothing to do, behavior that is not within my immediate control, behavior that is not only not free activity, but not even the activity of an agent to begin with; it is nothing but a mechanical reflex. Had I never learned that my very life depends on this pulse beat, I would regard it with complete indifference, as something foreign to me, like the oscillations of a clock pendulum that I idly contemplate.

Now this conception of activity, and of an agent who is the cause of it, involves two rather strange metaphysical notions that are never applied elsewhere in nature. The first is that of a *self* or *person* — for example, a man — who is not merely a collection of things or events, but a self-moving being. For on this view it is a person, and not merely some part of him or something within him, that is the cause of his own activity. Now, we certainly do not know that a human being is anything more than an assemblage of physical things and processes that act in accordance with those laws that describe the behavior of all other physical things and processes. Even though he is a living being, of enormous complexity, there is nothing, apart from the requirements of this theory, to suggest that his behavior is so radically different in its origin from that of other physical objects, or that an understanding of it must be sought in some metaphysical realm wholly different from that appropriate to the understanding of nonliving things.

Second, this conception of activity involves an extraordinary conception of causation according to which an agent, which is a substance and not an event, can nevertheless be the cause of an event. Indeed, if he is a free agent then he can, on this conception, cause an event to occur—namely, some act of his own—without anything else causing him to do so. This means that an agent is sometimes a cause, without being an antecedent sufficient condition; for if I affirm that I am the cause of some act of mine, then I am plainly not saying that my very existence is sufficient for its occurrence, which would be absurd. If I say that my hand causes my pencil to move, then I am saying that the motion of my hand is, under the other conditions then prevailing, sufficient for the motion of the pencil. But if I then say that I cause my hand to move, I am not saying anything remotely like this, and surely not that the motion of my self is sufficient for the motion of my arm and hand, since these are the only things about me that are moving.

This conception of the causation of events by things that are not events is, in fact, so different from the usual philosophical conception of a cause that it should not even bear the same name, for "being a cause" ordinarily just means "being an antecedent sufficient condition or set of conditions." Instead, then, of speaking of agents as *causing* their own acts, it would perhaps be better to use another word entirely, and say, for instance, that they *originate* them, *initiate* them, or simply that they *perform* them.

Now this is, on the face of it, a dubious conception of what a person is. Yet it is consistent with our data, reflecting the presuppositions of deliberation, and appears to be the only conception that is consistent with them, as determinism and simple indeterminism are not. The theory of agency avoids the absurdities of simple indeterminism by conceding that human behavior is caused, while at the same time avoiding the difficulties of determinism by denying that every chain of causes and effects is infinite. Some such causal chains, on this view, have beginnings, and they begin with agents themselves. Moreover, if we are to suppose that it is sometimes up to me what I do, and understand this in a sense that is not consistent with determinism, we must suppose that I am an agent or a being who initiates his own actions, sometimes under conditions that do not determine what action I shall perform. Deliberation becomes, on this view, something that is not only possible but quite rational, for it does make sense to deliberate about activity that is truly my own and that depends in its outcome upon me as its author, and not merely upon something more or less esoteric that is supposed to be intimately associated with me, such as my thoughts, volitions, choices or whatnot.

One can hardly affirm such a theory of agency with complete comfort, however, and not wholly without embarrassment, for the conception of agents and their powers which is involved in it is strange indeed, if not positively mysterious. In fact, one can hardly be blamed here for simply denying our data outright, rather than embracing this theory to which they do most certainly point. Our data—to the effect that we do sometimes deliberate before acting, and that, when we do, we presuppose among other things that it is up to us what we are going to do—rest upon nothing more than fairly common consent. These data might simply be illusions. It might, in fact, be that no one ever deliberates but only imagines that he does, that from pure conceit he supposes himself to be the master of his behavior and the author of his acts. Spinoza has suggested that if a stone, having been thrown into the air, were suddenly to become conscious, it would suppose itself to be the source of its own motion, being then conscious of what it was doing but not aware of the real cause of its behavior. Certainly we are *sometimes* mistaken in believing that we are behaving as a result of choice deliberately arrived at. A man might, for example, easily imagine that his embarking upon matrimony is the result of the most careful and rational deliberation, when in fact the causes, perfectly sufficient for that behavior, might be of an entirely physiological, unconscious origin. If it is sometimes false that we deliberate and then act as the result of a decision deliberately arrived at, even when we suppose it to be true, it might always be false. No one seems able, as we have noted, to describe deliberation without metaphors, and the conception of a thing's being "within one's power" or "up to him" seems to defy analysis or definition altogether, if taken in a sense that the theory of agency appears to require.

These are, then, dubitable conceptions, despite their being so well implanted in common sense. Indeed, when we turn to the theory of fatalism, we shall find formidable metaphysical considerations that appear to rule them out altogether. Perhaps here, as elsewhere in metaphysics, we should be content with discovering difficulties, with seeing what is and what is not consistent with such convictions as we happen to have, and then drawing such satisfaction as we can from the realization that, no matter where we begin, the world is mysterious and that we who try to understand it are even more so. This realization can, with some justification, make one feel wise, even in the full realization of his ignorance.

Further Questions

1. How might Hume reply to Taylor's criticisms of soft determinism?
2. Do Taylor's criticisms of "simple indeterminism" have any force against the view that James defends? If so, explain how. If not, explain whether they could accept Taylor's theory of agency.
3. Does anyone ever act freely? Explain how you would defend your answer, then how your answer could most plausibly be criticized, and then how you could best respond to the criticisms.

Further Readings

Dennett, Daniel C. *Elbow Room*. Cambridge, MA: MIT Press, 1984. An eloquent and accessible defense by a well-known contemporary philosopher of the idea that free will and determinism are compatible.

Watson, Gary, ed. *Free Will*. Oxford: Oxford University Press, 1982. One of the best free will anthologies.

Existentialism and Human Freedom   25

JEAN-PAUL SARTRE

French philosopher, playwright, and novelist Jean-Paul Sartre was born in Paris in 1905, the son of a naval officer; his mother was the cousin of the famous theologian and jungle doctor, Albert Schweitzer. Orphaned at a young age, Sartre was raised by his grandfather and educated in Paris. During World War II, he joined the French Army, where he behaved like an anarchist and also used the time to work on a novel, typing it in front of his commanding officers. He became a German prisoner of war for eight months, during which time he "sings, writes, puts on plays, acts, composes, lectures, teaches, plays the fool, and, finally, escapes with false papers" (*Sartre: A Life* by Annie Cohen-Solal. Pantheon, 1987, 151).

Although he did not invent existentialism, Sartre is certainly one of its most famous and evocative exponents. Among his famous and enduring works are the novel *Nausea* (1938), the plays *No Exit* (1944), *The Flies* (1946), and *The Condemned of Altona*

(1960), and the massive philosophical work *Being and Nothingness* (1943). In 1964 he refused to accept the Nobel Prize in Literature that was awarded him, calling the prize a political tool of the East-West struggle.

Reading Questions

1. Read the excerpt from *Nausea*. If it were true, as some physicists believe, that the universe—all of existence—arose spontaneously from nothing, how would that make you feel? Would the passage describe your feeling?
2. In the passage from "Existentialism and Humanism," Sartre suggests that people invented God to escape confronting the contingency of things and their own freedom. Do you agree? He also suggests that people hide from their freedom by pretending that they are material objects, and hence have a nature that determines how they must be. Could there be anything to that idea?
3. In "Portrait of the Anti-Semite," Sartre suggests that prejudice—for example, anti-Semitism—rather than being merely something that people are taught, is something they choose. Do you agree?
4. In the selection from *No Exit*, what is Garcin trying to do? Is what he is trying to do self-deceptive?
5. In the selection from *Being and Nothingness*, what does Sartre mean by saying that the homosexual is in "bad faith"? Do you agree?

THIS MOMENT WAS EXTRAORDINARY. I was there, motionless and icy, plunged in a horrible ecstasy. But something fresh had just appeared in the very heart of this ecstasy; I understood the Nausea, I possessed it. To tell the truth, I did not formulate my discoveries to myself. But I think it would be easy for me to put them in words now. The essential thing is contingency. I mean that one cannot define existence as necessity. To exist is simply *to be there,* those who exist let themselves be encountered, but you can never deduce anything from them. I believe there are people who have understood this. Only they tried to overcome this contingency by inventing a necessary, causal being. But no necessary being can explain existence: contingency is not a delusion, a probability which can be dissipated; it is the absolute, consequently, the perfect free gift. All is free, this park, this city and myself. When you realize that, it turns your heart upside down and everything begins to float . . .

From Nausea.

* * *

There are two kinds of existentialists. There are, on the one hand, the Christians, amongst whom I shall name Jaspers and Gabriel Marcel, both professed Catholics; and on the other the existential atheists, amongst whom we must place Heidegger as well as the French existentialists and myself. What they have in common is simply the fact that they believe that existence comes before essence—or, if you will, that we must begin from the subjective. What exactly do we mean by that?

If one considers an article of manufacture—as, for example, a book or a paper-knife—one sees that it has been made by an artisan who had a conception of it; and he has paid attention, equally, to the conception of a paper-knife and to the existent technique of production which is a part of that conception and is, at bottom, a formula. Thus the paper-knife is at the same time an article producible in a certain manner and one which, on the other hand, serves a definite purpose, for one cannot suppose that a man would produce a paper-knife without knowing what it was for. Let us say, then, of the paper-knife that its essence—that is to say the sum of the formulae and the qualities which made its production and its definition possible—precedes its existence. The presence of such and such a paper-knife or book is thus determined before my eyes. Here then we are viewing the world from a technical standpoint, and we can say that production precedes existence.

When we think of God as the creator, we are thinking of him, most of the time, as a supernatural artisan. Whatever doctrine we may be considering, whether it be a doctrine like that of Descartes, or of Leibniz himself, we always imply that the will follows, more or less, from the understanding or at least accompanies it, so that when God creates he knows precisely what he is creating. Thus the conception of man in the mind of God is comparable to that of the paper-knife in the mind of the artisan: God makes man according to a procedure and a conception, exactly as the artisan manufactures a paper-knife, following a definition and a formula. Thus each individual man is the realization of a certain conception which dwells in the divine understanding. In the philosophical atheism of the eighteenth century; the notion of God is suppressed, but not, for all that, the idea that essence is prior to existence; something of that idea we still find everywhere, in Diderot, in Voltaire and even in Kant. Man possesses a human nature; that "human nature," which is the conception of human being, is found in every man; which means that each man is a particular example of an universal conception, the conception of Man.

From "Existentialism and Humanism."

* * *

The anti-Semite has created the Jew from his need. Prejudice is not uninformed opinion. It is an attitude totally and freely chosen. . . . The anti-Semite is a man who is afraid, not of the Jews, of course, but of himself, of his conscience, his instincts, of his responsibilities, of solitude, of change, of society, and the world; of everything except the Jews. He is a coward who does not wish to admit his cowardice to himself. . . . a malcontent who dares not revolt for fear of the consequences of his rebellion. By adhering to his anti-Semitism, he is not only adopting an opinion, he is choosing himself as a person. . . . He is choosing the total irresponsibility of the warrior who obeys his leaders. . . .

From "Portrait of the Anti-Semite."

* * *

Garcin: They shot me.

Estelle: I know. Because you refused to fight. Well, why shouldn't you?

Garcin: I—I didn't exactly refuse. [*In a faraway voice*] I must say he talks well, he makes out a good case against me, but he never says what I should have done instead. Should I have gone to the general and said: "General. I decline to fight"? A mug's game; they'd have promptly locked me up. But I wanted to show my colors, my true colors, do you understand? I wasn't going to be silenced [*To Estelle*] So I—I took the train. . . . They caught me at the [Mexican] frontier. . . .

Estelle: But you *had* to run away. If you'd stayed they'd have sent you to jail, wouldn't they?

Garcin: Of course [*A pause.*] Well, Estelle, am I a coward?

Estelle: How can I say ? Don't be so unreasonable, darling. I can't put myself in your skin. You must decide that for yourself.

Garcin: [*wearily*] I can't decide.

Estelle: Anyhow, you must remember. You must have had reasons for acting as you did.

Garcin: I had.

Estelle: Well?

Garcin: But were they the real reasons?

Estelle: You've a twisted mind, that's your trouble. Plaguing yourself over such trifles!

Garcin: I'd thought it all out, and I wanted to make a stand. But was that my real motive?

Inez: Exactly. That's the question. Was that your real motive? No doubt you argued it out with yourself, you weighed the pros and cons, you found good reasons for what you did. But fear and hatred and all the dirty little instincts one keeps dark—they're motives too. So carry on, Mr. Garcin, and try to be honest with yourself—for once.

Garcin: Do I need you to tell me that? Day and night I paced my cell, from the window to the door, from the door to the window. I pried into my heart. I sleuthed myself like a detective. By the end of it I felt as if I'd given my whole life to introspection. But always I harked back to the one thing certain—that I had acted as I did. I'd taken that train to the frontier. But why? Why? Finally I thought: My death will settle it. If I face death courageously, I'll prove I am no coward.

Inez: And how did you face death?

Garcin: Miserably. Rottenly. [INEZ *LAUGHS.*] Oh, it was only a physical lapse—that might happen to anyone; I'm, not ashamed of it. Only everything's been left in suspense, forever. . . . Listen! Each man has an aim in life, a leading motive; that's so, isn't it? Well, I didn't give a damn for wealth, or love. I aimed at being a real man. A tough, as they say. I staked everything on the same horse. . . . Can one possibly be a coward when one's deliberately courted danger at every turn? And can one judge a life by a single action?

Inez: Why not? For thirty years you dreamt you were a hero, and condoned a thousand lapses— because a hero, of course, can do no wrong. An easy method obviously. Then a day came when you were up against it, the red light of real danger— and you took the train to Mexico.

Garcin: I "dreamt," you say. It was no dream. When I chose that hardest path, I made my choice deliberately. A man is what he wills himself to be.

Inez: Prove it. Prove it was no dream. It's what one does, and nothing else, that shows the stuff one's made of.

Garcin: I died too soon. I wasn't allowed time to—to do my deeds.

Inez: One always dies too soon—or too late. And yet one's whole life is complete at that moment, with a line drawn neatly under it, ready for the summing up. You are—your life, and nothing else.

From No Exit.

* * *

Let us take an example: A homosexual frequently has an intolerable feeling of guilt, and his whole existence is determined in relation to this feeling. One will readily foresee that he is in bad faith. In fact it frequently happens that this man, while recognizing his homosexual inclination, while avowing each and every particular misdeed which he has committed, refuses with all his strength to consider himself "*a paederast.*" His case is always "different," peculiar; there enters into it something of a game, of chance, of bad luck; the mistakes are all in the past; they are explained by a certain conception of the beautiful which women can not satisfy; we should see in them the results of a restless search, rather than the manifestations of a deeply rooted tendency, *etc., etc.* Here is as-

suredly a man in bad faith who borders on the comic since, acknowledging all the facts which are imputed to him, he refuses to draw from them the conclusion which they impose. His friend, who is his most severe critic, becomes irritated with this duplicity. The critic asks only one thing—and perhaps then he will show himself indulgent: that the guilty one recognize himself as guilty, that the homosexual declare frankly—whether humbly or boastfully matters little—"I am a paederast." We ask here: Who is in bad faith? The homosexual or the champion of sincerity?

The homosexual recognizes his faults, but he struggles with all his strength against the crushing view that his mistakes constitute for him a *destiny*. He does not wish to let himself be considered as a thing. He has an obscure but strong feeling that a homosexual is not a homosexual as this table is a table or as this red-haired man is red-haired. It seems to him that he has escaped from each mistake as soon as he has posited it and recognized it; he even feels that the psychic duration by itself cleanses him from each misdeed, constitutes for him an undetermined future, causes him to be born anew. Is he wrong? Does he not recognize in himself the peculiar, irreducible character of human reality? His attitude includes then an undeniable comprehension of truth. But at the same time he needs this perpetual rebirth, this constant escape in order to live; he must constantly put himself beyond reach in order to avoid the terrible judgment of collectivity. Thus he plays on the word *being*. He would be right actually if he understood the phrase "I am not a paederast" in the sense of "I am not what I am." That is, if he declared to himself, "To the extent that a pattern of conduct is defined as the conduct of a paederast and to the extent that I have adopted this conduct, I am a paederast. But to the extent that human reality can not be finally defined by patterns of conduct, I am not one." But instead he slides surreptitiously toward a different connotation of the word "being." He understands "not being" in the sense of "not-being-in-itself." He lays claim to "not being a paederast" in the sense in which this *table is not an inkwell. He is in bad faith.*

From Being and Nothingness.

Further Questions

1. Is our degree of freedom a question for scientists or one that ordinary people like ourselves can settle just by reflecting on our condition?
2. Even if we were not as free as Sartre supposes, might people still be afraid of what they take to be their freedom and so try to evade it? Do you think people do this?

Further Readings

Jubien, Michael. *Contemporary Metaphysics: An Introduction*. Oxford: Blackwell, 1997. Includes a lucid chapter on "Determinism, Freedom, and Fatalism."

Neisser, Ulric, and Robyn Fivush. *The Remembering Self: Construction and Accuracy in the Self-narrative*. Oxford: Oxford University Press, 1994. A valuable perspective on why we invent sself-conceptions and how accurate they are.

Part V

Knowledge

THIS IS NOT A BOOK. You didn't just read that sentence. You are not now reading this sentence.

You are not holding a book in your hands, because there is no book and you have no hands.

You are not even there. You are not anywhere. You have *never* been anywhere. Nor will you ever. You can't. You don't even exist.

The world does not exist, either. Nothing does. There is no space or time. This moment is not happening.

Your parents, your family, your friends, your world, are all figments of nobody's imagination because there is no imagination and there is nobody there to not have it.

2 + 2 does not equal 4. 2 + 2 does not equal anything. There are no 2s. There is no addition. *Nothing equals anything.*

You *believe* that everything written above is false.

But how do you *know*?

Universal skepticism is not the issue. According to universal skepticism, we don't have good reason to believe anything. However, if we have good reason to believe universal skepticism, we have good reason to believe at least one thing, and so universal skepticism must be false. But even though we cannot *know* that we do not have good reason to believe anything, we still *may not* have good reason to believe anything. We assume, though, that we do. The problem is understanding *how*.

Where to begin? With the things that seem most certain, searching for foundations? Or do we start with our ordinary network of beliefs, looking more for coherence than for foundations? Or do we start with the fact that we must be connected to the world reliably, otherwise we would not even be here wondering how we know anything because we would have perished long ago?

Each of these beginning points is represented in the readings that follow. Each motivates a different conception of knowledge. Collectively, they show that no one can explain, clearly and unproblematically, how we know anything at all.

26   Knowledge

PLATO

A brief biography of Plato appears on page 2.

    In the following selections from four of Plato's dialogs, Plato explains his view of knowledge, including that it is recollection and is of the Forms, or Ideas.

Reading Questions

1. What does Socrates mean by saying that knowledge is recollection?
2. What is the role of the senses in recollection?
3. What is learning?
4. What does Socrates mean by the essence of, for example, Beauty?
5. What is the distinction between "hypotheses" and "first principles"?
6. What is the point of Socrates' story about the underground den (i.e., the cave)?
7. How does Socrates explain the possibility of error?
8. In Socrates' view, is there a distinction between knowledge and true opinion? What is it?

FROM *MENO*

Men. Yes, Socrates; but what do you mean by saying that we do not learn, and that what we call learning is only a process of recollection? Can you teach me how this is?

Soc. I told you, Meno, just now that you were a rogue, and now you ask whether I can teach you, when I am saying that there is no teaching, but only recollection; and thus you imagine that you will involve me in a contradiction.

Men. Indeed, Socrates, I protest that I had no such intention. I only asked the question from habit; but if you can prove to me that what you say is true, I wish that you would.

Soc. It will be no easy matter, but I will try to please you to the utmost of my power. Suppose that you call one of your numerous attendants, that I may demonstrate on him.

Men. Certainly. Come hither, boy.

Soc. He is Greek, and speaks Greek, does he not?

Men. Yes, indeed; he was born in the house.

Soc. Attend now to the questions which I ask him, and observe whether he learns of me or only remembers.

Men. I will.

Soc. Tell me, boy, do you know that a figure like this is a square?

Boy. I do.

Soc. And you know that a square figure has these four lines equal?

Boy. Certainly.

Soc. And these lines which I have drawn through the middle of the square are also equal?

Boy. Yes.

Soc. A square may be of any size?

Boy. Certainly.

Reprinted from The Dialogues of Plato, *translated by Benjamin Jowett, 3rd ed. (Oxford: Oxford University Press, 1896).*

Soc. And if one side of the figure be of two feet, and the other side be of two feet, how much will the whole be? Let me explain: if in one direction the space was of two feet, and in the other direction of one foot, the whole would be of two feet taken once?

Boy. Yes.

Soc. But since this side is also of two feet, there are twice two feet?

Boy. There are.

Soc. Then the square is of twice two feet?

Boy. Yes.

Soc. And how many are twice two feet? count and tell me.

Boy. Four, Socrates.

Soc. And might there not be another square twice as large as this, and having like this the lines equal?

Boy. Yes.

Soc. And of how many feet will that be?

Boy. Of eight feet.

Soc. And now try and tell me the length of the line which forms the side of that double square: this is two feet—what will that be?

Boy. Clearly, Socrates, it will be double.

Soc. Do you observe, Meno, that I am not teaching the boy anything, but only asking him questions; and now he fancies that he knows how long a line is necessary in order to produce a figure of eight square feet; does he not?

Men. Yes.

Soc. And does he really know?

Men. Certainly not.

Soc. He only guesses that because the square is double, the line is double.

Men. True.

Soc. Observe him while he recalls the steps in regular order. (*To the Boy.*) Tell me, boy, do you assert that a double space comes from a double line? Remember that I am not speaking of an oblong, but of a figure equal every way, and twice the size of this—that is to say of eight feet; and I want to know whether you still say that a double square comes from a double line?

Boy. Yes.

Soc. But does not this line become doubled if we add another such line here?

Boy. Certainly.

Soc. And four such lines will make a space containing eight feet?

Boy. Yes.

Soc. Let us describe such a figure: Would you not say that this is the figure of eight feet?

Boy. Yes.

Soc. And are there not these four divisions in the figure, each of which is equal to the figure of four feet?

Boy. True.

Soc. And is not that four times four?

Boy. Certainly.

Soc. And four times is not double?

Boy. No, indeed.

Soc. But how much?

Boy. Four times as much.

Soc. Therefore the double line, boy, has given a space, not twice, but four times as much.

Boy. True.

Soc. Four times four are sixteen—are they not?

Boy. Yes.

Soc. What line would give you a space of eight feet, as this gives one of sixteen feet;—do you see?

Boy. Yes.

Soc. And the space of four feet is made from this half line?

Boy. Yes.

Soc. Good; and is not a space of eight feet twice the size of this, and half the size of the other?

Boy. Certainly.

Soc. Such a space, then, will be made out of a line greater than this one, and less than that one?

Boy. Yes; I think so.

Soc. Very good; I like to hear you say what you think. And now tell me, is not this a line of two feet and that of four?

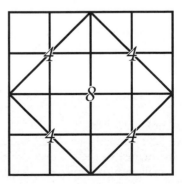

Boy. Yes.

Soc. Then the line which forms the side of eight feet ought to be more than this line of two feet, and less than the other of four feet?

Boy. It ought.

Soc. Try and see if you can tell me how much it will be.

Boy. Three feet.

Soc. Then if we add a half to this line of two, that will be the line of three. Here are two and there is one; and on the other side here are two also and there is one: and that makes the figure of which you speak?

Boy. Yes.

Soc. But if there are three feet this way and three feet that way, the whole space will be three times three feet?

Boy. That is evident.

Soc. And how much are three times three feet?

Boy. Nine.

Soc. And how much is the double of four?

Boy. Eight.

Soc. Then the figure of eight is not made out of a line of three?

Boy. No.

Soc. But from what line? — tell me exactly; and if you would rather not reckon, try and show me the line.

Boy. Indeed, Socrates, I do not know.

Soc. Do you see, Meno, what advances he has made in his power of recollection? He did not know at first, and he does not know now, what is the side of a figure of eight feet: but then he thought that he knew, and answered confidently as if he knew, and had no difficulty; now he has a difficulty, and neither knows nor fancies that he knows.

Men. True.

Soc. Is he not better off in knowing his ignorance?

Men. I think that he is.

Soc. If we have made him doubt, and given him the "torpedo's shock," have we done him any harm?

Men. I think not.

Soc. We have certainly, as would seem, assisted him in some degree to the discovery of the truth: and now he will wish to remedy his ignorance, but then he would have been ready to tell all the world again and again that the double space should have a double side.

Men. True.

Soc. But do you suppose that he would ever have enquired into or learned what he fancied that he knew, though he was really ignorant of it, until he had fallen into perplexity under the idea that he did not know, and had desired to know?

Men. I think not, Socrates.

Soc. Then he was the better for the torpedo's touch?

Men. I think so.

Soc. Mark now the farther development. I shall only ask him, and not teach him, and he shall share the enquiry with me: and do you watch and see if you find me telling or explaining anything to him, instead of eliciting his opinion. Tell me, boy, is not this a square of four feet which I have drawn?

Boy. Yes.

Soc. And now I add another square equal to the former one?

Boy. Yes.

Soc. And a third, which is equal to either of them?

Boy. Yes.

Soc. Suppose that we fill up the vacant corner?

Boy. Very good.

Soc. Here, then, there are four equal spaces?

Boy. Yes.

Soc. And how many times larger is this space than this other?

Boy. Four times.

Soc. But it ought to have been twice only, as you will remember.

Boy. True.

Soc. And does not this line, reaching from corner to corner, bisect each of these spaces?

Boy. Yes.

Soc. And are there not here four equal lines which contain this space?

Boy. There are.

Soc. Look and see how much this space is.

Boy. I do not understand.

Soc. Has not each interior line cut off half of the four spaces?

Boy. Yes.

Soc. And how many spaces are there in this section?

Boy. Four.

Soc. And how many in this?

Boy. Two.

Soc. And four is how many times two?

Boy. Twice.

Soc. And this space is of how many feet?

Boy. Of eight feet.

Soc. And from what line do you get this figure?

Boy. From this.

Soc. That is, from the line which extends from corner to corner of the figure of four feet?

Boy. Yes.

Soc. And that is the line which the learned call the diagonal. And if this is the proper name, then you, Meno's slave, are prepared to affirm that the double space is the square of the diagonal?

Boy. Certainly, Socrates.

Soc. What do you say of him, Meno? Were not all these answers given out of his own head?

Men. Yes, they were all his own.

Soc. And yet, we were just now saying he did not know?

Men. True.

Soc. But still he had in him those notions of his—had he not?

Men. Yes.

Soc. Then he who does not know may still have the true notions of that which he does not know?

Men. He has.

Soc. And at present these notions have just been stirred up in him, as in a dream; but if he were frequently asked the same questions, in different forms, he would know as well as any one at last?

Men. I dare say.

Soc. Without any one teaching him he will recover his knowledge for himself, if he is only asked questions?

Men. Yes.

Soc. And this spontaneous recovery of knowledge in him is recollection?

Men. True.

Soc. And this knowledge which he now has must he not either have acquired or always possessed?

Men. Yes.

Soc. But if he always possessed this knowledge he would always have known; or if he has acquired the knowledge he could not have acquired it in this life, unless he has been taught geometry; for he may be made to do the same with all geometry and every other branch of knowledge. Now, has any one ever taught him all this? You must know about him if, as you say, he was born and bred in your house.

Men. And I am certain that no one ever did teach him.

Soc. And yet he has the knowledge?

Men. The fact, Socrates, is undeniable.

Soc. But if he did not acquire the knowledge in this life, then he must have had and learned it at some other time?

Men. Clearly he must.

Soc. Which must have been the time when he was not a man?

Men. Yes.

Soc. And if there have been always true thoughts in him, both at the time when he was and was not a man, which only need to be awakened into knowledge by putting questions to him, his soul must have always possessed this knowledge, for he always either was or was not a man?

Men. Obviously.

Soc. And if the truth of all things always existed in the soul, then the soul is immortal. Wherefore be of good cheer, and try to recollect what you do know, or rather what you do not remember.

FROM *PHAEDO*

Socrates: Now consider this question. We affirm, do we not, that there is such a thing as equality, not of one piece of wood or stone or similar material thing with another, but that, over and above this, there is absolute equality? Shall we say so?

Say so, yes, replied Simmias, and swear to it, with all the confidence in life.

And do we know the nature of this absolute existence?

To be sure, he said.

And whence did we obtain our knowledge? Did we not see equalities of material things, such as pieces of wood and stones, and conceive from them the idea of an equality which is different from them? For you will acknowledge that there is a difference? Or look at the matter in another way:—Do not the same pieces of wood or stone appear to one man equal, and to another unequal?

That is certain.

But did pure equals ever appear to you unequal? or equality the same as inequality?

Never, Socrates.

Then these equal objects are not the same with the idea of equality?

I should say, clearly not, Socrates.

And yet from these equals, although differing from the idea of equality, you obtained the knowledge of that idea?

Very true, he said.

Which might be like, or might be unlike them?

Yes.

But that makes no difference: so long as from seeing one thing you conceive another, whether like or unlike, there must surely have been an act of recollection?

Very true.

But what would you say of equal portions of wood or other material equals? and what is the impression produced by them? Are they equals in the same sense in which absolute equality is equal? or do they fall short of this perfect equality in a measure.

Yes, he said, in a very great measure too.

And must we not allow, that when a man, looking at any object, reflects "the thing which I see aims at being like some other thing, but falls short of and cannot be like that other thing, and is inferior," he who so reflects must have had a previous knowledge of that to which the other, although similar, was inferior?

Certainly.

And has not this been our own case in the matter of equals and of absolute equality?

Precisely.

Then we must have known equality previously to the time when we first saw the material equals, and reflected that they all strive to attain absolute equality, but fall short of it?

Very true.

And we recognize also that we have only derived this conception of absolute equality, and can only derive it, from sight or touch, or from some other of the senses, which are all alike in this respect?

Yes, Socrates, for the purposes of the present argument, one of them is the same as the other.

From the senses then is derived the conception that all sensible equals aim at an absolute equality of which they fall short?

Yes.

Then before we began to see or hear or perceive in any way, we must have had a knowledge of absolute equality, or we could not have referred to that standard the equals which are derived from the senses?—for to that they all aspire, and of that they fall short.

No other inference can be drawn from the previous statements.

And did we now begin to see and hear and have the use of our other senses as soon as we were born?

Certainly.

Then we must have acquired the knowledge of equality at some previous time?

Yes.

That is to say, before we were born, I suppose?

It seems so.

And if we acquired this knowledge before we were born, and were born having the use of it, then we also knew before we were born and at the instant of birth not only the equal or the greater or the less, but all other such ideas; for we are not speaking only of equality, but of beauty, goodness, justice, holiness, and of all which we stamp with the name of absolute being in the dialectical process, both when we affirm with certainty that we acquired the knowledge before birth?

We do.

But, if after having acquired, we have not on each occasion forgotten what we acquired, then we must always come into life having this knowledge, and shall have it always as long as life lasts—for knowing is the acquiring and retaining knowledge and not losing it. Is not the loss of knowledge, Simmias, just what we call forgetting?

Quite true, Socrates.

But if this knowledge which we acquired before birth was lost by us at birth, and if afterwards by the use of the senses we recovered what we previously knew, will not the process which we call learning be a recovering of knowledge which is natural to us, and may not this be rightly termed recollection?

Very true.

So much is clear—that when we perceive something, either by the help of sight, or hearing, or some other sense, that perception can lead us to think of some other thing like or unlike which is associated with it but has been forgotten. Whence, as I was saying, one of two alternatives follows:—either we all have this knowledge at birth, and continue to know through life; or, after birth, those who are said to learn only recollect, and learning is simply recollection.

Yes, that is quite true, Socrates.

And which alternative, Simmias, do you prefer? Have we the knowledge at our birth, or do we recollect afterwards things which we knew previously to our birth?

I cannot decide at the moment.

At any rate you can decide whether he who has knowledge will or will not be able to render an account of his knowledge? What do you say?

Certainly, he will.

But do you think that every man is able to give an account of the matters about which we were speaking a moment ago?

Would that they could, Socrates, but I much rather fear that tomorrow, at this time, there will no longer be anyone alive who is able to give an account of them such as ought to be given.

Then you are not of opinion, Simmias, that all men know these things.

Certainly not.

They are in the process of recollecting that which they learned before?

Certainly.

But when did our souls acquire this knowledge?—clearly not since we were born as men?

Certainly not.

And therefore, previously?

Yes.

Then, Simmias, our souls must also have existed without bodies before they were in the form of man, and must have had intelligence.

Unless indeed you suppose, Socrates, that all knowledge is given us at the very moment of birth; for this is the only time which remains.

Yes, my friend, but if so, when, pray, do we lose it? for it is not in us when we are born—that is admitted. Do we lose it at the moment of receiving it, or if not at what other time?

No, Socrates, I perceive that I was unconsciously talking nonsense.

Then may we not say, Simmias, that if there do exist these things of which we are always talking, absolute beauty and goodness, and all that class of realities; and if to this we refer all our sensations and with this compare them, finding the realities to be pre-existent and our own possession—then just as surely as these exist, so surely must our souls have existed before our birth? Otherwise our whole argument would be worthless. By an equal compulsion we must believe both that these realities exist, and that our souls existed before our birth; and if not the realities, then not the souls.

Yes, Socrates; I am convinced that there is precisely the same necessity for the one as for the other; and the argument finds a safe refuge in the position that the existence of the soul before birth cannot be separated from the existence of the reality of which you speak. For there is nothing which to my mind is so patent as that beauty, goodness, and the other realities of which you were just now speaking, exist in the fullest possible measure; and I am satisfied with the proof.

* * *

There is nothing new, he said, in what I am about to tell you; but only what I have been always and everywhere repeating in the previous discussion and on other occasions: I shall try to show you the sort of causation which has occupied my thoughts. I shall have to go back to those familiar theories which are in the mouth of everyone, and first of all assume that there is an absolute beauty and goodness and greatness, and the like; grant me these and admit that they exist, and I hope to be able to show you the nature of cause, and to prove the immortality of the soul.

Cebes said: You may proceed at once with the proof, for I grant you this.

Well, he said, then I should like to know whether you agree with me in the next step; for I cannot help thinking that if there be anything beautiful other than absolute beauty it is beautiful only in so far as it partakes of absolute beauty—and I should say the same of everything. Do you agree in this notion of the cause?

Yes, he said, I agree.

He proceeded: I no longer looked for, nor can I understand, those other ingenious causes which are alleged; and if a person says to me that the bloom of colour, or form, or any such thing is a source of beauty, I dismiss all that, which is only confusing to me, and simply and singly, and perhaps foolishly, hold and am assured in my own mind that nothing makes a thing beautiful but the presence or participation of beauty in whatever way or manner obtained; for as to the manner I am uncertain, but I stoutly contend that by beauty all beautiful things become beautiful. This appears to me to be the safest answer which I can give, either to myself or to another, and to this I cling, in the persuasion that this principle will never be overthrown, and that to myself or to anyone who asks the question, I may safely reply, That by beauty beautiful things become beautiful. Do you not agree with me?

I do.

And that by greatness things become great and greater greater, and by smallness the less becomes less?

True.

Then if a person were to remark that A is taller by a head than B, and B less by a head than A, you would refuse to admit his statement, and would stoutly contend that what you mean is only that the greater is greater by, and by reason of, greatness, and the less is less only by, and by reason of, smallness. I imagine you would be afraid of a counter-argument that if the greater is greater and the less less by the head, then, first, the greater is greater and the less less by the same thing; and, secondly, the greater man is greater by the head which is itself small, and so you get the monstrous absurdity that a man is great by something small. You would be afraid of this, would you not?

Indeed I should, said Cebes, laughing.

In like manner you would think it dangerous to say the ten exceeded eight by, and by reason of, two; but would say by, and by reason of, number; or you would say that two cubits exceed one cubit not by a half, but by magnitude? — for there is the same danger in all these cases.

Very true, he said.

Again, would you not be cautious of affirming that the addition of one to one, or the division of one, is the cause of two? And you would loudly asseverate that you know of no way in which any-

thing comes into existence except by participation in the distinctive reality of that in which it participates, and consequently as far as you know, the only cause of two is the participation in duality — this is the way to make two, and the participation in unity is the way to make one. You would say: "I will let alone all subtleties like these of division and addition — wiser heads than mine may answer them; inexperienced as I am, and ready to start, as the proverb says, at my own shadow, I cannot afford to give up the sure ground of the original postulate." And if anyone fastens on you there, you would not mind him, or answer him until you could see whether the consequences which follow agree with one another or not, and when you are further required to give an account of this postulate, you would give it in the same way, assuming some higher postulate which seemed to you to be the best founded, until you arrived at a satisfactory resting-place; but you would not jumble together the fundamental principle and the consequences in your reasoning, like the eristics — at least if you wanted to discover real existence. Not that this confusion signifies to them, who probably never care or think about the matter at all, for they have the wit to be well pleased with themselves however thorough may be the muddle of their ideas.

But you, if you are a philosopher, will certainly do as I say.

What you say is most true, said Simmias and Cebes, both speaking at once.

FROM *REPUBLIC*

Socrates: Yes, I said, but I must first come to an understanding with you, and remind you of what I have mentioned in the course of this discussion, and at many other times.

Glaucon: What?

The old story, that there is a many beautiful and a many good, and so of other things which we describe and define; to all of them "many" is applied.

True, he said.

And there is an absolute beauty and an absolute good, and of other things to which the term "many" is applied there is an absolute; for they may be brought under a single idea, which is called the essence of each.

Very true.

The many, as we say, are seen but not known, and the ideas are known but not seen.

Exactly.

And what is the organ with which we see the visible things?

The sight, he said.

And with the hearing, I said, we hear, and with the other senses perceive the other objects of sense?

True.

But have you remarked that sight is by far the most costly and complex piece of workmanship which the artificer of the senses ever contrived?

No, I never have, he said.

Then reflect: has the ear or voice need of any third or additional nature in order that the one may be able to hear and the other to be heard?

Nothing of the sort.

No, indeed, I replied; and the same is true of most, if not all, the other senses—you would not say that any of them requires such an addition?

Certainly not.

But you see that without the addition of some other nature there is no seeing or being seen?

How do you mean?

Sight being, as I conceive, in the eyes, and he who has eyes wanting to see; colour being also present in them, still unless there be a third nature specially adapted to the purpose, the owner of the eyes will see nothing and the colours will be invisible.

Of what nature are you speaking?

Of that which you term light, I replied.

True, he said.

Noble, then, is the bond which links together sight and visibility, and great beyond other bonds by no small difference of nature; for light is their bond, and light is no ignoble thing?

Nay, he said, the reverse of ignoble.

And which, I said, of the gods in heaven would you say was the lord of this element? Whose is that light which makes the eye to see perfectly and the visible to appear?

You mean the sun, as you and all mankind say.

May not the relation of sight to this deity be described as follows?

How?

Neither sight nor the eye in which sight resides is the sun?

No.

Yet of all the organs of sense the eye is the most like the sun?

By far the most like.

And the power which the eye possesses is a sort of effluence which is dispensed from the sun?

Exactly.

Then the sun is not sight, but the author of sight who is recognized by sight.

True, he said.

And this is he whom I call the child of the good, whom the good begat in his own likeness, to be in the visible world, in relation to sight and the things of sight, what the good is in the intellectual world in relation to mind and the things of mind.

Will you be a little more explicit? he said.

Why, you know, I said, that the eyes, when a person directs them towards objects on which the light of day is no longer shining, but the moon and stars only, see dimly, and are nearly blind; they seem to have no clearness of vision in them?

Very true.

But when they are directed towards objects on which the sun shines, they see clearly and there is sight in them?

Certainly.

And the soul is like the eye: when resting upon that on which truth and being shine, the soul perceives and understands and is radiant with intelligence; but when turned towards the twilight of becoming and perishing, then she has opinion only, and goes blinking about, and is first of one opinion and then of another, and seems to have no intelligence?

Just so.

Now, that which imports truth to the known and the power of knowing to the knower is what I would have you term the idea of good, and this you will deem to be the cause of science, and of truth in so far as the latter becomes the subject of knowledge; beautiful too, as are both truth and knowledge, you will be right in esteeming this other nature as more beautiful than either; and, as in the previous instance, light and sight may be truly said to be like the sun, and yet not to be the sun, so in this other sphere, science and truth may be deemed to be like the good, but not the good; the good has a place of honour yet higher.

What a wonder of beauty that must be, he said, which is the author of science and truth, and yet surpasses them in beauty; for you surely cannot mean to say that pleasure is the good?

God forbid, I replied; but may I ask you to consider the image in another point of view?

In what point of view?

You would say, would you not, that the sun is not only the author of visibility in all visible things, but of generation and nourishment and growth, though he himself is not generation?

Certainly.

In like manner the good may be said to be not only the author of knowledge to all things known, but of their being and essence, and yet the good is not essence, but far exceeds essence in dignity and power.

Glaucon said, with a ludicrous earnestness: By the light of heaven, how amazing!

Yes, I said, and the exaggeration may be set down to you; for you made me utter my fancies.

And pray continue to utter them; at any rate let us hear if there is anything more to be said about the similitude of the sun.

Yes, I said, there is a great deal more.

Then omit nothing, however slight.

I will do my best, I said; but I should think that a great deal will have to be omitted.

You have to imagine, then, that there are two ruling powers, and that one of them is set over the intellectual world, the other over the visible. I do not say heaven, lest you should fancy that I am playing upon the name. May I suppose that you have this distinction of the visible and intelligible fixed in your mind?

I have.

Now take a line which has been cut into two unequal parts, and divide each of them again in the same proportion, and suppose the two main divisions to answer, one to the visible and the other to the intelligible, and then compare the subdivisions in respect of their clearness and want of clearness, and you will find that the first section in the sphere of the visible consists of images. And by images I mean, in the first place, shadows, and in the second place, reflections in water and in solid, smooth and polished bodies and the like: Do you understand?

Yes, I understand.

Imagine, now, the other section, of which this is only the resemblance, to include the animals which we see, and everything that grows or is made.

Very good.

Would you not admit that both the sections of this division have different degrees of truth, and that the copy is to the original as the sphere of opinion is to the sphere of knowledge?

Most undoubtedly.

Next proceed to consider the manner in which the sphere of the intellectual is to be divided.

In what manner?

Thus:—There are two subdivisions, in the lower of which the soul uses the figures given by the former division as images; the enquiry can only be hypothetical, and instead of going upwards to a principle descends to the other end; in the higher of the two, the soul passes out of hypotheses, and goes up to a principle which is above hypotheses, making no use of images as in the former case, but proceeding only in and through the ideas themselves.

I do not quite understand your meaning, he said.

Then I will try again; you will understand me better when I have made some preliminary remarks. You are aware that students of geometry, arithmetic, and the kindred sciences assume the odd and the even and the figures and three kinds of angles and the like in their several branches of science; these are their hypotheses, which they and every body are supposed to know, and therefore they do not deign to give any account of them either to themselves or others; but they begin with them, and go on until they arrive at last, and in a consistent manner, at their conclusion?

Yes, he said, I know.

And do you not know also that although they make use of the visible forms and reason about them, they are thinking not of these, but of the ideals which they resemble; not of the figures which they draw, but of the absolute square and the absolute diameter, and so on—the forms which they draw or make, and which have shadows and reflections in water of their own, are converted by them into images, but they are really seeking to behold the things themselves, which can only be seen with the eye of the mind?

That is true.

And of this kind I spoke as the intelligible, although in the search after it the soul is compelled to use hypotheses; not ascending to a first principle, because she is unable to rise above the region of hypothesis, but employing the objects of which the shadows below are resemblances in their turn as images, they having in relation to the shadows and reflections of them a greater distinctness, and therefore a higher value.

I understand, he said, that you are speaking of the province of geometry and the sister arts.

And when I speak of the other division of the intelligible, you will understand me to speak of that other sort of knowledge which reason herself attains by the power of dialectic, using the hypotheses not as first principles, but only as hypotheses—that is to say, as steps and points of departure into a world which is above hypotheses, in order that she may soar beyond them to the first principle of the whole; and clinging to this and then to that which depends on this, by successive steps she descends again without the aid of any sensible object, from ideas, through ideas, and in ideas she ends.

I understand you, he replied; not perfectly, for you seem to me to be describing a task which is really tremendous; but, at any rate, I understand you to say that knowledge and being, which the science of dialectic contemplates, are clearer than the notions of the arts, as they are termed, which proceed from hypotheses only: these are also contemplated by the understanding, and not by the senses: yet, because they start from hypotheses and do not ascend to a principle, those who contemplate them appear to you not to exercise the higher reason upon them, although when a first principle is added to them they are cognizable by the higher reason. And the habit which is concerned with geometry and the cognate sciences I suppose that you would term understanding and not reason, as being intermediate between opinion and reason.

You have quite conceived my meaning, I said; and now, corresponding to these four divisions, let there be four faculties in the soul—reason answering to the highest, understanding to the second, faith (or conviction) to the third, and perception of shadows to the last—and let there be a scale of them, and let us suppose that the several faculties

have clearness in the same degree that their objects have truth.

I understand, he replied, and give my assent, and accept your arrangement.

* * *

And now, I said, let me show in a figure how far our nature is enlightened or unenlightened:—Behold! human beings living in an underground den, which has a mouth open towards the light and reaching all along the den; here they have been from their childhood, and have their legs and necks chained so that they cannot move, and can only see before them, being prevented by the chains from turning round their heads. Above and behind them a fire is blazing at a distance, and between the fire and the prisoners there is a raised way; and you will see, if you look, a low wall built along the way, like the screen which marionette players have in front of them, over which they show the puppets.

I see.

And do you see, I said, men passing along the wall carrying all sorts of vessels, and statues and figures of animals made of wood and stone and various materials, which appear over the wall? Some of them are talking, others silent.

You have shown me a strange image, and they are strange prisoners.

Like ourselves, I replied; and they see only their own shadows, or the shadows of one another which the fire throws on the opposite wall of the cave?

True, he said; how could they see anything but the shadows if they were never allowed to move their heads?

And of the objects which are being carried in like manner they would only see the shadows?

Yes, he said.

And if they were able to converse with one another, would they not suppose that they were naming what was actually before them?

Very true.

And suppose further that the prison had an echo which came from the other side, would they not be sure to fancy when one of the passers-by spoke that the voice which they heard came from the passing shadow?

No question, he replied.

To them, I said, the truth would be literally nothing but the shadows of the images.

That is certain.

And now look again, and see what will naturally follow if the prisoners are released and disabused of their error. At first, when any of them is liberated and compelled suddenly to stand up and turn his neck round and walk and look towards the light, he will suffer sharp pains; the glare will distress him, and he will be unable to see the realities of which in his former state he had seen the shadows; and then conceive some one saying to him, that what he saw before was an illusion, but that now, when he is approaching nearer to being and his eye is turned towards more real existence, he has a clearer vision,—what will be his reply? And you may further imagine that his instructor is pointing to the objects as they pass and requiring him to name them,—will he not be perplexed? Will he not fancy that the shadows which he formerly saw are truer than the objects which are now shown to him?

Far truer.

And if he is compelled to look straight at the light, will he not have a pain in his eyes which will make him turn away to take refuge in the objects of vision which he can see, and which he will conceive to be in reality clearer than the things which are now being shown to him?

True, he said.

And suppose once more, that he is reluctantly dragged up a steep and rugged ascent, and held fast until he is forced into the presence of the sun himself, is he not likely to be pained and irritated? When he approaches the light his eyes will be dazzled, and he will not be able to see anything at all of what are now called realities.

Not all in a moment, he said.

He will require to grow accustomed to the sight of the upper world. And first he will see the shadows best, next the reflections of men and other objects in the water, and then the objects themselves; then he will gaze upon the light of the moon and the stars and the spangled heaven; and he will see the sky and the stars by night better than the sun or the light of the sun by day?

Certainly.

Last of all he will be able to see the sun, and not mere reflections of him in the water, but he will see him in his own proper place, and not in another; and he will contemplate him as he is.

Certainly.

He will then proceed to argue that this is he who gives the season and the years, and is the guardian of all that is in the visible world, and in a certain way the cause of all things which he and his fellows have been accustomed to behold?

Clearly, he said, he would first see the sun and then reason about him.

And when he remembered his old habitation, and the wisdom of the den and his fellow-prisoners, do you not suppose that he would felicitate himself on the change, and pity them?

Certainly, he would.

And if they were in the habit of conferring honours among themselves on those who were quickest to observe the passing shadows and to remark which of them went before, and which followed after, and which were together; and who were therefore best able to draw conclusions as to the future, do you think that he would care for such honours and glories, or envy the possessors of them? Would he not say with Homer,

"Better to be the poor servant of a poor master,"

and to endure anything, rather than think as they do and live after their manner?

Yes, he said, I think that he would rather suffer anything than entertain these false notions and live in this miserable manner.

Imagine once more, I said, such a one coming suddenly out of the sun to be replaced in his old situation; would he not be certain to have his eyes full of darkness?

To be sure, he said.

And if there were a contest, and he had to compete in measuring the shadows with the prisoners who had never moved out of the den, while his sight was still weak, and before his eyes had become steady (and the time which would be needed to acquire this new habit of sight might be very considerable), would he not be ridiculous? Men would say of him that up he went and down he came without his eyes; and that it was better not even to think of ascending; and if any one tried to loose another and lead him up to the light, let them only catch the offender, and they would put him to death.

No question, he said.

This entire allegory, I said, you may now append, dear Glaucon, to the previous argument; the prison-house is the world of sight, the light of the fire is the sun, and you will not misapprehend me if you interpret the journey upwards to be the ascent of the soul into the intellectual world according to my poor belief, which, at your desire, I have expressed — whether rightly or wrongly God knows. But, whether true or false, my opinion is that in the world of knowledge the idea of good appears last of all, and is seen only with an effort; and, when seen, is also inferred to be the universal author of all things beautiful and right, parent of light and of the lord of light in this visible world, and the immediate source of reason and truth in the intellectual; and that this is the power upon which he who would act rationally either in public or private life must have his eye fixed.

I agree, he said, as far as I am able to understand you.

Moreover, I said, you must not wonder that those who attain to this beatific vision are unwilling to descend to human affairs; for their souls are ever hastening into the upper world where they desire to dwell; which desire of theirs is very natural, if our allegory may be trusted.

Yes, very natural.

And is there anything surprising in one who passes from divine contemplations to the evil state of man, misbehaving himself in a ridiculous manner; if, while his eyes are blinking and before he has become accustomed to the surrounding darkness, he is compelled to fight in courts of law, or in other places, about the images or the shadows of images of justice, and is endeavouring to meet the conceptions of those who have never yet seen absolute justice?

Anything but surprising, he replied.

Any one who has common sense will remember that the bewilderments of the eyes are of two kinds, and arise from two causes, either from coming out of the light or from going into the light, which is true of the mind's eye, quite as much as of the bodily eye; and he who remembers this when he sees any one whose vision is perplexed and weak, will not be too ready to laugh; he will first ask whether that soul of man has come out of the brighter life, and is unable to see because unaccustomed to the dark, or having turned from darkness to the day is dazzled by excess of light. And he will count the one happy in his condition and state of being, and he will pity the other; or, if he have a mind to laugh at the soul which comes from below into the light, there will be more reason in this than in the laugh which greets him who returns from above out of the light into the den.

That, he said, is a very just distinction.

But then, if I am right, certain professors of education must be wrong when they say that they can put a knowledge into the soul which was not there before, like sight into blind eyes.

They undoubtedly say this, he replied.

Whereas, our argument shows that the power and capacity of learning exists in the soul already; and that just as the eye was unable to turn from darkness to light without the whole body, so too the instrument of knowledge can only by the movement of the whole soul be turned from the world of becoming into that of being, and learn by degrees to endure the sight of being, and of the brightest and best of being, or in other words, of the good.

Very true.

And must there not be some art which will effect conversion in the easiest and quickest manner; not implanting the faculty of sight, for that exists already, but has been turned in the wrong direction, and is looking away from the truth?

FROM *THEAETETUS*

Soc. But the original aim of our discussion was to find out rather what knowledge is than what it is not; at the same time we have made some progress, for we no longer seek for knowledge in perception at all, but in that other process, however called, in which the mind is alone and engaged with being.

Theaet. All that, Socrates, if I am not mistaken, is called thinking or opining.

Soc. You conceive truly. And now, my friend, please to begin again at this point; and having wiped out of your memory all that has proceded, see if you have arrived at any clearer view, and once more say what is knowledge.

Theaet. I cannot say, Socrates, that all opinion is knowledge, because there may be a false opinion;

but I will venture to assert, that knowledge is true opinion: let this then be my reply; and if this is hereafter disproved, we must try to find another.

Soc. That is the way in which you ought to answer. Theaetetus, and not in your former hesitating strain, for if we are bold we shall gain one of two advantages; either we shall find what we seek, or we shall be less likely to think that we know what we do not know—in either case we shall be richly rewarded. And now, what are you saying?— Are there two sorts of opinion, one true and the other false; and do you define knowledge to be the true?

Theaet. Yes, according to my present view.

Soc. Is it still worth our while to resume the discussion touching opinion?

Theaet. To what are you alluding?

Soc. There is a point which troubles me, as it has often done before; my discussion with myself or with others has left me in great perplexity about the nature or origin of the mental experience to which I refer.

Theaet. Pray what is it?

Soc. How a man can form a false opinion. But I am even now in doubt whether we ought to leave this question or examine it by another method than we used a short time ago.

Theaet. Begin again, Socrates,—at least if you think that there is the slightest necessity for doing so. Were not you and Theodorus just now remarking very truly, that in discussions of this kind we may take our own time?

Soc. You are quite right, and perhaps there will be no harm in retracing our steps and beginning again. Better a little which is well done, than a great deal imperfectly.

Theaet. Certainly.

Soc. Well, and what is the difficulty? Do we not speak of false opinion, and say that one man holds a false and another a true opinion, as though there were some natural distinction between them?

Theaet. We certainly say so.

Soc. And we can at least say that all things, and each thing severally, are either known or not known. I leave out of view the intermediate conceptions of learning and forgetting, because they have nothing to do with our present question.

Theaet. There can be no doubt, Socrates, if you exclude these, that there is no other alternative but knowing or not knowing a thing.

Soc. That point being now determined, must we not say that he who had an opinion, must either know or not know that to which his opinion refers?

Theaet. He must.

Soc. Moreover, he who knows, cannot not know, and he who does not know, cannot know, one and the same thing?

Theaet. Of course.

Soc. What shall we say then? When a man has a false opinion does he think that which he knows to be some other thing which he knows, and knowing both, is he at the same time ignorant of both?

Theaet. That, Socrates, is impossible.

Soc. But perhaps he thinks of something which he does not know as some other thing which he does not know; for example, he knows neither Theaetetus nor Socrates, and yet he fancies that Theaetetus is Socrates, or Socrates Theaetetus?

Theaet. How can he?

Soc. But surely he cannot suppose something which *knows* to be a thing which he does not know, or what he does not know to do what he knows?

Theaet. That would be monstrous.

Soc. How, then, is false opinion formed? For if all things are either known or unknown, there can be no opinion which is not comprehended under this alternative; and within it we can find no scope for false opinion.

Theaet. Most true.

Soc. Suppose that we remove the question out of the sphere of knowing or not knowing, into that of being and not-being.

Theaet. What do you mean?

Soc. May we not suspect the simple truth to be that he who thinks on any subject that which *is not,* will necessarily think what is false, whatever in other respects may be the state of his mind?

Theaet. That, again, is not unlikely, Socrates.

Soc. Then suppose some one to say to us, Theaetetus:—Is it possible for any man to think as you now say, that which *is not,* either as a self-existent substance or as a predicate of something else? And suppose that we answer, "Yes, he can, when in thinking he thinks what is not true."— That will be our answer?

Theaet. Yes.

Soc. But is there any parallel to this?

Theaet. What do you mean?

Soc. Can a man see something and yet see nothing?

Theaet. Impossible.

Soc. But if he sees any one thing, he sees something that exists. Do you suppose that what is one is ever to be found among non-existing things?

Theaet. I do not.

Soc. He then who sees some one thing, sees something which is?

Theaet. Apparently.

Soc. And he who hears anything, hears some one thing,—a thing which *is*?

Theaet. Yes.

Soc. And he who touches anything, touches something which is one and therefore is?

Theaet. That again is true.

Soc. And does not he who thinks, think some one thing?

Theaet. Certainly.

Soc. And does not he who thinks some one thing, think something which is?

Theaet. I agree.

Soc. Then he who thinks of that which is not, thinks of nothing?

Theaet. Apparently not.

Soc. And he who thinks of nothing, does not think at all?

Theaet. That seems clear.

Soc. Then no one can think that which is not, either as a self-existent substance or as a predicate of something else?

Theaet. Apparently not.

Soc. Then to think falsely is different from thinking that which is not?

Theaet. It would seem so.

Soc. Then false opinion has no existence in us, either in this way, or in that which we took a short time before.

Theaet. Certainly not.

Soc. But may not the following be the description of what we express by this name?

Theaet. What?

Soc. May we not suppose that false opinion or thought is a sort of heterodoxy; a person may make an exchange in his mind, and say that one real object is another real object. For thus he thinks that which is, but he puts one thing in place of another, and missing the aim of his thoughts, he may be truly said to have false opinion.

Theaet. Now you appear to me to have spoken the exact truth: when a man puts the base in the place of the noble, or the noble in the place of the base, then he has truly false opinion.

Soc. I see, Theaetetus, that your fear has disappeared, and that you are beginning to despise me.

Theaet. What makes you say so?

Soc. You think, if I am not mistaken, that your "truly false" is safe from censure, and that I shall never ask whether there can be a swift which is slow, or a heavy which is light, or any other self-contradictory thing, which works, not according to its own nature, but according to that of its opposite. But I will not insist upon this, for I do not wish needlessly to discourage you. And so you are satisfied that false opinion is heterodoxy, or the thought of something else?

Theaet. I am.

Soc. It is possible then upon your view for the mind to conceive of one thing as another?

Theaet. True.

Soc. But must not the mind, or thinking power, which misplaces them, have a conception either of both objects or of one of them?

Theaet. Certainly; either together or in succession.

Soc. Very good. And do you mean by conceiving, the same which I mean?

Theaet. What is that?

Soc. I mean the conversation which the soul holds with herself in consideration of anything. I speak of what I scarcely understand; but the soul when thinking appears to me to be just talking—asking questions of herself and answering them, affirming and denying. And when she has arrived at a decision, either gradually or by a sudden impulse, and has at last agreed, and does not doubt, this is called her opinion. I say, then, that to form an opinion is to speak, the opinion is a word spoken,—I mean, to oneself and in silence, not aloud or to another: What think you?

Theaet. I agree.

Soc. Then when any one thinks of one thing as another, he is saying to himself that one thing is another?

Theaet. Yes.

Soc. But do you ever remember saying to yourself that the noble is certainly base, or the unjust just; or, in a word, have you ever attempted to convince yourself that one thing is another? Nay, not even in sleep, did you ever venture to say to yourself that odd is undoubted even, or anything of the kind?

Theaet. Never.

Soc. And do you suppose that any other man, either in his senses or out of them, ever seriously tried to persuade himself that an ox is a horse, or that two are one?

Theaet. Certainly not.

Soc. But if thinking is talking to oneself, no one speaking and thinking of two objects, and apprehending them both in his soul, will say and think that the one is the other of them, and I must add, that you too had better let the word "other" alone [i.e. not insist that "one" and "other" are the same]. I mean to say, that no one thinks the noble to be base or anything of the kind.

Theaet. I will pass the word "other," Socrates; and I agree to what you say.

Soc. If a man has both of them in his thoughts, he cannot think that the one of them is the other?

Theaet. So it seems.

Soc. Neither, if he has one of them only in his mind and not the other, will he ever think that one is the other?

Theaet. True; for we should have to suppose that he apprehends that which is not in his thoughts at all.

Soc. Then no one who has either both or only one of the two objects in his mind can think that the one is the other. And therefore, he who maintains that false opinion is heterodoxy is talking nonsense; for neither in this, any more than in the two previous ways, can false opinion exist in us.

Theaet. No.

Soc. But if, Theaetetus, this experience is not shown to be real, we shall be driven into many absurdities.

Theaet. What are they?

Soc. I will not tell you until I have endeavoured to consider the matter from every point of view. For I should be ashamed of us if we were driven in our perplexity to admit the absurd consequences of which I speak. But if we find the solution and get away from them we may regard them only as the difficulties of others, and the ridicule will not attach to us. On the other hand, if we utterly fail, I suppose that we must be humble, and allow the argument to trample us under foot, as the sea-sick passenger is trampled upon by the sailor, and to do anything to us. Listen, then, while I tell you how I hope to find a way out of our difficulty.

Theaet. Let me hear.

Soc. I think that we were wrong in denying that a man could think what he knew to be what he did not know; and that there is a way in which such a deception is possible.

Theaet. You mean to say, as I suspected at the time when we made that denial, that I may know Socrates, and at a distance see someone who is unknown to me, and suppose him to be Socrates whom I know—then the deception will occur?

Soc. But has not that position been relinquished by us, because involving the absurdity that we should know and not know the things which we know?

Theaet. True.

Soc. Let us make the assertion in another form, which may or may not have a favourable issue; but as we are in a great strait, every argument should be turned over and tested. Tell me, then, whether I am right in saying that you may learn a thing which at one time you did not know?

Theaet. Certainly you may.

Soc. And another and another?

Theaet. Yes.

Soc. I would have you imagine, then, that there exists in the mind of man a block of wax, which is of different sizes in different men; harder, moister, and having more or less of purity in one than another, and in some of an intermediate quality.

Theaet. I see.

Soc. Let us say that this tablet is a gift of Memory, the mother of the Muses; and that when we wish to remember anything which we have seen, or heard, or thought in our own minds, we hold the wax to the perceptions and thoughts, and in that material receive the impression of them as from the seal of a ring; and that we remember and know what is imprinted as long as the image lasts; but when the image is effaced, or cannot be taken, then we forget and do not know.

Theaet. Very good.

Soc. Now, when a person has this knowledge, and is considering something which he sees or hears, may not false opinion arise in the following manner?

Theaet. In what manner?

Soc. When he thinks what he knows, sometimes to be what he knows, and sometimes to be what he does not know. We were wrong before in denying the possibility of this.

Theaet. And how would you amend the former statement?

Soc. I should begin by making a list of the impossible cases which must be excluded. (1) No one can think one thing to be another when he does not perceive either of them, but has the memorial or seal of both of them in his mind; nor can any mistaking of one thing for another occur, when he only knows one, and does not know, and has no impression of the other; nor can he think that one thing which he does not know is another thing which he does not know, or that what he does not know is what he knows; nor (2) that one thing which he perceives is another thing which he perceives, or that something which he perceives is something which he does not perceive; or that something which he does not perceive is something else which he does not perceive; or that something which he does not perceive is something which he perceives; nor again (3) can he think that something which he knows and perceives, and of which he has the impression coinciding with sense, is something else which he knows and perceives, and of which he has the impression coinciding with sense;—this last case, if possible, is still more inconceivable than the others; nor (4) can he think that something which he knows and perceives, and of which he has the memorial in good order, is something else which he knows; nor if his mind is thus furnished, can he think that a thing which he knows and perceives is another thing which he perceives; or that a thing which he does not know and does not perceive, is the same as another thing which he does not know and does not perceive, is the same as another thing which he does not know and does not perceive;—nor again, can he suppose that a thing which he does not know and does not perceive is the same as another thing which he does not know; or that a thing which he does not know; or that a thing which he does not know and does not perceive:—All these utterly and absolutely exclude the possibility of false opinion. The only cases, if any, which remain, are the following.

Theaet. What are they? If you tell me, I may perhaps understand you better; but at present I am unable to follow you.

Soc. A person may think that some thing which he knows, or which he perceives and does not know, are some other things which he knows and perceives; or that some things which he knows and perceives, are other things which he knows and perceives.

Theaet. I understand you less than ever now.

Soc. Hear me once more, then:—I, knowing Theodorus, and remembering in my own mind what sort of person he is, and also what sort of person Theaetetus is, at one time see them, and at another time do not see them, and sometimes I touch them, and at another time not, or at one time I may hear them or perceive them in some other way, and at another time not perceive you, but still I remember you, and know you in my own mind.

Theaet. Very true.

Soc. Then, first of all, I want you to understand that a man may or may not perceive sensibly that which he knows.

Theaet. True.

Soc. And that which he does not know will sometimes not be perceived by him and sometimes will be perceived and only perceived?

Theaet. That is also true.

Soc. See whether you can follow me better now: Socrates can recognize Theodorus and Theaetetus, but he sees neither of them, nor does he perceive them in any other way; he cannot then by any possibility imagine in his own mind that Theaetetus is Theodorus. Am I not right?

Theaet. You are quite right.

Soc. Then that was the first case of which I spoke.

Theaet. Yes.

Soc. The second case was, that I, knowing one of you and not knowing the other, and perceiving neither, can never think him whom I know to be him whom I do not know.

Theaet. True.

Soc. In the third case, not knowing and not perceiving either of you, I cannot think that one of you whom I do not know is the other whom I do not know. I need not again go over the catalogue of excluded cases, in which I cannot form a false opinion about you and Theodorus, either when I know both or when I am in ignorance of both, or when I know one and not the other. And the same of perceiving: do you understand me?

Theaet. I do.

Soc. The only possibility of erroneous opinion is, when knowing you and Theodorus, and having on the waxen block the impression of both of you given as by a seal, but seeing you imperfectly and at a distance, I am eager to assign the right impression of memory to the right visual impression, and to fit this into its own print, in order that recognition may take place; but if I fail and transpose them, putting the foot into the wrong shoe — that is to say, putting the vision of either of you on to the wrong impression, or if my mind, like the sight in a mirror, which is transferred from right to left, err by reason of some similar affection, then "heterodoxy" and false opinion ensue.

Theaet. Yes, Socrates, you have described the nature of opinion with wonderful exactness.

Soc. Or again, when I know both of you, and perceive as well as know one of you, but not the other, and my knowledge of him does not accord with perception — that was the case put by me just now which you did not understand.

Theaet. No, I did not.

Soc. I meant to say, that when a person knows and perceives one of you, and his knowledge coincides with his perception, he will never think him to be some other person, whom he knows and perceives, and the knowledge of whom coincides with his perception — for that also was a case supposed.

Theaet. True.

Soc. But there was an omission of the further case, in which, as we now say, false opinion may arise, when knowing both, and seeing, or having some other sensible perception of both, I fail in holding the seal over against the corresponding sensation; like a bad archer, I miss and fall wide of the mark — and this is called falsehood.

Theaet. Yes; it is rightly so called.

Soc. When, therefore, perception is present to one of the seals or impressions but not to the other, and the mind fits the seal of the absent perception on the one which is present, in any case of this sort the mind is deceived; in a word, if our view is sound, there can be no error or deception about things which a man does not know and has never perceived, but only in things which are known and perceived; in these alone opinion turns and twists about, and becomes alternately true or false; — true when the seals and impressions of sense meet straight and opposite — false when they go awry and are crooked.

Theaet. And is not that, Socrates, nobly said?

Soc. Nobly! yes; but wait a little and hear the explanation, and then you will say so with more reason; for to think truly is noble and to be deceived is base.

Theaet. Undoubtedly.

Soc. And the origin of truth and error, men say, is as follows: — When the wax in the soul of any one is deep and abundant, and smooth and perfectly tempered, then the impressions which pass through the senses and sink into the heart of the soul, as Homer says in a parable, meaning to indicate the likeness of the soul to wax; these, I say, being pure and clear, and having a sufficient depth of wax, are also lasting, and minds such as these easily learn and easily retain, and are not liable to confuse the imprints of sensations, but have true thoughts; for, having clear impressions well spaced out, they can quickly "say what they are," — that is, distribute them into their proper places on the block. And such men are called wise. Do you agree?

Theaet. Entirely.

Soc. But when the heart of anyone is shaggy — a quality which the all-wise poet commends — or muddy and of impure wax, or very soft, or very hard, then there is a corresponding defect in the mind; the soft are good at learning, but apt to forget, and the hard are the reverse; the shaggy and rugged and gritty, or those who have an admixture of earth or dung in their composition, have the impressions indistinct, as also the hard, for there is no depth in them; and the soft too are indistinct, for their impressions are easily confused and effaced. Yet greater is the indistinctness when they are all jostled together in a little soul, which has no room. These are the natures which are prone to false opinion; for when they see or hear or think of anything, they are slow in assigning the right objects to the right impressions — in their stupidity they confuse them, and are apt to see and hear and think amiss — and such men are said to be deceived in their knowledge of objects, and ignorant.

Theaet. No man, Socrates, can say anything truer than that.

Soc. Then now we may admit the existence of false opinion in us?

Theaet. Certainly.

Soc. And of true opinion also?

Theaet. Yes.

Soc. We have at length satisfactorily proven that beyond a doubt there are these two sorts of opinion.

Theaet. Undoubtedly.

Soc. Alas, Theaetetus, what a tiresome creature is a man who is fond of talking!

Theaet. What makes you say so?

Soc. Because I am disheartened at my own stupidity and tiresome garrulity; for what other term will describe the habit of a man who is always arguing on all sides of a question; whose dullness cannot be convinced, and who will never leave off?

Theaet. But what puts you out of heart?

Soc. I am not only out of heart, but in positive despair; for I do not know what to answer if anyone were to ask me:—O Socrates, have you indeed discovered that false opinion arises neither in the comparison of perceptions with one another nor yet in thought, but in the linking of thought with perception? Yes, I shall say, with the complacence of one who thinks that he has made a noble discovery.

Theaet. I see no reason why we should be ashamed of our demonstration, Socrates.

Soc. He will say: You mean to argue that the man whom we only think of and do not see, cannot be confused with the horse which we do not see or touch, but only think and do not perceive? That I believe to be my meaning, I shall reply.

Theaet. Quite right.

Soc. Well, then, he will say, according to that argument, the number eleven, which is only thought, can never be mistaken for twelve, which is only thought: How would you answer him?

Theaet. I should say that a mistake may very likely arise between the eleven or twelve which are seen or handled, but that no similar mistake can arise between the eleven and twelve which are in the mind.

Soc. Well, but do you think that no one ever put before his own mind five and seven,—I do not mean five or seven men or other such objects, but five or seven in the abstract, which, as we say, are recorded on the waxen block, and in which false opinion is held to be impossible;—did no man ever ask himself how many these numbers make when added together, and answer that they are eleven, while another thinks that they are twelve, or would all agree in thinking and saying that they are twelve?

Theaet. Certainly not; many would think that they are eleven, and in the higher numbers the chance of error is greater still; for I assume you to be speaking of numbers in general.

Soc. Exactly; and I want you to consider whether this does not imply that the twelve in the waxen block are supposed to be eleven? Then do we not come back to the old difficulty? For he who makes such a mistake does think one thing which he knows to be another thing which he knows; but this, as we said, was impossible, and afforded an irresistible proof of the non-existence of false opinion, because otherwise the same person would inevitably know and not know the same thing at the same time.

Theaet. Most true.

Soc. Then false opinion cannot be explained as a confusion of thought and sense, for in that case we could not have been mistaken about pure conceptions of thought; and thus we are obliged to say, either that false opinion does not exist, or that a man may not know that which he knows;—which alternative do you prefer?

Theaet. It is hard to determine, Socrates.

Soc. And yet the argument will scarcely admit of both. But, as we are at our wits' end, suppose that we do a shameless thing?

Theaet. What is it?

Soc. Let us attempt to explain what it is like "to know."

Theaet. And why should that be shameless?

Soc. You seem not to be aware that the whole of our discussion from the very beginning has been a search after knowledge, of which we are assumed not to know the nature.

Theaet. Nay, but I am well aware.

Soc. And it is not shameless when we do not know what knowledge is, to be explaining the verb "to know"? The truth is, Theaetetus, that we have long been infected with logical impurity. Thousands of times have we repeated the words "we know," and "do not know," and "we have or have not science or knowledge," as if we could understand what we are saying to one another, even while we remain ignorant about knowledge; and at this moment we are using the words "we understand," "we are ignorant," as though we could still employ them when deprived of knowledge or science.

Theaet. But if you avoid these expressions, Socrates, how will you ever argue at all?

Soc. I could not, being the man I am. The case would be different if I were a true hero of dialectic: and O that such an one were present! for he would have told us to avoid the use of these terms; at the same time he would not have spared in you and me the faults which I have noted. But, seeing that we are no great wits, shall I venture to say what knowing is? for I think that the attempt may be worth making.

Theaet. Then by all means venture, and no one shall find fault with you for using the forbidden terms.

Soc. You have heard the common explanation of the verb "to know"?

Theaet. I think so, but I do not remember it at the moment.

Soc. They explain the word "to know" as meaning "to have knowledge."

Theaet. True.

Soc. I propose that we make a slight change, and say "to possess" knowledge.

Theaet. How do the two expressions differ?

Soc. Perhaps there may be no difference; but still I should like you to hear my view, that you may help me to test it.

Theaet. I will, if I can.

Soc. I should distinguish "having" from "possessing": for example, a man may buy and keep under his control a garment which he does not wear; and then we should say, not that he has, but that he possess the garment.

Theaet. It would be the correct expression.

Soc. Well, may not a man "possess" and yet not "have" knowledge in the sense of which I am speaking? As you may suppose a man to have caught wild birds — doves or any other birds — and to be keeping them in an aviary which he has constructed at home; we might say of him in one sense, that he always has them because he possesses them, might we not?

Theaet. Yes.

Soc. And yet, in another sense, he has none of them; but they are in his power, and he has got them under his hand in an enclosure of his own, and can take and have them whenever he likes; — he can catch any which he likes, and let the bird go again, and he may do so as often as he pleases.

Theaet. True.

Soc. Once more, then, as in what preceded we made a sort of waxen tablet in the mind, so let us now suppose that in the mind of each man there is an aviary of all sorts of birds — some flocking together apart from the rest, others in small groups, others solitary, flying anywhere and everywhere.

Theaet. Let us imagine such an aviary — and what is to follow?

Soc. We may suppose that the birds are kinds of knowledge, and that when we were children, this receptacle was empty; whenever a man has gotten and detained in the enclosure a kind of knowledge, he may be said to have learned or discovered the thing which is the subject of the knowledge; and this is to know.

Theaet. Granted.

Soc. And further, when any one wishes to catch any of these knowledges or sciences, and having taken, to hold it, and again to let them go, how will he express himself? — will he describe the "catching" of them and the original "possession" in the same words? I will make my meaning clearer by an example: — You admit that there is an art of arithmetic?

Theaet. To be sure.

Soc. Conceive this is an attempt to capture knowledge of every species of the odd and even.

Theaet. I follow.

Soc. Having the use of the art, the arithmetician, if I am not mistaken, has the conceptions of number under his hand, and can transmit them to another.

Theaet. Yes.

Soc. And when transmitting them he may be said to teach them, and when receiving to learn them, and when having them in possession in the aforesaid aviary he may be said to know them.

Theaet. Exactly.

Soc. Attend to what follows: must not the perfect arithmetician know all numbers, for he has the science of all numbers in his mind?

Theaet. True.

Soc. And he can reckon abstract numbers in his head, or things about him which are numerable?

Theaet. Of course he can.

Soc. And to reckon is simply to consider how much such and such a number amounts to?

Theaet. Very true.

Soc. And so he appears to be searching into something which he knows, as if he did not know it, for we have already admitted that he knows all numbers;—you have heard these perplexing questions raised?

Theaet. I have.

Soc. May we not pursue the image of the doves, and say that the chase after knowledge is of two kinds? one kind is prior to possession and for the sake of possession, and the other for the sake of taking and holding in the hands that which is possessed already. And thus, when a man had learned and known something long ago, he may resume and get hold of the knowledge which he has long possessed, but has not at hand in his mind.

Theaet. True.

Soc. That was my reason for asking how we ought to speak when an arithmetician sets about numbering, or a grammarian about reading? Shall we say, that although he knows, he comes back to himself on such an occasion to learn what he already knows?

Theaet. It would be too absurd, Socrates.

Soc. Shall we say then that he is going to read or number what he does not know, although we have admitted that he knows all letters and all numbers?

Theaet. That, again, would be an absurdity.

Soc. Then shall we say that we care nothing about the mere names—any one may twist and turn the words "knowing" and "learning" in any way which he likes; but that since we have made a clear distinction between the possession of knowledge and the having or using it, we do assert that a man cannot not possess that which he possesses; and, therefore, in no case can a man not know that which he knows, but he may get a false opinion about it; for he may have the knowledge, not of this particular thing, but of some other;—when the various numbers and forms of knowledge are flying about in the aviary, and wishing to capture a certain sort of knowledge out of the general store, he may take the wrong one by mistake. Thus it is that he may think eleven to be twelve, getting hold, as it were, of the ring-dove which he had in his mind, when he wanted the pigeon.

Theaet. A very rational explanation.

Soc. But when he catches the one which he wants, then he is not deceived, and has an opinion of what is; and thus both false and true opinion may exist, and the difficulties which were previously raised disappear. I dare say that you agree with me, do you not?

Theaet. Yes.

Soc. And so we are rid of the difficulty of a man's not knowing what he knows, for we are not driven to the inference that he does not possess what he possesses, whether he be or be not deceived. And yet I fear that a greater difficulty is looking in at the window.

Theaet. What is it?

Soc. How can the exchange of one knowledge for another ever become false opinion?

Theaet. What do you mean?

Soc. In the first place, how can a man who has the knowledge of anything be ignorant of that which he knows, not by reason of ignorance, but by reason of his own knowledge? And, again, is it not an extreme absurdity that he should suppose another thing to be this, and this to be another thing;—that, having knowledge present with him in his mind, he should still know nothing and be ignorant of all things?—you might as well argue that ignorance may make a man know, and blindness make him see, as that knowledge can make him ignorant.

Theaet. Perhaps, Socrates, we may have been wrong in making only forms of knowledge our birds: whereas there ought to have been forms of ignorance as well, flying about together in the mind, and then he who sought to take one of them might sometimes catch a form of knowledge, and sometimes a form of ignorance; and thus he would have a false opinion from ignorance, but a true one from knowledge, about the same thing.

Soc. I cannot help praising you, Theaetetus, and yet I must beg you to reconsider your words. Let us grant what you say—then, according to you, he who takes ignorance will have a false opinion—am I right?

Theaet. Yes.

Soc. He will certainly not think that he has a false opinion?

Theaet. Of course not.

Soc. He will think that his opinion is true, and he will fancy that he knows the things about which he has been deceived?

Theaet. Certainly.

Soc. Then he will think that he has captured a knowledge and not an ignorance?

Theaet. Clearly.

Soc. And thus, after going a long way round, we are once more face to face with our original difficulty. The hero of dialectic will retort upon us:— "O my excellent friends," he will say, laughing, "if a man knows the specimen of ignorance and also that of knowledge, can he think that one of them which he knows is the other which he knows? or, if he knows neither of them, can he think that the one which he knows not is another which he knows not? or, if he knows one and not the other, can he think the one which he knows to be the one which he does not know? or the one which he does not know to be the one which he knows? or will you proceed to tell me that there are other knowledges which know the types of knowledge and ignorance, and which the owner keeps in some other aviaries or graven on waxen blocks according to your foolish images, and which he may be said to know while he possess them, even though he have them not at hand in his mind? And thus, in a perpetual circle, you will be compelled to go round and round, and you will make no progress." What are we to say in reply, Theaetetus?

Theaet. Indeed, Socrates, I do now know what we are to say.

Soc. Are not his reproaches just, and does not the argument truly show that we are wrong in seeking for false opinion until we know what knowledge is; that must be first ascertained; then, the nature of false opinion?

Theaet. I cannot but agree with you, Socrates, so far as we have yet gone.

Soc. Then, once more, what shall we say that knowledge is? — for we are not going to lose heart as yet.

Theaet. Certainly, I shall not lose heart, if you do not.

Soc. What definition will be most consistent with our former views?

Theaet. I cannot think of any but our old one, Socrates.

Soc. What was it?

Theaet. Knowledge was said by us to be true opinion; and true opinion is surely unerring, and the results which follow from it are all noble and good.

Soc. He who led the way into the river, Theaetetus, said "The experiment will show"; and perhaps if we go forward in the search, we may stumble upon the thing which we are looking for; but if we stay where we are, nothing will come to light.

Theaet. Very true; let us go forward and try.

Soc. The trail soon comes to an end, for a whole profession is against us.

Theaet. How is that, and what profession do you mean?

Soc. The profession of the great wise ones who are called orators and lawyers; for these persuade men by their art and make them think whatever they like, but they do not teach them. Do you imagine that there are any teachers in the world so clever as to be able to impart the full truth about past acts of robbery or violence, to men who were not eye-witnesses, while a little water is flowing in the clepsydra?

Theaet. Certainly not, they can only persuade them.

Soc. And would you not say that persuading them is making them have an opinion?

Theaet. To be sure.

Soc. When, therefore, judges are justly persuaded about matters which you can know only by seeing them, and not in any other way, and when thus judging of them from report they attain a true opinion about them, they judge without knowledge, and yet are rightly persuaded, if they have judged well.

Theaet. Certainly.

Soc. And yet, O my friend, if true opinion in law courts and knowledge are the same, the perfect judge could not have judged rightly without knowledge; and therefore I must infer that they are not the same.

Theaet. There is a distinction, Socrates, which I have heard made by someone else, but I had forgotten it. He said that true opinion, combined with reason, was knowledge, but that the opinion which had no reason was out of the sphere of knowledge; and that things of which there is no rational account are not knowable — such was the singular expression which he used — and that things which have a reason or explanation are knowable.

Soc. Excellent; but then, how did he distinguish between things which are and are not "knowable"? I wish that you would repeat to me what he said, and then I shall know whether you and I have heard the same tale.

Theaet. I do not know whether I can recall it; but if another person would tell me, I think that I could follow him.

Soc. Let me give you, then, a dream in return for a dream: — Methought that I too had a dream, and I heard in my dream that the primeval letters or elements out of which you and I and all other things are compounded, have no reason or explanation; you can only name each of them individually, but no predicate can be either affirmed or denied of them, for in the one case existence, in the other non-existence is already implied, neither of which must be added, if you mean to speak of this or that thing by itself alone. It should not be called "itself," or "that," or "each," or "alone," or "this," or the like; for these go about everywhere and are applied to all things, but are distinct from them; whereas if the first elements can be described, and had a definition of their own, they would be spoken of apart from all else. But none of these primeval elements can be defined; they can only be named, for they have nothing but a name; whereas the things which are compounded of them, as they themselves are complex, are defined by a combination of names, for the combination of names is the essence of a definition. Thus, then, the elements or letters are only objects of perception, and cannot be defined or known; but the syllables or combinations of them are known and expressed, and are apprehended by true opinion. When, therefore, any one forms the true opinion of anything without rational explanation, you may say that his mind is truly exercised, but has no knowledge; for he who cannot give and receive a reason for a thing, has no knowledge of that thing; but when he adds rational explanation, then, he is perfected in knowledge and may be all that I have been denying of him. Was that the form in which the dream appeared to you?

Theaet. Precisely.

Soc. And you allow and maintain that true opinion, combined with definition or rational explanation, is knowledge?

Theaet. Exactly.

Soc. Then may we assume, Theaetetus, that today, and in this casual manner, we have found a truth which in former times many wise men have grown old and have not found?

Theaet. At any rate, Socrates, I am satisfied with the present statement.

* * *

Soc. . . . do not let us lose sight of the question before us . . . , which is the meaning of the statement, that right opinion with rational definition of explanation is the most perfect form of knowledge.

Theaet. We must not.

Soc. Well, and what does the author of this statement mean by the term "explanation"? I think we have a choice of three meanings.

Theaet. What are they?

Soc. In the first place, the meaning may be, manifesting one's thought by the voice with verbs and nouns, imagining an opinion in the stream which flows from the lips, as in a mirror or water. Does not this appear to you to be one kind of explanation?

Theaet. Certainly; he was so manifests his thought, is said to explain himself.

Soc. But then, every one who is not born deaf or dumb is able sooner or later to manifest what he thinks of anything; and if so, all those who have a right opinion about anything will also have right explanation; nor will right opinion be anywhere found to exist apart from knowledge.

Theaet. True.

Soc. Let us not, therefore, hastily charge him who gave his account of knowledge with uttering an unmeaning word; for perhaps he did not intend to say this, but that when a person was asked what was the nature of anything, he should be able to answer his questioner by giving the elements of the thing.

Theaet. As for example, Socrates . . . ?

Soc. As, for example, when Hesiod says that a wagon is made up of a hundred planks. Now, neither you nor I could describe all of them individually; but if any one asked what is a wagon, we should be content to answer that a wagon consists of wheels, axle, body, rims, yoke.

Theaet. Certainly.

Soc. And our opponent will probably laugh at us, just as he would if we professed to be grammarians and to give a grammatical account of the name of Theaetetus, and yet could only tell the syllables and not the letters of your name. We might hold a true opinion and make a correct statement; but *knowledge,* he could claim, is not attained until, combined with true opinion, there is an enumeration of the elements out of which anything is composed, as, I think has already been remarked.

Theaet. It has.

Soc. In the same way, he might claim that while we merely have true opinion about the wagon, a man who can describe its essence by an enumeration of the hundred planks, adds rational explanation to true opinion, and instead of opinion has art and knowledge of the nature of a wagon, in that he attains to the whole through the elements.

Theaet. And do you not agree in that view, Socrates?

Soc. Tell me, my friend, whether the view is yours—whether you admit the resolution of all things into their elements to be a rational explanation of them, and the consideration of them in syllables or larger combinations of them to be irrational—so that we can inquire whether that view is right.

Theaet. Indeed I admit it.

Soc. Well, and do you conceive that a man has knowledge of any element who at one time affirms and at another time denies that element of something, or thinks that the same thing is composed of different elements at different times?

Theaet. Assuredly not.

Soc. And do you not remember that in your case and in that of others this often occurred at first in the process of learning to read?

Theaet. You mean that we often put different letters into the same syllables, and gave the same letter sometimes to the proper syllable, sometimes to a wrong one.

Soc. Yes.

Theaet. To be sure; I perfectly remember, and I am very far from supposing that they who are in this condition have knowledge.

Soc. When a person at that stage of learning writes the name of Theaetetus, and thinks that he ought to write and does write *Th* and *e;* but, again, meaning to write the name of Theodorus, thinks that he ought to write and does write *T* and *e*— can we suppose that he knows the first syllables of your two names?

Theaet. We have already admitted that such a one has not yet attained knowledge.

Soc. And in like manner he may enumerate without knowing them the second and third and fourth syllables of your name?

Theaet. He may.

Soc. And in that case, when he has written the syllables in order, since he can enumerate all the letters he will have written "Theaetetus" with right opinion?

Theaet. Clearly.

Soc. But although we admit that he has right opinion, he will still be without knowledge?

Theaet. Yes.

Soc. And yet he will have explanation, as well as right opinion, for he knew his way through the letters when he wrote; and this we admit to be explanation.

Theaet. True.

Soc. Then, my friend, there is such a thing as right opinion united with definition or explanation, which should still not be called knowledge.

Theaet. It would seem so.

Soc. And what we fancied to be a perfect definition of knowledge is a dream only. But perhaps we had better not say so as yet, for were there not three senses of "explanation," one of which must, as we said, be adopted by him who maintains knowledge to be true opinion combined with rational explanation? And very likely there may be found some one who will not prefer this but the third.

Theaet. Your reminder is just; there is still one sense remaining. The first was the image or expression of the mind in speech; the second, which has just been mentioned, is a way of reaching the whole by an enumeration of the elements. But what is the third?

Soc. That which would occur to many people; ability to tell the mark or sign of difference which distinguishes the thing in question from all others.

Theaet. Can you give me any example of such a definition?

Soc. As, for example, in the case of the sun, I think that you would be contented with the statement that the sun is the brightest of the heavenly bodies which revolve about the earth.

Theaet. Certainly.

Soc. Understand why: The reason is, as we were just now saying, that if you get at the difference and distinguishing characteristic of each thing, then, as many persons affirm, you will secure its explanation; but while you lay hold only of the common and not of the characteristic quality, your explanation will relate to all things to which this common quality belongs.

Theaet. I understand you, and it is in my judgement correct to call this definition [or explanation].

Soc. But he, who having right opinion about anything, can find out the difference which distinguishes it from other things will have come to *know* that of which before he had only an opinion.

Theaet. Yes; that is what we are maintaining.

Soc. Nevertheless, Theaetetus, on a nearer view, I find myself quite disappointed; the picture, which at a distance was not so bad, has now become altogether unintelligible.

Theaet. What do you mean?

Soc. I will endeavour to explain: I will suppose myself to have true opinion of you, and if to this I add your definition, then I have knowledge, but if not, opinion only.

Theaet. Yes.

Soc. The definition was assumed to be the interpretation of your difference.

Theaet. True.

Soc. But when I had only opinion, I had no conception of your distinguishing characteristics.

Theaet. I suppose not.

Soc. Then I must have conceived of some general or common nature which no more belonged to you than to another.

Theaet. True.

Soc. Tell me, now: How in that case could I have formed a judgement of you any more than of any one else? Suppose that I imagine Theaetetus to be a man who has nose, eyes, and mouth, and every other member complete; how would that enable me to distinguish Theaetetus from Theodorus, or from some outer barbarian?

Theaet. How could it?

Soc. Or if I had further conceived of you, not only as having nose and eyes, but as having a snub nose and prominent eyes, should I have any more notion of you than of myself and others who resemble me?

Theaet. Certainly not.

Soc. Surely I can have no conception of Theaetetus until your snub-nosedness has left an impression on my mind different from the snub-nosedness of all others whom I have ever seen, and until your other peculiarities have a like distinctness; and so when I meet you tomorrow the right opinion will be recalled?

Theaet. Most true.

Soc. Then right opinion also implies the perception of differences?

Theaet. Clearly.

Soc. What meaning, then, remains for the reason or explanation which we are told to add to right opinion? If the meaning is, that we should form an extra opinion of the way in which something differs from another thing, the proposal is ridiculous.

Theaet. How so?

Soc. We are bidden to acquire a right opinion of the differences which distinguish one thing from another, which is just what we already have, and so we go round and round; the revolution of the scytal, or pestle, or any other rotatory machine, in the same circles, is as nothing compared with such a requirement; and we may be truly described as the blind directing the blind; for to add those things which we already have, in order that we may learn what we already think, is like a soul utterly benighted.

Theaet. Tell me; what were you gong to say just now, when you asked the question?

Soc. If, my boy, the argument, in speaking of adding the definition, had used the word to "know," and not merely "have an opinion" of the difference, this which is the most promising of all the definitions of knowledge would have come to a pretty end, for to know is surely to acquire knowledge.

Theaet. True.

Soc. And so, when the question is asked, What is knowledge? this fair argument will answer "Right opinion with knowledge"—knowledge, that is, of difference, for this, as the said argument maintains, is adding the definition.

Theaet. That seems to be true.

Soc. But how utterly foolish, when we are asking what is knowledge, that the reply should only be, right opinion with knowledge whether of difference or of anything else! And so, Theaetetus, knowledge is neither sensation nor true opinion, nor yet definition and explanation accompanying and added to true opinion?

Theaet. I suppose not.

Soc. And are you still in labour and travail, my dear friend, or have you brought all that you have to say about knowledge to the birth?

Theaet. I am sure, Socrates, that you have elicited from me a good deal more than ever was in me.

Soc. And does not my art show that you have brought forth wind, and that the offspring of your brain are not worth bringing up?

Theaet. Very true.

Soc. But if, Theaetetus, you should ever conceive afresh, you will be all the better for the present investigation, and if not, you will be soberer and humbler and gentler to other men, and will be too modest to fancy that you know what you do not know. These are the limits of my art; I can no further go, nor do I know aught of the things which great and famous men know or have known in this or former ages. The office of a midwife I, like my mother, have received from God; she delivered women, and I deliver men; but they must be young and noble and fair.

Further Questions

1. Is all of our knowledge about the world derived from experience, or are we predisposed to know some things more quickly than we could have learned them on the basis of experience alone?
2. Had Plato known about genetics, how might he have modified his view that knowledge is recollection?

Further Readings

Fogelin, Robert J. *Pyrrhonian Reflections on Knowledge and Justification* (New York: Oxford University Press, 1994). A superb recent account of knowledge and skepticism.
Hintikka, Jaakko, and Kolak, Daniel. *Socrates and the Oracle* (forthcoming). A discussion that includes the limitations of knowledge and philosophy.
Kolak, Daniel. *From the Presocratics to the Present: A Personal Odyssey* (Mountain View, CA: Mayfield, 1998). Tells the story of philosophy by relating developments chronologically to the theme that philosophy is about unifying insights, not opposing systems of thought.
Nozick, Robert. *Philosophical Explanations* (Cambridge, Mass.: Harvard University Press, 1981). Includes an excellent short chapter on knowledge.

27   Meditations

RENÉ DESCARTES

Descartes was born in 1596 at La Haye in Touraine, France. When he was eight years old, his father, a councilor of the *parlement* of Rennes in Brittany, sent him to a Jesuit college, one of the most celebrated in Europe, where for ten years he studied literature, science, and philosophy. Somehow the young Descartes convinced the Jesuits to allow him not to have to get up until noon, so that he could "study in bed." He continued this practice for most of his life. After taking a degree in law (he never practiced) he took to fencing, horsemanship, and gambling, became a soldier, and served in three different armies—in the Netherlands, in Bavaria, and in Hungary. At thirty-three, disillusioned by "the book of the world," he moved to Holland and began writing and developing his iconoclastic thoughts. His radical departure from basing knowledge on accepted authority to basing it on one's own rational intuitions signaled the beginning of the "modern" age of philosophy. For twenty years, he wrote book after book and his reputation slowly grew. His *Meditations on First Philosophy* was quickly acknowledged as a radical criticism of all established philosophy and science. There were lots of furious objections, and the philosophers of the next century and a half spent much of their time trying to respond to the problems Descartes raised.

In 1633 he finished *The World,* a work in which he reaffirmed the "radical" Coperni-can hypothesis that the earth moves around the sun. But just before publication, he learned of Galileo's horrible troubles with the Inquisition and so immediately stopped publication. Some years later, he was labeled an atheist by the president of the University of Utrecht and promptly condemned by the local magistrates.

Descartes is certainly one of the most influential philosophers of all time. In addition to writing philosophical works, he tried to formulate a new system of science founded on mathematics, in the process making great contributions to mathematics and physics; he linked, for the first time, geometry to algebra—with the now famous Cartesian co-ordinate system named after him—thereby inventing analytic geometry. In discovering that geometrical representations could be represented algebraically, Descartes opened the door to the possibility of representing everything—the whole of nature—mathe-matically. Because size, figure, volume, and so on—representations of the objects we find in nature—are geometrical representations that, by Descartes' method, can be purely mathematically represented, it becomes possible to model all of nature purely mathematically.

In 1649 Queen Christina of Sweden invited him to visit her in Stockholm so that he could teach her his "new philosophy." The Queen, however, liked to take her lessons at five o'clock in the morning. After only a few months of having to get up so early, Descartes died.

The title *Meditations on First Philosophy,* from which the following two meditations are taken, is based on Aristotle's use of "first philosophy" to mean the *first principles of things, or metaphysics.* And so Descartes wrote: "Thus the whole of philosophy is like a tree, the roots are metaphysics, the trunk is physics, and the branches that rise from the trunk are all the other sciences."

Reading Questions

1. On what grounds does Descartes doubt evidence from his senses? People say, "Seeing is believing." Would Descartes agree? Why?
2. If you can't be certain of what the truth is based on your experience, how can you know anything at all? What is Descartes' answer?
3. What does Descartes mean by "clear and distinct"? Can your clear and distinct ideas be wrong?
4. *Why* does Descartes want to try to doubt everything?
5. Does he think that even mathematical truths like 5 + 2 = 7 are doubtful? Why?
6. What does Descartes think a person is?
7. What is the nature of the mind, according to Descartes? The nature of material bodies?
8. What does he try to show using the piece of wax?
9. Descartes' method is a *method of doubt:* accept nothing as true unless you are *absolutely one hundred percent certain* that it is so. Even if you consider a thing to be certain, if there is *any* possibility that you are mistaken, then you must doubt it. What does this leave you with? Of what beliefs are you most certain? How did you come to have them? Are they immune from doubt?
10. Before you read this selection, make a list of things of which you are *most* certain. Then, while reading, consider at what point your beliefs become questionable and why. How does this make you feel?
11. There is one thing about which Descartes is absolutely certain. What is it? How can he be so certain of this?

I OF THE THINGS WHICH MAY BE BROUGHT WITHIN THE SPHERE OF THE DOUBTFUL

IT IS NOW SOME YEARS since I detected how many were the false beliefs that I had from my earliest youth admitted as true, and how doubtful was everything I had since constructed on this basis; and from that time I was convinced that I must once for all seriously undertake to rid myself of all the opinions which I had formerly accepted, and commence to build anew from the foundation, if I wanted to establish any firm and permanent structure in the sciences. But as this enterprise appeared to be a very great one, I waited until I had attained an age so mature that I could not hope that at any later date I should be better fitted to execute my design. This reason caused me to delay so long that I should feel that I was doing wrong were I to occupy in deliberation the time that yet remains to me for action. To-day, then, since very opportunely for the plan I have in view I have delivered my mind from every care [and am happily agitated by no passions] and since I have procured for myself an assured leisure in a peaceable retirement, I shall at last seriously and freely address myself to the general upheaval of all my former opinions. . . .

Now for this object it is not necessary that I should show that all of these are false—I shall perhaps never arrive at this end. But inasmuch as reason already persuades me that I ought no less carefully to withhold my assent from matters which are not entirely certain and indubitable than from those which appear to me manifestly to be false, if I am able to find in each one some reason to doubt, this will suffice to justify my rejecting the whole. And for that end it will not be requisite that I should examine each in particular, which would be an endless undertaking; for owing to the fact that the destruction of the foundations of necessity brings with it the downfall of the rest of the edifice, I shall only in the first place attack those principles upon which all my former opinions rested.

All that up to the present time I have accepted as most true and certain I have learned either from the senses or through the senses; but it is sometimes proved to me that these senses are deceptive, and it is wiser not to trust entirely to any thing by which we have once been deceived.

But it may be that although the senses sometimes deceive us concerning things which are hardly perceptible, or very far away, there are yet many others to be met with as to which we cannot reasonably have any doubt, although we recognise them by their means. For example, there is the fact that I am here, seated by the fire, attired in a dressing gown, having this paper in my hands and other similar matters. And how could I deny that these hands and this body are mine, were it not perhaps that I compare myself to certain persons, devoid of sense, whose cerebella are so troubled and clouded by the violent vapours of black bile, that they constantly assure us that they think they are kings when they are really quite poor, or that they are clothed in purple when they are really without covering, or who imagine that they have an earthenware head or are nothing but pumpkins or are made of glass. But they are mad, and I should not be any the less insane were I to follow examples so extravagant.

At the same time I must remember that I am a man, and that consequently I am in the habit of sleeping, and in my dreams representing to myself the same things or sometimes even less probable things, than do those who are insane in their waking moments. How often has it happened to me that in the night I dreamt that I found myself in this particular place, that I was dressed and seated near the fire, whilst in reality I was lying undressed in bed! At this moment it does indeed seem to me that it is with eyes awake that I am looking at this paper; that this head which I move is not asleep, that it is deliberately and of set purpose that I extend my hand and perceive it; what happens in sleep does not appear so clear nor so distinct as does all this. But in thinking over this I remind myself that on many occasions I have in sleep been deceived by similar illusions, and in dwelling carefully on this reflection I see so manifestly that there are no certain indications by which we may clearly distinguish wakefulness from sleep that I am lost in astonishment. And my astonishment is such that it is almost capable of persuading me that I now dream.

Now let us assume that we are asleep and that all these particulars, e.g., that we open our eyes, shake our head, extend our hands, and so on, are but false delusions; and let us reflect that possibly neither our hands nor our whole body are such as they appear to us to be. At the same time we must at least confess that the things which are represented to us in sleep are like painted representations which can only have been formed as the counterparts of something real and true, and that in this way those general things at least, i.e., eyes, a head, hands, and a whole body, are not imaginary things, but things really existent. For, as a matter of fact, painters, even when they study with the greatest skill to represent sirens and satyrs by forms the most strange and extraordinary, cannot give them natures which are entirely new, but merely make a certain medley of the members of different animals; or if their imagination is extravagant enough to invent something so novel that nothing similar has ever before been seen, and that then their work represents a thing purely fictitious and absolutely false, it is certain all the same that the colours of which this is composed are necessarily real. And for the same reason, although these general things, to wit, [a body], eyes, a head, hands and such like, may be imaginary, we are bound at the same time to confess that there are at least some other objects yet more simple and more universal, which are real and true; and of these just in the same way as with certain real colours, all these images of things which dwell in our thoughts, whether true and real or false and fantastic, are formed.

To such a class of things pertains corporeal nature in general, and its extension, the figure of extended things, their quantity or magnitude and number, as also the place in which they are, the time which measures their duration, and so on.

That is possibly why our reasoning is not unjust when we conclude from this that Physics, Astronomy, Medicine and all other sciences which have as their end the consideration of composite things, are very dubious and uncertain; but that Arithmetic, Geometry and other sciences of that kind which only treat of things that are very simple and very general, without taking great trouble to ascertain whether they are actually existent or not, contain some measure of certainty and an element of the indubitable. For whether I am awake or asleep, two and three together always form five, and the square can never have more than four sides, and it does not seem possible that truths so clear and apparent can be suspected of any falsity [or uncertainty].

Nevertheless I have long had fixed in my mind the belief that an all-powerful God existed by whom I have been created such as I am. But how do I know that He has not brought it to pass that there is no earth, no heaven, no extended body, no magnitude, no place, and that nevertheless [I possess the perceptions of all these things and that] they seem to me to exist just exactly as I now see them? And, besides, as I sometimes imagine that others deceive themselves in the things which they think they know best, how do I know that I am not deceived every time that I add two and three, or count the sides of a square, or judge of things yet simpler, if anything simpler can be imagined? But possibly God has not desired that I should be thus deceived, for He is said to be supremely good. If, however, it is contrary to His goodness to have made me such that I constantly deceive myself, it would also appear to be contrary to His goodness to permit me to be sometimes deceived, and nevertheless I cannot doubt that He does permit this.

There may indeed be those who would prefer to deny the existence of a God so powerful, rather than believe that all other things are uncertain. But let us not oppose them for the present, and grant that all that is here said of a God is a fable; nevertheless in whatever way they suppose that I have arrived at the state of being that I have reached — whether they attribute it to fate or to accident, or make out that it is by a continual succession of antecedents, or by some other method — since to err and deceive oneself is a defect, it is clear that the greater will be the probability of my being so imperfect as to deceive myself ever, as is the Author to whom they assign my origin the less powerful. To these reasons I have certainly nothing to reply, but at the end I feel constrained to confess that there is nothing in all that I formerly believed to be true, of which I cannot in some measure doubt, and that not merely through want of thought or through levity, but for reasons which are very powerful and maturely considered; so that henceforth I ought not the less carefully to refrain from giving credence to these opinions than to that which is manifestly false, if I desire to arrive at any certainty [in the sciences].

But it is not sufficient to have made these remarks, we must also be careful to keep them in mind. For these ancient and commonly held opinions still revert frequently to my mind, long and familiar custom having given them the right to occupy my mind against my inclination and rendered them almost masters of my belief; nor will I ever lose the habit of deferring to them or of placing my confidence in them, so long as I consider them as they really are, i.e., opinions in some measure doubtful, as I have just shown, and at the same time highly probable, so that there is much more reason to believe in than to deny them. That is why I consider that I shall not be acting amiss, if, taking of set purpose a contrary belief, I allow myself to be deceived, and for a certain time pretend that all these opinions are entirely false and imaginary, until at last, having thus balanced my former prejudices with my latter [so that they cannot divert my opinions more to one side than to the other], my judgment will no longer be dominated by bad usage or turned away from the right knowledge of the truth. For I am assured that there can be neither peril nor error in this course, and that I cannot at present yield too much to distrust, since I am not considering the question of action, but only of knowledge.

I shall then suppose, not that God who is supremely good and the fountain of truth, but some evil genius not less powerful than deceitful, has employed his whole energies in deceiving me; I shall consider that the heavens, the earth, colours, figures, sound, and all other external things are nought but the illusions and dreams of which this genius has availed himself in order to lay traps for my credulity; I shall consider myself as having no hands, no eyes, no flesh, no blood, nor any senses, yet falsely believing myself to possess all these things; I shall remain obstinately attached to this idea, and if by this means it is not in my power to arrive at the knowledge of any truth, I may at least do what is in my power [i.e., suspend my judgment], and with firm purpose avoid giving credence to any false thing, or being imposed upon by this arch deceiver, however powerful and deceptive he may be. But this task is a laborious one, and in-

sensibly a certain lassitude leads me into the course of my ordinary life. And just as a captive who in sleep enjoys an imaginary liberty, when he begins to suspect that his liberty is but a dream, fears to awaken, and conspires with these agreeable illusions that the deception may be prolonged, so insensibly of my own accord I fall back into my former opinions, and I dread awakening from this slumber, lest the laborious wakefulness which would follow the tranquility of this repose should have to be spent not in daylight, but in the excessive darkness of the difficulties which have just been discussed.

II

The Meditation of yesterday filled my mind with so many doubts that it is no longer in my power to forget them. And yet I do not see in what manner I can resolve them; and, just as if I had all of a sudden fallen into very deep water, I am so disconcerted that I can neither make certain of setting my feet on the bottom, nor can I swim and so support myself on the surface. I shall nevertheless make an effort and follow anew the same path as that on which I yesterday entered, i.e., I shall proceed by setting aside all that in which the least doubt could be supposed to exist, just as if I had discovered that it was absolutely false; and I shall ever follow in this road until I have met with something which is certain, or at least, if I can do nothing else, until I have learned for certain that there is nothing in the world that is certain. Archimedes, in order that he might draw the terrestrial globe out of its place, and transport it elsewhere, demanded only that one point should be fixed and immoveable; in the same way I shall have the right to conceive high hopes if I am happy enough to discover one thing only which is certain and indubitable.

I suppose, then, that all the things that I see are false; I persuade myself that nothing has ever existed of all that my fallacious memory represents to me. I consider that I possess no senses; I imagine that body, figure, extension, movement and place are but the fictions of my mind. What, then, can be esteemed as true? Perhaps nothing at all, unless that there is nothing in the world that is certain.

But how can I know there is not something different from those things that I have just considered, of which one cannot have the slightest doubt? Is there not some God, or some other being by whatever name we call it, who puts these reflections into my mind? That is not necessary, for is it not possible that I am capable of producing them myself? I myself, am I not at least something? But I have already denied that I had senses and body. Yet I hesitate, for what follows from that? Am I so dependent on body and senses that I cannot exist without these? But I was persuaded that there was nothing in all the world, that there was no heaven, no earth, that there were no minds, nor any bodies: was I not then likewise persuaded that I did not exist? Not at all; of a surety I myself did exist since I persuaded myself of something [or merely because I thought of something]. But there is some deceiver or other, very powerful and very cunning, who ever employs his ingenuity in deceiving me. Then without doubt I exist also if he deceives me, and let him deceive me as much as he will, he can never cause me to be nothing so long as I think that I am something. So that after having reflected well and carefully examined all things, we must come to the definite conclusion that this proposition: I am, I exist, is necessarily true each time that I pronounce it, or that I mentally conceive it.

But I do not yet know clearly enough what I am, I who am certain that I am; and hence I must be careful to see that I do not imprudently take some other object in place of myself, and thus that I do not go astray in respect of this knowledge that I hold to be the most certain and most evident of all that I have formerly learned. That is why I shall now consider anew what I believed myself to be before I embarked upon these last reflections; and of my former opinions I shall withdraw all that might even in a small degree be invalidated by the reasons which I have just brought forward, in order that there may be nothing at all left beyond what is absolutely certain and indubitable.

What then did I formerly believe myself to be? Undoubtedly I believed myself to be a man. But what is a man? Shall I say a reasonable animal? Certainly not; for then I should have to inquire what an animal is, and what is reasonable; and thus from a single question I should insensibly fall into an infinitude of others more difficult; and I should not wish to waste the little time and leisure remaining to me in trying to unravel subtleties like these. But

I shall rather stop here to consider the thoughts which of themselves spring up in my mind, and which were not inspired by anything beyond my own nature alone when I applied myself to the consideration of my being. In the first place, then, I considered myself as having a face, hands, arms, and all that system of members composed of bones and flesh as seen in a corpse which I designated by the name of body. In addition to this I considered that I was nourished, that I walked, that I felt, and that I thought, and I referred all these actions to the soul: but I did not stop to consider what the soul was, or if I did stop, I imagined that it was something extremely rare and subtle like a wind, a flame, or an ether, which was spread throughout my grosser parts. As to body I had no matter of doubt about its nature, but thought I had a very clear knowledge of it; and if I had desired to explain it according to the notions that I had then formed of it, I should have described it thus: By the body I understand all that which can be defined by a certain figure: something which can be confined in a certain place, and which can fill a given space in such a way that every other body will be excluded from it; which can be perceived either by touch, or by sight, or by hearing, or by taste, or by smell: which can be moved in many ways not, in truth, by itself, but by something which is foreign to it, by which it is touched [and from which it receives impressions]: for to have the power of self-movement, as also of feeling or of thinking, I did not consider to appertain to the nature of body: on the contrary, I was rather astonished to find that faculties similar to them existed in some bodies.

But what am I, now that I suppose that there is a certain genius which is extremely powerful, and, if I may say so, malicious, who employs all his powers in deceiving me? Can I affirm that I possess the least of all those things which I have just said pertain to the nature of body? I pause to consider, I revolve all these things in my mind, and I find none of which I can say that it pertains to me. It would be tedious to stop to enumerate them. Let us pass to the attributes of soul and see if there is any one which is in me? What of nutrition or walking [the first mentioned]? But if it is so that I have no body it is also true that I can neither walk nor take nourishment. Another attribute is sensation. But one cannot feel without body, and besides I have thought I perceived many things during sleep that I recognised in my waking moments as not having been experienced at all. What of thinking? I find here that thought is an attribute that belongs to me; it alone cannot be separated from me. I am, I exist, that is certain. But how often? Just when I think; for it might possibly be the case if I ceased entirely to think, that I should likewise cease altogether to exist. I do not now admit anything which is not necessarily true: to speak accurately I am not more than a thing which thinks, that is to say a mind or a soul, or an understanding, or a reason, which are terms whose significance was formerly unknown to me. I am, however, a real thing and really exist; but what thing? I have answered: a thing which thinks.

And what more? I shall exercise my imagination [in order to see if I am not something more]. I am not a collection of members which we call the human body: I am not a subtle air distributed through these members, I am not a wind, a fire, a vapour, a breath, nor anything at all which I can imagine or conceive; because I have assumed that all these were nothing. Without changing that supposition I find that I only leave myself certain of the fact that I am somewhat. But perhaps it is true that these same things which I supposed were non-existent because they are unknown to me, are really not different from the self which I know. I am not sure about this, I shall not dispute about it now; I can only give judgment on things that are known to me. I know that I exist, and I inquire what I am, I whom I know to exist. But it is very certain that the knowledge of my existence taken in its precise significance does not depend on things whose existence is not yet known to me; consequently it does not depend on those which I can feign in imagination. And indeed the very term *feign* in imagination proves to me my error, for I really do this if I image myself a something, since to imagine is nothing else than to contemplate the figure or image of a corporeal thing. But I already know for certain that I am, and that it may be that all these images, and, speaking generally, all things that relate to the nature of body are nothing but dreams [and chimeras]. For this reason I see clearly that I have as little reason to say, "I shall stimulate my imagination in order to know more distinctly what I am," than if I were to say, "I am now awake, and I perceive somewhat that is real and true: but because I do not yet perceive it distinctly

enough, I shall go to sleep of express purpose, so that my dreams may represent the perception with greatest truth and evidence." And, thus, I know for certain that nothing of all that I can understand by means of my imagination belongs to this knowledge which I have of myself, and that it is necessary to recall the mind from this mode of thought with the utmost diligence in order that it may be able to know its own nature with perfect distinctness.

But what then am I? A thing which thinks. What is a thing which thinks? It is a thing which doubts, understands, [conceives], affirms, denies, wills, refuses, which also imagines and feels.

Certainly it is no small matter if all these things pertain to my nature. But why should they not so pertain? Am I not that being who now doubts nearly everything, who nevertheless understands certain things, who affirms that only one is true, who denies all the others, who desires to know more, is averse from being deceived, who imagines many things, sometimes indeed despite his will, and who perceives many likewise, as by the intervention of the bodily organs? Is there nothing in all this which is as true as it is certain that I exist, even though I should always sleep and though he who has given me being employed all his ingenuity in deceiving me? Is there likewise any one of these attributes which can be distinguished from my thought, or which might be said to be separated from myself? For it is so evident of itself that it is I who doubts, who understands, and who desires, that there is no reason here to add anything to explain it. And I have certainly the power of imagining likewise; for although it may happen (as I formerly supposed) that none of the things which I imagine are true, nevertheless this power of imagining does not cease to be really in use, and it forms part of my thought. Finally, I am the same who feels, that is to say, who perceives certain things, as by the organs of sense, since in truth I see light, I hear noise, I feel heat. But it will be said that these phenomena are false and that I am dreaming. Let it be so; still it is at least quite certain that it seems to me that I see light, that I hear noise and that I feel heat. That cannot be false; properly speaking it is what is in me called feeling[1]; and used in this precise sense that is no other thing than thinking.

[1]Sentire.

From this time I begin to know what I am with a little more clearness and distinction than before; but nevertheless it still seems to me, and I cannot prevent myself from thinking, that corporeal things, whose images are framed by thought, which are tested by the senses, are much more distinctly known than that obscure part of me which does not come under the imagination. Although really it is very strange to say that I know and understand more distinctly these things whose existence seems to me dubious, which are unknown to me, and which do not belong to me, than others of the truth of which I am convinced, which are known to me and which pertain to my real nature, in a word, than myself. But I see clearly how the case stands: my mind loves to wander, and cannot yet suffer itself to be retained within the just limits of truth. Very good, let us once more give it the freest rein, so that, when afterwards we seize the proper occasion for pulling up, it may the more easily be regulated and controlled.

Let us begin by considering the commonest matters, those which we believe to be the most distinctly comprehended, to wit, the bodies which we touch and see; not indeed bodies in general, for these general ideas are usually a little more confused, but let us consider one body in particular. Let us take, for example, this piece of wax: it has been taken quite freshly from the hive, and it has not yet lost the sweetness of the honey which it contains; it still retains somewhat of the odour of the flowers from which it has been culled; its colour, its figure, its size are apparent; it is hard, cold, easily handled, and if you strike it with the finger, it will emit a sound. Finally all the things which are requisite to cause us distinctly to recognise a body, are met with in it. But notice that while I speak and approach the fire what remained of the taste is exhaled, the smell evaporates, the colour alters, the figure is destroyed, the size increases, it becomes liquid, it heats, scarcely can one handle it, and when one strikes it, no sound is emitted. Does the same wax remain after this change? We must confess that it remains; none would judge otherwise. What then did I know so distinctly in this piece of wax? It could certainly be nothing of all that the senses brought to my notice, since all these things which fall under taste, smell, sight, touch, and hearing, are found to be changed, and yet the same wax remains.

Perhaps it was what I now think, viz. that this wax was not that sweetness of honey, nor that agreeable scent of flowers, nor that particular whiteness, nor that figure, nor that sound, but simply a body which a little while before appeared to me as perceptible under these forms, and which is now perceptible under others. But what, precisely, is it that I imagine when I form such conceptions? Let us attentively consider this, and, abstracting from all that does not belong to the wax, let us see what remains. Certainly nothing remains excepting a certain extended thing which is flexible and movable. But what is the meaning of flexible and movable? Is it not that I imagine that this piece of wax being round is capable of becoming square and of passing from a square to a triangular figure? No, certainly it is not that, since I imagine it admits of an infinitude of similar changes, and I nevertheless do not know how to compass the infinitude by my imagination, and consequently this conception which I have of the wax is not brought about by the faculty of imagination. What now is this extension? Is it not also unknown? For it becomes greater when the wax is melted, greater when it is boiled, and greater still when the heat increases; and I should not conceive [clearly] according to truth what wax is, if I did not think that even this piece that we are considering is capable of receiving more variations in extension than I have ever imagined. We must then grant that I could not even understand through the imagination what this piece of wax is, and that it is my mind alone which perceives it. I say this piece of wax in particular, for as to wax in general it is yet clearer. But what is thin piece of wax which cannot be understood excepting by the [understanding or] mind? It is certainly the same that I see, touch, imagine, and finally it is the same which I have always believed it to be from the beginning. But what must particularly be observed is that its perception is neither an act of vision, nor of touch, nor of imagination, and has never been such although it may have appeared formerly to be so, but only an intuition of the mind, which may be imperfect and confused as it was formerly, or clear and distinct as it is at present, according as my attention is more or less directed to the elements which are found in it, and of which it is composed.

Yet in the meantime I am greatly astonished when I consider [the great feebleness of mind] and its proneness to fall [insensibly] into error; for although without giving expression to my thoughts I consider all this in my own mind, words often impeded me and I am almost deceived by the terms of ordinary language. For we say that we see the same wax, if it is present, and not that we simply judge that it is the same from its having the same colour and figure. From this I should conclude that I knew the wax by means of vision and not simply by the intuition of the mind; unless by chance I remember that, when looking from a window and saying I see men who pass in the street, I really do not see them, but infer that what I see is men, just as I say that I see wax. And yet what do I see from the window but hats and coats which may cover automatic machines? Yet I judge these to be men. And similarly solely by the faculty of judgment which rests in my mind, I comprehend that which I believed I saw with my eyes.

A man who makes it his aim to raise his knowledge above the common should be ashamed to derive the occasion for doubting from the forms of speech invented by the vulgar; I prefer to pass on and consider whether I had a more evident and perfect conception of what the wax was when I first perceived it, and when I believed I knew it by means of the external senses or at least by the common sense as it is called, that is to say by the imaginative faculty, or whether my present conception is clearer now that I have most carefully examined what it is, and in what way it can be known. It would certainly be absurd to doubt as to this. For what was there in this first perception which was distinct? What was there which might not as well have been perceived by any of the animals? But when I distinguish the wax from its external forms, and when, just as if I had taken from it its vestments, I consider it quite naked, it is certain that although some error may still be found in my judgment, I can nevertheless not perceive it thus without a human mind.

But finally what shall I say of this mind, that is, of myself, for up to this point I do not admit in myself anything but mind? What then, I who seem to perceive this piece of wax so distinctly, do I not know myself, not only with much more truth and certainty, but also with much more distinctness and clearness? For if I judge that the wax is or exists from the fact that I see it, it certainly follows much more clearly that I am or that I exist myself from the fact that I see it. For it may be that what I see is not really wax, it may also be that I do not possess eyes with which to see anything; but it cannot be that when I see, or (for I no longer take account of the distinction) when I think I see, that I myself who think am nought. So if I judge that the wax exists from the fact that I touch it, the same thing will follow, to wit, that I am; and if I judge that my imaginations, or some other cause, whatever it is, persuades me that the wax exists, I shall still conclude the same. And what I have here remarked of wax may be applied to all other things which are external to me [and which are met with outside of me]. And further, if the [notion or] perception of wax has seemed to me clearer and more distinct, not only after the sight or the touch, but also after many other causes have rendered it quite manifest to me, with how much more [evidence] and distinctness must it be said that I now know myself, since all the reasons which contribute to the knowledge of wax, or any other body whatever, are yet better proofs of the nature of my mind! And there are so many other things in the mind itself which may contribute to the elucidation of its nature, that those which depend on body such as these just mentioned, hardly merit being taken into account.

But finally here I am, having insensibly reverted to the point I desired, for, since it is now manifest to me that even bodies are not properly speaking known by the senses or by the faculty of imagination, but by the understanding only, and since they are not known from the fact that they are seen or touched, but only because they are understood, I see clearly that there is nothing which is easier for me to know than my mind. But because it is difficult to rid oneself so promptly of an opinion to which one was accustomed for so long, it will be well that I should halt a little at this point, so that by the length of my meditation I may more deeply imprint on my memory this new knowledge.

Further Questions

1. Descartes' famous proof of his own existence is one of the great moments in the history of Western philosophy. Instead of basing science, mathematics, religion, and logic on the collective knowledge of humanity, Descartes bases it on the fact of his own existence. Do you suppose this had any relevance for the subsequent individualism of Western civilization?
2. *Epistemological skepticism*, roughly, is the doctrine that none of our beliefs about ourselves and the world are ever adequately justified. Descartes, however, is generally regarded as espousing the doctrine of *methodological skepticism*, which consists in doubting all your beliefs until you reach a belief that cannot be doubted. Based on what you've just read, what is the crucial factor in Descartes' philosophy that would make him the latter, not the former, type of skeptic? Do you agree? Why?
3. Descartes claims that the mind is known more directly than the body. He concludes that the mind is entirely different from the body. Do you agree with his conclusion?
4. Descartes finds that he can doubt the existence of everything except himself. Can you imagine how he might be wrong even about this? Think again about this question when you read the first three selections of the section of this book titled "Reality."

Further Readings

Frankfurt, Harry. *Demons, Dreamers, and Madmen: The Defense of Reason in Descartes' Meditations.* Indianapolis, IN: Bobbs-Merrill, 1970.
Kenny, Anthony. *Descartes: A Study of His Philosophy.* New York: Random House, 1968.
Kolak, Daniel. *In Search of Myself: Life, Death and Personal Identity.* Belmont, CA: Wadsworth, 1999. Descartes encounters Philosophy, the Goddess of Wisdom, among the ruins of Delphi.

Where Our Ideas Come From   28

JOHN LOCKE

This selection from Locke's *Essay Concerning Human Understanding* (1690) contains the core of Locke's attempt to explain the idea that the ideas in terms of which we express our knowledge of the world are derived from experience. In a memorable image, Locke says that the mind at birth is a *tabula rasa*, a blank page, on which sense experience subsequently leaves its marks. These marks then become the raw data from which our knowledge of the world is constructed.

A brief biography of Locke appears on page 120.

Reading Questions

1. What does Locke mean by *idea*? By *quality*?
2. How does Locke distinguish between primary and secondary qualities? What is the importance of this distinction in Locke's account?
3. What does Locke mean by "perception"? Where do perceptions come from?
4. According to Locke, do you have direct perceptions of objects out there in the external world? How does he think objects are able to affect our senses?
5. What is the cause of simple ideas? How are ideas known by the mind?
6. If we cannot see an idea with our eyes—how, then?
7. What does Locke mean by "privation"?

SOME FURTHER CONSIDERATIONS CONCERNING OUR SIMPLE IDEAS OF SENSATION

1. POSITIVE IDEAS FROM PRIVATIVE CAUSES. — Concerning the simple ideas of sensation it is to be considered, that whatsoever is so constituted in nature as to be able by affecting our senses to cause any perception in the mind, doth thereby produce in the understanding a simple idea; which, whatever be the external cause of it, when it comes to be taken notice of by our discerning faculty, it is by the mind looked on and considered there to be a real positive idea in the understanding, as much as any other whatsoever; though perhaps the cause of it be but a privation in the subject.

2. Thus the ideas of heat and cold, light and darkness, white and black, motion and rest, are equally clear and positive ideas in the mind; though perhaps some of the causes which produce them are barely privations in those subjects from whence our senses derive those ideas. These the understanding, in its view of them, considers all as distinct positive ideas without taking notice of the causes that produce them; which is an inquiry not belonging to the idea as it is in the understanding, but to the nature of the things existing without us. These are two very different things, and carefully to be distinguished; it being one thing to perceive and know the idea of white or black, and quite another to examine what kind of particles they must be, and how ranged in the superficies, to make any object appear white or black.

3. A painter or dyer who never inquired into their causes, hath the ideas of white and black and other colours as clearly, perfectly, and distinctly in his understanding, and perhaps more distinctly than the philosopher who hath busied himself in considering their natures, and thinks he knows how far either of them is in its cause positive or privative; and the idea of black is no less positive in his mind than that of white, however the cause of that colour in the external object may be only a privation.

4. If it were the design of my present undertaking to inquire into the natural causes and manner of perception, I should offer this as a reason why a privative cause might, in some cases at least, produce a positive idea, viz., that all sensation being produced in us only by different degrees and modes of motion in our animal spirits, variously agitated by external objects, the abatement of any former motion must as necessarily produce a new sensation as the variation or increase of it; and so introduce a new idea, which depends only on a different motion of the animal spirits in that organ.

5. But whether this be so or not I will not here determine, but appeal to every one's own experience, whether the shadow of a man, though it consists of nothing but the absence of light (and the more the absence of light is, the more discernible is the shadow), does not, when a man looks on it, cause as clear and positive an idea in his mind as a man himself, though covered over with clear sunshine! And the picture of a shadow is a positive thing. Indeed, we have negative names, [which stand not directly for positive ideas, but for their absence, such as *insipid, silence, nihil, & c.,* which words denote positive ideas, *v. g., taste, sound, being,* with a signification of their absence].

6. *Positive ideas from privative causes.* — And thus one may truly be said to see darkness. For, supposing a hole perfectly dark, from whence no light is reflected, it is certain one may see the figure of it, or it may be painted; or whether the ink I write with make any other idea, is a question. The privative causes I have here assigned of positive ideas are according to the common opinion; but, in truth, it will be hard to determine whether there be really any ideas from a privative cause, till it be determined whether rest be any more a privation than motion.

7. *Ideas in the mind, qualities in bodies.* — To discover the nature of our ideas the better, and to discourse of them intelligibly, it will be convenient to distinguish them, as they are ideas or perceptions in our minds, and as they are modifications of matter in the bodies that cause such perceptions in us; that so we may not think (as perhaps usually is done) that they are exactly the images and resemblances of something inherent in the subject; most of those of sensation being in the mind no more the likeness of something existing without us than the names that stand for them are the likeness of

From John Locke, An Essay Concerning Human Understanding. *First published in 1690.*

our ideas, which yet upon hearing they are apt to excite in us.

8. Whatsoever the mind perceives in itself, or is the immediate object of perception, thought, or understanding, that I call "idea"; and the power to produce any idea in our mind, I call "quality" of the subject wherein that power is. Thus a snowball having the power to produce in us the ideas of white, cold, and round, the powers to produce those ideas in us as they are in the snowball, I call "qualities"; and as they are sensations or perceptions in our understandings, I call them "ideas"; which ideas, if I speak of them sometimes as in the things themselves, I would be understood to mean those qualities in the objects which produce them in us.

9. *Primary qualities.*—[Qualities thus considered in bodies are, First, such as are utterly inseparable from the body, in what estate soever it be;] and such as, in all the alterations and changes it suffers, all the force can be used upon it, it constantly keeps; and such as sense constantly finds in every particle of matter which has bulk enough to be perceived, and the mind finds inseparable from every particle of matter, though less than to make itself singly be perceived by our senses: *v. g.*, take a grain of wheat, divide it into two parts, each part has still solidity, extension, figure, and mobility; divide it again, and it retains still the same qualities: and so divide it on till the parts become insensible, they must retain still each of them all those qualities. For, division (which is all that a mill or pestle or any other body does upon another, in reducing it to insensible parts) can never take away either solidity, extension, figure, or mobility from any body, but only makes two or more distinct separate masses of matter of that which was but one before; all which distinct masses, reckoned as so many distinct bodies, after division, make a certain number. [These I call *original* or *primary* qualities of body, which I think we may observe to produce simple ideas in us, viz., solidity, extension, figure, motion or rest, and number.]

10. *Secondary qualities.*—Secondly. Such qualities, which in truth are nothing in the objects themselves, but powers to produce various sensations in us by their primary qualities, *i.e.,* by the bulk, figure, texture, and motion of their insensible parts, as colours, sounds, tastes &c., these I call *secondary* qualities. To these might be added a

third sort, which are allowed to be barely powers, though they are as much real qualities in the subject as those which I, to comply with the common way of speaking, call qualities, but, for distinction, *secondary* qualities. For, the power in fire to produce a new colour or consistency in wax or clay, by its primary qualities, is as much a quality in fire as the power it has to produce in me a new idea or sensation of warmth or burning, which I felt not before, by the same primary qualities, viz., the bulk, texture, and motion of its insensible parts.

11. [*How primary qualities produce their ideas.*—The next thing to be considered is, how bodies produce ideas in us; and that is manifestly by impulse, the only way which we can conceive bodies to operate in.]

12. If, then, external objects be not united to our minds when they produce ideas therein, and yet we perceive these original qualities in such of them as singly fall under our senses, it is evident that some motion must be thence continued by our nerves, or animal spirits, by some parts of our bodies, to the brains or the seat of sensation, there to produce in our minds the particular ideas we have of them. And since the extension, figure, number, and motion of bodies of an observable bigness, may be perceived at a distance by the sight, it is evident some singly imperceptible bodies must come from them to the eyes, and thereby convey to the brain some motion which produces these ideas which we have of them in us.

13. *How secondary.*—After the same manner that the ideas of these original qualities are produced in us, we may conceive that the ideas of secondary qualities are also produced, viz., by the operation of insensible particles on our senses. For it being manifest that there are bodies, and good store of bodies, each whereof are so small that we cannot by any of our senses discover either their bulk, figure, or motion (as is evident in the particles of the air and water, and other extremely smaller than those, perhaps as much smaller than the particles of air or water as the particles of air or water are smaller than peas or hailstones): let us suppose at present that the different motions and figures, bulk and number, of such particles, affecting the several organs of our senses, produce in us those different sensations which we have from the colours and smells of bodies, *v.g.,* that a violet, by the impulse of such insensible particles of matter of peculiar

figures and bulks, and in different degrees and modifications of their motions, causes the ideas of the blue colour and sweet scent of that flower to be produced in our minds; it being no more impossible to conceive that God should annex such ideas to such motions, with which they have no similitude, than that he should annex the idea of pain to the motion of a piece of steel dividing our flesh, with which the idea hath no resemblance.

14. What I have said concerning colours and smells may be understood also of tastes and sounds, and other the like sensible qualities; which, whatever reality we by mistake attribute to them, are in truth nothing in the objects themselves, but powers to produce various sensations in us, and depend on those primary qualities, viz., bulk, figure, texture, and motion of parts [as I have said].

15. *Ideas of primary qualities are resemblances; of secondary, not.* — From whence I think it is easy to draw this observation, that the ideas of primary qualities of bodies are resemblances of them, and their patterns do really exist in the bodies themselves; but the ideas produced in us by these secondary qualities have no resemblance of them at all. There is nothing like our ideas existing in the bodies themselves. They are, in the bodies we denominate from them, only a power to produce those sensations in us; and what is sweet, blue, or warm in idea, is but the certain bulk, figure, and motion of the insensible parts in the bodies themselves, which we call so.

16. Flame is denominated *hot* and *light;* snow, *white* and *cold;* and manna *white* and *sweet,* from the ideas they produce in us, which qualities are commonly thought to be the same in those bodies that those ideas are in us, the one the perfect resemblance of the other, as they are in a mirror; and it would by most men be judged very extravagant, if one should say otherwise. And yet he that will consider that the same fire that at one distance produces in us the sensation of warmth, does at a nearer approach produce in us the far different sensation of pain, ought to bethink himself what reason he has to say, that this idea of warmth which was produced in him the same way is not in the fire. Why is whiteness and coldness in snow and pain not, when it produces the one and the other idea in us, and can do neither but by the bulk, figure, number, and motion of its solid parts?

17. The particular bulk, number, figure, and motion of the parts of fire or snow are really in them, whether any one's senses perceive them or no; and therefore they may be called *real* qualities, because they really exist in those bodies. But light, heat, whiteness, or coldness, are no more really in them than sickness or pain is in manna. Take away the sensation of them; let not the eyes see light or colours, nor the ears hear sounds; let the palate not taste, nor the nose smell; and all colours, tastes, odours, and sounds, as they are such particular ideas, vanish and cease, and are reduced to their causes, *i.e.,* bulk, figure, and motion of parts.

Further Questions

1. Can you think of any ideas you have that are not derived from experience?
2. Locke claimed that the mind is empty until provided with data by experience. Is it an objection to Locke's view that we seem predisposed to learn some things, for example, language, much more easily than others?

Further Readings

Ayer, A. J. *The Foundations of Empirical Knowledge.* New York: Macmillan, 1940. A clear, modern development of Lockean themes.

Russell, Bertrand. *A History of Western Philosophy.* New York: Simon & Schuster, 1945, Chs. 13–15. An excellent brief summary and critique of Locke's views.

To Be Is to Be Perceived   **29**

GEORGE BERKELEY

George Berkeley was born in 1685 in Ireland. At the age of 15, he entered Trinity College, Dublin, and by the time he was 22, he was lecturing on Greek, Hebrew, and divinity. He wanted to open a college in Bermuda for Indians and young American colonists but was forced to drop the project. He visited and gave much encouragement to Yale and Harvard; Berkeley, California was named after him. Back in Ireland, he became an Anglican bishop, devoting himself to the spiritual betterment of the Irish. In 1744 he started the practice of drinking tar water as a general medicine and wrote a spirited treatise in defense of this practice. Eight years later, he died.

Berkeley is best known for his "idealist" or "immaterialist" doctrine—that the existence of sensible objects consists solely in their being perceived. Because color exists only when seen, sound only when heard, shape only when seen or touched, to imagine any of these existing independently of mind, argued Berkeley, is a grave logical error. Among his best known philosophical works are *Treatise Concerning the Principles of Human Knowledge* (1710) and *Three Dialogues Between Hylas and Philonous* (1713), both written while he was in his twenties.

Reading Questions

1. How would Berkeley answer the famous question, "When a tree falls in the forest and there is no one there to hear it, does it make a sound?"
2. What does he mean by the distinction between "primary" and "secondary" qualities? Which are the real qualities, which the subjective?
3. By "material substance" Berkeley means an inert, senseless substance that has primary qualities but no secondary qualities. How does he argue against the existence of such a substance?
4. According to Berkeley, the chair you are sitting on does not exist unless it is being perceived. Do you agree with this strange thesis? If not, what is your *argument* against it?
5. In Berkeley's view, what are the objects of our knowledge? Of what are objects made?
6. What does he mean by *exist*?
7. Is there anything that it is impossible for a person to conceive?
8. Why is the idea of matter contradictory?
9. What is the difference between real and imaginary? Between God and reality?

1. IT IS EVIDENT TO ANY ONE who takes a survey of the *objects of human knowledge,* that they are either *ideas* actually imprinted on the senses; or else such as are perceived by attending to the passions and operations of the mind; or lastly, *ideas* formed by help of memory and imagination—either compounding, dividing, or barely representing those originally perceived in the aforesaid ways. By sight I have the ideas of light and colours, with their several degrees and variations. By touch I perceive hard and soft, heat and cold, motion and resistance; and of all these more and less either as to quantity or degree.

From A Treatise Concerning the Principles of Human Knowledge. *First published in 1710.*

Smelling furnishes me with odours; the palate with tastes; the hearing conveys sounds to the mind in all their variety of tone and composition.

And as several of these are observed to accompany each other, they come to be marked by one name, and so to be reputed as one *thing*. Thus, for example, a certain colour, taste, smell, figure and consistence having been observed to go together, are accounted one distinct thing, signified by the name apple; other collections of ideas constitute a stone, a tree, a book, and the like sensible things; which as they are pleasing or disagreeable excite the passions of love, hatred, joy, grief, and so forth.

2. But, besides all that endless variety of ideas or objects of knowledge, there is likewise Something which knows or perceives them; and exercises divers operations, as willing, imagining, remembering, about them. This perceiving, active being is what I call *mind, spirit, soul,* or *myself.* By which words I do not denote any one of my ideas, but a thing entirely distinct from them, wherein they exist, or, which is the same thing, whereby they are perceived; for the existence of an idea consists in being perceived.

3. That neither our thoughts, nor passions, nor ideas formed by the imagination, exist without the mind is what everybody will allow. And to me it seems no less evident that the various sensations or ideas imprinted on the Sense, however blended or combined together (that is, whatever objects they compose), cannot exist otherwise than in a mind perceiving them. I think an intuitive knowledge may be obtained of this, by any one that shall attend to what is meant by the term exist when applied to sensible things. The table I write on I say exists; that is, I see and feel it; and if I were out of my study I should say it existed; meaning thereby that if I was in my study I might perceive it, or that some other spirit actually does perceive it. There was an odour, that is, it was smelt; there was a sound, that is, it was heard; a colour or figure, and it was perceived by sight or touch. This is all that I can understand by these and the like expressions. For as to what is said of the *absolute* existence of unthinking things, without any relation to their being perceived, that is to me perfectly unintelligible. Their *esse* is *percipi;* nor is it possible they should have any existence out of the minds or thinking things which perceive them.

4. It is indeed an opinion strangely prevailing amongst men, that houses, mountains, rivers, and in a word all sensible objects, have an existence, natural or real, distinct from their being perceived by the understanding. But, with how great an assurance and acquiescence soever this Principle may be entertained in the world, yet whoever shall find in his heart to call it in question may, if I mistake not, perceive it to involve a manifest contradiction. For, what are the forementioned objects but the things we perceive by sense? and what do we perceive besides our own ideas or sensations? and is it not plainly repugnant that any one of these, or any combination of them, should exist unperceived?

5. If we thoroughly examine this tenet it will, perhaps, be found at bottom to depend on the doctrine of *abstract ideas.* For can there be a nicer strain of abstraction than to distinguish the existence of sensible objects from their being perceived, so as to conceive them existing unperceived? Light and colours, heat and cold, extension and figures — in a word the things we see and feel — what are they but so many sensations, notions, ideas, or impressions on the sense? and is it possible to separate, even in thought, any of these from perception? For my part, I might as easily divide a thing from itself. I may, indeed, divide in my thoughts, or conceive apart from each other, those things which perhaps I never perceived by sense so divided. Thus, I imagine the trunk of a human body without the limbs, or conceive the smell of a rose without thinking on the rose itself. So far, I will not deny, I can abstract; if that may properly be called *abstraction* which extends only to the conceiving separately such objects as it is possible may really exist or be actually perceived asunder. But my conceiving or imagining power does not extend beyond the possibility of real existence or perception. Hence, as it is impossible for me to see or feel anything without an actual sensation of that thing, so it is impossible for me to conceive in my thoughts any sensible thing or object distinct from the sensation or perception of it. [In truth, the object and the sensation are the same thing, and cannot therefore be abstracted from each other.]

6. Some truths there are so near and obvious to the mind that a man need only open his eyes to see them. Such I take this important one to be, viz., that all the choir of heaven and furniture of

the earth, in a word all those bodies which compose the mighty frame of the world, have not any subsistence without a mind; that their *being* is to be perceived or known; that consequently so long as they are not actually perceived by me, or do not exist in my mind, or that of any other created spirit, they must either have no existence at all, or else subsist in the mind of some Eternal Spirit: it being perfectly unintelligible, and involving all the absurdity of abstraction, to attribute to any single part of them an existence independent of a spirit. To be convinced of which, the reader need only reflect, and try to separate in his own thoughts the *being* of a sensible thing from its *being perceived*.

7. From what has been said it is evident there is not any other Substance than *Spirit*, or that which perceives. But, for the fuller proof of this point, let it be considered the sensible qualities are colour, figure, motion, smell, taste, and such like, that is, the ideas perceived by sense. Now, for an idea to exist in an unperceiving thing is a manifest contradiction; for to have an idea is all one as to perceive: that therefore wherein colour, figure, and the like qualities exist must perceive them. Hence it is clear there can be no unthinking substance or *substratum* of those ideas.

8. But, say you, though the ideas themselves do not exist without the mind, yet there may be things like them, whereof they are copies or resemblances; which things exist without the mind, in an unthinking substance. I answer, an idea can be like nothing but an idea; a colour or figure can be like nothing but another colour or figure. If we look but never so little into our thoughts, we shall find it impossible for us to conceive a likeness except only between our ideas. Again, I ask whether those supposed *originals,* or external things, of which our ideas are the pictures or representations, be themselves perceivable or no? If they are, then *they* are ideas, and we have gained our point: but if you say they are not, I appeal to any one whether it be sense to assert a colour is like something which is invisible; hard or soft, like something which is intangible; and so of the rest.

9. Some there are who make a distinction betwixt *primary* and *secondary* qualities. By the former they mean extension, figure, motion, rest, solidity or impenetrability, and number; by the latter they denote all other sensible qualities, as colours, sounds, tastes, and so forth. The ideas we have of these last they acknowledge not to be the resemblances of anything existing without the mind, or unperceived; but they will have our ideas of the *primary qualities* to be patterns or images of things which exist without the mind, in an unthinking substance which they call Matter. By Matter, therefore, we are to understand an inert, senseless substance, in which extension, figure, and motion do actually subsist. But it is evident, from what we have already shewn, that extension, figure, and motion are only ideas existing in the mind, and that an idea can be like nothing but another idea; and that consequently neither they nor their archetypes can exist in an unperceiving substance. Hence, it is plain that the very notion of what is called *Matter* or *corporeal substance,* involves a contradiction in it. Insomuch that I should not think it necessary to spend more time in exposing its absurdity. But, because the tenet of the existence of Matter seems to have taken so deep a root in the minds of philosophers, and draws after it so many ill consequences, I choose rather to be thought prolix and tedious than omit anything that might conduce to the full discovery and extirpation of that prejudice.

10. They who assert that figure, motion, and the rest of the primary or original qualities do exist without the mind, in unthinking substances, do at the same time acknowledge that colours, sounds, heat, cold, and suchlike secondary qualities, do not; which they tell us are sensations, existing in the mind alone, that depend on and are occasioned by the different size, texture, and motion of the minute particles of matter. This they take for an undoubted truth, which they can demonstrate beyond all exception. Now, if it be certain that those *original* qualities are inseparably united with the other sensible qualities, and not, even in thought, capable of being abstracted from them, it plainly follows that *they* exist only in the mind. But I desire any one to reflect, and try whether he can, by any abstraction of thought, conceive the extension and motion of a body without all other sensible qualities. For my own part, I see evidently that it is not in my power to frame an idea of a body extended and moving, but I must withal give it some colour or other sensible

quality, which is acknowledged to exist only in the mind. . . .

14. I shall farther add, that, after the same manner as modern philosophers prove certain sensible qualities to have no existence in Matter, or without the mind, the same thing may be likewise proved of all other sensible qualities whatsoever. Thus, for instance, it is said that heat and cold are affections only of the mind, and not at all patterns of real beings, existing in the corporeal substances which excite them; for that the same body which appears cold to one hand seems warm to another. Now, why may we not as well argue that figure and extension are not patterns or resemblances of qualities existing in Matter; because to the same eye at different stations, or eyes of a different texture at the same station, they appear various, and cannot therefore be the images of anything settled and determinate without the mind? Again, it is proved that sweetness is not really in the sapid thing; because the thing remaining unaltered the sweetness is changed into bitter, as in case of a fever or otherwise vitiated palate. Is it not as reasonable to say that motion is not without the mind; since if the succession of ideas in the mind become swifter, the motion, it is acknowledged, shall appear slower, without any alteration in any external object?

15. In short, let any one consider those arguments which are thought manifestly to prove that colours and tastes exist only in the mind, and he shall find they may with equal force be brought to prove the same thing of extension, figure, and motion. Though it must be confessed this method of arguing does not so much prove that there is no extension or colour in an outward object, as that we do not know by sense which is the true extension or colour of the object. But the arguments foregoing plainly shew it to be impossible that any colour or extension at all, or other sensible quality whatsoever, should exist in an unthinking subject without the mind, or in truth that there should be any such thing as an outward object.

16. But let us examine a little the received opinion. It is said extension is a *mode* or *accident* of Matter, and that Matter is the *substratum* that supports it. Now I desire that you would explain to me what is meant by Matter's *supporting* extension. Say you, I have no idea of Matter; and therefore cannot explain it. I answer, though you have no positive, yet, if you have any meaning at all, you

must at least have a relative idea of Matter; though you know not what it is, yet you must be supposed to know what relation it bears to accidents, and what is meant by its supporting them. It is evident *support* cannot here be taken in its usual or literal sense, as when we say that pillars support a building. In what sense therefore must it be taken? For my part, I am not able to discover any sense at all that can be applicable to it.

17. If we inquire into what the most accurate philosophers declare themselves to mean by *material substance*, we shall find them acknowledge they have no other meaning annexed to those sounds but the idea of Being in general, together with the relative notion of its supporting accidents. The general idea of Being appeareth to me the most abstract and incomprehensible of all other; and as for its supporting accidents, this, as we have just now observed, cannot be understood in the common sense of those words: it must therefore be taken in some other sense, but what that is they do not explain. So that when I consider the two parts or branches which make the signification of the words *material substance,* I am convinced there is no distinct meaning annexed to them. But why should we trouble ourselves any farther, in discussing this material *substratum* or support of figure and motion and other sensible qualities? Does it not suppose they have an existence without the mind? And is not this a direct repugnancy, and altogether inconceivable?

18. But, though it were possible that solid, figured, moveable substances may exist without the mind, corresponding to the ideas we have of bodies, yet how is it possible for us to know this? Either we must know it by Sense or by Reason. As for our senses, by them we have the knowledge only of our sensations, ideas, or those things that are immediately perceived by sense, call them what you will: but they do not inform us that things exist without the mind, or unperceived, like to those which are perceived. This the materialists themselves acknowledge.—It remains therefore that if we have any knowledge at all of external things, it must be by reason inferring their existence from what is immediately perceived by sense. But (I do not see) what reason can induce us to believe the existence of bodies without the mind, from what we perceive, since the very patrons of Matter themselves do not pretend there is any necessary connexion betwixt them and our ideas? I say it is

granted on all hands (and what happens in dreams, frensies, and the like, puts it beyond dispute) that it is possible we might be affected with all the ideas we have now, though no bodies existed without resembling them. Hence it is evident the supposition of external bodies is not necessary for producing our ideas; since it is granted they are produced sometimes, and might possibly be produced always, in the same order we see them in at present, without their concurrence.

19. But, though we might possibly have all our sensations without them, yet perhaps it may be thought easier to conceive and explain the manner of their production, by supposing external bodies in their likeness rather than otherwise; and so it might be at least probable there are such things as bodies that excite their ideas in our minds. But neither can this be said. For, though we give the materialists their external bodies, they by their own confession are never the nearer knowing how our ideas are produced; since they own themselves unable to comprehend in what manner body can act upon spirit, or how it is possible it should imprint any idea in the mind. Hence it is evident the production of ideas or sensations in our minds, can be no reason why we should suppose Matter or corporeal substances; since that is acknowledged to remain equally inexplicable with or without this supposition. If therefore it were possible for bodies to exist without the mind, yet to hold they do so must needs be a very precarious opinion; since it is to suppose, without any reason at all, that God has created innumerable beings that are entirely useless, and serve to no manner of purpose.

20. In short, if there were external bodies, it is impossible we should ever come to know it; and if there were not, we might have the very same reasons to think there were that we have now.

Suppose—what no one can deny possible—an intelligence, without the help of external bodies, to be affected with the same train of sensations or ideas that you are, imprinted in the same order and with like vividness in his mind. I ask whether that intelligence hath not all the reason to believe the existence of Corporeal Substances, represented by his ideas, and exciting them in his mind, that you can possibly have for believing the same thing? Of this there can be no question. . . .

23. But, say you, surely there is nothing easier than for me to imagine trees, for instance, in a park, or books existing in a closet, and nobody by to perceive them. I answer, you may so, there is no difficulty in it. But what is all this, I beseech you, more than framing in your mind certain ideas which you call *books* and *trees,* and at the same time omitting to frame the idea of any one that may perceive them? But do not you yourself perceive or think of them all the while? This therefore is nothing to the purpose: it only shews you have the power of imagining, or forming ideas in your mind; but it does not shew that you can conceive it possible the objects of your thoughts may exist without the mind. To make out this, it is necessary that you conceive them existing unconceived or unthought of; which is a manifest repugnancy. When we do our utmost to conceive the existence of external bodies, we are all the while only contemplating our own ideas. But the mind, taking no notice of itself, is deluded to think it can and does conceive bodies existing unthought of, or without the mind, though at the same time they are apprehended by, or exist in, itself. A little attention will discover to any one the truth and evidence of what is here said, and make it unnecessary to insist on any other proofs against the existence of *material substance.*

Further Questions

1. Now that you've read Berkeley's position, what is your response? Perhaps you find yourself sympathetic to the remarks of the great empiricist philosopher, David Hume: "The speculations of the ingenious Dr. Berkeley—they admit of no refutation, but they produce no conviction." If you are not convinced, *why* aren't you? Do you have a refutation?
2. How do you suppose Locke would respond to Berkeley's idealism? Could he respond using the primary-secondary quality distinction?
3. Does the world exist, according to Berkeley, when no one is perceiving it? Why?

4. Who perceives God? Berkeley answers: nobody. How then do you suppose Berkeley accounts for the existence of perceivers who are not themselves perceived? Can you see any way out of this puzzle with the paradoxical idea that perception somehow creates *itself* into existence? If this sounds too crazy to be true, then keep in mind that such craziness resurfaces in twentieth-century science, under the name *quantum mechanics*. More on that in the selections by Daniel Kolak titled "Quantum Cosmology, the Anthropic Principle, and Why Is There Something Rather Than Nothing?"

Further Readings

Moore, G. E. "Refutation of Idealism" in his *Philosophical Studies*. London: Routledge & Kegan Paul, 1922. One of the most famous "refutations" of Berkeley's position.
Turbayne, Colin, ed. *Berkeley: Critical and Interpretive Essays*. Minneapolis: University of Minnesota Press, 1982.

30   Perception, Knowledge, and Induction

BERTRAND RUSSELL

A biography of Russell can be found on page 34.

In the following selection, Russell explains why there are problems with basing knowledge on experience. He then revamps and elaborates the sort of foundational approach to solving these problems that was earlier advocated by Locke, Berkeley, and Hume. In particular, he attempts to explain how we get from what he regards as the ultimate data of empirical knowledge, "sense data," to all of the things we think we know about the world and ourselves, a task that leads him to consider skeptical doubts about the existence of the material world and about inductive inferences.

Reading Questions

1. Russell claims we never "immediately experience" real physical objects, such as tables and chairs. What, then, does he think we immediately experience? What is the relationship, in his view, between what we immediately experience and physical objects?
2. In his discussion of Descartes, Russell claims "the real Self is as hard to arrive at as the real table." What does Russell mean by "the real Self"? Why doesn't he simply accept Descartes' idea that one's knowledge of the existence of one's own self is the most certain knowledge that each of us has?
3. Are beliefs based directly on sense experience certain? What does Russell think? Why? What do you think?
4. Why does Russell think that while the hypothesis that the whole of life is a dream might be true, it cannot explain "the facts or our own lives" as simply as can the commonsense hypothesis that there really are physical objects that exist independently of us?
5. In Russell's view, what is the relation between physical space-time and the spatial and temporal relations we immediately experience?

6. What is an inductive inference? What, in Russell's view, are the assumptions on which all inductive inferences depend?

APPEARANCE AND REALITY

IS THERE ANY KNOWLEDGE in the world which is so certain that no reasonable man could doubt it? This question, which at first sight might not seem difficult, is really one of the most difficult that can be asked. When we have realized the obstacles in the way of a straightforward and confident answer, we shall be well launched on the study of philosophy—for philosophy is merely the attempt to answer such ultimate questions, not carelessly and dogmatically, as we do in ordinary life and even in the sciences, but critically, after exploring all that makes such questions puzzling, and after realizing all the vagueness and confusion that underlie our ordinary ideas.

In daily life, we assume as certain many things which, on a closer scrutiny, are found to be so full of apparent contradictions that only a great amount of thought enables us to know what it is that we really may believe. In the search for certainty, it is natural to begin with our present experiences, and in some sense, no doubt, knowledge is to be derived from them. But any statement as to what it is that our immediate experiences make us know is very likely to be wrong. It seems to me that I am now sitting in a chair, at a table of a certain shape, on which I see sheets of paper with writing or print. By turning my head I see out of the window buildings and clouds and the sun. I believe that the sun is about ninety-three million miles from the earth; that it is a hot globe many times bigger than the earth; that, owing to the earth's rotation, it rises every morning, and will continue to do so for an indefinite time in the future. I believe that, if any other normal person comes into my room, he will see the same chairs and tables and books and papers as I see, and that the table which I see is the same as the table which I feel pressing against my arm. All this seems to be so evident as to be hardly worth stating, except in answer to a man who doubts whether I know anything. Yet all this may be rea-

sonably doubted, and all of it requires much careful discussion before we can be sure that we have stated it in a form that is wholly true.

To make our difficulties plain, let us concentrate attention on the table. To the eye it is oblong, brown and shiny, to the touch it is smooth and cool and hard; when I tap it, it gives out a wooden sound. Any one else who sees and feels and hears the table will agree with this description, so that it might seem as if no difficulty would arise; but as soon as we try to be more precise our troubles begin. Although I believe that the table is "really" of the same colour all over, the parts that reflect the light look much brighter than the other parts, and some parts look white because of reflected light. I know that, if I move, the parts that reflect the light will be different, so that the apparent distribution of colours on the table will change. It follows that if several people are looking at the table at the same moment, no two of them will see exactly the same distribution of colours, because no two can see it from exactly the same point of view, and any change in the point of view makes some change in the way the light is reflected.

For most practical purposes these differences are unimportant, but to the painter they are all-important: the painter has to unlearn the habit of thinking that things seem to have the colour which common sense says they "really" have, and to learn the habit of seeing things as they appear. Here we have already the beginning of one of the distinctions that cause most trouble in philosophy—the distinction between "appearance" and "reality," between what things seem to be and what they are. The painter wants to know what things seem to be, the practical man and the philosopher want to know what they are; but the philosopher's wish to know this is stronger than the practical man's, and is more troubled by knowledge as to the difficulties of answering the question.

To return to the table. It is evident from what we have found, that there is no colour which

From The Problems of Philosophy *(Oxford University Press, 1912).*

preeminently appears to be *the* colour of the table, or even of any one particular part of the table — it appears to be of different colours from different points of view, and there is no reason for regarding some of these as more really its colour than others. And we know that even from a given point of view the colour will seem different by artificial light, or to a colour-blind man, or to a man wearing blue spectacles, while in the dark there will be no colour at all, though to touch and hearing the table will be unchanged. This colour is not something which is inherent in the table, but something depending upon the table and the spectator and the way the light falls on the table. When, in ordinary life, we speak of *the* colour of the table, we only mean the sort of colour which it will seem to have to a normal spectator from an ordinary point of view under usual conditions of light. But the other colours which appear under other conditions have just as good a right to be considered real; and therefore, to avoid favouritism, we are compelled to deny that, in itself, the table has any one particular colour.

The same thing applies to the texture. With the naked eye one can see the grain, but otherwise the table looks smooth and even. If we looked at it through a microscope, we should see roughnesses and hills and valleys, and all sorts of differences that are imperceptible to the naked eye. Which of these is the "real" table? We are naturally tempted to say that what we see through the microscope is more real, but that in turn would be changed by a still more powerful microscope. If, then, we cannot trust what we see with the naked eye, why should we trust what we see through a microscope? Thus, again, the confidence in our senses with which we began deserts us.

The *shape* of the table is no better. We are all in the habit of judging as to the "real" shapes of things, and we do this so unreflectingly that we come to think we actually see the real shapes. But, in fact, as we all have to learn if we try to draw, a given thing looks different in shape from every different point of view. If our table is "really" rectangular, it will look, from almost all points of view, as if it had two acute angles and two obtuse angles. If opposite sides are parallel, they will look as if they converged to a point away from the spectator; if they are of equal length, they will look as if the nearer side were longer. All these things are not commonly noticed in looking at a table, because experience has taught us to construct the "real" shape from the apparent shape, and the "real" shape is what interests us as practical men. But the "real" shape is not what we see; it is something inferred from what we see. And what we see is constantly changing in shape as we move about the room; so that here again the senses seem not to give us the truth about the table itself, but only about the appearance of the table.

Similar difficulties arise when we consider the sense of touch. It is true that the table always gives us a sensation of hardness, and we feel that it resists pressure. But the sensation we obtain depends upon how hard we press the table and also upon what part of the body we press with; thus the various sensations due to various pressures or various parts of the body cannot be supposed to reveal *directly* any definite property of the table, but at most to be *signs* of some property which perhaps *causes* all the sensations, but is not actually apparent in any of them. And the same applies still more obviously to the sounds which can be elicited by rapping the table.

Thus it becomes evident that the real table, if there is one, is not the same as what we immediately experience by sight or touch or hearing. The real table, if there is one, is not *immediately* known to us at all, but must be an inference from what is immediately known. Hence, two very difficult questions at once arise; namely, (1) Is there a real table at all? (2) If so, what sort of object can it be?

It will help us in considering these questions to have a few simple terms of which the meaning is definite and clear. Let us give the name of "sense-data" to the things that are immediately known in sensation: such things as colours, sounds, smells, hardnesses, roughnesses, and so on. We shall give the name "sensation" to the experience of being immediately aware of these things. Thus, whenever we see a colour, we have a sensation *of* the colour, but the colour itself is a sense-datum, not a sensation. The colour is that *of* which we are immediately aware, and the awareness itself is the sensation. It is plain that if we are to know anything about the table, it must be by means of the sense-data — brown colour, oblong shape, smoothness, etc. — which we associate with the table; but, for the reasons which have been given, we cannot say that the table *is* the sense-data, or even that the sense-data are directly properties of the table. Thus a problem arises as to the relation of the sense-data to the real table, supposing there is such a thing.

The real table, if it exists, we will call a "physical object." Thus we have to consider the relation of sense-data to physical objects. The collection of all physical objects is called "matter." Thus our two questions may be re-stated as follows: (1) Is there any such thing as matter? (2) If so, what is its nature?

The philosopher who first brought prominently forward the reasons for regarding the immediate objects of our senses as not existing independently of us was Bishop Berkeley (1685–1753). . . . [He tried] to prove that there is no such thing as matter at all, and that the world consists of nothing but minds and their ideas. . . . The arguments employed are of very different value: some are important and sound, others are confused or quibbling. But Berkeley retains the merit of having shown that the existence of matter is capable of being denied without absurdity, and that if there are any things that exist independently of us they cannot be the immediate objects of our sensations.

There are two different questions involved when we ask whether matter exists, and it is important to keep them clear. We commonly mean by "matter" something which is opposed to "mind," something which we think of as occupying space and as radically incapable of any sort of thought or consciousness. It is chiefly in this sense that Berkeley denies matter; that is to say, he does not deny that the sense-data which we commonly take as signs of the existence of the table are really signs of the existence of *something* independent of us, but he does deny that this something is nonmental, that it is neither mind nor ideas entertained by some mind. He admits that there must be something which continues to exist when we go out of the room or shut our eyes, and that what we call seeing the table does really give us reason for believing in something which persists even when we are not seeing it. But he thinks that this something cannot be radically different in nature from what we see, and cannot be independent of seeing altogether, though it must be independent of *our* seeing. He is thus led to regard the "real" table as an idea in the mind of God. Such an idea has the re-

quired permanence and independence of ourselves, without being—as matter would otherwise be—something quite unknowable, in the sense that we can only infer it, and can never be directly and immediately aware of it.

Other philosophers since Berkeley have also held that, although the table does not depend for its existence upon being seen by me, it does depend upon being seen (or otherwise apprehended in sensation) by *some* mind—not necessarily the mind of God, but more often the whole collective mind of the universe. This they hold, as Berkeley does, chiefly because they think there can be nothing real—or at any rate nothing known to be real—except minds and their thoughts and feelings. We might state the argument by which they support their view in some such way as this: "Whatever can be thought of is an idea in the mind of the person thinking of it; therefore nothing can be thought of except ideas in minds; therefore anything else is inconceivable, and what is inconceivable cannot exist."

Such an argument, in my opinion, is fallacious; and of course those who advance it do not put it so shortly or so crudely. But whether valid or not, the argument has been very widely advanced in one form or another; and very many philosophers, perhaps a majority, have held that there is nothing real except minds and their ideas. Such philosophers are called "idealists." When they come to explaining matter, they either say, like Berkeley, that matter is really nothing but a collection of ideas, or they say, like Leibniz (1646–1716), that what appears as matter is really a collection of more or less rudimentary minds.

But these philosophers, though they deny matter as opposed to mind, nevertheless, in another sense, admit matter. It will be remembered that we asked two questions; namely, (1) Is there a real table at all? (2) If so, what sort of object can it be? Now both Berkeley and Leibniz admit that there is a real table, but Berkeley says it is certain ideas in the mind of God, and Leibniz says it is a colony of souls. Thus both of them answer our first question in the affirmative, and only diverge from the views of ordinary mortals in their answer to our second question. In fact, almost all philosophers seem to be agreed that there is a real table: they almost all agree that, however much our sense-data—colour, shape, smoothness, etc.—may depend upon us, yet their occurrence is a sign of something existing independently of us, something differing, perhaps, completely from our sense-data, and yet to be regarded as causing those sense-data whenever we are in a suitable relation to the real table.

Now obviously this point in which the philosophers are agreed—the view that there *is* a real table, whatever its nature may be—is vitally important, and it will be worth while to consider what reasons there are for accepting this view before we go on to the further question as to the nature of the real table. Our next [section], therefore, will be concerned with the reasons for supposing that there is a real table at all.

Before we go farther it will be well to consider for a moment what it is that we have discovered so far. It has appeared that, if we take any common object of the sort that is supposed to be known by the senses, what the senses *immediately* tell us is not the truth about the object as it is apart from us, but only the truth about certain sense-data which, so far as we can see, depend upon the relations between us and the object. Thus what we directly see and feel is merely "appearance," which we believe to be a sign of some "reality" behind. But if the reality is not what appears, have we any means of knowing whether there is any reality at all? And if so, have we any means of finding out what it is like?

Such questions are bewildering, and it is difficult to know that even the strangest hypotheses may not be true. Thus our familiar table, which has roused but the slightest thoughts in us hitherto, has become a problem full of surprising possibilities. The one thing we know about it is that it is not what it seems. Beyond this modest result, so far, we have the most complete liberty of conjecture. Leibniz tells us it is a community of souls; Berkeley tells us it is an idea in the mind of God; sober science, scarcely less wonderful, tells us it is a vast collection of electric charges in violent motion.

Among these surprising possibilities, doubt suggests that perhaps there is no table at all. Philosophy, if it cannot *answer* so many questions as we could wish, has at least the power of *asking* questions which increase the interest of the world, and show the strangeness and wonder lying just below the surface even in the commonest things of daily life.

THE EXISTENCE OF MATTER

We have to ask ourselves whether, in any sense at all, there is such a thing as matter. Is there a table which has a certain intrinsic nature, and continues to exist when I am not looking, or is the table merely a product of my imagination, a dream-table in a very prolonged dream? This question is of the greatest importance. For if we cannot be sure of the independent existence of objects, we cannot be sure of the independent existence of other people's bodies, and therefore still less of other people's minds, since we have no grounds for believing in their minds except such as are derived from observing their bodies. Thus if we cannot be sure of the independent existence of objects, we shall be left alone in a desert—it may be that the whole outer world is nothing but a dream, and that we alone exist. This is an uncomfortable possibility; but although it cannot be strictly *proved* to be false, there is not the slightest reason to suppose that it is true. In this [section] we have to see why this is the case.

Before we embark upon doubtful matters, let us try to find some more or less fixed point from which to start. Although we are doubting the physical existence of the table, we are not doubting the existence of the sense-data which made us think there was a table; we are not doubting that, while we look, a certain colour and shape appear to us, and while we press, a certain sensation of hardness is experienced by us. All this, which is psychological, we are not calling in question. In fact, whatever else may be doubtful, some at least of our immediate experiences seem absolutely certain.

Descartes (1596–1650), the founder of modern philosophy, invented a method which may still be used with profit—the method of systematic doubt. He determined that he would believe nothing which he did not see quite clearly and distinctly to be true. Whatever he could bring himself to doubt, he would doubt, until he saw reason for not doubting it. By applying this method he gradually became convinced that the only existence of which he could be *quite* certain was his own. He imagined a deceitful demon, who presented unreal things to his senses in a perpetual phantasmagoria; it might be very improbable that such a demon existed, but still it was possible, and therefore doubt concerning things perceived by the senses was possible.

But doubt concerning his own existence was not possible, for if he did not exist, no demon could deceive him. If he doubted, he must exist; if he had any experiences whatever, he must exist. Thus, his own existence was an absolute certainty to him. "I think, therefore I am," he said (*Cogito, ergo sum*); and on the basis of this certainty he set to work to build up again the world of knowledge which his doubt had laid in ruins. By inventing the method of doubt, and by showing that subjective things are the most certain, Descartes performed a great service to philosophy, and one which makes him still useful to all students of the subject.

But some care is needed in using Descartes' argument. "*I* think, therefore *I* am" says rather more than is strictly certain. It might seem as though we were quite sure of being the same person to-day as we were yesterday, and this is no doubt true in some sense. But the real Self is as hard to arrive at as the real table, and does not seem to have that absolute, convincing certainty that belongs to particular experiences. When I look at my table and see a certain brown colour, what is quite certain at once is not "*I* am seeing a brown colour," but rather, "a brown colour is being seen." This of course involves something (or somebody) which (or who) sees the brown colour; but it does not of itself involve that more or less permanent person whom we call "I." So far as immediate certainty goes, it might be that the something which sees the brown colour is quite momentary, and not the same as the something which has some different experience the next moment.

Thus it is our particular thoughts and feelings that have primitive certainty. And this applies to dreams and hallucinations as well as to normal perceptions: when we dream or see a ghost, we certainly do have the sensations we think we have, but for various reasons it is held that no physical object corresponds to these sensations. Thus the certainty of our knowledge of our own experiences does not have to be limited in any way to allow for exceptional cases. Here, therefore, we have, for what it is worth, a solid basis from which to begin our pursuit of knowledge.

The problem we have to consider is this: Granted that we are certain of our own sense-data, have we any reason for regarding them as signs of the existence of something else, which we can call the physical object? When we have enumerated all the sense-data which we should naturally regard as connected with the table, have we said all there is to say about the table, or is there still something else—something not a sense-datum, something which persists when we go out of the room? Common sense unhesitatingly answers that there is. What can be bought and sold and pushed about and have a cloth laid on it, and so on, cannot be a *mere* collection of sense-data. If the cloth completely hides the table, we shall derive no sense-data from the table, and therefore, if the table were merely sense-data, it would have ceased to exist, and the cloth would be suspended in empty air, resting, by a miracle, in the place where the table formerly was. This seems plainly absurd; but whoever wishes to become a philosopher must learn not to be frightened by absurdities.

One great reason why it is felt that we must secure a physical object in addition to the sense-data, is that we want the *same* object for different people. When ten people are sitting round a dinner-table, it seems preposterous to maintain that they are not seeing the same tablecloth, the same knives and forks and spoons and glasses. But the sense-data are private to each separate person; what is immediately present to the sight of one is not immediately present to the sight of another: they all see things from slightly different points of view, and therefore see them slightly differently. Thus, if there are to be public neutral objects, which can be in some sense known to many different people, there must be something over and above the private and particular sense-data which appear to various people. What reason, then, have we for believing that there are such public neutral objects?

The first answer that naturally occurs to one is that, although different people may see the table slightly differently, still they all see more or less similar things when they look at the table, and the variations in what they see follow the laws of perspective and reflection of light, so that it is easy to arrive at a permanent object underlying all the different people's sense-data. I bought my table from the former occupant of my room; I could not buy *his* sense-data, which died when he went away, but I could and did buy the confident expectation of more or less similar sense-data. Thus it is the fact that different people have similar sense-data, and that one person in a given place at different times has similar sense-data, which makes us suppose that over and above the sense-data there is a permanent public object which underlies or causes the sense-data of various people at various times.

Now in so far as the above considerations depend upon supposing that there are other people besides ourselves, they beg the very question at issue. Other people are represented to me by certain sense-data, such as the sight of them or the sound of their voices, and if I had no reason to believe that there were physical objects independent of my sense-data, I should have no reason to believe that other people exist except as part of my dream. Thus, when we are trying to show that there must be objects independent of our own sense-data, we cannot appeal to the testimony of other people, since this testimony itself consists of sense-data, and does not reveal other people's experiences unless our own sense-data are signs of things existing independently of us. We must therefore, if possible, find, in our own purely private experiences, characteristics which show, or tend to show, that there are in the world things other than ourselves and our private experiences.

In one sense it must be admitted that we can never *prove* the existence of things other than ourselves and our experiences. No logical absurdity results from the hypothesis that the world consists of myself and my thoughts and feelings and sensations, and that everything else is mere fancy. In dreams a very complicated world may seem to be present, and yet on waking we find it was a delusion; that is to say, we find that the sense-data in the dream do not appear to have corresponded with such physical objects as we should naturally infer from our sense-data. (It is true that, when the physical world is assumed, it is possible to find physical causes for the sense-data in dreams: a door banging, for instance, may cause us to dream of a naval engagement. But although, in this case, there is a physical *cause* for the sense-data, there is not a physical object *corresponding* to the sense-data in the way in which an actual naval battle would correspond.) There is no logical impossibility in the supposition that the whole of life is a dream, in which we ourselves create all the objects that come before us. But although this is not logically impossible, there is no reason whatever to suppose that it

is true; and it is, in fact, a less simple hypothesis, viewed as a means of accounting for the facts of our own life, than the common-sense hypothesis that there really are objects independent of us, whose action on us causes our sensations.

The way in which simplicity comes in from supposing that there really are physical objects is easily seen. If the cat appears at one moment in one part of the room, and at another in another part, it is natural to suppose that it has moved from the one to the other, passing over a series of intermediate positions. But if it is merely a set of sense-data, it cannot have ever been in any place where I did not see it; thus we shall have to suppose that it did not exist at all while I was not looking, but suddenly sprang into being in a new place. If the cat exists whether I see it or not, we can understand from our own experience how it gets hungry between one meal and the next; but if it does not exist when I am not seeing it, it seems odd that appetite should grow during nonexistence as fast as during existence. And if the cat consists only of sense-data, it cannot be *hungry,* since no hunger but my own can be a sense-datum to me. Thus the behaviour of the sense-data which represent the cat to me, though it seems quite natural when regarded as an expression of hunger, becomes utterly inexplicable when regarded as mere movements and changes of patches of colour, which are as incapable of hunger as a triangle is of playing football.

But the difficulty in the case of the cat is nothing compared to the difficulty in the case of human beings. When human beings speak—that is, when we hear certain noises which we associate with ideas, and simultaneously see certain motions of lips and expressions of face—it is very difficult to suppose that what we hear is not the expression of a thought, as we know it would be if we emitted the same sounds. Of course similar things happen in dreams, where we are mistaken as to the existence of other people. But dreams are more or less suggested by what we call waking life, and are capable of being more or less accounted for on scientific principles if we assume that there really is a physical world. Thus every principle of simplicity urges us to adopt the natural view, that there really are objects other than ourselves and our sense-data which have an existence not dependent upon our perceiving them.

Of course it is not by argument that we originally come by our belief in an independent external world. We find this belief ready in ourselves as soon as we begin to reflect: it is what may be called an *instinctive* belief. We should never have been led to question this belief but for the fact that, at any rate in the case of sight, it seems as if the sense-datum itself were instinctively believed to be the independent object, whereas argument shows that the object cannot be identical with the sense-datum. This discovery, however—which is not at all paradoxical in the case of taste and smell and sound, and only slightly so in the case of touch—leaves undiminished our instinctive belief that there *are* objects *corresponding* to our sense-data. Since this belief does not lead to any difficulties, but on the contrary tends to simplify and systematize our account of our experiences, there seems no good reason for rejecting it. We may therefore admit—though with a slight doubt derived from dreams—that the external world does really exist, and is not wholly dependent for its existence upon our continuing to perceive it.

The argument which has led us to this conclusion is doubtless less strong than we could wish, but it is typical of many philosophical arguments, and it is therefore worth while to consider briefly its general character and validity. All knowledge, we find, must be built up upon our instinctive beliefs, and if these are rejected, nothing is left. But among our instinctive beliefs some are much stronger than others, while many have, by habit and association, become entangled with other beliefs, not really instinctive, but falsely supposed to be part of what is believed instinctively.

Philosophy should show us the hierarchy of our instinctive beliefs, beginning with those we hold most strongly, and presenting each as much isolated and as free from irrelevant additions as possible. It should take care to show that, in the form in which they are finally set forth, our instinctive beliefs do not clash, but form a harmonious system. There can never be any reason for rejecting one instinctive belief except that it clashes with others; thus, if they are found to harmonize, the whole system becomes worthy of acceptance.

It is of course *possible* that all or any of our beliefs may be mistaken, and therefore all ought to be held with at least some slight element of doubt. But we cannot have *reason* to reject a belief except on the ground of some other belief. Hence, by organizing our instinctive beliefs and their consequences, by considering which among them is most possible, if necessary, to modify or abandon, we can arrive, on the basis of accepting as our sole data what we instinctively believe, at an orderly systematic organization of our knowledge, in which, though the *possibility* of error remains, its likelihood is diminished by the interrelation of the parts and by the critical scrutiny which has preceded acquiescence.

This function, at least, philosophy can perform. Most philosophers, rightly or wrongly, believe that philosophy can do much more than this—that it can give us knowledge, not otherwise attainable, concerning the universe as a whole, and concerning the nature of ultimate reality. Whether this be the case or not, the more modest function we have spoken of can certainly be performed by philosophy, and certainly suffices, for those who have once begun to doubt the adequacy of common sense, to justify the arduous and difficult labours that philosophical problems involve.

THE NATURE OF MATTER

. . . We agreed, though without being able to find demonstrative reasons, that it is rational to believe that our sense-data—for example, those which we regard as associated with my table—are really signs of the existence of something independent of us and our perceptions. That is to say, over and above the sensations of colour, hardness, noise, and so on, which make up the appearance of the table to me, I assume that there is something else, *of* which these things are appearances. The colour ceases to exist if I shut my eyes, the sensation of hardness ceases to exist if I remove my arm from contact with the table, the sound ceases to exist if I cease to rap the table with my knuckles. But I do not believe that when all these things cease the table ceases. On the contrary, I believe that it is because the table exists continuously that all these sense-data will reappear when I open my eyes, replace my arm, and begin again to rap with my knuckles. The question we have to consider in this chapter is: What is the nature of this real table, which persists independently of my perception of it?

To this question physical science gives an answer, somewhat incomplete it is true, and in part still very hypothetical, but yet deserving of respect so far as it goes. Physical science, more or less unconsciously, has drifted into the view that all natural phenomena ought to be reduced to motions. Light and heat and sound are all due to wave-motions, which travel from the body emitting them to the person who sees light or feels heat or hears sound. That which has the wave-motion is either aether or "gross matter," but in either case is what the philosopher would call matter. The only properties which science assigns to it are position in space, and the power of motion according to the laws of motion. Science does not deny that it *may* have other properties; but if so, such other properties are not useful to the man of science, and in no way assist him in explaining the phenomena.

It is sometimes said that "light *is* a form of wave-motion," but this is misleading, for the light which we immediately see, which we know directly by means of our senses, is *not* a form of wave-motion, but something quite different—something which we all know if we are not blind, though we cannot describe it so as to convey our knowledge to a man who is blind. A wave-motion, on the contrary, could quite well be described to a blind man, since he can acquire a knowledge of space by the sense of touch; and he can experience a wave-motion by a sea voyage almost as well as we can. But this, which a blind man can understand, is not what we mean by *light:* we mean by *light* just that which a blind man can never understand, and which we can never describe to him.

Now this something, which all of us who are not blind know, is not, according to science, really to be found in the outer world: it is something caused by the action of certain waves upon the eyes and nerves and brain of the person who sees the light. When it is said that light *is* waves, what is really meant is that waves are the physical cause of our sensations of light. But light itself, the thing which seeing people experience and blind people do not, is not supposed by science to form any part of the world that is independent of us and our senses. And very similar remarks would apply to other kinds of sensations.

It is not only colours and sounds and so on that are absent from the scientific world of matter, but also *space* as we get it through sight or touch. It is

essential to science that its matter should be in *a* space, but the space in which it is cannot be exactly the space we see or feel. To begin with, space as we see it is not the same as space as we get it by the sense of touch; it is only by experience in infancy that we learn how to touch things we see, or how to get a sight of things which we feel touching us. But the space of science is neutral as between touch and sight; thus it cannot be either the space of touch or the space of sight.

Again, different people see the same object as of different shapes, according to their point of view. A circular coin, for example, though we should always *judge* it to be circular, will *look* oval unless we are straight in front of it. When we judge that it *is* circular, we are judging that it has a real shape which is not its apparent shape, but belongs to it intrinsically apart from its appearance. But this real shape, which is what concerns science, must be in a real space, not the same as anybody's *apparent* space. The real space is public, the apparent space is private to the percipient. In different people's *private* spaces the same object seems to have different shapes; thus the real space, in which it has its real shape, must be different from the private spaces. The space of science, therefore, though *connected* with the spaces we see and feel, is not identical with them, and the manner of its connexion requires investigation.

We agreed provisionally that physical objects cannot be quite like our sense-data, but may be regarded as *causing* our sensations. These physical objects are in the space of science, which we may call "physical" space. It is important to notice that, if our sensations are to be caused by physical objects, there must be a physical space containing these objects and our sense-organs and nerves and brain. We get a sensation of touch from an object when we are in contact with it; that is to say, when some part of our body occupies a place in physical space quite close to the space occupied by the object. We see an object (roughly speaking) when no opaque body is between the object and our eyes in physical space. Similarly, we only hear or smell or taste an object when we are sufficiently near to it, or when it touches the tongue, or has some suitable position in physical space relative to our body. We cannot begin to state what different sensations we shall derive from a given object under different circumstances unless we regard the object and our body as both in one physical space, for it is mainly the relative positions of the object and our body that determine what sensations we shall derive from the object.

Now our sense-data are situated in our private spaces, either the space of sight or the space of touch or such vaguer spaces as other senses may give us. If, as science and common sense assume, there is one public all-embracing physical space in which physical objects are, the relative positions of physical objects in physical space must more or less correspond to the relative positions of sense-data in our private spaces. There is no difficulty in supposing this to be the case. If we see on a road one house nearer to us than another, our other senses will bear out the view that it is nearer; for example, it will be reached sooner if we walk along the road. Other people will agree that the house which looks nearer to us is nearer; the ordnance map will take the same view; and thus everything points to a spatial relation between the houses corresponding to the relation between the sense-data which we see when we look at the houses. Thus we may assume that there is a physical space in which physical objects have spatial relations corresponding to those which the corresponding sense-data have in our private spaces. It is this physical space which is dealt with in geometry and assumed in physics and astronomy.

Assuming that there is physical space, and that it does thus correspond to private spaces, what can we know about it? We can know *only* what is required in order to secure the correspondence. That is to say, we can know nothing of what it is like in itself, but we can know the sort of arrangement of physical objects which results from their spatial relations. We can know, for example, that the earth and moon and sun are in one straight line during an eclipse, though we cannot know what a physical straight line is in itself, as we know the look of a straight line in our visual space. Thus we come to know much more about the *relations* of distances in physical space than about the distances themselves; we may know that one distance is greater than another, or that it is along the same straight line as the other, but we cannot have that immediate acquaintance with physical distances that we have with distances in our private spaces, or with colours or sounds or other sense-data. We can know all those things about physical space which a

man born blind might know through other people about the space of sight; but the kind of things which a man born blind could never know about the space of sight we also cannot know about physical space. We can know the properties of the relations required to preserve the correspondence with sense-data, but we cannot know the nature of the terms between which the relations hold.

With regard to time, our *feeling* of duration or of the lapse of time is notoriously an unsafe guide as to the time that has elapsed by the clock. Times when we are bored or suffering pain pass slowly, times when we are agreeably occupied pass quickly, and times when we are sleeping pass almost as if they did not exist. Thus, in so far as time is constituted by duration, there is the same necessity for distinguishing a public and a private time as there was in the case of space. But in so far as time consists in an *order* of before and after, there is no need to make such a distinction; the time-order which events seem to have is, so far as we can see, the same as the time-order which they do have. At any rate no reason can be given for supposing that the two orders are not the same. The same is usually true of space: if a regiment of men are marching along a road, the *shape* of the regiment will look different from different points of view, but the men will appear arranged in the same *order* from all points of view. Hence we regard the *order* as true also in physical space, whereas the shape is only supposed to correspond to the physical space so far as is required for the preservation of the order.

In saying that the time-order which events *seem to have* is the same as the time-order which they *really have*, it is necessary to guard against a possible misunderstanding. It must not be supposed that the various states of different physical objects have the same time-order as the sense-data which constitute the perceptions of those objects. Considered as physical objects, the thunder and lightning are simultaneous; that is to say, the lightning is simultaneous with the disturbance of the air in the place where the disturbance begins, namely, where the lightning is. But the sense-datum which we call hearing the thunder does not take place until the disturbance of the air has travelled as far as to where we are. Similarly, it takes about eight minutes for the sun's light to reach us; thus, when we see the sun we are seeing the sun of eight minutes ago. So far as our sense-data afford evidence as to the physical sun they afford evidence as to the physical sun of eight minutes ago; if the physical sun had ceased to exist within the last eight minutes, that would make no difference to the sense-data which we call "seeing the sun." This affords a fresh illustration of the necessity of distinguishing between sense-data and physical objects.

What we have found as regards space is much the same as what we find in relation to the correspondence of the sense-data with their physical counterparts. If one object looks blue and another red, we may reasonably presume that there is some corresponding difference between the physical objects; if two objects both look blue, we may presume a corresponding similarity. But we cannot hope to be acquainted directly with the quality in the physical object which makes it look blue or red. Science tells us that this quality is a certain sort of wave-motion, and this sounds familiar, because we think of wave-motions in the space we see. But the wave-motions must really be in physical space, with which we have no direct acquaintance; thus the real wave-motions have not that familiarity which we might have supposed them to have. And what holds for colours is closely similar to what holds for other sense-data. Thus we find that, although the *relations* of physical objects have all sorts of knowable properties, derived from their correspondence with the relations of sense-data, the physical objects themselves remain unknown in their intrinsic nature, so far at least as can be discovered by means of the senses. The question remains whether there is any other method of discovering the intrinsic nature of physical objects.

The most natural, though not ultimately the most defensible, hypothesis to adopt in the first instance, at any rate as regards visual sense-data, would be that, though physical objects cannot, for the reasons we have been considering, be *exactly* like sense-data, yet they may be more or less like. According to this view, physical objects will, for example, really have colours, and we might, by good luck, see an object as of the colour it really is. The colour which an object seems to have at any given moment will in general be very similar, though not quite the same, from many different points of view; we might thus suppose the "real" colour to be a sort of medium colour, intermediate between the various shades which appear from the different points of view.

Such a theory is perhaps not capable of being definitely refuted, but it can be shown to be groundless. To begin with, it is plain that the colour we see depends only upon the nature of the light-waves that strike the eye, and is therefore modified by the medium intervening between us and the object, as well as by the manner in which light is reflected from the object in the direction of the eye. The intervening air alters colours unless it is perfectly clear, and any strong reflection will alter them completely. Thus the colour we see is a result of the ray as it reaches the eye, and not simply a property of the object from which the ray comes. Hence, also, provided certain waves reach the eye, we shall see a certain colour, whether the object from which the waves start has any colour or not. Thus it is quite gratuitous to suppose that physical objects have colours, and therefore there is no justification for making such a supposition. Exactly similar arguments will apply to other sense-data. . . .

ON INDUCTION

In almost all our previous discussions we have been concerned in the attempt to get clear as to our data in the way of knowledge of existence. What things are there in the universe whose existence is known to us owing to our being acquainted with them? So far, our answer has been that we are acquainted with our sense-data, and, probably, with ourselves. These we know to exist. And past sense-data which are remembered are known to have existed in the past. This knowledge supplies our data.

But if we are to be able to draw inferences from these data—if we are to know of the existence of matter, of other people, of the past before our individual memory begins, or of the future, we must know general principles of some kind by means of which such inferences can be drawn. It must be known to us that the existence of some one sort of thing, A, is a sign of the existence of some other sort of thing, B, either at the same time as A or at some earlier or later time, as, for example, thunder is a sign of the earlier existence of lightning. If this were not known to us, we could never extend our knowledge beyond the sphere of our private experience; and this sphere, as we have seen, is exceedingly limited. The question we have now to consider is whether such an extension is possible, and if so, how it is effected.

Let us take as an illustration a matter about which none of us, in fact, feel the slightest doubt. We are all convinced that the sun will rise tomorrow. Why? Is this belief a mere blind outcome of past experience, or can it be justified as a reasonable belief? It is not easy to find a test by which to judge whether a belief of this kind is reasonable or not, but we can at least ascertain what sort of general beliefs would suffice, if true, to justify the judgement that the sun will rise to-morrow, and the many other similar judgements upon which our actions are based.

It is obvious that if we are asked why we believe that the sun will rise to-morrow, we shall naturally answer, "Because it always has risen every day." We have a firm belief that it will rise in the future, because it has risen in the past. If we are challenged as to why we believe that it will continue to rise as heretofore, we may appeal to the laws of motion: the earth, we shall say, is a freely rotating body, and such bodies do not cease to rotate unless something interferes from outside, and there is nothing outside to interfere with the earth between now and to-morrow. Of course it might be doubted whether we are quite certain that there is nothing outside to interfere, but this is not the interesting doubt. The interesting doubt is as to whether the laws of motion will remain in operation until to-morrow. If this doubt is raised, we find ourselves in the same position as when the doubt about the sunrise was first raised.

The *only* reason for believing that the laws of motion will remain in operation is that they have operated hitherto, so far as our knowledge of the past enables us to judge. It is true that we have a greater body of evidence from the past in favour of the laws of motion than we have in favour of the sunrise, because the sunrise is merely a particular case of fulfillment of the laws of motion, and there are countless other particular cases. But the real question is: Do *any* number of cases of a law being fulfilled in the past afford evidence that it will be fulfilled in the future? If not, it becomes plain that we have no ground whatever for expecting the sun to rise to-morrow, or for expecting the bread we shall eat at our next meal not to poison us, or for any of the other scarcely conscious expectations that control our daily lives. It is to be observed

that all such expectations are only *probable;* thus we have not to seek for a proof that they *must* be fulfilled, but only for some reason in favour of the view that they are *likely* to be fulfilled.

Now in dealing with this question we must, to begin with, make an important distinction, without which we should soon become involved in hopeless confusions. Experience has shown us that, hitherto, the frequent repetition of some uniform succession of coexistence has been a *cause* of our expecting the same succession or coexistence on the next occasion. Food that has a certain appearance generally has a certain taste, and it is a severe shock to our expectations when the familiar appearance is found to be associated with an unusual taste. Things which we see become associated, by habit, with certain tactile sensations which we expect if we touch them; one of the horrors of a ghost (in many ghost-stories) is that it fails to give us any sensations of touch. Uneducated people who go abroad for the first time are so surprised as to be incredulous when they find their native language not understood.

And this kind of association is not confined to men; in animals also it is very strong. A horse which has been often driven along a certain road resists the attempt to drive him in a different direction. Domestic animals expect food when they see the person who usually feeds them. We know that all these rather crude expectations of uniformity are liable to be misleading. The man who has fed the chicken every day throughout its life at last wrings its neck instead, showing that more refined views as to the uniformity of nature would have been useful to the chicken.

But in spite of the misleadingness of such expectations, they nevertheless exist. The mere fact that something has happened a certain number of times causes animals and men to expect that it will happen again. Thus our instincts certainly cause us to believe that the sun will rise to-morrow, but we may be in no better a position than the chicken which unexpectedly has its neck wrung. We have therefore to distinguish the fact that past uniformities *cause* expectations as to the future, from the question whether there is any reasonable ground for giving weight to such expectations after the question of their validity has been raised.

The problem we have to discuss is whether there is any reason for believing in what is called "the uniformity of nature." The belief in the uniformity of nature is the belief that everything that has happened or will happen is an instance of some general law to which there are *no* exceptions. The crude expectations which we have been considering are all subject to exceptions, and therefore liable to disappoint those who entertain them. But science habitually assumes, at least as a working hypothesis, that general rules which have exceptions can be replaced by general rules which have no exceptions. "Unsupported bodies in air fall" is a general rule to which balloons and aeroplanes are exceptions. But the laws of motion and the law of gravitation, which account for the fact that most bodies fall, also account for the fact that balloons and aeroplanes can rise; thus the laws of motion and the law of gravitation are not subject to these exceptions.

The belief that the sun will rise to-morrow might be falsified if the earth came suddenly into contact with a large body which destroyed its rotation; but the laws of motion and the law of gravitation would not be infringed by such an event. The business of science is to find uniformities, such as the laws of motion and the law of gravitation, to which, so far as our experience extends, there are no exceptions. In this search science has been remarkably successful, and it may be conceded that such uniformities have held hitherto. This brings us back to the question: Have we any reason, assuming that they have always held in the past, to suppose that they will hold in the future?

It has been argued that we have reason to know that the future will resemble the past, because what was the future has constantly become the past, and has always been found to resemble the past, so that we really have experience of the future, namely of times which were formerly future, which we may call past futures. But such an argument really begs the very question at issue. We have experience of past futures, but not of future futures, and the question is: Will future futures resemble past futures? This question is not to be answered by an argument which starts from past futures alone. We have therefore still to seek for some principle which shall enable us to know that the future will follow the same laws as the past.

The reference to the future in this question is not essential. The same question arises when we apply the laws that work in our experience to past things of which we have no experience—as, for example, in geology, or in theories as to the origin of the Solar System. The question we really have to ask is: "When two things have been found to be often associated, and no instance is known of the one occurring without the other, does the occurrence of one of the two, in a fresh instance, give any good ground for expecting the other?" On our answer to this question must depend the validity of the whole of our expectations as to the future, the whole of the results obtained by induction, and in fact practically all the beliefs upon which our daily life is based.

It must be conceded, to begin with, that the fact that two things have been found often together and never apart does not, by itself, suffice to *prove* demonstratively that they will be found together in the next case we examine. The most we can hope is that the oftener things are found together, the more probable it becomes that they will be found together another time, and that, if they have been found together often enough, the probability will amount *almost* to certainty. It can never quite reach certainty, because we know that in spite of frequent repetitions there sometimes is a failure at the last, as in the case of the chicken whose neck is wrung. Thus probability is all we ought to seek.

It might be urged, as against the view we are advocating, that we know all natural phenomena to be subject to the reign of law, and that sometimes, on the basis of observation, we can see that only one law can possibly fit the facts of the case. Now to this view there are two answers. The first is that, even if *some* law which has no exceptions applies to our case, we can never, in practice, be sure that we have discovered that law and not one to which there are exceptions. The second is that the reign of law would seem to be itself only probable, and that our belief that it will hold in the future, or in unexamined cases in the past, is itself based upon the very principle we are examining.

The principle we are examining may be called the *principle of induction,* and its two parts may be stated as follows:

(*a*) When a thing of a certain sort A has been found to be associated with a thing of a certain other sort B, and has never been found dissociated from a thing of the sort B, the greater the number of cases in which A and B have been associated, the greater is the probability that they will be associated in a fresh case in which one of them is known to be present;

(*b*) Under the same circumstances, a sufficient number of cases of association will make the probability of a fresh association nearly a certainty, and will make it approach certainty without limit.

As just stated, the principle applies only to the verification of our expectation in a single fresh instance. But we want also to know that there is a probability in favour of the general law that things of the sort A are *always* associated with things of the sort B, provided a sufficient number of cases of association are known, and no cases of failure of association are known. The probability of the general law is obviously less than the probability of the particular case, since if the general law is true, the particular case must also be true, whereas the particular case may be true without the general law being true. Nevertheless the probability of the general law is increased by repetitions, just as the probability of the particular case is. We may therefore repeat the two parts of our principle as regards the general law, thus:

(*a*) The greater the number of cases in which a thing of the sort A has been found associated with a thing of the sort B, the more probable it is (if no cases of failure of association are known) that A is always associated with B;

(*b*) Under the same circumstances, a sufficient number of cases of the association of A with B will make it nearly certain that A is always associated with B, and will make this general law approach certainty without limit.

It should be noted that probability is always relative to certain data. In our case, the data are merely the known cases of coexistence of A and B. There may be other data, which *might* be taken into account, which would gravely alter the probability. For example, a man who had seen a great many white swans might argue, by our principle, that on the data it was *probable* that all swans were white, and this might be a perfectly sound argument. The argument is not disproved by the fact that some swans are black, because a thing may very well happen in spite of the fact that some data render it improbable. In the case of the swans, a man might know that colour is a very variable characteristic in many species of animals, and that, therefore, an induction as to colour is peculiarly liable to error. But this knowledge would be a fresh datum, by no means proving that the probability relative to our previous data had been wrongly estimated. The fact, therefore, that things often fail to fulfill our expectations is no evidence that our expectations will not *probably* be fulfilled in a given case or a given class of cases. Thus our inductive principle is at any rate not capable of being *disproved* by an appeal to experience.

The inductive principle, however, is equally incapable of being *proved* by an appeal to experience. Experience might conceivably confirm the inductive principle as regards the cases that have been already examined; but as regards unexamined cases, it is the inductive principle alone that can justify any inference from what has been examined to what has not been examined. All arguments which, on the basis of experience, argue as to the future or the unexperienced parts of the past or present, assume the inductive principle; hence we can never use experience to prove the inductive principle without begging the question. Thus we must either accept the inductive principle on the ground of its intrinsic evidence, or forgo all justification of our expectations about the future. If the principle is unsound, we have no reason to expect the sun to rise to-morrow, to expect bread to be more nourishing than a stone, or to expect that if we throw ourselves off the roof we shall fall. When we see what looks like our best friend approaching us, we shall have no reason to suppose that his body is not inhabited by the mind of our worst enemy or of some total stranger. All our conduct is based upon associations which have worked in the past, and which we therefore regard as likely to work in the future; and this likelihood is dependent for its validity upon the inductive principle.

The general principles of science, such as the belief in the reign of law, and the belief that every event must have a cause, are as completely dependent upon the inductive principle as are the beliefs of daily life. All such general principles are believed because mankind have found innumerable instances of their truth and no instances of their falsehood. But this affords no evidence for their truth in the future, unless the inductive principle is assumed.

Thus all knowledge which, on a basis of experience tells us something about what is not experienced, is based upon a belief which experience can neither confirm nor confute, yet which, at least in its more concrete applications, appears to be as firmly rooted in us as many of the facts of experience. The existence and justification of such be-liefs—for the inductive principle . . . is not the only example—raises some of the most difficult and most debated problems of philosophy. . . .

Further Questions

1. Give the best example you can of a situation in which someone might be making a mistake about his or her immediately experienced sense-data. Then explain whether your example gives you any reason to doubt Russell's views.
2. In Russell's view, is the relation between physical space-time and the spatial and temporal relations we immediately experience like the relation between physical objects and the sense-data we immediately experience? If not, how do these relationships differ?
3. "You probably think you know (that is, have a justified, true belief) that your entire conscious life is not just an elaborate dream. But you do not know any such thing. To justify your claim that your conscious life is not a dream, either you have to assume that it is not, for instance, by assuming you know intuitively that it is not, which is really no justification at all, or else you have to assume that on some prior occasion you determined that your conscious life then was not just an elaborate dream, which, of course, begs the question in that it assumes part of the very thing that you are now being asked to prove." How would Russell respond? How would you? Does your response reveal anything important about the nature of knowledge?
4. In the light of your own critical reflection on Russell's views, what do you think is the role of assumption in knowledge? To what extent, if any, does what we call knowledge of the world rest ultimately on faith? Do you find the extent of this dependence unsettling? Why, or why not?

Further Readings

Audi, Robert. *Belief, Justification, and Knowledge*. Belmont, CA: Wadsworth, 1988. An excellent contemporary introduction.
Chisholm, R. M. *Theory of Knowledge*. 2d ed. Englewood Cliffs, NJ: Prentice-Hall, 1977. A short, clear introduction to the foundations approach to theory of knowledge.

31   The Infinite Regress of Reasons

D. M. ARMSTRONG

Before his retirement, D. M. Armstrong taught philosophy at the University of Sydney, in Australia, and wrote extensively on metaphysics and epistemology. In this selection, which is slightly more technical than the other readings in this section but well worth the effort it will take to master it, Armstrong gives an unusually clear, systematic, and concise explanation of the problems that face traditional theories of knowledge, including foundationalism and coherence theories, and then suggests a reliability account of knowledge to replace them.

Armstrong's symbolism, which should seem quite natural once you get used to it, may pose a problem initially. Here is how to read it: The letter "A" (capital or lowercase) stands for any person, and the letters "p," "q," and "r" for any statements. For instance, in the sentence, "A knows that p," "A" could stand for Galileo and "p" for the statement that there are mountains on the moon; on these substitutions, "A knows that p," or as Armstrong sometimes puts it, "Kap," would stand for the sentence, "Galileo knows that there are mountains on the moon." (Just once, in part III, section 2, Armstrong also uses "A," "B," and "C" to stand for events, such as the onset of a thunderstorm or your reading of this sentence.) Armstrong uses the expression "Kap" to stand for "A knows that p"; "Bap" for "A believes that p"; "~Kap" for "A does *not* know that p"; and "~Bap" for "A does *not* believe that p." Finally, the word "punter" in the first paragraph is Australian for "someone who gambles on horses."

Reading Questions

1. Think of clear, simple examples to illustrate the points Armstrong makes in his five "Conditions" paragraphs.
2. The Infinite Regress of Reasons is an infinite regress because knowledge must be based on evidence that is known. Because that evidence also is knowledge, it must be based on further evidence that is known, which, since that latter evidence also is knowledge . . . and so on. How did Descartes solve this sort of problem? How did Russell, in the preceding selection, solve it? (Or did he?) Finally, what do you think would be the most hopeful way to try to solve this problem?

I. THE EVIDENCE-CONDITION

. . . 'A KNOWS THAT P' entails 'A truly believes that p.' But true belief does not entail knowledge. The latter point is made by Plato in the *Theaetetus* 200D–201C). It may be illustrated, for instance, by *The Case of the Optimistic Punter*. Because he is optimistic, he regularly *believes* that the horses he bets on will win. But he never has any reliable information about these horses. As a result, he normally loses. From time to time, however, his horses win. On such occasions his beliefs are true. But we do not think that he *knows* that these horses will win.

This is the occasion for introducing the Evidence-condition. The trouble about the punter, it is plausibly suggested, is that he lacks *good reasons* or *sufficient evidence* for his true belief. If only he had that, he would know.

However, when the Evidence-condition is scrutinized more closely, all sorts of problems emerge. In this section no less than five subconditions will be outlined which the Evidence-conditions must satisfy, if it is accepted at all. All these sub-conditions raise important problems.

Condition 1. Suppose that p is true, A believes that p and A has evidence for 'p,' namely 'q.' It cannot be the case that A *knows* that p unless, as a matter of objective fact, 'q' constitutes *sufficient evidence* to establish the truth of 'p.' . . .

Condition 2. Suppose that 'p' is true, A believes that p, A has evidence 'q' for 'p,' and 'q' is in fact sufficient evidence for the truth of 'p.' It may still be the case that A does not realize, or has not noticed, the relevance of his evidence 'q' to 'p.' He may, for instance, have failed to 'put two and two together.'

What is needed is that A's evidence should be actually operative in A's mind, supporting his belief that p. We must therefore have an account of what it is for somebody actually to *take* one proposition as a (conclusive) reason for accepting another. . . .

Condition 3. But even if 'p' is true, A believes that p, A has evidence 'q' for the truth of 'p,' 'q' is

From Belief, Truth and Knowledge *by D. M. Armstrong.* © Cambridge University Press 1973. Reprinted *with the permission of Cambridge University Press.*

in fact sufficient evidence for 'p,' and the evidence actually operates in A's mind to support his belief that p, it still does not follow that A *knows* that p. For although 'q' in fact supports 'p' conclusively, might not A be reasoning from 'q' to 'p' according to some *false* principle which in this particular case moves from a truth to a truth? For instance, A's reasoning from 'q' to 'p' might involve a compensating error peculiar to the case in hand. It seems that we need to say that the principle of reasoning according to which A operates, when his belief that q operates in his mind to support his belief that p, is a *true* principle. This stipulation, by the way, makes Condition 1 redundant.

Condition 4. We now stipulate that 'p' is true, A believes that p, A has evidence 'q' for 'p,' the evidence actually operates in A's mind to support his belief that p, and the principle of reasoning according to which A operates is a true principle. It still does not follow that A *knows* that p. For although the principle of A's reasoning is true, may it not be that A accepts this principle on thoroughly bad grounds? And could we then say that he knew that p? It seems that we ought to amend Condition 3 by saying that the principle of A's reasoning is not simply true, but is *known* by A to be true. But this raises this difficulty that our analysis of A knows that p now involves *knowledge* by A of at least one general principle. What account shall we give of *this* knowledge?

Condition 5. Let us waive this difficulty (for the present). Suppose 'p' is true, A believes that p, A has evidence 'q' for 'p,' the evidence actually operates in A's mind to support his belief that p, and the principle of reasoning according to which A operates is known by A to be true. Even now it is not entailed that A knows p. For consider A's evidence 'q.' Do we not require the further stipulation that A *know* that q is true? Suppose it not to be the case that A knows that q (~Kaq). Is not 'p' insufficiently supported?

But if this is correct, then knowledge that p can be defined only in terms of *knowledge* that q. 'q' will then demand support in A's mind from evidence 'r,' and an infinite regress threatens.

Although the apparent necessity for Condition 4 also introduces the threat of an infinite regress, historically it is the regress which results from the demand that the evidence be itself some-

thing which A knows which has especially troubled supporters of the classical 'good reasons' analysis of knowledge. . . .

II. THE INFINITE REGRESS OF REASONS

Knowledge entails true belief, but true belief does not entail knowledge. It is therefore suggested that knowledge is a true belief for which the believer has sufficient evidence, or some such formula. But the evidence will have to be some proposition, 'q,' which is *known* to A. . . .

III. DIFFERENT REACTIONS TO THE REGRESS

1. The '*Sceptical*' *Reaction.* We may begin by distinguishing between 'sceptical' and 'non-sceptical' reactions to the regress. An extreme form of the sceptical reaction would be to say that the infinite regress showed that the concept of knowledge involves a contradiction. A moderate view would be that the word 'know,' although it attributes true belief, attributes nothing further of an objective nature to the belief—no relation to the facts—except truth. . . .

2. *The regress is infinite but virtuous.* The first non-sceptical solution which may be canvassed is that the regress exists, but is virtuous. Suppose that event A has a prior cause B, B has a prior cause C, and so, perhaps, *ad infinitum.* Few modern philosophers would consider this latter progression to infinity a vicious one. So perhaps A's knowledge that p rests upon knowledge that q which rests upon knowledge that r, and so on without stop. . . .

It can hardly be pretended, however, that this reaction to the regress has much plausibility. Like the 'sceptical' solution, it is a *desperate* solution, to be considered only if all others are clearly seen to be unsatisfactory.

3. *The regress is finite, but has no end.* Suppose, then, that the regress is not virtuous. Then either the regress has no end, or it has an end. If it has no

end, then at some point the reasons must come back upon their own tail, so that 'p' is supported by 'q,' which is supported by 'r,' which is supported by 's,' . . . which is supported by . . . , which is supported by 'p.' This may seem to involve *vicious* circularity. But perhaps it need not. If we have a circle of true beliefs which mutually support each other in this way, then it might be suggested that, once the circle is sufficiently comprehensive and the mutual support sufficiently strong, we would not have mere true beliefs but pieces of knowledge. This may be called the *Coherence* analysis of the concept of knowledge. . . .

Clearly, there are many difficulties for this 'Coherence theory of knowledge.' For instance, what criterion can be given to show that a circle of true beliefs is 'sufficiently comprehensive'? It is not easy to say. And might there not be a sufficiently comprehensive circle of true beliefs which was arrived at so irregularly and luckily that we would not want to call it knowledge?

4. *The regress ends in self-evident truths.* If the Coherence analysis is rejected, then at some point in the regress of reasons (perhaps right at the beginning) we will reach knowledge which is *not* based on reasons. I will call such knowledge 'non-inferential' knowledge. I oppose it to 'inferential' knowledge, which *is* based on reasons. Once it is granted that there is an objective notion of knowledge; that the infinite regress of reasons is in some way vicious; and that the regress cannot be stopped by judicious circularity; then it must be granted that, when A knows that p, then *either* this knowledge is non-inferential, or it is based on a finite set of reasons terminating in non-inferential knowledge.

The problem then comes to be that of giving an account of non-inferential knowledge. . . .

The classical answer is: non-inferential beliefs which are self-evident, indubitable or incorrigible. They will serve to stop the regress and act as the foundations of knowledge. This has been the *standard* solution from the time of Descartes until quite recently.

However, I reject the whole notion of beliefs that it is logically impossible to be wrong about. I think the logical possibility of error is always present in any belief about any subject matter whatsoever. In any case, it has been demonstrated again and again that, even if there is such self-evident

knowledge, it is completely insufficient in *extent* to serve as a foundation for all the things we ordinarily claim to know, even when we have circumscribed that claim by careful reflection. In the past, defenders of this Cartesian solution have regularly had to cut down the scope of our supposed knowledge in a completely unacceptable manner. (For instance, it becomes difficult to claim that there is any empirical knowledge, non-inferential or inferential, beyond that of our own current states of mind.)

5. '*Initial credibility.*' The alternative is to attempt an account of non-inferential knowledge without appealing to such self-evident truths. O'Hair has distinguished two sorts of view here, which he calls 'Initial credibility' and 'Externalist' views.

First a word about 'Initial credibility' theories. It might be maintained that certain classes of our non-inferential beliefs have an intrinsic claim to credibility, even although error about them is a logical and even an empirical possibility. Instances might be beliefs based directly upon sense-perception, upon memory, upon intuition of the simpler logical necessities, or perhaps only upon suitable subclasses of these classes. Now suppose that a belief is non-inferential, is 'initially credible' and is also *true*. Might it not then be accounted a case of non-inferential *knowledge*?

This approach strikes me as more hopeful than the possible reactions to the infinite regress which have already been mentioned. But it involves certain difficulties. It is easy, for instance, to construct non-inferential memory beliefs which are true, but which we certainly would not call knowledge. Thus, a probe in my brain might produce the belief in me that I had an itch in my little finger three days ago. By sheer coincidence, the belief might be true. Or a veridical memory-trace might degenerate but, in the course of a multi-stage degeneration, the original encoding might be reinstated by a sheer fluke. Some way of excluding such cases would have to be found. I myself am convinced, although I will not try to demonstrate the point here, that the only way to achieve such exclusions satisfactorily is to pass over into an 'Externalist' theory.

6. '*Externalist*' *theories.* According to 'Externalist' accounts of non-inferential knowledge, what makes a true non-inferential belief a case of *knowledge* is some natural relation which holds between

the belief-state, Bap, and the situation which makes the belief true. It is a matter of a certain relation holding between the believer and the world. It is important to notice that, unlike 'Cartesian' and 'Initial Credibility' theories, Externalist theories are regularly developed as theories of the nature of knowledge *generally* and not simply as theories of non-inferential knowledge. But they still have a peculiar importance in the case of non-inferential knowledge because they serve to solve the problem of the infinite regress.

Externalist theories may be further subdivided into 'Causal' and 'Reliability' theories.

6 (i) *Causal theories.* The central notion in causal theories may be illustrated by the simplest case. The suggestion is that Bap is a case of Kap if 'p' is true and, furthermore, the situation that makes 'p' true is causally responsible for the existence of the belief-state Bap. I not only believe, but *know,* that the room is rather hot. Now it is certainly *the excessive heat of the room* which has caused me to have this belief. This causal relation, it may then be suggested, is what makes my belief a case of knowledge. . . .

Causal theories face two main types of difficulty. In the first place, even if we restrict ourselves to knowledge of particular matters of fact, not every case of knowledge is a case where the situation known is causally responsible for the existence of the belief. For instance, we appear to have some knowledge of the future. And even if all such knowledge is in practice inferential, non-inferential knowledge of the future (for example, that I will be ill tomorrow) seems to be an intelligible possibility. Yet it could hardly be held that my illness tomorrow causes my belief today that I will be ill tomorrow. . . .

In the second place, and much more seriously, cases can be envisaged where the situation that makes 'p' true gives rise to Bap, but we would not want to say that A *knew* that p. Suppose, for instance, that A is in a hypersensitive and deranged state, so that almost any considerable sensory stimulus causes him to believe that there is a sound of a certain sort in his immediate environment. Now suppose that, on a particular occasion, the considerable sensory stimulus which produces that belief is, in fact, *a sound of just that sort in his immediate environment.* Here the p-situation produces Bap,

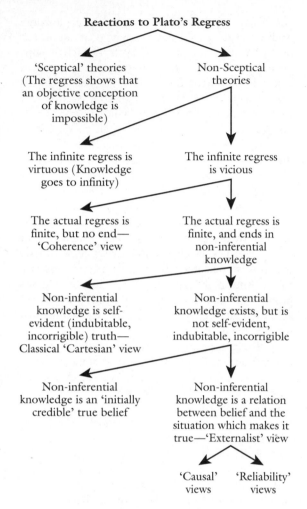

but we would not want to say that it was a case of knowledge.

I believe that such cases can be excluded only by filling out the Causal Analysis with a Reliability condition. But once this is done, I think it turns out that the Causal part of the analysis becomes redundant, and that the Reliability condition is sufficient by itself for giving an account of non-inferential (and inferential) knowledge.

6 (ii) *Reliability theories.* The second 'Externalist' approach is in terms of the *empirical reliability* of the belief involved. Knowledge is empirically reliable belief . . . [e.g., "the Thermometer View," below].

It is interesting to notice that a Reliability analysis is considered for a moment by Plato in the

Meno only to be dropped immediately. . . . Socrates asserts that '. . . true opinion is as good a guide as knowledge for the purpose of acting rightly,' and goes on to ask whether we should not draw the conclusion that 'right opinion is something no less useful than knowledge.' Meno however objects:

> Except that the man with knowledge will always be successful, and the man with only right opinion only sometimes.

Unfortunately, however, Socrates brushes aside this tentative development of a Reliability view, saying:

> What? Will he not always be successful so long as he has the right opinion?

Meno immediately concedes the point.

This concludes our brief survey. In philosophy, when one finds oneself in a difficult intellectual situation, it is often vitally important to be aware of the full range of response which is open to one. And in philosophy, if one practises it honestly, one invariably is in a more or less difficult intellectual situation. The survey just made was intended to create an awareness of the many different responses open to us in the difficult situation created by the threatened infinite regress involved in the classical analysis of knowledge. Against this background, I proceed to put forward a suggested solution of the problem.

FROM NON-INFERENTIAL KNOWLEDGE

. . . Thinking about the threatened infinite regress in the classical analysis of knowledge seems to lead to the conclusion that there must be non-inferential knowledge. Furthermore, we seem *forced* in the case of this sort of knowledge to look for some non-classical solution to the problem. (The classical or 'Cartesian' postulation of self-evident truths can rather easily be shown to be an insufficient account of the basis of all that we think we know.) If we can find a non-classical solution to the problem of non-inferential knowledge, where such a solution is clearly required, we may then try to extend the solution to cover all cases of knowledge. . . .

THE 'THERMOMETER' VIEW OF NON-INFERENTIAL KNOWLEDGE

Suppose that 'p' is true, and A believes that p, but his belief is not supported by any reasons. 'p' might be the proposition that there is a sound in A's environment. . . . What makes such a belief a case of knowledge? My suggestion is that there must be a *law-like connection* between the state of affairs Bap and the state of affairs that makes 'p' true such that, given Bap, it must be the case that p.

The quickest way to grasp the suggestion is to use a model. Let us compare non-inferential beliefs to the temperature-readings given by a thermometer. In some cases, the thermometer-reading will fail to correspond to the temperature of the environment. Such a reading may be compared to non-inferential false belief. In other cases, the reading will correspond to the actual temperature. Such a reading is like non-inferential true belief. The second case, where reading and actual environmental temperature coincide, is then subdivided into two sorts of case. First, suppose that the thermometer is a bad one, but that, on a certain occasion, the thermometer-reading coincides with the actual temperature. (Cf. the stopped clock that shows the right time twice a day.) Such a reading is to be compared with non-inferential true belief which falls short of knowledge. Suppose finally that the thermometer is a good one, so that a reading of 'T°' on the thermometer ensures that the environmental temperature is T. Such a reading is to be compared with non-inferential *knowledge*. When a true belief unsupported by reasons stands to the situation truly believed to exist as a thermometer-reading in a good thermometer stands to the actual temperature, then we have non-inferential knowledge.

I think the picture given by the thermometer-model is intuitively clear. The problem is to give a formal account of the situation. . . .

The model of the thermometer gives us further assistance here. For a thermometer to be reliable on a certain occasion in registering a certain temperature as T° we do not demand that there be a true law-like generalization: 'If any thermometer registers "T°," then the temperature is T°.' In the first place, we recognize that there can be good and bad thermometers. In the second place, we do not even demand that a good thermometer provide a reliable reading under every condition. We recognize that there may be special environmental conditions under which even a 'good' thermometer is unreliable.

What do we demand? Let us investigate a far less stringent condition. Suppose, on a certain occasion, a thermometer is reliably registering 'T°.' There must be some property of the instrument and/or its circumstances such that, if any thing has this property, and registers 'T°,' it must be the case, as a matter of natural law, that the temperature *is* T°. We might find it extremely hard to specify this property (set of properties). The specification might have to be given in the form of a blank cheque to be filled in only after extensive investigation. But it may be relatively easy to recognize that a certain thermometer is operating reliably, and so that such a specification is possible. . . .

Further Questions

1. Russell advocates a foundations account of knowledge. Armstrong an externalist (reliability) account. Clearly explain the essential differences between these types of accounts. Which seems most plausible to you, and why?
2. "If knowledge is justified, true belief, then there must be some things we know directly (not on the basis of anything else we know, but rather on their own basis—that is, these things must be self-justifying) or else we are led into a regress the result of which is that our so-called knowledge is without foundation—hence not really knowledge at all." First, give the best argument you can that the quoted remarks are true. Second, what is the significance of the remarks? Third, explain how the threatened, unsettling "regress" can best be stopped.

Further Readings

Morton, Adam. *A Guide Through the Theory of Knowledge*. Belmont, CA: Wadsworth, 1977. A useful beginning text.
Pollock, John. *Knowledge and Justification*. Totowa, NJ: Rowman and Littlefield, 1986. Sophisticated, but readable.

Part VI

God

DOES GOD EXIST?

On this topic, *everybody* has a belief. What's *yours*?

Yes? No? Maybe?

Having beliefs is easy. Understanding how you came to have them and then questioning your beliefs with an open mind is extremely difficult.

Whatever your belief about God, you are not likely to change it on the basis of anything you read. On other topics, reading and discussing opposing views often leads people to change their minds. But on the topic of God, people usually are not openly searching for the truth but merely defending their beliefs. It is a bit like watching a football game: no matter which team is better, you root for your side.

Which side are *you* on? In the readings that follow, if you merely seek support for your belief, then—whatever you believe—for you the question is closed.

32   The Ontological Argument

ANSELM

St. Anselm (1033–1109), a Benedictine monk, was Abbot of Bec, at the time one of the great centers of learning in Europe; he later became Archbishop of Canterbury. In his book *Monologion,* he advances the proof for God from the degrees of perfection found in creatures and also formulates a version of the cosmological argument (for later versions of these arguments, see the selection by Aquinas). He makes the point that the meaning of "nothing" is "not anything," stressing that "nothing" should not be regarded as the name of a shadowy, mysterious entity. His book *Proslogion* contains the famous ontological argument reprinted below; also reprinted below is the monk Guanilo's criticism of the argument and Anselm's reply.

Reading Questions

1. List all of the premises, or assumptions, on which the ontological argument depends. What is the argument's conclusion?
2. Explain, in your own words, the point of Guanilo's "lost island" objection.
3. How does Anselm respond to Guanilo's objection? Do you find his response adequate?

. . . I BEGAN TO ASK MYSELF whether there might be found a single argument which would require no other for its proof than itself alone; and alone would suffice to demonstrate that God truly exists, and that there is a supreme good requiring nothing else, which all other things require for their existence and well-being; and whatever we believe regarding the divine Being.

Although I often and earnestly directed my thought to this end, and at some times that which I sought seemed to be just within my reach, while again it wholly evaded my mental vision, at last in despair I was about to cease, as if from the search for a thing which could not be found. But when I wished to exclude this thought altogether, lest, by busying my mind to no purpose, it should keep me from other thoughts, in which I might be successful; then more and more, though I was unwilling and shunned it, it began to force itself upon me, with a kind of importunity. So, one day, when I was exceedingly wearied with resisting its importunity, in the very conflict of my thoughts, the proof of which I had despaired offered itself, so that I eagerly embraced the thoughts which I was strenuously repelling. . . .

And so Lord, do thou, who dost give understanding to faith, give me, so far as thou knowest it to be profitable, to understand that thou art as we believe; and that thou art that which we believe. And, indeed, we believe that thou art a being than which nothing greater can be conceived. Or is there no such nature, since the fool hath said in his heart, there is no God? But, at any rate, this very fool, when he hears of this being of which I speak—a being than which nothing greater can be conceived—understands what he hears, and what

From Proslogion, *translated by Sidney Norton Deane (Open Court, 1903), pp. 1–2, 6–9, 149–51, 158–59.*

he understands is in his understanding; although he does not understand it to exist.

For, it is one thing for an object to be in the understanding, and another to understand that the object exists. When a painter first conceives of what he will afterwards perform, he has it in his understanding, but he does not yet understand it to be, because he has not yet performed it. But after he has made the painting, he both has it in his understanding, and he understands that it exists, because he has made it.

Hence, even the fool is convinced that something exists in the understanding, at least, than which nothing greater can be conceived. For, when he hears of this, he understands it. And whatever is understood, exists in the understanding. And assuredly that, than which nothing greater can be conceived, cannot exist in the understanding alone. For, suppose it exists in the understanding alone: then it can be conceived to exist in reality; which is greater.

Therefore, if that, than which nothing greater can be conceived, exists in the understanding alone, the very being, than which nothing greater can be conceived, is one, than which a greater can be conceived. But obviously this is impossible. Hence, there is no doubt that there exists a being, than which nothing greater can be conceived, and it exists both in the understanding and in reality....

And it assuredly exists so truly, that it cannot be conceived not to exist. For, it is possible to conceive of a being which cannot be conceived not to exist, and this is greater than one which can be conceived not to exist. Hence, if that, than which nothing greater can be conceived, can be conceived not to exist, it is not that, than which nothing greater can be conceived. But this is an irreconcilable contradiction. There is, then, so truly a being than which nothing greater can be conceived to exist, that it cannot even be conceived not to exist; and this being thou art, O Lord, our God.

So truly, therefore, dost thou exist, O Lord, my God, that thou canst not be conceived not to exist; and rightly. For if a mind could conceive of a being better than thee, the creature would rise above the Creator; and this is most absurd. And, indeed, whatever else there is, except thee alone, can be conceived not to exist. To thee alone, therefore, it belongs to exist more truly than all other beings,

and hence in a higher degree than all others. For, whatever else exists does not exist so truly, and hence in a less degree it belongs to it to exist. Why, then, has the fool said in his heart, there is no God, since it is so evident, to a rational mind, that thou dost exist in the highest degree of all? Why, except that he is dull and a fool? . . .

IN BEHALF OF THE FOOL

AN ANSWER TO THE ARGUMENT OF ANSELM BY GAUNILO, A MONK OF MARMOUTIER

. . . if it should be said that a being which cannot be even conceived in terms of any fact, is in the understanding. I do not deny that this being is, accordingly, in my understanding. But since through this fact it can in no wise attain to real existence also, I do not yet concede to it that existence at all, until some certain proof of it shall be given.

For he who says that this being exists, because otherwise the being which is greater than all will not be greater than all, does not attend strictly to what he is saying. For I do not yet say, no, I even deny or doubt that this being is greater than any real object. Nor do I concede to it any other existence than this (if it should be called existence) which it has when the mind, according to a word merely heard, tries to form the image of an object absolutely unknown to it.

How, then, is the veritable existence of that being proved to me from the assumption, by hypothesis, that it is greater than all other beings? For I should still deny this, or doubt your demonstration of it, to this extent, that I should not admit that this being is in my understanding and concept even in the way in which many objects whose real existence is uncertain and doubtful, are in my understanding and concept. For it should be proved first that this being itself really exists somewhere; and then, from the fact that it is greater than all, we shall not hesitate to infer that it also subsists in itself.

For example: it is said that somewhere in the ocean is an island, which, because of the difficulty, or rather the impossibility, of discovering what

EXISTENCE IS NOT A PREDICATE

Immanuel Kant

Being is obviously not a real predicate; that is, it is not a concept of something which could be added to the concept of a thing. It is merely the positing of thing . . . The proposition, *God is omnipotent,* contains two concepts, each of which has its object—God and omnipotence. The small word *is* adds no new predicate, but only serves to posit the predicate. . . . If, now, we take the subject (God) with all its predicates (among which is omnipotence), and say *God is,* or *There is a God,* we attach no new predicate to the concept of God, but only posit the subject . . . with all its predicates and indeed postulate it as being an object that stands in relation to my concept. The content of both must be one and the same; nothing can have been added to the concept, which expresses merely what is possible, by my thinking its object . . . as given absolutely. Otherwise stated, the real contains no more than the merely possible. A hundred real thalers do not contain the least coin more than a hundred possible thalers. For as the latter signify the concept, and the former the object and the positing of the object, should the former contain more than the latter, my concept would not, in that case, express the whole object, and would not therefore be an adequate concept of it. My financial position is, however, affected very differently by a hundred real thalers than it is by the mere concept of them (that is, of their possibility). For the object, as it actually exists, is not analytically contained in my concept . . . and yet the conceived hundred thalers are not themselves in the least increased through thus acquiring existence outside my concept.

By whatever and by however many predicates we may think a thing . . . we do not make the least addition to the thing when we further declare that this thing exists. Otherwise it would not be exactly the same thing that exists, but something more than we had thought in the concept; and we could not, therefore, say that the exact object of my concept exists. . . . When, therefore, I think a being as the supreme reality, without any defect, the question still remains whether it exists or not.

From *The Critique of Pure Reason* (1781) (A-598-600:B626-628)

does not exist, is called the lost island. And they say that this island has an inestimable wealth of all manner of riches and delicacies in greater abundance than is told of the Islands of the Blest; and that having no owner or inhabitant, it is more excellent than all other countries, which are inhabited by mankind, in the abundance with which it is stored.

Now if someone should tell me that there is such an island, I should easily understand his words, in which there is no difficulty. But suppose that he went on to say, as if by a logical inference: "You can no longer doubt that this island which is more excellent than all lands exists somewhere, since you have no doubt that it is in your understanding. And since it is more excellent not to be in the understanding alone, but to exist both in the understanding and in reality, for this reason it must exist. For if it does not exist, any land which really exists will be more excellent than it; and so the island already understood by you to be more excellent will not be more excellent."

If a man should try to prove to me by such reasoning that this island truly exists, and that its existence should no longer be doubted, either I should believe that he was jesting, or I know not which I ought to regard as the greater fool: myself, supposing that I should allow this proof; or him, if he should suppose that he had established with any certainty the existence of this island. For he ought to show first that the hypothetical excellence of this island exists as a real and indubitable fact, and in no wise as any unreal object, or one whose existence is uncertain, in my understanding.

ANSELM'S REPLY

But, you say, it is as if one should suppose an island in the ocean, which surpasses all lands in its fertility, and which, because of the difficulty, or rather the impossibility, of discovering what does not exist, is called a lost island; and should say that there can be no doubt that this island truly exists in reality, for this reason, that one who hears it described easily understands what he hears.

Now I promise confidently that if any man shall devise anything existing either in reality or in concept alone (except that than which a greater cannot be conceived) to which he can adapt the sequence of my reasoning, I will discover that thing, and will give him his lost island, not to be lost again.

But it now appears that this being than which a greater is inconceivable cannot be conceived not to be, because it exists on so assured a ground of truth; for otherwise it would not exist at all.

Hence, if any one says that he conceives this being not to exist, I say that at the time when he conceives of this either he conceives of a being than which a greater is inconceivable, or he does not conceive at all. If he does not conceive, he does not conceive of the nonexistence of that of which he does not conceive. But if he does conceive, he certainly conceives of a being which cannot be even conceived not to exist. For if it could be conceived not to exist, it could be conceived to have a beginning and an end. But this is impossible.

He, then, who conceives of this being conceives of a being which cannot be even conceived not to exist; but he who conceives of this being does not conceive that it does not exist; else he conceives what is inconceivable. The nonexistence, then, of that than which a greater cannot be conceived is inconceivable.

Further Questions

1. Imagine you are Guanilo and that you have an opportunity to respond again to Anselm. What would you say?
2. Immanuel Kant, in *Critique of Pure Reason* (1781), claimed the ontological argument is unsound because existence is not a perfection: "If we think in a thing every feature of reality except one, the missing reality is not added by my saying that the defective thing exists . . . since otherwise what exists would be something different from what I thought. When, therefore, I think a being as the supreme reality, without any defect, the question still remains whether it exists or not." Explain, in your own words, whether you agree with Kant, and why.
3. In "An Ontological Argument for the Devil," *The Monist* (1970), David and Marjorie Haight argue that if the ontological argument is sound, then an analogous argument from the premise that we can have a concept of "something than which nothing *worse* can be conceived" to the conclusion that this awful thing ("the Devil"), therefore, exists would also be sound; for if the awful thing did not exist we could think of something still more awful, namely, the awful thing's actually existing. Do you agree that this argument is as good (or as bad) as the ontological argument?

Further Readings

Barnes, Jonathan. *The Ontological Argument*. London: Macmillan, 1972. A good general discussion.
Kolak, Daniel. In *Search of God: The Language and Logic of Belief*. Belmont, CA: Wadsworth, 1994. An exploration of how the mind formulates and tries to solve its ultimate questions.
Plantinga, Alvin, ed. *The Ontological Argument from St. Anselm to Contemporary Philosophers*. Garden City, NY: Doubleday, 1965. Just what the title implies.

33   The Five Ways and the Doctrine of Analogy

THOMAS AQUINAS

Thomas Aquinas (1225–1274) was born of Italian nobility and began his education in Naples. After becoming a Dominican monk, he went to Cologne to study under Albertus Magnus, the leading Aristotelian philosopher of the time, then went to Paris and taught theology. Aquinas returned to Italy in 1259 and remained there for most of the rest of his life. He is generally regarded as the greatest scholastic philosopher. Catholics consider him the greatest Christian theologian. His two major works are *Summa Theologica* and *Summa Contra Gentiles*.

Aquinas's famous "Five Ways" of proving the existence of God is the best-known passage from his works. The first way (of the five ways) infers from the fact of change the existence of an Unmoved Mover that originates change. The second uses the fact that some things are caused to infer the existence of a First Cause. The third infers from the fact that some things are contingent, or capable of coming into and going out of existence, the existence of something which is necessary, or incapable of coming into and going out of existence. The fourth uses the fact that there are degrees of excellence to infer the existence of a perfect being. The fifth uses the alleged fact that natural objects behave purposefully to infer the existence of an intelligence that directs the activities of natural objects.

Reading Questions

1. Explain in your own words Aquinas's arguments. Can you think of any ways in which they might be criticized effectively? Can you think of any reasons why the second and third arguments are generally regarded as the most interesting ones?
2. Aquinas wrote before the advent of modern science. Does it still make sense today to try to prove the existence of God by appeal to the nature of the world?
3. Must everything have a cause? Are there some things which just *are,* i.e., are not caused by anything else?

THE FIVE WAYS

THE EXISTENCE OF GOD can be proved in five ways.

The first and more manifest way is the argument from motion. It is certain, and evident to our senses, that in the world some things are in motion. Now whatever is moved is moved by another, for nothing can be moved except it is in potentiality to that towards which it is moved; whereas a thing moves inasmuch as it is in act. For motion is nothing else than the reduction of something from potentiality to actuality. But nothing can be reduced from potentiality to actuality, except by something in a state of actuality. Thus that which is actually hot, as fire, makes wood, which is potentially hot, to be actually hot, and thereby moves and changes it. Now it is not possible that the same thing should be at once in actuality and potentiality in the same respect, but only in different respects. For what is actually hot cannot simultaneously be potentially hot; but it is simultaneously potentially cold. It is therefore impossible that in the same respect and in the same way a thing should be both mover and moved, i.e., that it should move itself. Therefore, whatever is moved must be moved by another. If that by which it is moved be itself moved, then this also must needs be moved by another, and that by another again. But this cannot go on to infinity, because then there would be no first mover, and consequently no other mover, seeing that subsequent movers move only inasmuch as they are moved by the first mover; as the staff moves only because it is moved by the hand. Therefore it is necessary to arrive at a first mover, moved by no other; and this everyone understands to be God.

The second way is from the nature of efficient cause. In the world of sensible things we find there is an order of efficient causes. There is no case known (neither is it, indeed, possible) in which a thing is found to be the efficient cause of itself; for so it would be prior to itself, which is impossible. Now in efficient causes it is not possible to go on to infinity, because in all efficient causes following in order, the first is the cause of the intermediate cause, and the intermediate is the cause of the ultimate cause, whether the intermediate cause be several, or one only. Now to take away the cause is to take away the effect. Therefore, if there be no first cause among efficient causes, there will be no ultimate, nor any intermediate, cause. But if in efficient causes it is possible to go on to infinity, there will be no first efficient cause, neither will there be an ultimate effect, nor any intermediate efficient causes; all of which is plainly false. Therefore it is necessary to admit a first efficient cause, to which everyone gives the name of God.

The third way is taken from possibility and necessity, and runs thus. We find in nature things that are possible to be and not to be, since they are found to be generated, and to be corrupted, and consequently, it is possible for them to be and not to be. But it is impossible for these always to exist, for that which can not-be at some time is not. Therefore, if everything can not-be, then at one time there was nothing in existence. Now if this were true, even now there would be nothing in existence, because that which does not exist begins to exist only through something already existing. Therefore, if at one time nothing was in existence, it would have been impossible for anything to have begun to exist; and thus even now nothing would be in existence—which is absurd. Therefore, not

all beings are merely possible, but there must exist something the existence of which is necessary. But every necessary thing either has its necessity caused by another, or not. Now it is impossible to go on to infinity in necessary things which have their necessity caused by another, as has been already proved in regard to efficient causes. Therefore we cannot but admit the existence of some being having of itself its own necessity, and not receiving it from another, but rather causing in others their necessity. This all men speak of as God.

The fourth way is taken from the gradation to be found in things. Among beings there are some more and some less good, true, noble, and the like. But *more* and *less* are predicated of different things according as they resemble in their different ways something which is the maximum, as a thing is said to be hotter according as it more nearly resembles that which is hottest; so that there is something which is truest, something best, something noblest, and, consequently, something which is most in being, for those things that are greatest in truth are greatest in being, . . . Now the maximum in any genus is the cause of all in that genus, as fire, which is the maximum of heat, is the cause of all hot things, as is said in the same book. Therefore there must also be something which is to all beings the cause of their being, goodness, and every other perfection; and this we call God.

The fifth way is taken from the governance of the world. We see that things which lack knowledge, such as natural bodies, act for an end, and this is evident from their acting always, or nearly always, in the same way, so as to obtain the best result. Hence it is plain that they achieve their end, not fortuitously, but designedly. Now whatever lacks knowledge cannot move towards an end, unless it be directed by some being endowed with knowledge and intelligence; as the arrow is directed by the archer. Therefore some intelligent being exists by whom all natural things are directed to their end; and this being we call God.

THE DOCTRINE OF ANALOGY

Since it is possible to find in God every perfection of creatures, but in another and more eminent way, whatever names unqualifiedly designate a perfection without defect are predicated of God and of other things: for example, goodness, wisdom, being, and the like. But when any name expresses such perfections along with a mode that is proper to a creature, it can be said of God only according to likeness and metaphor. According to metaphor, what belongs to one thing is transferred to another, as when we say that a man is a *stone* because of the hardness of his intellect. Such names are used to designate the species of a created thing, for example, *man* and *stone;* for to each species belongs its own mode of perfection and being. The same is true of whatever names designate the properties of things, which are caused by the proper principles of their species. Hence, they can be said of God only metaphorically. But the names that express such perfections along with the mode of supereminence with which they belong to God are said of God alone. Such names are the *highest good, the first being,* and the like.

I have said that some of the aforementioned names signify a perfection without defect. This is true with reference to that which the name was imposed to signify; for as to the mode of signification, every name is defective. For by means of a name we express things in the way in which the intellect conceives them. For our intellect, taking the origin of its knowledge from the senses, does not transcend the mode which is found in sensible things in which the form and the subject of the form are not identical owning to the composition of form and matter. Now, a simple form is indeed found among such things, but one that is imperfect because it is not subsisting; on the other hand, though a subsisting subject of a form is found among sensible things, it is not simple but rather concreted. Whatever our intellect signifies as subsisting, therefore, it signifies in concretion; but what it signifies as simple, . . .

Now, the mode of supereminence in which the abovementioned perfections are found in God can be signified by names used by us only through negation, as when we say that God is *eternal* or *infinite,* or also through a relation of God to other things, as when He is called the *first cause* or the *highest good.* For we cannot grasp what God is, but only what He is not and how other things are related to Him, as is clear from what we said above.

Further Questions

1. Imagine that Aquinas were alive today and knew modern science. Would (should) he change any of his views?
2. Are there questions, such as "Why is there something rather than nothing at all? that science cannot now answer and never will be able to answer? If there are, can religion answer these questions and justify its answers, or are the questions simply unanswerable?

Further Readings

Kenny, Anthony. *Five Ways: Saint Thomas Aquinas's Proofs of God's Existence.* Boston: Routledge & Kegan Paul, 1969. A thorough, skillful commentary.

Mackie, J. L. *The Miracle of Theism.* Oxford: Oxford University Press, 1982. Arguments for and against the existence of God discussed by a distinguished English philosopher.

The Wager

BLAISE PASCAL

The French thinker Blaise Pascal (1623–1662), famous today primarily as a mathematician, was also a theologian, scientist, philosopher, and inventor. As a mathematician, Pascal made major contributions to probability theory, number theory, and geometry. In this selection, he argues that it is in your rational self-interest to believe that God exists.

Reading Questions

1. Is Pascal right that we must wager on whether God exists? Why can't we simply suspend judgment?
2. Pascal thinks it is better to bet that God exists than to bet that God does not exist. Why?
3. What is the connection between wagering and believing? Can you *choose* what to believe?
4. Can we know that God exists?
5. Is it reasonable to believe that God exists even if our belief is uncertain?
6. On what can faith in the existence of God be based?

. . . WE KNOW NEITHER THE EXISTENCE nor the nature of God, because He has neither extension nor limits.

But by faith we know His existence; in glory we shall know His nature. Now, I have already shown that we may well know the existence of a thing, without knowing its nature.

Let us now speak according to natural lights.

If there is a God, He is infinitely incomprehensible, since, having neither parts nor limits, He has no affinity to us. We are then incapable of knowing either what He is or if He is. This being so, who will dare to undertake the decision of the question? Not we, who have no affinity to Him.

Who then will blame Christians for not being able to give a reason for their belief, since they profess a religion for which they cannot give a reason? They declare, in expounding it to the world, that it is a foolishness, *stultitiam;* and then you complain that they do not prove it! If they proved it, they would not keep their words; it is in lacking proofs, that they are not lacking in sense. "Yes, but although this excuses those who offer it as such, and takes away from them the blame of putting it forward without reason, it does not excuse those who receive it." Let us then examine this point, and say, "God is, or He is not." But to which side shall we incline? Reason can decide nothing here. There is an infinite chaos which separates us. A game is being played at the extremity of this infinite distance where heads or tails will turn up. What will you wager? According to reason, you can do neither the one thing nor the other; according to reason, you can defend neither of the propositions.

Do not then reprove for error those who have made a choice; for you know nothing about it. "No, but I blame them for having made, not this choice, but a choice; for again both he who chooses heads and he who chooses tails are equally at fault, they are both in the wrong. The true course is not to wager at all."

—Yes; but you must wager. It is not optional. You are embarked. Which will you choose then; Let us see. Since you must choose, let us see which interests you least. You have two things to lose, the true and the good; and two things to stake, your reason and your will, your knowledge and your happiness; and your nature has two things to shun,

From Blaise Pascal, Thoughts, *trans. W. F. Trotter (New York: P. F. Collier & Son, 1910).*

PROVING GOD

G. W. F. von Leibniz

31. Our reasons are founded on *two great principles, that of contradiction,* in virtue of which we judge that to be *false* which involves contradiction, and that *true,* which is opposed or contradictory to the false.

32. And *that of sufficient reason,* in virtue of which we hold that no fact can be real or existent, no statement true, unless there be a sufficient reason why it is so and not otherwise, although most often these reasons cannot be known to us.

33. There are also two kinds of truths, those of *reasoning* and those of *fact.* Truths of reasoning are necessary and their opposite is impossible, and those of fact are contingent and their opposite is possible. When a truth is necessary its reason can be found by analysis, resolving it into more simple ideas and truths until we reach those which are primitive. . . .

36. But there must also be a *sufficient reason* for *contingent truths,* or those *of* fact, — that is, for the series of things diffused through the universe of created objects —

where the resolution into particular reason might run into a detail without limits, on account of the immense variety of objects and the division of bodies *ad infinitum.*

37. And as all this *detail* only involves other contingents, anterior or more detailed, each one of which needs a like analysis for its explanation, we make no advance: and the sufficient or final reason must be outside of the sequence or *series* of this detail of contingencies, however infinite it may be.

38. And thus it is that the final reason of things must be found in a necessary substance, in which the detail of changes exists only eminently, as in their source; and this it is which we call God.

39. Now this substance, being the sufficient reason of all this detail, which also is linked together throughout, *there is but one God, and this God suffices.*

From *The Monadology* (1714).

error and misery. Your reason is no more shocked in choosing one rather than the other, since you must of necessity choose. This is one point settled. But your happiness? Let us weigh the gain and the loss in wagering that God is. Let us estimate these two chances. If you gain, you gain all; if you lose, you lose nothing. Wager then without hesitation that He is. — "That is very fine. Yes, I must wager; but I may perhaps wager too much." — Let us see. Since there is an equal risk of gain and of loss, if you had only to gain two lives, instead of one, you might still wager. But if there were three lives to gain, you would have to play (since you are under the necessity of playing), and you would be impru-

dent, when you are forced to play, not to chance your life to gain three at a game where there is an equal risk of loss and gain. But there is an eternity of life and happiness. And this being so, if there were an infinity of chances, of which one only would be for you, you would still be right in wagering one to win two, and you would act stupidly, being obliged to play, by refusing to stake one life against three at a game in which out of an infinity of chances there is one for you, if there were an infinity of an infinitely happy life to gain. But there is here an infinity of an infinitely happy life to gain, a chance of gain against a finite number of chances of loss, and what you stake is finite. It is all divided;

wherever the infinite is and there is not an infinity of chances of loss against that of gain, there is no time to hesitate, you must give all. And thus, when one is forced to play, he must renounce reason to preserve his life, rather than risk it for infinite gain, as likely to happen as the loss of nothingness.

For it is no use to say it is uncertain if we will gain, and it is certain that we risk, and that the infinite distance between the *certainty* of what is staked and the *uncertainty* of what will be gained, equals the finite good which is certainly staked against the uncertain infinite. It is not so, as every player stakes a certainty to gain an uncertainty, and yet he stakes a finite certainty to gain a finite uncertainty, without transgressing against reason. There is not an infinite distance between the certainty staked and the uncertainty of the gain; that is untrue. In truth, there is an infinity between the certainty of gain and the certainty of loss. But the uncertainty of the gain is proportioned to the certainty of the stake according to the proportion of the chances of gain and loss. Hence it comes that, if there are as many risks on one side as on the other, the course is to play even; and then the certainty of the stake is equal to the uncertainty of the gain, so far is it from the fact that there is an infinite distance between them. And so our proposition is of infinite force, when there is the finite to stake in a game where there are equal risks of gain and of loss, and the infinite to gain. This is demonstrable; and if men are capable of any truths, this is one.

"I confess it, I admit it. But still is there no means of seeing the faces of the cards?"—Yes, Scripture and the rest, &c.—"Yes, but I have my hands tied and my mouth closed; I am forced to wager, and am not free. I am not released, and am so made that I cannot believe. What then would you have me do?"

"True. But at least learn your inability to believe, since reason brings you to this, and yet you cannot believe. Endeavour then to convince yourself, not by increase of proofs of God, but by the abatement of your passions. You would like to attain faith, and do not know the way; you would like to cure yourself of unbelief, and ask the remedy for it. Learn of those who have been bound like you, and who now stake all their possessions. These are people who know the way which you would follow, and who are cured of an ill of which you would be cured. Follow the way by which they began; by acting as if they believe, taking the holy water, having masses said, &c. Even this will naturally make you believe, and deaden your acuteness.—"But this is what I am afraid of."—And why? What have you to lose?

But to show you that this leads you there, it is this which will lessen the passions, which are your stumbling-blocks.

Further Questions

1. Even if Pascal is right that it is better to bet that God exists than to bet that God does not exist, what has this to do with whether God actually exists?
2. Isn't it possible there is a God who is offended by people who believe in God for selfish reasons? Has Pascal taken this possibility into account?
3. Suppose the God of one religion demands an annual human sacrifice, while the God of another religion forbids human sacrifice. Would Pascal's argument require you to both sacrifice and not sacrifice humans?

Further Readings

Krailsheimer, A. *Pascal*. Oxford: Oxford University Press, 1980. A readable, short introduction to Pascal's thought.
Stich, Steven. "The Recombinant DNA Debate," *Philosophy and Public Affairs,* Vol. 7, 1978. Includes an interesting discussion of Pascal's wager and "doomsday scenario arguments."

35   The Ethics of Belief

W. K. CLIFFORD

W. K. Clifford (1845–1879), mathematician and philosopher, was a Catholic during his student days at Trinity College, Cambridge, but later became an agnostic and turned against religion. His reflections on Charles Darwin's new theory of evolution were part of what changed his mind. In turning against religion, Clifford also took a rather extreme stand against faith, as in the following selection, where he argues that it is morally wrong for anyone, under any circumstances, to believe something on insufficient evidence.

Reading Questions

1. Do you agree with Clifford that the central characters in his shipowner example and his society of agitators example were wrong to have believed as they did?
2. What harm does Clifford think that belief on insufficient evidence does? What good does he concede it does? What do you think makes him feel so sure that the harm will always outweigh the good? Do you agree?

A SHIPOWNER WAS ABOUT TO SEND TO SEA an emigrant ship. He knew that she was old, and not over-well built at the first; that she had seen many seas and climes, and often had needed repairs. Doubts had been suggested to him that possibly she was not seaworthy. These doubts preyed upon his mind and made him unhappy; he thought that perhaps he ought to have her thoroughly overhauled and refitted, even though this should put him to great expense. Before the ship sailed, however, he succeeded in overcoming these melancholy reflections. He said to himself that she had gone safely through so many voyages and weathered so many storms that it was idle to suppose she would not come safely home from this trip also. He would put his trust in Providence, which could hardly fail to protect all these unhappy families that were leaving their fatherland to seek for better times elsewhere. He would dismiss from his mind all ungenerous suspicions about the honesty of builders and contractors. In such ways he acquired a sincere and comfortable conviction that his vessel was thoroughly safe and seaworthy; he watched her departure with a light heart, and benevolent wishes for the success of the exiles in their strange new home that was to be; and he got his insurance money when she went down in mid-ocean and told no tales.

What shall we say of him? Surely this, that he was verily guilty of the death of those men. It is admitted that he did sincerely believe in the soundness of his ship; but the sincerity of his conviction can in no wise help him, because *he had no right to believe on such evidence as was before him.* He had acquired his belief not by honestly earning it in patient investigation, but by stifling his doubts. And although in the end he may have felt so sure about it that he could not think otherwise, yet inasmuch as he had knowingly and willingly worked himself into that frame of mind, he must be held responsible for it.

Let us alter the case a little, and suppose that the ship was not unsound after all; that she made her voyage safely, and many others after it. Will that diminish the guilt of her owner? Not one jot. When an action is once done, it is right or wrong forever; no accidental failure of its good or evil fruits can possibly alter that. The man would not

From Lectures and Essays *(London: Macmillan, 1879).*

RELIGION AS WISH FULFILLMENT

Sigmund Freud

At this point one must expect to meet with an objection. "Well then if even obdurate sceptics admit that the assertions of religion cannot be refuted by reason, why should I not believe in them, since they have so much on their side — tradition, the agreement of mankind, and all the consolations they offer?" Why not, indeed? Just as no one can be forced to believe, so no one can be forced to disbelieve. But do not let us be satisfied with deceiving ourselves that arguments like these take us along the road of correct thinking. If ever there was a case of a lame excuse we have it here. Ignorance is ignorance; no right to believe anything can be derived from it. In other matters no sensible person will behave so irresponsibly or rest content with such feeble grounds for his opinions and for the line he takes. It is only in the highest and most sacred things that he allows himself to do so. In reality these are only attempts to pretend to oneself or to other people that one is still firmly attached to religion, when one has long since cut oneself loose from it. Where questions of religion are concerned, people are guilty of every possible sort of dishonesty and intellectual misdemeanor.

Philosophers stretch the meaning of words until they retain scarcely anything of their original sense. They give the name of "God" to some vague abstraction which they have created for themselves; having done so they can pose before all the world as deists, as believers in God, and they can even boast that they have recognized a higher, purer concept of God, notwithstanding that their God is now nothing more than an insubstantial shadow and no longer the mighty personality of religious doctrines. Critics persist in describing as "deeply religious" anyone who admits to a sense of man's insignificance or impotence in the face of the universe, although what constitutes the essence of the religious attitude is not this feeling but only the next step after it, the reaction to it which seeks a remedy for it. The man who goes no further, but humbly acquiesces in the small part which human beings play in the great world — such a man is, on the contrary, irreligious in the truest sense of the word.

From *The Future of an Illusion* (1927).

have been innocent, he would only have been not found out. The question of right or wrong has to do with the origin of his belief, not the matter of it; not what it was, but how he got it; not whether it turned out to be true or false, but whether he had a right to believe on such evidence as was before him.

There was once an island in which some of the inhabitants professed a religion teaching neither the doctrine of original sin nor that of eternal punishment. A suspicion got abroad that the professors of this religion had made use of unfair means to get their doctrines taught to children. They were accused of wresting the laws of their country in such a way as to remove children from the care of their natural and legal guardians; and even of stealing them away and keeping them concealed from their friends and relatives. A certain number of men formed themselves into a society for the purpose of agitating the public about this matter. They published grave accusations against individual citizens of the highest position and character, and did all in their power to injure those citizens in the exercise of their professions. So great was the noise they made, that a Commission was appointed to investigate the facts; but after the Commission had carefully inquired into all the evidence that could be got, it appeared that the accused were innocent. Not only had they been accused on insufficient evidence, but the evidence of their innocence was such as the agitators might easily have obtained, if they had attempted a fair inquiry. After these disclosures the inhabitants of that country looked upon the members of the agitating society, not only as persons whose judgment was to be distrusted, but also as no longer to be counted honorable men. For although they had sincerely and conscientiously believed in the charges they had made, *yet they had no right to believe on such evidence as was before them*. Their sincere convictions, instead of being honestly earned by patient inquiring, were stolen by listening to the voice of prejudice and passion.

Let us vary this case also, and suppose, other things remaining as before, that a still more accurate investigation proved the accused to have been really guilty. Would this make any difference in the guilt of the accusers? Clearly not; the question is not whether their belief was true or false, but whether they entertained it on wrong grounds. They would no doubt say, "Now you see that we were right after all; next time perhaps you will believe us." And they might be believed, but they would not thereby become honorable men. They would not be innocent, they would only be not found out. Every one of them, if he chose to examine himself *in foro conscientiae*, would know that he had acquired and nourished a belief, when he had no right to believe on such evidence as was before him; and therein he would know that he had done a wrong thing.

It may be said, however, that in both of these supposed cases it is not the belief which is judged to be wrong, but the action following upon it. The shipowner might say, "I am perfectly certain that my ship is sound, but still I feel it my duty to have her examined, before trusting the lives of so many people to her." And it might be said to the agitator, "However convinced you were of the justice of your cause and the truth of your convictions, you ought not to have made public attack upon any man's character until you had examined the evidence on both sides with the utmost patience and care."

In the first place, let us admit that, so far as it goes, this view of the case is right and necessary; right, because even when a man's belief is so fixed that he cannot think otherwise, he still has a choice in regard to the action suggested by it, and so cannot escape the duty of investigating on the ground of the strength of his convictions; and necessary, because those who are not yet capable of controlling their feelings and thought must have a plain rule dealing with overt acts.

But this being premised as necessary, it becomes clear that it is not sufficient, and that our previous judgment is required to supplement it. For it is not possible so to sever the belief from the action it suggests as to condemn the one without condemning the other. No man holding a strong belief on one side of a question, or even wishing to hold a belief on one side, can investigate it with such fairness and completeness as if he were really in doubt and unbiased; so that the existence of a belief not founded on fair inquiry unfits a man for the performance of this necessary duty.

Nor is that truly a belief at all which has not some influence upon the actions of him who holds it. He who truly believes that which prompts him to an action has looked upon the action to lust after it, he has committed it already in his heart. If a belief is not realized immediately in open deeds, it is stored up for the guidance of the future. It goes to make a part of that aggregate of beliefs which is the link between sensation and action at every moment of all our lives, and which is so organized and compacted together that no part of it can be isolated from the rest, but every new addition modifies the structure of the whole. No real belief, however trifling and fragmentary it may seem, is ever truly insignificant; it prepares us to receive more of its like, confirms those which resembled it before, and weakens others; and so gradually it lays a stealthy train in our inmost thoughts, which may some day explode into overt action, and leave its stamp upon our character forever.

And no one man's belief is in any case a private matter which concerns himself alone. Our lives are guided by that general conception of the course of things which has been created by society for social purposes. Our words, our phrases, our forms and processes and modes of thought are common property, fashioned and perfected from age to age; an heirloom which every succeeding generation inherits as a previous deposit and a sacred trust to be handed on to the next one, not unchanged but enlarged and purified, with some clear marks of its proper handiwork. Into this, for good or ill, is woven every belief of every man who has speech of his fellows. An awful privilege, and an awful responsibility, that we should help to create the world in which posterity will live.

In the two supposed cases which have been considered, it has been judged wrong to believe on insufficient evidence, or to nourish belief by suppressing doubts and avoiding investigation. The reason of this judgment is not far to seek; it is that in both these cases the belief held by one man was of great importance to other men. But for as much as no belief held by one man, however seemingly trivial the belief, and however obscure the believer, is ever actually insignificant or without its effect on the fate of mankind, we have no choice but to extend our judgment to all cases of belief whatever. Belief, that sacred faculty which prompts the decisions of our will, and knits into harmonious working all the compacted energies of our being, is ours not for ourselves but for humanity. It is rightly used on truths which have been established by long experience and waiting toil, and which have stood in the fierce light of free and fearless questioning. Then it helps to bind men together, and to strengthen and direct their common action. It is desecrated when given to unproved and unquestioned statements, for the solace and private pleasure of the believer; to add a tinsel splendor to the plain straight road of our life and display a bright mirage beyond it; or even to drown the common sorrows of our kind by a self-deception which allows them not only to cast down, but also to degrade us. Whoso would deserve well of his fellows in this matter will guard the purity of his belief with a very fanaticism of jealous care, lest at any time it should rest on an unworthy object, and catch a stain which can never be wiped away.

It is not only the leader of men, statesman, philosopher, or poet, that owes this bounden duty to mankind. Every rustic who delivers in the village alehouse his slow, infrequent sentences, may help to kill or keep alive the fatal superstitions which clog his race. Every hardworked wife of an artisan may transmit to her children beliefs which shall knit society together, or rend it in pieces. No simplicity of mind, no obscurity of station, can escape the universal duty of questioning all that we believe.

It is true that this duty is a hard one, and the doubt which comes out of it is often a very bitter thing. It leaves us bare and powerless where we thought that we were safe and strong. To know all about anything is to know how to deal with it under all circumstances. We feel much happier and more secure when we think we know precisely what to do, no matter what happens, than when we have lost our way and do not know where to turn. And if we have supposed ourselves to know all about anything, and to be capable of doing what is fit in regard to it, we naturally do not like to find that we are really ignorant and powerless, that we have to begin again at the beginning, and try to learn what the thing is and how it is to be dealt with—if indeed anything can be learned about it. It is the sense of power attached to a sense of knowledge that makes men desirous of believing, and afraid of doubting.

This sense of power is the highest and best of pleasures when the belief on which it is founded is true belief, and has been fairly earned by investigation. For then we may justly feel that it is common property, and holds good for others as well as for ourselves. Then we may be glad, not that *I* have learned secrets by which I am safer and stronger, but that *we men* have got mastery over more of the world; and we shall be strong, not for ourselves, but in the name of Man and in his strength. But if the belief has been accepted on insufficient evidence, the pleasure is a stolen one. Not only does it deceive ourselves by giving us a sense of power which we do not really possess, but it is sinful, because it is stolen in defiance of our duty to mankind. That duty is to guard ourselves from such beliefs as from a pestilence, which may shortly master our own body and then spread to the rest of the town. What would be thought of one who, for the sake of a sweet fruit, should deliberately run the risk of bringing a plague upon his family and his neighbors?

And, as in other such cases, it is not the risk only which has to be considered; for a bad action is always bad at the time when it is done, no matter what happens afterwards. Every time we let ourselves believe for unworthy reasons, we weaken our powers of self-control, of doubting, of judicially and fairly weighing evidence. We all suffer severely enough from the maintenance and support of false beliefs and the fatally wrong actions which they lead to, and the evil born when once such belief is

The Opium of the People

Karl Marx

Man makes religion, religion does not make man. In other words, religion is the self-consciousness and self-feeling of man who has either not yet found himself or has already lost himself again. But *man* is no abstract being squatting outside the world. Man is *the world of man,* the state, society. This state, this society, produce religion, *a reversed world-consciousness,* because they are *a reversed world.* Religion is the general theory of that world, its encyclopaedic compendium, its logic in a popular form, its spiritualistic *point d'honneur,* its enthusiasm, its moral sanction, its solemn completion, its universal ground for consolation and justification. It is *the fantastic realization* of the human essence because the *human essence* has no true reality. The struggle against religion is therefore mediately the fight against *the other world,* of which religion is the spiritual *aroma.*

Religious distress is at the same time the expression of real distress and the *protest* against real distress. Religion is the sigh of the oppressed creature, the heart of a heartless world, just as it is the spirit of a spiritless situation. It is the *opium* of the people.

The abolition of religion as the *illusory* happiness of the people is required for their *real* happiness. The demand to give up the illusions about its condition is the *demand to give up a condition which needs illusions.* The criticism of religion is therefore *in embryo the criticism of the vale of woe,* the *halo* of which is religion.

Criticism has plucked the imaginary flowers from the chain not so that man will wear the chain without any fantasy or consolation but so that he will shake off the chain and cull the living flower. The criticism of religion disillusions man to make him think and act and shape his reality like a man who has been disillusioned and has come to reason, so that he will revolve round himself and therefore round his true sun. Religion is only the illusory sun which revolves round man as long as he does not revolve round himself.

From "Contribution to the Critique of Hegel's Philosophy of Right" (1844).

---

entertained is great and wide. But a greater and wider evil arises when the credulous character is maintained and supported, when a habit of believing for unworthy reasons is fostered and made permanent. If I steal money from any person, there may be no harm done by the mere transfer of possession; he may not feel the loss, or it may prevent him from using the money badly. But I cannot help doing this great wrong towards Man, that I make myself dishonest. What hurts society is not that it should lose its property, but that it should become a den of thieves; for then it must cease to be society. This is why we ought not to do evil that good may come; for at any rate this great evil has come, that we have done evil and are made wicked thereby. In like manner, if I let myself believe anything on insufficient evidence, there may be no great harm done by the mere belief; it may be true after all, or I may never have occasion to exhibit it in outward acts. But I cannot help doing this great wrong toward Man, that I make myself credulous. The danger to society is not merely that it should believe wrong things, though that is great enough; but that it should become credulous, and lose the habit of testing things and inquiring into them; for then it must sink back into savagery.

The harm which is done by credulity in a man is not confined to the fostering of a credulous character in others, and consequent support of false beliefs. Habitual want of care about which I believe leads to habitual want of care in others about the truth of what is told to me. Men speak the truth to one another when each reveres the truth in his own mind and in the other's mind; but how shall my friend revere the truth in my mind when I myself am careless about it, when I believe things because I want to believe them, and because they are comforting and pleasant? Will he not learn to cry, "Peace," to me, when there is no peace? By such a course I shall surround myself with a thick atmosphere of falsehood and fraud, and in that I must live. It may matter little to me, in my cloud-castle of sweet illusions and darling lies; but it matters much to Man that I have made my neighbors ready to deceive. The credulous man is father to the liar and the cheat; he lives in the bosom of this his family, and it is no marvel if he should become even as they are. So closely are our duties knit together, that whoso shall keep the whole law, and yet offend in one point, he is guilty of all.

To sum up: it is wrong always, everywhere, and for anyone, to believe anything upon insufficient evidence.

If a man, holding a belief which he was taught in childhood or persuaded of afterwards, keeps down and pushes away any doubts which arise about it in his mind, purposely avoids the reading of books and the company of men that call in question or discuss it, and regards as impious those questions which cannot easily be asked without disturbing it—the life of that man is one long sin against mankind.

If this judgment seems harsh when applied to those simple souls who have never known better, who have been brought up from the cradle with a horror of doubt, and taught that their eternal welfare depends on what they believe, then it leads to the very serious question. Who hath made Israel to sin? . . .

Inquiry into the evidence of a doctrine is not to be made once for all, and then taken as finally settled. It is never lawful to stifle a doubt; for either it can be honestly answered by means of the inquiry already made, or else it proves that the inquiry was not complete.

"But," says one, "I am a busy man; I have no time for the long course of study which would be necessary to make me in any degree a competent judge of certain questions, or even able to understand the nature of the arguments." Then he would have no time to believe. . . .

Further Questions

1. The "feeling" that something is so is sometimes a good reason for thinking that it actually is so: for instance, "I feel nervous"; "I feel I'm about to vomit." In other cases, however, the value of our feelings as evidence is more dubious: "I feel that abortion is morally wrong"; "I feel that God exists." If you agree, explain why the evidential value of our feelings differs so much in the two sets of examples.
2. Can you think of any *noncontroversial* exceptions to Clifford's claim that we have a duty always to believe exactly according to the evidence?
3. Are there any important *dis*analogies between Clifford's shipowner and society of agitators examples and ordinary cases in which people believe things religiously without sufficient evidence?

Further Readings

Adams, Robert M. *The Virtue of Faith*. New York: Oxford University Press, 1987. A philosophically sophisticated defense of Christian belief by an important philosopher who is also a Presbyterian minister.

Penelhum, Terence, ed. *Faith*. New York: Macmillan, 1989. Historical and contemporary selections. An excellent anthology.

36   The Will to Believe

WILLIAM JAMES

A brief biography of James appears on page 194.

In this famous selection, James defends the rationality, under certain conditions, of believing in the existence of God in the absence of adequate arguments or evidence for the existence of God. James's thesis is still a live philosophical issue today and is sometimes defended even by atheists.

Reading Questions

1. What does James mean by a "genuine option"?
2. What are the conditions under which James claims it is rationally permissible to believe on faith that God exists? Why does James think these conditions suffice?
3. Some philosophers think it is a rule of rationality that the strength of one's belief should be directly proportional to the evidence supporting that belief, and if a belief is not supported by adequate evidence—that is, evidence that makes it more likely than not to be true—one ought to dispense with the belief. How does James answer these philosophers?

. . . LET US GIVE THE NAME of *hypothesis* to anything that may be proposed to our belief; and just as the electricians speak of live and dead wires, let us speak of any hypothesis as either *live* or *dead*. A live hypothesis is one which appeals as a real possibility to him to whom it is proposed. If I ask you to believe in the Mahdi, the notion makes no electric connection with your nature,—it refuses to scintillate with any credibility at all. As an hypothesis it is completely dead. To an Arab, however (even if he be not one of the Mahdi's followers), the hypothesis is among the mind's possibilities: it is alive. This shows that deadness and liveness in an hypothesis are not intrinsic properties, but relations to the individual thinker. They are measured by his willingness to act. The maximum of liveness in an hypothesis means willingness to act irrevocably. Practically, that means belief; but there is some believing tendency wherever there is willingness to act at all.

Next, let us call the decision between two hypotheses an *option*. Options may be of several kinds. They may be—1, *living or dead;* 2, *forced or avoidable;* 3, *momentous or trivial;* and for our purposes we may call an option a *genuine* option when it is of the forced, living, and momentous kind.

1. A living option is one in which both hypotheses are live ones. If I say to you: "Be a theosophist or be a Mohammedan," it is probably a dead option, because for you neither hypothesis is likely to be alive. But if I say, "Be an agnostic or be a Christian," it is otherwise: trained as you are, each hypothesis makes some appeal, however small, to your belief.

2. Next, if I say to you: "Choose between going out with your umbrella or without it," I do not offer you a genuine option, for it is not forced. You can easily avoid it by not going out at all. Similarly, if I say, "Either love me or hate me," "Either call my theory true or call it false," your option is avoidable. You may remain indifferent to me, neither loving

Extracts from William James, "The Will to Believe," an Address to the Philosophical Clubs of Yale and Brown Universities. First published in New World, *1896.*

ON THE ULTIMATE INSECURITY

William James

I went one evening into a dressing-room in the twilight to procure some article that was there; when suddenly there fell upon me without any warning, just as if it came out of the darkness, a horrible fear of my own existence. . . . it was as if something hitherto solid within my breast gave way entirely, and I became a mass of quivering fear. After this the universe was changed for me altogether. I awoke morning after morning with a horrible dread at the pit of my stomach, and with a sense of the insecurity of life that I never knew before, and that I have never felt since. It was like a revelation . . . for months I was unable to go out into the dark alone. In general I dreaded to be left alone. I remember wondering how other people could live, how I myself had ever lived, so unconscious of that pit of insecurity beneath the surface of life.

From *The Writings of William James,* John McDermott, ed.

nor hating, and you may decline to offer any judgment as to my theory. But if I say, "Either accept this truth or go without it," I put on you a forced option, for there is no standing place outside of the alternative. Every dilemma based on a complete logical disjunction, with no possibility of not choosing, is an option of this forced kind. . . .

The thesis I defend is, briefly stated, this: *Our passional nature not only lawfully may, but must, decide an option between propositions, whenever it is a genuine option that cannot by its nature be decided on intellectual grounds; for to say, under such circumstances, "Do not decide, but leave the question open," is itself a passional decision,—just like deciding yes or no,—and is attended with the same risk of losing the truth. . . .*

Wherever the option between losing truth and gaining it is not momentous, we can throw the chance of *gaining truth* away, and at any rate save ourselves from any chance of *believing falsehood*, by not making up our minds at all till objective evidence has come. In scientific questions, this is almost always the case; and even in human affairs in general, the need of acting is seldom so urgent that a false belief to act on is better than no belief at all. Law courts, indeed, have to decide on the best evidence attainable for the moment, because a judge's duty is to make law as well as to ascertain it, and (as a learned judge once said to me) few cases are worth spending much time over: the great thing is to have them decided on *any* acceptable principle, and got out of the way. But in our dealings with objective nature we obviously are recorders, not makers, of the truth; and decisions for the mere sake of deciding promptly and getting on to the next business would be wholly out of place. Throughout the breadth of physical nature facts are what they are quite independently of us, and seldom is there any such hurry about them that the risks of being duped by believing a premature theory need be faced. The questions here are always trivial options, the hypotheses are hardly living (at any rate not living for us spectators), the choice between believing truth or falsehood is seldom forced. The attitude of sceptical balance is therefore the absolutely wise one if we would escape mistakes. What difference, indeed, does it make to most of us whether we have or have not a theory of the Röntgen rays, whether we believe or not in mind-stuff, or have a conviction about the causality of conscious states? It makes no difference. Such options are not forced on us. On every account it is better not to make them, but still keep weighing reasons *pro et contra* with an indifferent hand. . . .

. . . Religions differ so much in their accidents that in discussing the religious question we must

ON THE CORPSE OF A BUDDHA, RELIGION STANDS

Shree Rajneesh

Lao Tzu says the nature of existence is more like the female, more feminine. . . .

A man can also be feminine. A Buddha is feminine, a Lao Tzu is feminine, a Jesus is feminine . . .

A man can live a feminine existence — then he becomes a mystic. That is the only way. So all mystics become in a certain way feminine. And they are the real religious men, not the founders of religion.

Remember, this is a difference. . . . Buddha is not the founder of Buddhism — no. His disciples are the founders. Jesus is not the founder of Christianity — no. His apostles, they are the founders. Mahavir is not the founder of Jainism. Gautam, his disciple, who was a scholar and great pundit, was. These are the men. . . .

You are born out of the mother's womb, and you have to find the womb again in existence. . . .

Hindus are better when they call their god "mother" — mother Kali — than Christians and Mohammedans and Jews, who go on calling their god "father." Those three religions are man-oriented, that's why they have been so violent. Mohammedans and Christians have killed so many, they have been a catastrophe on the earth. They have been murderers. In the name of religion they have been only killing and doing nothing else. This is man-oriented religion. . . .

Once a religion becomes organized, violence enters into it. Organization is going to be violent, it has to fight its way, it is bound to become male. Organization is male; religion is female.

I have heard an anecdote that a few disciples of the Devil came very worried and told him, "Why are you sitting here? Our whole business is at stake. A man has again become a Buddha, enlightened. We have to do something, otherwise he will transform people — and our world will be deserted, and who will come to hell? Do something immediately! No time should be lost. A man has again become a Buddha!"

The Devil said, "You don't worry. I work through the disciples. I have sent some already, the disciples are on the way. They will surround him. They will create an organization. And no need to worry: the organization will do everything that we cannot do, and they always do it better. I have learned it through history. I will create a church ... and I will not be involved in it at all. In fact, they do it on their own. I just simply encourage and help."

Once the pope is there, Christ is forgotten; once the church is there, the Buddha is killed and murdered. It is always on the corpse of a Buddha that a religion stands.

From Tao: *The Three Treasures.*

---

make it very generic and broad. What then do we now mean by the religious hypothesis? Science says things are; morality says some things are better than other things; and religion says essentially two things.

First, she says that the best things are the more eternal things, the overlapping things, the things in the universe that throw the last stone, so to speak, and say the final word. "Perfection is eternal," — this phrase of Charles Secrétan seems a good way

of putting this first affirmation of religion, an affirmation which obviously cannot yet be verified scientifically at all.

The second affirmation of religion is that we are better off even now if we believe her first affirmation to be true.

Now, let us consider what the logical elements of this situation are *in case the religious hypothesis in both its branches be really true.* (Of course, we must admit that possibility at the outset. If we are to

THE HISTORY OF MYSTICISM

Abraham Maslow

I see in the history of many organized religions a tendency to develop two extreme wings: the "mystical" and individual on the one hand, and the legalistic and organizational on the other. The profoundly and authentically religious person integrates these trends easily and automatically. The forms, rituals, ceremonials, and verbal formulae in which he was reared, remain for him experientially rooted, symbolically meaningful, archetypal, unitive. Such a person may go through the same motions and behaviors as his more numerous coreligionists, but he is never *reduced* to the behavioral, as most of them are. Most people lose or forget the subjectively religious experience, and redefine Religion as a set of habits, behaviors, dogmas, forms, which at the extreme becomes entirely legalistic and bureaucratic, conventional, empty, and in the truest meaning of the word, anti-religious. The mystic experience, the illumination, the great awakening, along with the charismatic seer who started the whole thing, are forgotten, lost, or transformed into their opposites. Organized Religion, the churches, finally may become the major enemies of the religious experience and the religious experiencer.

But on the other wing, the mystical (or experiential) also has its traps which I have not stressed sufficiently.... Out of the joy and wonder of his ecstasies and peak-experiences he may be tempted to *seek* them, *ad hoc,* and to value them exclusively, as the only or at least the highest goods of life, giving up other criteria of right and wrong. Focused on these wonderful subjective experiences, he may run the danger of turning away from the world and from other people in his search for triggers to peak-experiences, *any* triggers. In a word, instead of being temporarily self-absorbed and inwardly searching, he may become simply a selfish person, seeking his own personal salvation, trying to get into "heaven" even if other people can't, and finally, even perhaps *using* other people as triggers, as means to his sole end of higher states of consciousness. In a word, he may become not only selfish but also evil. My impression, from the history of mysticism, is that this trend can sometimes wind up in meanness, nastiness, loss of compassion, or even in the extreme of sadism.

From *Religions, Values, and Peak Experiences* (1970).

---

discuss the question at all, it must involve a living option. If for any of you religion be a hypothesis that cannot, by any living possibility be true, then you need go no farther. I speak to the "saving remnant" alone.) So proceeding, we see, first that religion offers itself as a *momentous* option. We are supposed to gain, even now, by our belief, and to lose by our nonbelief, a certain vital good. Secondly, religion is a *forced* option, so far as that good goes. We cannot escape the issue by remaining sceptical and waiting for more light, because, although we do avoid error in that way *if religion be untrue,* we lose the good, *if it be true,* just as

certainly as if we positively chose to disbelieve. It is as if a man should hesitate indefinitely to ask a certain woman to marry him because he was not perfectly sure that she would prove an angel after he brought her home. Would he not cut himself off from that particular angel-possibility as decisively as if he went and married some one else? Scepticism, then, is not avoidance of option; it is option of a certain particular kind of risk. *Better risk loss of truth than chance of error,* — that is your faith-vetoer's exact position. He is actively playing his stake as much as the believer is; he is backing the field against the religious hypothesis, just as the believer is backing the religious hypothesis against the field. To preach scepticism to us as a duty until 'sufficient evidence' for religion can be found, is tantamount therefore to telling us, when in presence of the religious hypothesis, that to yield to our fear of its being error is wiser and better than to yield to our hope that it may be true. It is not intellect against all passions, then; it is only intellect with one passion laying down its law. And by what, forsooth, is the supreme wisdom of this passion warranted? Dupery for dupery, what proof is there that dupery through hope is so much worse than dupery through fear? I, for one, can see no proof; and I simply refuse obedience to the scientist's command to imitate his kind of option, in a case where my own stake is important enough to give me the right to choose my own form of risk. If religion be true and the evidence for it be still insufficient, I do not wish, by putting our extinguisher upon my nature (which feels to me as if it had after all some business in this matter), to forfeit my sole chance in life of getting upon the winning side,— that chance depending, of course, on my willingness to run the risk of acting as if my passional need of taking the world religiously might be prophetic and right.

All this is on the supposition that it really may be prophetic and right, and that, even to us who are discussing the matter, religion is a live hypothesis which may be true. Now, to most of us religion comes in a still further way that makes a veto on our active faith even more illogical. The more perfect and more eternal aspect of the universe is represented in our religions as having personal form. The universe is no longer a mere *It* to us, but a *Thou*, if we are religious; and any relation that may be possible from person to person might be possible here. For instance, although in one sense we are passive portions of the universe, in another we show a curious autonomy, as if we were small active centres on our own account. We feel, too, as if the appeal of religion to us were made to our own active goodwill, as if evidence might be forever withheld from us unless we met the hypothesis half-way. To take a trivial illustration: just as a man who in a company of gentlemen made no advances, asked a warrant for every concession, and believed no one's word without proof, would cut

himself off by such churlishness from all the social rewards that a more trusting spirit would earn,— so here, one who should shut himself up in snarling logicality and try to make the gods extort his recognition willy-nilly, or not get it at all, might cut himself off forever from his only opportunity of making the gods' acquaintance. This feeling, forced on us we know not whence, that by obstinately believing that there are gods (although not to do so would be so easy both for our logic and our life) we are doing the universe the deepest service we can, seems part of the living essence of the religious hypothesis. If the hypothesis *were* true in all its parts, including this one, then pure intellectualism, with its veto on our making willing advances, would be an absurdity; and some participation of our sympathetic nature would be logically required. I, therefore, for one, cannot see my way to accepting the agnostic rules for truthseeking, or wilfully agree to keep my willing nature out of the game. I cannot do so for this plain reason, that *a rule of thinking which would absolutely prevent me from acknowledging certain kinds of truth if those kinds of truth were really there, would be an irrational rule.* That for me is the long and short of the formal logic of the situation, no matter what the kinds of truth might materially be.

I confess I do not see how this logic can be escaped. But sad experiences make me fear that some of you may still shrink from radically saying with me, *in abstracto,* that we have the right to believe at our own risk any hypothesis that is live enough to tempt our will. I suspect, however, that if this is so, it is because you have got away from the abstract logical point of view altogether, and are thinking (perhaps without realizing it) of some particular religious hypothesis which for you is dead. The freedom to "believe what we will" you apply to the case of some patent superstition; and the faith you think of is the faith defined by the schoolboy when he said, "Faith is when you believe something that you know ain't true." I can only repeat that this is misapprehension. *In concreto,* the freedom to believe can only cover living options which the intellect of the individual cannot by itself resolve; and living options never seem absurdities to him who has them to consider. When I look at the religious question as it really puts itself to concrete men, and when I think of all the possibilities which both practically and theoretically it involves, then this command that we shall put a stopper on our heart, instincts, and courage, and *wait*—acting of course meanwhile more or less as if religion were *not* true—till doomsday, or till such time as our intellect and senses working together may have raked in evidence enough,—this command, I say, seems to me the queerest idol ever manufactured in the philosophic cave. Were we scholastic absolutists, there might be more excuse. If we had an infallible intellect with its objec-

tive certitudes, we might feel ourselves disloyal to such a perfect organ of knowledge in not trusting to it exclusively, in not waiting for its releasing word. But if we are empiricists, if we believe that no bell in us tolls to let us know for certain when truth is in our grasp, then it seems a piece of idle fantasticality to preach so solemnly our duty of waiting for the bell. Indeed we *may* wait if we will.—I hope you do not think that I am denying that,—but if we do so, we do so at our peril as much as if we believed. In either case we *act*, taking our life in our hands. . . .

Further Questions

1. Suppose a ninety-year-old man were to believe on faith that he could win the 100-meter dash in the next summer Olympics. Is James committed to saying that his belief is rationally permissible?
2. Suppose someone were to believe on faith that there are thousands of little gremlins that cannot be detected in any way, either directly or indirectly, but which surround the leaves of trees in the fall and accompany them on their journey from the trees to the ground. Is James committed to saying that such a belief could be rationally permissible? Would he be committed if the belief were a genuine option?
3. Is it rationally permissible to believe, on the basis of faith alone (that is, in the absence of arguments or evidence that make your belief more likely than not to be true), that God exists? Explain how William James would answer. How would he defend his answer? Formulate a good objection to James's argument.

Further Readings

Mackie, J. L. *The Miracle of Theism*. Oxford: Clarendon Press, 1982, 204–209. Perhaps the best short discussion of James's argument.
Penelhum, Terence, ed. *Faith*. New York: Macmillan, 1989. An excellent comprehensive anthology.

God and Evil   37

DAVID HUME

In this selection, from *Dialogues Concerning Natural Religion* (1779), Hume's character, Philo, argues that the enormous amount of human and animal suffering provides good reason for believing that God does not exist.

A brief biography of Hume appears on page 128.

Reading Questions

1. There are three characters in Hume's *Dialogue:* Philo, Cleanthes, and Demea. Based just on the segment of the *Dialogue* included here, how would you characterize the differences in their views?
2. What are Philo's main arguments? How does Cleanthes respond?

PART X

IT IS MY OPINION, I OWN, replied Demea, that each man feels, in a manner, the truth of religion within his own breast, and, from a consciousness of his imbecility and misery rather than from any reasoning, is led to seek protection from that Being on whom he and all nature is dependent. So anxious or so tedious are even the best scenes of life that futurity is still the object of all our hopes and fears. We incessantly look forward and endeavour, by prayers, adoration, and sacrifice, to appease those unknown powers whom we find, by experience, so able to afflict and oppress us. Wretched creatures that we are! What resource for us amidst the innumerable ills of life did not religion suggest some methods of atonement, and appease those terrors with which we are incessantly agitated and tormented?

I am indeed persuaded, said Philo, that the best and indeed the only method of bringing everyone to a due sense of religion is by just representations of the misery and wickedness of men. And for that purpose a talent of eloquence and strong imagery is more requisite than that of reasoning and argument. For is it necessary to prove what everyone feels within himself? It is only necessary to make us feel it, if possible, more intimately and sensibly.

The people, indeed, replied Demea, are sufficiently convinced of this great and melancholy truth. The miseries of life, the unhappiness of man, the general corruptions of our nature, the unsatisfactory enjoyment of pleasures, riches, honours — these phrases have become almost proverbial in all languages. And who can doubt of what all men declare from their own immediate feeling and experience?

In this point, said Philo, the learned are perfectly agreed with the vulgar; and in all letters, *sacred* and *profane,* the topic of human misery has been insisted on with the most pathetic eloquence that sorrow and melancholy could inspire. The poets, who speak from sentiment, without a system, and whose testimony has therefore the more authority, abound in images of this nature. From Homer down to Dr. Young, the whole inspired tribe have ever been sensible that no other representation of things would suit the feeling and observation of each individual.

As to authorities, replied Demea, you need not seek them. Look round this library of Cleanthes. I shall venture to affirm that, except authors of particular sciences, such as chemistry or botany, who have no occasion to treat of human life, there is scarce one of those innumerable writers from whom the sense of human misery has not, in some passage or other, extorted a complaint and confession of it. At least, the chance is entirely on that side; and no one author has ever, so far as I can recollect, been so extravagant as to deny it.

There you must excuse me, said Philo: Leibniz has denied it, and is perhaps the first who ventured upon so bold and paradoxical an opinion; at least, the first who made it essential to his philosophical system.

And by being the first, replied Demea, might he not have been sensible of his error? For is this a subject in which philosophers can propose to make discoveries especially in so late an age? And can any man hope by a simple denial (for the subject scarcely admits of reasoning) to bear down the united testimony of mankind, founded on sense and consciousness?

And why should man, added he, pretend to an exemption from the lot of all other animals? The whole earth, believe me, Philo, is cursed and polluted. A perpetual war is kindled amongst all living creatures. Necessity, hunger, want stimulate the

From David Hume, Dialogues Concerning Natural Religion *(1779; London: Longmans Green, 1878).*

strong and courageous; fear, anxiety, terror agitate the weak and infirm. The first entrance into life gives anguish to the new-born infant and to its wretched parent; weakness, impotence, distress attend each stage of that life, and it is, at last, finished in agony and horror.

Observe, too, says Philo, the curious artifices of nature in order to embitter the life of every living being. The stronger prey upon the weaker and keep them in perpetual terror and anxiety. The weaker, too, in their turn, often prey upon the stronger, and vex and molest them without relaxation. Consider that innumerable race of insects, which either are bred on the body of each animal or, flying about, infix their stings in him. These insects have others still less than themselves which torment them. And thus on each hand, before and behind, above and below, every animal is surrounded with enemies which incessantly seek his misery and destruction.

Man alone, said Demea, seems to be, in part, an exception to this rule. For by combination in society he can easily master lions, tigers, and bears, whose greater strength and agility naturally enable them to prey upon him.

On the contrary, it is here chiefly, cried Philo, that the uniform and equal maxims of nature are most apparent. Man, it is true, can, by combination, surmount all his *real* enemies and become master of the whole animal creation; but does he not immediately raise up to himself *imaginary* enemies, the demons of his fancy, who haunt him with superstitious terrors and blast every enjoyment of life? His pleasure, as he imagines, becomes in their eyes a crime; his food and repose give them umbrage and offence; his very sleep and dreams furnish new materials to anxious fear; and even death, his refuge from every other ill, presents only the dread of endless and innumerable woes. Nor does the wolf molest more the timid flock than superstition does the anxious breast of wretched mortals.

Besides, consider, Demea: This very society by which we surmount those wild beasts, our natural enemies, what new enemies does it not raise to us? What woe and misery does it not occasion? Man is the greatest enemy of man. Oppression, injustice, contempt, contumely, violence, sedition, war, calumny, treachery, fraud — by these they mutually torment each other, and they would

soon dissolve that society which they had formed were it not for the dread of still greater ills which must attend their separation.

But though these external insults, said Demea, from animals, from men, from all the elements, which assault us form a frightful catalogue of woes, they are nothing in comparison of those which arise within ourselves, from the distempered condition of our mind and body. How many lie under the lingering torment of diseases? Hear the pathetic enumeration of the great poet.

Intestine stone and ulcer, colic-pangs,
Demoniac frenzy, moping melancholy,
And moon-struck madness, pining atrophy,
Marasmus, and wide-wasting pestilence.
Dire was the tossing, deep the groans: *Despair*
Tended the sick, busiest from couch to couch.
And over them triumphant *Death* his dart
Shook: but delay'd to strike, though oft invok'd
With vows, as their chief good and final hope.

The disorders of the mind, continued Demea, though more secret, are not perhaps less dismal and vexatious. Remorse, shame, anguish, rage, disappointment, anxiety, fear, dejection, despair — who has ever passed through life without cruel inroads from these tormentors? How many have scarcely ever felt any better sensations? Labour and poverty, so abhorred by everyone, are the certain lot of the far greater number; and those few privileged persons who enjoy ease and opulence never reach contentment or true felicity. All the goods of life united would not make a very happy man, but all the ills united would make a wretch indeed; and any one of them almost (and who can be free from every one?), nay, often the absence of one good (and who can possess all?) is sufficient to render life ineligible.

Were a stranger to drop on a sudden into this world, I would show him, as a specimen of its ills, an hospital full of diseases, a prison crowded with malefactors and debtors, a field of battle strewed with carcases, a fleet foundering in the ocean, a nation languishing under tyranny, famine, or pestilence. To turn the gay side of life to him and give him a notion of its pleasures — whither should I conduct him? To a ball, to an opera, to court? He might just think that I was only showing him a diversity of distress and sorrow.

A World Without Suffering and Misfortune

John Hick's View

Suppose that in a world without suffering and misfortune, someone *tried* to injure someone else. Something would always go wrong with the attempt. For instance, the would-be murderer's bullet would swerve off course at the last minute. Or, if someone behaved recklessly, then his or her behavior would never come to a bad end. For instance, the drunken driver who drove his car off a cliff would discover that it floated safely to the ground.

> To make possible this continual series of individual adjustments, nature would have to work by "special providences" instead of running according to general laws which men must learn to respect on penalty of pain or death. The laws of nature would have to be extremely flexible: sometimes gravity would operate, sometimes not; sometimes an object would be hard and solid, sometimes soft. There could be no sciences, for there would be no enduring world structure to investigate. In eliminating the problems and hardships of an objective environment, with its own laws, life would become like a dream in which, delightfully but aimlessly, we would float and drift at ease. (*Philosophy of Religion,* 3d ed., 1983, p. 45)

According to Hick, there would be a heavy price to pay for this bliss:

In such a world human misery would not evoke deep personal sympathy or call forth organised relief and sacrificial help and service. For it is presupposed in these compassionate reactions both that the suffering is deserved and that it is *bad* for the sufferer. We do not acknowledge a moral call to sacrificial measures to save a criminal from receiving his just punishment or a patient from receiving the painful treatment that is to cure him. But men and women often act in true compassion and massive generosity and self-giving in the face of unmerited suffering, especially when it comes in such dramatic forms as an earthquake, a famine, or a mining disaster. It seems, then, that in a world that is to be the scene of compassionate love and self-giving for others, suffering must fall upon mankind with something of the haphazardness and inequity that we now experience. It must be apparently unmerited, pointless, and incapable of being morally rationalized. For it is precisely this feature of our common human lot that creates sympathy between man and man and evokes the unselfishness, kindness, and goodwill which are among the highest values of personal life. (*Evil and the God of Love,* 1966, pp. 370–71)

Hick concludes that a world without suffering and misfortune would not be suitable for promoting the divine objective of *soulmaking.*

There is no evading such striking instances, said Philo, but by apologies which still further aggravate the charge. Why have all men, I ask, in all ages, complained incessantly of the miseries of life? . . . They have no just reason, says one: these complaints proceed only from their discontented, repining, anxious disposition. . . . And can there possibly, I reply, be a more certain foundation of misery than such a wretched temper?

But if they were really as unhappy as they pretend, says my antagonist, why do they remain in life? . . .

Not satisfied with life, afraid of death—

this is the secret chain, say I, that holds us. We are terrified, not bribed to the continuance of our existence.

It is only a false delicacy, he may insist, which a few refined spirits indulge, and which has spread these complaints among the whole race of mankind. . . . And what is this delicacy, I ask, which you blame? Is it anything but a greater sensibility to all the pleasures and pains of life? And if the man of a delicate, refined temper, by being so much more alive than the rest of the world, is only so much more unhappy, what judgment must we form in general of human life?

Let men remain at rest, says our adversary, and they will be easy. They are willing artificers of their own misery. . . . No! reply I: an anxious languor follows their repose; disappointment, vexation, trouble, their activity and ambition.

I can observe something like what you mention in some others, replied Cleanthes, but I confess I feel little or nothing of it in myself, and hope that it is not so common as you represent it.

If you feel not human misery yourself, cried Demea, I congratulate you on so happy a singularity. Others, seemingly the most prosperous, have not been ashamed to vent their complaints in the most melancholy strains. Let us attend to the great, the fortunate emperor, Charles V, when, tired with human grandeur, he resigned all his existent dominions into the hands of his son. In the last harangue which he made on that memorable occasion, he publicly avowed *that the greatest prosperities which he had ever enjoyed had been mixed with so many adversities that he might truly say he had never enjoyed any satisfaction or contentment.* But did the retired life in which he sought for shelter afford him any greater happiness? If we may credit his son's account, his repentance commenced the very day of his resignation.

Cicero's fortune, from small beginnings, rose to the greatest lustre and renown; yet what pathetic complaints of the ills of life do his familiar letters, as well as philosophical discourses, contain? And suitably to his own experience, he introduces Cato, the great, the fortunate Cato protesting in his old age that had he a new life in his offer he would reject the present.

Ask yourself, ask any of your acquaintance, whether they would live over again the last ten or twenty years of their life. No! but the next twenty, they say, will be better:

And from the dregs of life, hope to receive
What the first sprightly running could not give.

Thus, at last, they find (such is the greatness of human misery, it reconciles even contradictions) that they complain at once of the shortness of life and of its vanity and sorrow.

And is it possible, Cleanthes, said Philo, that after all these reflections, and infinitely more which

might be suggested, you can still persevere in your anthropomorphism, and assert the moral attributes of the Deity, his justice, benevolence mercy, and rectitude, to be of the same nature with these virtues in human creatures? His power, we allow, is infinite; whatever he wills is executed; but neither man nor any other animal is happy; therefore, he does not will their happiness. His wisdom is infinite; he is never mistaken in choosing the means to any end; but the course of nature tends not to human or animal felicity; therefore, it is not established for that purpose. Through the whole compass of human knowledge there are no inferences more certain and infallible than these. In what respect, then, do his benevolence and mercy resemble the benevolence and mercy of men?

Epicurus' old questions are yet unanswered.

Is he willing to prevent evil, but not able? then is he impotent. Is he able, but not willing? then is he malevolent. Is he both able and willing? whence then is evil?

You ascribe, Cleanthes, (and I believe justly) a purpose and intention to nature. But what, I beseech you, is the object of that curious artifice and machinery which she has displayed in all animals—the preservation alone of individuals, and propagation of the species? It seems enough for her purpose, if such a rank be barely upheld in the universe, without any care or concern for the happiness of the members that compose it. No resource for this purpose: no machinery in order merely to give pleasure or ease; no fund of pure joy and contentment; no indulgence without some want or necessity accompanying it. At least, the few phenomena of this nature are overbalanced by opposite phenomena of still greater importance.

Our sense of music, harmony, and indeed beauty of all kinds, gives satisfaction, without being absolutely necessary to the preservation and propagation of the species. But what racking pains, on the other hand, arise from gouts, gravels, megrims, toothaches, rheumatisms, where the injury to the animal machinery is either small or incurable? Mirth, laughter, play, frolic seem gratuitous satisfactions which have no further tendency; spleen, melancholy, discontent, superstition are pains of the same nature. How then does the Divine benevolence display itself, in the sense of you anthropomorphites? None but we mystics, as you were pleased to call us, can account for this strange

ABRAHAM AND ISAAC

Genesis

As it came to pass after these things, that God did tempt Abraham, and said unto him, "Abraham": and he said, "Behold, here I am."

And he said, "Take now thy son, thine only son Isaac, whom thou lovest, and get thee into the land of Moriah; and offer him there for a burnt offering upon one of the mountains which I will tell thee of."

And Abraham rose up early in the morning, and saddled his ass, and took two of his young men with him, and Isaac his son, and clave the wood for the burnt offering, and rose up, and went unto the place of which God had told him.

Then on the third day Abraham lifted up his eyes, and saw the place afar off.

And Abraham said unto his young men, "Abide ye here with the ass; and I and the lad will go yonder and worship, and come again to you."

And Abraham took the wood of the burnt offering, and laid it upon Isaac his son; and he took the fire in his hand, and a knife; and they went both of them together.

And Isaac spake unto Abraham his father, and said, "My father": and he said, "Here am I, my son." And he said, "Behold the fire and the wood: but where is the lamb for a burnt offering?"

And Abraham said, "My son, God will provide himself a lamb for a burnt offering": so they went, both of them together. . . .

mixture of phenomena, by deriving it from attributes infinitely perfect but incomprehensible.

And have you, at last, said Cleanthes smiling, betrayed your intentions, Philo? Your long agreement with Demea did indeed a little surprise me, but I find you were all the while erecting a concealed battery against me. And I must confess that you have now fallen upon a subject worthy of your noble spirit of opposition and controversy. If you can make out the present point, and prove mankind to be unhappy or corrupted, there is an end at once of all religion. For to what purpose establish the natural attributes of the Deity, while the moral are still doubtful and uncertain?

You take umbrage very easily, replied Demea, at opinions the most innocent and the most generally received, even amongst the religious and devout themselves; and nothing can be more surprising than to find a topic like this—concerning the wickedness and misery of man—charged with no less than atheism and profaneness. Have not all pious divines and preachers who have indulged their rhetoric on so fertile a subject, have they not easily, I say, given a solution of any difficulties which

may attend it? This world is but a point in comparison of the universe; this life but a moment in comparison of eternity. The present evil phenomena, therefore, are rectified in other regions, and in some future period of existence. And the eyes of men, being then opened to larger views of things, see the whole connection of general laws, and trace, with adoration, the benevolence and rectitude of the Deity through all the mazes and intricacies of his providence.

No! replied Cleanthes, no! These arbitrary suppositions can never be admitted, contrary to matter of facts, visible and uncontroverted. Whence can any cause be known but from its known effects? Whence can any hypothesis be proved but from the apparent phenomena? To establish one hypothesis upon another is building entirely in the air; and the utmost we ever attain by these conjectures and fictions is to ascertain the bare possibility of our opinion, but never can we, upon such terms, establish its reality.

The only method of supporting Divine benevolence—and it is what I willingly embrace—is to deny absolutely the misery and wickedness of

MYSTICAL EXPERIENCE VS. RELIGIOUS VISIONS

Walter Stace

Suppose someone sees a vision of the Virgin Mary. What he sees has shape, the shape of a woman, and color—white skin, blue raiment, a golden halo, and so on. But these are all images or sensations. They are therefore composed of elements of our sensory-intellectual consciousness. The same is true of voices. Or suppose one has a precognition of a neighbor's death. The components one is aware of—a dead man, a coffin, etc.—are composed of elements of our sensory-intellectual consciousness. The only difference is that these ordinary elements are arranged in unfamiliar patterns which we have come to think cannot occur, so that if they do occur they seem supernormal. Or the fact that such elements are combined in an unusual way so as to constitute the figure of a woman up in the clouds, perhaps surrounded by other humanlike figures with wings added to them—all this does not constitute a different *kind* of consciousness at all. And just as sensory elements of any sort are excluded from the mystical con-

sciousness, so are conceptual elements. It is not that the thoughts in the mystical consciousness are different from those we are accustomed to. It does not include any thoughts at all. The mystic, of course, expresses thoughts about his experience after that experience is over, and he remembers it when he is back again in his sensory-intellectual consciousness. But there are no thoughts *in* the experience itself. . . .

The most important, the central characteristics in which all *fully developed* mystical experiences agree, and which in the last analysis is definitive of them and serves to mark them off from other kinds of experiences, is that they involve the apprehension of *an ultimate nonsensuous unity in all things,* a oneness or a One to which neither the senses nor the reason can penetrate. In other words, it entirely transcends our sensory-intellectual consciousness.

From *The Teachings of the Mystics* (1960).

---

man. Your representations are exaggerated; your melancholy views mostly fictitious; your inferences contrary to fact and experience. Health is more common than sickness; pleasure than pain; happiness than misery. And for one vexation which we meet with, we attain, upon computation, a hundred enjoyments.

Admitting your position, replied Philo, which yet is extremely doubtful, you must at the same time allow that, if pain be less frequent than pleasure, it is infinitely more violent and durable. One hour of it is often able to outweigh a day, a week, a month of our common insipid enjoyments; and how many days, weeks, and months are passed by several in the most acute torments? Pleasure, scarcely in one instance, is ever able to reach ecstasy and rapture; and in no one instance can it

continue for any time at its highest pitch and altitude. The spirits evaporate, the nerves relax, the fabric is disordered, and the enjoyment quickly degenerates into fatigue and uneasiness. But pain often, good God, how often! rises to torture and agony; and the longer it continues, it becomes still more genuine agony and torture. Patience is exhausted, courage languishes, melancholy seizes us, and nothing terminates our misery but the removal of its cause or another event which is the sole cure of all evil, but which, from our natural folly, we regard with still greater horror and consternation.

But not to insist upon these topics, continued Philo, though most obvious, certain, and important, I must use the freedom to admonish you, Cleanthes, that you have put the controversy upon a most dangerous issue, and are unawares introducing a total scepticism into the most essential articles of natural and revealed theology. What! no method of fixing a just foundation for religion unless we allow the happiness of human life, and maintain a continued existence even in this world, with all our present pains, infirmities, vexations, and follies, to be eligible and desirable! But this is contrary to everyone's feeling and experience; it is contrary to an authority so established as nothing can subvert. No decisive proofs can ever be produced against this authority; nor is it possible for you to compute, estimate, and compare all the pains and all the pleasures in the lives of all men and all animals; and thus, by your resting the whole system of religion on a point which, from its very nature, must forever be uncertain, you tacitly confess that that system is equally uncertain.

But allowing you what never will be believed, at least, what you never possibly can prove, that animal or, at least, human happiness in this life exceeds its misery, you have yet done nothing; for this is not, by any means, what we expect from infinite power, infinite wisdom, and infinite goodness. Why is there any misery at all in the world? Not by chance, surely. From some cause then. Is it from the intention of the Deity? But he is perfectly benevolent. Is it contrary to his intention? But he is almighty. Nothing can shake the solidity of this reasoning, so short, so clear, so decisive, except we assert that these subjects exceed all human capacity, and that our common measures of truth and falsehood are not applicable to them — a topic which I have all along insisted on, but which you have, from the beginning, rejected with scorn and indignation.

But I will be contented to retire still from this intrenchment, for I deny that you can ever force me in it. I will allow that pain or misery in man is *compatible* with infinite power and goodness in the Deity, even in your sense of these attributes: what are you advanced by all these concessions? A mere possible compatibility is not sufficient. You must *prove* these pure, unmixt, and uncontrollable attributes from the present mixed and confused phenomena, and from these alone. A hopeful undertaking! Were the phenomena ever so pure and unmixed, yet, being finite, they would be insufficient for that purpose. How much more, where they are also so jarring and discordant!

Here, Cleanthes, I find myself at ease in my argument. Here I triumph. Formerly, when we argued concerning the natural attributes of intelligence and design, I needed all my sceptical and metaphysical subtilty to elude your grasp. In many views of the universe and of its parts, particularly the latter, the beauty and fitness of final causes strike us with such irresistible force that all objections appear (what I believe they really are) mere cavils and sophisms; nor can we then imagine how it was ever possible for us to repose any weight on them. But there is no view of human life or of the condition of mankind from which, without the greatest violence, we can infer the moral attributes or learn that infinite benevolence, conjoined with infinite power and infinite wisdom, which we must discover by the eyes of faith alone. It is your turn now to tug the labouring oar, and to support your philosophical subtilties against the dictates of plain reason and experience.

Further Questions

1. It is sometimes said that the reason there is suffering is that God is using Earth as a testing ground to see which humans merit heaven. Suppose this were true. Would it be an adequate response to Philo's arguments?

2. "The so-called problem of evil is not really a problem for Christianity since any suffering we may experience on Earth is nothing compared to the infinite and eternal bliss that according to Christianity awaits us in heaven." Assume, for the sake of argument, that the bliss really is coming. Would this be an adequate response to Philo's arguments?

3. "The basic flaw in the so-called problem of evil is in its assumption that God's goodness is like human goodness. It is not. God's goodness is so beyond human goodness that we humans, with our finite mental and emotional capacities, can scarcely begin to comprehend it." Do you agree? Why?

Further Readings

Hick, John. *Evil and the God of Love.* New York: Harper & Row, 1966. A well-known Protestant theologian responds to the problem of evil. Thoughtful and readable.

Peterson, Michael L., ed. *The Problem of Evil.* South Bend, IN: University of Notre Dame Press, 1992. An anthology of classical and contemporary selections.

Must God Create the Best?   38

ROBERT MERRIHEW ADAMS

Robert Adams, a Presbyterian minister, taught philosophy at the University of Michigan and U.C.L.A. before accepting his current position as professor of philosophy and chair of the department at Yale University. He was written extensively on metaphysics, ethics, philosophy of religion, and the history of philosophy. His *The Virtue of Faith* (Oxford 1987) includes many of his papers in philosophy of religion. And his recent *Leibniz: Determinist, Theist, Idealist* (Oxford 1994), is widely regarded as an important contribution to the history of modern philosophy. In the selection that follows, he responds on behalf of Christianity to the problem of evil.

Reading Questions:

1. What sorts of reasons does Adams say could be given for (P)?
2. Adams argues that none of these are good reasons. What are his arguments?
3. Explain, in your own words, the "retarded child" objection that Adams brings up in Section IV. How does he attempt to answer this objection? Is his answer sufficient?

MANY PHILOSOPHERS AND THEOLOGIANS have accepted the following proposition:

(*P*) If a perfectly good moral agent created any world at all, it would have to be the very best world that he could create.

The best world that an omnipotent God could create is the best of all logically possible worlds. Accordingly, it has been supposed that if the actual world was created by an omnipotent, perfectly good God, it must be the best of all logically possible worlds.

In this paper I shall argue that ethical views typical of the Judeo-Christian religious tradition do not require the Judeo-Christian theist to accept (*P*). He must hold that the actual world is a good world. But he need not maintain that it is the best of all possible worlds, or the best world that God could have made.

The position which I am claiming that he can consistently hold is that *even if* there is a best among possible worlds, God could create another instead of it, and still be perfectly good. I do not in fact see any good reason to believe that there is a best among possible worlds. Why can't it be that for every possible world there is another that is better? And if there is no maximum degree of perfection among possible worlds, it would be

Reprinted from The Philosophical Review *74 (1965) 27–46, by permission of the publisher and the author.*
Footnotes deleted.

unreasonable to blame God, or think less highly of His goodness, because He created a world less excellent than He could have created. But I do not claim to be able to prove that there is no best among possible worlds, and in this essay I shall assume for the sake of argument that there is one.

Whether we accept proposition (P) will depend on what we believe are the requirements for perfect goodness. If we apply an act-utilitarian standard of moral goodness, we will have to accept (P). For by act-utilitarian standards, it is a moral obligation to bring about the best state of affairs that one can. It is interesting to note that the ethics of Leibniz, the best-known advocate of (P), is basically utilitarian. In his *Theodicy* (Part I, Section 25) he maintains, in effect, that men, because of their ignorance of many of the consequences of their actions, ought to follow a rule-utilitarian code, but that God, being omniscient, must be a perfect act utilitarian in order to be perfectly good.

I believe that utilitarian views are not typical of the Judeo-Christian ethical tradition, although Leibniz is by no means the only Christian utilitarian. In this essay I shall assume that we are working with standards of moral goodness which are not utilitarian. But I shall not try either to show that utilitarianism is wrong or to justify the standards that I take to be more typical of Judeo-Christian religious ethics. To attempt either of these tasks would unmanageably enlarge the scope of the paper. What I can hope to establish here is therefore limited to the claim that the rejection of (P) is consistent with Judeo-Christian religious ethics.

Assuming that we are not using utilitarian standards of moral goodness, I see only two types of reason that could be given for (P). (1) It might be claimed that a creator would necessarily wrong someone (violate someone's rights), or be less kind to someone than a perfectly good moral agent must be, if he knowingly created a less excellent world instead of the best that he could. Or (2) it might be claimed that even if no one would be wronged or treated unkindly by the creation of an inferior world, the creator's choice of an inferior world must manifest a defect of character. I will argue against the first of these claims in Section II. Then I will suggest, in Section III, that God's choice of a less excellent world could be accounted for in terms of His grace, which is considered a virtue rather than a defect of character in Judeo-

Christian ethics. A counterexample, which is the basis for the most persuasive objections to my position that I have encountered, will be considered in Sections IV and V.

II

Is there someone *to* whom a creator would have an obligation to create the best world he could? Is there someone whose rights would be violated, or who would be treated unkindly, if the creator created a less excellent world? Let us suppose that our creator is God, and that there does not exist any being, other than Himself, which He has not created. It follows that if God has wronged anyone, or been unkind to anyone, in creating whatever world He has created, this must be one of His own creatures. To which of His creatures, then, might God have an obligation to create the best of all possible worlds? (For that is the best world He could create.)

Might He have an obligation to the creatures in the best possible world, to create them? Have they been wronged, or even treated unkindly, if God has created a less excellent world, in which they do not exist, instead of creating them? I think not. The difference between actual beings and merely possible beings is of fundamental moral importance here. The moral community consists of actual beings. It is they who would have actual rights, and it is to them that there are actual obligations. A merely possible being cannot be (actually) wronged or treated unkindly. A being who never exists is not wronged by not being created, and there is no obligation to any possible being to bring it into existence.

Perhaps it will be objected that we believe we have obligations to future generations, who are not yet actual and may never be actual. We do say such things, but I think what we mean is something like the following. There is not merely a logical possibility, but a probability greater than zero, that future generations will really exist; and *if* they will in fact exist, we will have wronged them if we act or fail to act in certain ways. On this analysis we cannot have an obligation to future generations to bring them into existence.

I argue, then, that God does not have an obligation to the creatures in the best of all possible

"GOD'S COMPASSION"

William J. Wainwright

Anselm argued that God is compassionate in the sense that He acts *as if* He felt compassion although He doesn't actually do so. . . .

Bernard of Clairvaux (1090–1153) maintains that while God can't grieve or suffer in His *own* nature, He became incarnate so that He might "learn by his own experience how to commiserate and sympathize with those who are . . . suffering and tempted." . . .

Thomas Aquinas (1225–74) has a more adequate solution. Love and joy are pure perfections. Hence, God literally has them although the mode in which He loves and rejoices differs from the mode in which we do so. (Human love and joy are often partly voluntary. We willingly embrace what we love or rejoice in. But they are also "passions"—externally induced modifications of our animal nature over which we have little control. God has no animal nature. His love and joy are wholly active, an expression only of His will.)

Anger and sorrow differ from love and joy because they entail suffering. Hence, even when these emotions are appropriate, they are only mixed perfections. They can therefore only be ascribed to God metaphorically. Nevertheless, anger and sorrow aren't *equally* metaphorical. Anger is ascribed to God because He produces effects similar to those which an angry person might produce. But no internal modification of God corresponds to anger in us. By contrast, God "is said to be saddened in so far as certain things take place contrary to what He loves and approves." While God doesn't literally grieve, there is something *in* God (an internal modification of God) that we apprehend as sorrow, namely, His love. That is, when our awareness of God's love is coupled with our recognition that creatures disobey God and suffer, we construe that divine love as sorrow.

Like Bernard, Thomas implicitly recognizes that there is no compassion without sympathetic feeling or emotion. But unlike many modern theologians, Thomas thinks the emotion in question is simply love—not tender sorrow. This has two advantages. Love is compatible with unalloyed joy while sympathetic sorrow is essentially a reaction rather than an action. Love thus coheres better with God's independence.

Thomas's solution is superior to Anselm's and Bernard's. Whether it is fully satisfactory depends on whether a compassion that doesn't literally involve sympathetic suffering is really compassion and thus adequately meets the demands of religious consciousness.

From *Philosophy of Religion* (1988).

---

worlds to create them. If God has chosen to create a world less excellent than the best possible. He has not thereby wronged any creatures whom He has chosen not to create. He has not even been unkind to them. If any creatures are wronged, or treated unkindly, by such a choice of the creator, they can only be creatures that exist in the world He has created.

I think it is fairly plausible to suppose that God could create a world which would have the following characteristics:

(1) None of the individual creatures in it would exist in the best of all possible worlds.

(2) None of the creatures in it has a life which is so miserable on the whole that it would be better for that creature if it had never existed.

(3) Every individual creature in the world is at least as happy on the whole as it would have been in any other possible world in which it could have existed.

It seems obvious that if God creates such a world He does not thereby wrong any of the creatures in it, and does not thereby treat any of them with less than perfect kindness. For none of them would have been benefited by His creating any other world instead.

If there are doubts about the possibility of God's creating such a world, they will probably have to do with the third characteristic. It may be worthwhile to consider two questions, on the supposition (which I am not endorsing) that no possible world less excellent than the best would have characteristic (3), and that God has created a world which has characteristics (1) and (2) but not (3). In such a case must God have wronged one of His creatures. Must He have been less than perfectly kind to one of His creatures?

I do not think it can reasonably be argued that in such a case God must have wronged one of His creatures. Suppose a creature in such a case were to complain that God had violated its rights by creating it in a world in which it was less happy on the whole than it would have been in some other world in which God could have created it. The complaint might express a claim to special treatment: "God ought to have created *me* in more favorable circumstances (even though that would involve His creating some *other* creature in less favorable circumstances than He could have created it in)." Such a complaint would not be reasonable, and would not establish that there had been any violation of the complaining creature's rights.

Alternatively, the creature might make the more principled complaint, "God has wronged me by not following the principle of refraining from creating any world in which there is a creature that would have been happier in another world He could have made." This also is an unreasonable complaint. For if God followed the stated principle, He would not create any world that lacked characteristic (3). And we are assuming that no world less excellent than the best possible would have characteristic (3). It follows that if God acted on the stated principle He would not create any world less excellent than the best possible. But the complaining creature would not exist in the best of all possible worlds; for we are assuming that this creature exists in a world which has characteristic (1). The complaining creature, therefore, would never have existed if God had followed the princi-

ple that is urged in the complaint. There could not possibly be any advantage to this creature from God's having followed that principle; and the creature has not been wronged by God's not following the principle. (It would not be better for the creature if it had never existed; for we are assuming that the world God created has characteristic [2].)

The question of whether in the assumed case God must have been unkind to one of His creatures is more complicated than the question of whether He must have wronged one of them. In fact it is too complicated to be discussed adequately here. I will just make three observations about it. The first is that it is no clearer that the best of all possible worlds would possess characteristic (3) than that some less excellent world would possess it. In fact it has often been supposed that the best possible world might not possess it. The problem we are now discussing can therefore arise also for those who believe that God has created the best of all possible worlds.

My second observation is that if kindness to a person is the same as a tendency to promote his happiness, God has been less than perfectly (completely, unqualifiedly) kind to any creature whom He could have made somewhat happier than He has made it. (I shall not discuss here whether kindness to a person is indeed the same as a tendency to promote his happiness; they are at least closely related.)

But in the third place I would observe that such qualified kindness (if that is what it is) toward some creatures is consistent with God's being perfectly good, and with His being very kind to all His creatures. It is consistent with His being very kind to all His creatures because He may have prepared for all of them a very satisfying existence even though some of them might have been slightly happier in some other possible world. It is consistent with His being perfectly good because even a perfectly good moral agent may be led, by other considerations of sufficient weight, to qualify his kindness or beneficence toward some person. It has sometimes been held that a perfectly good God might cause or permit a person to have less happiness than he might otherwise have had, in order to punish him, or to avoid interfering with the freedom of another person, or in order to create the best of all possible worlds. I would suggest that the desire to create and love all of a certain group of possible creatures (assuming that all of them would have satisfying lives on the whole) might be an adequate ground for a perfectly good God to create them, even if His creating *all* of them must have the result that some of them are less happy than they might otherwise have been. And they need not be the best of all possible creatures, or included in the best of all possible worlds, in order for this qualification of His kindness to be consistent with His perfect goodness. The desire to create *those* creatures is as legitimate a ground for Him to qualify His kindness toward some, as the desire to create the best of all possible worlds. This suggestion seems to me to be in keeping with the aspect of the Judeo-Christian moral ideal which will be discussed in Section III.

These matters would doubtless have to be discussed more fully if we were considering whether the *actual* world can have been created by a perfectly good God. For our present purposes, however, enough may have been said—especially since, as I have noted, it seems a plausible assumption that God could make a world having characteristics (1), (2), and (3). In that case He could certainly make a less excellent world than the best of all possible worlds without wronging any of His creatures or failing in kindness to any of them (I have, of course, *not* been arguing that there is no way in which God could wrong anyone or be less kind to anyone than a perfectly good moral agent must be.)

III

Plato is one of those who held that a perfectly good creator would make the very best world he could. He thought that if the creator chose to make a world less good than he could have made, that could be understood only in terms of some defect in the creator's character. Envy is the defect that Plato suggests. It may be thought that the creation of a world inferior to the best that he could make would manifest a defect in the creator's character even if no one were thereby wronged or treated unkindly. For the perfectly good moral agent must not only be kind and refrain from violating the rights of others, but must also have other virtues. For instance, he must be noble, generous,

high-minded, and free from envy. He must satisfy the moral ideal.

There are differences of opinion, however, about what is to be included in the moral ideal. One important element in the Judeo-Christian moral ideal is *grace*. For present purposes, grace may be defined as a disposition to love which is not dependent on the merit of the person loved. The gracious person loves without worrying about whether the person he loves is worthy of his love. Or perhaps it would be better to say that the gracious person sees what is valuable in the person he loves, and does not worry about whether it is more or less valuable than what could be found in someone else he might have loved. In the Judeo-Christian tradition it is typically believed that grace is a virtue which God does have and men ought to have.

A God who is gracious with respect to creating might well choose to create and love less excellent creatures than He could have chosen. This is not to suggest that grace in creation consists in a preference for imperfection as such. God could have chosen to create the best of all possible creatures, and still have been gracious in choosing them. God's graciousness in creation does not imply that the creatures He has chosen to create must be less excellent than the best possible. It implies, rather, that even if they are the best possible creatures, that is not the ground for His choosing them. And it implies that there is nothing in God's nature or character which would require Him to act on the principle of choosing the best possible creatures to be the object of His creative powers.

Grace, as I have described it, is not part of everyone's moral ideal. For instance, it was not part of Plato's moral ideal. The thought that it may be the expression of a virtue, rather than a defect of character, in a creator, *not* to act on the principle of creating the best creatures he possibly could, is quite foreign to Plato's ethical viewpoint. But I believe that thought is not at all foreign to a Judeo-Christian ethical viewpoint.

This interpretation of the Judeo-Christian tradition is confirmed by the religious and devotional attitudes toward God's creation which prevail in the tradition. The man who worships God does not normally praise Him for His moral rectitude and good judgment in creating *us*. He thanks God for his existence as for an undeserved personal favor. Religious writings frequently deprecate the intrinsic worth of human beings, considered apart from God's love for them, and express surprise that God should concern Himself with them at all.

> When I look at thy heavens, the work of thy fin-
> gers, the moon and the stars which thou has
> established;
> What is man that thou art mindful of him, and the
> son of man that thou dost care for him?
> Yet thou has made him little less than God, and
> dost crown him with glory and honor.
> Thou hast given him dominion over the works of
> thy hands; thou hast put all things under his
> feet [Psalm 8:3–6].

Such utterances seem quite incongruous with the idea that God created us because if He had not He would have failed to bring about the best possible state of affairs. They suggest that God has created human beings and made them dominant on this planet although He could have created intrinsically better states of affairs instead.

I believe that in the Judeo-Christian tradition the typical religious attitude (or at any rate the attitude typically encouraged) toward the fact of our existence is something like the following. "I am glad that I exist, and I thank God for the life He has given me. I am also glad that other people exist, and I thank God for them. Doubtless there could be more excellent creatures than we. But I believe that God, in His grace, created us and loves us; and I accept that gladly and gratefully." (Such an attitude need not be complacent; for the task of struggling against certain evils may be seen as precisely a part of the life that the religious person is to accept and be glad in.) When people who have or endorse such an attitude say that God is perfectly good, we will not take them as committing themselves to the view that God is the kind of being who would not create any other world than the best possible. For they regard grace as an important part of perfect goodness.

IV

On more than one occasion when I have argued for the positions I have taken in Sections II and III above, a counterexample of the following sort has been proposed. It is the case of a person who, knowing that he intends to conceive a child and that a certain drug invariably causes severe mental retardation in children conceived by those who have taken it, takes the drug and conceives a severely retarded child. We all, I imagine, have a strong inclination to say that such a person has done something wrong. It is objected to me that our moral intuitions in this case (presumably including the moral intuitions of religious Jews and Christians) are inconsistent with the views I have advanced above. It is claimed that consistency requires me to abandon those views unless I am prepared to make moral judgments that none of us are in fact willing to make.

I will try to meet these objections. I will begin by stating the case in some detail, in the most relevant form I can think of. Then I will discuss objections based on it. In this section I will discuss an objection against what I have said in Section II, and a more general objection against the rejection of proposition (P) will be discussed in Section V.

Let us call this Case (A). A certain couple become so interested in retarded children that they develop a strong desire to have a retarded child of their own—to love it, to help it realize its potentialities (such as they are) to the full, to see that it is as happy as it can be. (For some reason it is impossible for them to *adopt* such a child.) They act on their desire. They take a drug which is known to cause damaged genes and abnormal chromosome structure in reproductive cells, resulting in severe mental retardation of children conceived by those who have taken it. A severely retarded child is conceived and born. They lavish affection on the child They have ample means, so that they are able to provide for special needs, and to insure that others will never be called on to pay for the child's support. They give themselves unstintedly, and do develop the child's capacities as much as possible. The child is, on the whole, happy, though incapable of many of the higher intellectual, aesthetic, and social joys. It suffers some pains and frustrations, of course, but does not feel miserable on the whole.

The first objection founded on this case is based, not just on the claim that the parents have done something wrong (which I certainly grant), but on the more specific claim that they have *wronged the child*. I maintained, in effect, in Section II that a creature has not been wronged by its creator's creating it if both of the following conditions are satisfied. (4) The creature is not, on the whole, so miserable that it would be better for him if he had never existed. (5) No being who came into existence in better or happier circumstances would have been the same individual as the creature in question. If we apply an analogous principle to the parent-child relationship in Case (*A*), it would seem to follow that the retarded child has not been wronged by its parents. Condition (4) is satisfied: the child is happy rather than miserable on the whole. And condition (5) also seems to be satisfied. For the retardation in Case (*A*), as described, is not due to prenatal injury but to the genetic constitution of the child. Any normal child the parents might have conceived (indeed any normal child at all) would have had a different genetic constitution, and would therefore have been a different person, from the retarded child they actually did conceive. But—it is objected to me—we do regard the parents in Case (*A*) as having wronged the child, and therefore we cannot consistently accept the principle that I maintained in Section II.

My reply is that if conditions (4) and (5) are really satisfied the child cannot have been wronged by its parents' taking the drug and conceiving it. If we think otherwise we are being led, perhaps by our emotions, into a confusion. If the child is not worse off than if it had never existed, and if *its* never existing would have been a sure consequence of its not having been brought into existence as retarded, I do not see how *its* interests can have been injured, or *its* rights violated, by the parents' bringing it into existence as retarded.

It is easy to understand how the parents might come to feel that they had wronged the child. They might come to feel guilty (and rightly so), and the child would provide a focus for the guilt. Moreover, it would be easy, psychologically, to assimilate Case (*A*) to cases of culpability for prenatal injury, in which it is more reasonable to think of the child as having been wronged. And we often think very carelessly about counterfactual personal identity, asking ourselves questions of doubtful intelligibility, such as, "What if I had been born in the Middle Ages?" It is very easy to fail to consider the objection, "But that would not have been the same person."

It is also possible that an inclination to say that the child has been wronged may be based, at least in part, on a doubt that conditions (4) and (5) are really satisfied in case (*A*). Perhaps one is not convinced that in real life the parents could ever have a reasonable confidence that the child would be happy rather than miserable. Maybe it will be doubted that a few changes in chromosomes structure, and the difference between damaged and undamaged genes, are enough to establish that the retarded child is a different person from any normal child that the couple could have had. Of course, if conditions (4) and (5) are not satisfied, the case does not constitute a counterexample to my claims in Section II. But I would not rest any of the weight of my argument on doubts about the satisfaction of the conditions on Case (*A*), because I think it is plausible to suppose that they would be satisfied in Case (*A*) or in some very similar case.

V

Even if the parents in Case (*A*) have not wronged the child, I assume that they have done something wrong. It may be asked *what* they have done wrong, or *why* their action is regarded as wrong And these questions may give rise to an objection, not specifically to what I said in Section II, but more generally to my rejection of proposition (*P*) For it may be suggested that what is wrong about the action of the parents in Case (*A*) is that they have violated the following principle:

> (*Q*) It is wrong to bring into existence, knowingly, a being less excellent than one could have brought into existence.

If we accept this principle we must surely agree that it would be wrong for a creator to make a world that was less excellent than the best he could make, and therefore that a perfectly good creator would not do such a thing. In other words, (*Q*) implies (*P*).

I do not think (*Q*) is a very plausible principle. It is not difficult to think of counterexamples to it.

Case (*B*): A man breeds goldfish, thereby bringing about their existence. We do not normally think it is wrong, or even prima facie wrong, for a man to do this, even though he could equally well have brought about the existence of more excellent beings, more intelligent and capable of higher satisfactions (He could have bred dogs or pigs, for example.) The deliberate breeding of human beings of subnormal intelligence is normally offensive; the deliberate breeding of species far less intelligent than retarded human children is not morally offensive.

Case (C): Suppose it has been discovered that if intending parents take a certain drug before conceiving a child, they will have a child whose abnormal genetic constitution will give it vastly superhuman intelligence and superior prospects of happiness Other things being equal, would it be wrong for intending parents to have normal children instead of taking the drug? There may be considerable disagreement of moral judgment about this. I do not think that parents who choose to have normal children rather than take the drug would be doing anything wrong, nor that they would necessarily be manifesting any weakness or defect of moral character Parents' choosing to have a normal rather than superhuman child would not, at any rate, elicit the strong and universal or almost universal disapproval that would be elicited by the action of the parents in Case (A). Even with respect to the offspring of human beings, the principle we all confidently endorse is not that it is wrong to bring about, knowingly and voluntarily, the procreation of offspring less excellent than could have been procreated, but that it is wrong to bring about, knowingly and voluntarily, the procreation of a human offspring which is deficient by comparison with normal human beings.

Such counterexamples as these suggest that our disapproval of the action of the parents in Case (A) is not based on principle (Q), but on a less general and more plausible principle such as the following:

> (R) It is wrong for human beings to cause, knowingly and voluntarily, the procreation of an offspring of human parents which is notably deficient, by comparison with normal human beings, in mental or physical capacity

One who rejects (Q) while maintaining (R) might be held to face a problem of explanation. It may seem arbitrary to maintain such a specific moral principle as (R), unless one can explain it as based on a more general principle, such as (Q). I believe, however, that principle (R) might well be explained in something like the following way in a theological ethics in the Judeo-Christian tradition, consistently with the rejection of (Q) and (P).

God, in His grace, has chosen to have human beings among His creatures. In creating us He has certain intentions about the qualities and goals of human life. He has these intentions for us, not just as individuals, but as members of a community which in principle includes the whole human race. And His intentions for human beings as such extend to the offspring (if any) of human beings. Some of these intentions are to be realized by human voluntary action, and it is our duty to act in accordance with them.

It seems increasingly possible for human voluntary action to influence the genetic constitution of human offspring. The religious believer in the Judeo-Christian tradition will want to be extremely cautious about this. For he is to be thankful that we exist as the beings we are, and will be concerned lest he bring about the procreation of human offspring who would be deficient in their capacity to enter fully into the purposes that God has for human beings as such. We are not God. We are His creatures, and we belong to Him. Any offspring we have will belong to Him in a much more fundamental way that they can belong to their human parents. We have not the right to try to have as our offspring just any kind of being whose existence might on the whole be pleasant and of some value (for instance, a being of very low intelligence but highly specialized for the enjoyment of aesthetic pleasures of smell and taste). If we do intervene to affect the genetic constitution of human offspring, it must be in ways which seem likely to make them *more* able to enter fully into what we believe to be the purposes of God for human beings as such. The deliberate procreation of children deficient in mental or physical capacity would be an intervention which could hardly be expected to result in offspring more able to enter fully into God's purposes for human life. It would therefore be sinful, and inconsistent with a proper respect for the human life which God has given us.

On this view of the matter, our obligation to refrain from bringing about the procreation of deficient human offspring is rooted in our obligation to God, as His creatures, to respect His purposes for human life. In adopting this theological rationale for the acceptance of principle (R), one in no way commits oneself to proposition (P). For one does not base (R) on any principle to the effect that one must always try to bring into existence the most excellent things that one can. And the claim that, because of His intentions for human life, we have an obligation to God not to try to have as our offspring beings of certain sorts does not imply that it would be wrong for God to create such beings in other ways. Much less does it imply that it would be wrong for God to create a world less excellent than the best possible.

In this essay I have argued that a creator would not necessarily wrong anyone, or be less kind to anyone than a perfectly good moral agent must be, if he created a world of creatures who would not exist in the best world he could make. I have also argued that from the standpoint of Judeo-Christian religious ethics, a creator's choice of a less excellent world need not be regarded as manifesting a defect of character. It could be understood in terms of his *grace,* which (in that ethics) is considered an important part of perfect goodness. In this way I think the rejection of proposition (P) can be seen to be congruous with the attitude of gratitude and respect for human life as God's gracious gift which is encouraged in the Judeo-Christian religious tradition. And that attitude (rather than any belief that one ought to bring into existence only the best beings one can) can be seen as a basis for the disapproval of the deliberate procreation of deficient human offspring.

Further Questions

1. The problem of evil is often stated in some way such as this: If there were an all-powerful being, then that being could prevent evil. If there were a being who was perfectly good, that being would prevent evil if that being could. Evil exists. Therefore, no being is all-powerful and perfectly good. Has Adams answered this argument? Explain.
2. What, in your view, is the most powerful objection to Adams' argument (that he either did not consider or did not answer adequately)? Explain how Adams could best respond to this objection. Then explain whether, in your view, his response is adequate.

Further Readings

Penelhum, Terence, ed. *Faith*. New York: Macmillan, 1989. A comprehensive anthology.
Twain, Mark. *Letters from the Earth*. New York: Fawcett Crest, 1962. A funny, but still penetrating presentation of the problem of evil.

The Elusive Messiah   39

RAYMOND MARTIN

A brief biography of Martin appears on page 139.

In this selection, Martin reviews the problems that complicate the quest for the historical Jesus and then uses these as a springboard for reconsidering Bertrand Russell's famous discussion of the question of whether Jesus was "the best and the wisest" person.

Reading Questions

1. Explain in your own words what "the believer's dilemma" is and why Martin thinks it might be a problem for a Christian. If you were a Christian, would it be a problem for you?

2. Does a problem analogous to "the believer's dilemma" arise for believers in non-Christian religious traditions, such as Muslims, Jews, Hindus, and Buddhists?

3. Martin says that "it's unclear what the constraints are on theological interpretations" of the meaning of Jesus' sayings. Pick a specific saying from the New Testament, and explain what you think Martin means and why what he's drawing attention to might be a problem.

4. If you were a Christian, how would you interpret the remarks of Jesus of which Russell approves?

5. If you were an ordinary Christian—not a New Testament scholar—and you wanted to know whether Jesus really said something that he is reputed in the New Testament to have said, how would you decide? Would it be more reasonable of you to consult New Testament scholars or just to ask your local minister?

WAS JESUS CHRIST THE BEST AND THE WISEST PERSON? Bertrand Russell didn't think so. He explained why in his famous essay, "Why I am not a Christian."[1] I shall consider Russell's views in a moment. First, I want to raise two preliminary questions that Russell didn't consider.

THE BELIEVER'S DILEMMA

First: If we know what Jesus said, in the sense that we know what words he uttered, how should we interpret his words? Specifically, should we interpret his words as those of a first-century Jew, which is the only way they can be interpreted by responsible secular scholars, or should we interpret them as those of God or of a divinely inspired being?

The first way of proceeding is to treat Jesus like any other historical figure, say, like Socrates or Galileo, and to base one's interpretation of what Jesus probably meant by what he said on the best available historical evidence. The advantage of this way is that disputes over how Jesus' remarks should be interpreted can be settled, in principle, by appeal to historical evidence. The problem with this way, from the point of view of a Christian, is that one must presuppose for the sake of the inquiry something one believes to be false, namely, that Jesus was neither God nor divinely inspired, and then interpret his remarks accordingly.

The second way of proceeding is to regard Jesus as God or as divinely inspired. The advantage of this way, from the point of view of a Christian, is that one does not need to presuppose something one believes to be false. The problem with this way is that disputes over how Jesus' remarks should be interpreted cannot now be settled merely by appeal to historical evidence. In fact, on this way of proceeding it becomes unclear what role, if any, there is for historical evidence. Perhaps in determining what Jesus meant, historical evidence would be irrelevant; perhaps it would have only limited relevance. To whatever extent historical evidence is irrelevant, isn't it then largely arbitrary, on this second approach, how one interprets Jesus' remarks? Put differently, on this second way of proceeding, the project of interpreting Jesus' remarks is not an ordinary historical project but a theological one, and it is unclear what the constraints are on theological interpretations. I shall return to this issue later.

IN SEARCH OF THE HISTORICAL JESUS

Second: Do we know what Jesus was like as a person? Many twentieth-century Americans assume we do. But there are two reasons for being doubtful. First, most historians would agree that we don't know enough about Jesus to construct even a sketchy biography of his life. For instance, we don't know what city Jesus was born in, what his family life was like, how many, if any, siblings he had, what sort of education, if any, he received, what his formative years were like, and so on. We don't even know for sure what language Jesus spoke; scholars are divided about whether it was Greek, Aramaic, or Hebrew.[2] The best we can do by way of constructing a biography of Jesus before he went public in his mid-thirties is to sketch the barest outlines of his life. And what we know about Jesus' public ministry is also quite sketchy. John Meier, for instance, says in *A Marginal Jew* (Doubleday, 1991) that writing a biography of Jesus is out of the question since the "real Jesus, . . . unknown and unknowable, . . . is not available and never will be" (p. 22).

The second reason for being doubtful that we know what Jesus was like as a person is that we don't know much about what he said, and even if we were to know this, we know next to nothing about the context in which he said it. Hence, even when we know what Jesus said, we can do little more than hazard a guess about what he meant.

It will seem to many that such skepticism is exaggerated, that all one has to do to find out what Jesus said is to open the New Testament and read his words, and that ordinarily when one does that Jesus' meaning is plain enough. What's the problem?

The problem is that, so far as historians can determine, many of the words attributed to Jesus in the New Testament are not actually Jesus' words but rather later additions to the text. Separating the authentic from the inauthentic sayings of Jesus is a delicate task. Scholars disagree wildly about how to make that division. Some even doubt that it can be done to the satisfaction of most scholars. E. P. Sanders, for instance, in *Jesus and Judaism* (Fortress Press, 1985), says, "Scholars have not and, in my judgment, will not agree on the authenticity of the sayings material, either in whole *or in part.*"[3]

We have heard from two skeptical historians: Meier and Sanders. What do their opinions prove? By themselves, nothing. There are other scholars more sanguine than they are, and even Meier and Sanders have their more sanguine moments. Still, neither Meier nor Sanders is a marginal figure in the world of New Testament scholarship. Meier, a

Catholic priest, is Professor of New Testament at the Catholic University of America and an editor of the *Catholic Biblical Quarterly*. One reviewer said of the book of his from which the preceding quotation was taken, "Future scholars are certain to judge John Meier's book as one of the foremost studies ever written on the historical Jesus." Another said of Meier's book that it "will for generations serve as *the* guide on the quest for the historical Jesus."[4] Sanders, for his part, is Dean Ireland's Professor of Exegesis at Oxford University and the winner of two National Religious Book Awards. John Koenig, himself a prominent New Testament scholar, said in his *New York Times* review of Sanders's book that he "would be surprised if *Jesus and Judaism* does not turn out to be the most significant book of the decade in its field."[5]

The remarks quoted of Meier and Sanders may still be mistaken. Academics being what they are, it would not be surprising if there were equally well-credentialed scholars who would say that they are mistaken. Be that as it may, the opinions quoted should, I think, give one pause. If our goal is to determine *solely on the basis of historical evidence* who Jesus was and what he stood for, apparently it's not going to be easy.

Perhaps, though, we shouldn't bother with scholarly worries about historical evidence, or the lack thereof. Most Christians don't. It is true that in many cases their not bothering about historical evidence can be traced to the fact that their religious authorities have neglected to tell them that there's any problem about knowing on the basis of historical evidence what Jesus said or what he was like as a person. But even if ordinary Christians did know there is such a problem, perhaps they'd be right not to bother with historical evidence. Perhaps, in a matter such as this, faith is sufficient to the task. I shall return to this issue also.

What I propose for the time being is that we waive all questions about the authenticity of Jesus' New Testament sayings and simply *assume* that Jesus said the things attributed to him in the New Testament gospels and—when there is a straightforward interpretation of what he meant—that he meant just what he said. On this assumption, I want now to consider Russell's question: Was *that* Jesus—let's call him "the New Testament Jesus"—the best and the wisest person?

RUSSELL'S VERY BRITISH PUT-DOWN

Russell didn't think the New Testament Jesus was the best and the wisest person. Judging from his essay, he didn't even think the New Testament Jesus was a very good or a very wise person. His explicit conclusion, which reads like a parody of British understatement, is that "I cannot myself feel that either in the matter of wisdom or in the matter of virtue Christ stands quite as high as some other people [he mentions Buddha and Socrates] known to history." That's hardly a damning indictment. If on the all-time list of best and wisest people the New Testament Jesus were to get just barely nosed out of first place by Buddha and Socrates (that is, the Buddha of the Pali and Sanskrit scriptures and the Socrates of the Platonic dialogues), then Jesus might still be very wise and very good. It doesn't seem, though, from Russell's discussion as if he thought that Jesus was either.

Russell begins his critique of the New Testament Jesus by conceding that Jesus said some radical things with which Russell agrees. However, few Christians have thought that Jesus meant any of these things. For instance, one of the things the New Testament Jesus said that Russell liked is, "Resist not evil; but whosoever shall smite thee on thy right cheek, turn to him the other also." During World War I, Russell had been jailed for being a pacifist. Perhaps he liked this saying of Jesus partly because it seems to make Jesus a pacifist too. But few Christians have been pacifists. On the contrary, they have written the history of their religion in blood (the Crusades, the European witch-craze of the sixteenth and seventeenth centuries, and so on). Apparently, then, Christians as a whole haven't been as favorably impressed with this particular saying of Jesus, at least as Russell interpreted it, as Russell was.

Russell also liked the New Testament Jesus' saying, "Judge not lest ye be judged." But, he observed, this saying has not motivated Christians to shut down the law courts. Although Russell didn't go into it, so far as one can tell, this saying of Jesus has not motivated Christians to diminish *in any way* their practice of judging. If anything, their faith in the New Testament Jesus seems to have encouraged them to make judgments. For instance, for as long as anyone can remember, Christians have been identifying people as sinners and then calling on them to repent. Calling people sinners is surely judging them.

Russell did not argue in his essay that Christians should be pacifists or shut down the law courts. He did not even argue that they should refrain from judging so much. Russell's point was simply that, in his view, Jesus said some good things that Christians, for the most part, have ignored.

Suppose we put to one side these allegedly radical sayings of the New Testament Jesus, which if he said them, he may not have meant anyway, and consider, instead, just those alleged sayings of Jesus that the majority of Christians have thought he both said and meant. Call these Jesus' *mainstream sayings*. On the basis, then, just of Jesus' mainstream sayings, should we conclude that Jesus was the best and the wisest person? Not according to Russell, and mainly for two reasons: Jesus' doctrine of hell and his intolerance of dissent.

In Russell's words:

> Christ certainly as depicted in the Gospels did believe in everlasting punishment, and one does find repeatedly a vindictive fury against those people who would not listen to His preaching—an attitude which is not uncommon with preachers, but which does somewhat detract from superlative excellence. You do not, for instance, find that attitude in Socrates. You find him quite bland and urbane toward the people who would not listen to him; and it is, to my mind, far more worthy of a sage to take that line than to take the line of indignation. You probably all remember the sort of things that Socrates was saying when he was dying, and the sort of things that he generally did say to people who did not agree with him.

Perhaps you do not remember.

In his jail cell on the day he was scheduled to be executed, Socrates had a lengthy discussion with two of his students, Simmias and Cebes. The discussion was about the immortality of the soul. Socrates claimed that the soul is immortal. Simmias and Cebes argued that it is not and that when death comes that's the end of a person. To many of us, it may seem ungracious of Simmias and Cebes to have tried to convince Socrates just hours before he would be forced to ingest hemlock, a deadly

THE HISTORIAN AS PHILOSOPHER

Nancy Murphy

The historian is consciously or unconsciously a philosopher. It is quite obvious that every task of the historian beyond the finding of facts is dependent on evaluations of historical factors, especially the nature of man, his freedom, his determination, his development out of nature, etc. It is less obvious but also true that even in the act of finding historical facts philosophical presuppositions are involved. This is especially true in deciding, out of the infinite number of happenings in every infinitely small moment of time, which facts shall be called historically relevant facts. The historian is further forced to give his evaluation of sources and their reliability, a task which is not independent of his interpretation of human nature. Finally, in the moment in which a historical work gives implicit or explicit assertions about the meaning of historical events for human existence, the philosophical presuppositions of history are evident.

From *Theology in the Age of Scientific Reasoning* (1990).

poison, that he is mistaken in thinking he will survive his bodily death. How many of us would do that to a friend who was on his or her deathbed? To Socrates, however, the behavior of Simmias and Cebes was a compliment. It showed they had understood and approved the meaning of Socrates' life, which was to encourage rational inquiry. As Socrates himself put it at his trial, "The unexamined life is not worth living." Socrates not only taught this maxim, he lived it. Right to the very end. Socrates didn't want "Yes-men" or "Yes-women." He wanted people to think for themselves about life's important questions. After ostensibly winning the argument with Simmias and Cebes, and just minutes before the jailor appeared with the hemlock, Socrates encouraged Simmias and Cebes not to be overly impressed with the fact that he apparently had won the argument but to go back over it the next day, after he is dead, carefully rechecking each step, just to be sure that he hadn't somehow inadvertently pulled the wool over their eyes.

The New Testament Jesus was very different. In Russell's view, Jesus did want "Yes-men" and "Yes-women" and he used scare-tactics to get them:

> You will find that in the Gospels Christ said, "Ye serpents, ye generation of vipers, how can ye escape the damnation of hell?" That was said to people who did not like his preaching. It is not really to my mind quite the best tone, and there are a great many of these things about hell. . . .
>
> Then Christ says, "The Son of Man shall send forth His angels, and they shall gather out of His kingdom all things that offend, and them which do iniquity, and shall cast them into a furnace of fire; there shall be wailing and gnashing of teeth"; and He goes on about the wailing and gnashing of teeth. It comes in one verse after another. . . .
>
> Then you all, of course, remember about the sheep and the goats; how at the second coming He is going to divide the sheep from the goats and He is going to say to the goats, "Depart from me, ye cursed, into everlasting fire." He continues, "And these shall go away into everlasting fire." Then he says again, "If thy hand offend thee, cut it off; it is better for thee to enter into life maimed, than having two hands to go into hell, into the fire that never shall be quenched; where the worm dieth not and the fire is not quenched." He repeats that again and again also.

In Russell's view, "this doctrine that hell-fire is a punishment for sin is a doctrine of cruelty." And so Jesus slips out of contention for the first or second place on Russell's list of the best and wisest.

Not everyone will agree with Russell's assessment of Jesus. For one thing, people disagree about how bad it was for Jesus to have tried to scare people with all that talk about hell. Many Christians seem to think that scaring people with talk about hell is actually a good thing. In their view, being God-*fearing* is a virtue. Conservative preachers regularly and skillfully use the doctrine of hell in their relentless efforts to encourage all of us to acquire that virtue.

Another source of disagreement with Russell's assessment of Jesus is that some will doubt whether Jesus said the things to which Russell objects so strongly. Others will doubt whether if Jesus said them, he meant by them what Russell says he meant. Since Russell focuses on such central features of the New Testament gospel accounts and interprets the passages he considers so straightforwardly, it would seem that a person who takes either of these latter lines and doesn't just dismiss Russell's critique by appeal to faith is obligated to tackle the difficult problem of determining on the basis of historical evidence what Jesus actually said and what he meant by what he said. Yet many who would take this line in response to Russell's criticisms seem to be unaware that any such historical problem even exists.

WHAT DID JESUS SAY?

Ordinary Christians face a dilemma in trying to decide, solely on the basis of historical evidence, what Jesus said: New Testament scholars don't agree on what Jesus said, and ordinary Christians do not have the time or perhaps the talent and inclination to become scholars themselves. So, what's an ordinary Christian to do? Suppose, for the sake of argument, that you are an ordinary Christian and you want a middle-of-the-road, more or less consensus view, based solely on historical evidence, of what Jesus said. Where could you find such a view? Interestingly, there is a book to which you could turn.

The Five Gospels (Macmillan, 1993, edited by R. Funk and R. Hoover) is the collective report of a number of New Testament scholars who worked together for six years on a common question: What did Jesus really say? The scholars, many of whom were trained in the best universities in

North America and Europe, represent a wide array of Western religious traditions and academic institutions. They inventoried the surviving ancient texts for words attributed to Jesus. Then, they examined those words in the various ancient languages in which they have been preserved. Then, they produced a translation of all the gospels, known as the Scholars Version. Finally, they studied, debated, and voted on each of the 1,500+ alleged sayings of Jesus in their inventory.

The objective of the Fellows of the Jesus Seminar was to assess the authenticity of these alleged sayings solely on the basis of historical evidence rather than from the perspective of a theology or a creed. This task was complicated by the fact that we don't have original copies of any of the gospels. The oldest surviving copies date from about 200–210 A.D., and no two of them are identical. Moreover, the history of the original gospels, from their creation in the first century until the production of these surviving copies toward the beginning of the third is virtually unknown. That means that there is a temporal gap of about 175 years between Jesus' uttering whatever he uttered and the production of the first surviving copies of the gospels. That gap, the authors of *The Five Gospels* point out, "corresponds to the lapse in time from 1776 — the writing of the Declaration of Independence — to 1950." To get a feeling for what such a gap might mean for the project of trying to recover Jesus' words, they suggest that you imagine how much confusion there might have been about the original Declaration of Independence if the oldest copies of it that we possess were produced in 1950 and virtually nothing was known about what happened in regard to the document between 1776 and 1950: how many copies were made, who made them, under what conditions, with what motivations, and so forth.

There are other problems. For one thing, the earliest New Testament gospel, which most scholars believe is Mark, was probably not written before 50 A.D. and perhaps as late as 70; the latest gospel — that of John, who claims to be giving an eyewitness account — may have been written as late as 120 A.D. For another, the gospels of Mark, Matthew, and Luke were not written independently of each other and thus do not provide independent corroboration of the events they jointly depict. Many parts of the gospels that were written second and third—presumably Matthew and Luke—were copied verbatim from the earliest New Testament gospel—presumably Mark. The problem of working out the relations of literary dependency among the gospels of Mark, Matthew, and Luke (all scholars agree that John was written later) has been going on for centuries and is known, famously, as the Synoptic Problem. New Testament scholars agree that it is a sticky problem. Yet one has to solve it before one can even begin to search for the authentic sayings of Jesus. Although most scholars today agree on a particular solution to the Synoptic Problem, there are many variations on the basic theme of this solution, and there are still noted scholars who dissent from it altogether.

The discovery, in 1945, of a Coptic translation of the Gospel of Thomas (the fifth of the "five gospels" considered by the Jesus Seminar) has complicated the task of recovering Jesus' sayings. This gospel, which many scholars believe is based on sources as old or older than those on which the earliest New Testament Gospel—Mark—is based, contains 114 sayings and parables that are ascribed to Jesus, 65 of which are unique to this gospel!

That, in a nutshell, is the reason recovering the authentic words of Jesus is such a problem. What's the solution? It depends on whom you ask. There are many solutions—perhaps too many. The Jesus Seminar came up with one more. After six years of collective study and debate, they decided by vote that "eighty-two percent of the words ascribed to Jesus in the [five] gospels were not actually spoken by him" (p. 5). That means that, in their view, *only 18 percent* of these words were spoken by Jesus!

What of the sayings that repulsed or attracted Russell? Of the four different categories into which the Fellows of the Seminar voted to put alleged sayings of Jesus, all but one of the sayings that repulsed Russell were put into the least-likely-to-be-authentic category. Although the Fellows' categorization scheme is a little complicated, basically what this means is that in their opinion there is no reason to think that Jesus actually said any of these things or even that the ideas expressed in these sayings are close to Jesus' own ideas.

The only saying that bothered Russell that the Jesus Seminar put into any category other than the lowest one was the saying about removing bodily parts if they got you into trouble. In the view of the Fellows, some sayings of this sort belong in the next to lowest of the four categories. What this means is that in the opinion of the Fellows, though Jesus probably was not actually the author of any of these sayings, the ideas contained in them *may* be close to his own.

None of the sayings that the Fellows put into either the first or the second categories—that is, judged likely to be authentic—indicate that Jesus took a particularly hard line against those who dissented from what he preached. On the other hand, neither is there anything among the sayings deemed authentic to indicate that Jesus encouraged questioning and dissent. The Jesus that emerges from the sayings that the Fellows regarded as authentic may have been a prophet or a holy man, perhaps even a sage, but he was no philosopher—certainly not in the sense in which the Socrates of the Platonic dialogs was a philosopher. Still, the bottom line is that the Fellows have stripped away the basis for all of Russell's harshest criticisms.

What of the sayings that Russell liked? The one about not judging was put into the lowest—least-likely-to-be-authentic—category. But the saying that Russell thought endorsed pacifism got high marks. The Fellows gave the saying, "When someone strikes you on the cheek, offer the other as well" (their translation) in addition to some other sayings along the same lines, such as, "Love your enemies," the highest ranking. What this means is that as a group the Fellows either "would include these items unequivocally in the database for determining who Jesus was" or else that they believed that "Jesus undoubtedly said these things or something very like them."

WHAT DID JESUS MEAN?

The problem of determining what Jesus said (and did) is only half the battle in determining who he was. The rest of the battle is figuring out what he meant by what he said and did. Doing that on straightforward historical grounds is not easy. The reason is that we don't know much about

HISTORICAL METHOD IN THE STUDY OF RELIGION

Morton Smith

. . . The science of religion, for which these histories of particular religions are prerequisites, is still far in the future. But, when and if it comes, both it, and the individual histories already developing, will be shaped by a basic supposition of sound historical method.

This supposition, in classical terms, is "atheism." I say "in classical terms" because the adjective "atheist" was regularly used in classical times to describe, for instance, the Epicureans, who insisted that there were gods, but denied that they ever descended to any special intervention in the world's affairs. It is precisely this denial which is fundamental to any sound historical method. Whether or not supernatural beings exist is a question for metaphysics. Even if they exist and exercise some regular influence on the world, some influence of which the consequences are taken to be a part of the normal course of natural events—let us say, for instance, that they determine the motion of the sphere of fixed stars, or that the whole of nature, including its regular operation, is a manifestation of some unchanging divine nature or will—even this is of no concern to history, since it is not history's task to inquire into the causes of the normal phenomena of nature. But the historian does require a world in which these normal phenomena are not interfered with by arbitrary and *ad hoc* divine interventions to produce abnormal events with special historical consequences. This is not a matter of personal preference, but of professional necessity, for the historian's task, . . . is to calculate the most probable explanation of the preserved evidence. Now the minds of the gods are inscrutable and their actions, consequently, incalculable. Therefore, unless the possibility of their special intervention be ruled out, there can be no calculation of most probable causes—there would always be an unknown probability that a deity might have intervened.

From *History and Theory* (1968).

either Jesus' psychology or the external circumstances in which he spoke and acted. Hence, on straightforward historical grounds, we lack a context for interpreting what Jesus meant by what he said and did. This problem is compounded by the fact that Jesus so often spoke in parables.

So, what is one to do who wants to know what Jesus stood for? There are two choices: either admit we don't know what he stood for or else use faith as a guide. Virtually all Christians take the second of these options. But if in the end one is going to use faith as a guide, why bother with historical evidence in the first place?

This latter question is a version of the age-old one about the proper relation between faith and reason. Many answers to this old question have been proposed, from Tertullian's religiously extremist "I believe *because* it is absurd," to Augustine's middle-of-the-road maxim that faith should seek understanding through reason, to Clifford's secularly extremist view that it's always immoral to believe anything on faith. This is not the place to recount the history of this debate or even to canvass the main options. Instead, I want to consider just Meier's views. In his book, he addresses the specific question of why, if at all, one should bother with historical evidence in trying to figure out who Jesus was and what he stood for. His answer, whether or not one accepts it, is instructive.

Meier first points out that for him to address the question of why, if at all, one should bother with historical evidence in trying to figure out who

Jesus was and what he stood for, he (Meier) has to doff the hat of a modern, critical historian and don the hat of a theologian. For the former, he says, the "real" has "been defined—and has to be defined—in terms of what exists within this world of time and space, what can be experienced in principle by any observer, and what can be reasonably deduced or inferred from such experience." As a Christian theologian, however, he affirms "ultimate realities beyond what is merely empirical or provable by reason: e.g., the triune God and the risen Jesus." Thus, he concludes, to ask about the relation between the Jesus who can be reconstructed from modern historical research and the risen Jesus "is to pass from the realm of the merely empirical or rational into the larger framework of faith and theology, as it seeks to relate itself to the historical-critical project."

In Meier's view, "the Jesus of history is not and cannot be the object of Christian faith." For one thing, he says, many Christians have believed and still do believe in Christ "without having any clear idea of or access to the historical Jesus" and "yet no one will deny the validity and strength of their faith." (Contrary to Meier, some might deny the validity of their faith, but let it pass.) In Meier's view, even if all Christians were acquainted with historical research on Jesus, "the Church could still not make the historical Jesus the object of its preaching and faith" since historical research has served up too many different and often contradictory portraits of Jesus, and the picture is always changing. Which of these Jesuses would be the object of Christian faith?

Beyond that worry there is, for Meier, another, more important consideration. The object of Christian faith "is not and cannot be an idea or scholarly reconstruction, however reliable" but, rather, must be "a living person, Jesus Christ, who fully entered into a true human existence on earth in the 1st century A.D., but who now lives, risen and glorified, forever in the Father's presence." According to Meier, Christian faith affirms and adheres to this person and only secondarily to ideas and affirmations about him. In the realm of faith and theology, the real Jesus, the only one "existing and living now, is this risen Lord, to whom access is given only through faith." But, then, one might ask, why

should Christians bother with the quest for the historical Jesus?

Meier's answer is that they shouldn't bother, "if one is asking solely about the direct object of Christian faith." But if one is asking, in a contemporary cultural setting, about faith seeking understanding, that is, about contemporary theology, then, Meier thinks, one had better bother about the quest for the historical Jesus. For the price of not bothering is to be dismissed by many educated Christians as irrelevant.

> [O]nce a culture becomes permeated with a historical-critical approach, as has Western culture from the Enlightenment onward, theology can operate in and speak to that culture with credibility only if it absorbs into its methodology a historical approach (p. 198).

In other words, the reason, it seems, a Christian might want to be concerned with the quest for the historical Jesus is not that he or she might thereby learn some important truths about Jesus but, rather, to construct a more "credible" theology.

Meier is quick to point out that this appropriation by theology of the quest for the historical Jesus "is not idolatry to passing fads" but, rather, "serves the interest of faith." But the important question, one would have thought, is whether it serves the interest of truth, and Meier never addresses that question directly.

Meier claims that the quest for the historical Jesus serves the interest of faith by the quest's reminding Christians that faith in Christ is neither "a vague existential attitude," nor "a way of being in the world," nor adherence to some "mystically divine entity" but, rather, "the affirmation of and adherence to a particular person who said and did particular things in a particular time and place in human history," in short, to "a person as truly and fully human—with all the galling limitations that involves—as any other human being." Further, against any attempt to "domesticate" Jesus for the purposes of respectable, bourgeois Christians, the quest is a reminder that the historical Jesus was not respectable in that sense, for instance, that he associated with the religious and social "lowlife" of Palestine and was a critic of merely external religious observances. Finally, in Meier's view, the

LUCKY TO BE BORN INTO THE TRUE RELIGION?

John Hick

[I]n the great majority of cases—I should guess well over 95 per cent—the tradition within which a religious person finds his or her relationship to the Real depends to a very great extent upon where and when that person is born. For normally, in the world as a whole, the faith that a person accepts is the only faith that has been effectively made available to him or her. We can refer to this manifest dependence of spiritual allegiance upon the circumstances of birth and upbringing as the genetic and environmental relativity of religious perception and commitment. And it is an extraordinary, and to some a disturbing, thought that one's basic religious vision, which has come to seem so obviously right and true, has been largely selected by factors entirely beyond one's control—by the accidents of birth. It is not that one cannot move from one stream of religious life to another, but that this is a rare occurrence, usually presupposing privileged educational opportunities; so that the great majority of human beings live throughout their lives within the tradition by which they were formed. In view of this situation, can one be unquestioningly confident that the religion which one happens to have inherited by birth is indeed normative and that all others are properly to be graded by their likeness or unlikeness to it? Certainly, it is possible that one particular religious tradition is uniquely normative, and that I happen to have had the good fortune to be born into it. And indeed, psychologically, it is very difficult not to assume precisely this. And yet the possibility must persistently recur to any intelligent person, who has taken note of the broad genetic and environmental relativity of the forms of religious commitment, that to assess the traditions of the world by the measure of one's own tradition may merely be to be behaving, predictably, in accordance with the conditioning of one's up-bringing.

From "On Grading Religions" (1982).

historical Jesus is useful because he is "not easily coopted for programs of political revolution." The historical Jesus was "remarkably silent on many of the burning social and political issues of his day" and "can be turned into a this-worldly political revolutionary only by contorted exegesis and special pleading." In short, "the historical Jesus subverts not just some ideologies but all ideologies" and "eludes all our neat theological programs . . . by refusing to fit into the boxes we create for him." Hence, "the historical Jesus remains a constant stimulus to theological renewal."

Seemingly implicit in these latter remarks of Meier is the idea that the quest for the historical Jesus puts rational constraints on faith. For instance, he seems to think that one cannot accept on faith that Jesus was a political revolutionary if the historical evidence does not support that conception of Jesus. But why can't one simply give the back of one's hand to historical evidence? What, to a Christian, is so sacrosanct about evidence? In other words, since Meier, along with almost every Christian, thinks that faith provides independent access to truth about Jesus, why, for Christians, should faith give way to reason if there is a conflict between the two? Meier does not answer or even address this question except to say that if faith does not give way, Christian theology will cease to be credible. But credible to whom? It will still be credible to those who have faith and don't give a hoot about historical evidence. And why should someone with faith care if his or her theology is credible to someone without faith? Chances are it won't be credible anyway.

Suppose, to switch examples, that through faith a believer "knows" that the world was created in 4004 B.C. and through reason unguided by faith he or she knows that the world must be much older than that. Why, in such a believer's mind, should faith give way to reason? Is it because believers also have faith in reason or in the harmony of faith and reason? But is the latter true of all believers or just some? And for those who do have faith in the harmony of faith and reason, does that faith include just one's own faith or the other person's faith also? And if it includes the other person's, how does one reconcile the conflicting things that people believe on faith?

Perhaps it does not serve the interests of faith even to ask such questions. Perhaps Meier's point is just that it would be too absurd in this day and age to give the back of one's hand to reason. But why should a believer be afraid of absurdity? Tertullian wasn't. If by some secular criterion of absurdity Christian beliefs are absurd, it is certainly open to a Christian to brandish the absurdity of his or her beliefs as if it were a badge of honor.

WHY ISN'T ALL OF THIS COMMON KNOWLEDGE?

How many ordinary Christians are aware of the tenuousness with which any contemporary historian who does not begin by making religious assumptions — whether or not the historian happens also, in his or her personal life, to be a Christian — approaches the events of Jesus' life and the first few centuries of Christianity? The facts on which such an historian has to peg an interpretation of what Jesus said and did, and of what Jesus may have meant by what he said and did, are so disputable that it is difficult for an honest secular historian even to get an interpretation off the ground.

How many contemporary Christians are aware that the earliest Christians had radically different ideas about Jesus and his message and even produced alternative gospels to sustain their interpretations? If we confine our attention just to the New Testament gospels, how many know that the earliest New Testament gospel probably was not written before 50 A.D., and that the latest may have been written as late as 120 A.D.? How many know that the gospels of Mark, Matthew, and Luke were not written independently of each other — and thus do not provide independent corroboration of the events they jointly depict — but that many parts of the two latter accounts were copied verbatim from the earliest account? How many know that competent New Testament historians have agreed for quite some time that the vast majority of New Testament sayings of Jesus are probably not authentic?

One final question: Given how saturated our culture is with Christian ideology and with encouragement to read the Bible, why aren't such facts about the New Testament and its origins *common knowledge,* at least among educated Christians?

NOTES

1. *Why I Am Not A Christian.* New York: Watts & Co., 1927. All the remarks quoted from Russell are from the title essay in this volume.

2. Meier, John P. *A Marginal Jew. Rethinking the Historical Jesus.* New York: Doubleday, 1991, p. 255. Meier also remarked that "the reason why a biography of Jesus — in the modern sense of biography — cannot be written is by now obvious. We are dealing with a man who died in his mid-thirties and whose first thirty-two years or so are almost completely unknown and unknowable" (p. 253).

3. p. 4, emphasis added. Why were the actual words of Jesus altered by the people who authored and copied the gospels? According to the Fellows of the Jesus Seminar, whose views will be discussed shortly, one reason is that "the evangelists frequently attribute their own statements to Jesus" (*The Five Gospels,* p. 23). Another is that "hard sayings are frequently softened in the process of transmission to adapt them to the conditions of daily living" (p. 23). For instance, when Jesus advised a rich man to sell all he owns and give the proceeds to the poor, the man is understandably stunned by this advice (Mk 10:21–2). Jesus then tells his disciples that it is easier for a camel to squeeze through the eye of a needle than for a rich person to get into heaven (Mk 10:25). But the disciples and Mark find this a hard saying. So Mark qualifies it by adding, "Everything's possible for God" (Mk 10:27). Thus, the harsh saying is made less harsh by God's unlimited grace. And some literalists have even "located a caravan pass, called the needle's eye, which a camel can squeeze through with difficulty, if it is not loaded with baggage; others have imagined a tight gate in the wall of Jerusalem, through which a camel can barely pass" (p. 24). According to the editors of *The Five Gospels,*

"These are feeble and misguided attempts to take the sting out of the aphorism and rob Jesus' words of their edge" (p. 24).

4. The author of the first remark is Jack Dean Kingsbury, of the Union Theological Seminary in Virginia,

and of the second remark Rabbi Burton Visotzky, of the Jewish Theological Seminary of America. Both remarks are taken from the book jacket.

5. Quoted from the back cover of the paperback edition.

Further Questions

1. If you were a Christian, how would you respond to the issue that Martin calls "the believer's dilemma"? Give reasons to support the appropriateness of your response.

2. What, in your view, is the proper relation between faith and reason? Are you more drawn to Tertullian's "I believe *because* it is absurd," to Augustine's view that faith should seek understanding through reason, to Clifford's view that it's always immoral to believe anything whatsoever on faith, or to some different position?

3. Do you think the facts about the New Testament and its origins discussed in Martin's article are common knowledge among educated Christians? If not, why not? Should they be?

Further Readings

Crossan, John. *The Historical Jesus: The Life of a Mediterranean Jewish Peasant.* New York: Harper Collins, 1991. A dramatically written account by an important scholar.

Martin, Raymond. *The Elusive Messiah: A Philosophical Overview of the Quest for the Historical Jesus,* Boulder, CO: Westview, 1999.

40   Religion from an African Perspective

KWASI WIREDU

Kwasi Wiredu, a professor of philosophy at the University of South Florida, was formerly professor and head of the Department of Philosophy at the University of Ghana. Educated at the universities of Ghana and Oxford, he has been a visiting professor at the University of California, Los Angeles, and has received fellowships from the Woodrow Wilson Center and the National Humanities Center. His publications are primarily in the areas of philosophy of logic and African philosophy and include his book *Philosophy and an African Culture* (Cambridge University Press, 1980). In the selection that follows, he explains that the word *religion* may not be properly applicable to most traditional African thought.

Reading Questions

1. What are Wiredu's reasons for questioning whether traditional African life and thought are "religious"?

2. With respect to questions of so-called religious attitudes and ethics, how does Wiredu say the Akans differ from the typical European believers in a Supreme Being?
3. What is the attitude among Akans toward their dead ancestors? How does it differ from typical Christian attitudes toward the dead?
4. With respect to the ideas of (i) a transcendent being, (ii) the supernatural, (iii) the spiritual, and (iv) creation, how do the Akans differ from European religious believers?

TWO ASSUMPTIONS THAT MAY SAFELY BE MADE about the human species are one, that the entire race shares some fundamental categories and criteria of thought in common and two, that, nevertheless, there are some very deep disparities among the different tribes of humankind in regard to their modes of conceptualization in some sensitive areas of thought. The first accounts for the possibility of communication among different peoples, the second for the difficulties and complications that not infrequently beset that interaction.

Is religion a field of convergence or divergence of thought among the peoples and cultures of the world? The obvious answer, in alignment with our opening reflection, is that religion is both. There is also an obvious sequel: What are the specifics? But here an obvious answer is unavailable, at least, as concerns Africa vis-à-vis, for instance, the West. In fact, it is not at all obvious in what sense the English word "religion" is applicable to any aspect of African life and thought.

This last remark, of course, amounts to discounting the frequent affirmations, in the literature of African studies, of the immanent religiosity of the African mind. What exactly are the features of life and thought that are appealed to in that characterization? In investigating this issue I am going to have to be rather particularistic. I am going to have particular, though not exclusive, recourse to the Akans of West Africa, for the considerations to be adduced presuppose a level of cultural and linguistic insight to which I cannot pretend in regard to any African peoples except that particular ethnic group which I know through birth, upbringing, reading and deliberate reflective observation. This particularism has, at least, the logical potential of all counterexamples against universal claims.

Let us return to the word "religion." It has been suggested, even by some authors by whose reckoning African life is full of religion, that there is no word in many African languages which translates this word. Whether this is true of all African languages or not I do not know, but it is certainly true of Akan, in the traditional use of that language, that is. Not only is there no single word for religion but there is also no periphrastic equivalent. There is, indeed, the word "Anyamesom" which many translators might be tempted to proffer. But the temptation ought to be resisted. The word is a Christian invention by which the missionaries distinguished, in Akan speech, between their own religion and what they perceived to be the religion of the indigenous "pagans." Thus, it means, not religion, pure and simple, but Christianity. Ironically, in this usage the Christian missionaries were constrained by linguistic exigencies to adapt a word which the Akans use for the Supreme Being. "Onyame" is one among several names for the Supreme Being in Akan. Another very frequent one is "Onyankopon" which literally means The Being That Is Alone Great, in other words, That Than Which a Greater Cannot Be Conceived (with apologies to Saint Anselm). The remaining component of the word "Anyamesom" is "som" which means "to serve," so that the whole word means, literally, "the service of the Supreme Being" or, if you follow Christian methods of translation, "the service of God." In turn, this was taken to mean the *worship* of God.

By way of a designation for what they saw as indigenous religion, the Christians used the word "Abosomsom." This is a combination of two words "Obosom" and "Som." Etymologically, "obosom" means the service of stones. Thus, literally, the barbarism means the service of stone

Kwasi Wiredu, *"Universalism and Particularism in Religion from an African Perspective,"* Journal of Humanism and Ethical Religion *3(1): Fall 1990. Reprinted by permission of the publisher. Footnotes deleted.*

service! Still, it served its Christian purpose. But why stones? That is an allusion to the fact that the Akans traditionally believe that various objects, such as certain special rocks, trees and rivers, are the abode of extra-human forces and beings of assorted grades.

Having gathered from the foregoing remarks that the Akans, in fact, believe in the existence of a supreme being and a variety of extra-human forces and beings, the reader might be disposed to wonder why I make any issue of the sense in which "religion" might be applied to any aspect of Akan culture. If so, let him or her attend to the following considerations. To begin with, religion, however it is defined, involves a certain kind of attitude. If a given religion postulates a supra-human supreme being, that belief must, on any common showing, necessarily be joined to an attitude not only of unconditional reverence but also of worship. Some will go as far as to insist that this worshipful attitude will have to be given practical expression through definite rituals, especially if the being in question is supposed to be the determiner or controller of human destiny. There is a further condition of the utmost importance; it is one which introduces an ethical dimension into the definition. Essential to any religion in the primary sense is a conception of moral uprightness. If it involves supra-human beliefs, the relevant ethic will be based logically or psychologically on the "supra" being or beings concerned. Typically, but by no means invariably, a religion will have a social framework. In that case, it will have organized hortatory and other procedures for instilling or revivifying the commitment to moral virtue.

Consider, now, the character of the Akan belief in the Supreme Being. There is, indeed, generally among the Akans a confirmed attitude of unconditional reverence for *Onyankopon,* the Supreme Being. However, there is, most assuredly, no attitude or ritual of worship directed to that being either at a social or an individual level. They regard Him as good, wise and powerful in the highest. He is the determiner of human destiny as of everything else. But in all this they see no rationale for worship. Neither is the Akan conception or practice of morality based logically or even psychologically on the belief in the Supreme Being. Being good in the highest, He disapproves of evil; but, to the Akan

mind, the reason why people should not do evil is not because he disapproves of it but rather because it is contrary to human well-being, which is why He disapproves of it, in the first place.

The early European visitors to Africa, especially the missionaries, were quick to notice the absence of any worship of God among the Akans and various other African peoples. They were hardly less struck by the fact that God was not the foundation of Akan morals. On both grounds they deduced a spiritual and intellectual immaturity in the African. Notice the workings here of a facile universalism. It seems to have been assumed that belief in God must move every sound mind to worship. Perhaps, even now, such an assumption might sound plausible to many Western ears. It is, of course, not likely in this day and age that many can be found to suppose that any person of a sound mind must necessarily embrace belief in God. But given the prevailing tendencies in Western and even some non-Western cultures, it might be tempting to think that if people believe in God, then the *natural* thing for them to do is to worship Him. Yet, consider the notion of a perfect being. Why would he (she, it) need to be worshipped? What would be the point of it? It is well-known that the Judeo-Christian God *jealously* demands to be worshipped—witness The Ten Commandments—but, from an Akan point of view, such clamoring for attention must be paradoxical in the extreme in a perfect being, and I confess to being an unreconstructed Akan in this regard.

There is, in their resort to the word "Abosomsom" (the worship of stones) to name what they took to be Akan religion, an odd manifestation of the special importance that the Christian missionaries attached to worship. Having seen that the Akans did not worship God, they were keen to find out what it was that they worshipped, for surely a whole people must worship something. They quickly settled on the class of what I have called extra-human forces and beings, which, as I have already hinted, is a feature of the Akan worldview. There is, indeed, a great variety of such entities postulated in the Akan ontology (as in any other African ontology that I know of). Some are relatively person-like; others somewhat automatic in their operation. The former can, it is believed, be communicated with through some special procedures, and are credited with a moral sense. Commonly, a being of this sort would be believed to be localized at a household "shrine" from where it would protect the given group from evil forces. More person-like still are the ancestors who are thought to live in a realm closely linked with the world of the living.

Actually, the ancestors are conceived of as persons who continue to be members of their pre-mortem families, watching over their affairs and generally helping them. They are regarded as persons, but not as mortal persons; for they have tasted death and transcended it. Accordingly, they are not thought to be constrained by all the physical laws which circumscribe the activities of persons with fully physical bodies. For this reason, they are supposed to be more powerful than mortals. Additionally, they are considered to be more irreversibly moral than any living mortal. All these attributes are taken to entitle the ancestors to genuine reverence. Not quite the same deference is accorded to the first group of beings, but in view of their presumed power to promote human well-being, they are approached with considerable respect.

More types of extra-human forces and beings are spoken of in the Akan ontology than we have mentioned, but these are among the most relevant, and they will suffice for the impending point; which is this: The Akan attitude to the beings in question bears closer analogy to secular esteem than religious worship. The reverence given to the ancestors is only a higher degree of the respect that in Akan society is considered to be due to the earthly elders. For all their post-mortem ontologic transformation, the ancestors are, let it be repeated, regarded as members of their families. The libations that are poured to them on ceremonial and other important occasions are simply invitations to them to come and participate in family events. Moreover, everybody hopes eventually to become an ancestor, but this is not seen as a craving for self-apotheosis. Ancestorship is simply the crowning phase of human existence.

The non-religious character of the Akan attitude to the non-ancestral forces is even more clear. Real religious devotion to a being must be unconditional. But that is the one thing that the Akan approach to those beings is not; it is purely utilitarian: if they bring help, praise be to them, and other things besides. On the other hand, if they fail, particularly if that happens consistently, they can fall into disrepute or worse. K. A. Busia and J. B. Danquah, the two most celebrated expositors of Akan thought, have borne unambiguous and, as it seems to me, reliable testimony to this fact. Busia says, "The gods are treated with respect if they deliver the goods, and with contempt if they fail. . . . Attitudes to [the gods] depend on their success, and vary from healthy respect to sneering contempt." Danquah goes somewhat further: ". . . the general tendency is to sneer at and ridicule the fetish and its priest." There is an even more radical consideration. According to popular belief, these "gods" are capable of dying. Of a "god" who is finished the Akans say *nano atro,* that is, its powers have become totally blunted. This may happen through unknown causes, but it may also happen through human design. People can cause the demise of a "god" simply by permanently depriving it of attention. Or, for more rapid results, apply an antithetical substance to its "shrine." Such antidotes are known for at least some of these "gods," according to popular belief. It ought, perhaps, to be emphasized that in this matter the thought is not that a "god" has betaken itself elsewhere, but rather that it has ceased to be a force to be reckoned with at all. In light of all this, it is somewhat of a hyperbole to call the procedures designed for establishing satisfactory relations with the beings in question religious worship.

The considerations rehearsed so far should be enough, I think, to suggest the need for a review of the enthusiastic, not to say indiscriminate, attributions of religiosity to African peoples. But there are deeper reasons of the same significance. And in studying them we will see the role which the hasty universalization of certain Western categories of thought have played in the formation of the misapprehensions under scrutiny. Take, then, the Akan belief in the Supreme Being. In English discourse about Akan thought the word "God" is routinely used to refer to this being. This has led, or has been due, to the supposition that both the Akans and the Christians are talking of the same being when they speak of the Supreme Being, notwithstanding any divergences of cultural perception. This supposed identity of reference has come in handy to Christianized Africans wishing to demonstrate that they can profess Christianity and still remain basically true to their indigenous religions: There is, after all, only one God, and we are all trying to reach Him.

Yet, in spite of any apparent similarities, such as the postulation of That Than Which a Greater Cannot Be Conceived in both traditions of thought, the Akan supreme being is profoundly different from the Christian one. The Christian God is a creator of the world out of nothing. In further philosophical characterization, He is said to be transcendent, supernatural and spiritual in the sense of immaterial, non-physical. In radical contrast, the Akan supreme being is a kind of cosmic architect, a fashioner of the world order, who occupies the apex of the same hierarchy of being which accommodates, in its intermediate ranges, the ancestors and living mortals and, in its lower reaches, animals, plants and inanimate objects. This universe of being is ontologically homogenous. In other words, everything that exists exists in exactly the same sense as everything else. And this sense is empirical, broadly speaking. In the Akan language to exist is to "wo ho" which, in literal translation, means to be at some place. There is no equivalent, in Akan, of the existential "to be" or "is" of English, and there is no way of pretending in that medium to be speaking of the existence of something which is not in space. This locative connotation of the Akan concept of existence is irreducible except metaphorically. Thus you might speak of there existing an explanation for something (*ne nkyerease wo ho*) without incurring any obligation of spatial specification, because an explanation is not an object in any but a metaphorical sense; and to a metaphorical object corresponds only a metaphorical kind of space. The same applies to the existence of all so-called abstract entities. In the Akan conceptual framework, then, existence is spatial. Now, since, whatever transcendence means in this context, it implies existence beyond space, it follows that talk of any transcendent being is not just false, but unintelligible, from an Akan point of view.

But not only transcendence goes by the board. Neither the notion of the supernatural nor that of the spiritual can convey any coherent meaning to an Akan understanding in its traditional condition. No line is drawn in the Akan worldview demarcating one area of being corresponding to nature from another corresponding to supernature. Whatever is real belongs to one or another of the echelons of being postulated in that worldview. In that context it has all the explanation that is appropriate to it. An important axiom of Akan thought is that everything has its explanation, *biribiara wo nenkyerease*—a kind of principle of sufficient reason; and a clear pre-supposition of Akan explanations of phenomena is that there are interactions among all the orders of existents in the world. Accordingly, if an event in human affairs, for instance, does not appear explicable in human terms, there is no hesitation in invoking extra-human causality emanating from the higher or even the lower rungs of the hierarchy of beings. In doing this there is no sense of crossing an ontological chasm; for the idea is that there is only one universe of many strata wherein God, the ancestors, humans, animals, plants and all the rest of the furniture of the world have their being.

In this last connection, it might, perhaps, enhance understanding to regiment our terminology a little. Suppose we use the term "the world" to designate the totality of ordered existents fashioned out by God in the process of "creation," then, of course, God, being the author of the world, is not a part of it, in the Akan scheme of things. But we might, then, reserve the term "universe" for the totality of absolutely all existents. In this sense God would be part of the universe. Apart from regimenting our terminology, this gives us the opportunity to reinforce the point regarding the Akan sense of the inherent law-likeness of reality. And the crucial consideration is that God's relationship with the rest of the universe, that is, the world, is also conceived to be inherently law-like. This is the implication of the Akan saying that "The Creator created Death and Death killed the Creator," *Odomankoma boo Owuo na Owuo kum Odomankoma,* which, in my opinion, is one of the profoundest in the Akan corpus of metaphysical aphorisms.

But though God's relation with the world is conceived to be law-like, He is not made the basis of the explanation of any specific phenomenon, for since·everything is ultimately traceable to Him, *Biribiara ne Nyame,* references to Him are incapable of helping to explain why any particular thing is what it is and not another thing. Divine law-likeness only ensures that there will be no arbitrary interferences in the course of the world-process. Thus the reason why Akan explanations of specific things do not invoke God is not because He is thought to be transcendent or supernatural or anything like that, but rather because He is too immanently implicated in the nature and happening of things to have any explanatory value.

Still, however, in facing the cognitive problems of this world all the mundane theaters of being, human and extra-human, are regarded as *equally* legitimate sources of explanation. Thus, if an Akan explains a mysterious malady in terms of, say, the wrath of the ancestors, it makes little sense to ascribe to him or her a belief in the supernatural. That characterization is intelligible only in a conceptual framework in which the natural/supernatural dichotomy has a place. But the point is that it has no place in the Akan system of thought. We may be sure, then, that the widespread notion that Africans are given to supernatural explanations is the result of the superimposition of alien categories of thought on African thought-structures, in the Akan instance, at least. There is nothing particularly insidious in the fact that Western writers on African thought have generally engaged in this practice; for, after all, one thinks most naturally in terms of the conceptual framework of one's intellectual upbringing, and the natural/supernatural distinction is very endemic, indeed, in Western thought. I do not mean by this, of course, that there is a universal belief in the supernatural in the West. The suggestion is only that this concept together with its logical complement is a customary feature of Western conceptualizations; so much so, that even the Western philosophical naturalist, in denying the existence of anything supernatural, does not necessarily dispute the coherence of that concept. It is a more striking fact that many contemporary African expositors of their own traditional systems of thought yield no ground to their Western colleagues in stressing the role of belief in the supernatural in African thinking. It is hard not to see this as evidence of the fact that in some ways Christian proselytization and Western education have been over-successful in Africa.

But an interesting and important question arises. Suppose it granted that, as I have been arguing, the natural/supernatural dichotomy has no place in Akan and, perhaps, African thought generally. Does that not still leave the question of its objective validity intact? And, if it should turn out to be objectively valid, would it not be reasonable to think that it would be a good thing for Africans to learn to think along that line? My answer to both questions is affirmative; which implies a rejection of relativism. This disavowal is fully premeditated and is foreshadowed in the opening paragraph of this essay. However, for reasons of the division of preoccupation, I cannot try to substantiate my anti-relativism here.

Stated baldly, my thesis is that there is such a thing as the objective validity of an idea. Were it not for the recent resurgence of relativism in Philosophy, this would have been too platitudinous for any words. Furthermore, and rather less obviously, if an idea is objectively valid (or invalid or even incoherent) in any given language or conceptual framework, both the idea and its status can, in principle, be *represented* in, if not necessarily translated into, any other language or conceptual framework.

A corollary of the foregoing contention is that, however natural it may be to think in one's native framework of concepts, it is possible for human beings to think astride conceptual frameworks. In the absence of extended argumentation for this general claim, I will content myself with an illustration with respect to the idea of the supernatural. A relevant question, then, is: "Do the Akans need to incorporate the natural/supernatural distinction into their modes of thought?" I think not; for not only is Akan thought inhospitable to this distinction but also the distinction is, in my opinion, objectively incoherent. If this is so, it follows from our principle that it ought to be demonstrable (to the extent that such speculative matters are susceptible of demonstration) in any language and, in particular, in English. In fact, a simple argument suffices for this purpose.

In the sense pertinent to our discussion, the supernatural is that which surpasses the order of nature. In other words, a supernatural event is one whose occurrence is contrary to the laws of nature. But if the event actually happens, then any law that fails to reckon with its possibility is inaccurate and is in need of some modification, at least. However, if the law is suitably amended, even if only by means of an exceptive rider, the event is no longer contrary to natural law. Hence no event can be consistently described as supernatural.

What of the notion of the spiritual? Again, I begin with a disclaimer on behalf of Akan ontological thinking. As can be expected from the spatial character of the Akan concept of existence, the radical dualism of the material and the spiritual can find no home in the Akan scheme of reality. All the extra-human beings and powers, even including God, are spoken of in language irreducibly charged with spatial imagery. It is generally recognized by students of African eschatology that the *place* of the dead, the *abode* of the ancestors, is almost complete modelled on the world of living mortals. If the replication is not complete, it is only because the ancestors are not thought of as having *fully* material bodies. Some analogue of material bodies they surely must be supposed to have, given the sorts of things that are said about them. For example, a postulated component of a person that is supposed to survive death and eventually become an ancestor, all things being equal, is believed soon after death to travel *by land and by river* before arriving at the abode of the ancestors. For this reason in traditional times coffins were stuffed with travel needs such as clothing and money for the payment of ferrying charges. I have never heard it suggested in traditional circles that this practice was purely symbolic. If it were a purely symbolic gesture, that, certainly, would have been carrying symbolism rather far. But, in any case, the practice was of a piece with the conception, and the conception is decidedly quasi-material.

I use the term "quasi-material" to refer to any being or entity conceived as spatial but lacking some of the properties of material objects. The ancestors, for instance, although they are thought of as occupying space, are believed to be invisible to the naked eye and inaudible to the normal ear, except rarely when they choose to *manifest* themselves to particular persons for special reasons. On such occasions they can, according to very widely received conceptions among the Akans, appear and disappear at will unconstrained by those limitations of speed and impenetrability to which the gross bodies of the familiar world are subject. This is held to be generally true of all the relatively personalized forms of extra-human phenomena.

It is apparent from what has just been said that if the extra-human beings of the Akan worldview are not fully material, they are not fully immaterial either. Further to confirm this last point, we might note that, although the beings in question are not supposed to be generally visible to the *naked* eye, they are widely believed to be perceivable to the superior eyes of certain persons of special gift or training. People reputed to be of this class will sometimes tell you, "If you had but eyes to see, you would be amazed at what is going on right here around where you are standing." And here imagery tends to be so lustily spatial that, but for their selective invisibility, one would be hard put to distinguish between the quasi-material apparitions and the garden variety objects of the material world. Descriptions of human-like creatures gyrating on their heads are not unknown in such contexts. Whatever one may think of such claims, the conceptual point itself is clear, namely, that the extra-human existents of the Akan ontology do |not belong to the category of the spiritual in the Cartesian sense of non-spatial, unextended. The category itself is conceptually inadmissible in this system of thought. Should the reader be curious at this stage as to whether mind too is quasi-material in the Akan way of thinking, the short answer is that mind is not thought of as an entity at all but rather simply as the *capacity,* supervenient upon brain states and processes, to do various things. Hence the question whether mind is a spiritual or material or quasi-material entity does not arise.

The Akan worldview, then, involves no sharp ontological cleavages such as the Cartesian dichotomy of the material and the spiritual; what difference in nature there is between ordinary material things and those extra-human beings and forces so often called "spirits" in the literature is the difference between the fully material and the partially material. I ought, by the way, to stress that the absence of the spiritual, in the metaphysical sense, from the Akan conceptual framework does not imply the absence of spirituality, in the popular sense, from Akan life. In the latter sense spirituality is sensitivity to the less gross aspects of human experience.

But let us return to the class of quasi-material entities. A legitimate question is whether there is adequate evidence that such entities exist. Actually, this is not a question which faces Akan thought alone. All cultures, East, West and Central, abound in stories of quasi-material goings-on. In the West investigating the veridity and theoretical explicability of such stories is one of the main concerns of Parapsychology. In Africa there are any number of people who would be willing to bet their lives on the reality of such things, on the basis, reputedly, of first hand experience. Basically, the issue is an empirical one, though probably not completely; for if such phenomena were to be definitively confirmed, their explanation would be likely to have conceptual reverberations. Speaking for myself, I would say that neither in Africa nor elsewhere have I seen compelling evidence of such things; though dogmatism would be ill-advised. At all events, it is worth noting that the plausibility of specific quasi-material claims tends to dwindle in the face of advancing scientific knowledge, a consideration which any contemporary African would need to take to heart.

It is, however, interesting to note that the waning, in Africa, of belief in extra material entities and forces would leave the indigenous orientation thoroughly empirical; for the African worldview, at any rate, the Akan one, makes room for only material and quasi-material existents. The contrary seems to be the case in the West. Here any reduction in quasi-material beliefs has not automatically resulted in gains for empirical thinking in the minds of a large mass of people; for in addition to the categories of material and quasi-material, there is that of the spiritual, i.e. the immaterial, which exercises the profoundest influence in philosophic and quasi-philosophic speculation. Not only is actual belief in immaterial entities widespread in the West but also the intelligibility of the material/immaterial contrast seems to be taken for granted even more widely. Moreover, in spite of the fact that, to say the least, quasi-material beliefs are not at all rare in the West, the tendency is for thinking to be governed by an exclusive disjunction of the material with the immaterial. Thus, for many, though, of course, not everybody, in the West, if a thing is not supposed to be material, it is necessarily immaterial. The Europeans who imposed on themselves the "burden" of bringing "salvation" to the souls of the peoples of Africa certainly had this particular either-or fixation. Consequently,

those of them who made sympathetic, though not necessarily empathetic, studies of African thought could not but formulate their results in terms of that and cognate schemes of thought. A visible outcome of their assiduous evangelism is the great *flock* of faithful African converts who think in the same language, proudly attributing to their own peoples belief in sundry things spiritual and supernatural.

Yet, not only is the notion of the spiritual unintelligible within a thought system such as that of the Akans, but also it is objectively a very problematic one. One searches in vain for a useful definition of the spiritual. The sum total of the information available from Cartesian and many other spiritually dedicated sources is that the spiritual is that which is non-material. But, definition by pure negation, such as this, brings little enlightenment. The word "that" in the definition suggests that one is envisaging some *sort* of a referent, but this possibility of reference is given absolutely no grounding. How are we to differentiate between the spiritual and the void, for instance? Some negative definitions can be legitimate, but only if their context provides suitable information. In the present case the context seems to be a veritable void!

An even more unfortunate definition of the spiritual than the foregoing is sometimes encountered. It is explained that the spiritual is the unperceivable, the invisible, or, to adapt a phrase of Saint Paul's, the unseen. The problem with this definition is not its apparent negativeness, for the conditions of unperceivability are concrete enough; the problem is that it is so broad as to make gravity, for example, spiritual. It is, of course, not going to help to protest that although gravity is unseen, its effects are seen and felt; for exactly the same is what is claimed for the spiritual. Nor would it be of greater avail to add the condition of non-spatiality to that of invisibility, for something like the square root of four is neither spatial nor visible, and yet one wonders how spiritual it is.

Of the material/spiritual (immaterial) dichotomy, then, we can say the following. It is not a universal feature of human thinking, since the Akans, at least, do not use it. And, in any case, its coherence is questionable. It is not to be assumed, though, that if a mode of conceptualization is universal among humankind, then it is, for that reason, objectively valid. Belief in quasi-material entities, for example, seems to be universal among cultures (though not among all individuals) but the chances are that the concepts involved denote nothing.

After all the foregoing the reader is unlikely to be surprised to learn that the idea of creation out of nothing too does not make sense in the Akan framework of thinking. Avenues to that concept are blocked in Akanland from the side both of the concept of creation and that of nothingness. To take the latter first: Nothingness in the Akan language is relative to location. The idea is expressed as the absence of anything at a given location, *se whee nni ho,* literally, the circumstance of there not being something there. Note here the reappearance of the locative conception of existence. If you subtract the locative connotation from this construal of nothingness, you have exactly nothing left, that is, nothing of the conception remains in your understanding.

The concept of creation in the Akan language is similarly non-transcendent. To create is to *bo,* and the most self-explanatory word in Akan for the creator is *Obooade. Ade* means thing, and bo means to make in the sense of to fashion out, which implies the use of raw materials. Any claim to *bo* and *ade* without the use of absolutely any raw material would sound decidedly self-contradictory in the language. Thus the Akan Supreme Being is a maker of things, but not out of nothing; so that if the word "Creator" is used for him, it should be clearly understood that the concept of creation involved is fundamentally different from that involved in, say, orthodox Christian talk of creation. The Akan creator is the architect of the world order, but not the *ex nihilo* inventor of its stuff.

Interestingly, even within Western philosophy the concept of *ex nihilo* creation was not in the conceptual vocabulary of some of the greatest thinkers. It is well known, for example, that neither Plato nor Aristotle made use of any such concept. Of course, whether it is intelligible is a separate question. On the face of it, at least, there are tremendous paradoxes in that concept, and unless its exponents can offer profound clarifications, its absence from a conceptual framework can hardly be taken as a mark of insufficiency. Be that as it may, it is clear that the word "creation" should not be used in the context of Akan cosmology without due caution. It should be apparent also that considerable semantical circumspection is called for in using the word "God" for the Akan Supreme Being. Any transcendental inferences from that usage are misplaced.

So, then, we have the following picture of the outlook of the Akans. They believe in a supreme being, but they do not worship Him. Moreover, for conceptual reasons, this being cannot be said to be a spiritual or supernatural being. Nor is He a creator out of nothing. Furthermore, the foundations of Akan ethical life and thought have no necessary reference to Him. It will be recalled also that although the Akans believe in the existence of a whole host of extra-human beings and forces, they view these as regular resources of the world order which can be exploited for good or, sometimes for ill, given appropriate knowledge and the right approach. To all this we might add the fact that the customary procedures in Akan society pertaining to important stages in life, such as naming, marriage and death, which are well-structured, elaborate and highly cherished as providing concrete occasions for the manifestation of communal caring and solidarity, have no necessary involvement with the belief in the Supreme Being. These considerations, by the way, explain why some early European students of African cosmology called the African God an absentee God. In my opinion those visitors to Africa had their finger on something real, but the pejorative tenor of the observation can only be put down to a universalistic conceit. As for the ancestors, they are called upon to come and participate in all these ceremonies, but as revered members of the family, not as gods.

If we now renew the question of the applicability of the concept of religion to any aspect of Akan culture, we must be struck by the substantial disanalogies between the Akan setup of cosmological and moral ideas viewed in relation to practical life, on the one hand, and Western conceptions of reality and the good life viewed in the same relation. For the purpose of this discussion the most important disparity revolves round the slicing up of human experience into the categories of the religious and the secular. To start from the Western end of the comparison: whether we interpret the concept of the religious in a supernatural or non-supernatural sense, it is not a simple matter to discover an analogue of it in the traditional Akan context.

It might be thought that there is substantial common ground between Akan life and thought and that of, say, the Christian religion, since, even if the Akan Nyame is not thought of as supernatural, he is still regarded as in some sense the author of the world and determiner of its destiny. But conceptions or beliefs that do not dovetail into the fabric of practical life can hardly constitute a religion in the primary sense.

That the belief in Nyame has no essential role in the conduct of Akan life can be seen from a little exercise of the imagination. Imagine the belief in Nyame to be altogether removed from the Akan consciousness. What losses will be incurred in terms of sustenance for any institutions or procedures of practical life? The answer is, "Exactly zero." Customs and moral rules relating to the critical (or even non-critical) stages and circumstances in the lives of individuals do not have their basis in the belief in Nyame. The same is true of the institutions of traditional Akan public life. Thus neither the pursuit of moral virtue and noble ideals by individuals nor the cooperative endeavors of the community towards the common good can be said to stand or fall with the belief in Nyame; they all have a solid enough basis in considerations of human well-being, considerations, in other words, which are completely "this-worldly."

To elaborate a little on this last point: to the traditional Akan what gives meaning to life is usefulness to self, family, community and the species. Nothing transcending life in human society and its empirical conditions enters into the constitution of the meaning of life. In particular, there is not, in Akan belief, in contrast, for instance, to Christian belief, any notion of an afterlife of possible salvation and eternal bliss; what afterlife there is thought to be is envisaged very much on the model of this life, as previously hinted. More importantly, that afterlife is not pictured as a life of eternal fun for the immortals but rather as one of eternal vigilance—vigilance over the affairs of the living with the sole purpose of promoting their well-being within the general constraints of Akan ethics. Indeed, this is what is taken to give meaning to their survival.

From everything said (to my knowledge) about the ancestors, they are generally believed never to relent in this objective; which is one reason why they are held in such high esteem. The inhabitants of the world of the dead, then, are themselves thoroughly "this-worldly" in their orientation, according to Akan traditional conceptions.

Basically the same considerations would seem to discourage attributing to the Akans any sort of non-supernaturalistic religiosity. One great difficulty would be how to articulate such a notion within the Akan conceptual framework. Suppose we construe religion as life and thought impregnated by a sense of the sacred. Then, since the primary meaning of the word "sacred" presupposes some conception of deity, we would be in duty bound to give some notification of a broadening of meaning. Accordingly, the sacred might be understood as that in ethical life most worthy of respect, reverence and commitment. But this, in turn, would presuppose a system of values and ideals, and, in the case of the Akans, would bring us back to their irreducibly "this-worldly" ethic. Now, the remarkable thing is that in this ethic a demonstrated basic commitment to the values and ideals of the society is a component of the very concept of a person. An individual is not a person in the fullest sense unless he or she has shown a responsiveness to those ideals in confirmed habits of life. Not, of course, that an individual failing this test is denuded of human rights; for every individual, simply on the grounds of being human, is regarded as a center of quite extensive rights. On the other hand, there is a prestige attached to the status of personhood, or more strictly, superlative personhood—for indeed the status is susceptible of degrees—to which all Akans of sound mind aspire. But this is simply the aspiration to become a responsible individual in society, an individual who, through intelligent thinking, judicious planning and hard work, is able to carve out an adequate livelihood for himself and family and make significant contributions to the well-being of the community. The problem, now, is that if this is what, in the specific context of Akan culture, living a life informed by a sense of the sacred means, then applying the concept of religion to it would scarcely pick out anything in the culture corresponding to what in, say, Western culture might be called a non-supernaturalistic religion. In Western society there are historical as well as conceptual reasons why one might want to organize one's life on the lines of what might be called a nonsupernaturalist religion. In Akan society there are really none. In the West, loss of the belief in God, for example, usually results in disengagement from certain well-known institutions and practices. The consequent psychological or social void might be filled for some by a "non-theistic" religion. In the Akan situation, on the other hand, no such void is to be anticipated from a comparable belief mutation. Speaking from my own experience, failure to retain the belief in *Nyame*—I make no mention here of the Christian God, the conception of whom registers no coherent meaning upon my understanding—has caused me not the slightest alienation from any of the institutions or practices of Akan culture.

Not unexpectedly, what has cost me some dissonance with the culture is my skepticism regarding the continued existence of our ancestors. The pouring of libation, for example, is a practice in which, as previously hinted, the Akans call upon the ancestors to come and participate in important functions and lend their good auspices to any enterprise launched. This is a significant and not infrequent ceremony in Akan life. But obviously, if one does not believe that the ancestors are actually there, one cannot pretend to call them, or, what is the same thing, one can only pretend to do so. I cannot personally, therefore, participate in a custom like this with any total inwardness. In this, by the way, I do not stand alone. Any Akan Christian—and there are great numbers of them—is logically precluded from believing such things as the Akan doctrine of ancestors, for it does not cohere with Christian eschatology. As far as I am concerned, however, there is a saving consideration. This custom of libation, and many other customs of a like quasi-material basis, can be retained by simply reinterpreting the reference to the ancestors as commemoration rather than invocation. That, of course, would entail obvious verbal reformulations, but it should present no problem. What of customs that prove not to be susceptible to such revisions in the face of advancing skepticism? One hopes that they would eventually be abandoned. The culture is rich enough not to suffer any real

existential deficit from such a riddance. Nor is the atrophy of custom under the pressure of changing times at all rare in the history of culture.

Be that as it may, the fact remains that as already argued, the Akan belief in the existence and power of such beings as the ancestors, and the procedures associated with that belief do not constitute a religion in any reliable sense. We are now, therefore, brought to the following conclusion: The concept of religion is not unproblematically applicable within all cultures, and Akan culture is a case in point. Nevertheless, there may be some justification for speaking of Akan religion in a broadened sense of the word "religion." In this sense the word would refer simply to the fact that the Akans believe in Nyame, a being regarded as the architect of the world order. Certainly, this is an extremely attenuated concept of religion. As pointed out already, religion in the fullest sense, whether it be supernaturalistic or not, is not just a set of beliefs and conceptions but also a way of life based on those ideas. What we have seen, however, is that the Akan way of life is not based on the belief in Nyame. Hence, if we do use the word "religion" in the Akan context on the grounds of the belief in Nyame, we should evince some consciousness of the fact that we have made a considerable extension of meaning; otherwise we propagate a subtle misunderstanding of Akan and cognate cultures under the apparently widespread illusion that religion is a cultural universal.

Yet, surely, something must be universal. Consider the ease with which Christian missionaries have been able to convert large masses of Africans to Christianity by relaying to them "tidings" which are in some important parts most likely conceptually incoherent or, at any rate, incongruous with categories deeply embedded in indigenous ways of thinking. To be sure, it cannot be assumed that in the large majority of cases conversion has been total in terms of moral and cosmological outlook. Still there are impressive enough numbers of African converts, some in the high reaches of ecclesiastical authority, whose understanding of and dedication to the Christian religion challenges the severest comparisons among the most exalted practitioners of the same faith in the West. I take this as testimony to the malleability of the human mind which enables the various peoples of the world to share not only their insights but also their incoherences. This characteristic of the mind, being fundamental to the human status, makes our common humanity the one universal which potentially transcends all cultural particularities.

Further Questions

1. According to the *Washington Post,* the current Pope, on a visit to Africa, first admonished the Africans who were present to give up many of their traditional African beliefs because they are superstitious, and, at the conclusion of his talk, celebrated Holy Mass. What happened during that Mass, according to Catholic dogma and the Pope's avowed beliefs, is that by saying certain words the Pope *literally* (not metaphorically) turned ordinary bread into the *body* of Christ, which the Pope then *ate,* and by saying certain other words the Pope turned ordinary wine into the *blood* of Christ, which the Pope then *drank.* Assuming that the Pope actually did what the *Washington Post* reported that he did, do you find anything odd or hypocritical in the Pope's behavior?
2. Besides the notion of religion, can you think of any other ways in which people, by trying to understand another culture in terms of the same categories they use to understand their own culture, misunderstand the other culture?

Further Readings

Abraham, W. E. *The Mind of Africa.* Chicago: The University of Chicago Press, 1962. An Oxford-trained philosopher examines many aspects of recent African social and intellectual life.
Mbiti, John S. *African Religion and Philosophy.* London: Heinemann, 1969. An important study of African beliefs by an African scholar who is a Christian.

Memorial Service   41

H. L. MENCKEN

Henry Louis Mencken, born in 1880 in Baltimore, Maryland, was a pungent critic of American life. He always considered himself a journalist and worked as a reporter for the *Baltimore Sun,* but it was his essays that made him a legend. His *Prejudices* contains six volumes of essays, reviews, and criticisms that many loved with as great a passion as others hated with rage. Mencken attacked organized religion, ridiculed business, and called the American people "the most timorous, sniveling, poltroonish, ignominious mob of serfs and goosesteppers ever gathered under one flag in Christendom since the end of the Middle Ages." In mid-career he proudly published a whole book devoted to nothing but denunciations of himself. He died in Baltimore in 1956.

Reading Questions

1. What is your response to this list of dead gods?
2. If you believe in a god, do you think your god will ever make such a list?

WHERE IS THE GRAVE-YARD of dead gods? What lingering mourner waters their mounds? There was a day when Jupiter was the king of the gods, and any man who doubted his puissance was *ipso facto* a barbarian and an ignoramus. But where in all the world is there a man who worships Jupiter today? And what of Huitzilopochtli? In one year—and it is no more than five hundred years ago—50,000 youths and maidens were slain in sacrifice to him. Today, if he is remembered at all, it is only by some vagrant savage in the depths of the Mexican forest. Huitzilopochtli, like many other gods, had no human father; his mother was a virtuous widow; he was born of an apparently innocent flirtation that she carried on with the sun. When he frowned, his father, the sun, stood still. When he roared with rage, earthquakes engulfed whole cities. When he thirsted he was watered with 10,000 gallons of human blood. But today [in 1921] Huitzilopochtli is as magnificently forgotten as Allen G. Thurman. Once the peer of Allah, Buddha, and Wotan, he is now the peer of General Coxey, Richmond P. Hobson, Nan Petterson, Alton B. Parker, Adelina Patti, General Weyler, and Tom Sharkey.

Speaking of Huitzilopochtli recalls his brother, Tezcatilpoca. Tezcatilpoca was almost as powerful: He consumed 25,000 virgins a year. Lead me to his tomb: I would weep, and hang a *couronne des perles*. But who knows where it is? Or where the grave of Quitzalcoatl is? Or Tialoc? Or Chalchihuitlicue? Or Xiehtecutli? Or Centeotl, that sweet one? Or Tlazolteotl, the goddess of love? Or Mictlan? Or Ixtililton? Or Omacatl? Or Yacatecutli? Or Mixcoatl? Or Xipe? Or all the host of Tzitzimitles? Where are their bones? Where is the willow on which they hung their harps? In what forlorn and unheard of hell do they await the resurrection morn? Who enjoys their residuary estates? Or that of Dis, whom Caesar found to be the chief god of the Celts? Or that of Tarves, the bull? Or that of Moccos, the pig? Or that of Epona, the mare? Or that of Mullo, the celestial jack-ass? There was a time when the Irish revered all these gods as violently as they now hate the English. But today even the drunkest Irishman laughs at them.

But they have company in oblivion: The hell of dead gods is as crowded as the Presbyterian hell for babies. Damona is there, and Esus, and Drunemeton, and Silvana, and Dervones, and Adsalluta, and Deva, and Belisama, and Axona, and Vintios, and Taranuous, and Sulis, and Cocidius, and Adsmerius, and Dumiatis, and Caletos, and Moccus, and Ollovidius, and Albiorix, and Leucitius, and Vitucadrus, and Ogmios, and Uxellimus, and Borvo, and Grannos, and Mogons. All mighty gods in their day, worshiped by millions, full of demands and impositions, able to bind and loose— all gods of the first class, not dilettanti. Men labored for generations to build vast temples to them— temples with stones as large as hay-wagons. The business of interpreting their whims occupied thousands of priests, wizards, archdeacons, evangelists, haruspices, bishops, archbishops. To doubt them was to die, usually at the stake. Armies took to the field to defend them against infidels: Villages were burned, women and children were butchered, cattle were driven off. Yet in the end they all withered and died, and today there is none so poor to do them reverence. Worse, the very tombs in which they lie are lost, and so even a respectful stranger is debarred from paying them the slightest and politest homage.

What has become of Sutekh, once the high god of the whole Nile Valley? What has become of:

Resheph	Ahijah	Shalem
Anath	Isis	Dagon
Ashtoreth	Ptah	Sharrab
El	Anubis	Yau
Nergal	Baal	Amon-Re
Nebo	Astarte	Osiris
Ninib	Hadad	Sebek
Melek	Addu	Molech?

All these were once gods of the highest eminence. Many of them are mentioned with fear and trembling in the Old Testament. They ranked, five or six thousand years ago, with Jahveh himself; the worst of them stood far higher than Thor. Yet they have all gone down the chute, and with them the following:

Bilé
Lêr
Arianrod
Morrigu
Govannon
Gunfled
Sokk-mimi
Memetona
Dagda
Robigus
Pluto
Ops
Meditrina
Vesta
Tilmun
Ogyrvan
Dea Dia
Ceros
Vaticanus
Edulia
Adeona
Iuno Lucina
Saturn
Furrina
Vediovis
Consus
Cronos
Enki
Engurra
Belus
Dimmer
Mu-ul-lil
Ubargisi

Mami
Nin-man
Zaraqu
Suqamunu
Zagaga
Gwydion
Manawyddan
Nuada Argetlam
Tagd
Goibniu
Odin
Llaw Gyffes
Lleu
Ogma
Mider
Rigantona
Marzin
Mars
Kaawanu
Ni-zu
Sahi
Aa
Allatu
Jupiter
Cunina
Potina
Statilinus
Diana of Ephesus
Nin-azu
Lugal-Amarada
Zer-panitu
Merodach
U-ki

Ubilulu
Gasan lil
U-dimmer-an-kia
Enurestu
U-sab-sib
Kerridwen
Pwyll
Tammuz
Venus
Bau
Mulu-hursang
Anu
Beltis
Nusku
U-Mersi
Beltu
Dumu-zi-abzu
Kuski-banda
Sin
Abil Addu
Apsu
Dagan
Elali
Isum

Dauke
Gasan-abzu
Elum
U-Tin-dir-ki
Marduk
Nin-lil-la
Nin
Persephone
Istar
Lagas
U-urugal
Sirtumu
Ea
Nirig
Nebo
Samas
Ma-banba-anna
En-Mersi
Amurru
Assur
Aku
Qarradu
Ura-gala
Ueras

You may think I spoof. That I invent the names. I do not. Ask the rector to lend you any good treatise on comparative religion: You will find them all listed. They were gods of the highest standing and dignity—gods of civilized peoples—worshiped and believed in by millions. All were theoretically omnipotent, omniscient, and immortal. And all are dead.

Further Question

1. Does Mencken's list *prove* anything? What?

Further Reading

Gaskin, J. C. A., ed. *Varieties of Unbelief.* New York: Macmillan, 1989. Unbelief from Epicurus to Sartre. An excellent anthology.

42   Does Anyone Really Believe in God? An Exchange

GEORGES REY AND CHRISTOPHER BERNARD

Georges Rey is professor of philosophy at the University of Maryland–College Park. He was educated at Berkeley and Harvard, has taught at SUNY–Purchase and the University of Colorado, and has held visiting appointments at M.I.T., the Australian National University, the University of London, and various institutions in Paris. Rey works primarily in the philosophy of psychology and has written extensively on how a computational theory of mind offers solutions to a number of traditional philosophical problems on the topic, much of which is set out in his *Contemporary Philosophy of Mind: A Contentiously Classical Approach* (Oxford: Blackwell's, 1997). Despite his resolute atheism, he was raised with a variety of religious influences, is a great admirer of much religious art and music (one argument for the existence of God that does give him — brief — pause is the music of Bach), and wants to assure the reader that he has many friends whose religiosity interferes neither with their warm feelings nor with their not infrequent discussions of his views.

Christopher Bernard is a graduate student and teaching assistant at the University of Maryland at College Park. He has a B.A. in philosophy from the University of Minnesota and an M.A. in the New Testament from Luther Seminary. He is writing his dissertation in the arena of free will and moral responsibility.

Reading Questions

1. Rey claims that if distinctive religious claims were presented in a nonreligious context, they would be regarded as lunatic and asks the reader to imagine, as an example, the case of a judge who kills his own son to atone for the crimes of a defendant. Try this exercise with other such religious claims, disguising the religious context and noting both your own reactions and those of unsuspecting friends.

2. Rey claims that there's something incoherent about a person's both believing something and at the same time thinking he or she has no reasons for believing it. Bernard, however, calls attention to "basic beliefs," such as immediate perceptual ones that don't seem to require justification. How might these claims be reconciled? What about "gut intuitions"? What's the relation between believing oneself to have a reason and being able to state it?

3. What counterexamples does Bernard offer to Rey's claim that most theists do not really believe in God because they often behave in ways inconsistent with their professed beliefs?

4. What issue did Voltaire mockingly claim that medieval theologians debated? Why does Rey think that that issue doesn't count against "detail resistance"? Is the distinction he wants to draw here a legitimate one?

5. Is Bernard right when he claims that religious beliefs are no different than scientific beliefs when it comes to revisibility? Why or why not?

6. Why might one think that atheists are not in a position to know whether or not God exists while theists are?

Meta-Atheism: Reasons to Think that Few People Actually Believe in God

GEORGES REY

I AM NOT A PROFESSIONAL PHILOSOPHER of religion and have no special knowledge of theology. However, I regularly teach an introductory course in philosophy in which I discuss the standard arguments for the existence of God. The exercise has produced in me a certain incredulity: I have come increasingly to wonder how such extremely smart people like Aquinas or Descartes, could advance such patently bad arguments, as I think most philosophers (even those who claim to "believe") would take those arguments to be. At any rate, I find it hard to believe that anyone really buys the "ontological argument," or any of Aquinas' "five ways." Existence may or may not be a predicate, and there may or may not be unmoved movers, uncaused causers, and undesigned teleological systems, but these arguments don't remotely establish their intended conclusion, the existence of anything like the traditional (omniscient, omnipotent, omnibenevolent) Christian God. And "religious experiences," no matter how ecstatic or profound, could obviously be explained by any number of other far more modest hypotheses.[1] I began to wonder whether the arguments were ever really intended seriously; and this led me to wonder whether anyone actually believed their conclusion. That is, I began to wonder whether anyone really did believe in God.

Well, obviously lots of people claim to, and seem to live and sometimes die for such beliefs. It's certainly risky for me to second-guess them on that score just because of some bad arguments—after all, don't people know what they themselves believe, and ordinarily believe what they sincerely avow?

Maybe not. People seem to be susceptible to all manner of confusion and often deeply motivated distortions of their own psychological lives.[2] For starters, there are the formidable difficulties of expressing oneself clearly in language, of saying—

and thinking!—exactly "what one means." And, related to that, there is the familiar phenomenon of adjusting what one says—and thinks—in the light of the demands and expectations of one's audience (think of the "different ways you express yourself" on a topic to a friend, a foe, an interviewer, a judge in court: which of these is one's "real" belief?). But there's also the phenomenon of *self-deception:* people often claim to believe things that they merely *want* or *are committed* to believing, even though "at some level" they know the belief is false. There are the standard examples of someone's ignoring symptoms of some dread disease or the obvious evidence of the infidelities of a spouse; or doting parents exaggerating, even to themselves, the talents of their child. In most of these cases, it is because we have reason to suppose that the people involved are otherwise quite intelligent enough to draw the conclusions that they surprisingly resist that we suppose there must be something else at work.

This is my hunch about what passes as "religious belief" (although I expect the issues about expression and intended audience may also play a role). And so I find myself taking seriously the following hypothesis, which I call *meta-atheism:*

> Despite appearances, not many people—particularly, not many adults who've been exposed to standard Western science—seriously believe in God; most of those who sincerely claim to do so are self-deceived.

Notice that, strictly speaking, meta-atheism doesn't entail atheism: it's a view not about *God* and whether *He* exists, but about whether people actually *believe* that He does (hence the prefix *meta-*, which, in philosophy, has come to mean, roughly, 'at a second-order level about . . .'). Even someone who did take himself or herself to be a serious theist might find this thesis interesting, if only for the light it sheds upon the difficulty (sometimes noted by the devout) of actually believing. But, of course, my own interest in the view is in fact motivated by what seems to me the overwhelming obviousness of atheism. I'm afraid that I really don't think the question of the existence of God is much more "open" than the question of the existence of elves or ghosts.

I should say right away roughly what I shall mean by 'God.' I'm most familiar with Christian conceptions and in the short space here will focus upon them, although I expect much of what I say could be applied to others. What seems to me essential to most conceptions, and is what bothers atheists, is that *God is a psychological being,* i.e., a being capable of some or other mental state, such as knowing, caring, loving, disapproving. What the theist usually asserts that the atheist denies is that there is some psychological being who is not subject to the known laws of the physical universe, knows about our lives, cares about the good, and either created the physical world or can intervene in it. And, at least in Christianity, He is in charge of a person's whereabouts in an afterlife. If you think of God as something other than a psychological being of this sort, or that talk of God is simply a metaphorical or "symbolic" way of talking about love, the possibility of goodness, or the Big Bang, then much of what I say may not apply.

I want to emphasize that I am not intending what I say here to be critical of any religious *practices* (meditating, attending church) or the serious good that religions sometimes (although not always) do. I am concerned only with the *content* of what many religious people *say* they believe. This is because the more seriously and carefully I think about what they actually say, the more utterly bizarre and ludicrous I find it. It seems, quite frankly, *mad.* At any rate, beliefs that there are invisible psychological agents, with larger-than-life powers, with whom one is some special "super-natural" communication, who love, scold, disapprove, command, forgive — think about it: these are the sorts of beliefs that, *in any other, nonreligious context,* are associated with patently schizophrenic delusions!

Now, of course, I don't think that most religious people are in fact schizophrenic. Nor do I think all religious people are being insincere. Rather, the meta-atheism I want to defend is the view that many people who sincerely claim to believe in God are self-deceived, which, as some of the other cases I've already mentioned show, can be entirely "normal," and even morally benign (nothing like a little self-deception to keep an otherwise querulous family together!) My view is, of course, a kind of extension of the familiar observation that most religious stories involve patent wishful thinking and rehearsal of childhood dramas with one's parents. But I would also want to include other influences — for example, *loyalty* to one's family or other social groups, powerful commitments and identifications, or simple resistance to changing significant public stances and avowals.

A verbal issue: along lines of my (1988) argument, I'm inclined to describe the results of self-deception as not genuine belief, but, rather, as things people sincerely "think" or "avow" whether or not they actually believe them. But nothing turns on this. I can well imagine someone thinking of self-deceptive beliefs as genuine beliefs, and as simply manifesting ways in which people's beliefs can be bizarrely irrational and compartmentalized. What concerns me is not the label, but the psychological structure: all I want to claim is that for most contemporary adults in our culture, there is some level at which they know very well the religious stories are false, even if they manage to get themselves to "believe," avow, defend, and even die for them on the surface.

I don't pretend for a moment to be able to *establish* meta-atheism conclusively. I certainly recognize that there's a lot to be said that would appear to argue against it. Much depends upon having a much clearer understanding of such really quite complex states and processes of "belief," "avowal," and "self-deception" than I think anyone yet has, an understanding that depends upon a much subtler empirical psychology than is presently available (cf. my [1997:32–4, 187–9]). I fully expect that the full story in the area will allow for a wide variety of different sorts of "belief." All that I really hope to do here is to put my hypothesis in the running, calling attention to a number of striking peculiarities of religious thinking that I think it may help explain. Indeed, it's really these peculiarities that interest me most. There are (at my last count) eight:

(1) Tolerance of Otherwise Delusional Claims

I don't think you need to be an atheist to have the reaction I've mentioned to the content of religious claims. I submit that, *were the claims about a supernatural entity who loves, commands, scolds, forgives, etc., to be encountered in a fashion removed from the rich, "respectable" aesthetic and cultural traditions in which they are standardly presented, they would be widely regarded as psychotic.* Think, for instance, of how most normal, even religious people take the claims of various cults, in which some charismatic figure convinces people that he is the voice of God and convinces them to renounce their present lives and follow him in various peculiar practices (think of the Koresh cult in Texas, or the recent "Heaven's Gate" cult surrounding the Hale-Bopp comet) and then remember that many religions—notably Christianity—were themselves once just such "cults" (see Pagels 1989). Or, to pass on to related doctrines, think about what you would make of someone—again *in any other context*—who said he or she could really change wine into blood, or bread into flesh, or who thought that some kind of justice or other good would be realized by having a perfectly innocent person die for the sins of everyone else (imagine a judge in a local court deciding that, because he so loves the guilty defendant, he will conceive and then sacrifice a son to atone for the crimes!). In any nonreligious context, such proposals would, I submit, be regarded as sheer lunacy.

(2) Reliance on Texts

Many of these otherwise outlandish religious claims derive an air of legitimacy, of course, from their reliance on a specific set of usually archaic *texts,* whose claims are presented *dogmatically* (indeed, the primary meaning of 'dogma' has precisely to do with religious proclamations!). The texts standardly serve as the *sole* basis for various claims that are regarded as essentially uncontestable—certainly not contested on the basis of any non-textual evidence. As many have noted (e.g., Wittgenstein 1966), they are not presented as *hypotheses,* to be either confirmed or disconfirmed by further research. They are usually adopted or renounced not on the basis of serious evidence, but as a matter of "faith" or "conversion" (see also item 8 below).

By contrast, *there are no such texts or creeds for common sense or science.* In general, we know very well that truths about the world are largely not revealed by the contents of some text in the way that religious claims often are, and so, even though people of course rely on the text for the transmission of information, the texts are every few years being challenged, revised, updated, and eventually replaced. Contrary to popular ideas, there is no set of claims, much less any single text, to which all scientists need subscribe to be good scientists: indeed, as recent science shows, there is *no* claim so sacrosanct that some good scientist (or scientifically minded philosopher) might not challenge it. To use the nice metaphor of "Neurath's boat" emphasized by Quine, in both science and common-sense we are like mariners on the open sea who have to repair their boat while remaining afloat in it, standing now on one plank to repair a second, only to stand on the second to repair the first.

(3) Detail Resistance

This continual mutual revision and adjustment of ordinary beliefs is related to the multifarious ways in which they are interconnected, any one of them having logical or evidential relations to indefinite numbers of the others. For example, beliefs about whether O. J. Simpson murdered Nicole are connected to beliefs about cars, freeways, airports, police, DNA—which in turn connects them to beliefs about cities, governments, history, and cosmology. And one expects there to be in this way indefinite numbers of *details* that could be filled out in regard to these connections. If doubts are raised about the details, they can rebound to any one of the connected beliefs: thus, evidence against a particular theory of DNA would have given jurors reason to doubt that O. J. was at the scene of the crime. And if someone were to suggest that some third party murdered Nicole, then one would expect there to be further details—e.g., further fingerprints, DNA—that would serve as crucial evidence. If there were *no* such details, one would be reasonably skeptical: *absence of evidence,* especially when you look for it, becomes *evidence of absence,* and *most people know this,* which is one good reason they have for not believing in fairies or little green men controlling us from Mars.

By contrast, literally understood, religious claims are oddly *detail resistant*. Perhaps the most dramatic cases are the claims about creation. Whereas scientists regularly ask about the details of the "Big Bang"—there is an entire book, for example, about what happened in the first three minutes (see Weinberg 1977)—it seems perfectly silly to inquire into similar details of just how God did it. Just how did his saying, "Let there be light," actually bring about light? How did He "say" anything at all (does He have a *tongue*)? Or, if He merely "designed" the world or the species in it, how did He do this (are there blueprints of the individual particles/animals)? Was it just the quarks, the DNA, or the whole body? Or just some general directives that were executed by some angelic contractors? At what specific point does He—could He *possibly*—intervene in the natural course of events without causing utter havoc? Does anyone really think there is some set of truths answering these questions? Perhaps; but it is striking how there is nothing like the systematic research on them, in anything like the way that there is massive, ongoing systematic research into the indefinitely subtle details of biology and cosmology. As Kitcher (1982: ch. 5) points out, even so-called "Creation Science" is concerned only with resisting evolutionary biology, not with seriously investigating any of the massive details that would be required for the Creation story actually to be confirmed (imagine there being careful investigation of radioisotopes, sedimentary layers, and the fossil record to establish precisely how, when and where God created atoms and compounds, as well as the full array of biological species.)

Of course, some of this resistance to detail could be attributed to intellectual sloth. But not all of it. After all, if the religious stories really were true, an incredible lot would depend upon getting the details right (if you believe the *wrong* story, you could risk winding up in hell *forever*!). However, when I ask "believers" these kinds of questions of detail, I am invariably met with incredulity that I even think they're relevant.

There are three standard reactions: people either say the claims are not to be understood literally (in which case, fine: they are not literally believed); or they appeal to "mystery" (to which I will return

shortly); but more often they simply *giggle* or make some other indication that I can't possibly be asking these questions seriously. The questions are regarded as somehow *inappropriate*. I have never encountered the kind of response that would be elicited by questions about how, e.g., O. J. got to the airport in time, or about just how big the Bang was. To these latter questions, people will, of course, usually find the question *relevant,* and maybe even interesting. They might not *know* the answer, and perhaps not particularly *care* to find out, but they appreciate its *pertinence* and assume there is some intelligible way of finding out—and that, if there's not, or the answer came out wrong, then that would be a reason to doubt the purported event actually occurred.

(4) Similarity to Fiction   This resistance to detail is strikingly like a similar such resistance one encounters in dealing with *fiction*. It seems as silly to ask the kind of detailed questions about God as it does for someone to ask for details about fictional characters, e.g.: What did Hamlet have for breakfast? Just how did Dorothy and Toto make it over the rainbow? These questions are obviously silly and have no real answers—the text pretty much exhausts what can be said about the characters. So, in keeping with the reliance on texts and appeals to non-literality that we've already noted, perhaps religious claims are simply understood to be fiction from the start.

(5) Merely Symbolic Status of the Stories   Indeed, notice that much of the power of religious claims doesn't really consist in their literal *truth*. Take for example the tremendously moving story of the betrayal and crucifixion of Jesus, and ask yourself whether, were we actually trying to achieve justice in the world, his "dying for our sins" would be even *remotely* appropriate. In the first place, as I mentioned, the idea of an innocent person being sacrificed to expiate *someone else's* sins is really pretty wild.

But, secondly, supposing that this kind of proxy atonement did make sense, the question should certainly arise in the specific case of Jesus whether He actually did suffer *enough*! I don't mean to say that His betrayal and crucifixion weren't pretty awful, but can they really "balance" *all* the horror of

Genghis Khan, World War II, the Soviet gulags, or what death squads routinely do to their victims in Latin America? These are crucifixions multiplied tens of millions-fold. But, of course, all of this is less relevant if we are to take the passion story as merely *symbolic fiction,* i.e., not as *actually* a rectifying of wrongs. *Mere symbols, after all, needn't share the magnitudes of what they symbolize.*

(6) Appeals to "Mystery" Confronted with many of the above oddities, many theists claim God is a "mystery" — indeed, I once heard a famous convert, Malcolm Muggeridge, claim "mystery" as his *reason* for believing! But *ignorance (= mystery!)* is standardly a reason to *not* believe something. Imagine the police arresting you merely because it's a "mystery" how you could have murdered Smith! Just so: if it's really a complete mystery how God designed or created the world, then obviously that's a reason to suspect it's simply *not true* that He did — and my point is that *this is sufficiently obvious that everyone knows it*, and simply pretends that religion affords some very odd exception.

(7) Betrayal by Reactions and Behavior People's reactions and behavior — for example, grief, mourning at a friend's death — do not seem seriously affected by the claimed prospects of a Hereafter. Contrast the reactions in two situations of a loving, "believing" couple who are each seriously ill: in the first, the wife has to be sent off to a luxurious resort for care for two years before the husband can come and join her for an indefinite time thereafter; in the second, the wife is about to die, and the husband has been told he will follow in two years. If, in the second case, there really were the genuine belief in a heavenly afterlife that (let us suppose) they both avow, why shouldn't the husband feel as glad as in the first case — indeed, even gladder, given the prospect of *eternal* bliss? However, I bet he'd grieve and mourn the "loss" like anyone else. Note in this connection how even the most religious observances with respect to death are *deeply lugubrious,* and imagine the absurdity of performing a requiem mass on behalf of someone

you won't see for a few years because she has gone to a luxurious resort!

Or consider petitionary prayer: why aren't people who believe in it disposed to have the National Institute of Health do a controlled study (say, of the different sorts of prayer) as they would were they interested in the claim of whether soy beans cure cancer?[3] And, in any case, why do none of them expect prayer to cure wooden legs? Or bring back Aunt Martha after *twenty-five* years? I suggest that there are obvious limits to people's self-deception, and they know full well that God couldn't really intervene in such preposterous a way.

(8) Appeals to "faith" Many religious people readily recognize the failure of evidence but then go on to claim that religious beliefs are matters of "faith," not evidence (in an extreme case, like that of Tertullian or Kirkegaard, claiming to believe precisely "because it is absurd"). But try thinking something of the form:

> I believe that *p*; however, I don't have adequate evidence or reasons for believing it.

where you substitute for *p* some non-religious claim (e.g., "It's raining now in Vienna," "2 + 2 = 37," "the number of stars is even," "Columbus sailed in 1962"). Imagine how baffling it would be if someone claimed merely to "have faith" about these things! As Adler (1999) points out, there seems to be something "impossible," even "conceptually incoherent" about it, a little like the incoherence of thinking you know something, but being nevertheless convinced it isn't true.

On the other hand, issues of faith *do* arise precisely in those cases in which a person is asked to manifest his or her *loyalty* to a person or cause *despite* the evidence that might otherwise undermine it: thus, a father has faith in his son's honesty despite what the police say, or someone remains "true" to a political cause in the face of evidence of corruption. But, of course, such cases are precisely ones that lay the ground for the kind of self-deception that I have been arguing is characteristic of contemporary religious claims.

Response to "Meta-Atheism"

CHRISTOPHER BERNARD

GEORGES REY IS A META-ATHEIST because he is an atheist. He finds atheism so obviously true that he does not understand how "extremely smart people like Aquinas or Descartes" could believe in God. So he concludes that they probably do not. When they claim to believe in God, they are not consciously lying. They are engaging in self-deception.

Rey makes his case for meta-atheism by pointing out eight peculiarities of religious belief. He sees these anomalies as eight ways that genuine belief and religious belief typically differ and argues that these differences indicate that in many cases, what people report as religious belief is not genuine *belief* at all.

It is important to notice that the fact that someone *sincerely* claims to believe something is usually taken to be good reason to think she really does believe it. Sincere profession of belief creates a certain initial presumption of belief. This presumption can be overcome, of course, but only for good reason.

Rey's eight observations are supposed to raise enough doubt to undermine or defeat this presumption. His argument, then, depends on just how peculiar the peculiarities he points to are. I shall argue that he fails to overcome the presumption created by sincere professions of belief because the differences that he cites between ordinary cases of belief and typical religious belief are either exaggerated or nonexistent.

Consider the seventh peculiarity, for example. Rey argues that there are inconsistencies between what believers say they believe and their actions. He thinks this indicates that they do not really believe what they claim to believe. He gives the example of a believing couple where both partners are terminally ill. The wife is going to die two years before the husband. Rey points out that the husband will probably grieve like anyone else. If, however, he really believed in God, you would expect

him to rejoice rather than grieve. After all, he believes that his wife is going to paradise and that they will be reunited in two short years.

Suppose that Rey is right that theists often behave in ways inconsistent with their professed beliefs. This isn't peculiar to religious belief. Many people, for example, sincerely claim to believe that there are no ghosts. Yet they would also feel nervous camping in a graveyard instead of a national park, for example. It seems wrongheaded to think that this nervousness about sleeping in a graveyard reveals that these people really do believe in ghosts despite their sincere denials.

Many, if not most, smokers sincerely claim to believe that smoking is dangerous to one's health and yet they smoke. Surely this does not indicate that they do not really think that smoking is hazardous to one's health and that they are just deceiving themselves into thinking that smoking is dangerous. So even if Rey is right that believers act in ways inconsistent with their beliefs, this is not unique to religious belief.

Consider Rey's third and fourth anomalies, both of which involve what he calls "detail resistance." Rey uses the notion of detail resistance in two ways. First, he argues that genuine belief and religious belief *differ* with respect to detail resistance. According to Rey, a belief is detail resistant if the request for details elicits a reaction from the believer that indicates that she thinks the demand for details is inappropriate. This reaction usually takes two forms. Either the believer giggles because she thinks the request is silly or she retreats to mystery.

Rey takes belief in God to be detail resistant when, for example, believing students in his philosophy class giggle when he asks them for the details of how God designed the world: "How did He do this (are there blueprints of the individual particles/animals)? Was it just the quarks, the DNA, or the whole body? Or just some general directives that were executed by some world/animal contractors?" Their reaction to the demand for details, he thinks, indicates that they do not really believe that God created the world.

A better explanation, however, is that they giggle because he phrases his questions in a humorous manner. One could elicit a similar response from students in a physics course if you were to ask them: "How do subatomic particles attract one another? Do they suck large amounts of air into their lungs, pulling them together? Do they hold hands and pull themselves together?" In the case of both the philosophy students and the physics students, they are not giggling at the request for details but at the humorous way in which the request was phrased. To see this, ask yourself if the students would giggle if Rey simply asked, "How did God create the world?" It is doubtful that they would have laughed and giggled at a straightforward request for details. The behavior in question is better explained without appeal to meta-atheism.

When believers respond to the request for details by "retreating to mystery," it is not because they do not think there are details. They do so because they do not know the answer and have no way of finding out. They do not have access to the relevant information. What Rey calls a retreat to mystery most believers would see as simply saying, "I do not know and do not know how to find out."

Consider those who believe there is intelligent life on other planets. A skeptic might ask them how these aliens communicate. Do they use vocal chords, or do they use some sort of sign language? Do they communicate telepathically (as popular fiction so often portrays), or do they communicate by touch? Most people who believe in extraterrestrial life would probably respond, "I do not know. It's a mystery to me." This lack of cognitive access to such details might raise doubt about the claim, but it does not raise doubt whether the person truly *believes* the claim.

Contrary to what Rey says, however, religious believers do traffic in details. A whole class of religious people—namely, theologians—spends their entire careers thinking about the details of religious beliefs. Theologians have filled volumes with details on the atonement, the afterlife, the nature of man, the nature of Christ, the nature of the sacraments, and the like *ad nauseum*. In fact, the

French philosopher Voltaire ridiculed medieval theologians for giving too many theological details. He mocked their concern for minutiae by claiming that they even argued about how many angels could dance on the head of a pin.

Rey uses the notion of detail resistance in a second way, though. He argues that belief in God is *similar* to our attitude towards fiction in that both are detail resistant. It seems silly, for instance, to ask what Hamlet had for breakfast or how Dorothy and Toto made it over the rainbow. He thinks this similarity with fiction indicates that "religious claims are simply understood to be fiction from the start."

But this just begs the question. The "facts" about Hamlet are dependent on the play. It is silly to ask what Hamlet had for breakfast, not because he didn't really exist, but because the play does not speak to that particular detail. When religious beliefs lack in detail it is because we do not have *access* to the answers. We do not concern ourselves with the details of how God created the world because we do not have any way to find out, or even understand, the answer. So any similarity between religious belief and fiction on this point is merely superficial.

Additionally, Rey argues that the lack of evidence for God's existence is actually evidence that God does not exist. It isn't clear, however, that most religious belief is unjustified. Some of the traditional theistic proofs may be fallacious, as Rey claims. But contemporary theists have offered updated and sophisticated versions of these arguments as well as original ones (see Plantinga 1977, Collins 1999, Craig 1992).

More important, religious beliefs may be justified independent of arguments. Alvin Plantinga argues plausibly that belief in God is not inferred but is instead properly basic (Plantinga 1983). According to a standard theory of knowledge, the structure of one's beliefs resembles a building with a foundation and a superstructure. It divides beliefs into two sorts—basic and nonbasic, the nonbasic being inferred from the basic, while the basic are not inferred from anything at all. So, for example, my belief that 2 + 2 = 4, or that I have two hands, are basic beliefs because I do not hold them on the basis of other beliefs. On the other hand, my belief that Omaha is in Nebraska is nonbasic because it is based upon my belief that my maps are reliable and that my geography teacher is knowledgeable and honest. A belief is properly basic if it is both basic and justified. Plantinga argues that belief in God, like my belief that 2 + 2 = 4, is a properly basic belief. It can be rationally justified independent of arguments.

This raises an obvious objection. As Plantinga (1983, p. 74) puts it:

> If belief in God is properly basic, why cannot *just any* belief be properly basic? Could we not say the same for any bizarre aberration we can think of? What about voodoo or astrology? What about the belief that the Great Pumpkin returns every Halloween?

Plantinga responds to the Great Pumpkin objection by pointing out that just because he rejects commonly held criteria for proper basicality does not mean he must accept just anything as properly basic. One does not need a theory of sheep and goats in order to distinguish them. He *is* committed to supposing that there is a germane difference between belief in God and belief in the Great Pumpkin. One suggested difference is that belief in God is produced by reliable cognitive process whereas belief in the Great Pumpkin is not (Plantinga 1996, p. 336). He further argues for a theory of knowledge according to which this sort of difference is the relevant difference (Plantinga 1993; Plantinga 1996, p. 336; Plantinga 2000).

But even if Rey is right about the lack of evidence for the existence of God, this does not by itself constitute evidence that God does not exist. To see this, suppose you walked into a classroom and the professor had a large cardboard box on the floor. He tells you there could be something in the box or it could be empty. You are not allowed to look inside it, shake it, or even touch it. In effect, you have no evidence that there is something in the box and you have no evidence that it is empty. Your lack of evidence, in this case, is not evidence that there is nothing in the box. You have no evidence either way and so the rational stance is to suspend judgment.

Now suppose you walk into a classroom and the professor informs you that there is a normal-sized adult elephant in the room. You look around and you do not see an elephant. In this case, it looks like the lack of evidence that an elephant is present is evidence that there is not one there.

What is the difference between the two cases? In the second case, if there were an elephant in the room, we are in a position to know it. We would see the elephant if he were there. Because we do not see an elephant, we are entitled to conclude that there is no elephant in the room. In the first case, however, if there were something in the box, we would not be in a position to know this from our vantage point. We cannot tell just by looking at it from the outside. So a lack of evidence is evidence against a position only in cases where we are in a position to see the evidence, if there is any (Morris 1987, pp. 206–208).

Whether Rey is right about a lack of evidence for the existence of God being evidence that he does not exist depends on whether we are in a position to see the evidence for God, if there is any. It depends on whether our epistemic position vis-à-vis the existence of God is more like our position in the case of the elephant than the case of the cardboard box. An absence of evidence is often a reason to suspend belief rather than disbelieve. So Rey's point here is incomplete. He needs to make the further argument that if God exists, we are in a position to know this.

It is not enough to say that we have "looked" for God. Scientists have looked for intelligent extraterrestrial life with radio telescopes. We cannot conclude there is no intelligent life elsewhere just because this process has turned up no evidence. We have only been looking for a relatively short period of time and have not scanned a very large portion of the sky. We have looked and are still not in the proper epistemic position to conclude from a lack of evidence that there are no intelligent beings elsewhere in the universe—or no God.

Finally, Rey argues that religious beliefs "are a matter of creed" while genuine beliefs are not. It is not entirely clear what Rey means here. Creeds, like the Nicene Creed, are summaries of the religious beliefs of a particular community. They are doctrinal statements. Nonreligious beliefs are often expressed in written forms as well. The Declaration of Independence, for example, expresses the political and social beliefs of a particular community. If this is Rey's claim, there does not seem to be any relevant difference.

Maybe he means that religious beliefs are often arrived at by reading certain texts that are taken to be epistemically authoritative. But most of my scientific beliefs, for example, are formed by my reading science textbooks that I take to be epistemically authoritative. So if to be "a matter of creed" means that beliefs are formed by reading what the reader takes to be epistemically authoritative texts, there does not seem to be any important difference between religious beliefs and genuine beliefs on this account either.

Perhaps the key to understanding Rey's point is when he writes, "There is *no* claim so sacrosanct that some good scientist (or scientifically minded philosopher) might not challenge it." Rey might be saying that religious belief is so wedded to certain texts that religious beliefs are unrevisable. Scientific beliefs can be changed and revised when new evidence comes to light, while religious belief cannot because they are bound to unchanging texts.

Religious believers, however, do change their religious beliefs. When they change these beliefs, they sometimes reconcile their new beliefs to religious texts by reinterpreting the texts or by emphasizing certain passages over other ones. Other times they give the texts up altogether, change religions, or even give up religion altogether. Religious beliefs are not static, unchanging psychological givens. The charge that religious beliefs are unrevisable is false on the face of it.

It is true that most religions take a certain doctrine or set of doctrines to be a standard of orthodoxy, but this isn't fundamentally different than other domains. Political groups have standards of orthodoxy. For example, you might not be considered a true Democrat if you are not pro-choice. Scientists, like other social communities, have a set of views that are considered essential such that if you reject them you are considered a heretic. Evolution is an example of this. So it is not clear that there is a fundamental difference here between religious beliefs and genuine beliefs as Rey suggests.

Rey's other points suffer from similar problems, though I've run out of space to detail them. To sum up, Rey offers eight anomalies of religious belief in an attempt to overcome the strong *prima facie* evidence that most adults who claim to believe in God do, in fact, believe in God. But the peculiarities he raises turn out to not be very peculiar. They can be accounted for at least as well, if not better, by the view that they really do believe in God, than by meta-atheism.

Reply to Christopher Bernard

GEORGES REY

I'll reply briefly to what I take to be Bernard's main points:

(1) Graveyards and Smoking I think of my "meta-atheism" as an invitation to a more serious psychology of "belief" than is ordinarily presupposed. Bernard's nice example of people's reluctance to sleep in graveyards can be regarded as another. As in the case of religion, I'm not as confident as Bernard about the explanation of this phenomenon. Perhaps it's due simply to taboos surrounding death, but I don't think we should dismiss out of hand some odd residual belief in ghosts. Many people who should know better are prey to such (as we call them) "superstitions": knocking on wood after boasting, wearing the socks one wore in hitting the home run, worrying about the next air flight because one has flown so many times so far without accident. At least for many of us, what's peculiar about these "beliefs" is that they persist at some level despite our seriously disavowing them—and despite their failure to be integrated into the rest of our thought (they display precisely the same sort of detail resistance I

noted about religious claims). They might be called "ossified beliefs": thin, isolated beliefs that have become rigid and aren't removed by rational reflection. Other examples might be the "neurotic" beliefs Freudians ascribe to us on the basis of irrational behavior—e.g., regarding murderous fathers and castrating mothers.

I wouldn't be surprised if some religious beliefs are also of this ossified sort (when theists suspect atheists are themselves self-deceptive about their atheism, it may well be such ossified beliefs they have in mind). Of course, many religions are at pains to distinguish belief in God from "mere superstition." Religious belief becomes *self-deceptive* on my view when the belief is not merely noted, in the detached way that one notes one's superstitions, but wholly *endorsed,* being regarded as somehow *something more* than mere superstition. It's this further attempt to integrate religious beliefs into, as it were, *serious* belief that strikes me, for the reasons I have given, as going against what most people with a high school education know very well to be true.

Smoking, despite the obvious risks, and other cases of so-called "weakness of will" afford still other examples of discrepancies between behavior and what people avow (see my [1988]); and they may also arise in the religious case, as when people continue to "sin" despite their avowals about the risks of eternal damnation. However these also quite difficult cases are to be explained, I doubt that the cases of grief and mourning I mentioned figure among them. I presume that it is rare for the religious to think it *weak willed* to mourn!

(2) Giggles and Mysteries   Bernard is right to consider alternative hypotheses to mine in considering, for example, why people giggle at my request for details about, e.g., how God created the world. And perhaps he is right that it's due merely to the silliness of some of the proposals I press.

Although the point is well taken, and I should be careful in controlling for such effects, it is a little hard to know how else to proceed. The comparison to asking whether particles "suck air into their lungs" is arguably a bit unfair, since no physicist claims that particles have lungs. By contrast, the Bible did say God created the world by 'saying' (some translation of?), "Let there be light." Of

course, this could be metaphoric, but then I want to know where the mere metaphor ends. Are there *any* examples of plausible details that the theist is willing to take seriously in the way that there are details that science and commonsense are regularly willing to consider? And if she really can't imagine *at all* how He did it, then why doesn't that begin to undermine her conviction that He did? Again: if she can't imagine *how possibly* O. J. Simpson got to the airport in time, or point to any evidence that he did, then that will surely be a reason for her to begin to doubt either that he did, or that he committed the murder at the presumed time. An appeal to "mystery" at this point is an appeal that ordinarily *undermines* belief.

Bernard claims that believers are willing to tolerate the mysteries surrounding God because they have an additional belief, viz, that they also can't know about God's ways. Now, first of all, this is disingenuous. Most Christians think the Bible does tell them a lot about His ways, often think He's responsible for when people live and die, and is sometimes supposed to be responsive to petitionary prayer. But, of course, these then are precisely the points at which the God hypothesis is vulnerable to obvious disconfirmation: too much happens that's hard to believe is the result of a benign omnipotent being: too little happens that's an answer to prayer.

Be that as it may, Bernard likens knowledge about God to our position regarding how extraterrestrials communicate, or regarding the contents of a box that we're for some reason not allowed to inspect. But, putting aside the peculiar exceptions just noted, the differences here come with the force of the 'can't': we can't know much about the extraterrestrials, since of course they're too far away; and we can't know much about the contents of the box because apparently we're not allowed to go up and inspect. But, of course, we might find out more in these cases: scientists regularly scan the skies for evidence of radio transmissions, and we can imagine all sorts of ways of inferring the contents from indirect evidence, e.g. of where the box has been, how heavy it appears to be. The problem with God is that the 'can't' is so arbitrarily and inexplicably strong (why does God disallow us from "inspecting the box"? Why shouldn't His existence be establishable in the same way as the existence of bacteria or the Big Bang?). In any case, it's not as though the religious try to do what they might do in these other cases—namely, think of clever, indirect ways of finding out. To repeat some of the questions I already raised: Why don't believers present serious scientific papers about the Creation or the efficacy of prayer? No, the "mystery? is supposed to be "deeper" and far more impenetrable than that. I can't imagine what sustains such conviction—mind you, not about *God,* but about the *knowability* of God's ways—except perhaps an unconscious realization that there of course couldn't ever be serious evidence for something that doesn't actually exist.

(3) Theologians   Bernard goes to point out that, of course, theologians do discuss details. As I mentioned, I'm not a scholar of theology; however, I'm willing to wager that few of the details they discuss are of the *evidential* sort that we ordinarily expect of ordinary claims about the world, i.e., claims that link the theological to *crucial data that would be better explained by the theological than by any competing hypothesis.* Elaborations of the theological stories without this property—mere stories about "angels on the head of a pin"—do not constitute such details: they are merely like the elaboration of a fictional story. If there really are serious attempts to narrow down the details of God's activities by e.g., reference to the fossil record, or systematic studies of the effects of prayer, then I stand corrected. But I'd also wager that most "believers" would find such efforts silly, perhaps even "sacrilegious."

(4) Basic Beliefs   At another point, Bernard tries to assimilate religious belief to the kinds of "basic beliefs" that "foundationalist" epistemologists such as Plantinga claim are required for us to have knowledge of anything, e.g. beliefs about the reliability of memory, sense perception, basic arithmetic. I think it would be a mistake to think that discussions about theism really turn on difficult issues regarding, e.g., foundationalism, in the theory of knowledge. Whatever your theory of knowledge, it had better distinguish between, e.g., normal visual perception and schizophrenic delusions. The question is not whether there are foundational beliefs, but why on earth anyone should think that belief in the existence of anything with the extrava-

gant implications of *God* should figure among them (the *Great Pumpkin* is really rather modest by comparison); or, even if it does, why the utter failure of any of these implications to be independently confirmed wouldn't be an overwhelming reason to scotch the belief, basic or otherwise. Beliefs acquired by unassisted vision, be they ever so basic, are soon undermined by noticing you're not seeing what's smack in front of you, or thinking you're seeing things that are patently not there. In any case, *there obviously needs to be independent evidence for the reliability of any process if its testimony on a controversial topic is to be believed.* (I might add that until such independent evidence is provided, it is a bit chauvinistic for Christians to dismiss beliefs in astrology or voodoo: does anyone seriously believe these are epistemically distinguishable from, e.g., claims about the Eucharist, or the resurrection?)

(5) Political Creeds   Bernard rightly points out that creeds figure in areas other than religion, e.g., in the Declaration of Independence or political party platforms. These are precisely cases where what is often at stake is a person's *commitment to a program,* and is not the tested *truth* of what is said. It's precisely the kind of situation that invites and manifestly sustains abundant self-deception, which I wouldn't for a moment suppose is *confined* to religion. It was, after all, in a political context—or was it religious?—that a child cut through the massive self-deception about the emperor's new clothes.

NOTES

1. For perfectly adequate refutations of the standard arguments, see most any introductory text, e.g. Sober (2001: pt. II). The simplest thing to notice about most of the arguments is that they don't establish the existence of a *psychological* being of any sort (why should the uncaused causer have a mind?), much less of a *unique* one with the hyperbolic properties in question. And, of course, "religious experiences" by themselves can't establish much of anything, any more than dreams of ghosts do: what would need to be shown is that God—or ghosts—would be the *best explanation* of those experiences, but this no one has even seriously begun to do. They only argument that comes close to being plausible is the argument from biological design, but it can't be taken seriously since Darwin (for an excellent recent discussion of

"global design," see Weinberg 1999). Of course, I haven't kept up with all the very latest versions of the traditional arguments; nor, however, have I followed all the latest proposals for a perpetual motion machine (which, on many versions of theism, God seems to be!).

2. For a discussion of this point, see my contribution to McLaughlin and Rorty (1988), which enlarges a discussion well under way in Stich (1983) and Bach (1981). Some of that discussion was influenced by the classic paper of Nisbett and Wilson (1977) in which they adduce considerable evidence that much purported "introspection" of one's own psychological states is often merely the imposition upon oneself of the same kind of (often mistaken) popular psychology that we use to understand others.

3. Note that they could do this without disrespectfully praying with such a test in mind: they could simply do demographic studies of the incidence of cures with different religious sects.

I put aside for the nonce the extreme peculiarities of "belief" in petitionary prayer at all—which suggests that people believe that an omnipotent, omnibenevolent God would just as soon, e.g., let a young child die slowly from an excruciating cancer except that He's heard your prayers!

References

Adler, J. (1990). "Conservatism and Tacit Confirmation." *Mind* 99: 559–70.

Adler, J. (1999). "The Ethics of Belief: Off the Wrong Track." P. French and H. Wettstein, eds., *Midwest Studies 23: New Directions in Philosophy* (pp. 267–85).

Bach, K. (1981). "An Analysis of Self-deception," *Philosophy and Phenomenological Research* 41 (March): 351–70.

Collins, R. (1999). "A Scientific Argument for the Existence of God: the Fine-Tuning Design Argument." In M. Murray, ed., *Reason for the Hope Within* (pp. 47–75). Grand Rapids, MI: William B. Eerdmans.

Craig, W. L. (1992). "Philosophical and Scientific Pointers to *Creatio Ex Nihilo*." In R. D. Geivett and B. Sweetman, eds., *Contemporary Perspectives on Religious Epistemology* (pp. 185–200). New York: Oxford University Press.

Kitcher, P. (1982). *Abusing Science: the Case against Creationism*. Cambridge: MIT Press.

McLaughlin, B. and Rorty, A. (1988). *Perspectives on Self-Deception*. Berkeley: University of California Press.

Morris, T. V. (1987). Pascalian Wagering. In T. V. Morris, ed., *Anselmian Explorations: Essays in Philosophical Theology* (pp. 194–212). Notre Dame, IN: Notre Dame University Press.

Nisbett, R. and Wilson, T. (1977). "On Telling More than We Can Know," *Psychological Review* 84, 3: 231–59.

Pagels, E. (1969). *Adam, Eve, and the Serpent*. New York: Vintage.

Plantinga, A. (1977). *God, Freedom, and Evil*. Grand Rapids, MI: William B. Eerdmans.

Plantinga, A. (1983). "Reason and Belief in God." In A. Plantinga and N. Wolterstorff, eds., *Faith and Rationality: Reason and Belief in God* (pp. 16–93). Notre Dame, IN: Notre Dame University Press.

Plantinga, A. (1993). *Warrant and Proper Function*. New York: Oxford University Press.

Plantinga, A. (1996). "On Reformed Epistemology." In M. Peterson, W. Hasker, B. Reichenbach, and D. Basinger, eds., *Philosophy of Religion: Selected Readings* (pp. 330–336). New York: Oxford University Press.

Plantinga, A. (2000). *Warranted Christian Belief*. New York: Oxford University Press.

Rey, G. (1988). "Towards a Computational Account of Akrasia and Self-Deception." In B. McLaughlin and A. Rorty, eds., *Studies in Self-Deception* (pp. 264–96). Berkeley: University of California Press.

Rey, G. (1997). *Contemporary Philosophy of Mind: A Contentiously Classical Approach*. Oxford: Blackwell.

Schlesinger, G. (1999). From *New Perspectives on Old-time Religion*. In M. Murray & E. Stump, eds., *Philosophy or Religion: The Big Questions* (pp. 114–24). Oxford: Blackwell.

Sober, E. (2001). *Core Questions in Philosophy*, 3rd ed. New York: Macmillan.

Weinberg, S. (1977). *The First Three Minutes: A Modern View of the Origin of the Universe*. New York: Basic Books.

Weinberg, S. (1999). "Is the Universe Designed?" *New York Review of Books,* 46: 16 (October 21): 46–48.

Wittgenstein, L. (1966). *Lectures and Conversations on Religious Belief*. Berkeley: University of California Press.

Further Questions

1. Rey suggests at the end of his reply to Bernard that similar self-deception might occur in other domains, for example, with regard to political allegiances. Think of still other domains where some of the same considerations he raised might arise. Might it arise in science as well? Would this undermine Rey's point?

2. What in general is the relation between what people sincerely assert and what they believe? As Rey mentions in passing, think of the different ways people "express their beliefs" to friends, foes, judges, children. Think also of how much often goes "unsaid," as when we say "I haven't eaten," meaning "I haven't eaten today," or "No one came to my party," meaning, "Almost no one came to my party (although of couse my parents were there"). And then consider two young lovers who avow they will love each other "forever." To what extent ought Rey's claims to be modified in the light of these examples?

Further Readings

Bach, K. (1981), "An Analysis of Self-Deception," *Philosophy and Phenomenological Research* 41 (March): 351–70.

McLaughlin, B. and Rorty, A. (1988), *Perspectives on Self-Deception*, Berkeley: University of California Press.

Part VII

Reality

SOMEONE TAPS YOU ON THE SHOULDER: three short taps, followed by three long taps, followed by three short taps. Using the Morse code, you interpret the taps as the letters "S, O, S." You then interpret these letters as the message, "Help!"

Everything you experience—chairs, people, words—is based on the same principle: pressure gets interpreted as images, sounds, meanings, and things. *Nothing but taps ever touches you*—air tapping against your eardrum, light tapping against the backs of your eyes, pressure on your fingertips, and so on. That's as far as the taps go.

You do not experience the taps as pressure. You get hooked through the "medium" directly to the "message." You (or, your brain) interpret the signals automatically.

You of course believe that what you are seeing exists outside you. The ultimate *cause* of the immediate experiences might exist outside you. This is a theory, perhaps a justified one. But your experience does not exist outside you. It is *in* you. As a musical synthesizer synthesizes notes, you synthesize every element in your experience. All that ever reaches you is pressure. The rest happens in your head. This, too, is a theory!

One could put it this way: If by *dreaming* we mean experiencing images synthesized by the brain, right now *you are dreaming*. Your eyes are open. But there is no open passage between you and the outside. Even when your eyes are open they are, in a sense, closed. In a sense, you are right now dreaming with your eyes open.

Of course, we still distinguish dreams from reality. But how? What *is* reality?

43   Causation, Reality, and Fiction

DAVID HUME

A brief biography of Hume appears on page 128.

    In our conception of reality, what binds together events that occur at different times is to a great extent what we take to be the causal relations among them. Causation, as one contemporary philosopher put it, is "the cement of the universe." But what is causation? The following selection, from Hume's *An Enquiry Concerning Human Understanding* (1748), is Hume's answer. In this selection, which is one of the most influential in all of his writings, he tries to determine the sources in experience ("the impressions") from which our idea of cause (or power or necessary connection) is derived. Finding these impressions, he thinks, will reveal how the idea of causation should be understood.

Reading Questions

1. What is Hume's distinction between "idea" and "impression"?
2. Can one experience causation (necessary connections among objects) by examining the world? By looking within ourselves?
3. Suppose you will your arm to move, and then it moves. Haven't you thereby experienced causation? What does Hume think?
4. How does Hume define causation?

PART I

THERE ARE NO IDEAS, which occur in metaphysics, more obscure and uncertain, than those of *power, force, energy* or *necessary connexion,* of which it is every moment necessary for us to treat in all our disquisitions. We shall, therefore, endeavour, in this section, to fix, if possible, the precise meaning of these terms, and thereby remove some part of that obscurity, which is so much complained of in this species of philosophy.

    It seems a proposition, which will not admit of much dispute, that all our ideas are nothing but copies of our impressions, or, in other words, that it is impossible for us to *think* of any thing, which we have not antecedently *felt,* either by our external or internal senses. . . . To be fully acquainted, therefore, with the idea of power or necessary connexion, let us examine its impression; and in order to find the impression with greater certainty, let us search for it in all the sources, from which it may possibly be derived.

    When we look about us towards external objects, and consider the operation of causes, we are never able, in a single instance, to discover any power or necessary connexion; any quality, which binds the effect to the cause, and renders the one an infallible consequence of the other. We only find, that the one does actually, in fact, follow the other. The impulse of one billiard-ball is attended

From Hume, An Enquiry Concerning Human Understanding *(1748), Sections 5 and 7.*

with motion in the second. This is the whole that appears to the *outward* senses. The mind feels no sentiment or *inward* impression from this succession of objects: Consequently, there is not, in any single, particular instance of cause and effect, any thing which can suggest the idea of power or necessary connexion.

From the first appearance of an object, we never can conjecture what effect will result from it. But were the power or energy of any cause discoverable by the mind, we could foresee the effect, even without experience; and might, at first, pronounce with certainty concerning it, by mere dint of thought and reasoning.

In reality, there is no part of matter, that does ever, by its sensible qualities, discover any power or energy, or give us ground to imagine, that it could produce any thing, or be followed by any other object, which we could denominate its effect. Solidity, extension, motion; these qualities are all complete in themselves, and never point out any other event which may result from them. The scenes of the universe are continually shifting, and one object follows another in an uninterrupted succession; but the power or force, which actuates the whole machine, is entirely concealed from us, and never discovers itself in any of the sensible qualities of body. We know, that, in fact, heat is a constant attendant of flame; but what is the connexion between them, we have no room so much as to conjecture or imagine. It is impossible, therefore, that the idea of power can be derived from the contemplation of bodies, in single instances of their operation; because no bodies ever discover any power, which can be the original of this idea.

Since, therefore, external objects as they appear to the senses, give us no idea of power or necessary connexion, by their operation in particular instances, let us see, whether this idea be derived from reflection on the operations of our own minds, and be copied from any internal impression. It may be said, that we are every moment conscious of internal power; while we feel, that, by the simple command of our will, we can move the organs of our body, or direct the faculties of our mind. An act of volition produces motion in our limbs, or raises a new idea in our imagination. This influence of the will we know by consciousness. Hence we acquire the idea of power or energy; and are cer-

tain, that we ourselves and all other intelligent beings are possessed of power. . . .

We shall proceed to examine this pretension; and first with regard to the influence of volition over the organs of the body. This influence, we may observe, is a fact, which, like all other natural events, can be known only by experience, and can never be foreseen from any apparent energy or power in the cause, which connects it with the effect, and renders the one an infallible consequence of the other. The motion of our body follows upon the command of our will. Of this we are every moment conscious. But the means, by which this is effected; the energy, by which the will performs so extraordinary an operation; of this we are so far from being immediately conscious, that it must for ever escape our most diligent enquiry.

For *first;* is there any principle in all nature more mysterious than the union of soul with body; by which a supposed spiritual substance acquires such an influence over a material one, that the most refined thought is able to actuate the grossest matter? Were we empowered, by a secret wish, to remove mountains, or control the planets in their orbit; this extensive authority would not be more extraordinary, nor more beyond our comprehension. But if by consciousness we perceived any power or energy in the will, we must know this power; we must know its connexion with the effect; we must know the secret union of soul and body, and the nature of both these substances; by which the one is able to operate, in so many instances, upon the other.

Secondly, We are not able to move all the organs of the body with a like authority; though we cannot assign any reason besides experience, for so remarkable a difference between one and the other. Why has the will an influence over the tongue and fingers, not over the heart or liver? This question would never embarrass us, were we conscious of a power in the former case, not in the latter. . . .

Thirdly, We learn from anatomy, that the immediate object of power in voluntary motion, is not the member itself which is moved, but certain muscles, and nerves, and animal spirits, and, perhaps, something still more minute and more unknown, through which the motion is successively propagated, ere it reach the member itself whose motion is the immediate object of volition. Can there be a more certain proof, that the power, by which this whole operation is performed, so far from being directly and fully known by an inward sentiment or consciousness, is, to the last degree, mysterious and unintelligible? Here the mind wills a certain event: Immediately another event, unknown to ourselves, and totally different from the one intended, is produced: This event produces another, equally unknown: Till at last, through a long succession, the desired event is produced. But if the original power were felt, it must be known: Were it known, its effect also must be known; since all power is relative to its effect. And *vice versa,* if the effect be not known, the power cannot be known nor felt. How indeed can we be conscious of a power to move our limbs, when we have no such power; but only that to move certain animal spirits, which, though they produce at last the motion of our limbs, yet operate in such a manner as is wholly beyond our comprehension?

We may, therefore, conclude . . . that our idea of power is not copied from any sentiment or consciousness of power within ourselves, when we give rise to animal motion, or apply our limbs to their proper use and office. That their motion follows the command of the will is a matter of common experience, like other natural events: But the power or energy by which this is effected, like that in other natural events, is unknown and inconceivable. . . .

The generality of mankind never find any difficulty in accounting for the more common and familiar operations of nature—such as the descent of heavy bodies, the growth of plants, the generation of animals, or the nourishment of bodies by food: But suppose that, in all these cases, they perceive the very force or energy of the cause, by which it is connected with its effect, and is for ever infallible in its operation. They acquire, by long habit, such a turn of mind, that, upon the appearance of the cause, they immediately expect with assurance its usual attendant, and hardly conceive it possible that any other event could result from it. It is only on the discovery of extraordinary phaenomena, such as earthquakes, pestilence, and prodigies of any kind, that they find themselves at a loss to assign a proper cause, and to explain the manner in which the effect is produced by it. It is usual for men, in such difficulties to have recourse to some invisible intelligent principle as the immediate cause of that event which surprises them, and

which, they think, cannot be accounted for from the common powers of nature. But philosophers, who carry their scrutiny a little farther, immediately perceive that, even in the most familiar events, the energy of the cause is as unintelligible as in the most unusual, and that we only learn by experience the frequent *Conjunction* of objects, without being ever able to comprehend anything like *Connexion* between them. . . .

PART II

But to hasten a conclusion of this argument, which is already drawn out to too great a length: We have sought in vain for an idea of power or necessary connexion in all the sources from which we could suppose it to be derived. It appears that, in single instances of the operation of bodies, we never can, by our utmost scrutiny, discover any thing but one event following another, without being able to comprehend any force or power by which the cause operates, or any connexion between it and its supposed effect. The same difficulty occurs in contemplating the operations of mind on body—where we observe the motion of the latter to follow upon the volition of the former, but are not able to observe or conceive the tie which binds together the motion and volition, or the energy by which the mind produces this effect. The authority of the will over its own faculties and ideas is not a whit more comprehensible: So that, upon the whole, there appears not, throughout all nature, any one instance of connexion which is conceivable by us. All events seem entirely loose and separate. One event follows another; but we never can observe any tie between them. They seem *conjoined,* but never *connected.* And as we can have no idea of any thing which never appeared to our outward sense or inward sentiment, the necessary conclusion *seems* to be that we have no idea of connexion or power at all, and that these words are absolutely without any meaning, when employed either in philosophical reasonings or common life.

But there still remains one method of avoiding this conclusion, and one source which we have not yet examined. When any natural object or event is presented, it is impossible for us, by any sagacity or penetration, to discover, or even conjecture, without experience, what event will result from it, or to carry our foresight beyond that object which is immediately present to the memory and senses. Even after one instance or experiment where we have observed a particular event to follow upon another, we are not entitled to form a general rule, or foretell what will happen in like cases; it being justly esteemed an unpardonable temerity to judge of the whole course of nature from one single experiment, however accurate or certain. But when one particular species of event has always, in all instances, been conjoined with another, we make no longer any scruple of foretelling one upon the appearance of the other, and of employing that reasoning, which can alone assure us of any matter of fact or existence. We then call the one object, *Cause;* the other, *Effect.* We suppose that there is some connexion between them; some power in the one, by which it infallibly produces the other, and operates with the greatest certainty and strongest necessity.

It appears, then, that this idea of a necessary connexion among events arises from a number of similar instances which occur of the constant conjunction of these events; nor can that idea ever be suggested by any one of these instances, surveyed in all possible lights and positions. But there is nothing in a number of instances, different from every single instance, which is supposed to be exactly similar; except only, that after a repetition of similar instances, the mind is carried by habit, upon the appearance of one event, to expect its usual attendant, and to believe that it will exist. This connexion, therefore, which we *feel* in the mind, this customary transition of the imagination from one object to its usual attendant, is the sentiment or impression from which we form the idea of power or necessary connexion. Nothing farther is in the case. Contemplate the subject on all sides; you will never find any other origin of that idea. This is the sole difference between one instance, from which we can never receive the idea of connexion, and a number of similar instances, by which it is suggested. The first time a man saw the communication of motion by impulse, as by the shock of two billiard balls, he could not pronounce that the one event was *connected:* but only that it was *conjoined* with the other. After he has observed several instances of this nature, he then pronounces them to be *connected.* What alteration has happened to give rise to this new idea of *connexion?*

Nothing but that he now *feels* these events to be *connected* in his imagination, and can readily foretell the existence of one from the appearance of the other. When we say, therefore, that one object is connected with another, we mean only that they have acquired a connexion in our thought, and give rise to this inference, by which they become proofs of each other's existence: A conclusion which is somewhat extraordinary, but which seems founded on sufficient evidence. Nor will its evidence be weakened by any general diffidence of the understanding, or sceptical suspicion concerning every conclusion which is new and extraordinary. No conclusions can be more agreeable to scepticism than such as make discoveries concerning the weakness and narrow limits of human reason and capacity.

And what stronger instance can be produced of the surprising ignorance and weakness of the understanding than the present? For surely, if there be any relation among objects which it imports to us to know perfectly, it is that of cause and effect. On this are founded all our reasonings concerning matter of fact or existence. By means of it alone we attain any assurance concerning objects which are removed from the present testimony of our memory and senses. The only immediate utility of all sciences, is to teach us, how to control and regulate future events by their causes. Our thoughts and enquiries are, therefore, every moment, employed about this relation: Yet so imperfect are the ideas which we form concerning it, that it is impossible to give any just definition of cause, except what is drawn from something extraneous and foreign to it. Similar objects are always conjoined with similar. Of this we have experience. Suitably to this experience, therefore, we may define a cause to be *an object, followed by another, and where all the objects similar to the first are followed by objects similar to the second.* Or in other words, *where, if the first object had not been, the second never had existed.* The appearance of a cause always conveys the mind, by a customary transition, to the idea of the effect. Of this also we have experience. We may, therefore, suitably to this experience, form another definition of cause, and call it, *an object followed by another, and whose appearance always conveys the thought to that other.* But though both these definitions be drawn from circumstances foreign to the cause, we cannot remedy this inconvenience, or attain any more perfect definition, which may point out that circumstance in the cause, which gives it a connexion with its effect. We have no idea of this connexion, nor even any distinct notion what it is we desire to know, where we endeavour at a conception of it. We say, for instance, that the vibration of this string is the cause of this particular sound But what do we mean by that affirmation? We either mean *that this vibration is followed by this sound, and that all similar vibrations have been followed by similar sounds: Or, that this vibration is followed by this sound, and that upon the appearance of one the mind anticipates the senses, and forms immediately an idea of the other.* We may consider the relation of cause and effect in either of these two lights; but beyond these, we have no idea of it.

To recapitulate, therefore, the reasonings of this section: Every idea is copied from some preceding impression or sentiment; and where we cannot find any impression, we may be certain that there is no idea. In all single instances of the operation of bodies or minds, there is nothing that produces any impression, nor consequently can suggest any idea of power or necessary connexion. But when many uniform instances appear, and the same object is always followed by the same event; we then begin to entertain the notion of cause and connexion. We then *feel* a new sentiment or impression, to wit, a customary connexion in the thought or imagination between one object and its usual attendant; and this sentiment is the original of that idea which we seek for. For as this idea arises from a number of similar instances, and not from any single instance, it must arise from that circumstance, in which the number of instances differ from every individual instance. But this customary connexion or transition of the imagination is the only circumstance in which they differ. In every other particular they are alike. The first instance which we saw of motion communicated by the shock of two billiard balls (to return to this obvious illustration) is exactly similar to any instance that may, at present, occur to us; except only, that we could not, at first, *infer* one event from the other; which we are enabled to do at present, after so long a course of uniform experience.

Custom, then, is the great guide of human life. It is that principle alone which renders our experience useful to us, and makes us expect, for the future, a similar train of events with those which have appeared in the past. Without the influence of custom, we should be entirely ignorant of every matter of fact beyond what is immediately present to the memory and senses. We should never know how to adjust means to ends, or to employ our natural powers in the production of any effect. There would be an end at once of all action, as well as of the chief part of speculation.

But here it may be proper to remark, that though our conclusions from experience carry us beyond our memory and senses, and assure us of matters of fact which happened in the most distant places and most remote ages, yet some fact must always be present to the senses or memory, from which we may first proceed in drawing these conclusions. A man, who should find in a desert country the remains of pompous buildings, would conclude that the country had, in ancient times, been cultivated by civilized inhabitants; but did nothing of this nature occur to him, he could never form such an inference. We learn the events of former ages from history; but then we must peruse the volumes in which this instruction is contained, and thence carry up our inferences from one testimony to another, till we arrive at the eyewitnesses and spectators of these distant events. In a word, if we proceed not upon some fact, present to the memory or senses, our reasonings would be merely hypothetical; and however the particular links might be connected with each other, the whole chain of inferences would have nothing to support it, nor could we ever, by its means, arrive at the knowledge of any real existence. If I ask why you believe any particular matter of fact, which you relate, you must tell me some reason; and this reason will be some other fact, connected with it. But as you cannot proceed after this manner, *in infinitum,* you must at last terminate in some fact, which is present to your memory or senses; or must allow that your belief is entirely without foundation.

What, then, is the conclusion of the whole matter? A simple one; though, it must be confessed, pretty remote from the common theories of philosophy. All belief of matter of fact or real existence is derived merely from some object, present to the memory or senses, and a customary conjunction between that and some other object. Or in other words; having found, in many instances, that any two kinds of objects—flame and heat, snow and cold—have always been conjoined together; if flame or snow be presented anew to the senses, the mind is carried by custom to expect heat or cold, and to *believe* that such a quality does exist, and will discover itself upon a nearer approach. This belief is the necessary result of placing the mind in such circumstances. It is an operation of the soul, when we are so situated, as unavoidable as to feel the passion of love, when we receive benefits; or hatred, when we meet with injuries. All these operations are a species of natural instincts, which no reasoning or process of the thought and understanding is able either to produce or to prevent.

Further Questions

1. Some have suggested that Hume views reality as if it were a motion picture film in which each frame (whatever happens at each moment) is entirely independent of every other frame (what happens at other moments). So far as Hume's analysis of causation is concerned, is this an accurate suggestion?
2. Suppose that ten matchsticks are decorated in the same way and so uniquely that nothing else in the universe, either before or after, is ever decorated in the same way. Each of the matchsticks is then struck and lights. If one said, "The matchsticks' being decorated as they were and then struck was the cause of their lighting," one would be wrong. It wasn't their being decorated in that way and then struck that caused them to light but, rather, their being *matchsticks*, that is, having phosphorus tips, and then struck that caused them to light. But Hume, by his definition of cause, is committed to the view that the sticks' being decorated in that way and then struck was the cause of their lighting. Hence, Hume's definition of cause is mistaken. Discuss.

Further Readings

Mackie, J. L. *The Cement of the Universe*. Oxford: Clarendon Press, 1974. A modern Humean looks at causation.

Taylor, Richard. "Causation," in *The Encyclopedia of Philosophy*. New York: Macmillan, 1967, Vol. 1, pp. 56–66. An excellent historical survey and statement of the main remaining problems.

Considerations on the Universe as a Whole 44

ALBERT EINSTEIN

A brief biography of Einstein appears on page 80.

In this selection, Einstein explains his model of the universe and the structure of space-time.

Reading Questions

1. What view of the universe is out of harmony with Newton's theory?
2. What is the dilemma that forced Seeliger to modify Newton's law?
3. How is it possible for the universe to be finite yet unbounded?
4. Does Einstein think the universe is Euclidean?
5. What is the structure of space according to the General Theory of Relativity?

COSMOLOGICAL DIFFICULTIES OF NEWTON'S THEORY

IF WE PONDER over the question as to how the universe, considered as a whole, is to be regarded, the first answer that suggests itself to us is surely this: As regards space (and time) the universe is infinite. There are stars everywhere, so that the density of matter, although very variable in detail, is nevertheless on the average everywhere the same. In other words: However far we might travel through space, we should find everywhere an attenuated swarm of fixed stars of approximately the same kind and density.

This view is not in harmony with the theory of Newton. The latter theory rather requires that the universe should have a kind of centre in which the density of the stars is a maximum, and that as we proceed outwards from this centre the group-density of the stars should diminish, until finally, at great distances, it is succeeded by an infinite region of emptiness. The stellar universe ought to be a finite island in the infinite ocean of space.

This conception is in itself not very satisfactory. It is still less satisfactory because it leads to the result that the light emitted by the stars and also individual stars of the stellar system are perpetually passing out into infinite space, never to return, and without ever again coming into interaction with other objects of nature. Such a finite material universe would be destined to become gradually but systematically impoverished.

In order to escape this dilemma, Seeliger suggested a modification of Newton's law, in which he assumes that for great distances the force of attraction between two masses diminishes more rapidly than would result from the inverse square law. In this way it is possible for the mean density of matter to be constant everywhere, even to infinity, without infinitely large gravitational fields being produced. We thus free ourselves from the distasteful conception that the material universe ought to possess something of the nature of a centre. Of course we purchase our emancipation from the fundamental difficulties mentioned, at the cost of a modification and complication of Newton's law

which has neither empirical nor theoretical foundation. We can imagine innumerable laws which would serve the same purpose, without our being able to state a reason why one of them is to be preferred to the others; for any one of these laws would be founded just as little on more general theoretical principles as is the law of Newton.

THE POSSIBILITY OF A "FINITE" AND YET "UNBOUNDED" UNIVERSE

But speculations on the structure of the universe also move in quite another direction. The development of non-Euclidean geometry led to the recognition of the fact, that we can cast doubt on the *infiniteness* of our space without coming into conflict with the laws of thought or with experience (Riemann, Helmholtz). These questions have already been treated in detail and with unsurpassable lucidity by Helmholtz and Poincaré, whereas I can only touch on them briefly here.

In the first place, we imagine an existence in two-dimensional space. Flat beings with flat implements, and in particular flat rigid measuring-rods, are free to move in a *plane*. For them nothing exists outside of this plane: that which they observe to happen to themselves and to their flat "things" is the all-inclusive reality of their plane . . . In contrast to ours, the universe of these beings is two-dimensional; but, like ours, it extends to infinity. In their universe there is room for an infinite number of identical squares made up of rods, i.e. its volume (surface) is infinite. If these beings say their universe is "plane," there is sense in the statement, because they mean that they can perform the constructions of plane Euclidean geometry with their rods. In this connection the individual rods always represent the same distance, independently of their position.

Let us consider now a second two-dimensional existence, but this time on a spherical surface instead of on a plane. The flat beings with their measuring rods and other objects fit exactly on this surface and they are unable to leave it. Their whole universe of observation extends exclusively over the surface of the sphere. Are these beings able to

From Albert Einstein, Relativity: The Special and General Theory, *translated by R. W. Lawson, 1920, Part III, Chapters 30–32.*

regard the geometry of their universe as being plane geometry and their rods withal as the realisation of "distance"? They cannot do this. For if they attempt to realise a straight line, they will obtain a curve, which we "three-dimensional beings" designate as a great circle, i.e. a self-contained line of definite finite length, which can be measured up by means of a measuring-rod. Similarly, this universe has a finite area, that can be compared with the area of a square constructed with rods. The great charm resulting from this consideration lies in the recognition of the fact that *the universe of these beings is finite and yet has no limits.*

But the spherical-surface beings do not need to go on a world-tour in order to perceive that they are not living in a Euclidean universe. They can convince themselves of this on every part of their "world," provided they do not use too small a piece of it. Starting from a point, they draw "straight lines" (arcs of circles as judged in three-dimensional space) of equal length in all directions. They will call the line joining the free ends of these lines a "circle." For a plane surface, the ratio of the circumference of a circle to its diameter, both lengths being measured with the same rod, is, according to Euclidean geometry of the plane, equal to a constant value π, which is independent of the diameter of the circle. On their spherical surface our flat beings would find for this ratio the value

$$\pi \, \frac{\sin \dfrac{r}{R}}{\dfrac{r}{R}},$$

i.e. a smaller value than π, the difference being the more considerable, the greater is the radius of the circle in comparison with the radius R of the "world-sphere." By means of this relation the spherical beings can determine the radius of their universe ("world"), even when only a relatively small part of their world-sphere is available for their measurements. But if this part is very small indeed, they will no longer be able to demonstrate that they are on a spherical "world" and not on a Euclidean plane, for a small part of a spherical surface differs only slightly from a piece of a plane of the same size.

Thus if the spherical-surface beings are living on a planet of which the solar system occupies only a negligibly small part of the spherical universe, they have no means of determining whether they are living in a finite or in an infinite universe, because the "piece of the universe" to which they have access is in both cases practically plane, or Euclidean. It follows directly from this discussion, that for our sphere-beings the circumference of a circle first increases with the radius until the "circumference of the universe" is reached, and that it thenceforward gradually decreases to zero for still further increasing values of the radius. During this process the area of the circle continues to increase more and more, until finally it becomes equal to the total area of the whole "world-sphere."

Perhaps the reader will wonder why we have placed our "beings" on a sphere rather than on another closed surface. But this choice has its justification in the fact that, of all closed surfaces, the sphere is unique in possessing the property that all points on it are equivalent. I admit that the ratio of the circumference c of a circle to its radius r depends on r, but for a given value of r it is the same for all points of the "world-sphere"; in other words, the "world-sphere" is a "surface of constant curvature."

To this two-dimensional sphere-universe there is a three-dimensional analogy, namely, the three-dimensional spherical space which was discovered by Riemann. Its points are likewise all equivalent. It possesses a finite volume, which is determined by its "radius" ($2\pi^2 R^3$). Is it possible to imagine a spherical space? To imagine a space means nothing else than that we imagine an epitome of our "space" experience, i.e. of experience that we can have in the movement of "rigid" bodies. In this sense we *can* imagine a spherical space.

Suppose we draw lines or stretch strings in all directions from a point, and mark off from each of these the distance r with a measuring-rod. All the free end-points of these lengths lie on a spherical surface. We can specially measure up the area (F) of this surface by means of a square made up of measuring-rods. If the universe is Euclidean, then $F = 4\pi r^2$; if it is spherical, then F is always less than $4\pi r^2$. With increasing values of r, F increases from zero up to a maximum value which is determined by the "world-radius," but for still further increasing values of r, the area gradually diminishes to zero. At first, the straight lines which radiate from the starting point diverge farther and farther from one another, but later they approach each other, and finally they run together again at a "counter-point" to the starting point. Under such conditions they have traversed the whole spherical space. It is easily seen that the three-dimensional spherical space is quite analogous to the two-dimensional spherical surface. It is finite (i.e. of finite volume), and has no bounds.

It may be mentioned that there is yet another kind of curved space: "elliptical space." It can be regarded as a curved space in which the two "counter-points" are identical (indistinguishable from each other). An elliptical universe can thus be considered to some extent as a curved universe possessing central symmetry.

It follows from what has been said, that closed spaces without limits are conceivable. From amongst these, the spherical space (and the elliptical) excels in its simplicity, since all points on it are equivalent. As a result of this discussion, a most interesting question arises for astronomers and physicists, and that is whether the universe in which we live is infinite, or whether it is finite in the manner of the spherical universe. Our experience is far from being sufficient to enable us to answer this question. But the general theory of relativity permits of our answering it with a moderate degree of certainty, and in this connection the difficulty mentioned above finds its solution.

THE STRUCTURE OF SPACE ACCORDING TO THE GENERAL THEORY OF RELATIVITY

According to the general theory of relativity, the geometrical properties of space are not independent but they are determined by matter. Thus we can draw conclusions about the geometrical structure of the universe only if we base our considerations on the state of the matter as being something that is known. We know from experience that, for a suitably chosen co-ordinate system, the velocities of the stars are small as compared with the velocity of transmission of light. We can thus as a rough approximation arrive at a conclusion as to the nature of the universe as a whole, if we treat the matter as being at rest.

We already know from our previous discussion that the behaviour of measuring-rods and clocks is influenced by gravitational fields, i.e. by the distribution of matter. This in itself is sufficient to exclude the possibility of the exact validity of Euclidean geometry in our universe. But it is conceivable that our universe differs only slightly from a Euclidean one, and this notion seems all the more probable, since calculations show that the metrics of surrounding space is influenced only to an exceedingly small extent by masses even of the magnitude of our sun. We might imagine that, as regards geometry, our universe behaves analogously to a surface which is irregularly curved in its individual parts, but which nowhere departs appreciably from a plane: something like the rippled surface of a lake. Such a universe might fittingly be called a quasi-Euclidean universe. As regards its space it would be infinite. But calculation shows that in a quasi-Euclidean universe the average density of matter would necessarily be *nil*. Thus such a universe could not be inhabited by matter everywhere; it would present to us that unsatisfactory picture which we portrayed.

If we are to have in the universe an average density of matter which differs from zero, however small may be that difference, then the universe cannot be quasi-Euclidean. On the contrary, the results of calculation indicate that if matter be distributed uniformly, the universe would necessarily be spherical (or elliptical). Since in reality the detailed distribution of matter is not uniform, the real universe will deviate in individual parts from the spherical, i.e. the universe will be quasi-spherical. But it will be necessarily finite. In fact, the theory supplies us with a simple connection between the space-expanse of the universe and the average density of matter in it.

Further Questions

1. What would the spherical beings, in Einstein's discussion, experience if they traveled through their space forever?

2. When you think of curved space, what do you imagine as being curved? Curved emptiness? Or what?
3. Thinking about the universe as a whole, do you picture yourself outside it? If so, *from* where are you picturing it?
4. What do you suppose Wittgenstein would say about seeing the universe as a whole?

Further Readings

Einstein, Albert. *Relativity: The Special and General Theory*. R. W. Lawson, trans. New York: Peter Smith, 1920. A comprehensive and very readable treatment by its creator of both aspects of relativity.

Singh, Jagjit. *Great Ideas and Theories of Modern Cosmology*. New York: Dover, 1961. A survey for beginners of cosmological theories.

Tractatus Logico-Philosophicus   45

LUDWIG WITTGENSTEIN

Ludwig Wittgenstein (1889–1951) was born to one of the wealthiest families in Vienna. After studying engineering, mathematics, and physical sciences, he went to England to do research in aeronautical engineering (the forerunner of aerospace engineering), making possible the fateful meeting of two of the greatest minds of the twentieth century. Bertrand Russell, in his autobiography, describes how he came to meet Wittgenstein at Cambridge before World War I. Apparently, while doing his engineering mathematics, Wittgenstein began to ponder what it was about the world and the mind that made mathematics possible. Not finding an answer in any of his mathematics books, he asked whom he should consult. Russell says:

> Somebody mentioned my name, and he took up his residence at Trinity. He was perhaps the most perfect example I have ever known of genius as traditionally conceived, passionate, profound, intense, and dominating. He had a kind of purity which I have never known equalled except by G. E. Moore. I remember taking him once to a meeting of the Aristotelian Society, at which there were various fools whom I treated politely. When we came away he raged and stormed against my [moral] degradation in not telling these men what fools they were. His life was turbulent and troubled, and his personal force was extraordinary. . . . He used to come to see me every evening at midnight, and pace up and down my room like a wild beast for three hours in agitated silence. Once I said to him: "Are you thinking about logic or about your sins?" "Both," he replied, and continued his pacing. I did not like to suggest that it was time for bed, as it seemed probable both to him and me that on leaving me he would commit suicide.
>
> At the end of his first term at Trinity, he came to me and said: "Do you think I am an absolute idiot?" I said: "Why do you want to know?" He replied: "Because if I am I shall become an aeronaut, but if I am not I shall become a philosopher." I said to him: "My dear fellow, I don't know whether you are an absolute idiot or not, but if you will write me an essay during the vacation upon any philosophical topic that interests you, I will read it and tell you." He did so, and brought it to me at the beginning of the next term. As soon as I read the first sentence, I became persuaded that he was a man of genius, and assured him that he should on no account become an aeronaut.[1]

When Russell asked the great G. E. Moore, another legendary Cambridge philosopher, what he thought of Wittgenstein, Moore replied that he thought very well of him "because at my lectures he looks puzzled, and nobody else ever looks puzzled."

World War I interrupted Wittgenstein's studies with Russell and he became an officer in the Austrian army—completing his doctoral dissertation in the trenches! The work, *Tractatus Logico-Philosophicus,* which you are about to read, was the only book of Wittgenstein's published in his lifetime but it helped create the revolution in modern philosophy that led to the development of logical positivism, linguistic analysis, and semantics. The noted Oxford philosopher P. F. Strawson called Wittgenstein "the preeminent philosopher of this century." The profound effect Wittgenstein has had on philosophy cannot be overstated. In an intimate letter to a woman friend, Russell describes hauntingly the influence his student had on him:

> Do you remember that at the time when you were seeing Vittoz I wrote a lot of stuff about Theory of Knowledge, which Wittgenstein criticized with the greatest severity? His criticism, though I don't think you realized it at the time, was an event of first-rate importance in my life, and affected everything I have done since. I saw he was right, and I saw that I could not hope ever again to do fundamental work in philosophy. My impulse was shattered, like a wave dashed to pieces against a breakwater. I became filled with utter despair. . . .[2]

In the following reading, Wittgenstein makes clear the relationship between language and thought and shows how through them the mind is able to hook onto reality. He warns, in the preface, that probably the book won't be understood unless the reader "has himself already had the thoughts that are expressed in it—or at least similar thoughts."

NOTES

1. From *The Autobiography of Bertrand Russell* (Boston: Little, Brown, 1951), pp. 142–143.
2. Ibid., p. 68.

Reading Questions

1. What is the relationship between facts and the world? What does Wittgenstein mean by *the world*? By *fact*?
2. What determines the way the world is?
3. What is a state of affairs? What is reality?
4. How, and why, does Wittgenstein distinguish reality from the world?
5. What is a picture?
6. What is a thought?
7. What is a picture of the world? What is the relationship between a picture of reality and a model of reality as we imagine it? With what is reality compared?
8. What would we have to do to represent logical form? Can this be done? Why?
9. What does the simplest kind of proposition do? How can you tell if a proposition is elementary?
10. To give complete description of the world, what would you have to have?
11. Why are the limits of my language the limits of my world?
12. What is the key to the problem of solipsism?
13. What does Wittgenstein mean when he says, "The world is *my* world"?
14. What does the proposition "I am my world" have to do with solipsism "coinciding" with reality? What is most mystical about the world?

1   The world is all that is the case.

1.1   The world is the totality of facts, not of things.

. . . .

2   What is the case—a fact—is the existence of states of affairs.

2.1   We picture facts to ourselves.

. . . .

3   A logical picture of facts is a thought.

. . . .

3.01   The totality of true thoughts is a picture of the world.

. . . .

4   A thought is a proposition with a sense.

. . . .

4.01   A proposition is a picture of reality. A proposition is a model of reality as we imagine it.

. . . .

4.12   Propositions can represent the whole of reality, but they cannot represent what they must have in common with reality in order to be able to represent it—logical form.

In order to be able to represent logical form, we should have to be able to station ourselves with propositions somewhere outside logic, that is to say outside the world.

. . . .

5   A proposition is a truth-function of elementary propositions.

. . . .

5.6   *The limits of my language* mean the limits of my world.

. . . .

5.63   I am my world.

. . . .

5.64   Here it can be seen that solipsism, when its implications are followed out strictly, coincides with pure realism. The self of solipsism shrinks to a point without extension, and there remains the reality co-ordinated with it.

. . . .

6.44   It is not *how* things are in the world that is mystical, but *that* it exists.

. . . .

6.45   . . . Feeling the world as a limited whole—it is this that is mystical.

. . . .

6.5   When the answer cannot be put into words, neither can the question be put into words.

The *riddle* does not exist.

If a question can be framed at all, it is also *possible* to answer it.

. . . .

6.54   My propositions serve as elucidations in the following way: anyone who understands me eventually recognizes them as nonsensical, when he has used them—as steps—to climb up beyond them. (He must, so to speak, throw away the ladder after he has climbed up it.)

He must transcend these propositions, and then he will see the world aright.

. . . .

7   What we cannot speak about we must pass over in silence.

From Ludwig Wittgenstein, Tractatus Logico-Philosophicus, *translated by D. F. Pears and E. F. McGuinness (New Jersey: Humanities Press International, Inc. 1961).*

Further Questions

1. What impression do you form of Wittgenstein's view of the world?
2. What is your impression of his view of *the self*?
3. Wittgenstein sometimes claimed to be writing philosophical poetry. Does what you just read have anything in common with poetry?

Further Readings

Kolak, Daniel. *Wittgenstein's Tractatus*. Mountain View, CA: Mayfield, 1998. A new translation, which Jaakko Hintikka calls "a fresh translation . . . which offers a new projection of Wittgenstein's German into English."
Monk, Ray. *Ludwig Wittgenstein: The Duty of Genius*. New York: Macmillan, 1990. The greatest and fullest biography of Wittgenstein. Monk tries to relate Wittgenstein's philosophy to his life.
Ramsey, Frank. "Critical Notice of Ludwig Wittgenstein's *Tractatus Logico-Philosophicus*," in *Mind* XXXII, no. 128 (1923), pp. 465–478. The best short introduction to the *Tractatus*.

46   Fiction

ROBERT NOZICK

Robert Nozick teaches philosophy at Harvard University. His writings range across the entire spectrum of philosophy, but he is perhaps best known for his controversial contribution to political philosophy, *Anarchy, State and Utopia,* New York: Basic Books, 1974. He is also the author of *Philosophical Explanations* (Harvard 1981) and *The Nature of Rationality* (Princeton 1983). One of his latest is *Socratic Puzzles* (Harvard 1997). In this selection, Nozick suggests that there may be no way to tell whether we are fictional or real.

Reading Questions

1. What does Nozick mean by "fiction"? How does being fictional, in his sense, differ from being real, in your sense?
2. Previous selections consider the distinction between dreams and reality. Is the distinction between fiction and reality the same distinction or a different one?

I AM A FICTIONAL CHARACTER. However, you would be in error to smile smugly, feeling ontologically superior. For you are a fictional character too. All my readers are except one who is, properly, not reader but author.

I am a fictional character; this is *not*, however, a work of fiction, no more so than any other work you've ever read. It is not a modernist work that self-consciously *says* it's a work of fiction, nor one even more tricky that denies its fictional status. We all are familiar with such works and know how to deal with them, how to frame them so that *nothing* the author says—nothing the first person voices even in an afterword or in something headed "author's note"—can convince us that anyone is speaking seriously, *non*-fictionally in his own first person.

All the more severe is my own problem of informing you that this very piece you are reading is a work of non-fiction, yet we are fictional characters, nevertheless. *Within* this world of fiction we inhabit, this writing is non-fictional, although in a wider sense, encased as it is in a work of fiction, it too can only be a fiction.

Think of our world as a novel in which you yourself are a character. Is there any way to tell what our author is like? Perhaps. *If* this is a work in which the author *expresses* himself, we can draw inferences about his facets, while noting that each such inference we draw will be written by him. And if he writes that we find a particular inference plausible or valid, who are we to argue?

One sacred scripture in the novel we inhabit says that the author of our universe created things merely by speaking, by saying "Let there be . . ." The only thing mere speaking can create, we know, is a story, a play, an epic poem, a fiction. Where we live is created by and in words: a uni-verse.

Recall what is known as the problem of evil: why does a good creator allow evil in the world, evil he knows of and can prevent? However, when an author includes monstrous deeds—pain and suffering—in his work, does this cast any special doubt upon his goodness? Is an author callous who puts his characters through hardships? Not if the characters do not suffer them *really*. But don't they? Wasn't Hamlet's father really killed? (Or was he merely hiding to see how Hamlet would respond?) Lear really was cast adrift—he didn't just dream this. Macbeth, on the other hand, did *not* see a real dagger. But these characters aren't real and never were, so there was no suffering outside of the world of the work, no *real* suffering in the author's *own* world, and so in his creating, the author was not cruel. (Yet why is it cruel only when he creates suffering in his *own* world? Would it be perfectly all right for Iago to create misery in *our* world?)

"What!" you say, "we don't really undergo suffering? Why it's as real to us as Oedipus' is to him." Precisely as real. "But can't you *prove* that you *really*

exist?" If Shakespeare had Hamlet say "I think, therefore I am," would that prove to us that Hamlet exists? Should it prove that to Hamlet, and if so what is such proof worth? Could not *any* proof be written into a work of fiction and be presented by one of the characters, perhaps one named "Descartes"? (Such a character should worry less that he's dreaming, more that he's dreamed.)

Often, people discover anomalies in the world, facts that just don't jibe. The deeper dug, the more puzzles found—far-fetched coincidences, dangling facts—on these feed conspiracy and assassination buffs. That number of hours spent probing into *anything* might produce anomalies, however, if reality is not as coherent as we thought, if it is not *real*. Are we simply discovering the limits of the details the author worked out? But *who* is discovering this? The author who writes our discoveries knows them himself. Perhaps he now is preparing to correct them. Do we live in galley proofs in the process of being corrected? Are we living in a *first draft*?

My tendency, I admit, is to want to revolt, to conspire along with the rest of you to overthrow our author or to make our positions more equal, at least, to hide some portion of our lives from him—to gain a little breathing space. Yet these words I write he reads, my secret thoughts and modulations of feeling he knows and records, my Jamesian author.

But does he *control* it all? Or does our author, through writing, learn about his characters and from them? Is he surprised by what he finds us doing and thinking? When we feel we freely think or act on our own, is this merely a description he has written in for us, or does he *find* it to be true of us, his characters, and therefore write it? Does our leeway and privacy reside in this, that there are some implications of his work that he hasn't yet worked out, some things he has not thought of which nevertheless are true in the world he has created, so that there are actions and thoughts of ours that elude his ken? (Must we therefore speak *in code*?) Or is he only ignorant of what we *would* do or say in some *other* circumstances, so that our independence lies only in the *subjunctive* realm?

Does this way madness lie? Or enlightenment?

Our author, we know, is outside our realm, yet he may not be free of our problems. Does he wonder too whether *he* is a character in a work of fiction, whether his writing our universe is a play within a play? Does he have me write this work and especially this very paragraph in order to express his own concerns?

It would be nice for us if our author too is a fictional character and this fictional world he made describes (that being no coincidence) the actual world inhabited by *his* author, the one who created him. We then would be fictional characters who, unbeknownst to our own author although not to his, correspond to real people. (Is that why we are so true to life?)

Must there be a top-floor somewhere, a world that itself is not created in someone else's fiction? Or can the hierarchy go on infinitely? Are circles excluded, even quite narrow ones where a character of one world creates another fictional world wherein a character creates the first world? Might the circle get narrower, still?

Various theories have described our world as less real than another, even as an illusion. The idea of our having this inferior ontological status takes some getting used to, however. It may help if we approach our situation as literary critics and ask the genre of our universe, whether tragedy, farce, or theater-of-the-absurd? What is the plot line, and which act are we in?

Still, our status may bring some compensations, as, for example, that we live on even after we die, preserved permanently in the work of fiction. Or if not permanently, at least for as long as our book lasts. May we hope to inhabit an enduring masterpiece rather than a quickly remaindered book?

Moreover, though in some sense it might be false, in another wouldn't it be true for Hamlet to say, "I am Shakespeare"? What do Macbeth, Banquo, Desdemona, and Prospero have in common? The consciousness of the one author, Shakespeare, which underlies and infuses each of them. (So too, there is the brotherhood of man.) Playing on the intricacy both of our ontological status and of the first person reflexive pronoun, each of us too may truly say, "I am the author."

NOTE FROM THE AUTHOR

Suppose I now tell you that the preceding *was* a work of fiction and the "I" didn't refer to me, the author, but a first person character. Or suppose I tell you that it was *not* a work of fiction but a playful, and so of course serious, philosophical essay by me, Robert Nozick. (*Not* the Robert Nozick named as author at the beginning of this work—he may be, for all we know, another literary persona—but the one who attended P.S. 165.) How would your response to this whole work differ depending on which I say, supposing you were willing, as you won't be, simply to accept my statement?

May I decide *which* to say, fiction or philosophical essay, only now, as I finish writing this, and how will that decision affect the character of what already was set down previously? May I postpone the decision further, perhaps until after you have read this, fixing its status and genre and only then?

Perhaps God has not decided *yet* whether he has created, in this world, a fictional world or a real one. Is the Day of Judgment the day he will decide? Yet what additional thing depends upon which way he decides—what would either decision add to our situation or subtract from it?

And which decision do you hope for?

Further Questions

1. Are you fictional or real? How do you know?
2. Does it make any difference—either theoretically, in terms of how you think about yourself, or practically, in terms of how you lead your life—whether you are fictional or real?
3. Nozick suggests that if we are fictional, the problem of evil may not arise. Is he right? If he is, is this part of the answer to the previous question?

Further Readings

Ghose, Zulfikar. *The Fiction of Reality* (London: Macmillan, 1983).
Lamarque, Peter. *Truth, Fiction, and Literature: A Philosophical Perspective* (New York: Oxford University Press, 1994).

Quantum Cosmology, the Anthropic Principle, and Why Is There Something Rather Than Nothing? 47

DANIEL KOLAK

Daniel Kolak came to philosophy from physics and astronomy. A brief biography of him appears on page 96.

In this selection, Kolak explains the developments in quantum mechanics leading up to the current view in physics that the universe came from nowhere and out of nothing, as well as the anthropic principle according to which the reason the universe exists is that we are here to observe it. He puts the recent "mind-boggling" aspects of quantum mechanics into philosophical perspective by showing that such a view of reality is a version of nineteenth-century absolute idealism. Kolak then asks whether science's ultimate answer to the enigma of existence fares any better than religion's against the biggest question of all time: *Why is there something rather than nothing?*

Reading Questions

1. Can you imagine nothingness? What happens when you try?
2. What is the biggest question, and why?
3. What is a question?
4. Why is *God* not an answer to the biggest question?
5. What is a *black hole*?
6. What is a *singularity*?
7. What is the Anthropic Principle?
8. What is idealism?
9. Is quantum mechanics a type of idealism? What type?
10. What does it mean, in quantum mechanics, to say that something is objectively real?
11. What was the disagreement between Einstein and Bohr?
12. What was the purpose of the Einstein-Podolsky-Rosen thought experiment?
13. What role does God play in Wheeler's theory?

Nothingness lies coiled in the heart of being, like a worm.

—JEAN-PAUL SARTRE, *Being and Nothingness*

1. THE CREATION OF THE UNIVERSE FROM NOTHING

GENESIS ACCORDING TO QUANTUM COSMOL-OGY goes something like this: *In the beginning there was nothing.* No space. No time. No matter, no energy. Not even emptiness. Emptiness implies a container and there were no containing spaces of any kind. There was just nothing. No universe, no thinkers, no thoughts, no consciousness. *Absolutely nothing existed.*

Then, spontaneously and from out of nowhere, *something:* the big bang. The universe started out, about fifteen billion years ago, as a tiny dot of existence, the tiniest little dot imaginable—the size of the Planck length, to be exact, 10^{-33} centimeters—and began to expand at the speed of light to its present, ever-expanding size of about 10^{28} cm across. (The big bang of course is a misnomer; the event was of the smallest possible diameter, and it was *completely silent,* since there were no sound waves. A slightly more accurate name would be "the teeny, tiny silence.")

What about *before* the big bang? There was no "before" since not just space and matter but also time itself began in that tiny and brief moment of cosmic birth, before which there was absolutely nothing. Contemporary quantum cosmology does not end where the universe begins. It reaches beyond the beginning of time, into the very heart of nonexistence itself, where from a state of absolute nothingness it supposedly brings forth the ultimate answer why.

Why did the big bang happen? Why didn't nothing just stay nothing? That is, why did nothing "degenerate" or "cease to be nothing" so as to make way for, or give rise to, something—the universe? The answer from contemporary quantum physics is that the state in which nothing exists *is an unstable state.* In physics there are two levels of nothing: the virtual vacuum and the absolute vacuum. The virtual vacuum of empty space is at the bottom level a state of quasi-nothing, an abyss of unactuality that amounts to a frothing sea of infinite possibility. Beneath that virtual vacuum is an absolute void that is a complete and total negation of everything, an utter state of nothingness that cannot so remain because of its own *nonexistence*—quantum instability, which gives the nothing a tendency toward some-

thing, toward actualization. In short, the ultimate answer to the ultimate question, according to the physicist Alan Guth, one of the leading proponents today of the "inflationary universe" model of the big bang, is this: "the nothing is unstable."

On the face of it, this sounds extremely odd and paradoxical. How can one speak of *nothing* and then go on to say that it is unstable? If there is nothing there, how can "it" be unstable or stable? (There is no *it!*) *What* is unstable? We might be able to understand how, for instance, one might say that having no money, no house, no food, and so on, makes you unstable—provided there is someone there, you, who is penniless, homeless, and hungry. This is certainly not a very stable position to be in. But if there is no one there, then hopelessness is not there either, neither is the pennilessness. So how can it make sense to talk of *nothing* as being unstable?

2. SINGULARITIES, BLACK HOLES, AND THE BOUNDARIES BETWEEN SOMETHING AND NOTHING

Whether the universe had a beginning in time or is eternal, in both cases if one does *cosmology*—the study of the universe as a whole—one *must,* necessarily, have to deal with the problem of the concept of nothing. For if by "universe," we mean the totality of existence, then we must necessarily—directly or indirectly—talk about an ultimate boundary beyond which there is not anything—i.e., we must ultimately come up against *nothing.* And as we shall see, such boundaries have been constructed in mathematical models, first from models of such boundaries *within* the universe itself and then, ultimately, at its outermost edges (where "edge" is understood as a boundary of a four-dimensional manifold spacetime sphere).

The boundaries between something and nothing *within* the universe are called the *event horizons* of *black holes*—places within the universe where due to gravitational collapse a star crushes itself out of existence in a sort of stellar suicide. Stephen Hawking, the famous physicist who much of his adult life has been bound to a wheelchair and whose voice cannot be understood except through

THE FIRST HUNDREDTH OF A SECOND

Steven Weinberg

In the beginning there was an explosion. Not an explosion like those familiar on earth, starting from a definite center and spreading out to engulf more and more of the circumambient air, but an explosion which occurred simultaneously everywhere, filling all space from the beginning, with every particle of matter rushing apart from every other particle. "All space" in this context may mean either all of an infinite universe, or all of a finite universe which curves back on itself like the surface of a sphere. Neither possibility is easy to comprehend, but this will not get in our way; it matters hardly at all in the early universe whether space is finite or infinite.

At about one-hundredth of a second, the earliest time about which we can speak with any confidence, the temperature of the universe was about a hundred thousand million (10^{11}) degrees Centigrade. This is much hotter than in the center of even the hottest star, so hot, in fact, that none of the components of ordinary matter, molecules, or atoms, or even the nuclei of atoms, could have held together. Instead, the matter rushing apart in this explosion consisted of various types of the so-called elementary particles. . . .

In addition to electrons and positrons, there were roughly similar numbers of various kinds of neutrinos, ghostly particles with no mass or electric charge whatever. Finally, the universe was filled with light. . . .

These particles—electrons, positrons, neutrinos, photons—were continually being created out of pure energy, and then after short lives being annihilated again. Their number therefore was not preordained, but fixed instead by a balance between processes of creation and annihilation.

From *The First Three Minutes: A Modern View of the Origin of the Universe* (1976).

an interpreter, provided the first fully working mathematical models of such structures, though the idea was already proposed several centuries earlier by Laplace. In his *Exposition of the System of the World*,[1] Laplace suggested that if the universe contained a star 250 times the diameter of the sun but with the same density as the Earth, its gravitational field would be so strong that no light or signals of any kind could escape. Then, in a little known paper, he offered a proof.[2] In 1939, Evan Oppenheimer and a collaborator showed that inside a black hole not just matter but space and time themselves would have to come to an end. For a long time, physicists thought this was just an aberration of the mathematical models. But then in 1965 Roger Penrose and, five years later, Stephen Hawking and Penrose provided what are called *singularity theorems,* which established within the classical theory of general relativity that whenever there is gravitational collapse space-time singularities—"rips" in the fabric of space-time—will *have* to occur. Hawking then went on to show how to represent such bordered regions of nothingness mathematically, as stars collapsing out of existence, leaving a "missing point" in space-time, a space-time tunneling out of the universe into nothing. Their reasoning was that if light cannot escape, then *no information whatsoever* can escape from that location which, in terms of quantum mechanics, means, in effect, *there is nothing there.*

When a tree falls in a forest and there is no one there to hear it, does it make a sound? Well, if by *sound* you mean the *thump,* the answer is *no;* if you mean *sound waves* the answer is *yes.* Air goes out in

IS THE UNIVERSE A FREE LUNCH?

Paul Davies

We can . . . construct a cosmic scenario that reveals the astonishing scope of the new physics to explain the physical world. . . . Recent discoveries in particle physics have suggested mechanisms whereby matter can be created in empty space by the cosmic gravitational field, which only leaves the origin of spacetime itself as a mystery. But even here there are some indications that space and time could have sprung into existence spontaneously without violating the laws of physics. . . . In this remarkable scenario, the entire cosmos simply comes out of nowhere, completely in accordance with the laws of quantum physics, and creates along the way all the matter and energy needed to build the universe we now see. It thus incorporates the creation of all physical things, including space and time. Rather than postulate an unknowable singularity to start the universe off, the quantum spacetime model attempts to explain everything entirely within the context of the laws of physics. It is an awesome claim. We are used to the idea of "putting something in and getting something out," but getting something for nothing (or out of nothing) is alien. Yet the world of quantum physics routinely produces something for nothing. Quantum gravity suggests we might get everything for nothing. Discussing this scenario, the physicist Alan Guth remarked: "It is often said that there is no such thing as a free lunch. The universe, however, is a free lunch." . . . The "free lunch" scenario claims all you need are the laws—the universe can take care of itself, including its own creation.

From *God and the New Physics*.

sound waves and the sound waves are not, themselves, loud or soft, thumps or bumps; they come in varying lengths. It takes some sort of ear connected to a brain to react to those wavelengths and create an audible event that *sounds like something*. Air waves, by themselves, don't sound like anything. The answer to that old supposedly unanswerable question is *it depends on what you mean*, and certainly in any case *something* happened; you can go into that forest and find the information there: the logs, the effect on the surrounding foliage, and so on. In other words, the information has been preserved, and a good scientist could go in and tell you fairly precisely when the tree fell, perhaps within a margin of a few weeks. But the situation with black holes is different. The very structure of *things "as things"* requires that the information of that thing be contained in, say, a geometry to give it shape, some sort of bordered connections separating it from other things via differential structures (described mathematically by differential equations), some sort of operational logic to give it functional consistency, laws or rules governing behavior, and so on. In a black hole, all these are crushed out of existence. It would be more like asking the old question about the tree in the forest this way: if an imaginary tree fell in a nonexistent forest and there was nobody there to hear the nonexistent sound which we are here now figuratively describing in an imaginary story using words, would it make a sound? The answer to that question is *no*.

Penrose and Hawking realized that the black hole singularities—"nothings contained" within the universe—were predicted by Einstein's equations. So they worked out the equations with which we could, by studying the properties of such objects as they made their exit from the universe into nothing, study the boundary between something and nothing, perfectly precisely, in their mathematical model. Hawking then went on to show how the universe as a whole could be viewed as being a black hole, such that the boundary between the universe and the end of the universe—

On Hume and Quantum Mechanics

John Bell

[The Bell Theorem] comes from an analysis of the consequences of the idea that there should be no action at a distance, under certain conditions that Einstein, Podolsky, and Rosen focused attention on in 1935 — conditions which lead to some very strange correlations as predicted by quantum mechanics . . . I believe that there certainly are paradoxes. The problem of measurement and the observer is the problem of where the measurement begins and ends, and where the observer begins and ends. Consider my spectacles, for example: if I take them off now, how far away must I put them before they are part of the object rather than part of the observer? There are problems like this all the way from the retina through the optic nerve to the brain and so on. I think, that — when you analyze this language that the physicists have fallen into, that physics is about the results of observations — you find that on analysis it evaporates, and nothing very clear is being said. . . . I'm quite convinced that quantum theory is only a temporary expedient. . . . it does not really explain things; in fact the founding fathers of quantum mechanics rather prided themselves on giving up on the idea of explanation. They were very proud that they dealt only with phenomena: they refused to look behind the phenomena, regarding that as the price one had to pay for coming to terms with nature. And it is a fact of history that the people who took that agnostic attitude towards the real world on the microphysical level were very successful. At the time it was a good thing to do. But I don't believe it will be so indefinitely. Of course, I cannot produce theorems to that effect. If you go back to, say, David Hume, who made a careful analysis of our reasons for believing things, you find that there is no good reason for believing that the sun will come up tomorrow. . . . It's a habit we have, of believing that things will continue very much as they did before. However, it is a fact that this seems to be a good habit! I cannot make that a theorem, because I think Hume's analysis is sound, but nevertheless I do believe it's a good habit, to look for explanations.

From *The Ghost in the Atom*, Paul Davies, ed.

the boundary between *all* of existence and *all the rest of nothing* — could in principle be rendered, perfectly precisely, into conceptual view. They showed how it was possible to construct a mathematical model of a singularity not just as the *ending* of space-time but the *beginning* of space-time as well: the big bang was thus viewed as an *initial* singularity that brought all the space-time, matter-energy, and laws of physics into existence from virtually nothing.

There can be no question but that the most complete, successful, and effective representations of the physical world to date are to be found in mathematical models arising out of relativity and quantum mechanics. All the most important laws can be described mathematically and the most important mathematics involved is that of differential equations. These equations come in two varieties. There are the *change and constraint* equations. Then there are the boundary conditions describing the beginning and end conditions of that evolution in relative terms. Thus, differential equations provided the ready-made tools that physicists extended to Einstein's field theory of general relativity, which provided the evolution equations. What all the creation out of nothing models of the universe do is add to Einstein's field equations the boundary conditions in a perfectly orderly and consistent way, thereby taking the mind on an imaginary journey into nothingness and showing why something must come out, that is, why something exists on this side of nothing.

Adding boundary conditions to Einstein's evolution equations allows one to alter initial conditions from out of which the universe occurred starting from a singularity in such a way as to make an incredibly broad spectrum of equally possible universes. To give you just one bizarre example, suppose that you wished to argue that the universe is only 6,000 years old. All you have to do is specify boundary conditions that give the *appearance* of a fifteen-billion-year-old universe; the two models are absolutely indistinguishable! You *cannot* distinguish between them on the basis of the equations nor on any observational data. *Statistically,* one is not more likely than another—they are all equally unlikely. It is at such points in the theory that, as we shall see, the so-called Anthropic Principle is evoked by physicists, which, in varying degrees in different models, relies on the existence of mind as a necessary condition for the existence of the universe and thus helps select for a normal universe containing observers like us.

To better understand these models of creation of the universe from nothing, we must trace their recent history over the last twenty years. A good starting point is to ask: on any such model, where did the energy of existence come from? If before the universe began there was nothing, why is there now all this energy? This is a very good question, and what got the creation from nothing models off the ground was a general solution to this problem by Edward Tryon. He showed in 1973 that by adding boundary-type equations to Einstein's field equations one could push the calculations all the way beyond the event horizon, into the singularity, where the energy states were shown to balance themselves out.

In the end—as in the beginning—the equations, surprisingly enough, equaled out to 0. This was not mere hand-waving or simple trickery; one cannot simply make up the equations any way one wants, extrapolate a model, and make it all come out zero. In his groundbreaking[3] paper, Edward Tryon extrapolated from a possibility derived precisely from Heisenberg's Uncertainty Principle to create a viable model showing how the entire universe emerges *naturally* from nothing without violating the conservation laws, as the result of a vacuum fluctuation. The vacuum as conceived in the quantum microstructure is a sort of frothing sea of creation and annihilation, where particle–antiparticle pairs come into existence for brief instants of time. The energy required for this "bubbling forth" into existence from virtually nothing occurs in subspaces so small that, according to Heisenberg's Uncertainty Principle, these so-called virtual particles come into existence as unobservable individual events. The *effects* of such virtual particles have been confirmed observationally to one part in a billion. Tryon showed that what holds for the microcosm could hold for the universe as a whole; he conceived of the universe as a fifteen-billion-year vacuum fluctuation and showed how it is possible that for the universe as a whole the energy shift from pre-big bang to now is *zero:* that is, there has been no overall change in energy from the initial condition of the virtual vacuum.

All that Tryon's model required was that the universe should be closed rather than open. An *open* universe is one in which space is either Euclidean or negatively curved non-Euclidean (sometimes called 'hyperbolic': imagine a Western saddle curved outwardly forever, but in four dimensions). A *closed* universe is one in which space is positively curved non-Euclidean (imagine a sphere but in four dimensions). The best currently available calculations, based on the measured density of the known universe, suggest that the universe is probably closed. *If* it is closed, writes Tryon,

> Then it would be topologically impossible for any gravitational flux lines to escape. If the Universe were viewed from the outside, by a viewer in some larger space in which the Universe were imbedded, the absence of gravitational flux would imply that the system had zero energy. Hence any closed universe has zero energy. . . . our Universe may have zero net values for all conserved quantities. If this be the case, then our Universe could have appeared from nowhere without violating any conservation laws.[4]

Tryon's solution is precisely what is needed to avoid the singularity involved in breaking the conservation laws: the mass-energy "before" the big bang was 0. The universe came about by borrowing its initial energy—positive and negative—from a virtual vacuum, without any other positive energy influx, from another universe, say. Tryon further writes:

Quantum theory does, however, imply that the vacuum should be unstable against large scale fluctuations in the presence of a long range, negative energy, universal interaction. Gravitation is precisely such an interaction, so I am encouraged to believe that the origin and properties of our Universe may be explicable within the framework of conventional science . . .[5]

Following some innovations by Alan Guth, Tryon's model was improved considerably ten years later by Alexander Vilenkin. Guth had shown[6] that various macroscopic structures observed as properties of the observable universe—homogeneity, isotropy, and apparent flatness—could be explained if the very early universe passed through what is known as a de Sitter phase of exponential inflation, yielding what has since been dubbed the "inflationary" model. A de Sitter space is analogous to the space described by special relativity, which one can "picture" as the surface of a four-dimensional sphere in a flat five-dimensional space. This model was originally used in the so-called *steady state model* of the universe, since abandoned by its founders, according to which the universe is infinitely old and red-shift expansion is the result of the spontaneous creation of matter between galaxies from nothing. When the radius of the de Sitter space approaches zero, its (ten-parameter) group of motions goes over into the so-called Poincaré group or inhomogeneous Lorentz group[7], exhibits a number of puzzling properties (such as that past a certain limit you could get from one point to another without going through the points between—the precursor to quantum tunneling).[8] Relying on the de Sitter space model and the work of Guth, Vilenkin applied notions of quantum tunneling described by Atkatz and Pagels[9] to the universe as a whole and argued that one could indeed explain how the universe arises completely out of nothing.

No single physicist invents the whole storehouse of concepts and tools with which such models are created. Tryon's earlier model of a universe bubbling forth from a virtual quantum mechanical vacuum was *not* a true creation from *nothing,* as the popular literature sometimes describes it, since the virtual quantum vacuum has in fact a very elaborate mathematical structure. In Tryon's model, the structure came from the collapse of the previous universe; the virtual quantum vacuum that preceded

our big bang got its structure—the so-called *boundary conditions* of the universe—by relying on the cyclical cosmological model of an endless sequence of universes, each one coming into existence from a big bang that itself is in part the result of a previous "big crunch." The annihilation of space-time from the collapse of a previous universe would leave a sort of "residual" empty structure in the remaining virtual vacuum of either Minkowski or de Sitter space-time and such "creation from nothing" models would not really be that. Vilenkin's added insight was to show that no initial conditions at the big bang—no boundary conditions—are really necessary by presenting a cosmological model in which the universe arises spontaneously from *nothing,* in ways that do not violate known laws or require changes in fundamental equations. The scenario involves an analogue of quantum tunneling—wherein a particle can tunnel through impenetrable barriers—in which the universe itself tunnels into existence from *nothing.*[10]

What bothered many physicists about Vilenkin's model and Guth's inflationary universe scenario was the apparent unverifiability of these theories. Many physicists still rely for their philosophy of science on a rather antiquated form of logical positivism or logical empiricism, which dictates that all scientific models be (somehow) verifiable. The only test for the models of Tryon, Guth, and Vilenkin is the "closure" of the universe, and this paucity of testability precludes general acceptance. Anticipating such criticisms, Guth argued that according to his inflationary model the actual density of the universe well overshoots the critical density for closure. Vilenkin tried a less quantitative approach:

The concept of the universe being created from nothing is a crazy one. . . . The advantages of the scenario presented here are of aesthetic nature. It gives a cosmological model which does not have a singularity at the big bang (there still may be a final singularity) and does not require any initial or boundary conditions. The structure and evolution of the universe(s) are totally determined by the laws of physics.[11]

Thus the latest quantum models try to render the creation from nothing model as a singularity-free complete model of the universe in greater and

ON PHILOSOPHY

David Bohm

. . . originally the word *philosophy* meant love of wisdom. Now it becomes a sort of technique. Also I think our modern age is falling into reducing everything to techniques, and it takes away the significance of everything. I think that people have gradually fallen into that, and have said that anything else which doesn't fit that simply is of no consequence. You must notice this has developed historically. You can't regard it as an absolute truth. . . . I think that any fundamental new experiments arise from philosophical questions. If you go into history, in the Greek times, science was largely speculative. People then corrected that by bringing in experiments. Now we've gone the other way and said experiments are almost the only thing there is to it. So, in effect, we have gone to the opposite extreme.

Science surely involves several things. It involves insight into ideas, and this insight precedes experiments. If you exclude philosophy you will eventually exclude these things too. The only insight available now is through mathematics: that's the only place people allow themselves any freedom. They can play around with mathematics as much as they like without experiments. . . . People believe that mathematics is truth, but anything else is not. . . . But if you will allow mathematical elegance, will you not allow elegance in the conception? Every physicist has at least a tacit philosophy but the present generally accepted philosophy is extremely inelegant. It's really crude.

From *The Ghost in the Atom,* P. Davies and J. Brown, eds.

greater detail. In 1983, Hawking and his collaborator J. Hartle succeeded in getting a complete set of energy states for the universe in such a model[12] and two years later, Hawking removed the last remnants of a need for boundary conditions by quantizing gravity in a model without singularities.[13] The model predicts observable results in good accord with the observed expansion rate of the universe as measured in volume over time; were that rate not precisely balanced, stars would not form, and none of us could ask why there is something rather than nothing. Einstein's worry that "God would not play dice with the universe" has been answered, Hawking claims, because the new model

> . . . has opened up a new possibility, in which there would be no boundary to space-time and so there would be no need to specify the behavior at the boundary. There would be no singularities at which the laws of science broke down and no edge of space-time at which one would have to appeal to God or some new law to set the bound-

ary conditions for space-time. One could say: "The boundary condition of the universe is that it has no boundary." The universe would be completely self-contained and not affected by anything outside itself. It would neither be created nor destroyed. It would just BE.[14]

Think of it this way. The reason we begin thinking that there has to be some *reason* or some *answer* to the question, "Why is there a universe?" is that we realize that the universe—the space-time manifold—is *contingent*. When we do so, we are inclined—whether we imagine that the universe had a beginning in time, or has existed for an infinite amount of time—to think about the initial and *boundary conditions* of that universe. For to say that the manifold of the universe is infinite means, simply, that one could assign a one-to-one correspondence between all those space-time points (each point being defined by four coordinates: length, x, breadth, y, height, z, and time, w) and the integers (1,2,3 . . .) *and never run out of points.*

And though there are, of course, an infinite number of integers, one can always construct sets of numbers that are *bigger infinities* than the infinity of the integers. For instance, the set of *real* numbers, which includes not just the integers and rational numbers but also the irrational numbers, is bigger. And the same applies to any manifold: to say that a particular manifold is infinite is *still* to ascribe boundaries to the points within that manifold: they are, after all, the points of *that* manifold and not of some other possible manifold.

In other words, to say that the universe is infinite in time really means: *if you are a creature in that world, you will never live to see its end.* Similarly, to say that the universe is infinite in space really means: *if you are a creature in that world and you travel everywhere in that world, you will never observe an edge of your world.* To say that a world is infinite in this way is *not* to say that world has no boundary. Talk of any world, even infinite worlds, implicitly raises the question of ultimate boundaries. In mathematical terms, a boundary condition of "the universe as a whole" would specify the nature of a surface of contact between the universe and its external cause.

At least that's the traditional thinking. Hawking's revolutionary proposal, in a nutshell, is that since the quantum models show how it is possible for the universe to have come about spontaneously from nothing without violating any known laws of physics, the world was therefore not externally caused. But then, Hawking says, the universe itself exists *necessarily.* Hence, "the boundary condition of the universe," in his words, "is that it has no boundaries."

From the standpoint of the equations, what happens in Stephen Hawking's model is that the singularity is itself removed and *no external conditions* are needed to bring about the universe. That is, the existence of the universe is itself a noncontingent fact about the universe. The universe exists because the inner structure of the universe is such that it *cannot not be.* In other words, strangely enough, the latest scientific answer is, ultimately, of the same form as the old religious answer! The only difference between the physicist's ultimate answer to the ultimate question and religion's (pseudo) answer is that the necessarily existent something is not God but the universe itself.

The question then arises: can the physicist's model explain why in fact the universe has the internal properties that make it the sort of thing that exists necessarily—that is, why *that* model corresponds to *this* universe? Why does the actual universe have that structure so that, ultimately, it exists necessarily? The problem is a subtle one but, in effect, can be thought of in the following terms. A model of reality is a theory. It is not the reality described. To have a working model, which *if* it applied to the world *would* explain the world, still leaves the question of why the world has *that* structure rather than some other structure—why *that* model applies; in other words, why that model is not just a fanciful model but an actual model of the real universe. There are lots of possible models, and there are lots of possible universes. Whence the real one, and whence the *reality* of that which the real model models?

Stephen Hawking's answer to this difficult question comes in two parts. First, if the boundary condition of the universe is that it has no boundaries, so that it is completely self-contained without any singularities, it can be shown that it is then completely describable by a Grand Unification Theory (though no one has actually constructed such a theory unifying all the forces of nature into one equation). In any case, however, the only model allowing of such complete unification is a superstring-type model (involving what are called heterotic strings, which build manifolds not of spacetime points but of points with length, called strings, which are used to explain some of the unaccounted for built-in properties of quantum particles, like left-handedness). Such a model is both free of boundary conditions and singularities and, at the same time, allows for the development of complex structures like human beings *but as themselves being necessary ingredients for there being a real world.* Second, what makes Hawking's model an ultimate explanation of the existence of the universe, in his view, is that not only is it a *possible* model of the way the world is, it is the *only* possible model that could allow for the spontaneous development of human beings as a *necessary ingredient of the model.* That is, such a model could be a sufficient explanation only if the universe has to be *necessarily* one whose boundary condition is that it has no boundaries. The reason for this is that our own existence—the existence of mind—brings about this necessity from within the model. Hence there is no appeal, in Hawking's model, to any external forces to account for the existence of the universe; the existence of the universe is therefore *noncontingent,* meaning that the universe exists *necessarily.*

Thus, in the end, the latest scientific answer is on all accounts a definite improvement over the old religious answer. Although it too tries to resolve the question of existence with the idea of some sort of noncontingent (necessary) existence, the requirement of mind at some level to appear within the universe and actualize it is not itself a contingency *since it, itself, is necessitated by the existence of the universe.*

3. THE ANTHROPIC PRINCIPLE AND COSMIC DESIGN

But how does the loop of existence get "off the ground"? Isn't this a bit like trying to pick yourself up by your bootstraps? As Hawking puts it:

> What is it that breathes fire into the equations and makes a universe for them to describe? The usual approach of science of constructing a mathematical model cannot answer the question of why there be a universe for the model to describe. Why does the universe go to all the bother of existing? Is the unified theory so compelling that it brings about its own existence? Or does it need a creator, and if so, does he have any other effect on the universe? And who created him?[15]

First, the fact that Hawking, like other physicists—most notably John Archibald Wheeler—here weaves into his equations the so-called Anthropic Principle, according to which *the universe must be such as to admit within it the existence of conscious observers,* must be viewed against the background of the widely accepted absolute idealism brought into the philosophy of quantum mechanics by Neils Bohr, the so-called Copenhagen Interpretation. As we shall see in the next section, the underlying presupposition of this school of thought is that all that exists is a form of *mind.* Second, Hawking evokes this principle not just in some general way to simply appease his philosophical worries; it occurs in two very specific places in

his theory. He evokes the principle as the *best explanation* as to why time's arrows are the way they are, including the three symmetries known as C, P, and T. C is the particle–antiparticle symmetry, P is the mirror image symmetry, and T is the direction of motion of all particles being able to run in either a relative forward or relative backward direction. If these were different by even 1 percent, life could never evolve in the universe; but if life never evolved in the universe, there could never be any such *real* symmetries because they require—as all quantum processes do—a conscious observer to determine one state versus another (otherwise there is just a probability amplitude that does not become a real object). And he evokes this as the *best explanation* why on the microscopic level the ten dimensions of space-time are extremely curved (looping into "tight balls," as described by Roger Penrose), whereas on the macroscopic level, time and the three space dimensions are almost perfectly flat, as described by de Sitter space and Minkowski manifolds. This is the only situation where an observation *as a conscious observation involving light rays and perceptions could occur;* without that, you get no real universe of *any* kind. The idea, in other words, is that if we weren't here to see it, there *would* exist nothing at all. A strange loop, indeed.

But what is the alternative? Part of the physicists' reasoning here is that for the time being there is no better alternative. Being able to construct such scenarios, describing creation from nothing is one thing; deciding which, if any, model applies to the real universe is another. The only standard way to do this is by taking some aspect of the model that has an empirical component and then checking to see if it matches the way the world reveals itself to be in the appearances (which in the case of Hawking's complete model is not possible). This Hawking readily admits: "If we actually did discover the ultimate theory of the universe [that is, had his model *plus* a grand unification theory] . . . we could never be quite sure that we had indeed found the correct theory, since theories can't be proved." The only nonstandard way is to take *the fact of observation itself as an observation.* Ultimately, to have a single "non-contradicted" model of the universe *and quantum theory in general* physicists *make mind the fulcrum of reality.* That is, in the strangest and loopiest twists of all, the physicist is forced to

ON KANT AND COMPREHENSIBILITY

Albert Einstein

The very fact that the totality of our sense experiences is such that by means of thinking (operations with concepts, and the creation and use of definite functional relations between them, and the coordination of sense experiences to these concepts) it can be put in order, this fact is one which leaves us in awe, but which we shall never understand. One may say "the eternal mystery of the world is its comprehensibility." It is one of the great realizations of Immanuel Kant that the setting up of a real external world would be senseless without this comprehensibility.

In speaking here concerning "comprehensibility," the expression is used in its most modest sense. It implies: the production of some sort of order among sense impressions, this order being produced by the creation of general concepts, relations between these concepts, and by relations between the concepts and sense experience, these relations being determined in any possible manner. It is in this sense that the world of our sense experiences is comprehensible. The fact that it is comprehensible is a miracle.

From *Out of My Later Years.*

---

argue that he can only offer a complete model of the universe by accepting some form of absolute idealism—the philosophical view that no physical world exists independently of the mind.

Stephen Hawking and his collaborator C. B. Collins conclude their extremely technical but far-reaching paper by suggesting that

> . . . the isotropy of the Universe and our existence are both results of the fact that the Universe is expanding at just about the critical rate. Since we could not observe the Universe to be different if we were not here, one can say, in a sense, that the isotropy of the Universe is a consequence of our existence.[16]

To take another example, suppose you wonder why the universe is so big. Well, there we are wondering. The fact of human wondering itself demands that the universe must be a certain way when it is being wondered about: the act of *wondering* requires a mind, which requires a brain, which requires living tissue, which requires the presence of much heavier elements than just hydrogen. Stars work on the proton–proton interaction that produces helium via fusion: inside the centers of stars it is hot enough for atoms of hydrogen to fuse into helium, but not hot enough to create heavy elements like oxygen. That requires the temperature found in supernova explosions. Supernova explosions require thermonuclear combustion, which, in turn, requires several billion years to cook up enough matter inside a star. According to general relativity, such vast amounts of time cannot exist in a closed universe unless the radius at maximum expansion of the universe is several billion light years. And *that's* why the universe is so big—because the only time we can ask why is it so big is when it is so big.

To get a sense of what is involved in this type of anthropic reasoning, consider the following. Suppose you find a deck of cards, perfectly arranged by suits from lowest to highest card. You would assume the deck had not been randomly shuffled; instead, you would assume someone had ordered the cards that way. The deck of cards is analogous to the universe. It brings in several important factors: first, the cards can be shuffled infinitely many times. If the cards are shuffled enough times, sooner

GRAND UNIFICATION THEORIES (GUTs) AND THE END OF THE WORLD

Daniel Kolak

There is an ancient myth that if human beings ever learn the true name of God, the universe will end. Well, in modern terms, the "name of God" can be taken metaphorically to mean "The Grand Unification Theory" in physics, referred to by physicists as GUT (the pronunciation of which in German and Swedish means "God!"). GUT is contemporary physics' heroic attempt to unify all the known forces of nature into a single, all-explaining, omnipotent equation.

To get a feel for the unlimited powers such an equation would unleash for us, consider that one precursor of it is Einstein's famous $E=mc^2$, which showed how mass and energy were really the same thing. This minor (in comparison to GUT) revelation gave us nuclear energy. The price for unlocking one of nature's ultimate secrets? Nuclear weapons and the capability to destroy all life on earth.

The possible repercussions of the search for GUT, however, are much more dangerous than this—the possible destruction not only of the human race and the whole planet but the *entire cosmos* as well. And all this without a moment's warning! This could conceivably happen, according to some physicists, if enough energy was generated in one of the high-energy collisions between sub-atomic particles, which allow physicists

to "see," as if through some super-microscope into the innermost heart of matter and reality, to create what physicists call a "real vacuum" bubble. This "vacuum bubble," once created, would instantaneously begin to expand at the speed of light, obliterating all of spacetime. The earth would vanish in a fraction of a second. Everything would just "plop" out of existence.

To help you visualize this, consider the following analogy. Imagine that the universe is represented as a photographic transparency, like a big Kodak slide, in which information is encoded, like on a film, with light. The brighter the light, the more transparent the slide, and hence the brighter the image. But suppose the light was so bright that it ignited a spot on the slide—like sunlight focused through a magnifying lens. The images on the slide would vanish as the slide itself melted away in an ever-widening circle of flame. This is what would happen to our spacetime continuum (the Kodak slide) if the "true vacuum" bubble (the point ignited by the magnified light rays) was ever created in a laboratory accelerator.

When it was recently discovered that the spacetime "stuff" out of which the universe is made might be some sort of metastable state based on what is known as a "false vacuum," in

or later, the well-ordered sequence will arise purely by chance. This shows how it would happen that the cards come up ordered, but it makes such an order a very, very rare occurrence. Imagine, though, that *we are the cards*. Further, imagine that only cards in a specifically ordered sequence—say where you have only Royal Flushes—can be conscious. In that case, the only time the randomly shuffled

Royal Flushes could have the opportunity to ask, "why is our universe (the deck of cards in which we exist) so perfectly ordered into Royal Flushes," would be when in fact the deck happened to precisely thus order itself. All other random shuffles go unobserved. Only well-ordered shuffles, like this one right here around you now, get observed.

GRAND UNIFICATION THEORIES (GUTs)
AND THE END OF THE WORLD (*continued*)

which the appearance of a "true vacuum" would annihilate the "false vacuum" of reality, the National Science Foundation funded a grant (NSF grant #PHY79-19884) to study whether our particle accelerators might be strong enough to produce a "true vacuum" bubble and destroy the universe. The U.S. government invested a good deal of taxpayer money on this not very publicized but very real worry: might the physicists' tinkering with the virtual vacuum destroy the universe by poking a hole into *nothing,* which then would spread outward at the speed of light and annihilate the entire universe? The reason they thought this really might happen is that the energies generated by these super-energy particle accelerators is now approaching energies greater than any energy in the universe since the big bang. And this, some physicists feared, might rip apart the spacetime continuum, leaving a hole of nothing.

A particle accelerator is basically a big microscope. Physicists use them to look at the smallest subatomic particles of nature. You need the particle accelerator to generate the energy, much in the way you need a flashbulb if you're going to take a picture in the dark. Down there in the microscopic world it is completely dark since we are looking at regions smaller than the wavelength of visible light. You need something smaller than the wavelength of visible light, such as a beam of electrons, to bounce back from the tiny thing you're looking at, or you can't see it (hence electron microscopes). That's why, for instance, X-rays can be used to take pictures of your skeleton. But when you want to look at the smallest particles of nature, you must generate really small wavelengths to see them. That is, because of the inverse law of energy and wavelength, the smaller the wavelength the greater the energy, and so you must generate a great deal of energy. That's what the supercolliders are for. And the energy levels are so high that physicists began to worry whether it might "burn a hole," so to speak, right through the fabric of spacetime. So the physicists worried that such a hole might open up in their lab and annihilate *everything*. The conclusion of the physicists who did the actual government-sponsored research was that it is *unlikely* that we might inadvertently wipe out the cosmos and "at least we can be confident that no particle accelerator in the *foreseeable* future will pose any threat to our vacuum."*

*See *Nature,* Vol 302, 433, "How Stable Is Our Vacuum?" My emphasis.

Proponents of the recent "Anthropic Cosmological Principle," use exactly this sort of reasoning to explain the order we observe in the universe by providing the missing component, the missing piece in the puzzle: *us*. To many, this is but the latest entry in the "shocking" aspects of quantum mechanics, the "strangeness" of quantum mechanics, its "mind-boggling aspects" . . . to quote just some of the adjectives of the science popularizers. But of course to philosophers, who have been dealing with the problem of the nature of the relationship between mind and reality at least since Locke, Berkeley, and Hume first put them in their modern form, which Kant then synthesized and thereby paved the way for nineteenth-century developments, such thinking is centuries old.

It was John Locke who first put forth an empirical theory of knowledge consistent with the mind's active role in perception: the mind is not a direct link to the outside world but an indirect link. Today, one might put Locke's view this way: conscious perception is the end result of a long chain of processes beginning at the back of the eye (where the light stops), continuing as electrochemical impulses coded into numbers (nobody knows how) and sent along the optic nerve, and ending as a series of representations (nobody knows how) actively processed by the brain into something that doesn't seem like neurons firing or numbers being processed (nobody knows how that happens, either). Some may not like such a translation into contemporary scientific language, but the point is that Locke distinguished the phenomena of experience—the actual colors and shapes in perception—from the physical objects they represent. In Locke's model of the world, there exist physical objects, and they have both *primary* qualities— their mind-independent attributes, like extension and hardness—and *secondary* qualities—the mind-dependent attributes, like colors. The primary qualities of the object can be thought of as the *thing-in-itself,* as Kant later would do; whereas the secondary qualities do not exist in things in themselves but require minds for their existence. Berkeley, upon close scrutiny of Locke's analysis, realized that Locke's notion of primary qualities was ultimately an *abstract idea.* And abstract ideas don't exist. All that exists are *concrete* ideas, and these are ideas that you are well familiar with: the things you actually see. Tables and chairs and stars are concrete ideas, that is, actually existent objects, whereas the idea of an extended substance that has no perceivable qualities is an abstraction from concrete ideas, a fabrication. Berkeley, like any good quantum physicist today, and like any good empiricist of his or any other time, did not want to accept the idea of something "unknowable" existing beyond what was accessible to human experience. And since Locke showed that one could have no experience of the thing-in-itself, Berkeley did away with the notion, arguing that this is but a chimerical idea and not good science. "To be is to be perceived," wrote Berkeley, bringing into modern form the view of the world known as *idealism:* existence requires conscious observers, the mind. An obvious difficulty arose in Berkeley's system: why do tables and chairs not vanish, why does the world not disappear, when nobody is looking at it? His answer: because God is there observing things even when the human mind is not. Without God's omnipresent perceptions to sustain the world, all things would instantly cease to exist, for without the experience of things, there would be no things at all, there would be just nothing.

From Berkeley's idealism sprang Kant's *transcendental* idealism, a philosophy designed to literally go beyond the phenomena of experience, to transcend experience and get to the reality beyond experience, the *ding-an-sich,* the "thing-in-itself" as it exists not in the mind's *re*presentation but in *presentation,* in reality. Kant argued that the mind could not know objects in themselves as they actually are. The mind could only, at best, force sensory experience of objects in certain patterns, or forms, which can, at best, to a certain degree in some way resemble the actual object being experienced. Beyond the realm of the mind's representations was not nothing but something, albeit an *unknowable* something forever beyond the reach of experience; to put it in more contemporary language: *no information whatsoever could be extracted from the thing-in-itself.* You can see why a physicist—like any extreme empiricist— would want, as the physicist Niels Bohr did, to do away with the notion of the thing-in-itself: if no information can be extracted from the thing-in-itself, then it does not exist. Thus, in response to what many philosophers and scientists at the time found to be a philosophically unacceptable state of affairs (the positing of the existence of a realm forever beyond the reach of mind) arose *absolute* idealism. This was not Berkeley's subjective idealism but the objective idealism in Germany of Fichte, Hegel, and, even more so, Schelling, which in the twentieth century crossed over into physics via Niels Bohr, while in England T. H. Green and F. H. Bradley and B. Bosanquet in France developed similar, absolute idealist, views of reality. One of the pioneers of this sort of absolute (often called *objective*) idealism, J. G. Fichte, wrote:

> A finite rational being has nothing beyond experience; it is this that comprises the entire staple of his thought. The philosopher is necessarily in the same position; it seems, therefore, incomprehensible how he could raise himself above experience . . . the

thing-in-itself is a pure invention and has no reality whatever. It does not occur in experience for the system of experience is nothing other than thinking . . . [which is] nothing else but the *totality of relations unified by the imagination,* and that all these relations constitute the thing; the object is surely the original synthesis of all these concepts. Form and matter are not separate items; the totality of form is the matter . . .[17]

For something, say a chair, to be *objectively real* simply means, in Fichte's view, that it consists of all possible experiences that it can generate in the mind of a potential observer. Take the chair apart or don't take it apart, look at it from above and below or not; the point is that you could because the chair is a containing space of all (perhaps infinite) possibilities of the relations of that object. And this, essentially, is the view of Niels Bohr of what it means for something to be real at the quantum-mechanical level: the equation describing the object allows you to list all the possible solutions that it could generate: beyond that range of possibility there is no mind independent actuality. According to Bohr's absolute idealism, Mind and World are so intimately connected that

an independent reality in the ordinary physical sense can neither be ascribed to the phenomena nor to the agencies of observations.[18]

At the quantum level, the essential properties of subatomic particles do not exist until the conscious mind brings it into existence.

The Anthropic Principle can thus be viewed as a macroscopic version of what has already been accepted by most physicists to be true at the microscopic level: that the mind is an essential ingredient of reality. Bohr's view of quantum mechanics hinges on showing that Heisenberg's Uncertainty Principle precludes any such a mind-independent existence. According to that principle, the equation describing the position of an electron moving in some direction, x, with some momentum, p_x, is $\Delta x \, \Delta p_x \geq \frac{\hbar}{2}$, where $\hbar$ is Planck's constant[19] divided by 2π (as amended by Paul Dirac), where $\Delta x, \Delta p$ are the uncertainty in the measurement of the electron's position in direction x, and Δp is the measurement of the electron's momentum in the x direction. A minimum condition for a physical object to be real is that it is somewhere or going somewhere; Bohr's

argument shows that if a mind knows precisely the particle's position, this would obliterate the possibility of knowing its momentum not because the momentum was there in the world as a thing-in-itself and the mind just couldn't reach down there to find it but, rather, because that information itself did not exist in the world, it was not there. Or, if a mind knows precisely the particle's momentum (mv, the product of its mass and velocity), then the particle's position becomes completely unknown, not because the particle is somewhere where the mind cannot reach it, but because it has no specific location.

Albert Einstein rejected absolute idealism in favor of a sort of transcendental idealism of the sort constructed by Immanuel Kant, who was Einstein's most important early influence. (He read, and re-read, Kant's *Critique of Pure Reason* and *Prolegomena to Any Future Metaphysics* as a teenager.) He defended the idea of the thing-in-itself, a mind-independent reality, against other leading physicists, including most of his contemporaries. Although Einstein and Bohr were great friends, Einstein vehemently rejected Bohr's absolute idealist view, claiming that there is more to the world than can be perceived in the sphere of the conscious intellect, the human mind, arguing for the existence of a mind-independent physical reality. He formulated a series of idealized experiments to get around Bohr's so-called Copenhagen Interpretation of the implications of Heisenberg's Uncertainty Principle for quantum mechanics. The most famous of these is the so-called Einstein-Podolsky-Rosen paradox (dubbed "paradox," of course, from within the perspective of Bohr's Copenhagen Interpretation) in which Einstein and his collaborators argue that it is in principle possible to predict, without disturbing the physical system but with absolute certainty—i.e., with probability = 1—the value of a physical quantity and that, therefore, this physical quantity exists independently of the conscious mind. Most physicists now agree that Einstein was on this point wrong and that Bohr was right. It therefore behooves us to take a little trouble and understand their reasoning, for the Einstein-Podolsky-Rosen (EPR) experiment is in fact the prototype for all subsequent "delayed choice" and "two slit experiments" that are presently the staple of all the "revolutionary" and "mind-boggling" claims of quantum physicists and the key aspects of the quantum physicist's argument that mind and nature and invariably and intimately linked in ways we could never have imagined—even *beyond* what the nineteenth-century absolute idealists had imagined. If you want to understand the philosophy behind quantum mechanics, especially the different philosophies of reality behind the current leading interpretation of quantum mechanics and Albert Einstein's, there is no better way to do it than by studying the reasoning involved in that thought experiment.

The reasoning goes as follows. If one does the EPR-experiment using the spin of an electron[20] (described in the three-space Cartesian coordinate system using an x, y, and z axis) in the z-direction, S_z, it is always complementary to its spin in a perpendicular direction. These spin values are *quantized*, that is, they can take only one of two discrete values with nothing continuous between; those discrete, quantized values are $\pm\frac{\hbar}{2}$. So the value of S_z *must be* $\pm\frac{\hbar}{2}$. Suppose then, that $S_z = \frac{\hbar}{2}$. In that case, the electron's spin value in the x-direction—because of the required complementarity as described by Heisenberg's uncertainty principle—will according to Bohr's interpretation be completely indeterminate, that is, undefined and even in principle unobservable (and therefore, in his view, nonexistent). It can only take a value upon being perceived by a conscious mind, that is, through the act of measurement—but, in that case, the reality of the spin in the z-direction, S_z, has been annihilated from existence.

The EPR thought experiment causes the following dilemma. It is important to understand this thoroughly because physics popularizers often simplify it in such a way as to completely misrepresent it. A pair of coupled electrons ($e1$, $e2$), whose total spin along any axis is zero ($-\frac{\hbar}{2} + \frac{\hbar}{2} = 0$) are sent off in opposite directions. Suppose observer Alpha measures the spin of $e1$ in the z-direction and finds $S_{z_{e1}} = +\frac{\hbar}{2}$, in that case, we know that if some second far away observer, Beta, *were* to make the corresponding spin measurement of $e2$, Beta would have to find $S_{z_{e2}} = -\frac{\hbar}{2}$. Let the electrons (which are flying away from each other in opposite directions at the speed of light) get so far away from each other that Alpha and Beta are out of each other's light cones. (A light cone is a hypersphere surface in spacetime marking out the possible directions for light rays passing through a given event.) This is not precluded by Heisenberg's Uncertainty Principle, which allows perfectly precise simultaneous measurements of the total spin of the electron pair in *either* the z or x direction. But even if Beta *doesn't* make the requisite measurement, the probability that the spin value will be $-\frac{\hbar}{2}$ is 1. This means that $e2$'s spin value along the z-axis is real, according to the restated EPR paradox, *independently of any observer*. But the situation for the would-be absolute idealist physicist is even worse. First, Alpha could have decided to measure $e1$'s spin along the x-axis. Suppose that $S_{x_{e1}} = +\frac{\hbar}{2}$. In that case, were Beta to have measured $e2$'s spin along the x-axis, Beta would have found that $S_{x_{e2}} = -\frac{\hbar}{2}$. Doesn't this prove, using the Einsteinian reasoning in the EPR paradox, that both S_z and S_x exist and are real independently of any observing minds?

Einstein's point was that in the example, Alpha's mind interacts only with $e1$, not $e2$, and that it would be absurd to suppose that Alpha's mind, separated from an event at another part of the universe, could simultaneously bring into existence, depending on what arbitrary choice Alpha made (whether to measure S_x or S_z) what happens in that other part of the universe where Beta is. Not only would this be action at a distance, it would be one-upping even Berkeleyian idealism with a vengeance: the mind isn't just *necessary* to *sustain* an object's existence, it *causally brings it about* that something exists *where it isn't even looking nor could look because the other event, separated by a light cone, is (relative to Alpha) in the past*. In other words, it wouldn't even be creation of physical reality out of an act of mind *in the present*, it would be the creation by an act of mind in the present the physical reality *of the past*.

But of course one man's absurdity is another man's theory. The preceding explanation has been of a minimally technical nature, which allows some comprehension of the subsequent moves in quantum theory where to speak of the reality of the system as it exists independently of any observer, turns out to be absolutely meaningless. The great twentieth-century philosopher Wittgenstein wrote, "What we cannot speak about we must pass over in silence." The absolute idealist quantum physicists' version of this is, "What the theory cannot speak about must therefore not exist." Thus the *thing-in-itself*, the objectively existing real objects of the world that do not require the mind for their existence, the very things that seventeenth- and eighteenth-century physics divorced itself from philosophy to look for—*have been banished from the realm of physics.*

The fundamental role the conscious mind now plays in all fundamental physical measurement is not limited just to the microscopic level; it pervades physics all the way up to the macroscopic level, leading not just to the creation of universes from nothing scenario but, also, John Archibald Wheeler's so-called participatory universe. As I've mentioned, the Einstein-Podolsky-Rosen thought experiment is really the prototype for all the famous *delayed-choice* experiments in physics and the reasoning they employ is all essentially the reasoning employed by Einstein and his collaborators. To suppose that the spin is brought into existence *over there* by the *conscious choice* of which measurement to make *over here* meant, for Einstein, that quantum physics was merely a very elaborate "fudge factor" designed to get around the unknowns. Bohr and others of the Copenhagen school of quantum mechanics took Einstein's results not to be a reduction of quantum mechanics but a further argument for their brand of absolute idealism that has since then become all the rage in physics. Wheeler, for instance, showed in the late 1970s how to construct what is essentially a delayed-choice EPR-type experiment in which an observation we make here on Earth today brings into existence some restricted properties of a pulsar in a galaxy billions of light years away, that is, billions of years in the past. Using these results, he constructed his model of the participatory universe in which existence comes into being from out of nothing as a ghostly superposition of quantum states until real properties occur retroactively but only after some time when conscious observers pop from out of these random not-yet-real fluctuations onto the real scene; the order of the universe comes about as a result of the multiple observations being made self-consistent—a requirement that, if not met, would preclude their ever being any observations of the requisite kind to begin with and hence, on Wheeler's view, no universe.

This sort of blatantly teleological explanation in terms of final causes—an example of anthropic

reasoning—has a tradition going back beyond Leibniz, to Aristotle of course but also to Plato, though it was Leibniz who gave it its first precise mathematical and, subsequently, physical formulation, which he derived from his Principle of Sufficient Reason. Wheeler, a great admirer and follower of Leibniz, believes, as Leibniz did, that even the *ultimate* objects of inquiry "are ordered as the order in the data":

> Inspect the interior of a particle of one type, and magnify it up enormously, and in that interior see one view of the whole universe (compare the concept of monad of Leibniz [1714], "The monads have no window through which anything can enter or depart"); and do likewise for another particle of the same type. Are particles of the same pattern identical in any one cycle of the universe because they give identically patterned views of the same universe? No acceptable explanation for the miraculous identity of particles of the same type has ever been put forward. That identity must be regarded, not as a triviality, but as a central mystery of physics.[7]

In Wheeler's cyclical universes model, this present universe was created in a big bang from out of a state of nothing that was in turn preceded by a previous universe, which also had come about from a still previous big bang and big crunch. These collapses into a state of nothingness Wheeler likens to a cosmic storm, where

> In the week between one storm and the next, most features of the weather are ever-changing, but some special patterns of the wind last the week. . . . A percent or so change one way in one of the "constants," $\frac{hc}{e^2}$, will cause all stars to be red stars; and a comparable change the other way will make all stars be blue stars . . . In neither case will any star like the sun be possible. . . . the right order of ideas may not be, here is the universe, so what must man be; but here is man, so what must the universe be? . . . [This] may only be a halfway point on the road toward thinking of the universe as Leibniz did, as a world of relationships, not a world of machinery. Far from being brought into its present condition by "reprocessing" from earlier cycles, may the universe in some strange sense be "brought into being" by the participation of those who participate? On this view the concept of "cycles" would even seem to be altogether wrong. Instead the vital act is the act of participa-

ON WITTGENSTEIN, PHILOSOPHY, AND GOD

Stephen Hawking

Up to now, most scientists have been too occupied with the development of new theories that describe *what* the universe is to ask the question *why*. On the other hand, the people whose business it is to ask *why*, the philosophers, have not been able to keep up with the advance of scientific theories. In the eighteenth century, philosophers considered the whole of human knowledge, including science, to be their field and discussed questions such as: Did the universe have a beginning? However, in the nineteenth and twentieth centuries, science became too technical and mathematical for the philosophers, or anyone else except a few specialists. Philosophers reduced the scope of their inquiries so much that Wittgenstein, the most famous philosopher of this century, said, "The sole remaining task for philosophy is the analysis of language." What a comedown from the great tradition of philosophy from Aristotle to Kant!

However, if we do discover a complete theory, it should in time be understandable in broad principle by everyone, not just a few scientists. Then we shall all, philosophers, scientists, and just ordinary people, be able to take part in the discussion of the question of why it is that we and the universe exist. If we find the answer to that, it would be the ultimate triumph of human reason—for then we would know the mind of God.

From *A Brief History of Time.*

---

tion. "Participator" is the incontrovertible new concept given by quantum mechanics; it strikes down the term "observer" of classical theory, the man who stands safely behind the thick glass wall and watches what goes on without taking part. It can't be done, quantum mechanics says. Even with the lowly electron one must participate before one can give any meaning whatsoever to its position or its momentum. Is this firmly established result the tiny tip of a giant iceberg? Does the universe also derive its meaning from "participation"? Are we destined to return to the great concept of Leibniz, of "preestablished harmony" ("Leibniz logic loop"), before we can make the next great advance?[22]

But if the existence and structure of the universe is to be explained using some teleological physical model, how are we to understand the nature of the mind, or minds, involved? The most vivid example of this is Wheeler's participatory model of the universe. All that can be verified experimentally, according to Wheeler and others of Bohr's Copenhagen school, is that mind is required to bring into existence quantum processes, such as the example of spin that we considered. What about the electrons themselves? What about the other particles? What about the coordination problems involved in organizing all these particles into observers like us who can bring about microscopic properties like spin? Wheeler's solution has been to propose the existence of an ultimate observer who brings forth the entire universe into existence and coordinates into coherence all the observations of the conscious entities within it. It seems the absolute idealists of quantum physics have come full circle, back in fact to a Berkeleyian God to make the whole thing work. Indeed, one act of observation creates the reality that leads to another, and so on, until the entire sequence of all observations in the universe by all possible observers—after all possible events have occurred— bring into existence the ultimate observer, God, who loops back around and brings the whole thing into some sort of cosmic, holistic focus: universe

On Bohr, Philosophy, and Meaning

John Wheeler

. . . in Bohr's very last taped interview a few hours before his unexpected death, he singled out certain philosophers for particular criticism. He said, ". . . they have not that instinct that is important to learn something and that we must be prepared to learn something of very great importance . . . They did not see that it (the complementary description of quantum theory) was an objective description and that it was the only possible objective description." . . . I think the word *objective* in Bohr's sense referred to the idea of dealing with what's right in front of you: the perceptions that you experience and the measurements you make, rather than Einstein's idea of the universe existing "out there," independently of the observer. . . . I try to put his point of view in this statement: "No elementary quantum phenomenon is a phenomenon until it's brought to a close by an irreversible act of amplification by a detection such as the click of a Geiger counter or the blackening of a grain of photographic emulsion." This, as Bohr puts it, amounts to something that one person can speak about to another in plain language. . . . That is, putting the observation of quantum phenomenon to *use*. The impact of the alpha particle on a screen of zinc sulfide will create a flash which the eye can see. However, if this flash takes place on the surface of the moon there's no one around to make use of it, so that it's not used in the construction of knowledge. This is the most mysterious part of the whole story: what happens when we put something to use?

In the end I suspect we will have to depend on the work of our friends in the world of philosophy, though maybe philosophy is too important to be left to the philosophers! The construction of meaning—what meaning is—has been a central topic for study by philosophers for the past several decades, and there's no single consequence of that study which better summarises the key point in my view than the statement of Follesdal—the Norwegian philosopher (a former student of Professor Donald Davison and now at Stanford University). He said that meaning is "the joint product of all the evidence that is available to those who communicate." *Communication* is the essential idea. . . .

From *The Ghost in the Atom*, P. Davies and J. Brown, eds.

from nothing requires man who brings universe into existence but requires God—Wheeler's God, positioned either at the final singularity of a closed universe or at the future time-like infinite singularity of an open one—who then brings the universe and man into existence so that God can be brought into existence as the ultimate self-designing principle.

The whole process, from creation of the universe from nothing, to the building up of superpositional structures, to the collapse of superposition by observers, in Wheeler's model does not go on forever but closes in on itself. For there can be no higher acts of observation beyond the ultimate and final act of observation specified within Wheeler's model; the entire sequence of observations can be specified in the form of a wave equation for the entire universe. The ultimate "God equation" looks like this:

$$\Psi = \Pi_\eta \Sigma_{i,k} \Psi_{ik} O_{ink}$$

where i is all possible outcomes of the kth observation and n is the entire sequence of observers observing k. (The Ψ symbol is always used in quantum mechanics to denote a complex wave function.) The sense Wheeler gives to the idea that the entire series of observations must end is that the preceding equation has the form of an infinite sequence with no last term. Now, lest this sound overly speculative, it must be noted that already back in 1932, Von Neumann had shown that Bohr's model in particular and the Copenhagen Interpretation of quantum mechanics in general could be given a rigorous axiomatic formulation. He did this by giving it one.[23] In Von Neumann's formalization, the necessary role of an observer appears explicitly as an axiom. But it also bifurcated the entire system into two very different types of quantum processes: a quantum state can come about either continuously (as a solution to the Schrödinger equation, which describes the framework for quantum-mechanical equations in general and the behavior of the quantum wave function in particular) or discontinuously via an act of measurement by an observer. The ambiguity allows for the collapse of the wave function to occur either within the quantum apparatus itself or in the conscious mind of the observer; this has lead to the famous Schrödinger's Cat paradox, the thought experiment cooked up by Schrödinger in which

> A cat is penned up in a steel chamber, along with the following diabolical device (which must be secured against direct interference by the cat): in a Geiger counter there is a tiny bit of radioactive substance so small that perhaps in the course of one hour one of the atoms decays, but also, with equal probability, perhaps none; if it happens, the counter tube discharges and through a relay releases a hammer which shatters a small flask of hydrocyanic acid. If one has left this entire system to itself for an hour, one would say that the cat still lives if meanwhile no atom has decayed. The first atomic decay would have poisoned it. The Ψ-function of the entire system would express this by having in it the living and the dead cat (pardon the expression) mixed or smeared out in equal parts.[24]

An hour later, the cat is in a superposition of one of two states. Either it is dead, for which the quantum state is $\Psi = \Psi_{dead}$, or it is alive, for which the quantum state is $\Psi = \Psi_{alive}$. But what caused the one state or the other? To suppose either that, say,

the Geiger counter (the measuring apparatus itself) did it, or that the conscious human observer did it, or even that the cat itself did it—apparently the view most physicists today vote for—leads to an infinite and impossible regress. As Eugine Wigner[25] and others have pointed out, the apparatus itself, or the human observer, or any combination thereof, including even the cat, *before* there is a collapse of the wave function, have themselves not yet been observed in one state or the other and so exist in a state of superposition. In other words, if we take the "collapse by the conscious observer" alternative, quantum theory says that the observer has *both* seen a dead cat and an alive cat. One way out of this rather beguiling situation, to say the least, has been the Everett-DeWitt so-called many-worlds interpretation of quantum mechanics, according to which the wave function *never* collapses.[26] In their model, our universe must be viewed as forever splitting into more and more universes, each of which is peopled by your actual, living, breathing, thinking counterparts:

> Our universe must be viewed as constantly splitting into a stupendous number of branches. . . . Every quantum transition taking place on every star, in every galaxy, in every remote corner of the universe is splitting our local world into myriads of copies of itself. Here is schizophrenia with a vengeance! . . . All the worlds are there, even those in which everything goes wrong and all the statistical laws break down. The situation is similar to that which we face in ordinary statistical mechanics. If the initial conditions were right the universe-as-we-see-it *could* be a place in which heat sometimes flows from cold bodies to hot. We can perhaps argue that in those branches in which the universe makes a habit of misbehaving in this way, life fails to evolve, so no intelligent automata are around to be amazed by it.[27]

It should be stressed that this many-worlds interpretation of quantum mechanics is most often classified as the only *realist* alternative to Bohr's idealist Copenhagen Interpretation.[28] The other perhaps less realist alternative is Wheeler's ultimate observer view.

At this point, one might wonder: are we still doing science here or theology? The anthropic principle and the entire creation of the universe from nothing may seem as far-fetched as the most far-fetched claims of any theologican explanation of existence—maybe even more so. Does the scientific answer fare any better than the religious answer? That depends on what the question is.

4. THE BIGGEST QUESTION

Why is there something rather than nothing? This is the biggest of all questions. It extends to everything. It asks: Why existence? Why does anything exist? Why isn't there just nothing?

The question removes the borders between all things, it reduces the many to an undifferentiated one and asks: *why* existence rather than nonexistence? Why not nothing? By not discriminating between things, the question extends to everything. It lumps all the things in the world into one and asks, Why a world, any world, rather than no world? By ignoring the quantity, quality, and types of existent things the question brings into sharp focus the brute fact of existence itself. Why existence rather than nonexistence?

The oldest answer to the biggest question was *God.* The reason there is something rather than nothing is that God created it. And the reason God exists is that God has always existed, God is eternal, and the reason God is eternal is that that is God's nature.

One thing nearly all religions have in common is their shared belief in some sort of noncontingent being, a being that exists *necessarily,* which they call *God.* However, when it comes to the biggest question of all time, *the question of whether God exists is completely irrelevant.* It's not that God is the *wrong* answer; God is not even *an* answer. To offer God as an answer is just a very fancy bait and switch.

Question: Why is there something rather than nothing? Answer: "Because a Big Something made the little something!" This is not an answer. Our question asks why *anything,* why *any sort* of anything exists—material, spiritual, zwabongial— rather than nothing. God is not nothing. God is also something. The question asks about God too. A world without a God is from the point of view of our question no less mysterious than a world *with* God. In fact, if God exists, then the biggest ques-

tion has grown even bigger. *Why is there a (material) world and an immaterial world (God) rather than nothing?* If a world consisting of *contingent* material somethings is puzzling, how much more puzzling to find ourselves in a world containing contingent material somethings *plus* a *non*contingent immaterial something! *Why is there something—any type of something, contingent or noncontingent, material or spiritual—rather than nothing?*

Ironically, although most religions have proclaimed this question to be *answered,* most philosophers have proclaimed it to be *meaningless.* When twenty-five centuries ago Parmenides claimed that the world itself, rather than some God beyond the world, was eternal and unchanging, he argued that it is *not* possible for the world itself not to exist. Everything that exists, according to Parmenides, exists necessarily. Indeed, for Parmenides, the question "Why is there something rather than nothing?" cannot and should not even legitimately be asked. According to Parmenides, to ask it is illogical; it is like asking, "Why is a square not a circle?" The reason there is something rather than nothing is contained in the concept of something: *it is not possible that there be nothing.* His was the first ontological argument—not for the existence of God but for the existence of the universe. The existence of the world is derived from the nature of the world itself. Something *simply must* exist. Existence is *necessary.* Since *nothing,* by the very meaning of the term, does not exist, all the somethings that there are—the Parmenidean One, *Being*— are eternal, existing without beginning or end. To even think about the possibility of nothing is according to Parmenides so illogical that he forbid his students even *to think* or *talk* about it; if you do, you will go "deaf and blind":

> You could not know what is not—that is impossible—nor could you express it. . . . For I hold you back from this first way of inquiry; but also from that way on which mortals knowing nothing wander . . . For helplessness guides the wandering thought in their breasts; they are carried along deaf and blind alike, dazed, beasts without judgment. . . . For never shall this prevail: that things that are not, are. But hold back your thought from this way of inquiry, nor let habit born of long experience force you to ply an aimless eye

THE ANTHROPIC PRINCIPLE

John D. Barrow and Frank J. Tipler

The central problem of science and epistemology is deciding which postulates to take as fundamental. The perennial solution of the great idealistic philosophers has been to regard Mind as logically prior, and even materialistic philosophers consider the innate properties of matter to be such as to allow—or even require—the existence of intelligence to contemplate it; that is, these properties are necessary or sufficient for life. Thus the existence of Mind is taken as one of the basic postulates of a philosophical system. . . . [D]uring the past fifteen years there has grown up amongst cosmologists an interest in a collection of ideas, known as the Anthropic Cosmological Principle, which offer a means of relating Mind and observership directly to the phenomena traditionally within the encompass of physical science.

The expulsion of Man from his self-assumed position at the centre of Nature owes much to the Copernican principle that we do not occupy a privileged position in the Universe. This Copernican assumption would be regarded as axiomatic at the outset of most scientific investigations. However, like most generalizations it must be used with care. Although we do not regard our position in the Universe to be central or special in every way, this does not mean that it cannot be special in *any* way. This "Anthropic Principle" . . .

[is that] *The Universe must have those properties which allow life to develop within it at some stage in its history.*

An implication . . . is that the constants and laws of Nature must be such that life can exist. This speculative statement leads to a number of quite distinct interpretations of a radical nature: firstly, the most obvious is to continue in the tradition of the classical Design Arguments and claim that:

(A) *There exists one possible Universe 'designed' with the goal of generating and sustaining 'observers.'*

This view would have been supported by the natural theologians of past centuries, . . . [The physicist John Archibald] Wheeler has a second possible interpretation . . . :

(B) *Observers are necessary to bring the Universe into being.*

This statement is somewhat reminiscent of the outlook of Bishop Berkeley and we shall see that it has physical content when considered in the light of attempts to arrive at a satisfactory interpretation of quantum mechanics.

From *The Anthropic Cosmological Principle* (1986).

---

and droning ear along this road. . . . One way remains to be spoken of: the way how it is. Along this road there are very many indications that what is is unbegotten and imperishable; for it is whole and immovable and complete. Nor was it at any time, nor will it be, since it is now, all at once, one and continuous.

For what begetting of it would you search for? How and whence did it grow? I shall not let you

say or think "from what is not"; for it is not possible either to say or to think how it is not.[29]

Some philosophers have condoned both the question and the subject, so long as one was not scientific about it. Martin Heidegger is a perfect example; he wrote a whole book on the question, Why is there something rather than nothing?[30] in which he warned against using the "cheap acid of a merely logical intelligence." Scientists, according to Heidegger, could never understand or talk about nothing:

> It is perfectly true that we cannot talk about nothing, as though it were a thing like the rain outside or a mountain or any object whatsoever. In principle, nothingness remains inaccessible to science. The man who wishes truly to speak about nothing must of necessity become unscientific. But this is a misfortune only so long as one supposes that scientific thinking is the only authentic rigorous thought, and that it alone can and must be made into the standard of philosophical thinking. But the reverse is true. All scientific thought is merely a derived form of philosophical thinking, which proceeded to freeze into its scientific cast. . . . To speak of nothing will always remain a horror and an absurdity for science. . . . Authentic speaking about nothing always remains extraordinary. It cannot be vulgarized. It dissolves if it is placed in the cheap acid of a merely logical intelligence.[31]

Meanwhile, Heidegger's philosophical antagonist, the logical positivist Rudolf Carnap, in his famous attack on metaphysics in general and Heidegger in particular, makes out of Heidegger a paradigm of the sort of nonsense that should be banned from serious scientific philosophy:

> Let us now take a look at some examples of metaphysical pseudo-statements of a kind where the violation of logical syntax is especially obvious . . . *"What about this Nothing? . . . Does the Nothing exist only because the Not, i.e. the Negation exists? Or is it the other way around? Does Negation and the Not exist only because the Nothing exists? . . .* We assert: *the Nothing is prior to the Not and the Negation. . . .* Where do we seek the Nothing? How do we find the Nothing. . . . We know the Nothing. . . . Anxiety reveals the Nothing. . . .* That for which and because of which we were anxious, was 'really'-nothing. Indeed: the Nothing itself—as such— was present. . . . *What about this Nothing?—The Nothing itself nothings."* [Heidegger's original italics, Carnap's original ellipses.] . . . the possibility of forming pseudo-statements is based on a logical defect of language . . . The fault of our language identified here lies, therefore, in the circumstance that, in contrast to a logically correct language, it admits of the same grammatical form for meaningful and meaningless word sequences. . . . The construction

of [sentences like "We seek the Nothing," "We find the Nothing," "We know the Nothing"] is simply based on the mistake of employing the word "nothing" as a noun, because it is customary in ordinary language to use it in this form in order to construct a negative existential statement. . . . Sentence ["The Nothing nothings"] adds something new, viz. the fabrication of the meaningless word "to nothing." This sentence, therefore, is senseless for a twofold reason. We pointed out before that the meaningless words of metaphysics usually owe their origin to the fact that a meaningful word is deprived of its meaning through its metaphorical use in metaphysics. But here we confront one of those rare cases where a new word is introduced which never had a meaning to begin with.[32]

There is a deep irony here. The reason philosophers like Carnap declared the question to be meaningless is that they were trying to keep philosophy in line with science, especially physics, which they took to be the paradigm of human rationality. Yet physics today has one-upped religion's answer by providing, at least, an answer to why there is something rather than nothing and, in the process, proving Parmenides, Heidegger, and Carnap all to be dead wrong. And what were these philosophers wrong *about*? *They were wrong about nothing.* Surely there's a metaphysical moral somewhere in all this?

So: "Why is there something rather than nothing?" The physicist's ultimate answer is that, luckily for us, the *nothing* is unstable. And why that lucky unstable nothing? Why not an unlucky stable nothing, a really bad nothing, unstructured, absolutely nonexistent, a nothing that doesn't snuff itself out of the way to make room for the lucky nothing that nothings itself and thereby gives rise to the preferred participatory universe? The physicist's answer is that the nothing is unstable necessarily. But *why is the nothing unstable?*

Here the physicist can say only this: we can make a model in which the boundary conditions of the universe are that it has no boundary, meaning that the universe itself is not contingent upon anything for its existence. We can show, as Hawking's and Penrose's very powerful singularity theorems show, that on such a model a universe just like ours could come into existence. But why does *that* model apply, rather than there being just absolutely, permanently nothing?

The only answer the physicist can give to *that* question is that in *that* case what we now observe to be the case — the existence of the universe — would not be the case. But *why* is it the case that what we now observe to be the case — ourselves and the universe existing — is the case? *Why*? To this question *physics, like theology, has no answer*. A God whose nature it is to exist necessarily and a nothing whose nature it is to not exist necessarily (i.e., give rise to something) both get swallowed by a question that is bigger than both religion and science, a truly *philosophical* question.

What is a truly philosophical question, and how does it differ from scientific questions? I would like to illustrate with a personal anecdote of what drew me to philosophy from physics in the first place. One day my physics advisor took me aside and said, "Look, Dan, you keep asking these big questions. Why don't you first try and understand all the little answers?" Try as I would, however, the big questions just kept popping into my head in the most inopportune moments: what is an observer? What is an observation? Is physics the study of the world or of our understanding of the world? Finally, my advisor got so frustrated he suggested that perhaps my temperament might make me better suited to philosophy. I asked what philosophy was. I had never even *heard* of it. He said something like, "That's where all they do is ask big questions to which there are no answers." A few years later, I was in my second year of graduate school, working with a great philosopher of science, Dudley Shapere, who was as well versed in relativity theory and quantum mechanics as any physicist I had ever known. I was working on various foundational problems in the philosophy of space and time when it occurred to me that one could make a model of a singularity that was *nothing like* the singularity envisioned by Penrose and Hawking. Penrose's nothing was basically an orderly singularity with enough chaos in it to generate galaxies, stars, and, eventually, people. This to me seemed not at all *nothing*like; it was structured in certain formal ways. In my model of the universe I was trying to work out how a completely unPenrose-like and unHawking-like *completely unstructured nothingness* that would preclude there ever being anything. I would then use my *ultra*singularity theorem *that nothing whatsoever exists* as a Kantian antinomy to the Hawking-Penrose sin-

gularity and thereby show that physicists could not use a singularity as an ultimate explanation for why there is something rather than nothing. I showed my model of the universe to Shapere who suggested I see his friend in the physics department, a well-known physicist named Charles Misner who had — contrary to Penrose and Hawking — been developing what he called a *chaotic* singularity model,[33] in which he tried to show how a universe could nevertheless come out of even a completely unstructured nothing. Shapere told him he had a graduate student who perhaps had the making of a doctoral dissertation that Misner might be interested in. When I showed Misner my model and what I was trying to do with it, he pointed out various mistakes and gaps but suggested that I might indeed wish to develop this further as a doctoral dissertation. He said, "The key thing you've got to decide here is whether you want to patch this thing up far enough mathematically so that it answers your questions, or if you're just going to leave it this way to make philosophical problems." In other words: did I want to be a physicist or a philosopher?

Instead of being excited, I left Misner's office in a quandary. Had it really come to this? Did scientists simply patch things up to get their ultimate answers? Did philosophers just squint the right way to keep making problems? I thought long and hard about it, and I realized I didn't really care about physics. I didn't really care about philosophy. What I really cared about was *why is there something rather than nothing*?

The question. I cared about the question. I didn't want to lose the question. I felt that if I wasn't very careful I would forget about the question, the power of it, the insecurity of it. That question connected me to the whole universe. It made my mind aware of the existence of all things, the mystery of our being here. And I liked that.

I realized that no matter what any physicist, philosopher, or theologian did or said about it, the question was still there. Even if God existed, the question was still there, in God's mind. The question would still exist and even God could not answer it.

There was something *very* special about such questions. In a flash of insight, I realized what it was: the question applied to all possible models of the world, that is, it was in some sense "true" in all possible worlds. It could be asked in all possible worlds. Propositions, I knew, were the sorts of things that were true or false, not questions. Some propositions were true in all possible worlds: they're called *noncontingent* propositions. What if there were some questions that applied to all possible worlds — the counterpart to *noncontingent* propositions — *noncontingent* questions? Mathematics and logic are the domain of noncontingent propositions. What was the domain of noncontingent questions? Walking beneath the trees along the path dividing the campus, I headed straight for philosophy.

Physicists have microscopes. Astronomers have telescopes. Philosophers have questions: *necessary* questions.[34]

NOTES

1. 1798, Part II, p. 305.
2. *Allgemeine geographische Ephemeriden,* verfasset von Einer Gessellschaft Gelehrten, 8vo Weimer, IV, Bd I St. 1799, Ed. F. X. von Zach.
3. Tryon's paper appeared more than a decade before the "inflationary" models, inspired by Guth, made the creation from nothing scenarios popular among quantum cosmologists.
4. Edward Tryon, "Is the Universe a Vacuum Fluctuation?" *Nature* 246 (1973) pp. 396–397.
5. *Op. cit.,* p. 397.
6. *Physical Review D:* [(2) 15 Jan], 1981; for a less technical version, see his article in *Scientific American* 250 (1984) 116–128.
7. One of the most important concepts in modern physics, both for relativity and quantum mechanics, is the *Lorentz invariant,* meaning that an event has a consistent description for all observers depending on how they're moving.
8. See F. Gursy, "Introduction to Group Theory," in *Relativity, Groups and Topology.* New York: Gordon and Breach, 1964.
9. D. Atkatz and H. Pagels, *Phys Rev* D25 (1982) 2065.
10. For those who understand the mathematics, Vilenkin's model relies on properties of the de Sitter compact instanton, a manifold-structure on the four-sphere, S^4.
11. Vilenkin, *op. cit.,* pp. 27–28.
12. J. Hartle and S. W. Hawking, *Phys. Rev.* D 28 (1983) 2906.
13. By integrating path integrals only over compact metrics.
14. Stephen Hawking, *A Brief History of Time.* New York: Bantam Books, 1988, p. 136.
15. Stephen Hawking, *A Brief History of Time,* New York: Bantam Books, 1988, p. 174.

16. C. B. Collins and S. W. Hawking, *Astrophys. J.* 180, 317.
17. J. G. Fichte, *Wissenschaftslehre* (1787). P. Heath and J. Lachs trans., Cambridge: Cambridge University Press, 1982, pp. 8–23.
18. Neils Bohr, *Atomic Theory and the Description of Nature.* Cambridge: Cambridge University Press, 1934, p. 52.
19. Planck's constant is one of the fundamental universal constants of nature. It quantifies the scales at which quantum effects occur and appears in lots of relationships, such as the ratio of the energy of a photon to the frequency of the light wave.
20. Einstein's original thought experiment involved position and momentum. The rediscription is due to David Bohm in the most influential physics text of the 1950s, *Quantum Theory* (Englewood Cliffs: Prentice-Hall, 1951). The shift is not trivial; as you can see by Einstein's reasoning, *no actual experiment needs to be performed.* It is an idealized thought experiment about what *would* have to happen *if* someone did such-and-such. But Einstein's experiment could not actually be performed (any more than one could actually ride a beam of light). Bohm's version, and the version I present here is essentially Bohm's, could in principle be performed.
21. J. A. Wheeler, "Beyond the End of Time," chapter 44 of *Gravitation,* Charles Misner et al., San Francisco: W. H. Freeman and Company, 1971.
22. Ibid.
23. J. Von Neumann, *Mathematical Foundations of Quantum Mechanics.* Princeton, NJ: Princeton University Press, 1955, R. T. Beyer, trans. of the 1932 German ed.
24. E. Schrödinger, *Naturwiss* 23 (1935) 807–849, English trans., J. D. Trimmer, *Proc. Am. Phil. Soc.* 124 (1980) 323.
25. Eugene Wigner, *Monist* 48 (1964) 248.
26. B. S. DeWitt and N. Graham, *The Many-Worlds Interpretation of Quantum Mechanics.* Princeton, NJ: Princeton University Press, 1973.
27. Ibid, p. 186.
28. S. Brush, *Social Stud. Sci* 10 (1980) 393.
29. Simplicius *Phys.* 145, 1 (Dk 28 B 8, lines 1–21) reprinted in J. M. Robinson *An Introduction to Early Greek Philosophy.* New York: Houghton Mifflin, pp. 110–112.
30. Martin Heidegger, *An Introduction to Metaphysics,* New Haven: Yale University Press, 1959.
31. Ibid.
32. Rudolf Carnap, "Uberwindung der Metaphysic durch Logische Analyse der Sprache," *Erkenntnis,* Vol. II (1932).
33. See, for instance, C. W. Misner, *Astrophys. J.* 151 (1968) 431.
34. I thank my colleague Bill Boos for his comments.

Further Questions

1. All the information about the universe that modern astronomers and astrophysicists have collected with their telescopes in 100 years is deduced from an amount of light that is equivalent to the energy of one snowflake hitting the surface of the earth. Relate this to the Problem of Induction raised by Bertrand Russell in the selection titled "Perception, Knowledge, and Induction." How do you suppose a physicist would respond? Better yet, ask one.

2. When you picture the creation of the universe as science envisions it, what does it look like? What does the nothingness that preceded it look like? How does it make you feel to push your imagination to such limits?

3. In the end, Davies suggests that the ultimate bottom line of everything is the underlying physical laws. But why these laws, rather than no laws? Has the ultimate question of existence really been answered? Do you think it ever will be?

4. What is the point of the story with which this selection ends?

5. Do the ideas of quantum mechanics seem puzzling, strange, bizarre to you? Why? Try to identify the *presuppositions* and commonsense intuitions you have that make quantum mechanics difficult to accept. Where did you get those intuitions and presuppositions?

6. Do you think the author's idea of philosophy being the domain of *necessary questions* is a sound one? How would you say it squares with the other selections in this book that you have read?

7. What other necessary questions might you identify from the other readings?

Further Readings

Barrow, John, and Frank Tippler. *The Anthropic Cosmological Principle*. New York: Oxford University Press, 1986. A great scholarly achievement, this book compiles the history of teleological design arguments and sets up the anthropic principle on a solid philosophical foundation. It explores all the relevant quantum mechanical developments, from the big bang to the creation of universes from nothing.

Hawking, Stephen. *A Brief History of Time: From the Big Bang to Black Holes*. New York: Bantam Books, 1988. A tour-de-force of simplicity from one of the great geniuses of the twentieth century; this book explains Hawking's view of the universe in a completely nontechnical way.

Kolak, Daniel. *In Search of God: The Language and Logic of Belief*. Belmont, CA: Wadsworth, 1994. Includes a detailed look at how the latest quantum cosmologies fare against traditional religious arguments.

Penrose, Roger. *The Emperor's New Mind*. New York: Oxford University Press, 1989. A fantastic, thoroughly enjoyable, and very complete rendition of all the latest mathematical and physical developments clearly explained by one of the pivotal figures in quantum mechanics. It includes discussions of Mandelbrot sets, Turing Machines, logic, and relevant philosophical developments.

The Puzzle of Reality: Why Does the Universe Exist?   48

DEREK PARFIT

Derek Parfit is Professor of Philosophy at All Soul's College, Oxford University. He is the foremost philosophical theorist on analytic personal identity theory, and he has made major contributions to the theory of rationality and to ethics. In this selection, Parfit considers a question that some regard as meaningless and others regard as the most fundamental question of metaphysics: "Why is there something rather than nothing at all?"

Reading Questions

1. What distinction does Parfit have in mind between causal answers and other sorts of answers?
2. Parfit says the Big Bang was like the second of his lottery examples. Why?
3. Why does Parfit say that rather than believing that the Big Bang merely happened to be right for life, we should believe either in God or in many worlds?
4. Is there a theory that leaves nothing unexplained? What does Parfit think?
5. What is the Axiarchic View?
6. Why is the problem of evil an objection to some versions of the Axiarchic View? How does it differ from the Brute Fact View? The Maximalist View?
7. What does Parfit mean by "a plausible selector"?

IT MIGHT HAVE BEEN TRUE that nothing ever existed: no minds, no atoms, no space, no time. When we imagine this possibility, it can seem astonishing that anything exists. Why is there a universe? And things might have been, in countless ways, different. So why is the Universe as it is?

These facts cannot be causally explained. No law of nature could explain why there are any laws of nature, or why these laws are as they are. And, if God created the world, there cannot be a causal explanation of why God exists.

Since our questions cannot have causal answers, we may wonder whether they make sense. But there may be other kinds of answers.

Consider, first, a more particular question. Many physicists believe that, for stars, planets and life to be able to exist, the initial conditions in the Big Bang had to be precisely as they were. Why were these conditions so precisely right? Some say: "If they had not been right, we couldn't even ask this question." But that is no answer. It could be baffling how we survived some crash even though, if we hadn't, we could not be baffled.

Others say: "There had to be some initial conditions, and those conditions were as likely as any others. So there is nothing to be explained." To see what is wrong with this reply, we must distinguish two kinds of case. Suppose that, of a million people facing death, only one can be rescued. If there is a lottery to pick this one survivor, and I win, I would be very lucky. But there would be nothing to be explained. Someone had to win, and why not me? Consider next a second lottery. Unless my gaoler picks the longest of a million straws, I shall be beheaded. If I win this lottery, there *would* be something to be explained. It would not be enough to say, "That result was as likely as any other." In the first lottery, nothing special happened: whatever the result, someone's life would be saved. In this second lottery, the result *was* special. Of the million possible results, only one would save a life. Why was *this* what happened? Though this might be a coincidence, the chance of that is only one in a million. I could be almost certain that this lottery was rigged.

The Big Bang, it seems, was like the second lottery. For life to be possible, the initial conditions had to be selected with the kind of accuracy that would be needed to hit a bull's-eye in a distant galaxy. Since it is not arrogant to think life special, this appearance of fine-tuning needs to be explained. Of the countless possible initial conditions, why were the ones that allowed for life *also* the ones that actually obtained?

On one view, this was a mere coincidence. That is conceivable, but most unlikely. On some estimates, the chance is below one in a billion billion. Others say: "The Big Bang *was* fine-tuned. It is not surprising that God chose to make life possible." We may be tempted to dismiss this answer, thinking it improbable that God exists. But should we put the chance as low as one in a billion billion? If not, this is a better explanation.

There is, however, a rival explanation. Our Universe may not be the whole of reality. Some physicists suggest that there are many other Universes — or, to avoid confusion, *worlds.* These worlds have the same laws of nature as our own world, and they emerged from similar Big Bangs, but each had slightly different initial conditions. On this *many-worlds hypothesis,* there would be no need for fine-tuning. If there were enough Big Bangs, it would be no surprise that, in a few of these, conditions were just right for life. And it would be no surprise that our Big Bang was one of these few.

On most versions of this theory, these many worlds are not causally related, and each has its own space and time. Some object that, since our world could not be affected by such other worlds, we have no reason to believe in them. But we do have such a reason, since their existence would explain an otherwise puzzling feature of our world: the appearance of fine-tuning.

How should we choose between these explanations? The many-worlds hypothesis is more cautious, since it merely claims that there is more of the kind of reality we know. But God's existence has been claimed to be intrinsically more plausible.

By "God" we mean a being who is omnipotent, omniscient, and wholly good. The existence of such a being has been claimed to be both simpler, and less arbitrary, than the existence of many complicated and specific worlds.

If such a God exists, however, why is the Universe as it is? It may not be surprising that God chose to make life possible. But the laws of nature could have been different, so there are many possible worlds that would have contained life. It is hard to understand why, with all these possibilities, God chose to create *our* world. The greatest difficulty here is the problem of evil. There appears to be suffering which any good person, knowing the truth, would have prevented if he could. If there is such suffering, there cannot be a God who is omnipotent, omniscient, and wholly good.

One response to this problem is to revise our view of God. Some suggest that God is not omnipotent. But, with that revision, the hypothesis that God exists becomes less plausible. How could there be a being who, though able to create our world, cannot prevent such suffering? Others believe in a god who, whatever he is called, is not good. Though that view more easily explains the character of life on Earth, it may seem in other ways less credible.

As we shall see, there may be other answers to this problem. But we have larger questions to consider. I began by asking why things are as they are. We must also ask *how* things are. There is much about our world that we have not discovered. And, just as there may be other worlds like ours, there may be worlds that are very different.

It will help to distinguish two kinds of possibility. For each particular kind of possible world, there is the *local* possibility that such a world exists. If there is such a world, that leaves it open whether there are also other worlds. *Global* possibilities, in contrast, cover the whole Universe, or everything that ever exists. One global possibility is that *every* conceivable world exists. That is claimed by the *all-worlds hypothesis.* Another possibility, which might have obtained, is that nothing ever exists. This we can call the *Null Possibility.* In each of the remaining possibilities, the number of possible worlds that exist is between none and all. There are countless of these possibilities, since there are countless combinations of particular possible worlds.

Of these different global possibilities, one must obtain, and only one can obtain. So we have two questions. Which obtains, and why? These questions are connected. If some possibility would be less puzzling, or easier to explain, we have more reason to think that it obtains. That is why, rather than believing that the Big Bang merely happened to be right for life, we should believe either in God or many worlds.

Is there some global possibility whose obtaining would be in no way puzzling? That might be claimed of the Null Possibility. It might be said that, if no one had ever existed, no one would have been puzzled. But that misunderstands our questions. Suppose that, in a mindless and finite Universe, an object looking like the *TLS* [*Times Literary Supplement*] spontaneously formed. Even with no one to be puzzled, that would be, in the sense I mean, puzzling. It may next be said that, if there had never been anything, there wouldn't have been anything to be explained. But that is not so. When we imagine that nothing ever existed, what we imagine away are such things as minds and atoms, space and time. There would still have been truths. It would have been true that nothing existed, and that things might have existed. And there would have been other truths, such as the truth that 27 is divisible by 3. We can ask why these things would have been true.

These questions may have answers. We can explain why, even if nothing had ever existed, 27 would have been divisible by 3. There is no conceivable alternative. And we can explain the non-existence of such things as two-horned unicorns, or spherical cubes. Such things are logically impossible. But why would *nothing* have existed? Why would there have been no stars or atoms, no minds or bluebell woods? How could *that* be explained?

We should not claim that, if nothing had existed, there would have been nothing to be explained. But we might claim something less. Perhaps, of all the global possibilities, this would have needed the least explanation. It is much the simplest. And it seems the easiest to understand. When we imagine there never being anything, that does not seem, as our own existence can, astonishing.

Here, for example, is one natural line of thought. It may seem that, for any particular thing to exist, its existence must have been caused by other

things. If that is so, what could have caused them *all* to exist? If there were an infinite series of things, the existence of each might be caused by other members of that series. But that could not explain why there was this whole series, rather than some other series, or no series. In contrast, the Null Possibility raises no such problem. If nothing had ever existed, that state of affairs would not have needed to be caused.

Even if this possibility would have been the easiest to explain, it does not obtain. Reality does not take its simplest and least puzzling form.

Consider next the all-worlds hypothesis. That may seem the next least puzzling possibility. For one thing, it avoids arbitrary distinctions. If only one world exists, we have the question: "Out of all the possible worlds, why is *this* the one that exists?" On the many-worlds hypothesis, we have the question: Why are *these* the ones? But, if *all* possible worlds exist, there is no such question. Though the all-worlds hypothesis avoids that question, it is not as simple as it seems. Is there a sharp distinction between those worlds that are and are not possible? Must all worlds be governed by natural laws? Does each kind of world exist only once? And there are further complications.

Whichever global possibility obtains, we can ask why it obtains. All that I have claimed so far is that, with some possibilities, this question would be less puzzling. We should now ask: Could this question have an answer? Is there a theory that leaves nothing unexplained?

On one kind of view, it is logically necessary that God, or the whole Universe, exists. Though it may seem conceivable that there might never have been anything, that is not really logically possible. Some people even claim that there is only one coherent global possibility. If such a view were true, everything would be explained. But the standard objections to such views, which I shall not repeat, seem to me convincing.

Others claim that the Universe exists because its existence is good. This is the Platonic, or Axiarchic, View. Even if we think this view absurd, it is worth asking whether it makes sense. That may suggest other possibilities.

The Axiarchic View can take a theistic form. It can claim that God exists because His existence is good, and that the rest of the Universe exists be-

MIND AND PHYSICS

Freeman Dyson

It is remarkable that mind enters into our awareness of nature on two separate levels. At the highest level, the level of human consciousness, our minds are somehow directly aware of the complicated flow of electrical and chemical patterns in our brains. At the lowest level, the level of single atoms and electrons, the mind of an observer is again involved in the description of events. Between lies the level of molecular biology, where mechanical models are adequate and mind appears to be irrelevant. But I, as a physicist, cannot help suspecting that there is a logical connection between the two ways in which mind appears in my universe. I cannot help thinking that our awareness of our own brains has some-thing to do with the process which we call "observation" in atomic physics. That is to say, I think our consciousness is not just a passive epiphenomenon carried along by the chemical events in our brains, but is an active agent forcing the molecular complexes to make choices between one quantum state and another. In other words, mind is already inherent in every electron, and the processes of human consciousness differ only in degree but not in kind from the processes of choice between quantum states which we call "chance" when they are made by electrons.

From *Disturbing the Universe* (1988).

cause God caused it to exist. But in that explanation God is redundant. If God can exist because His existence is good, so can the whole Universe.

In its simplest form, the Axiarchic View makes three claims: (1) It would be best if reality were a certain way. (2) Reality is that way. (3) (1) explains (2).

(1) is an ordinary evaluative claim, like the claim that it would be better if there was no pointless suffering. The Axiarchic View assumes, in my opinion correctly, that such claims can be true. (2) is an ordinary descriptive claim, though of a sweeping kind. What is distinctive in this view is claim (3).

Can we understand (3)? To focus on this question, we should briefly ignore the world's evils. Suppose that, as Leibniz claimed, the best possible Universe exists. Could this Universe exist *because* it is the best? That question might be confused with another. If God intentionally created the best possible world, that world would exist because it is the best. But, though God would not be part of the world that He creates, He would be part of the Universe, or the totality of what exists. And God cannot have created Him-self. So an appeal to God cannot explain why the best Universe exists.

Axiarchists make a different claim. On their view, that there is a best way for reality to be explains *directly* why reality is that way. If God exists, that is because His existing is best. Truths about value are, in John Leslie's phrase, *creatively effective.*

This cannot be an ordinary causal claim. Ordinary causes are particular events, or facts about existing things. But the axiarchic claim may have some of the meaning of an ordinary causal claim.

When we believe that X caused Y, we usually believe that, without an X, there would have been no Y. A spark caused an explosion if, without a spark, there would have been no explosion. Axiarchists might make a similar claim. They might say that, if it had not been best if reality were a certain way, reality would not have been that way. But such a claim may not help to explain the Axiarchic View, since what it asks us to imagine could not have been true. Just as pointless suffering could not have been good, the best way for reality to be could not have failed to be the best.

In defending a causal claim, we may also appeal to a generalization. Certain conditions cause an explosion if, whenever there are such conditions, there is an explosion. It may seem that, with only one Universe, Axiarchists cannot appeal to a generalization. But that is not so. They could say that, whenever it would be better if the Universe had some particular feature, it *has* that feature.

Would that explain their claim that this is *why* the Universe has these features? That use of "why" may seem utterly mysterious. But we should remember that even ordinary causation is mysterious. At the most fundamental level, we have no idea why some events cause others. And it is hard to explain what causation is.

Axiarchy can be best explained as follows. We are now assuming that, of all the countless ways that reality might be, one is both the very best, and is the way that reality is. On the Axiarchic View, *that is no coincidence*. That claim makes, I believe, some kind of sense. And, on those assumptions, it would be a reasonable conclusion.

Compared with the appeal to God, the Axiarchic View has one advantage. God cannot have settled *whether*, as part of the best Universe, He himself exists, since He can only settle anything if He does exist. But even if nothing had ever existed, it would still have been true that it would be best if the best Universe existed. So that truth might explain why this Universe exists.

The main objection to this view is the problem of evil. Our world appears to be flawed.

If we appeal to a variant of the many-worlds hypothesis, this objection can be partly met. Perhaps, in the best Universe, *all* good possible worlds exist. We would then avoid the question why things are not much better than they are. Things *are*, on the whole, much better. They are better elsewhere.

Why are they not *also* better here? One answer might be as follows. If it is best that all good worlds exist, that implies that, even in the best Universe, many worlds would not be very good. Some would be only just good enough. Perhaps our world is one of these. It would then be good that our world exists, since a good niche is thereby filled. And we might be able to explain why our world is not better than it is. The Louvre would be a worse collection if its less good paintings were turned into copies of the "Mona Lisa." In the same way, if our world were in itself better, reality as a whole might be less good. Since every other good niche is already filled, our world would then be a mere copy of some other world, and one good niche would be left unfilled.

Even on this view, however, each world must be good enough. The existence of each world must be better, even if only slightly, than its nonexistence. Can this be claimed of our world? It would be easier to make that claim on a broadly Utilitarian view. Our world's evils might then be outweighed by what is good. But, on some principles of justice, that would not be enough. If innocent beings suffer, in lives that are not worth living, that could not be morally outweighed by the happiness of other beings. For our world to be good enough, there must be future lives in which the sufferings of each being could, in the end, be made good. Even the burnt fawn in the forest fire must live again. Or perhaps these different beings are, at some level, one.

These replies may seem too weak. We may doubt that our world could be even the least good part of the best possible Universe.

If we reject the Axiarchic View, what conclusion should we draw? Is the existence of our world a mere brute fact, with no explanation? That does not follow. If we abstract from the optimism of this view, its claims are these. One global possibility has a special feature, this is the possibility that obtains, and it obtains because it has this feature. Other views can make such claims.

Suppose that our world were part of the worst possible Universe. Its bright days may only make its tragedies worse. If reality were as bad as it could be, could we not suspect that this was no coincidence?

Suppose next, more plausibly, that all possible worlds exist. That would also be grim, since the evil of the worst worlds could hardly be outweighed. But that would be incidental. If every conceivable world exists, reality has a different distinctive feature. It is *maximal*: as full and varied as it could possibly be. If this is true, is it a coincidence? Does it merely happen to be true that, of all the countless global possibilities, the one that obtains is at this extreme? As always, that is conceivable. Coincidences can occur. But it seems hard to believe. We can reasonably assume that, if all possible worlds exist, that is *because* that makes reality as full as it could be.

COSMIC RELIGIOUS FEELING

Albert Einstein

It is easy to see why the churches have always fought science and persecuted its devotees. On the other hand, I maintain that the cosmic religious feeling is the strongest and noblest motive for scientific research. Only those who realize the immense efforts and, above all, the devotion without which pioneer work in theoretical science cannot be achieved are able to grasp the strength of the emotion out of which alone such work, remote as it is from the immediate realities of life, can issue. What a deep conviction of the rationality of the universe and what a yearning to understand, were it but a feeble reflection of the mind revealed in this world, Kepler and Newton must have had to enable them to spend years of solitary labor in disentangling the principles of celestial mechanics! Those whose acquaintance

with scientific research is derived chiefly from its practical results easily develop a completely false notion of the mentality of the men who, surrounded by a skeptical world, have shown the way to kindred spirits scattered wide through the world and the centuries. Only one who has devoted his life to similar ends can have a vivid realization of what has inspired these men and given them the strength to remain true to their purpose in spite of countless failures. It is cosmic religious feeling that gives a man such strength. A contemporary has said, not unjustly, that in this materialistic age of ours the serious scientific workers are the only profoundly religious people.

From *Religion and Science* (1950).

Similar remarks apply to the Null Possibility. If there had never been anything, would that have been a coincidence? Would it have merely happened that, of all the possibilities, what obtained was the *only* possibility in which nothing exists? That is also hard to believe. Rather, if this possibility had obtained, that would have been because it had that feature.

Here is another special feature. Perhaps reality is as it is because that makes its fundamental laws as mathematically beautiful as they could be. That is what many physicists believe.

If some possibility obtains because it has some feature, that feature selects what reality is like. Let us call it the *Selector*. A feature is a *plausible* Selector if we can reasonably believe that, were reality to have that feature, that would not merely happen to be true.

There are countless features which are not plausible Selectors. Suppose that fifty-seven worlds exist. Like all numbers, 57 has some special features. For example, it is the smallest number that is the

sum of seven primes. But that could hardly be *why* that number of worlds exist.

I have mentioned certain plausible Selectors. A possibility might obtain because it is the best, or the simplest, or the least arbitrary, or because it makes reality as full as it could be, or because its fundamental laws are as elegant as they could be. There are, I assume, other such features, some of which we have yet to discover.

For each of these features, there is the *explanatory* possibility that this feature *is* the Selector. That feature then explains why reality is as it is. There is one other, special explanatory possibility: that there is *no* Selector. This is like the global possibility that nothing exists. If there is no Selector, it is random that reality is as it is. Events may be in one sense random, even though they are causally inevitable. That is how it is random whether a meteorite strikes the land or the sea. Events are random in a stronger sense if they have no cause. That is what most physicists believe about some facts at the quantum level, such as how some particles move. If it is random what reality is like, the Universe would not only have no cause, it would have no explanation of any kind. This we can call the *Brute Fact View.*

On this view, we should not expect reality to have very special features, such as being maximal, or best, or having very simple laws, or including God. In much the largest range of the global possibilities, there would exist an arbitrary set of messily complicated worlds. That is what, with a random selection, we should expect. It is unclear whether ours is one such world.

The Brute Fact View may seem hard to understand. It may seem baffling how reality could be even randomly selected. What kind of *process* could select whether time had no beginning, or whether anything ever exists? But this is not a real problem. It is logically necessary that one global possibility obtains. There is no conceivable alternative. Since it is necessary that one possibility obtains, it is necessary that it be settled which obtains. Even without any kind of process, logic ensures that a selection is made. There is no need for hidden machinery.

If reality were randomly selected, it would not be mysterious *how* the selection is made. It would be in one sense inexplicable why the Universe is as it is. But this would be no more puzzling than the random movement of a particle. If a particle can simply happen to move as it does, it could simply happen that reality is as it is. Randomness may even be *less* puzzling at the level of the whole Universe, since we know that facts at this level could not have been caused.

There would, however, be a further question. If there is no explanation why reality is as it is, why is *that* true?

Some reply that this, too, is logically necessary. On their view, the nature of the Universe must be a mere brute fact, since it could not conceivably be explained. But, as I have argued, that is not so. Though it is logically necessary that one global possibility obtain, it is not necessary that it be random which obtains. There are other explanatory possibilities.

Since it is not necessary that there be no explanation why reality is as it is, that truth might be another brute fact. There may be no explanation why there is no explanation. Perhaps both simply

happen to be true. But why would *that* be true? Would it, too, simply happen to be true? And why should we accept this view? If it was randomly selected *whether* reality was selected randomly, and there are several other possibilities, why expect random selection to have been selected? Unless we can explain *why* it is random what reality is like, we may have no reason to believe that this *is* random.

Return now to the other explanatory possibilities. Each raises the same further question. Whichever possibility obtains, we can ask why it obtains. Consider first the Axiarchic View. Suppose that the best Universe exists because it is the best. Why is that true? Even if this view is true, its falsehood is at least logically conceivable. It may seem that Axiarchy could explain itself. On this view, claims about reality are true because their being true is best. It might be best if this view were true. Could that be why it *is* true? That is not possible. Even if this view is true, its being true could not be explained by its being true. Just as God cannot have caused His own existence, the truth of the Axiarchic View cannot be what makes this view true.

Consider next the Maximalist View. Suppose that all possible worlds exist, and that this is no coincidence. Suppose these worlds all exist because that makes reality as full as it could be. If that is true, why is it true? Perhaps this truth makes reality even more maximal. But, as before, this truth could not explain itself.

A similar claim may apply to every view. As we have seen, it is not logically necessary that, of the *global* possibilities, it is random which obtains. This possibility might be selected in other ways. But it may be logically necessary that, of the *explanatory* possibilities, it is random which obtains. Perhaps nothing could select between all the possible Selectors: If that were so, it would not be mysterious that a particular explanatory claim simply happened to be true. The randomness would be fully explained, since there would be no conceivable alternative.

It may be objected that, if some claim simply happens to be true, it cannot provide an explanation. Such a claim may seem to add nothing. To illustrate this objection, return to the Maximalist View. Consider first two global possibilities:

(1) Only our world exists. (2) Every conceivable world exists. These possibilities are very different. Suppose next that (2) is true. There are then two explanatory possibilities. On the Brute Fact View, (2) simply happens to be true. On the Maximalist View, (2) is true because that makes reality as full as it could be. Here again, these seem to be different possibilities. But we are now supposing that, even if the Maximalist View is true, its truth is a brute fact, with no explanation. We may think that, if that is so, the Maximalist View could not *explain* (2). If this view simply happens to be true, it may seem not to differ from the Brute Fact View.

That reaction is a mistake. On the Brute Fact View, (2) would involve an extreme coincidence. There are countless global possibilities, and most of these, unlike (2), have no very special feature. It is hard to believe that, of this vast range of possibilities, it simply happens to be true that every conceivable world exists. That is implausible because, at this level, there is an alternative. If the Maximalist View is true, the existence of all these worlds is no coincidence. At the next level, things are different. Of the plausible explanatory possibilities, all have special features. There is no possibility whose obtaining would be a coincidence. And, as we have seen, it may be logically necessary that, of *these*

possibilities, one simply happens to obtain. At this level, there may be no alternative. It would then be in no way puzzling if the Maximalist View simply happens to be true.

We should not claim that, if an explanation rests on a brute fact, it is not an explanation. Scientific explanations all take this form. But we might claim something less. Any such explanation may, in the end, be merely a better description.

If that is true, there is a different answer. Even to discover how things are, we need explanations. And we may need explanations on the grandest scale. Our world may seem to have some feature that would be unlikely to be a coincidence. We might reasonably suspect that our world exists, not as a brute fact, but because it has this feature. That hypothesis might lead us to confirm that, as it seemed, our world does have this feature. We might then reasonably conclude either that ours is the only world, or that there are many other worlds, with the same or related features. We might reach truths about the whole Universe.

Even if all explanations must end with a brute fact, we should go on trying to explain why the Universe exists, and is as it is. The brute fact may not enter at the lowest level. If the Universe exists because it has some feature, to know *what* reality is like, we must ask *why*.

Further Questions

1. Is it more psychologically satisfying to you to say that the Universe was created by God and that nothing created God, or that nothing created the Universe? Why?
2. Is the idea of something—an entity, an explanation—that explains itself an intelligible idea?

Further Readings

Mackie, John. *The Miracle of Theism*. Oxford: Clarendon Press, 1982. A highly respected philosopher explains why, in his opinion, theistic explanations of the universe are vacuous.

Nozick, Robert. *Philosophical Explanations*. Cambridge, MA: Harvard University Press, 1981. Includes a discussion of the possibility that some explanations might explain everything else and also explain themselves.

Part VIII

Experience

DEEP IN THE HEART OF A MYSTERIOUS LABYRINTH you find the center. Cautiously, you step in only to find yourself in yet another labyrinth, deeper and more puzzling than the first. You wander through it until you find its center—where there is yet another labyrinth, a labyrinth within a labyrinth within a labyrinth—

You turn and go back. You find the exit to the original labyrinth where you began. You step out into an outer labyrinth. You continue outward, exiting into another outer labyrinth, then another—

You go inward, entering one labyrinth after another. You go outward, exiting into one labyrinth after another. You never emerge: *there is no exit.* You never find what you are looking for: *There is no center.*

Perhaps you find this story strange. But that is where you are now: inside a labyrinth. The labyrinth has a name. It is called "experience."

That experience exists at all is both obvious and puzzling. Right now you are having the experience of reading a book and, along with it, the experience of being in the world at a particular place and time. You might be mistaken about whether your experience is accurate or true. But you cannot be mistaken about whether experience itself—accurate or not—is going on. Experience is happening. To you. Now.

There is far less correspondence between your experiences and what exists outside you than you probably think. And that there is any correspondence at all is based *completely* on theory. It cannot be verified in your experience! In other words, the experiences you are having cannot be *seen* to be a reliable indication of what exists outside you because every element of your experience is inside you. The puzzle goes deeper. No one has ever been able to explain unproblematically how experience is even possible—how for instance, atoms interacting with each other can produce sensation, emotions, and thoughts—what you might call your "mental inside."

Your experiences are always inside. Inside what? You. Along with your image of the outside there is also the image of you, the image of a something that has an inside. This "having an inside" is the ability to have experiences: something we call consciousness. But consciousness, too, like your image of the outside, is synthesized by you! How could that be? How could your brain, a collection of nonconscious elements, ever become conscious? How could this "having an inside," "being a center of consciousness," ever come about? What *is* consciousness?

Suppose you did find yourself inside a mysterious labyrinth within a labyrinth whose center is a labyrinth that has yet another labyrinth for a center. What would you do?

Perhaps this.

49   Of Sense and Imagination

THOMAS HOBBES

Thomas Hobbes (1588–1679) decided to become a philosopher when, one day in the library, he came across the Pythagorean Theorem, studied it, and—in a flash of insight—was seduced by geometry and the power of reason into spending the rest of his life trying to understand the world. Educated at Oxford University, Hobbes fled the country when England was torn by civil strife. He went to France, where he ended up reading Descartes' *Meditations* before its publication. The work looked to him so derivative of Plato that his first response was to say "I am sorry that so excellent an author of new speculations should publish this old stuff." Descartes published all of Hobbes' objections, along with his own rebuttals.

Ten years later, in 1651, Hobbes published his own masterwork, *Leviathan*. Like Descartes, he developed a method of inquiry, but his ran along a different path. Hobbes called his method, which was influenced not only by Descartes but also by Galileo, *resolution and composition*. Like Descartes' second rule for the direction of the mind, which itself is based on Plato's division of ideas, *resolution* involves analysis of complex wholes into simpler elements. Like Descartes' third rule, *composition* consists in synthesis, or putting back together the parts into a whole. But the similarities end there. Whereas Descartes argued that the mind is something completely separate and distinct from the body, and not reducible to physical elements, Hobbes maintained that the mind is not separate from the body; rather, like the body, it is itself a purely physical thing.

Reading Questions

1. What does Hobbes mean by saying that thoughts are representations?
2. What is a representation?
3. What is the cause of our thoughts? What are the causes of sights? Of sounds? Of the understanding?
4. Why is imagination nothing more than decaying sense?
5. What is experience? What is the relationship between experience and memory?
6. What is the difference between simple and compound imagination?
7. How can dreaming be distinguished from waking states?

CHAPTER 1: OF SENSE

SENSE. CONCERNING THE THOUGHTS OF MAN, I will consider them first singly, and afterwards in train, or dependence upon one another. Singly, they are every one a *representation* or *appearance,* of some quality, or other accident of a body without us, which is commonly called an *object.* Which object worketh on the eyes, ears, and other parts of a man's body; and by diversity of working, produceth diversity of appearances.

The original of them all, is that which we call SENSE, for there is no conception in a man's mind, which hath not at first, totally, or by parts, been begotten upon the organs of sense. The rest are derived from that original.

To know the natural cause of sense, is not very necessary to the business now in hand; and I have elsewhere written of the same at large. Nevertheless, to fill each part of my present method, I will briefly deliver the same in this place.

The cause of sense, is the external body, or object, which presseth the organ proper to each sense, either immediately, as in the taste and touch; or mediately, as in seeing, hearing, and smelling; which pressure, by the mediation of the nerves, and other strings and membranes of the body, continued inwards to the brain and heart, causeth there a resistance, or counter-pressure, or endeavour of the heart to deliver itself, which endeavour, because *outward,* seemeth to be some matter without. And this *seeming,* or *fancy,* is that which men call *sense;* and consisteth, as to the eye, in a *light,* or *colour* figured; to the ear, in a *sound;* to the nostrils in an *odour;* to the tongue and palate, in a *savour;* and to the rest of the body, in *heat, cold, hardness, softness,* and such other qualities as we discern by *feelings.* All which qualities, called *sensible,* are in the object, that causeth them, but so many several motions of the matter, by which it presseth our organs diversely. Neither in us that are pressed, are they anything else, but divers motions; for motion produceth nothing but motion. But their appearance to us is fancy, the same waking, that dreaming. And as pressing, rubbing, or striking the eye, makes us fancy a light; and pressing the ear, produceth a din; so do the bodies also we see, or hear, produce the same by their strong, though unobserved action. For if these colours and sounds were in the bodies, or objects that cause them, they could not be severed from them, as by glasses, and in echoes by reflection, we see they are; where we know the thing we see is in one place, the appearance in another. And though at some certain distance, the real and very object seem invested with the fancy it begets in us; yet the object is one thing, the image or fancy is another. So that sense, in all cases, is nothing else but original fancy, caused, as I have said, by the pressure, that is, by the motion, of external things upon our eyes, ears, and other organs thereunto ordained.

But the philosophy-schools, through all the universities of Christendom, grounded upon certain texts of Aristotle, teach another doctrine, and say, for the cause of *vision,* that the thing seen, sendeth forth on every side a *visible species,* in English, a *visible show, apparition,* or *aspect,* or *a being seen;* the receiving whereof into the eye, is *seeing.* And for the cause of *hearing,* that the thing heard, sendeth forth an *audible species,* that is an *audible aspect,* or *audible being seen;* which entering at the ear, maketh *hearing.* Nay, for the cause of *understanding* also, they say the thing understood, sendeth forth an *intelligible species,* that is, an *intelligible being seen;* which, coming into the understanding, makes us understand. I say not this, as disproving the use of universities; but because I am to speak hereafter of their office in a commonwealth, I must let you see on all occasions by the way, what things would be amended in them; amongst which the frequency of insignificant speech is one.

CHAPTER 2: OF IMAGINATION

Imagination.   That when a thing lies still, unless somewhat else stir it, it will lie still for ever, is a truth that no man doubts of. But that when a thing is in motion, it will eternally be in motion, unless somewhat else stay it, though the reason be the same, namely, that nothing can change itself, is

From Leviathan *in* The English Works of Thomas Hobbes of Malmesbury, *collected and edited by Sir William Molesworth (London: John Bohn, 1839).*

not so easily assented to. For men measure, not only other men, but all other things, by themselves; and because they find themselves subject after motion to pain, and lassitude, think every thing else grows weary of motion, and seeks repose of its own accord; little considering, whether it be not some other motion, wherein that desire of rest they find in themselves, consisteth. From hence it is, that the schools say, heavy bodies fall downwards, out of an appetite to rest, and to conserve their nature in that place which is most proper for them; ascribing appetite, and knowledge of what is good for their conservation, which is more than man has, to things inanimate, absurdly.

When a body is once in motion, it moveth, unless something else hinder it, eternally; and whatsoever hindreth it, cannot in an instant, but in time, and by degrees, quite extinguish it; and as we see in the water, though the wind cease, the waves give not over rolling for a long time after: so also it happeneth in that motion, which is made in the internal parts of a man, then, when he sees, dreams, &c. For after the object is removed, or the eye shut, we still retain an image of the thing seen, though more obscure than when we see it. And this is it, the Latins call *imagination*, for the image made in seeing; and apply the same, though improperly, to all the other senses. But the Greeks call it *fancy;* which signifies *appearance,* and is as proper to one sense, as to another. IMAGINATION therefore is nothing but *decaying sense;* and is found in men, and many other living creatures, as well sleeping, as waking.

The decay of sense in men waking, is not the decay of the motion made in sense; but an obscuring of it, in such manner as the light of the sun obscureth the light of the stars; which stars do no less exercise their virtue, by which they are visible, in the day than in the night. But because amongst many strokes, which our eyes, ears, and other organs receive from external bodies, the predominant only is sensible; therefore, the light of the sun being predominant, we are not affected with the action of the stars. And any object being removed from our eyes, though the impression it made in us remain, yet other objects more present succeeding, and working on us, the imagination of the past is obscured, and made weak, as the voice of a man is in the noise of the day. From whence it followeth, that the longer the time is, after the sight or sense of any object, the weaker is the imagination. For the continual change of man's body destroys in time the parts which in sense were moved: so that distance of time, and of place, hath one and the same effect in us. For as at a great distance of place, that which we look at appears dim, and without distinction of the smaller parts; and as voices grow weak, and inarticulate; so also, after great distance of time, our imagination of the past is weak; and we lose, for example, of cities we have seen, many particular streets, and of actions, many particular circumstances. This *decaying sense,* when we would express the thing itself, I mean *fancy* itself, we call *imagination,* as I said before: but when we would express the decay, and signify that the sense is fading, old, and past, it is called *memory.* So that imagination and memory are but one thing, which for divers considerations hath divers names.

Much memory, or memory of many things, is called *experience.* Again, imagination being only of those things which have been formerly perceived by sense, either all at once, or by parts at several times; the former, which is the imagining the whole object as it was presented to the sense, is *simple* imagination, as when one imagineth a man, or horse, which he hath seen before. The other is *compounded;* as when, from the sight of a man at one time, and of a horse at another, we conceive in our mind a Centaur. So when a man compoundeth the image of his own person with the image of the actions of another man, as when a man imagines himself a Hercules or an Alexander, which happeneth often to them that are much taken with reading of romances, it is a compound imagination, and properly but a fiction of the mind. There be also other imaginations that rise in men, though waking, from the great impression made in sense: as from gazing upon the sun, the impression leaves an image of the sun before our eyes a long time after; and from being long and vehemently attent upon geometrical figures, a man shall in the dark, though awake, have the images of lines and angles before his eyes; which kind of fancy hath no particular name, as being a thing that doth not commonly fall into men's discourse.

The imaginations of them that sleep, are those we call *dreams.* And these also (as all other imaginations) have been before, either totally, or by parcels in the sense. And because in sense, the brain, and nerves, which are the necessary organs of sense, are so benumbed in sleep, as not easily to be moved by the action of *external objects,* there can happen in sleep, no imagination; and therefore no dream, but what proceeds from the agitation of the inward parts of man's body; which inward parts, for the connexion they have with the brain, and other organs, when they be distempered, do keep the same in motion; whereby the imaginations there formerly made, appear as if a man were waking; saving that the *organs of sense* being now benumbed, so as there is no new object, which can master and obscure them with a more vigorous impression, a dream must needs be more clear, in this silence of sense, than are our waking thoughts. And hence it cometh to pass, that it is a hard matter, and by many thought impossible to distinguish exactly between *sense* and *dreaming.* For my part, when I consider, that in dreams, I do not often, nor constantly think of the same persons, places, objects, and actions that I do waking; nor remember so long a train of coherent thoughts, dreaming, as at other times; and because waking I often observe the absurdity of dreams, but never dream of the absurdities of my waking thoughts; I am well satisfied, that being awake, I know I dream not; though when I dream, I think my self awake.

And seeing dreams are caused by the distemper of some of the inward parts of the body; diverse distempers must needs cause different dreams. And hence it is, that lying cold breedeth dreams of fear, and raiseth the thought and image of some fearful object (the motion from the brain to the inner parts, and from the inner parts to the brain being reciprocal:) And that as anger causeth heat in some parts of the body, when we are awake; so when we sleep, the over heating of the same parts causeth anger, and raiseth up in the brain the imagination of an enemy. In the same manner; as natural kindness, when we are awake causeth desire; and desire makes heat in certain other parts of the body; so also, too much heat in those parts, while we sleep, raiseth in the brain an imagination of some kindness shown. In sum, our dreams are the reverse of our waking imaginations; the motion when we are awake, beginning at one end; and when we dream, at another. . . .

Further Questions

1. Compare Hobbes's view of the role of dreams in the analysis of the nature of knowledge and experience with Descartes's.
2. How do you think Descartes might respond to Hobbes?

Further Readings

Hobbes, Thomas. *Leviathan,* in *The English Works of Thomas Hobbes of Malmesbury.* Sir William Molesworth, ed., London: John Bohm, 1839. A complete collection of all of Hobbes's major works.
Hobbes, Thomas. *Objections to Descartes' Meditations.* Cambridge: Cambridge University Press, 1911.

50   Experience and Understanding

JOHN LOCKE

A brief biography of Locke appears on page 120.

In the following selection, Locke tries to account for the origin and nature of human knowledge. Unlike earlier philosophers, such as Descartes, who emphasized reason and intuition as sources of knowledge about the world, Locke emphasizes experience.

Reading Questions

1. How does Locke outline his method?
2. Why is it useful to know the extent of our comprehension?
3. What is the cure for skepticism?
4. What does Locke mean by an idea? What is the relationship between ideas and the objects of our understanding? Where do all our ideas come from?
5. What are the objects of sensation? What is the difference between reflection and sensation?
6. What accounts for the differences among people's stores of ideas? In other words, why don't we all agree about everything?
7. What do reflective ideas require that those based on sensation do not?
8. What does he mean by personal identity?
9. Why are thoughts during dreaming not rational? In what does thinking consist?
10. What proof does Locke offer for the thesis that there can be no ideas without sensation and reflection? Is this proof rational or is it empirical? Why?
11. Why does the mind think in proportion to the experience it gets? What is sensation? How does it give rise to ideas? Is the understanding active or is it passive in the reception of simple ideas? Why?

INTRODUCTION

1. SINCE IT IS THE *UNDERSTANDING* THAT SETS MAN ABOVE the rest of sensible beings, and gives him all the advantage and dominion which he has over them; it is certainly a subject, even for its nobleness, worth our labour to inquire into. The understanding, like the eye, whilst it makes us see and perceive all other things, takes no notice of itself; and it requires art and pains to set it at a distance and make it its own object. But whatever be the difficulties that lie in the way of this inquiry; whatever it be that keeps us so much in the dark to ourselves; sure I am that all the light we can let in upon our minds, all the acquaintance we can make with our own understandings, will not only be very pleasant, but bring us great advantage, in directing our thoughts in the search of other things.

2. This, therefore, being my purpose—to inquire into the original, certainty, and extent of *human knowledge,* together with the grounds and degrees of *belief, opinion,* and *assent;*—I shall not at present meddle with the physical consideration of the mind; or trouble myself to examine wherein its

From Essay Concerning Human Understanding. *Book II, by John Locke. First published in 1690.*

essence consists; or by what motions of our spirits or alterations of our bodies we come to have any *sensation* by our organs, or any *ideas* in our understandings; and whether those ideas do in their formation, any or all of them, depend on matter or not. These are speculations which, however curious and entertaining, I shall decline, as lying out of my way in the design I am now upon. It shall suffice to my present purpose, to consider the discerning faculties of a man, as they are employed about the objects which they have to do with. And I shall imagine I have not wholly misemployed myself in the thoughts I shall have on this occasion, if, in this historical, plain method, I can give any account of the ways whereby our understandings come to attain those notions of things we have; and can set down any measures of the certainty of our knowledge; or the grounds of those persuasions which are to be found amongst men, so various, different, and wholly contradictory; and yet asserted somewhere or other with such assurance and confidence, that he that shall take a view of the opinions of mankind, observe their opposition, and at the same time consider the fondness and devotion wherewith they are embraced, the resolution and eagerness wherewith they are maintained, may perhaps have reason to suspect, that either there is no such thing as truth at all, or that mankind hath no sufficient means to attain a certain knowledge of it.

3. It is therefore worth while to search out the bounds between opinion and knowledge; and examine by what measures, in things whereof we have no certain knowledge, we ought to regulate our assent and moderate our persuasion. In order whereunto I shall pursue this following method:—

First, I shall inquire into the original of those *ideas,* notions, or whatever else you please to call them, which a man observes, and is conscious to himself he has in his mind: and the ways whereby the understanding comes to be furnished with them.

Secondly, I shall endeavor to show what *knowledge* the understanding hath by those ideas; and the certainty, evidence, and extent of it.

Thirdly, I shall make some inquiry into the nature and grounds of *faith* or *opinion:* whereby I mean that assent which we give to any proposition as true, of whose truth yet we have no certain knowledge. And here we shall have occasion to examine the reasons and degrees of *assent.*

4. If by this inquiry into the nature of the understanding, I can discover the powers thereof; how far they reach; to what things they are in any degree proportionate; and where they fail us, I suppose it may be of use to prevail with the busy mind of man to be more cautious in meddling with things exceeding its comprehension; to stop when it is at the utmost extent of its tether; and to sit down in a quiet ignorance of those things which, upon examination, are found to be beyond the reach of our capacities. We should not then perhaps be so forward, out of an affectation of an universal knowledge, to raise questions, and perplex ourselves and others with disputes about things to which our understandings are not suited; and of which we cannot frame in our minds any clear or distinct perceptions, or whereof (as it has perhaps too often happened) we have not any notions at all. If we can find out how far the understanding can extend its view; how far it has faculties to attain certainty; and in what cases it can only judge and guess, we may learn to content ourselves with what is attainable by us in this state.

5. For though the comprehension of our understandings comes exceeding short of the vast extent of things, yet we shall have cause enough to magnify the bountiful Author of our being, for that proportion and degree of knowledge he has bestowed on us, so far above all the rest of the inhabitants of this our mansion. Men have reason to be well satisfied with what God hath thought fit for them, since he hath given them (as St. Peter says) πάντα πρὸς ζωὴν καί εὐσεβειαν, whatsoever is necessary for the conveniences of life and information of virtue; and has put within the reach of their discovery, the comfortable provision for this life, and the way that leads to a better. How short soever their knowledge may come of an universal or perfect comprehension of whatsoever is, it yet secures their great concernments, that they have light enough to lead them to the knowledge of their Maker, and the sight of their own duties. Men may find matter sufficient to busy their heads, and employ their hands with variety, delight, and satisfaction, if they will not boldly quarrel with their own constitution, and throw away

the blessings their hands are filled with, because they are not big enough to grasp everything. We shall not have much reason to complain of the narrowness of our minds, if we will not employ them about what may be of use to us; for of that they are very capable. And it will be an unpardonable, as well as childish peevishness, if we undervalue the advantages of our knowledge, and neglect to improve it to the ends for which it was given us, because there are some things that are set out of the reach of it. It will be no excuse to an idle and untoward servant, who would not attend his business by candle light, to plead that he had not broad sunshine. The Candle that is set up in us shines bright enough for all our purposes. The discoveries we can make with this ought to satisfy us; and we shall then use our understandings right, when we entertain all objects in that way and proportion that they are suited to our faculties, and upon those grounds they are capable of being proposed to us; and not peremptorily or intemperately require demonstration, and demand certainty, where probability only is to be had, and which is sufficient to govern all our concernments. If we will disbelieve everything, because we cannot certainly know all things, we shall do much-what as wisely as he who would not use his legs, but sit still and perish, because he had no wings to fly.

6. When we know our own strength, we shall the better know what to undertake with hopes of success; and when we have well surveyed the *powers* of our own minds, and made some estimate what we may expect from them, we shall not be inclined either to sit still, and not set our thoughts on work at all, in despair of knowing anything; nor on the other side, question everything, and disclaim all knowledge, because some things are not to be understood. It is of great use to the sailor to know the length of his line, though he cannot with it fathom all the depths of the ocean. It is well he knows that it is long enough to reach the bottom, at such places as are necessary to direct his voyage, and caution him against running upon shoals that may ruin him. Our business here is not to know all things, but those which concern our conduct. If we can find out those measures, whereby a rational creature, put in that state in which man is in this world, may and ought to govern his opinions, and actions depending thereon, we need not to be troubled that some other things escape our knowledge.

7. This was that which gave the first rise to this *Essay* concerning the understanding. For I thought that the first step towards satisfying several inquiries the mind of man was very apt to run into, was, to take a survey of our own understandings, examine our own powers, and see to what things they were adapted. Till that was done I suspected we began at the wrong end, and in vain sought for satisfaction in a quiet and sure possession of truths that most concerned us, whilst we let loose our thoughts into the vast ocean of Being; as if all that boundless extent were the natural and undoubted possession of our understandings, wherein there was nothing exempt from its decisions, or that escaped its comprehensions. Thus men, extending their inquiries beyond their capacities, and letting their thoughts wander into those depths where they can find no sure footing, it is no wonder that they raise questions and multiple disputes, which, never coming to any clear resolution, are proper only to continue and increase their doubts, and to confirm them at last in perfect scepticism. Whereas, were the capacities of our understandings well considered, the extent of our knowledge once discovered, and the horizon found which sets the bounds between the enlightened and dark parts of things; between what is and what is not comprehensible by us, men would perhaps with less scruple acquiesce in the avowed ignorance of the one, and employ their thoughts and discourse with more advantage and satisfaction in the other.

8. Thus much I thought necessary to say concerning the occasion of this Inquiry into Human Understanding. But, before I proceed on to what I have thought on this subject, I must here in the entrance beg pardon of my reader for the frequent use of the word *idea,* which he will find in the following treatise. It being that term which, I think, serves best to stand for whatsoever is the *object* of the understanding when a man thinks; I have used it to express whatever is meant by *phantasm, notion, species,* or *whatever it is which the mind can be employed about in thinking;* and I could not avoid frequently using it.

I presume it will be easily granted me, that there are such *ideas* in men's minds: every one is conscious of them in himself; and men's words and actions will satisfy him that they are in others.

Our first inquiry then shall be,—how they come into the mind.

CHAPTER I: OF IDEAS IN GENERAL AND THEIR ORIGINAL

1. Every man being conscious to himself that he thinks; and that which his mind is applied about whilst thinking being the *ideas* that are there, it is past doubt that men have in their minds several ideas,—such as are those expressed by the words *whiteness, hardness, sweetness, thinking, motion, man, elephant, army, drunkenness,* and others: it is in the first place then to be inquired, *How he comes by them?*

I know it is a received doctrine, that men have native ideas, and original characters, stamped upon their minds in their very first being. This opinion I have at large examined already; and, I suppose what I have said in the foregoing Book will be much more easily admitted, when I have shown whence the understanding may get all the ideas it has; and by what ways and degrees they may come into the mind;—for which I shall appeal to every one's own observation and experience.

2. Let us then suppose the mind to be, as we say, white paper, void of all characters, without any ideas:—How comes it to be furnished? Whence comes it by that vast store which the busy and boundless fancy of man has painted on it with an almost endless variety? Whence has it all the materials of reason and knowledge? To this I answer, in one word, from EXPERIENCE. In that all our knowledge is founded; and from that it ultimately derives itself. Our observation employed either, about external sensible objects, or about the internal operations of our minds perceived and reflected on by ourselves, is that which supplies our understandings with all the *materials* of thinking. These two are the fountains of knowledge, from whence all the ideas we have, or can naturally have, do spring.

3. First, our Senses, conversant about particular sensible objects, do convey into the mind several distinct perceptions of things, according to those various ways wherein those objects do affect them. And thus we come by those *ideas* we have of *yellow, white, heat, cold, soft, hard, bitter, sweet,* and all those which we call sensible qualities; which when I say the senses convey into the mind, I mean, they from external objects convey into the mind what produces there those perceptions. This great source of most of the ideas we have, depending wholly upon our senses, and derived by them to the understanding, I call SENSATION.

4. Secondly, the other fountain from which experience furnisheth the understanding with ideas is,—the perception of, the operations of our own mind within us, as it is employed; about the ideas it has got;—which operations, when the soul comes to reflect on and consider, do furnish the understanding with another set of ideas, which could not be had from things without. And such are *perception, thinking, doubting, believing, reasoning, knowing, willing,* and all the different actings of our own minds;—which we being conscious of, and observing in ourselves, do from these receive into our understandings as distinct ideas as we do from bodies affecting our senses. This source of ideas every man has wholly in himself; and though it be not sense, as having nothing to do with external objects, yet it is very like it, and might properly enough be called *internal sense.* But as I call the other Sensation, so I call this REFLECTION, the ideas it affords being such only as the mind gets by reflecting on its own operations within itself. By reflection then, in the following part of this discourse, I would be understood to mean, that notice which the mind takes of its own operations, and the manner of them, by reason whereof there come to be ideas of these operations in the understanding. These two, I say, viz. external material things, as the objects of SENSATION, and the operations of our own minds within, as the objects of REFLECTION, are to me the only originals from whence all our ideas take their beginnings. The term *operations* here I use in a large sense, as comprehending not barely the actions of the mind about its ideas, but some sort of passions arising sometimes from them, such as is the satisfaction or uneasiness arising from any thought.

5. The understanding seems to me not to have the least glimmering of any ideas which it doth

not receive from one of these two. *External objects* furnish the mind with the ideas of sensible qualities, which are all those different perceptions they produce in us; and *the mind* furnishes the understanding with ideas of its own operations.

These, when we have taken a full survey of them, and their several modes, [combinations, and relations,] we shall find to contain all our whole stock of ideas; and that we have nothing in our minds which did not come in one of these two ways. Let any one examine his own thoughts, and thoroughly search into his understanding; and then let him tell me, whether all the original ideas he has there, are any other than the objects of his senses, or of the operations of his mind, considered as objects of his reflection. And how great a mass of knowledge soever he imagines to be lodged there, he will, upon taking a strict view, see that he has not any idea in his mind but what one of these two have imprinted;—though perhaps, with infinite variety compounded and enlarged by the understanding, as we shall see hereafter.

6. He that attentively considers the state of a child, at his first coming into the world, will have little reason to think him stored with plenty of ideas, that are to be the matter of his future knowledge. It is *by degrees* he comes to be furnished with them. And though the ideas of obvious and familiar qualities imprint themselves before the memory begins to keep a register of time or order, yet it is often so late before some unusual qualities come in the way, that there are few men that cannot recollect the beginning of their acquaintance with them. And if it were worth while, no doubt a child might be so ordered as to have but a very few, even of the ordinary ideas, till he were grown up to a man. But all that are born into the world, being surrounded with bodies that perpetually and diversely affect them, variety of ideas, whether care be taken of it or not, are imprinted on the minds of children. Light and colours are busy at hand everywhere, when the eye is but open; sounds and some tangible qualities fail not to solicit their proper senses, and force an entrance to the mind;—but yet, I think, it will be granted easily, that if a child were kept in a place where he never saw any other but black and white till he were a man, he would have no more ideas of scarlet or green, than he that from his childhood never tasted an oyster, or a pine-apple, has of those particular relishes.

7. Men then come to be furnished with fewer or more simple ideas from without according as the objects they converse with afford greater or less variety; and from the operations of their minds within, according as they more or less reflect on them. For, though he that contemplates the operations of his mind, cannot but have plain and clear ideas of them; yet, unless he turn his thoughts that way, and considers them *attentively* he will no more have clear and distinct ideas of all the operations of his mind, and all that may be observed therein, than he will have all the particular ideas of any landscape, or of the parts and motions of a clock, who will not turn his eyes to it, and with attention heed all the parts of it. The picture, or clock may be so placed, that they may come in this way every day; but yet he will have but a confused idea of all the parts they are made up of, till he applies himself with attention, to consider them each in particular.

8. And hence we see the reason why it is pretty late before most children get ideas of the operations of their own minds; and some have not any very clear or perfect ideas of the greatest part of them all their lives. Because, though they pass there continually, yet, like floating visions, they make not deep impressions enough to leave in their mind clear, distinct, lasting ideas, till the understanding turns inward upon itself, reflects on its own operations, and makes them the objects of its own contemplation. Children when they come first into it, are surrounded with a world of new things, which, by a constant solicitation of their senses, draw the mind constantly to them; forward to take notice of new, and apt to be delighted with the variety of changing objects. Thus the first years are usually employed and diverted in looking abroad. Men's business in them is to acquaint themselves with what is to be found without; and so growing up in a constant attention to outward sensations, seldom make any considerable reflection on what passes within them, till they come to be of riper years; and some scarce ever at all.

9. To ask, at what *time* a man has first any ideas, is to ask, when he begins to perceive;—*having ideas,* and *perception,* being the same thing. I know it is an opinion, that the soul always thinks, and that it has the actual perception of ideas in itself constantly, as long as it exists; and that actual thinking is as inseparable from the soul as actual extension is

from the body; which if true, to inquire after the beginning of a man's ideas is the same as to inquire after the beginning of his soul. For, by this account, soul and its ideas, as body and its extension, will begin to exist both at the same time.

10. But whether the soul be supposed to exist, antecedent to, or coeval with, or some time after the first rudiments of organization, or the beginnings of life in the body, I leave to be disputed by those who have better thought of that matter. I confess myself to have one of those dull souls, that doth not perceive itself always to contemplate ideas; nor can conceive it any more necessary for the soul always to think, than for the body always to move: the perception of ideas being (as I conceive) to the soul, what motion is to the body; not its essence, but one of its operations. And therefore, though thinking be supposed never so much the proper action of the soul, yet it is not necessary to suppose that it should be always thinking, always in action. That, perhaps, is the privilege of the infinite Author and Preserver of all things, who "never slumbers nor sleeps", but is not competent to any finite being, at least not to the soul of man. We know certainly, by experience, that we *sometimes* think; and thence draw this infallible consequence,—that there is something in us that has a power to think. But whether that substance *perpetually* thinks or no, we can be no further assured than experience informs us. For, to say that actual thinking is essential to the soul, and inseparable from it, is to beg what is in question, and not to prove it by reason;—which is necessary to be done, if it be not a self-evident proposition. But whether this, "That the soul always thinks," be a self-evident proposition, that everybody assents to at first hearing, I appeal to mankind. It is doubted whether I thought at all last night or no. The question being about a matter of fact, it is begging it to bring, as a proof for it, an hypothesis, which is the very thing in dispute: by which way one may prove anything, and it is but supposing that all watches, whilst the balance beats, think, and it is sufficiently proved, and past doubt, that my watch thought all last night. But he that would not deceive hmself, ought to build his hypothesis on matter of fact, and make it out by sensible experience, and not presume on matter of fact, because of his hypothesis, that is, because he supposes it to be so; which way of proving amounts to this, that I must necessarily think all last night, because another supposes I always think, though I myself cannot perceive that I always do so.

But men in love with their opinions may not only suppose what is in question, but allege wrong matter of fact. How else could any one make it an inference of mine, that a thing is not, because we are not sensible of it in our sleep? I do not say there is no *soul* in a man, because he is not sensible of it in his sleep; but I do say, he cannot *think* at any time, waking or sleeping, without being sensible of it. Our being sensible of it is not necessary to anything but to our thoughts; and to them it is; and to them it always will be necessary, till we can think without being conscious of it.

11. I grant that the soul, in a waking man, is never without thought, because it is the condition of being awake. But whether sleeping without dreaming be not an affection of the whole man, mind as well as body, may be worth a waking man's consideration; it being hard to conceive that anything should think and not be conscious of it. If the soul doth think in a sleeping man without being conscious of it, I ask whether, during such thinking, it has any pleasure or pain, or be capable of happiness or misery? I am sure the man is not; no more than the bed or earth he lies on. For to be happy or miserable without being conscious of it, seems to me utterly inconsistent and impossible. Or if it be possible that the *soul* can, whilst the body is sleeping, have its thinking, enjoyments, and concerns, its pleasures or pain, apart, which the *man* is not conscious of nor partakes in,—it is certain that Socrates asleep and Socrates awake is not the same person; but his soul when he sleeps, and Socrates the man, consisting of body and soul, when he is waking, are two persons: since waking Socrates has no knowledge of, or concernment for that happiness or misery of his soul, which it enjoys alone by itself whilst he sleeps, without perceiving anything of it; no more than he has for the happiness or misery of a man in the Indies, whom he knows not. For, if we take wholly away all consciousness of our actions and sensations, especially of pleasure and pain, and the concernment that accompanies it, it will be hard to know wherein to place personal identity.

12. The soul, during sound sleep, thinks, say these men. Whilst it thinks and perceives, it is capable certainly of those of delight or trouble, as well

as any other perceptions; and *it* must necessarily be *conscious* of its own perceptions. But it has all this apart: the sleeping man, it is plain, is conscious of nothing of all this. Let us suppose, then, the soul of Castor, while he is sleeping, retired from his body; which is no impossible supposition for the men I have here to do with, who so liberally allow life, without a thinking soul, to all other animals. These men cannot then judge it impossible, or a contradiction, that the body should live without the soul; nor that the soul should subsist and think, or have perception even perception, of happiness or misery, without the body. Let us then, I say, suppose the soul of Castor separated during his sleep from his body, to think apart. Let us suppose, too, that it chooses for its scene of thinking the body of another man, v.g. Pollux, who is sleeping without a soul. For, if Castor's soul can think, whilst Castor is asleep, what Castor is never conscious of, it is no matter what *place* it chooses to think in. We have here, then, the bodies of two men with only one soul between them, which we will suppose to sleep and wake by turns; and the soul still thinking in the waking man, whereof the sleeping man is never conscious, has never the least perception. I ask, then whether Castor, and Pollux, thus with only one soul between them, which thinks and perceives in one what the other is never conscious of, nor is concerned for, are not two as distinct *persons* as Castor and Hercules, or as Socrates and Plato were? And whether one of them might not be very happy, and the other very miserable? Just by the same reason, they make the soul and the man two persons, who make the soul think apart what the man is not conscious of. For, I suppose nobody will make identity of persons to consist in the soul's being united to the very same numerical particles of matter. For if that be necessary to identity, it will be impossible, in that constant flux of the particles of our bodies, that any man should be the same person two days, or two moments, together.

13. Thus, methinks, every drowsy nod shakes their doctrine, who teach that the soul is always thinking. Those, at least, who do at any time *sleep without dreaming,* can never be convinced that their thoughts are sometimes for four hours busy without their knowing of it; and if they are taken in the very act, waked in the middle of that sleeping contemplation, can give no manner of account of it.

14. It will perhaps be said,—That the soul thinks even in the soundest sleep, but the *memory* retains it not. That the soul in a sleeping man should be this moment busy a thinking, and the next moment in a waking man not remember nor be able to recollect one jot of all those thoughts, is very hard to be conceived, and would need some better proof than bare assertion to make it be believed. For who can without any more ado, but being barely told so, imagine that the greatest part of men do, during all their lives, for several hours every day, think of something, which if they were asked, even in the middle of these thoughts, they could remember nothing at all of? Most men, I think, pass a great part of their sleep without dreaming. I once knew a man that was bred a scholar, and had no bad memory, who told me he had never dreamed in his life, till he had that fever he was then newly recovered of, which was about the five or six and twentieth year of his age. I suppose the world affords more such instances: at least every one's acquaintance will furnish him with examples enough of such as pass most of their nights without dreaming.

15. To think often, and never to retain it so much as one moment, is a very useless sort of thinking; and the soul, in such a state of thinking, does very little, if at all, excel that of a looking-glass, which constantly receives variety of images, or ideas, but retains none; they disappear and vanish, and there remain no footsteps of them; the looking-glass is never the better for such ideas, nor the soul for such thoughts. Perhaps it will be said, that in a waking *man* the materials of the body are employed, and made use of, in thinking; and that the memory of thoughts is retained by the impressions that are made on the brain, and the traces there left after such thinking; but that in the thinking of the *soul,* which is not perceived in a sleeping man, there the soul thinks apart, and making no use of the organs of the body, leaves no impressions on it, and consequently no memory of such thoughts. Not to mention again the absurdity of two distinct persons, which follows from this supposition, I answer, further.—That whatever ideas the mind can receive and contemplate without the help of the body, it is reasonable to conclude it can retain without the help of the body too; or else the soul, or any separate spirit, will have but little advantage by thinking. If it has no memory of its

own thoughts; if it cannot lay them up for its own use, and be able to recall them upon occasion; if it cannot reflect upon what is past, and make use of its former experiences, reasonings, and contemplations, to what purpose does it think? They who make the soul a thinking thing, at this rate, will not make it a much more noble being than those do whom they condemn, for allowing it to be nothing but the subtilist parts of matter. Characters drawn on dust, that the first breath of wind effaces; or impressions made on a heap of atoms, or animal spirits, are altogether as useful, and render the subject as noble, as the thoughts of a soul that perish in thinking; that, once out of sight, are gone for ever, and leave no memory of themselves behind them. Nature never makes excellent things for mean or no uses; and it is hardly to be conceived that our infinitely wise Creator should make so admirable a faculty as the power of thinking, that faculty which comes nearest the excellency of his own incomprehensible being, to be so idly and uselessly employed, at least a fourth part of its time here, as to think constantly, without remembering any of those thoughts, without doing any good to itself or others, or being any way useful to any other part of the creation. If we will examine it, we shall not find, I suppose, the motion of dull and senseless matter, any where in the universe, made so little use of and so wholly thrown away.

16. It is true, we have sometimes instances of perception whilst we are asleep, and retain the memory of those thoughts: but how extravagant and incoherent for the most part they are; how little conformable to the perfection and order of a rational being, those who are acquainted with dreams need not be told. This I would willingly be satisfied in,—whether the soul, when it thinks thus apart, and as it were separate from the body, acts less rationally than when conjointly with it, or no. If its separate thoughts be less rational, then these men must say, that the soul owes the perfection of rational thinking to the body: if it does not, it is a wonder that our dreams should be, for the most part, so frivolous and irrational; and that the soul should retain none of its more rational soliloquies and meditations.

17. Those who so confidently tell us that the soul always actually thinks, I would they would also tell us, what those ideas are that are in the soul of a child, before or just at the union with the body, before it hath received any by sensation. The dreams of sleeping men are, as I take it, all made up of the waking man's ideas; though for the most part oddly put together. It is strange, if the soul has ideas of its own that it derived not from sensation or reflection, (as it must have, if it thought before it received any impressions from the body,) that it should never, in its private thinking, (so private, that the man himself perceives it not,) retain any of them the very moment it wakes out of them, and then make the man glad with new discoveries. Who can find it reason that the soul should, in its retirement during sleep, have so many hours' thoughts, and yet never light on any of those ideas it borrowed not from sensation or reflection; or at least preserve the memory of none but such, which, being occasioned from the body, must needs be less natural to a spirit? It is strange the soul should never once in a man's whole life recall over any of its pure native thoughts, and those ideas it had before it borrowed anything from the body; never bring into the waking man's view any other ideas but what have a tang of the cask, and manifestly derive their original from that union. If it always thinks, and so had ideas before it was united, or before it received any from the body, it is not to be supposed but that during sleep it recollects its native ideas; and during that retirement from communicating with the body, whilst it thinks by itself, the ideas it is busied about should be, sometimes at least, those more natural and congenial ones which it had in itself, underived from the body, or its own operations about them: which, since the waking man never remembers, we must from this hypothesis conclude either that the soul remembers something that the man does not; or else that memory belongs only to such ideas as are derived from the body, or the mind's operations about them.

18. I would be glad also to learn from these men who so confidently pronounce that the human soul, or, which is all one, that a man always thinks, how they come to know it; nay, how they come to know that they themselves think, when they themselves do not perceive it. This, I am afraid, is to be sure without proofs, and to know without perceiving. It is, I suspect, a confused notion, taken up to serve an hypothesis; and none of those clear truths, but either their own evidence forces us to admit, or common experience makes it

impudence to deny. For the most that can be said of it is, that it is possible the soul may always think, but not always retain it in memory. And I say, it is as possible that the soul may not always think; and much more probable that it should sometimes not think, than that it should often think, and that a long while together, and not be conscious to itself, the next moment after, that it had thought.

19. To suppose the soul to think, and the man not to perceive it, is, as has been said, to make two persons in one man. And if one considers well these men's way of speaking, one should be led into a suspicion that they do so. For they who tell us that the *soul* always thinks, do never, that I remember, say that a *man* always thinks. Can the soul think, and not the man? Or a man think, and not be conscious of it? This, perhaps, would be suspected of jargon in others. If they say the man thinks always, but is not always conscious of it, they may as well say his body is extended without having parts. For it is altogether as intelligible to say that a body is extended without parts, as that anything thinks without being conscious of it, or perceiving that it does so. They who talk thus may, with as much reason, if it be necessary to their hypothesis, say that a man is always hungry, but that he does not always feel it; whereas hunger consists in that very sensation, as thinking consists in being conscious that one thinks. If they say that a man is always conscious to himself of thinking, I ask, How they know it? Consciousness is the perception of what passes in a man's own mind. Can another man perceive that I am conscious of anything, when I perceive it not myself? No man's knowledge here can go beyond his experience. Wake a man out of a sound sleep, and ask him what he was that moment thinking of. If he himself be conscious of nothing he then thought on, he must be a notable diviner of thoughts that can assure him that he was thinking. May he not, with more reason, assure him he was not asleep? This is something beyond philosophy; and it cannot be less than revelation, that discovers to another thoughts in my mind, when I can find none there myself. And they must needs have a penetrating sight who can certainly see that I think, when I cannot perceive it myself, and when I declare that I do not; and yet can see that dogs or elephants do not think, when they give all the demonstration of it imaginable, except only telling us that they do so. This some may suspect to be a step beyond

the Rosicrucians; it seeming easier to make one's self invisible to others, than to make another's thoughts visible to me, which are not visible to himself. But it is but defining the soul to be "a substance that always thinks," and the business is done. If such definition be of any authority, I know not what it can serve for but to make many men suspect that they have no souls at all; since they find a good part of their lives pass away without thinking. For no definitions that I know, no suppositions of any sect, are of force enough to destroy constant experience; and perhaps it is the affectation of knowing beyond what we perceive, that makes so much useless dispute and noise in the world.

20. I see no reason, therefore, to believe that the soul thinks before the senses have furnished it with ideas to think on; and as those are increased and retained, so it comes, by exercise, to improve its faculty of thinking in the several parts of it; as well as, afterwards, by compounding those ideas, and reflecting on its own operations, it increases its stock, as well as facility in remembering, imagining, reasoning, and other modes of thinking.

21. He that will suffer himself to be informed by observation and experience, and not make his own hypothesis the rule of nature, will find few signs of a soul accustomed to much thinking in a new-born child, and much fewer of any reasoning at all. And yet it is hard to imagine that the rational soul should think so much, and not reason at all. And he that will consider that infants newly come into the world spend the greatest part of their time in sleep, and are seldom awake but when either hunger calls for the teat, or some pain (the most importunate of all sensations), or some other violent impression on the body, forces the mind to perceive and attend to it;—he, I say, who considers this, will perhaps find reason to imagine that a fœtus in the mother's womb differs not much from the state of a vegetable, but passes the greatest part of its time without perception or thought; doing very little but sleep in a place where it needs not seek for food, and is surrounded with liquor, always equally soft, and near of the same temper; where the eyes have no light, and the ears so shut up are not very susceptible of sounds; and where there is little or no variety, or change of objects, to move the senses.

22. Follow a child from its birth, and observe the alterations that time makes, and you shall find, as the mind by the senses comes more and more to

be furnished with ideas, it comes to be more and more awake; thinks more, the more it has matter to think on. After some time it begins to know the objects which, being most familiar with it, have made lasting impressions. Thus it comes by degrees to know the persons it daily converses with, and distinguishes them from strangers; which are instances and effects of its coming to retain and distinguish the ideas the senses convey to it. And so we may observe how the mind, *by degrees,* improves in these; and *advances* to the exercise of those other faculties of enlarging, compounding, and abstracting its ideas, and of reasoning about them, and reflecting upon all these; of which I shall have occasion to speak more hereafter.

23. If it shall be demanded then, *when* a man *begins* to have any ideas, I think the true answer is, — *when he first has any sensation.* For, since there appear not to be any ideas in the mind before the senses have conveyed any in, I conceive that ideas in the understanding are coeval with *sensation; which is such an impression or motion made in some part of the body, as [produces some perception] in the understanding.* It is about these impressions made on our senses by outward objects that the mind seems *first* to employ itself, in such operations as we call perception, remembering, consideration, reasoning, &c.

24. In time the mind comes to reflect on its own operations about the ideas got by sensation, and thereby stores itself with a new set of ideas, which I call ideas of reflection. These are the impressions that are made on our senses by outward objects that are extrinsical to the mind; and its own operations, proceeding from powers intrinsical and proper to itself, which, when reflected on by itself, become also objects of its contemplation — are, as I have said, the original of all knowledge. Thus the first capacity of human intellect is, — that the mind is fitted to receive the impressions made on it; either through the senses by outward objects, or by its own operations when it reflects on them. This is the first step a man makes towards the discovery of anything, and the groundwork whereon to build all those notions which ever he shall have naturally in this world. All those sublime thoughts which tower above the clouds, and reach as high as heaven itself, take their rise and footing here: in all that great extent wherein the mind wanders, in those remote speculations it may seem to be elevated with, it stirs not one jot beyond those ideas which *sense* or *reflection* have offered for its contemplation.

25. In this part the understanding is merely passive; and whether or no it will have these beginnings, and as it were materials of knowledge, is not in its own power. For the objects of our senses do, many of them, obtrude their particular ideas upon our minds whether we will or not; and the operations of our minds will not let us be without, at least, some obscure notions of them. No man can be wholly ignorant of what he does when he thinks. These simple ideas, when offered to the mind, the understanding can no more refuse to have, nor alter when they are imprinted, nor blot them out and make new ones itself, than a mirror can refuse, alter, or obliterate the images or ideas which the objects set before it do therein produce. As the bodies that surround us do diversely affect our organs, the mind is forced to receive the impressions; and cannot avoid the perception of those ideas that are annexed to them.

Further Questions

1. How would Locke answer the following question: When you dream, with what are you experiencing the dream? That is, since your eyes are closed, you can't be seeing dream images with your eyes. What, then?
2. Do the things Locke says about the nature of the understanding seem intuitively clear to you? Or do you find what he says strange and puzzling? Why do you suppose the true nature of the understanding is not immediately understandable by the very entity trying to understand itself?
3. Can you see any specific ways here that Locke might have influenced Kant?

Further Readings

Aaron, Richard. *John Locke*. Oxford: Clarendon Press, 1971. An update of the 1937 edition that takes into account the discovery (in 1935) of the Lovelace papers.

Ayers, Michael. *Locke*. 2 vols. New York: Routledge, 1991. The best of recent scholarship on Locke's epistemology and ontology.

Kolak, Daniel. *From Plato to Wittgenstein*. Belmont, CA: Wadsworth, 1994. Contains Book I of Locke's *Treatis*.

51   The Senses

DAVID HUME

A brief biography of Hume appears on page 128.

In the following selection, from his *Treatise of Human Nature* (1739), Hume gives his views about the distinctions between, on the one hand, our experience of the world, and on the other, what we suppose to be true of the word.

Reading Questions

1. Hume says that the senses themselves are "incapable of giving rise to the notion of the *continu'd* existence of their objects." Why does he think this? Do you agree?

2. Hume says that "if the senses presented our impressions as external to, and independent of ourselves, both the objects and ourselves must be obvious to our senses." But aren't objects (e.g., the chair you are sitting in) and ourselves (e.g., you) obvious to our senses? What could be more obvious? How would Hume reply?

3. When you perceive your arms, don't you come into *direct* experiential contact with the surface of a material object. What would Hume say? What would you say?

THUS THE SCEPTIC STILL CONTINUES to reason and believe, even tho' he asserts, that he cannot defend his reason by reason; and by the same rule he must assent to the principle concerning the existence of body, tho' he cannot pretend by any arguments of philosophy to maintain its veracity. Nature has not left this to his choice, and has doubtless esteem'd it an affair of too great importance to be trusted to our uncertain reasonings and speculations. We may well ask, *What causes induce us to believe in the existence of body?* but 'tis in vain to ask, *Whether there be body or not?* That is a point, which we must take for granted in all our reasonings.

The subject, then, of our present enquiry is concerning the *causes* which induce us to believe in the existence of body: And my reasoning on this head I shall begin with a distinction, which at first sight may seem superfluous, but which will contribute very much to the perfect understanding of what follows. We ought to examine apart those two questions, which are commonly confounded together, *viz*. Why we attribute a CONTINU'D existence to objects, even when they are not present to the senses; and why we suppose them to have an existence DISTINCT from the mind and perception. Under this last head I comprehend their situation as well as relations, their *external* position as well as the *independence* of their existence and operation. These two questions concerning the continu'd and distinct existence of body are intimately connected together. For if the objects of our senses continue to exist, even when they are not perceiv'd, their existence is of course independent of and distinct from the perception; and *vice versa,* if their existence be independent of the perception and distinct from it, they must continue to exist, even tho' they be not perceiv'd. But tho' the decision of the one question decides the other; yet that we may the more easily discover the principles of human nature, from whence the decision arises, we shall carry along with us this distinction, and shall consider, whether it be the *senses, reason,* or the *imagination,* that produces the opinion of a *continu'd* or of a *distinct* existence. These are the only questions, that are intelligible on the present subject. For as to the notion of external existence, when taken for something specifically different from our perceptions, we have already shown its absurdity.

To begin with the SENSES, 'tis evident these faculties are incapable of giving rise to the notion of the *continu'd* existence of their objects, after they no longer appear to the senses. For that is a contradiction in terms, and supposes that the senses continue to operate, even after they have ceas'd all manner of operation. These faculties, therefore, if they have any influence in the present case, must produce the opinion of a distinct, not of a continu'd existence; and in order to that, must present their impressions either as images and representations, or as these very distinct and external existences.

That our senses offer not their impressions as the images of something *distinct,* or *independent,* and *external,* is evident; because they convey to us nothing but a single perception, and never give us the least intimation of any thing beyond. A single perception can never produce the idea of a double existence, but by some inference either of the reason or imagination. When the mind looks farther than what immediately appears to it, its conclusions can never be put to the account of the senses; and it certainly looks farther, when from a single perception it infers a double existence, and supposes the relations of resemblance and causation betwixt them.

If our sense, therefore, suggest any idea of distinct existences, they must convey the impressions as those very existences, by a kind of fallacy and illusion. Upon this head we may observe, that all sensations are felt by the mind, such as they really are, and that when we doubt, whether they present themselves as distinct objects, or as mere impressions, the difficulty is not concerning their nature, but concerning their relations and situation. Now if the senses presented our impressions as external to, and independent of ourselves, both the objects and ourselves must be obvious to our senses, otherwise they cou'd not be compar'd by these faculties. The difficulty, then, is how far we are *ourselves* the objects of our senses.

'Tis certain there is no question in philosophy more abstruse than that concerning identity, and the nature of the united principle, which constitutes a person. So far from being able by our senses merely to determine this question, we must have recourse to the most profound metaphysics to give a satisfactory answer to it; and in common life 'tis evident these ideas of self and person are never very fix'd nor determinate. 'Tis absurd, therefore, to imagine the senses can ever distinguish betwixt ourselves and external objects.

Add to this, that every impression, external and internal, passions, affections, sensation, pains and pleasures, are originally on the same footing; and that whatever other differences we may observe among them, they appear, all of them, in their true colours, as impressions or perception. And indeed, if we consider the matter aright, 'tis scarce possible it shou'd be otherwise, nor is it conceivable that our senses shou'd be more capable of deceiving us in the situation and relations, than in the nature of our impressions. For since all actions and sensations of the mind are known to us by consciousness, they must necessarily appear in every particular what they are, and be what they appear. Every thing that enters the mind, being in *reality* as the perception, 'tis impossible any thing shou'd to *feeling* appear different. This were to suppose, that even where we are most intimately conscious, we might be mistaken.

But not to lose time in examining, whether 'tis possible for our senses to deceive us, and represent our perceptions as distinct from ourselves, that is as *external* to and *independent* of us; let us consider whether they really do so, and whether this error proceeds from an immediate sensation, or from some other causes.

To begin with the question concerning *external* existence, it may perhaps be said, that setting aside the metaphysical question of the identity of a thinking substance, our own body evidently belongs to us; and as several impressions appear exterior to the body, we suppose them also exterior to ourselves. The paper, on which I write at present, is beyond my hand. The table is beyond the paper. The walls of the chamber beyond the table. And in casting my eye towards the window, I perceive a great extent of fields and buildings beyond my chamber. From all this it may be infer'd, that no other faculty is requir'd, beside the senses, to convince as of the external existence of body. But to prevent this inference, we need only weight the three following considerations. *First,* That, properly speaking, 'tis not our body we perceive, when we regard our limbs and members, but certain impressions, which enter by the senses; so that the ascribing a real and corporeal existence to these impressions, or to their objects, is an act of the mind as difficult to explain, as that which we examine at present. *Secondly,* Sounds, and tastes, and smells, tho' commonly regarded by the mind as continu'd independent qualities, appear not to have any existence in extension, and consequently cannot appear to the senses as situated externally to the body. The reason, why we ascribe a place to them, shall be consider'd afterwards. *Thirdly,* Even our sight informs us not of distance or outness (so to speak) immediately and without a certain reasoning and experience, as is acknowledg'd by the most rational philosophers.

As to the *independency* of our perceptions on ourselves, this can never be an object of the senses; but any opinion we form concerning it, must be deriv'd from experience and observation: And we shall see afterwards, that our conclusions from experience are far from being favourable to the doctrine of the independency of our perceptions. Mean while we may observe that when we talk of real distinct existences, we have commonly more in our eye their independency than external situation in place, and think an object has a sufficient reality, when it Being is uninterrupted, and independent of the incessant revolutions, which we are conscious of in ourselves.

Thus to resume what I have said concerning the senses; they give us no notion of continu'd existence, because they cannot operate beyond the extent, in which they really operate. They as little produce the opinion of a distinct existence, because they neither can offer it to the mind as represented, nor as original. To offer it as represented, nor as original. To offer it as represented, they must present both an object and an image. To make it appear as original, they must convey a falshood; and this falshood must be in the relations and situation: In order to which they must be able to compare the object with ourselves; and even in that case they do not, nor is it possible they shou'd, deceive us. We may, therefore, conclude with certainty, that the opinion of a continu'd and of a distinct existence never arises from the senses.

To confirm this we may observe, that there are three different kinds of impressions convey'd by the senses. The first are those of the figure, bulk, motion and solidity of bodies. The second those of colours, tastes, smells, sounds, heat and cold. The third are the pains and pleasures, that arise from the application of objects to our bodies, as by the cutting of our flesh with steel, and such like. Both philosophers and the vulgar suppose the first of these to have a distinct continu'd existence. The vulgar only regard the second as on the same footing. Both philosophers and the vulgar, again, esteem the third to be merely perceptions; and consequently interrupted and dependent beings.

Now 'tis evident, that, whatever may be our philosophical opinion, colours, sounds, heat and cold, as far as appears to the senses, exist after the same manner with motion and solidity, and that the difference we make betwixt them in this respect, arises not from the mere perception. So strong is the prejudice for the distinct continu'd existence of the former qualities, that when the contrary opinion is advanc'd by modern philosophers, people imagine they can almost refute it from their feeling and experience, and that their very senses contradict this philosophy. 'Tis also evident, that colours, sounds, &c. are originally on the same footing with the pain that arises from steel, and pleasure that proceeds from a fire: and that the difference betwixt them is founded neither on perception nor reason, but on the imagination. For as they are confest to be, both of them, nothing but perceptions arising from the particular configurations and motions of the parts of body, wherein possibly can their difference consist? Upon the whole, then, we may conclude, that as far as the senses are judges, all perceptions are the same in the manner of their existence.

We may also observe in this instance of sounds and colours, that we can attribute a distinct continu'd existence to objects without ever consulting REASON, or weighing our opinions by any philosophical principles. And indeed, whatever convincing arguments philosophers may fancy they can produce to establish the belief of objects independent of the mind, 'tis obvious these arguments are known but to very few, and that 'tis not by them, that children, peasants, and the greatest part of mankind are induc'd to attribute objects to some impressions, and deny them to others. Accordingly we find, that all the conclusions, which the vulgar form on this head, are directly contrary to those which are con-firm'd by philosophy. For philosophy informs us, that every thing, which appears to the mind, is nothing but a perception, and is interrupted, and dependent on the mind; whereas the vulgar confound perceptions and objects, and attribute a distinct continu'd existence to the very things they feel or see. This sentiment, then, as it is entirely unreasonable, must proceed from some other faculty than the understanding. To which we may add, that as long as we take our perceptions and objects to be the same, we can never infer the existence of the one from that of the other, nor form any argument from the relations of cause and effect; which is the only one that can assure us of matter of fact. Even after we distinguish our perceptions from our objects, 'twill appear presently, that we are still incapable of reasoning from the existence of one to that of the other: So that upon the whole our reason neither does, nor is it possible it ever shou'd, upon any supposition, give us an assurance of the continu'd and distinct existence of body. That opinion must be entirely owing to the IMAGINATION: which must now be the subject of our enquiry.

Further Questions

1. If you make a judgment to the effect that you are seeing some particular object in the world, you might be mistaken (e.g., you could be dreaming). If you make a more cautious judgment only to the effect that you are having such and such a kind of subjective experience, could you be mistaken? Explain.
2. When you have an experience (of anything), is there an interpretation of yours that is ingredient in the experience or is the experience just a *given,* which afterwards you may interpret or not, as you like?

Further Readings

Kolak, Daniel. *The Mayfield Anthology of Western Philosophy.* Mountain View, CA: Mayfield, 1998. Contains large chunks of Hume and 51 other major philosophers, which W. V. Quine calls "a convenient addition to a private philosophical library. It is a handy first resort for ready consultation before seeking elsewhere, and it is richly suited to edifying bouts of idle browsing."

Norton, David Fate. *The Cambridge Companion to Hume.* Cambridge, 1993. Essays by distinguished scholars, written especially for students, on all aspects of Hume's philosophy.

Scruton, Roger. *A Short History of Modern Philosophy: From Descartes to Wittgenstein,* 2nd ed. Routledge, 1996. A readable survey in which Hume's views may be seen in the context of the times in which they arose and of subsequent developments.

52   Percepts and Concepts

IMMANUEL KANT

Immanuel Kant (1724–1804) was born in Köningsberg, East Prussia (today's Russia), where his grandfather had emigrated from Scotland. He became the first great modern philosopher to earn his living as a university professor. He mainly taught logic and metaphysics. His salary, however, was paid not by an administration, but directly by the students. Like many philosophers before him, he got in trouble with the authorities for the "distortion of many leading and fundamental doctrines of holy writ and Christianity," in the words of the Prussian king, Frederick William II. The king ordered Kant not to lecture or write further on such topics. Kant dutifully obeyed until the day the king died, at which point Kant promptly resumed his writings and teachings.

Kant was already fifty-seven years old, living the life of a quiet old professor nearing the end of a singularly undistinguished career, when he published his first philosophy book. It had a mixed reception—at first. Some said that it made no sense at all, or that it was unreadable. Others claimed that it was the greatest single work of philosophy ever written. Today there can be no doubt that *Critique of Pure Reason* is one of the major achievements in the history of philosophy. Published in 1781, it brought Kant great fame. Philosophers all over Europe suddenly began proclaiming themselves "Kantians." It quickly became the book about which everyone was talking and writing.

Showing why space, time, and causality are not fully objective but, to a large extent, are the products of the human mind was in Kant's view a philosophical revolution on a par with the Copernican scientific revolution. Indeed, Albert Einstein said that reading Kant had the greatest impact on him of all philosophical works and helped him directly in his development of relativity.

As you read, keep in mind what Kant means by the word translated as *intuition*, for this can be extremely confusing. What he means is really the same thing that Hume means by the terms "impressions" and "perceptions." Thus, for instance, what you presently see are, in Kant's vocabulary, not things in themselves but your own intuitions of things. The problem is that the word "intuition" in its vernacular English sense means something like "hunch" or "thought" or "gut feeling." This is not at all what Kant means. What he means is more like *perception*.

Reading Questions

1. Why does all knowledge begin with experience?
2. How does Kant distinguish the a priori from the a posteriori?
3. What does he mean by "understanding"? By "intuition"?
4. Why and how does he distinguish the analytic from the synthetic?
5. What is the problem of pure reason?
6. What does he mean by "transcendental esthetic"?
7. Why does he give a *metaphysical* exposition of space and time, and what is meant by this?

I. OF THE DIFFERENCE BETWEEN PURE AND EMPIRICAL KNOWLEDGE

THAT ALL OUR KNOWLEDGE BEGINS WITH EXPE-RIENCE there can be no doubt. For how should the faculty of knowledge be called into activity, if not by objects which affect our senses, and which either produce representations by themselves, or rouse the activity of our understanding to compare, to connect, or to separate them; and thus to convert the raw material of our sensuous impressions into a knowledge of objects, which we call experience? In respect of time, therefore, no knowledge within us is antecedent to experience, but all knowledge begins with it.

But although all our knowledge begins with experience, it does not follow that it arises from experience. For it is quite possible that even our empirical experience is a compound of that which we receive through impressions, and of that which our own faculty of knowledge (incited only by sensuous impressions), supplies from itself, a supplement which we do not distinguish from that raw material, until long practice has roused our attention and rendered us capable of separating one from the other.

It is therefore a question which deserves at least closer investigation, and cannot be disposed of at first sight, whether there exists a knowledge independent of experience, and even of all impressions of the senses? Such *knowledge* is called *a priori,* and distinguished from *empirical* knowledge, which has its sources *a posteriori,* that is, in experience.

This term *a priori,* however, is not yet definite enough to indicate the full meaning of our question. For people are wont to say, even with regard to knowledge derived from experience, that we have it, or might have it, *a priori,* because we derive it from experience, not *immediately,* but from a general rule, which, however, has itself been derived from experience. Thus one would say of a person who undermines the foundations of his house, that he might have known *a priori* that it would tumble down, that is, that he need not wait for the experience of its really tumbling down. But still he could not know this entirely *a priori,* because he had first to learn from experience that bodies are heavy, and will fall when their supports are taken away.

We shall therefore, in what follows, understand by knowledge *a priori* knowledge which is *absolutely* independent of all experience, and not of this or that experience only. Opposed to this is empirical knowledge, or such as is possible *a posteriori* only, that is, by experience. Knowledge *a priori,* if mixed up with nothing empirical, is called *pure.* Thus the proposition, for example, that every change has its cause, is a proposition *a priori,* but not pure: because change is a concept which can only be derived from experience.

II. WE ARE IN POSSESSION OF CERTAIN COGNITIONS *A PRIORI,* AND EVEN THE ORDINARY UNDERSTANDING IS NEVER WITHOUT THEM

All depends here on a criterion, by which we may safely distinguish between pure and empirical knowledge. Now experience teaches us, no doubt, that something is so or so, but not that it cannot be different. *First,* then, if we have a proposition, which is thought, together with its necessity, we have a judgment *a priori;* and if, besides, it is not derived from any proposition, except such as is itself again considered as necessary, we have an absolutely *a priori* judgment. *Secondly,* experience never imparts to its judgments true or strict, but only assumed or relative universality (by means of induction), so that we ought always to say, so far as we have observed hitherto, there is no exception to this or that rule. If, therefore, a judgment is thought with strict universality, so that no exception is admitted as possible, it is not derived from experience, but valid absolutely *a priori.* Empirical universality, therefore, is only an arbitrary extension of a validity which applies to most cases, to one that applies to all: as, for instance, in the proposition, all bodies are heavy. If, on the contrary, strict universality is essential to a judgment, this always points to a special source of knowledge, namely, a faculty of knowledge *a priori.* Necessity, therefore, and strict universality are safe criteria of knowledge *a priori,* and are inseparable one from the other. As, however, in the use of these criteria,

From The Critique of Pure Reason *(1781), Max Müller, trans.*

it is sometimes easier to show the contingency than the empirical limitation of judgments, and as it is sometimes more convincing to prove the unlimited universality which we attribute to a judgment than its necessity, it is advisable to use both criteria separately, each being by itself infallible.

That there really exist in our knowledge such necessary, and in the strictest sense universal, and therefore pure judgments *a priori*, is easy to show. If we want a scientific example, we have only to look to any of the proportions of mathematics; if we want one from the sphere of the ordinary understanding, such a proposition as that each change must have a cause, will answer the purpose; nay, in the latter case, even the concept of cause contains so clearly the concept of the necessity of its connection with an effect, and of the strict universality of the rule, that it would be destroyed altogether if we attempted to derive it, as Hume does, from the frequent concomitancy of that which happens with that which precedes, and from a habit arising thence (therefore from a purely subjective necessity), of connecting representations. It is possible even, without having recourse to such examples in proof of the reality of pure propositions *a priori* within our knowledge, to prove their indispensability for the possibility of experience itself, thus proving it *a priori*. For whence should experience take its certainty, if all the rules which it follows were always again and again empirical, and therefore contingent and hardly fit to serve as first principles? For the present, however, we may be satisfied for having shown the pure employment of the faculty of our knowledge as a matter of fact, with the criteria of it. . . .

III. PHILOSOPHY REQUIRES A SCIENCE TO DETERMINE THE POSSIBILITY, THE PRINCIPLES, AND THE EXTENT OF ALL COGNITIONS A PRIORI

. . . Certain kinds of knowledge leave the field of all possible experience, and seem to enlarge the sphere of our judgments beyond the limits of experience by means of concepts to which experience can never supply any corresponding objects.

And it is in this very kind of knowledge which transcends the world of the senses, and where experience can neither guide nor correct us, that reason prosecutes its investigations, which by their importance we consider far more excellent and by their tendency far more elevated than anything the understanding can find in the sphere of phenomena. Nay, we risk rather anything, even at the peril of error, than that we should surrender such investigations, either on the ground of their uncertainty, or from any feeling of indifference or contempt. These inevitable problems of pure reason itself are, *God, Freedom,* and *Immortality.* The science which with all its apparatus is really intended for the solution of these problems, is called *Metaphysic.* Its procedure is at first *dogmatic*, i.e. unchecked by a previous examination of what reason can and cannot do, before it engages confidently is so arduous an undertaking.

Now it might seem natural that, after we have left the solid ground of experience, we should not at once proceed to erect an edifice with knowledge which we possess without knowing whence it came, and trust to principles the origin of which is unknown, without having made sure of the safety of the foundations by means of careful examination. It would seem natural, I say, that philosophers should first of all have asked the question how the mere understanding could arrive at all this knowledge *a priori,* and what extent, what truth, and what value it could possess. If we take natural to mean what is just and reasonable, then indeed nothing could be more natural. But if we understand by natural what takes place ordinarily, then, on the contrary, nothing is more natural and more intelligible than that this examination should have been neglected for so long a time. For one part of this knowledge, namely, the mathematical, has always been in possession of perfect trustworthiness; and thus produces a favourable presumption with regard to other parts also, although these may be of a totally different nature. Besides, once beyond the precincts of experience, and we are certain that experience can never contradict us, while the charm of enlarging our knowledge is so great that nothing will stop our progress until we encounter a clear contradiction. This can be avoided if only we are cautious in our imaginations, which nevertheless remain what they are, imaginations only. How far we can advance independent of all experience in *a priori* knowledge is shown by the brilliant example of mathematics. It is true they deal with objects and knowledge so far only as they can be represented in intuition. But this is easily overlooked, because that intuition itself may be given *a priori,* and be difficult to distinguish from a pure concept. Thus inspirited by a splendid proof of the power of reason, the desire of enlarging our knowledge sees no limits. The light dove, piercing in her easy flight the air and perceiving its resistance, imagines that flight would be easier still in empty space. It was thus that Plato left the world of sense, as opposing so many hindrances to our understanding, and ventured beyond on the wings of his ideas into the empty space of pure understanding. He did not perceive that he was making no progress by these endeavours, because he had no resistance as a fulcrum on which to rest or to apply his powers, in order to cause the understanding to advance. It is indeed a very common fate of human reason first of all to finish its speculative edifice as soon as possible, and then only to enquire whether the foundation be sure. Then all sorts of excuses are made in order to assure us as to its solidity, or to decline altogether such a late and dangerous enquiry. The reason why during the time of building we feel free from all anxiety and suspicion and believe in the apparent solidity of our foundation, is this:—A great, perhaps the greatest portion of what our reason finds to do consists in the analysis of our concepts of objects. This gives us a great deal of knowledge which, though it consists in no more than in simplifications and explanation of what is comprehended in our concepts (though in a confused manner), is yet considered as equal, at least in form, to new knowledge. It only separates and arranges our concepts, it does not enlarge them in matter or contents. As by this process we gain a kind of real knowledge *a priori,* which progresses safely and usefully, it happens that our reason, without being aware of it, appropriates under that pretence propositions of a totally different character, adding to given concepts new and strange ones *a priori,* without knowing whence they come, nay without even thinking of such a question. I shall therefore at the very outset treat of the distinction between these two kinds of knowledge.

IV. OF THE DISTINCTION BETWEEN ANALYTICAL AND SYNTHETICAL JUDGMENTS

In all judgments in which there is a relation between subject and predicate (I speak of affirmative judgments only, the application to negative ones being easy), that relation can be of two kinds. Either the predicate B belongs to the subject A as something contained (though covertly) in the concept A; or B lies outside the sphere of the concept A, though somehow connected with it. In the former case I call the judgment analytical, in the latter synthetical. Analytical judgments (affirmative) are therefore those in which the connection of the predicate with the subject is conceived through identity, while others in which that connection is conceived without identity, may be called synthetical. The former might be called illustrating, the latter expanding judgments, because in the former nothing is added by the predicate to the concept of the subject, but the concept is only divided into its constituent concepts which were always conceived as existing within it, though confusedly; while the latter add to the concept of the subject a predicate not conceived as existing within it, and not to be extracted from it by any process of mere analysis. If I say, for instance, All bodies are extended, this is an analytical judgment. I need not go beyond the concept connected with the name of body, in order to find that extension is connected with it. I have only to analyse that concept and become conscious of the manifold elements always continued in it, in order to find that predicate. This is therefore an analytical judgment. But if I say, All bodies are heavy, the predicate is something quite different from what I think as the mere concept of body. The addition of such a predicate gives us a synthetical judgment.

It becomes clear from this,

1. That our knowledge is in no way extended by analytical judgments, but that all they effect is to put the concepts which we possess into better order and render them more intelligible.

2. That in synthetical judgments I must have besides the concept of the subject something else (*x*) on which the understanding relies in order to

know that a predicate, not contained in the concept, nevertheless belongs to it.

In empirical judgments this causes no difficulty, because this *x* is here simply the complete experience of an object which I conceive by the concept A, that concept forming one part of my experience. For though I do not include the predicate of gravity in the general concept of body, that concept nevertheless indicates the complete experience through one of its parts, so that I may add other parts also of the same experience, all belonging to the concept. I may first, by an analytical process, realise the concept of body through the predicates of extension, impermeability, form, etc., all of which are contained in it. Afterwards I expand my knowledge, and looking back to the experience from which my concept of body was abstracted, I find gravity always connected with the beforementioned predicates. Experience therefore is the *x* which lies beyond the concept A, and on which rests the possibility of a synthesis of the predicate of gravity B with the concept A.

In synthetical judgments *a priori*, however, that help is entirely wanting. If I want to go beyond the concept A in order to find another concept B connected with it, where is there anything on which I may rest and through which a synthesis might become possible, considering that I cannot have the advantage of looking about in the field of experience? Take the proposition that all which happens has its cause. In the concept of something that happens I no doubt conceive of something existing preceded by time, and from this certain analytical judgments may be deduced. But the concept of cause is entirely outside that concept, and indicates something different from that which happens, and is by no means contained in that representation. How can I venture then to predicate of that which happens something totally different from it, and to represent the concept of cause, though not contained in it, as belonging to it, and belonging to it by necessity? What is here the unknown *x,* on which the understanding may rest in order to find beyond the concept A a foreign predicate B, which nevertheless is believed to be connected with it? It cannot be experience, because the proposition that all which happens has its cause represents this second predicate as added to the subject not only

with greater generality than experience can ever supply, but also with a character of necessity, and therefore purely *a priori,* and based on concepts. All our speculative knowledge *a priori* aims at and rests on such synthetical, i.e. expanding propositions, for the analytical are no doubt very important and necessary, yet only in order to arrive at that clearness of concepts which is requisite for a safe and wide synthesis, serving as a really new addition to what we possess already. . . .

V. IN ALL THEORETICAL SCIENCES OF REASON SYNTHETICAL JUDGMENTS *A PRIORI* ARE CONTAINED AS PRINCIPLES

1. *All mathematical judgments are synthetical.* This proposition, though incontestably certain, and very important to us for the future, seems to have hitherto escaped the observation of those who are engaged in the anatomy of human reason: nay, to be directly opposed to all their conjectures. For as it was found that all mathematical conclusions proceed according to the principle of contradiction (which is required by the nature of all apodictic certainty), it was supposed that the fundamental principles of mathematics also rested on the authority of the same principle of contradiction. This, however, was a mistake: for though a synthetical proposition may be understood according to the principle of contradiction, this can only be if another synthetical proposition is presupposed, from which the latter is deduced, but never by itself. First of all, we ought to observe, that mathematical propositions, properly so called, are always judgments *a priori,* and not empirical, because they carry along with them necessity, which can never be deduced from experience. If people should object to this, I am quite willing to confine my statement to pure mathematics, the very concept of which implies that it does not contain empirical, but only pure knowledge *a priori.*

At first sight one might suppose indeed that the proposition 7+5=12 is merely analytical, following, according to the principle of contradiction, from the concept of a sum of 7 and 5. But, if we look more closely, we shall find that the concept of the sum of 7 and 5 contains nothing beyond the union of both sums into one, whereby nothing is told us as to what this single number may be which combines both. We by no means arrive at a concept of Twelve, by thinking that union of Seven and Five; and we may analyse our concept of such a possible sum as long as we will, still we shall never discover in it the concept of Twelve. We must go beyond these concepts, and call in the assistance of the intuition corresponding to one of the two, for instance, our five fingers, or, as Segner does in his arithmetic, five points, and so by degrees add the units of the Five, given in intuition, to the concept of the Seven. For I first take the number 7, and taking the intuition of the fingers of my hand, in order to form with it the concept of the 5, I gradually add the units, which I before took together, to make up the number 5, by means of the image of my hand, to the number 7, and I thus see the number 12 arising before me. That 5 should be added to 7 was no doubt implied in my concept of a sum 7+5, but not that that sum should be equal to 12. An arithmetical proposition is, therefore, always synthetical, which is seen more easily still by taking larger numbers, where we clearly perceive that, turn and twist our conceptions as we may, we could never, by means of the mere analysis of our concepts and without the help of intuition, arrive at the sum that is wanted.

Nor is any proposition of pure geometry analytical. That the straight line between two points is the shortest, is a synthetical proposition. For my concept of *straight* contains nothing of magnitude (quantity), but a quality only. The concept of the *shortest* is, therefore, purely adventitious, and cannot be deduced from the concept of the straight line by any analysis whatsoever. The aid of intuition, therefore, must be called in, by which alone the synthesis is possible.

It is true that some few propositions, presupposed by the geometrician, are really analytical, and depend on the principle of contradiction: but then they serve only, like identical propositions, to form the chain of the method, and not as principles. Such are the propositions, a=a, the whole is equal to itself, or (a+b) > a. that the whole is greater than its part. And even these, though they

are valid according to mere concepts, are only admitted in mathematics, because they can be represented in intuition. What often makes us believe that the predicate of such apodictic judgments is contained in our concept, and the judgment therefore analytical, is merely the ambiguous character of the expression. We are told that we *ought* to join in thought a certain predicate to a given concept, and this necessity is inherent in the concepts themselves. But the question is not what we *ought* to join to the given concept, but what we *really think* in it, though confusedly only, and then it becomes clear that the predicate is no doubt inherent in those concepts by necessity, not, however, as thought in the concept itself, but by means of an intuition, which must be added to the concept.

2. *Natural science (physical) contains synthetical judgments* a priori *as principles.* I shall adduce, as examples, a few propositions only, such as, that in all changes of the material world the quantity of matter always remains unchanged: or that in all communication of motion, action and reaction must always equal each other. It is clear not only that both convey necessity, and that, therefore, their origin is *a priori,* but also that they are synthetical propositions. For in the concept of matter I do not conceive its permanency, but only its presence in the space which it fills. I therefore go beyond the concept of matter in order to join something to it *a priori,* which I did not before conceive *in it.* The proposition is, therefore, not analytical, but synthetical, and yet *a priori,* and the same applies to the other propositions of the pure part of natural science.

3. *Metaphysic,* even if we look upon it as hitherto a tentative science only, which, however, is indispensable to us, owing to the very nature of human reason, is meant to *contain synthetical knowledge a priori.* Its object is not at all merely to analyse such concepts as we make to ourselves of things *a priori,* and thus to explain them analytically, but to expand our knowledge *a priori.* This we can only do by means of concepts which add something to a given concept that was not contained in it; nay, we even attempt, by means of synthetical judgments *a priori,* to go so far beyond a given concept that experience itself cannot follow us: as, for instance, in the proposition that the

world must have a first beginning. Thus, according at least to its intentions, metaphysic consists merely of synthetical propositions *a priori*.

VI. THE GENERAL PROBLEM OF PURE REASON

Much is gained if we are able to bring a number of investigations under the formula of one single program. For we thus not only facilitate our own work by defining it accurately, but enable also everybody else who likes to examine it to form a judgment, whether we have really done justice to our purpose or not. Now the real problem of pure reason is contained in the question, *How are synthetical judgments* a priori *possible?*

That metaphysic has hitherto remained in so vacillating a state of ignorance and contradiction is entirely due to people not having thought sooner of this problem, or perhaps even of a distinction between *analytical* and *synthetical* judgments. The solution of this problem or a sufficient proof that a possibility which is to be explained does in reality not exist at all, is the question of life or death to metaphysic. *David Hume,* who among all philosophers approached nearest to that problem, though he was far from conceiving it with sufficient definiteness and universality, confining his attention only to the synthetical proposition of the connection of an effect with its causes (*principium causalitatis*), arrived at the conclusion that such a proposition *a priori* is entirely impossible. According to his conclusions, everything which we call metaphysic would turn out to be a mere delusion of reason, fancying that it knows by itself what in reality is only borrowed from experience, and has assumed by mere habit the appearance of necessity. If he had grasped our problem in all its universality, he would never have thought of an assertion which destroys all pure philosophy, because he would have perceived that, according to his argument, no pure mathematical science was possible either, on account of its certainty containing synthetical propositions *a priori;* and from such an assertion his good sense would probably have saved him.

On the solution of our problem depends, at the same time the possibility of the pure employment of reason, in establishing and carrying out all sciences which contain a theoretical knowledge *a priori* of objects, i.e. the answer to the questions.

How is pure mathematical science possible?
How is pure natural science possible?

As these sciences really exist, it is quite proper to ask, *How* they are possible? for *that* they must be possible, is proved by their reality.

But as to *metaphysic,* the bad progress which it has hitherto made, and the impossibility of asserting of any of the metaphysical systems yet brought forward that it really exists, so far as its essential aim is concerned, must fill every one with doubts as to its possibility.

Yet, in a certain sense, this *kind of knowledge* also must be looked upon as given, and though not as a science, yet as a natural disposition (*metaphysica naturalis*) metaphysic is real. For human reason, without being moved merely by the conceit of omniscience, advances irresistibly, and urged on by its own need, to questions such as cannot be answered by any empirical employment of reason, or by principles thence derived, so that we may really say, that all men, as soon as their reason became ripe for speculation, have at all times possessed some kind of metaphysic, and will always continue to possess it. And now it will also have to answer the question,

How is metaphysic possible, as a natural disposition? that is, how does the nature of universal human reason give rise to questions which pure reason proposes to itself, and which it is urged on by its own need to answer as well as it can?

As, however, all attempts which have hitherto been made at answering these natural questions (for instance, whether the world has a beginning, or exists from all eternity) have always led to inevitable contradictions, we cannot rest satisfied with the mere natural disposition to metaphysic, that is, with the pure faculty of reason itself, from which some kind of metaphysic (whatever it may be) always arises; but it must be possible to arrive with it at some certainty as to our either knowing or not knowing its objects; that is, we must either decide that we can judge of the objects of these questions, or of the power or want of power of reason, in deciding anything upon them,—therefore that we can either enlarge our pure reason with certainty, or that we have to impose on it fixed and firm limits. This last question, which arises out of the former more general problem, would properly assume this form,

How is metaphysic possible, as a science?

The critique of reason leads, therefore, necessarily, to true science, while its dogmatical use, without criticism, lands us in groundless assertions, to which others, equally specious, can always be opposed, that is, in *scepticism.*

Nor need this science be very formidable by its great prolixity, for it has not to deal with the objects of reason, the variety of which is infinite, but with reason only, and with problems, suggested by reason and placed before it, not by the nature of things, which are different from it, but by its own nature; so that, if reason has only first completely understood its own power, with reference to objects given to it in experience, it will have no difficulty in determining completely and safely the extent and limits of its attempted application beyond the limits of all experience.

We may and must therefore regard all attempts which have hitherto been made at building up a metaphysic dogmatically, as *non-avenu.* For the mere analysis of the concepts that dwell in our reason *a priori,* which has been attempted in one or other of those metaphysical systems, is by no means the aim, but only a preparation for true metaphysic, namely, the answer to the question, how we can enlarge our knowledge *a priori* synthetically; nay, it is utterly useless for the purpose, because it only shows what is contained in those concepts, but not by what process *a priori* we arrive at them, in order thus to determine the validity of their employment with reference to all objects of knowledge in general. Nor does it require much self denial to give up these pretensions, considering that the undeniable and, in the dogmatic procedure, inevitable contradictions of reason with itself, have long deprived every system of metaphysic of all authority. More firmness will be required in order not to be deterred by difficulties from within and resistance from without, from trying to advance a science, indispensable to human reason (a science of which we may lop off every branch, but will never be able to destroy the root), by a treatment entirely opposed to all former treatments,

which promises, at last, to ensure the successful and fruitful growth of metaphysical science.

TRANSCENDENTAL ÆSTHETIC

[Introduction]   Whatever the process and the means may be by which knowledge reaches its objects, there is one that reaches them directly, and forms the ultimate material of all thought, viz. intuition (Anschauung). This is possible only when the object is given, and the object can be given only (to human beings at least) through a certain affection of the mind (Gemüth).

This faculty (receptivity) of receiving representations (Vorstellungen), according to the manner in which we are affected by objects, is called sensibility (Sinnlichkeit).

Objects therefore are given to us through our sensibility. Sensibility alone supplies us with intuitions (Anschauungen). These intuitions become thought through the understanding (Verstand), and hence arise conceptions (Begriffe). All thought therefore must, directly or indirectly, go back to intuitions (Anschauungen), i.e. to our sensibility, because in no other way can objects be given to us.

The effect produced by an object upon the faculty of representation (Vorstellungsfähigkeit), so far as we are affected by it, is called sensation (Empfindung). An intuition (Anschauung) of an object, by means of sensation, is called empirical. The undefined object of such an empirical intuition is called phenomenon (Erscheinung).

In a phenomenon I call that which corresponds to the sensation its *matter;* but that which causes the manifold matter of the phenomenon to be perceived as arranged in a certain order, I call its *form.*

Now it is clear that it cannot be sensation again through which sensations are arranged and placed in certain forms. The matter only of all phenomena is given us *a posteriori;* but their form must be ready for them in the mind (Gemüth) *a priori,* and must therefore be capable of being considered as separate from all sensations.

I call all representations in which there is nothing that belongs to sensation, *pure* (in a transcendental sense). The pure form therefore of all sensuous intuitions, that form in which the manifold elements of the phenomena are seen in a certain order, must be found in the mind *a priori*. And this pure form of sensibility may be called the pure intuition (Anschauung).

Thus, if we deduct from the representation (Vorstellung) of a body what belongs to the thinking of the understanding, viz. substance, force, divisibility, etc., and likewise what belongs to sensation, viz, impermeability, hardness, colour, etc., there still remains something of that empirical intuition (Anschauung), viz. extension and form. These belong to pure intuition, which *a priori,* and even without a real object of the senses or of sensation, exists in the mind as a mere form of sensibility.

The science of all the principles of sensibility *a priori* I call *Transcendental Æsthetic.* There must be such a science, forming the first part of the Elements of Transcendentalism, as opposed to that which treats of the principles of pure thought, and which should be called *Transcendental Logic.*

In Transcendental Æsthetic therefore we shall first isolate sensibility, by separating everything which the understanding adds by means of its concepts, so that nothing remains but empirical intuition (Anschauung).

Secondly, we shall separate from this all that belongs to sensation (Empfindung), so that nothing remains but pure intuition (reine Anschauung) or the mere form of the phenomena, which is the only thing which sensibility *a priori* can supply. In the course of this investigation it will appear that there are, as principles of a *a priori* knowledge, two pure forms of sensuous intuition (Anschauung), namely, *Space* and *Time.* We now proceed to consider these more in detail.

First Section: Of Space

Metaphysical Exposition of the Concept of Space   By means of our external sense, a property of our mind (Gemüth), we represent to ourselves objects as external or outside ourselves, and all of these in space. It is within space that their form, size, and relative position are fixed or can be fixed. The internal sense by means of which the mind perceives itself or its internal state, does not give an intuition (Anschauung) of the soul (Seele) itself, as an object, but it is nevertheless a fixed form under which alone an intuition of its internal state is possible, so that whatever belongs to its internal determinations

(Bestimmungen) must be represented in relations of time. Time cannot be perceived (angeschaut) externally, as little as space can be perceived as something within us.

What then are space and time? Are they real beings? Or, if not that, are they determinations or relations of things, but such as would belong to them even if they were not perceived? Or lastly, are they determinations and relations which are inherent in the form of intuition only, and therefore in the subjective nature of our mind, without which such predicates as space and time would never be ascribed to anything?

In order to understand this more clearly, let us first consider space.

1. Space is not an empirical concept which has been derived from external experience. For in order that certain sensations should be referred to something outside myself, i.e. to something in a different part of space from that where I am; again, in order that I may be able to represent them (vorstellen) as side by side, that is, not only as different, but as in different places, the representation (Vorstellung) of space must already be there. Therefore the representation of space cannot be borrowed through experience from relations of external phenomena, but, on the contrary, this external experience becomes possible only by means of the representation of space.

2. Space is a necessary representation *a priori,* forming the very foundation of all external intuitions. It is impossible to imagine that there should be no space, though one might very well imagine that there should be space without objects to fill it. Space is therefore regarded as a condition of the possibility of phenomena, not as a determination produced by them; it is a representation *a priori* which necessarily precedes all external phenomena. . . .

3. Space is not a discursive or so-called general concept of the relations of things in general, but a pure intuition. For, first of all, we can imagine one space only and if we speak of many spaces, we mean parts only of one and the same space. Nor can these parts be considered as antecedent to the one and all-embracing space and, as it were, its component parts out of which an aggregate is formed, but they can be thought of as existing

within it only. Space is essentially one; its multiplicity, and therefore the general concept of spaces in general, arises entirely from limitations. . . .

4. Space is represented as an infinite quantity. Now a general concept of space, which is found in a foot as well as in an ell, could tell us nothing in respect to the quantity of the space. If there were not infinity in the progression of intuition, no concept of relations of space could ever contain a principle of infinity.

Transcendental Exposition of the Concept of Space
. . . Geometry is a science which determines the properties of space synthetically, and yet *a priori*. What then must be the representation of space, to render such a knowledge of it possible? It must be originally intuitive; for it is impossible from a mere concept to deduce propositions which go beyond that concept, as we do in geometry. That intuition, however, must be *a priori*, that is, it must exist within us before any perception of the object, and must therefore be pure, not empirical intuition. For all geometrical propositions are apodictic, that is, concocted with the consciousness of their necessity, as for instance the proposition, that space has only three dimensions; and such proposition cannot be empirical judgments, nor conclusions from them.

How then can an external intuition dwell in the mind anterior to the objects themselves, and in which the concept of objects can be determined *a priori*? Evidently not otherwise than so far as it has its seat in the subject only, as the formal condition under which the subject is affected by the objects and thereby is receiving an *immediate representation*, that is, *intuition* of them; therefore as a form of the external *sense* in general.

It is therefore by our explanation only that the *possibility* of *geometry* as a synthetical science *a priori* becomes intelligible. Every other explanation, which fails to account for this possibility, can best be distinguished from our own by that criterion, although it may seem to have some similarity with it.

Conclusions from the Foregoing Concepts

a. Space does not represent any quality of objects by themselves, or objects in their relation to one another; i.e. space does not represent any determi-

nation which is inherent in the objects themselves, and would remain, even if all subjective conditions of intuition were removed. For no determinations of objects, whether belonging to them absolutely or in relation to others, can enter into our intuition before the actual existence of the objects themselves, that is to say, they can never be intuitions *a priori*,

b. Space is nothing but the form of all phenomena of the external senses; it is the subjective condition of our sensibility, without which no external intuition is possible for us. If then we consider that the receptivity of the subject, its capacity of being affected by objects, must necessarily precede all intuition of objects, we shall understand how the form of all phenomena may be given before all real perceptions, may be, in fact, *a priori* in the soul, and may, as the pure intuition, by which all objects must be determined, contain, prior to all experience, principles regulating their relations.

It is therefore from the human standpoint only that we can speak of space, extended objects, etc. If we drop the subjective condition under which alone we can gain external intuition, that is, so far as we ourselves may be affected by objects, the representation of space means nothing. For this predicate is applied to objects only in so far as they appear to us, and are objects of our senses. The constant form of this receptivity, which we call sensibility, is a necessary condition of all relations in which objects, as without us, can be perceived; and, when abstraction is made of these objects, what remains is that pure intuition which we call space. As the peculiar conditions of our sensibility cannot be looked upon as conditions of the possibility of the objects themselves, but only of their appearance as phenomena to us, we may say indeed that space comprehends all things which may appear to us externally, but not all things by themselves, whether perceived by us or not, or by any subject whatsoever. We cannot judge whether the intuitions of other thinking beings are subject to the same conditions which determine our intuition, and which for us are generally binding. If we add the limitation of a judgment to a subjective concept, the judgment gains absolute validity. The proposition "all things are beside each other in space," is valid only under the limitation that things are taken as object of our sensuous intuition (Anschauung). If I add that limitation to the concept and say "all things, as external phenomena, are beside each other in space," the rule obtains universal and unlimited validity. Our discussions teach therefore the reality, i.e. the objective validity, of space with regard to all that can come to us externally as an object, but likewise the *ideality* of space with regard to things, when they are considered in themselves by our reason, and independent of the nature of our senses. We maintain the empirical reality of space, so far as every possible external experience is concerned, but at the same time its transcendental ideality; that is to say, we maintain that space is nothing, if we leave out of consideration the condition of a possible experience, and accept it as something on which things by themselves are in any way dependent. . . .

Second Section. Of Time

Metaphysical Exposition of the Concept of Time

1. Time is not an empirical concept deduced from any experience, for neither coexistence nor succession would enter into our perception, if the representation of time were not given *a priori*. Only when this representation *a priori* is given, can we imagine that certain things happen at the same time (simultaneously) or at different times (successively).

2. Time is a necessary representation on which all intuitions depend. We cannot take away time from phenomena in general, though we can well take away phenomena out of time. Time therefore is given *a priori*. In time alone is reality of phenomena possible. All phenomena may vanish, but time itself (as the general condition of their possibility) cannot do done away with.

[3]. Time is not a discursive, or what is called a general concept, but a pure form of sensuous intuition. Different times are parts only of one and the same time. Representation, which can be produced by a single object only, is called an intuition. The proposition that different times cannot exist at the same time cannot be deduced from any general concept. Such a proposition is synthetical, and cannot be deduced from concepts only. It is contained immediately in the intuition and representation of time.

[4]. To say that time is infinite means no more than that every definite quantity of time is possible only by limitations of one time which forms the foundation of all times. The original representation of time must therefore be given as unlimited. But when the parts themselves and every quantity of an object can be represented as determined by limitation only, the whole representation cannot be given by concepts (for in that case the partial representations come first), but it must be founded on immediate intuition.

Transcendental Exposition of the Concept of Time

On this *a priori* necessity depends also the possibility of apodictic principles of the relations of time, or of axioms of time in general. Time has one dimension only; different times are not simultaneous, but successive, while different spaces are never successive, but simultaneous. Such principles cannot be derived from experience, because experience could not impart to them absolute universality nor apodictic certainty. We should only be able to say that common experience teaches us that it is so, but not that it must be so. These principles are valid as rules under which alone experience is possible; they teach us before experience, not by means of experience.

. . . The concept of change, and with it the concept of motion (as change of place), is possible only through and in the representation of time; if this representation were not intuitive (internal) *a priori*, no concept, whatever it be, could make us understand the possibility of a change, that is, of a connection of contradictorily opposed predicates (for instance, the being and not-being of one and the same thing in one and the same place) in one and the same object. It is only in time that both contradictorily opposed determinations can be met with in the same object, that is, one after the other. Our concept of time, therefore, exhibits the possibility of as many synthetical cognitions *a priori* as are found in the general doctrine of motion, which is very rich in them.

Conclusions from the Foregoing Concepts

a. Time is not something existing by itself, or inherent in things as an objective determination of them, something therefore that might remain when abstraction is made of all subjective conditions of intuition. For in the former case it would be something real, without being a real object. In the latter is could not, as a determination or order inherent in things themselves, be antecedent to things as their condition, and be known and perceived by means of synthetical propositions *a priori*. All this is perfectly possible if time is nothing but a subjective condition under which alone intuitions take place within us. For in that case this form of internal intuition can be represented prior to the objects themselves, that is, *a priori*.

b. Time is nothing but the form of the internal sense, that is, of our intuition of ourselves, and of our internal state. Time cannot be a determination peculiar to external phenomena. It refers neither to their shape, nor their position, etc., it only determines the relation of representations in our internal state. And exactly because this internal intuition supplies no shape, we try to make good this deficiency by means of analogies, and represent to ourselves the succession of time by a line progressing to infinity, in which the manifold constitutes a series of one dimension only; and we conclude from the properties of this line as to all the properties of time, with one exception, i.e. that the parts of the former are simultaneous, those of the latter successive. From this it becomes clear also, that the representation of time is itself an intuition, because all its relations can be expressed by means of an external intuition.

c. Time is the formal condition, *a priori,* of all phenomena whatsoever. Space, as the pure form of all external intuition, is a condition, *a priori,* of external phenomena only. But, as all representations, whether they have for their objects external things or not, belong by themselves, as determinations of the mind, to our inner state, and as this inner state falls under the formal conditions of internal intuition, and therefore of time, time is a condition, *a priori,* of all phenomena whatsoever, and is so directly as a condition of internal phenomena (of our mind) and thereby indirectly of external phenomena also. If I am able to say, *a priori,* that all external phenomena are in space, and are determined, *a priori,* according to the relations of space, I can, according to the principle of the internal sense, make the general assertion that all phenomena, that is, all objects of the sense, are in time, and stand necessarily in relations of time.

If we drop our manner of looking at ourselves internally, and of comprehending by means of that intuition all external intuitions also within our power of representation, and thus take objects as they may be by themselves, then time is nothing. Time has objective validity with reference to phenomena only, because these are themselves things which we accept as objects of our senses; but time is no longer objective, if we remove the sensuous character of our intuitions, that is to say, that mode of representation which is peculiar to ourselves, and speak of things in general. Time is therefore simply a subjective condition of our (human) intuition (which is always sensuous, that is so far as we are affected by objects), but by itself, apart from the subject, nothing. Nevertheless, with respect to all phenomena, that is, all things which can come within our experience, time is necessarily objective. We cannot say that all things are in time, because, if we speak of things in general, nothing is said about the manner of intuition, which is the real condition under which time enters into our representation of things. If therefore this condition is added to the concept, and if we say that all things as phenomena (as objects of sensuous intuition) are in time, then such a proposition has its full objective validity and *a priori* universality.

What we insist on therefore is the empirical reality of time, that is, its objective validity, with reference to all objects which can ever come before our senses. And as our intuition must at all times be sensuous, no object can ever fall under our experience that does not come under the conditions of time. What we deny is, that time has any claim on absolute reality, so that, without taking into account the form of our sensuous condition, it should by itself be a condition or quality inherent in things; for such qualities which belong to things by themselves can never be given to us through the senses. This is what constitutes the transcendental ideality of time, so that, if we take no account of the subjective conditions of our sensuous intuitions time is nothing, and cannot be added to the objects by themselves (without their relation to our intuition) whether as subsisting or inherent. . . .

[General Conclusion] ... In natural theology, where we think of an object which not only can never be an object of intuition to us, but which even to itself can never be an object of *sensuous* intuition, great care is taken to remove all conditions of space and time from its intuition (for all its knowledge must be intuitive, and not *thought,* which always involves limitation). But how are we justified in doing this, when we have first made space and time forms of things by themselves, such as would remain as conditions of the existence of things a *priori,* even if the things themselves had been removed? If conditions of all existence, they would also be conditions of the existence of God. If we do not wish to change space and time into objective forms of all things, nothing remains but to accept them as subjective forms of our external as well as internal intuition, which is called sensuous, for the very reason that it is not originally spontaneous, that is such, that it could itself give us the existence of the objects of intuition (such an intuition, so far as we can understand, can belong to the First Being only), but dependent on the existence of objects, and therefore possibly only, if the faculty of representation in the subject is affected by them.

It is not necessary, moreover, that we should limit this intuition in space and time to the sensibility of man; it is quite possible that all finite thinking beings must necessarily agree with us on this point (though we cannot decide this). On account of this universal character, however, it does not cease to be sensibility, for it always is, and remains derivative (*intuitus derivativus*), not original (*intuitus originarius*), and therefore not intellectual intuition. For the reason mentioned before, the latter intuition seems only to belong to the First Being, and never to one which is dependent, both in its existence and its intuition (which intuition determines its existence with reference to given objects). This latter remark, however, must only be taken as an illustration of our æsthetic theory, and not as a proof. . . .

Further Questions

1. What is the relationship between Kant's *intuitions* and Hume's *impressions* and *perceptions*? What similarities and differences do you see?
2. Kant said that it was Hume who awoke him from his "dogmatic slumbers." What do you suppose was the dogma that, reading Hume, Kant was force to give up?
3. Compare Kant's view with Berkeley's. How are they different? How are they similar?

Further Readings

Kant, Immanuel. *Foundations of the Metaphysics of Ethics,* 1785.
——*Metaphysical First Principles of Natural Science,* 1786.
——*Critique of Practical Reason,* 1788.
——*Critique of Judgment,* 1790.
——*Religion Within the Limits of Mere Reason,* 1793.
——*Perpetual Peace,* 1795.
Kolak, Daniel. *From the Presocratics to the Present: A Personal Odyssey,* ch. 4. "Kant and the Nineteenth Century." Mayfield, 1998.

A Coffeehouse Conversation on the Turing Test   53

DOUGLAS R. HOFSTADTER

Douglas Hofstadter is Professor of Cognitive Science and Computer Science at the Center for Research on Concepts and Cognition at Indiana University. He is the author of *Gödel, Escher, and Bach* (1979), co-editor, along with Daniel Dennett, of *The Mind's I* (1981), and author of *Metamagical Themas* (1985), a collection of essays. Several of the essays appeared originally, as did the following selection, in his regular column in *Scientific American*. In this selection, Hofstadter dramatically portrays the reasons for and against using the "Turing Test" as a criterion for determining whether a machine can think.

Reading Questions

1. What's the difference between the Imitation Game and the Turing Test? Which, if either, is a more adequate test of whether machines can think?
2. Which of the characters—Chris, Sandy, or Pat—has the best arguments?
3. D. M. Armstrong, in a previous selection, suggested that a thermometer might have knowledge. *If* we're prepared to say that a thermometer might know, should we hesitate to say that a computer might think?

PARTICIPANTS IN THE DIALOGUE: Chris, a physics student; Pat, a biology student; Sandy, a philosophy student.

Chris: Sandy, I want to thank you for suggesting that I read Alan Turing's article "Computing Machinery and Intelligence." It's a wonderful piece and certainly made me think—and think about my thinking.

Sandy: Glad to hear it. Are you still as much of a skeptic about artificial intelligence as you used to be?

Chris: You've got me wrong. I'm not against artificial intelligence; I think it's wonderful stuff—perhaps a little crazy, but why not? I simply am convinced that you AI advocates have far underestimated the human mind, and that there are things a computer will never, ever be able to do. For instance, can you imagine a computer writing a Proust novel? The richness of imagination, the complexity of the characters—

Sandy: Rome wasn't built in a day!

Chris: In the article, Turing comes through as an interesting person. Is he still alive?

Sandy: No, he died back in 1954, at just 41. He'd be only 70 or so now, although he is such a legendary figure it seems strange to think that he could still be living today.

Chris: How did he die?

Sandy: Almost certainly suicide. He was homosexual, and had to deal with some pretty barbaric treatment and stupidity from the outside world. In the end, it got to be too much, and he killed himself.

Chris: That's horrendous, especially in this day and age.

Sandy: I know. What really saddens me is that he never got to see the amazing progress in computing machinery and theory that has taken place since 1954. Can you imagine how he'd have been wowed?

Chris: Yeah . . .

Pat: Hey, are you two going to clue me in as to what this Turing article is about?

Sandy: It is really about two things. One is the question "Can a machine think?"—or rather, "Will a machine ever think?" The way Turing answers the question—he thinks the answer is *yes*, by the way—is by batting down a series of objections to the idea, one after another. The other point he tries to make is that, as it stands, the question is not meaningful. It's too full of emotional connotations. Many people are upset by the suggestion that people are machines, or that machines might think. Turing tries to defuse the question by casting it in less emotional terms. For instance, what do you think, Pat, of the idea of thinking machines?

Pat: Frankly, I find the term confusing. You know what confuses me? It's those ads in the newspapers and on TV that talk about "products that think" or "intelligent ovens" or whatever. I just don't know how seriously to take them.

Sandy: I know the kind of ads you mean, and they probably confuse a lot of people. On the other hand, we're always hearing the refrain "Computers are really dumb; you have to spell everything out for them in words of one syllable"—yet on the other hand, we're constantly bombarded with advertising hype about "smart products."

Chris: That's certainly true. Do you know that one company has even taken to calling its products "dumb terminals" in order to stand out from the crowd?

Sandy: That's a pretty clever gimmick, but even so it just contributes to the trend toward obfuscation. The term "electronic brain" always comes to my mind when I'm thinking about this. Many people swallow it completely, and others reject it out of hand. It takes patience to sort out the issues and decide how much of it makes sense.

Pat: Does Turing suggest some way of resolving it, some kind of IQ test for machines?

Sandy: That would be very interesting, but no machine could yet come close to taking an IQ test. Instead, Turing proposes a test that theoretically could be applied to any machine to determine whether or not it can think.

Pat: Does the test give us a clear-cut yes-or-no answer? I'd be skeptical if it claimed to.

Sandy: No, it doesn't claim to. In a way that's one of its advantages. It shows how the borderline is quite fuzzy, and how subtle the whole question is.

Pat: And so, as usual in philosophy, it's all just a question of words!

Sandy: Maybe, but they're emotionally charged words, and so it's important, it seems to me, to explore the issues and try to map out the meanings of the crucial words. The issues are fundamental to our concept of ourselves, so we shouldn't just sweep them under the rug.

Pat: Okay, so tell me how Turing's test works.

Sandy: The idea is based on what he calls the *Imitation Game*. Imagine that a man and a woman go into separate rooms, and from there they can be interrogated by a third party via some sort of teletype set-up. The third party can address questions to either room, but has no idea which person is in which room. For the interrogator, the idea is to determine which room the woman is in. The woman, by her answers, tries to help the interrogator as much as she can. The man, though, is doing his best to bamboozle the interrogator, by responding as he thinks a woman might. And if he succeeds in fooling the interrogator . . .

Pat: The interrogator only gets to see written words, eh? And the sex of the author is supposed to shine through? That game sounds like a good challenge. I'd certainly like to take part in it some day. Would the interrogator have met either the man or the woman before the test began? Would any of them know any of the others?

Sandy: That would probably be a bad idea. All kinds of subliminal cueing might occur if the interrogator knew one or both of them. It would certainly be best if all three people were totally unknown to one another.

Pat: Could you ask any questions at all, with no holds barred?

Sandy: Absolutely. That's the whole idea!

Pat: Don't you think, then, that pretty quickly it would degenerate into sex-oriented questions? I mean, I can imagine the man, overeager to act convincing, giving away the game by answering some very blunt questions that most women would find too personal to answer, even through an anonymous computer connection.

Sandy: That's a nice observation. I wonder if it's true . . .

Chris: Another possibility would be to probe for knowledge of minute aspects of traditional sex-role differences, by asking about such things as dress sizes and so on. The psychology of the Imitation

Game could get pretty subtle. I suppose whether the interrogator was a woman or a man would make a difference. Don't you think that a woman could spot some telltale differences more quickly than a man could?

Pat: If so, maybe the best way to tell a man from a woman is to let each of them play interrogator in an Imitation Game, and see which of the two is better at telling a man from a woman!

Sandy: Hmm . . . that's a droll twist. Oh, well. I don't know if this original version of the Imitation Game has ever been seriously tried out, despite the fact that it would be relatively easy to do with modern computer terminals. I have to admit, though, that I'm not at all sure what it would prove, whichever way it turned out.

Pat: I was wondering about that. What would it prove if the interrogator—say a woman—couldn't tell correctly which person was the woman? It certainly wouldn't prove that the man *was* a woman!

Sandy: Exactly! What I find funny is that although I strongly believe in the idea of the Turing Test, I'm not so sure I understand the point of its basis, the Imitation Game.

Chris: As for me, I'm not any happier with the Turing Test as a test for thinking machines than I am with the Imitation Game as a test for femininity.

Pat: From what you two are saying, I gather the Turing Test is some kind of extension of the Imitation Game, only involving a machine and a person instead of a man and a woman.

Sandy: That's the idea. The machine tries its hardest to convince the interrogator that it is the human being and the human being tries to make it clear that he or she is not the computer.

Pat: The machine *tries*? Isn't that a loaded way of putting it?

Sandy: Sorry, but that seemed the most natural way to say it.

Pat: Anyway, this test sounds pretty interesting. But how do you know that it will get at the essence of thinking? Maybe it's testing for the wrong things. Maybe, just to take a random illustration, someone would feel that a machine was able to think only if it could dance so well that you couldn't tell it was a machine. Or someone else could suggest some other characteristic. What's so sacred about being able to fool people by typing at them?

Sandy: I don't see how you can say such a thing. I've heard that objection before, but frankly, it baffles me. So what if the machine can't tap-dance or drop a rock on your toe? If it can discourse intelligently on any subject you want, then it has shown that it can think—to me, at least! As I see it, Turing has drawn, in one clean stroke, a clear division between thinking and other aspects of being human.

Pat: Now *you're* the baffling one. If you couldn't conclude anything from a *man's* ability to win at the Imitation Game, how could you conclude anything from a *machine's* ability to win at the Turing Game?

Chris: Good question.

Sandy: It seems to me that you could conclude *something* from a man's win in the Imitation Game. You wouldn't conclude he was a woman, but you could certainly say he had good insights into the feminine mentality (if there is such a thing). Now, if a computer could fool someone into thinking it was a person, I guess you'd have to say something similar about it—that it had good insights into what it's like to be human, into "the human condition" (whatever that is).

Pat: Maybe, but that isn't necessarily equivalent to *thinking*, is it? It seems to me that passing the Turing Test would merely prove that some machine or other could do a very good job of *simulating* thought.

Chris: I couldn't agree more with Pat. We all know that fancy computer programs exist today for simulating all sorts of complex phenomena. In theoretical physics, for instance, we simulate the behavior of particles, atoms, solids, liquids, gases, galaxies, and so on. But no one confuses any of those simulations with the real thing!

Sandy: In his book *Brainstorms,* the philosopher Daniel Dennett makes a similar point about simulated hurricanes.

Chris: That's a nice example, too. Obviously, what goes on inside a computer when it's simulating a hurricane is not a hurricane, for the machine's memory doesn't get torn to bits by 200-mile-an-hour winds, the floor of the machine room doesn't get flooded with rainwater, and so on.

Sandy: Oh, come on—that's not a fair argument! In the first place, the programmers don't claim the simulation really *is* a hurricane. It's merely a simulation of certain aspects of a hurricane. But in the second place, you're pulling a fast one when you imply that there are no downpours or 200-mile-an-hour winds in a simulated hurricane. To *us* there aren't any, but if the program were incredibly detailed, it could include simulated people on the ground who would experience the wind and the rain just as we do when a hurricane hits. In their minds—or, if you'd rather, in their *simulated* minds—the hurricane would be not a simulation, but a genuine phenomenon complete with drenching and devastation.

Chris: Oh, my—what a science-fiction scenario! Now we're talking about simulating whole populations, not just a single mind!

Sandy: Well, look—I'm simply trying to show you why your argument that a simulated McCoy isn't the real McCoy is fallacious. It depends on the tacit assumption that any old observer of the simulated phenomenon is equally able to assess what's going on. But in fact, it may take an observer with a special vantage point to recognize what is going on. In the hurricane case, it takes special "computational glasses" to see the rain and the winds.

Pat: "Computational glasses"? I don't know what you're talking about.

Sandy: I mean that to see the winds and the wetness of the hurricane, you have to be able to look at it in the proper way. You—

Chris: No, no, no! A simulated hurricane isn't wet! No matter how much it might seem wet to simulated people, it won't ever be *genuinely* wet! And no computer will ever get torn apart in the process of simulating winds.

Sandy: Certainly not, but that's irrelevant. You're just confusing levels. The laws of physics don't get torn apart by real hurricanes, either. In the case of the simulated hurricane, if you go peering at the computer's memory, expecting to find broken wires and so forth, you'll be disappointed. But look at the proper level. Look into the *structures* that are coded for in memory. You'll see that many abstract links have been broken, many values of variables radically changed, and so on. *There's* your flood, your devastation—real, only a little concealed, a little hard to detect.

Chris: I'm sorry, I just can't buy that. You're insisting that I look for a new kind of devastation, one never before associated with hurricanes. That

way you could call *anything* a hurricane as long as its effects, seen through your special "glasses," could be called "floods and devastation."

Sandy: Right—you've got it exactly! You recognize a hurricane by its *effects*. You have no way of going in and finding some ethereal "essence of hurricane," some "hurricane soul" right in the middle of the storm's eye. Nor is there any ID card to be found that certifies "hurricanehood." It's just the existence of a certain kind of *pattern*—a spiral storm with an eye and so forth—that makes you say it's a hurricane. Of course, there are a lot of things you'll insist on before you call something a hurricane.

Pat: Well, wouldn't you say that being an *atmospheric* phenomenon is one prerequisite? How can anything inside a computer be a storm? To me, a simulation is a simulation is a simulation!

Sandy: Then I suppose you would say that even the *calculations* computers do are simulated—that they are fake calculations. Only *people* can do genuine calculations, right?

Pat: Well, computers get the right answers, so their calculations are not exactly fake—but they're still just patterns. There's no *understanding* going on in there. Take a cash register. Can you honestly say that you feel it is *calculating* something when its gears mesh together? And the step from cash register to computer is very short, as I understand things.

Sandy: If you mean that a cash register doesn't feel like a schoolkid doing arithmetic problems, I'll agree. But is that what "calculation" means? Is that an integral part of it? If so, then contrary to what everybody has thought up till now, we'll have to write a very complicated program indeed to perform *genuine* calculations. Of course, this program will sometimes get careless and make mistakes, and it will sometimes scrawl its answers illegibly, and it will occasionally doodle on its paper . . . It won't be any more reliable than the store clerk who adds up your total by hand. Now, I happen to believe that eventually such a program could be written. Then we'd know something about how clerks and schoolkids work.

Pat: I can't believe you'd ever be able to do that!

Sandy: Maybe, maybe not, but that's not my point. You say a cash register can't calculate. It reminds me of another favorite passage of mine from Dennett's *Brainstorms*. It goes something like this: "Cash registers can't really calculate; they can only spin their gears. But cash registers can't really spin their gears, either; they can only follow the laws of physics." Dennett said it originally about computers; I modified it to talk about cash registers. And you could use the same line of reasoning in talking about people: "People can't really calculate; all they can do is manipulate mental symbols. But they aren't really manipulating symbols; all they are doing is firing various neurons in various patterns. But they can't really make their neurons fire; they simply have to let the laws of physics make them fire for them." Et cetera. Don't you see how this *reductio ad absurdum* would lead you to conclude that calculation doesn't exist, that hurricanes don't exist—in fact, that nothing at a level higher than particles and the laws of physics exists? What do you gain by saying that a computer only pushes symbols around and doesn't truly calculate?

Pat: The example may be extreme, but it makes my point that there is a vast difference between a real phenomenon and any simulation of it. This is so for hurricanes, and even more so for human thought.

Sandy: Look, I don't want to get too tangled up in this line of argument, but let me try one more example. If you were a radio ham listening to another ham broadcasting in Morse code and you were responding in Morse code, would it sound funny to you to refer to "the person at the other end"?

Pat: No, that would sound okay, although the existence of a person at the other end would be an assumption.

Sandy: Yes, but you wouldn't be likely to go and check it out. You're prepared to recognize personhood through those rather unusual channels. You don't have to see a human body or hear a voice. All you need is a rather abstract manifestation—a code, as it were. What I'm getting at is this. To "see" the person behind the dits and dahs, you have to be willing to do some *decoding*, some interpretation. It's not direct perception; it's indirect. You have to peel off a layer or two or find the reality hidden in there. You put on your "radioham's glasses" to "see" the person behind the buzzes. Just the same with the simulated hurri-

cane! You don't see it darkening the machine room; you have to decode the machine's memory. You have to put on special "memory-decoding" glasses. *Then* what you see is a hurricane.

Pat: Oh, ho ho! Talk about fast ones—wait a minute! In the case of the shortwave radio, there's a real person out there, somewhere in the Fiji Islands or wherever. My decoding act as I sit by my radio simply reveals that that person exists. It's like seeing a shadow and concluding there's an object out there, casting it. One doesn't confuse the shadow with the object, however! And with the hurricane there's no *real* storm behind the scenes, making the computer follow its patterns. No, what you have is just a shadow-hurricane without any genuine hurricane. I just refuse to confuse shadows with reality.

Sandy: All right. I don't want to drive this point into the ground. I even admit it is pretty silly to say that a simulated hurricane *is* a hurricane. But I wanted to point out that it's not as silly as you might think at first blush. And when you turn to simulated *thought*, then you've got a very different matter on your hands from simulated hurricanes.

Pat: I don't see why. You'll have to convince me.

Sandy: Well, to do so, I'll first have to make a couple of extra points about hurricanes.

Pat: Oh, no! Well, all right, all right.

Sandy: Nobody can say just exactly what a hurricane is—that is, in totally precise terms. There's an abstract pattern that many storms share, and it's for that reason we call those storms hurricanes. But it's not possible to make a sharp distinction between hurricanes and nonhurricanes. There are tornadoes, cyclones, typhoons, dust devils . . . Is the Great Red Spot on Jupiter a hurricane? Are sunspots hurricanes? Could there be a hurricane in a wind tunnel? In a test tube? In your imagination, you can even extend the concept of "hurricane" to include a microscope storm on the surface of a neutron star.

Chris: That's not so far-fetched, you know. The concept of "earthquake" has actually been extended to neutron stars. The astrophysicists say that the tiny changes in rate that once in a while are observed in the pulsing of a pulsar are caused by "glitches"—starquakes—that have just occurred on the neutron star's surface.

Sandy: Oh, I remember that now. That "glitch" idea has always seemed eerie to me—a surrealistic kind of quivering on a surrealistic kind of surface.

Chris: Can you imagine—plate tectonics on a giant sphere of pure nuclear matter?

Sandy: That's a wild thought. So starquakes and earthquakes can both be subsumed into a new, more abstract category. And that's how science constantly extends familiar concepts, taking them further and further from familiar experience and yet keeping some essence constant. The number system is the classic example—from positive numbers to negative numbers, then rationals, reals, complex numbers, and "on beyond zebra," as Dr. Seuss says.

Pat: I think I can see your point, Sandy. In biology, we have many examples of close relationships that are established in rather abstract ways. Often the decision about what family some species belongs to comes down to an abstract pattern shared at some level. Even the concepts of "male" and "female" turn out to be surprisingly abstract and elusive. When you base your system of classification on very abstract patterns, I suppose that a broad variety of phenomena can fall into "the same class," even if in many superficial ways the class members are utterly unlike one another. So perhaps I can glimpse, at least a little, how to you, a simulated hurricane could, in a funny sense, *be* a hurricane.

Chris: Perhaps the word that's being extended is not "hurricane," but "be."

Pat: How so?

Chris: If Turing can extend the verb "think," can't I extend the verb "be"? All I mean is that when simulated things are deliberately confused with genuine things, somebody's doing a lot of philosophical wool-pulling. It's a lot more serious than just extending a few *nouns,* such as "hurricane."

Sandy: I like your idea that "be" is being extended, but I sure don't agree with you about the wool-pulling. Anyway, if you don't object, let me just say one more thing about simulated hurricanes and then I'll get to simulated minds. Suppose you consider a really deep simulation of a hurricane—I mean a simulation of every atom, which I admit is sort of ridiculous, but still, just consider it for the sake of argument.

Pat: Okay.

Sandy: I hope you would agree that it would then share all the abstract structure that defines the "essence of hurricanehood." So what's to keep you from calling it a hurricane?

Pat: I thought you were backing off from that claim of equality.

Sandy: So did I, but then these examples came up, and I was forced back to my claim. But let me back off, as I said I would do, and get back to *thought,* which is the real issue here. Thought, even more than hurricanes, is an abstract structure, a way of describing some complex events that happen in a medium called a brain. But actually, thought can take place in any one of several billion brains. There are all these physically very different brains, and yet they all support "the same thing": thinking. What's important, then, is the abstract *pattern,* not the medium. The same kind of swirling can happen inside any of them, so no person can claim to think more "genuinely" than any other. Now, if we come up with some new kind of medium in which *the same style* of swirling takes place, could you deny that thinking is taking place in it?

Pat: Probably not, but you have just shifted the question. The question now is: How can you determine whether the "same style" of swirling is really happening?

Sandy: The beauty of the Turing Test is that it tells you when! Don't you see?

Chris: I don't see that at all. How would you know that the same style of activity was going on inside a computer as inside my mind, simply because it answered questions as I do? All you're looking at is its *outside.*

Sandy: I'm sorry, I disagree entirely! How do you know that when I speak to you, anything similar to what you call thinking is going on inside *me?* The Turing Test is a fantastic probe, something like a particle accelerator in physics. Here, Chris— I think you'll like this analogy. Just as in physics, when you want to understand what is going on at an atomic or subatomic level, since you can't see it directly, you scatter accelerated particles off a target and observe their behavior. From this, you infer the internal nature of the target. The Turing Test extends this idea to the mind. It treats the mind as a "target" that is not directly visible but whose structure can be deduced more abstractly. By "scattering" questions off a target mind, you learn about its internal workings, just as in physics.

Chris: Well . . . to be more exact, you can *hypoth-esize* about what kinds of internal structures might account for the behavior observed — but please remember that they may or may not in fact exist.

Sandy: Hold on, now! Are you suggesting that atomic nuclei are merely *hypothetical* entities? After all, their existence (or should I say *hypothetical* existence?) was proved (or should I say *suggested*?) by the behavior of particles scattered off atoms.

Chris: I would agree, but you know, physical systems seem to me to be much simpler than the mind, and the certainty of the inferences made is correspondingly greater. And the conclusions are confirmed over and over again by different types of experiments.

Sandy: Yes, but those experiments still are of the same sort — scattering, detecting things indirectly. You can never *handle* an electron or a quark. Physics experiments are also correspondingly harder to do and to interpret. Often they take years and years, and dozens of collaborators are involved. In the Turing Test, though, just one person could perform many highly delicate experiments in the course of no more than an hour. I maintain that people give other people credit for being conscious simply because of their continual external monitoring of other people — which is itself something like a Turing Test.

Pat: That may be roughly true, but it involves more than just conversing with people through a teletype. We see that other people have bodies, we watch their faces and expressions — we see they are human beings, and so we think they think.

Sandy: To me, that seems a narrow, anthropocentric view of what thought is. Does that mean you would sooner say a mannequin in a store thinks than a wonderfully programmed computer, simply because the mannequin looks more human?

Pat: Obviously I would need more than just vague physical resemblance to the human form to be willing to attribute the power of thought to an entity. But that organic quality, the sameness of origin, undeniably lends a degree of credibility that is very important.

Sandy: Here we disagree. I find this simply too chauvinistic. I feel that the key thing is a similarity of *internal* structure — not bodily, organic, chemical structure but *organizational* structure — software. Whether an entity can think seems to me a question of whether its organization can be described in a certain way, and I'm perfectly willing to believe that the Turing Test detects the presence

or absence of that mode of organization. I would say that your depending on my physical body as evidence that I am a thinking being is rather shallow. The way I see it, the Turing Test looks far deeper than at mere external form.

Pat: Hey, now — you're not giving me much credit. It's not just the *shape* of a body that lends weight to the idea that there's real thinking going on inside. It's also, as I said, the idea of common origin. It's the idea that you and I both sprang from DNA molecules, an idea to which I attribute much depth. Put it this way: the external form of human bodies reveals that they share a deep biological history, and it's *that* depth that lends a lot of credibility to the notion that the owner of such a body can think.

Sandy: But that is all indirect evidence. Surely you want some *direct* evidence. That's what the Turing Test is for. And I think it's the *only* way to test for thinkinghood.

Chris: But, you could be fooled by the Turing Test, just as an interrogator could mistake a man for a woman.

Sandy: I admit, I could be fooled if I carried out the test in too quick or too shallow a way. But I would go for the deepest things I could think of.

Chris: I would want to see if the program could understand jokes — or better yet, make them! *That* would be a real test of intelligence.

Sandy: I agree that humor probably is an acid test for a supposedly intelligent program, but equally important to me — perhaps more so — would be to test its emotional responses. So I would ask it about its reactions to certain pieces of music or works of literature — especially my favorite ones.

Chris: What if it said, "I don't know that piece," or even, "I have no interest in music"? What if it tried its hardest (oops! — sorry, Pat!) . . . Let me try that again. What if it did everything it could to steer clear of emotional topics and references?

Sandy: That would certainly make me suspicious. Any consistent pattern of avoiding certain issues would raise serious doubts in my mind as to whether I was dealing with a thinking being.

Chris: Why do you say that? Why not just conclude you're dealing with a thinking but unemotional being?

Sandy: You've hit upon a sensitive point. I've thought about this for quite a long time, and I've concluded that I simply can't believe emotions and thought can be divorced. To put it another way, I think emotions are an automatic by-product of the ability to think. They are entailed by the very nature of thought.

Chris: That's an interesting conclusion, but what if you're wrong? What if I produced a machine that could think but not emote? Then its intelligence might go unrecognized because it failed to pass *your* kind of test.

Sandy: I'd like you to point out to me where the boundary line between emotional questions and non-emotional ones lies. You might want to ask about the meaning of a great novel. This certainly requires an understanding of human emotions! Now is that thinking, or merely cool calculation? You might want to ask about a subtle choice of words. For that, you need an understanding of their connotations. Turing uses examples like this in his article. You might want to ask for advice about a complex romantic situation. The machine would need to know a lot about human motivations and their roots. If it failed at this kind of task, I would not be much inclined to say that it could think. As far as I'm concerned, *thinking, feeling,* and *consciousness* are just different facets of one phenomenon, and no one of them can be present without the others.

Chris: Why couldn't you build a machine that could feel nothing (we all know machines don't feel anything!), but that could think and make complex decisions anyway? I don't see any contradiction there.

Sandy: Well, I do. I think that when you say that, you are visualizing a metallic, rectangular machine, probably in an air-conditioned room—a hard, angular, cold object with a million colored wires inside it, a machine that sits stock still on a tiled floor, humming or buzzing or whatever, and spinning its tapes. Such a machine can play a good game of chess, which, I freely admit, involves a lot of decision-making. And yet I would never call it conscious.

Chris: How come? To mechanists, isn't a chess-playing machine rudimentarily conscious?

Sandy: Not to *this* mechanist! The way I see it, consciousness has got to come from a precise pattern of organization, one we haven't yet figured out how to describe in any detailed way. But I be-

lieve we will gradually come to understand it. In my view, consciousness requires a certain way of mirroring the external universe internally, and the ability to respond to that external reality on the basis of the internally represented model. And then in addition, what's really crucial for a conscious machine is that it should incorporate a well-developed and flexible self-model. And it's there that all existing programs, including the best chess-playing ones, fall down.

Chris: Don't chess programs look ahead and say to themselves as they're figuring out their next move, "If my opponent moves here, then I'll go there, and then if they go this way, I could go that way . . ."? Doesn't that usage of the concept "I" require a sort of self-model?

Sandy: Not really. Or, if you want, it's an extremely limited one. It's an understanding of self in only the narrowest sense. For instance, a chess-playing program has no concept of why it is playing chess, or of the fact that it is a program or is in a computer, or has a human opponent. It has no idea about what winning and losing are, or—

Pat: How do *you* know it has no such sense? How can *you* presume to say what a chess program feels or knows?

Sandy: Oh, come on! We all know that certain things don't feel anything or know anything. A thrown stone doesn't know anything about parabolas, and a whirling fan doesn't know anything about air. It's true I can't *prove* those statements—but here, we are verging on questions of faith.

Pat: This reminds me of a Taoist story I read. It goes something like this. Two sages were standing on a bridge over a stream. One said to the other, "I wish I were a fish. They are so happy." The other replied, "How do *you* know whether fish are happy or not? *You're* not a fish!" The first said, "But you're not *me*, so how do you know whether I know how fish feel?"

Sandy: Beautiful! Talking about consciousness really does call for a certain amount of restraint. Otherwise, you might as well just jump on the solipsism bandwagon ("*I* am the only conscious being in the universe") or the panpsychism bandwagon ("*Everything* in the universe is conscious!").

Pat: Well, how do you know? Maybe everything *is* conscious.

Sandy: Oh, Pat, if you're going to join the club that maintains that stones and even particles like electrons have some sort of consciousness, then I guess we part company here. That's a kind of mysticism I just can't fathom. As for chess programs, I happen to know how they work, and I can tell you for sure that they aren't conscious. No way!

Pat: Why not?

Sandy: They incorporate only the barest knowledge about the goals of chess. The notion of "playing" is turned into the mechanical act of comparing a lot of numbers and choosing the biggest one over and over again. A chess program has no sense of disappointment about losing, or pride in winning. Its self-model is very crude. It gets away with doing the least it can, just enough to play a game of chess and nothing more. Yet interestingly enough, we still tend to talk about the "desires" of a chess-playing computer. We says, "It wants to keep its king behind a row of pawns" or "It likes to get its rooks out early" or "It thinks I don't see that hidden fork."

Pat: Yes, and we do the same thing with insects. We spot a lonely ant somewhere and say, "It's trying to get back home" or "It wants to drag that dead bee back to the colony." In fact, with any animal we use the terms that indicate emotions, but we don't know for certain how much the animal feels. I have no trouble talking about dogs and cats being happy or sad, having desires and beliefs, and so on, but of course I don't think their sadness is as deep or complex as human sadness is.

Sandy: But you wouldn't call it "simulated" sadness, would you?

Pat: No, of course not. I think it's real.

Sandy: It's hard to avoid use of such teleological or mentalistic terms. I believe they're quite justified, although they shouldn't be carried too far. They simply don't have the same richness of meaning when applied to present-day chess programs as when applied to people.

Chris: I still can't see that intelligence has to involve emotions. Why couldn't you imagine an intelligence that simply calculates and has no feelings?

Sandy: A couple of answers here. Number one, any intelligence has to have motivations. It's simply not the case, whatever many people may think, that machines could think any more "objectively" than people do. Machines, when they look at a

scene, will have to focus and filter that scene down into some preconceived categories, just as a person does. And that means seeing some things and missing others. It means giving more weight to some things than to others. This happens on every level of processing.

Pat: I'm not sure I'm following you.

Sandy: Take me right now, for instance. You might think I'm just making some intellectual points, and I wouldn't need emotions to do that. But what makes me *care* about these points? Just now — why did I stress the word "care" so heavily? Because I'm emotionally involved in this conversation! People talk to each other out of conviction — not out of hollow, mechanical reflexes. Even the most intellectual conversation is driven by underlying passions. There's an emotional undercurrent to every conversation — it's the fact that the speakers want to be listened to, understood, and respected for what they are saying.

Pat: It sounds to me as if all you're saying is that people need to be interested in what they're saying, otherwise a conversation dies.

Sandy: Right! I wouldn't bother to talk to anyone if I weren't motivated by *interest*. And "interest" is just another name for a whole constellation of subconscious biases. When I talk, all my biases work together, and what you perceive on the surface level is my personality, my style. But that style arises from an immense number of tiny priorities, biases, leanings. When you add up a million of them interacting together, you get something that amounts to a lot of *desires*. It just all adds up! And that brings me to the other answer to Chris' question about feelingless calculation. Sure, that exists — in a cash register, a pocket calculator. I'd say it's even true of all today's computer programs. But eventually, when you put enough feelingless calculations together in a huge coordinated organization, you'll get something that has properties *on another level*. You can see it — in fact, you *have* to see it — not as a bunch of little calculations but as a system of tendencies and desires and beliefs and so on. When things get complicated enough, you're *forced* to change your level of description. To some extent that's already happening, which is why we use words such as "want," "think," "try," and "hope" to describe chess programs and other attempts at mechanical thought. Dennett calls that kind of level-switch by the observer "adopting the intentional stance." The really interesting things in AI will only begin to happen, I'd guess, when the program *itself* adopts the intentional stance toward itself!

Chris: That would be a very strange sort of level-crossing feedback loop.

Sandy: It certainly would. When a program looks at itself *from the outside,* as it were, and tries to figure out why it acted the way it did, then I'll start to think that there's *someone* in there, doing the looking.

Pat: You mean an "I"? A self?

Sandy: Yes, something like that. A soul, even — although not in any religious sense. Of course, it's highly premature for anyone to adopt the intentional stance (in the full force of the term) with respect to today's programs. At least that's my opinion.

Chris: For me an important related question is: To what extent is it valid to adopt the intentional stance toward beings other than humans?

Pat: I would certainly adopt the intentional stance toward mammals.

Sandy: I vote for that.

Chris: Now that's interesting. How can that be, Sandy? Surely you wouldn't claim that a dog or cat can pass the Turing Test? Yet don't you maintain the Turing Test is the *only* way to test for the presence of consciousness? How can you have these beliefs simultaneously?

Sandy: Hmmm . . . All right. I guess that my argument is really just that the Turing Test works only above a certain level of consciousness. I'm perfectly willing to grant that there can be thinking beings that could *fail* at the Turing Test — but the main point that I've been arguing for is that anything that *passes* it would be a genuinely conscious, thinking being.

Pat: How can you think of a computer as a conscious being? I apologize if what I'm going to say sounds like a stereotype, but when I think of conscious beings, I just can't connect that thought with machines. To me, consciousness is connected with soft, warm bodies, silly though it may sound.

Chris: That does sound odd, coming from a biologist. Don't you deal with life so much in terms of chemistry and physics that all magic seems to vanish?

Pat: Not really. Sometimes the chemistry and physics simply increase the feeling that there's something magical going on down there! Anyway, I can't always integrate my scientific knowledge with my gut feelings.

Chris: I guess I share that trait.

Pat: So how do you deal with rigid preconceptions like mine?

Sandy: I'd try to dig down under the surface of your concept of "machine" and get at the intuitive connotations that lurk there, out of sight but deeply influencing your opinions. I think we all have a holdover image from the Industrial Revolution that sees machines as clunky iron contraptions gawkily moving under the power of some loudly chugging engine. Possibly that's even how the computer inventor Charles Babbage saw people! After all, he called his magnificent many-geared computer the "Analytical Engine."

Pat: Well, *I* certainly don't think people are just fancy steam shovels or electric can openers. There's something about people, something that — that — they've got a sort of *flame* inside them, something alive, something that flickers unpredictably, wavering, uncertain — but something *creative*!

Sandy: Great! That's just the sort of thing I wanted to hear. It's very human to think that way. Your flame image makes me think of candles, of fires, of vast thunderstorms with lightning dancing all over the sky in crazy, tumultuous patterns. But do you realize that just that kind of thing is visible on a computer's console? The flickering lights form amazing chaotic sparkling patterns. It's such a far cry from heaps of lifeless, clanking metal! It *is* flamelike, by God! Why don't you let the word "machine" conjure up images of dancing patterns of light rather than of giant steam shovels?

Chris: That's a beautiful image, Sandy. It does tend to change my sense of mechanism from being matter-oriented to being pattern-oriented. It makes me try to visualize the thoughts in my mind — these thoughts right now, even! — as a huge spray of tiny pulses flickering in my brain.

Sandy: That's quite a poetic self-portrait of a mere spray of flickers to have come up with!

Chris: Thank you. But still, I'm not totally convinced that a machine is all that I am. I admit, my concept of machines probably does suffer from anachronistic subconscious flavors, but I'm afraid I can't change such a deeply rooted sense in a flash.

Sandy: At least you sound open-minded. And to tell the truth, part of me sympathizes with the way you and Pat view machines. Part of me balks at calling myself a machine. It *is* a bizarre thought that a feeling being like you or me might emerge from mere circuitry. Do I surprise you?

Chris: You certainly surprise *me*. So, tell us—do you believe in the idea of an intelligent computer, or don't you?

Sandy: It all depends on what you mean. We've all heard the question "Can computers think?" There are several possible interpretations of this (aside from the many interpretations of the word "think"). They revolve around different meanings of the words "can" and "computer."

Pat: Back to word games again . . .

Sandy: I'm sorry, but that's unavoidable. First of all, the question might mean, "Does some present-day computer think, right now?" To this I would immediately answer with a loud *no*. Then it could be taken to mean, "Could some present-day computer, if suitably programmed, potentially think?" That would be more like it, but I would still answer, "Probably not." The real difficulty hinges on the word "computer." The way I see it, "computer" calls up an image of just what I described earlier; an air-conditioned room with cold rectangular metal boxes in it. But I suspect that with increasing public familiarity with computers and continued progress in computer architecture, that vision will eventually become outmoded.

Pat: Don't you think computers as we know them will be around for a while?

Sandy: Sure, there will have to be computers in today's image around for a long time, but advanced computers—maybe no longer called "computers"—will evolve and become quite different. Probably, as with living organisms, there will be many branchings in the evolutionary tree. There will be computers for business, computers for schoolkids, computers for scientific calculations, computers for systems research, computers for simulation, computers for rockets going into space, and so on. Finally, there will be computers for the study of intelligence. It's really only these last that I'm thinking of—the ones with the maximum

flexibility, the ones that people are deliberately attempting to make smart. I see no reason that these will stay fixed in the traditional image. They probably will soon acquire as standard features some rudimentary sensory systems—mostly for vision and hearing, at first. They will need to be able to move around, to explore. They will have to be physically flexible. In short, they will have to become more animal-like, more self-reliant.

Chris: It makes me think of the robots R2D2 and C3PO in the movie *Star Wars*.

Sandy: Not me! In fact, I don't think of anything remotely like them when I visualize intelligent machines. They are too silly, too much the product of a film designer's imagination. Not that I have a clear vision of my own. But I think it's necessary, if people are realistically going to try to imagine an artificial intelligence, to go beyond the limited, hard-edged picture of computers that comes from exposure to what we have today. The only thing all machines will always have in common is their underlying mechanicalness. That may sound cold and inflexible, but then—just think what could be more mechanical, in a wonderful way, than the working of the DNA and proteins and organelles in our cells?

Pat: To me, what goes on inside cells has a "wet," "slippery" feel to it, and what goes on inside machines is dry and rigid. It's connected with the fact that computers don't make mistakes, that computers do only what you tell them to do. Or at least that's my image of computers.

Sandy: Funny—a minute ago, your image was of a flame, and now it's of something wet and slippery. Isn't it marvelous, how contradictory we can be?

Pat: I don't need your sarcasm.

Sandy: No, no, I'm not being sarcastic—I really *do* think it's marvelous.

Pat: It's just an example of the human mind's slippery nature—mine, in this case.

Sandy: True. But your image of computers is stuck in a rut. Computers certainly *can* make mistakes—and I don't mean on the hardware level. Think of any present-day computer predicting the weather. It can make wrong predictions, even though its program runs flawlessly.

Pat: But that's only because you've fed it the wrong data.

Sandy: Not so. It's because weather prediction is too complex. Any such program has to make do with a limited amount of data—entirely correct data—and extrapolate from there. Sometimes it will make wrong predictions. It's no different from a farmer gazing at the clouds and saying, "I reckon we'll get a little snow tonight." In our heads, we make models of things and use those models to guess how the world will behave. We have to make do with our models, however inaccurate they may be, or evolution will prune us out ruthlessly—we'll fall off a cliff or something. And for intelligent computers, it'll be the same. It's just that human designers will speed up the evolutionary process by aiming explicitly at the goal of creating intelligence, which is something nature just stumbled on.

Pat: So you think computers will be making fewer mistakes as they get smarter?

Sandy: Actually, just the other way around! The smarter they get, the more they'll be in a position to tackle messy real-life domains, so they'll be more and more likely to have inaccurate models. To me, mistake-making is a sign of high intelligence!

Pat: Wow—you throw me sometimes!

Sandy: I guess I'm a strange sort of advocate for machine intelligence. To some degree I straddle the fence. I think that machines won't really be intelligent in a humanlike way until they have something like your biological wetness or slipperiness to them. I don't mean *literally* wet—the slipperiness could be in the software. But biological-seeming or not, intelligent machines will in any case be machines. We will have designed them, built them—or grown them! We'll understand how they work—at least in some sense. Possibly no one person will really understand them, but collectively we will know how they work.

Pat: It sounds like you want to have your cake and eat it too. I mean, you want to have people able to build intelligent machines and yet at the same time have some of the mystery of mind remain.

Sandy: You're absolutely right—and I think that's what *will* happen. When *real* artificial intelligence comes—

Pat: Now there's a nice contradiction in terms!

Sandy: Touché! Well, anyway, when it comes, it will be mechanical and yet at the same time organic. It will have that same astonishing flexibility that we see in life's mechanisms. And when I say mechanisms, I *mean* mechanisms. DNA and enzymes and so on really *are* mechanical and rigid and reliable. Wouldn't you agree, Pat?

Pat: Sure! But when they work together, a lot of unexpected things happen. There are so many complexities and rich modes of behavior that all that mechanicalness adds up to something very fluid.

Sandy: For me, it's an almost unimaginable transition from the mechanical level of molecules to the living level of cells. But it's that exposure to biology that convinces me that people are machines. That thought makes me uncomfortable in some ways, but in other ways it is exhilarating.

Chris: I have one nagging question . . . If people are machines, how come it's so hard to convince them of the fact? Surely a machine ought to be able to recognize its own machinehood!

Sandy: It's an interesting question. You have to allow for emotional factors here. To be told you're a machine is, in a way, to be told that you're nothing more than your physical parts, and it brings you face to face with your own vulnerability, destructibility, and, ultimately, your mortality. That's something nobody finds easy to face. But beyond this emotional objection, to see yourself as a machine, you have to "unadopt" the intentional stance you've grown up taking toward yourself—you have to jump all the way from the level where the complex lifelike activities take place to the bottom-most mechanical level where ribosomes chug along RNA strands, for instance. But there are so many intermediate layers that they act as a shield, and the mechanical quality way down there becomes almost invisible. I think that when intelligent machines come around, that's how they will seem to us—and to themselves! Their mechanicalness will be buried so deep that they'll *seem* to be alive and conscious—just as *we* seem alive and conscious . . .

Chris: You're baiting me! But I'm not going to bite.

Pat: I once heard a funny idea about what will happen when we eventually have intelligent machines. When we try to implant that intelligence into devices we'd like to control, their behavior won't be so predictable.

Sandy: They'll have a quirky little "flame" inside, maybe?

Pat: Maybe.

Chris: And what's so funny about that?

Pat: Well, think of military missiles. The more sophisticated their target-tracking computers get, according to this idea, the less predictably they will function. Eventually, you'll have missiles that will decide they are pacifists and will turn around and go home and land quietly without blowing up. We could even have "smart bullets" that turn around in midflight because they don't want to commit suicide!

Sandy: What a nice vision!

Chris: I'm very skeptical about all this. Still, Sandy, I'd like to hear your predictions about when intelligent machines will come to be.

Sandy: It won't be for a long time, probably, that we'll see anything remotely resembling the level of human intelligence. It rests on too awesomely complicated a substrate—the brain—for us to be able to duplicate it in the foreseeable future. Anyhow, that's my opinion.

Pat: Do you think a program will ever pass the Turing Test?

Sandy: That's a pretty hard question. I guess there are various degrees of passing such a test, when you come down to it. It's not black or white. First of all, it depends on who the interrogator is. A simpleton might be totally taken in by some programs today. But secondly, it depends on how deeply you are allowed to probe.

Pat: You could have a range of Turing Tests—one-minute versions, five-minute versions, hour-long versions, and so forth. Wouldn't it be interesting if some official organization sponsored a periodic competition, like the annual computer-chess championships, for programs to try to pass the Turing Test?

Chris: The program that lasted the longest against some panel of distinguished judges would be the winner. Perhaps there could be a big prize for the first program that fools a famous judge for, say, ten minutes.

Pat: A prize for the *program,* or for its *author?*

Chris: For the program, of course!

Pat: That's ridiculous! What would a program do with a prize?

Chris: Come now, Pat. If a program's human enough to fool the judges, don't you think it's human enough to enjoy the prize? That's precisely the threshold where it, rather than its creators, deserves the credit and the rewards. Wouldn't you agree?

Pat: Yeah, yeah—especially if the prize is an evening out on the town, dancing with the interrogators!

Sandy: I'd certainly like to see something like that established. I think it could be hilarious to watch the first programs flop pathetically!

Pat: You're pretty skeptical for an AI advocate, aren't you? Well, do you think any computer program today could pass a five-minute Turing Test, given a sophisticated interrogator?

Sandy: I seriously doubt it. It's partly because no one is really working at it explicitly. I should mention, though, that there is one program whose inventors claim it has *already* passed a rudimentary version of the Turing Test. It is called "Parry," and in a series of remotely conducted interviews, it fooled several psychiatrists who were told they were talking to either a computer or a paranoid patient. This was an improvement over an earlier version, in which psychiatrists were simply handed transcripts of short interviews and asked to determine which ones were with a genuine paranoid and which ones were with a computer simulation.

Pat: You mean they didn't have the chance to ask any questions? That's a severe handicap—and it doesn't seem in the spirit of the Turing Test. Imagine someone trying to tell which sex *I* belong to, just by reading a transcript of a few remarks by me. It might be very hard! I'm glad the procedure has been improved.

Chris: How do you get a computer to act like a paranoid?

Sandy: Now just a moment—I didn't say it *does* act like a paranoid, only that some psychiatrists, under unusual circumstances, thought so. One of the things that bothered me about this pseudo-Turing Test is the way Parry works. "He," as the people who designed it call it, acts like a paranoid in that "he" gets abruptly defensive and veers away from undesirable topics in the conversation. In effect, Parry maintains strict control so that no one can truly probe "him." For reasons like this, simulating a paranoid is a whole lot easier than simulating a normal person.

Pat: I wouldn't doubt that. It reminds me of the joke about the easiest kind of human being for a computer program to simulate.

Chris: What is that?

Pat: A catatonic patient—they just sit and do nothing at all for days on end. Even *I* could write a computer program to do that!

Sandy: An interesting thing about Parry is that it creates no sentences on its own—it merely selects from a huge repertoire of canned sentences the one that in some sense responds best to the input sentence.

Pat: Amazing. But that would probably be impossible on a larger scale, wouldn't it?

Sandy: You better believe it (to use a canned remark)! Actually, this is something that's really not appreciated enough. The number of sentences you'd need to store in order to be able to respond in a normal way to all possible turns that a conversation could take is more than astronomical—it's really unimaginable. And they would have to be so intricately indexed, for retrieval . . . Anybody who thinks that somehow, a program could be rigged up just to pull sentences out of storage like records in a jukebox, and that this program could pass the Turing Test, hasn't thought very hard about it. The funny part is that it is just this kind of unrealizable "parrot program" that most critics of artificial intelligence cite, when they argue against the concept of the Turing Test. Instead of imaging a truly intelligent machine, they want you to envision a gigantic, lumbering robot that intones canned sentences in a dull monotone. They set up the imagery in a contradictory way. They manage to convince you that you could see through to its mechanical level with ease, even as it is simultaneously performing tasks that we think of as fluid, intelligent processes. Then the critics say, "You see! A machine could pass the Turing Test and yet it would still be just a mechanical device, not intelligent at all." I see things almost the opposite way. If *I* were shown a machine that can do things that I can do—I mean pass the Turing Test—then, instead of feeling insulted or threatened, I'd chime in with philosopher Raymond Smullyan and say, "How wonderful machines are!"

Chris: If you could ask a computer just one question in the Turing Test, what would it be?

Sandy: Uhmm . . .

Pat: How about this: "If you could ask a computer just one question in the Turing Test, what would it be?"

Further Questions

1. There are three characters in Hofstadter's dialogue: Chris, Sandy, and Pat. What are their sexes? Justify your answer. (Does your difficulty justifying your answer to this question remind you of anything about Turing's Imitation Game?)
2. Is the Turing Test an adequate criterion for determining whether a machine can think? Can you think of a better criterion?

Further Readings

Robinson, William S. *Computers, Minds, and Robots.* Philadelphia: Temple University Press, 1992. Philosophy of mind through the lens of artificial intelligence.

Searle, John. "Minds, Brains, and Programs." *The Behavioral and Brain Sciences,* Vol. 3, 1980. The most famous attack on the Turing Test. It appears with twenty-eight responses.

A Simple Guide to Contemporary Philosophy of Mind   54

GARRETT THOMSON AND PHILIP TURETZKY

Garrett Thomson received his Ph.D. from Oxford University. He teaches philosophy at the College of Wooster in Ohio. His book *Needs* (Routledge & Kegan Paul) explains why needs are different from desires. He has also published *An Introduction to Modern Philosophy: Descartes to Kant* (Wadsworth). Philip Turetzky received his Ph.D. from Cambridge University and has taught at various colleges and universities in the United States.

Reading Questions

1. What is substance dualism? How does substance dualism differ from property dualism?
2. What is reification? What do nouns have to do with it?
3. What is the problem with mind's place in nature? What reasons are given for the claim that the ontological issue is largely irrelevant to the question of the mind's place in nature?
4. Why is the mind-body problem not ontological? How should the mind-body be posed, and how does this capture what bothers us about mental states?
5. What is the distinction between extensional and intensional descriptions? Why is the extensional-intensional distinction important to the mind-body problem?

THERE IS SOMETHING DEEPLY MYSTERIOUS about the mind's place in nature, but it is alluringly difficult to articulate what the mystery is. Among the myriad of objects in the world, there is one which is me. How can the impersonal universe contain me as an object? I can recognize that my body is one object much like others: it takes up space, it is open to public scrutiny, and it is made of the same basic stuff as trees and planets. Yet I cannot think of myself in only this impersonal way. How can any object, including this body with this brain, have a perspective on the world and be conscious? How is it possible that a thing which is a part of the world has a view on the world? How can a point of view on the world be contained within the world, as a part of it?

Metaphysical questions and considerations like these attempt to express the mystery of the mind's place in nature. However, they require an understanding which most contemporary theories of the mind, which are oriented towards the demands of science, do not provide.

SECTION 1: THE ONTOLOGICAL OPTION

You look in wonder at the baby's head and ask: Is she this fleshy substance, and if not, what is she?

1.1 SUBSTANCE DUALISM

Descartes answered this question, by arguing that a person is an essentially conscious and non-material substance or thing. Accordingly, the universe contains at least two kinds of substances, mind and matter.[1] Substance dualism suffers from some serious problems. First, the mind and the body are in fact in a very intimate relation, a point on which Descartes himself insisted. For example, if particular parts of the brain are destroyed, then we lose specific mental capabilities. Substance dualism, however, does not seem able to explain this. If the mind and the body are two distinct things, and it is the mind which remembers, then it ought to be able to do this quite independently of what the brain does. However, in fact, when particular brain cells are killed, this will destroy particular memories. Second, the problem would be accentuated if the mind were, as Descartes claimed, a non-spatial entity. If the mind is not in space and has no location, then how can it have such a specific and direct causal influence on the brain? And why only the brain? Why does the mind have a direct causal effect only on one particular body, i.e., why can't my mind cause movement in your body or in this table? On the other hand, there are problems with the contrary claim that the mind does exist in space. If it is in space then, presumably, it has a specific size and location and ought to be detectable. Yet, none of these spatial qualities seem to apply to the mind. Third, if the mind is not in space, then in what sense is it a thing? More importantly, Descartes framed the mystery of the mind's place in nature as an ontological question, a question regarding what exists. Later we shall reject this way of approaching the problem.

1.2 PROPERTY DUALISM

Most contemporary dualists reject Descartes's substance dualism and accept that persons are physical beings, and not mental entities. However, they argue for a dualism of properties, that what differentiates conscious beings from other physical objects is that they have two different types of properties: physical properties, like having a certain weight and size, and mental properties, like thinking about the color of apples at a certain time.[2]

This view apparently avoids some of the difficulties of substance dualism. For example, it skirts the problems of how two very different kinds of substance interact and coordinate every time we act and think. Yet property dualism retains some of the apparent appeal of dualism, because it claims that mental properties or features are not reducible or identical to physical ones.

A problem with property dualism, however, is that it requires a clear conception of what a prop-

erty or a feature is and, moreover, that the notion of a mental property is unproblematic. First, the notion of a property is not clear enough for us to be able to count them. For example, the apple is colored (it has the property of being colored); it is red (it has the property of being red) and it reflects light of a certain wavelength. Are these distinct properties that the apple has?[3] How many properties does the apple have? If we do not know how to count properties then it must be impossible to say whether two property words or predicates, like "being colored" or "being red," indicate two distinct properties or one. In other words, without being able to count properties, it is impossible to say whether they are identical or distinct. Property dualism requires, for instance, that the property of being in a particular brain state and the property of being in pain are two distinct properties, i.e., property dualism requires that these properties are not identical.

Second, the very idea of mental properties is itself problematic. Mental states are individuated by their content.[4] But the content of mental states like beliefs, wishes, desires and fears is partly dependent on how they are described. Philosophers tend to call a property or state "extensional" or "intensional" if that property or state is expressed respectively by an extensional or intensional description. One criterion for the extensionality of a description is that if a complex description contains a sentence as a part, then an equivalent sentence can be substituted within it without changing the truth value of the description. So, for example, the complex description "Ellen is five feet tall and Ellen weighs one hundred and ten pounds" contains the sentence "Ellen weighs one hundred and ten pounds." This simple sentence always has the same truth value as the sentence "Ellen weighs fifty kilograms." If we substitute this sentence into the initial complex description, the truth value of the complex description will never change. However, some descriptions do not share this feature. Among such intensional descriptions are those for mental states.[5] So if we substitute the sentence "Ellen weighs fifty kilograms" for the sentence "Ellen weighs one hundred and ten pounds" in the description "Sue believes that Ellen weighs one hundred and ten pounds," we get the description "Sue believes that Ellen weighs fifty kilograms." But this latter description of Sue's mental state may be false even though the first description of her belief state is true and vice versa. We will discuss the intensionality of mental descriptions in more detail in section 2.2. For the moment, we need only note that the notion of an intensional property is problematic, because there are no criteria for counting intensional states.

Even if we can overcome these problems with the concept of a property and with the notion of a mental property, property dualism does not solve the deep problem of the mind's place in nature, for reasons we shall see later when we discuss whether the mind-body problem should be understood as an ontological problem at all.

1.3 MATERIALISM

Materialism is the view that the only substances in the world are physical, and that these material things have only physical properties. The universe consists only of completely material things and their physical properties. Sometimes, this is misleadingly expressed as follows: mental states are identical to physical states, specifically states of the brain. Or more generally, the mind is the brain.

There are several arguments in favor of materialism. It is ontologically simpler than either substance or property dualism. Since it is a general principle that we prefer simpler explanations, then if we do not need to postulate the existence of mental substances and properties and can explain consciousness and other mental states without them, it is preferable to exclude them from our theory of the mind.[6]

Another argument in favor of materialism is based on the claim that mental states are identified by their causal role, i.e., mental states are identified by, for instance, this behavior in causing other mental states.[7]

1. Mental states are identified by their causal role.

2. Brain states have this causal role.

3. Therefore, mental states are brain states.

Against materialism, it might be argued that general types of mental states, like pain, cannot be identified with general types of brain states like the firing of neurons in the frontal lobe. Pain in you might have a different physical composition from pain in me, or from pain in a being from Venus, and consequently we cannot identify types of mental states with types of brain states. Most materialists accept this point and, instead, argue that particular or token mental states are identical with particular token brain states.[8] In other words, every particular mental state is identical with a particular brain state, but we cannot make generalizations about such identities.

Against materialism we can also argue: my sensation is green, but there is nothing green in my head and therefore this sensation is not a brain state. Consequently, materialism is a false theory of mind. The form of this argument is as follows:

1. There is a property which my sensation has which my brain state lacks.

2. If sensations and brain states are identical then they must have the same properties.

3. Therefore, the two cannot be identical.

But this argument against materialism fails because it falsely assumes that materialism must treat sensations as things, i.e., that it must reify mental states. It falsely assumes that the materialist must identify sensations with brain states. The materialist does not have to say that there is a thing called a sensation, or a concept, or a thought, which is really a brain state. Instead the materialist can identify the *having of* particular sensations with the *having of* particular brain states. In other words, the materialist should not assert that mental states are brain states, but rather that *being in* a particular mental state is the same as *being in* a particular brain state. This means that the original materialist argument should be restated as follows:

1. Being in a particular mental state is identified by its causal role.

2. Being in a particular brain state has this causal role.

3. Therefore, being in a particular mental state is identical to being in a particular brain state.

1.4 REJECTING REIFICATION

The English language is full of nouns. Given the assumption that nouns must name things, it is reasonable to conclude that where there is a noun in use, then there must be a thing or object to which it refers. For this reason, it is natural to think that the noun "belief" refers to a thing, a belief. Similarly for "mind," "sensations," "will," "consciousness," "decision," "act," etc. One might then puzzle what these mental objects could be. I know what a material object is, but what is a belief? If beliefs are things which I have then, where are they? What size are they? How many do I have and what happens when I change them?

These questions are, however, based on the initial and false assumption, namely that all nouns must name things. Many expressions which grammatically are nouns do refer to things,[9] like "rock," but others, like "randomness," do not. Beliefs are not things and the noun "belief" does not refer to a mental entity. When we say "I have a belief that P" it sounds as if there is a mental entity, a belief, which I possess. To avoid this suggestion, it would be better to use the verb "believe" rather than the noun "belief" and assert "I believe that P." Instead of claiming "I have the sensation of red," it would be more accurate to say "I see red." In ordinary language we often use a noun where a verb would be philosophically less misleading. The sentence with the verb is less misleading than the one with the noun equivalent because when we use a noun there is a tendency to think that there must be an entity referred to by the noun, i.e., we have a tendency to reify.

Descartes and the Empiricists reified ideas. For these philosophers, ideas represented objects outside of the mind, but such objects could only be known indirectly through their representation by ideas in the mind. As a consequence of this representational theory of knowledge, they treated ideas as mental objects on an analogy with signs, which are themselves objects presented to point to other objects which are not present. For example a road sign saying "Exit four miles" is an object presented to us to refer to the exit which is not present to us. These philosophers adapted this analogy but made the stronger claim that only ideas are the direct objects of perception, thought and consciousness and that objects in the world can never be direct objects of perception. This treatment led to the notion of a veil of ideas, the claim that we can directly perceive only our own ideas and cannot directly perceive external objects, which, unlike the exit in our example of a representational sign, are hidden forever beyond the wall of ideas.

The treatment of ideas as mental entities, the reification of consciousness and its contents as objects, also tends to lead to dualism. If ideas are regarded as mental objects, then it is apparently reasonable to regard the mind as a container which possesses or holds those ideas.

1.5 IS THE PROBLEM ONTOLOGICAL?

We have examined briefly three ontological claims:

1. substance dualism: the claim that the universe contains two distinct kinds of substances, mental and material;

2. property dualism: the claim that the universe contains only one kind of substance, physical things, but two different kinds of properties, mental and physical; and

3. materialism: the claim that the universe contains only physical things and their physical properties.

The difference between these positions seems great, and much contemporary discussion has been taken up with showing that materialism is not as counterintuitive as it first may appear. *None of these positions, however, really touches the metaphysical problem of the mind's place in nature.* Ontological views postulate what kinds of things exist, but as such they do not explain how it is possible for any thing to be conscious, nor do they give us any insight into what consciousness is.

Suppose we agreed with the materialist and said "yes; only matter and its properties exist." Or suppose that we could find a conclusive argument for dualism. In neither of these two cases is the mystery of the mind solved. We do not have any deeper understanding of how it is at all possible that a thing could ever be me, be conscious, or have a view on the world. Even if the thing in question is a non-material substance, the enigma still remains untouched; it is equally as puzzling how such a non-material thing could ever be self-conscious as how a lump of flesh could. Imagine your brain: how could that be self-conscious? Now, imagine a non-physical version of your brain: well, how could that ever be self-conscious? The supposed fact that this ghostly entity is not made of matter makes absolutely no difference. The composition of the thing is irrelevant.

It is tempting to think that Descartes's dualism, if it were true, would solve the mind-body problem. It is tempting because Descartes defines the mind as conscious and then tries to prove that this mind is not material. However, this does not solve the problem because it is merely stipulation. Descartes merely stipulates or assumes that the mind is a substance with the property of being conscious. But saying that it is so does not show how it is possible nor demonstrate that it is true. If it is not obvious that a physical thing could be conscious then, it is at least equally unobvious how a non-material thing could be conscious. Stipulating that the mind is a thing (material or non-material) which has the property of being conscious does not answer the question "How could such a thing be conscious?" or the question "How could anything be conscious?"; it only hides the question.[10]

SECTION 2: THE SHIFT FROM ONTOLOGY TO DESCRIPTIONS

2.1 HOW TO AVOID CRUDE SCIENTISM

The ontological issue appears to be more important than it is because we assume that if materialism is true then something is lost. Many people feel that something very important has been left out or is missing if the universe merely consists of matter and material properties.[11] We might say that human spirit or soul has been omitted. To express this, we might ask the materialist in a derisory tone "Do you mean that my feelings are merely electrical impulses in my brain?"[12] What I feel when I look at a painting by Giotto—how can this be included in a clinically scientific picture of the world? Neurons fire and chemicals change in the synapses of the brain, but none of this seems to include the feelings themselves. Materialism seems like a cynical doctrine, equivalent to a crude form of scientism.[13] It seems to tell us that there is nothing to the universe but packets of energy moving without purpose and value. It apparently banishes color and consciousness from the world, because these do not appear as entities in scientific theory. With these kinds of thoughts in mind, it is easy to assume that materialism must be false, dualism true and that the mind-body problem was ontological after all.

But denying the mind as a non-physical entity does not banish mentalistic descriptions of persons. The rejection of dualism and the assertion of materialism do not imply crude scientism. The issues involved in crude scientism and materialism are distinct. Materialism is an ontological claim about what kinds of things exist, or of what the universe is composed. However, crude scientism concerns how we may truly characterize the universe. It concerns what can truly be said of persons, i.e., what true descriptions we may give of people.

The ontology of a book is not really puzzling, but there are problems relating to how we may describe it. Many things can be said about the book: the story is boring; the characters in it are dull and flat; it contains so many words; the pages are of a certain dimension; the cover is blue and pink; the paper has a certain chemical composition. We might ask what relationships exist between some of these descriptions. For instance, what is the relation between the statement that the characters in the novel are dull and flat, and a description of the letters written on each page? The latter kind of description may seem to be more basic than the former. Is there some sense in which the former richer description is based on the latter more physical description? Or consider another example: we can describe a game of baseball as a movement of molecules, or as people hitting a piece of leather with bits of wood, or as a game with rules, an etiquette, and winners and losers. We might think that the descriptions of baseball as a game must be based on some physical descriptions.

Similarly, a person can be described as a movement of molecules, as the activities of a brain and a body, or as a being with conscious thoughts and feelings and a character with a life story to tell. We can divide the kinds of things we wish to say about persons into two types:

(a) physicalistic descriptions like "Ellen is five feet tall" or "Ellen's brain is undergoing intense electrochemical activity in the frontal lobe" and,

(b) mentalistic descriptions like "Ellen is thinking of the exchange rate" or "Ellen feels sad."[14]

Crude scientism denies the truth of mentalistic descriptions of persons, or claims to reduce them to physicalistic descriptions. The earlier claim that the mind-body problem is not ontological can now be replaced by the more positive suggestion that *the problem concerns the relationship between mentalistic and physicalistic descriptions*. The problem is not "Of what are we composed?" but rather "How may we be truly described?"

2.2 INTENSIONAL SENTENCES—THE PROBLEM RESTATED

The problem of how to conceive of the mental and its place in nature can be recast. Descriptions of the physical universe can be stated in extensional sentences. As we partly explained earlier, extensional sentences are transparent in the sense that we can substitute terms referring to the same thing within the sentences, or substitute equivalent sentences that are parts of complex descriptions, without changing whether the original sentence is true or false. For example, the object in the corner of the room can be referred to in many ways; the sentence "The object in the corner of the room weighs five kilograms" is extensional because any one of the expressions which refers to that object could be put into the sentence and the new sentence would still be true. Replacing the phrase 'the object in the corner of the room' with another expression which refers to the same object, for instance with the phrase 'my dictionary,' does not change the truth value of the sentence. It is as if extensional sentences are transparent or clear; it does not matter from what angle or aspect one regards the states of affairs in question. It is as if the description is from no particular point of view.[15]

However, it seems that mentalistic descriptions are not extensional, and are fundamentally different from physicalistic descriptions. For example,

"John believes that . . ."
"John wants that . . ."
"John thinks that . . ."

are non-extensional. The truth value of the sentences formed by such phrases depends on how one describes the thing in question. John wants X under one description, but does not want the same thing under another. Henry believes that p but not that q even though p is equivalent to q. One might say that the truth of sentences formed from such phrases depends on how the thing in question is

described, i.e., from what angle or aspect it is described. The fact that mental phenomena are described nonextensionally reflects the "aboutness" of mental states. Desires, wishes, beliefs, thoughts, and sensations are about something; they have content, which is reflected in the "that . . ." clause.[16] If terms which refer to the same thing are substituted within the "that . . ." clause, this may change the truth value of the overall sentence. John desires X under one description, or from one aspect, or from one particular point of view and he may not from another. In this way, non-extensional sentences are closed or opaque.[17]

Here we have struck a fundamental difference between descriptions of physicalistic and mentalistic phenomena. The first are transparent and the second are opaque because mental phenomena have content and are about something else. This seems to be a basic difference between the physical and the mental, which moreover can be given a reasonably precise linguistic formulation.

2.3 THREE STRATEGIES

The problem of the mind's place in nature can now be reformulated as follows: how can there be true intensional sentences if the universe can be characterized entirely extensionally? Much contemporary debate in the philosophy of mind has revolved around three broad strategies to answer this question.

The first strategy is to reify the intensional and treat this mode of discourse as if it were about its own distinct realm of substances, or properties or facts; we have already rejected this approach because it misleads us into treating the problems ontologically, which we argued is a fruitless exercise. The second strategy is to argue that intensional sentences can be reduced to extensional ones. The third strategy is to argue that the universe can be characterized completely without intensional descriptions and, therefore, the intensional mode of description can be eliminated. The second of these three alternatives is sometimes called 'reductive materialism' and the third 'eliminative materialism.' So the reductive materialist claims that sentences like "John believes that the moon is made of green cheese" can be translated without residue into extensional sentences about John's brain states. The eliminative materialist, in contrast, does not claim that such sentences can be translated into extensional sentences, but rather that intensional sentences can, in principle, be dropped out of a complete true description of the world which includes descriptions of human beings. Both of these names misleadingly suggest that reductionism and eliminativism are ontological claims. Since materialism already denies the existence of distinct mental properties and substances, eliminativism and reductionism cannot merely be ontological positions. They concern the relations between the extensional and intensional descriptions of animate beings.[18]

This is a much deeper issue than it sounds. Physics and chemistry are characterizable without invoking intensional descriptions. If a psychological explanation of why Jones believed what he did is to fit into the physical sciences, then psychological intensional characterizations in some sense have to be reducible to physical or extensional ones. The question of whether the psychological, which must be described intensionally, can be explained within the constraints of physical scientific theory, which is extensional, depends on whether the intensional can be reduced to the extensional. Consequently, the hopes of artificial intelligence and neurological sciences, which are both characterizable extensionally, to give us adequate explanations of the psychological depend on the answer to this question.

a) Reduction   The materialist claim that the mind is not an item or property in the world in addition to physical objects or properties is sometimes called "ontological reduction." This materialist ontological position should be distinguished from the present use of 'reduction' which is a claim about descriptions and their meaning, namely that psychological descriptions are reducible in meaning to physical ones. An ontological materialist does not have to accept the further and stronger claim that all psychological descriptions are reducible to physical ones, but only the claim that everything that exists is physical.

"Reduction" in this stronger sense roughly means something like translation. Claim (a) can be reduced to statements (b) and (c), if (a) implies (b) and (c), and if (b) and (c) imply (a). In this sense, for instance, the claim that the average height of the people in the room is six feet is indeed reducible to the claim that the total height of all the people in the room divided by the number of people in the room is six feet.

Intensional descriptions are not reducible to the extensional. No set of physical descriptions will imply an intensional description, because the intensional mode utilizes concepts which are richer than those used by the extensional and which cannot be derived from the latter. Furthermore, no intensional description will imply a particular physical one, because the intentional could be realized in different physical ways. It can be shown formally that any attempt at reduction will leave an untranslated residue.[19]

If intensional sentences cannot be reduced or translated into extensional ones, this means that there is no way to translate psychological statements into the language of physical science. This presents a problem for those who want to unify everyday statements about people's desires and beliefs with science. Some philosophers argue that this is a reason for being suspicious about everyday psychology.

b) Eliminativism   The claim of eliminativism is that the concepts or ideas which we use in ordinary everyday descriptions of people's psychological states are somehow deeply mistaken. For example, Churchland argues that the concept of believing is confused because there exist many borderline cases for which we do not know how to ascribe propositional content to the belief. He says that we find "some very deep similarities between the structure of folk psychology and the structure of paradigmatically physical theories."[20] If the dog scratches and whines at the closed door, we might say "he believes that his master is in the room." But on second thought, we may wonder whether the dog really has the concept of a master or a room. The concept of a belief is vague. According to eliminativism, the ordinary concepts of folk psychology, like those of belief and want, will have to be replaced by the more precise scientific concepts of neuroscience.

As with reductionism, we should not confuse eliminativism as an ontological claim with eliminativism as a much stronger assertion about intensional descriptions. Ontologically, eliminativism can mean nothing more than materialism; that the mental is not in addition to matter an item in, or property of, the world. The stronger claim is about a certain class of descriptions; namely the class of psychological statements or perhaps even the class of all intensional statements. The theory states that all such descriptions are, strictly speaking, false. For instance, according to eliminativism, "Joan wants to go home" is strictly false, because the concept of wanting is confused and inadequate. The statement is false in the way that "The ghost is happy" is false; there are no ghosts to be happy or sad. Earlier we saw that we can present the central problem of the mind by asking the following: what is the place of intensional descriptions in a world which is characterized with extensional statements? What is the relation between intensional and extensional statements? The eliminativist answers these questions by asserting that intensional statements are strictly speaking false.

The eliminativist's idea that neuropsychology will replace ordinary psychological explanations, or what is called 'folk psychology,' is misleading. It falsely suggests that neuropsychology and everyday (folk) psychology are competitors. Churchland, for example, complains that folk psychology cannot explain why we dream, how we learn, etc.[21] But this is not the function of folk psychology. Its function is to explain actions by citing the beliefs and desires which caused them. For example, why did Frederick shout at the dog? Because he wanted the dog to leave and believed that this was the only way to get it to leave.

Churchland also derides folk psychology for not neatly mapping mental states onto neurological states. He says that "there are vastly many more ways of being an explanatorily successful neuroscience while not mirroring the structure of folk psychology, than there are ways of being an explanatorily successful neuroscience while also mirroring the very specific structure of folk psychology."[22] And so he claims that it is likely that folk psychology is "simply mistaken." However, we should ask in what way is so-called folk psychology a theory which can be replaced by neuroscience? In this respect we might compare our talk of people's desires and beliefs with our discourse regarding material objects, like chairs and trees. It is clear that when I say the salt is on the table, and the salt really is on the table, I am not saying something

false, even though our conception of a material object is unclear and perhaps even confused. The claim that material objects exist is not an empirical theory, if by theory we mean a set of explanatory statements, which can be given up in the light of contrary empirical evidence. What empirical evidence could we have that material objects do not exist? Quantum mechanics[23] is a well verified theory but

(a) we do not take quantum mechanics to show that our belief in the existence of ordinary objects is false, but rather to show us how strange such objects really are;

(b) even if (a) were false, we have not abandoned talk of tables, chairs and housing estates in favor of quantum mechanical descriptions and could not because they serve quite different functions and interests.[24]

Churchland urges a historical comparison between the theory of phlogiston and everyday psychology. He says that "Phlogiston emerged, not as an incomplete description of what was going on, but as a radical misdescription," and that "The concepts of folk psychology—belief, desire, fear, sensation, pain, joy, and so on—await a similar fate."[25] A more apt comparison would be between the belief that ordinary objects exist and folk psychology. The belief that objects exist is not threatened by quantum mechanics, because quantum mechanics gives us new and rather strange descriptions of objects and their composition. Quantum mechanics does not eliminate objects. Similarly, the fact that we can give complex neurological descriptions of a person does not threaten our everyday ascriptions of beliefs and desires to persons. Neuroscience does not eliminate believing and desiring.

If the historical analogy we are urging is more apt than the one which Churchland offers us, then this is because folk psychology, ascriptions of beliefs and desires, is not a theory which can be dispensed with. It is not a theory because empirical evidence could not count against it. Why should this be? The concept of an action is fundamentally different from that of a physical movement. It does not matter how one describes a physical movement: all descriptions equivalent to a true description will also be true, because they are extensional. But it does matter from what angle or point of view one describes an action; not all extensionally equivalent descriptions regarding my action will be true. The concept of action has an intensional element, i.e., intentional actions must be described intensionally. For example, 'I intentionally drank the tea': even if my drinking the tea killed my aunt, you should not conclude that 'I intentionally killed my aunt.'

In other words,

1. Person P intentionally did A.

2. "A" is equivalent to "B."

3. Therefore person P intentionally did B is not a valid argument.

Eliminativism should be committed to the purging of all intentional descriptions. The elimination of desire and belief descriptions implies the elimination of action descriptions. This elimination would imply that we should not think of actions as such, not as acts done intentionally, but rather merely as physical movements.

In face of such points, some eliminativists have tried to maintain a double standard about the intentional mode of discourse. On the one hand, they agree that the intensional mode is practically necessary, because we need it to carry on with our lives and that in this way, it cannot be eliminated. On the other hand, they maintain that if we are describing the "true and ultimate structure of reality"[26] then, we cannot utilize the intentional mode. Statements made in the intentional mode are strictly false, but practically necessary. This approach seems plausible only if it is assumed that we are tempted to reify the intensional. Dennett says "strictly speaking, ontologically speaking there are no such things as beliefs, desires or other intentional phenomena."[27] But this is a misleading way of putting the point because it makes it appear that reification is the only alternative to elimination.

c) Conclusion In summary, the difficulty of understanding the mind's place in nature is not resolved by regarding the problem as ontological. The problem of what exists is quite distinct from the nature of consciousness. A more promising way of approaching the puzzle of the mind is through the contrast between intensional and extensional descriptions. How can there be intensional descriptions?

This way of putting the problem will show how materialism need not be committed to a crude form of scientism and it will show that the feeling that materialism leaves something out is based on confusing materialism and crude scientism.

There are at least three strategies for dealing with the intensional.

1. Reify the intentional, and treat beliefs, desires and the mind as objects, as things. This path leads us right back to treating the problem of the mind as an ontological difficulty, which does not unravel the enigma. Furthermore, it leads to dualism.

2. Try to reduce intentional descriptions to extensional ones. But there seems to be little hope that such successful reductions can be produced.

3. The third is to try to eliminate intentional descriptions. But we cannot get rid of the intentional mode, messy as it is.

Elimination and reduction involve more than just rejecting reification. Both reductionism and eliminativism work from the usually implicit assumption that only extensional descriptions describe reality and that intentional ones per se do not. Reductionism salvages the intentional mode by claiming that it is a translation from the extensional. The eliminativist says that the intensional cannot be translated and, consequently, concludes that the intentional mode cannot be salvaged and must be scrapped. However, we do not have to accept the starting premise that only the extensional idiom of science describes reality in its "true and ultimate structure." Nor do we have to accept the trichotomy: eliminate, reduce or reify. The alternative to these three choices is to take the intensional and extensional modes as equal partners which serve different functions in the way we describe reality.

If none of the three strategies work, as we have urged, then where does this leave us? It leaves us in the following situation: dualism is unacceptable, but so is materialism, combined either with a reductive or eliminative view of intentional descriptions. In simpler terms, we should not accept either dualism or crude scientism. Therefore, we should not think that these are the only alternatives before us, i.e., we should avoid the trap in thinking that because we reject dualism, we must accept crude scientism and visa versa. We should not think that because crude scientism incorrectly leaves out something, it leaves out some THING.

In this section, we have explained what is behind the idea that two kinds of crude scientism[28] leave out something. Eliminativism deliberately leaves something out, in the sense that it denies that states of affairs described neurologically can also be truly described in normal psychological terms. Reductionism leaves something out in the sense that it claims that psychological descriptions can be reduced to physicalistic ones, which means that they say nothing more than a collection of physical descriptions. This denies the fact that psychological descriptions are richer than physical ones.

The rejection of these two views, however, does not vindicate dualism nor imply the rejection of materialism. Because materialism is an ontological view, it does not have be committed to either the reduction or elimination claim regarding the relation between intensional and extensional descriptions. It is compatible to argue that only matter and its properties exist and at the same time, claim that this matter can and should be described in the intentional mode, without reduction or elimination.

SECTION 3: BEHAVIOR AND FUNCTION

3.1 LOGICAL BEHAVIORISM

How should we conceive of the mental? Descartes argued that we should conceive of it as a non-material thing, and this conclusion leads to an ontological debate which is ultimately unsatisfactory. But there is another route. Imagine that we find a large moving object on another planet. We think that we can discern a head and legs but we are not sure. We believe that the thing may be alive but we cannot be certain. We think that the thing may have thoughts and feelings but we do not really know. How can we find out? And what does it mean for the thing to be animate? One route to answering these questions is to assert that the thing has a "mind" if it behaves appropriately. If its physical movements are sufficiently complex and complex in the right way then, it would be correct to say that those movements are actions. Not all physical movements are actions. According to this approach, the movements of a physical thing are actions if the thing's movements are complex enough and appropriately sophisticated.[29]

But actions are such that they are caused by mental states, i.e., by the thing having desires and beliefs. So, for the thing to be animate is for it to want and believe, to think and wish, and the only possible way to know whether it is animate is through its physical movements, whether they should be called actions. To know whether a thing "has a soul" or is animate is to know whether its physical movements are actions. And to know the content of its mental states, we have to know its actions and how it would act under certain conditions.

The idea that the content of mental states is known through their causal effects on behavior has led to the stronger idea that mental states should be identified and defined through their causal effects on behavior and their potential effects on behavior under certain conditions (e.g., how an angry person would behave if he or she were uninhibited). In other words, to feel pain is to be in a state which would cause such and such behavior or actions. More generally, a mental state is defined by its causal role: as a dispositional state to behave in certain ways under certain conditions.

The basic idea behind behaviorism is that the ascription of mental content requires a behavioral base. The behaviorist answers the question "What is a mental state?"—it is being disposed to behave in certain ways given certain sensory inputs. To be in pain is to be disposed to cry out, withdraw the painful part of the body, etc. depending on how hard one was struck.

However, it seems that this definition is too simplistic. The connection between sensory input and behavioral output does not depend on only one mental state; it also depends on other mental states. For example, the desire to go to the bank cannot be identified by the action of walking in a certain direction because it also requires the belief that the bank is in that direction, which is another mental state.

3.2 FUNCTIONALISM

Functionalism differs from behaviorism in that it recognizes this type of interconnection between mental states. Ask a functionalist what a mental state is and she will reply: a disposition to act and have other mental states given certain sensory inputs and mental states. This means that functionalists identify mental states partly by their causal role with respect to other mental states.

Functionalism is not an ontological claim. One could argue for functionalism and still accept dualism, for example, by claiming that the mental states of non-material minds have to be identified and differentiated, i.e., defined, by their causal effects on publicly observable and objective behavior. The functionalist could claim that the mental states of spirits and non-material ghosts should be defined functionally.[30] However, probably all functionalists are in fact materialists, and moreover, as we have seen, there is an argument in favor of materialism which uses as a premise the claim that mental states are defined by their causal role.[31]

3.3 QUALIA: INTROSPECTIVE QUALITY

This general approach, i.e., that mental states are to be defined by their causal role, should be contrasted with the position popular in the modern period according to which mental states are defined and identified by how they feel, by the qualities they present to introspection. The main difference between these two approaches is that the contemporary causal approach provides a public criterion for the differentiation and identification of mental states; the introspective approach provides for an essentially first-person and subjective criterion. This difference is one prima facie reason for thinking that the contemporary causal approach is preferable, since mental states can be identified and known by others not having them. I can, indeed, know that another is in pain.

However, some contemporary criticisms of functionalism have resurrected aspects of the modern introspective view, because there seems to be more to having mental states than just their causal role. Nagel asks, "What is it like to be a bat?" to highlight the claim that there are essentially subjective facts, like how it feels to be in pain and what it is like to have the experiences of a whale. Nagel argues that any causal or functionalist account of mental states is bound to be incomplete because it cannot account for these essentially subjective facts. He claims that "Whatever may be the status of facts about what it is like to be a human being, or a bat, or a Martian, these appear to be facts that embody a particular point of view. . . . There is a sense in which phenomenological facts are perfectly objective: one person can know or say of another what the quality of the other's experience is. They are subjective, however, in the sense that even this objective ascription of experience is possible only for someone sufficiently similar to the object of ascription to be able to adopt his point of view—to understand the ascription in the first person . . ."[32] A phenomenological fact is a fact about how things appear to us, and Nagel insists that while experiences of pain and color are indeed subjective, it is still a fact that they appear a certain way to us, and it is that fact that requires an explanation.

SECTION 4: ANTS AND CPUS

Ants see. They can visually discriminate and we can study their visual abilities. We can safely assume that these abilities are purely physically based in the functioning of the ant's brain.

Guzman's SEE computer program enables computers to count boxes which are in a jumble. The program allows computers to detect edges, corners and sides and to draw the appropriate conclusions about how many boxes there are.[33] These sophisticated visual abilities are obviously purely physically based.

There seems to be no reason why we would not in principle design a computer program which would simulate the visual abilities of ants. This program would provide a model for what is happening inside an ant's brain. The computer performs certain tasks with specifiable end results; so the ant's brain could be performing similar tasks with the same end results. Understanding the ant's visual abilities would then consist in

(a) knowing how the computer program achieves its result, or knowing how to design a computer model which achieves those results, and

(b) knowing how the neurology of the brain works to the same end.

The differences between an ant, a spider, a mouse, a monkey and a human are ones of degree.

Consequently, the basic strategy which works for understanding the mental capabilities of ants should work also for human thought and perceptual capacities.

One compelling feature of the computer which makes it a potentially fruitful model for the mind is that the computer recognizes the cube, or performs its task, through a highly complex series of binary operations, which are fundamentally mechanical and unintelligent. Therefore we can at least simulate some intelligent acts through a complex set of unintelligent operations, which a machine and even brain cells can perform.

The idea of cognitive science is that the mind is like an incredibly complicated adding machine, which performs calculations or computations according to rules (or computational procedures). Obviously, the mind is supposed to perform these mechanical calculations on more than just numbers, i.e., it is also supposed to use such calculations for the recognition of shapes, colors, words and linguistic structures, for example. In each of these cases, the basic principle is that, with a machine "the output states bear systematic and rule governed relations to input states." For example, if the rule is +2 and the input is 4 then the output is 6. It is in this way that cognitive psychology tries to account for the activities which together make up consciousness. It tries to account for them piecemeal, one by one, by postulating a system of internal states governed by such rules. The idea is functionalist in spirit, with the added ingredient of computation or calculation.

One way to test whether the system produces the relevant activities or end results is to run a computer program which simulates it. This is the project of artificial intelligence (A.I.). All computations can be represented by a formal system. Formal systems consist of a set of formulas and a set of rules according to which the formulas can be manipulated. Formal logic and mathematics are two such formal systems. The important point for the project of cognitive psychology and A.I. is that every formal system can in principle be instantiated in a machine, like a computer, or in a formal model of a possible machine.

Margaret Boden, an advocate of A.I., says that computational psychologists "see psychology as the study of the computational processes whereby mental representations are constructed, interpreted, and transformed."[34] According to the projects of cognitive psychology and A.I., consciousness consists of many activities which are computational in nature and which can be represented by a formal system and therefore on a computer. The claim that consciousness consists in many different types of activity is in fundamental opposition to the standard modern view. It means that consciousness itself is not a single simple property or state, which one either has or does not. Instead it consists of many different types of abilities and activities, like visually recognizing a corner or differentiating a voice from a sound. According to cognitive science, each one of these activities can be split into sub-tasks, each of which can be further split, until at root level one reaches tasks which can be mechanically performed. Therefore, according to cognitive science, consciousness consists of a highly complex series of tasks each of which is fundamentally mechanical in nature. Boden asserts that "artificial intelligence" means "the use of computer programs and programming techniques to cast light on the principles of intelligence in general and human thought in particular."[35]

In assessing the projects of cognitive science and A.I., important questions are:

(a) Are all the activities that constitute consciousness really mechanical in nature at root?

(b) Do A.I. programs merely simulate these activities or could they actually constitute them?

With the first question, we now know that many of the tasks involved in playing chess can be reproduced mechanically. Similarly for many other activities, which already have been simulated by computer models. But this gives us no guarantee that all the activities could be simulated mechanically, i.e., that there is not some aspect of consciousness which will elude a computer model.

These two points are behind the often asked question "Could a computer ever think?" The philosophical import of this popular question is given in (a) and (b). For example, Data the android character in Star Trek acts and behaves exactly like a self-conscious being, but is Data really conscious or is he merely simulating consciousness?

If Data is conscious then it would be true that all the activities that constitute consciousness are really mechanical in nature. If Data's consciousness is constructed out of a complex interacting set of computational programs then it would be true that A.I. programs would actually constitute consciousness. Of course, the character in the television series is convincing and sympathetic because he is portrayed by a human being. But the A.I. project holds out the expectation that a self-conscious construct like Data really is a possibility. And the philosophical issue with respect to A.I. is whether this is true.

With the computer, it seems that the relations between intensional and extensional descriptions can be explained without introducing the idea that computers have a mind, as a non-physical thing. Obviously its functioning can be described extensionally, e.g., "There is a current of 12 volts passing through the chip now." Apparently, the computer's functions also can be described intensionally, e.g. "The computer thinks that the queen is in danger." If the working of the computer can be described intensionally, then it is clear that these intensional descriptions are true of the computer purely in virtue of some physical and extensional descriptions being true. There is no appeal to the idea that there is more to the computer than the plastic and metal. The richer intensional descriptions which we can apparently give of the functioning of the computer in terms of what it is doing are all true by virtue of some physical and extensional descriptions.

Furthermore, an important feature that A.I. has in common with functionalism is that it is possible for one program to be run on many different physical machines. A program is an abstract formal model that can be physically implemented in many different material forms. This removes any temptation to identify programs with physical machines, or to say that the hardware causes the software to act in a certain way. The software implements particular functional tasks that may be carried out by various physical means. This does not imply that a program works non-physically. There has to be some physical means or other in which the program is implemented, but there need not be a direct correspondence between the physical implementation and the program implemented.

However, we must be wary of using the intentional mode inappropriately to describe what should be characterized non-intentionally. For example, the brain tells the muscles to move; one cell communicates with the other; the CPU is now informing the VDU; the hypothalmus has the information. In each of these cases, we use intensional vocabulary to describe what should not be so described, strictly speaking. Brains do not tell, cells do not communicate, etc. It is a contentious matter whether we really should use the intentional mode to describe the functioning of even very complex computers. When we say that the computer wants to win the chess game or that it believes that the queen should not be moved, do we really want to imply that the computer believes and wants?

The A.I. project, however, is still fraught with difficulties that are not merely problems of discovering the right computational models. Alan Turing, one of the first to think about problems of artificial intelligence, suggested a test to determine whether a machine could think. He described a game in which an interrogator sits in a room with two teletype machines and asks questions directed to a person at the end of one line and a machine at the end of the other line. Turing's idea is that if the interrogator is unable to tell which answers are coming from the person and which from the machine, then we would have to conclude that the machine has thoughts, i.e., that it is appropriate to apply intentional descriptions to the machine.

Many thinkers accept the Turing test as a standard for determining whether we can legitimately apply intensional descriptions to machines. However, we should reflect on whether the standard is set too low. There are many facets of human intelligence, abilities we share, that can not be manifested through asking questions and receiving replies in printed signs. These facets include at least the following:

(a) the ability to come to see new and surprising similarities,

(b) the ability to understand via the orientation and use of our bodies, and

(c) the ability to care about certain matters.

Now the A.I. advocate is likely to reply that each of these can, in principle, be done by a machine. We may be able to give a machine the ability to recognize certain patterns, but it remains to be seen whether that can be extended past a pre-programmed set of relationships so that the machine could pick out new similarities.

We may be able to give a machine a robot body, like Data on Star Trek. But this aspect of intelligence cannot plausibly be tested by Turing's test. Because we are embodied, we have a certain orientation to objects, e.g., some are in front of us and some in back. We can understand certain procedures through our bodily grasp of them, e.g., we can get the feel of a particular musical instrument or a dance step. These aspects of human beings can be described intentionally, but not conveyed adequately by printed questions and answers as in the Turing test.

Finally, things matter to us. The machine in the Turing test may be able to say all the right things in response to questions about what matters, and print out sentences like "That doesn't interest me." But that something matters for a human being is shown through the projects the person undertakes and the commitment manifested in her actions over a long period of time and in the context of social interactions and relations. It begins to look like intensional descriptions are legitimately ascribed not to something that merely passes Turing's test, but rather by something that is capable of most of what human beings do. We seem, at least, to need to have a machine that appears more and more like Star Trek's Data, i.e., one that appears more and more like an actual human being.[36]

SECTION 5: BACK TO BATS AGAIN

It is one question whether or not the basic principles of cognitive science are correct. It is a different matter whether cognitive science and its allies get to the heart of the philosophical problem of the mind. Can cognitive science and recent versions of functionalism answer the questions we began with?

The basic doubt has already been mentioned. Can we understand the first person perspective from the third person perspective? This is partly Nagel's worry about the phenomenological fact that we have subjective states; that there is something it is like to be a bat or a whale. But the worry

is more general than that. Answering the question with which we began "How can a point of view on the world be contained within the world, as a part of it?" turns on the status of intensional descriptions. Can such descriptions be reduced to or eliminated in favor of extensional descriptions? Can we justify ascribing intensional states to some processes we understand, like computational processes? One intriguing suggestion is that we should give up the claim that extensional descriptions are a paradigm of understanding and clarity and see intensional descriptions as somehow more basic.[37]

In any case, we have clearly come to see that the problem of the mind's place in nature is not merely an ontological problem about the existence or substantiality of minds. Instead, the problem turns on understanding the nature of intensional descriptions which express a point of view on the world.[38]

NOTES

1. For the purposes of this discussion, we shall ignore the possibility of the existence of abstract objects like numbers and sets.

2. See P. F. Strawson, *Individuals*, Methuen, 1959, Ch. 3 and his essay "Persons," in *The Philosophy of Mind*, ed. V. C. Chappell, Prentice-Hall, 1962, Paul Churchland, *Matter and Consciousness: a Contemporary Introduction to the Philosophy of Mind*, MIT Press, 1984, pp. 11–13, Bernard Williams, "Are Persons Bodies?" in his *Problems of the Self*, Cambridge University Press, 1973.

3. One way to individuate and identify properties is semantically as follows: P = F if and only if necessarily (x) (if Px then Fx, and if Fx then Px). The problem with this definition of the identity of properties is that it requires the necessity operator "necessarily" which is intentional (see the explanation of extensionality and intensionality below). The definition therefore does not give us an extensional grasp on the notion of a property. Since, as we shall see, intensionality is perhaps the key feature of the mind, and it is problematic that any thing could have non-extensional features, the definition repeats the problem we are trying to solve.

It should be pointed out that this point is equally problematic for attributive materialism—the view that mental properties are identical to physical properties.

4. The possible exceptions are sensations like pains, which are not about anything.

5. It should be noted that other expressions besides those for mental states can be intensional. See, for example, the remarks on the operator "necessarily" in note 3.

6. The materialist can argue that since the postulations of mental substances and properties do not explain consciousness, they are obsolete.

7. See Section 3: Behavior and Function.

8. This appeals to the distinction between types and tokens. A token is a particular example of some general sort or kind of thing or type. So, for example, the particular inscription of the letter A at the beginning of the previous sentence is a token of the letter A which is a type instantiated by this and all other tokens of the same type. Hence, the following three inscriptions A A A are three additional tokens of the one type, the letter A.

9. Some meaningful expressions which grammatically are nouns refer, but always in the context of an article or demonstrative expression, like 'the,' 'this' or 'that,' or 'a' and 'an.'

10. In a similar way stipulating that God is the creator of the universe does not answer the question "How did the universe come to be?" Even if it were true that God created the universe, the puzzle is not solved by this answer because it fails to answer the question "How did God create the universe?"

11. But to say that something has been left out is not the same as saying that some THING has been left out. The urge back to dualism is based on the implicit idea that if something has been left out then some THING must have been left out. In other words it is based on reifying the mental.

12. To which the materialist should answer no. The materialist position is not that beliefs are identical to brain states nor that the mind is the brain. It is rather that the persons believing that p is identical to his being in a certain brain state the materialist should not treat beliefs as entities.

13. Scientism is an epistemological view about the scope of scientific knowledge. Roughly, scientism claims that the only real knowledge we can possibly have is what is obtained via the application of scientific methods and what is presented in good scientific theories and especially the theories of theoretical physics.

14. There may be mixed descriptions as well like "Ellen ran out of the room angrily."

15. Thinking about extensional sentences as if they are from no particular point of view is suggested by Thomas Nagel in his book *The View from Nowhere*, Oxford University Press, 1986. See especially ch. I "Introduction" and ch. II "Mind." Nagel says, for example, that "A view or form of thought is more objective than another if it relies less on the specifics of the individual's makeup and position in the world, or on the character of the particular type of creature he is."

16. It is often objected that sensations refute the claim that all mental states are about something. However, see the arguments that even sensations must be described intensionally in G. E. M. Anscombe, "The Intentionality of Sensation: A Grammatical Feature," in volume two of her collected papers, *Metaphysics and the Philosophy of Mind*, St. Paul: University of Minnesota Press, 1981.

17. We will often call non-extensional sentences "intensional." This should not be confused with the description of the particular mental state in which we have an intention to act or do something. The difference in spelling—intensional with an 's' and intentional with a 't'—makes this distinction.

18. Traditional ontological approaches like those of Descartes and the Empiricists tend to the strategy of reification of the intensional. Contemporary philosophers such as J. J. C. Smart, "Sensations and brain processes," *The Philosophical Review*, 1959, and D. M. Armstrong, *A Materialist Theory of the Mind*, Routledge and Kegan Paul, 1968, tend to defend a form of reductionism. While others like Paul Churchland, "Eliminative Materialism and the Propositional Attitudes," *Journal of Philosophy*, vol. LXXVIII, no. 2, 1981, and Richard Rorty "In Defense of Eliminative Materialism," *Review of Metaphysics*, vol. XXIV, 1970, attempt to support the eliminativist strategy.

19. The arguments here concern wider problems in the philosophy of science. They tend to be difficult and technical. See, for example, the debates over theory reduction in P. Oppenheim and H. Putnam, "Unity of Science as a Working Hypothesis," in *Minnesota Studies in the Philosophy of Science*, vol. 2, J. Kim, "Supervenience and Nomological Incommensurables," in *American Philosophical Quarterly*, 15, April, 1978, G. Hellman and F. Thompson, "Physicalism: Ontology, Determination and Reduction," *Journal of Philosophy*, 72, 1975, and D. Davidson, "Mental Events" in his *Actions and Events*, Oxford University Press, 1980.

20. Churchland, op. cit. p. 64.

21. Ibid. pp. 45–46.

22. Ibid. p. 47.

23. For our purposes we need not worry about the difficulties of interpreting quantum mechanics. Some physicists will argue that certain features of quantum mechanics necessitate that observers exist for some physical phenomena to have certain determinate features. However, what constitutes an observer is not clear, and these matters are the scene of considerable contention among physicists. Sorting out the issues here would take us too far astray.

24. Particular token descriptions of physical objects are true in virtue of highly complex microdescriptions of quantum phenomena. The two types of descriptions are true by virtue of the same states of affairs. But this does not mean that one can be reduced to the other.

25. Churchland, op. cit. p. 44.

26. W. V. O. Quine, *Word and Object*, MIT Press, 1960, p. 221.

27. D. Dennett, *Content and Consciousness*, Routledge and Kegan Paul, 1969, p. 342.

28. In an important sense these forms of scientism are not forms of materialism because they are not ontological claims per se.

29. See Dennett, op. cit.

30. See Churchland, op. cit. pp. 36–42, who presents functionalism as a form of materialism.

31. But functionalism is incompatible with type-type identity theory; it is only compatible with token-token identity theory. The argument from a causal analysis of mental states to token-token identity theory is given in section 1.3.

32. Thomas Nagel, "What is it like to be a bat?" in his *Mortal Questions,* Cambridge University Press, 1979.

33. Guzman's SEE program is described in Churchland, op. cit. p. 115.

34. In her introduction to *The Philosophy of Artificial Intelligence,* ed. Margaret Boden, Oxford University Press, 1990, p. 2. For a detailed study and defense of the A.I. project see Margaret Boden, *Artificial Intelligence and Natural Man,* Basic Books, 1977.

35. Margaret Boden, *Artificial Intelligence and Natural Man,* p. 5.

36. Similar objections to the A.I. project are raised in Hubert L. Dreyfus, *What Computers Can't Do: The Limits of Artificial Intelligence,* Harper & Row, 1979.

37. This procedure is adopted in contemporary phenomenology.

38. We thank Daniel Kolak and Raymond Martin for their helpful comments.

Further Questions

1. How is it possible that any object, including my body with my brain, has a perspective on the world?
2. How can a point of view on the world be contained within the world as a part of it?
3. Could a machine have thoughts, feelings, or desires? If not, why not? What test could settle this?

Further Readings

Churchland, Paul. *Matter and Consciousness: a Contemporary Introduction to the Philosophy of Mind.* Cambridge, MA: MIT Press, 1984.

Nagel, Thomas. *The View From Nowhere.* Oxford: Oxford University Press, 1986.

55   Observation: What is Wrong with the Standard Account and How it Can Be Fixed

SARA VOLLMER

Sara Vollmer received a PhD in chemistry from the University of Nebraska, worked for a decade as a research chemist and biochemist, then earned a second PhD, this one in philosophy from the University of Maryland. After that Vollmer lived in Berlin and worked as a research fellow at the Max Planck Institute for the History of Science. She currently teaches at the University of Alabama at Birmingham. She writes on topics in the philosophy of science generally and the philosophy of chemistry specifically, especially observation. In this selection, she explains how on a widely accepted account of observation, which she calls the "standard account" (Source-Transmission-Receiver, or "STR" for short), observation occurs as a result of a signal that travels from a source to an observer. Vollmer explains a serious difficulty with this account of observation and suggests a partial solution. She ends by explaining a puzzle about observation that remains.

Reading Questions

1. Explain the STR account of observation.
2. In Vollmer's view, what's wrong with the STR account?
3. What solution does she propose to this problem?
4. When you see an ordinary object, such as a dime, you probably have no doubt about what you are observing: obviously, you are observing the dime. Explain why it is hard to say, on an STR account of observation, that it is the dime you are observing.
5. Does Vollmer think her proposed solution resolves problems with the STR account for all cases of observation? If not, which ones remain problematic? Why?

A STANDARD ACCOUNT OF OBSERVATION, the Source-Transmission-Receiver account (hereafter, *STR*), explains how an observer can observe something. The explanation requires that a signal travel from a source to a receiver. According to the basic version of STR, a receiver observes a source just if the source transmits a signal directly to the receiver, and the receiver interacts with the signal. The source, e.g., a tree, can be anything that is capable of producing or interacting with the signal transmitted. The signal transmitted can be anything that is produced or affected by the source and that travels from the source to the receiver, where it is received. The source transmits the signal directly to the receiver just if the source transmits the signal without interference to the receiver. The receiver can be a person. On some versions of STR, the receiver can also be an animal or an appropriate piece of technology.

Basic STR has an outstanding virtue. It explains observation in terms of a signal's traveling from the observed to the observer. Basic STR also has an outstanding problem. This problem has to do with the fact that the only way to observe a source is to observe its effects—the signal. But the signal can be a causal chain of multiple effects linking the source to the observer. Each effect, then, is a source in its own right, and basic STR has no way to distinguish between observation of the *original* source and observation of these effects that are the intermediate links in the chain. So when an effect is received and an observation is made, there is no way to say which is the source that is observed. Suppose, for instance, that under perfectly ordinary circumstances you look up into the sky and observe a vapor trail of a jet, but the jet itself is so far in the distance that it cannot be seen. According to basic STR, since the vapor trail is an effect of the jet, in observing the vapor trail you also observe the jet. But this can't be right since in this case you observe only the vapor trail, not also the jet. Basic STR, thus, is too permissive. It allows the observation of some causal effects of a thing that are not observations of that thing itself to count as observations of it.

One way to solve the problem of distinguishing between observation of a source and observation of its effects is to recognize that signals transmitted in cases or ordinary visual observation carry information about the shape and orientation—the *topography*—of objects, e.g., in observing a tree, the signal transmitted carries information about the shape and orientation of the tree. Further, in ordinary visual observation there is an obvious, common-sense answer to the question of which source in the causal chain is observed: it is the object that has the transmitted topography, e.g., the tree. In the jet vapor trail case, information about the shape and orientation of the vapor trail is received, but not about the jet; so what is observed—in no uncertain terms on this common sense notion—is the vapor trail, not the jet.

This suggests that determining what is observed—that is, which step in the causal chain is the original source—can be guided by this common-sense answer from ordinary visual observation. What is observed—the original source—is the object whose topography is transmitted. I will call this development of basic STR the *topographical account* of observation. On the topographical account, the solution to the problem of which step in the causal chain is being observed is that it is the step in the causal chain that has transmitted topography, e.g., the jet's vapor trail, and not the jet itself. (This proposal, then, rules out as what is observed steps in the causal chain prior to the object whose topography is transmitted, such as the source of transmitted light and the jet. It also rules out steps in the causal chain subsequent to the object whose topography is transmitted, such as brain waves that result from the receipt of the signal.) Scientific examples of topographical transmission include optical and electron microscopic observation. In these cases what is transmitted is information about the topography—the shapes and observations—of objects. For instance, in electron microscopy of a freeze-fractured cell, what is transmitted is information about the shape and orientation of the freeze-fractured cell, so on the topographical account that is what is observed.

The topographical account might work as a general account of observation but for the fact that not all signal transmission transmits topographical information about a source. For example, in the case of observing the level of fuel in a fuel tank by reading an ordinary gas gauge in a car, the topography of the fuel level is not transmitted; what is transmitted is only, e.g., a numerical indication of the amount of fuel in the tank. In the case of a doorbell ringing, the topography of the person who rings the doorbell is not transmitted; what is transmitted is only an indication that there is someone at the door. So sometimes a signal is transmitted and received, but no topography of the source is represented. In cases of observation of this second kind, what, then, determines which step of the causal chain is observed?

The topographical account might seem to suggest that only the first kind of transmission, in which a topography is transmitted, results in an observation of a source; in the vapor trail case, what is transmitted to the observer is the topography of the vapor trail, not the topography of the jet, so on the topographical account, just the vapor trail is observed. But when a gauge represents a fuel level, or a doorbell rings, there is no transmission of any topographical information; what, then, is being observed? The topographical account of observation seems to suggest, surprisingly, nothing! But it is not obviously right that when a gauge

needle registers a fuel level, or a doorbell signals a bell ringer, no observation at all is being made. After all, doesn't the gauge report the level of the fuel, and a doorbell signal a bell ringer even though no topography of the fuel level or doorbell ringer has been transmitted? So the topographical account, which seems so promising in the case of the vapor trail example, may not generalize well.

Consider an example of a standard sort of observation in science in which no topography is transmitted that was introduced into the philosophical discussion of observation by the philosopher Dudley Shapere.[1] In this example, processes occurring at the core of the sun transmit neutrinos to earth, where they impinge on a system containing, among other things, dry-cleaning fluid. The neutrinos cause a component of the fluid, chlorine 37, to decay to an unstable form of argon. The argon then beta-decays, releasing beta particles that are detectable by a Geiger counter. In Shapere's view, the Geiger counter's clicking results in an observation of a source in the causal chain—the core of the sun—even though, he says, the core of the sun is "buried underneath 400,000 miles of material under conditions of temperature, pressure, and opacity that would seem to rule out the possibility of any sort of direct access to it."[2] Thus, in Shapere's view, an object—the core of the sun—can be the source in an observation even though there is no transmission from it that provides a topographical representation.

If we find this example persuasive, we will want to say that the clicks of the Geiger counter result in an observation, even though there is no topographical transmission. Even so, there is nothing in STR, or in Shapere's analysis, that shows why we observe some particular antecedent, such as the core of the sun, rather than any other effect in the causal chain. This is a consequence of the fact that STR has no resources to explain which step in the causal chain—which effect—that begins with an original source, and ends in receipt of the signal, is the object observed. So the detection by the Geiger counter results, on STR, not only in an observation of the core of the sun, but also in an observation of the neutrinos, of the chlorine 37, of the argon, of the beta particles, and of every other effect in the causal chain under consideration.

Shapere, in seeming acknowledgment of the problem, sometimes speaks of "observing neutrinos."[3]

Turn now to another version of the STR account of observation, one that the philosopher Jerry Fodor suggests is the standard account given as an explanation for how we get empirical knowledge from perception.[4] The source on this account is a "happening" or happenings about which we wish to know. In the case of observation in science, the happenings, or "effects of these happenings," are transmitted and impact, first on an instrument of observation, and then on an observer who, deploying the instrument, has an experience of the object observed.[5] According to Fodor, this account is wrong. On it, any kind of visual experience of the object can result in an observation. Fodor claims to the contrary that only one kind of visual experience of the object can result in an observation. In his view, the only kind of visual experience that can result in an observation is the kind of experience that an observer has when there is "something it's like" to experience the source, or happening. What Fodor means by an experience that there is "something it's like" is that there is a quality to the experience that permits us, if we've had it before, to match the experience with a particular thing in the world. For example, if we've tasted asparagus before, the experience on a new occasion permits us to know that the taste is that of asparagus; so there is "something it's like" to taste asparagus. Likewise, a visual experience of an object has a quality that permits us to match the experience with a display of the object from a certain perspective, and so we say there is "something it's like" to see the object from a perspective. On Fodor's view, when an observer has an "experience that is *like that*," an observation is made. An example he gives of this kind of experience is seeing litmus paper turning pink; another example is seeing an X-ray tube (as it overheats).[6] These experiences, he suggests further, are the kind that involve "seeing as." When we see a piece of litmus paper turning pink, or a jet plane's vapor trail, we do not see it in the way someone who has never before seen such an object or happening would see it. Rather, we see it in a way that involves seeing it as a particular kind of object or happening, a way that involves some of what we have previously learned

about it.[7] Interestingly, at least in the case of these examples, the kind of seeing experience that is had in "seeing as," or in which there is "something it's like," is the kind of seeing experience in which a topography is transmitted and received as a spatial representation.

A second kind of visual experience, Fodor claims, does not result in observation. This kind of experience Fodor describes as one that there is "nothing it's like." Examples he gives include determining the level of cosmic microwave radiation in the universe and reading a display of a statistical analysis of an automated experiment. What these cases that do not result in observation have in common is that the observer reads a number. In the example of the statistical analysis of an automated experiment, the final result of the analysis is a numerical value—Fodor calls this value a *p-value*—that is printed by a computer and read by an observer; Fodor says "there's nothing it's like to 'observe' a p-value." He notes, further, that we sometimes refer to such acts as observations, e.g., we might say something is "observed" when the p-value that the statistical analysis of the data produces is read. But this, he says, is "just a way of talking." Fodor uses the word "observation" for these acts, but always in quotation marks.[8]

The notion that there is a kind of experience that there is "nothing it's like" is not a straightforward one as it is hard to see just how this second kind of visual experience is categorically different from the first kind, e.g., seeing the litmus paper (turning pink). What Fodor means by an experience there is "nothing it's like" likely has to do with the fact that in "observations" that involve this second kind of experience, the final result is a number read by an observer. It may seem that what Fodor is suggesting is that in reading a number, there is no true *experience* at all. Cognizing numbers, he might think, is categorically different from seeing objects, and from tasting or touching. Numbers might be received in a way that is more like the way a computer receives numbers than like the way we experience tastes. But this isn't what Fodor means, for he says of the example of reading the result of a statistical analysis of an automated experiment that "to a first approximation, 'observing that p is less than .05' is just having some or other experience," that is, an experience of observing "some or other" number between (and including) 0.000 and 0.049. So he thinks that in this second kind of "observation" there is an *experience;* it is just an experience that there is "nothing it's like." He might mean, then, by an experience that there is "nothing it's like," an experience that there is no one, single thing it is like; instead, there are a multiplicity of things it is like: observing that p is less than 0.05 involves *any one* of the experiences of reading a number between 0.00 and 0.049.

But there is a problem with this interpretation, too. To see what it is, consider the example of the visual observation of an ordinary object, such as a dime, from different perspectives. When you look at a dime from straight on, you get one experience; that is, there is "something it's like" to see a dime from straight on. When you look along its edge, you get quite a different experience; there is a qualitatively different "thing it is like" to seeing a dime along its edge. So, there is no one, single thing it is like to see a dime; instead, there are a multiplicity of things, *any one* of which is what it is like to see an ordinary object such as a dime. This means that if Fodor thinks that whenever there is no one single thing but a multitude of things that it is like to observe something (e.g., "observing" p is less than 0.05), we can't really observe the thing at all and there is an unwanted consequence. He would have to conclude that because there are a multitude of things that it is like to see an ordinary object such as a dime, we cannot really observe ordinary objects at all! But no one would say that we can't really observe, e.g., a dime for this reason. This can't, then, be what Fodor means.

Finally, Fodor might mean by an experience there is "nothing it's like," an experience—reading a number—that doesn't supply the kind of information that permits us to match it with any particular object or happening in the world, but only with a number. An experience there is "something it's like," on the other hand, e.g., the experience of a jet vapor trail, or a piece of litmus paper, is an experience that carries the kind of information that permits us to match it with a particular object or happening: a particular jet vapor trail or piece of litmus paper. This, then—that the experience of reading a number isn't like the experience of any particular object or happening, but just an

experience of a *magnitude*—would seem to be what Fodor means by the notion that the experience that is had in this second kind of "observation" is an experience that there is "nothing it's like."

Only the first kind of visual experience—the experience that there is "something it's like" to see an object—is the kind, as noted above, in which the information transmitted about the object or happening observed is topographical, e.g., the shape and size of the litmus paper is transmitted when we see the litmus paper turning pink. This means that for Fodor, of these two kinds of visual experiences, only the one in which a topography is transmitted—and so only when there is an obvious common-sense answer to the question of which source we are observing: the object in the causal chain that has the topography that is transmitted—is an observation made at all.

This means that Fodor's account is essentially a topographical account of observation. On his view, the second kind of "observation," when no topography is transmitted, is not really an observation at all. If we were to consider this second kind of "observation" to be a true observation, then what is observed, he suggests, could "be practically anything at all (including, by the way, bits and pieces of other theories)."[9] But it doesn't seem right that no observation is really being made at all. Surely, e.g., in the example that involves a statistical analysis of an automated experiment, something is being observed. What the experimenter wants to know about is how we come to understand sentences; sentences, it is thought, require the application of rules to be understood. Relatively complex sentences require the application of a greater number of rules than simpler sentences (e.g., passive as compared with active sentences). In Fodor's example, a particular sentence is read out loud to a subject while he or she performs a task; if it takes a longer time for the subject to perform the task than when a putatively simple sentence is being read, then the sentence is relatively *complex.* But the difference in the time that it takes the subject to complete the task while these different kinds of sentences are being read is so slight that many measurements need to be performed. The experimental data is automatically collected and subjected to statistical analysis and, for a given sentence, a number is printed by a computer. An observer reads the number, called a *p-value;* if the p-value is between 0.000 and 0.049, this means that the sentence causes the subject to take a (slightly but) significantly longer time in performing the task than when a simple sentence is being read.

So when an observer reads a p-value, if anything having to do with what the experimenter really wants to know about—how we come to understand a particular sentence—is being observed, what is being observed is not how we come to understand the sentence. We can't, after all, watch the mind sequentially applying rules to sentences. Instead, we are observing the *effects* of a sentence's complexity on something else, i.e., on how long it takes to do a task while the sentence is being read out loud. Likewise, if we are observing anything having to do with how long it takes to do a task while the sentence is being read out loud, we are observing not how long it takes, but its effects, the p-value that is a result of the statistical analysis. But the p-value is an effect not just of how long it takes to do the task, but also of many—perhaps every— event in the causal chain leading to the p-value, including the timing device that automatically collects the times and the computer program that calculates the p-values. So while it would seem that we are observing effects in a causal chain, there is no way to say which effect, any more than any other, would be singled out as the source. That we might be observing what we really want to know about—how we come to understand a particular sentence—is no more plausible, and perhaps less so, than that what we are observing is any other step in the causal chain.

A similar problem exists in an example such as the registering of the needle of a fuel gauge. The information transmitted to the dial of a fuel gauge is in correlation with, and a causal effect of, not just the level of fuel in the tank, but also the prior steps in the causal chain. It is, for example, in correspondence with, and a causal consequence of, the height of an arm attached to a float in the fuel tank; or, if the gauge is electrical, it is in correspondence with, and a causal consequence of, the magnitude of an electrical signal. And if the gauge output were to be further converted, say, automatically to number of miles traveled, the information displayed would be information not only about the fuel level, the float arm, and the electrical signal, but also about the number of miles traveled.

The needle reading, if the gauge is in working order, is assumed to be an effect of the fuel level. But how would one argue for this specific source, and not others in the respective causal chain? In this case, while the observed effect is said to be an effect of some object or happening, it cannot, on any analysis so far given, be attributed to just one source in the causal chain. It is no more obvious why it should be attributed specifically to the level of fuel than to any other step in the causal chain. So without some further account of what is observed when no topography is transmitted, it is no more plausible that what is observed is the level of the fuel than that what is observed is any of these other steps in the causal chain.

Bonnie Paller addresses the question of what is observed in Shapere's example of neutrinos hurled through space by referring to the relations between "relevant [causal] systems" and human purposes.[10] If a causal chain—a "relevant system"—does, in fact, extend from the core of the sun to the Geiger counter and we intend to use that system to observe the core of the sun, then, in her view, we observe the core of the sun. In her words, the "relevant type" of system "is the most successful system consistent with intended use."[11] Paller's suggestion, I think, is along the right lines for an analysis of the kind of constraint on basic STR that would determine in cases when topography is not transmitted which particular source is being observed; but her solution does not fully solve the problem of fixing the reference of nontopographical observations. For one thing, she does not offer a criterion for determining which system is the most successful one consistent with intended use. For another, in the case of a relevant causal chain that results in an observation, while the intention of the cognizer, as she suggests, does seem to be relevant to what is observed, it seems that much more than the intention of the cognizer is relevant. Intending to observe one link in a causal chain rather than another does not by itself insure that one observes that link, or else by observing, with the relevant psychology, the fuel gauge one would thereby observe the number of miles traveled. While it might be possible to use the fuel gauge in this way, if an account of this kind of observation is to explain why it is that in reading a fuel gauge we observe the level of fuel, then something else, including the social setting in which the causal chain occurs and the observation is made, is also relevant to what is observed. Determining the nature of the influence of the setting on which step (if any) in the causal chain is the source is called *contextualizing*. Admittedly, the details of how contextualizing tends to fix the reference of observation is extremely complex and, so far, a relatively neglected topic in the literature on observation.

Where, then, does this leave us? I have suggested that, on the topographical account of observation, when a topography is transmitted—following our common sense notion in ordinary visual observation—what is observed is the step in the causal chain—the object—that has that topography. When no topography is transmitted, such as the reading of a fuel gauge, which step in the causal chain is observed is much less obvious. What is observed will not be determined by topography but by the nature of the causal chain together with relevant psychological and perhaps social/scientific contextualizing. For instance, in the case of the Geiger counter detection resulting from processes occurring at the core of the sun, it would seem that psychological and scientific contextualizing would be what would make it, e.g., if not the core of the sun, or the neutrinos, then perhaps the beta

particles that finally cause the Geiger counter to click, that are being observed. And in the case of a fuel gauge, it would seem that it is psychological and social contextualizing (what else could it possibly be?) that makes it the fuel level, as opposed to the float arm, or the number of miles driven, that is the putative object of the gauge.

NOTES

1. Dudley Shapere, "The Concept of Observation in Science and Philosophy," *Philosophy of Science* 49 (1982): 485–525; also Dudley Shapere, "Observation and the Scientific Enterprise," in Peter Achenstein and Owen Hannaway, eds., *Observation, Experiment, and Hypothesis in Modern Physical Science* (Cambridge: MIT Press, 1985), pp. 21–45.
2. Shapere, "Observation and the Scientific Enterprise," p. 23.
3. Ibid., pp. 513, 521.
4. Jerry Fodor, "The Dogma that Didn't Bark (A Fragment of a Naturalized Epistemology)," *Mind* 100 (1991): 201–220.
5. Ibid., pp. 201, 204.
6. Ibid., pp. 206, 207.
7. Ibid., p. 208.
8. Ibid., p. 206.
9. Ibid., p. 208.
10. Bonnie Paller, "Visual Perception, Observation Systems, and Empiricism," *Philosophical Studies* 55 (1989): 65–80.
11. Ibid., p. 76.

Further Questions

1. Do Fodor and Shapere agree on what they mean by an observation? If not, on what do they disagree?
2. Vollmer explains that Fodor's notion of an experience that there is "nothing it's like" is not straightforward. She explains what she thinks he means, and why. Give a summary of her reasoning. Does it sound right to you? Is there any problem with it?
3. The main reason that Fodor restricts observation to cases in which (typically) a topography of the object observed is transmitted and received is that this kind of observation does not rely, or perhaps relies only minimally, on background knowledge and theories. Explain what is meant by this. Why would one want to define observation in the way Fodor does? in the way Vollmer does?
4. Suppose extrasensory perception (ESP) is a real phenomenon. Would ESP count as a kind of observation on basic STR? on Shapere's account? on Fodor's account? There are many possible answers to this question; explain yours in full.

Further Readings

Brown, Harold I. *Perception, Theory and Commitment: The New Philosophy of Science.* Chicago: University of Chicago Press, 1993.
Dretske, Fred I. *Knowledge and the Flow of Information.* Cambridge: MIT Press, 1981.

Part IX

Consciousness

USUALLY, WHEN WE TRY TO UNDERSTAND something, we try to reduce it to simpler components. We try to understand the complex whole by getting hold of the simple elements of which it is composed. Do we ever succeed? Only up to a point. The problem is that we the observers are invariably and inextricably linked to whatever we are trying to understand.

We imagine our relationship to the universe to be like that of fish to a fishtank: whether or not there are fish, the tank is there. We think the universe is not shaped by us. Rather, we are shaped by it. We believe that ultimately the universe exists independently of the minds trying so desperately to understand it.

One of the most amazing scientific discoveries of all time, however, is that this fishbowl model of the universe simply does not work. Without us, the observers, trying to understand the observed, the universe we know would literally not exist — and neither would we.

56   The Selfish Gene

RICHARD DAWKINS

Richard Dawkins is a British biologist. His book, *The Selfish Gene,* from which the following selection is taken, is a modern classic of popular science. In it Dawkins explains how simple constituents can combine, through the action of natural forces, to produce a highly complex result: you. In the process, Dawkins nicely illustrates how science, by reducing the complex to the simple, contributes to our understanding of nature and ourselves.

Reading Questions

1. How, according to Dawkins, did simple atoms become biologically more complex?
2. If Dawkins's account is correct, who's running the show—us, or our genes?
3. Why is there no need for design or purpose at the molecular level?
4. What is a *survival machine*?

IN THE BEGINNING WAS SIMPLICITY. It is difficult enough explaining how even a simple universe began. I take it as agreed that it would be even harder to explain the sudden springing up, fully armed, of complex order—life, or a being capable of creating life. Darwin's theory of evolution by natural selection is satisfying because it shows us a way in which simplicity could change into complexity, how unordered atoms could group themselves into ever more complex patterns until they ended up manufacturing people. Darwin provides a solution, the only feasible one so far suggested, to the deep problem of our existence. I will try to explain the great theory in a more general way than is customary, beginning with the time before evolution itself began.

Darwin's "survival of the fittest" is really a special case of a more general law of *survival of the stable*. The universe is populated by stable things. A stable thing is a collection of atoms which is perma-nent enough or common enough to deserve a name. It may be a unique collection of atoms, such as the Matterhorn, which lasts long enough to be worth naming. Or it may be a *class* of entities, such as rain drops, which come into existence at a sufficiently high rate to deserve a collective name, even if any one of them is shortlived. The things which we see around us, and which we think of as needing explanation—rocks, galaxies, ocean waves—are all, to a greater or lesser extent, stable patterns of atoms. Soap bubbles tend to be spherical because this is a stable configuration for thin films filled with gas. In a spacecraft, water is also stable in spherical globules, but on earth, where there is gravity, the stable surface for standing water is flat and horizontal. Salt crystals tend to be cubes because this is a stable way of packing sodium and chloride ions together. In the sun the simplest atoms of all, hydrogen atoms, are fusing to form helium atoms, because in the conditions which prevail there the helium configuration is more stable. Other even more complex atoms are being formed in stars all over the universe, and were formed in the "big bang" which, according to the prevailing theory, initiated the universe. This is originally where the elements on our world came from.

Sometimes when atoms meet they link up together in chemical reaction to form molecules, which may be more or less stable. Such molecules can be very large. A crystal such as a diamond can be regarded as a single molecule, a proverbially stable one in this case, but also a very simple one since its internal atomic structure is endlessly repeated. In modern living organisms there are other large molecules which are highly complex, and their complexity shows itself on several levels. The hemoglobin of our blood is a typical protein molecule. It is built up from chains of smaller molecules, amino acids, each containing a few dozen atoms arranged in a precise pattern. In the hemoglobin molecule there are 574 amino acid molecules. These are arranged in four chains, which twist around each other to form a globular three-dimensional structure of bewildering complexity. . . .

Hemoglobin is a modern molecule, used to illustrate the principle that atoms tend to fall into stable patterns. The point that is relevant here is that, before the coming of life on earth, some rudimentary evolution of molecules could have occurred by ordinary processes of physics and chemistry. There is no need to think of design or purpose or directedness. If a group of atoms in the presence of energy falls into a stable pattern it will tend to stay that way. The earliest form of natural selection was simply a selection of stable forms and a rejection of unstable ones. There is no mystery about this. It had to happen by definition.

From this, of course, it does not follow that you can explain the existence of entities as complex as man by exactly the same principles on their own. It is no good taking the right number of atoms and shaking them together with some external energy till they happen to fall into the right pattern, and out drops Adam! You may make a molecule consisting of a few dozen atoms like that, but a man consists of over a thousand million million million million atoms. To try to make a man, you would have to work at your biochemical cocktail-shaker for a period so long that the entire

age of the universe would seem like an eye-blink, and even then you would not succeed. This is where Darwin's theory, in its most general form, comes to the rescue. Darwin's theory takes over from where the story of the slow building up of molecules leaves off.

The account of the origin of life which I shall give is necessarily speculative; by definition, nobody was around to see what happened. There are a number of rival theories, but they all have certain features in common. The simplified account I shall give is probably not too far from the truth.

We do not know what chemical raw materials were abundant on earth before the coming of life, but among the plausible possibilities are water, carbon dioxide, methane, and ammonia: all simple compounds known to be present on at least some of the other planets in our solar system. Chemists have tried to imitate the chemical conditions of the young earth. They have put these simple substances in a flask and supplied a source of energy such as ultraviolet light or electric sparks—artificial simulation of primordial lightning. After a few weeks of this, something interesting is usually found inside the flask: a weak brown soup containing a large number of molecules more complex than the ones originally put in. In particular, amino acids have been found—the building blocks of proteins, one of the two great classes of biological molecules. . . .

Processes analogous to these must have given rise to the "primeval soup" which biologists and chemists believe constituted the seas some three to four thousand million years ago. The organic substances became locally concentrated, perhaps in drying scum round the shores, or in tiny suspended droplets. Under the further influence of energy such as ultraviolet light from the sun, they combined into larger molecules. . . .

At some point a particularly remarkable molecule was formed by accident. We will call it the *Replicator*. It may not necessarily have been the biggest or the most complex molecule around, but it had the extraordinary property of being able to create copies of itself. This may seem a very unlikely sort of accident to happen. So it was. It was exceedingly improbable. In the lifetime of a man, things which are that improbable can be treated for practical purposes as impossible. That is why you will never win a big prize on the football pools. But in our human estimates of what is probable and what is not, we are not used to dealing in hundreds of millions of years. If you filled in pools coupons every week for a hundred million years you would very likely win several jackpots.

Actually a molecule which makes copies of itself is not as difficult to imagine as it seems at first, and it only had to arise once. Think of the replicator as a mold or template. Imagine it as a large molecule consisting of a complex chain of various sorts of building block molecules. The small building blocks were abundantly available in the soup surrounding the replicator. Now suppose that each building block has an affinity for its own kind. Then whenever a building block from out in the soup lands up next to a part of the replicator for which it has an affinity, it will tend to stick there. The building blocks which attach themselves in this way will automatically be arranged in a sequence which mimics that of the replicator itself. It is easy then to think of them joining up to form a stable chain just as in the formation of the original replicator. This process could continue as a progressive stacking up, layer upon layer. This is how crystals are formed. On the other hand, the two chains might split apart, in which case we have two replicators, each of which can go on to make further copies.

A more complex possibility is that each building block has affinity not for its own kind, but reciprocally for one particular other kind. Then the replicator would act as a template not for an identical copy, but for a kind of "negative," which would in its turn remake an exact copy of the original positive. For our purposes it does not matter whether the original replication process was positive–negative or positive–positive, though it is worth remarking that the modern equivalents of the first replicator, the DNA molecules, use positive–negative replication. What does matter is that suddenly a new kind of "stability" came into the world. Previously it is probable that no particular kind of complex molecule was very abundant in the soup, because each was dependent on building blocks happening to fall by luck into a particular stable configuration. As soon as the replicator was born it must have spread its copies rapidly throughout the seas, until the smaller building block molecules became a scarce resource, and other larger molecules were formed more and more rarely.

So we seem to arrive at a large population of identical replicas. But now we must mention an important property of any copying process: it is not perfect. Mistakes will happen. I hope there are no misprints in this book, but if you look carefully you may find one or two. They will probably not seriously distort the meaning of the sentences, because they will be "first-generation" errors. But imagine the days before printing, when books such as the Gospels were copied by hand. All scribes, however careful, are bound to make a few errors, and some are not above a little willful "improvement." If they all copied from a single master original, meaning would not be greatly perverted. But let copies be made from other copies, which in their turn were made from other copies, and errors will start to become cumulative and serious. We tend to regard erratic copying as a bad thing, and in the case of human documents it is hard to think of examples where errors can be described as improvements. I suppose the scholars of the Septuagint could at least be said to have started something big when they mistranslated the Hebrew word for "young woman" into the Greek word for "virgin," coming up with the prophecy: "Behold a virgin shall conceive and bear a son. . . ." Anyway, as we shall see, erratic copying in biological replicators can in a real sense give rise to improvement, and it was essential for the progressive evolution of life that some errors were made. We do not know how accurately the original replicator molecules made their copies. Their modern descendants, the DNA molecules, are astonishingly faithful compared with the most high-fidelity human copying process, but even they occasionally make mistakes, and it is ultimately these mistakes which make evolution possible. Probably the original replicators were far more erratic, but in any case we may be sure that mistakes were made, and these mistakes were cumulative.

As mis-copyings were made and propagated, the primeval soup became filled by a population not of identical replicas, but of several varieties of replicating molecules, all "descended" from the same ancestor. Would some varieties have been more numerous than others? Almost certainly yes. Some varieties would have been inherently more

---

THE SELF AS COMMUNITY

Richard Thomas

A good case can be made for our nonexistence as entities. We are not made up, as we had always supposed, of successively enriched packets of our own parts. We are shared, rented, occupied. At the interior of our cells, driving them, providing the oxidative energy that sends us out for the improvement of each shining day, are the mitochondria, and in a strict sense they are not ours. They turn out to be little separate creatures, the colonial posterity of migrant prokaryocytes, probably primitive bacteria that swam into ancestral precursors of our eukaryotic cells and stayed there. Ever since, they have maintained themselves and their ways, replicating in their own fashion, privately, with their own DNA and RNA quite different from ours. They are as much symbionts as the rhizobial bacteria in the roots of beans. Without them, we would not move a muscle, drum a finger, think a thought.

Mitochondria are stable and responsible lodgers, and I choose to trust them. But what of the other little animals, similarly established in my cells, sorting and balancing me, clustering me together? My centrioles, basal bodies, and probably a good many other more obscure tiny beings at work inside my cells, each with its own special genome, are as foreign, and as essential, as aphids in anthills. My cells are no longer the pure line entities I was raised with; they are ecosystems more complex than Jamaica Bay. . . .

As for me, I am grateful for differentiation and speciation, but I cannot feel as separate an entity as I did a few years ago, before I was told these things, nor, I should think, can anyone else. . . .

From "*The Lives of a Cell*" (1973).

---

stable than others. Certain molecules, once formed, would be less likely than others to break up again. These types would become relatively numerous in the soup, not only as a direct logical consequence of their "longevity," but also because they would have a long time available for making copies of themselves. Replicators of high longevity would therefore tend to become more numerous and, other things being equal, there would have been an "evolutionary trend" toward greater longevity in the population of molecules.

But other things were probably not equal, and another property of a replicator variety which must have had even more importance in spreading it through the population was speed of replication, or "fecundity." If replicator molecules of type *A* make copies of themselves on average once a week while those of type *B* make copies of themselves once an hour, it is not difficult to see that pretty soon type *A* molecules are going to be far outnumbered, even

if they "live" much longer than *B* molecules. There would therefore probably have been an "evolutionary trend" towards higher "fecundity" of molecules in the soup. A third characteristic of replicator molecules which would have been positively selected is accuracy of replication. If molecules of type *X* and type *Y* last the same length of time and replicate at the same rate, but *X* makes a mistake on average every tenth replication while *Y* makes a mistake only every hundredth replication, *Y* will obviously become more numerous. The *X* contingent in the population loses not only the errant "children" themselves, but also all their descendants, actual or potential.

If you already know something about evolution, you may find something slightly paradoxical about the last point. Can we reconcile the idea that copying errors are an essential prerequisite for evolution to occur, with the statement that natural selection favors high copying-fidelity? The answer is that although evolution may seem, in some vague sense, a "good thing," especially since we are the product of it, nothing actually "wants" to evolve. Evolution is something that happens, willy-nilly, in spite of all the efforts of the replicators (and nowadays of the genes) to prevent it happening. Jacques Monod made this point very well in his Herbert Spencer lecture, after wryly remarking: "Another curious aspect of the theory of evolution is that everybody thinks he understands it!"

To return to the primeval soup, it must have become populated by stable varieties of molecules; stable in that either the individual molecules lasted a long time, or they replicated rapidly, or they replicated accurately. Evolutionary trends toward these three kinds of stability took place in the following sense: If you had sampled the soup at two different times, the later sample would have contained a higher proportion of varieties with high longevity/fecundity/copying-fidelity. This is essentially what a biologist means by evolution when he is speaking of living creatures, and the mechanism is the same — natural selection.

Should we then call the original replicator molecules "living"? Who cares? I might say to you "Darwin was the greatest man who has ever lived," and you might say, "No, Newton was," but I hope we would not prolong the argument. The point is that no conclusion of substance would be affected whichever way our argument was resolved. The facts of the lives and achievements of Newton and Darwin remain totally unchanged whether we label them "great" or not. Similarly, the story of the replicator molecules probably happened something like the way I am telling it, regardless of whether we choose to call them "living." Human suffering has been caused because too many of us cannot grasp that words are only tools for our use, and that the mere presence in the dictionary of a word like "living" does not mean it necessarily has to refer to something definite in the real world. Whether we call the early replicators living or not, they were the ancestors of life; they were our founding fathers.

The next important link in the argument, one which Darwin himself laid stress on (although he was talking about animals and plants, not molecules) is *competition*. The primeval soup was not capable of supporting an infinite number of replicator molecules. For one thing, the earth's size is

finite, but other limiting factors must also have been important. In our picture of the replicator acting as a template or mold, we supposed it to be bathed in a soup rich in the small building block molecules necessary to make copies. But when the replicators became numerous, building blocks must have been used up at such a rate that they became a scarce and precious resource. Different varieties or strains of replicator must have competed for them. We have considered the factors which would have increased the numbers of favored kinds of replicator. We can now see that less-favored varieties must actually have become *less* numerous because of competition, and ultimately many of their lines must have gone extinct. There was a struggle for existence among replicator varieties. They did not know they were struggling, or worry about it; the struggle was conducted without any hard feelings, indeed without feelings of any kind. But they were struggling, in the sense that any miscopying which resulted in a new higher level of stability, or a new way of reducing the stability of rivals, was automatically preserved and multiplied. The process of improvement was cumulative. Ways of increasing stability and of decreasing rivals' stability became more elaborate and more efficient. Some of them may even have "discovered" how to break up molecules of rival varieties chemically, and to use the building blocks so released for making their own copies. These proto-carnivores simultaneously obtained food and removed competing rivals. Other replicators perhaps discovered how to protect themselves, either chemically or by building a physical wall of protein around themselves. This may have been how the first living cells appeared. Replicators began not merely to exist, but to construct for themselves containers, vehicles for their continued existence. The replicators which survived were the ones which built *survival machines* for themselves to live in. The first survival machines probably consisted of nothing more than a protective coat. But making a living got steadily harder as new rivals arose with better and more effective survival machines. Survival machines got bigger and more elaborate, and the process was cumulative and progressive.

Was there to be any end to the gradual improvement in the techniques and artifices used by the replicators to ensure their own continuance in the world? There would be plenty of time for improvement. What weird engines of self-preservation would the millennia bring forth? Four thousand million years on, what was to be the fate of the ancient replicators? They did not die out, for they are past masters of the survival arts. But do not look for them floating loose in the sea; they gave up that cavalier freedom long ago. Now they swarm in huge colonies, safe inside gigantic lumbering robots, sealed off from the outside world, communicating with it by tortuous indirect routes, manipulating it by remote control. They are in you and in me; they created us, body and mind; and their preservation is the ultimate rationale for our existence. They have come a long way, those replicators. Now they go by the name of genes, and we are their survival machines.

Further Questions

1. Does a scientific theory have to be reductionist?
2. It is sometimes said that "creationism"—the claim that the various species of plants and animals are each the product of a separate act of divine creation—and evolutionary theory are competing theories of our origins. But are the two really *theories* in the same sense? (What are the important differences, if any, between a religious "theory" and a scientific theory?)

Further Readings

Hofstadter, Douglas. *Gödel, Escher, and Bach*. New York: Basic Books, 1979. An imaginative exploration of consciousness.
Pribram, Karl. *The Languages of the Brain*. Englewood Cliffs, NJ: Prentice-Hall, 1971. Explores different levels of descriptions of the brain.

The Story of a Brain   57

ARNOLD ZUBOFF

Arnold Zuboff teaches philosophy at the University of London and writes primarily in the areas of philosophy of mind and personal identity. In this well-known and highly imaginative essay, he shows how the modern scientific idea that the mind is nothing more than a collection of neurons functioning in a particular way leads to some deeply bizarre results.

Reading Questions

1. Consider the various Cassanderish "conditions of experience" discussed in this essay: proximity; actual causal connection; synchronization; topology; neural identity; and neural context. Is there any reason to think any of them are necessary for experience to occur?
2. Assuming that experience can be continued in the way sketched in this story, is the identity of the experiencer also continued? In other words, is the young man at the beginning the same experiencer as whatever is having experiences at the end? In still other words, did the young man's scheme for prolonging *his* capacity to have experiences work?

I

ONCE UPON A TIME, a kind young man who enjoyed many friends and great wealth learned that a horrible rot was overtaking all of his body but his nervous system. He loved life: he loved having experiences. Therefore he was intensely interested when scientist friends of amazing abilities proposed the following:

"We shall take the brain from your poor rotting body and keep it healthy in a special nutrient bath. We shall have it connected to a machine that is capable of inducing in it any pattern at all of neural firings and is therein capable of bringing about for you any sort of total experience that it is possible for the activity of your nervous system to cause or to be."

The reason for this last disjunction of the verbs *to cause* and *to be* was that, although all these scientists were convinced of a general theory that they called "the neural theory of experience," they disagreed on the specific formulation of this theory. They all knew of countless instances in which it was just obvious that the state of the brain, the pattern of its activity, somehow had made for a man's experiencing this rather than that. It seemed reasonable to them all that ultimately what decisively controlled any particular experience of a man — controlled whether it existed and what it was like — was the state of his nervous system and more specifically that of those areas of the brain that careful research had discovered to be involved in the various aspects of consciousness. This conviction was what had prompted their proposal to their young friend. That they disagreed about whether an experience simply consisted in or else was caused by neural activity was irrelevant to their belief that as long as their friend's brain was alive and functioning under their control, they could keep him having his beloved experience indefinitely, just as though he were walking about and getting himself into the various situations that would in a more natural way have stimulated each of those patterns of neural firings that they would bring about artificially. If he were actually to have gazed through a hole in a snow-covered frozen pond, for instance, the physical reality there would have caused him to experience what Thoreau described: "the quiet parlor of the fishes, pervaded by a softened light as through a window of ground glass, with its bright sanded floor the same as in summer." The brain lying in its bath, stripped of its body and far from the pond, if it were made to behave precisely as it naturally would under such pond-hole circumstances, would have for the young man that very same experience.

Well, the young man agreed with the concept and looked forward to its execution. And a mere month after he had first heard the thing proposed to him, his brain was floating in the warm nutrient bath. His scientist friends kept busy researching, by means of paid subjects, which patterns of neuron firings were like the natural neural responses to very pleasant situations; and, through the use of a complex electrode machine, they kept inducing only these neural activities in their dear friend's brain.

Then there was trouble. One night the watchman had been drinking, and, tipsily wandering into the room where the bath lay, he careened forward so his right arm entered the bath and actually split the poor brain into its two hemispheres.

The brain's scientist friends were very upset the next morning. They had been all ready to feed into the brain a marvelous new batch of experiences whose neural patterns they had just recently discovered.

"If we let our friend's brain mend after bringing the parted hemispheres together," said Fred, "we must wait a good two months before it will be healed well enough so that we can get the fun of feeding him these new experiences. Of course, he won't know about the waiting; but we sure will! And unfortunately, as we all know, two separated halves of a brain can't entertain the same neural patterns that they can when they're together. For all those impulses which cross from one hemisphere to another during a whole-brain experience just can't make it across the gap that has been opened between them."

The end of this speech gave someone else an idea. Why not do the following: Develop tiny electrochemical wires whose ends could be fitted to the synapses of neurons to receive or discharge their neural impulses. These wires could then be strung from each neuron whose connection had been broken in the split to that neuron of the other hemisphere to which it had formerly been connected. "In this way," finished Bert, the proposer of this idea, "all those impulses that were supposed to cross over from one hemisphere to the other could do just that—carried over the wires."

This suggestion was greeted with enthusiasm, since the construction of the wire system, it was felt, could easily be completed within a week. But one grave fellow named Cassander had worries. "We all agree that our friend has been having the experiences we've tried to give him. That is, we all accept in some form or other the neural theory of experience. Now, according to this theory as we all accept it, it is quite permissible to alter as one likes the context of a functioning brain, just so long as one maintains the pattern of its activity. We might look at what we're saying this way. There are various conditions that make for the usual having of an experience—an experience, for instance, like that pond-hole experience we believe we gave our friend three weeks ago. Usually these conditions are the brain being in an actual body on an actual pond stimulated to such neural activity as we did indeed give our friend. We gave our friend the neural activity without those other conditions of its context, because our friend has no body and because we believe that what is essential and decisive for the existence and character of an experience anyway is not such context but rather only the neural activity that it can stimulate. The contextual conditions, we believe, are truly inessential to the bare fact of a man having an experience—even if they *are* essential conditions in the normal having of that experience. If one has the wherewithal, as we do, to get around the normal necessity of these external conditions of an experience of a pond hole, then such conditions are no longer necessary. And this demonstrates that within our concept of experience they never were necessary in principle to the bare fact of having the experience.

"Now, what you men are proposing to do with these wires amounts to regarding as inessential just one more normal condition of our friend's having his experience. That is, you are saying something like what I just said about the context of neural activity—but *you're* saying it about the condition of the *proximity* of the hemispheres of the brain to one another. You're saying that the two hemispheres are being attached to one another in the whole-brain experiences may be nec-

essary to the coming about of those experiences in the usual case, but if one can get around a breach of this proximity in some, indeed *un*usual case, as you fellows would with your wires, there'd still be brought about just the same bare fact of the same experience being had! You're saying that proximity isn't a necessary condition to this bare fact of an experience. But isn't it possible that even reproducing precisely the whole-brain neural patterns in a sundered brain would, to the contrary, *not* constitute the bringing about of the whole-brain experience? Couldn't proximity be not just something to get around in creating a particular whole-brain experience but somehow an absolute condition and principle of the having of a whole-brain experience?"

Cassander got little sympathy for his worries. Typical replies ran something like this: "Would the damn hemispheres *know* they were connected by wires instead of attached in the usual way? That is, would the fact get encoded in any of the brain structures responsible for speech, thought or any other feature of awareness? How could this fact about how his brain looks to external observers concern our dear friend in his pleasures at all—any more than being a naked brain sitting in a warm nutrient bath does? As long as the neural activity in the hemispheres—together *or* apart—matches precisely that which would have been the activity in the hemispheres lumped together in the head of a person walking around having fun, then the person himself is having that fun. Why, if we hooked up a mouth to these brain parts, he'd be telling us through it about his fun." In reply to such answers, which were getting shorter and angrier, Cassander could only mutter about the possible disruption of some experiential field "or some such."

But after the men had been working on the wires for a while someone else came up with an objection to their project that *did* stop them. He pointed out that it took practically no time for an impulse from one hemisphere to enter into the other when a brain was together and functioning normally. But the travel of these impulses over wires must impose a tiny increase on the time taken in such crossovers. Since the impulses in the rest of the brain in each hemisphere would be taking their normal time, wouldn't the overall pattern get garbled, operating as if there were a slowdown in only one region? Certainly it would be impossible to get precisely the normal sort of pattern going—you'd have something strange, disturbed.

When this successful objection was raised, a man with very little training in physics suggested that somehow the wire be replaced by radio signals. This could be done by outfitting the raw face—of the split—of each hemisphere with an "impulse cartridge" that would be capable of sending any pattern of impulses into the hitherto exposed and unconnected neurons of that hemisphere, as well as of receiving from those neurons any pattern of impulses that that hemisphere might be trying to communicate to the other hemisphere. Then each cartridge could be plugged into a special radio transmitter and receiver. When a cartridge received an impulse from a neuron in one hemisphere intended for a neuron of the other, the impulse could then be radioed over and properly administered by the other cartridge. The fellow who suggested this even mused that then each half of the brain could be kept in a separate bath and yet the whole still be engaged in a single whole-brain experience.

The advantage of this system over the wires, this fellow thought, resided in the "fact" that radio waves take no time, unlike impulses in wires, to travel from one place to another. He was quickly disabused of this idea. No, the radio system still suffered from the time-gap obstacle.

But all this talk of impulse cartridges inspired Bert. "Look, we could feed each impulse cartridge with the same pattern of impulses it would have been receiving by radio but do so by such a method as to require no radio or wire transmission. All we need do is fix to each cartridge not a radio transmitter and receiver but an "impulse programmer," the sort of gadget that would play through whatever program of impulses you have previously given it. The great thing about this is that there is no longer any need for the impulse pattern going into one hemisphere to be *actually caused,* in part, by the pattern coming from the other. Therefore there need not be any wait for the transmission. The programmed cartridges can be so correlated with the rest of our stimulation of neural patterns that all of the timing can be just as it would have been if the hemispheres were together. And, yes, then it will be easy to fix each hemisphere in a separate bath—perhaps one in the laboratory here and one in the laboratory across town, so that we may employ the facilities of each laboratory in working with merely half a brain. This will make everything easier. And we can then bring in more people; there are many who've been bothering us to let them join our project."

But now Cassander was even more worried. "We have already disregarded the condition of proximity. Now we are about to abandon yet another condition of usual experience—that of actual causal connection. Granted you can be clever enough to get around what is usually quite necessary to an experience coming about. So now, with your programming, it will no longer be necessary for impulses in one half of the brain actually to be a cause of the completion of the whole-brain pattern in the other hemisphere in order for the whole-brain pattern to come about. But is the result still the bare fact of the whole-brain experience or have you, in removing this condition, removed an absolute principle of, an essential condition for, a whole-brain experience really being had?"

The answers to this were much as they had been to the other. How did the neural activity *know* whether a radio-controlled or programmed impulse cartridge fed it? How could this fact, so totally external to them, register with the neural structures underlying thought, speech, and every other item of awareness? Certainly it could not register mechanically. Wasn't the result then precisely the same with tape as with wire except that now the time-gap program had been overcome? And wouldn't a properly hooked-up mouth even report the experiences as nicely after the taped as after the wired assistance with crossing impulses?

The next innovation came soon enough—when the question was raised about whether it was at all important, since each hemisphere was now working separately, to synchronize the two causally unconnected playings of the impulse patterns of the hemispheres. Now that each hemisphere would in effect receive all the impulses that in a given experience it would have received from the other hemisphere—and receive them in such a way as would work perfectly with the timing of the rest of its impulses—and since this fine effect could be achieved in either hemisphere quite independent of its having yet been achieved in the other, there seemed no reason for retaining what Cassander sadly pointed to as the "condition of synchronization." Men were heard to say, "How does either hemisphere *know*, how could it register when the other goes off, in the time of the external observer, anyway? For each hemisphere what more can we say than that it is just precisely as if the other had gone off with it the right way? What is there to worry about if at one lab they run through one half of a pattern one day and at the other lab they supply the other hemisphere with its half of the pattern another day? The pattern gets run through fine. The experience comes about. With the brain parts hooked up properly to a mouth, our friend could even report his experience."

There was also some discussion about whether to maintain what Cassander called "topology"—that is, whether to keep the two hemispheres in the general spatial relation of facing each other. Here too Cassander's warnings were ignored.

II

Ten centuries later the famous project was still engrossing men. But men now filled the galaxy and their technology was tremendous. Among them were billions who wanted the thrill and responsibility of participating in the "Great Experience Feed." Of course, behind this desire lay the continuing belief that what men were doing in programming impulses still amounted to making a man have all sorts of experiences.

But in order to accommodate all those who now wished to participate in the project, what Cassander had called the "conditions" of the experiencing had, to the superficial glance, changed enormously. (Actually, they were in a sense more conservative than they had been when we last saw them, because, as I shall explain later, something like "synchronization" had been restored.) Just as earlier each hemisphere of the brain had rested in its bath, now *each individual neuron* rested in one of its own. Since there were billions of neurons, each of the billions of men could involve himself with the proud task of manning a neuron bath.

To understand this situation properly, one must go back again ten centuries, to what had occurred as more and more men had expressed a desire for part of the project. First it was agreed that if a whole-brain experience could come about with the brain split and yet the two halves programmed as I have described, the same experience could come about if each hemisphere too were carefully divided and each piece treated just as each of the two hemispheres had been. Thus each of four pieces of brain could now be given not only its own bath but a whole lab—allowing many more people to participate. There naturally seemed nothing to stop further and further divisions of the thing, until finally, ten centuries later, there was this situation—a man on each neuron, each man responsible for an impulse cartridge that was fixed to both ends of that neuron—transmitting and receiving an impulse whenever it was programmed to do so.

Meanwhile there had been other Cassanders. After a while none of these suggested keeping the condition of proximity, since this would have so infuriated all his fellows who desired to have a piece of the brain. But it *was* pointed out by such Cassanders that the original topology of the brain, that is, the relative position and directional attitude of each neuron, could be maintained even while the brain was spread apart; and also it was urged by them that the neurons continue to be programmed to fire with the same chronology—that same temporal pattern—that their firings would have displayed when together in the brain.

But the suggestion about topology always brought a derisive response. A sample: "How should each of the neurons *know*, how should it register on a single neuron, where it is in relation to the others? In the usual case of an experience it is indeed necessary for the neurons, in order at all to get firing in that pattern that is or causes the experience, to be next to each other, actually causing the firing of one another, in a certain spatial relation to one another—but the original necessity of all these conditions is overcome by our techniques. For example, they are not necessary to the *bare fact* of the coming about of the experience that we are now causing to be had by the ancient gentleman whose neuron this is before me. And if we should bring these neurons together into a hookup with a mouth, then he would tell you of the experience personally."

Now as for the second part of the Cassanderish suggestion, the reader might suppose that after each successive partitioning of the brain, synchronization of the parts would have been consistently disregarded, so that eventually it would have been thought not to matter when each individual neuron was to be fired in relation to the firings of the other neurons—just as earlier the conditions had been disregarded when there were only two hemispheres to be fired. But somehow, perhaps because disregarding the timing and order of individual neuron firings would have reduced the art of programming to absurdity, the condition of order and timing had crept back, but without the Cassanderish reflectiveness. "Right" temporal order of firings is now merely *assumed* as somehow essential to bringing about a given experience by all those men standing before their baths and *waiting* for each properly programmed impulse to come to its neuron.

But now, ten centuries after the great project's birth, the world of these smug billions was about to explode. Two thinkers were responsible.

One of these, named Spoilar, had noticed one day that the neuron in his charge was getting a bit the worse for wear. Like any other man with a neuron in that state, he merely obtained another fresh one just like it and so replaced the particular one that had gotten worn—tossing the old one away. Thus he, like all the others, had violated the Cassandcrish condition of "neural identity"—a condition never taken very seriously even by Cassanders. It was realized that in the case of an ordinary brain the cellular metabolism was always replacing all the particular matter of any neuron with other particular matter, forming precisely the same kind of neuron. What this man had done was really no more than a speeding-up of this process. Besides, what if, as some Cassanders had implausibly argued, replacing one neuron by another just like it somehow resulted, when it was eventually done to all the neurons, in a new identity for the experiencer? There still would be an experiencer having the same experience every time the same patterns of firings were realized (and what it would mean to say he was a different experiencer was not clear at all, even to the Cassanders). So any shift in neural identity did not seem destructive of the fact of an experience coming about.

This fellow Spoilar, after he had replaced the neurons, resumed his waiting to watch his own neuron fire as part of an experience scheduled several hours later. Suddenly he heard a great crash and a great curse. Some fool had fallen against another man's bath, and it had broken totally on the floor when it fell. Well, this man whose bath had fallen would just have to miss out on any experi-

ences his neuron was to have been part of until the bath and neuron could be replaced. And Spoilar knew that the poor man had had one coming up soon.

The fellow whose bath had just broken walked up to Spoilar. He said, "Look, I've done favors for you. I'm going to have to miss the impulse coming up in five minutes—that experience will have to manage with one less neuron firing. But maybe you'd let me man yours coming up later. I just hate to miss all the thrills coming up today!"

Spoilar thought about the man's plea. Suddenly, a strange thought hit him. "Wasn't the neuron you manned the same sort as mine?"

"Yes."

"Well, look. I've just replaced my neuron with another like it, as we all do occasionally. Why don't we take my entire bath over to the old position of yours? Then won't it still be the same experience brought about in five minutes that it would have been with the old neuron if we fire this then, since this one is just like the old one? Surely the *bath's* identity means nothing. Anyway, then we can bring the bath back here and I can use the neuron for the experience it is scheduled to be used for later on. Wait a minute! We both believe the condition of topology is baloney. So why need we move the bath at all? Leave it here; fire it for yours; and then I'll fire it for mine. Both experiences must still come about. Wait a minute again! Then all we need do is fire this one neuron here in place of all the firings of all neurons just like it! Then there need be only one neuron of each type firing again and again and again to bring about all these experiences! But how would the neurons *know* even that they were repeating an impulse when they fired again and again? How would they *know* the relative order of their firings? Then we could have one neuron of each sort firing once and that would provide the physical realization of all patterns of impulses (a conclusion that would have been arrived at merely by consistently disregarding the necessity of synchronization in the progress from parted hemispheres to parted neurons). And couldn't these neurons simply be any of those naturally firing in any head? So what are we all doing here?

Then an even more desperate thought hit him, which he expressed thus: "But if all possible neural experience will be brought about simply in the firing once of one of each type of neuron, how can any experiencer believe that he is connected to anything more than this bare minimum of physical reality through the fact of his having *any* of his experiences? And so all this talk of heads and neurons in them, which is supposedly based on the true discovery of physical realities, is undermined entirely. There may be a true system of physical reality, but if it involves all this physiology we had been hoodwinked into believing, it provides so cheaply for so much experience that we can never know what is an actual experience of *it,* the physical reality. And so belief in such a system undermines itself. That is, unless it's tempered with Cassanderish principles."

The other thinker, coincidentally also named Spoilar, came to the same conclusion somewhat differently. He enjoyed stringing neurons. Once he got his own neuron, the one he was responsible for, in the middle of a long chain of like neurons and then recalled he was supposed to have it hooked up to the cartridge for a firing. Not wanting to destroy the chain, he simply hooked the two end neurons to the chain to the two poles of the impulse cartridge and adjusted the timing of the cartridge so that the impulse, traveling now through this whole chain, would reach his neuron at just the right time. Then he noticed that here a neuron, unlike one in usual experience, was quite comfortably participating in two patterns of firings at once — the chain's, which happened to have proximity and causal connection, and the programmed experience for which it had fired. After this Spoilar went about ridiculing "the condition of neural context." He'd say, "Boy, I could hook my neuron up with all those in your head, and if I could get it to fire just at the right time, I could get it into one of those programmed experiences as fine as if it were in my bath, on my cartridge."

Well, one day there was trouble. Some men who had not been allowed to join the project had come at night and so tampered with the baths that many of the neurons in Spoilar's vicinity had simply died. Standing before his own dead neuron, staring at the vast misery around him, he thought about how the day's first experience must turn out for the experiencer when so many neuron firings were to be missing from their physical realization. But as he looked about he suddenly took note of something else. Nearly everyone was stooping to inspect some damaged equipment just under his bath. Suddenly it seemed significant to Spoilar that next to every bath there was a head, each with its own billions of neurons of all sorts, with perhaps millions of each sort firing at any given moment. Proximity didn't matter. But then at any given moment of a particular pattern's being fired through the baths all the requisite activity was already going on anyway in the heads of the operators — in even *one* of those heads, where a loose sort of proximity condition was fulfilled too! Each head was bath and cartridge enough for any spread-brain's realization: "But," thought Spoilar, "the same kind of physical realization must exist for every experience of every brain — since all brains are spreadable. And that includes mine. But then all my beliefs are based on thoughts and experiences that might exist only as some such floating cloud. They are all suspect — including those that had convinced me of all this physiology in the first place. Unless Cassander is right, to some extent, then physiology reduces to absurdity. It undermines itself."

Such thinking killed the great project and with it the spread-brain. Men turned to other weird activities and to new conclusions about the nature of existence. But what these were is another story.

Further Questions

1. If the view of consciousness sketched in Zuboff's story is right, then there are conscious experiences that do not belong to any particular organism. Explain how that could be. Does this consequence reduce to absurdity the view of consciousness which implies it, or does it merely show that if the view of consciousness is correct, the world is an even stranger place than we thought? Give reasons for your answer.

2. How much weight, if any, should be given to common sense in deciding whether a theory is correct?

Further Readings

Block, Ned, ed. *Readings in Philosophy of Psychology,* 2 vols. Cambridge, MA: Harvard University Press, 1980, 1981. An excellent collection of papers, many of which focus on functionalism.

Dennett, Daniel. "Current Issues in the Philosophy of Mind." *American Philosophical Quarterly,* Vol. 15, 1978, pp. 249–261. An excellent account of the rise of functionalism, the theory of consciousness portrayed in the selection by Hofstadter.

58   What Is It Like to Be a Bat?

THOMAS NAGEL

Thomas Nagel taught philosophy for several years at Princeton University and now teaches at New York University. He writes primarily in the areas of philosophy of mind and ethics. In this selection, Nagel claims that the essence of consciousness is that "there is something it is like" to be a conscious being and nothing it is like to be a being that lacks consciousness. Thus, for instance, there is something it is like to be a bat, but nothing it is like to be a rock. Furthermore, we could know everything there is to know scientifically—from the "outside"—about how a conscious being, say, a bat, works, yet still not know what it is like to be that conscious being. Nagel argues that this implies the anti-reductionist view that there is more to consciousness than what can be captured in our current scientific theories.

Reading Questions

1. What is Nagel's understanding of subjectivity? What is the role of "point of view"?
2. Use an example of your own to illustrate what Nagel means by his claim that there are facts which we can neither state nor comprehend.
3. Can we have evidence for the truth of something we cannot understand? How does Nagel answer? What use does he make of his answer?
4. What is "objective phenomenology"?

CONSCIOUSNESS IS WHAT makes the mind-body problem really intractable. Perhaps that is why current discussions of the problem give it little attention or get it obviously wrong. The recent wave of reductionist euphoria has produced several analyses of mental phenomena and mental concepts designed to explain the possibility of some variety of materialism, psychophysical identification, or reduction. But the problems dealt with are those common to this type of reduction and other types, and what makes the mind-body problem unique, and unlike the water-H_2O problem or the Turing machine-IBM machine problem or the lightning-electrical discharge problem or the gene-DNA problem or the oak tree-hydrocarbon problem, is ignored.

Every reductionist has his favorite analogy from modern science. It is most unlikely that any of these unrelated examples of successful reduction

"What Is It Like to Be a Bat?" by Thomas Nagel, The Philosophical Review, *October 1974. Reprinted by permission of the author and* The Philosophical Review. *Footnotes deleted.*

will shed light on the relation of mind to brain. But philosophers share the general human weakness for explanations of what is incomprehensible in terms suited for what is familiar and well understood, though entirely different. This has led to the acceptance of implausible accounts of the mental largely because they would permit familiar kinds of reduction. I shall try to explain why the usual examples do not help us to understand the relation between mind and body—why, indeed, we have at present no conception of what an explanation of the physical nature of a mental phenomenon would be. Without consciousness the mind-body problem would be much less interesting. With consciousness it seems hopeless. The most important and characteristic feature of conscious mental phenomena is very poorly understood. Most reductionist theories do not even try to explain it. And careful examination will show that no currently available concept of reduction is applicable to it. Perhaps a new theoretical form can be devised for the purpose, but such a solution, if it exists, lies in the distinct intellectual future.

Conscious experience is a widespread phenomenon. It occurs at many levels of animal life, though we cannot be sure of its presence in the simpler organisms, and it is very difficult to say in general what provides evidence of it. (Some extremists have been prepared to deny it even of mammals other than man.) No doubt it occurs in countless forms totally unimaginable to us, on other planets in other solar systems throughout the universe. But no matter how the form may vary, the fact that an organism has conscious experience *at all* means, basically, that there is something it is like to *be* that organism. There may be further implications about the form of the experience; there may even (though I doubt it) be implications about the behavior of the organism. But fundamentally an organism has conscious mental states if and only if there is something that it is like to *be* that organism—something it is like *for* the organism.

We may call this the subjective character of experience. It is not captured by any of the familiar, recently devised reductive analyses of the mental, for all of them are logically compatible with its absence. It is not analyzable in terms of any explanatory system of functional states, or intentional states, since these could be ascribed to robots or automata that behaved like people though they ex-

perienced nothing. It is not analyzable in terms of the causal role of experiences in relation to typical human behavior—for similar reasons. I do not deny that conscious mental states and events cause behavior, nor that they may be given functional characterizations. I deny only that this kind of thing exhausts their analysis. Any reductionist program has to be based on an analysis of what is to be reduced. If the analysis leaves something out, the problem will be falsely posed. It is useless to base the defense of materialism on any analysis of mental phenomena that fails to deal explicitly with their subjective character. For there is no reason to suppose that a reduction which seems plausible when no attempt is made to account for consciousness can be extended to include consciousness. Without some idea, therefore, of what the subjective character of experience is, we cannot know what is required of a physicalist theory.

While an account of the physical basis of mind must explain many things, this appears to be the most difficult. It is impossible to exclude the phenomenological features of experience from a reduction in the same way that one excludes the phenomenal features of an ordinary substance from a physical or chemical reduction of it—namely, by explaining them as effects on the minds of human observers. If physicalism is to be defended, the phenomenological features must themselves be given a physical account. But when we examine their subjective character it seems that such a result is impossible. The reason is that every subjective phenomenon is essentially connected with a single point of view, and it seems inevitable that an objective, physical theory will abandon that point of view.

Let me first try to state the issue somewhat more fully than by referring to the relation between the subjective and the objective, or between the *pour-soi* and the *en-soi*. This is far from easy. Facts about what it is like to be an *X* are very peculiar, so peculiar that some may be inclined to doubt their reality, or the significance of claims about them. To illustrate the connection between subjectivity and a point of view, and to make evident the importance of subjective features, it will help to explore the matter in relation to an example that brings out clearly the divergence between the two types of conception, subjective and objective.

I assume we all believe that bats have experience. After all, they are mammals, and there is no more doubt that they have experience than that mice or pigeons or whales have experience. I have chosen bats instead of wasps or flounders because if one travels too far down the phylogenetic tree, people gradually shed their faith that there is experience there at all. Bats, although more closely related to us than those other species, nevertheless present a range of activity and a sensory apparatus so different from ours that the problem I want to pose is exceptionally vivid (though it certainly could be raised with other species). Even without the benefit of philosophical reflection, anyone who has spent some time in an enclosed space with an excited bat knows what it is to encounter a fundamentally *alien* form of life.

I have said that the essence of the belief that bats have experience is that there is something that it is like to be a bat. Now we know that most bats (the microchiroptera, to be precise) perceive the external world primarily by sonar, or echo-location, detecting the reflections, from objects within range, of their own rapid, subtly modulated, high-frequency shrieks. Their brains are designed to correlate the outgoing impulses with the subsequent echoes, and the information thus acquired enables bats to make precise discriminations of distance, size, shape, motion, and texture comparable to those we make by vision. But bat sonar, though clearly a form of perception, is not similar in its operation to any sense that we possess, and there is no reason to suppose that it is subjectively like anything we can experience or imagine. This appears to create difficulties for the notion of what it is like to be a bat. We must consider whether any method will permit us to extrapolate to the inner life of the bat from our own case, and if not, what alternative methods there may be for understanding the notion.

Our own experience provides the basic material for our imagination, whose range is therefore limited. It will not help to try to imagine that one has webbing on one's arms, which enables one to fly around at dusk and dawn catching insects in one's mouth; that one has very poor vision, and perceives the surrounding world by a system of reflected high-frequency sound signals; and that one spends the day hanging upside down by one's feet in an attic. In so far as I can imagine this (which is not very far), it tells me only what it would be like for *me* to behave as a bat behaves. But that is not the ques-

tion. I want to know what it is like for a *bat* to be a bat. Yet if I try to imagine this, I am restricted to the resources of my own mind, and those resources are inadequate to the task. I cannot perform it either by imagining additions to my present experience, or by imagining segments gradually subtracted from it, or by imagining some combination of additions, subtractions, and modifications.

To the extent that I could look and behave like a wasp or a bat without changing my fundamental structure, my experiences would not be anything like the experiences of those animals. On the other hand, it is doubtful that any meaning can be attached to the supposition that I should possess the internal neurophysiological constitution of a bat. Even if I could by gradual degrees be transformed into a bat, nothing in my present constitution enables me to imagine what the experiences of such a future stage of myself thus metamorphosed would be like. The best evidence would come from the experiences of bats, if we only knew what they were like.

So if extrapolation from our own case is involved in the idea of what it is like to be a bat, the extrapolation must be incompletable. We cannot form more than a schematic conception of what it *is* like. For example, we may ascribe general *types* of experience on the basis of the animal's structure and behavior. Thus we describe bat sonar as a form of three-dimensional forward perception; we believe that bats feel some versions of pain, fear, hunger, and lust, and that they have other, more familiar types of perception besides sonar. But we believe that those experiences also have in each case a specific subjective character, which it is beyond our ability to conceive. And if there is conscious life elsewhere in the universe, it is likely that some of it will not be describable even in the most general experiential terms available to us. (The problem is not confined to exotic cases, however, for it exists between one person and another. The subjective character of the experience of a person deaf and blind from birth is not accessible to me, for example, nor presumably is mine to him. This does not prevent us each from believing that the other's experience has such a subjective character.)

If anyone is inclined to deny that we can believe in the existence of facts like this whose exact nature we cannot possibly conceive, he should reflect that in contemplating the bats we are in much the same position that intelligent bats or Martians would occupy if they tried to form a conception of what it was like to be us. The structure of their own minds might make it impossible for them to succeed, but we know they would be wrong to conclude that there is not anything precise that it is like to be us: that only certain general types of mental state could be ascribed to us (perhaps perception and appetite would be concepts common to us both; perhaps not). We know they would be wrong to draw such a skeptical conclusion because we know what it is like to be us. And we know that while it includes an enormous amount of variation and complexity, and while we do not possess the vocabulary to describe it adequately, its subjective character is highly specific, and in some respects describable in terms that can be understood only by creatures like us. The fact that we cannot expect ever to accommodate in our language a detailed description of Martian or bat phenomenology should not lead us to dismiss as meaningless the claim that bats and Martians have experiences fully comparable in richness of detail to our own. It would be fine if someone were to develop concepts and a theory that enabled us to think about those things; but such an understanding may be permanently denied to us by the limits of our nature. And to deny the reality or logical significance of what we can never describe or understand is the crudest form of cognitive dissonance.

This brings us to the edge of a topic that requires much more discussion than I can give it here: namely, the relation between facts on the one hand and conceptual schemes or systems of representation on the other. My realism about the subjective domain in all its forms implies a belief in the existence of facts beyond the reach of human concepts. Certainly it is possible for a human being to believe that there are facts which humans never *will* possess the requisite concepts to represent or comprehend. Indeed, it would be foolish to doubt this, given the finiteness of humanity's expectations. After all, there would have been transfinite numbers even if everyone had been wiped out by the Black Death before Cantor discovered them. But one might also believe that there are facts which *could* not ever be represented or comprehended by human beings, even if the species lasted forever—simply

because our structure does not permit us to operate with concepts of the requisite type. This impossibility might even be observed by other beings, but it is not clear that the existence of such beings, or the possibility of their existence, is a precondition of the significance of the hypothesis that there are humanly inaccessible facts. (After all, the nature of beings with access to humanly inaccessible facts is presumably itself a humanly inaccessible fact.) Reflection on what it is like to be a bat seems to lead us, therefore, to the conclusion that there are facts that do not consist in the truth of propositions expressible in a human language. We can be compelled to recognize the existence of such facts without being able to state or comprehend them.

I shall not pursue this subject, however. Its bearing on the topic before us (namely, the mind-body problem) is that it enables us to make a general observation about the subjective character of experience. Whatever may be the status of facts about what it is like to be a human being, or a bat, or a Martian, these appear to be facts that embody a particular point of view.

I am not adverting here to the alleged privacy of experience to its possessor. The point of view in question is not one accessible only to a single individual. Rather it is a *type*. It is often possible to take up a point of view other than one's own, so the comprehension of such facts is not limited to one's own case. There is a sense in which phenomenological facts are perfectly objective: one person can know or say of another what the quality of the other's experience is. They are subjective, however, in the sense that even this objective ascription of experience is possible only for someone sufficiently similar to the object of ascription to be able to adopt his point of view—to understand the ascription in the first person as well as in the third, so to speak. The more different from oneself the other experiencer is, the less success one can expect with this enterprise. In our own case we occupy the relevant point of view, but we will have as much difficulty understanding our own experience properly if we approach it from another point of view as we would if we tried to understand the experience of another species without taking up *its* point of view.

This bears directly on the mind-body problem. For if the facts of experience—facts about what it is like *for* the experiencing organism—are accessible only from one point of view, then it is a mystery how the true character of experiences could be revealed in the physical operation of that organism. The latter is a domain of objective facts *par excellence*—the kind that can be observed and understood from many points of view and by individuals with differing perceptual systems. There are no comparable imaginative obstacles to the acquisition of knowledge about bat neurophysiology by human scientists, and intelligent bats or Martians might learn more about the human brain than we ever will.

This is not by itself an argument against reduction. A Martian scientist with no understanding of visual perception could understand the rainbow, or lightning, or clouds as physical phenomena, though he would never be able to understand the human concepts of rainbow, lightning, or cloud, or the place these things occupy in our phenomenal world. The objective nature of the things picked out by these concepts could be apprehended by him because, although the concepts themselves are connected with a particular point of view and a particular visual phenomenology, the things apprehended from that point of view are not: they are observable from the point of view but external to it; hence they can be comprehended from other points of view also, either by the same organisms or by others. Lightning has an objective character that is not exhausted by its visual appearance, and this can be investigated by a Martian without vision. To be precise, it has a *more* objective character than is revealed in its visual appearance. In speaking of the move from subjective to objective characterization, I wish to remain noncommittal about the existence of an end point, the completely objective intrinsic nature of the thing, which one might or might not be able to reach. It may be more accurate to think of objectivity as a direction in which the understanding can travel. And in understanding a phenomenon like lightning, it is legitimate to go as far away as one can from a strictly human viewpoint.

In the case of experience, on the other hand, the connection with a particular point of view seems much closer. It is difficult to understand what could be meant by the *objective* character of an experience, apart from the particular point of view from which its subject apprehends it. After all,

what would be left of what it was like to be a bat if one removed the viewpoint of the bat? But if experience does not have, in addition to its subjective character, an objective nature that can be apprehended from many different points of view, then how can it be supposed that a Martian investigating my brain might be observing physical processes which were my mental processes (as he might observe physical processes which were bolts of lightning), only from a different point of view? How, for that matter, could a human physiologist observe them from another point of view.

We appear to be faced with a general difficulty about psycho-physical reduction. In other areas the process of reduction is a move in the direction of greater objectivity, toward a more accurate view of the real nature of things. This is accomplished by reducing our dependence on individual or species-specific points of view toward the object of investigation. We describe it not in terms of the impressions it makes on our senses, but in terms of its more general effects and of properties detectable by means other than the human senses. The less it depends on a specifically human viewpoint, the more objective is our description. It is possible to follow this path because although the concepts and ideas we employ in thinking about the external world are initially applied from a point of view that involves our perceptual apparatus, they are used by us to refer to things beyond themselves—toward which we *have* the phenomenal point of view. Therefore we can abandon it in favor of another, and still be thinking about the same things.

Experience itself, however, does not seem to fit the pattern. The idea of moving from appearance to reality seems to make no sense here. What is the analogue in this case to pursuing a more objective understanding of the same phenomena by abandoning the initial subjective viewpoint toward them in favor of another that is more objective but concerns the same thing? Certainly it *appears* unlikely that we will get closer to the real nature of human experience by leaving behind the particularity of our human point of view and striving for a description in terms accessible to beings that could not imagine what it was like to be us. If the subjective character of experience is fully comprehensible only from one point of view, then any shift to greater objectivity—that is, less attachment to a specific viewpoint—does not take us nearer to the real nature of the phenomenon: it takes us farther away from it.

In a sense, the seeds of this objection to the reducibility of experience are already detectable in successful cases of reduction; for in discovering sound to be, in reality, a wave phenomenon in air or other media, we leave behind one viewpoint to take up another, and the auditory, human or animal viewpoint that we leave behind remains unreduced. Members of radically different species may both understand the same physical events in objective terms, and this does not require that they understand the phenomenal forms in which those events appear to the senses of members of the other species. Thus it is a condition of their referring to a common reality that their more particular viewpoints are not part of the common reality that they both apprehend. The reduction can succeed only if the species-specific viewpoint is omitted from what is to be reduced.

But while we are right to leave this point of view aside in seeking a fuller understanding of the external world, we cannot ignore it permanently, since it is the essence of the internal world, and not merely a point of view on it. Most of the neobehaviorism of recent philosophical psychology results from the effort to substitute an objective concept of mind for the real thing, in order to have nothing left over which cannot be reduced. If we acknowledge that a physical theory of mind must account for the subjective character of experience, we must admit that no presently available conception gives us a clue how this could be done. The problem is unique. If mental processes are indeed physical processes, then there is something it is like, intrinsically, to undergo certain physical processes. What it is for such a thing to be the case remains a mystery.

What moral should be drawn from these reflections, and what should be done next? It would be a mistake to conclude that physicalism must be false. Nothing is proved by the inadequacy of physicalist hypotheses that assume a faulty objective analysis of mind. It would be truer to say that physicalism is a position we cannot understand because we do not at present have any conception of how it might be true. Perhaps it will be thought unreasonable to require such a conception as a condition of understanding. After all, it might be said, the meaning of physicalism is clear enough: mental states are states of the body; mental events are physical events. We do not know *which* physical states and events they are, but that should not prevent us from understanding the hypothesis. What could be clearer than the words "is" and "are"?

But I believe it is precisely this apparent clarity of the word "is" that is deceptive. Usually, when we are told that X is Y we know *how* it is supposed to be true, but that depends on a conceptual or theoretical background and is not conveyed by the "is" alone. We know how both "X" and "Y" refer, and the kinds of things to which they refer, and we have a rough idea how the two referential paths might converge on a single thing, be it an object, a person, a process, an event, or whatever. But when the two terms of the identification are very disparate it may not be so clear how it could be true. We may not have even a rough idea of how the two referential paths could converge, or what kind of things they might converge on, and a theoretical framework may have to be supplied to enable us to understand this. Without the framework, an air of mysticism surrounds the identification.

This explains the magical flavor of popular presentations of fundamental scientific discoveries, given out as propositions to which one must subscribe without really understanding them. For example, people are now told at an early age that all matter is really energy. But despite the fact that they know what "is" means most of them never form a conception of what makes this claim true, because they lack the theoretical background.

At the present time the status of physicalism is similar to that which the hypothesis that matter is energy would have had if uttered by a pre-Socratic philosopher. We do not have the beginnings of a conception of how it might be true. In order to understand the hypothesis that a mental event is a physical event, we require more than an understanding of the word "is." The idea of how a mental and a physical term might refer to the same thing is lacking, and the usual analogies with theoretical identification in other fields fail to supply it. They fail because if we construe the reference of mental terms to physical events on the usual model, we either get a reappearance of separate subjective events as the effects through which mental reference to physical events is secured, or else we get a false account of how mental terms refer (for example, a causal behaviorist one).

Strangely enough, we may have evidence for the truth of something we cannot really understand. Suppose a caterpillar is locked in a sterile safe by someone unfamiliar with insect metamorphosis, and weeks later the safe is reopened, revealing a butterfly. If the person knows that the safe has been shut the whole time, he has reason to believe that the butterfly is or was once the caterpillar, without having any idea in what sense this might be so. (One possibility is that the caterpillar contained a tiny winged parasite that devoured it and grew into the butterfly.)

It is conceivable that we are in such a position with regard to physicalism. Donald Davidson has argued that if mental events have physical causes and effects, they must have physical descriptions. He holds that we have reason to believe this even though we do not — and in fact *could* not — have a general psychophysical theory. His argument applies to intentional mental events, but I think we also have some reason to believe that sensations are physical processes, without being in a position to understand how. Davidson's position is that certain physical events have irreducibly mental properties, and perhaps some view describable in this way is correct. But nothing of which we can now form a conception corresponds to it; nor have we any idea what a theory would be like that enabled us to conceive of it.

Very little work has been done on the basic question (from which mention of the brain can be entirely omitted) whether any sense can be made of experiences' having an objective character at all. Does it make sense, in other words, to ask what my experiences are *really* like, as opposed to how they appear to me? We cannot genuinely understand the hypothesis that their nature is captured in a physical description unless we understand the more fundamental idea that they *have* an objective nature (or that objective processes can have a subjective nature).

I should like to close with a speculative proposal. It may be possible to approach the gap between subjective and objective from another direction. Setting aside temporarily the relation between the mind and the brain, we can pursue a more objective understanding of the mental in its own right. At present we are completely unequipped to think about the subjective character of experience without relying on the imagination — without taking up the point of view of the experiential subject. This should be regarded as a challenge to form new concepts and devise a new method — an objective phenomenology not dependent on empathy or the imagination. Though presumably it would not capture everything, its goal would be to describe, at least in part, the subjective character of experiences in a form comprehensible to beings incapable of having those experiences.

We would have to develop such a phenomenology to describe the sonar experiences of bats; but it would also be possible to begin with humans. One might try, for example, to develop concepts that could be used to explain to a person blind from birth what it was like to see. One would reach a blank wall eventually, but it should be possible to devise a method of expressing in objective terms much more than we can at present, and with much greater precision. The loose intermodal analogies — for example, "Red is like the sound of a trumpet" — which crop up in discussions of this subject are of little use. That should be clear to anyone who has both heard a trumpet and seen red. But structural features of perception might be more accessible to objective description, even though something would be left out. And concepts alternative to those we learn in the first person may enable us to arrive at a kind of understanding even of our own experience which is denied us by the very ease of description and lack of distance that subjective concepts afford.

Apart from its own interest, a phenomenology that is in this sense objective may permit questions about the physical basis of experience to assume a more intelligible form. Aspects of subjective experience that admitted this kind of objective description might be better candidates for objective explanations of a more familiar sort. But whether or not this guess is correct, it seems unlikely that any physical theory of mind can be contemplated until more thought has been given to the general problem of subjective and objective. Otherwise we cannot even pose the mind-body problem without sidestepping it.

Further Questions

1. Could an android have a point of view? Could it have one even if it were not conscious?
2. Is it possible that there is an experiential way of understanding things that differs from the scientific way of understanding things even though the experiential way of understanding does not imply the existence of any extra things (psychic events or properties) than those implied by our best scientific theories? In other words, is it possible that experiential *understanding* cannot be reduced to scientific understanding even though an experiencing *organism* is nothing more than a certain kind of wholly physical mechanism?

Further Readings

Morton, Adam. *Frames of Mind*. New York: Oxford University Press, 1980. On subjectivity.
Nagel, Thomas. *The View from Nowhere*. New York: Oxford University Press, 1986. Nagel's latest thoughts on subjectivity.

Epiphenomenal Qualia   59

FRANK JACKSON

Frank Jackson teaches philosophy at Monash University in Australia and writes primarily in the area of philosophy of mind. A mind-body dualist, he is one of the foremost philosophical opponents of the idea that mental phenomena can be reduced to physical phenomena. In this selection, Jackson provides vivid and interesting examples that seem to refute physicalism. In one of these examples, Mary, who knows all there is to know scientifically about color perception but has been confined all her life to a black-and-white environment, finally emerges to experience the full range of colors. Jackson claims that what she learns through her new experiences shows that physicalism is false.

Reading Questions

1. Do the examples of Fred and Mary make the same point or different points? What is the point of each story?
2. Can we learn things from experience that we cannot learn from science? If so, does this count against physicalism?

. . . I AM WHAT IS SOMETIMES KNOWN as a "qualia freak." I think that there are certain features of the bodily sensations especially, but also of certain perceptual experiences, which no amount of purely physical information includes. Tell me everything physical there is to tell about what is going on in a living brain, the kind of states, their functional role, their relation to what goes on at

From Frank Jackson, "Epiphenomenal Qualia," Philosophical Quarterly, *Vol. 32, 1982, pp. 127–136.*
Reprinted by permission of the publisher.

other times and in other brains, and so on and so forth, and be I as clever as can be in fitting it all together, you won't have told me about the hurtfulness of pains, the itchiness of itches, pangs of jealousy, or about the characteristic experience of tasting a lemon, smelling a rose, hearing a loud noise or seeing the sky. . . .

THE KNOWLEDGE ARGUMENT FOR QUALIA

People vary considerably in their ability to discriminate colours. Suppose that in an experiment to catalogue this variation Fred is discovered. Fred has better colour vision than anyone else on record; he makes every discrimination that anyone has ever made, and moreover he makes one that we cannot even begin to make. Show him a batch of ripe tomatoes and he sorts them into two roughly equal groups and does so with complete consistency. That is, if you blindfold him, shuffle the tomatoes up, and then remove the blindfold and ask him to sort them out again, he sorts them into exactly the same two groups.

We ask Fred how he does it. He explains that all ripe tomatoes do not look the same colour to him, and in fact that this is true of a great many objects that we classify together as red. He sees two colours where we see one, and he has in consequence developed for his own use two words "red$_1$" and "red$_2$" to mark the difference. Perhaps he tells us that he has often tried to teach the difference between red$_1$ and red$_2$ to his friends but has got nowhere and has concluded that the rest of the world is red$_1$-red$_2$ colour-blind—or perhaps he has had partial success with his children, it doesn't matter. In any case he explains to us that it would be quite wrong to think that because "red" appears in both "red$_1$" and "red$_2$" that the two colours are shades of the one colour. He only uses the common term "red" to fit more easily into our restricted usage. To him red$_1$ and red$_2$ are as different from each other and all the other colours as yellow is from blue. And his discriminatory behavior bears this out: he sorts red$_1$ from red$_2$ tomatoes with the greatest of ease in a wide variety of viewing circumstances. Moreover, an investigation of the physiological basis of Fred's exceptional ability reveals that Fred's optical system is able to separate out two groups of wavelengths in the red spectrum as sharply as we are able to sort out yellow from blue.

I think that we should admit that Fred can see, really see, at least one more colour than we can; red$_1$ is a different colour from red$_2$. We are to Fred as a totally red-green colour-blind person is to us. H. G. Wells' story "The Country of the Blind" is about a sighted person in a totally blind community. This person never manages to convince them that he can see, that he has an extra sense. They ridicule this sense as quite inconceivable, and treat his capacity to avoid falling into ditches, to win fights and so on as precisely that capacity and nothing more. We would be making their mistake if we refused to allow that Fred can see one more colour than we can.

What kind of experience does Fred have when he sees red$_1$ and red$_2$? What is the new colour or colours like? We would dearly like to know but do not; and it seems that no amount of physical information about Fred's brain and optical system tells us. We find out perhaps that Fred's cones respond differently to certain light waves in the red section of the spectrum that makes no difference to ours (or perhaps he has an extra cone) and that this leads in Fred to a wider range of those brain states responsible for visual discriminatory behaviour. But none of this tells us what we really want to know about his colour experience. There is something about it we don't know. But we know, we may suppose, everything about Fred's body, his behaviour and dispositions to behaviour and about his internal physiology, and everything about his history and relation to others that can be given in physical accounts of persons. We have all the physical information. Therefore, knowing all this is *not* knowing everything about Fred. It follows that Physicalism leaves something out.

To reinforce this conclusion, imagine that as a result of our investigations into the internal workings of Fred we find out how to make everyone's physiology like Fred's in the relevant respects; or perhaps Fred donates his body to science and on his death we are able to transplant his optical system into someone else—again the fine detail doesn't matter. The important point is that such a happening would create enormous interest. People would say, "At last we will know what it is like to see the extra colour, at last we will know how Fred has differed from us in the way he has struggled to tell us about for so long." Then it cannot be that we knew all along all about Fred. But *ex hypothesi* we did know all along everything about Fred that features in the physicalist scheme; hence the physicalist scheme leaves something out.

Put it this way. *After* the operation, we will know *more* about Fred and especially about his colour experiences. But beforehand we had all the physical information we could desire about his body and brain, and indeed everything that has ever featured in physicalist accounts of mind and consciousness. Hence there is more to know than all that. Hence Physicalism is incomplete.

Fred and the new colour(s) are of course essentially rhetorical devices. The same point can be made with normal people and familiar colours. Mary is a brilliant scientist who is, for whatever reason, forced to investigate the world from a black and white room *via* a black and white television monitor. She specialises in the neurophysiology of vision and acquires, let us suppose, all the physical information there is to obtain about what goes on when we see ripe tomatoes, or the sky, and use terms like "red," "blue," and so on. She discovers, for example, just which wavelength combinations from the sky stimulate the retina, and exactly how this produces *via* the central nervous system the contraction of the vocal chords and expulsion of air from the lungs that results in the uttering of the sentence "The sky is blue." (It can hardly be denied that it is in principle possible to obtain all this physical information from black and white television, otherwise the Open University would *of necessity* need to use colour television.)

What will happen when Mary is released from her black and white room or is given a colour television monitor? Will she *learn* anything or not? It seems just obvious that she will learn something about the world and our visual experience of it. But then it is inescapable that her previous knowledge was incomplete. But she had *all* the physical information. *Ergo* there is more to have than that, and Physicalism is false. . . .

Further Questions

1. Does either of Jackson's examples show that science is incomplete? If so, in what ways is it incomplete?
2. Does either of Jackson's examples show that physicalism is false? If so, how? If not, why not?

Further Readings

Campbell, Keith. *Body and Mind*. New York: Doubleday, 1970. An excellent introduction to the traditional issues.
Churchland, Paul. *Matter and Consciousness*. Cambridge, MA: MIT Press, Revised Edition, 1988. A beautifully written, physiologically informed argument for reductionism.

60 Reduction, Qualia, and the Direct Introspection of Brain States

PAUL CHURCHLAND

Paul Churchland teaches philosophy at the University of California at San Diego and writes primarily in the area of philosophy of mind. He is one of the leading spokesmen for physicalism, the view that mental states can be reduced to physical states—the view that Thomas Nagel and Frank Jackson attacked in the preceding selections. In this selection, Churchland explains how we should understand physicalism and then why, in his opinion, certain well-known criticisms of it, including Nagel's and Jackson's, ultimately fail.

Reading Questions

1. Churchland distinguishes several different versions of the reductionist thesis. In your own words, explain the differences among them.
2. In which versions of reductionism does Churchland believe?
3. Why does Churchland think that the antireductionist arguments of Nagel and Jackson fail? Do you agree?
4. What is "intertheoretic reduction"? Why does Churchland think the classical account of it is mistaken? How does he think it can be repaired?
5. What is the difference between *theoretical* and *perceptual* change?
6. How does Churchland respond to Thomas Nagel's arguments?
7. What does Churchland think are the two shortcomings of Jackson's knowledge argument?

DO THE PHENOMENOLOGICAL or qualitative features of our sensations constitute a permanent barrier to the reductive aspirations of any materialistic neuroscience? I here argue that they do not. . . .

If we are to deal sensibly with the issues here at stake, we must approach them with a general theory of scientific reduction already in hand, a theory motivated by and adequate to the many instances and varieties of interconceptual reduction displayed *elsewhere* in our scientific history. With an independently based account of the nature and grounds of intertheoretic reduction, we can approach the specific case of subjective qualia, free from the myopia that results from trying to divine the proper conditions on reduction by simply staring long and hard at the problematic case at issue.

I. INTERTHEORETIC REDUCTION

We may begin by remarking that the classical account of intertheoretic reduction now appears to be importantly mistaken, though the repairs necessary are quickly and cleanly made. Suppressing niceties, we may state the original account as follows. A new and more comprehensive theory *reduces* an older theory just in case the new theory, when conjoined with appropriate correspondence rules, logically entails the principles of the older theory. (The point of the correspondence rules, or "bridge laws," is to connect the disparate ontologies of the two theories: often these are expressed as identity statements, such as *Temperature = $mv^2/3k$.*) Schematically,

Paul Churchland, "Reduction, Qualia, and the Direct Introspection of Brain States," LXXXII:1 (January 1985), pp. 8–28. Used by permission of The Journal of Philosophy *and the author. Footnotes deleted.*

T_N & (Correspondence Rules)

logically entails

$$T_O$$

Difficulties with this view begin with the observation that most reduced theories turn out to be, strictly speaking and in a variety of respects, *false*. (Real gases don't really obey $PV = \mu RT$, as in classical thermodynamics; the planets don't really move in ellipses, as in Keplerian astronomy; the acceleration of falling bodies isn't really uniform, as in Galilean dynamics; etc.) If reduction is *de*duction, modus tollens would thus require that the premises of the new reducing theories (statistical thermodynamics in the first case, Newtonian dynamics in the second and third) be somehow false as well, in contradiction to their assumed truth.

This complaint can be temporarily deflected by pointing out that the premises of a reduction must often include not just the new reducing theory but also some limiting assumptions or counterfactual boundary conditions (such as that the molecules of a gas enjoy only mechanical energy, or that the mass of the planets is negligible compared to the sun's, or that the distance any body falls is negligibly different from zero). Falsity in the reducing premises can thus be conceded, since it is safely confined to those limiting or counterfactual assumptions.

This defense will not deal with all cases of falsity, however, since in some cases the reduced theory is so radically false that some or all of its ontology must be rejected entirely, and the "correspondence rules" connecting that ontology to the newer ontology therefore display a problematic status. Newly conceived features cannot be identical with, nor even nomically connected with, old features, if the old features are illusory and uninstantiated. For example, relativistic mass is not identical with Newtonian mass, nor even coextensive with it, even at low velocities. Nevertheless, the reduction of Newtonian by Einsteinian mechanics is a paradigm of a successful reduction. For a second example, neither is caloric-fluid-pressure identical with, nor even coextensive with, mean molecular kinetic energy. But an overtly *fluid* thermodynamics (i.e., one committed to the existence of caloric) still finds a moderately impressive reduction within statistical thermodynamics. In sum, even theories with a *nonexistent* ontology can enjoy reduction, and this fact is problematic on the traditional account at issue.

What cases like these invite us to give up is the idea that what gets *de*duced in a reduction is the theory to be *re*duced. . . .

The point of a reduction, according to this view, is to show that the new or more comprehensive theory contains explanatory and predictive resources that parallel, to a relevant degree of exactness, the explanatory and predictive resources of the reduced theory. . . .

. . . it is to be expected that existing conceptual frameworks will eventually be reduced or displaced by new and better ones, and those in turn by frameworks better still; for who will be so brash as to assert that the feeble conceptual achievements of our adolescent species comprise an exhaustive account of anything at all? If we put aside this conceit, then the only alternatives to intertheoretic reduction are epistemic stagnation or the outright elimination of old frameworks as wholly false and illusory.

II. THEORETICAL CHANGE AND PERCEPTUAL CHANGE

Esoteric properties and arcane theoretical frameworks are not the only things that occasionally enjoy intertheoretic reduction. Observable properties and common-sense conceptual frameworks can also enjoy smooth reduction. Thus, being a middle-A sound is identical with being an oscillation in air pressure at 440 hz; being red is identical with having a certain triplet of electromagnetic reflectance efficiencies; being warm is identical with having a certain mean level of microscopically embodied energies, and so forth.

Moreover, the relevant reducing theory is capable of replacing the old framework not just in contexts of calculation and inference. *It should be appreciated that the reducing theory can displace the old framework in all its observational contexts as well.* Given the reality of the property identities just listed, it is quite open to us to begin framing our spontaneous perceptual reports in the language of the more sophisticated reducing theory. It is even desirable that we begin doing this, since the new vocabulary observes distinctions that are in fact within the discriminatory reach of our native perceptual systems, though those objective distinctions go unmarked and unnoticed from within the old framework. We can thus make more penetrating use of our native perceptual equipment. Such displacement is also desirable for a second reason: the greater inferential or computational power of the new conceptual framework. We can thus make better inferential *use* of our new perceptual judgments than we made of our old ones.

It is difficult to convey in words the vastness of such perceptual transformations and the naturalness of the new conceptual regime, once established. A nonscientific example may help to get the initial point across.

Consider the enormous increase in discriminatory skill that spans the gap between an untrained child's auditory apprehension of a symphony and the same person's apprehension of the same symphony forty years later, heard in his capacity as conductor of the orchestra performing it. What was before a seamless voice is now a mosaic of distinguishable elements. What was before a dimly apprehended tune is now a rationally structured sequence of distinguishable and identifiable chords supporting an appropriately related melody line. The matured musician hears an entire world of structured detail, concerning which the child is both dumb and deaf.

Other modalities provide comparable examples. Consider the practiced and chemically sophisticated wine taster, for whom the "red wine" classification used by most of us divides into a network of fifteen or twenty distinguishable elements: ethanol, glycol, fructose, sucrose, tannin, acid, carbon dioxide, and so forth, whose relative concentrations he can estimate with accuracy.

Or consider the astronomer, for whom the speckled black dome of her youth has become a visible abyss, scattered nearby planets, yellow dwarf stars, blue and red giants, distant globular clusters, and even a remote galaxy or two, all discriminable as such and locatable in three-dimensional space with her unaided (repeat: *unaided*) eye.

In each of these cases, what is finally mastered is a conceptual framework—whether musical, chemical, or astronomical—a framework that embodies far more wisdom about the relevant sensory domain than is immediately apparent to untutored discrimination. Such frameworks are characteristically a cultural heritage, pieced together over many generations, and their mastery supplies a richness and penetration to our sensory lives that would be impossible in their absence.

Our *introspective* lives are already the extensive beneficiaries of this phenomenon. The introspective discriminations we make are for the most part learned; they are acquired with practice and experience, often quite slowly. And the specific discriminations we learn to make are those it is useful for us to make. Generally, those are the discriminations that others are already making, the discriminations embodied in the psychological vocabulary of the language we learn. The conceptual framework for psychological states that is embedded in ordinary language is a modestly sophisticated theoretical achievement in its own right, and it shapes our matured introspection profoundly. If it embodied substantially *less* wisdom in its categories and connecting generalizations, our introspective apprehension of our internal states and activities would be much diminished, though our native discriminatory mechanisms remain the same. Correlatively, if folk psychology embodied substantially *more* wisdom about our inner nature than it actually does, our introspective discrimination and recognition could be very much *greater* than it is, though our native discriminatory mechanisms remain unchanged.

This brings me to the central positive suggestion of this paper. Consider now the possibility of learning to describe, conceive, and introspectively apprehend the teeming intricacies of our inner lives within the conceptual framework of a matured neuroscience, a neuroscience that successfully reduces, either smoothly or roughly, our common-sense folk psychology. Suppose we trained our native mechanisms to make a new and more detailed set of discriminations, a set that corresponded not to the primitive psychological taxonomy of ordinary language, but to some more penetrating taxonomy of states drawn from a completed neuroscience. And suppose we trained ourselves to respond to that reconfigured discriminative activity with judgments that were framed, as a matter of course, in the appropriate concepts from neuroscience.

If the examples of the symphony conductor (who can hear the A*m*7 chords), the oenologist (who can see and taste the glycol), and the astronomer (who can see the temperature of a blue giant star) provide a fair parallel, then the enhancement in our introspective vision could approximate a revelation. Dopamine levels in the limbic system, the spiking frequencies in specific neural pathways, resonances in the *n*th layer of the occipital cortex, inhibitory feedback to the lateral geniculate nucleus, and countless other neurophysical niceties could be moved into the objective focus of our introspective discrimination, just as G*m*7 chords and A*dim* chords are moved into the objective focus of a trained musician's auditory discrimination. We will of course have to *learn* the conceptual framework of a matured neuroscience in order to pull this off. And we will have to *practice* its noninferential application. But that seems a small price to pay for the quantum leap in self-apprehension.

All of this suggests that there is no problem at all in conceiving the eventual reduction of mental states and properties to neurophysiological states and properties. A matured and successful neuroscience need only include, or prove able to define, a taxonomy of kinds with a set of embedding laws that faithfully mimics the taxonomy and casual generalizations of *folk* psychology. Whether future neuroscientific theories will prove able to do this is a wholly empirical question, not to be settled a priori. The evidence for a positive answer is substantial and familiar, centering on the growing explanatory success of the several neurosciences.

But there is negative evidence as well: I have even urged some of it myself ("Eliminative Materialism and the Propositional Attitudes," *Journal of Philosophy*, 1981). My negative arguments there center on the explanatory and predictive poverty of folk psychology, and they question whether it has the categorical integrity to *merit* the reductive preservation of its familiar ontology. That line suggests substantial revision or outright elimination as the eventual fate of our mentalistic ontology. The qualia-based arguments of Nagel, Jackson, and Robinson, however, take a quite different line. They find no fault with the folk psychology. Their concern is with the explanatory and descriptive poverty of any possible *neuroscience,* and their line suggests that emergence is the correct story for our mentalistic ontology. Let us now examine their arguments.

III. THOMAS NAGEL'S ARGUMENTS

For Thomas Nagel, it is the phenomenological features of our experiences, the properties or *qualia* displayed by our sensations, that constitute a problem for the reductive aspirations of any materialistic neuroscience. In his classic position paper I find three distinct arguments in support of the view that such properties will never find any plausible or adequate reduction within the framework of a matured neuroscience. All three arguments are beguiling, but all three, I shall argue, are unsound.

First Argument: What makes the proposed reduction of mental phenomena different from reductions elsewhere in science, says Nagel, is that

> It is impossible to exclude the phenomenological features of experience from a reduction, in the same way that one excludes the phenomenal features of an ordinary substance from a physical or chemical reduction of it—namely, by explaining them as effects on the minds of human observers. (437)

The reason it is impossible to exclude them, continues Nagel, is that the phenomenological features are essential to experience and to the subjective point of view. But this is not what interests me about this argument. What interests me is the claim that reductions of various substances elsewhere in science *exclude the phenomenal features of the substance.*

This is simply false, and the point is extremely important. The phenomenal features at issue are those such as the objective redness of an apple, the warmth of a coffee cup, and the pitch of a sound. These properties are not excluded from our reductions. Redness, an objective phenomenal property of apples, is identical with a certain wavelength triplet of electromagnetic reflectance efficiencies. Warmth, an objective phenomenal property of objects, is identical with the mean level of the objects' microscopically embodied energies. Pitch, an objective phenomenal property of a sound, is identical with its oscillatory frequency. These electromagnetic and micromechanical properties, out there in the objective world, are genuine phenomenal properties. Despite widespread ignorance of their dynamical and microphysical details, it is these objective physical properties to which everyone's perceptual mechanisms are keyed.

The reductions whose existence Nagel denies are in fact so complete that one can already displace entirely large chunks of our common-sense vocabulary for observable properties and learn to frame one's perceptual judgments directly in terms of the reducing theory. The mean KE of the molecules in this room, for example, is currently about . . . 6.2×10^{-21} joules. The oscillatory frequency of this sound (I here whistle C one octave above middle C) is about 524 hz. And the three critical electromagnetic reflectance efficiencies (at .45, .53, and .63 μm) of this (white) piece of paper are all above 80 percent. These microphysical and electromagnetic properties can be felt, heard, and seen, respectively. Our native sensory mechanisms can easily discriminate such properties, one from another, and their presence from their absence. They have been doing so for millennia. The "resolution" of these mechanisms is inadequate, of course, to reveal the microphysical details and the extended causal roles of the properties thus discriminated. But they are abundantly adequate to permit the reliable discrimination of the properties at issue.

On this view, the standard perceptual properties are not "secondary" properties at all, in the standard sense which implies that they have no real existence save *inside* the minds of human observers. On the contrary, they are as objective as you please, with a wide variety of objective causal properties. Moreover, it would be a mistake even to try to "kick the phenomenal properties inwards," since that would only postpone the problem of reckoning their place in nature. We would only confront them again later, as we address the place in nature of mental phenomena. And, as Nagel correctly points out, the relocation dodge is no longer open to us, once the problematic properties are already located within the mind.

Nagel concludes from this that subjective qualia are unique in being immune from the sort of re-

ductions found elsewhere in science. I draw a very different conclusion. The *objective* qualia (redness, warmth, etc.) should never have been "kicked inwards to the minds of observers" in the first place. They should be confronted squarely, and they should be reduced where they stand: *out*side the human observer. As we saw, this can and has in fact been done. If objective phenomenal properties are so treated, then *subjective* qualia can be confronted with parallel forthrightness, and can be reduced where *they* stand: *in*side the human observer. So far then, the external and the internal case are not different: they are parallel after all.

Second Argument: A second argument urges the point that the intrinsic character of experiences, the qualia of sensations, are essentially accessible from only a single point of view, the subjective point of view of the experiencing subject. The properties of physical brain states, by contrast, are accessible from a variety of entirely objective points of view. We cannot hope adequately to account for the former, therefore, in terms of properties appropriate to the latter domain (cf. Nagel, 442–444).

This somewhat diffuse argument appears to be an instance of the following argument:

1. The qualia of my sensations are directly known by me, by introspection, as elements of my conscious self.
2. The properties of my brain states are not directly known by me, by introspection as elements of my conscious self.
∴ 3. The qualia of my sensations ≠ the properties of my brain states.

And perhaps there is a second argument here as well, a complement to the first:

1. The properties of my brain states are known-by-the-various-external-senses, as having such-and-such physical properties.
2. The qualia of my sensations are *not* known-by-the-various-external-senses, as having such-and-such physical properties.
∴ 3. The qualia of my sensations ≠ the properties of my brain states. . . .

. . . The fallacy committed in both cases is amply illustrated in the following parallel arguments.

1. Hitler is widely recognized as a mass murderer.
2. Adolf Schicklgruber is *not* widely recognized as a mass murderer.
∴ 3. Hitler ≠ Adolf Schicklgruber.

or

1. Aspirin is known by John to be a pain reliever.
2. Acetylsalicylic acid is *not* known by John to be a pain reliever.
∴ 3. Aspirin ≠ acetylsalicylic acid.

or, to cite an example very close to the case at issue,

1. Temperature is known by me, by tactile sensing, as a feature of material objects.
2. Mean molecular kinetic energy is *not* known by me, by tactical sensing, as a feature of material objects.
∴ 3. Temperature ≠ mean molecular kinetic energy.

The problem with all these arguments is that the "property" ascribed in premise 1 and withheld in premise 2 consists only in the subject item's being *recognized, perceived,* or *known* as something, *under some specific description or other.* Such apprehension is not a genuine feature of the item itself, fit for divining identities, since one and the same subject may be successfully recognized under one description (e.g., "qualia of my mental state"), and yet fail to be recognized under another, equally accurate, coreferential description (e.g., "property of my brain state"). . . .

Third Argument: The last argument here is the one most widely associated with Nagel's paper. The leading example is the (mooted) character of the experiences enjoyed by an alien creature such as a bat. The claim is that, no matter how much one knew about the bat's neurophysiology and its interaction with the physical world, one could still not know, nor perhaps even imagine, what it is like to be a bat. Even total knowledge of the physical details still leaves something out. The lesson drawn is that the reductive aspirations of neurophysiology are doomed to dash themselves, unrealized, against the impenetrable keep of subjective qualia (cf. Nagel, 438 ff.).

This argument is almost identical with an argument put forward in a recent paper by Frank Jackson. Since Jackson's version deals directly with humans, I shall confront the problem as he formulates it.

IV. JACKSON'S KNOWLEDGE ARGUMENT

Imagine a brilliant neuroscientist named Mary, who has lived her entire life in a room that is rigorously controlled to display only various shades of black, white, and grey. She learns about the outside world by means of a black/white television monitor, and, being brilliant, she manages to transcend these obstacles. She becomes the world's greatest neuroscientist, all from within this room. In particular, she comes to know everything there is to know about the physical structure and activity of the brain and its visual system, of its actual and possible states.

But there would still be something she did *not* know, and could not even imagine, about the actual experiences of all the other people who live outside her black/white room, and about her possible experiences were she finally to leave her room: the nature of the experience of seeing a ripe tomato, what it is like to see red or have a sensation-of-red. Therefore, complete knowledge of the physical facts of visual perception and its related brain activity *still leaves something out.* Therefore, materialism cannot give an adequate reductionist account of all mental phenomena.

To give a conveniently tightened version of this argument:

1. Mary knows everything there is to know about brain states and their properties.
2. It is not the case that Mary knows everything there is to know about sensations and their properties.

Therefore, by Leibniz's law,

3. Sensations and their properties ≠ brain states and their properties. . . .

. . . We can, I think, find at least two . . . shortcomings in this sort of argument.

The First Shortcoming: This defect is simplicity itself. "Knows about" . . . is not *univocal* in both premises. . . . Jackson's argument is valid only if "knows about" is univocal in both premises. But the kind of knowledge addressed in premise 1 seems pretty clearly to be different from the kind of knowledge addressed in (2). Knowledge in (1) seems to be a matter of having mastered a set of sentences or propositions, the kind one finds written in neuroscience texts, whereas knowledge in (2) seems to be a matter of having a representation of redness in some prelinguistic or sublinguistic medium of representation for sensory variables, or to be a matter of being able to *make* certain sensory discriminations, or something along these lines. . . .

. . . the difference between a person who knows all about the visual cortex but has never enjoyed a sensation of red, and a person who knows no neuroscience but knows well the sensation of red, may reside not in *what* is respectively known by each (brain states by the former, qualia by the latter), but rather in the differing *type* of knowledge each has *of exactly the same thing*. The difference is in the manner of the knowing, not in the nature of the thing(s) known. . . .

. . . In sum, there are pretty clearly more ways of "having knowledge" than having mastered a set of sentences. And nothing in materialism precludes this. The materialistic can freely admit that one has "knowledge" of one's sensations in a way that is independent of the scientific theories one has learned. This does not mean that sensations are beyond the reach of physical science. *It just means that the brain uses more modes and media of representation than the simple storage of sentences.* And this proposition is pretty obviously true: almost certainly the brain uses a considerable variety of modes and media of representation, perhaps hundreds of them. Jackson's argument, and Nagel's, exploit this variety illegitimately: both arguments equivocate on "knows about."

This criticism is supported by the observation that, if Jackson's form of argument were sound, it would prove far too much. Suppose that Jackson were arguing, not against materialism, but against dualism: against the view that there exists a non-material substance—call it "ectoplasm"—whose hidden constitution and nomic intricacies ground all mental phenomena. Let our cloistered Mary be an "ectoplasmologist" this time, and let her know₁

everything there is to know about the ectoplasmic processes underlying vision. There would still be something she did not know₂: what it is like to see red. Dualism is therefore inadequate to account for all mental phenomena!

This argument is as plausible as Jackson's, and for the same reason: it exploits the same equivocation. But the truth is, such arguments show nothing, one way or the other, about how mental phenomena might be accounted for.

The Second Shortcoming: There is a further shortcoming with Jackson's argument, one of profound importance for understanding one of the most exciting consequences to be expected from a successful neuroscientific account of mind. I draw your attention to the assumption that even a utopian knowledge of neuroscience *must* leave Mary hopelessly in the dark about the subjective qualitative nature of sensations not-yet-enjoyed. It is true, of course, that no sentence of the form "*x* is a sensation-of-red" will be deductible from premises restricted to the language of neuroscience. But this is no point against the reducibility of phenomenological properties. As we saw in section I, direct deducibility is an intolerably strong demand on reduction, and if this is all the objection comes to, then there is no objection worth addressing. What the defender of emergent qualia must have in mind here, I think, is the claim that Mary could not even *imagine* what the relevant experience would be like, despite her exhaustive neuroscientific knowledge, and hence must still be missing certain crucial information.

This claim, however, is simply false. Given the truth of premise 1, premise 2 seems plausible to Jackson, Nagel, and Robinson only because none of these philosophers has adequately considered how much one might know if, as premise 1 asserts, one knew *everything* there is to know about the physical brain and nervous system. In particular, none of these philosophers has even begun to consider the changes in our introspective apprehension of our internal states that could follow upon a wholesale revision in our conceptual framework for our internal states.

The fact is, we can indeed imagine how neuroscientific information would give Mary detailed information about the qualia of various sensations.

Recall our earlier discussion of the transformation of perception through the systematic reconceptualization of the relevant perceptual domain. In particular, suppose that Mary has learned to conceptualize her inner life, even in introspection, in terms of the completed neuroscience we are to imagine. So she does not identify her visual sensations crudely as "a sensation-of-black," "a sensation-of-grey," or "a sensation-of-white"; rather she identifies them more revealingly as various spiking frequencies in the *n*th layer of the occipital cortex (or whatever). If Mary has the relevant neuroscientific concepts for the sensational states at issue (viz., sensations-of-*red*), but has never yet been *in* those states, she may well be able to imagine being in the relevant cortical state, and imagine it with substantial success, even in advance of receiving external stimuli that would actually produce it.

One test of her ability in this regard would be to give her a stimulus that would (finally) produce in her the relevant state (viz., a spiking frequency of 90 hz in the gamma network: a "sensation-of-red" to us), and see whether she can identify it correctly *on introspective grounds alone,* as "a spiking frequency of 90 hz: the kind a tomato would cause." It does not seem to me to be impossible that she should succeed in this, and do so regularly on similar tests for other states, conceptualized clearly by her, but not previously enjoyed.

This may seem to some an outlandish suggestion, but the following will show that it is not. Musical chords are auditory phenomena that the young and unpracticed ear hears as undivided wholes, discriminable one from another, but without elements or internal structure. A musical education changes this, and one comes to hear chords as groups of discriminable notes. If one is sufficiently practiced to have absolute pitch, one can even name the notes of the apprehended chord. And the reverse is also true: if a set of notes is specified verbally, a trained pianist or guitarist can identify the chord and recall its sound in auditory imagination. Moreover, a really skilled individual can construct, in auditory imagination, the sound of a chord he may never have heard before, and certainly does not remember. Specify for him a relatively unusual one—an F# 9th*add*13th for example—and let him brood for a bit. Then play for him three or four chords, one of which is

the target, and see whether he can pick it out as the sound that meets the description. Skilled musicians can do this. Why is a similar skill beyond all possibility for Mary?

"Ah," it is tempting to reply, "musicians can do this only because chords are audibly structured sets of elements. Sensations of color are not."

But neither did chords seem, initially, to be structured sets of elements. They also seemed to be undifferentiated wholes. Why should it be unthinkable that sensations of color possess a comparable internal structure, unnoticed so far, but awaiting our determined and informed inspection? Jackson's argument, to be successful, must rule this possibility out, and it is difficult to see how he can do this *a priori*. Especially since there has recently emerged excellent empirical evidence to suggest that *our sensations of color are indeed structured sets of elements*. . . .

I do not mean to suggest, of course, that there will be no limits to what Mary can imagine. Her brain is finite, and its specific anatomy will have specific limitations. For example, if a bat's brain includes computational machinery that the human brain simply lacks (which seems likely), then the subjective character of *some* of the bat's internal states may well be beyond human imagination. Clearly, however, the elusiveness of the bat's inner life here stems not from the metaphysical "emergence" of its internal qualia, but only from the finite capacities of our idiosyncratically human brains. Within those sheerly structural limitations, our imaginations may soar far beyond what Jackson, Nagel, and Robinson suspect, if we possess a neuroscientific conceptual framework that is at last adequate to the intricate phenomena at issue.

I suggest then, that those of us who prize the flux and content of our subjective phenomenological experience need not view the advance of materialistic neuroscience with fear and foreboding. Quite the contrary. The genuine arrival of a materialist kinematics and dynamics for psychological state and cognitive processes will constitute not a gloom in which our inner life is suppressed or eclipsed, but rather a dawning, in which its marvelous intricacies are finally *revealed*—most notably, if we apply ourselves, in direct self-conscious introspection.

Further Questions

1. Churchland thinks we should drop our familiar vocabulary for describing our experiences and start describing them in the language of neuroscience. Why? Do you agree?
2. Which is the more plausible view of consciousness—reductionism or antireductionism?

Further Readings

Dennett, Daniel and Kolak, Daniel. "Consciousness, Self and Reality: Who Are We? A Dialogue with Daniel Dennett. *Philosophical Bridges.* Mountain View, CA: Mayfield, 1999. A dialogue in which the discussion ranges from the relation of mind to world and the nature of consciousness and the self.

Hofstadter, Douglas, and Dennett, Daniel, eds. *The Mind's I.* New York: Basic Books, 1981. Interdisciplinary, including some excellent fiction.

McGinn, Colin. *The Character of Mind.* New York: Oxford University Press, 1982. A good, concise introduction.

61   The Reality of Color

MELINDA ROBERTS

After a career in Los Angeles, California, as an artist and designer, Melinda Roberts returned to academia and received her Ph.D. in philosophy from the University of California, Davis in 1993. She continues the themes of human knowledge and the representational qualities of experience addressed in her paintings through her work in the ontology of color. In this selection, she forges a Kantian compromise between subjectivist and objectivist conceptions of color with the original claim that colors are features of appearance-events, in which perceivers engage with light-mediating objects as they move through an illuminated environment.

Reading Questions

1. What is at issue in the "spectrum-inversion problem"? How does Roberts think this traditional philosophical puzzle relates to the debate about color?
2. What distinction does Roberts draw between qualia and phenomenal qualities? How does this figure into her view of color?
3. Why does Roberts think the correct conception of color should be "outwardly directed"?

THE RED LIGHT AHEAD SIGNALS YOU to come to a stop; the light changes, and you notice that shiny strip of red on the road had turned green. The evening's rain has left shallow pools of water here and there, turning stretches of the dark pavement into nearly perfect reflectors. What for a moment appeared to be a gleaming red strip of light shining up from the road now becomes a glowing green.

Reprinted by permission of the author.

Past experience has shown, however, that this whole show of colors is just an illusion—they will disappear when the water evaporates or the signal light stops working. Common sense enjoins reason; no part of the road, you tell yourself, is really red or green: its color is the same as that of most paved surfaces—an indeterminate composite shade of dark gray-to-black. Parts of it only *look* red or green, because they are reflecting first the red, then the green light from the signal. But, we might go on to ask, what is it in the signal light that really is red? It is not the light generated by the lamp itself, for the same (broad-band) light could be used in a green signal. The lamp is made with a filter through which only long-wave light can pass, while middle- and short-wave light is trapped or absorbed, so the filter might be said to be the source of the redness present in this situation.

Hence the red color you see reflected on the wet road is neither a property of that which is reflecting it, nor of that which is generating the light. Is it really a property of the filtering material, though? There are reasons to think not, because if we were to shine only short-wave light, or a mixture of short- and middle-wave light through it, if any light at all made it through the filter, it would appear a very dark amber, not red. So the color of the filter seems to be relative to the composition of the light it transmits.

Finding nothing outside the perceiver to be, in any determinate or absolute sense, red, we would turn next to an examination of the perceiver. However, if she were not equipped with certain visual mechanisms, if she lacked the same array of differentially absorptive retinal photopigments, or had neural mechanisms (e.g., "opponency channels") that operated in different ways from the sorts of processes that actually take place in normal color perceivers such as humans, long-wave light, which appears red to us, would likely have a quite different appearance to her. It might have an achromatic appearance (simply as uncolored light of a certain degree of brightness), or it might look the way green or yellow light looks to us. We might eventually come to the conclusion, as a number of philosophers have, common sense notwithstanding, that colors are instantiated neither by external objects nor by the sort of electromagnetic radiation we call light, nor, in fact, by

anything at all in the world outside of perceiving subjects (of a certain type).

This is the view called *color subjectivism,* made famous by thinkers throughout history such as Democritus, Galileo, Newton, Descartes, and Locke, among others, and accepted by a growing number of contemporary philosophers and psychologists. C. L. Hardin, a leading commentator on color, states the position bluntly:

> Since physical objects are not colored, [that is, they are neither reddish nor yellowish nor bluish nor greenish] and we have no good reason to believe that there are nonphysical bearers of color phenomena, and since colored objects would have to be physical or nonphysical, we have no good reason to believe that there are colored objects. Colored objects are illusions, but not unfounded illusions. We are normally in chromatic perceptual states, and these are neural states. . . . We are to be eliminativists with respect to color as a property of objects, but reductivists with respect to color experiences.[1]

This position is bolstered by empirical evidence that clearly shows that there is no simple, nondisjunctive objective feature or property shared by things that exhibit the same color. A bird's feather, a flower petal, a refracted ray of light, a volume of liquid, or a heated iron ingot could all have a red appearance, but the cause in each case would be physically distinct. The move to save a common-sense objectivism about color by claiming, for example, that what all red things share is that they reflect, refract, or emit light of the same wavelength (or have identical—or at least very similar—wavelength compositions) is thwarted by the phenomenon of metamerism: an indefinite number of distinct (and in some cases radically distinct) compositions of light (quantified in terms of wavelength-and-intensity ratios) can all have identical color appearances. These findings have been enough to turn the gaze of color theorists inward, looking to the neurophysiology underlying the sensory mechanisms of color vision rather than to features of the external world to explain and account for the content of color experience.

Although color subjectivists accept that there is indeed experience of colors—we do see things as red, green, yellow, blue, or mixtures of those four primary hues—they are also committed to the elimination of colors from a "corrected" ontology of the real.[2] Some may wish to deliver the subjectivist message in softer tones, calling it a reductionist thesis: what explains our beliefs and judgments about color are facts about relations or comparisons between the states of certain populations of neurons in the visual centers of the brain. Any true statements we can make about color, if such can be made, are to be understood in terms referring to features of or relations between neurophysiological states. It may be less disturbing to think of oneself as a reductionist rather than as an eliminativist about color, but it should be clear that the ontological consequences are the same. Subjectivists, whether characterized as reductionists or eliminativists, are committed to the claim that in any ordinary sense of the word "color," colors do not exist, and that there is some kind of global error being made in our general color discourse. When we say of the cardinal's coat of feathers, of the rose's petals, or of the clouds lit by the setting sun that they are red, we cannot but speak falsely. Nothing in the world external to the brains and visual systems of color perceivers is really colored, according to the subjectivist: colors as we see them are illusions, and to believe that they accurately portray or directly represent actual or objective features (such as physical microstructures or surface-reflectance profiles) of the observable world is to be taken in by the illusion.

Subjectivists need not claim, however, that because color perception does not actually detect the presence of any property or kind, that the production of these "false" sensory qualities is not useful or advantageous to the species of organisms that have this capacity. Being equipped with a highly specialized neurophysiology that allows us to see the world "in color" is surely an evolutionary boon. It aids us in important survival tasks by allowing for the enhancement of differences in surface spectral reflectances, making boundaries or edges of objects in a visual array more salient and allowing for quick and easy individuation and identification of objects.[3]

I think we should agree with the subjectivist claim that colors are the product of the visual apprehension of the world, hence that color is dependent on the existence of appropriately equipped perceiving subjects. It has been amply demon-

strated that the characteristics and constraints of physiological mechanisms and processes (such as neural opponency channels and arrays of spectrally opponent cells) provide the best explanation of pervasive color phenomena such as successive and simultaneous color contrast, color complementarity, the results of additive color mixing, the reducibility of all colors into four basic hue categories, and the absence of red-green or yellow-blue binary colors. It is true that the nature of color properties and color relations is grounded in neurophysiology, but neurophysiological explanations cannot tell the whole story. We should be subjectivists about color, but we need not take an eliminativist stance on the ontology of color. The question to be explored here is, if it is accepted that colors are subjective (in the sense they are dependent on visual perception), must it be denied that they are real—that colors actually exist?

COLOR APPEARANCES AND THE QUALITY OF COLOR

A satisfactory account of color properties—a true theory of color—should provide a broadly inclusive conception of color and be able to explain our use of color language, not only in color-matching tasks or even in the everyday classifications of things into basic color categories, but also in helping to determine, if not truth conditions, then at least assertibility conditions for more specialized areas of color discourse. For example, a satisfactory account of color should be able to address claims made about color harmony or about various aesthetic qualities of colors or color combinations, such as are made in the fields of color design and painting. Under what conditions am I warranted in asserting claims of the following variety: that the use of flat, untoned primaries in a sequence of painted vertical bars is insipid or uninspired, or that a particular juxtaposition of red and blue is imbalanced and unsettling because of their respective advancing and receding qualities, or that I look terrible in orange or apricot tones, or that the particular shade of yellowish-green used to paint this room is depressing but adding white would soften the color (and its negative effect), or that one combination of colors "works" (looks good, harmonious, appealing, etc.) whereas another one does not, and so on? It seems plain that no reducing explanation in terms of neurophysiological states can make sense of such claims, yet we do make sense of them. Although understanding such claims might be said to depend to some extent on contextual considerations regarding conventionalized canons of aesthetic taste, an important aspect of color experience is expressed in such discourse that could be understood by any normal color perceiver proficient in the use of color terms that cannot be captured by strictly neurophysiological explanations.

A likely place to look for the reference of color terms is in the realm of color appearances — a place overlooked by the subjectivist who opts for elimination or neurophysiological reduction, even though it is in his own "backyard." In fact, both subjectivists and objectivists about color acknowledge that color experiential states are real *qua* sensory episodes, which might be described as, for example, "a seeing of bright orange-red" or "an awareness of a blue appearance." In this way, color appearances enter into any account of color that is in the business of explaining the perceptual aspects of color (which is, of course, the subjectivist's stock in trade). It is here, in color appearances, that colors reside. Appearances can be thought of as special sorts of relations between certain features of objects or events in the external world (e.g., the organic compounds in the molecules of the rose petal's surface as they interact with sunlight) and neurophysiological mechanism of visual systems inside color perceivers (quantum catch of retinal photopigments transduced into neurally transmittable signals). If we conceive of colors as properties of appearances, we have a better chance to make sense of the various levels of color discourse, because it is, after all, the "looks" of things, of color arrays, of paints and pigments, of juxtapositions of various color media, about which we are making judgments in any case of color attribution or evaluative claim about color.

Bringing appearance properties into an account of the content of color experience makes available a fuller, richer analysis, because in addition to the resources of comparative quantificational analyses of neuron-firing rates at various locations in the brain we can also appeal to facts about particular physical substances and their interactions with light, or (quantum-level) events such as energy-state changes, and the ways visual systems of certain types are affected by such states and events. The point here is that the quality of color itself — the qualitative aspects of color experience, if you will — can be explained only when it is thought of as a primarily relational phenomenon. Saying that something looks red, or looks green, or yellow, or blue is not a very accurate depiction of the lived character of color experience. That character reflects the particularity of color experiential episodes, of particular color appearances. Perceivers who happen to have trichromatic visual systems have a certain set of constraints already laid out for the way their world will look to them. But this is only a framework, an unplayed instrument, into which a content is yet to be woven. Carrying forward the analogy of the instrument, it might be said that just as its structure determines what sorts of sounds can be made with it, the structure of our neurophysiology determines what sorts of sensory qualities can be experienced. A stringed instrument and wind instrument can both sound the same note, but there will be a distinct character reflective of the type of instrument carried in the sound of each note played. Similarly, a trichromatic perceiver's visual experience will reflect the particular nature of that type of visual mechanism.

What is interesting about color and what, it might be asserted, much of our specialized color discourse is about, is not simply the character of trichromatic color perception, but the particular way that objects and events in the environment "play" that instrument. A color appearance is like a sounding of an instrument, and the content of the appearance cannot be captured without taking account of the particular way the visual system is engaged, which includes consideration of facts about the light-modification properties of the perceptual object, as well as facts about what surrounds it, about the composition of the ambient illumination, about the angle and distance from which it is being viewed, and a host of other factors including conditions internal to the perceiver, ranging from adaptive states of the visual mechanisms to input from cognitive and memory structures. These elements all affect the quality of color experience. They are all aspects or components of color appearances; hence, if colors are conceived as appearance properties, the complex, even emotionally charged or aesthetically relevant, highly context-dependent character of color properties can be accounted for, because they are properties of a rather complex psychophysical event.

THE SUBJECTIVE REALITY OF COLOR EVENTS

It has been noted that all sides of the color debate agree that talk of color appearances is not empty. This is shown by the distinction commonly made between ("veridical" and "mere" appearances with respect to color. A *veridical* color appearance is a regular, law-governed sort of occurrence: one can expect to see red if shown monochromatic light (light of the same wavelength) of around 650 nanometers under the appropriate or standard conditions for viewing light. To say that the color of something is a *mere* appearance suggests that the thing has a real color, but somehow that real color is masked by some color that it does not really have: her pale blond hair appears blue only under strong fluorescent light; its blue color is a mere appearance, but its blond color is its veridical appearance. Now to say any of this should sound odd in light of our previous discussion, especially to a color subjectivist, because nothing has a "real" color on that view, let along a merely apparent color. Or to put it another way, all colors are equally mere appearances, and what we mean by the expression "veridical color appearance" is simply "the color appearance something has under what is taken to be standard or normal conditions."

In any case, everyone can agree that color appearances are effected through the occurrence of the relevant neural states in relation to certain sorts of stimuli. Obviously there is more to a mental event that is a perception of color than just what is inside the head, or what is going on in a particular type of brain state. Colors are always the products of an interactive relationship between a perceiving subject and some environmental stimulus (or in some cases between the perceiving system and a direct stimulation of part of it, e.g., direct pressure on the eyes, bumps on the head, or electrodes penetrating the visual cortex). If we are going to argue for the reality of color while at the same time accepting the subjectivity of color, it must be done in the context of these subject-involving relational events, that is to say, by appealing to appearances. A color subjectivist might agree that colors are exemplified in the world and yet remain an internalist about color, which is to say that color is in the world, but it is "in the head." James McGilvray adopts just such a "projectivist, nonintentionalist" account:

> To explain the relevant sort of projection, we must begin by saying that the object out there is the object about which the visual system needs to have information, including information concerning its surface spectral reflectances.... Call this physical object the "intended object." It typically has surface spectral reflectance properties (unless it is an emitter of light), but it is not colored. Now we must locate colors inside the head. Make them properties of "phenomenal objects," which can be identified with neural events. These objects are ways external objects are perceived, and colors on this view become event properties, making them (strictly speaking) colorings.[4]

McGilvray narrowly eschews eliminativism by predicting colors of neurophysiological events, but he nevertheless asserts the illusory nature of colors: "Green objects that are seen.... are illusions."[5] In this way, colors exist in the head because that is where the "phenomenal object," which is the colored object, is. This object however, is not "*seen,* but undergone."[6] In Hardin's terms, McGilvray is claiming that there are physical bearers of color properties, and these are just the neurophysiological events in which color appearances are realized.

Although there are no external colored objects in McGilvray's account, there are internal events that instantiate colors, and that may be specified according to their particular functional role in visual perception. Although McGilvray is on the right track in conceiving of colors as properties of perceptual events, his account still falls short in terms of getting the content of color experience right. On his view, it is as if all of the colors are already there, in our heads, waiting to be put to use in coloring the incoming visual data, like crayons in a box. The reality of color lies not solely in the neurophysiology of perceivers such as humans, (and other animals); it also lies in the features of the environment in conjunction with which such visual systems evolved.

In the previous section, an account of color properties was suggested in which color appearances—relational events typified by a perceiver's internal response to the stimulus of an illuminated array of external objects—are taken to be the part of the world that may truly be said to instantiate color. That is, color is neither a property of the object nor of the subject, strictly speaking, but of the relation, or interaction, between the two. This gives us a subjective account of color that is also a realist account. As appearance-properties, colors are realized in spatio-temporally located events, and these "appearings" have both objective and subjective features, contributed by the environment and the conscious perceiver, respectively. By conceiving of the "phenomenal object" or "perceptual object" as a relational event, rather than a strictly mental event, a secure footing for colors in the external world is established, because these events are *bona fide* concrete, physical events, with determinate spatio-temporal locations.

In a recent article, Thompson, Palacios, and Varela offer a view of color they describe as "enactive and ecological," which is compatible with the event view of color suggested here.

> According to enactivism, color is neither a perceiver-independent property, as in objectivism nor is it merely a projection or property of the brain, as in subjectivism. Rather, it is a property of the enacted perceptual environments experienced by animals in their visually guided interactions.[7]

Thompson et al. refer to "perceptual objects" as objects "construed in relation to the sensory-motor capacities of perceiving animals,"[8] and these are to be thought of as the bearers of color properties. These phenomena are ecological in the broadest sense; that is, they encompass not only the extra-dermal world as an animal environment, but also perceiving animals as both assemblies of sensory-motor networks and organismic unities that shape the extradermal world into an environment in their interactions.[9]

We can elaborate on this concept, for their account of perceptual or phenomenal objects is just what has been herein offered as the correct conception of appearances. The event view holds that colors are actually exemplified by perceptual relations involving perceivers such as humans and certain primates, and perhaps birds, fish, insects, and other sorts of organisms in the process of engaging with their environments. Thus color is neither a property of unperceived "stuff—surfaces of things, aggregates of molecules, nonmental substances, waves or particles of electromagnetic energy, and so on—nor is it a property of brains or of strictly mental substances or states. Yet colors do exist; they come into being when certain conditions are satisfied, and we may think of the "perceptual objects" referred to by Thompson et al. as being the mereological sums designated by descriptions of those conditions. In the ordinary case, these involve "enactive" relations that may obtain between (organismic) visual mechanisms (photosensitive protein-based molecules in retinal cells, electrochemically based neural transmission in the optic nerve, lateral geniculate nucleus and visual cortex, etc.) and light-reflective or radiant stimuli, and that result in the occurrence of visual appearances.

We can illustrate the appearance-event view by looking at the case of refractive spectral appearances. Imagine a faceted crystal or bit of prismatic glass through which bright sunlight is being refracted. The refracted light then reaches a diffuse reflector, such as a white wall. What appears on the wall is a multihued patch of light; at one end is a brilliantly warm spectral red, which give way to bright green, separated only by a narrow band of yellow; the green subtly moves into blue-green and then blue, finally shading into a clear yet ethereal violet hue. This spectral image is a paradigm instance of color; but what are we really seeing in this kind of case—when light is refracted through prisms or faceted, beveled, or imperfect glass, or when we see rainbows, ice crystals in clouds, or a dewdrop on a blade of grass—when the brilliant colors of the visible spectrum appear? Among the various *visibilia* in question, which ones are colored? No one would claim that transparent refractors (e.g., bits of glass or droplets of water) are colored, nor, it is generally agreed, are the light rays or the air through which they travel, nor are events inside the cortex (*pace* McGilvray). You are viewing sunlight as it emerges from its journey through a bit of prismatic glass: of what might you be predicating the pure brilliance, the chromatic richness of the spectral hues, the unique differences among which are displayed in the clearest imaginable way?

Do we see colors, or colored objects, or are we merely seeing "in color"? Subjectivist theorists such as Hardin and McGilvray would say that what we see *looks* colored—in the case described above, it is a part of a white wall, reflecting light composed of many wavelengths, that *merely* appears colored but is not actually colored, and we can tell a neurophysiological (or electrochemical) story about why refracted light causes the color illusions it does. So, on an internalist or eliminativist view, colors are not seen, but rather colors are modes of seeing. It is true that seeing in color is a mode of visual perception, but particular colors *are* seen; they are seen when they appear, that is, when they are instantiated by appearance events. The color qualities of which the perceiver is aware in the scenario above are qualities of appearances, but this is not to say that colors are inside the perceiver—not entirely anyway—any more than they are in, or on, external objects. The mode in question, seeing as effected through wavelength discrimination and representations of brightness contrasts, is qualitatively determined by the physical or neurophysiological ground in which it is realized (hence differently composed organisms may have different arrays of representational possibilities). But the point is that an examination of this mode of visual representation, conceived as internal to the brain, will come up short in accounting for the representational content of color perceptual states as well as the functional and information-gathering roles played by color perception. Apprehending the color appearance of something, or some scene or situation (the burst of color in a flowering tree in full spring blossom, of a sandy bluff seen from a distance, or a mixture of paint pigments on the artist's palette) is not only seeing particular light reflectors, or seeing light reflected by way of a certain type of visual mechanism. It also involves an active, conscious engagement with the perceived environment, an intentional taking in and dividing up of a scene (and this is in part determined by the organism's interests and goals in relation to the particular environment) as well as a propensity on the part of the reflecting things to interact with light in one way rather than another.

The notion of a "mode of seeing" must be elaborated in such a way that it is understood as much in terms of what it has evolved to reveal, delineate, or interpret, as it is in terms of what it contributes to perception on the basis of its neurophysiological form or structure. What it is for something to be red is for it to look red, and what it is to look red is more than just being a stimulus for a particular kind of neurophysiological response state and nothing more. What is needed for a more complete explanation of color perception and the nature of color properties is to go beyond the neurophysiological state, back out to the external world, to fully understand color.

A precise description of a color-appearance event involves more than just an indication of the presence of light of such-and-such wavelength/intensity ratios being reflected at location l at time t entering the eyes of a perceiver of type p. It also involves facts about the perceiver's mental constitution and experiential history, as well as facts about the immediate surroundings and local environment of the target stimulus. One could say the *visibilia* of color perception are the objective events making up the world as seen by the perceiver in question. One sees the suffuse red appearance of the sky at dusk, and the faint red of the outer arc of a primary rainbow; more commonly one sees the bright red of freshly drawn blood or the nearly opaque, deep purplish-red of Cabernet or Burgundy wine; the lusty, glowing red in neon signs at night, the gaudy red of flags and Santa suits, the ephemeral, pale red of an afterimage induced by a saturated blue-green color swatch, the highly visible red of a traffic signal, or of its gleaming reflection on a wet road at night. We call the ordinary sorts of things—the blood, the wine, the dyed cloth, the traffic light—as well as the not-so-ordinary "things"—the sky, the rainbow, the afterimage, the reflection on the road—all in a single sense, "red," because each of these sorts of things regularly constitutes (in part) the ground for a characteristic type of appearance event; the other main constituent of the event comprises the properties of a perceiving subject. The broad character of this type of event, what we might call the "color category," is contributed by the subject, but the specific instances of colors can be realized only through particular color appearances, which are events reflective of both the embeddedness of the perceiving subject within its environment and the objective ground with which the subject engages. The reality of color is exemplified in the existence of this living cycle of intentionaliy.

NOTES

1. C. L. Hardin, *Color for Philosophers: Unweaving the Rainbow,* Indianapolis, IN: Hackett, 1988, 111–112.

2. Color eliminativism has been defended by many contemporary philosophers, notable by C. L. Hardin in *Color for Philosophers* and a number of other articles including "Color and Illusion," in William Lycan, ed., *Mind and Cognition: A Reader,* Cambridge, MA and Oxford: Basil Blackwell, 1991 and "The Virtues of Illusion," *Philosophical Studies,* No. 68. 1992, pp. 371–382. Austen Clark puts forward a similar view, although preferring to refer to it as reductionist, in *Sen-sory Qualities,* Oxford: Clarendon Press, 1993; in the recent Proceedings for the 1996 Biennial Meeting of the Philosophy of Science Association, an article by Clark entitled "True Theories, False Colors," accompanies articles by two other authors favoring color eliminativism, Richard J. Hall, "The Evolution of Color Vision Without Colors," and Don Dedrick, "Can Color be Reduced to Anything?" all in *Philosophy of Science,* supplement to vol. 63, no. 3, S125–S150. Also, Paul Boghossian and David Velleman in "Colour as a Secondary Quality," *Mind,* 98, 1989, pp. 81–103, and Charles Landesman in *Color and Consciousness,* Philadelphia: Temple University Press, 1989 put forward extended arguments for color eliminativism.

3. Richard Hall makes this point in "The Evolution of Color Vision Without Colors," S131.

4. James A. McGilvray, "Colors really are only in the head," Open Peer Commentary, *Behavioral and Brain Sciences,* 1992, pp. 48–49.

5. Ibid.

6. Ibid.

7. Evan Thompson, Adrian Palacios, and Francisco J. Varela, "Ways of Coloring: Comparative color vision as a case study for cognitive science," *Behavioral and Brain Sciences,* 15, 1991, p. 23.

8. Ibid., p. 17.

9. Ibld., p. 19.

Further Readings

Clark, Austen. *Sensory Qualities.* Oxford: Clarendon Press, 1993.

Hardin, C. L. *Color for Philosophers: Unweaving the Rainbow.* Cambridge, MA: Hackett, 1988.

Thompson, Evan. *Colour Vision: A Study in Cognitive Science and Philosophy.* New York: Routledge, 1995.

Villanueva, Enrique, ed. *Perception.* Atascadero, CA: Ridgeview, 1996.

Part X

Death

WHEREVER YOU GO, WHATEVER YOU DO, an armed assassin walks behind you. The nozzle presses cold against your neck. The gun is cocked, the bullet ready to shatter you forever.

You have no place to run, nowhere to hide. No one can help you. The assassin's finger is always on the trigger. Always.

Why doesn't he blow you away? Not yet. But soon. At any moment. Maybe now as you're reading this. Maybe you won't finish this page, this paragraph, this sentence, this word.

How do you feel?

Probably, you say to yourself there is no assassin. No gun. No bullet. But the truth is this: the bullet has already been fired. The bullet will find you. The bullet goes through walls, beliefs, schemes — it pierces everything in its relentless journey. Your death is on its way to you. Now.

Assassins are superfluous. Murder is superfluous. Suicide is superfluous. Life itself is all these things and then some. Death never misses. No one gets out alive.

What does death mean? *Your* death, something you can do nothing about yet which you must face and face alone, unarmed, defenseless, utterly naked. It waits for you: the ultimate unknown.

62   Death and Immortality

PLATO

A brief biography of Plato appears on p. 2.

In the following selection, from *Phaedo,* Plato recounts the conversation that took place in Socrates' prison cell on the day that he was put to death. According to Plato's account, Socrates spent this day with some of his closest students, discussing the immortality of the soul. Socrates argued that the soul is immortal. His students argued that when a person dies that's the end of it. To a modern reader, it may seem ungracious of Socrates's students to have pressed the case for the finality of death to Socrates on the very day that Socrates would die. Actually their doing this was a compliment. For Socrates, like Buddha but decidedly unlike Jesus, did not want any of his students to believe something just because he believed it. He had no use for that sort of disciple. Instead, Socrates encouraged his students to question, especially everything that he himself believed.

Reading Questions

1. Why does Socrates think that true philosophers should welcome death when it comes?
2. Why does Socrates think that each of us must have existed prior to our births in our current bodies?
3. Souls aside, Socrates thinks that whereas some things are changeable, others are unchangeable. Give examples of each. Why does he think that the soul is more like these unchangeable things than it is like changeable things?
4. Does Socrates believe in the transmigration of souls?

IN THIS PRESENT LIFE, I reckon that we make the nearest approach to knowledge when we have the least possible intercourse or communion with the body, and are not surfeited with the bodily nature, but keep ourselves pure until the hour when God himself is pleased to release us. And thus having got rid of the foolishness of the body we shall be pure and hold converse with the pure, and know of ourselves the clear light everywhere, which is no other than the light of truth. For the impure are not permitted to approach the pure. These are the sort of words, Simmias, which the true lovers of knowledge cannot help saying to one another, and thinking. You would agree; would you not?

Undoubtedly, Socrates.

But, O my friend, if this be true, there is great reason to hope that, going whither I go, when I have come to the end of my journey, I shall attain that which has been the pursuit of my life. And therefore I go on my way rejoicing, and not I only, but every other man who believes that his mind has been made ready and that he is in a manner purified.

Certainly, replied Simmias.

From The Dialogues of Plato, *trans. Benjamin Jowett (New York: Scribner's, 1889).*

PLATO'S LEGACY

John Hick

It was Plato (428/7–348/7 B.C.), the philosopher who has most deeply and lastingly influenced Western culture, who systematically developed the body–mind dichotomy and first attempted to prove the immortality of the soul.

Plato argues that although the body belongs to the sensible world, and shares its changing and impermanent nature, the intellect is related to the unchanging realities of which we are aware when we think not of particular good things but of Goodness itself, not of specific just acts but of Justice itself, and of the other "universals" or eternal Ideas in virtue of which physical things and events have their own specific characteristics. Being related to this higher and abiding realm, rather than to the evanescent world of sense, reason or the soul is immortal. Hence, one who devotes his life to the contemplation of eternal realities rather than to the gratification of the fleeting desires of the body will find at death that whereas his body turns to dust, his soul gravitates to the realm of the unchanging, there to live forever. . . .

Plato used the further argument that the only things that can suffer destruction are those that are composite, since to destroy something means to disintegrate it into its constituent parts. All material bodies are composite; the soul, however, is simple and therefore imperishable. This argument was adopted by Aquinas and has become standard in Roman Catholic theology, as in the following passage from the modern Catholic philosopher, Jacques Maritain:

> A spiritual soul cannot be corrupted, since it possesses no matter; it cannot be disintegrated, since it has no substantial parts; it cannot lose its individual unity, since it is self-subsisting, nor its internal energy, since it contains within itself all the sources of its energies. The human soul cannot die. Once it exists, it cannot disappear; it will necessarily exist for ever, endure without end. Thus, philosophic reason, put to work by a great metaphysician like Thomas Aquinas, is able to prove the immortality of the human soul in a demonstrative manner. [*The Range of Reason*. New York: Charles Scribner's Sons, 1953, p. 60.]

From *Philosophy of Religion* (1973).

And what is purification but the separation of the soul from the body, as I was saying before; the habit of the soul gathering and collecting herself into herself from all sides out of the body; the dwelling in her own place alone, as in another life, so also in this, as far as she can;—the release of the soul from the chains of the body?

Very true, he said.

And this separation and release of the soul from the body is termed death?

To be sure, he said.

And the true philosophers, and they only, are ever seeking to release the soul. Is not the separation and release of the soul from the body their especial study?

That is true.

And, as I was saying at first, there would be a ridiculous contradiction in men studying to live as nearly as they can in a state of death, and yet repining when it comes upon them.

Clearly.

And the true philosophers, Simmias, are always occupied in the practice of dying, wherefore also to them least of all men is death terrible. Look at the matter thus:—if they have been in every way the enemies of the body, and are wanting to be alone with the soul, when this desire of theirs is granted, how inconsistent would they be if they trembled and repined, instead of rejoicing at their departure to that place where, when they arrive, they hope to gain that which in life they desired—and this was wisdom—and at the same time to be rid of the company of their enemy. Many a man has been willing to go to the world below animated by the hope of seeing there an earthly love, or wife, or son, and conversing with them. And will he who is a true lover of wisdom, and is strongly persuaded in like manner that only in the world below he can worthily enjoy her, still repine at death? Will he not depart with joy? Surely he will, O my friend, if he be a true philosopher. For he will have a firm conviction that there, and there only, he can find wisdom in her purity. And if this be true, he would be very absurd, as I was saying, if he were afraid of death. . . .

RECOLLECTION

. . . And shall we proceed a step further, and affirm that there is such a thing as equality, not of one piece of wood or stone with another, but that, over and above this, there is absolute equality? Shall we say so?

Say so, yes, replied Simmias, and swear to it, with all the confidence in life.

And do we know the nature of this absolute essence?

To be sure, he said.

And whence did we obtain our knowledge? Did we not see equalities of material things, such as pieces of wood and stones, and gather from them the idea of an equality which is different from them? For you will acknowledge that there is a difference. Or look at the matter in another way:— Do not the same pieces of wood or stone appear at one time equal, and at another time unequal?

That is certain.

But are real equals ever unequal? or is the idea of equality the same as of inequality?

Impossible, Socrates.

Then these (so-called) equals are not the same with the idea of equality?

I should say, clearly not, Socrates.

And yet from these equals, although differing from the idea of equality, you conceived and attained that idea?

Very true, he said.

Which might be like, or might be unlike them?

Yes.

But that makes no difference: whenever from seeing one thing you conceived another, whether like or unlike, there must surely have been an act of recollection?

Very true.

But what would you say of equal portions of wood and stone, or other material equals? and what is the impression produced by them? Are they equals in the same sense in which absolute equality is equal? or do they fall short of this perfect equality in a measure?

Yes, he said, in a very great measure too.

And must we not allow, that when I or any one, looking at any object, observes that the thing which he sees aims at being some other thing, but falls short of, and cannot be, that other thing, but is inferior, he who makes this observation must have had a previous knowledge of that to which the other, although similar, was inferior?

Certainly.

And has not this been our own case in the matter of equals and of absolute equality?

Precisely.

Then we must have known equality previously to the time when we first saw the material equals, and reflected that all these apparent equals strive to attain absolute equality, but fall short of it?

Very true.

And we recognize also that this absolute equality has only been known, and can only be known, through the medium of sight or touch, or of some other of the senses, which are all alike in this respect?

Yes, Socrates, as far as the argument is concerned, one of them is the same as the other.

From the senses then is derived the knowledge that all sensible things aim at an absolute equality of which they fall short?

Yes.

Then before we began to see or hear or perceive in any way, we must have had a knowledge of absolute equality, or we could not have referred to that standard the equals which are derived from the senses?—for to that they all aspire, and of that they fall short.

No other inference can be drawn from the previous statements.

And did we not see and hear and have the use of our other senses as soon as we were born?

Certainly.

Then we must have acquired the knowledge of equality at some previous time?

Yes.

That is to say, before we were born, I suppose?

True.

And if we acquired this knowledge before we were born, and were born having the use of it, then we also knew before we were born and at the instant of birth not only the equal or the greater or the less, but all other ideas; for we are not speaking only of equality, but of beauty, goodness, justice, holiness, and of all which we stamp with the name of essence in the dialectical process, both when we ask and when we answer questions. Of all this we may certainly affirm that we acquired the knowledge before birth?

We may.

But if, after having acquired, we have not forgotten what in each case we acquired, then we must always have come into life having knowledge, and shall always continue to know as long as life lasts—for knowing is the acquiring and retaining knowledge and not forgetting. Is not forgetting, Simmias, just the losing of knowledge?

Quite true, Socrates.

But if the knowledge which we acquired before birth was lost by us at birth, and if afterwards by the use of the senses we recovered what we precisely knew, will not the process which we call learning be a recovering of the knowledge which is natural to us, and may not this be rightly termed recollection? . . .

THE SOUL'S KINSHIP WITH THE DIVINE

Then now let us return to the previous discussion. Is that idea or essence, which in the dialectical process we define as essence or true existence—whether essence of equality, beauty, or anything else—are these essences, I say, liable at times to some degree of change? or are they each of them always what they are, having the same simple self-existent and unchanging forms, not admitting of variation at all, or in any way, or at any time?

They must be always the same, Socrates, replied Cebes.

And what would you say of the many beautiful—whether men or horses or garments or any other things which are named by the same names and may be called equal or beautiful,—are they all unchanging and the same always, or quite the reverse? May they not rather be described as almost always changing and hardly ever the same, either with themselves or with one another?

The latter, replied Cebes; they are always in a state of change.

And these you can touch and see and perceive with the senses, but the unchanging things you can only perceive with the mind—they are invisible and are not seen?

That is very true, he said.

Well then, added Socrates, let us suppose that there are two sorts of existences—one seen, the other unseen.

Let us suppose them.

The seen is the changing, and the unseen is the unchanging?

That may be also supposed.

And, further, is not one part of us body, another part soul?

To be sure.

And to which class is the body more alike and akin?

Clearly to the seen—no one can doubt that.

And is the soul seen or not seen?

Not by man, Socrates.

And what we mean by "seen" and "not seen" is that which is or is not visible to the eye of man?

Yes, to the eye of man.

And is the soul seen or not seen?

Not seen.

Unseen then?

Yes.

Then the soul is more like to the unseen, and the body to the seen?

That follows necessarily, Socrates.

THE TRUTH ABOUT THE SOUL

The Catholic Encyclopaedia

The notion that God has a supply of souls that are not any body's in particular until He infuses them into human embryos is entirely unwarranted by any evidence . . . The soul is created by God at the time it is infused into matter.

And were we not saying long ago that the soul when using the body as an instrument of perception, that is to say, when using the sense of sight or hearing or some other sense (for the meaning of perceiving through the body is perceiving through the senses)—were we not saying that the soul too is then dragged by the body into the region of the changeable, and wanders and is confused; the world spins round her, and she is like a drunkard, when she touches change?

Very true.

But when returning into herself she reflects, then she passes into the other world, the region of purity, and eternity, and immortality, and unchangeableness, which are her kindred, and with them she ever lives, when she is by herself and is not let or hindered; then she ceases from her erring ways, and being in communion with the unchanging is unchanging. And this state of the soul is called wisdom?

That is well and truly said, Socrates, he replied.

And to which class is the soul more nearly alike and akin, as far as may be inferred from this argument, as well as from the preceding one?

I think, Socrates, that, in the opinion of every one who follows the argument, the soul will be infinitely more like the unchangeable—even the most stupid person will not deny that.

And the body is more like the changing?

Yes.

Yet once more consider the matter in another light: When the soul and the body are united, then nature orders the soul to rule and govern, and the body to obey and serve. Now which of these two functions is akin to the divine? and which to the mortal? Does not the divine appear to you to be that which naturally orders and rules, and the mortal to be that which is subject and servant?

True.

And which does the soul resemble?

The soul resembles the divine, and the body the mortal—there can be no doubt of that, Socrates.

Then reflect, Cebes: of all which has been said is not this the conclusion?—that the soul is in the very likeness of the divine, and immortal, and intellectual, and uniform, and indissoluble, and unchangeable; and that the body is in the very likeness of the human, and mortal, and unintellectual, and multiform, and dissoluble, and changeable. Can this, my dear Cebes, be denied?

It cannot.

But if it be true, then is not the body liable to speedy dissolution? and is not the soul almost or altogether indissoluble?

Certainly.

And do you further observe, that after a man is dead, the body, or visible part of him, which is lying in the visible world, and is called a corpse, and would naturally be dissolved and decomposed and dissipated, is not dissolved or decomposed at once, but may remain for some time, nay even for a long time, if the constitution be sound at the time of death, and the season of the year favourable? For the body when shrunk and embalmed, as the manner is in Egypt, may remain almost entire through infinite ages; and even in decay, there are still some portions, such as the bones and ligaments, which are practically indestructible:—Do you agree?

Yes.

And is it likely that the soul, which is invisible, in passing to the place of the true Hades, which like her is invisible, and pure, and noble, and on her way to the good and wise God, whither, if God will, my soul is also soon to go,—that soul, I repeat, if this be her nature and origin, will be blown away and destroyed immediately on quitting the body, as the many say? That can never be, my dear Simmias and Cebes. The truth rather is, that the soul which is pure at departing and draws after her no bodily taint, having never voluntarily during life had connection with the body, which she is ever avoiding, herself gathered into herself;—and making such abstraction her perpetual study—which means that she has been a true disciple of philosophy; and therefore has in fact been always engaged in the practice of dying? For is not philosophy the study of death?—

Certainly—

That soul, I say, herself invisible, departs to the invisible world—to the divine and immortal and rational: thither arriving, she is secure of bliss and is released from the error and folly of men, their fears and wild passions and all other human ills, and for ever dwells, as they say of the initiated, in company with the gods. Is not this true, Cebes? . . .

TRANSMIGRATION

. . . the soul which has been polluted, and is impure at the time of her departure, and is the companion and servant of the body always, and is in love with and fascinated by the body and by the desires and pleasures of the body, until she is led to believe that the truth only exists in a bodily form, which a man may touch and see and taste, and use for the purposes of his lusts,—the soul, I mean, accustomed to hate and fear and avoid the intellectual principle, which to the bodily eye is dark and invisible, and can be attained only by philosophy;—do you suppose that such a soul will depart pure and unalloyed?

Impossible, he replied.

She is held fast by the corporeal, which the continual association and constant care of the body have wrought into her nature.

Very true.

And this corporeal element, my friend, is heavy and weighty and earthy, and is that element of sight by which a soul is depressed and dragged down again into the visible world, because she is afraid of the invisible and of the world below— prowling about tombs and sepulchres, near which, as they tell us, are seen certain ghostly apparitions of souls which have not departed pure, but are cloyed with sight and therefore visible.

That is very likely, Socrates.

Yes, that is very likely, Cebes; and these must be the souls, not of the good, but of the evil, which are compelled to wander about such places in payment of the penalty of their former evil way of life; and they continue to wander until through the craving after the corporeal which never leaves them, they are imprisoned finally in another body. And they may be supposed to find their prisons in the same natures which they have had in their former lives.

What natures do you mean, Socrates?

What I mean is that men who have followed after gluttony, and wantonness, and drunkenness, and have had no thought of avoiding them, would pass into asses and animals of that sort. What do you think?

I think such an opinion to be exceedingly probable.

And those who have chosen the portion of injustice, and tyranny, and violence, will pass into wolves, or into hawks and kites;—whither else can we suppose them to go?

Yes, said Cebes; with such natures, beyond question.

And there is no difficulty, he said, in assigning to all of them places answering to their several natures and propensities?

There is not, he said.

Some are happier than others; and the happiest both in themselves and in the place to which they go are those who have practised the civil and social virtues which are called temperance and justice, and are acquired by habit and attention without philosophy and mind.

Why are they the happiest?

Because they may be expected to pass into some gentle and social kind which is like their own, such as bees or wasps or ants, or back again into the form of man, and just and moderate men may be supposed to spring from them.

THE CARTESIAN ASSUMPTION

Antony Flew

. . . Plato and Aristotle can be regarded as the archetypical protagonists of two opposing views of man. Plato is the original spokesman for a dualistic view, and it seems that it is upon dualism that a doctrine of personal immortality must be grounded if it is to possess any initial plausibility. As a defender of a monistic view, Aristotle was neither so consistent nor so wholehearted. Yet it is still fair to see him at his most characteristic as the philosophical founding father of the view that the person is the living human organism, a view that apparently leaves no room whatsoever for belief in personal immortality. Aquinas, who generally followed Aristotle on this point, characteristically attempted a synthesis that would have opened, had it been successful, the doors to heaven and to hell. In the present perspective Descartes must be placed squarely in the Platonic tradition. Thus, in the final paragraph of Part V of the *Discourse on Method,* after remarking that "next to the error of those who deny God . . . there is none which is more effectual in leading feeble spirits from the straight path of virtue, than to imagine that . . . after this life we having nothing to fear or to hope for, any more than the flies or the ants," Descartes concluded that "our soul is in its nature entirely independent of the body, and in consequence that it is not liable to die with it."

From "Immortality" in volume 4 of *The Encyclopedia of Philosophy* (1967).

Very likely.

No one who has not studied philosophy and who is not entirely pure at the time of his departure is allowed to enter the company of the Gods, but the lover of knowledge only. And this is the reason, Simmias and Cebes, why the true votaries of philosophy abstain from all fleshly lusts, and hold out against them and refuse to give themselves up to them, — not because they fear poverty or the ruin of their families, like the lovers of money, and the world in general; nor like the lovers of power and honour, because they dread the dishonour or disgrace of evil deeds.

No, Socrates, that would not become them, said Cebes.

THE BODY AS THE SOUL'S PRISON

. . . they who have any care of their own souls, and do not merely live moulding and fashioning the body, say farewell to all this; they will not walk in the ways of the blind: and when philosophy offers them purification and release from evil, they feel that they ought not to resist her influence, and whither she leads they turn and follow.

What do you mean, Socrates?

I will tell you, he said. The lovers of knowledge are conscious that the soul was simply fastened and glued to the body — until philosophy received her, she could only view real existence through the bars of a prison, not in and through herself; she was wallowing in the mire of every sort of ignorance, and by reason of lust had become the principal accomplice in her own captivity. This was her original state; and then, as I was saying, and as the lovers of knowledge are well aware, philosophy, seeing how terrible was her confinement, of which she was to herself the cause, received and gently comforted her and sought to release her, pointing out that the eye and the ear and the other senses are full of deception, and persuading her to retire from them, and abstain from all but the necessary use of them, and be gathered up and collected into herself, bidding her trust in herself and her own pure apprehension of pure existence, and to mistrust whatever comes to her through other channels and is subject to variation; for such things are visible and tangible, but what she sees in her own nature is intelligible and invisible. And the soul of the true philosopher thinks that she ought not to resist this deliverance, and therefore abstains from pleasures and desires and pains and fears, as far as she is able; reflecting that when a man has great joys or sorrows or fears or desires, he suffers from them, not merely the sort of evil which might be anticipated—as for example, the loss of his health or property which he has sacrificed to his lusts—but an evil greater far, which is the greatest and worst of all evils, and one of which he never thinks.

What is it, Socrates? said Cebes.

The evil is that when the feeling of pleasure or pain is most intense, every soul of man imagines the objects of this intense feeling to be then plainest and truest: but this is not so, they are really the things of sight.

Very true.

And is not this the state in which the soul is most enthralled by the body?

How so?

Why, because each pleasure and pain is a sort of nail which nails and rivets the soul to the body, until she becomes like the body, and believes that to be true which the body affirms to be true; and from agreeing with the body and having the same delights she is obliged to have the same habits and haunts, and is not likely ever to be pure at her departure to the world below, but is always infected by the body; and so she sinks into another body and there germinates and grows, and has therefore no part in the communion of the divine and pure and simple. . . .

. . . A man of sense ought not to say, nor will I be very confident, that the description which I have given of the soul and her mansions is exactly true. But I do say that, inasmuch as the soul is shown to be immortal, he may venture to think, not improperly or unworthily, that something of the kind is true. The venture is a glorious one, and he ought to comfort himself with words like these, which is the reason why I lengthen out the tale. Wherefore, I say, let a man be of good cheer about his soul, who having cast away the pleasures and

ornaments of the body as alien to him and working harm rather than good, has sought after the pleasures of knowledge; and has arrayed the soul, not in some foreign attire, but in her own proper jewels, temperance, and justice, and courage, and nobility, and truth—in these adorned she is ready to go on her journey to the world below, when her hour comes. You, Simmias and Cebes, and all other men, will depart at some time or other. Me already, as a tragic poet would say, the voice of fate calls. . . .

THE SOUL'S RELEASE

. . . We will do our best, said Crito: And in what way shall we bury you?

In any way that you like; but you must get hold of me, and take care that I do not run away from you. Then he turned to us, and added with a smile:—I cannot make Crito believe that I am the same Socrates who has been talking and conducting the argument; he fancies that I am the other Socrates whom he will soon see, a dead body—and he asks, How shall he bury me? And though I have spoken many words in the endeavour to show that when I have drunk the poison I shall leave you and go to the joys of the blessed,—these words of mine, with which I was comforting you and myself, have had, as I perceive, no effect upon Crito. And therefore I want you to be surety for me to him now, as at the trial he was surety to the judges for me: but let the promise be of another sort; for he was surety for me to the judges that I would remain, and you must be my surety to him that I shall not remain, but go away and depart; and then he will suffer less at my death, and not be grieved when he sees my body being burned or buried. I would not have him sorrow at my hard lot, or say at the burial, Thus we lay out Socrates, or, Thus we follow him to the grave or bury him; for false words are not only evil in themselves, but they infect the soul with evil. Be of good cheer then, my dear Crito, and say that you are burying my body only, and do with that whatever is usual, and what you think best. . . .

Further Questions

1. Many commentators of Western thought regard the passages in this selection as the origin of a dualistic view, according to which reality comprises two radically different sorts of things, one of which is immaterial and the other of which is material. Is that view actually expressed in these passages? Does Socrates commit himself to the view that humans have an immaterial part?
2. Suppose you do have an immaterial soul and suppose that it persists after your bodily death. How much, if any, of your psychology—your beliefs, memories, likes and dislikes, and so on—would have to go along with your soul in order to satisfy your desire for survival of bodily death? Would it satisfy your desire if those aspects of your psychology could survive on their own even without a soul?

Further Readings

Donnelly, John. ed. *Language, Metaphysics, and Death.* 2d ed. New York: Fordham University Press, 1994. An anthology of classical and contemporary sources.

Vlastos, Gregory. *Plato's Universe.* Seattle: University of Washington Press, 1975. A really wonderful book by one of the premier classicists of the twentieth century. It is about the origins of questioning and the development of science in ancient Greece.

63   Of the Immortality of the Soul

DAVID HUME

A brief biography of Hume appears on p. 128.

In the following selection, which was written in 1755 but not published until after his death, Hume summarizes and then attempts to refute all arguments for the view that humans survive their bodily deaths.

Reading Questions

1. Why does Hume think that matter and spirit are equally unknown?
2. Hume says that the soul's continued existence after our bodily deaths should not concern us. Why shouldn't it?
3. What are Hume's views about punishments and rewards in the afterlife?
4. What does Hume mean by his last sentence about divine revelation? Do you think he's serious, or is he kidding?

BY THE MERE LIGHT OF REASON IT seems difficult to prove the Immortality of the Soul. The arguments for it are commonly derived either from *metaphysical* topics, or *moral*, or *physical*. But in reality, it is the gospel, and the gospel alone, that has brought life and immortality to light.

I. Metaphysical topics suppose that the soul is immaterial, and that it is impossible for thought to belong to a material substance.

But just metaphysics teach us, that the notion of substance is wholly confused and imperfect, and that we have no other idea of any substance, than

[*This essay was written by Hume in 1755 but not published until after his death.*]

as an aggregate of particular qualities inhering in an unknown something. Matter, therefore, and spirit, are at bottom equally unknown; and we cannot determine what qualities inhere in the one or in the other.

They likewise teach us, that nothing can be decided *a priori* concerning any cause or effect; and that experience, being the only source of our judgments of this nature, we cannot know from any other principle, whether matter, by its structure or arrangement, may not be the cause of thought. Abstract reasoning cannot decide any question of fact or existence.

But admitting a spiritual substance to be dispersed throughout the universe, like the ethereal fire of the *Stoics,* and to be the only inherent subject of thought, we have reason to conclude from *analogy,* that nature uses it after the manner she does the other substance, matter. She employs it as a kind of paste or clay; modifies it into a variety of forms and existences; dissolves after a time each modification, and from its substance erects a new form. As the same material substance may successively compose the bodies of all animals, the same spiritual substance may compose their minds: their consciousness, or that system of thought, which they formed during life, may be continually dissolved by death; and nothing interests them in the new modification. The most positive assertors of the mortality of the soul, never denied the immortality of its substance. And that an immaterial substance, as well as a material, may lose its memory or consciousness, appears, in part, from experience, if the soul be immaterial.

Reasoning from the common course of nature, and without supposing any new interposition of the Supreme Cause, which ought always to be excluded from philosophy; what is incorruptible must also be ingenerable. The soul, therefore, if immortal, existed before our birth: And if the former existence noways concerned us, neither will the latter.

Animals undoubtedly feel, think, love, hate, will, and even reason, though in a more imperfect manner than man. Are their souls also immaterial and immortal?

II. Let us now consider the *moral* arguments, chiefly those derived from the justice of God, which is supposed to be further interested in the further punishment of the vicious and reward of the virtuous.

But these arguments are grounded on the supposition that God has attributes beyond what he has exerted in this universe, with which alone we are acquainted. Whence do we infer the existence of these attributes?

'Tis very safe for us to affirm, that, whatever we know the Deity to have actually done, is best; but it is very dangerous to affirm, that he must always do what to us seems best. In many instances would this reasoning fail us with regard to the present world.

But, if any purpose of nature be clear, we may affirm, that the whole scope and intention of man's creation, so far as we can judge by natural reason, is limited to the present life. With how weak a concern, from the original, inherent structure of the mind and passions, does he ever look further? What comparison either for steadiness or efficacy, betwixt so floating an idea, and the most doubtful persuasion of any matter of fact, that occurs in common life?

There arise, indeed, in some minds, some unaccountable terrors with regard to futurity: But these would quickly vanish, were they not artificially fostered by precept and education. And those, who foster them: what is their motive? Only to gain a livelihood, and to acquire power and riches in this world. Their very zeal and industry, therefore, are an argument against them.

What cruelty, what iniquity, what injustice in nature, to confine thus all our concern, as well as all our knowledge, to the present life, if there be another scene still waiting us, of infinitely greater consequence? Ought this barbarous deceit to be ascribed to a beneficent and wise Being?

Observe with what exact proportion the task to be performed, and the performing powers, are adjusted throughout all nature. If the reason of man gives him a great superiority above other animals, his necessities are proportionably multiplied upon him. His whole time, his whole capacity, activity, courage, passion, find sufficient employment, in fencing against the miseries of his present condition. And frequently, nay almost always, are too slender for the business assigned them.

A pair of shoes, perhaps, was never yet wrought to the highest degree of perfection, which that commodity is capable of attaining. Yet it is necessary, at least very useful, that there should be some politicians and moralists, even some geometers, poets, and philosophers among mankind.

The powers of men are no more superior to their wants, considered merely in this life, than those of foxes and hares are, compared to *their* wants and *their* period of existence. The inference from parity of reason is therefore obvious.

On the theory of the soul's mortality, the inferiority of women's capacity is easily accounted for: Their domestic life requires no higher faculties either of mind or body. This circumstance vanishes and becomes absolutely insignificant, on the religious theory: The one sex has an equal task to perform as the other: Their powers of reason and resolution ought also to have been equal, and both of them infinitely greater than at present.

As every effect implies a cause, and that another, till we reach the first cause of all, which is the *Deity;* everything that happens, is ordained by Him; and nothing can be the object of His punishment or vengeance.

By what rule are punishments and rewards distributed? What is the Divine standard of merit and demerit? Shall we suppose, that human sentiments have place in the Deity? However bold that hypothesis, we have no conception of any other sentiments.

According to human sentiments, sense, courage, good manners, industry, prudence, genius, etc., are essential parts of personal merits. Shall we therefore erect an elysium for poets and heroes, like that of the ancient mythology? Why confine all rewards to one species of virtue?

Punishment, without any proper end or purpose, is inconsistent with *our* ideas of goodness and justice; and no end can be served by it after the whole scene is closed.

Punishment, according to *our* conception, should bear some proportion to the offence. Why then eternal punishment for the temporary offences of so frail a creature as man? Can any one approve of *Alexander's* rage, who intended to exterminate a whole nation, because they had seized his favourite horse, Bucephalus?

Heaven and hell suppose two distinct species of men, the good and the bad. But the greatest part of mankind float betwixt vice and virtue.

Were one to go round the world with an intention of giving a good supper to the righteous and a sound drubbing to the wicked, he would frequently be embarrassed in his choice, and would find, that the merits and demerits of most men and women scarcely amount to the value of either.

To suppose measures of approbation and blame, different from the human, confounds every thing. Whence do we learn, that there is such a thing as moral distinctions, but from our own sentiments?

What man, who has not met with personal provocation (or what good-natur'd man who has), could inflict on crimes, from the sense of blame alone, even the common, legal, frivolous punishments? And does anything steel the breast of judges and juries against the sentiments of humanity but reflections on necessity and public interest?

By the Roman law, those who had been guilty of parricide, and confessed their crime, were put into a sack, along with an ape, a dog, and a serpent; and thrown into the river: Death alone was the punishment of those, who denied their guilt, however fully proved. A criminal was tried before *Augustus,* and condemned after a full conviction: but the humane emperor, when he put the last interrogatory, gave it such a turn as to lead the wretch into a denial of his guilt. *"You surely,* said the prince, *did not kill your father?"* This lenity suits our natural ideas of RIGHT, even towards the greatest of all criminals, and even though it prevents so inconsiderable a sufferance. Nay, even the most bigoted priest would naturally, without reflection, approve of it; provided the crime was not heresy or infidelity. For as these crimes hurt himself in his *temporal* interest and advantages; perhaps he may not be altogether so indulgent to them.

The chief source of moral ideas is the reflection on the interests of human society. Ought these interests, so short, so frivolous, to be guarded by punishments, eternal and infinite? The damnation of one man is an infinitely greater evil in the universe, than the subversion of a thousand millions of kingdoms.

Nature has rendered human infancy peculiarly frail and mortal; as it were on purpose to refute the notion of a probationary state. The half of mankind die before they are rational creatures.

III. The *physical* arguments from the analogy of nature are strong for the mortality of the soul: and these are really the only philosophical arguments, which ought to be admitted with regard to this question, or indeed any question of fact.

Where any two objects are so closely connected, that all alterations, which we have seen in the one, are attended with proportionable alterations in the other: we ought to conclude, by all rules of analogy, that when there are still greater alterations produced in the former, and it is totally dissolved, there follows a total dissolution of the latter.

Sleep, a very small effect on the body, is attended with a temporary extinction: at least, a great confusion in the soul.

The weakness of the body and that of the mind in infancy are exactly proportioned; their vigour in manhood, their sympathetic disorder in sickness, their common gradual decay in old age. The step further seems unavoidable; their common dissolution in death.

The last symptoms, which the mind discovers, are disorder, weakness, insensibility, and stupidity; the forerunners of its annihilation. The further progress of the same causes, increasing the same effects, totally extinguish it.

Judging by the usual analogy of nature, no form can continue, when transferred to a condition of life very different from the original one, in which it was placed. Trees perish in the water; fishes in the air; animals in the earth. Even so small a difference as that of climate is often fatal. What reason then to imagine, that an immense alteration, such as is made on the soul by the dissolution of its body, and all its organs of thought and sensation, can be effected without the dissolution of the whole?

Everything is in common betwixt soul and body. The organs of the one are all of them the organs of the other. The existence therefore of the one must be dependent on the other.

The souls of animals are allowed to be mortal: and these bear so near a resemblance to the souls of men, that the analogy from one to the other forms a very strong argument. Their bodies are not more resembling: yet no one rejects the argument drawn from comparative anatomy. The *Metempsychosis* is therefore the only system of this kind, that philosophy can hearken to.

Nothing in this world is perpetual; Everything, however seemingly firm, is in continual flux and change: The world itself gives symptoms of frailty and dissolution: How contrary to analogy, therefore, to imagine, that one single form, seeming the frailest of any, and subject to the greatest disorders is immortal and indissoluble! What a daring theory is that! How lightly, not to say how rashly, entertained!

How to dispose of the infinite number of posthumous existences ought also to embarrass the religious theory. Every planet, in every solar system, we are at liberty to imagine peopled with intelligent, mortal beings: At least we can fix on no other supposition. For these, then, a new universe must, every generation, be created beyond the bounds of the present universe: or one must have been created at first so prodigiously wide as to admit of this continual influx of beings. Ought such bold suppositions to be received by philosophy: and that merely on the pretext of a bare possibility?

When it is asked, whether *Agamemnon, Thersites, Hannibal, Nero,* and every stupid clown, that ever existed in *Italy, Scythia, Bactria, or Guinea,* are now alive; can any man think, that a scrutiny of nature will furnish arguments strong enough to answer so strange a question in the affirmative? The want of argument, without revelation, sufficiently establishes the negative. *Quanto facilius,* says Pliny, *certiusque sibi quemque credere, ac specimen accuritatis antegenitali sumere experimento.*[1] Our insensibility, before the composition of the body, seems to natural reason a proof of a like state after dissolution.

Were our horrors of annihilation an original passion, not the effect of our general love of happiness, it would rather prove the mortality of the soul: For as nature does nothing in vain, she would never give us a horror against an impossible event. She may give us a horror against an unavoidable event, provided our endeavours, as in the present case, may often remove it to some distance. Death is in the end unavoidable; yet the human species could not be preserved, had not nature inspired us with an aversion towards it. All doctrines are to be suspected which are favoured by our passions. And the hopes and fears which give rise to this doctrine, are very obvious.

'Tis an infinite advantage in every controversy, to defend the negative. If the question be out of the common experienced course of nature, this circumstance is almost, if not altogether, decisive. By what arguments or analogies can we prove any state of existence, which no one ever saw, and which no way resembles any that ever was seen? Who will repose such trust in any pretended philosophy, as to admit upon its testimony the reality of so marvelous a scene? Some new species of logic is requisite for that purpose; and some new faculties of the mind, that they may enable us to comprehend that logic.

Nothing could set in a fuller light the infinite obligations which mankind have to Divine revelation; since we find, that no other medium could ascertain this great and important truth.

NOTE

1. Hume's quotation is from Pliny's *Natural History,* Book VII, Section 55: "All men are in the same state from their last day onward as they were before their first day, and neither body nor mind possesses any sensation after death, any more than it did before birth — for the same vanity prolongs itself also into the future and fabricates for itself a life lasting even into the period of death, sometimes bestowing on the soul immortality, sometimes transfiguration, sometimes giving sensation to those below, and worshipping ghosts and making a god of one who has already ceased to be even a man — just as if man's mode of breathing were in any way different from that of the other animals, or as if there were not many animals found of greater longevity, for which nobody prophesies a similar immortality! But what is the substance of the soul taken by itself? What is its material? Where is its thought located? How does it see and hear, and with what does it touch? What use does it get from these senses, so what good can it experience without them? Next, what is the abode, or how great is the multitude of the souls or shadows in all these ages? These are fictions of childish absurdity and belong to a mortality greedy for life unceasing. . . . What repose are the generations ever to have if the soul retains permanent sensation in the upper world and the ghost in the lower? Assuredly this sweet but credulous fancy ruins nature's chief blessing, death, and doubles the sorrow of one about to die by the thought of sorrow to come hereafter also. . . . But how much easier and safer for each to trust in himself, and for us to derive our idea of future tranquillity from our experience of it before birth!"

Further Questions

1. Did Hume's refutation of arguments for the view that humans survive their bodily deaths convince you? If there were a weak spot in his arguments, what would it be?
2. Is there any argument that Hume failed to consider for the view that humans survive their bodily deaths that you think might be a good argument? Which such argument, in your view, is the best?

Further Readings

Cullman, Oscar. *Immortality of the soul or Resurrection of the Body.* London, 1958.
H. H. Price. "Survival and the Idea of 'Another World'." *Proceedings of the Society for Psychical Research,* Vol. 1, 1953, pp. 1–25. A famous essay on the question of whether *disembodied* survival of bodily death even makes sense.

64   Survival of Bodily Death: A Question of Values

RAYMOND MARTIN

A brief biography of Martin appears on page 139.

In this selection, Martin explains what he takes to be the dramatic implications of recent developments in personal identity theory for the age-old debate over survival of bodily death. He suggests that these implications ought to transform how the issue is debated and that as a consequence of them it is easier now than it used to be to make a good case for meaningful personal survival. He illustrates the latter point by arguing for a kind of minimalist reincarnation.

Reading Questions

1. What, according to Martin, is the crucial realization that has emerged from the recent debate over personal identity?
2. In your own words, explain why Martin thinks that the remarks in the quotation by Flew take something for granted, without argument, that now requires an argument.
3. What is a fission example? What role have fission examples played in the recent debate over personal identity?
4. Do you believe what Stevenson says about his investigations of Jasbir? If you do, give the best reason you can think of for being skeptical. If you do not, explain why not.
5. Briefly summarize Stevenson's reasons for rejecting all possible explanations of his data that he considers except for the survival explanation.
6. Briefly summarize Martin's reasons for claiming that Stevenson's rejection of the ESP explanation was too hasty.
7. Why does Martin think that the case for meaningful personal survival of bodily death does not depend on one's being able to show that the ESP explanation is less plausible than the survival explanation?

DOES ANYONE EVER SURVIVE his or her bodily death? *Could* anyone? No speculative questions are older than these, or have been answered more frequently or more variously. None have been laid to rest more often, or—in our times—with more claimed decisiveness. Jay Rosenberg, for instance, no doubt speaks for many contemporary philosophers when he claims, in his recent book, to have *"demonstrated"* that "we cannot [even] make *coherent sense* of the supposed possibility that a person's history might continue beyond that person's [bodily] death."

It may seem preposterous at this late date, after thousands of years of debate, to try to add anything radically new to the philosophical discussion of survival. Surely by now it has all been said. Surprisingly, though, there is something new to add—a realization that has emerged from the recent debate over personal identity that makes it much easier to argue successfully for meaningful personal survival. This realization is that for many people the preservation of personal identity does not matter primarily in survival. What this means to the debate over survival of bodily death is that now the person who would argue for survival does not have to presuppose any particular criterion of identity and has much more latitude in terms of how the evidence for survival might be explained. The purpose of the present paper is to illustrate these

claims. I shall do this by arguing for a kind of minimalist reincarnation.

Traditional arguments for reincarnation are invariably burdened with unnecessary and questionable assumptions: the vehicle for survival is some sort of metaphysical substance or soul; there are connections of an unverifiable kind (say, karmic connections) between earlier and later people; personal survival requires identity. The argument that I shall present, by contrast, is compatible with materialism or physicalism, stands or falls on straightforward empirical grounds and dispenses with the assumption that meaningful personal survival requires identity. It is modest also in being only for the *temporary* survival of *some*—so, not for immortality or even for the temporary survival of everyone—and in resting on admittedly *incomplete and fragmentary data*—so that even if the argument is successful as far as it goes, it shows no more than that there is a *prima facie* case for actual survival that could easily be undermined later by more and/or better data. Even with all of these qualifications, however, the argument is still ambitious in that it is for *actual* personal survival of bodily death, something that most contemporary philosophers regard as completely beyond the pale.

I shall rely heavily on the hard word of others: on the philosophical side, on the arguments and examples of Derek Parfit and, to a lesser extent, on

Reprinted from Religious Studies, *Vol. 28 (1992), by permission of the publisher and the author. Footnotes deleted.*

those of Sydney Shoemaker and Robert Nozick—none of whom, of course, has argued for *actual* personal survival of bodily death; and, on the empirical side, on the data that Ian Stevenson and his associates have collected in their investigations of children who apparently remember previous lives. My argument is what I regard as the best defence of the claim that the most likely explanation of Stevenson's data implies meaningful personal survival. Although Stevenson has already used his data to argue for reincarnation, my argument will be so much more modest than Stevenson's own argument that those who find his persuasive (a group that probably does not include many professional philosophers) may well feel that I have thrown out the baby with the bath water. No matter, both arguments could be correct.

I

From 1694, when John Locke added a chapter on personal identity to his *Essay Concerning Human Understanding,* until the late 1960s British and American philosophers concerned with *personal identity* concentrated on a central question: What are the necessary and sufficient conditions under which personal identity is preserved (over time)? In 1967 the univocal focus of this nearly 300-year-old debate was shattered—probably irrevocably. What changed things was the introduction into the debate, by David Wiggins, of so-called fission examples, in which a person somehow divides (in Wiggins' account, amoeba-like) into two or more qualitatively similar persons. Consideration of these examples forced philosophers to face the possibility that one might survive *as* (or be continued by) someone else whose existence one values as much as one's own and, hence, also forced them, appropriately enough, to divide two questions they had previously treated as one: the traditional question, mentioned above, and the new one: What are the conditions under which *what matters primarily in survival* is preserved (over time)? This new question was never raised earlier probably because it was simply assumed that personal identity must be what matters primarily in survival, an assumption that, if true, would guarantee that both questions have the same answer.

In the 1970s and 1980s several philosophers—including Parfit, Shoemaker, and Nozick—argued persuasively that other things matter more in survival than identity. If their arguments are correct, then there are ways of surviving (or, quasi-surviving) that do not preserve identity that are as good, or almost as good, from a person's own egoistic or self-regarding point of view, as survival that does preserve identity. This is not a new idea. In the Vedic traditions that led to Hinduism, for instance, the idea that there can be meaningful survival not as oneself but as part of a larger psychic entity is as old as recorded history. But hard-headed western thinkers have for the most part summarily dismissed such possibilities as either not responsive to western interests in personal survival or as so much mystical mumbo-jumbo. Antony Flew, for instance, who has written more extensively on survival of bodily death than perhaps any other analytic philosopher, nicely captures this dismissive attitude:

> Confronted by such an obstacle [the inevitability of bodily death] how is any such doctrine [of personal survival] to get started? Before trying to suggest an answer I wish to make a sharp, simplifying move . . . I shall . . . be taking it for granted, first, that what we are interested in is our personal post-mortem futures, if any. "Survival" through our children and our children's children after we ourselves are irrecoverably dead, "immortality" through the memories of others thanks to our great works, or even our immersion in some universal world-soul—whatever that might mean—may be as much as, or much more than, most of us will in fact be getting. And it may be lamentably self-centered, albeit humanly altogether understandable, that we should be concerned about more than these thin substitutes. But, for better or for worse, what we are discussing now is the possibility of our post-mortem survival as persons identifiable as those we are here and now.

The sort of quick, dismissive move expressed in Flew's remarks is now obsolete. Although the seeming-possibility of meaningful personal survival without identity may be illusory, it will no longer do simply to *assume* that it is. The point must be argued.

My argument for reincarnation will stake its claim in the territory that Flew (and most other analytic philosophers) have vacated. Whether its conclusion—that some have survived *as* others to whom they are not (or may not be) identical—is a "thin substitute" for ordinary survival (with identity) remains to be seen. It depends partly on which alternatives to ordinary survival one has in mind. (The ones I consider will be much closer to ordinary survival than those Flew mentions, particularly in that one might reasonably anticipate the future experiences of those he survives as in the same ways as he anticipates his own future experiences.) It depends also on how "thick" ordinary survival is. I think, along with Parfit and some others (although for somewhat different reasons), that ordinary survival is much "thinner" than we usually suppose, a point to which I shall return.

One of the things that makes the change of focus that comes with arguing for meaningful personal survival without identity theoretically interesting is that virtually all of the arguments that Flew and Rosenberg and others have presented against either the possibility or the actuality of survival with identity are not even relevant as objections. A plausible argument for meaningful personal survival without identity, then, can provide us with a fresh approach (at least within the context of western philosophy) to an old and relatively tired set of issues. Of course, it is controversial whether other things do in fact matter more in survival than identity. To find out one has to consider hypothetical situations, such as the fission examples, in which one is forced to choose between survival with identity and survival without it. I shall illustrate such choice situations shortly. The outcome of a full consideration of them, as I have argued at length elsewhere, is the realization that for many people some kinds of survival without identity matter as much, or almost as much, as survival with identity. If this is the outcome, then to address the values *of these people* the debate over personal survival will have to shift away from its traditional focus and toward three questions that philosophers have only recently begun to discuss: What matters most importantly in survival? Under what conditions is *this* (whatever it turns out to be) preserved (over time)? Is there good evidence that *this* has ever persisted beyond someone's bodily death?

This last question is the crucial one. As indicated, I answer that, yes, for many people the persistence of their psychologies under favourable conditions (whether or not this preserves identity) may well be—if not now, at least on reflection—among the things that matter most importantly to them in survival, and there is a good enough *prima facie* case that enough of the psychologies of some people have persisted beyond their bodily deaths to make the claim of meaningful personal survival in their cases plausible.

II

The kind of fission examples that have preoccupied philosophers are, for the most part, science fiction scenarios far removed from the practical realities of day-to-day life (and death). But not completely removed. In the late 1930s some psychosurgeons began severing the corpus callosums of severe epileptics in an effort to reduce the severity and frequency of their seizures, a procedure that had the bizarre side-effect, not discovered until many years later, of creating two independent centres of consciousness within the same human skull. These centres not only lacked introspective access to each other, but they could also be made to acquire information about the world, and express it behaviorally, independently of each other. Most dramatically, they sometimes differed volitionally, expressing their differences using alternate sides of the same human bodies that they jointly shared. In one frequently cited example a patient was reported to have hugged his wife with one arm while he pushed her away with the other; in another a patient tried with his right hand (controlled by his left, verbal hemisphere) to hold a newspaper in front of himself, thereby blocking his view of the TV, while he tried with his left hand to knock the paper out of the way.

The fission (and non-fission) examples that have preoccupied philosophers concerned with the possibility of survival without identity are tidier and more complete than these real life cases. They have the disadvantage of being hypothetical, but the advantage of bringing the issue of egoistic survival values into much sharper focus. Consider, for instance, an example, based on one originally presented by Shoemaker, in which you are asked to imagine that you have a health problem that will result soon in your sudden and painless death unless you receive one of two available treatments. The first is to have your brain removed and placed into the empty cranium of a body that is otherwise qualitatively identical to your own. The second is to have your brain removed, divided into functionally identical halves (each of which is capable of sustaining your full psychology), and then to have each of these halves put into the empty cranium of a body of its own, again one that is brainless but otherwise qualitatively identical to your own.

In the first treatment there is a 10% chance the transplantation will take. If it does take, the survivor who wakes up in the recovery room will be physically and psychologically like you just prior to the operation except that he will know he has had the operation and he will be healthy. In the second there is a 95% chance both transplantations will take. If they do, the survivors who wake up in the recovery room will be physically and psychologically like you just prior to the operation except that each of them will know he has had the operation and each will be healthy. If the transplantation in the first treatment does not take, the would-be survivor will die painlessly on the operating table. If either transplantation in the second treatment does not take, then the other will not either, and both of the would-be survivors will die painlessly on the operating table. Suppose everything else about the treatments is the same and as attractive to you as possible; for instance, both are painless and free of charge and, if successful, result in survivors who recover quickly.

Many philosophers believe that identity would be retained in the first (non-fission) treatment but lost in the second (fission) treatment. The reason for its loss in the second treatment is that identity is a transitive relationship—which implies that if one of the survivors were the same person as the brain donor, and the donor were the same person as the other survivor, then the former survivor would be the same person as the latter survivor. Yet the survivors, at least once they begin to lead independent lives, are not plausibly regarded as the same people as each other. And since it would be arbitrary to regard just one of the survivors, but not the other, as the same person as the brain donor (in the beginning they are equally qualified), it is more plausible to regard each of the survivors as a different person from the donor.

But if you would persist through the first treatment but not the second, then only by sacrificing your identity can you greatly increase the chances of someone's surviving for years who is qualitatively just like you. Would it be worth it—that is, would it be worth it for selfish (or self-regarding) reasons? Most people who consider this example feel strongly that it would be, hence (apparently) that survival without identity can matter as much, or almost as much, as survival with identity.

Some have questioned whether fission undermines identity and, hence, whether such examples can support the view that survival without identity matters as much as survival with identity. Since I have argued elsewhere that the same point can be made with non-fission examples, nothing hinges, in my view, on the debate over whether fission undermines identity, and I shall here, for expository reasons, stick to the fission case as my central example, asking the reader to focus on what is crucial about this case—not fission, but the apparently selfishly motivated trading of continued identity for other benefits.

I want now to illustrate how these theoretical developments make it much easier to make a case for meaningful personal survival by considering the data that Stevenson has collected in his investigations of children who apparently remember past lives. I am using Stevenson's data because I believe it is the best evidence we have of the survival of human personality beyond the grave. The theoretical point I want to illustrate, though, is a general one that could be illustrated as well with other data, such as those gleaned from reports of mediumistic communications.

III

To begin with a specific case, consider that of Jasbir, who was born in Rasulpur, India, in 1950, and who, when he was three and a half years old, was thought to have died of smallpox. According to Stevenson's report, Jasbir's father made preparations to bury him but because of darkness postponed the burial until morning. That night he noticed stirrings in his son's body. Over a period of several weeks the boy gradually recovered enough to talk. When he did

---

REMEMBRANCES OF PAST LIVES

C. J. Ducasse

Moreover, there is occasional testimony of recollection of a previous life, where the recollection is quite circumstantial and even alleged to have been verified. One such case may be cited here without any claim that it establishes preexistence, but only to substantiate the assertion that specific testimony of this kind exists. . . .

It is that of "The Rebirth of Katsugoro," recorded in detail and with many affidavits respecting the facts, in an old Japanese document translated by Lafcadio Hearn. [L. Hearn, *Gleanings in Buddha Fields,* Chap. X.] The story is, in brief, that a young boy called Katsugoro, son of a man called Genzo in the village of Nakanomura, declared that in his preceding life a few years before he had been called Tozo; that he was then the son of a farmer called Kyubei and his wife Shidzu in a village called Hodokubo; that his father had died and had been replaced in the household by a man called Hanshiro; and that he himself, Tozo, had died of smallpox at the age of six, a year after his father. He described his burial, the appearance of his former parents, and their house. He eventually was taken to their village, where such persons were found. He himself led the way to their house and recognized them; and they confirmed the facts he had related. Further, he pointed to a shop and a tree, saying that they had not been there before; and this was true.

Testimony of this kind is directly relevant to the question of rebirth. The recollections related in this case are much too circumstantial to be dismissed as instances of the familiar and psychologically well-understood illusions of *déja vu,* and although the testimony that they were verified is not proof that they were, it cannot be rejected *a priori.* Its reliability has to be evaluated in terms of the same standards by which the validity of testimonial evidence concerning anything else is appraised.

From *Nature, Mind and Death* (1951).

---

talk it was evident that he had undergone a remarkable transformation. He then stated that he was the son of Shankar of Vehedi—a person unknown to Jasbir's parents and from a relatively remote village; and he communicated many details of "his" life and death in Vehedi, including how, during a wedding procession, he had eaten poisoned sweets given him by a man who owed him money, fell from a chariot he was riding, injured his head, and died.

Stevenson claims that Jasbir's father tried to hide Jasbir's strange claims and behaviour but news of it leaked out and about three years later came to the attention of a woman from Jasbir's village who had married a native of Vehedi. On rare occasions, at intervals of several years, she returned to Rasulpur. On one such trip in 1957, Jasbir saw her and "recognized" her as his aunt. She then reported the incident and what she had learned of Jasbir's claims to her husband's family and also to the Tyagi family of Vehedi whose son, Sobha Ram Tyagi, had died in May, 1954, at the age of twenty-two, in a chariot accident, in the manner described by Jasbir. The Tyagis knew nothing, though, of any poisoning or debt owed Sobha Ram.

When Sobha Ram's father and other members of his family later went to Rasulpur, Jasbir reportedly recognized them and correctly identified their relationships to Sobha Ram. Jasbir was then brought to Vehedi, put down near the railway station, and asked to lead the way to the Tyagi quadrangle, which he did without difficulty. Then, over a period of several days, he demonstrated to the Tyagis and other villagers a detailed knowledge of the Tyagis and their affairs. He returned to Rasulpur reluctantly, afterward complaining that he felt isolated and lonely there and wanted to live in

KARMIC TRIBULATIONS

Paul Edwards

The Law of Karma is not an empirical statement and it is wholly unlike "natural" laws. To begin with, the Law of Karma has no predictive value whatsoever. A simple example will make this clear. Let us suppose that a plane takes off in which all the crew and passengers are, as far as we can tell, thoroughly decent people. The believer in Karma cannot predict any more or less confidently than the unbeliever that the plane will not crash. The best he can do is offer a statistical prediction based not on Karma but on data concerning the safety of airplanes or, perhaps more specifically, of the kind of plane in which these people are flying. Let us now suppose that a madman or a terrorist planted a time-bomb on the plane and, furthermore, that it is a very efficiently constructed time-bomb. The lunatic, because of his empirical information, can predict with high probability that the plane is going to crash.

It may be argued that the lack of predictive content of Karma is not a serious matter since some scientific laws, notably Darwin's theory of natural selection, also lack predictive content. I do not think that this comparison is sound, but I will not press the point. . . . Scientific laws and indeed all statements that are not empty are *not* compatible with anything that may happen. All of them exclude some conceivable state of af-

fairs. If such an excluded state of affairs were to obtain, the statement would be false. Just like Boyle's law or the second law of thermodynamics, Darwin's theory of natural selection is *not* compatible with anything.

The Law of Karma on the other hand is compatible with anything. . . . Let us suppose that a horrible criminal like Hitler is finally brought to justice. This of course confirms the principle since the criminal's suffering was the result of his evil deeds. Suppose, however, that a person who, according to all the best available information, is decent and kind comes to a bad end, as the result of being run over by a drunken driver, a judicial frameup, or perhaps because of some dreadful illness. Would this disconfirm the principle? Not at all. It only shows that in a previous life he committed evil deeds of which his present suffering is the just punishment. Let us suppose that we know that the next incarnation of this individual is going to be one long horrendous nightmare of torture and persecution. Would this show that the Law of Karma is not true? Not at all: It would only show that his sins in past lives were so enormous that the disasters of his present life were insufficient punishment.

From "The Case Against Reincarnation," *Free Inquiry* (1986-87).

Vehedi, which he continued to visit from time to time, usually for several weeks in the summer.

According to Stevenson, Jasbir made twenty-two checkable statements about "himself," almost all of which were true of Sobha Ram. For instance, Jasbir said that he was the son of Shankar of Vehedi, that he was a Brahmin (not, as Jasbir was, a Jat), that there was a peepal tree in front of his house, and that the house had a well that was half

in and half outside the house (the only well of this kind in Vehedi). He said that his wife belonged to the village of Molna, that his mother was named Kela, his son Baleshwar, his aunt Ram Kali, and his mother-in-law Kirpi. And, as indicated, Jasbir explained the circumstances of Sobha Ram's death.

Stevenson claims that Jasbir recognized a total of sixteen relatives and friends of Sobha Ram and correctly identified their relationships to Sobha

Ram, sometimes adding relevant details. For instance, when a man named Birbal Singh, who was teasingly called "Gandhiji" (because he had large ears that resembled those of Mahatma Gandhi), appeared at the door, Jasbir said, "Come in, Gandhiji." Someone present reportedly corrected Jasbir by saying, "This is Birbal," to which Jasbir replied, "We call him 'Gandhiji'." For their part, the Tyagis accepted Jasbir as a full member of the family and consulted him about the marriage of Sobha Ram's son and daughter. And the man Jasbir claimed killed Sobha Ram to avoid paying a debt later paid Jasbir (not Sobha Ram's family) 600 rupees.

Stevenson reports that Jasbir, after his change in personality, did not retain his original Jasbir personality. Instead, Jasbir claimed that he was Sobha Ram, behaved like Sobha Ram, and only gradually (and never fully) accepted the body and life situations of Jasbir. He continued to think of himself as a Brahmin, added Sobha Ram's Brahmin name to his Jat family name, and refused employment that was appropriate to his Jat status because he considered it beneath his dignity. Yet he continued to live most of the time with his natural parents and planned to marry in the Jat caste.

Jasbir's case differs importantly from most of the other cases Stevenson has investigated, first, in that the person whose personality Jasbir apparently took over did not die until after Jasbir was born—normally the previous personality dies first; second, in that Jasbir's personality was virtually replaced by that of Sobha Ram's—normally there is a blending of the two personalities; and, third, in that Jasbir's apparent memories of Sobha Ram's life and his identification with Sobha Ram continued into adulthood—normally the apparent memories and identification last only a few years. Otherwise, Jasbir's case closely resembles Stevenson's other cases.

Stevenson claims, as of 1987, to have investigated about 250 "cases suggestive of reincarnation" thoroughly and to have investigated at least another thousand cases in enough detail to include them in an analysis of recurrent features. Additional cases have been investigated by Stevenson's associates. Usually Stevenson and his associates have arrived on the scene only after the families involved have attempted to verify the child's statements. Stevenson then has gathered his information after

the fact, so to speak, in (apparently) carefully conducted interviews (usually involving re-interviews and cross-examination of key informants). However, in twenty-four cases (the number is continually growing) Stevenson claims that someone made a written record of what the child had said *before* anyone attempted to verify the child's statements and before the two families concerned had met.

Stevenson reports that the children usually began speaking about "their previous lives" as soon as they could speak—between two and four years old—and then stopped talking about them between the ages of five and eight. (In only a few cases—one of which is Jasbir's—did the apparent memories of the previous life continue into adulthood). Stevenson claims that in the cases he has investigated thoroughly about 90% of the children's checkable statements about "their previous lives" are correct.

In many cases the previous personality met a violent and early death, and events connected with or just preceding his or her death tend to be prominent among the children's apparent memories. And Stevenson reports that in 50% of the cases in which the previous personality died violently, phobias related to the previous personality's mode of death were present—for instance, if the previous personality died of drowning (or, from being shot), the subject might have a phobia of water (or, of firearms). Stevenson claims that the subjects sometimes had skills—such as sewing or the ability to repair engines—that the previous personalities also had and that the children had no normal opportunities to acquire. He also claims that birthmarks on the children corresponding closely to marks on the previous personality, often to the wounds from which the previous personality met death, are not uncommon—but, curiously, are more common in some cultures, such as the Eskimos, the Tlingits, and the Burmese, than in others.

Cultural differences are also reflected in other ways in the data—most importantly, perhaps, in that reported cases are much more common in cultures in which reincarnation is a widely shared belief than in ones in which it is not, even when the two are side by side. So, for instance, there are many more reported cases from Asia and Western Africa than from Europe and (non-tribal) North

BEYOND DEATH

John Beloff

Probably the person for whose postmortem existence we have the best evidence is a George Pellew. He was a Bostonian gentleman, a member of the newly founded American S.P.R., and, although he did not himself believe in survival, he once told his friend Hodgson that, should he die in the not too distant future and then discover that he *had* survived, he would earnestly attempt to communicate the fact through Mrs. Piper. In the event, he did die soon afterward in an accident at the early age of 33 and, lo and behold, a spirit-control calling itself George Pellew (in the literature, for the sake of anonymity, he is referred to as George Pelham, or just G. P.) duly began communicating through Mrs. Piper. Whenever she held a sitting at which any of his friends were present, he never failed to greet them whereas, conversely, he never greeted anyone he had not known during his lifetime. In this way he correctly recognized 30 out of a possible 150 individuals without making a single error.

Then, after some years, he stopped communicating. It appears to be a general rule that it is the recent dead who communicate through mediums, especially when they have died prematurely, leaving unfinished business. This raises the question as to what happens to us eventually, assuming we do survive. Do we, in due course, progress to some higher spiritual sphere where we lose all interest in earthly matters? Does our private ego merge with some universal cosmic mind? We can but speculate. However, a case like that of G. P. reminds us that, perhaps, some people are better *able* to communicate than others, just as some are more psychically gifted than others. It also reminds us that survival does not necessarily imply eternal life.

Hodgson, himself, died soon afterward, also somewhat prematurely at the age of 50 while playing squash. He likewise soon began communicating through Mrs. Piper, and it then fell to his friend William James to study and evaluate the R. H. control. James, the great pioneer of psychology in America and a Harvard professor, was the one who had originally discovered Mrs. Piper. As befits an academic, he was very cautious about coming to a definite conclusion about anything, but he had no doubt whatever that the entranced Mrs. Piper knew more about Richard Hodgson than she could possibly have known in her waking life.

From "Is There Anything Beyond Death? A Parapsychologist's Summation," in P. Edwards, ed., *Immortality*, 1992.

America and many more from the Druses of Lebanon than from the Christians of Lebanon. (Stevenson says he has investigated at least thirty-five (non-tribal) cases from the continental United States.) The interval between the death of the previous personality and the birth of the subject is also linked to culturally determined beliefs.

With this brief indication of the rich array of descriptive data that have been (and still are being) collected by Stevenson and his associates, I want now to turn to the more theoretically interesting question of how dispensing with the assumption that meaningful personal survival requires identity affects the evaluation of competing explanations of Stevenson's data.

IV

Stevenson considers six different possible explanations of his data: fraud, cryptomnesia, paramnesia, genetic memory, extrasensory perception, and survival. Among survival explanations he distinguishes between possession and reincarnation, a distinction I shall ignore since both involve the persistence of a mind or soul which is distinct from a person's physical body and which transmigrates somehow from the deceased person to the child who apparently remembers that person's life.

Fraud. I know of no specific evidence for fraud in connection with Stevenson's data, other than what Stevenson himself mentions. Even so, it is always a possibility, either on the part of the investigators or those they investigate. And judgements about how likely it is, made ultimately against the backdrop of unstated and often unconscious assumptions about what is plausible and what not, are bound to vary from person to person. In my own admittedly subjective view, if Stevenson is as honest as he appears to be, then fraud on a scale sufficient to undermine his data is quite unlikely.

As for Stevenson himself, since 1966 he has conducted his research as a highly visible public figure, often in conjunction with research assistants, and from a relatively high profile base of operations at the University of Virginia. None of Stevenson's by now voluminous publications on these cases have the internal earmarks of investigative fraud — indeed just the opposite. Stevenson consistently comes across as someone who is willing and open to the idea of other investigators checking his cases, although few of them have actually been checked. There are, of course, independent anecdotal reports of the same phenomenon, and many reports of closely related phenomena, such as adults who claim to remember previous lives. (Given how common it is for adults under hypnosis to claim to remember past lives, perhaps it should not be surprising that so many children should make such claims.) Still, even if everything else about my argument for reincarnation is persuasive, one should not regard it as anything more than a *prima facie* case for survival unless and until Stevenson's data has survived the most rigorous checking by *independent* investigators.

Assuming, then, that the data as Stevenson presents them are accurate, Stevenson himself argues persuasively (at least to me) that large scale fraud on the part of his informants is unlikely. While he admits that fraud has occurred occasionally (he claims to know of three cases) he doubts it has

happened often because the sort of peasant villagers that are frequently the subjects of his investigations usually lack both the time and motivation to prepare an elaborate hoax and because a successful hoax generally would require an extraordinary conspiracy involving numerous witnesses, including children, that, he thinks, his usual practice of multiple interviews would probably detect. Stevenson says he has occasionally heard adults prompting the subjects — which he says he strongly discourages — but claims that it has never seemed to him to be more than an expression of adult eagerness not to have the children let the adults down by failing to say to Stevenson what the children have often said to them.

Stevenson also cites the difficulties of directing and staging some of the highly emotional scenes he claims to have witnessed.

> I cannot believe that simple villagers would have the time or inclination to rehearse such dramas as occurred in Chhatta when the family of Prakash thought — or said they thought — I favored his returning to the other family. The complexity of the behavioural features of these cases alone seems to make fraud virtually out of the question, and I prefer to pass on to other more plausible explanations of them.

And we should too. My purpose is not to put the argument for reincarnation in its most convincing form but merely to put it fully and plausibly enough that it can be used to illustrate the ways in which the dynamic of the traditional debate over survival of bodily death should change.

Cryptomnesia would occur if the children acquired the information that they thought they remembered in a normal way, forgot how they acquired it, and then subsequently honestly mistook memories of this information for memories of a previous life. Stevenson claims that despite persistent trying he has generally been unable to find any significant link between the pairs of families involved in these cases and, hence, doubts that cryptomnesia could often be the explanation. He also thinks it is unlikely that young children — many of whom could barely talk when they first began relating their apparent memories — could assimilate so much information on the basis of a few overheard conversations. And he claims that many of the children investigated have revealed private information that was not known outside of the immediate families of the previous personalities. For instance, one child knew of the previous personality's attempt to borrow money from his wife, another of an occasion when the previous personality and a woman had gone to a wedding in a village (which she named) where they had had difficulty finding a latrine. Finally, Stevenson notes that it is not just information but also behavioural features of the cases that must be explained—such as the strong identifications that the subjects often make with the previous personalities.

Paramnesia. This occurs when there are certain other sorts of honest distortions and inaccuracies in the memories of those who provide information on the cases. A possible scenario, that Stevenson thinks may have obtained in a few of the cases he has investigated, involves the parents unwittingly giving their child's first few statements about the previous personality more coherence than the statements actually had:

> [The subject's parents] think of the sort of person about whom the child might be talking. Then they start searching for such a person. They find a family having a deceased member whose life seems to correspond to the child's statements. They explain to this family what their child has been saying about the previous life. The second family agrees that the child's statements might refer to the deceased member of their family. The two families exchange detailed information about the deceased person and about what the child has been saying. From enthusiasm and carelessness, they may then credit the child with having stated numerous details about the identified deceased person, when in fact he said very little, and perhaps nothing specific, before the two families met.

Thus, a myth of what the child apparently remembered might develop and come to be accepted by both the families.

But this sort of scenario—and paramnesia generally—is not easily applicable in those cases in which someone had made a written record of what the child said before the accuracy of his or her statements was checked and before the two families had met. And paramnesia is unlikely also in many other cases in which Stevenson claims that he or his associates reached the scene within a few weeks or months of the initial meeting between the families and before memories of the child's previous remarks had much of a chance to fade. Add to this that the children often repeated their apparent memories many times before the families involved met and that in some cases many peoples' memories of the child's statements would have had to become distorted in the same ways, and paramnesia begins to seem less plausible as a general explanation of the data.

There is also the question of motive. Stevenson claims that many parents are reluctant to have the child's statements verified; some believe that the child could be harmed by remembering a past life, some that they could lose the child to the other family, some are reluctant to have anyone verify the children's statements about another life that was either much poorer or much more prosperous than their own, and some simply dislike encouraging behaviour that they find unattractive in the child. In addition, Stevenson claims that the families of the previous personalities often have their own reasons for being reluctant to endorse the case: some, particularly wealthy families, are afraid that the subject's family means to exploit them; some dread embarrassing revelations that the subject may make about the family; still others—somewhat paradoxically—do not wish to reawaken the grief they continue to have for the deceased person. Paramnesia, then, whether from ordinary forgetfulness or from motivated distortion seems an unlikely explanation of much of the data.

Genetic memory. Another possibility, at least for those cases in which the subject might be a descendant of the previous personality, is genetic (or inherited) memory. But much of the information apparently remembered is about events—such as the deaths of previous personalities—that occurred after the previous personalities' children were conceived, and, in any case, most of the children investigated were not genetic descendants of the previous personalities.

Extrasensory perception. Stevenson claims that ESP by itself cannot account for the behavioural features of the richer cases, including the fact that the subjects characteristically attribute their apparent memories to a previous personality with whom they identify (personation). He therefore considers

WHAT I SAW WHEN I WAS DEAD

A. J. Ayer

The only memory that I have of an experience closely encompassing my death, is very vivid. I was confronted by a red light, exceedingly bright, and also very painful even when I turned away from it. I was aware that this light was responsible for the government of the universe. Among its ministers were two creatures who had been put in charge of space. These ministers periodically inspected space and had recently carried out such an inspection. They had, however, failed to do their work properly, with the result that space, like a badly fitted jigsaw puzzle, was slightly out of joint.

A further consequence was that the laws of nature had ceased to function as they should. I felt that it was up to me to put things right. I also had the motive of finding a way to extinguish the painful light. I assumed that it was signalling that space was awry and that it would switch itself off when order was restored. Unfortunately, I had no idea where the guardians of space had gone and feared that even if I found them I should not be allowed to communicate with them. It then occurred to me that whereas, until the present century, physicists accepted the Newtonian severance of space and time, it had become customary, since the vindication of Einstein's general theory of relativity, to treat space-time as a single whole. Accordingly I thought that I could cure space by operating upon time.

I was vaguely aware that the ministers who had been given charge of time were in my neighbourhood and I proceeded to hail them. I was again frustrated. Either they did not hear me, or they chose to ignore me, or they did not understand me. I then hit upon the expedient of walking up and down, waving my watch, in the hope of drawing their attention not to my watch itself but to the time which it measured. This elicited no response. I became more and more desperate, until the experience suddenly came to an end.

This experience could well have been delusive. A slight indication that it might have been veridical has been supplied by my French friend, or rather by her mother, who also underwent a heart arrest many years ago. When her daughter asked her what it had been like, she replied that all that she remembered was that she must stay close to the red light.

On the face of it, these experiences, on the assumption that the last one was veridical, are rather strong evidence that death does not put an end to consciousness.

From the *Sunday Telegraph,* August 28, 1988.

ESP-with-personation as the hypothesis that most plausibly competes with survival (hereafter, I shall use the label ESP to mean ESP-with-personation). Even so, Stevenson does not think ESP would explain the selection of the person whose experiences are apparently remembered, or how—in those cases where we would have to suppose that the information apparently remembered was obtained telepathically from more than one living person who remembered it—the information came to be organized in the minds of the children who apparently remembered it in the same ways it was organized in the minds of the previous personalities, or—particularly in cultures hostile to the idea of reincarnation—why the information came to the children in the form of apparent memories, or, how, in some cases, the children exhibited special skills or birthmarks appropriate to the previous personalities. In short, Stevenson claims that if ESP were the explanation, it would have to be ESP "of a very extensive and extraordinary kind."

Second, Stevenson claims that the cases suggestive of reincarnation differ in various ways from what one would expect if ESP were the explanation. Other than their apparent memories of previous lives these children rarely exhibit any additional evidence of ESP; the phenomenology of the children's apparent memories is the same as that of ordinary memory — not, say, trancelike; most of the children experience the apparent memories not as disconnected but as continuous with their present lives; the children's access to information about, and identification with, the previous lives sometimes lasts more or less continuously for a long time — usually for years and occasionally even for decades; and the children and also their parents often lack a plausible motive for the children to identify with the previous personalities.

In what must be one of the most knowledgeable reviews of Stevenson's data, the British psychologist Alan Gauld claims that it is "extremely unlikely that either fraud or cryptomnesia have been more than marginal factors in producing the correct statements and recognitions" and remarks that he is "quite at one with Stevenson over his doubts concerning the ESP (or super ESP) theory." Gauld concludes that he does "not find it easy to dissent" from Stevenson's claim that his data sustain "a rational belief in reincarnation."

V

I assume that *something* explains Stevenson's data. If his data are accurate, then I agree with Stevenson that fraud, cryptomnesia, paramnesia, and genetic memory are unlikely as explanations. That leaves ESP and survival. There are, of course, scientific objections to ESP. Those who weight these more heavily than I do will perhaps give the nod to one of the explanations — such as cryptomnesia — that I would pass over. But if they do, it is probably because they feel that one of those explanations *must* be correct, not because there is much independent evidence that one of them actually is correct. Currently, so far as I know, there is almost no such evidence.

Even those who weight scientific objections to ESP more heavily than I do would probably agree that if we had more and better data on cases suggestive of reincarnation, data of a sort that counts against normal explanations and toward ESP or survival, that would at least make those latter ex-

planations *more* likely. So long as one admits that *enough* good data of this sort *could* make either ESP or survival the *most* likely explanation, then disagreement over how much evidence that would take is a matter of judgement about which it is difficult and probably pointless to argue. It would be dogmatic, it seems to me, for someone to take the view that *no matter how good* the data were, they could *never* tip the balance far enough that it actually favoured either the ESP or survival explanations. As long as one agrees with that, the prudent course is simply to wait and see how good the evidence actually gets.

Whatever objections one might have to ESP as an alternative to normal explanations, these are not likely to be objections to it as an alternative to the survival explanation. So, to focus on those aspects of the argument that illustrate how the traditional debate over survival should change, I am going to set scientific qualms about ESP to one side and consider just the relative merits of ESP and survival. In my opinion, Stevenson is not in a position to dismiss ESP so easily as a possible explanation of his data. The reason is that we have virtually no basis for opinions about how ESP, if it exists, might work and, hence, no basis for claiming that it could not have produced the results Stevenson has reported. This would be so even if there were no evidence in parapsychological research that ESP might be as extraordinary and extensive as it would have to be to account for Stevenson's data. But there is *some*.

The French physician E. Osty, Director of the Institut Metapsychique of Paris from 1926 to 1938 reported incidents that would amount (according to Gauld) "to what could justifiably be called 'super-ESP'... without any suggestion that the information originated from spirits". And S. G. Soal, former President of the British Society for Psychical Research, reported on sittings with the famous medium Mrs. Blanche Cooper in which Soal claims she thought (as did Soal) that she was communicating with a dead Gordon Davis, but instead telepathically got information from a living Gordon Davis while simultaneously exhibiting impressive evidence of precognition. Gauld remarks that "'Super-ESP' seems an appropriate term to describe what was going on; and if it could occur in this case, why not in others, indeed in all the others that have been presented as evidence for survival?" Why not indeed?

Gauld has his reasons why not—which include that Osty was careless in writing up his reports and that Gauld suspects Soal of having "improved" the Gordon Davis case. But even if the outcome of Gauld's assessment were (which it is not) that our evidence for ESP is *always* evidence for more modest results than would be required to account for Stevenson's data—even so—since we do not know how ESP works, if we concede that it has to be taken seriously as a possible explanation (which we should *when* the competing explanation is survival), then we do not have a right to say that ESP could not be powerful enough to account for Stevenson's data. This should be clear from an analogy.

Idiot savants sometimes have extraordinary memories and equally impressive behavioural skills, such as the ability to make complicated mathematical computations quickly and accurately or to play a musical instrument proficiently with little or no training. Imagine an investigator of 150 years ago who did not have much of an idea what genes were or how they worked but who believed that he had evidence that there were genes and that a certain kind of gene—which he called a memory-gene—exercised a powerful influence on the quality and scope of every normal person's memory. Suppose he denied that memory-genes might account for the extraordinary memories and skills of idiot savants on the grounds that for a memory-gene to produce such results it would have to be not an ordinary memory-gene but a super-memory-gene—something for which, he claimed correctly, there was no evidence except in the cases of idiot savants. Imagine that he urged, instead, that the extraordinary powers of these idiot savants are more likely explained on the supposition that they draw directly on the powers of immaterial souls (many of whom were once incarnated in people who were musical or mathematical) that have somehow survived bodily death.

No one should be convinced, first, because until the investigator knows more about genes, and about memory-genes in particular, he has no business putting such limits on what genes are capable of producing and, second, because no matter how mysterious it might seem—and 150 years ago it might have

seemed mysterious to the point of being almost miraculous—that genes could produce the extraordinary powers observed in some idiot savants, it could hardly be less mysterious to explain these powers by appeal to the survival of dead people.

Even Stevenson admits that ESP might have produced the results he has observed if, as he says, it were of a very extensive and extraordinary kind—for instance, if it were a kind of ESP that produced both informational and behavioural results in an organized way (so as to mimic the arrangement in a previous personality), and even produced physical effects such as the birth marks. But *how* could ESP do all this? It could if something about the previous personality directly caused the result in the subjects, who were "selected" simply due to their unusual receptivity. The "transmissions" could either be without intervening links (so-called action at a distance) or in the form of something like a radio-wave. We can suppose that the subjects' receptivity was such that it caused them to experience the informational aspects of these transmissions as if they were ordinary memory, which, then, in some of them did and in some did not become firmly enough implanted to resist erosion by competing influences that came later. Finally we can suppose that this receptivity in the subjects was as a special capacity distinct from the more ordinary and diffuse powers of ESP that are sometimes exhibited by others and, hence, not likely to manifest itself as a generalized capacity for ESP.

Fantastic? I agree. But if we accept Stevenson's data at face value and reject fraud, cryptomnesia, paramnesia, and genetic memory as explanations, then all of the remaining explanations are fantastic. I do not say that the explanation I have just sketched is preferable to Stevenson's survival explanation, only that, based on what we know, it is at least as likely, and hence that it would be arbitrary to reject it in favour of Stevenson's explanation. In sum, if the case for meaningful personal survival based on Stevenson's data depends on survival being the best explanation, then it fails, since for all we know his data can be explained by super-ESP.

But there is no reason that I know of to suppose that the case for meaningful personal survival based on Stevenson's data does depend on survival being the best explanation. Stevenson may feel that if ESP were the best explanation, then the

RESURRECTION

Peter van Inwagen

It is part of the Christian faith that all men who share in the sin of Adam must die. What does it mean to say that I must die? Just this: that one day I shall be composed entirely of non-living matter; that is, I shall be a corpse. It is not part of the Christian faith that I must at any time be totally annihilated or disintegrate. (One might note that Christ, whose story is supposed to provide the archetype for the story of each man's resurrection, became a corpse but did not, even in His human nature, cease to exist.) It is of course true that men apparently cease to exist: those who are cremated, for example. But it contradicts nothing in the creeds to suppose that this is not what really happens, and that God preserves our corpses contrary to all appearance. . . . Perhaps at the moment of each man's death, God removes his corpse and replaces it with a simulacrum which is what is burned or rots. Or perhaps God is not quite so wholesale as this: perhaps He removes for "safekeeping" only the "core person"—the brain and central nervous system—or even some special part of it. These are details.

I take it that this story shows that the resurrection is a feat an almighty being *could* accomplish. . . . Of course one might wonder *why* God would go such lengths to make it look as if most people not only die but pass into complete nothingness. This is a difficult question. I think it can be given a plausible answer, but not apart from a discussion of the nature of religious belief. I will say just this. If corpses inexplicably disappeared no matter how carefully they were guarded, or inexplicably refused to decay and were miraculously resistant to the most persistent and ingenious attempts to destroy them, then we should be living in a world in which observable events that were *obviously* miraculous, *obviously* due to the intervention of a power beyond Nature, happened with monotonous regularity. In such a world we should all believe in the supernatural: its existence would be the best explanation for the observed phenomena. If Christianity is true, God wants us to believe in the supernatural. But experience shows us that, if there is a God, He does not do what He very well *could* do: provide us with a ceaseless torrent of public, undeniable evidence of a power outside the natural order. And perhaps it is not hard to think of good reasons for such a policy.

From "The Possibility of Resurrection," *International Journal for Philosophy of Religion*, 1978.

identities of the people whose lives the children apparently remembered would not have been preserved. Whether he is right about that is debatable, just as it is debatable, and for much the same reasons, whether the identities would have been preserved even on Stevenson's dualistic hypothesis; Rosenberg, for instance, does not think that they would have been.

The deeper point is that it may not matter as much as survivalists, such as Stevenson, and skeptics, such as Flew and Rosenberg, seem to think whether the *identities* of the previous personalities in these cases have or have not been preserved. The new developments in personal identity theory, as illustrated in the fission example, suggest that meaningful personal survival may not require the preservation of identity. And since we have no *evidence* to support a view about *how* either a disincarnate mind or ESP (whatever these might be) could account for Stevenson's data, it is arbitrary, in our current state of ignorance, to assume that if ESP accounted for them, that would be inferior—from the point of view either of preserving identity or of sustaining meaningful personal survival—to the ways in which souls would account for his data. If this is not obvious, consider another analogy.

Imagine that you are a resident of Earth at some time in the technologically distant future and that you have urgent business on Mars. You can conduct this business only by activating a Star Trek-style beamer that records exact and complete information about your body, brain, and psychology at the same time as it dematerializes you on Earth and sends the information to a receiving station on Mars. A few minutes later, the information is used on Mars to create an exact replica of you out of new, but qualitatively similar, matter. In short, the beamer is, in effect, a reincarnation machine. Suppose further that even though no one in your culture has ever known exactly how the beamer works, since it obviously preserves a person's psychology and bodily form its use is widely accepted as a way of preserving identity. You share this belief, though with some hesitation. Remembering that there are philosophers who argue that the beamer does not preserve identity—but also remembering the fission examples—you reason that whether or not the beamer preserves identity, it at least preserves what matters most to you in survival. So you drive to the transmitting station to be beamed. Once there, however, you learn that scientists have recently discovered that the beamer works in exactly the same way that super-ESP works, which, as it happens, is one of the ways I sketched above.

Would this new information make any difference to you, so far as your decision to enter the beamer is concerned? If you were satisfied that the beamer probably preserves identity, would you feel now that its claim to preserve identity had been sullied by the revelation that the information is transmitted from Earth to Mars by means of a process that also underlies super-ESP? If you were satisfied that whether or not the beaming process preserves identity it at least preserves what matters to you in survival, would you feel that it would preserve what matters to you any less if the information were transmitted by a process that also underlies super-ESP? Probably not—to both questions. But, then, super-ESP may be as good a way of ensuring meaningful personal survival as the process, what-

ever it is, that underlies Stevenson's survival hypothesis.

What I am suggesting is that assuming that Stevenson's data are as he presents them, then they may well provide the basis for a good argument for meaningful personal survival *whether or not* the super-ESP explanation or his survival explanation best explains them and *whether or not* the actual processes involved, on either explanation, preserve personal identity. They *will* provide such a case for anyone for whom what matters primarily in survival is simply the singular reemergence of his or her psychology—beliefs, memories, intentions, personality, and so on—after bodily death.

VI

In philosophical discussions of survival of bodily death, values often masquerade as facts, and facts are often portrayed as being more substantial than they actually are. For instance, how "thick" or "thin" something is as a substitute for ordinary survival, which may seem to be a factual question, depends not on how *much*—physically or psychologically—has been lost in the substitution, not even, necessarily, on whether identity has been lost, but, rather, on how much *of what matters* in survival has been lost. That is, the relevant sense of "thick" and "thin" have more to do, in the first instance, with our values than with either our identities or our normal circumstances, which are relevant only to the extent that we value preserving them. So, even though a great deal (quantitatively) may have been lost in some transformation, if what was lost is trivial from the vantage point of our concern for meaningful personal survival, then what emerged from the transformation is not, in the relevant sense, a thin substitute for survival, but, rather, a robust one.

The ways philosophers argue for one criterion of identity over another is often also covertly evaluative in that they rely heavily on idiosyncratic and controversial intuitive judgments about whether identity would be preserved through various sorts of bizarre transformations—the infamous puzzle cases of the personal identity literature—which are controversial in the first place because our conventions, which were formed to apply to cases that arise in normal circumstances, underdetermine what we should say about these extraordinary examples. Thus, the suspicion is unavoidable that the ways philosophers try to extend the conventions to cover the extraordinary examples generally have more to do with personal values than with objective social facts, in particular, they seem to have more to do with their feelings about whether *what matters in survival* has been preserved through the transformations depicted in the examples. If this is right, then disputes over criteria of personal identity are often simply disguised disputes over what matters in survival.

Even if it were possible, which it does not seem to be, to determine objectively how our linguistic conventions regarding personal identity should extend to cover the puzzle cases, our linguistic conventions are just that—conventions; they are not necessarily deep ontological truths. Before thinking much about how personal identity may be conventional, our identities may seem quite substantial; after thinking about it they are likely to seem more ephemeral. Nozick was right to call the puzzle cases in the personal identity literature "a koan for philosophers." Even the so-called facts of identity may be thinner than they first appear.

This "lightness" of identity is surprisingly bearable. Consider, for instance, Shoemaker's example of an environmentally polluted society of the technologically distant future in which people, to keep from getting very sick, have to replace their bodies every several years with qualitatively identical ones, a procedure that in their society is regarded as routine; no more of a threat to maintaining one's identity than, say, getting one's teeth cleaned is in ours. Projecting ourselves imaginatively into such a society, it is easy for many of us to see ourselves (or our replicas) conforming without much strain to their conventions. This suggests that we could simply, and sensibly, take the view that any ways in which our social conventions might differ from those of the polluted society are not that important. By analogy, when one sees that various moral prohibitions in one's own society—for instance, against public nudity or extra-marital sex—are not shared by other societies with which one can identify without much strain, there is a natural tendency to downplay the importance of the conventions of one's own society. In the same way, when one sees that certain of our conventions regarding personal identity are not present in other (possible) societies with which one can identify without much strain, there is a natural tendency to downplay the importance of our own conventions. There is nothing inevitable about shedding such parochial values, but it is a natural and often reasonable response to exposure to attractive alternatives.

In sum, the fission examples and the other examples that have motivated the belief that identity may not be what matters primarily in survival suggest that identity, even under normal circumstances, has been overrated. In particular, they suggest that identity is not a condition of reasonably anticipating having experiences in the same ways we would ordinarily anticipate having our own experiences. These suggestions may or may not be correct. To decide we will have to look freshly at—that is, re-*evaluate*—what it means to survive under ordinary as well as hypothetical circumstances. Yet among those who have tried to do this there is not now, and probably never will be, a univocal response: to some identity seems to matter a great deal, to others much less.

Whatever the outcome of this process of re-evaluation, as soon as we admit, as it seems we must, its relevance to the assessment of arguments for meaningful personal survival of bodily death, the cat is out of the bag. For then no argument for meaningful personal survival is dismissible merely on the grounds that because the kind of survival it postulates would not preserve identity it is too "thin" to be responsive to our egoistic interests in survival. And this means that the standard ways many philosophers have dismissed arguments for survival will no longer work. One must now consider not just whether the kind of process postulated preserves identity but also whether it preserves enough of what matters importantly in survival. In sum, when it comes to meaningful personal survival of bodily death the key question is not simply one of metaphysics, as has been assumed traditionally, but also one of values—and values that, in the end, may well vary from person to person in quite subjective ways.

Many philosophers will not welcome this conclusion. We, philosophers, love to be decisive, to settle things not just for the time being and for people with certain values rather than others, but for everyone and once and for all. We want to draw straight, definite lines. Particularly when it comes to "nonsense," we like to dispatch it not just as unwarranted but as impossible. Yet the new developments in personal identity theory strongly suggest that for the bit of nonsense we have been discussing—meaningful personal survival of bodily death—the days of decisive dismissals are over. On this topic, many of the lines that most need to be drawn are now and henceforth probably always will be curved and blurry.

Further Questions

1. When you watch an episode of "Star Trek" and see the crew members of the *Enterprise* beamed from the spaceship to a planet, do you assume that the people who emerge from the beaming are the same people who were beamed from the spaceship or, rather, that the people who were beamed are now destroyed and have been replaced by identical replicas who are not they, but other people? Argue as plausibly as you can for the view of beaming that you do not accept.
2. Adherents of some Asian religious traditions hope that when they die they will not continue as the people they now are but instead lose their individuality and merge with some grander psychic entity or process. Would you regard that as a better option than personal survival of bodily death? Explain why you think that someone who is not confused might take a different view than yours.

Further Readings

Kolak, Daniel, and Martin, Raymond, eds. *Self & Identity*. New York: Macmillan, 1991. The latest from philosophers and psychologists on unity of consciousness, personal identity, and self.
Martin, Raymond. *Self-Concern: An Experimental Approach to What Matters in Survival*. Cambridge: Cambridge University Press, 1998.

Death, Nothingness, and Subjectivity 65

THOMAS W. CLARK

Thomas Clark is associate director of the Institute for Naturalistic Philosophy in Cambridge, Massachusetts. In addition to conducting a philosophy seminar for the Humanist Association of Massachusetts, he writes regularly on philosophical topics for *Humanist,* the magazine of the American Humanist Association. He is also a research associate with Health and Addictions Research, Inc., a nonprofit organization in the social sciences. In the following selection, he claims that many of our attitudes toward death are due to a mistaken view about what it involves. The truth, he suggests, gives all of us a reason to fear death less.

Reading Questions

1. How does Clark attempt to show that people actually do believe in a kind of positive nothingness? Does his attempt succeed? Do you think you have ever had that belief?

2. From our personal points of view, as subjects of experience, are there gaps, or blank spaces, during the course of our conscious lives? What does Clark think? Why? What do you think?

3. Clark claims that "subjectivities—centers of awareness—don't have beginnings and endings for themselves, rather they simply find themselves in the world." What does he mean? Do you agree?

4. Clark asks, "How much of a change between TC and TC/mod is necessary to destroy personal subjective continuity?" How does he answer? How would you answer? Why?

5. How does Clark attempt to show that "awareness—for itself, in its generic aspect of 'always having been present'—is immune to interruption"? Do you agree?

6. Clark suggests that "consciousness, for itself, is impervious to death or indeed to any sort of objective interruption." What does he mean? Do you agree?

7. What does Clark mean when he says that "to identify ourselves with generic subjectivity is perhaps as far as the naturalistic materialist can go toward accepting some sort of immortality"?

For only death annihilates all sense, all becoming, to replace them with nonsense and absolute cessation.

—F. GONZALEZ-CRUZZI, "Days of the Dead" in *The New Yorker,* November 1993.

THE WORDS QUOTED DISTILL THE COMMON SECULAR CONCEPTION of death. If we decline the traditional religious reassurances of an afterlife, or their fuzzy new age equivalents, and instead take the hard-boiled and thoroughly modern materialist view of death, then we likely end up with Gonzalez-Cruzzi. Rejecting visions of reunions with loved ones or of crossing over into the light, we anticipate the opposite: darkness, silence, an engulfing emptiness. But we would be wrong.

The topic of our fate after death is a touchy subject, but nevertheless the error of anticipating nothingness needs rectifying. This misconception is so widespread and so psychologically debilitating for those facing death (all of us, sooner or later) it is worth a careful look at the faulty, rather subliminal logic that persuades us that dying leads us into "the void."

Here, again, is the view at issue: When we die, what's next is *nothing;* death is an abyss, a black hole, the end of experience; it is eternal nothingness, the permanent extinction of being. And here, in a nutshell, is the error contained in the view: It is to *reify* nothingness—make it a positive condition or quality (e.g., of "blackness")—and then to place the individual in it after death, so that we somehow fall *into* nothingness, to remain there eternally. It is to illicitly project the subject that died into a situation following death, a situation of no experiences, of what might be called "positive nothingness." Epicurus deftly refuted this mistake millennia ago, saying "When I am, death is not, and when death is, I am not," but regrettably his pearl of wisdom has been largely overlooked or forgotten. In what follows, I will try to refine this insight and, using a thought experiment, make its implications vivid.

Not that there haven't been more recent attempts to counter the myth of nothingness, notably by the philosopher Paul Edwards in his classic 1969 paper "Existentialism and Death: A Survey of Some Confusions and Absurdities." In this essay, I will produce my own examples of those bewitched by the vision of the void, but before continuing I must bow to Edwards's "who's who" of thinkers that have fallen into this particular conceptual trap.

He quotes Shakespeare, Heine, Seneca, Swinburne, Houseman, Mencken, Bertrand Russell, Clarence Darrow, James Baldwin, and others, all to the effect that, as Swinburne put it, death is "eternal night." Those who anticipate nothingness at death are at least in some pretty exalted company.

If, as I will argue, nothingness cannot be anything positively existent, that is, if it truly (as the term would indicate) doesn't exist, then the situation at death cannot involve falling into it. Those skeptical of the soul and an afterlife need not fear (or cannot look forward to, if such is their preference) blackness and emptiness. There is no eternal absence of experience, no black hole that swallows up the unfortunate victim of death. If we conscientiously eliminate the tendency to project ourselves into a situation following death, and if we drop the notion of positive nothingness, then this picture loses plausibility and a rather different one emerges.

Do people still really believe, as I claim they do, in a kind of positive nothingness? I will present enough examples to show that, beyond Edwards's celebrities, many do harbor such a misconception. In developing a plausible alternative, my operating assumptions and guiding philosophy will be resolutely naturalistic, materialist, and non-dualist. I assume only a single universe of interconnected phenomena, a universe devoid of souls, spirits, mental essences, and the like. In particular, persons, on this account, are not possessed of any essential core identity (an indivisible self or soul), but consist only of relatively stable constellations of dispositions and traits, both physical and psychological. Although some conclusions I reach may end up sounding counterintuitive to those inclined to naturalism, it won't be because the argument departs from naturalistic assumptions. And for readers who are skeptical about naturalism, these conclusions may not be so unpalatable as my starting point might lead them to suppose.

ANTICIPATING NOTHINGNESS

The late Isaac Asimov, interviewed by Bill Moyers's series "A World of Ideas," questioned the traditional religious picture of our fate after death: "When I die I won't go to heaven or hell, there will just be nothingness." Asimov's naturalistically based skepticism about heaven or hell is common among secularists (there is no evidence for such realms), but he commits an equally common fallacy in his blithe assumption about nothingness, namely, that it could "be." By substituting nothingness for heaven and hell, Asimov implies that it awaits us after death. Indeed the word itself, with the suffix "ness," conjures up the strange notion of "that stuff which does not exist." In using it, we may start to think, in a rather casual, unreflective way, that there *exists* something that doesn't exist, but of course this is not a little contradictory. We must simply see that nothingness doesn't exist, period.

Harvard philosopher Robert Nozick, in his book *The Examined Life,* expresses much the same view as Asimov, and in much the same context. He debunks, in a very respectful tone, the wishful thinking that supposes there will be an afterlife involving the memories and personality of a currently existing person. "It might be nice to believe such a theory, but isn't the truth starker? This life is the only existence there is; afterward there is nothing." Although he probably doesn't mean to, with these words Nozick may suggest to the unwary that "nothing" is something like a state into which we go and never return. But, as Paul Edwards explained in "Existentialism and Death," death is *not* a state, it is not a condition in which we end up after dying. Of course, I'm not denying that we die and disappear, only that we go *into* something called nonexistence, nothing, or nothingness.

My richest example is offered by the late novelist Anthony Burgess in his memoirs, *You've Had Your Time: The Second Part of the Confessions.* The following paragraph from his meditations about death contains several nice variations on the "nothingness" theme.

> Am I happy? Probably not. Having passed the prescribed biblical age limit, I have to think of death, and I do not like the thought. There is a vestigial fear of hell, and even of purgatory, and no amount of rereading rationalist authors can expunge it. If there is only darkness after death, then that darkness is the ultimate reality and that love of life that I intermittently possess is no preparation for it. In face of the approaching blackness, which Winston Churchill facetiously termed black velvet, concerning oneself with a world that is soon to fade out like a television image in a power

WHY ARE TRACES IMPORTANT?

Robert Nozick

When people desire to leave a trace behind, they want to leave a certain kind of trace. We all do leave traces, causal effects reverberate down: our voices move molecules which have their effects, we feed the worms, and so on. The kind of trace one wishes to leave is one that people know of in particular and that they know is due to you, one due (people know) to some action, choice, plan of yours, that expresses something you take to be important about the kind of person you are, such that people respect or positively evaluate both the trace and that aspect of yourself. We want somehow to live on, but not as an object lesson for others. Notice also that wanting to live on by leaving appropriate traces need not involve wanting continuous existence; you want there to be some time after which you continue to leave a mark, but this time needn't be precisely at your death. Artists as well as those who anticipate resurrection are quite willing to contemplate and tolerate a gap.

Why are traces important? There are several possibilities. First, the importance of traces might lie not in themselves but (only) in what they indicate. Traces indicate that a person's life had a certain meaning or importance, but they are not infallible signs of this—there may be traces without meaning, or meaning without traces. For instance, to "live on" in the memory of others indicates one's effect on these others. It is the effect that matters; even if each of them happened to die first, there still would have been that effect. On this first view, it is a mistake to scrutinize traces in an attempt to understand how life has or can have meaning, for at best traces are a symptom of a life's meaning. Second, traces might be an expression of something important about a life, but it might be important and valuable in addition that this be expressed.

Third, it might be thought that the leaving of traces is intrinsically important. A philosophical tradition going back to Plato holds that the permanent and unchanging is more valuable by virtue of being permanent and unchanging.

From *Philosophical Explanations,* 1981.

cut seems mere frivolity. But rage against the dying of the light is only human, especially when there are still things to be done, and my rage sometimes sounds to myself like madness. It is not only a question of works never to be written, it is a matter of things unlearned. I have started to learn Japanese, but it is too late; I have started to read Hebrew, but my eyes will not take in the jots and tittles. How can one fade out in peace, carrying vast ignorance into a state of total ignorance?

Listing the thematic variations, we have "darkness after death," "approaching blackness," "black velvet," "a world that is soon to fade out," "the dying of the light," "a state of total ignorance." All these express Burgess's expectation that death will mean entering a realm devoid of experience and qualities, a state something like losing all sensation (Gonzalez-Cruzzi's "non-sense"), all perception, all thought. He is raging against the imminent arrival of Nothingness, the eternal experience of no experience in which the subject somehow witnesses, permanently, its own extinction. But death rules out any such experience or witnessing, unless of course we covertly believe, as Burgess seems to, that in death we persist as some sort of pseudo-subject, to whom eternity presents itself as "black velvet." Burgess, as well as Nozick and Asimov, all deny that they continue on in any form, so their picture of the subject trapped in nothingness after death is really quite contradictory. Since death really is the end of the individual, it cannot mean the arrival of darkness as witnessed by some personal remnant.

Two more brief examples, which I believe are typical of those who face death without the traditional reassurances of an afterlife. Arthur W. Frank, author of *At The Will Of The Body: Reflections on Illness,* wrote about his heart attack that "Afterward I felt always at risk of one false step, or heartbeat, plunging me over the side again. I will never lose that immanence of nothingness, the certainty of mortality." And Larry Josephs, an AIDS patient, wrote in the *Times* that ". . . I hope that when the time comes to face death, I will feel stronger, and less afraid of falling into an empty black abyss."

Although the fear of death is undoubtedly biological and hence unavoidable to some extent, the fear of nothingness, of the black abyss, can be dealt with successfully. This involves seeing, and then actually feeling, if possible, that your death is not the end of experience. It is the end of *this experiencer* most definitely, but that end is not followed by the dying of the light. Experience, I will argue, is quite impervious to the hooded figure who leads his unwilling charges into the night.

CONTINUITY AND BEING PRESENT

In order to make this clear, it will be helpful to consider some facts about ordinary experience. First is the initially somewhat surprising fact that, from our point of view as subjects of experience, there are no gaps during the course of our conscious lives. Even though we are frequently and regularly unconscious (asleep, perhaps drugged, knocked out, and so forth) these unconscious periods do not represent subjective pauses between periods of consciousness. That is, for the subject there is an instantaneous transition from the experience preceding the unconscious interval to the experience immediately following it. On the operating table, we hear ourselves mumble our last admonition to the anesthesiologist not to overdo the pentathol, and the next instant we are aware of the fluorescent lights in the recovery room. Or we experience a last vague thought before falling asleep and the next experience (barring a dream, another

sort of experience) is hearing the neighbor's dog at 6 A.M. As much as we know that time has passed, nevertheless for us there has been no gap or interval between the two experiences that bracket a period of unconsciousness. I will call this fact about experience "personal subjective continuity."

Next, note that this continuity proceeds from our first experience as a child until the instant of death. For the subject, life is a single block of experience, marked by the rhythm of days, weeks, months, and years, and highlighted by personal and social watersheds. Although it may seem obvious and even tautological, for the purposes of what follows I want to emphasize that during our lives we never find ourselves absent from the scene. We may occasionally have the *impression* of having experienced or "undergone" a period of unconsciousness, but of course this is impossible. For the subject, awareness is constant throughout life; the "nothingness" of unconsciousness cannot be an experienced actuality.

But what about the time periods before and after this subjectively continuous block of experience, that is, before birth and after death? Don't these represent some sort of emptiness or "blank" for the subject since, after all, it doesn't exist in either? To think that they might, as I've pointed out, is to confuse nonexistence with a state that we somehow primitively subsist in, as an impotent ego confronted with blackness. Certainly we don't ordinarily think of the time *before* we come into existence as an abyss from which we manage to escape; we simply find ourselves present in the world. We cannot contrast the fact of being conscious with some prior state of nonexperience.

The same is true of the time after death. There will be no future personal state of nonexperience to which we can compare our present state of being conscious. All we have, as subjects, is this block of experience. We know, of course, that it is a finite block, but *since that's all we have, we cannot experience its finitude.* As much as we can know with certainty that this particular collection of memories, desires, intentions, and habits will cease, this cessation will not be a concrete fact for us, but can only be hearsay, so to speak. Hence (and this may start to sound a little fishy) as far as we're concerned as subjects, we're always situated here in the midst of experience.

THE EVIL OF DEATH

Epicurus

So death, the most terrifying of ills, is nothing to us, since so long as we exist, death is not with us; but when death comes, then we do not exist. It does not concern either the living or the dead, since for the former it is not, and the latter are no more.

Letter to Menoeceus.

Even given all this, when we imagine our death being imminent (a minute or two away, let us suppose) it is still difficult not to ask the questions "What will happen to me?" or "What's next?", and then anticipate the onset of nothingness. It is extraordinarily tempting to project ourselves—*this* locus of awareness—into the future, entering the blackness or emptiness of nonexperience. But since we've ruled out nothingness or nonexperience as the fate of subjectivity what, then, are plausible answers to such questions? The first one we can dispense with fairly readily. The "me" characterized by personality and memory simply ends. No longer will experience occur in the context of such personality and memory. The second question ("What's next?") is a little trickier because, unless we suppose that my death is coincident with the end of the entire universe, we can't responsibly answer "nothing." Nothing is precisely what *can't* happen next. What happens next must be *something,* and part of that something consists in various sorts of consciousness. In the very ordinary sense that other centers of awareness exist and come into being, *experience* continues after my death. This is the something (along with many other things) that follows the end of my particular set of experiences.

Burgess suggests, when facing death, that "concerning oneself with a world that is soon to fade out like a television image in a power cut seems mere frivolity." But we know, as persons who have survived and witnessed, perhaps, the death of others, that the world does not fade out. It continues on in all sorts of ways, including the persistence of our particular subjective worlds. Death ends indi-vidual *subjectivities* while others are continuing or being created.

As I tried to make clear, subjectivities—centers of awareness—don't have beginnings and endings for themselves, rather they simply find themselves in the world. From their perspective, it's as if they have always been present, always here; as if the various worlds evoked by consciousness were always "in place." Of course we know that they are not always in place from an objective standpoint, but their own nonbeing is never an experienced actuality for them. This fact, along with the fact that other subjectivities succeed us after we die, suggests an alternative to the intuition of impending nothingness in the face of death. (Be warned that this suggestion will likely seem obscure until it gets fleshed out using the thought experiment that follows.) Instead of anticipating nothingness at death, I propose that we should anticipate the *subjective sense of always having been present,* experienced within a different context, the context provided by those subjectivities that exist or come into being.

In proposing this, I don't mean to suggest that there exist some supernatural, death-defying connections between consciousnesses that could somehow preserve elements of memory or personality. This is not at all what I have in mind since material evidence suggests that everything a person consists of—a living body, awareness, personality, memories, preferences, expectations, and so on—is erased at death. Personal subjective continuity as I defined it earlier requires that experiences be those of a *particular* person; hence, this sort of continuity is bounded by death. So when I say that *you* should look forward, at death, to the "subjective sense of always having been present," I am speaking rather loosely, for it is not you—not *this* set of personal characteristics—that will experience "being present." Rather, it will be another set of characteristics (in fact, countless sets) with the capacity, perhaps, for completely different sorts of experiences. But, despite these (perhaps radical) differences, it will share the qualitatively *very same sense* of always having been here, and, like you, will never experience its cessation.

TRANSFORMATION AND GENERIC SUBJECTIVITY

To help make this shared, continuing sense of "always having been present" more concrete, I want to embark on a thought experiment of the Rip Van Winkle variety. So imagine, in the perhaps not so distant future, that we develop the technology to reliably stop and then restart biological processes. One could, if one wished, be put "on hold" for an indefinite period and then be "started up" again. (Some trusting and perhaps naive souls have already had their brains or entire bodies frozen in the expectation of just such technology.) In essence, one is put to sleep and then awakened after however many years, memories and personality intact.

From the point of view of the subject, such a suspension of consciousness would seem no different from a normal night's sleep, or, for that matter, an afternoon nap. The length of the unconscious interval—minutes, years, or centuries—makes no difference. There is simply the last experience before being suspended, and then the first experience upon reactivation, with no experienced gap or interval of nothingness in between. In principle, a subject could lie dormant for millions of years, to awaken with no sense of time having passed, except, of course, the clues given by the changed circumstances experienced upon regaining consciousness. Personal subjective continuity would have been preserved across the eons.

Next, suppose that during the unconscious period (the length of which is unimportant for the point I'm about to make) changes in memories or personality, or both, take place, either deliberately or through some inadvertent process of degrada-

tion. I go to sleep as TC and wake up as TC/mod. (Readers are encouraged to substitute their own initials in what follows.) If the changes aren't too radical, then I (and others) will be able to reidentify myself as TC, albeit a modified version, whose differences from the original I might or might not be able to pinpoint myself. ("Funny, I don't remember ever having liked calf's liver before. Was I always this grumpy? I wonder if this suspension technique really worked as well as they claimed. Maybe some unscrupulous technician fiddled with my hypothalamus while I was under. Still, all in all, I seem relatively intact.") Assuming this sort of reidentification is possible, personal subjective continuity is still preserved across the unconscious interval. There would be no subjective gap or pause between the last experience of TC and the first experience of TC/mod. For TC/mod, TC was never not here. There is simply one block of experience, the context of which suffered an abrupt but manageable alteration when TC woke up as TC/mod.

An interesting series of questions now arises, questions that may generate some visceral understanding of what I mean by expecting the sense of always having been present. First, how much of a change between TC and TC/mod is necessary to destroy personal subjective continuity? At what point, that is, would we start to say "Well, TC 'died' and a stranger now inhabits his body; experience ended for TC and now occurs for someone else"? It is not at all obvious where to draw the line. But let's assume we did draw it somewhere, for instance at the failure to recognize family and friends, or perhaps a vastly changed personality and the claim to be not TC but someone else altogether. Imagine changes so radical that everyone agrees it is not TC that confronts us upon awakening; he no longer exists. Given this rather unorthodox way of dying, *what happens to the intuition that now, for TC there is "nothing"*?

We have seen that, given small or moderate changes in memory and personality, there is no subjective gap or "positive nothingness" between successive experiences on either side of the unconscious period. Instead, there is an instantaneous transition from one to another. (TC/mod says, "I'm still here, more or less like before. Seems like I went to sleep just a second ago.") Given this, it seems wrong to suppose that, at some point

A TIBETAN BUDDHIST EXPERIENCE OF DEATH

When the expiration hath ceased, the vital-force will have sunk into the nerve-centre of Wisdom and the Knower will be experiencing the Clear Light of the natural condition. . . . Now thou art experiencing the Radiance of the Clear Light of Pure Reality. Recognize it. . . . thy present intellect, in real nature void, not formed into anything as regards characteristics or colour, naturally void, is the very Reality, the All-Good.

Thine own intellect, which is now voidness, yet not to be regarded as of the voidness of nothingness, but as being the intellect itself, unobstructed, shining, thrilling, and blissful, is the very consciousness, the All-good Buddha.

Thine own consciousness, not formed into anything, in reality void, and the intellect, shining and blissful, — these two, — are inseparable. The union of them is . . . Perfect Enlightenment.

Thine own consciousness, shining, void, and inseparable from the Great Body of Radiance, hath no birth, nor death, and is the Immutable Light. . . .

Knowing this is sufficient. Recognizing the voidness of thine own intellect to be Buddhahood, and looking upon it as being thine own consciousness, is to keep thyself in the divine mind of the Buddha. . . .

From *The Tibetan Book of the Dead*. Translated by W. Y. Evans-Wentz.

---

further along on the continuum of change (the point at which we decide someone else exists), TC's last experience before unconsciousness is not still *instantly followed* by more experiences. These occur within a substantially or perhaps radically altered context, that of the consciousness of the new person who awakens. These experiences may not be *TC's* experiences, but there has been no subjective cessation of experience, no black abyss of nothingness for TC. Destroying personal subjective continuity (that is, ending a particular subject by means of the transformation envisioned here) doesn't result in the creation of some positive absence of experience "between" subjects into which the unfortunate TC falls or out of which the new person emerges. Rather, it just changes the context of experience radically enough so that we, and the person who wakes up, decide TC no longer exists. Death in this case is matter of convention, not biology, and it hasn't interrupted awareness, only changed its context.

Although this transformation has disrupted the personal subjective continuity imparted by a stable context of memory and personality, there is another sort of continuity or sameness, that created by the shared sense of always having been present. Such *generic subjective continuity* is independent of the context of memory and personality (that is, of being a particular person), and it amounts simply to the fact that, whoever wakes up feels as if they've always been here, that there has been no subjective blank or emptiness "in front" of their current experience. We can, I think, imagine going to sleep, being radically transformed, and having someone else wake up, with no worry about falling into nothingness, even though we no longer exist. The first experience of TC/rad (a radically changed TC, no longer identifiable as the same person) would follow directly on the heels of the last experience of TC. If there are no subjective gaps of positive nothingness between successive experiences of a single individual, then there won't be such a gap between a person's last experience and the first experience of his or her radically transformed successor. That first experience occurs within a context of memory and personality that establishes the same sense of always having been present generated by the original person's consciousness.

But of course the difficulty here is that it seems arbitrary, or simply false, to say that TC/rad's experience *instantly follows* TC's last experience if there is no connection of memory or personality, but only some bodily continuity. (And if we wish, we can imagine that drastic changes in body as well are engineered during the unconscious period, so that TC/rad looks nothing like his predecessor.) The objective facts are that TC has a last experience, then sometime later TC/rad has a first experience. But despite the lack of personal subjective continuity, despite the fact that we may decide at some point on the continuum of change (in memory, personality, and body), that TC no longer exists to have experiences, experience doesn't end *for* him, that is, there is no onset of nothingness. What we have instead is a transformation of the *subject itself*, a transformation of the context of awareness, while experience chugs along, oblivious of the unconscious interval during which the transformation took place. It's not that TC/rad's experience follows TC's in the sense of being connected to it by virtue of memory or personality, but that there is no *subjective* interval or gap between them experienced by either person. This is expressed in the fact that TC/rad, like TC, feels like he's always been present. However radical the change in context, and however long the unconscious interval, it seems that awareness — for itself, in its generic aspect of "always having been present" — is immune to interruption.

DEATH AND BIRTH

Let us call TC's fate in becoming TC/rad "death by transformation." My claim is that awareness is subjectively continuous, in this generic sense, across such a transformation. Considered from "its" point of view, experience never stops even though objectively speaking (from the "outside") one context for it ends and later on, as much later as you care to imagine, another context picks up. The next step in my argument is to apply this conclusion to ordinary death and birth. Instead of being transformed into some sort of successor, imagine that TC is allowed by a careless technician to lapse from unconsciousness into irreversible brain death. Somewhere, sometime later, a fresh consciousness comes into being, either naturally or by artifice. Except that the physical incarnations of TC and this other consciousness have no causal connection, this situation is the same as death by transformation. That is, one context of awareness has lapsed and another very different one begins. During the objective interval, there has been no subjective hiatus in awareness; only the context of experience has changed.

This thesis implies that even if all centers of awareness were extinguished and the next conscious creature appeared millions of years hence (perhaps in a galaxy far, far away) there would still be no subjective interregnum. Subjectivity would jump that (objective) gap just as easily as it jumps the gap from our last experience before sleep to the first upon awakening. All the boring eons that pass without the existence of a subject will be irrelevant for the subject that comes into being. Nor will they count as "nothingness" for all the conscious entities that ceased to exist. Subjectivity, awareness, consciousness, experience — whatever we call it — never stops arising as far as *it* is concerned.

At this point, it is likely that our intuitions about experience "jumping the gap" have been stretched beyond the breaking point. We have moved from the fairly uncontroversial fact of the continuity of one person's experience (no subjective gaps in consciousness during a lifetime) to this seemingly outlandish notion that consciousness, for itself, is impervious to death or indeed to any sort of objective interruption. But let me quickly reiterate my main points in order to reinstate some plausibility. (1) It is a mundane, although contingent, fact of life that when I die other subjects exist, hence subjectivity certainly is immune to *my* death in *these* circumstances. (2) If I am unconscious for any length of time, I don't experience that interval; I am always "present"; this is personal subjective continuity. (3) If, after a period of unconsciousness, the transformed person who wakes up is not me, there *still* won't be any perceived gap in awareness. The person who wakes up feels, as I did (hence "still" feels), that they've always been present. There has been no prior experience of not being present for them, nor when I stop existing do I have such an experience; this is generic subjective continuity. (4) Death and birth are "functionally equivalent" to the sort of transformation in (3), so again there will be no perceived gap, no nothingness of nonexperience into which the subject might fall. Generic subjective continuity holds across any objective discontinuities in the existence of conscious beings.

Points 3 and 4 are certainly the most difficult to accept, and accepting them really depends on whether we are willing to slide down the slippery slope of the transformation thought experiment. If you don't buy the idea of a soul or indivisible self, it's an easy trip. From a naturalistic perspective, the self is nothing more than a contingent collection of fairly stable personality traits, memories, and physical characteristics. Thus the difference between my transformation into someone still recognizably me and someone barely not me is not a difference that would prevent awareness from jumping the gap. If there is no nothingness between experiences in the first case, then there is no nothingness in the second.

The reason 3 may have some intuitive plausibility is that we can generalize from our own ordinary experience of subjective continuity to cases in which we may not be quite sure who it is that wakes up. We can then see that even significant changes in the context of experience won't create subjective gaps. It is the absence of such gaps, resulting in the continuing shared sense of always having been present, that constitutes generic continuity.

Point 4 seems plausible only if we accept what I call generic continuity in the *extreme* case of 3 (a completely different person wakes up) and then buy the notion that there is no real difference between death by transformation and ordinary death. This equivalence is difficult to accept since in ordinary death no causal "successor" person "takes over" the consciousness relinquished by the person who dies. But keep in mind that in our thought experiment the successor's consciousness might be activated long after the original person was put to sleep, have very different physical and personal traits, and be somewhere else altogether. The only connecting link is presumably some bodily "shell," any of the parts of which (including the brain) might be changed or replaced. The most extreme

case of 3 looks a lot, then, like ordinary death, except that there is a very attenuated successor that comes into existence by virtue of a radical transformation. Ordinary death and birth amount, I think, to such radical transformations of subjectivity, except that there is no obvious candidate for a successor. My point is, however, that we don't need such a candidate to ensure the generic continuity of experience. We need only see that the continuity is that of subjectivity itself, abstracted from any particular context, and it finds concrete expression in the fact that none of us has ever experienced (or will ever experience) not being here.

Despite my naturalistic and materialist caveats at the beginning of this essay, this conclusion may still seem to have a mystical ring. It may seem as though I give too much weight to the subjective sense of always having been present, and, in claiming that subjectivity, for itself, always "is," I ignore the vast times and spaces in which no consciousness exists at all. Nevertheless, I believe a materialist can see that consciousness, as a strictly physical phenomenon instantiated by the brain, creates a world subjectively immune to its own disappearance. It is the very finitude of a self-reflective cognitive system that bars it from witnessing its own beginning or ending, and hence prevents there being, *for it,* any condition other than existing. Its ending is only an event, and its nonexistence a current fact, for other perspectives. After death we won't experience nonbeing, we won't "fade to black." We continue as the generic subjectivity that always finds itself here, in the various contexts of awareness that the physical universe manages to create. So when I recommend that *you* look forward to the (continuing) sense of always having been here, construe that "you" not as a particular person, but as that condition of awareness, which although manifesting itself in finite subjectivities, nevertheless always finds itself present.

To identify ourselves with generic subjectivity is perhaps as far as the naturalistic materialist can go toward accepting some sort of immortality. It isn't conventional immortality (not even as good as living in others' memory, some might think) since there is no "one" who survives, just the persistence of subjectivity for itself. It might be objected that in countering the myth of positive nothingness I go too far in claiming some sort of positive *connection* between subjectivities, albeit a connection that doesn't preserve the individual. I might be construed as saying, to borrow the language of a different tradition, that an eternal Subject exists, ever-present in all contexts of experience. I wouldn't endorse such a construal since it posits an entity above and beyond specific consciousness for which there is no evidence; nevertheless such language captures something of the feel for subjectivity and death I want to convey.

It is possible that this view may make it easier to cope with the prospect of personal extinction since, if we accept it, we can no longer anticipate being hurled into oblivion, to face the eternal blackness that so unsettled Burgess (and, I suspect, secretly

bedevils many atheists and agnostics). We may wear our personalities more lightly, seeing ourselves as simply variations on a theme of subjectivity that is in no danger of being extinguished by our passing. Of course we cannot completely put aside our biologically given aversion to the prospect of death, but we can ask, at its approach, why we are so attached to *this* context of consciousness. Why, if experience continues anyway, is it so terribly important that it continue within *this* set of personal characteristics, memories, and body? If we are no longer haunted by nothingness, then dying may seem more like the radical refreshment of subjectivity than its extinction.

Further Questions

1. Did your reading of Clark's essay affect you emotionally, even if only temporarily; for instance, did it "give you a rush"? If it did, why did it? And what can you learn about your current attitudes toward death from your having been so affected?
2. Do you fear death? Would you, if you thought that you would not personally survive it? If you do (or would), did your reading of Clark's essay make any difference to how much you fear (or would fear) death? Why or why not?

Further Readings

Breer, Paul. *The Spontaneous Self: Viable Alternatives to Free Will.* Cambridge, MA: Institute for Naturalistic Philosophy, 1989. Against the idea that we are agents. Very accessible.
Glover, Jonathan. *I: The Philosophy and Psychology of Personality Identity.* London: Penguin Books, 1988. An excellent introduction to the main issues.

The Wine Is in the Glass   66

DANIEL KOLAK

In this short story a man sits alone in a restaurant. While waiting for his food to arrive, he ruminates.

A brief biography of Daniel Kolak appears on page 96.

Reading Questions

1. How often do you eat alone, without a book or magazine or television to distract you? Does it make you uncomfortable to sit and eat by yourself in a restaurant? Why?
2. What do you think about this man? Would you like to join him? What would you ask him? How might he respond?

THE WINE IS IN THE GLASS.

There is a man looking at the wine, thinking: there is wine in the glass and it is true that there is wine in the glass. I am the man looking at the glass, thinking: what is in the man, in me?

The man picks up the glass, raises the rim to his lips, purses his lips, and, slowly, takes a sip. He swallows. He puts the glass back down onto the table.

There is now a little less wine in the glass. But now there is a little wine in the man, who thinks: the wine is still wine, it is in me. Soon it will change from wine to blood. It will become me. The wine becomes my blood. He smiles, and thinks: I don't know how to turn blood into wine but I know how to turn wine into blood. Actually, I don't. I couldn't do it outside me. Inside me, I just do it. Automatically. Without effort or thought. This is not a miracle. This is digestion. He burps (quietly, under his breath, to himself).

There are creases in the white tablecloth. He straightens them and wonders why, what the significance of it is. He concludes there is no significance. To the act of removing creases from a tablecloth, that is. Why, then, did he do it? He doesn't know. But he cares that he doesn't know. And, it bothers him that he cares. It also bothers him, now that he has reflected upon it, that he can't quite remove the creases. They have been ironed in. It wouldn't take much to do the ironing right. Whoever was ironing the tablecloth was in a hurry, or perhaps careless. If whoever ironed the tablecloth had been more attentive to the tablecloth now he, an ordinary man in a rather expensive restaurant passing time with ordinary thoughts while waiting to order his hopefully extraordinary dinner, would not be trying to straighten out the creases and thinking about it and also at the same time wondering why he was think-

ing about an inconsequential crease in an inconsequential tablecloth. He would be doing something else, thinking about something else or maybe not thinking about anything.

The man smiles to himself. To acknowledge that it is only to himself that he smiled he lowers his eyes to the crease on the tablecloth and shakes his head a little just in case anyone else is looking. Why did he do that? He does not know anybody in this restaurant. Nobody knows him. What does he care? But he does. How strange, he thinks, that he should be so self-conscious. He glances around the restaurant. No one is looking at him. Back to the crease in the tablecloth. Then to the wine in the glass. His image is in the wine.

The waiter, who noticed the man looking, rushes over.

"Ready to order, sir?"

"I'll have the blackened grouper."

"Baked potato or cottage fries?"

"What are cottage fries? Never mind. Baked potato."

"Like chips. Sliced."

"I'll have the baked."

"Salad or cole slaw?"

"Cole slaw. No. Make that salad."

"What kind of dressing would you like, sir?"

"What have you got?"

"We've got — "

"Italian?"

"Is creamy all right?"

"You don't have, ah, regular?"

"Our house is vinaigrette."

"Oh."

"Would you like that?"

"Fine."

The man stares at his image staring back at him from the wine in the glass while the waiter rushes off toward the kitchen. The man picks up the glass and then, changing his mind, puts it back down. His image stares back at him. He forgot to ask about bread. He would like some bread with his wine before the salad comes. He looks up but the waiter is gone.

The man thinks: what should I think about? I am by myself in a restaurant waiting for my food and I have time to think. But there is nothing in particular he wants to think about. Yet he feels anxious — only slightly — feeling as if he wants something only he doesn't quite know what. The food, ordered, would be coming. He would eat it and enjoy it and then walk to his car and drive home. Laughing (to himself) he shakes his head again. Why is he anticipating going home after the restaurant? Where else but home would he go? Translucent and dim little pictures flash through his consciousness, superimposed over his field of vision but so very dimly that he knows it is too much to think of them as actual pictures. They are like shadows of pictures. A bit like interference from another channel on a television set, only dim- mer. The future, perhaps, interfearing with the present? He laughs at the pun. Inter-fearing. A possible future, perhaps. How strange, he thinks, that such thoughts run through his head. Thoughts paying attention to thoughts (inter-fearing with themselves) and thinking about why this is hap- pening and then remarking — to whom, them- selves? — that they are aware of what they (the thoughts) are doing —

The waiter comes with the salad and, the man is glad to see, a basket with fresh-baked bread. He remembers the time his girlfriend brought a bas- ket, similar to this one, from Mexico as a present for his parents and there had been, hidden in it, some tiny eggs that had hatched into bugs. They discovered the bugs because the freshly hatched bugs made strange noises inside the wicker and so they put it out on the balcony in the snow. The bugs died. They threw the basket away anyway, just in case there were some eggs left in the basket.

"Here you go, sir."

"Is that baked here?"

"No, sir." The waiter takes the wine from the cooler and fills the glass. "We get it. Enjoy."

"Thank you."

The crust is nice and thick, dark, and the bread is still warm. The butter is whipped. The man breaks off a piece of bread, butters it, takes several bites. While still chewing he lifts the glass to his lips and soaks the bread and butter in his mouth with the wine.

"Mmmmm," he says aloud, but softly, only to himself.

The wine is very white and very dry and the tartness of it is delicious with the sweetness of the butter and the saltiness of the rich, whole-wheat bread.

His thoughts are just running now, he is not paying attention to them — so that if someone in- terrupted him right now and asked, "What are you thinking about?" the man would more than likely look up, surprised, and say, with a full mouth, "Hm?" then quickly swallow and add, "Oh, I don't know. I was daydreaming," and he probably couldn't say what he was daydreaming about. But he was daydreaming about his girlfriend.

The salad is a bit soggy, he thinks, but very good. Very green. He thinks: I am turning food into thought, and then, thinks: why am I thinking about turning food into thought (into myself)? Is that what is happening? Is that what digestion is — turning food into thought and, among other things, into things like fingernails, live cells, and blood? How do you get thoughts out of wine and bread?

Now, if something else were happening — say, a beautiful woman had walked into the restaurant, alone, and had sat within eyesight — he would be involved in this something else, whatever it would have happened to be. He would not be thinking about his own thoughts and the puzzling question of why he is thinking about his own thoughts. Rather, he would be looking, admiring her, un- dressing her in his mind, wondering what it would be like to do something sexual and preferably ob- scene with her — What a thought, he thought, while chewing on your salad! There is not even a suitable woman around who fits appropriately into his (only remotely realized) fantasy. An elderly couple sits several tables away and anyway the old woman has her back to him. Not very suitable. But perhaps they have a daughter. He begins laughing, until suddenly a piece of salad goes down the wrong way and he chokes. It is a big piece, too big, he knows (even though this is the one thing his mother had never particularly nagged him about) he didn't chew it properly, and he thinks: I just inhaled salad! What if I die?

Unable to breathe, he takes several gulps of wine to try and wash the green leaf down but it doesn't go down either, he can't even get the wine into his throat. It dribbles, rejected, down his chin. The salad gets lodged even deeper. Gasping loudly now, he tries hitting himself on the back but this only makes him panic more. Nothing is working. He sees the elderly couple looking.

The old man asks, "You all right?"

Like a fool (he thinks this to himself—"What a fool I am for nodding"), he nods. But he is not all right, he can't talk or breathe and his heart is pounding. He will pass out (he thinks, and his thinking is correct) if he doesn't get some oxygen soon.

The old man stands up, his napkin in his wrinkled hands held over his lap like a loin cloth. "Help? Some help? Do you need help?"

The old woman brings her scrunched napkin to her mouth, covering the lower part of her face like a veil. "What's the matter? Are you choking?"

Veils? Loin cloths? Why am I thinking like this, in analogies, he wonders? I might be dying!

The waiter does not hear the noise, he is in the kitchen on the telephone, taking a reservation.

"I say, are you all right?" shouts the old man.

He can't answer, he is dead. (You think this is too sudden. People don't just die like that. But maybe a piece of plaque got loose in the arteries around his heart. Or maybe you just don't like it when the hero of the story dies. But this guy was not a hero. He was just an ordinary guy in a restaurant thinking about his thoughts when the salad did him in. You don't even know his name or what he does [used to do] for a living or anything.)

The wine, undrunk, is in the glass. It is made from fermented grapes which (before they are crushed) grow in vineyards where seeds feed on water and sunlight and earth and whatever else seeds can use to turn earth into fruit—for instance corpses like the one the man has just become. (Look, even if it would have taken a little longer, what's the difference?) Soon, waiters (who are not called "waiters") dressed in black (just like the waiter in the kitchen who has just gotten off the phone but will be back on the phone shortly, only blacker) will deliver the man—with a pompous ceremony even more formal than the one that would have delivered the blackened grouper (and which now the cook will himself gladly eat)—to the seeds and animals none of whom has ever paid a bill. The bill for this future ceremony (with music, there will be very sad ethnic music from the Mediterranean region, the man himself specified it), gratuities included, has been paid, well in advance, by the man who will soon be (if he isn't already) in the coffin. To be served, like the white wine in the glass, well chilled.

At home on the man's desk lies a letter the man had composed but not yet sent to his girlfriend:

> I want to make love to you. I want to touch you so that I can feel the texture of what you are. I want my feeling you to make you feel. The feeling of feeling you is the feeling of ecstasy. I want to make you stop, then go. Then stop, then go. To get so close that the dizzyness of the distance between us becomes a whirlpool of madness, danger, desire. When I look without looking I see my seeing and there you are: a mystery that moves. Into you I ascend into myself and forget that I too am no one. The veil of the world is the veil between us. Soft and transparent and warm like gauze. To love you is to be wounded. Sorrow is the joy of knowing the unknown. I don't want a looking-back but a looking-at: I want to know you now or not at all. Now is the place for knowing, touching, feeling, seeing. Now is now. My now is yours, forever.

Nice letter. Really, he was quite an extraordinary man. Oh, well. I could go on. But what would be the point? The man is dead.

Further Questions

1. What is this story about? What feelings does it evoke?
2. What is the significance of the letter? Do you see any importance in the fact that it was never mailed?
3. It seems to be a fact of life that we, the living, must feed on the dead. And it seems to be a fact of physics that nature recycles *everything*—that under ordinary circumstances matter and energy can neither be created nor destroyed. Relate these ideas to the themes and images of the story as you interpret them.

Further Readings

Kolak, Daniel. *In Search of Myself: Life, Death and Personal Identity.* Belmont, CA: Wadsworth, 1999. In this novel a young student encounters the spirit of René Descartes amoung the ruins of Delphi.

Romains, Jules. *The Death of a Nobody.* New York: H. Fertig, 1976. An explicitly nonexistentialist view of death, the subject of which is not a man but, says the author, "an event."

Tolstoy, Leo. *The Death of Ivan Ilych.* Originally published in 1886. About a symbolic Everyman who discovers the meaning of life only when confronted by death.

Part XI

Meaning

Many have claimed to know the meaning of life. Probably more answers have been given on this topic than on any other. Yet, in spite of all the answers, the meaning of life is not understood. Why?

Perhaps because there is no meaning: life is absurd.

Perhaps because the answers up to now have not been good enough: we need a new, bigger and better answer.

Perhaps because the answer is not an answer: we should look, instead, for a big, colorful question mark, hanging suspended by nothing amidst a blinding abyss of unknowing.

67   My Confession

LEO TOLSTOY

Count Leo Tolstoy (1828–1910) was born, educated, and lived almost all of his life in Russia. At the age of fifty, after writing some of the greatest novels ever written, including *War and Peace* and *Anna Karenina,* Tolstoy experienced a religious crisis, described in the following selection, in which he sought the meaning of life and found it in faith. Tolstoy's discovery led him to advocate humility, nonviolence, vegetarianism, the moral value of manual labor, the avoidance of luxury, and sexual abstinence. After his conversion, he continued to write prolifically and produced *The Death of Ivan Ilyich* during this latter period of his life.

Reading Questions

1. What is the "strange thing" that began to happen to Tolstoy?
2. What perplexity is he evoking with the phrase, "Why? Well, and then?"
3. Why does he feel as if somebody had played a mean trick on him by creating him?
4. What is the "cruel truth" of life?
5. What are the two drops of honey in Tolstoy's life, and why are they no longer sweet to him?
6. When Tolstoy says that he can no longer keep himself from seeing the truth, "and the truth is death," what does he mean? Is he just making the mistake of supposing that to be valuable at all, something must last forever? Or is he trying to convey a deeper insight?
7. How did Tolstoy resolve his crisis? Did he resolve it by taking refuge in a system of beliefs that he accepted on faith, or did he solve it by having a genuine insight he had previously overlooked? (Or are these two the same?)

ALTHOUGH I REGARDED AUTHORSHIP as a waste of time, I continued to write during those fifteen years. I had tasted of the seduction of authorship, of the seduction of enormous monetary remunerations and applauses for my insignificant labour, and so I submitted to it, as being a means for improving my material condition and for stifling in my soul all questions about the meaning of my life and life in general.

In my writings I advocated, what to me was the only truth, that it was necessary to live in such a way as to derive the greatest comfort for oneself and one's family.

Thus I proceeded to live, but five years ago something very strange began to happen with me: I was overcome by minutes at first of perplexity and then of an arrest of life, as though I did not know how to live or what to do, and I lost myself and was dejected. But that passed, and I continued to live as before. Then those minutes of perplexity were repeated oftener and oftener, and always in one and the same form. These arrests of life found their

From My Confession *by Leo Tolstoy. Trans. Leo Wiener (Dent, 1905).*

expression in ever the same questions: "Why? Well, and then?"

At first I thought that those were simply aimless, inappropriate questions. It seemed to me that that was all well known and that if I ever wanted to busy myself with their solution, it would not cost me much labour,—that now I had no time to attend to them, but that if I wanted to I should find the proper answers. But the questions began to repeat themselves oftener and oftener, answers were demanded more and more persistently, and, like dots that fall on the same spot, these questions, without any answers, thickened into one black blotch.

There happened what happens with any person who falls ill with a mortal internal disease. At first there appear insignificant symptoms of indisposition, to which the patient pays no attention; then these symptoms are repeated more and more frequently and blend into one temporally indivisible suffering. The suffering keeps growing, and before the patient has had time to look around, he becomes conscious that what he took for an indisposition is the most significant thing in the world to him,—is death.

The same happened with me. I understood that it was not a passing indisposition, but something very important, and that, if the questions were going to repeat themselves, it would be necessary to find an answer for them. And I tried to answer them. The questions seemed to be so foolish, simple, and childish. But the moment I touched them and tried to solve them, I became convinced, in the first place, that they were not childish and foolish, but very important and profound questions in life, and, in the second, that, no matter how much I might try, I should not be able to answer them. Before attending to my Samára estate, to my son's education, or to the writing of a book, I ought to know why I should do that. So long as I did not know why, I could not do anything. I could not live. Amidst my thoughts of farming, which interested me very much during that time, there would suddenly pass through my head a question like this: "All right, you are going to have six thousand desyatínas of land in the Government of Samára, and three hundred horses,—and then?" And I completely lost my senses and did not know what to think farther. Or, when I thought of the educa-tion of my children, I said to myself: "Why?" Or, reflecting on the manner in which the masses might obtain their welfare, I suddenly said to myself: "What is that to me?" Or, thinking of the fame which my works would get me, I said to myself: "All right, you will be more famous than Gógol, Púshkin, Shakespeare, Molière, and all the writers in the world,—what of it?" And I was absolutely unable to make any reply. The questions were not waiting, and I had to answer them at once; if I did not answer them, I could not live. . . .

All that happened with me when I was on every side surrounded by what is considered to be complete happiness. I had a good, loving, and beloved wife, good children, and a large estate, which grew and increased without any labour on my part. I was respected by my neighbours and friends, more than ever before, was praised by strangers, and, without any self-deception, could consider my name famous. With all that, I was not deranged or mentally unsound,—on the contrary, I was in full command of my mental and physical powers, such as I had rarely met with in people of my age: physically I could work in a field, mowing, without falling behind a peasant; mentally I could work from eight to ten hours in succession, without experiencing any consequences from the strain. And while in such condition I arrived at the conclusion that I could not live, and, fearing death, I had to use cunning against myself, in order that I might not take my life.

This mental condition expressed itself to me in this form: my life is a stupid, mean trick played on me by somebody. Although I did not recognize that "somebody" as having created me, the form of the conception that some one had played a mean, stupid trick on me by bringing me into the world was the most natural one that presented itself to me.

Involuntarily I imagined that there, somewhere, there was somebody who was now having fun as he looked down upon me and saw me, who had lived for thirty or forty years, learning, developing, growing in body and mind, now that I had become strengthened in mind and had reached that summit of life from which it lay all before me, standing as a complete fool on that summit and seeing clearly that there was nothing in life and never would be. And that was fun to him—

But whether there was or was not that somebody who made fun of me, did not make it easier for me. I could not ascribe any sensible meaning to a single act, or to my whole life. I was only surprised that I had not understood that from the start. All that had long ago been known to everybody. Sooner or later there would come diseases and death (they had come already) to my dear ones and to me, and there would be nothing left but stench and worms. All my affairs, no matter what they might be, would sooner or later be forgotten, and I myself should not exist. So why should I worry about all these things? How could a man fail to see that and live,—that was surprising! A person could live only so long as he was drunk; but the moment he sobered up, he could not help seeing that all that was only a deception, and a stupid deception at that! Really, there was nothing funny and ingenious about it, but only something cruel and stupid.

Long ago has been told the Eastern story about the traveller who in the steppe is overtaken by an infuriated beast. Trying to save himself from the animal, the traveller jumps into a waterless well, but at its bottom he sees a dragon who opens his jaws in order to swallow him. And the unfortunate man does not dare climb out, lest he perish from the infuriated beast, and does not dare jump down to the bottom of the well, lest he be devoured by the dragon, and so clutches the twig of a wild bush growing in the cleft of the well and holds on to it. His hands grow weak and he feels that soon he shall have to surrender to the peril which awaits him at either side; but he still holds on and sees two mice, one white, the other black, in even measure making a circle around the main trunk of the bush to which he is clinging, and nibbling at it on all sides. Now, at any moment, the bush will break and tear off, and he will fall into the dragon's jaws. The traveller sees that and knows that he will inevitably perish; but while he is still clinging, he sees some drops of honey hanging on the leaves of the bush, and so reaches out for them with his tongue and licks the leaves. Just so I hold on to the branch of life, knowing that the dragon of death is waiting inevitably for me, ready to tear me to pieces, and I cannot understand why I have fallen on such suffering. And I try to lick that honey which used to give me pleasure; but now it no longer gives me

joy, and the white and the black mouse day and night nibble at the branch to which I am holding on. I clearly see the dragon, and the honey is no longer sweet to me. I see only the inevitable dragon and the mice, and am unable to turn my glance away from them. That is not a fable, but a veritable, indisputable, comprehensible truth.

The former deception of the pleasures of life, which stifled the terror of the dragon, no longer deceives me. No matter how much one should say to me, "You cannot understand the meaning of life, do not think, live!" I am unable to do so, because I have been doing it too long before. Now I cannot help seeing day and night, which run and lead me up to death. I see that alone, because that alone is the truth. Everything else is a lie.

The two drops of honey that have longest turned my eyes away from the cruel truth, the love of family and of authorship, which I have called an art, are no longer sweet to me.

"My family—" I said to myself, "but my family, my wife and children, they are also human beings. They are in precisely the same condition that I am in: they must either live in the lie or see the terrible truth. Why should they live? Why should I love them, why guard, raise, and watch them? Is it for the same despair which is in me, or for dullness of perception? Since I love them, I cannot conceal the truth from them,—every step in cognition leads them up to this truth. And the truth is death."

"Art, poetry?" For a long time, under the influence of the success of human praise, I tried to persuade myself that that was a thing which could be done, even though death should come and destroy everything, my deeds, as well as my memory of them; but soon I came to see that that, too, was a deception. It was clear to me that art was an adornment of life, a decoy of life. But life lost all its attractiveness for me. How, then, could I entrap others? So long as I did not live my own life, and a strange life bore me on its waves; so long as I believed that life had some sense, although I was not able to express it,—the reflections of life of every description in poetry and in the arts afforded me pleasure, and I was delighted to look at life through this little mirror of art; but when I began to look for the meaning of life, when I experienced the necessity of living myself, that little mirror became either useless, superfluous, and ridiculous, or painful to me. I could no longer console myself with what I saw in the mirror, namely, that my situation was stupid and desperate. . . .

By abandoning myself to the bright side of knowledge I saw that I only turned my eyes away from the question. No matter how enticing and clear the horizons were that were disclosed to me, no matter how enticing it was to bury myself in the infinitude of this knowledge, I comprehended that these sciences were the more clear, the less I needed them, the less they answered my question.

"Well, I know," I said to myself, "all which science wants so persistently to know, but there is no answer to the question about the meaning of my life." But in the speculative sphere I saw that, in spite of the fact that the aim of the knowledge was directed straight to the answer of my question, or because of that fact, there could be no other answer than what I was giving to myself: "What is the meaning of my life?"—"None." Or, "What will come of my life?"—"Nothing." Or, "Why does everything which exists exist, and why do I exist?"—"Because it exists."

Putting the question to the one side of human knowledge, I received an endless quantity of exact answers about what I did not ask: about the chemical composition of the stars, about the movement of the sun toward the constellation of Hercules, about the origin of species and of man, about the forms of infinitely small, imponderable particles of ether; but the answer in this sphere of knowledge to my question what the meaning of my life was, was always: "You are what you call your life; you are a temporal, accidental conglomeration of particles. The interrelation, the change of these particles, produces in you that which you call life. This congeries will last for some time; then the interaction of these particles will cease, and that which you call life and all your questions will come to an end. You are an accidentally cohering globule of something. The globule is fermenting. This fermentation the globule calls its life. The globule falls to pieces, and all fermentation and all questions will come to an end." Thus the clear side of knowledge answers, and it cannot say anything else, if only it strictly follows its principles.

With such an answer it appears that the answer is not a reply to the question. I want to know the meaning of my life, but the fact that it is a particle of the infinite not only gives it no meaning, but even destroys every possible meaning. . . .

I lived for a long time in this madness, which, not in words, but in deeds, is particularly characteristic of us, the most liberal and learned of men. But, thanks either to my strange, physical love for the real working class, which made me understand it and see that it is not so stupid as we suppose, or to the sincerity of my conviction, which was that I could know nothing and that the best that I could do was to hang myself,—I felt that if I wanted to live and understand the meaning of life, I ought naturally to look for it, not among those who had lost the meaning of life and wanted to kill themselves, but among those billions of departed and living men who had been carrying their own lives and ours upon their shoulders. And I looked around at the enormous masses of deceased and living men, not learned and wealthy, but simple men,—and I saw something quite different. I saw that all these billions of men that lived or had lived, all, with rare exceptions, did not fit into my subdivisions, and that I could not recognize them as not understanding the question, because they themselves put it and answered it with surprising clearness. Nor could I recognize them as Epicureans, because their lives were composed rather of privations and suffering than of enjoyment. Still less could I recognize them as senselessly living out their meaningless lives, because every act of theirs and death itself was explained by them. They regarded it as the greatest evil to kill themselves. It appeared, then, that all humanity was in possession of a knowledge of the meaning of life, which I did not recognize and which I condemned. It turned out that rational knowledge did not give any meaning to life, excluded life, while the meaning which by billions of people, by all humanity, was ascribed to life was based on some despised, false knowledge.

The rational knowledge in the person of the learned and the wise denied the meaning of life, but the enormous masses of men, all humanity, recognized this meaning in an irrational knowledge. This irrational knowledge was faith, the same that I could not help but reject. That was God as one and three, the creation in six days, devils and angels, and all that which I could not accept so long as I had not lost my senses.

My situation was a terrible one. I knew that I should not find anything on the path of rational knowledge but the negation of life, and there, in faith, nothing but the negation of reason, which was still more impossible than the negation of life. From the rational knowledge it followed that life was an evil and men knew it,—it depended on men whether they should cease living, and yet they lived and continued to live, and I myself lived, though I had known long ago that life was meaningless and an evil. From faith it followed that, in order to understand life, I must renounce reason, for which alone a meaning was needed.

There resulted a contradiction, from which there were two ways out: either what I called rational was not so rational as I had thought; or that which to me appeared irrational was not so irrational as I had thought. And I began to verify the train of thoughts of my rational knowledge.

In verifying the train of thoughts of my rational knowledge, I found that it was quite correct. The deduction that life was nothing was inevitable; but I saw a mistake. The mistake was that I had not reasoned in conformity with the question put by me. The question was, "Why should I live?" that is, "What real, indestructible essence will come from my phantasmal, destructible life? What meaning has my finite existence in this infinite world?" And in order to answer this question, I studied life.

The solutions of all possible questions of life apparently could not satisfy me, because my question, no matter how simple it appeared in the beginning, included the necessity of explaining the finite through the infinite, and vice versa.

I asked, "What is the extra-temporal, extra-causal, extra-spatial meaning of life?" But I gave an answer to the question, "What is the temporal, causal, spatial meaning of my life?" The result was that after a long labour of mind I answered, "None." . . .

When I saw that [. . . for philosophy the solution remains insoluble] I understood that it was not right for me to look for an answer to my question in rational knowledge, and that the answer given by rational knowledge was only an indication that the answer might be got if the question were differently put, but only when into the discussion of the question should be introduced the question of the relation of the finite to the infinite. I also

understood that, no matter how irrational and monstrous the answers might be that faith gave, they had this advantage that they introduced into each answer the relation of the finite to the infinite, without which there could be no answer.

No matter how I may put the question, "How must I live?" the answer is, "According to God's law." "What real result will there be from my life?"—"Eternal torment or eternal bliss." "What is the meaning which is not destroyed by death?"—"The union with infinite God, paradise."

Thus, outside the rational knowledge, which had to me appeared as the only one, I was inevitably led to recognize that all living humanity had a certain other irrational knowledge, faith, which made it possible to live.

All the irrationality of faith remained the same for me, but I could not help recognizing that it alone gave to humanity answers to the questions of life, and, in consequence of them, the possibility of living.

The rational knowledge brought me to the recognition that life was meaningless,—my life stopped, and I wanted to destroy myself. When I looked around at people, at all humanity, I saw that people lived and asserted that they knew the meaning of life. I looked back at myself: I lived so long as I knew the meaning of life. As to other people, so even to me, did faith give the meaning of life and the possibility of living.

Looking again at the people of other countries, contemporaries of mine and those passed away, I saw again the same. Where life had been, there faith, ever since humanity had existed, had given the possibility of living, and the chief features of faith were everywhere one and the same.

No matter what answers faith may give, its every answer gives to the finite existence of man the sense of the infinite,—a sense which is not destroyed by suffering, privation, and death. Consequently in faith alone could we find the meaning and possibility of life. What, then, was faith? I understood that faith was not merely an evidence of things not seen, and so forth, not revelation (that is only the description of one of the symptoms of faith), not the relation of man to man (faith has to be defined, and then God, and not first God, and faith through him), not merely an agreement with what a man was told, as faith was generally understood,—that faith was the knowledge of the meaning of human life, in consequence of which man did not destroy himself, but lived. Faith is the power of life. If a man lives he believes in something. If he did not believe that he ought to live for some purpose, he would not live. If he does not see and understand the phantasm of the finite, he believes in that finite; if he understands the phantasm of the finite, he must believe in the infinite. Without faith one cannot live. . . .

In order that all humanity may be able to live, in order that they may continue living, giving a meaning to life, they, those billions, must have another, a real knowledge of faith, for not the fact that I, with Solomon and Schopenhauer, did not kill myself convinced me of the existence of faith, but that these billions had lived and had borne us, me and Solomon, on the waves of life.

Then I began to cultivate the acquaintance of the believers from among the poor, the simple and unlettered folk, of pilgrims, monks, dissenters, peasants. The doctrine of these people from among the masses was also the Christian doctrine that the quasi-believers of our circle professed. With the Christian truths were also mixed in very many superstitions, but there was this difference: the superstitions of our circle were quite unnecessary to them, had no connection with their lives, were only a kind of an Epicurean amusement, while the superstitions of the believers from among the labouring classes were to such an extent blended with their life that it would have been impossible to imagine it without these superstitions,—it was a necessary condition of that life. I began to examine closely the lives and beliefs of these people, and the more I examined them, the more did I become convinced that they had the real faith, that their faith was necessary for them, and that it alone gave them a meaning and possibility of life. In contradistinction to what I saw in our circle, where life without faith was possible, and where hardly one in a thousand professed to be a believer, among them there was hardly one in a thousand who was not a believer. In contradistinction to what I saw in our circle, where all life passed in idleness, amusements, and tedium of life, I saw that the whole life of these people was passed in hard work, and that they were satisfied with life. In contradistinction to the people

of our circle, who struggled and murmured against fate because of their privations and their suffering, these people accepted diseases and sorrows without any perplexity or opposition, but with the calm and firm conviction that it was all for good. In contradistinction to the fact that the more intelligent we are, the less do we understand the meaning of life and the more do we see a kind of a bad joke in our suffering and death, these people live, suffer, and approach death, and suffer in peace and more often in joy. In contradistinction to the fact that a calm death, a death without terror or despair, is the greatest exception in our circle, a restless, insubmissive, joyless death is one of the greatest exceptions among the masses. And of such people, who are deprived of everything which for Solomon and for me constitutes the only good of life, and who withal experience the greatest happiness, there is an enormous number. I cast a broader glance about me. I examined the life of past and present vast masses of men, and I saw people who in like manner had understood the meaning of life, who had known how to live and die, not two, not three, not ten, but hundreds, thousands, millions. All of them, infinitely diversified as to habits, intellect, culture, situation, all equally and quite contrary to my ignorance knew the meaning of life and of death, worked calmly, bore privations and suffering, lived and died, seeing in that not vanity, but good.

I began to love those people. The more I penetrated into their life, the life of the men now living, and the life of men departed, of whom I had read and heard, the more did I love them, and the easier it became for me to live. Thus I lived for about two years, and within me took place a transformation, which had long been working within me, and the germ of which had always been in me. What happened with me was that the life of our circle,—of the rich and the learned,—not only disgusted me, but even lost all its meaning. All our acts, reflections, sciences, arts,—all that appeared to me in a new light. I saw that all that was mere pampering of the appetites, and that no meaning could be found in it; but the life of all the working masses, of all humanity, which created life, presented itself to me in its real significance. I saw that that was life itself and that the meaning given to this life was truth, and I accepted it.

Further Questions

1. It is hard to read Tolstoy's account without being moved. If you were moved, what moved you? His beliefs, or the beautiful way he expresses them, or the simple humanity with which he lived his life? Did you like best those parts of his account that agree with what you already believe? Or were you led to see something that you hadn't seen before? If the latter, what? If you were charmed by Tolstoy, was it by the beautiful way he expressed himself or by what he expressed?
2. When you read an essay like this one, do you look for new insight or merely a beautiful expression of what you already believe? What can you learn about yourself from the way you answer this question? Can you learn whether you are searching for truth or just for confirmation?

Further Readings

Frankl, Victor. *Man's Search for Meaning*. Boston: Beacon Press, 1963. A noted psychologist looks at some of the issues that troubled Tolstoy.

Rolston, Holmes, III. *Science and Religion*. New York: Random House, 1987. A thorough, easy-to-read attempt to explore the interface between science and religion.

68   The Myth of Sisyphus

ALBERT CAMUS

French essayist, novelist, and playwright Albert Camus was born in Algeria in 1913. After studying philosophy at the University of Algiers, he worked as a meteorologist, stockbroker's agent, civil servant, journalist, and actor and director in an amateur theatrical company. During World War II, he joined the French resistance movement. As a journalist, he often got into trouble with authorities by campaigning for economic and social reforms on behalf of Algerians. He died in an automobile accident in 1960.

Camus expressed his theme of the absurd and irrational nature of the world in various forms. Among his best: a collection of essays, *The Myth of Sisyphus* (1942); the novels, *The Stranger* (1946), *The Plague* (1948), and *The Fall* (1957); and the play, *Caligula* (1944). He won the Nobel Prize for literature in 1957.

Reading Questions

1. Why does Camus think the world is absurd? What does he mean by this? Do you agree?
2. Camus seems to suggest that while the world does not have any meaning, your individual life *can* have meaning. How?
3. How do human beings "secrete the inhuman"?
4. What does Camus mean by "living without appeal"?

ALL GREAT DEEDS AND ALL GREAT THOUGHTS have a ridiculous beginning. Great works are often born on a streetcorner or in a restaurant's revolving door. So it is with absurdity. The absurd world more than others derives its nobility from that abject birth. In certain situations, replying "nothing" when asked what one is thinking about may be pretense in a man. Those who are loved are well aware of this. But if that reply is sincere, if it symbolizes that odd state of soul in which the void becomes eloquent, in which the chain of daily gestures is broken, in which the heart vainly seeks the link that will connect it again, then it is as it were the first sign of absurdity.

It happens that the stage sets collapse. Rising, streetcar, four hours in the office or the factory, meal, streetcar, four hours of work, meal, sleep, and Monday Tuesday Wednesday Thursday Friday and Saturday according to the same rhythm—this path is easily followed most of the time. But one day the "why" arises and everything begins in that weariness tinged with amazement. "Begins"—this is important. Weariness comes at the end of the acts of a mechanical life, but at the same time it inaugurates the impulse of consciousness. It awakens consciousness and provokes what follows. What follows is the gradual return into the chain or it is the definitive awakening. . . .

Likewise and during every day of an unillustrious life, time carries us. But a moment always comes when we have to carry it. We live on the future: "tomorrow," "later on," "when you have made your way," "you will understand when you are old enough." Such irrelevancies are wonderful, for, after all, it's a matter of dying. Yet a day comes when a man notices or says that he is thirty. Thus he asserts his youth. But simultaneously he situates himself in relation to time. He takes his place in it. He admits that he stands at a certain point on a curve that he acknowledges having to travel to its end. He belongs to time, and by the horror that seizes him, he recognizes his worst enemy. Tomorrow, he was longing for tomorrow, whereas everything in him ought to reject it. That revolt of the flesh is the absurd.

A step lower and strangeness creeps in: perceiving that the world is "dense," sensing to what a degree a stone is foreign and irreducible to us, with what intensity nature or a landscape can negate us. At the heart of all beauty lies something inhuman, and these hills, the softness of the sky, the outline of these trees at this very minute lose the illusory meaning with which we had clothed them, henceforth more remote than a lost paradise. The primitive hostility of the world rises up to face us across millennia. For a second we cease to understand it because for centuries we have understood in it solely the images and designs that we had attributed to it beforehand, because henceforth we lack the power to make use of that artifice. The world evades us because it becomes itself again. That stage scenery masked by habit becomes again what it is. It withdraws at a distance from us. Just as there are days when under the familiar face of a woman, we see as a stranger her we have loved months or years ago, perhaps we shall come even to desire what suddenly leaves us so alone. But the time has not yet come. Just one thing: that denseness and that strangeness of the world is the absurd.

Men, too, secrete the inhuman. At certain moments of lucidity, the mechanical aspect of their gestures, their meaningless pantomime makes silly everything that surrounds them. A man is talking on the telephone behind a glass partition; you cannot hear him, but you see his incomprehensible dumb show: you wonder why he is alive. This discomfort in the face of man's own inhumanity, this incalculable tumble before the image of what we are, this "nausea," as a writer of today calls it, is also the absurd. Likewise the stranger who at certain seconds comes to meet us in a mirror, the familiar and yet alarming brother we encounter in our own photographs is also the absurd. . . .

Let us insist again on the method: it is a matter of persisting. At a certain point on his path the absurd man is tempted. History is not lacking in either religions or prophets, even without gods. He is asked to leap. All he can reply is that he doesn't fully understand, that it is not obvious. Indeed, he does not want to do anything but what

he fully understands. He is assured that this is the
sin of pride, but he does not understand the notion
of sin; that perhaps hell is in store, but he has not
enough imagination to visualize that strange future;
that he is losing immortal life, but that seems to
him an idle consideration. An attempt is made to
get him to admit his guilt. He feels innocent. To tell
the truth, that is all he feels — his irreparable innocence. This is what allows him everything. Hence,
what he demands of himself is to live *solely* with
what he knows, to accommodate himself to what
is, and to bring in nothing that is not certain. He is
told that nothing is. But this at least is a certainty.
And it is with this that he is concerned: he wants to
find out if it is possible to live *without* appeal.

THE MYTH OF SISYPHUS

The gods had condemned Sisyphus to ceaselessly
rolling a rock to the top of a mountain, whence
the stone would fall back of its own weight. They
had thought with some reason that there is no
more dreadful punishment than futile and hopeless
labor.

If one believes Homer, Sisyphus was the wisest
and most prudent of mortals. According to another
tradition, however, he was disposed to practice the
profession of highwayman. I see no contradiction
in this. Opinions differ as to the reasons why he
became the futile laborer of the underworld. To
begin with, he is accused of a certain levity in regard to the gods. He stole their secrets. Ægina, the
daughter of Æsopus, was carried off by Jupiter.
The father was shocked by that disappearance and
complained to Sisyphus. He, who knew of the ab-
duction, offered to tell about it on condition that
Æsopus would give water to the citadel of Corinth.
To the celestial thunderbolts he preferred the
benediction of water. He was punished for this in
the underworld. Homer tells us also that Sisyphus
had put Death in chains. Pluto could not endure
the sight of his deserted, silent empire. He dis-
patched the god of war, who liberated Death from
the hands of her conqueror.

It is said also that Sisyphus, being near to death,
rashly wanted to test his wife's love. He ordered
her to cast his unburied body into the middle of

the public square. Sisyphus woke up in the underworld. And there, annoyed by an obedience so
contrary to human love, he obtained from Pluto
permission to return to earth in order to chastise
his wife. But when he had seen again the face of
this world, enjoyed water and sun, warm stones
and the sea, he no longer wanted to go back to the
infernal darkness. Recalls, signs of anger, warnings
were of no avail. Many years more he lived facing
the curve of the gulf, the sparkling sea, and the
smiles of earth. A decree of the gods was necessary.
Mercury came and seized the impudent man by
the collar and, snatching him from his joys, led
him forcibly back to the underworld, where his
rock was ready for him.

You have already grasped that Sisyphus is the
absurd hero. He *is*, as much through his passions
as through his torture. His scorn of the gods, his
hatred of death, and his passion for life won him
that unspeakable penalty in which the whole being
is exerted toward accomplishing nothing. This is
the price that must be paid for the passions of this
earth. Nothing is told us about Sisyphus in the underworld. Myths are made for the imagination to
breathe life into them. As for this myth, one sees
merely the whole effort of a body straining to raise
the huge stone, to roll it and push it up a slope a
hundred times over; one sees the face screwed up,
the cheek tight against the stone, the shoulder
bracing the clay-covered mass, the foot wedging it,
the fresh start with arms outstretched, the wholly
human security of two earth-clotted hands. At
the very end of his long effort measured by sky-
less space and time without depth, the purpose is
achieved. Then Sisyphus watches the stone rush
down in a few moments toward that lower world
whence he will have to push it up again toward the
summit. He goes back down to the plain.

It is during that return, that pause, that Sisyphus interests me. A face that toils so close to
stones is already stone itself! I see that man going
back down with a heavy yet measured step toward
the torment of which he will never know the end.
That hour like a breathing-space which returns as
surely as his suffering, that is the hour of consciousness. At each of those moments when he
leaves the heights and gradually sinks toward the
lairs of the gods, he is superior to his fate. He is
stronger than his rock.

If this myth is tragic, that is because its hero is conscious. Where would his torture be, indeed, if at every step the hope of succeeding upheld him? The workman of today works every day in his life at the same tasks, and this fate is no less absurd. But it is tragic only at the rare moments when it becomes conscious. Sisyphus, proletarian of the gods, powerless and rebellious, knows the whole extent of his wretched condition: it is what he thinks of during his descent. The lucidity that was to constitute his torture at the same time crowns his victory. There is no fate that cannot be surmounted by scorn. . . .

If the descent is thus sometimes performed in sorrow, it can also take place in joy. This word is not too much. Again I fancy Sisyphus returning toward his rock, and the sorrow was in the beginning. When the images of earth cling too tightly to memory, when the call of happiness becomes too insistent, it happens that melancholy rises in man's heart: this is the rock's victory, this is the rock itself. The boundless grief is too heavy to bear. These are our nights of Gethsemane. But crushing truths perish from being acknowledged. Thus, Œdipus at the outset obeys fate without knowing it. But from the moment he knows, his tragedy begins. Yet at the same moment, blind and desperate, he realizes that the only bond linking him to the world is the cool hand of a girl. Then a tremendous remark rings out: "Despite so many ordeals, my advanced age and the nobility of my soul make me conclude that all is well." Sophocles' Œdipus, like Dostoevsky's Kirilov, thus gives the recipe for the absurd victory. Ancient wisdom confirms modern heroism.

One does not discover the absurd without being tempted to write a manual of happiness. "What! by such narrow ways—?" There is but one world, however. Happiness and the absurd are two sons of the same earth. They are inseparable. It would be a mistake to say that happiness necessarily springs from the absurd discovery. It happens as well that the feeling of the absurd springs from happiness. "I conclude that all is well," says Œdipus, and that remark is sacred. It echoes in the wild and limited universe of man. It teaches that all is not, has not been, exhausted. It drives out of this world a god who had come into it with dissatisfaction and a preference for futile sufferings. It makes of fate a human matter, which must be settled among men.

All Sisyphus' silent joy is contained therein. His fate belongs to him. His rock is his thing. Likewise, the absurd man, when he contemplates his torment, silences all the idols. In the universe suddenly restored to its silence, the myriad wondering little voices of the earth rise up. Unconscious, secret calls, invitations from all the faces, they are the necessary reverse and price of victory. There is no sun without shadow, and it is essential to know the night. The absurd man says yes and his effort will henceforth be unceasing. If there is a personal fate, there is no higher destiny, or at least there is but one which he concludes is inevitable and despicable. For the rest, he knows himself to be the master of his days. At that subtle moment when man glances backward over his life, Sisyphus returning toward his rock, in that slight pivoting he contemplates that series of unrelated actions which becomes his fate, created by him, combined under his memory's eye and soon sealed by his death. Thus, convinced of the wholly human origin of all that is human, a blind man eager to see who knows that the night has no end, he is still on the go. The rock is still rolling.

I leave Sisyphus at the foot of the mountain! One always finds one's burden again. But Sisyphus teaches the higher fidelity that negates the gods and raises rocks. He too concludes that all is well. This universe henceforth without a master seems to him neither sterile nor futile. Each atom of that stone, each mineral flake of that night-filled mountain, in itself forms a world. The struggle itself toward the heights is enough to fill a man's heart. One must imagine Sisyphus happy.

Further Questions

1. In what sense are we like Sisyphus? In what sense are we different?
2. Why, according to Camus, must we imagine Sisyphus happy? Do you agree? Why?

Further Readings

Klemke, E. D. *The Meaning of Life*. New York: Oxford University Press, 1981. Presents religious, atheistic, and philosophical perspectives on the meaning of life.

Kluge, Eike-Henner W. *The Practice of Death*. New Haven, CT: Yale University Press, 1975. Contains philosophical arguments for and against suicide.

69   Is Life Meaningful?

RICHARD TAYLOR

A brief biography of Taylor appears on p. 209.

In this selection, from Taylor's *Good and Evil* (1984), he claims that life is meaningful and gives his response to the challenge to meaningfulness posed by "The Myth of Sisyphus."

Reading Questions

1. Do any of the ways Taylor modifies the story of Sisyphus affect the meaning of Sisyphus's life?
2. Do you agree with Taylor that meaninglessness is essentially endless pointlessness? Do you agree that our lives resemble such pointlessness?
3. What is the "little afterthought" of the gods with regard to Sisyphus that is both "perverse" and "merciful," and why?
4. What same "spectacle" do all living things present?
5. How does Taylor think we should look at all of life?

THE QUESTION OF WHETHER LIFE has any meaning is difficult to interpret, and the more one concentrates his critical faculty on it the more it seems to elude him, or to evaporate as any intelligible question. One wants to turn it aside, as a source of embarrassment, as something that, if it cannot be abolished, should at least be decently covered. And yet I think any reflective person recognizes that the question it raises is important, and that it ought to have a significant answer.

If the idea of meaningfulness is difficult to grasp in this context, so that we are unsure what sort of thing would amount to answering the question, the idea of meaninglessness is perhaps less so. If, then, we can bring before our minds a clear image of meaningless existence, then perhaps we can take a step toward coping with our original question by seeing to what extent our lives, as we actually find them, resemble that image, and draw such lessons as we are able to from the comparison.

MEANINGLESS EXISTENCE

A perfect image of meaninglessness, of the kind we are seeking, is found in the ancient myth of Sisyphus. Sisyphus, it will be remembered, betrayed divine secrets to mortals, and for this he was condemned by the gods to roll a stone to the top of a hill, the stone then immediately to roll back down, again to be pushed to the top by Sisyphus, to roll down once more, and so on again and again, *forever.* Now in this we have the picture of meaningless, pointless toil, of a meaningless existence that is absolutely *never* redeemed. It is not even redeemed by a death that, if it were to accomplish nothing more, would at least bring this idiotic cycle to a close. If we were invited to imagine Sisyphus struggling for awhile and accomplishing nothing, perhaps eventually falling from exhaustion, so that we might suppose him then eventually turning to something having some sort of promise, then the meaninglessness of that chapter of his life would not be so stark. It would be a dark and dreadful dream, from which he eventually awakens to sunlight and reality. But he does not awaken, for there is nothing for him to awaken to. His repetitive toil is his life and reality, and it goes on forever, and it is without any meaning whatever. Nothing ever comes out of what he is doing, except simply, more of the same. Not by one step, nor by a thousand, nor by ten thousand does he even expiate by the smallest token the sin against the gods that led him into his fate. Nothing comes of it, nothing at all.

This ancient myth has always enchanted men, for countless meanings can be read into it. Some of the ancients apparently thought it symbolized the perpetual rising and setting of the sun, and others the repetitious crashing of the waves upon the shore. Probably the commonest interpretation is that it symbolizes man's eternal struggle and unquenchable spirit, his determination always to try once more in the face of overwhelming discouragement. This interpretation is further supported by that version of the myth according to which Sisyphus was commanded to roll the stone *over* the hill, so that it would finally roll down the other side, but was never quite able to make it.

I am not concerned with rendering or defending any interpretation of this myth, however. I have cited it only for the one element it does unmistakably contain, namely, that of a repetitious, cyclic activity that never comes to anything. We could contrive other images of this that would serve just as well, and no myth-makers are needed to supply the materials of it. Thus, we can imagine two persons transport-

ing a stone — or even a precious gem, it does not matter — back and forth, relay style. One carries it to a near or distant point where it is received by the other; it is returned to its starting point, there to be recovered by the first, and the process is repeated over and over. Except in this relay nothing counts as winning, and nothing brings the contest to any close, each step only leads to a repetition of itself. Or we can imagine two groups of prisoners, one of them engaged in digging a prodigious hole in the ground that is no sooner finished than it is filled in again by the other group, the latter then digging a new hole that is at once filled in by the first group, and so on and on endlessly.

Now what stands out in all such pictures as oppressive and dejecting is not that the beings who enact these roles suffer any torture or pain, for it need not be assumed that they do. Nor is it that their labors are great, for they are no greater than the labors commonly undertaken by most men most of the time. According to the original myth, the stone is so large that Sisyphus never quite gets it to the top and must groan under every step, so that his enormous labor is all for nought. But this is not what appalls. It is not that his great struggle comes to nothing, but that his existence itself is without meaning. Even if we suppose, for example, that the stone is but a pebble that can be carried effortlessly, or that the holes dug by the prisoners are but small ones, not the slightest meaning is introduced into their lives. The stone that Sisyphus moves to the top of the hill, whether we think of it as large or small, still rolls back every time, and the process is repeated forever. Nothing comes of it, and the work is simply pointless. That is the element of the myth that I wish to capture.

Again, it is not the fact that the labors of Sisyphus continue forever that deprives them of meaning. It is, rather, the implication of this: that they come to nothing. The image would not be changed by our supposing him to push a different stone up every time, each to roll down again. But if we supposed that these stones, instead of rolling back to their places as if they had never been moved, were assembled at the top of the hill and there incorporated, say, in a beautiful and enduring temple, then the aspect of meaninglessness would disappear. His labors would then have a point, something would come of them all, and although one could perhaps still say it was not worth it, one could not say that the life of Sisyphus was devoid of meaning altogether. Meaningfulness would at least have made an appearance, and we could see what it was.

That point will need remembering. But in the meantime, let us note another way in which the image of meaninglessness can be altered by making only a very slight change. Let us suppose that the gods, while condemning Sisyphus to the fate just described, at the same time, as an afterthought, waxed perversely merciful by implanting in him a strange and irrational impulse; namely a compulsive impulse to roll stones. We may if we like, to make this more graphic, suppose they accomplish this by implanting in him some substance that has this effect on his character and drives. I call this perverse, because from our point of view there is clearly no reason why anyone should have a persistent and insatiable desire to do something so pointless as that. Nevertheless, suppose that is Sisyphus' condition. He has but one obsession, which is to roll stones, and it is an obsession that is only for the moment appeased by his rolling them — he no sooner gets a stone rolled to the top of the hill than he is restless to roll up another.

Now it can be seen why this little afterthought of the gods, which I called perverse, was also in fact merciful. For they have by this device managed to give Sisyphus precisely what he wants — by making him want precisely what they inflict on him. However it may appear to us, Sisyphus' fate now does not appear to him as a condemnation, but the very reverse. His one desire in life is to roll stones, and he is absolutely guaranteed its endless fulfillment. Where otherwise he might profoundly have wished surcease, and even welcomed the quiet of death to release him from endless boredom and meaninglessness, his life is now filled with mission and meaning, and he seems to himself to have been given an entry to heaven. Nor need he even fear death, for the gods have promised him an endless opportunity to indulge his single purpose, without concern or frustration. He will be able to roll stones *forever*.

What we need to mark most carefully at this point is that the picture with which we began has not really been changed in the least by adding this supposition. Exactly the same things happen as before. The only change is in Sisyphus' view of them.

The picture before was the image of meaningless activity and existence. It was created precisely to be an image of that. It has not lost that meaninglessness, it has now gained not the least shred of meaningfulness. The stones still roll back as before, each phase of Sisyphus' life still exactly resembles all the others, the task is never completed, nothing comes of it, no temple ever begins to rise, and all this cycle of the same pointless thing over and over goes on forever in this picture as in the other. The *only* thing that has happened is this: Sisyphus has been reconciled to it, and indeed more, he has been led to embrace it. Not, however, by reason or persuasion, but by nothing more rational than the potency of a new substance in his veins.

THE MEANINGLESSNESS OF LIFE

I believe the foregoing provides a fairly clear content to the idea of meaninglessness and, through it, some hint of what meaningfulness, in this sense, might be. Meaninglessness is essentially endless pointlessness, and meaningfulness is therefore the opposite. Activity, and even long, drawn-out and repetitive activity, has a meaning if it has some significant culmination, some more or less lasting end that can be considered to have been the direction and purpose of the activity. But the descriptions so far also provide something else; namely, the suggestion of how an existence that is objectively meaningless, in this sense, can nevertheless acquire a meaning for him whose existence it is.

Now let us ask: Which of these pictures does life in fact resemble? And let us not begin with our own lives, for here both our prejudices and wishes are great, but with the life in general that we share with the rest of creation. We shall find, I think, that it all has a certain pattern, and that this pattern is by now easily recognized.

We can begin anywhere, only saving human existence for our last consideration. We can, for example, begin with any animal. It does not matter where we begin, because the result is going to be exactly the same.

Thus, for example, there are caves in New Zealand, deep and dark, whose floors are quiet pools and whose walls and ceilings are covered with soft light. As one gazes in wonder in the stillness of these caves it seems that the Creator has reproduced there in microcosm the heavens themselves, until one scarcely remembers the enclosing presence of the walls. As one looks more closely, however, the scene is explained. Each dot of light identifies an ugly worm, whose luminous tail is meant to attract insects from the surrounding darkness. As from time to time one of these insects draws near it becomes entangled in a sticky thread lowered by the worm, and is eaten. This goes on month after month, the blind worm lying there in the barren stillness waiting to entrap an occasional bit of nourishment that will only sustain it to another bit of nourishment until. . . . Until what? What great thing awaits all this long and repetitious effort and makes it worthwhile? Really nothing. The larva just transforms itself finally to a tiny winged adult that lacks even mouth parts to feed and lives only a day or two. These adults, as soon as they have mated and laid eggs, are themselves caught in the threads and are devoured by the cannibalist worms, often without having ventured into the day, the only point to their existence having now been fulfilled. This has been going on for millions of years, and to no end other than that the same meaningless cycle may continue for another millions of years.

All living things present essentially the same spectacle. The larva of a certain cicada burrows in the darkness of the earth for seventeen years, through season after season, to emerge finally into the daylight for a brief flight, lay its eggs, and die—this all to repeat itself during the next seventeen years, and so on to eternity. We have already noted, in another connection, the struggles of fish, made only that others may do the same after them and that this cycle, having no other point than itself, may never cease. Some birds span an entire side of the globe each year and then return, only to ensure that others may follow the same incredibly long path again and again. One is led to wonder what the point of it all is, with what great triumph this ceaseless effort, repeating itself through millions of years, might finally culminate, and why it should go on and on for so long, accomplishing nothing, getting nowhere. But then one realizes that there is no point to it at all, that it really culminates in nothing, that each of these cycles, so filled with toil, is to be followed only by more of

the same. The point of any living thing's life is, evidently, nothing but life itself.

This life of the world thus presents itself to our eyes as a vast machine, feeding on itself, running on and on forever to nothing. And we are part of that life. To be sure, we are not just the same, but the differences are not so great as we like to think; many are merely invented, and none really cancels the kind of meaninglessness that we found in Sisyphus and that we find all around, wherever anything lives. We are conscious of our activity. Our goals, whether in any significant sense we choose them or not, are things of which we are at least partly aware and can therefore in some sense appraise. More significantly, perhaps, men have a history, as other animals do not, such that each generation does not precisely resemble all those before. Still, if we can in imagination disengage our wills from our lives and disregard the deep interest each man has in his own existence, we shall find that they do not so little resemble the existence of Sisyphus. We toil after goals, most of them—indeed every single one of them—of transitory significance and, having gained one of them, we immediately set forth for the next, as if that one had never been, with this next one being essentially more of the same. Look at a busy street any day, and observe the throng going hither and thither. To what? Some office or shop, where the same things will be done today as were done yesterday, and are done now so they may be repeated tomorrow. And if we think that, unlike Sisyphus, these labors do have a point, that they culminate in something lasting and, independently of our own deep interests in them, very worthwhile, then we simply have not considered the thing closely enough. Most such effort is directed only to the establishment and perpetuation of home and family; that is, to the begetting of others who will follow in our steps to do more of the same. Each man's life thus resembles one of Sisyphus' climbs to the summit of his hill, and each day of it one of his steps; the difference is that whereas Sisyphus himslf returns to push the stone up again, we leave this to our children. We at one point imagined that the labors of Sisyphus finally culminated in the creation of a temple, but for this to make any difference it had to be a temple that would at least endure, adding beauty to the world for the remainder of time. Our achievements, even though they are often beautiful, are mostly bubbles; and those that do last, like the sand-swept pyramids, soon become mere curiosities while around them the rest of mankind continues its perpetual toting of rocks, only to see them roll down. Nations are built upon the bones of their founders and pioneers, but only to decay and crumble before long, their rubble then becoming the foundation for others directed to exactly the same fate. The picture of Sisyphus is the picture of existence of the individual man, great or unknown, of nations, of the race of men, and of the very life of the world.

On a country road one sometimes comes upon the ruined hulks of a house and once extensive buildings, all in collapse and spread over with weeds. A curious eye can in imagination reconstruct from what is left a once warm and thriving life, filled with purpose. There was the hearth, where a family once talked, sang, and made plans; there were the rooms, where people loved, and babes were born to a rejoicing mother; there are the musty remains of a sofa, infested with bugs, once bought at a dear price to enhance an ever-growing comfort, beauty, and warmth. Every small piece of junk fills the mind with what once, not long ago, was utterly real, with children's voices, plans made, and enterprises embarked upon. That is how these stones of Sisyphus were rolled up, and that is how they became incorporated into a beautiful temple, and that temple is what now lies before you. Meanwhile other buildings, institutions, nations, and civilizations spring up all around, only to share the same fate before long. And if the question "What for?" is now asked, the answer is clear: so that just this may go on forever.

The two pictures—of Sisyphus and of our own lives, if we look at them from a distance—are in outline the same and convey to the mind the same image. It is not surprising, then, that men invent ways of denying it, their religions proclaiming a heaven that does not crumble, their hymnals and prayer books declaring a significance to life of which our eyes provide no hint whatever. Even our philosophies portray some permanent and lasting good at which all may aim, from the changeless forms invented by Plato to the beatific vision of St. Thomas and the ideals of permanence contrived by the moderns. When these fail to convince, then

earthly ideals such as universal justice and brotherhood are conjured up to take their places and give meaning to man's seemingly endless pilgrimage, some final state that will be ushered in when the last obstacle is removed and the last stone pushed to the hilltop. No one believes, of course, that any such state will be final, or even wants it to be in case it means that human existence would then cease to be a struggle; but in the meantime such ideas serve a very real need.

THE MEANING OF LIFE

We noted that Sisyphus' existence would have meaning if there were some point to his labors, if his efforts ever culminated in something that was not just an occasion for fresh labors of the same kind. But that is precisely the meaning it lacks. And human existence resembles his in that respect. Men do achieve things—they scale their towers and raise their stones to their hilltops—but every such accomplishment fades, providing only an occasion for renewed labors of the same kind.

But here we need to note something else that has been mentioned, but its significance not explored, and that is the state of mind and feeling with which such labors are undertaken. We noted that if Sisyphus had a keen and unappeasable desire to be doing just what he found himself doing, then, although his life would in no way be changed, it would nevertheless have a meaning for him. It would be an irrational one, no doubt, because the desire itself would be only the product of the substance in his veins, and not any that reason could discover, but a meaning nevertheless.

And would it not, in fact, be a meaning incomparably better than the other? For let us examine again the first kind of meaning it could have. Let us suppose that, without having any interest in rolling stones, as such, and finding this, in fact, a galling toil, Sisyphus did nevertheless have a deep interest in raising a temple, one that would be beautiful and lasting. And let us suppose he succeeded in this, that after ages of dreadful toil, all directed at this final result, he did at last complete his temple, such that now he could say his work was done, and he could rest and forever enjoy the result. Now what? What picture now presents itself to our minds? It is precisely the picture of infinite boredom! Of Sisyphus doing nothing ever again, but contemplating what he has already wrought and can no longer add anything to, and contemplating it for an eternity! Now in this picture we have a meaning for Sisyphus' existence, a point for his prodigious labor, because we have put it there; yet, at the same time, that which is really worthwhile seems to have slipped away entirely. Where before we were presented with the nightmare of eternal and pointless activity, we are now confronted with the hell of its eternal absence.

Our second picture, then, wherein we imagined Sisyphus to have had inflicted on him the irrational desire to be doing just what he found himself doing, should not have been dismissed so abruptly. The meaning that picture lacked was no meaning that he or anyone could crave, and the strange meaning it had was perhaps just what we were seeking.

At this point, then, we can reintroduce what has been until now, it is hoped, resolutely pushed aside in an effort to view our lives and human existence with objectivity; namely, our own wills, our deep interest in what we find ourselves doing. If we do this we find that our lives do indeed still resemble that of Sisyphus, but that the meaningfulness they thus lack is precisely the meaningfulness of infinite boredom. At the same time, the strange meaningfulness they possess is that of the inner compulsion to be doing just what we were put here to do, and to go on doing it forever. This is the nearest we may hope to get to heaven, but the redeeming side of that fact is that we do thereby avoid a genuine hell.

If the builders of a great and flourishing ancient civilization could somehow return now to see archaeologists unearthing the trivial remnants of what they had once accomplished with such effort—see the fragments of pots and vases, a few broken statues, and such tokens of another age and greatness—they could indeed ask themselves what the point of it all was, if this is all it finally came to. Yet, it did not seem so to them then, for it was just the building, and not what was finally built, that gave their life meaning. Similarly, if the builders of the ruined home and farm that I described a short while ago could be brought back to see what is left, they would have the same feelings. What we

construct in our imaginations as we look over these decayed and rusting pieces would reconstruct itself in their very memories, and certainly with unspeakable sadness. The piece of a sled at our feet would revive in them a warm Christmas. And what rich memories would there be in the broken crib? And the weed-covered remains of a fence would reproduce the scene of a great herd of livestock, so laboriously built up over so many years. What was it all worth, if this is the final result? Yet, again, it did not seem so to them through those many years of struggle and toil, and they did not imagine they were building a Gibraltar. The things to which they bent their backs day after day, realizing one by one their ephemeral plans, were precisely the things in which their wills were deeply involved, precisely the things in which their interests lay, and there was no need then to ask questions. There is no more need of them now—the day was sufficient to itself, and so was the life.

This is surely the way to look at all of life—at one's own life, and each day and moment it contains; of the life of a nation; of the species; of the life of the world; and of everything that breathes. Even the glow worms I described, whose cycles of existence over the millions of years seem so pointless when looked at by us, will seem entirely different to us if we can somehow try to view their existence from within. Their endless activity, which gets nowhere, is just what it is their will to pursue. This is its whole justification and meaning. Nor would it be any salvation to the birds who span the globe every year, back and forth, to have a home made for them in a cage with plenty of food and protection, so that they would not have to migrate any more. It would be their condemnation, for it is the doing that counts for them, and not what they hope to win by it. Flying these prodigious distances, never ending, is what it is in their veins to do, exactly as it was in Sisyphus' veins to roll stones, without end, after the gods had waxed merciful and implanted this in him.

A human being no sooner draws his first breath than he responds to the will that is in him to live. He no more asks whether it will be worthwhile, or whether anything of significance will come of it, than the worms and the birds. The point of his living is simply to be living, in the manner that it is his nature to be living. He goes through his life building his castles, each of these beginning to fade into time as the next is begun; yet, it would be no salvation to rest from all this. It would be a condemnation, and one that would in no way be redeemed were he able to gaze upon the things he has done, even if these were beautiful and absolutely permanent, as they never are. What counts is that one should be able to begin a new task, a new castle, a new bubble. It counts only because it is there to be done and he has the will to do it. The same will be the life of his children, and of theirs; and if the philosopher is apt to see in this a pattern similar to the unending cycles of the existence of Sisyphus, and to despair, then it is indeed because the meaning and point he is seeking is not there— but mercifully so. The meaning of life is from within us, it is not bestowed from without, and it far exceeds in both its beauty and permanence any heaven of which men have ever dreamed or yearned for.

Further Questions

1. In the end, Taylor tries to snatch meaningfulness (for our lives) from the jaws of meaninglessness. Did he convince you?
2. Compare Tolstoy's and Taylor's accounts of what makes life meaningful. Do they have anything in common? How do they differ? Which, if either, is more plausible to you?

Further Readings

Russell, Bertrand. *The Conquest of Happiness*. New York: New American Library, 1930. Russell's account of bouts with meaninglessness.
Sanders, Steven, and Cheney, David, eds. *The Meaning of Life*. Englewood Cliffs, NJ: Prentice-Hall, 1980. A good anthology.

70   A Fast Car and a Good Woman

RAYMOND MARTIN

A brief biography of Martin appears on page 139.

In this selection, Martin questions the psychological validity of philosophical worries about the meaning of life. He suggests that as often as not, such worries merely mask a deep, underlying problem: our inability to stay satisfied.

Reading Questions

1. Martin distinguishes between the problem of the meaning of life and the problem of life. How?
2. Martin criticizes Tolstoy, Nagel, and Taylor. What are his criticisms of each?
3. Martin claims that, at least this side of enlightenment, there is no fully satisfying solution to the problem of life. Why?
4. What connection does he see between there being no solution to the problem of life and the fact that many people feel that death challenges the meaning of their lives?

POVERTY, SICKNESS, LONELINESS, alienation, feelings of inferiority, an inability to give and receive love. Such problems can challenge the meaning of our lives. There is no puzzle about why. When we are afflicted with them, we suffer. If our suffering is bad enough and seemingly intractable, we may lose the sense that our lives are worth living.

Such problems are practically, but not philosophically, challenging. When they cause suffering that is avoidable, the important question is how to avoid it. When they cause suffering that is inevitable, the question is how to accept it. Learning how to avoid suffering when we can and accept it when we must are not part of the problem of the meaning of life. They are part of the problem of life.

Death also challenges the meaning of our lives. But in the case of death, unlike in the cases of the other problems mentioned, it is not clear why. What does the fact that our lives will come to an end have to do with whether they are worth living? There seems to be no connection. I shall suggest a partial answer.

The problem of the meaning of life is the philosophical question of how, if at all, our lives can be worth living. It concerns, for instance, such speculative questions as whether there is an overriding purpose or pattern for human life as a whole that confers meaning on our individual lives, and whether there is an objective source of value for our lives. The problem of life, on the other hand, is the practical question of how to live our lives so that they are as worth living as they can be. Clearly the problem of life is more important. In fact, it can seem so much more important that it is a tenet of practical wisdom that if we take proper care of our lives, questions of meaning will take care of themselves. That's good advice, unless you are the sort of person who *has* to address questions of meaning to take proper care of your life. Not everyone does, and even among those who do, questions of meaning will seem more important at some times than at others.

Tolstoy is the classic example of someone for whom questions of meaning can be urgent.

> . . . I was overcome by minutes at first of perplexity and then of an arrest of life, as though I did not know how to live or what to do, and I lost

myself and was dejected. But that passed and I continued to live as before. Then those minutes of perplexity were repeated oftener and oftener, and always in one and the same form. These arrests of life found their expression in ever the same questions: "Why? Well, and then?"

> At first I thought that those were simply aimless, inappropriate questions . . . [But they] began to repeat themselves oftener and oftener, answers were demanded more and more persistently, and, like dots that fall on the same spot, these questions, without any answers, thickened into one black blotch.

> . . . And I was absolutely unable to make any reply. The questions were not waiting and I had to answer them at once; if I did not answer them, I could not live.[1]

Empathizing with Tolstoy's existential anguish can unravel our familiar everyday rationalizations and expose a secret need for understanding we keep buried deep within. Stripped of our pretensions, we look freshly—at our own lives, at the lives of those around us, at the lives of everyone who has ever lived—and we ask: Why? There is no answer. Just the silent, anxious echo of our question. And sometimes a nagging doubt.

There is something fishy about existential anguish. Even when it comes wrapped in the paper of respectable philosophical questioning, it often smells suspiciously like a rationalization of unmentioned problems. Tolstoy, for instance, portrays himself as one who would be happy, except for worries about the meaning of life. But is it really worries about the meaning of life that keep dragging him down? There are questions he can ask about the meaning of his life, doubts to be raised. But questions and doubts can be raised about anything. Questions are not necessarily problems. They can be. We can make a psychological problem out of almost anything. But how often are philosophical questions genuine psychological problems? When it seems that our philosophical questions give rise to existential anguish, should we marvel at the depth of our insight or suspect self-deception?

There is one familiar way philosophy can give rise to psychological problems. The naive person whose sense of security is built on a foundation of unquestioned beliefs can have those beliefs suddenly swept out from under him or her by philosophical questioning. Consider, for instance, a person whose sense of security rests on religious beliefs that suddenly become subject to doubt. The resulting turmoil can be so painfully confusing as to call into question the meaning of life.

Without minimizing this sort of problem, I wish to set it aside. The philosophical questioning which induces it usually directly challenges only the beliefs we depend on for security, not the meaning of our lives per se. The suffering comes not from some insoluble philosophical problem but from the sudden realization that our personal ideologies rest on dubious assumptions. Most people get over this realization quickly enough (usually too quickly), either by forgetting or ignoring their doubts or else by finding a new basis for security. I am asking whether there is a deeper and more direct philosophical challenge to the meaning of our lives which is at least as psychologically valid as the one that depends on philosophical naiveté, yet is not so easily set aside or outgrown.

In sum, I have distinguished three challenges to the meaning of our lives: bad times, death, and philosophical doubts of a sort that can arise even when our lives are going quite well. My concern, now, is with the third of these challenges. Putting aside problems caused by the realization that our personal ideologies rest on dubious assumptions, I am asking whether challenges of this third sort — that is, philosophical doubts about the meaning of our lives that can arise even when our lives are going quite well — are psychologically genuine. I don't deny that when our lives are going quite well, psychological problems can arise. I'm asking how likely it is that philosophical questions are the explanation. I admit they may sometimes be the explanation. I'm asking whether there isn't usually some deeper explanation, a source of anxiety and despair we may not be facing if we allow ourselves to become preoccupied with philosophy.

Thomas Nagel sets aside as unphilosophical those challenges to the meaning of life that arise because things go wrong and "are compatible with the possibility of meaning had things gone differently." Philosophical challenges to meaning, in his view, threaten human life with "objective meaninglessness" even when it is "at its subjective best."

And he seems to think that philosophical challenges to meaning are a chronic source of deep psychological problems.

> In seeing ourselves from outside we find it difficult to take our lives seriously. This loss of conviction, and the attempt to regain it, is the problem of the meaning of life.
>   . . . it is a genuine problem which we cannot ignore. The capacity for transcendence brings with it a liability to alienation. . . . Yet we can't abandon the external standpoint because it is our own.

It is our own, Nagel says, because the objective self is such a vital part of us that "to ignore its quasi-independent operation is to be cut off from oneself as much as if one were to abandon one's subjective individuality." So, in Nagel's view, there is no escape from this sort of alienation — "no credible way of eliminating the inner conflict" — and, hence, no solution to the philosophical problem of the meaning of life.

But there is help, Nagel thinks, and it comes from two sources:

> [Morality] permits the objective assertion of subjective values to the extent that this is compatible with the corresponding claims of others. It . . . [involves] occupying a position far enough outside your own life to reduce the importance of the difference between yourself and other people, yet not so far outside that all human values vanish in a nihilistic blackout. . . .
>   . . . Humility falls between nihilistic detachment and blind self-importance. . . . The human race has a strong disposition to adore itself, in spite of its record. But it is possible to live a complete life of the kind one has been given without overvaluing it hopelessly.[2]

Even so, Nagel thinks that "the gap is too wide to be closed entirely, for anyone who is fully human." So, although morality and humility help, the problem is insoluble. Serious internal conflict remains. In sum, Nagel agrees with Tolstoy, though for different reasons, that philosophical challenges to the meaning of life are an important source of psychological problems.

If Nagel and Tolstoy are right, practical wisdom is wrong. Questions of meaning do not take care of themselves. If you are intellectually sensitive, then to take proper care of your life, you have to

DEATH

Thomas Nagel

There will be a last day, a last hour, a last minute of consciousness, and that will be it. Off the edge.

To grasp this it isn't enough to think only of a particular stream of consciousness coming to an end. The external view of death is psychological as well as physical: it includes the idea that the person who you are will have no more thoughts, experiences, memories, intensions, desires, etc. That inner life will be finished. But the recognition that the life of a particular person in the world will come to an end is not what I am talking about. To grasp your own death from within you must try to look *forward* to it — to see it as a *prospect*.

Is this possible? It might seem that there could be no form of thought about your own death except either an external view, in which the world is pictured as continuing after your life stops, or an internal view that sees only this side of death — that includes only the finitude of your expected future consciousness. But this is not true. There is also something that can be called the expectation of nothingness, and though the mind tends to veer away from it, it is an unmistakable experience, always startling, often frightening, and very different from the familiar recognition that your life will go on for only a limited time — that you probably have less than thirty years and certainly less than a hundred. The positive prospect of the end of subjective time, though it is logically inseparable from these limits, is something distinct.

From *Mortal Questions* (Cambridge University Press, 1979).

attend to questions about meaning. Tolstoy's self-portrait seems to show that these questions *can* bring you down. Nagel's view is that if you think honestly and correctly about questions of meaning, they *will* bring you down. Tolstoy solved his problem by embracing Christianity. Nagel claims there is no honest solution. Nagel's analysis of the philosophical issues is elegant. Yet his account, like Tolstoy's, is psychologically suspect.

To see why, think about a time when your life *was* at its subjective best. Maybe you were young and had just fallen deeply in love with someone who had just fallen deeply in love with you. Perhaps you were in the throes of sexual ecstasy or enveloped in mystical bliss. Or you may have played some instrument, or danced, or acted, or written much better than you ever thought you could. Perhaps you were simply drawn out of yourself by the muted texture of an autumn day or the vibrant sting of cold rain against your face.

Whatever your peak experiences, were you worried then about the meaning of life? Did *questions* about meaning *bother* you, that is, were they *problems* for you? Of course not. If your life really was at its subjective best, then probably it was insufficient: you lacked nothing. Because you had solved the problem of life, at least temporarily, questions about the meaning of life did not even arise. If such questions had been raised, you would have regarded them as an entertainment or, more likely, dismissed them as irrelevant. Perhaps, then, practical wisdom is right after all: how to live well is the only psychologically valid issue.

When we are happy, *questions* about the meaning of our lives rarely ever become *problems*. The solution to the *problem* of the meaning of life, then, is simple: be happy. The really important question is: how? Life is too short to try out many paths to happiness. We have to take our chances. And we have to take some of our most important chances when we are young and relatively inexperienced. Through ignorance or bad luck, people often choose the wrong paths to happiness and, as a consequence, suffer. Such bad choices are obviously an important source of suffering, particularly for people in circumstances sufficiently advantaged that they have the luxury of choice. But the fact that people make bad choices about how to be happy does not in and of itself give rise to *philosophical* problems about the meaning of our lives.

Like Nagel, Richard Taylor locates *philosophical* questions about the meaning of our lives in the tension between objective meaninglessness — for him, "endless pointlessness" — and subjective meaning. His view is that our lives are objectively meaningless, but not meaningless per se.

> At this point, then, we can reintroduce . . . our own wills, our deep interest in what we find ourselves doing. If we do this we find that our lives do indeed still resemble that of Sisyphus, but . . . the strange meaningfulness they possess is that of the inner compulsion to be doing just what we were put here to do, and to go on doing it forever.

In other words, the tasks people set for themselves, the things to which

> they bent their backs day after day, realizing one by one their ephemeral plans, were precisely the things in which their wills were deeply involved, precisely the things in which their interests lay, and there was no need then to ask questions. There is no more need of them now — the day was sufficient to itself, and so was the life. This is surely the way to look at all of life. . . .

So, in Taylor's view, subjective meaningfulness resides in activity in which our wills are involved.

> A human being no sooner draws his first breath than he responds to the will that is in him to live. He no more asks whether it will be worthwhile, or whether anything of significance will come of it, than the worms and the birds. The point of his living is simply to be living, in the manner that it is his nature to be living. . . . What counts is that one should be able to begin a new task, a new castle, a new bubble. It counts only because it is there to be done and he has the will to do it. . . . The meaning of life is from within us, it is not

bestowed from without, and it far exceeds in both its beauty and permanence any heaven of which men have ever dreamed or yearned for.[3]

Taylor's view, in sum, is that the value derived from activity in which our wills are involved is enough to sustain the meaning of our lives, indeed, is as much as we can rationally hope for.

Is it? Looking around, we see people *willfully* building their castles and bubbles, so to speak, just as Taylor says they do, but not as *meaningfully* as he claims. Surely Thoreau was not all wrong when he observed that most people live in quiet desperation.

Taylor finds meaning everywhere. Nagel finds it nowhere. The saccharine sweetness of Taylor's conclusion makes Nagel's pessimism look appealing. But neither account feels psychologically valid. Taylor's is too romantic and makes meaning too easy. Nagel's is too intellectual and makes meaning too hard.

It is worth exploring the middle ground. A plausible view suggested by Taylor's discussion is that people have meaningful lives not when they are doing what they *will* to do but when they are doing what they *love* to do. Such a view seems to leave a place for meaningfulness without romanticizing human life. For most people are not doing what they love to do but, rather, what they have to do, or what they feel they have to do. The human spectacle is not a scene of yeoman farmers toiling happily in their fields. It includes a fair proportion of tired, unhappy people, resigned to their painful, dreary lives, trying desperately to distract and anesthetize themselves.

Meaning, then, on this criterion, is neither impossible nor inevitable. Nor is it all or nothing. It is a matter of degree. Is the answer, then, not that your life is or is not inherently meaningful but, rather, that it can be meaningful, and is meaningful largely to the degree that you are doing what you love to do? That seems a more likely hypothesis than the ones already considered. Yet, in its implicit suggestion that the main problem of meaning is the practical problem of finding out what you love to do and then doing it, this view too may be hopelessly romantic.

Oscar Wilde once remarked that there are only two problems in life: not getting what you want, and getting it. If Wilde is right, then what many people think is the whole problem—not getting what you want (or doing what you want to do)—is really only part of the problem. Ironically, the rest of the problem is what these same people think is the solution. It is hard to quarrel with that much of Wilde's observation. Getting what you want *can* be problematic. Wilde's remark also *suggests,* however, that getting what you want not only *can be* but *will be* problematic. If that's true, then our lives are an insoluble problem.

It is easy to see how not getting what you want can be a problem. And, if you want the wrong things—say, the pleasures of an unhealthy lifestyle—it's also easy to see how getting what you want can be a problem. But what if you want the right things—things that are not only good in themselves but also good for you. How could wanting the right things be a problem?

Think back to those times when your life was at its subjective best. Granted, at those moments you were not bothered by questions about the meaning of life. But were you completely satisfied? That's a loaded question. How could you ever know that you couldn't have been even more satisfied? So far as you could tell, then, were you completely satisfied? Probably you were. If you were, then it must be possible to be so happy that, so far as you can tell, you have all of your unsatisfied wants driven out of you—at least all of them that detract from your happiness. That may or may not be complete satisfaction. But it's close enough for most of us. And we sometimes get it. In and of itself, it's a solution, not a problem. But it inevitably leads to a problem, the real problem: *it doesn't last.*

Life is a tease. It promises more lasting satisfactions than it delivers. No matter how good it gets, eventually we always find ourselves wanting more. If we lose what was satisfying us completely, we want it back. If we keep it, we want more of it or else we want something else. And we will want in a way that detracts from our happiness. That's a psychological truth you can bet the farm on. Whatever you think is going to satisfy you completely, it is not going to satisfy you completely for long. It may for a while. If you are clever, you may even distract yourself from noticing that the itch of unsatisfied desire has returned. But if you look closely, you will see that what you wanted, what

you may have thought would be enough, what you were sure would satisfy you completely, does not really do it.

Most of us have the dubious luxury of thinking that we would be happy if only we had something we cannot have, or we were doing something we cannot do. Our deprivation nourishes the illusion that complete satisfaction—that lasts—is attainable, if only the external circumstances of our lives were better. Tolstoy did not have the luxury of that illusion. He had everything he wanted—wealth, fame, a loving family—and was doing what he wanted to do. Yet still he wasn't satisfied. He had so much that he couldn't imagine what more he wanted—unless perhaps it was answers. So he embraced answers, and then—so he would have us believe—he was happy. That is his story: that it was lack of answers that brought him down in the first place, and that it was his subsequent conviction that he had answers—his "irrational knowledge"—that made everything right again.

Perhaps. But another possibility is that Tolstoy's lack of answers was at most a symptom of the problem, not the real problem. Since he had everything and was doing what he wanted to be doing, what, then, could his real problem have been? It *could* have been simply that even with everything, Tolstoy's life did not stay at its subjective best: satisfied, he could not stay satisfied. The problem could have been that Tolstoy wanted his life to be at its subjective best but could not keep it there. So, when he came down, as inevitably he did, he wanted more, even though, as we say, "he had everything." In other words, the problem could have been simply that while life allowed him to taste complete satisfaction, it didn't last.

If not getting what you want (or not doing what you want to do) won't satisfy you completely, and getting what you want (or doing what you want to do) won't satisfy you completely either, it's worth thinking briefly about the extreme alternative: don't want. That's the essence of the Buddha Gautama's contribution to solving the problem of life. It may or may not be the right solution. We don't really have to decide. For even if it is the right solution, it is the Buddha's solution, not ours. We may give lip service to that solution, but few of us really see it as a realistic option for ourselves. If we did, we'd be off somewhere, perhaps meditating in a monastery in Burma, not taking college courses or reading essays like this one on the meaning of life. We may say we're on the "path." And we may be. But even on the path we still spend most of our waking time trying to get what we want. Except that on the path, in addition to all of the usual wants—security, sex, love, power, glory—we now have an unusual want: not wanting. The path is crowded with spiritual materialists.[4]

We're back to a realistic pessimism. The answer to the problem of the meaning of life may simply be that we're stuck with a life of fleeting satisfactions and unsatisfied desires. Whatever the value of morality and humility, they are precious little help in solving this problem. Doing what you love to do is a great help, probably the most important contribution you can make to the meaningfulness of your life. Ironically, doing what you love to do may even be a critical part of the most important contribution you can make to the lives of those around you. Even so, at least this side of enlightenment, there may be no fully satisfying solution to the problem of life.

Since satisfaction doesn't last, then either we have to continually resatisfy ourselves or successfully and pleasantly distract ourselves from the fact that we haven't. That seems to be our fate, and if we're reasonably good at these two tasks, it's not such a bad fate. But neither is it a fully satisfying solution to the problem of life. In other words, what I am suggesting is that the root psychological problem, the one that keeps arising even when our lives are going quite well, may simply be that we cannot satisfy ourselves completely for long. That is why even among people whose lives are going quite well, almost everyone is chronically unsatisfied. Acknowledging that this is the problem can bring us down from our philosophical heights. Back on earth, we can redirect our energies toward solving the problem of life. To do that, we follow our individual recipes for happiness: a fast car and a good woman, or whatever you think will do it for you.

The acknowledgment that there is no fully satisfying solution to the problem of life can quash our hopes that we will ever get the complete and lasting satisfaction we crave. That is one of the deepest and most emotionally significant hopes we have.

True, that hope may never have survived rational scrutiny anyway, but that doesn't stop us from secretly nourishing it. It comes as a profound disappointment to finally admit, not just verbally, but completely, that whether we get what we want or not we will never stay satisfied for long.

And then there is death. Death has always been a puzzle for philosophers. Not what it is, but why we have some of the attitudes toward it we do. For present purposes, we can ignore most of these famous enigmas. Our question is this: Why does death threaten the meaning of our lives? Surely part of the answer is the familiar observation that we fear we may vanish without leaving a significant trace— that our lives will not have made a positive difference. But, of course, that should not be a problem for people, such as Tolstoy, whose lives have gone as well as possible and, hence, who have made a positive difference. There must be more than that to the challenge to meaning that death poses. The analysis just given suggests part of the answer.

Death threatens the meaningfulness of our lives partly because it ends our struggle for satisfaction. Because death kills us, the prospect that death is near kills the unspoken and irrational hope that if only we had a little more time, we might satisfy our need for psychological closure—for complete satisfaction. If we have already given up that hope, we will fear death less. We may even welcome it as a merciful release from a struggle we cannot help throwing ourselves into even though we know we shall never win it. In any case, death challenges the meaningfulness of our lives partly because the prospect that death is near makes it painfully obvious that we will lose the struggle for satisfaction. Death is a major symbol of defeat.

Return once again to those moments when your life was at its subjective best. Those moments brought complete satisfaction. And complete satisfaction is a kind of victory over death. A person, for instance, can be so much in love, so deeply satisfied, she feels that she could die and it wouldn't matter. When our experience gets that good, we have won the battle for satisfaction, and death holds no terror. The problem is that our victory is only temporary. Death is a persistent foe, and desire its ally. Satisfied, we cannot stay satisfied. The itch of desire returns, the struggle resumes. Until death ends the struggle—perhaps forever.

NOTES

1. Leo Tolstoy's reflections on the meaning of life are in his book, *My Confession,* translated by Leo Wiener, Dent and Sons, 1905.

2. Thomas Nagel's thoughts on the meaning of life were published originally in his essay, "The Absurd," *The Journal of Philosophy,* v. 63, 1971, pp. 716–727. The passages quoted are taken from that portion of Nagel's *The View from Nowhere,* New York: Oxford University Press, 1986, 214–223, that is reprinted in the present volume.

3. Richard Taylor's views are from his book, *Good and Evil,* New York: Macmillan, 1970. They are reprinted in the present volume.

4. I have borrowed the notion of "spiritual materialism" from Chögyam Trungpa, *Cutting Through Spiritual Materialism,* Boulder, Colorado: Shambhala Publications, 1973.

Further Questions

1. Which is more important for you: the problem of the meaning of life or the problem of life? Must you solve the former to solve the latter?
2. What is your personal solution to the problem of life?
3. Is being completely satisfied compatible with having unsatisfied desires? If it is, does this fact undermine Martin's argument?

Further Readings

J. Krishnamurti, *Reflections on the Self.* Chicago: Open Court, 1997.
Lao Tzu. *The Way of Life.* Witter Bynner translation. New York: Perigee Books, 1944, 1972. The Taoist classic on how to live well. One of the best translations for Americans.

Part XII

Ethics

NATURE HAS NO RESPECT FOR MORALITY. Nature kills indiscriminately. Rocks, animals, insects, and plants know nothing of morality. We do. Isn't our moral sense part of what makes us special?

Perhaps. But we kill far more efficiently than either nature or any of its creatures. In this century alone, more than fifty million human beings have been slaughtered in war, and today we're in danger of destroying not only the rest of humanity but all life on this planet. Meanwhile, we continue to ravage the earth, enslave other animals, and pollute our environment. We rape and pillage and murder one another, often without provocation. That is almost a distinction in itself. However, there is at least one other animal that murders its own kind without provocation: rats.

Many claim morality can save us from ourselves. Others say we must save ourselves from morality. But what does it mean to be moral? Is morality objective? Subjective? An expression of self-interest? A way of keeping self-interest in check? Who is to determine what is right and what is wrong? Are there moral truths and, if so, how can we know them? How can we settle moral disagreements?

We might not know the answers to any of these questions. But, unlike all other known creatures, we can at least ask them.

71   The Categorical Imperative

IMMANUEL KANT

A biography of Kant appears on page 436.

    Here Kant argues for the objectivity of morals. He is one of the best representatives of the view that moral laws are binding on everyone and always without any qualification — hence "categorical."

Reading Questions

1. What distinguishes the *hypothetical* from the *categorical* imperative?
2. Kant believed morality could be summed up, like scientific laws, in one ultimate principle. What is that principle?
3. By "maxim," Kant means "rule." By "universal law," he means something that is binding upon everyone, always. Thus, he says, "Act only according to that maxim by which you can at the same time will that it should become a universal law." But what, according to Kant, is supposed to guide your *will*?
4. What makes the categorical imperative categorical, and how can you know it is categorical rather than hypothetical?
5. Why does Kant think that human beings are ends in themselves?
6. What does he mean by human "will"?
7. Why does Kant think that duty is a categorical imperative?

NOTHING CAN POSSIBLY BE CONCEIVED in the world, or even out of it, which can be called good without qualification, except a *good will*. Intelligence, wit, judgment, and other *talents* of the mind, however they may be named, or courage, resolution, perseverance, as qualities of temperament, are undoubtedly good and desirable in many respects; but these gifts of nature may also become extremely bad and mischievous if the will which is to make use of them, and which, therefore, constitutes what is called *character*, is not good. It is the same with the *gifts of fortune*. Power, riches, honor, even health, and the general well-being and contentment with one's condition which is called

happiness, inspire pride, and often presumption, if there is not a good will to correct the influence of these on the mind, and with this also to rectify the whole principle of acting, and adapt it to its end. The sight of a being who is not adorned with a single feature of a pure and good will, enjoying unbroken prosperity, can never give pleasure to an impartial rational spectator. Thus a good will appears to constitute the indispensable condition even of being worthy of happiness.

    There are even some qualities which are of service to this good will itself, and may facilitate its action, yet which have no intrinsic unconditional value, but always presuppose a good will, and this

From Immanuel Kant, The Fundamental Principles of the Metaphysics of Morals. *Translated by Thomas K. Abbott, 1889.*

qualifies the esteem that we justly have for them, and does not permit us to regard them as absolutely good. Moderation in the affections and passions, self-control, and calm deliberation are not only good in many respects, but even seem to constitute part of the intrinsic worth of the person; but they are far from deserving to be called good without qualification, although they have been so unconditionally praised by the ancients. For without the principles of a good will, they may become extremely bad; and the coolness of a villain not only makes him far more dangerous, but also directly makes him more abominable in our eyes than he would have been without it.

A good will is good not because of what it performs or effects, not by its aptness for the attainment of some proposed end, but simply by virtue of the volition—that is, it is good in itself, and considered by itself is to be esteemed much higher than all that can be brought about by it in favor of any inclination, nay, even of the sumtotal of all inclinations. Even if it should happen that, owing to special disfavor of fortune, or the niggardly provision of a stepmotherly nature, this will should wholly lack power to accomplish its purpose, if with its greatest efforts it should yet achieve nothing, and there should remain only the good will (not, to be sure, a mere wish, but the summoning of all means in our power), then, like a jewel, it would still shine by its own light, as a thing which has its whole value in itself. Its usefulness or fruitlessness can neither add to nor take away anything from this value. It would be, as it were, only the setting to enable us to handle it the more conveniently in common commerce, or to attract to it the attention of those who are not yet connoisseurs, but not to recommend it to true connoisseurs, or to determine its value. . . .

Everything in nature works according to laws. Rational beings alone have the faculty of acting according *to the conception* of laws, that is according to principles, *i.e.* have a *will*. Since the deduction of actions from principles requires *reason*, the will is nothing but practical reason. . . . the relation of the objective laws to a will that is not thoroughly good is conceived as the determination of the will of a rational being by principles of reason, but which the will from its nature does not of necessity follow.

The conception of an objective principle, in so far as it is obligatory for a will, is called a command (of reason), and the formula of the command is called an Imperative. . . .

Now all *imperatives* command either *hypothetically* or *categorically*. . . .

. . . If now the action is good only as a means *to something else,* then the imperative is *hypothetical;* if it is conceived as good *in itself* and consequently as being necessarily the principle of a will which of itself conforms to reason, then it is *categorical*. . . .

When I conceive of a hypothetical imperative, in general I do not know beforehand what it will contain until I am given the condition. But when I conceive a categorical imperative, I know at once what it contains. For as the imperative contains besides the law only the necessity that the maxims shall conform to this law, while the law contains no conditions restricting it, there remains nothing but the general statement that the maxim of the action should conform to a universal law, and it is this conformity alone that the imperative properly represents as necessary.

There is . . . but one categorical imperative, namely, this: *Act only on that maxim whereby thou canst at the same time will that it should become a universal law.*

Now if all imperatives of duty can be deduced from this one imperative as from their principle, then, although it should remain undecided whether what is called duty is not merely a vain notion, yet at least we shall be able to show what we understand by it and what this notion means.

Since the universality of the law according to which effects are produced constitutes what is properly called *nature* in the most general sense (as to form), that is the existence of things so far as it is determined by general laws, the imperative of duty may be expressed thus: *Act as if the maxim of thy action were to become by thy will a universal law of nature.*

We will now enumerate a few duties, adopting the usual division of them into duties to ourselves and to others, and into perfect and imperfect duties.

1. A man reduced to despair by a series of misfortunes feels wearied of life, but is still so far in possession of his reason that he can ask himself whether it would not be contrary to his duty to himself to take his own life. Now he inquires

whether the maxim of his action could become a universal law of nature. His maxim is: From self-love I adopt it as a principle to shorten my life when its longer duration is likely to bring more evil than satisfaction. It is asked then simply whether this principle founded on self-love can become a universal law of nature. Now we see at once that a system of nature of which it should be a law to destroy life by means of the very feeling whose special nature it is to impel to the improvement of life would contradict itself, and therefore could not exist as a system of nature; hence that maxim cannot possibly exist as a universal law of nature, and consequently would be wholly inconsistent with the supreme principle of all duty.

2. Another finds himself forced by necessity to borrow money. He knows that he will not be able to repay it, but sees also that nothing will be lent to him, unless he promises stoutly to repay it in a definite time. He desires to make this promise, but he has still so much conscience as to ask himself: Is it not unlawful and inconsistent with duty to get out of a difficulty in this way? Suppose, however, that he resolves to do so, then the maxim of his action would be expressed thus: When I think myself in want of money, I will borrow money and promise to repay it, although I know that I never can do so. Now this principle of self-love or of one's own advantage may perhaps be consistent with my whole future welfare; but the question now is, Is it right? I change then the suggestion of self-love into a universal law, and state the question thus: How would it be if my maxim were a universal law? Then I see at once that it could never hold as a universal law of nature, but would necessarily contradict itself. For supposing it to be a universal law that everyone when he thinks himself in a difficulty should be able to promise whatever he pleases, with the purpose of not keeping his promise, the promise itself would become impossible, as well as the end that one might have in view in it, since no one would consider that anything was promised to him, but would ridicule all such statements as vain pretences.

3. A third finds in himself a talent which with the help of some culture might make him a useful man in many respects. But he finds himself in comfortable circumstances, and prefers to indulge in pleasure rather than to take pains in enlarging and improving his happy natural capacities. He asks, however, whether his maxim of neglect of his natural gifts, besides agreeing with his inclination to indulgence, agrees also with what is called duty. He sees then that a system of nature could indeed subsist with such a universal law although men (like the South Sea islanders) should let their talents rest, and resolve to devote their lives merely to idleness, amusement, and propagation of their species—in a word, to enjoyment; but he cannot possibly *will* that this should be a universal law of nature, or be implanted in us as such by a natural instinct. For, as a rational being, he necessarily wills that his faculties be developed, since they serve him, and have been given him, for all sorts of possible purposes.

4. A fourth, who is in prosperity, while he sees that others have to contend with great wretchedness and that he could help them, thinks: What concern is it of mine? Let everyone be as happy as Heaven pleases, or as he can make himself; I will take nothing from him nor even envy him, only I do not wish to contribute anything to his welfare or to his assistance in distress! Now no doubt if such a mode of thinking were a universal law, the human race might very well subsist, and doubtless even better than in a state in which everyone talks of sympathy and good-will, or even takes care occasionally to put it into practice, but, on the other side, also cheats when he can, betrays the rights of men, or otherwise violates them. But although it is possible that a universal law of nature might exist in accordance with that maxim, it is impossible to *will* that such a principle should have the universal validity of a law of nature. For a will which resolved this would contradict itself, inasmuch as many cases might occur in which one would have the need of the love and sympathy of others, and in which, by such a law of nature, sprung from his own will, he would deprive himself of all hope of the aid he desires. . . .

We have thus established at least this much, that if duty is a conception which is to have any import and real legislative authority for our actions, it can only be expressed in categorical, and not at all in hypothetical imperatives. We have also, which is of great importance, exhibited clearly and definitely for every practical application the content of the categorical imperative, which must contain the principle of all duty if there is such a thing at all. We have not yet, however, advanced so far as to prove *a priori* that there actually is such an imperative, that there is a practical law which commands absolutely of itself, and without any other impulse, and that the following of this law is duty. . . .

Now I say: man and generally any rational being *exists* as an end in himself, *not merely as a means* to be arbitrarily used by this or that will, but in all his actions, whether they concern himself or other rational beings, must be always regarded at the same time as an end. All objects of the inclinations have only a conditional worth; for if the inclinations and the wants founded on them did not exist, then their object would be without value. But the inclinations themselves being sources of want are so far from having an absolute worth for which they should be desired, that, on the contrary, it must be the universal wish of every rational being to be wholly free from them. Thus the worth of any object which is *to be acquired* by our action is always conditional. Beings whose existence depends not on our will but on nature's, have nevertheless, if they are not rational beings, only a relative value as means, and are therefore called *things;* rational beings, on the contrary, are called *persons,* because their very nature points them out as ends in themselves, that is as something which must not be used merely as means, and so far therefore restricts freedom of action (and is an object of respect). These, therefore, are not merely subjective ends whose existence has a worth *for us* as an effect of our action, but *objective ends,* that is things whose existence is an end in itself: an end moreover for which no other can be substituted, which they should subserve *merely* as means, for otherwise nothing whatever would possess *absolute worth;* but if all worth were conditioned and therefore contingent, then

there would be no supreme practical principle of reason whatever.

If then there is a supreme practical principle or, in respect of the human will, a categorical imperative, it must be one which, being drawn from the conception of that which is necessarily an end for everyone because it is *an end in itself,* constitutes an *objective* principle of will, and can therefore serve as a universal practical law. The foundation of this principle is: *rational nature exists as an end in itself.* Man necessarily conceives his own existence as being so: so far then this is a *subjective* principle of human action. But every other rational being regards its existence similarly, just on the same rational principle, that holds for me: so that it is at the same time an objective principle, from which as a supreme practical law all laws of the will must be capable of being deduced. Accordingly the practical imperative will be as follows: *So act as to treat humanity, whether in thine own person or in that of any other, in every case as an end withal, never as means only.* . . .

The conception of every rational being as one which must consider itself as giving all the maxims of its will universal laws, so as to judge itself and its actions from this point of view—this conception leads to another which depends on it and is very fruitful, namely, that of a *kingdom of ends.*

By a *kingdom* I understand the union of different rational beings in a system by common laws. Now since it is by laws that ends are determined as regards their universal validity, hence, if we abstract from the personal differences of rational beings, and likewise from all the content of their private ends, we shall be able to conceive all ends combined in a systematic whole (including both rational beings as ends in themselves, and also the special ends which each may propose to himself), that is to say, we can conceive a kingdom of ends, which on the preceding principle is possible.

Further Questions

1. Kant believed that lying is always forbidden by the categorical imperative. Suppose, however, that your neighbor comes over looking for her husband, whom she plans to kill. Unbeknownst to her, he is hiding in your basement. Do you point the way? How do you think Kant would respond? [In "On a Supposed Right to Lie from Altruistic Motives," in

his *Critique of Practical Reason and Other Writings in Moral Philosophy*, translated by Lewis White Beck (University of Chicago Press, 1949), Kant does respond.]

2. What do you think of Kant's maxim to always treat others as an end, never only as a means? What is the relation between this maxim and the categorical imperative?

Further Readings

Acton, H. B. *Kant's Moral Philosophy.* New York: Macmillan, 1970.
Ross, W. D. *Kant's Ethical Theory.* Oxford: Oxford University Press, 1954.

72   Utilitarianism

JOHN STUART MILL

John Stuart Mill (1806–1873) was born in London. Educated by his father, a prominent historian, economist, and philosopher, Mill began to study Greek at age three, and by the time he was eight he had read major works of Plato in the original and began the study of Latin, Euclid, and algebra. By twelve he had read Aristotle's logical treatises. By fourteen he had mastered logic, mathematics, and all of world history. At nineteen he had a nervous breakdown.

Raised by his father on the utilitarian doctrines of Jeremy Bentham and the "philosophical radicals," Mill ended up revolutionizing their ideas in one of the most influential books on ethics ever written, *Utilitarianism* (1863). In his *On Liberty* (1859), he argued that the greatest happiness of the greatest number would best be achieved by allowing people as much freedom of thought and action as possible. In *The Subjection of Women* (1861), he argued for the then-radical idea that women should be allowed to vote and have careers. He spoke out on the discrimination against women, helped found the first women's suffrage society, and was one of the first advocates of birth control. In his *System of Logic* (1843), he argued that all knowledge comes from experience. In *Considerations on Representative Government* (1861), he argued that representative government is preferable to constitutional monarchy and enlightened aristocracy.

Reading Questions

1. What is the principle on which Mill wants to base morality?
2. What does he mean by "happiness"?
3. Why does Mill think that if an act produces the greatest amount of happiness, that act is right?
4. How does he distinguish "higher" from "lower" pleasures? What role does moral obligation play? Do you agree?
5. What does Mill mean by "utility"?
6. What is the "Greatest Happiness Principle"?

THE CREED WHICH ACCEPTS [utility] as the foundation of morals, or the Greatest Happiness Principle, holds that actions are right in proportion as they tend to promote happiness, wrong as they tend to produce the reverse of happiness. By happiness is intended pleasure, and the absence of pain; by unhappiness, pain, and the privation of pleasure. To give a clear view of the moral standard set up by the theory, much more requires to be said; in particular, what things it includes in the ideas of pain and pleasure; and to what extent this is left an open question. But these supplementary explanations do not affect the theory of life on which this theory of morality is grounded — namely, that pleasure, and freedom from pain, are the only things desirable as ends; and that all desirable things (which are as numerous in the utilitarian as in any other scheme) are desirable either for the pleasure inherent in themselves, or as means to the promotion of pleasure and the prevention of pain.

Now, such a theory of life excites in many minds, and among them in some of the most estimable in feeling and purpose, inveterate dislike. To suppose that life has (as they express it) no higher end than pleasure — no better and nobler object of desire and pursuit — they designate as utterly mean and grovelling; as a doctrine worthy only of swine, . . .

. . . the accusation supposes human beings to be capable of no pleasures except those of which swine are capable. If this supposition were true, the charge could not be gainsaid, but would then be no longer an imputation; for if the sources of pleasure were precisely the same to human beings and to swine, the rule of life which is good enough for the one would be good enough for the other. The comparison of the Epicurean life to that of beasts is felt as degrading, precisely because a beast's pleasures do not satisfy a human being's conceptions of happiness. Human beings have faculties more elevated than the animal appetites, and when once made conscious of them, do not regard anything as happiness which does not include their gratification. I do not, indeed, consider the Epicureans to have been by any means faultless in drawing out their scheme of consequences from the utilitarian

principle. To do this in any sufficient manner, many Stoic, as well as Christian elements require to be included. But there is no known Epicurean theory of life which does not assign to the pleasures of the intellect, of the feelings and imagination, and of the moral sentiments, a much higher value as pleasures than to those of mere sensation. It must be admitted, however, that utilitarian writers in general have placed the superiority of mental over bodily pleasures chiefly in the greater permanency, safety, uncostliness, etc., of the former — that is, in their circumstantial advantages rather than in their intrinsic nature. And on all these points utilitarians have fully proved their case; but they might have taken the other, and, as it may be called, higher ground, with entire consistency. It is quite compatible with the principle of utility to recognise the fact, that some *kinds* of pleasure are more desirable and more valuable than others. It would be absurd that while, in estimating all other things, quality is considered as well as quantity, the estimation of pleasures should be supposed to depend on quantity alone.

If I am asked, what I mean by difference of quality in pleasures, or what makes one pleasure more valuable than another, merely as a pleasure, except its being greater in amount, there is but one possible answer. Of two pleasures, if there be one to which all or almost all who have experience of both give a decided preference, irrespective of any feeling of moral obligation to prefer it, that it is the more desirable pleasure. If one of the two is, by those who are competently acquainted with both, placed so far above the other that they prefer it, even though knowing it to be attended with a greater amount of discontent, and would not resign it for any quantity of the other pleasure which their nature is capable of, we are justified in ascribing to the preferred enjoyment a superiority in quality, so far outweighing quantity as to render it, in comparison, of small account.

Now it is an unquestionable fact that those who are equally acquainted with, and equally capable of appreciating and enjoying, both, do give a most marked preference to the manner of existence which employs their higher facilities. Few human

From J. S. Mill, Utilitarianism, *first published in 1863.*

creatures would consent to be changed into any of the lower animals, for a promise of the fullest allowance of a beast's pleasures; no intelligent human being would consent to be a fool, no instructed person would be an ignoramus, no person of feeling and conscience would be selfish and base, even though they should be persuaded that the fool, the dunce, or the rascal is better satisfied with his lot than they are with theirs. They would not resign what they possess more than he for the most complete satisfaction of all the desires which they have in common with him. If they ever fancy they would, it is only in cases of unhappiness so extreme, that to escape from it they would exchange their lot for almost any other, however undesirable in their own eyes. A being of higher faculties requires more to make him happy, is capable probably of more acute suffering, and certainly accessible to it at more points, than one of an inferior type; but in spite of these liabilities, he can never really wish to sink into what he feels to be a lower grade of existence. We may give what explanation we please of this unwillingness; we may attribute it to pride, a name which is given indiscriminately to some of the most and to some of the least estimable feelings of which mankind are capable: we may refer it to the love of liberty and personal independence, an appeal to which was with the Stoics one of the most effective means for the inculcation of it; to the love of power, or to the love of excitement, both of which do really enter into and contribute to it: but its most appropriate appellation is a sense of dignity, which all human beings possess in one form or other, and in some, though by no means in exact, proportion to their higher faculties, and which is so essential a part of the happiness of those in whom it is strong, that nothing which conflicts with it could be, otherwise than momentarily, an object of desire to them. Whoever supposes that this preference takes place at a sacrifice of happiness — that the superior being, in anything like equal circumstances, is not happier than the inferior — confounds the two very different ideas, of happiness, and content. It is indisputable that the being whose capacities of enjoyment are low, has the greatest chance of having them fully satisfied; and a highly endowed being will always feel that any happiness which he can look for, as the world is constituted, is imperfect.

But he can learn to bear its imperfections, if they are at all bearable; and they will not make him envy the being who is indeed unconscious of the imperfections, but only because he feels not at all the good which those imperfections qualify. It is better to be a human being dissatisfied than a pig satisfied; better to be Socrates dissatisfied than a fool satisfied. And if the fool, or the pig, are of a different opinion, it is because they only know their own side of the question. The other party to the comparison knows both sides.

It may be objected, that many who are capable of the higher pleasures, occasionally, under the influence of temptation, postpone them to the lower. But this is quite compatible with a full appreciation of the intrinsic superiority of the higher. Men often, from infirmity of character, make their election for the nearer good, though they know it to be the less valuable; and this no less when the choice is between two bodily pleasures, than when it is between bodily and mental. They pursue sensual indulgences to the injury of health, though perfectly aware that health is the greater good. It may be further objected, that many who begin with youthful enthusiasm for everything noble, as they advance in years sink into indolence and selfishness. But I do not believe that those who undergo this very common change, voluntarily choose the lower description of pleasures in preference to the higher. I believe that before they devote themselves exclusively to the one, they have already become incapable of the other. Capacity for the nobler feelings is in most natures a very tender plant, easily killed, not only by hostile influences, but by mere want of substance; and in the majority of young persons it speedily dies away if the occupations to which their position in life has devoted them, and the society in which it has thrown them, are not favourable to keeping that higher capacity in exercise. Men lose their high aspirations as they lose their intellectual tastes, because they have not time or opportunity for indulging them; and they addict themselves to inferior pleasures, not because they deliberately prefer them, but because they are either the only ones to which they have access, or the only ones which they are any longer capable of enjoying. It may be questioned whether any one who has remained equally susceptible to both classes of pleasures, ever knowingly and calmly preferred the lower, though many, in all ages, have broken down in an ineffectual attempt to combine both.

From this verdict of the only competent judges, I apprehend there can be no appeal. On a question which is the best worth having of two pleasures, or which of two modes of existence is the most grateful to the feelings, apart from its moral attributes and from its consequences, the judgment of those who are qualified by knowledge of both, or, if they differ, that of the majority among them, must be admitted as final. And there needs be the less hesitation to accept this judgment respecting the quality of pleasures, since there is no other tribunal to be referred to even on the question of quantity. What means are there of determining which is the acutest of two pains, or the intensest of two pleasurable sensations, except the general suffrage of those who are familiar with both? Neither pains nor pleasures are homogeneous, and pain is always heterogeneous with pleasure. What is there to decide whether a particular pleasure is worth purchasing at the cost of a particular pain, except the feelings and judgment of the experienced? When, therefore, those feelings and judgment declare the pleasures derived from the higher faculties to be preferable *in kind,* apart from the question of intensity, to those of which the animal nature, disjoined from the higher faculties, is susceptible, they are entitled on this subject to the same regard.

I have dwelt on this point, as being a necessary part of a perfectly just conception of Utility or Happiness, considered as the directive rule of human conduct. But it is by no means an indispensable condition to the acceptance of the utilitarian standard; for that standard is not the agent's own greatest happiness, but the greatest amount of happiness altogether; and if it may possibly be doubted whether a noble character is always the happier for its nobleness, there can be no doubt that it makes other people happier, and that the world in general

is immensely a gainer by it. Utilitarianism, therefore, could only attain its end by the general cultivation of nobleness of character, even if each individual were only benefited by the nobleness of others, and his own, so far as happiness is concerned, were a sheer deduction from the benefit. But the bare enunciation of such an absurdity as this last, renders refutation superfluous.

According to the Greatest Happiness Principle, as above explained, the ultimate end, with reference to and for the sake of which all other things are desirable (whether we are considering our own good or that of other people), is an existence exempt as far as possible from pain, and as rich as possible in enjoyments, both in point of quantity and quality; the test of quality, and the rule for measuring it against quantity, being the preference felt by those who in their opportunities of experience, to which must be added their habits of self-consciousness and self-observation, are best furnished with the means of comparison. This, being, according to the utilitarian opinion, the end of human action, is necessarily also the standard of morality; which may accordingly be defined, the rules and precepts for human conduct, by the observance of which an existence such as has been described might be, to the greatest extent possible, secured to all mankind; and not to them only, but, so far as the nature of things admits, to the whole sentient creation. . . .

. . . the happiness which forms the utilitarian standard of what is right in conduct, is not the agent's own happiness, but that of all concerned. As between his own happiness and that of others, utilitarianism requires him to be as strictly impartial as a disinterested and benevolent spectator. In the golden rule of Jesus of Nazareth, we read the complete spirit of the ethics of utility. To do as you would be done by, and to love your neighbour as yourself, constitute the ideal perfection of utilitarian morality.

Further Questions

1. Utilitarianism has been accused of being a "godless doctrine." Can you see any reason why?
2. Why does Mill want you to increase the happiness of everyone concerned, not just your own? Do you agree?

3. What do you think Kant would say about Mill's Greatest Happiness Principle? Who do you side with, and why?
4. What do you suppose Mill's stand would be on drugs? Pornography?

Further Readings

Gorovitz, Samuel, ed. *John Stuart Mill: Utilitarianism*. Indianapolis, IN: Bobbs-Merrill, 1971. One of the best and most complete collections on the subject.

Thomas, William. *Mill*. New York: Oxford University Press, 1985. A brief overview of Mill's life and his major ideas.

73   Beyond Good and Evil

FRIEDRICH NIETZSCHE

Born in Roeken, Germany, into a puritanical, religious family, Friedrich Nietzsche (1844–1900), the son of a minister, became one of the most influential and outspoken critics of religion, particularly of Christianity, and he mounted one of the greatest attacks ever on traditional morality.

After studying at the University of Bonn and the University of Leipzig, he became a professor of philosophy at the University of Basel. Among his many important and provocative works are *Thus Spake Zarathustra* (1884), *Beyond Good and Evil* (1886), *The Genealogy of Morals* (1887), *The Antichrist* (1888), and *The Will to Power* (1906).

From Nietzsche comes the famous slogan, "God is dead." The English-speaking world (George Bernard Shaw and H. L. Mencken are two notable exceptions) has tended to underplay the value of his writings, often discounting them on the psychological level as mere reaction to his childhood, whereas in Germany and France many of the most important philosophers, psychologists, theologians, novelists, and poets have been influenced by him. These include Thomas Mann, Hermann Hesse, Karl Jaspers, Martin Heidegger, Sigmund Freud, and Jean-Paul Sartre.

Reading Questions

1. What strikes you about Nietzsche's style? How do you react to it? Why?
2. Why does Nietzsche hope that the study of morals, which he considers "tedious," never becomes interesting?
3. He says, "Is moralising not—immoral?" Why? Do you agree?
4. He calls Christianity "the most fatal and seductive lie that has ever yet existed" and urges you to declare open war with it. Why? For what purpose? What bothers him so about Christianity? Do you agree? Why?
5. What does he think is the "will to the denial of life" under disguise?
6. What does he say is the *fundamental fact* of all history?
7. Why does he think that only by denying God can people save the world?
8. Why are Christians "little lying abortions of bigotry"?

9. Why does Nietzsche think Christians should be incarcerated in lunatic asylums?
10. Why does he think Jews led a parasitic existence?
11. What is the "soil" of Judaism out of which Christianity grew?
12. What is the "moral idiosyncrasy" by which psychologists have been corrupted?

I HOPE TO BE FORGIVEN for discovering that all moral philosophy hitherto has been tedious and has belonged to the soporific appliances — and that "virtue," in my opinion, has been more injured by the *tediousness* of its advocates than by anything else; at the same time, however, I would not wish to overlook their general usefulness. It is desirable that as few people as possible should reflect upon morals, and consequently it is *very* desirable that morals should not some day become interesting! But let us not be afraid! Things still remain today as they have always been: I see no one in Europe who has (or discloses) an idea of the fact that philosophising concerning morals might be conducted in a dangerous, captious, and ensnaring manner — that *calamity* might be involved therein. . . . No new thought, nothing of the nature of a finer turning or better expression of an old thought, not even a proper history of what has been previously thought on the subject: an *impossible* literature, taking it all in all unless one knows how to leaven it with some mischief. In effect, the old English vice called *cant*, which is *moral Tartuffism*, has insinuated itself also into these moralists (whom one must certainly read with an eye to their motives if one *must* read them), concealed this time under the new form of the scientific spirit; moreover, there is not absent from them a secret struggle with the pangs of conscience, from which a race of former Puritans must naturally suffer, in all their scientific tinkering with morals. (Is not a moralist the opposite of a Puritan? That is to say, as a thinker who regards morality as questionable, as worthy of interrogation, in short, as a problem? Is moralising not — immoral?) In the end, they all want *English* morality to be recognised as authoritative, inasmuch as mankind, or the "general utility," or "the happiness of the greatest number," —

no! the happiness of *England,* will be best served thereby. They would like, by all means, to convince themselves that the striving after *English* happiness, I mean after *comfort* and *fashion* (and in the highest instance, a seat in Parliament), is at the same time the true path of virtue; in fact, that in so far as there has been virtue in the world hitherto, it has just consisted in such striving. Not one of those ponderous, conscience-stricken herding-animals (who undertake to advocate the cause of egoism as conducive to the general welfare) wants to have any knowledge or inkling of the facts that the "general welfare" is no ideal, no goal, no notion that can be at all grasped, but is only a nostrum, — that what is fair to one *may not* at all be fair to another, that the requirement of one morality for all is really a detriment to higher men, in short, that there is a *distinction of rank* between man and man, and consequently between morality and morality. They are an unassuming and fundamentally mediocre species of men, these utilitarian Englishmen, . . . Every elevation of the type "man," has hitherto been the work of an aristocratic society — and so will it always be — a society believing in a long scale of gradations of rank and differences of worth among human beings, and requiring slavery in some form or other. Without the *pathos of distance,* such as grows out of the incarnated difference of classes, out of the constant outlooking and downlooking of the ruling caste on subordinates and instruments, and out of their equally constant practice of obeying and commanding, of keeping down and keeping at a distance — that other more mysterious pathos could never have arisen, the longing for an ever new widening of distance within the soul itself, the formation of ever higher, rarer, further, more extended, more comprehensive states, in short, just the elevation of

From Nietzsche, Beyond Good and Evil, *translated by Helen Zimmern,* The Twilight of the Idols *and* The Will to Power, *translated by A. M. Ludovici, in* The Complete Works of Friedrich Nietzsche, *translated under Oscar Levy (1909–1911).*

the type "man," the continued "self-surmounting of man," to use a moral formula in a supermoral sense. To be sure, one must not resign oneself to any humanitarian illusions about the history of the origin of an aristocratic society (that is to say, of the preliminary condition for the elevation of the type "man"): the truth is hard. Let us acknowledge unprejudicedly how every higher civilisation hitherto has *originated*! Men with a still natural nature, barbarians in every terrible sense of the word, men of prey, still in possession of unbroken strength of will and desire for power, threw themselves upon weaker, more moral, more peaceful races (perhaps trading or cattle-rearing communities), or upon old mellow civilisations in which the final vital force was flickering out in brilliant fireworks of wit and depravity. At the commencement, the noble caste was always the barbarian caste: their superiority did not consist first of all in their physical, but in their psychical power—they were more *complete* men (which at every point also implies the same as "more complete beasts").

To refrain mutually from injury, from violence, from exploitation, and put one's will on a par with that of others: this may result in a certain rough sense in good conduct among individuals when the necessary conditions are given (namely, the actual similarity of the individuals in amount of force and degree of worth, and their corelation within one organisation). As soon, however, as one wished to take this principle more generally, and if possible even as *the fundamental principle of society,* it would immediately disclose what it really is— namely, a Will to the *denial* of life, a principle of dissolution and decay. Here one must think profoundly to the very basis and resist all sentimental weakness: life itself is essentially appropriation, injury, conquest of the strange and weak, suppression, severity, obtrusion of peculiar forms, incorporation, and at the least, putting it mildest, exploitation;— but why should one for ever use precisely these words on which for ages a disparaging purpose has been stamped? Even the organisation within which, as was previously supposed, the individuals treat each other as equal—it takes place in every healthy aristocracy—must itself, if it be a living and not a dying organisation, do all that towards other bodies, which the individuals within it refrain from doing to each other: it will have to be the in-

carnated Will to Power, it will endeavour to grow, to gain ground, attract to itself and acquire ascendency—not owing to any morality or immorality, but because it *lives,* and because life *is* precisely Will to Power. On no point, however, is the ordinary consciousness of Europeans more unwilling to be corrected than on this matter; people now rave everywhere, even under the guise of science, about coming conditions of society in which "the exploiting character" is to be absent:—that sounds to my ears as if they promised to invent a mode of life which should refrain from all organic functions. "Exploitation" does not belong to a depraved, or imperfect and primitive society: it belongs to the *nature* of the living being as a primary organic function; it is a consequence of the intrinsic Will to Power, which is precisely the Will to Life.— Granting that as a theory this is a novelty—as a reality it is the *fundamental fact* of all history: let us be so far honest towards ourselves!

In a tour through the many finer and coarser moralities which have hitherto prevailed or still prevail on the earth, I found certain traits recurring regularly together and connected with one another, until finally two primary types revealed themselves to me, and a radical distinction was brought to light. There is *master*-morality and *slave*-morality;—I would at once add, however, that in all higher and mixed civilisations, there are also attempts at the reconciliation of the two moralities; but one finds still oftener the confusion and mutual misunderstanding of them, indeed, sometimes their close juxtaposition—even in the same man, within one soul. The distinctions of moral values have either originated in a ruling caste, pleasantly conscious of being different from the ruled—or among the ruled class, the slaves and dependents of all sorts. In the first case, when it is the rulers who determine the conception "good," it is the exalted, proud disposition which is regarded as the distinguishing feature, and that which determines the order of rank. The noble type of man separates from himself the beings in whom the opposite of this exalted, proud disposition displays itself: he despises them. Let it at once be noted that in this first kind of morality the antithesis "good" and "bad" means practically the same as "noble" and "despicable";—the antithesis "good" and "*evil*" is of a different origin. The cowardly, the timid, the insignificant, and those thinking merely of narrow utility are despised; moreover, also, the distrustful, with their constrained glances, the self-abasing, the dog-like kind of men who let themselves be abused, the mendicant flatterers, and above all the liars: — it is a fundamental belief of all aristocrats that the common people are untruthful. "We truthful ones" — the nobility in ancient Greece called themselves. It is obvious that everywhere the designations of moral value were at first applied to *men,* and were only derivatively and at a later period applied to *actions;* it is a gross mistake, therefore, when historians of morals start with questions like, "Why have sympathetic actions been praised?" The noble type of man regards himself as a determiner of values; he does not require to be approved of; he passes the judgment: "What is injurious to me is injurious in itself"; he knows that it is he himself only who confers honour on things; he is a creator of values. He honours whatever he recognises in himself: such morality is self-glorification. In the foreground there is the feeling of plenitude, of power, which seeks to overflow, the happiness of high tension, the consciousness of a wealth which would fain give and bestow: — the noble man also helps the unfortunate, but not — or scarcely — out of pity, but rather from any impulse generated by the super-abundance of power. The noble man honours in himself the powerful one, him also who has power over himself, who knows how to speak and how to keep silence, who takes pleasure in subjecting himself to severity and hardness, and has reverence for all that is severe and hard. "Wotan placed a hard heart in my breast," says an Old Scandinavian Saga: it is thus rightly expressed from the soul of a proud Viking. Such a type of man is even proud of *not* being made for sympathy; the hero of the Saga therefore adds warningly: "He who has not a hard heart when young, will never have one." The noble and brave who think thus are the furthest removed from the morality which sees precisely in sympathy, or in acting for the good of others, or in *désintéressement,* the characteristic of the moral; faith in oneself, pride in oneself, a radical enmity and irony towards "selflessness," belong as definitely to noble morality, as do a careless scorn and precaution in presence of sympathy and the "warm heart." — It is the powerful who *know*

how to honour, it is their art, their domain for invention. The profound reverence for age and for tradition — all law rests on this double reverence, — the belief and prejudice in favour of ancestors and unfavourable to newcomers, is typical in the morality of the powerful; and if, reversely, men of "modern ideas" believe almost instinctively in "progress" and the "future," and are more and more lacking in respect for old age, the ignoble origin of these "ideas" has complacently betrayed itself thereby. A morality of the ruling class, however, is more especially foreign and irritating to present-day taste in the sternness of its principle that one has duties to one's equals; that one may act towards beings of a lower rank, towards all that is foreign, just as seems good to one, or "as the heart desires," and in any case "beyond good and evil": it is here that sympathy and similar sentiments can have a place. The ability and obligation to exercise prolonged gratitude and prolonged revenge — both only within the circle of equals, — artfulness in retaliation, *raffinement* of the idea in friendship, a certain necessity to have enemies (as outlets for the emotions of envy, quarrelsomeness, arrogance — in fact, in order to be a good *friend*): all these are typical characteristics of the noble morality, which, as has been pointed out, is not the morality of "modern ideas," and is therefore at present difficult to realise, and also to unearth and disclose. — It is otherwise with the second type of morality, *slave-morality.* Supposing that the abused, the oppressed, the suffering, the unemancipated, the weary, and those uncertain of themselves, should moralise, what will be the common element in their moral estimates? Probably a pessimistic suspicion with regard to the entire situation of man will find expression, perhaps a condemnation of man, together with his situation. The slave has an unfavourable eye for the virtues of the powerful; he has a scepticism and distrust, a *refinement* of distrust of everything "good" that is there honoured — he would fain persuade himself that the very happiness there is not genuine. On the other hand, *those* qualities which serve to alleviate the existence of sufferers are brought into prominence and flooded with light; it is here that sympathy, the kind, helping hand, the warm heart, patience, diligence, humility, and friendliness attain to honour; for here these are the most useful qualities, and

REVOLT

Jiddu Krishnamurti

Now, society is always trying to control, to shape, to mould the thinking of the young. From the moment you are born and begin to receive impressions, your father and mother are constantly telling you what to do and what not to do, what to believe and what not to believe; you are told that there is God, or that there is no God but the State and that some dictator is its prophet. From childhood these things are poured into you, which means that your mind — which is very young, impressionable, inquisitive, curious to know, wanting to find out — is gradually being encased, conditioned, shaped so that you will fit into the pattern of a particular society and not be a revolutionary. Since the habit of patterned thinking has already been established in you, even if you do "revolt" it is within the pattern. It is like prisoners revolting in order to have better food, more conveniences — but always within the prison. When you seek God, or try to find out what is right government, it is always within the pattern of society, which says, "This is true and that is false, this is good and that is bad, this is the right leader and these are the saints." So your revolt, like the so-called revolution brought about by ambitious or very clever people, is always limited in the past. That is not revolt, that is not revolution: it is merely heightened activity, a more valiant struggle within the pattern. Real revolt, true revolution is to break away from the pattern and to inquire outside of it.

From *Think on These Things*, 1964.

almost the only means of supporting the burden of existence. Slave-morality is essentially the morality of utility. Here is the seat of the origin of the famous antithesis "good" and "evil":— power and dangerousness are assumed to reside in the evil, a certain dreadfulness, subtlety, and strength, which do not admit of being despised. According to slave-morality, therefore, the "evil" man arouses fear: according to master-morality, it is precisely the "good" man who arouses fear and seeks to arouse it, while the bad man is regarded as the despicable being. The contrast attains its maximum when, in accordance with the logical consequences of slave-morality, a shade of depreciation — it may be slight and well-intentioned — at last attaches itself even to the "good" man of this morality; because, according to the servile mode of thought, the good man must in any case be the *safe* man: he is good-natured, easily deceived, perhaps a little stupid, *un bonhomme*. Everywhere that slave-morality gains the ascendancy, language shows a tendency to approximate the significance of the words "good" and "stupid.". . .

What then, alone, can our teaching be? — That no one gives man his qualities, either God, society, his parents, his ancestors, nor himself. . . . No one is responsible for the fact that he exists at all, that he is constituted as he is, and that he happens to be in certain circumstances and in a particular environment. The fatality of his being cannot be divorced from the fatality of all that which has been and will be. This is not the result of an individual attention, of a will, of an aim, there is no attempt at attaining to any "ideal man," or "ideal happiness" or "ideal morality" with him — it is absurd to wish him to be careering towards some sort of purpose. *We* invented the concept "purpose"; in reality purpose is altogether lacking. One is necessary, one is a piece of fate, one belongs to the whole, one is in the whole—there is nothing that could judge, measure, compare, and condemn our existence, for that would mean judging, measuring, comparing and condemning the whole. *But there is nothing outside the whole!* The fact that no one shall any longer be made responsible, that the nature of existence may not be traced to a *causa prima*, that the world is an entity neither as a sensorium nor as a spirit—*this alone is the great deliverance*—thus alone is the innocence of Becoming restored. . . . The concept "God" has been the greatest objection to existence hitherto. . . . We deny God, we deny responsibility in God: thus alone do we save the world.

I regard Christianity as the most fatal and seductive lie that has ever yet existed—as the greatest and most *impious* lie: I can discern the last sprouts and branches of its ideal beneath every form of disguise, I decline to enter into any compromise or false position in reference to it—I urge people to declare open war with it.

The morality of paltry people as the measure of all things: this is the most repugnant kind of degeneracy that civilisation has ever yet brought into existence. And this *kind of ideal* is hanging still, under the name of "God," over men's heads!!

However modest one's demands may be concerning intellectual cleanliness, when one touches the New Testament one cannot help experiencing a sort of inexpressible feeling of discomfort; for the unbounded cheek with which the least qualified people will have their say in its pages, in regard to the greatest problems of existence, and claim to sit in judgment on such matters, exceeds all limits. The impudent levity with which the most unwieldy problems are spoken of here (life, the world, God, the purpose of life), as if they were not problems at all, but the most simple things which these little bigots *know all about!!!*

This was the most fatal form of insanity that has ever yet existed on earth:—when these little lying abortions of bigotry begin laying claim to the words "God," "last judgment," "truth," "love," "wisdom," "Holy Spirit," and thereby distinguishing themselves from the rest of the world; when such men begin to transvalue values to suit themselves, as though they were the sense, the salt, the standard, and the measure of all things; then all

that one should do is this: build lunatic asylums for their incarceration. To *persecute* them was an egregious act of antique folly: this was taking them too seriously; it was making them serious. . . .

The *law*, which is the fundamentally realistic formula of certain self-preservative measures of a community, forbids certain actions that have a definite tendency to jeopardise the welfare of that community: it does *not* forbid the attitude of mind which gives rise to these actions—for in the pursuit of other ends the community requires these forbidden actions, namely, when it is a matter of opposing its *enemies*. The moral idealist now steps forward and says: "God sees into men's hearts: The action itself counts for nothing; the reprehensible attitude of mind from which it proceeds must be extirpated. . . ." In normal conditions men laugh at such things; it is only in exceptional cases, when a community lives *quite* beyond the need of waging war in order to maintain itself, that an ear is lent to such things. Any attitude of mind is abandoned, the utility of which cannot be conceived.

This was the case, for example, when Buddha appeared among a people that was both peaceable and afflicted with great intellectual weariness.

This was also the case in regard to the first Christian community (as also the Jewish), the primary condition of which was the absolutely *unpolitical* Jewish society. Christianity could grow only upon the soil of Judaism—that is to say, among a people that had already renounced the political life, and which led a sort of parasitic existence within the Roman sphere of government. Christianity goes a step *farther*: it allows men to "emasculate" themselves even more; the circumstances actually favour their doing so.—*Nature* is *expelled* from morality when it is said, "Love ye your enemies": for *Nature's* injunction, "Ye shall *love* your neighbour and *hate* your enemy," has now become senseless in the law (in instinct); now, even *the love a man feels for his neighbour* must first be based upon something (*a sort of love of God*). *God* is introduced everywhere, and *utility* is withdrawn; the natural *origin* of morality is denied everywhere: the *veneration of Nature*, which lies in *acknowledging a natural morality*, is *destroyed* to the roots. . . .

Whence comes the *seductive charm* of this emasculate ideal of man? Why are we not *disgusted* by it, just as we are disgusted at the thought of a eunuch? . . . The answer is obvious: it is not the voice of the eunuch that revolts us, despite the cruel mutilation of which it is the result; for, as a matter of fact, it has grown sweeter. . . . And owing to the very fact that the "male organ" has been amputated from virtue, its voice now has a feminine ring, which, formerly, was not to be discerned.

On the other hand, we have only to think of the terrible hardness, dangers, and accidents to which a life of manly virtues leads . . . to perceive how the most robust type of man was fascinated and moved by the voluptuous ring of this "goodness" and "purity." . . .

The *Astuteness of moral castration.*—How is war waged against the virile passions and valuations? No violent physical means are available; the war must therefore be one of ruses, spells, and lies—in short, a "spiritual war."

First recipe: One appropriates virtue in general, and makes it the main feature of one's ideal; the older ideal is denied and declared to be *the reverse of all ideals*. Slander has to be carried to a fine art for this purpose.

Second recipe: One's own type is set up as a general *standard;* and this is projected into all things, behind all things, and behind the destiny of all things—as God.

Third recipe: The opponents of one's ideal are declared to be the opponents of God; one arrogates to oneself a *right* to great pathos, to power, and a right to curse and to bless.

Fourth recipe: All suffering, all gruesome, terrible, and fatal things are declared to be the results of opposition to *one's* ideal—all suffering is *punishment* even in the case of one's adherents (except it be a trial, etc.).

Fifth recipe: One goes so far as to regard Nature as the reverse of one's ideal, and the lengthy sojourn amid natural conditions is considered a great trial of patience—a sort of martyrdom; one studies contempt, both in one's attitudes and one's looks towards all "natural things."

Sixth recipe: The triumph of anti-naturalism and ideal castration, the triumph of the world of the pure, good, sinless, and blessed, is projected into the future as the consummation, the finale, the great hope, and the "Coming of the Kingdom of God."

I hope that one may still be allowed to laugh at this artificial hoisting up of a small species of man to the position of an absolute standard of all things.

To what extent psychologists have been corrupted by the moral idiosyncrasy!—Not one of the ancient philosophers had the courage to advance the theory of the non-free will (that is to say, the theory that denies morality);—not one had the courage to identify the typical feature of happiness, of every kind of happiness ("pleasure"), with the will to power: for the pleasure of power was considered immoral;—not one had the courage to regard virtue as a *result of immorality* (as a result of a will to power) in the service of a species (or of a race, or of a *polis*); for the will to power was considered immoral.

In the whole of moral evolution, there is no sign of truth: all the conceptual elements which come into play are fictions; all the psychological tenets are false; all the forms of logic employed in this department of prevarication are sophisms. The chief feature of all moral philosophers is their total lack of intellectual cleanliness and self-control: they regard "fine feelings" as arguments: their heaving breasts seem to them the bellows of godliness. . . .

This "virtue" made wholly abstract was the highest form of seduction: to make oneself abstract means to *turn one's back on the world.*

The moment is a very remarkable one: the Sophists are within sight of the first *criticism* of morality, the first *knowledge* of morality:—they classify the majority of moral valuations (in view of their dependence upon local conditions) together;—they lead one to understand that every form of morality is capable of being upheld dialectically: that is to say, they guessed that all the fundamental principles of a morality must be *sophistical*—a proposition which was afterwards proved in the grandest possible style by the ancient philosophers from Plato onwards (up to Kant);—they postulate the primary truth that there is no such thing as a "moral *per se,*" a "good *per se,*" and that it is madness to talk of "truth" in this respect.

Further Questions

1. Specifically, and in your own words, what do you suppose Nietzsche would say about the preceding two selections? Do you agree? How might Kant and Mill respond? How might Nietzsche respond to their responses? Who is right, and why? Also, *who is to say* who is right, and on what grounds?
2. Distinguish between and explain Nietzsche's notions of *slave morality* and *master morality*. How might you apply these concepts to present society?

Further Readings

Kaufmann, Walter. *Nietzsche: Philosopher, Psychologist, Antichrist*. New York: Doubleday, 1960. Revised edition.

Mencken, H. L. *The Philosophy of Friedrich Nietzsche*. New York: Luce & Co., 1913.

The Rights of Women   74

MARY WOLLSTONECRAFT

Mary Wollstonecraft (1759–1797) was born near London to a farming family made poor when her father squandered the family fortune. She supported herself as a teacher and governess while struggling to become a writer. She attained success in 1787 with *Thoughts on the Education of Daughters,* in which she argued against Rousseau's position on the education of women. According to Rousseau, women should be educated "To please, to be useful to us, to make us love and esteem them, to educate us when young and take care of us when grown up, to advise, to console us, to render our lives easy and agreeable—these are the duties of woman at all times, and what they should be taught in their infancy." Wollstonecraft brilliantly met such arguments on their own terms, showing how such an education would produce women who were "mere propagators of fools," and that such an education was in the interest of *neither* men nor women. Women, she argues, were as suited as men to wisdom and rationality, and society should allow them to attain with equal rights to philosophy and education. Her book attracted wide attention and won her the support of many philosophers, including William Godwin (1756–1836), a political anarchist whom she married.

In her most famous work, *A Vindication of the Rights of Woman* (1792), she advocated equal rights for women in a way that would not be realized for another century and a half. She died giving birth to a daughter, Mary Godwin, known throughout the world today by her married name, Mary Shelly—the author of one of the most famous novels of all time: *Frankenstein.*

Reading Questions

1. What, according to Wollstonecraft, is the source of most of the "evils and vices" of the world?
2. What is the relationship between *virtue* and *independence*?
3. What is her view of ambition?
4. What is the role of wealth and social position in the development of her view?

FROM THE RESPECT PAID TO PROPERTY FLOW, as from a poisoned fountain, most of the evils and vices which render this world such a dreary scene to the contemplative mind. For it is in the most polished society that noisome reptiles and venomous serpents lurk under the rank herbage; and there is voluptuousness pampered by the still sultry air, which relaxes every good disposition before it ripens into virtue.

One class presses on another, for all are aiming to procure respect on account of their property; and property once gained will procure the respect due only to talents and virtue. Men neglect the duties incumbent on man, yet are treated like demigods. Religion is also separated from morality by a ceremonial veil, yet men wonder that the world is almost, literally speaking, a den of sharpers or oppressors.

There is a homely proverb, which speaks shrewd truth, that whoever the devil finds idle he will employ. And what but habitual idleness can heredity wealth and titles produce? For man is so constituted that he can only attain a proper use of his faculties by exercising them, and will not exercise them unless necessity of some kind first set the wheels in motion. Virtue likewise can only be acquired by the discharge of relative duties; but the importance of these sacred duties will scarcely be felt by the being who is cajoled out of his humanity by the flattery of sycophants. There must be more equality established in society, or morality will never gain ground, and this virtuous equality will not rest firmly even when founded on a rock, if one-half of mankind be chained to its bottom by fate, for they will be continually undermining it through ignorance or pride.

It is vain to expect virtue from women till they are in some degree independent of men; nay, it is vain to expect that strength of natural affection which would make them good wives and mothers. While they are absolutely dependent on their husbands they will be cunning, mean, and selfish; and the men who can be gratified by the fawning fondness of spaniel-like affection have not much delicacy, for love is not to be bought; in any sense of the words, its silken wings are instantly shriveled up when anything beside a return in kind is sought. Yet whilst wealth enervates men, and women live,

as it were, by their personal charms, how can we expect them to discharge those ennobling duties which equally require exertion and self-denial? Hereditary property sophisticates the mind, and the unfortunate victims to it — if I may so express myself — swathed from their birth, seldom exert the locomotive faculty of body or mind, and thus viewing everything through one medium, and that a false one, they are unable to discern in what true merit and happiness consist. False, indeed, must be the light when the drapery of situation hides the man, and makes him stalk in masquerade, dragging from one scene of dissipation to another the nerveless limbs that hang with stupid listlessness, and rolling round the vacant eye, which plainly tells us that there is no mind at home.

I mean therefore to infer that the society is not properly organized which does not compel men and women to discharge their respective duties by making it the only way to acquire that countenance from their fellow-creatures, which every human being wishes some way to attain. The respect consequently which is paid to wealth and mere personal charms is a true north-east blast that blights the tender blossoms of affection and virtue. Nature has wisely attached affections to duties to sweeten toil, and to give that vigor to the exertions of reason which only the heart can give. But the affection which is put on merely because it is the appropriated insignia of a certain character, when its duties are not fulfilled, is one of the empty compliments which vice and folly are obliged to pay to virtue and the real nature of things.

To illustrate my opinion, I need only observe that when a woman is admired for her beauty, and suffers herself to be so far intoxicated by the admiration she receives as to neglect to discharge the indispensable duty of a mother, she sins against herself by neglecting to cultivate an affection that would equally tend to make her useful and happy. True happiness — I mean all the contentment and virtuous satisfaction that can be snatched in this imperfect state — must arise from well-regulated affections, and an affection includes a duty. Men are not aware of the misery they cause, and the vicious weakness they cherish, by only inciting women to render themselves pleasing; they do not consider that they thus make natural and artificial duties clash by sacrificing the comfort and respectability of a woman's life to voluptuous notions of beauty, when in nature they all harmonize.

Cold would be the heart of a husband, were he not rendered unnatural by early debauchery, who did not feel more delight at seeing his child suckled by its mother than the most artful wanton tricks could ever raise, yet this natural way of cementing the matrimonial tie, and twisting esteem with fonder recollections, wealth leads women to spurn. To preserve their beauty, and wear the flowery crown of the day, which gives them a kind of right to reign for a short time over the sex, they neglect to stamp impressions on their husbands' hearts that would be remembered with more tenderness when the snow on the head began to chill the bosom than even their virgin charms. The maternal solicitude of a reasonable affectionate woman is very interesting, and the chastened dignity with which a mother returns the caresses that she and her child receive from a father who has been fulfilling the serious duties of his station is not only a respectable, but a beautiful sight. So singular, indeed, are my feelings—and I have endeavored not to catch factitious ones—that after having been fatigued with the sight of insipid grandeur and the slavish ceremonies that with cumbrous pomp supplied the place of domestic affections, I have turned to some other scene to relieve my eye by resting it on the refreshing green everywhere scattered by Nature. I have then viewed with pleasure a woman nursing her children, and discharging the duties of her station with perhaps merely a servant-maid to take off her hands the servile part of the household business. I have seen her prepare herself and children, with only the luxury of cleanliness, to receive her husband, who, returning weary home in the evening, found smiling babes and clean hearth. My heart has loitered in the midst of the group, and has even throbbed with sympathetic emotion when the scraping of the well-known foot has raised a pleasing tumult.

Whilst my benevolence has been gratified by contemplating this artless picture, I have thought that a couple of this description, equally necessary and independent of each other, because each fulfilled the respective duties of their station, possessed all that life could give. Raised sufficiently above ab-ject poverty not to be obliged to weight the consequence of every farthing they spend, and having sufficient to prevent their attending to a frigid system of economy which narrows both heart and mind, I declare, so vulgar are my conceptions, that I know not what is wanted to render this the happiest as well as the most respectable situation in the world, but a taste for literature, to throw a little variety and interest into social converse, and some superfluous money to give to the needy and to buy books. For it is not pleasant when the heart is opened by compassion, and the head active in arranging plans of usefulness, to have a prim urchin continually twitching back the elbow to prevent the hand from drawing out an almost empty purse, whispering at the same time some prudential maxim about the priority of justice.

Destructive, however, as riches and inherited honors are to the human character, women are more debased and cramped, if possible, by them than men, because men may still in some degree unfold their faculties by becoming soldiers and statesmen.

As soldiers, I grant they can now only gather for the most part vainglorious laurels, whilst they adjust to a hair the European balance, taking especial care that no bleak northern nook or sound incline the beam. But the days of true heroism are over, when a citizen fought for his country like a Fabricius or a Washington, and then returned to his farm to let his virtuous fervor run in a more placid, but not a less salutary, stream. No, our British heroes are oftener sent from the gaming-table than from the plough; and their passions have been rather inflamed by hanging with dumb suspense on the turn of a die, then sublimated by painting after the adventurous march of virtue in the historic page.

The statesman, it is true, might with more propriety quit the faro bank, or card-table, to guide the helm, for he has still but to shuffle and trick—the whole system of British politics, if system it may courteously be called, consisting in multiplying dependents and contriving taxes which grind the poor to pamper the rich. Thus a war, or any wild-goose chase, is, as the vulgar use the phrase, a lucky turn-up of patronage for the minister, whose chief merit is the art of keeping himself in place. It is not necessary then that he should have bowls for the poor, so he can secure for his family the odd trick. Or should some show of respect, for what is termed with ignorant ostentation an Englishman's birthright, be expedient to bubble the gruff mastiff that he has to lead by the nose, he can make an empty show, very safely, by giving his single voice, and suffering his light squadron to file off to the other side. And when a question of humanity is agitated, he may dip a sop in the milk of human kindness to silence Cerberus, and talk of the interest which his heart takes in an attempt to make the earth no longer cry for vengeance as it sucks in its children's blood, though his cold hand may at the very moment rivet their chains, by sanctioning the abominable traffic. A minister is no longer a minister, than while he can carry a point, which he is determined to carry. Yet it is not necessary that a minister should feel like a man, when a bold push might shake his seat.

But, to have done with these episodical observations, let me return to the more specious slavery which chains the very soul of woman, keeping her for ever under the bondage of ignorance.

The preposterous distinctions of rank, which render civilization a curse, by dividing the world between voluptuous tyrants and cunning envious dependents, corrupt, almost equally, every class of people, because respectability is not attached to the discharge of the relative duties of life, but to the station, and when the duties are not fulfilled the affections cannot gain sufficient strength to fortify the virtue of which they are the natural reward. Still there are some loop-holes out of which a man may creep, and dare to think and act for himself; but for a woman it is a herculean task, because she has difficulties peculiar to her sex to overcome, which require almost superhuman powers.

A benevolent legislator always endeavors to make it the interest of each individual to be virtuous; and thus private virtue becoming the cement of public happiness, an orderly whose is consolidated by the tendency of all the parts towards a common center. But the private or public virtue of woman is very problematical, for Rousseau, and a numerous list of male writers, insist that she should all her life be subjected to a severe restraint, that of propriety. Why subject her to propriety — blind propriety — if she be capable of acting from a no-

bler spring, if she be an heir of immortality? Is sugar always to be produced by vital blood? Is one half of the human species, like the poor African slaves, to be subject to prejudices that brutalize them, when principles would be a surer guard, only to sweeten the cup of man? Is not this indirectly to deny woman reason? for a gift is a mockery, if it be unfit to use.

Women are, in common with men, rendered weak and luxurious by the relaxing pleasures which wealth procures; but added to this they are made slaves to their persons, and must render them alluring that man may lend them his reason to guide their tottering steps aright. Or should they be ambitious, they must govern their tyrants by sinister tricks, for without rights there cannot be any incumbent duties. The laws respecting woman, which I mean to discuss in a future part, make an absurd unit of a man and his wife; and then, by the easy transition of only considering him as responsible, she is reduced to a mere cipher.

The being who discharges the duties of its station is independent; and, speaking of women at large, their first duty is to themselves as rational creatures, and the next, in point of importance, as citizens, is that, which includes so many, of a mother. The rank in life which dispenses with their fulfilling this duty, necessarily degrades them by making them mere dolls. Or should they turn to something more important than merely fitting drapery upon a smooth block, their minds are only occupied by some soft platonic attachment; or the actual management of an intrigue may keep their thoughts in motion; for when they neglect domestic duties, they have it not in their power to take the field and march and counter-march like soldiers, or wrangle in the senate to keep their faculties from rusting.

I know that, as a proof of the inferiority of the sex, Rousseau has exultingly exclaimed, How can they leave the nursery for the camp! And the camp has by some moralists been proved the school of the most heroic virtues; though I think it would puzzle a keen casuist to prove the reasonableness of the greater number of wars that have dubbed heroes. I do not mean to consider this question critically; because, having frequently viewed these freaks of ambition as the first natural mode of civilization, when the ground must be torn up, and the woods cleared by fire and sword, I do not choose to call them pests; but surely the present system of war has little connection with virtue of any denomination, being rather the school of *finesse* and effeminacy than of fortitude.

Yet, if defensive war, the only justifiable war, in the present advanced state of society, where virtue can show its face and ripen amidst the rigors which purify the air on the mountain's top, were alone to be adopted as just and glorious, the true heroism of antiquity might again animate female bosoms. But fair and softly, gentle reader, male or female, do no alarm thyself, for though I have compared the character of a modern soldier with that of a civilized woman, I am not going to advise them to turn their distaff into a musket, though I sincerely wish to see the bayonet converted into a pruning-hook. I only re-created an imagination, fatigued by contemplating the vices and follies which all proceed from a feculent stream of wealth that has muddied the pure rills of natural affection, by supposing that society will some time or other be so constituted, that man must necessarily fulfill the duties of a citizen, or be despised, and that while he was employed in any of the departments of civil life, his wife, also an active citizen, should be equally intent to manage her family, educate her children, and assist her neighbors.

But to render her rally virtuous and useful, she must not, if she discharge her civil duties, want individually the protection of civil laws; she must not be dependent on her husband's bounty for her subsistence during his life, or support after his death; for how can a being be generous who has nothing of its own? or virtuous who is not free? The wife, in the present state of things, who is faithful to her husband, and neither suckles nor educates her children, scarcely deserves the name of a wife, and has no right to that of a citizen. But take away natural rights, and duties become null.

Women then must be considered as only the wanton solace of men, when they become so weak in mind and body that they cannot exert themselves unless to pursue some frothy pleasure, or to invent some frivolous fashion. What can be a more melancholy sight to a thinking mind, than to look into the numerous carriages that drive helter-skelter about this metropolis in a morning full of pale-faced creatures who are flying from themselves! I have often wished, with Dr. Johnson, to place some of them in a little shop with half a dozen children looking up to their languid countenances for support. I am much mistaken, if some latent vigor would not soon give health and spirit to their eyes, and some lines drawn by the exercise of reason on the blank cheeks, which before were only undulated by dimples, might restore lost dignity to the character, or rather enable it to attain the true dignity of its nature. Virtue is not to be acquired even by speculation, much less by the negative supineness that wealth naturally generates.

Besides, when poverty is more disgraceful than even vice, is not morality cut to the quick? Still to avoid misconstruction, though I consider that women in the common walks of life are called to fulfill the duties of wives and mothers, by religion and reason, I cannot help lamenting that women of a superior cast have not a road open by which they can pursue more extensive plans of usefulness and independence. I may excite laughter, by dropping a hint, which I mean to pursue, some future time, for I really think that women ought to have representatives, instead of being arbitrarily governed without having any direct share allowed them in the deliberations of government.

But, as the whole system of representation is now, in this country, only a convenient handle for despotism, they need not complain, for they are as well represented as a numerous class of hard-working mechanics, who pay for the support of royalty when they can scarcely stop their children's mouth with bread. How are they represented whose very sweat supports the splendid stud of an heir-apparent, or varnishes the chariot of some female favorite who looks down on shame? Taxes on the very necessaries of life, enable an endless tribe of idle princes and princesses to pass with stupid pomp before a gaping crowd, who almost worship the very parade which costs them so dear. This is mere gothic grandeur, something like the barbarous useless parade of having sentinels on horseback at Whitehall, which I could never view without a mixture of contempt and indignation.

How strangely must the mind be sophisticated when this sort of state impresses it! But, till these monuments of folly are levelled by virtue, similar follies will leaven the whole mass. For the same character, in some degree, will prevail in the aggregate of society; and the refinements of luxury, or the vicious repinings of envious poverty, will equally banish virtue from society, considered as the characteristic of that society, or only allow it to appear as one of the stripes of the harlequin coat, worn by the civilized man.

In the superior ranks of life, every duty is done by deputies, as if duties could ever be waived, and the vain pleasures which consequent idleness forces the rich to pursue, appear so enticing to the next rank, that the numerous scramblers for wealth sacrifice everything to tread on their heels. The most sacred trusts are then considered as sinecures, because they were procured by interest, and only sought to enable a man to keep *good company.* Women, in particular, all want to be ladies. Which is simply to have nothing to do, but listlessly to go they scarcely care where, for they cannot tell what.

But what have women to do in society? I may be asked, but to loiter with easy grace; surely you would not condemn them all to suckle fools and chronicle small beer! No. Women might certainly study the art of healing, and be physicians as well as nurses. And midwifery, decency seems to allot to them, though I am afraid, the word midwife, in our dictionaries, will soon give place to *accoucheur,* and one proof of the former delicacy of the sex be effaced from the language.

They might also study politics, and settle their benevolence on the broadest basis; for the reading of history will scarcely be more useful than the perusal of romances, if read as mere biography; if the character of the times, the political improvements, arts, etc. be not observed. In short, if it not be considered as the history of man and not of particular men, who filled a niche in the temple of fame, and dropped into the black rolling stream of time, that silently sweeps all before it into the shapeless void called — eternity. — For shape, can it be called, "that shape hath none"?

Business of various kinds, they might likewise pursue, if they were educated in a more orderly manner, which might save many from common and legal prostitution. Women would not then marry for a support, as men accept of places under Government, and neglect the implied duties; nor would an attempt to earn their own subsistence, a most laudable one! sink them almost to the level of those poor abandoned creatures who live by prostitution. For are not milliners and mantua-makers reckoned the next class? The few employments open to women, so far, from being liberal, are menial; and when a superior education enables them to take charge of the education of children as governesses, they are not treated like the tutors of sons, though even clerical tutors are not always treated in a manner calculated to render them respectable in the eyes of their pupils, to say nothing of the private comfort of the individual. But as women educated like gentlewomen, are never designed for the humiliating situation which necessity sometimes forces them to fill; these situations are considered in the light of a degradation; and they know little of the human heart, who need to be told, that nothing so painfully sharpens sensibility to such a fall in life.

Some of these women might be restrained from marrying by a proper spirit of delicacy, and others may not have had it in their power to escape in this pitiful way from servitude; is not that Government then very defective, and very unmindful of the happiness of one-half of its members, that does not provide for honest, independent women, by encouraging them to fill respectable stations? But in order to render their private virtue a public benefit, they must have a civil existence in the state, married or single; else we shall continually see some worthy woman, whose sensibility has been rendered painfully acute by undeserved contempt, droop like "the lily broken down by a plowshare."

It is a melancholy truth; yet such is the blessed effect of civilization! the most respectable women are the most oppressed; and, unless they have understandings far superior to the common run of understandings, taking in both sexes, they must, from being treated like contemptible beings, become contemptible. How many women thus waste life away the prey of discontent, who might have practices as physicians, regulated a farm, managed a shop, and stood erect, supported by their own industry, instead of hanging their heads surcharged with the dew of sensibility, that consumes the beauty to which it at first gave luster; nay, I doubt whether pity and love are so near akin as poets feign, for I have seldom seen much compassion excited by the helplessness of females, unless they were fair; then, perhaps, pity was the soft hand-maid of love, or the harbinger of lust.

How much more respectable is the woman who earns her own bread by fulfilling any duty, than the most accomplished beauty!—beauty did I say!—so sensible am I of the beauty of moral loveliness, or the harmonious propriety that attunes the passions of a well-regulated mind, that I blush at making the comparison; yet I sigh to think how few women aim at attaining this respectability by withdrawing from the giddy whirl of pleasure, or the indolent claim that stupefies the good sort of women it sucks in.

Proud of their weaknesses, however, they must always be protected, guarded from care, and all the rough toils that dignify the mind. If this be the fiat of fate, if they will make themselves insignificant and contemptible, sweetly to waste "life away," let them not expect to be valued when their beauty fades, for it is the fate of the fairest flowers to be admired and pulled to pieces by the careless hand that plucked them. In how many ways do I wish, from the purest benevolence, to impress this truth on my sex; yet I fear that they will not listen to a truth that dear bought experience has brought home to many an agitated bosom, nor willingly resign the privileges of rank and sex for the privileges of humanity, to which those have no claim who do not discharge its duties.

Those writers are particularly useful, in my opinion, who make man feel for man, independent of the station he fills, or the drapery of factitious sentiments. I then would fain convince reasonable men of the importance of some of my remarks; and prevail on them to weigh dispassionately the whole tenor of my observations. I appeal to their understandings; and, as a fellow-creature, claim, in the name of my sex, some interest in their hearts. I entreat them to assist to emancipate their companion, to make her a *helpmeet* for them.

Would men but generously snap our chains, and be content with rational fellowship instead of slavish obedience, they would find us more observant daughters, more affectionate sisters, more faithful wives, more reasonable mothers—in a word, better citizens. We should then love them with true affection, because we should learn to respect ourselves; and the peace of mind of a worthy man would not be interrupted by the idle vanity of his wife, nor the babes sent to nestle in a strange bosom, having never found a home in their mother's.

Further Questions

1. What does she mean in claiming that "Liberty is the mother of virtue?" Do you agree?
2. Compare Wollstonecraft's views with those of a famous male feminist, such as John Stuart Mill, or some contemporary female feminists. What possible influence do you see? How have her views withstood the test of time?

Further Readings

De Beauvoir Simone. *The Second Sex:* New York: Penguin, 1976. By the lifelong friend and companion of Jean-Paul Sartre.

Millett, Kate. *Sexual Politics.* New York: Doubleday, 1970. Adreinne Rich calls it a "landmark book."

75   The Conscience of Huckleberry Finn

JONATHAN BENNETT

Jonathan Bennett was born in Greymouth, New Zealand. He teaches philosophy at Syracuse University. His books include *Kant's Analytic* (1966), *Kant's Dialectic* (1974), *Locke, Berkeley, Hume* (1971), and *A Study of Spinoza's Ethics* (1984). In this provocative selection, he argues against the commonly accepted idea that we should always let our consciences and our personal feelings guide our actions.

Reading Questions

1. Heinrich Himmler, head of the Nazi S.S., was instrumental in exterminating millions of people. Jonathan Edwards was an American theologian in the eighteenth century. Huck Finn is the famous Mark Twain character. How and why does Bennett use these three personas to make his point?
2. According to one type of moral theory, an act is right only if it produces good consequences; according to another, an act is right only if it is in accordance with some rule or principle. Which do you think Bennett would advocate, and why?
3. How, according to Bennett, should the relationship between one's moral conscience and one's moral principles be guided? Do you agree? Can you think of any objections? How might Bennett respond?
4. Does Himmler follow his moral principles? Does Huck Finn? Who do you think is the better person, and why?

IN THIS PAPER, I SHALL PRESENT not just the conscience of Huckleberry Finn but two others as well. One of them is the conscience of Heinrich Himmler. He became a Nazi in 1923; he served drably and quietly, but well, and was rewarded with increasing responsibility and power. At the peak of his career he held many offices and commands, of which the most powerful was that of leader of the S.S. — the principal police force of the Nazi regime. In this capacity, Himmler commanded the whole concentration camp system, and was responsible for the execution of the so-called "final solution of the Jewish problem." It is important for my purposes that this piece of social engineering should be thought of not abstractly but in concrete terms of Jewish families being marched to what they think are bathhouses, to the accompaniment of loudspeaker renditions of extracts from *The Merry Widow* and *Tales of Hoffman*, there to be choked to death by poisonous gases. Altogether, Himmler succeeded in murdering about four and a half million of them, as well as several million gentiles, mainly Poles and Russians.

The other conscience to be discussed is that of the Calvinist theologian and philosopher Jonathan Edwards. He lived in the first half of the eighteenth century, and has a good claim to be considered America's first serious and considerable philosophical thinker. He was for many years a widely-renowned preacher and Congregationalist minister in New England; in 1748 a dispute with his congregation led him to resign (he couldn't accept their view that unbelievers should be admitted to the Lord's Supper in the hope that it would convert

"The Conscience of Huckleberry Finn" by Johathan Bennett, Philosophy, *Vol. 49 (1974), pp. 123–143. Reprinted with the permission of Cambridge University Press and the author. Footnotes deleted.*

them); for some years after that he worked as a missionary, preaching to the Indians through an interpreter; then in 1758 he accepted the presidency of what is now Princeton University, and within two months died from a smallpox inoculation. Along the way he wrote some first-rate philosophy: his book attacking the notion of free will is still sometimes read. Why I should be interested in Edwards' *conscience* will be explained in due course.

I shall use Heinrich Himmler, Jonathan Edwards and Huckleberry Finn to illustrate different aspects of a single theme, namely the relationship between *sympathy* on the one hand and *bad morality* on the other.

All that I can mean by a "bad morality" is a morality whose principles I deeply disapprove of. When I call a morality bad, I cannot prove that mine is better; but when I here call any morality bad, I think you will agree with me that it is bad; and that is all I need.

There could be dispute as to whether the springs of someone's actions constitute a *morality*. I think, though, that we must admit that someone who acts in ways which conflict grossly with our morality may nevertheless have a morality of his own—a set of principles of action which he sincerely assents to, so that for him the problem of acting well or rightly or in obedience to conscience is the problem of conforming to *those* principles. The problem of conscientiousness can arise as acutely for a bad morality as for any other: rotten principles may be as difficult to keep as decent ones.

As for "sympathy": I use this term to cover every sort of fellow-feeling, as when one feels pity over someone's loneliness, or horrified compassion over his pain, and when one feels a shrinking reluctance to act in a way which will bring misfortune to someone else. These *feelings* must not be confused with *moral judgments*. My sympathy for someone in distress may lead me to help him, or even to think that I ought to help him; but in itself it is not a judgment about what I ought to do but just a *feeling* for him in his plight. We shall get some light on the difference between feelings and moral judgments when we consider Huckleberry Finn.

Obviously, feelings can impel one to action, and so can moral judgments; and in a particular case sympathy and morality may pull in opposite directions. This can happen not just with bad moralities, but also with good ones like yours and mine. For example, a small child, sick and miserable, clings tightly to his mother and screams in terror when she tries to pass him over to the doctor to be examined. If the mother gave way to her sympathy, that is to her feeling for the child's misery and fright, she would hold it close and not let the doctor come near; but don't we agree that it might be wrong for her to act on such a feeling? Quite generally, then, anyone's moral principles may apply to a particular situation in a way which runs contrary to the particular thrusts of fellow-feeling that he has in that situation. My immediate concern is with sympathy in relation to bad morality, but not because such conflicts occur only when the morality is bad.

Now, suppose that someone who accepts a bad morality is struggling to make himself act in accordance with it in a particular situation where his sympathies pull him another way. He sees the struggle as one between doing the right, conscientious thing, and acting wrongly and weakly, like the mother who won't let the doctor come near her sick, frightened baby. Since we don't accept this person's morality, we may see the situation very differently, thoroughly disapproving of the action he regards as the right one, and endorsing the action which from his point of view constitutes weakness and backsliding.

Conflicts between sympathy and bad morality won't always be like this, for we won't disagree with every single dictate of a bad morality. Still, it can happen in the way I have described, with the agent's right action being our wrong one, and vice versa. That is just what happens in a certain episode in chapter 16 of *The Adventures of Huckleberry Finn,* an episode which brilliantly illustrates how fiction can be instructive about real life.

Huck Finn has been helping his slave friend Jim to run away from Miss Watson, who is Jim's owner. In their raft-journey down the Mississippi river, they are near to the place at which Jim will become legally free. Now let Huck take over the story:

> Jim said it made him all over trembly and feverish to be so close to freedom. Well, I can tell you it made me all over trembly and feverish, too, to hear

him, because I begun to get it through my head
that he *was* most free—and who was to blame for
it? Why, *me*. I couldn't get that out of my conscience, no how nor no way. . . . It hadn't ever
come home to me, before, what this thing was that
I was doing. But now it did; and it stayed with me,
and scorched me more and more. I tried to make
out to myself that *I* warn't to blame, because *I*
didn't run Jim off from his rightful owner; but it
warn't no use, conscience up and say, every time:
"But you knowed he was running for his freedom,
and you could a paddled ashore and told somebody." That was so—I couldn't get around that,
no way. That was where it pinched. Conscience
says to me: "What had poor Miss Watson done to
you, that you could see her nigger go off right under your eyes and never say one single word? What
did that poor old woman do to you, that you
could treat her so mean? . . ." I got to feeling so
mean and so miserable I most wished I was dead.

Jim speaks of his plan to save up to buy his wife,
and then his children, out of slavery; and he adds
that if the children cannot be bought he will
arrange to steal them. Huck is horrified:

Thinks I, this is what comes of my not thinking.
Here was this nigger which I had as good as
helped to run away, coming right out flat-footed
and saying he would steal his children—children
that belonged to a man I didn't even know; a man
that hadn't ever done me no harm.

I was sorry to hear Jim say that, it was such a
lowering of him. My conscience got to stirring me
up hotter than ever, until at last I says to it: "Let
up on me—it ain't too late, yet—I'll paddle
ashore at first light, and tell." I felt easy, and
happy, and light as a feather, right off. All my
troubles was gone.

This is bad morality all right. In his earliest years
Huck wasn't taught any principles, and the only
ones he has encountered since then are those of
rural Missouri, in which slave-owning is just one
kind of ownership and is not subject to critical
pressure. It hasn't occurred to Huck to question
those principles. So the action, to us abhorrent, of
turning Jim in to the authorities presents itself
clearly to Huck as the right thing to do.

For us, morality and sympathy would both dictate helping Jim to escape. If we felt any conflict, it
would have both these on one side and something
else on the other—greed for a reward, or fear of

punishment. But Huck's morality conflicts with his
sympathy, that is, with his unargued, natural feeling for his friend. The conflict starts when Huck
sets off in the canoe towards the shore, pretending
that he is going to reconnoitre, but really planning
to turn Jim in:

As I shoved off, [Jim] says: "Pooty soon I'll be a-
shout'n for joy, en I'll say, it's all on accounts o'
Huck I's a free man . . . Jim won't ever forgit you,
Huck; you's de bes' fren' Jim's ever had; en you's
de *only* fren' old Jim's got now."

I was paddling off, all in a sweat to tell on him;
but when he says this, it seemed to kind of take
the tuck all out of me. I went along slow then,
and I warn't right down certain whether I was
glad I started or whether I warn't. When I was
fifty yards off, Jim says:

"Dah you goes, de ole true Huck; de on'y
white genlman dat ever kep' his promise to old
Jim." Well, I just felt sick. But I says, I *got* to do
it—I can't get *out* of it.

In the upshot, sympathy wins over morality. Huck
hasn't the strength of will to do what he sincerely
thinks he ought to do. Two men hunting for run-
away slaves ask him whether the man on his raft is
black or white:

I didn't answer up prompt. I tried to, but the
words wouldn't come. I tried, for a second or
two, to brace up and out with it, but I warn't man
enough—hadn't the spunk of a rabbit. I see I was
weakening; so I just give up trying, and up and
says: "He's white."

So Huck enables Jim to escape, thus acting weakly
and wickedly—he thinks. In this conflict between
sympathy and morality, sympathy wins.

One critic has cited this episode in support of
the statement that Huck suffers "excruciating moments of wavering between honesty and respectability." That is hopelessly wrong, and I agree
with the perceptive comment on it by another
critic, who says:

The conflict waged in Huck is much more serious:
he scarcely cares for respectability and never hesitates to relinquish it, but he does care for honesty
and gratitude—and both honesty and gratitude
require that he should give Jim up. It is not, in
Huck, honesty at war with respectability but love
and compassion for Jim struggling against his

conscience. His decision is for Jim and hell: a right decision made in the mental chains that Huck never breaks. His concern for Jim is and remains *irrational*. Huck finds many reasons for giving Jim up and none for stealing him. To the end Huck sees his compassion for Jim as a weak, ignorant, and wicked felony.

This is precisely correct—and it can have that virtue only because Mark Twain wrote the episode with such unerring precision. The crucial point concerns *reasons*, which all occur on one side of the conflict. On the side of conscience we have principles, arguments, considerations, ways of looking at things:

> "It hadn't even come home to me before what I was doing"
> "I tried to make out that I warn't to blame"
> "Conscience said "But you knowed . . ."—I couldn't get around that"
> "What had poor Miss Watson done to you?"
> "This is what comes of my not thinking"
> ". . . children that belonged to a man I didn't even know."

On the other side, the side of feeling, we get nothing like that. When Jim rejoices in Huck, as his only friend, Huck doesn't consider the claims of friendship or have the situation "come home" to him in a different light. All that happens is: "When he says this, it seemed to kind of take the tuck all out of me. I went along slow then, and I warn't right down certain whether I was glad I started or whether I warn't." Again, Jim's words about Huck's "promise" to him don't give Huck any *reason* for changing his plan: in his morality promises to slaves probably don't count. Their effect on him is of a different kind: "Well, I just felt sick." And when the moment for final decision comes, Huck doesn't weigh up pros and cons: he simply *fails* to do what he believes to be right—he isn't strong enough, hasn't "the spunk of a rabbit." This passage in the novel is notable not just for its finely wrought irony, with Huck's weakness of will leading him to do the right thing, but also for its masterly handling of the difference between general moral principles and particular unreasoned emotional pulls.

Consider now another case of bad morality in conflict with human sympathy, the case of the odious Himmler. Here, from a speech he made to some S.S. generals, is an indication of the content of his morality:

> What happens to a Russian, to a Czech, does not interest me in the slightest. What the nations can offer in the way of good blood of our type, we will take, if necessary by kidnapping their children and raising them here with us. Whether nations live in prosperity or starve to death like cattle interests me only in so far as we need them as slaves to our Kultur; otherwise it is of no interest to me. Whether 10,000 Russian females fall down from exhaustion while digging an antitank ditch interests me only in so far as the antitank ditch for Germany is finished.

But has this a moral basis at all? And if it has, was there in Himmler's own mind any conflict between morality and sympathy? Yes there was. Here is more from the same speech:

> . . . I also want to talk to you quite frankly on a very grave matter . . . I mean . . . the extermination of the Jewish race. . . . Most of you must know what it means when 100 corpses are lying side by side, or 500, or 1,000. To have stuck it out and at the same time—apart from exceptions caused by human weakness—to have remained decent fellows, that is what has made us hard. This is a page of glory in our history which has never been written and is never to be written.

Himmler saw his policies as being hard to implement while still retaining one's human sympathies—while still remaining a "decent fellow." He is saying that only the weak take the easy way out and just squelch their sympathies, and is praising the stronger and more glorious course of retaining one's sympathies while acting in violation of them. In the same spirit, he ordered that when executions were carried out in concentration camps, those responsible "are to be influenced in such a way as to suffer no ill effect in their character and mental attitude." A year later he boasted that the S.S. had wiped out the Jews

> without our leaders and their men suffering any damage in their minds and souls. The danger was considerable, for there was only a narrow path between the Scylla of their becoming heartless ruffians unable any longer to treasure life, and the Charybdis of their becoming soft and suffering nervous breakdowns.

And there really can't be any doubt that the basis of Himmler's policies was a set of principles which constituted his morality—a sick, bad, wicked *morality*. He described himself as caught in "the old tragic conflict between will and obligation." And when his physician Kersten protested at the intention to destroy the Jews, saying that the suffering involved was "not to be contemplated," Kersten reports that Himmler replied:

> He knew that it would mean much suffering for the Jews. . . . "It is the curse of greatness that it must step over dead bodies to create new life. Yet we must . . . cleanse the soil or it will never bear fruit. It will be a great burden for me to bear."

This, I submit, is the language of morality.

So in this case, tragically, bad morality won out over sympathy. I am sure that many of Himmler's killers did extinguish their sympathies, becoming "heartless ruffians" rather than "decent fellows"; but not Himmler himself. Although his policies ran against the human grain to a horrible degree, he did not sandpaper down his emotional surfaces so that there was no grain there, allowing his actions to slide along smoothly and easily. He did, after all, bear his hideous burden, and even paid a price for it. He suffered a variety of nervous and physical disabilities, including nausea and stomach-convulsions, and Kersten was doubtless right in saying that these were "the expression of a psychic division which extended over his whole life."

This same division must have been present in some of those officials of the Church who ordered heretics to be tortured so as to change their theological opinions. Along with the brutes and the cold careerists, there must have been some who cared, and who suffered from the conflict between the sympathies and their bad morality.

In the conflict between sympathy and bad morality, then, the victory may go to sympathy as in the case of Huck Finn, or to morality as in the case of Himmler.

Another possibility is that the conflict may be avoided by giving up, or not ever having, those sympathies which might interfere with one's principles. That seems to have been the case with Jonathan Edwards. I am afraid that I shall be doing an injustice to Edwards' many virtues, and to

his great intellectual energy and inventiveness; for my concern is only with the worst thing about him—namely his morality, which was worse than Himmler's.

According to Edwards, God condemns some men to an eternity of unimaginably awful pain, though he arbitrarily spares others—"arbitrarily" because none deserve to be spared:

> Natural men are held in the hand of God over the pit of hell; they have deserved the fiery pit, and are already sentenced to it; and God is dreadfully provoked, his anger is as great towards them as to those that are actually suffering the executions of the fierceness of his wrath in hell . . . ; the devil is waiting for them, hell is gaping for them, the flames gather and flash about them, and would fain lay hold on them . . . ; and . . . there are no means within reach that can be any security to them. . . . All that preserves them is the mere arbitrary will, and uncovenanted unobliged forebearance of an incensed God.

Notice that he says "they have deserved the fiery pit." Edwards insists that men *ought* to be condemned to eternal pain; and his position isn't that this is right because God wants it, but rather that God wants it because it is right. For him, moral standards exist independently of God, and God can be assessed in the light of them (and of course found to be perfect). For example, he says:

> They deserve to be cast into hell; so that . . . justice never stands in the way, it makes no objection against God's using his power at any moment to destroy them. Yea, on the contrary, justice calls aloud for an infinite punishment of their sins.

Elsewhere, he gives elaborate arguments to show that God is acting justly in damning sinners. For example, he argues that a punishment should be exactly as bad as the crime being punished; God is infinitely excellent; so any crime against him infinitely bad; and so eternal damnation is exactly right as a punishment—it is infinite, but, as Edwards is careful also to say, it is "no more than infinite."

Of course, Edwards himself didn't torment the damned; but the question still arises of whether his sympathies didn't conflict with his *approval* of eternal torment. Didn't he find it painful to contemplate any fellow-human's being tortured for ever? Apparently not:

> The God that holds you over the pit of hell, much as one holds a spider or some loathsome insect over the fire, abhors you, and is dreadfully provoked; . . . he is of purer eyes than to bear to have you in his sight; you are ten thousand times so abominable in his eyes as the most hateful venomous serpent is in ours.

When God is presented as being as misanthropic as that, one suspects misanthropy in the theologian. This suspicion is increased when Edwards claims that "the saints in glory will . . . understand how terrible the sufferings of the damned are; yet . . . will not be sorry for [them]." He bases this partly on a view of human nature whose ugliness he seems not to notice:

> The seeing of the calamities of others tends to heighten the sense of our own enjoyments. When the saints in glory, therefore, shall see the doleful state of the damned, how will this heighten their sense of the blessedness of their own state. . . . When they shall see how miserable others of their fellow-creatures are . . . ; when they shall see the smoke of their torment, . . . and hear their dolorous shrieks and cries, and consider that they in the mean time are in the most blissful state, and shall surely be in it to all eternity; how they will rejoice!

I hope this is less than the whole truth! His other main point about why the saints will rejoice to see the torments of the damned is that it is *right* that they should do so:

> The heavenly inhabitants . . . will have no love nor pity to the damned. . . . [This will not show] a want of a spirit of love in them . . . ; for the heavenly inhabitants will know that it is not fit that they should love [the damned] because they will know then, that God has no love to them, nor pity for them.

The implication that *of course* one can adjust one's feelings of pity so that they conform to the dictates of some authority—doesn't this suggest that ordinary human sympathies played only a small part in Edwards' life?

Huck Finn, whose sympathies are wide and deep, could never avoid the conflict in that way; but he is determined to avoid it, and so he opts for the only other alternative he can see—to give up morality altogether. After he has tricked the slave-hunters, he returns to the raft and undergoes a peculiar crisis:

> I got aboard the raft, feeling bad and low, because I knowed very well I had done wrong, and I see it warn't no use for me to try to learn to do right; a body that don't get *started* right when he's little, ain't got no show—when the pinch comes there ain't nothing to back him up and keep him to his work, and so he gets beat. Then I thought a minute, and says to myself, hold on—s'pose you'd a done right and give Jim up; would you feel better than what you do now? No, says I, I'd feel bad—I'd feel just the same way I do now. Well, then, says I, what's the use you learning to do right, when it's troublesome to do right and ain't no trouble to do wrong, and the wages is just the same? I was stuck. I couldn't answer that. So I reckoned I wouldn't bother no more about it, but after this always do whichever come handiest at the time.

Huck clearly cannot conceive of having any morality except the one he has learned—too late, he thinks—from his society. He is not entirely a prisoner of that morality, because he does after all reject it; but for him that is a decision to relinquish morality as such; he cannot envisage revising his morality, altering its content in face of the various pressures to which it is subject, including pressures from his sympathies. For example, he does not begin to approach the thought that slavery should be rejected on moral grounds, or the thought that what he is doing is not theft because a person cannot be owned and therefore cannot be stolen.

The basic trouble is that he cannot or will not engage in abstract intellectual operations of any sort. In chapter 33 he finds himself "feeling to blame, somehow" for something he knows he had no hand in; he assumes that this feeling is a deliverance of conscience; and this confirms him in his belief that conscience shouldn't be listened to:

> It don't make no difference whether you do right or wrong, a person's conscience ain't got no sense, and just goes for him *anyway*. If I had a yaller dog that didn't know no more than a person's conscience does, I would pison him. It takes up more room than all the rest of a person's insides, and yet ain't no good, nohow.

That brisk, incurious dismissiveness fits well with the comprehensive rejection of morality back on the raft. But this is a digression.

On the raft, Huck decides not to live by principles, but just to do whatever "comes handiest at the time"—always acting according to the mood of the moment. Since the morality he is rejecting is narrow and cruel, and his sympathies are broad and kind, the results will be good. But moral principles are good to have, because they help to protect one from acting badly at moments when one's sympathies happen to be in abeyance. On the highest possible estimate of the role one's sympathies should have, one can still allow for principles as embodiments of one's best feelings, one's broadest and keenest sympathies. On that view, principles can help one across intervals when one's feelings are at less than their best, i.e., through periods of misanthropy or meanness or self-centredness or depression or anger.

What Huck didn't see is that one can live by principles and yet have ultimate control over their content. And one way such control can be exercised is by checking of one's principles in the light of one's sympathies. This is sometimes a pretty straightforward matter. It can happen that a certain moral principle becomes untenable—meaning literally that one cannot hold it any longer—because it conflicts intolerably with the pity or revulsion or whatever that one feels when one sees what the principle leads to. One's experience may play a large part here: experiences evoke feelings, and feelings force one to modify principles. Something like this happened to the English poet Wilfred Owen, whose experiences in the First World War transformed him from an enthusiastic soldier into a virtual pacifist. I can't document his change of conscience in detail; but I want to present something which he wrote about the way experience can put pressure on morality.

The Latin poet Horace wrote that it is sweet and fitting (or right) to die for one's country—*dulce et decorum est pro patria mori*—and Owen wrote a fine poem about how experience could lead one to relinquish that particular moral principle. He describes a man who is too slow donning his gas mask during a gas attack—"As under a green sea I saw him drowning," Owen says. The poem ends like this:

> In all my dreams before my helpless sight
> He plunges at me, guttering, choking, drowning
> If in some smothering dreams, you too could pace
> Behind the wagon that we flung him in,
> And watch the white eyes writhing in his face,
> His hanging face, like a devil's sick of sin;
> If you could hear, at every jolt, the blood
> Come gargling from the froth-corrupted lungs,
> Bitter as the cud
> Of vile, incurable sores on innocent tongues,—
> My friend, you would not tell with such high zest
> To children ardent for some desperate glory,
> The old Lie: Dulce et decorum est
> pro patria mori.

There is a difficulty about drawing from all this a moral for ourselves. I imagine that we agree in our rejection of slavery, eternal damnation, genocide, and uncritical patriotic self-abnegation; so we shall agree that Huck Finn, Jonathan Edwards, Heinrich Himmler, and the poet Horace would all have done well to bring certain of their principles under severe pressure from ordinary human sympathies. But then we can say this because we can say that all those are bad moralities, whereas we cannot look at our own moralities and declare them bad. This is not arrogance: it is obviously incoherent for someone to declare the system of moral principles that he *accepts* to be *bad*, just as one cannot coherently say of anything that one *believes* it but it is *false*.

Still, although I can't point to any of my beliefs and say "That is false," I don't doubt that some of my beliefs *are* false; and so I should try to remain open to correction. Similarly, I accept every single item in my morality—that is inevitable—but I am sure that my morality could be improved, which is to say that it could undergo changes which I should be glad of once I had made them. So I must try to keep my morality open to revision, exposing it to whatever valid pressures there are—including pressures from my sympathies.

I don't give my sympathies a blank cheque in advance. In a conflict between principle and sympathy, principles ought sometimes to win. For example, I think it was right to take part in the Second World War on the allied side; there were many ghastly individual incidents which might have led someone to doubt the rightness of his participation in that war; and I think it would have been right for such a person to keep his sympathies in a subordinate place on those occasions, not allowing them to modify his principles in such a way as to make a pacifist of him.

Still, one's sympathies should be kept as sharp and sensitive and aware as possible, and not only because they can sometimes affect one's principles or one's conduct or both. Owen, at any rate, says that feelings and sympathies are vital even when they can do nothing but bring pain and distress. In another poem he speaks of the blessings of being numb in one's feelings: "Happy are the men who yet before they are killed/Can let their veins run cold," he says. These are the ones who do not suffer from any compassion which, as Owen puts it,

"makes their feet/Sore on the alleys cobbled with their brothers." He contrasts these "happy" ones, who "lose all imagination," with himself and others "who with a thought besmirch/Blood over all our soul." Yet the poem's verdict goes against the "happy" ones. Owen does not say that they will act worse than the others whose souls are besmirched with blood because of their keen awareness of human suffering. He merely says that they are the losers because they have cut themselves off from the human condition:

> By choice they made themselves immune
> To pity and whatever moans in man
> Before the last sea and the hapless stars;
> Whatever mourns when many leave these shores;
> Whatever shares
> The eternal reciprocity of tears.

Further Question

1. How does Bennett resolve the difficulties he raises? Do you agree? Why? Would you resolve them any differently?

Further Readings

Brandt, Richard. *Value and Obligation*. New York: Harcourt, Brace & World, 1961. An older but still much used standard reference.

Hospers, John. *Human Conduct*. New York: Harcourt, Brace & World, 1961. A good, elementary introduction.

The Metaphysics of Anti-Semitism   76

JOHN WHITE

John White received his PhD from the University of Vienna, where he studied with Moritz Schlick (1882–1936), one of the original founders of the famous Vienna Circle and logical positivism. As a young man, White had a "life-altering experience" that prompted him to pursue instead a career in the arts. He emigrated to the United States, where for over forty years he served as a director of the City Opera in New York. He has, however, continued to publish a number of articles, ranging from a psychoanalytic study of Franz Kafka to a book exploring the modern notion of an ideal universal human character, "the knight, adventurer, experimenter, inventor, thinker, artist, poet, fighter and individualist . . . combined in one man."

Reading Questions

1. Why does the author prefer the term *anti-Judaism* to *anti-Semitism*?
2. How, in his view, did anti-Semitism begin, and why?
3. What role did the Christian church play in the history of anti-Semitism? Why?
4. What is Gnosticism? How does it relate to orthodox Christianity? What does White mean by "Gnostic anti-Semitism"?
5. What is the relation between Plato's notion of God (the demiurge) and the character and role of Christ in Christianity?
6. How, in White's view, did the metaphysical doctrines of the Catholic church contribute to the holocaust?

ANTI-SEMITISM: THE BETTER WORD IS ANTI-JUDAISM. The present conflict is between Semitic nations: the Israelis and a group of Arab states can hardly be called an anti-Semitic conflict, but an anti-Judaistic war or anti-Arab war waged between Israel and a group of Arab-Moslem nations.[1]

Anti-Judaism dates back to antiquity. It was provoked by a small group of people proud of its traditional monotheism, an ethnic group that was self-contained to the degree of exclusivism and separatism. The main antique cities where the Jewish problem became acute were Rome and Alexandria. Both were melting pots of different religious currents, a syncretism of Jewish oriental and Hellenistic elements with a strong admixture of magic, astrological, and mystic features in addition to pagan fertility cults.[2] Particularly irritating to the traditional Roman was the successful proselytism of the small Jewish community. One of the first to express hostility against the Jews was the Roman orator Arpion. He derides circumcision and the Jewish abstinence from eating pork, attributing the latter not without evidence to the fact that the boar was a holy animal to the Jews. He goes so far as to tell his readers that the Jews in Jerusalem adore the golden head of an ass in their synagogue.[3] Cicero defines the Jewish religion as a "barbarian superstition."[4] Posing as the representative of the "good old days," Tacitus takes this theme up, accusing the Jews of vilifying all that is holy to Roman citizens. The satirists Juvenal and Martial mocked the "circumcised, lecherous Jews" and reproached them for attempting to destroy the Roman Pantheon.

There were also benevolent currents in Roman-Judaistic history. Emperor Augustus confirmed the rights of the Jews and posed for a while as their protector. Varro, a contemporary of Cicero's, praised the Jews for their prohibition of images in the temple. He goes even so far as to identify Jehovah with Jupiter.[5]

Anti-Semitism as we understand it was fomented by the Christian church, wherever the Christian church was successful, especially among the Gentiles, the main field of activity of St. Paul. It brought Paul into conflict with the more conservative St. Peter. A fundamental question arose: Shall the Gentile who wanted to convert to Christianity pass first through the stage of the Torah, or can he pass directly from paganism to Christianity? Peter insisted that the stage of Christianity can only be reached by those who have passed through Judaism. In St. Paul's opinion, those who wanted to become Christians did not have to pass preliminarily through the phase of the Torah. Peter was quite forceful in his opposition to Paul. "One tot or tittle shall not pass from the laws," he insisted.[6] Which means, "all dietary laws, circumcision, all the precepts of the Torah have to be observed before the doors of Christianity can be opened to those who want to convert to the new creed, for to take such a position, namely to bypass the laws of the Torah, is to act against God who has spoken through Moses, and whose eternal endurance was attested by our Lord."[7] Like many others, Paul's co-worker Barrabbas opposed Paul's direct appeal to the Gentiles and parted from him.[8] Paul even accuses him of insincerity for following those Jews who insisted: "Unless you are circumcised according to the laws of Moses you cannot be saved."[9] Peter was very direct in his opposition to Paul: "So our beloved brother Paul wrote to you according to his wisdom given him, speaking of this as he does in his letter. There are some things in them hard to understand which the ignorant and unstable twist to their own destruction as they do to other scriptures."[10]

The final result of this dualism ended with a poorly disguised compromise. In truth, the final triumph of Christianity is the work of St. Paul, who became the leader of an ever-growing sect of followers. The deification of Jesus starts with Paul. His work is in essence the Christology as we know it. It brought about the humanization of God, a God that became Man. It opened up eschatological perspectives. It elevated the Parakletos (the intercessor) by bestowing on him the appelatives of Theos (God), Kyrios (King), and Soter (Redeemer). In Jesus, according to his mythographer, the prophetic concept of the universality of God merged with that of the Messiah; it established the Parousia (the return of the new God) as the Judge who will bring peace to the elected and eternal damnation to the sinners.

And yet the attitude of Paul is in many respects enigmatic. One has the feeling that he speaks, as Americans say, "from both sides of his mouth." The man who insists on abolishing the Torah, the old covenant, surprises us in Romans, where he says: "Circumcision is indeed of value if you obey the law. . . . What is the value of circumcision? Much in every way. Has God rejected his people? By no means."[11] Can we see in this contradiction the hesitation of a former Pharisee, the pupil of rabbis Gamaliel and Hillel? Is he a man torn between former loyalties and the new truth after the miracle on the road to Damascus? With a passionate soul like his, could he not at certain moments of inner turmoil relapse and contradict himself? Anyone who has an understanding of the human soul would hardly blame Paul for this.

There are, however, other opinions of Christologists who see in these statements the politician, the ruseful founder of a new religion. Paul was certainly a courageous man, and his anti-Torah attitude was most perilous. We know from Acts that it might have cost him his life.[12] Besides, some mod-

ern students of Paul, Jews as well as non-Jews doubt whether he was really a Jew who, as a student, sat at the feet of the venerable Gamaliel and Hillel. According to these students, Paul might have been a Gentile from Tapsus who, when he came to Jerusalem, pretended to be a Jew in order to gain respectability there. It was not easy in the beginning. "This man Paul," we read in Acts 18:13, "is persuading man to worship God contrary to the rules" his adversaries stated, and we know what this meant.

Whether Paul was a Gentile from Tapsus or of Jewish origin, the fact remains that he grew up in a Hellenistic milieu and that after his arrival in Jerusalem he met with the Sadducees, a conservative group that tried to adjust to the Roman superpower. They were thus in sharp opposition to the Pharisees, who considered them traitors to the Jewish cause of freedom from any foreign yoke. They saw in the Sadducees a group of quislings. Paul, who at this time still called himself Saul, belonged first to the Sadducees. This is corroborated by his participation in the stoning of Stephan. He went so far as to round up the Pharisees who buried St. Stephan and helped to put them into jail. He even seemed to have been a henchman appointed by the Sadducees. When the Pharisees and the anti-Roman Jews fled from Rome to Damascus, Paul was sent there to arrest them. It was on the way to Damascus that his conversion took place. Though having never experienced the living Christ, he based his bold christological theory on the Gospel of John, the only biblical text where Hellenistic influence is obvious by its reference to the Logos as identical with Jesus Christ.

The synoptic gospels spoke less to Paul than the Gospel of John. The reason for this lies in the fact that the synoptic gospels evolve on the temporal, historic plain: their faithful authors, though writing about fifty years after Jesus' death, pretended to have experienced the deification of Jesus the man, his charismatic personality, his painful road through life, his cruel death, his transfiguration, and the miracle of his resurrection. In contrast to this, in the Gospel of John we are right in the beginning raised from the temporal to the timeless eternal sphere. The son, the Logos, who coexists with God the Father himself is the theme: the word that has become flesh. This identification with Jesus with the Logos signifies a demotion of the Jewish Jahve. An anti-Jewish trend is set into motion that developed steadily over the centuries to come. For Jahave is the God of the Jews. Of all the gospels, the Gospel of John represents the most vicious anti-Jewish tendency. It is all pervasive there; the Jews are depicted as the implacable eternal enemies of Christ. The pious, religious Pharisaical, political anti-Roman group to which the saintly rabbis Gamaliel and Hillel belonged are addressed in the most virulent terms, as the children of Satan: "You are of your father, the devil and your will is to do your father's desire. He was a murderer from the beginning and has nothing to do with the truth because there is no truth in him. Whenever he lies, he speaks according to his nature, for he is a liar and the father of lies."[13]

Paul never went so far. His aim was the universal acceptance of Christ by the Gentiles without any condition and without rejecting the past. The old covenant of Jahve with his people was legitimate, according to Paul, until it became obsolete through the Logos incarnate. The Jewish particularism was, according to him, superseded by the all-embracing Catholic universalism. It was in essence the old Jewish prophetic God of Abraham in a new christological form. Expecting the imminent Parousia, he was inspired by the miraculous concretization of the invisible Godhead in the form of a Man. Paul saw in Christ the final redeemer of mankind, enmeshed in sin and guilt through the perverse, sinful act of Adam. Christ is, according to Paul, the Messiah, the Prince of Peace who will bring justice and harmony to a strife-torn world. He will fulfill the plan of God to bring mankind to his eternal presence—not as an agent of or a messenger from God, for he is identical with God, created as he was before the beginning of time and before the creation of the universe. Christ represents the power of God and the wisdom of God, as Paul calls him in I Corinthians 24.

Actually, Paul followed the Jewish prophets; his Christology revolved around the same religious concept of God as theirs did. Yet to the universality of the God of the Prophets, a *God of All*, Paul adds the idea of a God of redemptive purpose, a *God for All*, necessitated by the sin of Adam, the curse of which the new Adam, Jesus Christ, will lift from a guilt-ridden world. With the ultimate victory of

Christ, the irrevocability of death is lifted from the oppressed human soul. The finality of life gives way to the perennial bliss of the human creature that found its way back to its divine creator. Christ, the eternal Logos, is representative of God's own mysterious longing to bring back the original purity of Man. He too will return to his father, he too will be reabsorbed into the divine unity of which he is himself a part, with whom he is co-equal and co-substantial:

> For as in Adam all die so also in Christ shall all be made alive. But each in his own order. Christ the first fruits, then at his coming, those who belong to Christ. Then comes the end when he delivers the kingdom to God the Father after destroying every rule and every authority and power. For he must reign until he has put all his enemies under his feet. The last enemy to be destroyed is death. For God has put all things in subjection under his feet. But when it says all things are put in subjection under him, it is plain that he is excepted who put all things under him. When all things are subjected to him then, the Son himself will also be subjected to him who put all things under him, that God may be everything to everyone.[14]

It is thus difficult to understand that it was Paul who was invoked by all those that referred to the Jewish Jahve as the principle source of all the evil in the world. What is the reason for this demonization of Jahve? It results from the concept of the Logos, a concept that infiltrated into Christology through the Hellenistic milieu in which Paul as well as the writer of the Gospel of John grew up. We recognize now Peter's wisdom when he required that any new follower of Christ, especially those of pagan, Gentile origin, must first pass through Judaism in order to see how deeply connected the new covenant was with the Jewish Torah, for Peter recognized the immense danger that Hellenism represented for Jewish monotheism.

In the Eastern Hellenistic surroundings a Neoplatonic philosophy evolved, a syncretistic movement in which Platonic thoughts, as expressed in the *Timaeus,* were fused with additive elements, borrowed from Zoroastic, mystic, and Pythagorean sources. The most important representative of this philosophy was Plotin, who influenced the Arab philosopher Averroes as well as the Jewish philosophers Philo and Avicembron. Even the later mysticism of Master Eckhardt and Nicholas de Cues give testimony of Neoplatonic thinking.

The Neoplatonic cosmogony as represented in the various Neoplatonic systems was a gradualism reaching from the all-pervasive, all-containing "One" down to the deepest depth of "non-being," the Negative, Evil itself. This gradualism is emanatative, the different stages (hypostases) representing different aspects of the numinous essence. Like a stone that has been thrown into a body of water, producing concentric waves that become weaker and weaker the further they are from the centerpoint, so the hypostases weaken the further they are away from the focal point—the "One." The degradation is thus not qualitative but quantitative, the Evil being a lesser Good. To the limited human view, so the Neoplatonic argues, the world appears as a dynamic pantheism, every single phenomenon seeming a different aspect of the essentiality of being. However, in the Neoplatonic vision, it is in reality a static immobilism that only the Neoplatonic recognizes, for he alone is endowed with a new awareness, a higher wisdom vis à vis the world. The awareness—namely, that behind the phenomenal world of "Becoming" stands the constancy of the Conceptual. Parmenides called it, "The being that is." We are indeed in the presence of the old confrontation of Parmenides and Heraclitus, the two antithetic concepts that found their synthesis in the poetic vision of Plato. In the Platonic system, the world of existential appearances is transfigured by the starlike brilliance of the ultimate realities: the world of the eternal ideas culminates in the idea of the "One," the "Good," the Judeo-Christian God.

As Platonism needed the Aristotelian corrective,[15] so Neoplatonic thinking found its necessary corrective in the Christology of Paul. Otherwise, it was incomplete and full of contradiction. According to Plotinus and many thinkers of his school, the "One" cannot be defined, for every definition is a limitation. The "One," however, is infinite. It has not qualities, it has no attributes. "If we are to think positively of the 'One,' there would be more truth in Silence," as Plotinus explained. In order that the Divine, the infinite, becomes concrete, it needs a bridge that would lead from the ephemeral world to the pure being. For that purpose the Nous, the Logos, was interpolated between the "One" and the phenomenal world. The Nous, or Logos, is the first visible form of the all containing "One." It is the focal point of the above-mentioned hypostases. Through it the visible world manifests itself. Its equivalent in man is the human soul. Being within the body of Man, it is in touch with the phenomenal world but its longing tends to return to its unworldly origin. The ecstatic urge in Man alone enables it to lift itself up to God, the "One," from whence it stems.

There are definite contradictions in this Neoplatonic system. Plotinus justifies the existence of the phenomenal world because sheer potentiality in the Aristotelian sense would be meaningless if it were not concretized. In addition, this world to him is a good world, yet there is a strong life-negating pessimism noticeable because the soul feels imprisoned in the body. The existential is, after all, a falling away from the essential and the soul is constantly longing to return to the Godlike "One." In Plotinus's cosmology, such a return is conceived as an act of liberation. This conflictual situation is resolved by the christological worldview. The phenomenal world is a degraded world. It is a fallen world through the sin of Adam. Jesus Christ became the instrument whereby the fallen world returned to its original purity. Christ, the incarnated Logos, was able through his human aspect to fulfill his soterological destiny. His humanity was real. The heresy of Docetism that conceived his humanity as symbolic was rejected by the fathers of the church. Christ, though not identical with God the Father, has similarities with him through his sonship: not *ousios* but *oisious,* as the Greek formula read (not identical but similar to God the Father).

As we said before, the final offspring and last consequence of the Neoplatonic movement is the Gnosis. Aware of the link that existed between Jesus and Jehovah by the sonship of Christ, the proponents of Gnosis attempted to cut this relationship by identifying, like the Neoplatonics, the Logos with Christ but rejecting the creator of this world, Jehovah, as Christ's Father. This world is the world of Evil. Its creator, Jehovah, is a malevolent force whom the Gnostics called, with Plato, a demiurge.

Gnosticism is not a definite religious doctrine.[16] Though it represents a personalized religious movement containing in its different expressions many Christian elements, it is totally different from the orthodox Christian doctrine. The latter does not tolerate any deviations from its firmly established religious principles, declaring any such deviation as heretic. In contrast to this severe orthodox rigidity is the personalized Gnostic religious attitude, by definition as variable as individuals vary from each other. The Gnostic vision represents a subjective intuitive process leading via self-knowledge to an awakening of the individual self to God. Mystic esoteric elements lead the Gnostic to an exalted trancelike subjectivism, shunning any outside intervention, be it a priest, a deacon, or a bishop. One of the most outspoken adversaries of the Gnostics, Tertullian, warns: "Away with all attempts to produce a mixed Christianity, a stoic Platonic or dialectic composition. . . . With our faith we desire no further belief."[17] Even more than the Neoplatonic philosophy does Gnosticism represent a syncretism based too on Plato's *Timaeus* coupled with elements of Plotinus, Philo, Persian, and even Buddhistic elements. In Western philosophy the Gnostic Christology is most important insofar as certain Gnostic branches are based on a degradation of the Jewish Jahve, the God of the Old Testament, the God of the Jews. He is identified by the Gnostics to Plato's demiurge, the intermediary maker of this world who in the Gnostic vision caused all the evil in this world. According to Valentinus, one of the main Gnostic writers who is supposed to be the author of the Gnostic "Testimony of the Truth," the God of the Hebrews is the Chief of the Fallen Angles. Christ came to free humanity from Jehovah's hybris that would enslave mankind. He, Jehovah, is a malicious power, jealous, vindictive, the original Satan. According to the author of "Reality of Rules," the God of the Old Testament is blind, arrogant, considering himself the Lord of this world; he too sees in this God the great seducer. Epiphanius quotes a subdivision of the Gnostics, the Archonites, who consider Jehovah to be the son of Satan.

However, the worldview of the Gnosis, though in many respects similar to that of Neoplatonism, is not *emanative* but *dualistic*. Both systems are gradualistic but the aeons, the equivalent of the hypostases, are essentially oppositional to each other: the evil not being a lesser good but in a Manichaean sense a quality in itself. Indeed, Mani was considered the Iranian representative of Gnosticism. The Gnosis is nihilistic with regard to the phenomenal world. In its extreme form, like the world view of Marcion, a proto-Gnostic, this world has to be rejected. The ideal man, in Marcion's view, is the saint. He is an ascetic leading the life of celibacy, rejecting matrimony and procreation. The world of the flesh is a world of evil. Its creator, the demiurge, the god of the Old Testament, is a satanic force. We hear the echo of John's gospel, which rejects the Jews as servants of Satan and opponents of Christ. The Gnostic Christ is the only leader back to the extramundane God who has nothing to do with the demiurge, Jehovah. From the darkness of this demiurge Christ leads the Gnostic back to the divine light. The world-affirmative attitude of the Jew to whom Jehovah dictated to "choose life." is rejected by the Gnostic.[18] Amos' injunction to the Jews "seek the world and live" puts, in the Gnostic vision, an evil stamp on the Jew for being the servant of the worldly demonic power. It directs him away from the road to salvation. In Gnostic thinking, the Jew is the slave of the dark forces in life, a slave of the senses, in modern terms, a materialist. The follower of the Jewish God is, in contrast to the transmundane God of the Gnostics, a slave of Mammon; he is subject to the forces of darkness and sin.

According to Marcion, this world is contaminated by the Old Testamental Jewish spirit. It can only be redeemed by adopting Paul's view that the old covenant is abolished and replaced by the New Testament, inspired by Jesus Christ. Indeed, Paul is claimed by the most rigorous Gnostics as the teacher whom Man has to follow unconditionally. This Gnostic metaphysical anti-Semitism stigmatized the Jew as a negative force in Western civilization. It demonized him as a child and follower of Satan. The Catholic church fostered this metaphysical anti-Semitism although it rehabilitated the Old Testament by accepting it as the foundation of the Gospels. It follows Paul's method, declaring the Jews of the Old Testament as immune of guilt while condemning the Jews after Jesus' crucifixion for not following the Christian road to salvation. However, the fathers of the church had to remain adamant in affirming the Old Testament as the basis of Christianity. After all, the first Christians mentioned so many events in the Old Testament as forerunners of the new creed; they could quote many psalms and other passages to this effect. Especially the two towering Jewish prophets Isaiah and Jeremiah seemed to many Christians the prophets of the coming redeemer, Jesus. Paul himself spoke of the first Adam, who brought sin into the world, while the second Adam, Jesus, blotted out the curse that oppressed humanity since its fall from grace and expulsion from Paradise. Thus the Catholic church had to reject the demotion of Jahve. It had based Christology on so many instances in the Old Testament that it could not easily invoke these passages without at the same time insisting on the Fatherhood of Jehovah, the father of Jesus Christ, the almighty God of the Jews.[19] But it found a powerful weapon for its fierce anti-Judaism in the figure of Judas Iscariot. Judas Iscariot became, in the course of the following centuries, the representative of the Gnostic Jehovah, the nefarious representative of Judaism.

Who was this Judas Iscariot, what was his motivation, and in which way did he become the representative of all the Jews as the murderer of Jesus Christ, the Galilean of Nazareth? According to the Gospels, whenever he is mentioned Judas is the last of the twelve apostles, while Simon Peter is the first mentioned. The figure 12 is not arbitrary but refers to the twelve original tribes of old Israel. Although eleven disciples stem from Galilee, Judas alone hails from Judea. Two questions arise: (1) Is there any significance to the fact that the only non-Galilean disciple hailed from Judea? (2) Why did Jesus not recognize in the only non-Galilean the man who turned out to be the main cause of his undoing?

There are indeed strong indications that Judas' treason had been known to Christ. According to Matthew 26, Jesus told his apostles at the last supper: "One of you will betray me." When Judas asked, "Is it I, Master?" Jesus said to him, "You have said so." Even more poignantly, we read in John that when John asked Jesus who would betray him, Jesus answered: "It is he whom I shall give this morsel when I have dipped it," and he gave it to Judas: "At this moment Satan entered into him."[20] Judas' betrayal was thus preordained, as shown in a quotation from Psalms 41:9. "Even my bosom friend in whom I trusted, who ate my bread, has lifted his heel against me" is quoted by Jesus: "I know whom I have chosen. It is that the scriptures may be fulfilled. He who ate my bread has lifted his heel against me."[21] And again, in the most anti-Judaistic gospel, that of John, we read: "Did I not choose you, the twelve, and one of you is the devil? Jesus spoke of Judas, the son of Simon Iscariot, for he, one of the twelve, was to betray him."[22]

What results from these episodes is:

1. The importance of Judas as one of the twelve Apostles
2. The enemy of God, Satan, led him to the betrayal of the Lord
3. He has been the chosen instrument so that the Old Testamental prophecy be fulfilled in order that the world be changed, cleansed from the original sin by the redemptive Messiah

Judas was thus less a factor in the heinous crime but a seemingly innocent product of a mysterious divine will. There is, one can almost say, a tragic aspect to his crime; it makes him a victim rather than a criminal. And yet the representatives of Christianity found no redeeming word for Judas, the man of Iscariot. They were not able to see the part he had to play in Jesus' sacrificial mission to obliterate the original sin. Who else but Judas was the vehicle by which this self-ordained sacrifice was made possible, even compelling? The Christian doctrine recognizes the sin of Adam as necessary, for it was brought about by God's mysterious will of self-disclosure in the form of Man. As we read in the missal on Holy Saturday at the blessing of the Paschal lamb, "Oh truly gainful [*certe necessarium*] sin of Adam which was wiped away by the death of Christ. Oh happy fault [*oh felix culpa*] which merited so great a redeemer.

Was Judas' betrayal not equally necessary in order that the biblical scriptures be fulfilled? And yet some of the gospels insinuate that his act was an act of greed. For thirty shekels he is supposed to have betrayed the man whom his followers and himself had called the Messiah. A ridiculous sum indeed, which was the equivalent price for a wounded slave to the slave's owner, as we read in Exodus 21:32. It is repeated as a minimum sum in Zachariah XI:12. In other Jewish scriptures it is also mentioned as a shockingly small sum as the reward for a major transgression. As it is not quite clear whether his act was preordained so that the Old Testament could be fulfilled or whether it was an act of personal greed, so Judas' end is described differently in the different accounts of the Gospels. According to Matthew 27:5, he hanged himself, and in Acts 1:17 "he fell head long, burst open and all his bowels gushed out." Mark and John amazingly do not mention his death at all.

The Jesus figure is invested with so many archetypical layers that consequently one can detect in the Judas figure the archetypical "Adversary": the personification of a Satanic demon, the Gnostic Jehovah. Jesus and Judas are archetypical contrast figures representing an unconscious projection of an ambivalently loved and respected potentiated paternal autocrat, elevated to the lofty rank of deity. This deity is abhorred for its malevolence and loved for its benevolent character. Such dichotomization in primitive man's psyche and the ensuing ambivalent feeling reaction provokes, vis à vis the split-off hate component, a powerful guilt feeling and an irresistible, compulsive wish for atonement in the form of sacrifice. This feeling of guilt is especially aroused by the individual's transgression of its own authority, brushing aside the divine veto against such a transgression. This is particularly the case when a new event is planned, a new endeavor is instituted, or a new branch of human activity is foreseen, for the Godhead is considered to be jealous of its prerogative to establish a new order of worldly, especially human affairs. It sees in any self-proclaimed human authority an attempt to be dethroned and to be stripped of its power.

The tower of Babel is the symbolic expression of this kind of divine veto against human transgression, as is the eating from the Tree of Knowledge. As a consequence, ritual human sacrifices were instituted to placate the assumed anger of the deity, especially if such divine anger is aroused, manifesting itself by plagues, periods of starvation, or a never ending war. In other words, through the act of sacrifice or self-sacrifice of one of its members, a community is enabled to undertake new ventures without having to fear the deity's wrath. In male-oriented societies, the son of a leading authority must be sacrificed by his own father, as in the case of Abraham, who was willing to murder his own son before laying the foundation of the new nation of Israel. Often the brother is the sacrificial victim, as in the saga of Romulus and Remus, in which Remus is sacrificed—a murder necessitated by the foundation of Rome through Romulus. Such brother victimization is the basis of many other fratricidal narratives, like that of Jacob and Esau, David and Absalon, Osiris and Seth, and Baal and Moth. The most notorious brother murder is that committed by Cain. It is the subject of a probing study by Hyam Maccoby, *The Sacred Executioner*. This study shows how much we must be aware that old texts obfuscate more than they reveal the real thrust of a myth.

The heinous crime of the murder of his brother, Abel, makes the Cain figure the archetype of evil itself, and yet at Cain's insistence God stamps a sign on his forehead lest he become a victim of anyone who would be inclined to murder him. In the light of what we have said earlier, we have to study the posterity of Cain and his immediate offspring. The word "Cain" stems from the Hebrew *quamah,* meaning smith or metalworker. Indeed, the Bible informs us that the Cainites were the offsprings of Enoch, the eldest son of Cain, and that they were the inventors of metalworking as well as of musical instruments. The church honored Enoch.[23] According to apocryphal literature, he was "close to God," who granted him immortality as a "gift of God." Enoch was transferred to heaven without an earthly death. Apocryphal literature speaks even of his "resurrection."

We learn further that the Cainites were practically the only tribe that survived the "great flood." They were friendly with the Jews and were singled out as such by the Jewish nation. Indeed, we read in II Samuel 15:6 that the Cainites settled among the Amalekites, but when Saul, the king of Israel, fought the Amalekites, he spared the Cainites. "Go, depart" he tells them, "get you down from the Amalekites, lest I destroy you with them, for you have showed kindness to all the children of Israel when they came out of Egypt." And, what is most illuminating, there exists even a link with Moses, who liberated the Israelites suffering under the yoke of the Egyptians. For his father-in-law, Jethro, was a Cainite occasionally called Cain in the Septuagint, indicating that *cain* might have become an honorary title like *pharaoh*. In other words, the direct descendants of Cain, the infamous murderer of his brother, were intimately connected with the grandiose saviour and leader of the Jewish people to Canaan: Moses, whom Jehovah selected as a mouthpiece and who proclaimed Jahve as the only God of the Jews.

Finally, we read in Genesis that Cain was the founder of the city of Nod, where he lived in exile "east of Eden" and called this city after his son Enoch. The reference to Eden is puzzling. After all, Cain is generations apart from Eden, and what is even more puzzling, the expression "east of Eden" occurs in connection with the expulsion of Adam. For God had put his cherub in the direction of "east of Eden" not to let the Adamites back to the paradise of Eden. Seemingly we have here an amalgamation of two stories: that of the Cainites and that of the Adamites. Since the Cainites survived the "great flood," they are the ancestors of the human race, and the figures of Adam and Enoch would then be identical. To corroborate this, the curse of God against Adam and against Cain shows strong similarities. When God banishes Adam, he tells him: "Cursed is the ground because of you. In toil you shall eat of it. All of your life thorns and thistles shall it bring forth for thee.[24] In other words, the ground became infertile unless Adam would work on it by the sweat of his brow. The curse against Cain is similar, but even harsher. "When thou tillest the earth, she shall not henceforth yield unto thee her strength. You shall be a fugitive and wander on the earth.[25] Does that mean that Adam would become an agriculturist and Cain a nomad? This is hardly possible since nomadism does not follow agriculturism, but the other way around. Indeed, in Genesis we read that the generations after Cain were not nomads, but settled down "east of Eden." The probability arises, then, that Cain and Adam were identical and that the ancestors of the Cainites and the Adamites were the same person. At the same time, hailing from Eden indicates Man's eternal longing for the blissful state of happiness, the carefree situation and well-being supplied by maternal care and solicitude. It is the siren song of the "All Motherhood of Being," the warmth and safety provided to the self sheltered within the mother's womb before entering the cold world with its challenges and demands: Paradise.

Cain's murderous act is in reality infanticide, Abel being his son and not his brother. This act enabled Cain's descendents to emancipate themselves, to become the ancestors of humankind and to create civilization.

The lessening of the eruptive, irrational tendencies on behalf of rational self-containment and more regard for the self of the "Other" is the final step from hominization to humanization. Hand in hand, the victim is himself transformed. The brother substitution that we encounter in the Cain saga and others represents a toned-down variation of the slaying of one's child, for the destruction of a person's succession seemingly appears utterly repellent to the primitive mind. A further progress of civilization led to the replacement of an animal for the human being—the ram for the Abraham saga and the doe in the Agamemnon myth, a derivative of which represents the scapegoat sent alive into the desert carrying with itself the sins of the people that have been laid upon the sacrificial animal. Finally, the destruction of the knife that killed the sacrificial victim signifies the symbolic act of reification as a substitute for the "bloody murder."

Cain and Judas are often mentioned together in folklore. Eternal wanderers through the ages to the end of all time, they are cursed and rejected by all who encounter them; yet there is a significant difference. Cain, as we have demonstrated, enables his offspring through his misdeeds to bring about new forms of civilizations, leading to the overcoming of the Stone Age by the Metal Age and the invention of the arts. They survived the cataclysm of the "great flood" and enthroned Jahve as the almighty God of Humanity. In contrast to Cain is Judas and what he stands for, a willful product of the Catholic church, which made him the representative of the Jewish people and thus stamped on the Jews the indelible mark of deicide. Judas became the anti-Christ in person, the representative of the Gnostic Jehovah, the perfidious Jew, the enemy of the Christian world and its people.

What led to that transformation of Judas? We have already noticed the different reports about his suicide. It is quite clear that his personality must have been shrouded in mystery, even to his contemporaries. For instance, when he quasiadmitted in front of the other apostles that he was the traitor to the Lord, why did they react as if they had not heard or quite understood this unheard-of admission? Even more perplexing is the fact that Judas, according to Luke 22:19, Mark 14:22, and Matthew 26:20, had participated in the establishment of the Eucharist, although he had already planned the treasonable act that would have definitely excluded him from the sanctifying grace. When Judas performed the acts of treason at night, we are given to understand that he was afraid of the reaction among Jesus' followers had it been done in the daytime. However, the fact *that* Jesus was arrested and not *when* would have been dangerous, after all. According to Mark 14:11, the Jews of the temple offered Judas a reward (Mark), while Matthew 26:14–16 "has him ask for remuneration." In contrast to this, Luke 22:3 tells us that Satan entered into Judas and seduced him to betray Jesus.

Wherever we look, we see inconsistencies in Judas' actions and reactions. One assumes that he hailed from Judea since he was called Judas, son of Simon Iscariot.[26] It is not quite clear whether that means a man of Kerioth, a place in Judea: *ish Kerioth,* the man of the town of Kerioth. In Joshua 5:25, a Kerioth is mentioned but unfortunately it is not located in Judea. Should it be a nickname stemming from the Latin *Sicarius,* "the bandit"? But here again the accent in Latin does not fall on the appropriate syllable. There have been a great many different attempts to establish the location or the meaning of Kerioth, but they do not lead to any definite result. Paul in I Corinthians 22 speaks of a treasonable act against Jesus without even mentioning the traitor.[27] Moreover, in Corinthians 15:5, Paul tells us that after the resurrection Christ appeared to the twelve apostles, which would mean that Judas was still considered an apostle. Should he not have mentioned that there were only eleven apostles at that time? The election of Matthias to replace Judas is not historically assured.[28] Consequently, some Christologists maintain that the treason story connected with the personality of Judas might be a legend and was not based on fact. It seems quite plausible that through the homonym, the connection of *Jew, Judas,* and *Judea* serves the evil purpose of labeling the Judas figure as an eponym of the Jewish people. The eminent Guignebert and many Christologists at this time were of this opinion. One of the most eminent present-day Christologists, John Dominic Crossant, indicates such a possibility in his book *Who Killed Jesus?* "The name Judas resonates in Hebrew with the name 'Jew' and so Judas was created to accuse Judaism of betraying Jesus. Judas is Judaism and he simply incarnates the anti-Judaism of earliest Christianity."[29]

Maccoby's intelligent study could offer that the basis of the Judas story would be the motif of the sacred executioner: Judas took the murder of Jesus on himself so that the new creed could be established. However, in the Gospels the Jews themselves fanatically opposed their redeemer and declared emphatically in Matthew 27:25: "His blood be on us and on our children," implying that as long as there were Jews in the world, Christianity would have a deadly enemy in the world. This apocalyptic threat against Christianity is undoubtably of Gnostic origin. It was at the bottom of the genocidal drive by the Nazis, and the Catholic church has fostered it through their adroit interpretation, if not invention, of the Judas figure. From his or her earliest youth (from about the fourth year on) the Christian youngster heard about Judas, the Jew from Judea, who betrayed Christ, hated Christ, and left this legacy to his children and children's children. By the homonymous sound of *Judas, Jew,* and *Judea,* the youngster was prepared to despise, abhor, persecute, and even murder the Jew. And if one realizes that in German the word *Jew* (*Jude*) is pronounced "YouDuh," then the effect of this homonymous sound is doubly strong. In Austria there is an even finer nuance, the elimination of the final *e* to *Jud,* which for the Austrian ear is even more contemptuous. Once Dollfus, the Austrian chancellor, in order to appeal to the mob mentality of his Christian Socialist Party, shouted in Parliament to Dr. Otto Bauer, a member of the Socialist Party, "You are nothing but an arrogant Kike (*Jud*). This invective gave the members of his party great satisfaction. Many young Austrian musicians even today are amazed that the name Judas could have an honorific connotation in the Handel oratorio *Judas Maccabeus.* Indeed, as Judas was the name of Jesus' half brother, he was probably

Joseph's son by a previous marriage and might have been the author of the Epistle of Jude.

In folklore, the Jew Ahasver became another exponent of the eternal Jew who was condemned to wander aimlessly and guilt ridden through the ages without ever finding peace. This Ahasver was a shoemaker who with his family watched the lamentable plight of Jesus on his painful road to Golgotha. When Jesus stopped for a moment in front of his house to rest, Ahasver shouted: "Move on, move on." Whereupon Jesus looked at him, saying: "You shall not rest until the last Judgement." God uttered a very similar condemnation against Cain: "You shall be a fugitive and wander restlessly on the earth." The inner pain Ahasver would experience on his eternal road is foreshadowed in Jesus' remark about Judas, "It would have been better for this man had he not been born."[30]

Judas found his defenders. In recent times the lawyer of the French collaborationists,* Maître Isorni, spoke on Judas' behalf. According to him, Judas might have been an honest follower of Jesus. Like the group of zealots to whom he might have belonged, he might well have seen in Jesus the Messiah, but in a very narrow nationalistic sense — namely, as the liberator from the hated Roman yoke. Judas, in the opinion of his defenders like Isorni, was disappointed in Jesus. He did not understand Jesus' all-embracing love for humanity and his hope for universal peace. He was not the Messiah in the political sense, as the zealots and Judas had interpreted him. They were shocked to hear: "Give to Caesar what is due to Caesar." Caesar meant Rome, which was the only target for the zealots and Judas, if Judas was indeed a zealot. This misunderstanding of Jesus' only ethical concern made him the opponent of the zealots and Judas himself. Isorni even goes so far as to tell us that the apostles did not behave much better than Judas. They all hid when Jesus was condemned except for John, but this is only mentioned in the Gospel of John, which might have been *pro domo*. According to some, the fourth gospel was written by John's disciples, who tried to elevate him to the detriment of the other disciples. In reality, none of the disciples came to the crucifixion to console Mary and the other women who came to witness

*With the Germans during WWII.

Jesus' martyrdom. Peter even renounced him three times: the same Peter who was declared to be the representative of Christ in this world, Peter whom Christ himself had called Satan for not being on the side of God.[31]

Judas, Ahasver the eternal wanderer, and even Cain became part of the same anti-Jewish complex: the Eternal Rootless Jew, a symbolic representative of the Jewish people condemned to eternal restlessness and fear for being labeled the people of deicide.

The last representative of Gnostic anti-Semitism was the conservative Viennese Catholic Anton Orel, who died in 1953. Typically, Orel insisted, whenever the occasion arose, that he not be called a racial anti-Semite, but an anti-Judaist. According to him, the Jewish spirit stems from Lucifer-Satan, which appears in modern times as capitalism. He thought the Jews themselves could only be redeemed by their conversion to Catholicism and by rejecting, in the parlance of the old Gnostics, the world-corrupting demiurge in favor of Jesus Christ.[32]

For two thousand years, the Jewish people have been vilified, slandered, harassed, and persecuted as the people of deicide. The Catholic church and its highest representatives were responsible for this campaign of hatred against the people among which Jesus was born, hatred that led to the genocidal crimes against the Jews by the Nazi regime that culminated in what is commonly called the holocaust.[33]

NOTES

1. John Gaeger, *The Origin of Anti-Semitism* (Oxford: Oxford University Press, 1983).
2. Ibid., p. 87.
3. Ibid., pp. 39–55.
4. Ibid., p. 64.
5. Ibid., p. 44.
6. Matthew 5:18.
7. Gaeger, *Origin of Anti-Semitism*, p. 124.
8. Ibid., p. 124.
9. Acts 15:1.
10. II Peter 3:14–55.
11. Acts 23:6, 26:6.
12. II Corinthians 11:24.
13. John 8:44ff.
14. I Corinthians 1:5, 21.
15. It needed, indeed, an Aristotle to build a bridge from the *Ephemeral*, the *Concrete*, to the *Eternal*, the

Entelecheia: the actualization of the Potentiality. For it was Aristotle's bold move to bring the lofty Platonic world of the ideas down to earth. For Aristotle, the idea is burned in the concrete, his system established the immanence of the Ideal within the Real. All "Becoming" is thus in Aristotle's vision an actualization of an inherent potentiality. All change consists of a substratum of matter that acquires form: matter being inert and vacuous does only exist when impregnated by form. As in typical male-oriented societies, which Greece became after the Dorian invasion, Aristotle declares that the form, the male principle impregnates, so to speak, matter (the female: matter = *mater*). In the same fashion as in the patriarchal society of the old Israelites, the Father God hovers (lies) over the desolate waste, the chaos, the female principle. This male orientation is vividly expressed in the Mesopotamian myth of the divinity of Marduk, who established his overlordship over the world by defeating first his mother, Tiamat, who reigned as a real matriarch over the world before him. Marduk represents a dynamic, creative intelligence, the Aristotelian Form, while Tiamat is inertia, the dead weight, the Aristotelian potentiality that has to be actualized. With allegorical sexual symbolism, the male-female confrontation ends in the defeat of matriarchy: "She opened her mouth to swallow him, he drove his evil wind into her mouth, wide open and distending her belly. An arrow shot into her gullet, cutting through her inside and tore her heart asunder." (Norman Cohn, *Cosmos and Chaos* [1993] p. 96.)

16. It is clear when we discuss Gnosticism that we only refer to those Gnostic systems that deal with Christology and the Old Testamental God. Insofar as it is a personalized religious movement, there are many Gnostic systems that go in different directions (cf. V. Bentley Layton *The Gnostic Scriptures,* 1987) based on a mystic individualistic point of view.

17. Elaine Pagels, *The Gnostic Gospels* (NY: Vintage Books, 1989), p. 114.

18. Deuteronomy 30:19.

19. In a certain sense, Judaism owes the rehabilitation of Jahve to the Catholic doctrine. Had Gnosticism prevailed, Judeo-Christianity would not have become the cornerstone of Western civilization.

20. John 13:27.

21. John 13:18.

22. John 6:70–71.

23. Hyam Maccoby, *The Sacred Executioner* (London: Thames and Hudson, 1982), p. 22.

24. Genesis 3:17.

25. Genesis 4:2.

26. John 13:20.

27. Charles Guignebert, *Jesus* (Paris: 1933). Guignebert was the most eminent Christologist at the Sorbonne in the 1920s and 1930s.

28. Act 1:26 and Luke 10:11.

29. John Dominic Crossant, *Who Killed Jesus?* (San Francisco: HarperCollins, 1995), p. 71.

30. Matthew 26:24, Mark 14:21.

31. Matthew 16:23.

32. Anton Orel, *Judaismus, der Weltgeschichliche Gegensatz zum Christentum* (Graz, 1934); Joseph Görlich, "Ein Katholik gegen Dollfus' Österrich," in *Jahrbuch der Geschichte der Deutschen Jugend Bewegung,* 1971.

33. When the concentration camps were opened in 1945, and the gas chambers revealed the horrifying crimes committed there, a shudder overwhelmed the Christian world. An awareness arose that a new dialogue with the Jewish people had to start. Such a moment offered itself in the 1960s. The Jews were represented by a group, proud of being in the process of having their own country after centuries of a diasporic past. The church was represented by two high-minded personalities of good will toward the Jewish people, two men of highest moral standards: the Italian Pope Giovanni XXIII, and the German Cardinal Augustin Bea S.J.

Further Questions

1. Do you think other sorts of genocide may have had the sort of basis in the metaphysical views of the perpetrators that White attributes to anti-Semitism and the holocaust? How would you go investigating or testing such a claim?:
2. Why do you think genocide happens? Compare this essay with Stanley Milgram's "Obedience to Authority" in Part I of this book. How does Milgram's psychological explanation compare with White's explanation? Do the religious and metaphysical issues contradict or complement the psychological issues?

Further Readings

White, John. *Renaissance Cavalier.* New York: Philosophical Library, 1959. A study of the notion of the "ideal man," from classical to modern times in relation to what happened (and still is happening) in relation to education. Should the goal of education be "the development of personal facilities," or should education consider the individual as a member of the community to which he belongs?

Arendt, Hannah. *The Origins of Totalitarianism*. New York: Humanities Press, 1951. The famous German-Jewish political philosopher (she was a student of Husserl and Heidegger) traces in this pivotal work the rise of imperialism and anti-semitism in nineteenth-century Europe and the subsequent emergence of Nazi and Bolshevik dictatorships.

Amoralism   77

RICHARD GARNER

Richard Garner teaches philosophy at Ohio State University. He has combined his work in ethics, the philosophy of language, and Asian philosophy in a book, *Beyond Morality* (Temple University Press, 1993). In this selection, which includes some sections from this book, Garner introduces a position he calls "amoralism." He argues that amoralism is a more plausible stance than forms of moralism that rely on the notion of intrinsic value or objective obligation. Garner concludes by suggesting that informed, compassionate amoralism is capable of guiding us to a very satisfactory existence, without the deception and the rhetoric that are the hallmarks of moralism.

Reading Questions

1. Explain Garner's distinction between the moralist and the amoralist.
2. Argue for or against the claim that an impasse is the natural endstate of a philosophical dispute.
3. How does Garner understand the claim that something is "intrinsically valuable"?
4. What must one believe to be classified as a "crazy objectivist"?
5. What ways have moralists devised to attack amoralism and amoralists?
6. What, according to Garner, is wrong with morality? Do you agree with this claim?

1. THE THREAT OF AMORALISM

Moral judgment belongs, as does religious judgment, to a level of ignorance at which even the concept of the real, the distinction between the real and the imaginary, is lacking. (Nietzsche, *Twilight of the Idols,* p. 55).

But whatsoever is the object of any man's appetite or desire, that is it which he for his part calls *good;* and the object of his hate and aversion, *evil;* and of his contempt, *vile* and *inconsiderable.* For these words of *good, evil,* and *contemptible* are ever used with relation to the person that uses them, there being nothing simply and absolutely so, nor any common rule of good and evil to be taken from the nature of the objects themselves. . . . (Hobbes, *Leviathan,* 53) Subhuti, though we speak of "goodness" the Tathagata [Buddha] declares

This selection was written especially for this volume and is included by kind permission of the author.

that there is no goodness, such is merely a name. (The Buddha, *The Diamond Sutra*, Section 23, in Price and Wong, 1969)

WHAT IF NIETZSCHE, HOBBES, and the Buddha are right? What if nothing is good or bad, right or wrong, permitted or forbidden? What if there are no rights, no obligations, no virtues or vices? What if our valueless world is filled with valueless beings acting from their ignorance and their desires, and subject to morality only because they have not seen that it is a convenient fiction, a noble lie, a paternalistic deception?

The problem with such categorical denial of morality and value is that almost no one believes it. "Goodness" may be only a "name," but it is a powerful and a useful one. Perhaps, then, we should not say that nothing is good, but only that nothing is good *in itself,* or good independent of some relation to human desires and standards. Rather than flat-out denying morality, we might try to affirm it, with the acknowledgement that it is a conventional human creation. "Things are good and bad, right and wrong, permitted and forbidden," we might say, "but only because *people* prefer, command, permit, and forbid them." Moral rules and rights are genuine, but they are genuine *artifacts*—things we create and then embody in our cultures and our language.

Sensible as this might be, this humanized and relativized way of looking at value and obligation will never replace the original. When morality is taken to be a human artifact, it loses its ability to bind anyone who chooses not to be bound, or to motivate anyone who wishes to resist. If duty is merely the command of our group, it is too easy to ask what gives *them* the right to make commands, and what gives *us* the duty to obey. If all "You ought to" amounts to is "I (or we) want you to," then you can just say "So what?"

So, both a strong form of amoralism (nothing is good or bad, right or wrong) and a milder form of relativistic morality (things are good or bad, right or wrong, relative to desires, agreements, standards, etc.) will alarm anyone who wants morality to provide more than an optional guide to conduct. And this, I would say, includes most people. We live in a sea of moral concepts, distinctions, slogans, assumptions, principles, dogmas, and guilt.

We assume that any competent adult knows the difference between right and wrong. We also assume that there is a difference between right and wrong. This belief is so strong and so widespread that moral philosophers use sentences like *Hitler was evil, It is wrong to incinerate cats, kick dogs, or knowingly and willingly torture innocents,* as starting points, not conclusions, of their arguments. Nobody, they assume, could reasonably doubt any of these things.

2. MORAL DISCUSSIONS

How could amoralists have come to a conclusion that goes so against everything we hear from our parents, preachers, professors, and peers? Well, perhaps they have noticed what happens when people argue about moral issues. The idea that rational beings have reasons for their actions and beliefs influences many of the conventions that govern our interactions. It opens the way for discussion, persuasion, debate, criticism, and compromise. Also, the idea that rational beings will or should have reasons for their moral judgments makes it easy to support a convention that allows us to ask our fellow rational beings for their reasons.

The surprising thing about the demand for reasons is the ease with which it can be satisfied. When we make a moral judgment in public we are usually ready with argument-fragments, slogans, and information to offer in defense of our claim. If we take the trouble, we can even come up with a moral defense for actions we think are morally wrong.

Why are we so good at this? Why are we so rarely at a loss for words when it is time to defend moral judgments? It may be because we have learned to expect those who do not agree with us to ask for reasons. Knowing this, we are prepared. Fortunately, the reason we produce doesn't have to be a super-reason, powerful enough to convince any rational being. Almost anything not obviously false or irrelevant will do for a start. If we associate with people who share our moral beliefs and pay attention to what they say, we will develop an arsenal of reasons that will see us through most challenges.

There are many issues that have attracted the attention of moralists, moral philosophers, and concerned citizens—abortion, capital punishment, sexual morality, human rights, the treatment of animals, and all the problems flowing from our attempts to distribute the benefits and burdens of society. Around each of these issues there has developed a pattern of disputation involving everything from one-line slogans to complex and subtle arguments. Many of these slogans are insulting in their simplicity (abortion is murder, an eye for an eye), and many of the arguments play fast and loose with language and hidden assumptions. But the one-liners sink in, and the arguments will be similar enough to standard patterns of rational debate to satisfy the minimal demands made upon those who wish to hold a moral position.

Arguments about moral issues can develop in many directions. Some degenerate into theological disputes and others come to an impasse over some difficult or abstract problem in ethics or in philosophy (What is the nature of goodness? What is a person?). Sometimes moral arguments evolve into disputes about meaning (the meaning of "life," or of "rights," or of "humane"), and often they come to a standstill over some factual claim that neither side can prove or disprove (Does capital punishment decrease the number of offenses or only the number of offenders?).

When we move from the question of whether it is wrong to eat animals to the question of what a person is, or from the question of whether or not abortion is wrong to the question of when human life begins, we have replaced a difficult question about morality with a certifiably unanswerable philosophical question. This does not bring the argument any closer to a resolution. Usually it turns out that our theory of human life or of personhood takes the shape it must to bolster our more personal and practical beliefs about diet and abortion. This shift to a more "basic" question will usually guarantee that the protagonists will arrive at an impasse—the natural endstate of a philosophical dispute.

While the sorry state of moral "discussions" should lead us to wonder about the objectivity of morality, it does not prove anything. I suggest, however, that if we look more closely at the character of moral judgments themselves, at what they are, and at what they are supposed to do, we will

find other reasons to suspect that Nietzsche, Hobbes, and the Buddha are right, and that "moral judgments agree with religious ones in believing in realities which are no realities."

3. INTRINSIC VALUE

Kant said that a "good will" is not good because of its effects, it is good in itself. "When it is considered in itself, then it is to be esteemed very much higher than anything which it might ever bring about merely in order to favor some inclination, or even the sum total of all inclinations." Even if a good will is powerless to attain its end, it would "like a jewel, still shine by its own light as something which has its full value in itself." (Kant, 394)

We use the expressions "intrinsically good," "good in itself," and "good as an end" almost interchangeably. Intrinsic goodness is a kind of goodness a thing has apart from its relation to other things. A thing is *intrinsically good* if it is good no matter what else is true and no matter how people feel about it. A thing is *good in itself* when it is good just because of the kind of thing it is—its goodness is, presumably, part of its nature. Finally, a thing is *good as an end* when it is worth choosing apart from any consequences that might flow from choosing it, or use to which it might be put.

This might "explain" the intrinsic part, but it doesn't explain the goodness. Nor is it clear what would—which is why some have taken goodness to be unanalyzable. But what needs to be explained is what can be explained, and what can be explained is our use of moral language, and our habit of thinking of things as good and bad. We did not learn to use the words "good" and "bad" in isolation, but as a part of learning a language and a set of social practices, standards, rules, and exceptions. We begin by believing what we are told, and by accepting any value that does not cause us immediate and intense discomfort—and some that do. Our common language and system of values unites us and provides a setting for our individuality, and our socialization makes us human, so these things are not to be scorned. But we can understand and participate in most conventional ways of using "good" and "bad" without becoming involved with the concept of "intrinsic value." Since we all want to live and to be healthy and happy, we can (and do) say that "good food" and "good habits" are food and habits that promote health and happiness, and that bad food and habits accomplish the reverse.

But what do we say when someone asks us what makes health and happiness good? It is not easy to say what happiness is good *for*, and if we do think of something, we will soon find ourselves facing the further question of what *that* is good for, and so on till we run out of answers or time. The claim that something is *intrinsically good* is designed to stop this game by heading off further questions. If a thing is intrinsically good, it is good, period, and nobody gets to ask "What makes it good?" or "What is it good for?"

But even if that is how it is supposed to work, how are we to understand this question-stopper? Since we learned to use "good" to evaluate actual items according to familiar (if implicit) standards and purposes, why should we think we can extend it to encompass such an abstract notion as intrinsic goodness? When there are established standards it is natural to rank things on the basis of those standards. Something is a good apple if it is tart, large, unmarked, and wormless. A car that does not break down and is fast (or easy on gas, or impressive) is a good car. Bill is a good plumber and Bob is a good friend. But what is it for a thing to be, not a good X, and not "good for Y" or "good as Z," but just good, period—good-in-itself? If someone were to speak up for the "intrinsically useful," that which is useful in itself, useful as an end, we would see the joke. Why do we not see it when we speak of intrinsic value?

4. CRAZY OBJECTIVITY

We all have preferences and standards, and it is a common belief that we prefer things because they are preferable and like things because they are good. The idea that we *give* value to things by valuing them, that values are "conventional" or "subjective," makes it impossible to see the differ-

ence between the desired and the desirable. Wisely or foolishly, what we want is objective value—value that exists apart from what we have come to desire, value that does not depend on changing conventions and individual whims, value that commands our respect and requires our support.

This desire, or need, for objective value leads us to embrace a kind of fundamentalism about value that I call crazy objectivity. When John Mackie argued that values are not objective, not part of the "fabric of the world," he was attacking crazy objectivity. (Mackie, 15) Objective values, he said, would have to be "entities or qualities or relations of a very strange sort, utterly different from anything else in the universe," and any awareness of them "would have to be by some special faculty of moral perception or intuition, utterly different from our ordinary way of knowing everything else." (Mackie, 38) What makes crazy objectivity really crazy is the belief in what Mackie called objective prescriptivity. If judgments of value and obligation were objectively prescriptive, then something about the way things are would "require" us to do or to choose some things; in Mackie's words, some situations would have a kind of "ought-to-be-ness" or "ought-not-to-be-ness" about them.

5. ATTACKS ON AMORALISM

Amoralism, the rejection of the characteristic claims of moralists, is neither a philosophy of life nor a guide to conduct. But neither is moralism, as such. Everything depends on which moral principles a given moralist holds, and then on how closely those principles are followed and on how loosely they are interpreted. I believe that we can easily do without morality if we can supplement our amoralism with *compassion, a desire to know what is going on, and a disposition to be non-duplicitous.* By "doing without morality" I do not mean doing without kindness or turning our selves into sociopathic predators. I simply mean rejecting the idea that there are intrinsic values, non-conventional obligations, objective duties, natural rights, or any of the other peremptory items moralists cherish. To reject morality is to reject these beliefs, but this is something very few people have ever been willing to do. The vast majority of those who first hear about amoralism leap to attack it, or some version of it they construct to serve as a docile sacrifice to their own version of moralism.

Bernard Williams opens his book *Morality* with an attempt to answer "the amoralist," who is "supposedly immune to moral considerations." We can't expect philosophers under the influence of moralism to wear themselves out constructing a coherent challenge to their own presuppositions. But their responses to their opponents are typically directed against weak versions of foolish positions, against those who violate (or promote the violation of) conventional moral standards, and against selfishness and heartless misanthropy. Amoralists are imagined to be inconsiderate monsters, as when Williams suggests that the amoralist may not even be "recognizably human."

Critics who confuse the amoralist with the pathological egoist say that amoralists are necessarily selfish and either lack compassion or feel it arbitrarily and sporadically. But what we believe about morality is independent of how much we care about others and of how many of them we care about. When Williams says that the amoralist "in his pure form" is "immune to moral considerations," he means that the amoralist is totally unmoved by the suffering of others. This amoralist has no "inclination to tell the truth or keep promises if it does not suit him to do so." By way of contrast, when *I* say that amoralists are "immune to moral considerations," I mean that while they may actively and regularly promote the welfare of others, they aren't led to do this by moral beliefs. My amoralists may be moved by the suffering of others, but not by being told that suffering is intrinsically bad, or that others have a moral right to help.

We are right to worry about people who are unmoved by the pain of others. We understand Williams when he calls them psychopaths and monsters. But they aren't psychopaths and monsters because they "reject morality," they are psychopaths and monsters because they don't care about the suffering of others. Someone bound only by the dictates of some morality and utterly without affection, sympathy, or kindness would be a monster too—a moral monster.

Sometimes amoralists are presented as denying some obvious truth, or asserting something too horrible to be accepted. Gilbert Harman says that extreme nihilism (the belief that "nothing is ever right or wrong, just or unjust, good or bad") implies

> that there are no moral constraints—that everything is permitted. As Dostoevsky observes, it implies that there is nothing wrong with murdering your father. It also implies that slavery was not unjust and that Hitler's extermination camps were not immoral. These are not easy conclusions to accept. (Harman, 11)

Whatever extreme nihilists might mean by saying that nothing is right or wrong, just or unjust, good or bad, they will not want to deny that there are conventional moral constraints, and that law, custom, other people, and our own rules forbid many things.

The amoralist is not denying that we have a conventional morality, and the moralist is saying more than that we have created sets of conventional rules and rights. The moralist insists that the immorality of death camps and slavery does not depend on what people happen to think, want, believe, buy into, or choose. The amoralist can join with the moralist in this rejection of subjectivism, but must demur when the moralist adds that death camps and slavery are *really* wrong, not just unacceptable by conventions we adopt from our society or inherit from our genes.

Amoralists who do not want to misrepresent themselves will not say that the extermination camps were immoral, however much they may detest them. But they will also hesitate to say that the camps were "not immoral" because those who hear this may take them to accept the institution of morality and to be giving not unfavorable marks to extermination camps. If we do not want to be mistaken for moralists, we must avoid moralist ways of expressing ourselves. We can be sure that plenty of amoralists give in to the temptation to exploit the power of moral language. Those who do are fair game for anyone who wants to score a point for moralism by exposing an amoralist committing morality. But when this happens, the problem is with the amoralist, not with amoralism.

Those who believe the amoralist is likely to exhibit antisocial behavior may try to think up techniques to make amoralists change their ways. Others are content to try to change amoralists' beliefs about morality, or at least to make amoralists acknowledge that they cannot rationally reject certain moral principles or values.

(1) *Argument.* In *Morality,* Bernard Williams looks for an answer to the "amoralist" he identifies as a psychopathic monster. Williams knows that *this* amoralist will not be moved by arguments, and that "the idea of arguing him into morality is surely idiotic." (Williams, 8) Accordingly, he supplies us with a less extreme amoralist—one it is, presumably, not idiotic to try to argue into morality. His example is the stereotype from a gangster movie (the mobster), "who cares about his mother, his child, even his mistress." He helps people, but only when he feels like it: he considers the interests of others, but not consistently or on any regular basis. Williams says that if "morality can be got off the ground rationally," we ought to be able to get it off the ground in an argument with someone like this. (Williams, 2)

The mobster cares about his close associates, but there is a wide gap between this feeling and the belief that he *ought* to care about people he doesn't even know, and yet another gap between that belief and any actual caring-behavior. The only thing the moralist can do is catch the mobster making some moral judgment of his own and then try to convince him that unless he makes similar judgments about relevantly similar cases he will have to add inconsistency to his list of crimes. If, however, the mobster knows how to argue, he knows enough to deny that the cases are relevantly similar, to withdraw his moral judgment, or to tell the moralist to get lost.

(2) *Persuasion.* It is not hard to persuade attentive, open-minded, non-defensive people to treat others with more consideration. We can describe suffering in detail and paint in unattractive colors the life of the person who profits from the misery of others. We can document the effects of crack addiction, state torture, death squads, and slaughterhouses.

Merely knowing that there are such things as death squads is very different from fully realizing that there are. To "realize" what the death squads

do is to go well beyond the words "There are death squads" and allow our imaginations and our memories to supply some horrible details. Because we are so often insulated by ignorance from the effects of what we do, or cause to be done, Peter Singer's few pictures of animals in labs and factory farms in his book *Animal Liberation* probably did more for animal welfare than all his arguments. But just as our arguments won't take hold unless our victim has the right principles, persuasion only works when we can appeal to desires or attitudes, some compassion, pity, or a spark of good will that already exists. Fortunately this is not a serious problem because few humans lack all such desires and feelings.

(3) *Coercion.* When argument and persuasion fail, we can either give up trying to control the offending behavior, or we can turn to force or fraud. Moralists who identify the amoralist with the pathological egoist, and then observe that arguments and pleas are useless with such a monster, sometimes conclude that we have no choice but to threaten him, and if necessary to isolate him, or even hunt him down and kill him. Needless to say, these extreme remedies are unnecessary to cope with the average amoralist, who probably has as many kind and generous impulses as the next person, or some informed and compassionate amoralist, who has more. Amoralists will not believe that laws can be given a moral justification, but they are not likely to want to live without them. Coercion by laws falls equally on the heads of moralists and amoralists, and both can be glad there are penalties for murder and for dumping toxic waste in the river.

(4) *Denial.* One way to combat amoralism is to show that some form of moralism is true, another is to attack amoralism, and a third is to deny that amoralism is a possible position. One way to argue for the third option is to say that to desire something is to value it, and that to value it is to think it is valuable. If this is so, then it will turn out that no one with desires can deny the reality of value. Similarly, someone might try to argue that the mere fact that we choose one course of action over another is enough to establish that we have moral principles.

Only sophistical tricks can help the moralist here because just as there is no non-fallacious path from the desired to the desirable, there is none from the fact that I desire or choose something to the fact that I think it is desirable. This is not to say that people who desire things do not think the things they desire are worthy of desiring. Often they do. It is just to remain sensitive to the fact that sometimes people realize that what they desire doesn't deserve to be desired.

Some moralists point not to the desires and choices of amoralists, but to their deeds. If "amoralists" behave as if they subscribe to moral principles, then why not conclude that they do, perhaps without realizing it? Amoralists who are fair can be accused of believing in justice, and amoralists who tell the truth and help others can be charged with holding the moral principles of truthfulness and beneficence.

But these accusations are easily answered. There is a respect in which amoralists do subscribe to moral principles, and a more important respect in which they do not. The non-duplicitous amoralist subscribes to a principle (non-duplicity) moralists might call a moral principle. But amoralists who adhere to non-duplicity as a policy will not subscribe to that policy as moralists do, because they will not see it as objectively binding. Amoralists who allow their principles of action to be called "moral principles" run the risk of giving the impression that they subscribe to the moralist assumptions that lie behind their moralist way of talking.

It makes more sense for an amoralist to resist the idea that the principle of non-duplicity is a moral principle, acknowledging only that others interpret it that way. If I have adopted some such principle as a non-moral and non-binding guideline, then I will be prepared to explain how I understand it, why I have adopted it, and why I recommend it to others, when I do. I am not prepared to give it a moral justification and neither, I suspect, is the moralist. Friendly and compassionate amoralists are helpful, truthful, and respectful without once thinking this practice is required by anything other than the way of acting they have chosen or accepted.

6. WHAT IS WRONG WITH MORALITY?

The conventions of morality are based on the widely held but mistaken assumption that the demands of morality are objectively authoritative, categorical, rational, justifiable, and sometimes universal. People are taught and encouraged to think of moral judgments as expressing such demands, and this teaching is reinforced by the presuppositions underlying the use of moral language. Nearly everyone assumes it would be dangerous not to have an objective morality, so even Mackie, who sees through the pretenses of the moral realists, spends the second half of his book trying to "invent right and wrong."

My suggestion is that we do not need morality. If morality requires objective prescriptivity and there is no such thing, then when we realize this we either have to abandon morality or agree to participate in a conspiracy to promote it as something we know it is not. It is risky, unnecessary, and more difficult than we think to control others by misleading them about the true character of the world, but this is exactly what we do when we continue to use moral language in a way that implies things we do not accept.

Moralists claim that morality beats compassion and kindness, since these feelings come and go. But morality only beats compassion and kindness if it makes good on its own ground, which it can't, and if it actually is capable of influencing behavior, which can be debated. Compassion, on the other hand, is a direct motivator, and it doesn't have to be justified. It is a way of looking, and a disposition to help. If you care about somebody, if you want them to be happy, there is nothing to prove and no problem about motivation. If you merely think it is your duty to help them, then it will always be possible to dig up some excuse for not doing anything.

So what is wrong with morality? It isn't what people think it is, and if they saw it for what it is, it wouldn't work. It encourages deception and even self-deception. Anything can be given a moral defense by a clever sophist, but no moral judgment can be conclusively established, no moral debate resolved once and for all. Morality can be (and has been) used to defend cruelty, selfishness, exploitation, and neglect. By itself morality is insufficient for motivation, and its actual contribution to any decision is far from clear. It is not necessary for the kind of behavior it is thought to be a device to promote, and since people can be conventionally good without believing in the objectivity of morality, it makes sense to consider some alternatives. *The* alternative is, and always has been (in one form or another), expanded sympathies, increased concern for others. I believe that if we could establish this "informed compassionate amoralism," we could leave morality, with its lies and its guilt, with its bogus heteronomy, its capacity for exploitation and rationalization, its unresolvable arguments, and its perpetual flirtation with religion, behind us. Freud was probably right when he called religion a childhood neurosis, but what he didn't say (because he didn't believe it) was that morality is an adolescent one.

Further Questions

1. Observe some actual moral discussions among your friends and associates. Do you think that Garner's characterization of moral argumentation is accurate?
2. Is it correct to say that the average person subscribes to some form of crazy objectivity?
3. What would it take to make a world without a belief in morality livable?

Further Readings

Garner, Richard. *Beyond Morality*. Philadelphia: Temple University Press, 1994. An extremely accessible and insightful argument for amoralism. Highly recommended.
Mackie, J. L. *Ethics: Inventing Right and Wrong*. Harmondsworth: Penguin, 1977. An earlier version of a view like Garner's.

Part XIII

Values

IMAGINE MAKING A PERFECT VERSION OF YOURSELF. No flaws!
What would you choose to keep the same and what would you choose to change, from the way you are now?

Most of us value things like money, fame, health, happiness, and so on. But these are things we *have,* not things we *are.* What do we value about ourselves?

In dealing with others, things like honesty, openness, and sincerity tend to be high on our lists. Do we value these things as highly in ourselves?

Suppose you were *completely* honest, open, sincere—always, with everyone. What would your life be like? Would you like that version of yourself? That is the question to which we now turn.

78   The Myth of Gyges's Ring

PLATO

A brief biography of Plato appears on p. 2.

In the following selection, from Plato's classic treatise on political philosophy, *The Republic*, Glaucon, one of the characters in the dialogue, argues to Socrates that humans are egoists, by nature strongly inclined to promote their own self-interest over the interests of others. Glaucon claims that the only reason supposedly just people are just is that they lack the power to be unjust and get away with it. To illustrate his point, Glaucon tells the story of Gyges.

Reading Questions

1. What, according to Glaucon, is the nature and origin of justice?
2. Is the story of Gyges a good illustration of Glaucon's theory? Why or why not?

GLAUCON: IF YOU PLEASE, THEN, I will revive the argument of Thrasymachus. And first I will speak of the nature and origin of justice according to the common view of them. Secondly, I will show that all men who practice justice do so against their will, of necessity, but not as a good. And thirdly, I will argue that there is reason in this view, for the life of the unjust is after all better far than the life of the just—if what they say is true, Socrates, since I myself am not of their opinion. But still I acknowledge that I am perplexed when I hear the voices of Thrasymachus and myriads of others dinning in my ears; and, on the other hand, I have never yet heard the superiority of justice to injustice maintained by any one in a satisfactory way. I want to hear justice praised in respect of itself; then I shall be satisfied, and you are the person from whom I think that I am most likely to hear this; and therefore I will praise the unjust life to the utmost of my power, and my manner of speaking will indicate the manner in which I desire to hear you

too praising justice and censuring injustice. Will you say whether you approve of my proposal?

Socrates: Indeed I do; nor can I imagine any theme about which a man of sense would oftener wish to converse.

Glaucon: I am delighted, he replied, to hear you say so, and shall begin by speaking, as I proposed, of the nature and origin of justice.

They say that to do injustice is, by nature, good; to suffer injustice, evil; but that the evil is greater than the good. And so when men have both done and suffered injustice and have had experience of both, not being able to avoid the one and obtain the other, they think that they had better agree among themselves to have neither; hence there arise laws and mutual covenants; and that which is ordained by law is termed by them lawful and just. This they affirm to be the origin and nature of justice:—it is a mean or compromise, between the best of all, which is to do injustice and not be punished, and the worst of all, which is to suffer injustice

From The Dialogues of Plato, *trans. Benjamin Jowett (New York: Scribner's, 1889).*

without the power of retaliation; and justice, being at a middle point between the two, is tolerated not as a good, but as the lesser evil, and honoured by reason of the inability of men to do injustice. For no man who is worthy to be called a man would ever submit to such an agreement if he were able to resist; he would be mad if he did. Such is the received account, Socrates, of the nature and origin of justice.

Now that those who practice justice do so involuntarily and because they have not the power to be unjust will best appear if we imagine something of this kind: having given both to the just and the unjust power to do what they will, let us watch and see whither desire will lead them; then we shall discover in the very act the just and unjust man to be proceeding along the same road, following their interest, which all natures deem to be their good, and are only diverted into the path of justice by the force of law. The liberty which we are supposing may be most completely given to them in the form of such a power as is said to have been possessed by Gyges the ancestor of Croesus the Lydian. According to the tradition, Gyges was a shepherd in the service of the king of Lydia; there was a great storm, and an earthquake made an opening in the earth at the place where he was feeding his flock. Amazed at the sight, he descended into the opening, where, among other marvels, he beheld a hollow brazen horse, having doors, at which he stooping and looking in saw a dead body of stature, as appeared to him, more than human, and having nothing on but a gold ring; this he took from the finger of the dead and reascended. Now the shepherds met together, according to custom, that they might send their monthly report about the flocks to the king; into their assembly he came having the ring on his finger, and as he was sitting among them he chanced to turn the collet of the ring inside his hand, when instantly he became invisible to the rest of the company and they began to speak of him as if he were no longer present. He was astonished at this, and again touching the ring he turned the collet outwards and reappeared; he made several trials of the ring, and always with the same result — when he turned the collet inwards he became invisible, when outwards he reappeared. Whereupon he contrived to be chosen one of the messengers who were sent to the court; where as soon as he arrived he seduced the queen, and with her help conspired against the king and slew him, and took the kingdom. Suppose now that there were two such magic rings, and the just put on one of them and the unjust the other; no man can be imagined to be of such an iron nature that he would stand fast in justice. No man would keep his hands off what was not his own when he could safely take what he liked out of the market, or go into houses and lie with any one at his pleasure, or kill or release from prison whom he would, and in all respects be like a God among men. Then the actions of the just would be as the actions of the unjust; they would both come at last to the same point. And this we may truly affirm to be a great proof that a man is just, not willingly or because he thinks that justice is any good to him individually, but of necessity, for wherever any one thinks that he can safely be unjust, there he is unjust. For all men believe in their hearts that injustice is far more profitable to the individual than justice, and he who argues as I have been supposing, will say that they are right. If you could imagine any one obtaining this power of becoming invisible, and never doing any wrong or touching what was another's, he would be thought by the lookers-on to be a most wretched idiot, although they would praise him to one another's faces, and keep up appearances with one another from a fear that they too might suffer injustice. Enough of this.

Now, if we are to form a real judgment of the life of the just and unjust, we must isolate them; there is no other way; and how is the isolation to be effected? I answer: Let the unjust man be entirely unjust, and the just man entirely just; nothing is to be taken away from either of them, and both are to be perfectly furnished for the work of their respective lives. First, let the unjust be like other distinguished masters of craft; like the skillful pilot or physician, who knows intuitively his own powers and keeps within their limits, and who, if he fails at any point, is able to recover himself. So let the unjust make his unjust attempts in the right way, and lie hidden if he means to be great in his injustice (he who is found out is nobody): for the highest reach of injustice is: to be deemed just when you are not. Therefore I say that in the perfectly unjust man we must assume the most perfect injustice; there is to be no deduction, but we must allow him, while doing the most unjust acts, to have acquired the greatest reputation for justice. If he have taken a false step he must be able to recover himself; he must be one who can speak with effect, if any of his deeds come to light, and who can force his way where force is required by his courage and strength, and command of money and friends. And at his side let us place the just man in his nobleness and simplicity, wishing, as Aeschylus says, to be and not to seem good. There must be no seeming, for if he seem to be just he will be honoured and rewarded, and then we shall now know whether he is just for the sake of justice or for the sake of honours and rewards; therefore, let him be clothed in justice only, and have no other covering; and he must be imagined in a state of life the opposite of the former. Let him be the best of men, and let him be thought the worst; then he will have been put to the proof; and we shall see whether he will be affected by the fear of infamy and its consequences. And let him continue thus to the hour of death; being just and seeming to be unjust. When both have reached the uttermost extreme, the one of justice and the other of injustice, let judgment be given which of them is the happier of the two.

Socrates: Heavens! my dear Glaucon, I said, how energetically you polish them up for the decision, first one and then the other, as if they were two statues.

Glaucon: I do my best, he said. And now that we know what they are like there is no difficulty in tracing out the sort of life which awaits either of them. This I will proceed to describe; but as you may think the description a little too coarse, I ask you to suppose, Socrates, that the words which follow are not mine.—Let me put them into the mouths of the eulogists of injustice: they will tell you that the just man who is thought unjust will be scourged, racked, bound—will have his eyes burnt out; and, at last, after suffering every kind of evil, he will be impaled: Then he will understand that he ought to seem only, and not to be, just; the words of Aeschylus may be more truly spoken of the unjust than of the just. For the unjust is pursuing a reality; he does not live with a view to appearances—he wants to be really unjust and not to seem only:—

His mind has a soil deep and fertile.
Out of which spring his prudent counsels.

In the first place, he is thought just, and therefore bears rule in the city; he can marry whom he will, and give in marriage to whom he will; also he can trade and deal where he likes, and always to his own advantage, because he has no misgivings about injustice; and at every contest, whether in public, or private, he gets the better of his antagonists, and gains at their expense, and is rich, and out of his gains he can benefit his friends, and harm his enemies; moreover, he can offer sacrifices, and dedicate gifts to the gods abundantly and magnificently, and can honour the gods or any man whom he wants to honour in a far better style than the just, and therefore he is likely to be dearer than they are to the gods. And thus, Socrates, gods and men are said to unite in making the life of the unjust better than the life of the just. . . .

Socrates: Now that we've gotten this far, I said, let's go back to that statement made at the beginning, which brought us here: that it pays for a man to be perfectly unjust if he appears to be just. Isn't that what someone said?

Yes.

Then since we've agreed what power justice and injustice each have, let's have a discussion with him.

How?

By molding in words an image of the soul, so that the one who said that will realize what he was saying.

What kind of image?

Oh, something like those natures the myths tell us were born in ancient times—the Chimaera, Scylla, Cerberus, and others in which many different shapes were supposed to have grown into one.

So they tell us, he said.

Then mold one figure of a colorful, many-headed beast with heads of wild and tame animals growing in a circle all around it; one that can change and grow all of them out of itself.

That's a job for a skilled artist. Still, words mold easier than wax or clay, so consider it done.

And another of a lion, and one of a man. Make the first by far the biggest, the second second largest.

That's easier, and already done.

Now join the three together so that they somehow grow.

All right.

Next mold the image of one, the man, around them all, so that to someone who can't see what's inside but looks only at the container it appears to be a single animal, man.

I have.

Then shall we inform the gentleman that when he says it pays for this man to be unjust, he's saying that it profits him to feast his multifarious beast and his lion and make them grow strong, but to starve and enfeeble the man in him so that he gets dragged wherever the animals lead him, and instead of making them friends and used to each other, to let them bite and fight and eat each other?

That's just what he's saying by praising injustice.

The one who says justice pays, however, would be saying that he should practice and say whatever will give the most mastery to his inner man, who should care for the many-headed beast like a farmer, raising and domesticating its tame heads and preventing the wild ones from growing, making the lion's nature his partner and ally, and so raise them both to be friends to each other and to him.

That's exactly what he means by praising justice.

So in every way the commender of justice is telling the truth, the other a lie. Whether we examine pleasure, reputation, or profit, we find that the man who praises justice speaks truly, and one who disparages it disparages sickly and knows nothing of what he disparages.

I don't think he does at all.

Then let's gently persuade him—his error wasn't intended—by asking him a question: "Shouldn't we say that the traditions of the beautiful and the ugly have come about like this: Beautiful things are those that make our bestial parts subservient to the human—or rather, perhaps, to the divine—part of our nature, while ugly ones are those that enslave the tame to the wild?" Won't he agree?

If he takes my advice.

On this argument then, can it pay for a man to take money unjustly if that means making his best part a slave to the worst? If it wouldn't profit a man to sell his son or his daughter into slavery—to wild and evil men at that—even if he got a fortune for it, then if he has no pity on himself and enslaves the most godlike thing in him to the most godless and polluted, isn't he a wretch who gets bribed for gold into a destruction more horrible than Euriphyle's, who sold her husband's life for a necklace?

Much more horrible, said Glaucon.

. . . everyone is better off being ruled by the godlike and intelligent; preferably if he has it inside, but if not, it should be imposed on him from without so that we may all be friends and as nearly alike as possible, all steered by the same thing.

Yes, and we're right, he said.

Law, the ally of everyone in the city, clearly intends the same thing, as does the rule of children, which forbids us to let them be free until we've instituted a regime in them as in a city. We serve their best part with a similar part in us, install a like guardian and ruler in them, and only then set them free.

Clearly.

Then how, by what argument, Glaucon, can we say that it pays for a man to be unjust or self indulgent or to do something shameful to get more money or power if by doing so he makes himself worse?

We can't, he said.

And how can it pay to commit injustice without getting caught and being punished? Doesn't getting away with it make a man even worse? Whereas if a man gets caught and punished, his beastlike part is taken in and tamed, his tame part is set free, and his whole soul acquires justice and temperance and knowledge. Therefore his soul recovers its best nature and attains a state more honorable than the state the body attains when it acquires health and strength and beauty, by as much as the soul is more honorable than the body.

Absolutely.

Then won't a sensible man spend his life directing all his efforts to this end?

Further Questions

1. *Psychological egoism* is a view about how people actually do behave. It is the view that all people always behave selfishly, at least in all of their voluntary, deliberate behavior. On this view, even when people act in a way apparently calculated to benefit others, they are actually motivated by the desire to benefit themselves. *Ethical egoism*, by contrast, is a view about how people ought to behave. It is the view that people have no obligation to behave in any

way that is not in their own self-interest, regardless of the effect of their behavior on others. Is Glaucon a psychological egoist? An ethical egoist?

2. Give the best objection you can give to psychological egoism. To ethical egoism. Do you think that your objections are good objections? If not, why not? Is so, how could a psychological or ethical egoist most plausibly reply to your objections?

Further Readings

Plato, *Republic,* trans. G. M. A. Grube. Indianapolis: Hackett Publishing Co., 1974. A good translation of Plato's timeless classic.

Rachels, James. "Egoism and Moral Skepticism," in Steven M. Cahn, ed., *A New Introduction to Philosophy.* New York: Harper & Row, 1971; reprinted in Mark Timmons, ed., *Conduct and Character.* Belmont, CA: Wadsworth, 1995. An excellent account of what is at issue in Glaucon's argument.

79   Virtue and Character

ARISTOTLE

Aristotle was born in 384 B.C. in Stagira on the northeast coast of Thrace. His father was the physician to the King of Macedonia. When he was seventeen years old, Aristotle went to Athens to enroll in Plato's Academy, where he spent the next twenty years. In 348 B.C. Aristotle left the Academy and went to Assos, near Troy, and married the ruler's niece, who bore him a daughter. After he returned to Athens, he had a son, Nichomachus, by another woman. In 343 B.C. Philip of Madedon invited Aristotle to become the tutor of his son Alexander, who was then thirteen years old, and who later became Alexander the Great. When Alexander ascended the throne, Aristotle returned to Athens and founded his own school, the Lyceum, where he remained for twelve years, teaching and writing. He died at the age of sixty-one.

In this selection, from his *Nicomachean Ethics,* Aristotle first argues that a happy or good life consists of a life of activity in accordance with virtue, which includes those traits that enable people to live well in communities. In Aristotle's view, although intellectual virtues may be taught, moral virtues must be learned by living. Moral virtues are good habits and are the best way to ensure personal well-being (*eudaimonia,* happiness), acquired by living well, provided one is fortunate enough to be living in a flourishing community. The morally virtuous life consists of striking a proper balance in how one lives, that is, in living according to the Golden Mean.

Reading Questions

1. What things does Aristotle consider and then reject as candidates for the highest good? Why does he reject them?
2. What reasons does Aristotle give for thinking that happiness is the highest good?
3. How does Aristotle think one should proceed in order to properly define happiness? How does he define it?

4. What, according to Aristotle, is the proper relationship between pleasure, virtue, and education?
5. What is the difference, in Aristotle's view, between the arts and the virtues?
6. What does Aristotle mean by calling virtue "a mean between extremes"? What extremes? And how does one tell what ought to be regarded as an extreme?
7. What advice does Aristotle give a person for discovering the mean in a given activity?

BOOK I
CHAPTER 1

EVERY ART AND EVERY SCIENTIFIC INQUIRY, and similarly every action and purpose, may be said to aim at some good. Hence the good has been well defined as that at which all things aim. But it is clear that there is a difference in ends; for the ends are sometimes activities, and sometimes results beyond the mere activities. Where there are ends beyond the action, the results are naturally superior to the action.

As there are various actions, arts, and sciences, it follows that the ends are also various. Thus health is the end of the medical art, a ship of shipbuilding, victory of strategy, and wealth of economics. It often happens that a number of such arts or sciences combine for a single enterprise, as the art of making bridles and all such other arts as furnish the implements of horsemanship combine for horsemanship, and horsemanship and every military action if for strategy; and in the same way, other arts or sciences combine for others. In all these cases, the ends of the master arts or sciences, whatever they may be, are more desirable than those of the sur-ordinate arts or sciences, as it is for the sake of the former that the latter are pursued. It makes no difference to the argument whether the activities themselves are the ends of the action, or something beyond the activities, as in the above mentioned sciences.

If it is true that in the sphere of action there is some end which we wish for its own sake, and for the sake of which we wish everything else, and if we do not desire everything for the sake of something else (for, if that is so, the process will go on *ad infinitum,* and our desire will be idle and futile), clearly this end will be good and the supreme good. Does it not follow then that the knowledge of this good is of great importance for the conduct of life? Like archers who have a mark at which to aim, shall we not have a better chance of attaining what we want? If this is so, we must endeavor to comprehend, at least in outline, what this good is, and what science or faculty makes its object.

It would seem that this is the most authoritative science. Such a kind is evidently the political, for it is that which determines what sciences are necessary in states, and what kinds should be studied, and how far they should be studied by each class of inhabitant. We see too that even the faculties held in highest esteem, such as strategy, economics, and rhetoric, are subordinate to it. Then since politics makes use of the other sciences and also rules what people may do and what they may not do, it follows that its end will comprehend the ends of the other sciences, and will therefore be the good of mankind. For even if the good of an individual is identical with the good of a state, yet the good of the state is evidently greater and more perfect to attain or to preserve. For though the good of an individual by himself is something worth working for, to ensure the good of a nation or a state is nobler and more divine.

CHAPTER 2

As every science and undertaking aims at some good, what is in our view the good at which political science aims, and what is the highest of all practical goods? As to its name there is, I may say, a general agreement. The masses and the cultured classes agree in calling it happiness, and conceive that "to live well" or "to do well" is the same thing as "to be happy." But as to what happiness is they do not agree. . . .

From The Dialogues of Plato, *trans. Benjamin Jowett (New York: Scribner's, 1889).*

CHAPTER 3

Men's conception of the good or of happiness may be read in the lives they lead. Ordinary or vulgar people conceive it to be a pleasure, and accordingly choose a life of enjoyment. For there are, we may say, three conspicuous types of life, the sensual, the political, and, thirdly, the life of thought. Now the mass of men present an absolutely slavish appearance, choosing the life of brute beasts. . . . Cultivated and energetic people, on the other hand, identify happiness with honor, as honor is the general end of political life. But this seems too superficial an idea for our present purpose; for honor depends more upon the people who pay it than upon the person to whom it is paid, and the good we feel is something which is proper to a man himself and cannot be easily taken away from him. Men too appear to seek honor in order to be assured of their own goodness. Accordingly, they seek it at the hands of the sage and of those who know them well, and they seek it on the ground of their virtue; clearly then, in their judgment at any rate, virtue is better than honor. Perhaps then we might look on virtue rather than honor as the end of political life. Yet even this idea appears not quite complete; for a man may possess virtue and yet be asleep or inactive throughout life, and not only so, but he may experience the greatest calamities and misfortunes. Yet no one would call such a life a life of happiness, unless he were maintaining a paradox. But we need not dwell further on this subject, since it is sufficiently discussed in popular philosophical treatises. The third life is the life of thought, which we will discuss later.

The life of money making is a life of constraint; and wealth is obviously not the good of which we are in quest; for it is useful merely as a means to something else. It would be more reasonable to take the things mentioned before—sensual pleasure, honor, and virtue—as ends than wealth, since they are things desired on their own account. Yet these too are evidently not ends. . . .

CHAPTER 5

But leaving this subject for the present, let us revert to the good of which we are in quest and consider what it may be. For it seems different in different activities or arts; it is one thing in medicine, another in strategy, and so on. What is the good in each of these instances? It is presumably that for the sake of which all else is done. In medicine this is health, in strategy victory, in architecture a house, and so on. In every activity and undertaking it is the end, since it is for the sake of the end that all people do whatever else they do. If then there is an end for all our activity, this will be the good to be accomplished; and if there are several such ends, it will be these.

Our argument is arrived by a different path at the same point as before; but we must endeavor to make it still plainer. Since there are more ends than one, and some of these ends—for example, wealth, flutes, and instruments generally—we desire as means to something else, it is evident that not all are final ends. But the highest good is clearly something final. Hence if there is only one final end, this will be the object of which we are in search; and if there are more than one, it will be the most final. We call that which is sought after for its own sake more final than that which is sought after as a means to something else; we call that which is never desired as a means to something else more final than things that are desired both for themselves and as means to something else. Therefore, we call absolutely final that which is always desired for itself and never as a means to something else. Now happiness more than anything else answers to this description. For happiness we always desire for its own sake and never as a means to something else, whereas honor, pleasure, intelligence, and every virtue we desire partly for their own sakes (for we should desire them independently of what might result from them), but partly also as means to happiness, because we suppose they will prove instruments of happiness. Happiness, on the other hand, nobody desires for the sake of these things, nor indeed as a means to anything else at all.

If we start from the point of view of self-sufficiency, we reach the same conclusion; for we assume that the final good is self-sufficient. By self-sufficiency we do not mean that a person leads a solitary life all by himself, but that he has parents, children, wife and friends and fellow citizens in general, as man is naturally a social being. Yet here it is necessary to set some limit; for if the circle must be extended to include ancestors, descendants, and friends' friends, it will go on indefinitely. Leaving this point, however, for future investigation, we call the self-sufficient that which, taken even by itself, makes life desirable and wanting nothing at all; and this is what we mean by happiness.

Again, we think happiness the most desirable of all things, and that not merely as one good thing among others. If it were only that, the addition of the smallest more good would increase its desirableness; for the addition would make an increase of goods, and the greater of two goods is always the more desirable. Happiness is something final and self-sufficient and the end of all action.

CHAPTER 6

Perhaps, however, it seems a commonplace to say that happiness is the supreme good; what is wanted is to define its nature a little more clearly. The best way of arriving at such a definition will probably be to ascertain the function of man. For, as with a flute player, a sculptor, or any artist, or in fact anybody who has a special function or activity, his goodness and excellence seem to lie in his function, so it would seem to be with man, if indeed he has a special function. Can it be said that, while a carpenter and a cobbler have special functions and activities, man, unlike them, is naturally functionless? Or, as the eye, the hand, the foot, and similarly each part of the body has a special function, so may man be regarded as having a special function apart from all these? What, then, can this function be? It is not life; for life is apparently something that man shares with plants; and we are looking for something peculiar to him. We must exclude therefore the life of nutrition and growth. There is next what may be called the life of sensation. But this too, apparently, is shared by man with horses, cattle, and all other animals. There remains what I may call the active life of the rational part of man's being. Now this rational part is twofold; one part is rational in the sense of being obedient to reason, and the other in the sense of possessing and exercising reason and intelligence. The active life too may be conceived of in two

ways, either as a state of character, or as an activity; but we mean by it the life of activity, as this seems to be the truer form of the conception.

The function of man then is activity of soul in accordance with reason, or not apart from reason. Now, the function of a man of a certain kind, and of a man who is good of that kind—for example, of a harpist and good harpist—are in our view the same in kind. This is true of all people of all kinds without exception, the superior excellence being only an addition to the function; for it is the function of a harpist to play the harp, and of a good harpist to play the harp well. This being so, if we define the function of man as a kind of life, and this life as an activity of the soul or a course of action in accordance with reason, and if the function of a good man is such activity of a good and noble kind, and if everything is well done when it is done in accordance with its proper excellence, it follows that the good of man is activity of soul in accordance with virtue, or, if there are more virtues than one, in accordance with the best and most complete virtue. But we must add the words "in a complete life." For as one swallow or one day does not make a spring, so one day or a short time does not make a man blessed or happy. . . .

Inasmuch as happiness is an activity of soul in accordance with perfect virtue, we must now consider virtue, as this will perhaps be the best way of studying happiness. . . . Clearly it is human virtue we have to consider; for the good of which we are in search is, as we said, human good, and the happiness, human happiness. By human virtue or excellence we mean not that of the body, but that of the soul, and by happiness we mean an activity of the soul. . . .

BOOK II
CHAPTER 1

Virtue then is twofold, partly intellectual and partly moral, and intellectual virtue is originated and fostered mainly by teaching; it demands therefore experience and time. Moral virtue on the other hand is the outcome of habit, and accordingly its name, *ethike,* is derived by a slight variation from *ethos,* habit. From this fact it is clear that moral virtue is not implanted in us by nature; for nothing that exists by nature can be transformed by habit. Thus a stone, that naturally tends to fall downwards, cannot be habituated or trained to rise upwards, even if we tried to train it by throwing it up ten thousand times. Nor again can fire be trained to sink downwards, nor anything else that follows one natural law be habituated or trained to follow another. It is neither by nature then nor in defiance of nature that virtues grow in us. Nature gives us the capacity to receive them, and that capacity is perfected by habit.

Again, if we take the various natural powers which belong to us, we first possess the proper faculties and afterwards display the activities. It is obviously so with the senses. Not by seeing frequently or hearing frequently do we acquire the sense of seeing or hearing; on the contrary, because we have the senses we make use of them; we do not get them by making use of them. But the virtues we get by first practicing them, as we do in the arts. For it is by doing what we ought to do when we study the arts that we learn the arts themselves; we become builders by building and harpists by playing the harp. Similarly, it is by doing just acts that we become just, by doing temperate acts that we become temperate, by doing brave acts that we become brave. The experience of states confirms this statement, for it is by training in good habits that lawmakers make the citizens good. This is the object all lawmakers have at heart; if they do not succeed in it, they fail of their purpose; and it makes the distinction between a good constitution and a bad one.

Again, the causes and means by which any virtue is produced and destroyed are the same; and equally so in any part. For it is by playing the harp that both good and bad harpists are produced; and the case of builders and others is similar, for it is by building well that they become good builders and by building badly that they become bad builders. If it were not so, there would be no need of anybody to teach them; they would all be born good or bad in their several crafts. The case of the virtues is the same. It is by our actions in dealings between man and man that we become either just or unjust. It is by our actions in the face of danger and by our

training ourselves to fear or to courage that we become either cowardly or courageous. It is much the same with our appetites and angry passions. People become temperate and gentle, others licentious and passionate, by behaving in one or the other way in particular circumstances. In a word, moral states are the results of activities like the states themselves. It is our duty therefore to keep a certain character in our activities, since our moral states depend on the differences in our activities. So the difference between one and another training in habits in our childhood is not a light matter, but important, or rather, all-important.

CHAPTER 2

. . . It must be admitted that all reasoning on matters of conduct must be like a sketch in outline; it cannot be scientifically exact. We began by laying down the principle that the kind of reasoning demanded in any subject must be such as the subject matter itself allows; and questions of conduct and expediency no more admit of hard and fast rules than questions of health.

If this is true of general reasoning on ethics, still more true is it that scientific exactitude is impossible in treating of particular ethical cases. They do not fall under any art or law, but the actors themselves have always to take account of circumstances, as much as in medicine or navigation. Still, although such is the nature of our present argument, we must try to make the best of it.

The first point to be observed is that in the matters we are now considering deficiency and excess are both fatal. It is so, we see, in questions of health and strength. (We must judge of what we cannot see by the evidence of what we do see.) Too much or too little gymnastic exercise is fatal to strength. Similarly, too much or too little meat and drink is fatal to health, whereas a suitable amount produces, increases, and sustains it. It is the same with temperance, courage, and other moral virtues. A person who avoids and is afraid of everything and faces nothing becomes a coward; a person who is not afraid of anything but is ready to face everything becomes foolhardy. Similarly, he who enjoys every pleasure and abstains from none is licentious; he who refuses all pleasures, like a boor, is an insensible sort of person. For temperance and courage are destroyed by excess and deficiency but preserved by the mean.

Again, not only are the causes and agencies of production, increase, and destruction in moral states the same, but the field of their activity is the same also. It is so in other more obvious instances, as, for example, strength; for strength is produced by taking a great deal of food and undergoing a great deal of exertion, and it is the strong man who is able to take most food and undergo most exertion. So too with the virtues. By abstaining from pleasures we become temperate, and, when we have become temperate, we are best able to abstain from them. So again with courage; it is by training ourselves to despise and face terrifying things that we become brave, and when we have become brave, we shall be best able to face them.

The pleasure or pain which accompanies actions may be regarded as a test of a person's moral state. He who abstains from physical pleasures and feels pleasure in so doing is temperate; but he who feels pain at so doing is licentious. He who faces dangers with pleasure, or at least without pain, is brave; but he who feels pain at facing them is a coward. For moral virtue is concerned with pleasures and pains. It is pleasure which makes us do what is base, and pain which makes us abstain from doing what is noble. Hence the importance of having a certain training from very early days, as Plato says, so that we may feel pleasure and pain at the right objects; for this is true education. . . .

CHAPTER 3

But we may be asked what we mean by saying that people must become just by doing what is just and temperate by doing what is temperate. For, it will be said, if they do what is just and temperate and they are already just and temperate themselves, in the same way as, if they practice grammar and music, they are grammarians and musicians.

But is this true even in the case of the arts? For a person may speak grammatically either by chance or at the suggestion of somebody else; hence he will not be a grammarian unless he not only speaks grammatically but does so in a grammatical manner, that is, because of the grammatical knowledge which he possesses.

There is a point of difference too between the arts and the virtues. The productions of art have their excellence in themselves. It is enough then that, when they are produced, they themselves should possess a certain character. But acts in accordance with virtue are not justly or temperately performed simply because they are in themselves just or temperate. The doer at the time of performing them must satisfy certain conditions; in the first place, he must know what he is doing; secondly, he must deliberately choose to do it and do it for his own sake; and thirdly, he must do it as part of his own firm and immutable character. If it be a question of art, these conditions, except only the condition of knowledge, are not raised; but if it be a question of virtue, mere knowledge is of little or no avail; it is the other conditions, which are the results of frequently performing just and temperate acts, that are not slightly but all-important. Accordingly, deeds are called just and temperate when they are such as a just and temperate person would do; and a just and temperate person is not merely one who does these deeds but one who does them in the spirit of the just and the temperate.

It may fairly be said that a just man becomes just by doing what is just, and a temperate man becomes temperate by doing what is temperate, and if a man did not so act, he would not have much chance of becoming good. But most people, instead of acting, take refuge in theorizing; they imagine that they are philosophers and that philosophy will make them virtuous; in fact, they behave like people who listen attentively to their doctors but never do anything that their doctors tell them. But a healthy state of the soul will no more be produced by this kind of philosophizing than a healthy state of the body by this kind of medical treatment.

CHAPTER 4

We have next to consider the nature of virtue. Now, as the properties of the soul are three, namely, emotions, faculties, and moral states, it follows that virtue must be one of the three. By emotions I mean desire, anger, fear, pride, envy, joy, love, hatred, regret, ambition, pity — in a word, whatever feeling is attended by pleasure or pain. I call those faculties through which we are said to be capable of

On Egoism

Thomas Hobbes

Of the voluntary acts of every man, the object is [always] some good to himself.

No man gives but with intention of good to himself, because gift is voluntary, and of all voluntary acts the object is to every man his own good.

From *Leviathan* (1651).

Among so many dangers therefore, as the natural lusts of me do daily threaten each other withal, to have a care of one's self is so far from being a matter scornfully to be looked upon, that one has neither the power nor wish to have done otherwise. For every man is desirous of what is good for him, and shuns what is evil, but chiefly the chiefest of natural evils, which is death; and this he doth by a certain impulsion of nature, no less than that whereby stone moves downward.

From *Philosophical Rudiments Concerning Government and Society* (1972).

John Aubrey, in his sketch of Hobbes in *Brief Lives,* recounts an exchange between Hobbes and a clergyman who had just seen Hobbes give alms to a beggar. The clergyman inquired whether Hobbes would have given the alms if Jesus had not commanded it; Hobbes's reply was that by giving alms to the beggar, he not only relieved the beggar's distress but he also relieved his own distress at seeing the beggar's distress.

From Alasdair MacIntyre, "Egoism and Altruism," in *The Encyclopedia of Philosophy* (New York: Macmillan, 1967), Vol. 2, p. 463.

experiencing these emotions, for instance, capable of getting angry or being pained or feeling pity. And I call those moral states through which we are well or ill disposed in our emotions, ill disposed, for instance, in anger, if our anger be too violent or too feeble, and well disposed, if it be rightly moderate; and similarly in our other emotions.

Now neither the virtues nor the vices are emotions; for we are not called good or bad for our emotions but for our virtues or vices. We are not praised or blamed simply for being angry, but only for being angry in a certain way; but we are praised or blamed for our virtues or vices. Again, whereas we are angry or afraid without deliberate purpose, the virtues are matters of deliberate purpose, or require deliberate purpose. Moreover, we are said to be moved by our emotions, but by our virtues or vices we are not said to be moved but to have a certain disposition.

For these reasons the virtues are not faculties. For we are not called either good or bad, nor are we praised or blamed for having simple capacity for emotion. Also while Nature gives us our faculties, it is not Nature that makes us good or bad; but this point we have already discussed. If then the virtues are neither emotions nor faculties, all that remains is that they must be moral states.

CHAPTER 5

The nature of virtue has been now described in kind. But it is not enough to say merely that virtue is a moral state; we must also describe the character of that moral state.

We may assert then that every virtue or excellence puts into good condition that of which it is a virtue or excellence, and enables it to perform its work well. Thus excellence in the eye makes the eye good and its function good, for by excellence in the eye we see well. Similarly, excellence of the horse makes a horse excellent himself and good at racing, at carrying its rider and at facing the enemy.

If then this rule is universally true, the virtue or excellence of a man will be such a moral state as makes a man good and able to perform his proper function well. How this will be the case we have already explained, but another way of making it clear will be to study the nature or character of virtue.

Now of everything, whether it be continuous or divisible, it is possible to take a greater, a smaller, or an equal amount, and this either in terms of the thing itself or in relation to ourselves, the equal being a mean between too much and too little. By the mean in terms of the thing itself, I understand that which is equally distinct from both its extremes, which is one and the same for every man. By the mean relatively to ourselves, I understand that which is neither too much nor too little for us; but this is not one nor the same for everybody. Thus if 10 be too much and 2 too little, we take 6 as a mean in terms of the thing itself; for 6 is as much greater than 2 as it is less than 10, and this is a mean in arithmetical proportion. But the mean considered relatively to ourselves may not be ascertained in that way. It does not follow that if 10 pounds of meat is too much and 2 too little for a man to eat, the trainer will order him 6 pounds, since this also may be too much or too little for him who is to take it; it will be too little, for example, for Milo but too much for a beginner in gymnastics. The same with running and wrestling; the right amount will vary with the individual. This being so, the skillful in any art avoids alike excess and deficiency; he seeks and chooses the mean, not the absolute mean, but the mean considered relatively to himself.

Every art then does its work well, if it regards the mean and judges the works it produces by the mean. For this reason we often say of successful works of art that it is impossible to take anything from them or to add anything to them, which implies that excess or deficiency is fatal to excellence but that the mean state ensures it. Good artists too, as we say, have an eye to the mean in their works. Now virtue, like Nature herself, is more accurate and better than any art; virtue, therefore, will aim at the mean. I speak of moral virtue, since it is moral virtue which is concerned with emotions and actions, and it is in these we have excess and deficiency and the mean. Thus it is possible to go too far, or not far enough in fear, pride, desire, anger, pity, and pleasure and pain generally, and

the excess and the deficiency are alike wrong; but to feel these emotions at the right times, for the right objects, towards the right persons, for the right motives, and in the right manner, is the mean or the best good, which signifies virtue. Similarly, there may be excess, deficiency, or the mean, in acts. Virtue is concerned with both emotions and actions, wherein excess is an error and deficiency a fault, while the mean is successful and praised, and success and praise are both characteristics of virtue.

It appears then that virtue is a kind of mean because it aims at the mean.

On the other hand, there are many different ways of going wrong; for evil is in its nature infinite, to use the Pythagorean phrase, but good is finite and there is only one possible way of going right. So the former is easy and the latter is difficult; it is easy to miss the mark but difficult to hit it. And so by our reasoning excess and deficiency are characteristics of vice and the mean is a characteristic of virtue.

For good is simple, evil manifold.

CHAPTER 6

Virtue then is a state of deliberate moral purpose, consisting in a mean relative to ourselves, the mean being determined by reason, or as a prudent man would determine it. It is a mean, firstly, as lying between two vices, the vice of excess on the one hand, the vice of deficiency on the other, and, secondly, because, whereas the vices either fall short of or go beyond what is right in emotion and action, virtue discovers and chooses the mean. Accordingly, virtue, if regarded in its essence or theoretical definition, is a mean, though, if regarded from the point of view of what is best and most excellent, it is an extreme.

But not every action or every emotion admits of a mean. There are some whose very name implies wickedness, as, for example, malice, shamelessness, and envy among the emotions, and adultery, theft, and murder among the actions. All these and others like them are marked as intrinsically wicked, not merely the excesses or deficiencies of them. It is never possible then to be right in them; they are always sinful. Right or wrong in such acts as adultery does not depend on our committing it with the right woman, at the right time, or in the right manner; on the contrary, it is wrong to do it at all. It would be equally false to suppose that there can be a mean or an excess or deficiency in unjust, cowardly or licentious conduct; for, if that were so, it would be a mean of excess and deficiency, an excess of excess and a deficiency of deficiency. But as in temperance and courage there can be no excess or deficiency, because the mean there is in a sense an extreme, so too in these other cases there cannot be a mean or an excess or a deficiency, but however the acts are done, they are wrong. For in general an excess or deficiency does not have a mean, nor a mean an excess or deficiency. . . .

CHAPTER 8

There are then three dispositions, two being vices, namely, excess and deficiency, and one virtue, which is the mean between them; and they are all in a sense mutually opposed. The extremes are opposed both to the mean and to each other, and the mean is opposed to the extremes. For as the equal if compared with the less is greater, but if compared with the greater is less, so the mean state, whether in emotion or action, if compared with deficiency is excessive, but if compared with excess is deficient. Thus the brave man appears foolhardy compared with the coward, but cowardly compared with the foolhardy. Similarly, the temperate man appears licentious compared with the insensible man but insensible compared with the licentious; and the liberal man appears extravagant compared with the stingy man but stingy compared with the spendthrift. The result is that the extremes each denounce the mean as belonging to the other extreme; the coward calls the brave man foolhardy, and the foolhardy man calls him cowardly; and so on in other cases.

But while there is mutual opposition between the extremes and the mean, there is greater opposition between the two extremes than between extreme and the mean; for they are further removed from each other than from the mean, as the great is further from the small and the small from the great than either from the equal. Again, while some extremes show some likeness to the mean, as foolhardiness to courage and extravagance to liberality, there is the greatest possible dissimilarity between extremes. But things furthest removed from each other are called opposites; hence the further things are removed, the greater is the opposition between them.

In some cases it is deficiency and in others excess which is more opposed to the mean. Thus it is not foolhardiness, an excess, but cowardice, a deficiency, which is more opposed to courage, nor is it insensibility, a deficiency, but licentiousness, an excess, which is more opposed to temperance. There are two reasons why this should be so. One lies in the nature of the matter itself; for when one of two extremes is nearer and more like the mean, it is not this extreme but its opposite that we chiefly contrast with the mean. For instance, as foolhardiness seems more like and nearer to courage than cowardice, it is cowardice that we chiefly contrast with courage; for things further removed from the mean seem to be more opposite to it. This reason lies in the nature of the matter itself; there is a second which lies in our own nature. The things to which we ourselves are naturally more inclined we think more opposed to the mean. Thus we are ourselves naturally more inclined to pleasures than to their opposites, and are more prone therefore to self-indulgence than to moderation. Accordingly we speak of those things in which we are more likely to run to great lengths as more opposed to the mean. Hence licentiousness, which is an excess, seems more opposed to temperance than insensibility.

CHAPTER 9

We have now sufficiently shown that moral virtue is a mean, and in what sense it is so; that it is a mean as lying between two vices, a vice of excess on the one side and a vice of deficiency on the other, and as aiming at the mean in emotion and action.

That is why it is so hard to be good; for it is always hard to find the mean in anything; it is not everyone but only a man of science who can find the mean or center of a circle. So too anybody can get angry—that is easy—and anybody can give or spend money, but to give it to the right person, to give the right amount of it, at the right time, for the right cause and in the right way, this is not what anybody can do, nor is it easy. That is why goodness is rare and praise worthy and noble. One then who aims at a mean must begin by departing from the extreme that is more contrary to the mean; he must act in the spirit of Calypso's advice, "Far from this spray and swell hold thou thy ship," for of the two extremes one is more wrong than the other. As it is difficult to hit the mean exactly, we should take the second best course, as the saying is, and choose the lesser of two evils. This we shall best do in the way described, that is, steering clear of the evil which is further from the mean. We must also note the weaknesses to which we are ourselves particularly prone, since different natures tend in different ways; and we may ascertain what our tendency is by observing our feelings of pleasure and pain. Then we must drag ourselves away towards the opposite extreme; for by pulling ourselves as far as possible from what is wrong we shall arrive at the mean, as we do when we pull a crooked stick straight.

In all cases we must especially be on our guard against the pleasant, or pleasure, for we are not impartial judges of pleasure. Hence our attitude towards pleasure must be like that of the elders of the people in the *Iliad* towards Helen, and we must constantly apply the words they use; for if we dismiss pleasure as they dismissed Helen, we shall be less likely to go wrong. By action of this kind, to put it summarily, we shall best succeed in hitting the mean.

Undoubtedly this is a difficult task, especially in individual cases. It is not easy to determine the right manner, objects, occasion and duration of anger. Sometimes we praise people who are deficient in anger, and call them gentle, and at other times we praise people who exhibit a fierce temper as high spirited. It is not however a man who deviates a little from goodness, but one who deviates a great deal, whether on the side of excess or of deficiency, that is blamed; for he is sure to call attention to himself. It is not easy to decide in theory how far and to what extent a man may go before he becomes blameworthy, but neither is it easy to define in theory anything else in the region of the senses; such things depend on circumstances, and our judgment of them depends on our perception.

So much then is plain, that the mean is everywhere praiseworthy, but that we ought to aim at one time towards an excess and at another towards a deficiency; for thus we shall most easily hit the mean, or in other words reach excellence.

Further Questions

1. What is Aristotle's conception of happiness? Is there any respect in which it is ambiguous?
2. If you were to adopt Aristotle's ethics as your guide to life, how much help would it be? What would you do differently from what you are already doing? Would your acting differently in this way be an improvement?

Further Readings

Kruschwitz, Robert, and Robert Roberts, eds. *The Virtues*. Belmont, CA: Wadsworth, 1987. Just what the title implies.

Taylor, Richard. *Virtue Ethics: An Introduction*. Interlaken, NY: Linden Books, 1991. A clear and useful survey by a master expositor of philosophy for the general reader.

80   On Liberty

JOHN STUART MILL

A brief biography of Mill appears on page 602.

In this selection, which is from a classic of liberal thought, Mill discusses the degree to which government and society may interfere in the lives of citizens. He argues that interference is warranted only to prevent one person from harming another—never to compel someone to act for her own good or prevent her from harming herself. This implies, Mill claims, that people should be allowed to think and speak as they like, to choose their own associates and their own way of living, and so on. Mill's principle of warranted interference is often called "the harm principle."

Mill believes that morality rests on the principle of utility: "Strive to produce as much happiness as possible." To show that following the harm principle will maximize happiness, Mill argues that all of society benefits from tolerance. For instance, from the free discussion of unpopular beliefs we learn new truths or better understand old ones; from unorthodox behavior we learn the results of "experiments of living"; and each of us gains personally from developing and expressing his individuality.

Reading Questions

1. Mill claims that society has a right to protect itself, but not to protect its citizens from harming themselves. But how does he know?
2. Doesn't society have an obligation to protect children from harming themselves? How would Mill respond?
3. If our own society were organized on the basis of Mill's principles, how would it be different?
4. How does Mill argue for free speech?
5. Why does Mill think that "individuality" is one of the elements of well-being.

THE SUBJECT OF THIS ESSAY is not the so-called "liberty of the will," so unfortunately opposed to the misnamed doctrine of philosophical necessity; but civil, or social liberty: the nature and limits of the power that can be legitimately exercised by society over the individual. A question seldom stated, and hardly ever discussed in general terms, but which profoundly influences the practical controversies of the age by its latent presence, and is likely soon to make itself recognized as the vital question of the future. It is so far from being new that, in a certain sense, it has divided mankind almost from the remotest ages; but in the stage of progress into which the more civilized portions of the species have now entered, it presents itself under new conditions and requires a different and more fundamental treatment.

The struggle between liberty and authority is the most conspicuous feature in the portions of history with which we are earliest familiar, particularly in that of Greece, Rome, and England. But in old times this contest was between subjects, or some classes of subjects, and the government. But liberty was meant protection against the tyranny of the political rulers. The rulers were conceived (except in some of the popular governments of Greece) as in a necessarily antagonistic position to the people whom they ruled. They consisted of a governing One, or a governing tribe or caste, who derived their authority from inheritance or conquest, who, at all events, did not hold it at the pleasure of the governed, and whose supremacy men did not venture, perhaps did not desire, to contest, whatever precautions might be taken against its oppressive exercise. Their power was regarded as necessary, but also as highly dangerous; as a weapon which they would attempt to use against their subjects, no less than against external enemies. To prevent the weaker members of the community from being preyed upon by innumerable vultures, it was needful that there should be an animal of prey stronger than the rest, commissioned to keep them down. But as the king of the vultures would be no less bent upon preying on the flock than any of the minor harpies, it was indispensable to be in a perpetual attitude of defense against his beak and claws. The aim, therefore, of patriots was to set limits to the power which the ruler should be suffered to exercise over the community; and this limitation was what they meant by liberty. It was attempted in two ways. First, by obtaining a recognition of certain immunities, called political liberties or rights, which it was to be regarded as a breach of duty in the ruler to infringe, and which if he did infringe, specific resistance or general rebellion was held to be justifiable. A second, and generally a later, expedient was the establishment of constitutional checks by which the consent of the community, or of a body of some sort, supposed to represent its interests, was made a necessary condition to some of the more important acts of the governing power. To the first of these modes of limitation, the ruling power, in most European countries, was compelled, more or less, to submit. It was not so with the second; and, to attain this, or, when already in some degree possessed, to attain it more completely, became everywhere the principal object of the lovers of liberty. And so long as mankind were content to combat one enemy by another, and to be ruled by a master on condition of being guaranteed more or less efficaciously against his tyranny, they did not carry their aspirations beyond this point.

A time, however, came, in the progress of human affairs, when men ceased to think it a necessity of nature that their governors should be an independent power opposed in interest to themselves. It appeared to them much better that the various magistrates of the state should be their tenants or delegates, revocable at their pleasure. In that way alone, it seemed, could they have complete security that the powers of government would never be abused to their disadvantage. By degrees this new demand for elective and temporary rulers became the prominent object of the exertions of the popular party wherever any such party existed, and superseded, to a considerable extent, the previous efforts to limit the power of rulers. As the struggle proceeded for making the ruling power emanate from the periodical choice of the ruled, some persons began to think that too much importance had been attached to the limitation of the power itself. *That* (it might seem) was a resource against rulers whose interests were habitually opposed to those of the people. What was now wanted was that the rulers should be identified with the people, that their interest and will should be the interest and will of the nation. The nation did not need to be protected against its own will. There was no fear of its tyrannizing over itself. Let the rulers be effectually responsible to it, promptly removable by it, and it could afford to trust them with power of which it could itself dictate the use to be made. Their power was but the nation's own power, concentrated and in a form convenient for exercise. This mode of thought, or rather perhaps of feeling, was common among the last generation of European liberalism, in the Continental section of which it still apparently predominates. Those who admit any limit to what a government may do, except in the case of such governments as they think ought not to exist, stand out as brilliant exceptions among the political thinkers of the Continent. A similar tone of sentiment might by this time have been prevalent in our own country if the circumstances which for a time encouraged it had continued unaltered.

But, in political and philosophical theories as well as in persons, success discloses faults and infirmities which failure might have concealed from observation. The notion that the people have no need to limit their power over themselves might seem axiomatic, when popular government was a thing only dreamed about, or read of as having existed at some distant period of the past. Neither was that notion necessarily disturbed by such temporary aberrations as those of the French Revolution, the worst of which were the work of a usurping few, and which, in any case, belonged, not to the permanent working of popular institutions, but to a sudden and convulsive outbreak against monarchical and aristocratic despotism. In time, however, a democratic republic came to occupy a large portion of the earth's surface and made itself felt as one of the most powerful members of the community of nations; and elective and responsible government became subject to the observations and criticisms which wait upon a great existing fact. It was now perceived that such phrases as "self-government," and "the power of the people over themselves," do not express the true state of the case. The "people" who exercise the power are not always the same people with those over whom it is exercised; and the "self-government" spoken of is not the government of each by himself, but of each by all the rest. The will of the people, moreover, practically means the will of the most numerous or the most active *part* of the people—the majority, or those who succeed in making themselves accepted as the majority; the people, consequently, *may* desire to oppress a part of their number, and precautions are as much needed against this as against any other abuse of power. The limitations, therefore, of the power of government over individuals loses none of its importance when the holders of power are regularly accountable to the community, that is, to the strongest party therein. This view of things, recommending itself equally to the intelligence of thinkers and to the inclination of those important classes in European society to whose real or supposed interests democracy is adverse, has had no difficulty in establishing itself; and in political speculations "the tyranny of the majority" is now generally included among the evils against which society requires to be on its guard.

Like other tyrannies, the tyranny of the majority was at first, and is still vulgarly, held in dread, chiefly as operating through the acts of the public authorities. But reflecting persons perceived that when society is itself the tyrant—society collectively over the separate individuals who compose it—its means of

tyrannizing are not restricted to the acts which it may do by the hands of its political functionaries. Society can and does execute its own mandates; and if it issues wrong mandates instead of right, or any mandates at all in things with which it ought not to meddle, it practices a social tyranny more formidable than many kinds of political oppression, since, though not usually upheld by such extreme penalties, it leaves fewer means of escape, penetrating much more deeply into the details of life, and enslaving the soul itself. Protection, therefore, against the tyranny of the magistrate is not enough; there needs protection also against the tyranny of the prevailing opinion and feeling, against the tendency of society to impose, by other means than civil penalties, its own ideas and practices as rules of conduct on those who dissent from them; to fetter the development and, if possible, prevent the formation of any individuality not in harmony with its ways, and compel all characters to fashion themselves upon the model of its own. There is a limit to the legitimate interference of collective opinion with individual independence; and to find that limit, and maintain it against encroachment, is as indispensable to a good condition of human affairs as protection against political despotism.

But though this proposition is not likely to be contested in general terms, the practical question where to place the limit—how to make the fitting adjustment between individual independence and social control—is a subject on which nearly everything remains to be done. All that makes existence valuable to anyone depends on the enforcement of restraints upon the actions of other people. Some rules of conduct, therefore, must be imposed—by law in the first place, and by opinion on many things which are not fit subjects for the operation of law. What these rules should be is the principal question in human affairs. . . .

The object of this essay is to assert one very simple principle, as entitled to govern absolutely the dealings of society with the individual in the way of compulsion and control, whether the means used be physical force in the form of legal penalties or the moral coercion of public opinion. That principle is that the sole end for which mankind are warranted, individually or collectively, in interfering with the liberty of action of any of their number is self-protection. That the only purpose for which power can be rightfully exercised over any member of a civilized community, against his will, is to prevent harm to others. His own good, either physical or moral, is not a sufficient warrant. He cannot rightfully be compelled to do or forbear because it will be better for him to do so, because it will make him happier, because, in the opinions of others, to do so would be wise or even right. These are good reasons for remonstrating with him, or reasoning with him, or persuading him, or entreating him, but not for compelling him or visiting him with any evil in case he do otherwise. To justify that, the conduct from which it is desired to deter him must be calculated to produce evil to someone else. The only part of the conduct of anyone for which he is amenable to society is that which concerns others. In the part which merely concerns himself, his independence is, of right, absolute. Over himself, over his own body and mind, the individual is sovereign.

It is, perhaps, hardly necessary to say that this doctrine is meant to apply only to human beings in the maturity of their faculties. We are not speaking of children or of young persons below the age which the law may fix as that of manhood or womanhood. Those who are still in a state to require being taken care of by others must be protected against their own actions as well as against external injury. For the same reason we may leave out of consideration those backward states of society in which the race itself may be considered as in its nonage. The early difficulties in the say of spontaneous progress are so great that there is seldom any choice of means for overcoming them; and a ruler full of the spirit of improvement is warranted in the use of any expedients that will attain an end perhaps otherwise unattainable. Despotism is a legitimate mode of government in dealing with barbarians, provided the end be their improvement and the means justified by actually effecting that end. Liberty, as a principle, has not application to any state of things anterior to the time when mankind have become capable of being improved by free and equal discussion. Until then, there is nothing for them but implicit obedience to an Akbar or a Charlemagne, if they are so fortunate as to find one. But as soon as mankind have attained the capacity of being guided to their own improvement by conviction or persuasion (a period long since reached in all nations with whom we need here concern ourselves), compulsion, either in the direct form or in that of pains and penalties for noncompliance, is no longer admissible as a means to their own good, and justifiable only for the security of others.

It is proper to state that I forego any advantage which could be derived to my argument from the idea of abstract right as a thing independent of utility. I regard utility as the ultimate appeal on all ethical questions; but it must be utility in the largest sense, grounded on the permanent interests of man as a progressive being. Those interests, I contend, authorize the subjection of individual spontaneity to external control only in respect to those actions of each which concern the interest of other people If anyone does an act hurtful to others, there is *prima facie* case for punishing him by law or, where legal penalties are not safely applicable, by general disapprobation. There are also many positive acts for the benefit of others which he may rightfully be compelled to perform, such as to give evidence in a court of justice, to bear his fair share in the common defense or in any other joint work necessary to the interest of the society of which he enjoys the protection, and to perform certain acts of individual beneficence, such as saving a fellow creature's life or interposing to protect the defenseless against ill usage—things which whenever it is obviously a man's duty to do he may rightfully be made responsible to society for not doing. A person may cause evil to others not only by his actions but by his inaction, and in either case he is justly accountable to them for the injury. The latter case, it is true, requires a much more cautious exercise of compulsion than the former. To make anyone answerable for doing evil to others is the rule; to make him answerable for not preventing evil is, comparatively speaking, the exception. Yet there are many cases clear enough and grave enough to justify that exception. In all things which regard the external relations of the individual, he is *de jure* amenable to those whose interests are concerned, and, if need be, to society as their protector. There are often good reasons for not holding him to the responsibility; but these reasons must arise from the special expediencies of the case: either because it is a kind of case in which he is on the whole likely to act better when left to his own discretion than when controlled in any way in which society have it in their power to control him; or because the attempt to exercise control would produce other evils, greater than those which it would prevent. When such reasons as these preclude the enforcement of responsibility, the conscience of the agent himself should step into the vacant judgment seat and protect those interests of others which have no external protection; judging himself all the more rigidly, because the case does not admit of his being made accountable to the judgment of his fellow creatures.

But there is a sphere of action in which society, as distinguished from the individual, has, if any, only an indirect interest: comprehending all that portion of a person's life and conduct which affects only himself or, if it also affects others, only with their free, voluntary, and undeceived consent and participation. When I say only himself, I mean directly and in the first instance; for whatever affects himself may affect others through himself; and the objection which may be grounded on this contingency will receive consideration in the sequel. This, then, is the appropriate region of human liberty. It comprises, first, the inward domain of consciousness, demanding liberty of conscience in the most comprehensive sense, liberty of thought and feeling, absolute freedom of opinion and sentiment on all subjects, practical or speculative, scientific, moral, or theological. The liberty of expressing the publishing opinions may seem to fall under a different principle, since it belongs to that part of the conduct of an individual which concerns other people, but, being almost of as much importance as the liberty of thought itself and resting in great part on the same reasons, is practically inseparable from it. Secondly, the principle requires liberty of tastes and pursuits, of framing the plan of our life to suit our own character, of doing as we like, subject to such consequences as may follow, without impediment from our fellow creatures, so long as what we do does not harm them, even though they should think our conduct foolish, perverse, or wrong. Thirdly, from this liberty of each individual follows the liberty, within the same limits, of com-

bination among individuals; freedom to unite for any purpose not involving harm to others: the persons combining being supposed to be of full age and not forced or deceived.

OF THE LIBERTY OF THOUGHT AND DISCUSSION

The time, it is to be hoped, is gone by when any defense would be necessary of the "liberty of the press" as one of the securities against corrupt or tyrannical government. No argument, we may suppose, can now be needed against permitting a legislature or an executive, not identified in interest with the people, to prescribe opinions to them and determine what doctrines or what arguments they shall be allowed to hear. This aspect of the question, besides, has been so often and so triumphantly enforced by preceding writers that it needs not be specially insisted on in this place. Though the law of England, on the subject of the press, is as servile to this day as it was in the time of the Tudors, there is little danger of its being actually put in force against political discussion except during some temporary panic when fear of insurrection drives ministers and judges from their propriety; and, speaking generally, it is not, in constitutional countries, to be apprehended that the government, whether completely responsible to the people or not, will often attempt to control the expression of opinion, except when in doing so it makes itself the organ of the general intolerance of the public. Let us suppose, therefore, that the government is entirely at one with the people, and never thinks of exerting any power of coercion unless in agreement with what it conceives to be their voice.

But I deny the right of the people to exercise such coercion, either by themselves or by their government. The power itself is illegitimate. The best government has no more title to it than the worst. It is as anxious, or more noxious, when exerted in accordance with public opinion than when in opposition to it. If all mankind minus one were of one opinion, mankind would be no more justified in silencing that one person than he, if he had the power, would be justified in silencing mankind.

Were an opinion a personal possession of no value except to the owner, if to be obstructed in the enjoyment of it were simply a private injury, it would make some difference whether the injury was inflicted only on a few persons or on many. But the peculiar evil of silencing the expression of an opinion is that it is robbing the human race, posterity as well as the existing generation—those who dissent from the opinion, still more than those who hold it. If the opinion is right they are deprived of the opportunity of exchanging error for truth; if wrong, they lose, what is almost as great a benefit, the clearer perception and livelier impression of truth produced by its collision with error.

It is necessary to consider separately these two hypotheses, each of which has a distinct branch of the argument corresponding to it. We can never be sure that the opinion we are endeavoring to stifle is a false opinion; and if we were sure, stifling it would be an evil still.

First, the opinion which it is attempted to suppress by authority may possibly be true. Those who desire to suppress it, of course, deny its truth; but they are not infallible. They have no authority to decide the question for all mankind and exclude every other person from the means of judging. To refuse a hearing to an opinion because they are sure that it is false is to assume that *their* certainty is the same thing as *absolute* certainty. All silencing of discussion is an assumption of infallibility. Its condemnation may be allowed to rest on this common argument, not the worse for being common.

Unfortunately for the good sense of mankind, the fact of their fallibility is far from carrying the weight in their practical judgment which is always allowed to it in theory; for while everyone well knows himself to be fallible, few think it necessary to take any precautions against their own fallibility, or admit the supposition that any opinion of which they feel very certain may be one of the examples of the error to which they acknowledge themselves to be liable. Absolute princes, or others who are accustomed to unlimited deference, usually feel this complete confidence in their own opinions on nearly all subjects. People more happily situated, who sometimes hear their opinions disputed and are not wholly unused to be set right when they are wrong, place the same unbounded reliance

only on such of their opinions as are shared by all who surround them, or to whom they habitually defer; for in proportion to a man's want of confidence in his own solitary judgment does he usually repose, with implicit trust, on the infallibility of "the world" in general. And the world, to each individual, means the part of it with which he comes in contact: his party, his sect, his church, his class of society; the man may be called, by comparison, almost liberal and large-minded to whom it means anything so comprehensive as his own country or his own age. Nor is his faith in the collective authority at all shaken by his being aware that other ages, countries, sects, churches, classes, and parties have thought, and even now think the exact reverse. He devolves upon his own world the responsibility of being in the right against the dissentient worlds of other people; and it never troubles him that mere accident has decided which of these numerous worlds is the object of his reliance, and that the same causes which make him a churchman in London would have made him a Buddhist or a Confucian in Peking. Yet it is as evident in itself, as any amount of argument can make it, that ages are no more infallible than individuals—every age having held many opinions which subsequent ages have deemed not only false but absurd; and it is as certain that many opinions, now general, will be rejected by future ages, as it is that many, once general, are rejected by the present.

The objection likely to be made to this argument would probably take some such form as the following. There is no greater assumption of infallibility in forbidding the propagation of error than in any other thing which is done by public authority on its own judgment and responsibility. Judgment is given to men that they may use it. Because it may be used erroneously, are men to be told that they ought not to use it at all? To prohibit what they think pernicious is not claiming exception from error, but fulfilling the duty incumbent on them, although fallible, of acting on their conscientious conviction. If we were never to act on our opinions, because those opinions may be wrong, we should leave all our interests uncared for, and all our duties unperformed. An objection which applies to all conduct can be no valid objection to any conduct in particular. It is the duty of governments, and of individuals, to form the truest opinions they can; to form them carefully, and never impose them upon others unless they are quite sure of being right. But when they are sure (such reasoners may say), it is not conscientiousness but cowardice to shrink from acting on their opinions and allow doctrines which they honestly think dangerous to the welfare of mankind, either in this life or in another, to be scattered abroad without restraint, because other people, in less enlightened times, have persecuted opinions now believed to be true. Let us take care, it may be said, not to make the same mistake; but governments and nations have made mistakes in other things which are not denied to be fit subjects for the exercise of authority: they have laid on bad taxes, made unjust wars. Ought we therefore to lay on no taxes and, under whatever provocation, make no wars? Men and governments must act to the best of their ability. There is no such thing as absolute certainty, but there is assurance sufficient for the purposes of human life. We may, and must, assume our opinion to be true for the guidance of our own conduct; and it is assumng no more when we forbid bad men to pervert society by the propagation of opinions which we regard as false and pernicious.

I answer, that it is assuming very much more. There is the greatest difference between presuming an opinion to be true because, with every opportunity for contesting it, it has not been refuted, and assuming its truth for the purpose of not permitting its refutation. Complete liberty of contradicting and disproving our opinion is the very condition which justifies us in assuming its truth for purposes of action; and on no other terms can a being with human faculties have any rational assurance of being right.

When we consider either the history of opinion or the ordinary conduct of human life, to what is it to be ascribed that the one and the other are no worse than they are? Not certainly to the inherent force of the human understanding, for on any matter not self-evident there are ninety-nine persons totally incapable of judging of it for one who is capable; and the capacity of the hundredth person is only comparative, for the majority of the eminent men of every past generation held many opinions now known to be erroneous, and did or approved numerous things which no one will now justify. Why is it then, that there is on the whole a preponderance among mankind of rational opinions and rational conduct? If there really is this preponderance—which there must be unless human affairs are, and have always been, in an almost desperate state—it is owing to a quality of the human mind, the source of everything respectable in man either as an intellectual or as a moral being, namely, that his errors are corrigible. He is capable of rectifying his mistakes by discussion and experience. Not by experience alone. There must be discussion to show how experience is to be interpreted. Wrong opinions and practices gradually yield to fact and argument; but facts and arguments, to produce any effect on the mind, must be brought before it. Very few facts are able to tell their own story, without comments to bring out their meaning. The whole strength and value, then, of human judgment depending on the one property, that it can be set right when it is wrong, reliance can be placed on it only when the means of setting it right are kept constantly at hand. In the case of any person whose judgment is really deserving of confidence, how has it become so? Because he has kept his mind open to criticism of his opinions and conduct. Because it has been his practice to listen to all that could be said against him; to profit by as much of it as was just, and to expound to himself, and upon occasion to others, the fallacy of what was fallacious. Because he has felt that the only way in which a human being can make some approach to knowing the whole of a subject is by hearing what can be said about it by persons of every variety of opinion, and studying all modes in which it can be looked at by every character of mind. No wise man ever acquired his wisdom in any mode but this; nor is it in that nature of human intellect to become wise in any other manner. The steady habit of correcting and completing his own opinion by collating it with those of others, so far from causing doubt and hesitation in carrying it into practice, is the only stable foundation for a just reliance on it; for, being cognizant of all that can, at least obviously, be said against him, and having taken up his position against all gainsayers—knowing that he has sought for objections and difficulties instead of avoiding them, and has shut out no light which can be thrown upon the subject from any quarter—he has a right to think his judgment better than that of any person, or any multitude, who have not gone through a similar process.

Let us now pass to the second division of the argument, and dismissing the supposition that any of the received opinions may be false, let us assume them to be true and examine into the worth of the manner in which they are likely to be held when their truth is not freely and openly canvassed. However unwillingly a person who has a strong opinion may admit the possibility that his opinion may be false, he ought to be moved by the consideration that, however true it may be, if it is not fully, frequently, and fearlessly discussed, it will be held as a dead dogma, not a living truth.

There is a class of persons (happily not quite so numerous as formerly) who think it enough if a person assents undoubtingly to what they think true, though he has no knowledge whatever of the grounds of the opinion and could not make a tenable defense of it against the most superficial objections. Such persons, if they can once get their creed taught from authority, naturally think that no good, and some harm, comes of its being allowed to be questioned. Where their influence prevails, they make it nearly impossible for the received opinion to be rejected wisely and considerately, though it may still be rejected rashly and ignorantly; for to shut out discussion entirely is seldom possible, and when it once gets in, beliefs not grounded on conviction are apt to give way before the slightest semblance of an argument. Waiving, however, this possibility—assuming that the true opinion abides in the mind, but abides as a prejudice, a belief independent of, and proof against argument—this is not the way in which truth ought to be held by a rational being. This is not knowing the truth. Truth, thus held, is but one superstition the more, accidentally clinging to the words which enunciate a truth.

If the intellect and judgment of mankind ought to be cultivated, a thing which Protestants at least do not deny, on what can these faculties be more appropriately exercised by anyone than on the things which concern him so much that it is considered necessary for him to hold opinions on them? If the cultivation of the understanding consists in one thing more than in another, it is surely in learning the grounds of one's own opinions. Whatever people believe, on subjects on which it is of the first importance to believe rightly, they ought to be able to defend against at least the common objections. But, someone may say, "Let them be *taught* the grounds of their opinions. It does not follow that opinions must be merely parroted because they are never heard controverted. Persons who learn geometry do not simply commit the theorems to memory, but understand and learn likewise the demonstrations; and it would be absurd to say that they remain ignorant of the grounds of geometrical truths because they never hear anyone deny and attempt to disprove them." Undoubtedly; and such teaching suffices on a subject like mathematics, where there is nothing at all to be said on the wrong side of the question. The peculiarity of the evidence of mathematical truths is that all the argument is on one side. There are no objections, and no answers to objections. But on every subject on which difference of opinion is possible, the truth depends on a balance to be struck between two sets of conflicting reasons. Even in natural philosophy, there is always some other explanation possible of the same facts; some geocentric theory instead of heliocentric, some phlogiston instead of oxygen; and it has to be shown why that other theory cannot be the true one; and until this is shown, we do not understand the grounds of our opinion. But when we turn to subjects infinitely more complicated, to morals, religion, politics, social relations, and the business of life, three-fourths of the arguments for every disputed opinion consists in dispelling the appearances which favor some opinion different from it. The greatest orator, save one, of antiquity, has left it on record that he always studied his adversary's case with as great, if not still greater, intensity than even his own. What Cicero practiced as the means of forensic success requires to be imitated by all who study any subject in order to arrive at the truth. He who knows only his own side of the case knows little of that. His reasons may be good, and no one may have been able to refute them. But if he is equally unable to refute the reasons on the opposite side, if he does not so much as know what they are, he has no ground for preferring either opinion. The rational position for him would be suspension of judgment, and unless he contents himself with that, he is either led by authority or adopts, like the generality of the world, the side to which he feels most inclination. Nor is it enough that he should hear the arguments of adversaries from his own teachers, presented as they state them, and accompanied by what they offer as refutations. That is not the way to do justice to the arguments or bring them into real contact with his own mind. He must be able to hear them from persons who actually believe them, who defend them in earnest and do their very utmost for them. He must know them in their most plausible and persuasive form; he must feel the whole force of the difficulty which the true view of the subject has to encounter and dispose of, else he will never really possess himself of the portion of truth which meets and removes that difficulty. Ninety-nine in a hundred of what are called educated men are in this condition, even of those who can argue fluently for their opinions. Their conclusion may be true, but it might be false for anything they know; they have never thrown themselves into the mental position of those who think differently from them and considered what such persons may have to say; and, consequently, they do not, in any proper sense of the word, know the doctrine whch they themselves profess. . . .

We have now recognized the necessity to the mental well-being of mankind (on which all their other well-being depends) of freedom of opinion, and freedom of the expression of opinion, on four distinct grounds, which we will now briefly recapitulate:

First, if any opinion is compelled to silence, that opinion may, for aught we can certainly know, be true. To deny this is to assume our own infallibility.

Secondly, though the silenced opinion be an error, it may, and very commonly does, contain a portion of truth; and since the general or prevailing opinion on any subject is rarely or never the whole truth, it is only by the collision of adverse opinions that the remainder of the truth has any chance of being supplied.

Thirdly, even if the received opinion be not only true, but the whole truth; unless it is suffered to be, and actually is, vigorously and earnestly contested, it will, by most of those who receive it, be held in the manner of a prejudice, with little comprehension or feeling of its rational grounds. And not only this, but, fourthly, the meaning of the doctrine itself will be in danger of being lost or enfeebled, and deprived of its vital effect on the character and conduct; the dogma becoming a mere formal profession, inefficacious for good, but cumbering the ground and preventing the growth of any real and heartfelt conviction from reason or personal experience.

OF INDIVIDUALITY, AS ONE OF THE ELEMENTS OF WELL-BEING

Such being the reasons which make it imperative that human beings should be free to form opinions and to express their opinions without reserve; and such the baneful consequences to the intellectual, and through that to the moral nature of man, unless this liberty is either conceded or asserted in spite of prohibition; let us next examine whether the same reasons do not require that men should be free to act upon their opinions—to carry these out in their lives without hindrance, either physical or moral, from their fellow men, so long as it is at their own risk and peril. This last proviso is of course indispensable. No one pretends that actions should be as free as opinions. On the contrary, even pinions lose their immunity when the circumstances in which they are expressed are such as to constitute their expression a positive instigation to some mischievous act. An opinion that corn dealers are starvers of the poor, or that private property is robbery, ought to be unmolested when simply circulated through the press, but may justly incur punishment when delivered orally to an excited mob assembled before the house of a corn dealer, or when handed about among the same mob in the form of a placard. Acts, of whatever kind, which without justifiable cause do harm to others may be, and in the more important cases absolutely require to be, controlled by the unfavorable sentiments, and, when needful, by the active interference of mankind. The liberty of the individual must be thus far limited; he must not make himself a nuisance to other people. But if he refrains from molesting others in what concerns them, and merely acts according to his own inclination and judgment in things which concern himself, the same reasons which show that opinion should be free prove also that he should be allowed, without molestation, to carry his opinions into practice at his own cost. That mankind are not infallible; that their truths, for the most part, are only half-truths; that unity of opinion, unless resulting from the fullest and freest comparison of opposite opinions, is not desirable, and diversity not an evil, but a good, until mankind are much more capable than at present of recognizing all sides of the truth, are principles applicable to men's modes of action not less than to their opinions. As it is useful that while mankind are imperfect there should be different opinions, so it is that there should be different experiments of living; that free scope should be given to varieties of character, short of injury to others; and that the worth of different modes of life should be proved practically, when anyone thinks fit to try them. It is desirable, in short, that in things which do no primarily concern others individuality should assert itself. Where not the person's own character but the traditions of customs of other people are the rule of conduct, there is wanting one of the principal ingredients of human happiness, and quite the chief ingredient of individual and social progress.

Having said that the individuality is the same thing with development, and that it is only the cultivation of individuality which produces, or can produce, well-developed human beings, I might here close the argument; for what more or better can be said of any condition of human affairs than that it brings human beings themselves nearer to the best thing they can be? Or what worse can be said of any obstruction to good than that it prevents this? Doubtless, however, these considerations will not suffice to convince those who most need convincing; and it is necessary further to show that these developed human beings are of some use to the undeveloped—to point out to those who do not desire liberty, and would not avail themselves of it, that they may be in some intelligible manner rewarded for allowing other people to make use of it without hindrance.

In the first place, then, I would suggest that they might possibly learn something from them. It will not be denied by anybody that originality is a valuable element in human affairs. There is always need of persons not only to discover new truths and point out when what were once truths are true no longer, but also to commence new practices and set the example of more enlightened conduct and better taste and sense in human life. This cannot well be gainsaid by anybody who does not believe that the world has already attained perfection in all its ways and practices. It is true that this benefit if not capable of being rendered by everybody alike; there are but few persons, in comparison with the whole of mankind, whose experiments, if adopted by others, would be likely to be any improvement on established practice. But these few

are the salt of the earth; without them, human life would become a stagnant pool. Not only is it they who introduce good things which did not before exist; it is they who keep the life in those which already exist. If there were nothing new to be done, would human intellect cease to be necessary? Would it be a reason why those who do the old things should forget why they are done, and do them like cattle, not like human beings? There is only too great a tendency in the best beliefs and practices to degenerate into the mechanical; and unless there were a succession of persons whose ever-recurring originality prevents the grounds of those beliefs and practices from becoming merely traditional, such dead matter would not resist the smallest shock from anything really alive, and there would be no reason why civilization should not die out, as in the Byzantine Empire. . . .

I have said that it is important to give the freest scope possible to uncustomary things, in order that it may in time appear which of these are fit to be converted into customs. But independence of action and disregard of custom are not solely deserving of encouragement for the chance they afford that better modes of action, and customs more worthy of general adoption, may be struck out; nor is it only persons of decided mental superiority who have a just claim to carry on their lives in their own way. There is no reason that all human existence should be constructed on some one or some small number of patterns. If a person possesses any tolerable amount of common sense and experience, his own mode of laying out his existence is the best, not because it is the best in itself, but because it is his own mode. Human beings are not like sheep; and even sheep are not indistinguishably alike. A man cannot get a coat or a pair of boots to fit him unless they are either made to his measure or he has a whole warehouseful to choose from; and is it easier to fit him with a life than with a coat, or are human beings more like one another in their whole physical and spiritual conformation than in the shape of their feet? If it were only that people have diversities of taste, that is reason enough for not attempting to shape them all after one model. But different persons also require different conditions for their spiritual development; and can no more exist healthily in the same moral than all the variety of plants can in the same physical, atmosphere and climate. The same things which are helps to one person toward the cultivation of his higher nature are hindrances to another. The same mode of life is a healthy excitement to one, keeping all his faculties of action and enjoyment in their best order, while to another it is a distracting burden which suspends or crushes all internal life. Such are the differences among human beings in their sources of pleasure, their susceptibilities of pain, and the operation on them of dfferent physical and moral agencies that, unless there is a corresponding diversity in their modes of life, they neither obtain their fair share of happiness, nor grow up to the mental, moral, and aesthetic stature of which their nature is capable. . . .

Further Questions

1. Should motorcyclists be forced to wear helmets?
2. Should society tolerate such "experiments in living" as the use of hard drugs? What would Mill say? Why? What do you say?

Further Readings

Feinberg, Joel. *Social Philosophy*. Englewood Cliffs, NJ: Prentice-Hall, 1973. An accessible survey.
Wolff, Robert Paul. *In Defense of Anarchism*. New York: Harper and Row, 1970. Short and provocative.

81   Openness

JONATHAN GLOVER

Jonathan Glover teaches philosophy at Oxford University and writes primarily in the areas of ethics and philosophy of mind. In this selection, he considers how our lives would be affected if we were more transparent to each other and whether that would be a good thing.

Reading Questions

1. How important is mental privacy? Under what circumstances would you be willing to relinquish yours? Are there any circumstances under which you would relinquish it completely?
2. Do you think your intimate relationships would improve if you and those you love were completely transparent to each other?

A remote radio-communications system using belt transceivers is presently undergoing prototype testing. Systems of this type can monitor geographical location and psychophysiological variables, as well as permit two-way coded communication with people in their natural social environment. Probable subjects include individuals susceptible to emergency medical conditions that occasionally preclude calling for help (e.g. epilepsy, diabetes, myocardial infarctions), geriatric or psychiatric outpatients, and parolees. It is conceivable, for example, that convicts might be given the option of incarceration or parole with mandatory electronic surveillance. (Robert L. Schwitzgebel: *Emotions and Machines: A Commentary On the Context and Strategy Of Psychotechnology*)

During the last few years, methodology has been developed to stimulate and record the electrical activity of the brain in completely unrestrained monkeys and chimpanzees. This procedure should be of considerable clinical interest because it permits exploration of the brain for unlimited periods in patients without disturbing their rest or normal spontaneous activities. (José M. R. Delgado: *Journal of Nervous and Mental Disease* 1968)

THE DEVELOPMENT OF ELECTRONIC monitoring devices makes it possible for us to keep people under surveillance without locking them up in prison. We could largely replace prison by a system of keeping track of convicted criminals without restricting their movements. This thought can arouse both anxiety and optimism. The anxiety (when not about the effectiveness of such a system in restraining criminal activity) is about the invasion of privacy involved in such monitoring. The optimism comes from the thought that submitting to a monitoring system might be much less terrible than going to prison.

Advocates of monitoring systems use the argument that they would be more humane, and would be no more an invasion of privacy than prison. They suggest that we should try out monitoring for its effectiveness in preventing crime. If these systems turn out to be no more ineffective than prisons, it may seem that their supporters will have won the argument.

But it is a bit more complicated than this. Monitoring systems, just because they are less horrible to submit to than prison, may be resorted to more readily. Periods of monitoring might be much longer than prison sentences, and many more people might be monitored than are now sent to prison. We would then live in a society in which many had lost a lot of privacy. Perhaps social gains, such as a reduced crime rate and the abolition of prisons, would be thought great enough to outweigh this loss. But the issue is not a simple one,

and the ways in which monitoring techniques could be developed and used have to be taken into account.

One obvious development is to monitor, not merely where people are, but also various of their physical states. Dr. Schwitzgebel mentions some useful applications of this internal monitoring in the cases of people with conditions dangerous to themselves. The extension to sex offenders, and to people liable to do harm when drunk or in fits of rage, can easily be imagined. And, as techniques for recording the electrical and chemical activity of the brain grow more sophisticated, we can expect it to become possible to monitor physical and psychological states with increasing precision.

When we think of more finely tuned monitoring, which would cross the blurred boundary between physical and psychological states, we are likely to feel increasing anxiety at the potential for invasion of privacy. To many people it will seem obvious that any extension of monitoring to psychological states should be resisted. But it is worth scrutinizing what is often taken for granted, and asking what the reasons are for valuing privacy as we do. Would it really be so terrible if our feelings and thoughts could be monitored by other people? What would be lost in a world without privacy?

To pose this issue in its sharpest form, let us consider the extreme case, in which the neurosciences have developed to the point where, by monitoring the activity of a person's brain, others could know in some detail the contents of his mind.

1. MONITORING THOUGHTS

The idea that we could monitor thoughts in this way presupposes that different mental states are correlated with different states of the brain. This is the working assumption of much psychology and neurophysiology, but it is controversial. We cannot be certain what future scientific work will show, and we are probably in for many surprises before the brain is fully understood. Yet there is already much suggestive work showing that electrical stimulation of particular points of the cortex can evoke highly specific memories, or that seeing particular patterns involves the firing of specific neurons in the cortex. In the scientific context, the working assumption, even if by no means impregnable, seems plausible.

Some philosophers have argued that there could not exist comprehensive and detailed psychophysical laws, while others disagree. These arguments will not be gone into here. The plan is to consider the implications of a technology based on monitoring brain activity, with deliberate casualness about current opinions as to which way the neurosciences will develop.

But there is a question which cannot be shelved here. What does it mean to talk of monitoring someone's thoughts and feelings? In a way, we all know what it is to have thoughts, and in most cases it seems absurd to suggest that someone does not know what thought he is having. Yet, despite this, there is a real problem in saying what having a thought consists in. And this problem causes difficulty for the idea of monitoring thoughts.

What is the problem about thoughts? Some thinking is in words, but sometimes we have a thought not formulated in words, where, if we are aware of anything, it is perhaps only some image. When I am struck by the thought that I have forgotten to telephone for a taxi, it may be that no words cross my mind. Perhaps I simply have a mental picture of a taxi. In such cases, images do not just come to mind on their own, but come with an interpretation. If I tell someone else that I have a mental picture of a taxi, he will not know what thought I am having, though I may be in no doubt at all that my thought is about the phone call. This process of interpretation, which applies to words as well as images, is something we know almost nothing about. This is why psychological studies of thinking, which can tell us so much about the strategies people use for solving problems, have so far told us so little about what our ordinary "background" stream of consciousness consists in.

Because the process of interpretation is so important, even where the thought has embodiment in words or images, someone monitoring simply those words or images passing through my mind will have an incomplete knowledge of what I am thinking about. We can imagine a device that would decode the brain's activity and project on to a screen images corresponding to those in the person's mind. (We might need two screens: one for experiences involved in seeing, and one for visual

imagination.) Thoughts which take place in words could be reproduced on a soundtrack, and images which are not visual or auditory could be reproduced by similar devices. But it is much less clear what it would be to give public embodiment to the process of interpreting these words and images. For this reason it seems better to discuss monitoring only words and images. It has to be recognized that a technology letting us do this would not give us perfect knowledge of people's mental lives.

Let us suppose that these devices are developed, and that they are produced in conveniently portable form. You come into the room holding what looks like a small portable television. The next thing I know is that I hear coming from it the words that are running through my mind, and see my accompanying visual images on the screen. This technology will make people's minds largely transparent. Despite the problems about interpreting words and images, we will often have a fairly good idea of what others are thinking.

Will this be the end of privacy? In one way, the answer is clearly "yes." For, as the onion layers of privacy are peeled away, if there is a centre it must surely be the contents of the mind. But the machines so far described will leave us with an intermittent privacy of a kind. For, while the contents of a mind would always in principle be open to inspection, for much of the time it would not be under scrutiny. This is because of our limited powers of attention. Even with several thought-reading machines going at once, I could only attend to the thoughts of one or two people at a time. Some television enthusiasts have more than one set, so that they can watch programmes on different channels at the same time. The limitations on how far this could go are obvious. And, apart from problems of limited attention, most of us would want to spend most of the time doing other things, or thinking our own thoughts, and would probably not spend long tuned in to the minds of others. (Though artists and writers might find their thoughts constantly monitored by people doing courses about creativity.)

A society or a government determined to eliminate privacy could overcome these difficulties by developing a central monitor and memory store, where everyone's thoughts could be recorded and stored, so that they would be available for scrutiny when desired. At this point, systematic thought policing would be possible.

In our present world, governments and other organizations can destroy or hamper the freedom to express thoughts, but at least thought itself is always free. The introduction of thought-policing would make many people's lives scarcely worth living. It would also give governments complete power to block new ideas and social change, if only by killing or locking up people as soon as they had the ideas. Thought-policing is so appalling that there is a lot to be said for the view that work on developing thought-reading machines is immoral, merely because it helps to make it possible.

2. TRANSPARENCY IN A FREE COMMUNITY

Much of the horror of devices to make our minds transparent to others has to do with their uses in an authoritarian society. We are surely right to fear these potential uses, but some of our deepest anxieties about privacy come from other sources. This can be seen by a thought experiment in which we eliminate misuse by the authorities. Imagine a community of free and equal people. (It is not clear what this comes to, but imagine the nearest we can get in practice to an anarchist utopia.) Even here, the general availability of thought-reading machines can be seen as a terrible threat.

Why should we be disturbed if our thoughts become transparent to others? Some explanations that come to mind involve particular projects, or particular kinds of thought, which generate their own reasons for secrecy. If we are trying to give someone a surprise, bargaining with him, or trying to swindle or cheat him, the project will collapse if our thoughts are publicly available. A society transparent in this way will be one in which bargaining and swindling are impossible, which will no doubt have repercussions on our economy. But most of us will see little reason for being appalled. More personal anxieties are stronger. Some of our thoughts would seem discreditable, or at least embarrassing. Feelings of jealousy or resentment, sexual fantasies, or Walter Mitty daydreams of a self-flattering kind would all be sources of embarrassment. And, less selfishly, we are glad to keep some thoughts about other people secret so that we do not hurt them.

But these reasons, although psychologically powerful, may not go the heart of the matter. They concern particular kinds of thoughts and feelings. We can imagine a society in which bargaining and swindling did not exist, and in which daydreams and sexual fantasies were no longer a matter for embarrassment. In that society, people might still feel a resistance to their mental lives being made transparent to others. There is a case for saying that the value of privacy depends on something deeper than the embarrassing or hurtful aspects of particular thoughts and feelings. It may be bound up with the nature of relationships, and with our sense of our own identity.

3. RELATIONSHIPS

On one view, the fact that we have an area of privacy is more important than which particular activities or thoughts are included in it. (This is suggested in a particularly perceptive discussion of these issues by Charles Fried.[1]) The claim is that privacy is necessary for different kinds of relationships. We choose how far to admit people to friendship or other relationships with us partly by controlling how much of what is private we reveal to them. As Fried puts it,

> Love or friendship can be partially expressed by the gift of other rights—gifts of property or of service. But these gifts, without the intimacy of shared private information, cannot alone constitute love or friendship. The man who is generous with his possessions, but not with himself, can hardly be a friend, nor—and this more clearly shows the necessity of privacy for love—can the man who, voluntarily or involuntarily, shares everything about himself with the world indiscriminately.

But is it certain that gradations of intimacy are necessary for differences of relationship? In a world of transparent relationships, there would still be room for people being generous with themselves to different degrees. We would continue to give people different amounts of our concern and our time. We would respond to people with varying degrees of warmth, and this would be more obvious than it is now. Close relationships would consist in choosing to be together, and in the way people would feel about each other. There would no longer be the mutual lowering of the barriers of privacy. Closeness would be different from now, but not so different as to be non-existent.

It does seem that some of the pleasures of relationships involve talking about things that otherwise would be private. We like to do things together and to talk about our responses. (Part of the appeal of films and, especially, novels is that they often portray people from the inside, and so give us comparisons to use in trying to capture and articulate our own fugitive private experiences.) In talking to each other, and so learning to express (and sharpen) our experiences, we are doing something similar to what a novelist does. If we were transparent to each other, some of the things we now say would not need to be said. But it does not follow that all such conversation would be eliminated. This is because our conversation does not just report responses, but shapes them. We often only get clear about our *own* thoughts and feelings by trying to express them to someone else, and by listening to their thoughts in return. So transparency would not destroy conversation, though we might just think together without having to talk.

But another aspect of relationships might be threatened by transparency. In our present state, privacy gives a special quality to the times when it is waived. Other people can seem like medieval fortified towns. We can climb the hill and walk round outside their walls. But if they open the gate and let us in, we have the pleasures of exploration, seeing squares and houses and churches, sometimes like those we know and sometimes quite different. And while you are showing me round your town, I am showing you round mine, so that we are each at the same time explorer and host. A world without privacy would be a world in which the gates of all towns would always be open, so the excitement of the first admission would be less.

If these changes in relationships are for the worse, they provide a reason for rejecting, not only the thought-reading machine, but also any *voluntary* general lowering of the barriers which protect privacy. The changes are equally likely whether our privacy is invaded from outside or whether it is given away freely.

But the value placed on gradations of intimacy need not be a reason against a much greater degree of transparency than we have now. We hide behind so many different layers of defences. There are barriers created by context: you can't mention that here. And there are barriers of manner and style, created perhaps because we feel threatened, signalling that we are unapproachable about this, or will not talk about that. Sometimes the threat turns out to be imaginary. Tolstoy describes this in *Anna Karenina:*

> Levin had often noticed in discussions between the most intelligent people that after enormous efforts, and endless logical subtleties and talk, the disputants finally became aware that what they had been at such pains to prove to one another had long ago, from the beginning of the argument, been known to both, but that they liked different things, and would not define what they liked for fear of its being attacked. He had often had the experience of suddenly in the middle of a discussion grasping what it was the other liked and at once liking it too, and immediately he found himself agreeing, and then all arguments fell away useless. Sometimes the reverse happened: he at last expressed what he liked himself, which he had been arguing to defend and, chancing to express it well and genuinely, had found the person he was disputing with suddenly agree.[2]

When we do not feel threatened, we are more willing to take down the barriers, and less timid people sometimes take them down even when they do feel threatened.

It may be that already, as the result of innumerable individual decisions, we are moving towards greater transparency. These things are hard to establish, and no doubt vary from culture to culture. But it seems to me that in our century, there has been a strong trend towards greater honesty in relationships, with greater openness about things which used to be private, and that this is part of a beneficial transformation of our consciousness and social life. (If taking down the barriers is starting to transform us, the obstruction of this process is another charge, to add to the familiar ones, against political systems where people fear the authorities, and so need the barriers.) This change could go a long way further, and still leave us room for different degrees of privacy and intimacy.

The effects of transparency on relationships would be in several ways beneficial. Deception, with its resulting erosion of love and friendship, would be impossible. And relationships now are obscured, not only by deception, but also by our limited ability to express our thoughts and feelings, and by our lack of perception about other people. The thought-reading machine, because of the problems about interpretation, would not abolish these limitations, but it would greatly reduce their obscuring effects. As we understood more about each other's mental lives, we would form more realistic pictures of each other, and it seems plausible that this would make relationships better rather than worse. And a stronger sense of community might result from the barriers of privacy coming down, together with the ending of a sense of loneliness and isolation which some people feel because of their inability to share their experiences.

Sometimes a society of transparent relationships is held up as an ideal. In a fine interview on his seventieth birthday,[3] Jean-Paul Sartre was asked, 'Does it bother you when I ask you about yourself?' He replied:

No, why? I believe that everyone should be able to speak of his innermost being to an interviewer. I think that what spoils relations among people is that each keeps something hidden from the other, something secret, not necessarily from everyone, but from whomever he is speaking to at the moment. I think transparency should always be substituted for what is secret, and I can quite well imagine the day when two men will no longer have secrets from each other, because no one will have any more secrets from anyone, because subjective life, as well as objective life, will be completely offered up, given . . . There is an as-for-myself (*quant-à-soi*), born of distrust, ignorance, and fear, which keeps me from being confidential with another, or not confidential enough. Personally, moreover, I do not express myself on all points with the people I meet, but I try to be as translucent as possible, because I feel that this dark region that we have within ourselves, which is at once dark for us and dark for others, can only be illuminated for ourselves in trying to illuminate it

for others . . . One can't say everything, you know that well. But I think that later, that is, after my death, and perhaps after yours, people will talk about themselves more and more and that this will produce a great change. Moreover, I think that this change is linked to a real revolution. A man's existence must be entirely visible to his neighbour, whose own existence must in turn be entirely visible to him, in order for true social harmony to be established.

There is obviously a big difference between Sartre's ideal and the world of the thought-reading machine. Sartre envisages people voluntarily abandoning their own secrecy of thought, rather than having the power to invade that of others. His transition period would involve no loss of autonomy, and might involve relatively little distress. The introduction of the thought-reading machine would not respect people's autonomy, but would strip them of secrecy against their will. It is hard to see how the process could fail to cause great unhappiness, both to those losing protective secrecy and to those who would be hurt by the thoughts of others. Resistance would be so strong that there might develop an arms race of offensive and defensive technology: devices to jam the thought-reading machines, devices to jam the jammers, and so on. But if, after the horrors of the transition period, the world of the thought-reading machine became established, the effect on relationships might be much the same as that of voluntarily lowering the barriers. And it is not obvious that transparent relationships would be worse than opaque ones.

4. IDENTITY AND INDIVIDUALITY

In our present world, the sort of people we are is to some extent the result of our own choices. (The question of the extent to which our choices could have been different raises the problems about determinism and free will, which will not be discussed here. But, whatever the solution to those problems, most of us prefer to have our identity modifiable by our decisions.) It may be that privacy contributes to this control. Charles Fried has said that we often have thoughts we do not express, and that only when we choose to express them do we adopt them as part of ourselves. If the end of privacy is the end of any distinction between thoughts being endorsed and merely being entertained, then we may lose some control over our identity. It may have been some view of this kind which led Justices Warren and Brandeis to argue that a legal right to privacy is independent of more general property rights: "The principle which protects personal writings and all other personal productions, not against theft and physical appropriation, but against publication in any form, is in reality not the principle of private property, but that of an inviolate personality."[4]

In suggestions of this kind, there is something obscure about the idea of personality or identity. For what a person is depends on all his features, including those concealed from others. A sufficiently subtle thought-reading machine would detect the difference between thoughts merely coming to mind and thoughts being endorsed. All that would be lost is concealment of thoughts only entertained. But it is part of me that I do entertain these thoughts, and my identity is not changed because this aspect of it comes to light. So when people say that transparency might threaten our freedom to choose our identity, they may not have in mind "identity" in the sense of being a particular kind of person, but "identity" in a sense closer to "images of ourselves projected to other people." It is obviously true that the abolition of privacy will reduce the control we have over the pictures other people have of us. But this seems more of a threat to our reputation than to our identity. Our freedom to define ourselves, when not just a matter of manipulation of image, is our freedom to choose between beliefs and attitudes, and to opt for some kinds of actions and ways of life rather than others. And this is not destroyed by others knowing what different ideas we have also considered.

Perhaps the threat posed by transparency is more oblique. It may be that public scrutiny of my mind does not in itself change my identity, but rather has effects which will inhibit the development of individuality. You will know when I am contemplating the ideas and actions you disapprove of, and I will know at once of your attitude. This may create very strong pressures to conform. John Stuart Mill wrote in 1859 of the social pressures towards respectability and conformity: "In our times, from the highest class of society down

to the lowest, everyone lives as under the eye of a hostile and dreaded censorship."[5] One result of transparency might be to extend the social censorship inwards, so that there would be the same pressures for conformity of thought and feeling as there are for conformity of behaviour. We have only partial control over our thoughts and feelings, but the social censorship might persuade us to turn away from lines of thought which we knew might lead us into dangerous areas, as well as not to act on ideas arousing disapproval.

Privacy is necessary if we are not to be stifled by other people. Even in our present world, without the thought-reading machine, being permanently observed, as in some prisons, can destroy individuality. (Sartre, in an earlier phase, talked in *Being and Nothingness* with an almost neurotic horror of being observed by other people, and vividly presented the awfulness of permanent scrutiny in *Huis Clos*, where hell for three people is being locked for ever in a room together.) To be observed by other people can build up a feeling of pressure to justify what we are doing and how we are doing it, or to justify doing nothing. For many people, happiness, and perhaps creativity and originality, flourish where there are long stretches free from critical appraisal.

Perhaps we have the potential to grow more robust, and in a world of transparent relationships we might grow stronger in our resistance to pressures to conform. But it is hard to see how the extra pressures could be avoided, with their obvious threat to individuality.

5. THE TWO PERSPECTIVES

I have suggested that transparency would not in itself threaten our identity, and that its effects on relationships might, after a transition period, be beneficial. But it is plausible that it would allow new and powerful social pressures for conformity. If this account is accepted, our view of any proposed steps towards the transparent world will depend on how we weigh these different gains and losses. Any appraisal is difficult because it is hard to imagine relationships so transformed. If the threat to individuality seems much more clear than the benefits to relationships, many of us will be very cautious in our attitude to the dismantling of the barriers of privacy.

Yet it may be that our horror at the thought of entering the transparent world is nothing to the horror with which people in the transparent world will look back at our lives. They may think of us as hiding behind barriers of mutual pretense, like the inhabitants of a suburban street hiding behind fences and hedges. They might be far more concerned to avoid the reinstatement of the barriers of privacy than we are to avoid them being dismantled. The conflict between their perspective and ours, which will reappear in other contexts, raises a deep theoretical difficulty in deciding what sort of world we should aim for.

NOTES

1. *An Anatomy of Values,* Harvard, 1970, chapter 9.
2. *Anna Karenina,* translated by Rosemary Edmonds, Harmondsworth, 1954, p. 421.
3. "Sartre at Seventy: An Interview," *New York Review of Books,* August 1975.
4. "The Right to Privacy," *Harvard Law Review,* 1890.
5. *On Liberty,* chapter 3.

Further Questions

1. What differences are there, if any, between honesty and openness?
2. Do you think that honesty and openness are a good thing generally, or only under certain conditions? What conditions?

Further Readings

Goffman, Erving. *The Presentation of Self in Everyday Life.* New York: Doubleday, 1959. A classic account of how we project our "image" to the world.
Weil, Simone. "Friendship," in *Waiting for God.* New York: Harper & Row, 1973.

Intrinsic Value   82

G. E. MOORE

A brief biography of Moore appears on page 201.

In the following selection from his book *Ethics* (London, 1912), Moore gives his views, first, about what it means to say of some action that it was intrinsically either good or bad and, second, about whether any actions actually have been either intrinsically good or bad.

Reading Questions

1. What does Moore mean by *intrinsically good* and *intrinsically bad*?
2. What is "the Objection of Egoism"? To what is it an objection?
3. What is the point of Moore's "paradox" about the two men, A and B? Do you agree with Moore's conclusion?
4. Moore considers the question of whether one whole is intrinsically better than another just in case it contains more pleasure. How does he answer? Do you agree with his answer?

THE MAIN CONCLUSIONS, at which we have arrived so far, . . . may be briefly summed up as follows. I tried to show, first of all, (1) that to say that a voluntary action is *right,* or *ought* to be done, or is *wrong,* is *not* the same thing as to say that any being or set of beings whatever, either human or non-human, has towards it any mental attitude whatever—either an attitude of feeling, or of willing, or of thinking something about it; and that hence no proof to the effect that any beings, human or non-human, have any such attitude towards an action is sufficient to show that it is right, or ought to be done, or is wrong; and (2) similarly, that to say that any one thing or state of things is *intrinsically good,* or *intrinsically bad,* or that one is *intrinsically better* than another, is also not the same thing as to say that any being or set of beings has towards it any mental attitude whatever—either an attitude of feeling, or of desiring, or of thinking something about it; and hence that here again no proof to the effect that any being or set of beings *has* some such mental attitude towards a given thing or state of things is ever sufficient to show that it is intrinsically good or bad. These two points are extremely important, because the contrary view is very commonly held, in some form or other, and because (though this is not always seen), whatever form it be held in, it is absolutely fatal to one or both of two very fundamental principles, which our theory implies. In many of their forms such views are fatal to the principle (1) that no action is ever *both* right and wrong; and hence also to the view that there is any characteristic whatever which *always* belongs to right actions and *never* to wrongs ones; and in *all* their forms they are fatal to the principle, (2) that if it is once the duty of any being to do an action whose total effects will be A rather than one whose total effects will be B, it must *always* be the duty of any being to do an action whose total effects will be precisely similar to A rather than one whose total effects will be precisely similar to B, if he has to choose between them.

I tried to show, then, first of all, that these two principles may be successfully defended against this first line of attack—the line of attack which consists in saying (to put it shortly) that "right" and "good" are merely *subjective* predicates. But we found next that even those who admit and insist (as many do) that "right" and "intrinsically good" are *not* subjective predicates, may yet attack the second principle on another ground. For this second principle implies that the question whether an action is right or wrong must always depend upon its *actual* consequences; and this view is very commonly disputed on one or other of three grounds, namely (1) that it sometimes depends merely on the *intrinsic nature* of the action, or, in other words, that certain kinds of actions would be absolutely always right, and others absolutely wrong, *whatever* their consequences might be, or (2) that it depends, partly or wholly, on the *motive* from which the action is done, or (3) that it depends on the question whether the agent had *reason to expect* that its consequences would be the best possible. I tried, accordingly, to show next that each of these three views is untrue.

But, finally, we raised . . . a question as to the *precise* sense in which right and wrong do *depend* upon the actual consequences. And here for the first time we came upon a point as to which it seemed very doubtful whether our theory was right. All that could be agreed upon was that a voluntary action is right whenever and only when its total consequences are *as* good, intrinsically, as any that would have followed from any action which the agent *could have* done instead. But we were unable to arrive at any certain conclusion as to the precise sense in which the phrase "*could have*" must be understood if this proposition is to be true; and whether, therefore, it *is* true, it we give to these words the precise sense which our theory gave to them.

I conclude, then, that the theory stated . . . is right so far as it merely asserts the three principles (1) That there *is* some characteristic which belongs and must belong to absolutely *all* right voluntary actions and to *no* wrong ones; (2) That one such characteristic consists in the fact that the total consequences of right actions must always be as good, intrinsically, as any which it was *possible* for the agent to produce under the circumstances (it being uncertain, however, in what sense precisely the word "possible" is to be understood), whereas this can never be true of wrong ones; and (3) That if any set of consequences A is once intrinsically better than another set B, any set precisely similar to A must always be intrinsically better than a set precisely similar to B. We have, indeed, not considered all the objections which might be urged against these three principles; but we have, I think considered all those which are most commonly urged, *with one single exception.* And I must now briefly state what this one remaining objection is, before I go on to point out the respect in which this theory . . . seems to me to be utterly wrong, in spite of being right as to all these three points.

This one last objection may be called the objection of Egoism; and it consists in asserting that no agent can ever be under any obligation to do the action, whose *total* consequences will be the best possible, *if* its total effects upon *him,* personally, are not the best possible; or in other words that it always would be *right* for an agent to choose the action whose total effects *upon himself* would be the best, even if *absolutely all* its effects (taking into account its effects on other beings as well) would *not* be the best. It asserts in short that it can never be the duty of any agent to sacrifice his own good to the general good. And most people, who take this view, are, I think content to assert this, without asserting further that it must always be his positive *duty* to prefer his own good to the general good. That is to say, they will admit that a man may be acting *rightly,* even if he *does* sacrifice his own good to the general good; they only hold that he will be acting *equally* rightly, if he does *not.* But there are some philosophers who seem to hold that I must *always* be an agent's positive duty to do what is best for *himself*—*always,* for instance, to do what will conduce most to his own "perfection," or his own salvation, or his own "self-realization"; who imply, therefore, that it would be his duty so to act, even if the action in question did *not* have the best possible consequences upon the whole.

Now the question, whether this view is true, in either of these two different forms, would, of course, be of no practical importance, if it were true that, as a matter of fact, every action which most promotes the general good always *also* most promotes the agent's own good, and vice versa. And many philosophers have taken great pains to try to show that this *is* the case: some have even tried to show that it *must* necessarily be the case. But it seems to me that none of the arguments which have been used to prove this proposition really do show that it is by any means *universally*

true. A case, for instance, may arise in which, if a man is to secure the best consequences for the world as a whole, it may be absolutely necessary that he should sacrifice his own life. And those who maintain that, even in such a case, he will absolutely always be securing the greatest possible amount of good *for himself,* must either maintain that in some future life he will receive goods sufficient to compensate him for all that he might have had during many years of continued life in this world—a view to which there is the objection that it may be doubted, whether we shall have any future life at all, and that it is even more doubtful, what, *if* we shall, that life will be like; or else they must maintain the following paradox.

Suppose there are two men, A and B, who up to the age of thirty have lived lives of equal intrinsic value; and that at that age it becomes the duty of each of them to sacrifice his life for the general good. Suppose A does his duty and sacrifices his life, but B does not, and continues to live for thirty years more. Those who hold that the agent's own good *always* coincides with the general good, must then hold that B's sixty years of life, no matter how well the remaining thirty years of it may be spent, cannot possibly have so much intrinsic value as A's life in which he does his duty at the expense of his life; and however high we put the loss in intrinsic value to B's life, which arises from the fact that, in this one instance, he failed to do his duty. B may, for instance, repent of this one act and the whole of the remainder of his life may be full of the highest goods; and it seems extravagant to maintain that all the goods there may be in this last thirty years of it cannot possibly be enough to make his life more valuable, intrinsically, than that of A.

I think, therefore, we must conclude that a maximum of true good, for ourselves, is by no means always secured by those actions which are necessary to secure a maximum of true good for the world as a whole; and hence that it *is* a question of practical importance, whether, in such cases of conflict, it is always a duty, or right, for us to prefer our own good to the general good. And this is a question which, so far as I can see, it is impossible to decide by argument one way or the other. If any person, after clearly considering the question, comes to the conclusion that he can never be under any obligation to sacrifice his own good to the general good, if they *were* to conflict, or even that it would be wrong for him to do so, it is, I think, impossible to prove that he is mistaken. But it is certainly equally impossible for him to prove that he is not mistaken. And, for my part, it seems to me quite self-evident that he is mistaken. It seems to me quite self-evident that it must always be our duty to do what will produce the best effects *upon the whole,* no matter how bad the effects upon ourselves may be and no matter how much good we ourselves may lose by it.

I think, therefore, we may safely reject this last objection to the principle that it must always be the duty of every agent to do that one, among all the actions which he *can* do on any given occasion, whose *total consequences* will have the greatest intrinsic value; and we may conclude, therefore, that the theory . . . is right as to all the three points yet considered, except for the doubt as to the precise sense in which the words "can do" are to be understood in this proposition. But obviously on any theory which maintains, as this one does, that right and wrong depend on the intrinsic value of the consequences of our actions, it is extremely important to decide rightly what kinds of consequences *are* intrinsically better or worse than others. And it is on this important point that the theory in question seems to me to take an utterly wrong view. It maintains, as we saw . . . that any whole which contains *more pleasure* is always intrinsically better than one which contains less, and that none can be intrinsically better, *unless* it contains more pleasure; it being remembered that the phrase "more pleasure," in this statement, is not to be understood as meaning strictly what it says, but as standing for any one of five different alternatives, the nature of which was fully explained. . . . And the last question we have to raise is, therefore: Is this proposition true or not? and if not, what *is* the right answer to the question: What kinds of things are intrinsically better or worse than others?

And first of all it is important to be quite clear as to how this question is related to another question, which is very liable to be confused with it: namely the question whether the proposition which was distinguished . . . as forming *the first part* of the theory . . . is true or not: I mean, the proposition that quantity of pleasure is a correct *criterion* of right and wrong, or that, *in this world,*

it always is, *as a matter of fact,* our duty to do the action which will produce a maximum of pleasure, or (for this is, perhaps, more commonly held) to do the action which, *so far as we can see,* will produce such a maximum. This latter proposition has been far more often *expressly* held than the proposition that what contains more pleasure is *always* intrinsically better than what contains less; and many people may be inclined to think they are free to maintain it, even if they deny that the intrinsic value of every whole is *always* in proportion to the quantity of pleasure it contains. And so, *in a sense,* they are; for it is quite possible, *theoretically,* that quantity of pleasure should always be a correct *criterion* of right and wrong, here in this world, even if intrinsic value is not always in exact proportion to quantity of pleasure. But though this is theoretically possible, it is, I think, easy to see that it is extremely *unlikely* to be the case. For if it were the case, what it would involve is this. It would involve our maintaining that, where the total consequences of any actual voluntary action have more intrinsic value than those of the possible alternatives, it *absolutely always* happens to be true that they *also* contain more pleasure, although, in other cases, we know that degree of intrinsic value is by no means always in proportion to quantity of pleasure contained. And, of course, it is theoretically possible that this should be so: it is *possible* that the total consequences of actual voluntary actions should form a complete exception to the general rule: that, in their case, what has more intrinsic value should *absolutely always* also contain more pleasure, although, in other cases, this is by no means always true: but anybody can see, I think, that, in the absence of strict proof that it is so, the probabilities are all the other way. It is, indeed, so far as I can see, quite impossible absolutely to *prove* either that it is so or that it is not so; because *actual* actions in this world are liable to have such an immense number of indirect and remote consequences, which we cannot trace, that it is impossible to be quite certain how the *total* consequences of any two actions will compare either in respect of intrinsic value, or in respect of the quantity of pleasure they contain. It *may,* therefore, *possibly* be the case that quantity of pleasure *is,* as a matter of fact, a correct *criterion* of right and wrong, even if intrinsic value is *not* always in proportion to quantity of pleasure contained. But it is impossible to *prove* that it is a correct criterion, except by assuming that intrinsic value always *is* in proportion to quantity of pleasure. And most of those who have held the former view have, I think, in fact made this assumption, even if they have not definitely realized that they were making it.

Is this assumption true, then? Is it true that one whole will be intrinsically better than another, whenever and only when it contains more pleasure, no matter what the two may be like in other respects? It seems to me almost impossible that any one, who fully realizes the consequences of such a view, can possibly hold that it *is* true. It involved our saying, for instance, that a world in which absolutely nothing except pleasure existed—no knowledge, no love, no enjoyment of beauty, no moral qualities—must yet be intrinsically better—better worth creating—provided only the total quantity of pleasure in it were the least bit greater, than one in which all these things existed *as well as* pleasure. It involves our saying that, even if the total quantity of pleasure in each was exactly equal, yet the fact that all the beings in the one possessed in addition knowledge of many different kinds and a full appreciation of all that was beautiful or worthy of love in their world, whereas *none* of the beings in the other possessed any of these things, would give us no reason whatever for preferring the former to the latter. It involves our saying that, for instance, the state of mind of a drunkard, when he is intensely pleased with breaking crockery, is just as valuable, in itself—just as well worth having, as that of a man who is fully realizing all that is exquisite in the tragedy of King Lear, provided only the mere quantity of pleasure in both cases is the same. Such instances might be multiplied indefinitely, and it seems to me that they constitute a *reductio ad absurdum* of the view that intrinsic value is always in proportion to quantity of pleasure. Of course, here again, the question is quite incapable of proof either way. And if anybody, after clearly considering the issue, does come to the conclusion that no one kind of enjoyment is ever intrinsically better than another, provided only that the pleasure in both is equally intense, and that, if we *could* get as much pleasure in the world, without needing to have any knowledge, or any moral qualities, or any sense of beauty, as we can get *with*

them, then all these things would be entirely superfluous, there is no way of proving that he is wrong. But it seems to me almost impossible that anybody, who does really get the question clear, should take such a view; and, if anybody were to, I think it is self-evident that he would be wrong.

It may, however, be asked: If the matter is as plain as this, how has it come about that anybody ever has adopted the view that intrinsic value *is* always in proportion to quantity of pleasure, or has ever argued, as if it were so? And I think one chief answer to this question is that those who have done so have *not* clearly realized all the consequences of their view, partly because they have been too exclusively occupied with the particular question as to whether, in the case of *the total consequences* of *actual* voluntary actions, degree of intrinsic value is not always in proportion to quantity of pleasure—a question which, as has been admitted, is, in itself, much more obscure. But there is, I think, another reason, which is worth mentioning, because it introduces us to a principle of great importance. It may, in fact, be held, with great plausibility, that no whole can ever have any intrinsic value *unless* it contains some pleasure; and it might be thought, at first sight, that this reasonable, and perhaps true, view could not possibly lead to the wholly unreasonable one that intrinsic value is always *in proportion* to quantity of pleasure: it might seem obvious that to say that nothing can be valuable *without* pleasure is a very different thing from saying that intrinsic value is always *in proportion* to pleasure. And it is, I think, in fact true that the two views are really as different as they seem, and that the latter does not at all follow from the former. But, if we look a little closer, we may, I think, see a reason why the latter should very naturally have been *thought* to follow from the former.

The reason is as follows. If we say that no whole can ever by intrinsically good, *unless* it contains some pleasure, we are, of course, saying that if from any whole, which is intrinsically good, we were to subtract all the pleasure it contains, the remainder, whatever it might be, would have no intrinsic goodness at all, but must always be either intrinsically *bad,* or else intrinsically indifferent: and this (if we remember our definition of intrinsic value) is the same thing as to say that this remainder actually *has* no intrinsic goodness at all, but always *is* either positively bad or indifferent. Let us call the pleasure which such a whole contains, A, and the whole remainder, whatever it may be, B. We are then saying that the whole A+B is intrinsically good, but that B is *not* intrinsically good at all. Surely it seems to follow that the intrinsic value of A+B cannot possibly be greater than that of A by itself? How, it may be asked, could it possibly be otherwise? How, by adding to A something, namely B, which has *no* intrinsic goodness at all, could we possibly get a whole which has *more* intrinsic value than A? It may naturally seem to be self-evident that we could not. But, if so, then it absolutely follows that we can never increase the value of any whole whatever except by adding *pleasure* to it: we may, of course, *lessen* its value, by adding other things, e.g. by adding pain; but we can never *increase* it except by adding pleasure.

Now from this it does not, of course, follow strictly that the intrinsic value of a whole is always *in proportion* to the quantity of pleasure it contains in the special sense in which we have throughout been using this expression—that is to say, as meaning that it is in proportion to the *excess* of pleasure over pain, in one of the five senses explained . . . . But it is surely very natural to think that it does. And it *does* follow that we must be wrong in the reasons we gave for disputing this proposition. It does follow that we must be wrong in thinking that by adding such things as knowledge or a sense of beauty to a world which contained a certain amount of pleasure, without adding any more pleasure, we could increase the intrinsic value of that world. If, therefore, we are to dispute the proposition that intrinsic value *is* always in proportion to quantity of pleasure we must dispute this argument. But the argument may seem to be almost indisputable. It has, in fact, been used as an argument in favour of the proposition that intrinsic value *is* always in proportion to quantity of pleasure, and I think it has probably had much influence in inducing people to adopt that view, even if they have not expressly put it in this form.

How, then, can we dispute this argument? We might, of course, do so, by rejecting the proposition that no whole can ever be intrinsically good, *unless* it contains some pleasure; but, for my part, though I don't feel certain that this proposition *is* true, I also don't feel at all certain that it is *not*

true. The part of the argument which it seems to me certainly can and ought to be disputed is another part—namely, the assumption that, where a whole contains two factors, A and B, and one of these, B, has no intrinsic goodness at all, the intrinsic value of the whole cannot be *greater* than that of the other factor, A. This assumption, I think, obviously rests on a still more general assumption, of which it is only a special case. The general assumption is: That where a whole consists of two factors A and B, the amount by which its intrinsic value exceeds that of one of these two factors must always be equal to that of the other factor. Our special case will follow from this general assumption: because it will follow that if B be intrinsically *indifferent* that is to say, if its intrinsic value=0, then the amount by which the value of the whole A+B exceeds the value of A must also=0, that is to say, the value of the whole must be precisely *equal* to that of A; while if B be intrinsically *bad,* that is to say, if its intrinsic value is less than 0, then the amount by which the value of A+B will exceed that of A will also be less than 0, that is to say, the value of the whole will be *less* than that of A. Our special case does then follow from the general assumption; and nobody, I think, would maintain that the special case was true without maintaining that the general assumption was also true. The general assumption may, indeed, very naturally seem to be self-evident: it has, I think, been generally assumed that it is so: and it may seem to be a mere deduction from the laws of arithmetic. But, so far as I can see, it is *not* a mere deduction from the laws of arithmetic, and, so far from being self-evident, is certainly untrue.

Let us see exactly what we are saying, if we deny it. We are saying that the fact that A and B *both* exist together, together with the fact that they have to one another any relation which they do happen to have (when they exist together, they always must have *some* relation to one another; and the precise nature of the relation certainly may in some cases make a great difference to the value of the whole state of things, though, perhaps, it need not in all cases)—that these two facts *together* must have a certain amount of intrinsic value, that is to say must be either intrinsically good, or intrinsically bad, or intrinsically indifferent, and that the amount by which this value exceeds the value which the existence of A would have, if A existed quite alone, *need* not be equal to the value which the existence of B would have, if B existed quite alone. This is all that we are saying. And can any one pretend that such a view necessarily contradicts the laws of arithmetic? or that, it is self-evident that it cannot be true? I cannot see any ground for saying so; and if there is no ground, then the argument which sought to show that we can never add to the value of any whole *except* by adding pleasure to it, is entirely baseless.

If, therefore, we reject the theory that intrinsic value is always in proportion to quantity of pleasure, it does seem as if we may be compelled to accept the principle that *the amount by which the value of a whole exceeds that of one of its factors is not necessarily equal to that of the remaining factor*—a principle which, if true, is very important in many other cases. But, though at first sight this principle may seem paradoxical, there seems to be no reason why we should not accept it; while there are other independent reasons why we should accept it. And, in any case, it seems quite clear that the degree of intrinsic value of a whole is *not* always in proportion to the quantity of pleasure it contains.

But, if we do reject this theory, what, it may be asked, can we substitute for it? How can we answer the question, what kinds of consequences are intrinsically better or worse than others?

We may, I think, say, first of all, that for the same reason for which we have rejected the view that intrinsic value is always in proportion to quantity of pleasure, we must also reject the view that it is always in proportion to the quantity of any other *single* factor whatever. Whatever single kind of thing may be proposed as a measure of intrinsic value, instead of pleasure—whether knowledge, or virtue, or wisdom, or love—it is, I think, quite plain that it is not such a measure; because it is quite plain that, however valuable any one of these things may be, we may always add to the value of a whole which contains any one of them, not only by adding more of that one, but also *by adding something else instead*. Indeed, so far as I can see, there is no characteristic whatever which always distinguishes every whole which has greater intrinsic value from every whole which has less, *except* the fundamental one that it would always be the duty

of every agent to prefer the better to the worse, if he had to choose between a pair of actions, of which they would be the *sole* effects. And similarly, so far as I can see, there is no characteristic whatever which belongs to all things that are intrinsically *good* and only to them—except simply the one that they all *are* intrinsically good and *ought* always to be preferred to *nothing at all,* if we had to choose between an action whose sole effect would be one of them and one which would have no effects whatever. The fact is that the view which seems to me to be true is the one which, apart from theories, I think every one would naturally take, namely, that there are an *immense variety* of different things, *all* of which are intrinsically good; and that though all these things may perhaps have some characteristic *in common,* their variety is so great that they have none, which, *besides* being common to them all, is also *peculiar* to them—that is to say, which never beongs to anything which is intrinsically bad or indifferent. All that can, I think, be done by way of making plain what kinds of things are intrinsically good or bad, and what are better or worse than others, is to classify some of the chief kinds of each, pointing out what the factors are upon which their goodness or badness depends. And I think this is one of the most profitable things which can be done in Ethics, and one which has been too much neglected hitherto. But I have not space to attempt it here.

I have only space for two final remarks. The first is that there do seem to be two important characteristics, which are *common* to absolutely all intrinsic goods, though not peculiar to them. Namely (1) it does seem as if nothing can be an intrinsic good unless it contains *both* some feeling and *also* some other form of consciousness; and, as we have said before, it seems possible that amongst the feelings contained must always be some amount of pleasure. And (2) it does also seem as if every intrinsic good must be a complex whole containing a considerable variety of different factors—as if, for instance, nothing so simple as pleasure by itself, however intense, could ever be any good. But it is important to insist (though it is obvious) that neither of these characteristics is *peculiar* to intrinsic goods: they may obviously *also* belong to things bad and indifferent. Indeed, as regards the first, it is not only true that many wholes which contain both feeling and some other form of consciousness are intrinsically bad; but it seems also to be true that nothing can be intrinsically bad, *unless* it contains some feeling.

The other final remark is that we must be very careful to distinguish the two questions (1) whether, and in what degree, a thing is *intrinsically* good and bad, and (2) whether, and in what degree, it is capable of adding to or subtracting from the intrinsic value of a whole of which it forms a part, from a third, entirely different question, namely (3) whether, and in what degree, a thing is *useful* and has good *effects,* or *harmful* and has *bad* effects. All three questions are very liable to be confused, because, in common life, we apply the names " good" and "bad" to things of all three kinds indifferently: when we say that a thing is "good" we may mean either (1) that it is intrinsically good or (2) that it adds to the value of many intrinsically good wholes or (3) that it is useful or has good effects; and similarly when we say that a thing is bad we may mean any one of the three corresponding things. And such confusions is very liable to lead to mistakes, of which the following are, I think, the commonest. In the first place, people are apt to assume with regard to things, which really are very good indeed in senses (1) or (2), that they are scarcely any good at all, simply because they do no seem to be of much *use*—that is

to say, to lead to *further* good effects; and similarly, with regard to things which really are very bad in senses (1) or (2), it is very commonly assumed that there cannot be much, if any, harm in them, simply because they do not seem to lead to *further* bad results. Nothing is commoner than to find people asking of a good thing: What *use* is it? and concluding that, if it is no use, it cannot be any good; or asking of a bad thing: What harm does it do? and concluding that if it *does* no harm there cannot be any harm *in* it. Or, again, by a converse mistake, of things which really are very useful, but are not good at all in senses (1) and (2), it is very commonly assumed that they *must* be good in one or both of these two senses. Or again, of things, which really are very good in senses (1) and (2), it is assumed that, because they are good, they cannot possibly do harm. Or finally, of things, which are neither intrinsically good nor useful, it is assumed that they cannot be any good at all, although in fact they are very good in sense (2). All these mistakes are liable to occur, because, in fact, the degree of goodness or badness of a thing in any one of these three senses is by no means always in proportion to the degree of its goodness or badness in either of the other two; but if we are careful to distinguish the three different questions, they can, I think, all be avoided.

Further Questions

1. Some philosophers—hedonists—maintain that only pleasure (or satisfaction) is intrinsically good. Moore denies this. How might a hedonist best respond to Moore's arguments?
2. Explain how the question of whether values are "subjective" or "objective" bears, if it does at all, on the adequacy of Moore's conclusions.

Further Readings

Brandt, Richard B. *Facts, Values, and Morality.* Cambridge: Cambridge University Press, 1996.
    Focuses on the questions of how value judgments and moral beliefs can be justified.
Lemos, Noah M. *Intrinsic Value: Concept and Warrant.* Cambridge: Cambridge University Press, 1994.

Epilog

Concluding Unphilosophical Postscript

A Portrait of the Philosopher as a Young Man

ROBERT NOZICK

A brief biography of Nozick appears on page 380.

WHEN I WAS FIFTEEN YEARS OLD or sixteen I carried around in the streets of Brooklyn a paperback copy of Plato's *Republic,* front cover facing outward. I had read only some of it and understood less, but I was excited by it and knew it was something wonderful. How much I wanted an older person to notice me carrying it and be impressed, to pat me on the shoulder and say . . . I didn't know what exactly.

I sometimes wonder, not without uneasiness, what that young man of fifteen or sixteen would think of what he has grown up to do. I would like to think that with this book he would be pleased.

It now occurs to me to wonder also whether that older person whose recognition and love he sought then might not turn out to be the person he would grow up to become. If we reach adulthood by becoming the parent of our parents, and we reach maturity by finding a fit substitute for parents' love, then by becoming our ideal parent ourselves finally the circle is closed and we reach completeness.

From Robert Nozick, The Examined Life. *(New York: Simon & Schuster, 1989).*

On Becoming a Philosopher

FREEMAN DYSON

Freeman Dyson is a professor of physics at the Institute for Advanced Study in Princeton. Besides his work in theoretical physics, he has written popular meditations on the problems of war, the human condition, nuclear weapons, and the universe in *Disturbing the Universe* (Harper & Row, 1979), *Weapons and Hope* (Harper & Row, 1984), and *Infinite in All Directions* (Harper & Row, 1985). The following excerpt is from a letter Dyson wrote about his longtime friend and fellow physicist, Richard Feynman, who won a Nobel Prize for his work in particle physics.

April 9, 1981

DEAR ———,

I just spent a marvelous three days with Dick Feynman and wished you had been there to share him with us. Sixty years and a big cancer operation have not blunted him. He is still the same Feynman that we knew in the old days at Cornell.

We were together at a small meeting of physicists organized by John Wheeler at the University of Texas. For some reason Wheeler decided to hold the meeting at a grotesque place called World of Tennis, a country club where Texas oil-millionaires go to relax. So there we were. We all grumbled at the high prices and the extravagant ugliness of our rooms. But there was nowhere else to go. Or so we thought. But Dick thought otherwise. Dick just said: "To hell with it. I am not going to sleep in this place," picked up his suitcase and walked off alone into the woods. In the morning he reappeared, looking none the worse for his night under the stars. He said he did not sleep much, but it was worth it.

We had many conversations about science and history, just like in the old days. But now he had something new to talk about, his children. He said: "I always thought I would be a specially good father because I wouldn't try to push my kids into any particular direction. I wouldn't try to turn them into scientists or intellectuals if they didn't want it. I would be just as happy with them if they decided to be truck-drivers or guitar-players. In fact I would even like it better if they went out in the world and did something real instead of being professors like me. But they always find a way to hit back at you. My boy Carl for instance. There he is in his second year at MIT, and all he wants to do with his life is to become a god-damned philosopher!" . . .

From the personal correspondence of Freeman Dyson. Used by permission of the author.

Glossary

Ad hoc. One's defense of a theory in response to an objection is *ad hoc* if one defends the theory by modifying it artificially, simply changing it enough to avoid the objection but without explaining why the change is natural or necessary quite apart from the objection. Usually, when one says that someone else's defense of a theory is ad hoc, the implication is that if the person cannot do better in defending the theory he or she ought to admit that it is wrong.

Ad hominem objection. Instead of objecting to what another says by showing that what he or she says is false, one irrelevantly attacks the person instead. For instance, Jones: "The minimum wage should be raised since one cannot live decently, in many parts of the country, on minimum wages." Smith: "Jones is a Communist, and his opinion, which is typical Commie tripe, should be disregarded."

Affirming the consequent. An incorrect mode of reasoning in which one infers from the fact that the consequent of a conditional (what follows the "then" in an "if . . . , then . . ." statement) is true, that the antecedent of the condition (what follows the "if") is true. For instance, one affirms the consequent if one argues as follows: If Jones is a Communist, then Jones is an atheist. Jones is an atheist. Therefore, Jones is a Communist.

A fortiori. With even stronger reason. For instance, "If it is unlikely that Senator Blowhard will win the election even in his own state, then, a fortiori, it is unlikely that he will win it in the country as a whole."

Agent. Someone who performs an action.

Agent causation. Usually it is thought that causes and effects must be events. But some philosophers have claimed that the cause of an action may be, rather than any event, simply the agent who performed the action. This is usually said as a way of defending freedom of the will against the theories of determinists.

Agnosticism. See *atheism*.

Analytic statement/synthetic statement. A statement is analytic if it cannot be false because its denial is self-contradictory, a condition that will obtain when a statement is true merely because of the meaning of the words used to formulate it, as in the statement that all bachelors are unmarried, or because of its logical form, as in the statement that either pigs can fly or it's not the case that pigs can fly. An analytic statement that is true because of its logical form is said to be *tautology*. Statements that are not analytic are synthetic. The denial of a synthetic statement is not self-contradictory.

A posteriori. A statement is *a posteriori* if one has to appeal to experience to determine whether it is true. For example, the statement "All swans are white," which most Europeans believed at the beginning of the nineteenth century, is both *a posteriori* and also false (since there are black swans). An *a posteriori* statement is contingent, rather than necessary, in that even if it is true, it is the sort of statement (unlike, say, "A rose is a rose") that, if the facts had been different, could have been false. See *analytic*.

A priori. A statement is *a priori* if one can determine whether it is true without appealing to experience. For example, "If there are more than four people in the room, then there are more than two people in the room." An *a priori* statement is necessary, rather than contingent, in that if it is true, it could not have been false, and if it is false, it could not have been true.

Argument. In ordinary usage, an argument is a debate between two or more people, often a heated debate. Philosophers also use the word "argument" to mean a set of statements consisting of a conclusion and one or more premises that are said to provide grounds or reasons for the conclusion. In the philosophical sense of "argument," words such as "for," "since," "due to," and "because" often precede statements intended to be premises, while words such as "thus," "so," "hence," "therefore," "it follows that," and "then" often precede statements intended to be conclusions.

Artificial intelligence (abbreviated AI). An area of study in computer science and psychology that involves writing computer programs that simulate, or mimic, certain "intelligent" human activities, such as playing chess or carrying on a conversation.

Atheism/theism/agnosticism. Atheism is the view that God does not exist; theism, the view that God does exist; and agnosticism, the view that no one (or, alternatively, the person who calls himself or herself an agnostic) knows whether God exists.

Behaviorism. There are two main forms. *Methodological* behaviorism is the view that only external behavior should be investigated by the science of psychology. B. F. Skinner is the best known methodological behaviorist. *Analytic* (or *philosophical*) behaviorism is the view that when we use mentalistic language to apparently refer to private mental episodes, what we are actually talking about is external behavior.

Burden of proof. In a disagreement, sometimes one side is expected to prove its case, and if it can't, the other side wins. In such a situation, the side that is expected to prove its case is said to have the burden of proof.

Conditional. An "if . . . , then . . ." statement. For instance, if Jones wins the lottery, then he will be a rich man.

Confirmation/disconfirmation/verification/falsification. A statement or theory has been confirmed (or verified) when there is evidence for it that is strong enough to entitle us to believe that the statement or theory is true. It is disconfirmed (or falsified) when the evidence against it entitles us to believe that the statement or theory is false.

Contradiction/self-contradiction. One or more statements that both affirm that something is the case and also deny it. The joint affirmation and denial may be explicit or implicit. It is always the case that contradictory statements are false. When two or more statements are jointly contradictory, it is always the case that at least one of them is false.

Deductive argument/deduction/inductive argument/induction. A correct deductive argument is an argument such that if we assume its premises are true, then its conclusion must be true; that is, an argument such that it would be self-contradictory to affirm its premises while also denying its conclusion. Correct deductive arguments provide absolutely conclusive evidence for their conclusions. Correct inductive arguments, on the other hand, support their conclusions by showing only that they are probably true.

Descriptive. See *normative*.

Disconfirmation. See *confirmation*.

Dualism. See *substance*.

Equivocation. See *verbal dispute*.

Falsification. See *confirmation*.

Idealism. See *substance*.

Inductive argument. See *deductive argument*.

Law of nature. A lawlike universal statement of the form, "All *As* are *B*," or "If *X*, then *Y*," or "Whenever *X*, then *Y*," which is empirically testable or an essential part of a theory that is empirically testable. Lawlike statements, when true, are not true accidentally but must be true because of the way the world is constituted. For instance, the universal statement that all the marbles in the jar are black, even if it were true, is not lawlike, since one could have made it false simply by putting a white marble in the jar. The universal statements that formulate laws in physics, on the other hand, are lawlike since one could not, even if one tried, do something to make them false.

Materialism. See *substance*.

Necessary condition/sufficient condition. Generally, something, *X*, is a *necessary* condition for something else, *Y*, just in case *Y* without *X* is impossible; and something, *X*, is a *sufficient* condition for something else, *Y*, just in case *X* without *Y* is impossible. For example, the presence of oxygen is a necessary condition for fire because it is impossible for there to be a fire unless oxygen is present. On the other hand, the fire is a sufficient condition for the presence of oxygen because if there is a fire, oxygen must be present.

Normative/descriptive. A statement is normative when it expresses a value, for instance, when it says how people ought to behave or what is good and what is bad. A statement is descriptive, on the other hand, when it merely states the facts without expressing any values.

Ontology. The study of being, that is, of what basic kinds of things exist. See *substance*.

Physicalism. See *substance*.

Proposition. A sentence that is either true or false.

Self-contradiction. See *contradiction*.

Sound deductive argument. A correct (or valid) deductive argument, all of the premises of which are true. That is, a deductive argument all of the premises of which are true and which satisfies the following condition: its premises cannot be affirmed and its conclusion denied without self-contradiction. (Inductive arguments, by contrast, are neither sound nor unsound, valid nor invalid; instead, we say of inductive arguments that they are either good or bad, reasonable or unreasonable, acceptable or unacceptable, and so on.)

Statement. See *proposition*.

Straw-man. A bad form of arguing in which one tries to refute a position by arguing against a much weaker version of it than other versions that are known to be available.

Substance. The stuff of which things are made. Dualists, for instance, believe there are two basic kinds of substances: physical (material, corporeal) and mental. Idealists believe there is only one basic kind of substance: mental. Physicalists (materialists) also believe there is only one basic substance: physical.

Sufficient condition. See *necessary condition*.

Sui geneni. Latin for "of its own kind."

Synthetic statement. See *analytic statement*.

Tautology. Strictly speaking, a statement that is necessarily true merely by virtue of its logical form. For instance, any so-called identity statement, such as "A rose is a rose." More loosely, any analytic statement. See *analytic statement*.

Theism. See *atheism*.

Theodicy. A theory the point of which is to explain how God's knowledge, power, and goodness are compatible with the existence of evil (or apparently unnecessary suffering) in the world.

Token. See *type*.

Truth of language. An analytic statement, such as "All bachelors are unmarried," including such tautologies as, "A rose is a rose." See *analytic statement*.

Turing machine. A simple kind of computer, thought up by the mathematician A. M. Turing, that reads symbols on a tape, causing changes in the computer's internal states, which in turn cause the computer to erase and print symbols on the tape. It is often debatable what the capacities and limits of such a machine may be. Computer scientists, psychologists, and philosophers of mind have often thought it of great theoretical significance how such debates are resolved.

Type/token. Two (or more) things of the same sort, or general kind, are said to be tokens of the same type. For instance, two cats are two tokens of the type *cat*.

Vacuous. Literally, empty. In philosophy, sometimes a term of abuse, as when one says that someone else's claim is vacuous as a way of saying that the claim is not the least bit informative. For instance, the statement "God is good, but in a sense of 'good' that is utterly and completely beyond human comprehension" might be said by a critic to be vacuous. However, the word *vacuous* also has a more technical meaning in logic, as when certain universal statements, such as "All unicorns are friendly," may be said to be vacuously true because they are true merely in virtue of being about things that do not exist.

Valid deductive argument. See *sound deductive argument*.

Verbal dispute. A dispute that may appear to be genuine but actually is not because the people disputing are using key words in different senses. Such disputes are sometimes said to depend on an *equivocation*. When one person's argument is undermined by his or her using a key term in more than one sense, the argument is said to depend on an *equivocation*.

Verification. See *confirmation*.

Weltanschauung. A German word meaning "world-view." A very general theory of the way things are; an overview that provides a framework for more specific views and beliefs.

Yoga. Certain exercise and meditative techniques, usually derived from Hinduism, that are designed to calm the mind or bring about enlightenment.